Quite a few dearly missed characters appear in this volume. I had to keep checking past volumes while drawing them because I'd forgotten some of their specs, which ended up taking way too long. Argh!!

—*Masashi Kishimoto, 2011*

岸本斉史

Author/artist Masashi Kishimoto was born in 1974 in rural Okayama Prefecture, Japan. After spending time in art college, he won the Hop Step Award for new manga artists with his manga **Karakuri** (Mechanism). Kishimoto decided to base his next story on traditional Japanese culture. His first version of **Naruto**, drawn in 1997, was a one-shot story about fox spirits; his final version, which debuted in **Weekly Shonen Jump** in 1999, quickly became the most popular ninja manga in Japan.

# NARUTO

## 3-in-1 Edition
## Volume 19
### SHONEN JUMP Manga Omnibus Edition
A compilation of the graphic novel volumes 55–57

## STORY AND ART BY MASASHI KISHIMOTO

Translation/Mari Morimoto
English Adaptation/Joel Enos
Touch-up Art & Lettering/Inori Fukuda Trant, Sabrina Heep
Design/Sam Elzway (Original Series and Omnibus Edition)
Editor/Megan Bates (Manga Edition)
Managing Editor/Erica Yee (Omnibus Edition)

Printed in Canada

Published by VIZ Media, LLC
P.O. Box 77010
San Francisco, CA 94107

10 9 8 7 6 5 4
Omnibus edition first printing, July 2017
Fourth printing, June 2022

VIZ MEDIA
viz.com

SHONEN JUMP

EDITION

# NARUTO

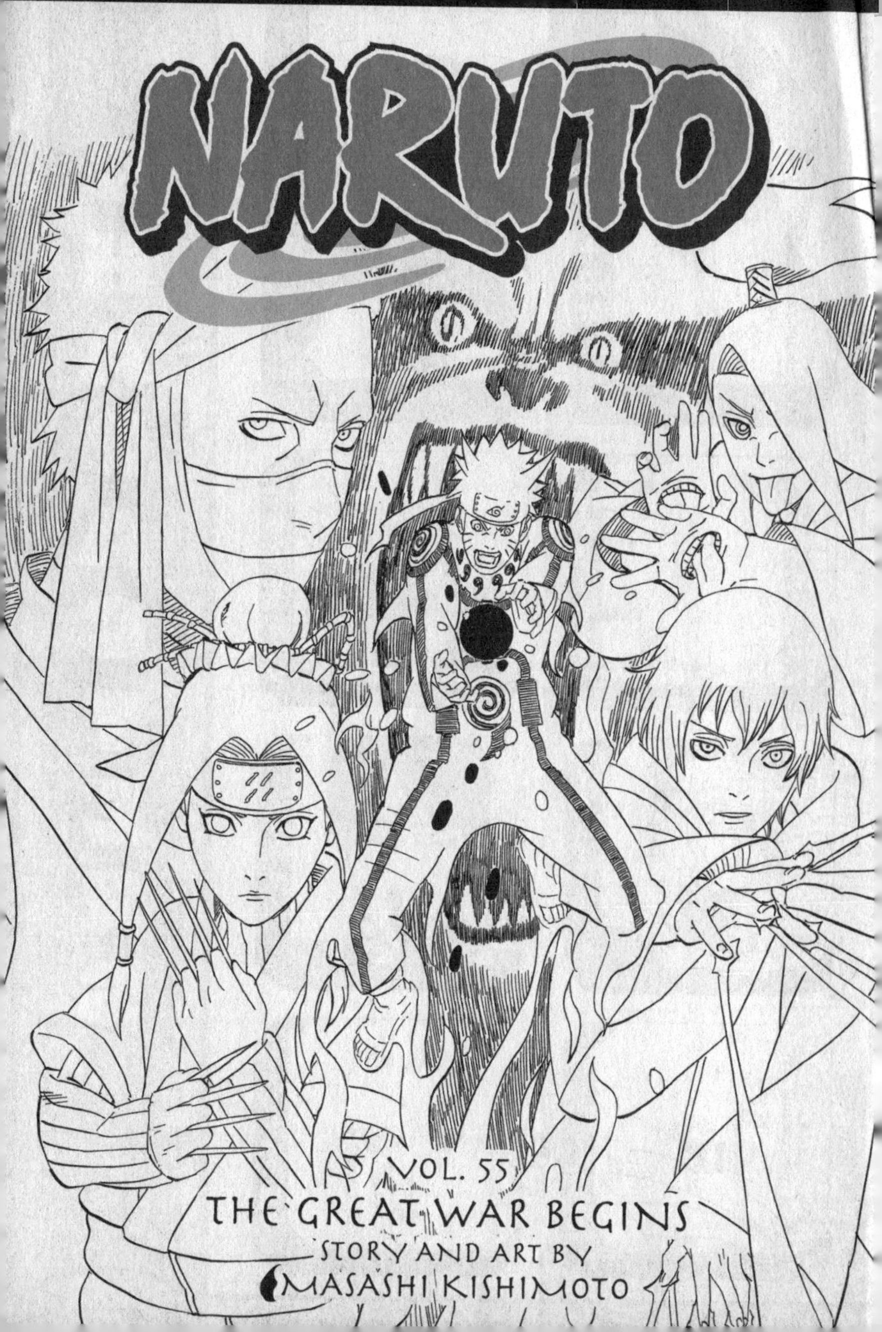

## VOL. 55

## THE GREAT WAR BEGINS

STORY AND ART BY

MASASHI KISHIMOTO

# CHARACTERS

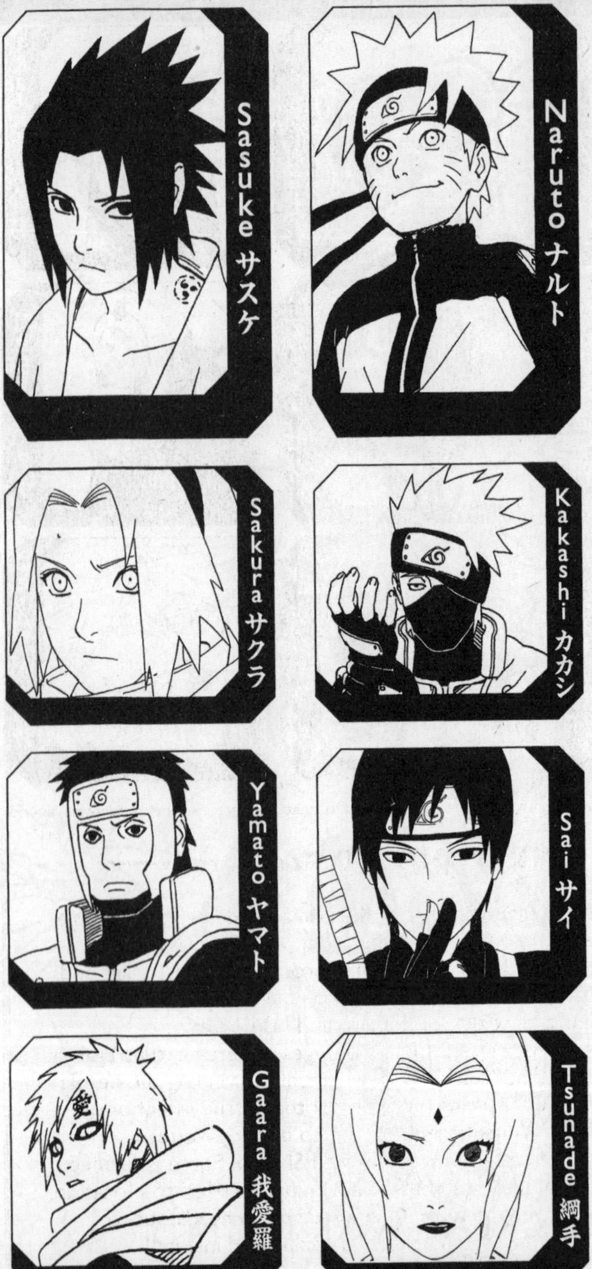
Naruto ナルト
Sasuke サスケ
Kakashi カカシ
Sakura サクラ
Sai サイ
Yamato ヤマト
Tsunade 綱手
Gaara 我愛羅

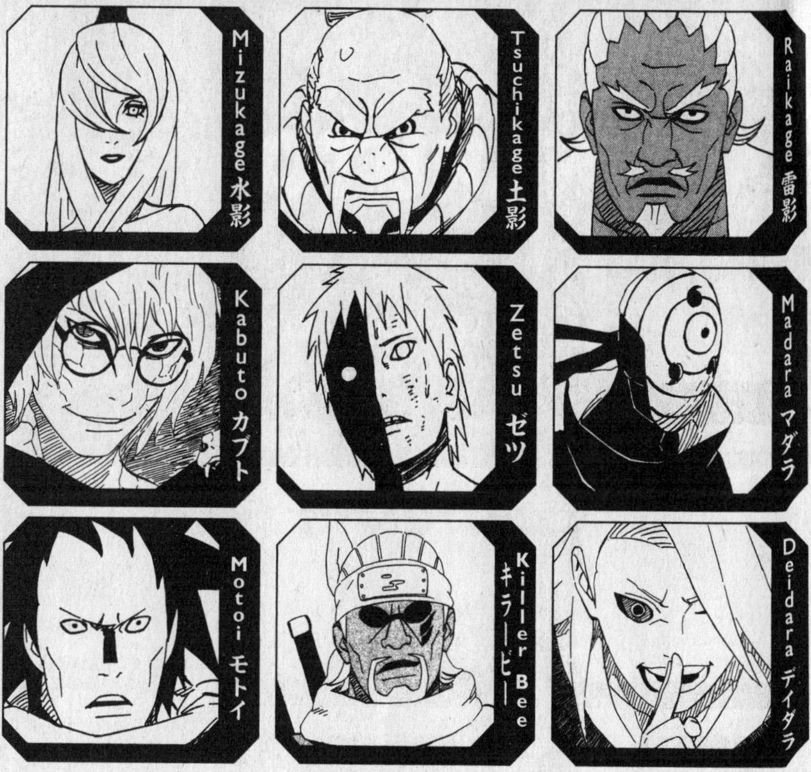
Raikage 雷影
Tsuchikage 土影
Mizukage 水影
Madara マダラ
Zetsu ゼツ
Kabuto カブト
Deidara デイダラ
Killer Bee キラービー
Motoi モトイ

## THE STORY SO FAR...

Naruto, the biggest troublemaker at the Ninja Academy in the Village of Konohagakure, finally becomes a ninja along with his classmates Sasuke and Sakura. They grow and mature through countless trials and battles. However, Sasuke, unable to give up his quest for vengeance, leaves Konohagakure to seek Orochimaru and his power…

Two years pass. Naruto grows up and engages in fierce battles against the Tailed Beast-targeting Akatsuki. Elsewhere, after winning the heroic battle against Itachi and learning his older brother's true intentions, Sasuke allies with the Akatsuki and sets out to destroy Konoha.

Upon Madara's declaration of war, an Allied Shinobi Force is formed. As tensions rise in both camps, the Akatsuki pinpoint Naruto's location. Madara directs Kabuto to capture Nine Tails. Yamato heads out to intercept Kabuto and protect Naruto, but is captured instead!

# NARUTO

## VOL. 55
## THE GREAT WAR BEGINS

## CONTENTS

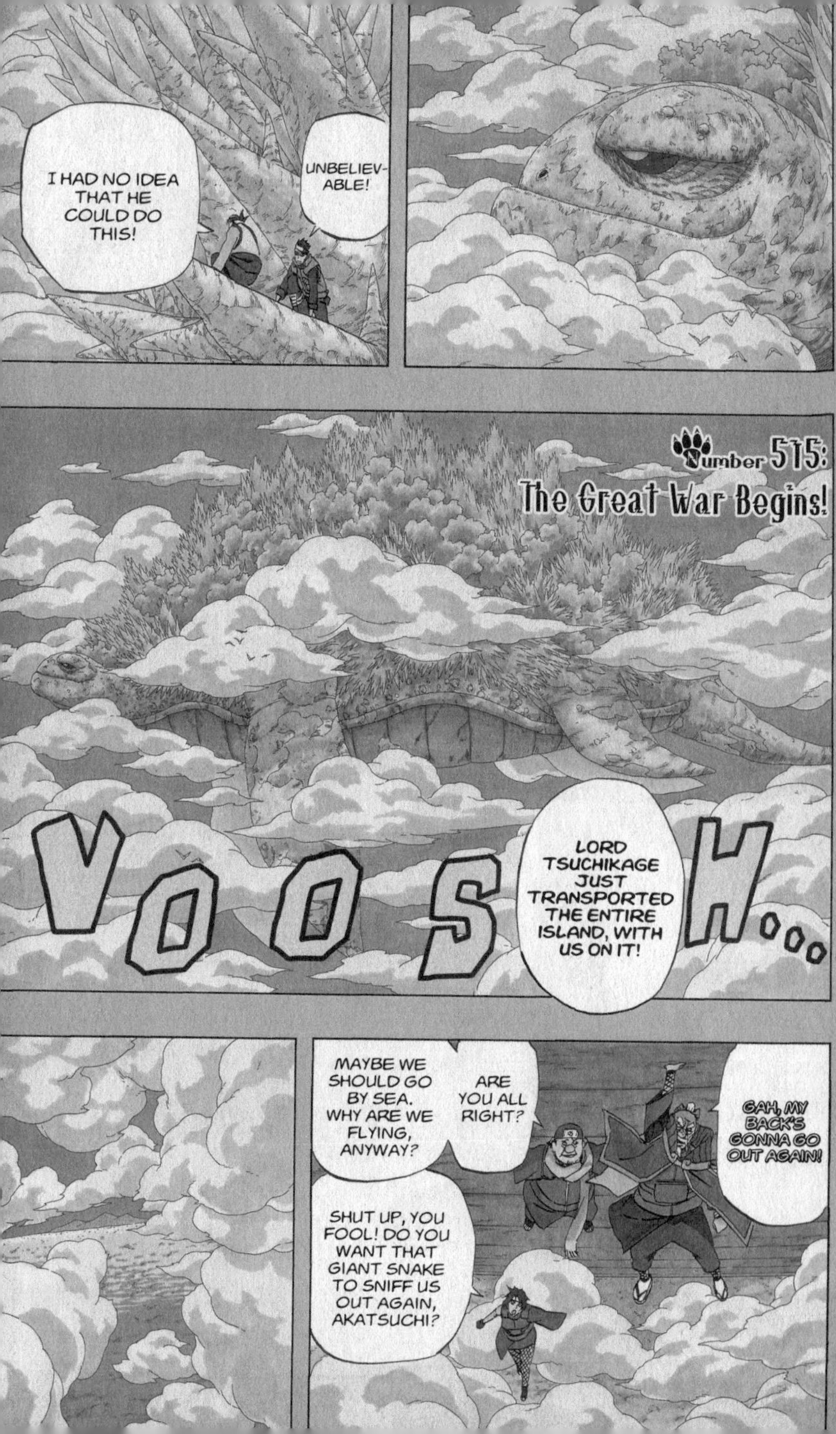
UNBELIEV-ABLE!
I HAD NO IDEA THAT HE COULD DO THIS!
Number 515: The Great War Begins!
LORD TSUCHIKAGE JUST TRANSPORTED THE ENTIRE ISLAND, WITH US ON IT!
VOOSH...
GAH, MY BACK'S GONNA GO OUT AGAIN!
ARE YOU ALL RIGHT?
MAYBE WE SHOULD GO BY SEA. WHY ARE WE FLYING, ANYWAY?
SHUT UP, YOU FOOL! DO YOU WANT THAT GIANT SNAKE TO SNIFF US OUT AGAIN, AKATSUCHI?

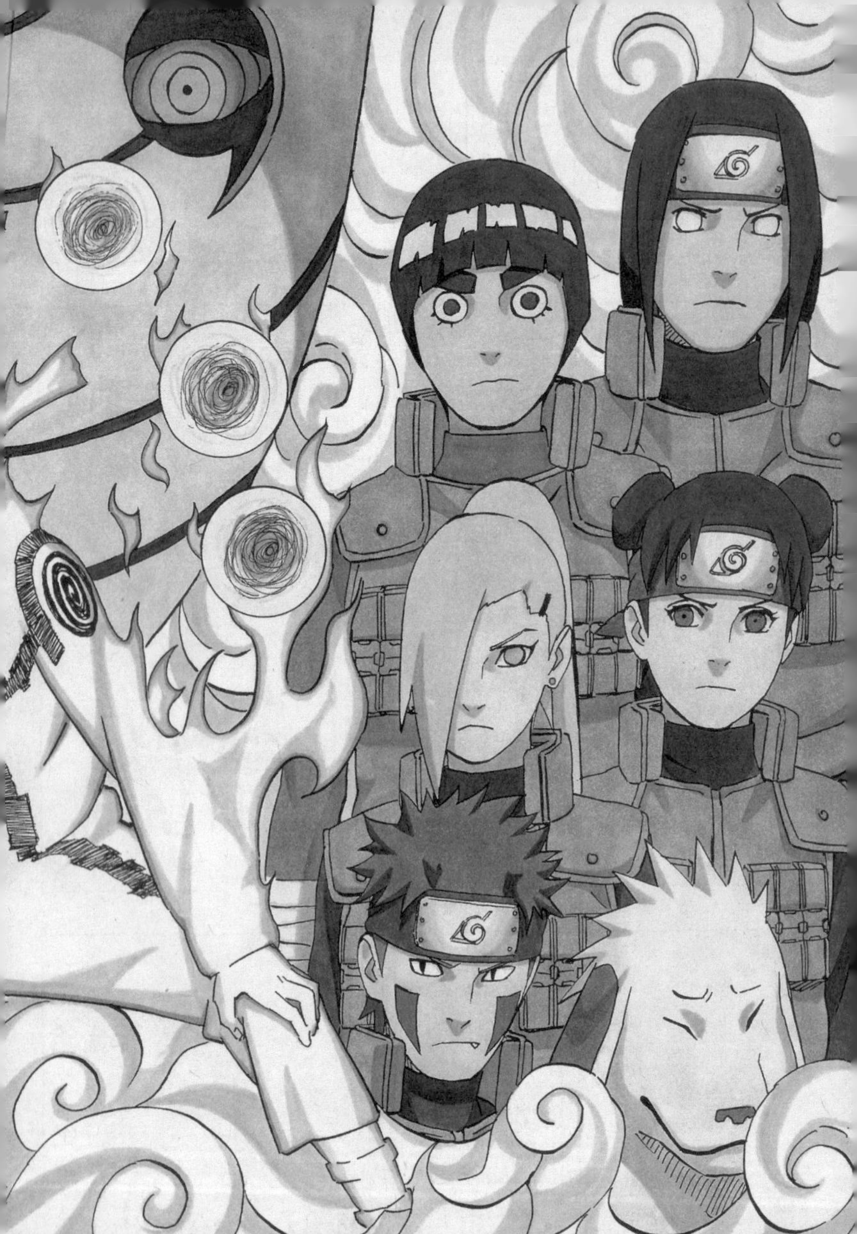

Number 515: The Great War Begins!

NARUTO

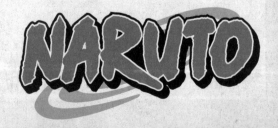

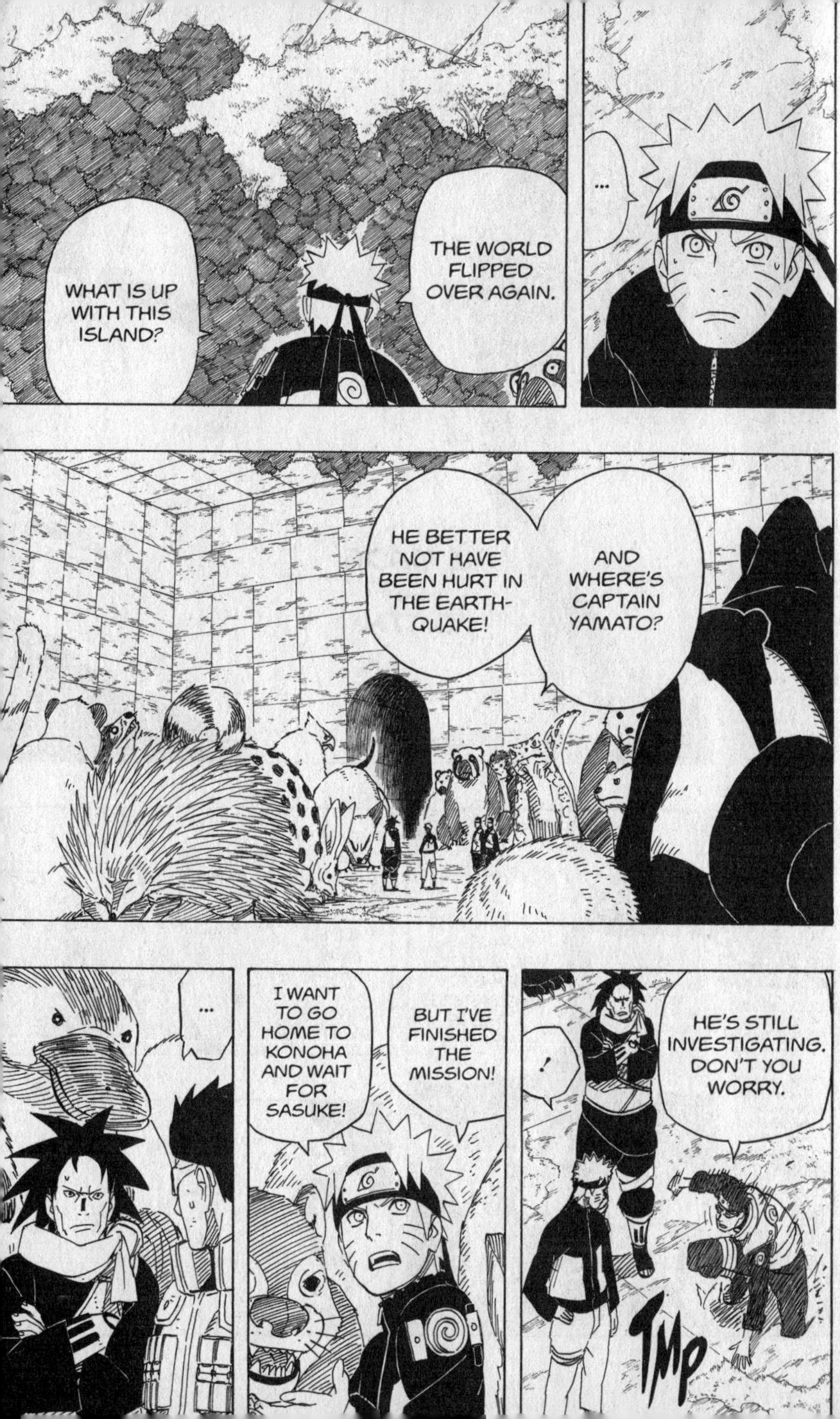
...
THE WORLD FLIPPED OVER AGAIN.
WHAT IS UP WITH THIS ISLAND?
AND WHERE'S CAPTAIN YAMATO?
HE BETTER NOT HAVE BEEN HURT IN THE EARTH-QUAKE!
HE'S STILL INVESTIGATING. DON'T YOU WORRY.
!
TMP
BUT I'VE FINISHED THE MISSION!
I WANT TO GO HOME TO KONOHA AND WAIT FOR SASUKE!
...

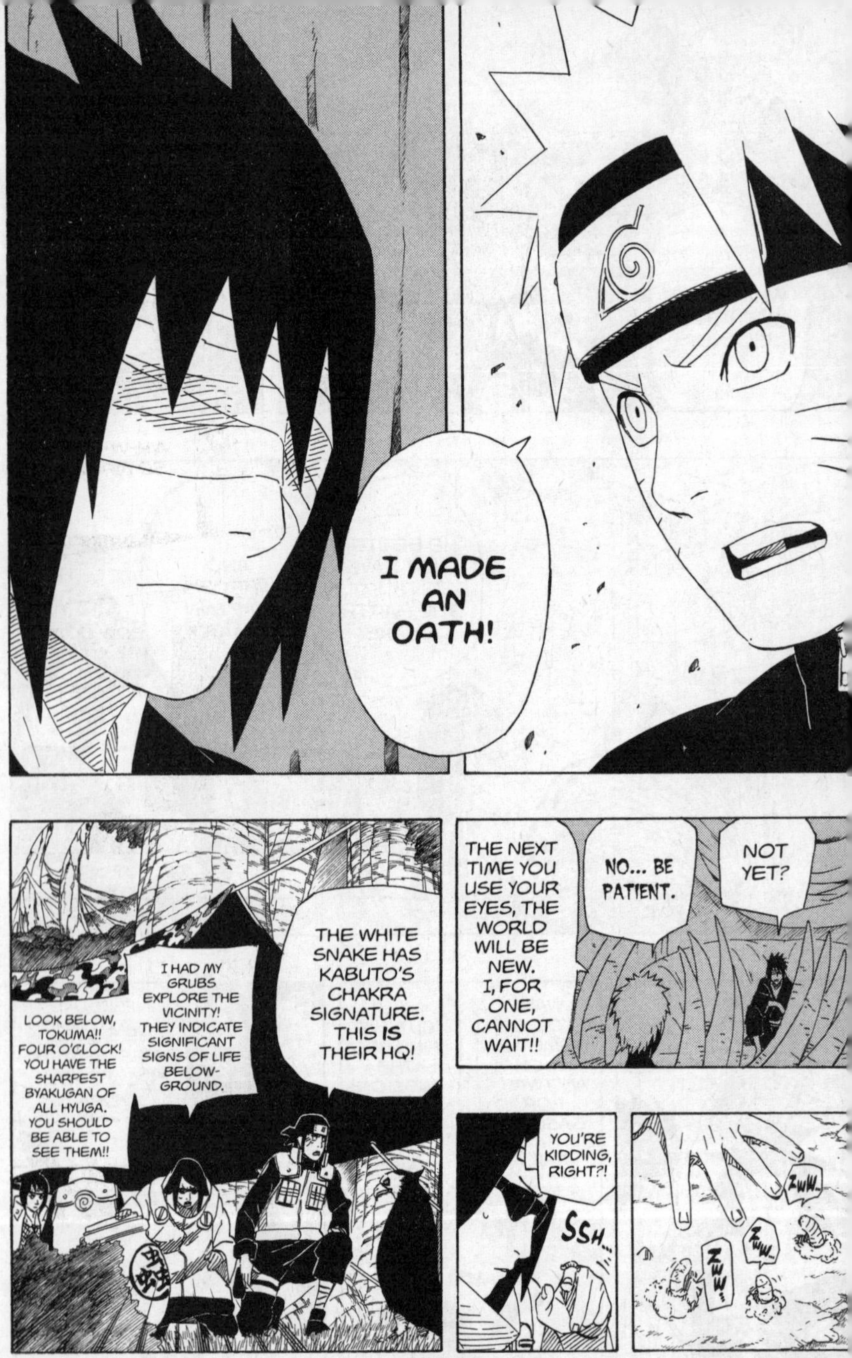
I MADE AN OATH!
NOT YET?
NO... BE PATIENT.
THE NEXT TIME YOU USE YOUR EYES, THE WORLD WILL BE NEW. I, FOR ONE, CANNOT WAIT!!
ZWW...
ZWW...
ZWW...
YOU'RE KIDDING, RIGHT?!
SSH...
THE WHITE SNAKE HAS KABUTO'S CHAKRA SIGNATURE. THIS IS THEIR HQ!
I HAD MY GRUBS EXPLORE THE VICINITY! THEY INDICATE SIGNIFICANT SIGNS OF LIFE BELOW-GROUND.
LOOK BELOW, TOKUMA!! FOUR O'CLOCK! YOU HAVE THE SHARPEST BYAKUGAN OF ALL HYUGA. YOU SHOULD BE ABLE TO SEE THEM!!

READ THIS WAY

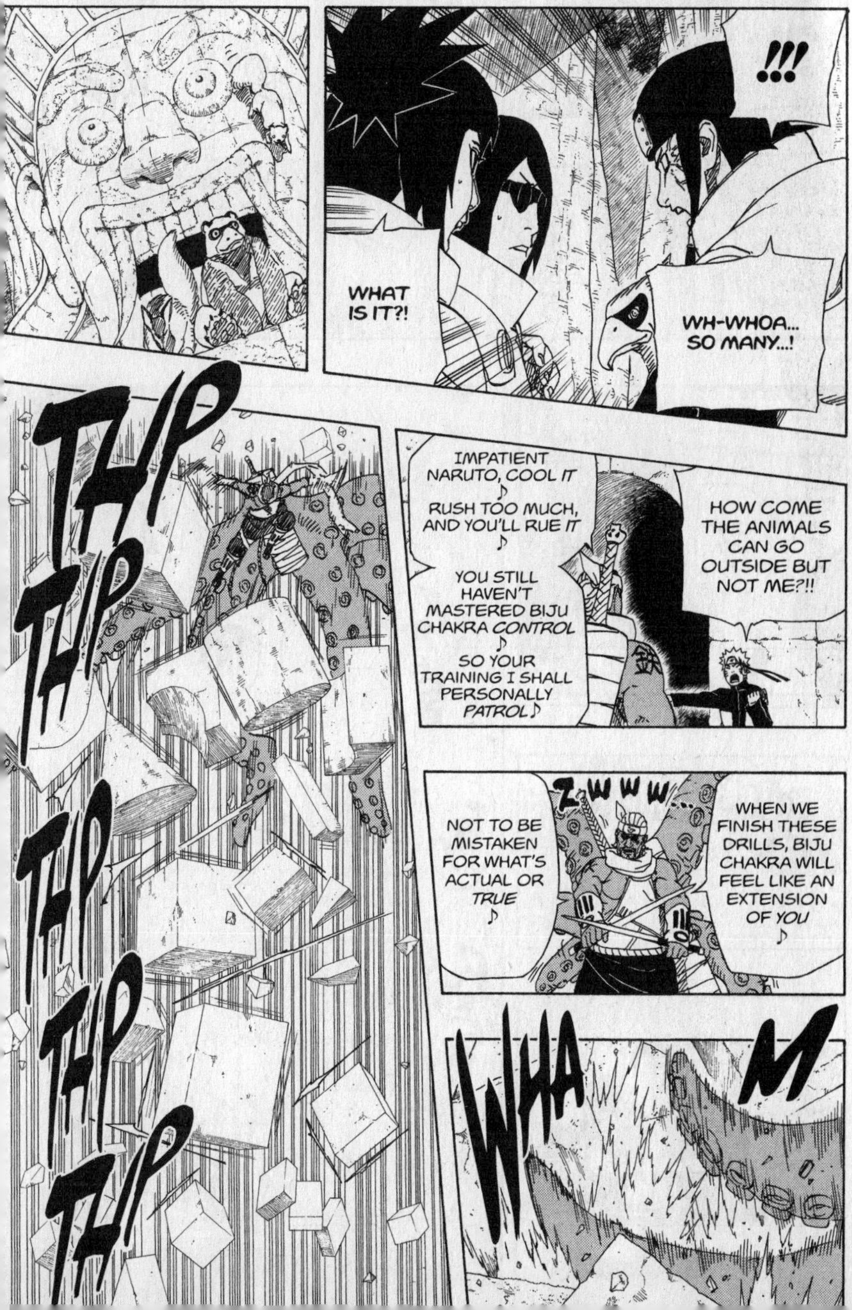
!!!
WH-WHOA... SO MANY...!
WHAT IS IT?!
HOW COME THE ANIMALS CAN GO OUTSIDE BUT NOT ME?!!
IMPATIENT NARUTO, COOL *IT* ♪
RUSH TOO MUCH, AND YOU'LL RUE *IT* ♪
YOU STILL HAVEN'T MASTERED BIJU CHAKRA *CONTROL* ♪
SO YOUR TRAINING I SHALL PERSONALLY *PATROL* ♪
WHEN WE FINISH THESE DRILLS, BIJU CHAKRA WILL FEEL LIKE AN EXTENSION OF *YOU* ♪
ZWWW...
NOT TO BE MISTAKEN FOR WHAT'S ACTUAL OR *TRUE* ♪
WHAM
THP THP THP THP THP

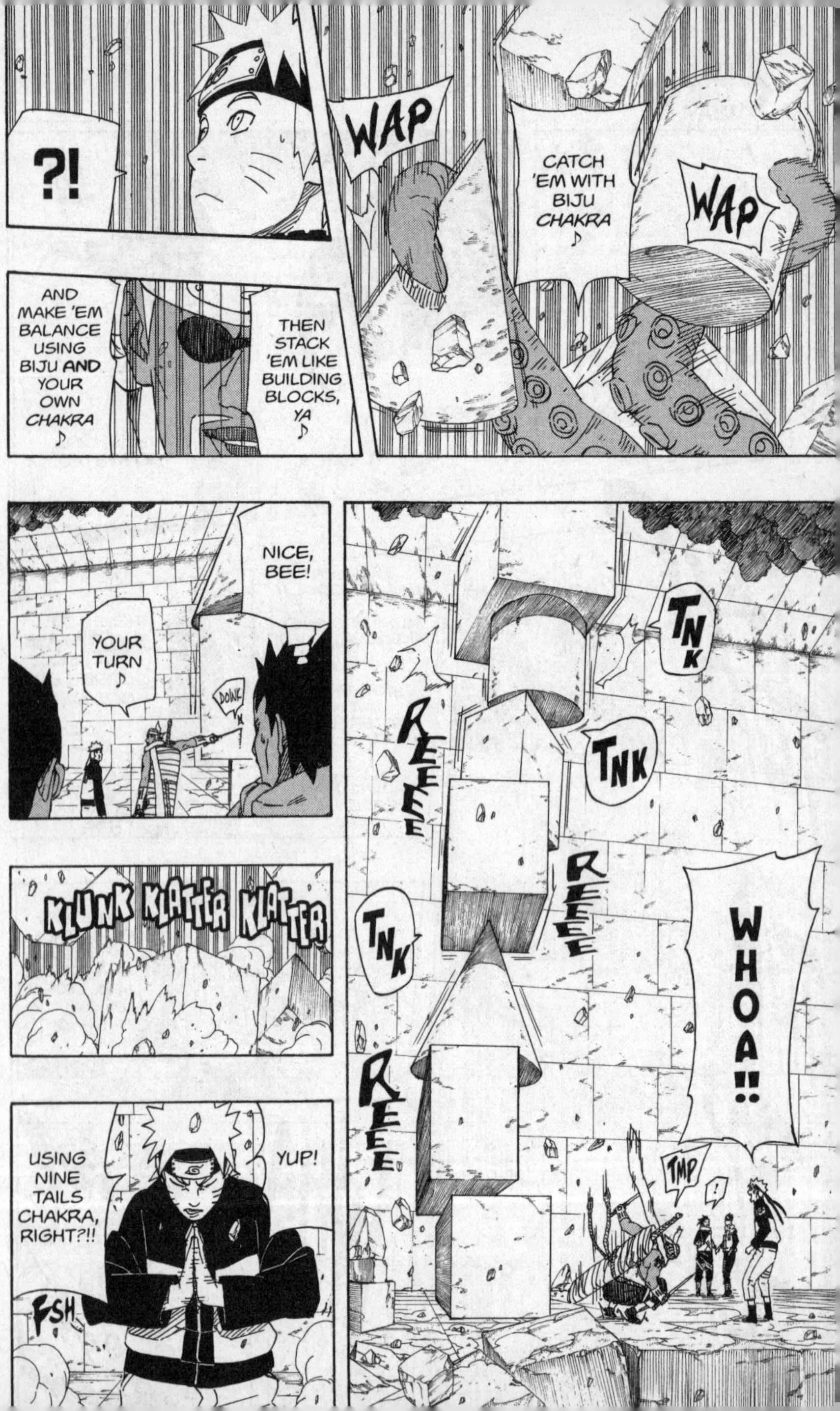
WAP
CATCH 'EM WITH BIJU CHAKRA ♪
WAP
?!
THEN STACK 'EM LIKE BUILDING BLOCKS, YA ♪
AND MAKE 'EM BALANCE USING BIJU AND YOUR OWN CHAKRA ♪
TNK
REEE
TNK
REEE
WHOA!!
TNK
REEE
TMP
!
NICE, BEE!
YOUR TURN ♪
DOINK
KLUNK KLATTER KLATTER
YUP!
USING NINE TAILS CHAKRA, RIGHT?!!
FSH

READ THIS WAY

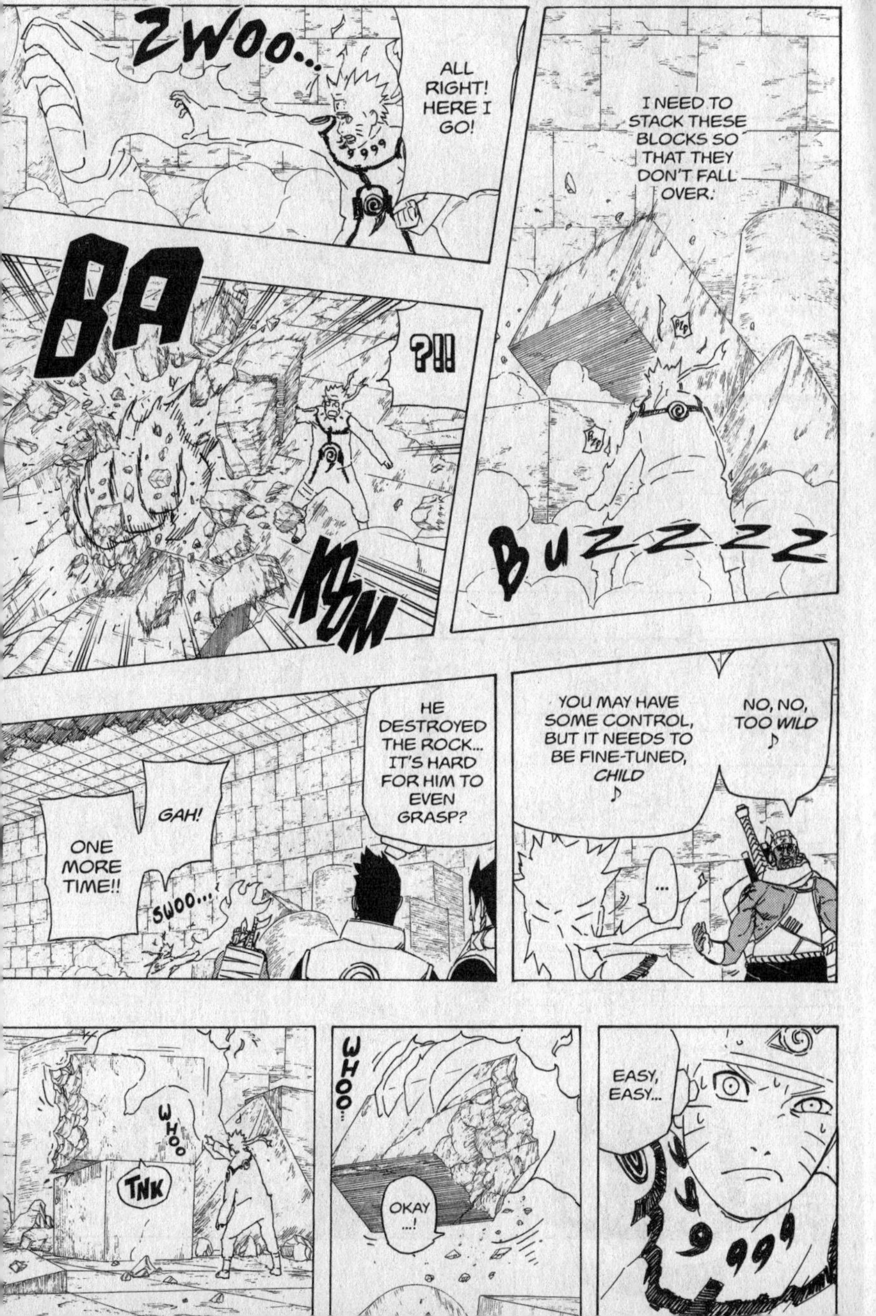
I NEED TO STACK THESE BLOCKS SO THAT THEY DON'T FALL OVER.
BUZZZZZ
ZWOO...
ALL RIGHT! HERE I GO!
BA
?!!
KBOM
NO, NO, TOO WILD ♪
YOU MAY HAVE SOME CONTROL, BUT IT NEEDS TO BE FINE-TUNED, CHILD ♪
...
HE DESTROYED THE ROCK... IT'S HARD FOR HIM TO EVEN GRASP?
GAH!
ONE MORE TIME!!
SWOO...
EASY, EASY...
WHOO...
OKAY ...!
WHOO
TNK

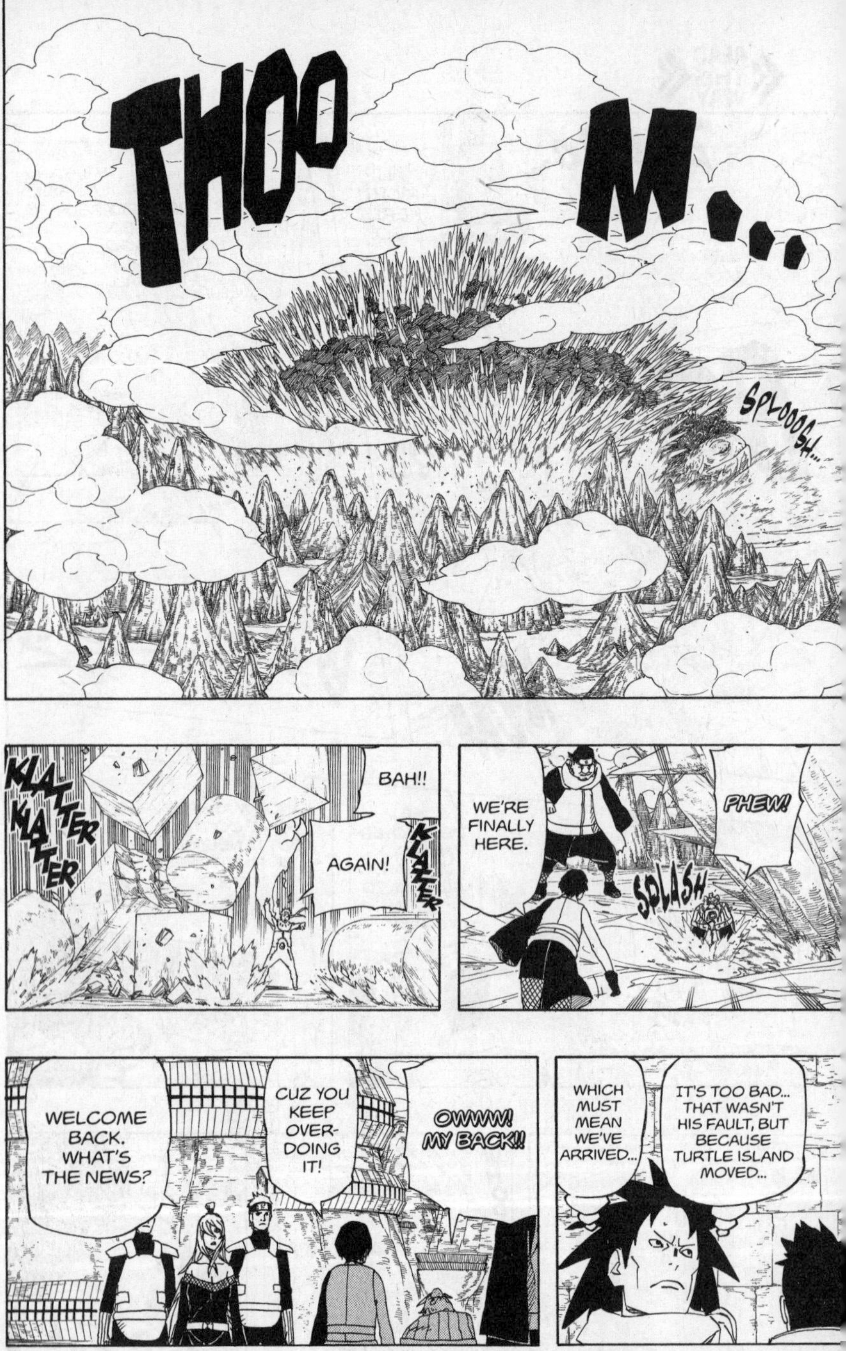
THOOM...
SPLOOOSH...
PHEW!
WE'RE FINALLY HERE.
SPLASH
BAH!!
AGAIN!
KLATTER
KLATTER
KLATTER
IT'S TOO BAD... THAT WASN'T HIS FAULT, BUT BECAUSE TURTLE ISLAND MOVED...
WHICH MUST MEAN WE'VE ARRIVED...
OWWW! MY BACK!!
CUZ YOU KEEP OVER-DOING IT!
WELCOME BACK. WHAT'S THE NEWS?

READ THIS WAY

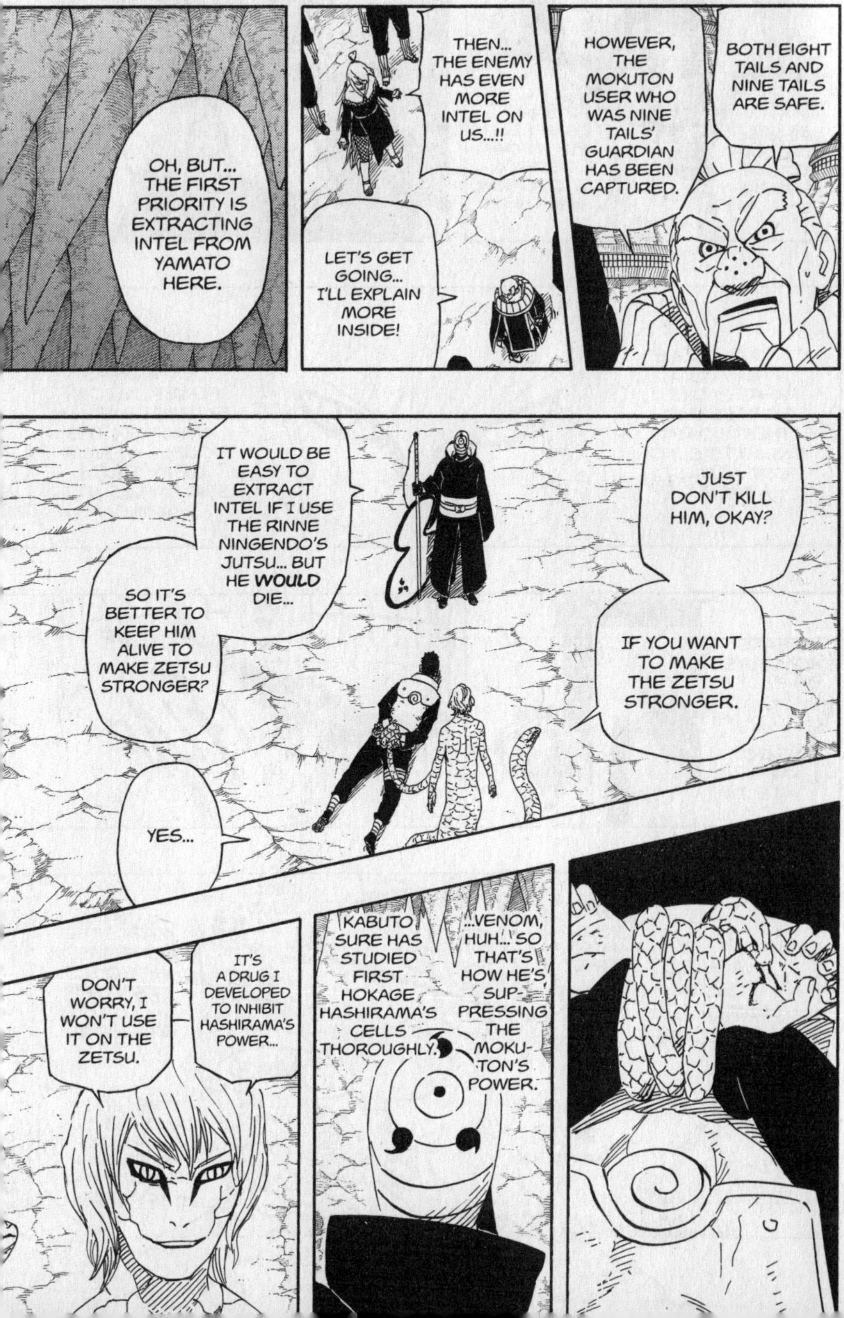
BOTH EIGHT TAILS AND NINE TAILS ARE SAFE.
HOWEVER, THE MOKUTON USER WHO WAS NINE TAILS' GUARDIAN HAS BEEN CAPTURED.
THEN... THE ENEMY HAS EVEN MORE INTEL ON US...!!
LET'S GET GOING... I'LL EXPLAIN MORE INSIDE!
OH, BUT... THE FIRST PRIORITY IS EXTRACTING INTEL FROM YAMATO HERE.
JUST DON'T KILL HIM, OKAY?
IF YOU WANT TO MAKE THE ZETSU STRONGER.
IT WOULD BE EASY TO EXTRACT INTEL IF I USE THE RINNE NINGENDO'S JUTSU... BUT HE **WOULD** DIE...
SO IT'S BETTER TO KEEP HIM ALIVE TO MAKE ZETSU STRONGER?
YES...
...VENOM, HUH... SO THAT'S HOW HE'S SUP-PRESSING THE MOKU-TON'S POWER.
KABUTO SURE HAS STUDIED FIRST HOKAGE HASHIRAMA'S CELLS THOROUGHLY.
IT'S A DRUG I DEVELOPED TO INHIBIT HASHIRAMA'S POWER...
DON'T WORRY, I WON'T USE IT ON THE ZETSU.

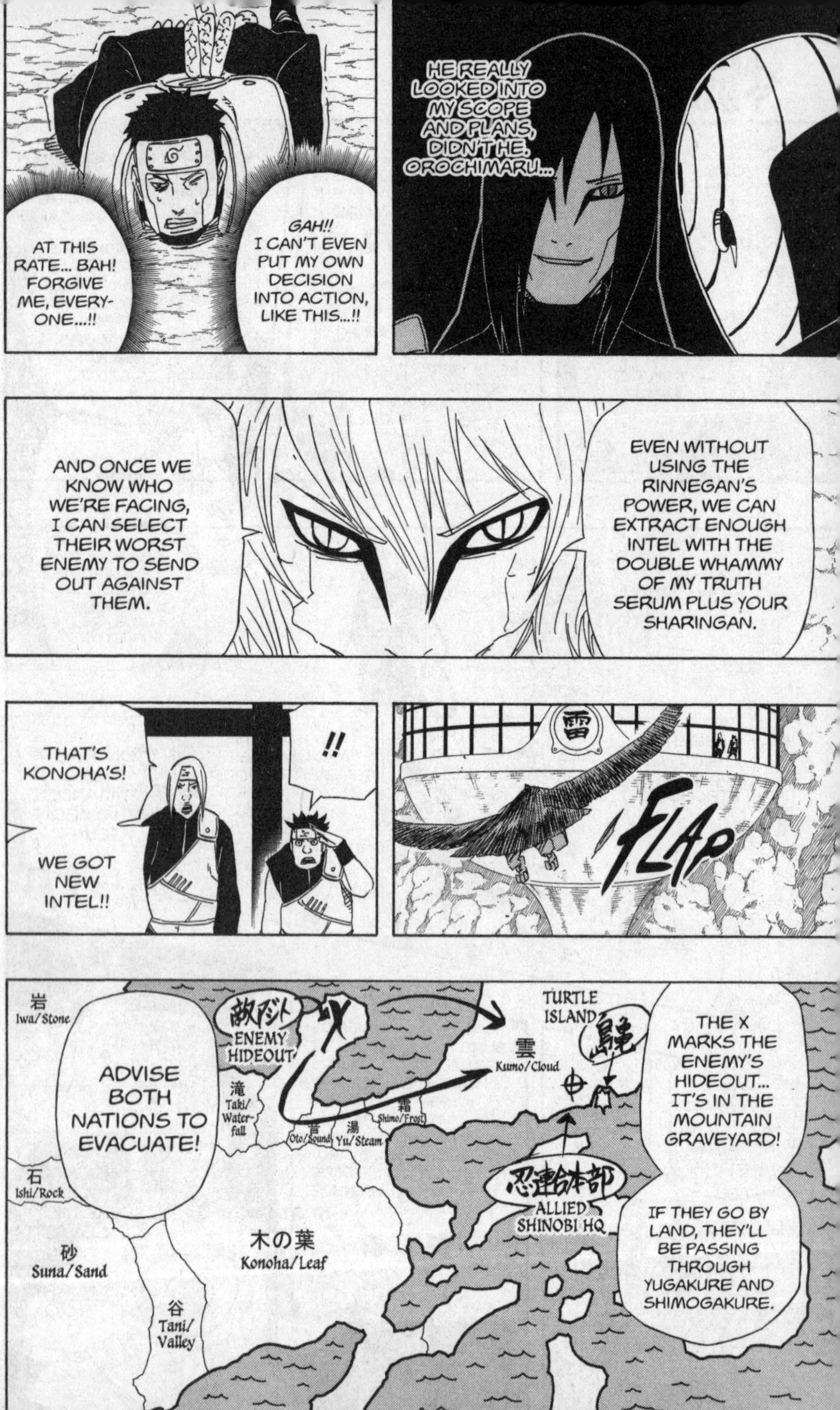
HE REALLY LOOKED INTO MY SCOPE AND PLANS, DIDN'T HE, OROCHIMARU...
GAH!! I CAN'T EVEN PUT MY OWN DECISION INTO ACTION, LIKE THIS...!!
AT THIS RATE... BAH! FORGIVE ME, EVERY-ONE...!!
EVEN WITHOUT USING THE RINNEGAN'S POWER, WE CAN EXTRACT ENOUGH INTEL WITH THE DOUBLE WHAMMY OF MY TRUTH SERUM PLUS YOUR SHARINGAN.
AND ONCE WE KNOW WHO WE'RE FACING, I CAN SELECT THEIR WORST ENEMY TO SEND OUT AGAINST THEM.
FLAP
!!
THAT'S KONOHA'S!
WE GOT NEW INTEL!!
THE X MARKS THE ENEMY'S HIDEOUT... IT'S IN THE MOUNTAIN GRAVEYARD!
IF THEY GO BY LAND, THEY'LL BE PASSING THROUGH YUGAKURE AND SHIMOGAKURE.
TURTLE ISLAND
敵アジト ENEMY HIDEOUT
雲 Kumo/Cloud
霜 Shimo/Frost
湯 Yu/Steam
音 Oto/Sound
滝 Taki/Waterfall
岩 Iwa/Stone
石 Ishi/Rock
忍連合本部 ALLIED SHINOBI HQ
木の葉 Konoha/Leaf
砂 Suna/Sand
谷 Tani/Valley
ADVISE BOTH NATIONS TO EVACUATE!

READ THIS WAY

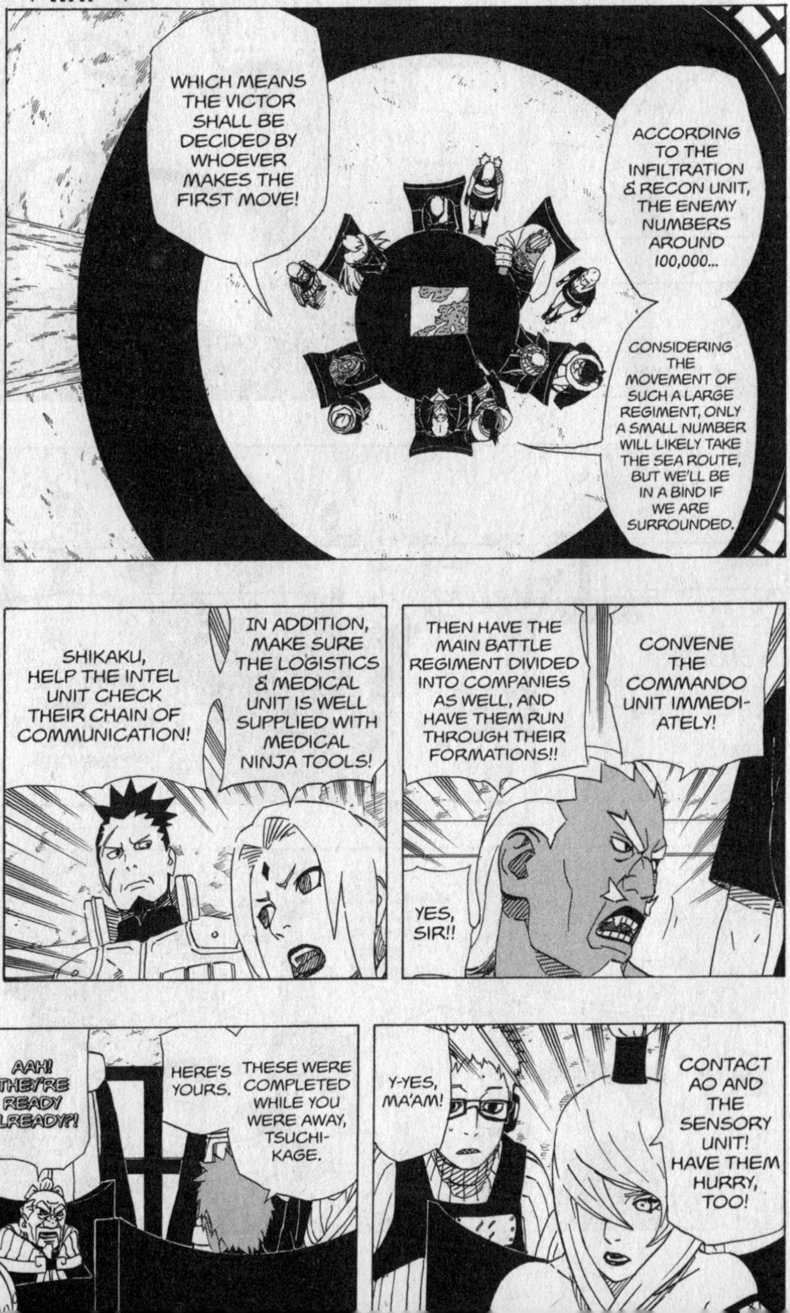
ACCORDING TO THE INFILTRATION & RECON UNIT, THE ENEMY NUMBERS AROUND 100,000...
CONSIDERING THE MOVEMENT OF SUCH A LARGE REGIMENT, ONLY A SMALL NUMBER WILL LIKELY TAKE THE SEA ROUTE, BUT WE'LL BE IN A BIND IF WE ARE SURROUNDED.
WHICH MEANS THE VICTOR SHALL BE DECIDED BY WHOEVER MAKES THE FIRST MOVE!
CONVENE THE COMMANDO UNIT IMMEDIATELY!
THEN HAVE THE MAIN BATTLE REGIMENT DIVIDED INTO COMPANIES AS WELL, AND HAVE THEM RUN THROUGH THEIR FORMATIONS!!
YES, SIR!!
IN ADDITION, MAKE SURE THE LOGISTICS & MEDICAL UNIT IS WELL SUPPLIED WITH MEDICAL NINJA TOOLS!
SHIKAKU, HELP THE INTEL UNIT CHECK THEIR CHAIN OF COMMUNICATION!
CONTACT AO AND THE SENSORY UNIT! HAVE THEM HURRY, TOO!
Y-YES, MA'AM!
THESE WERE COMPLETED WHILE YOU WERE AWAY, TSUCHIKAGE.
HERE'S YOURS.
AAH! THEY'RE READY ALREADY?!

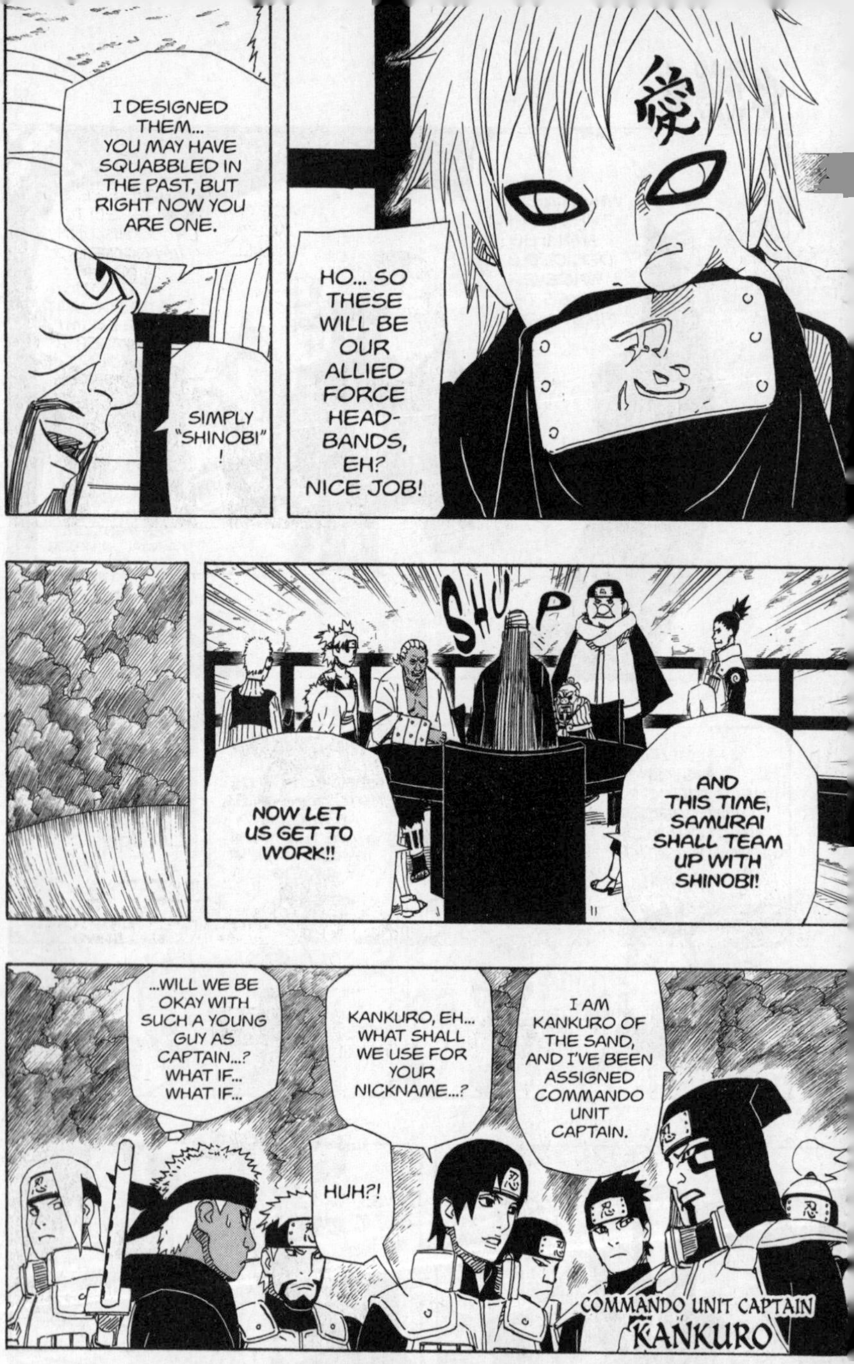
HO... SO THESE WILL BE OUR ALLIED FORCE HEAD-BANDS, EH? NICE JOB!
I DESIGNED THEM... YOU MAY HAVE SQUABBLED IN THE PAST, BUT RIGHT NOW YOU ARE ONE.
SIMPLY "SHINOBI"!
SHUP
AND THIS TIME, SAMURAI SHALL TEAM UP WITH SHINOBI!
NOW LET US GET TO WORK!!
I AM KANKURO OF THE SAND, AND I'VE BEEN ASSIGNED COMMANDO UNIT CAPTAIN.
COMMANDO UNIT CAPTAIN KANKURO
KANKURO, EH... WHAT SHALL WE USE FOR YOUR NICKNAME...?
HUH?!
...WILL WE BE OKAY WITH SUCH A YOUNG GUY AS CAPTAIN...? WHAT IF... WHAT IF...

READ THIS WAY

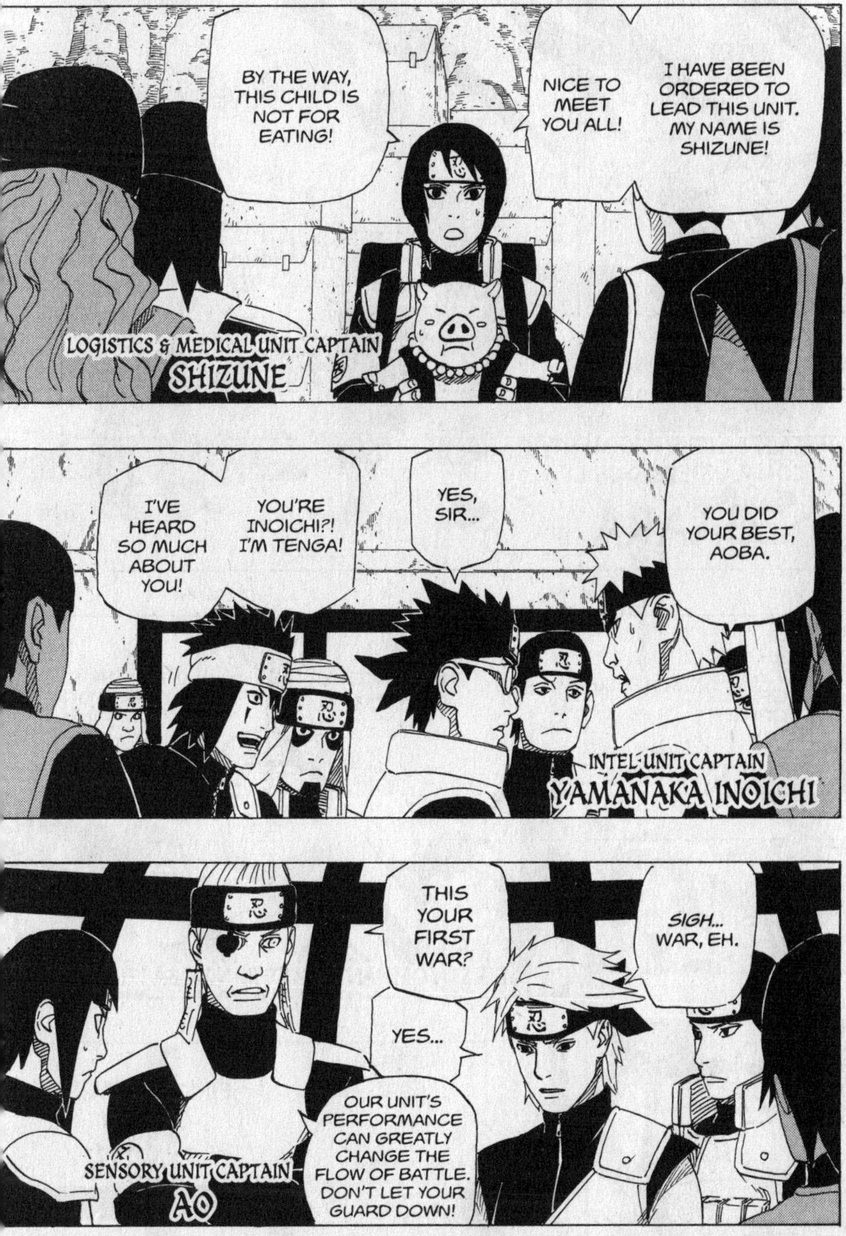

I HAVE BEEN ORDERED TO LEAD THIS UNIT. MY NAME IS SHIZUNE!
NICE TO MEET YOU ALL!
BY THE WAY, THIS CHILD IS NOT FOR EATING!
LOGISTICS & MEDICAL UNIT CAPTAIN
SHIZUNE
YOU DID YOUR BEST, AOBA.
YES, SIR...
YOU'RE INOICHI?! I'M TENGA!
I'VE HEARD SO MUCH ABOUT YOU!
INTEL UNIT CAPTAIN
YAMANAKA INOICHI
SIGH... WAR, EH.
THIS YOUR FIRST WAR?
YES...
OUR UNIT'S PERFORMANCE CAN GREATLY CHANGE THE FLOW OF BATTLE. DON'T LET YOUR GUARD DOWN!
SENSORY UNIT CAPTAIN
AO

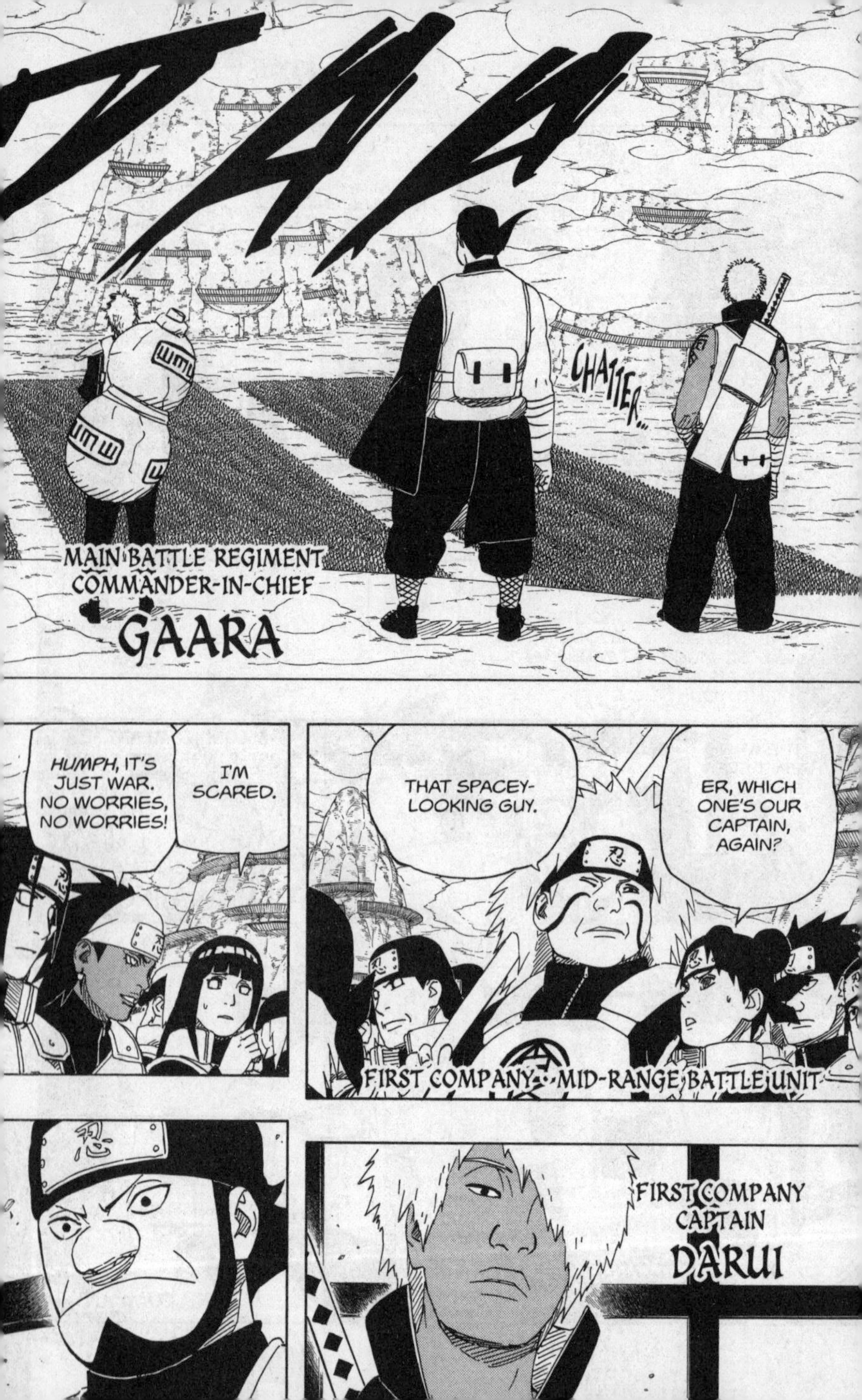
CHATTER...
MAIN BATTLE REGIMENT COMMANDER-IN-CHIEF
GAARA
ER, WHICH ONE'S OUR CAPTAIN, AGAIN?
THAT SPACEY-LOOKING GUY.
FIRST COMPANY • MID-RANGE BATTLE UNIT
I'M SCARED.
HUMPH, IT'S JUST WAR. NO WORRIES, NO WORRIES!
FIRST COMPANY CAPTAIN
DARUI

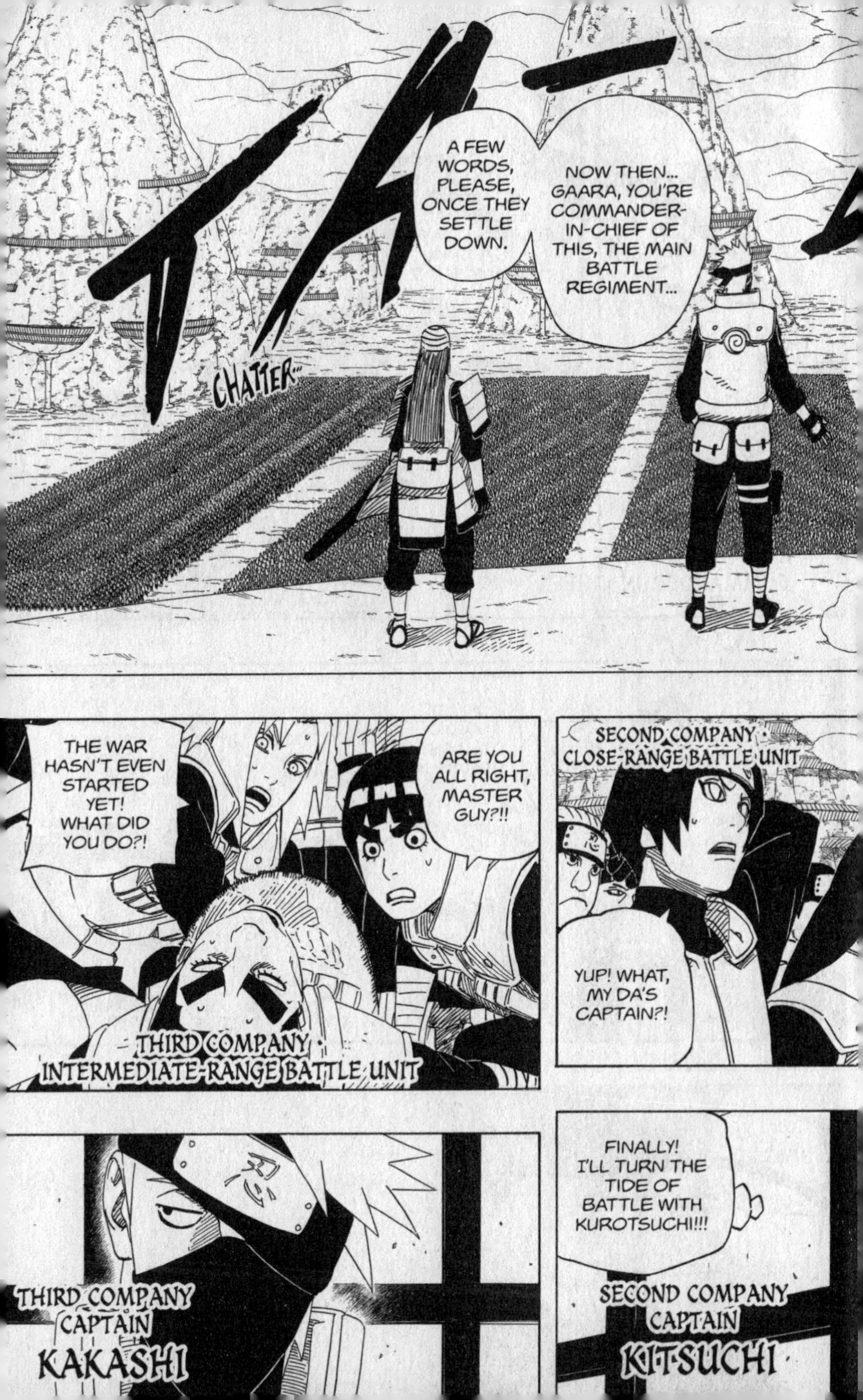
NOW THEN... GAARA, YOU'RE COMMANDER-IN-CHIEF OF THIS, THE MAIN BATTLE REGIMENT...
A FEW WORDS, PLEASE, ONCE THEY SETTLE DOWN.
CHATTER...
SECOND COMPANY · CLOSE-RANGE BATTLE UNIT
YUP! WHAT, MY DA'S CAPTAIN?!
ARE YOU ALL RIGHT, MASTER GUY?!!
THE WAR HASN'T EVEN STARTED YET! WHAT DID YOU DO?!
THIRD COMPANY · INTERMEDIATE-RANGE BATTLE UNIT
FINALLY! I'LL TURN THE TIDE OF BATTLE WITH KUROTSUCHI!!!
SECOND COMPANY CAPTAIN KITSUCHI
THIRD COMPANY CAPTAIN KAKASHI

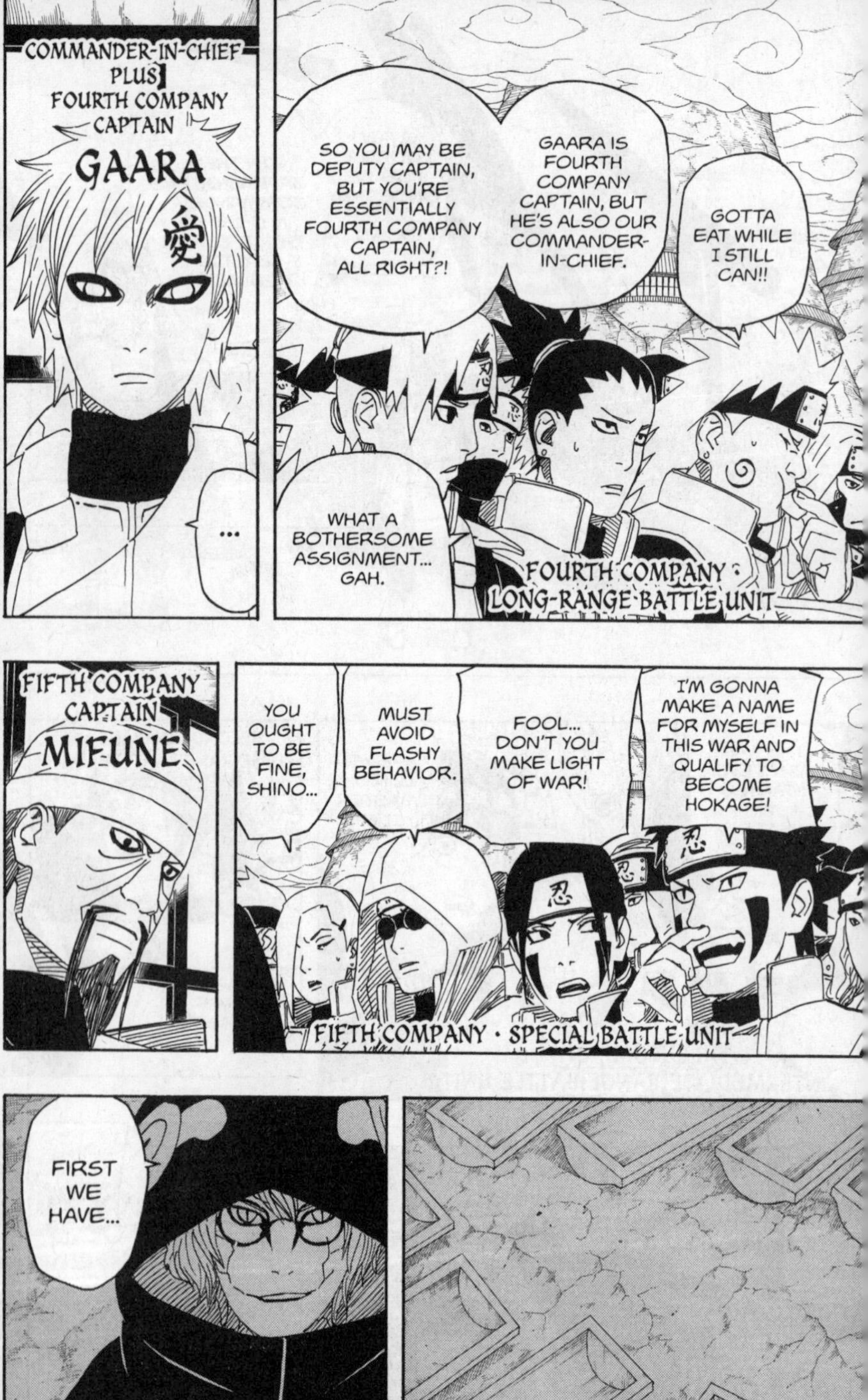
GOTTA EAT WHILE I STILL CAN!!
GAARA IS FOURTH COMPANY CAPTAIN, BUT HE'S ALSO OUR COMMANDER-IN-CHIEF.
SO YOU MAY BE DEPUTY CAPTAIN, BUT YOU'RE ESSENTIALLY FOURTH COMPANY CAPTAIN, ALL RIGHT?!
WHAT A BOTHERSOME ASSIGNMENT... GAH.
FOURTH COMPANY · LONG-RANGE BATTLE UNIT
COMMANDER-IN-CHIEF PLUS FOURTH COMPANY CAPTAIN
GAARA
...
I'M GONNA MAKE A NAME FOR MYSELF IN THIS WAR AND QUALIFY TO BECOME HOKAGE!
FOOL... DON'T YOU MAKE LIGHT OF WAR!
MUST AVOID FLASHY BEHAVIOR.
YOU OUGHT TO BE FINE, SHINO...
FIFTH COMPANY · SPECIAL BATTLE UNIT
FIFTH COMPANY CAPTAIN
MIFUNE
FIRST WE HAVE...

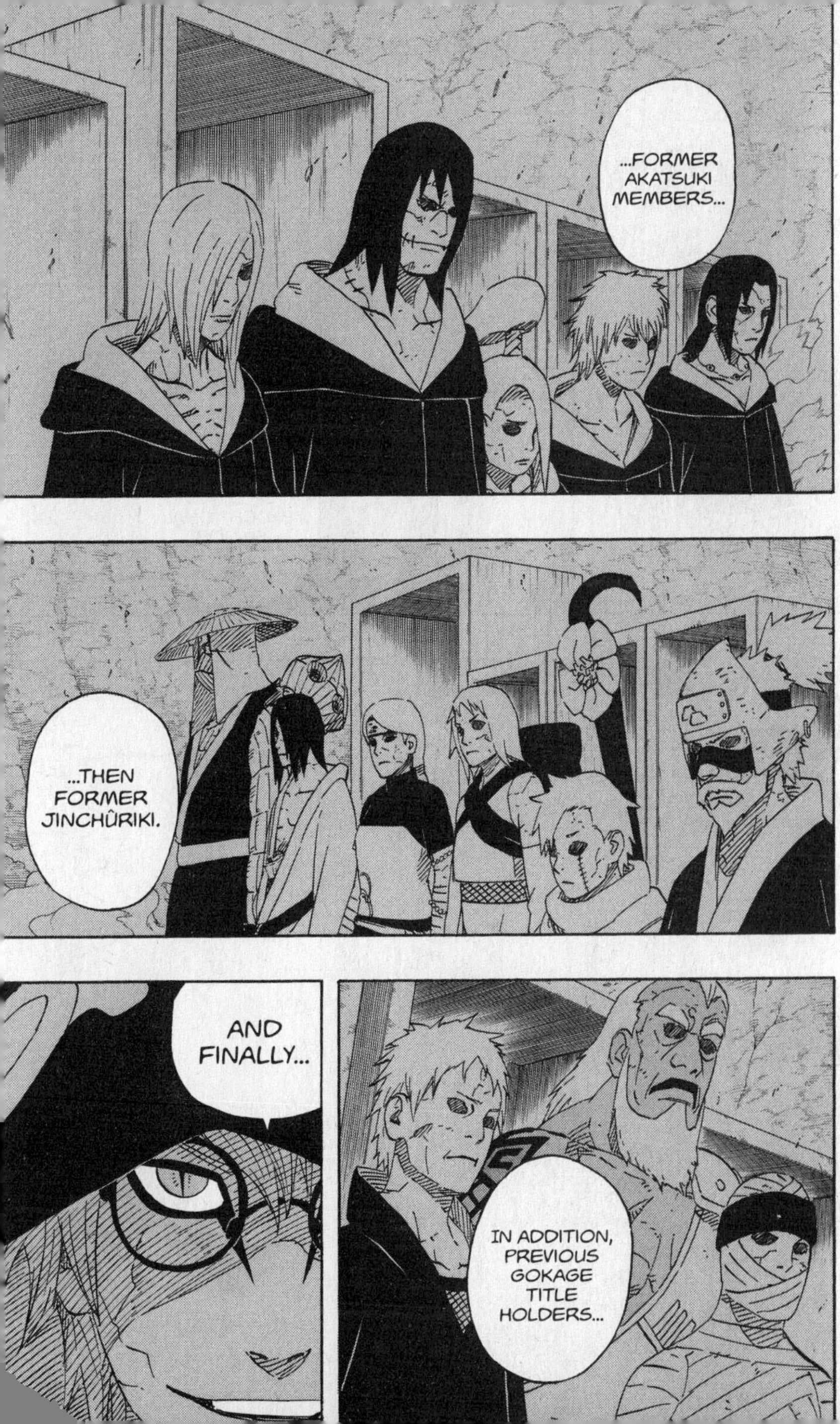
...FORMER AKATSUKI MEMBERS...
...THEN FORMER JINCHÛRIKI.
IN ADDITION, PREVIOUS GOKAGE TITLE HOLDERS...
AND FINALLY...

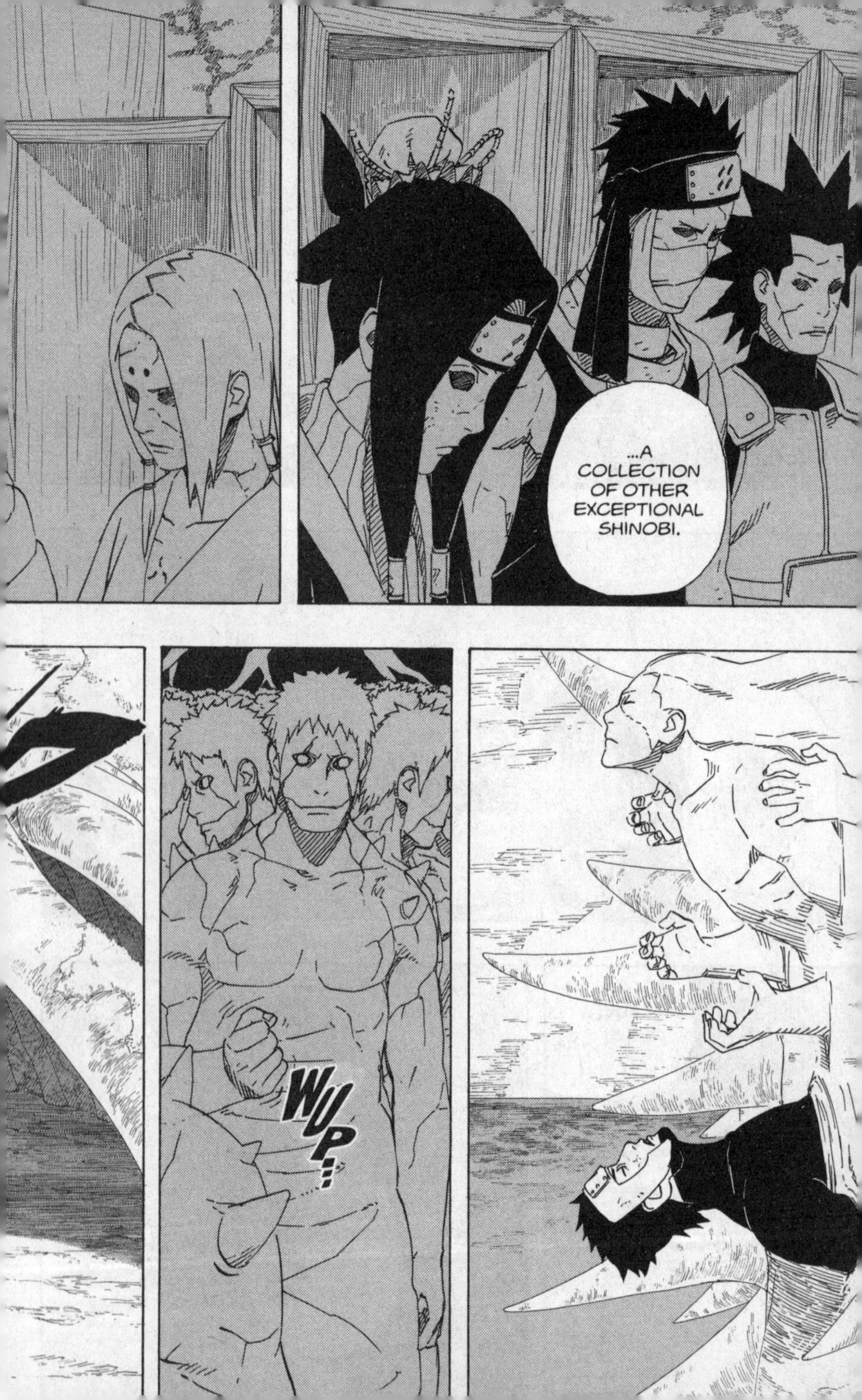
...A COLLECTION OF OTHER EXCEPTIONAL SHINOBI.
WUP...

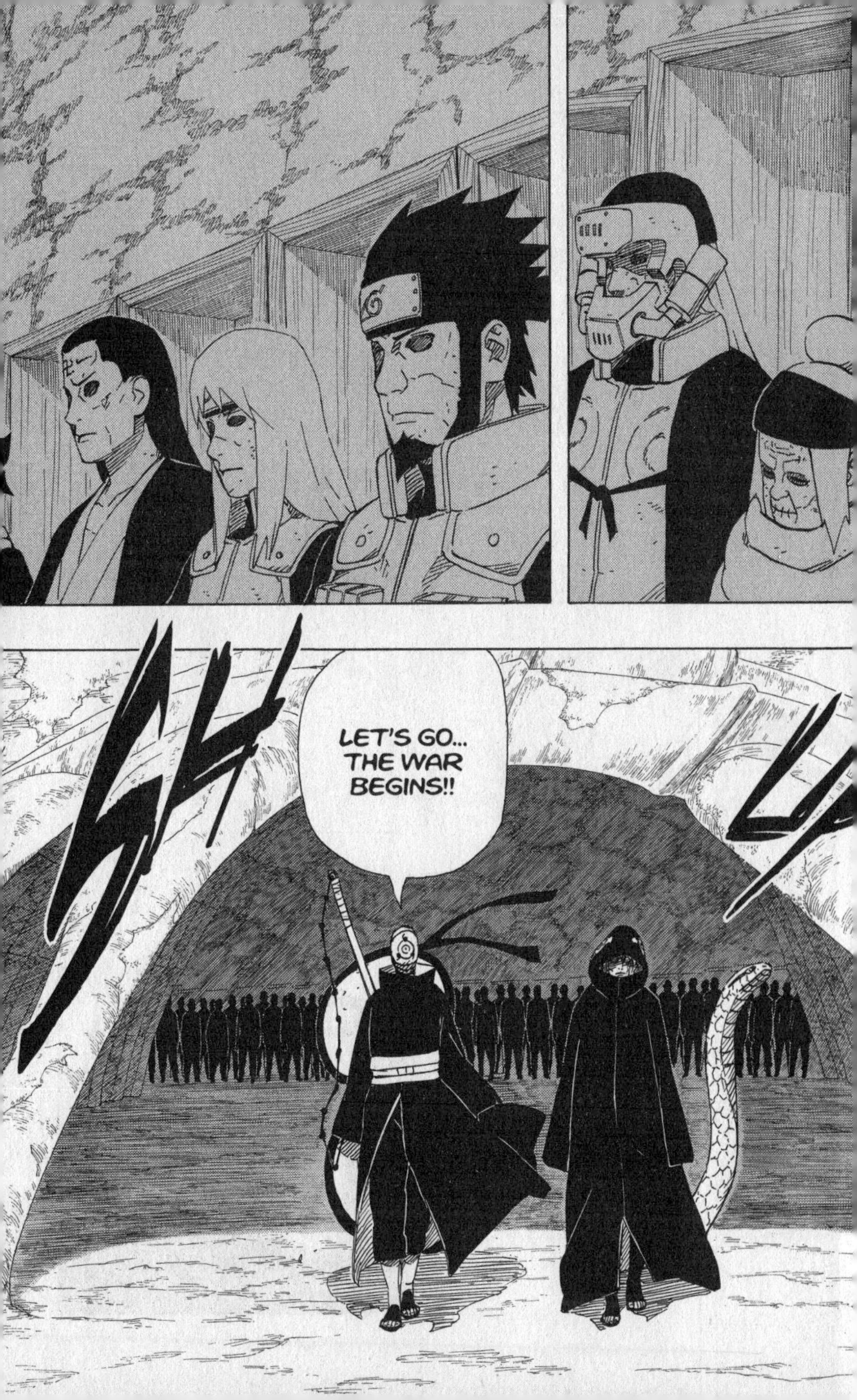
LET'S GO... THE WAR BEGINS!!

# Number 516: Gaara's Speech

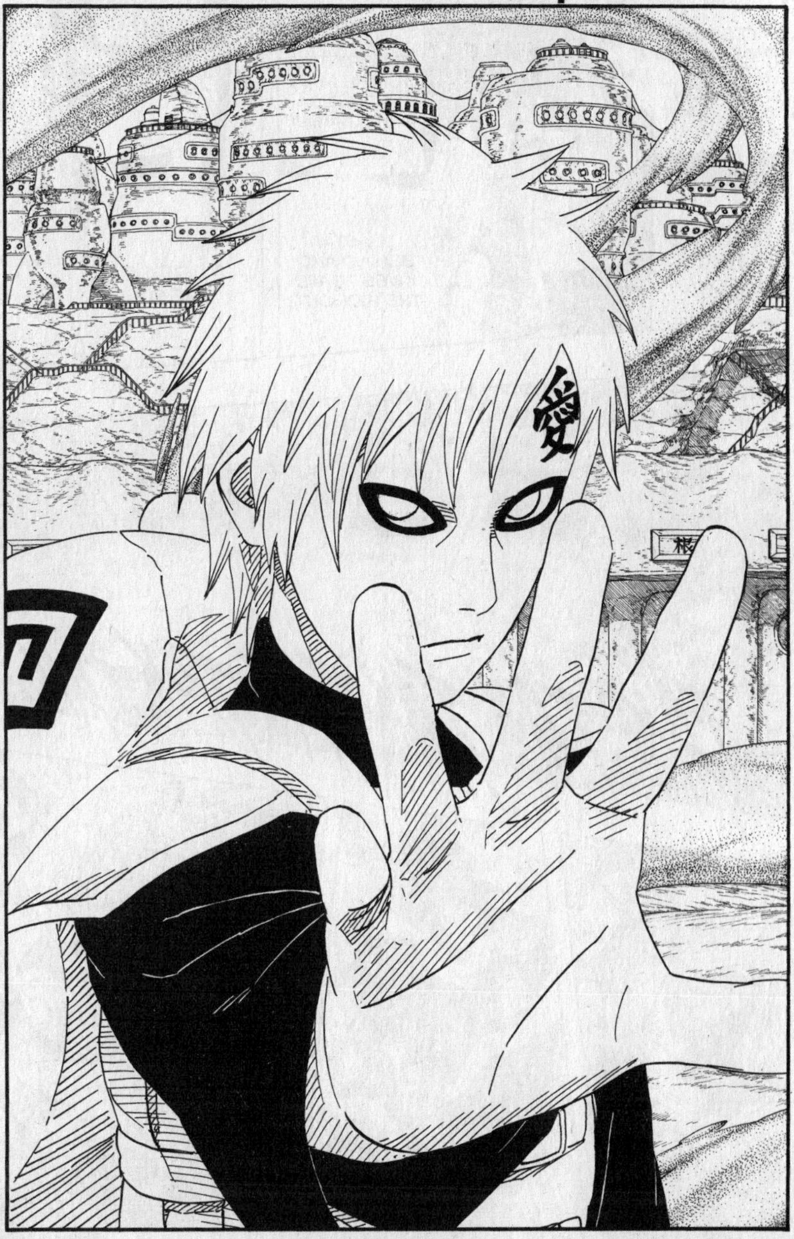

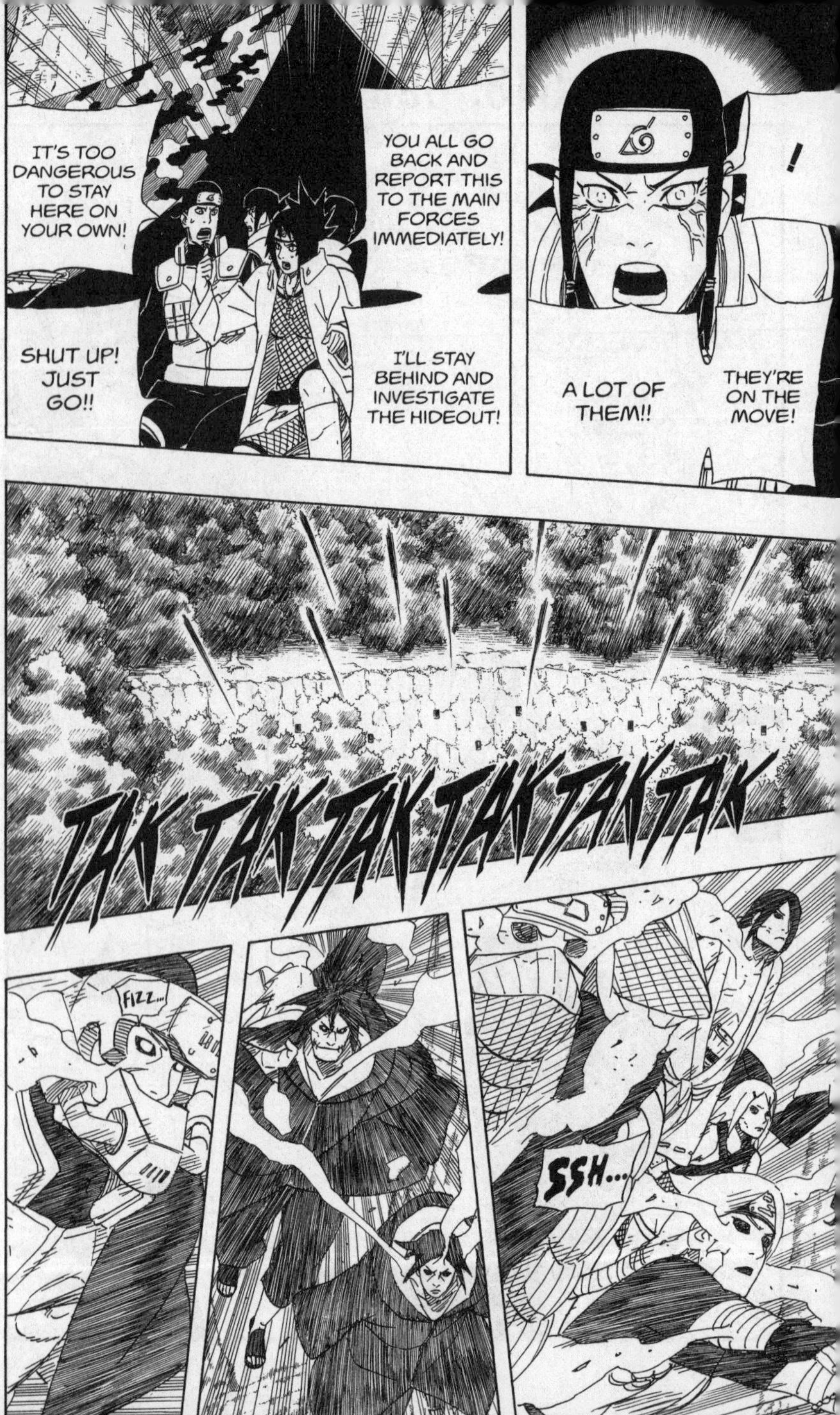
!
THEY'RE ON THE MOVE!
A LOT OF THEM!!
YOU ALL GO BACK AND REPORT THIS TO THE MAIN FORCES IMMEDIATELY!
I'LL STAY BEHIND AND INVESTIGATE THE HIDEOUT!
IT'S TOO DANGEROUS TO STAY HERE ON YOUR OWN!
SHUT UP! JUST GO!!
TAK TAK TAK TAK TAK TAK
SSH...
FIZZ...

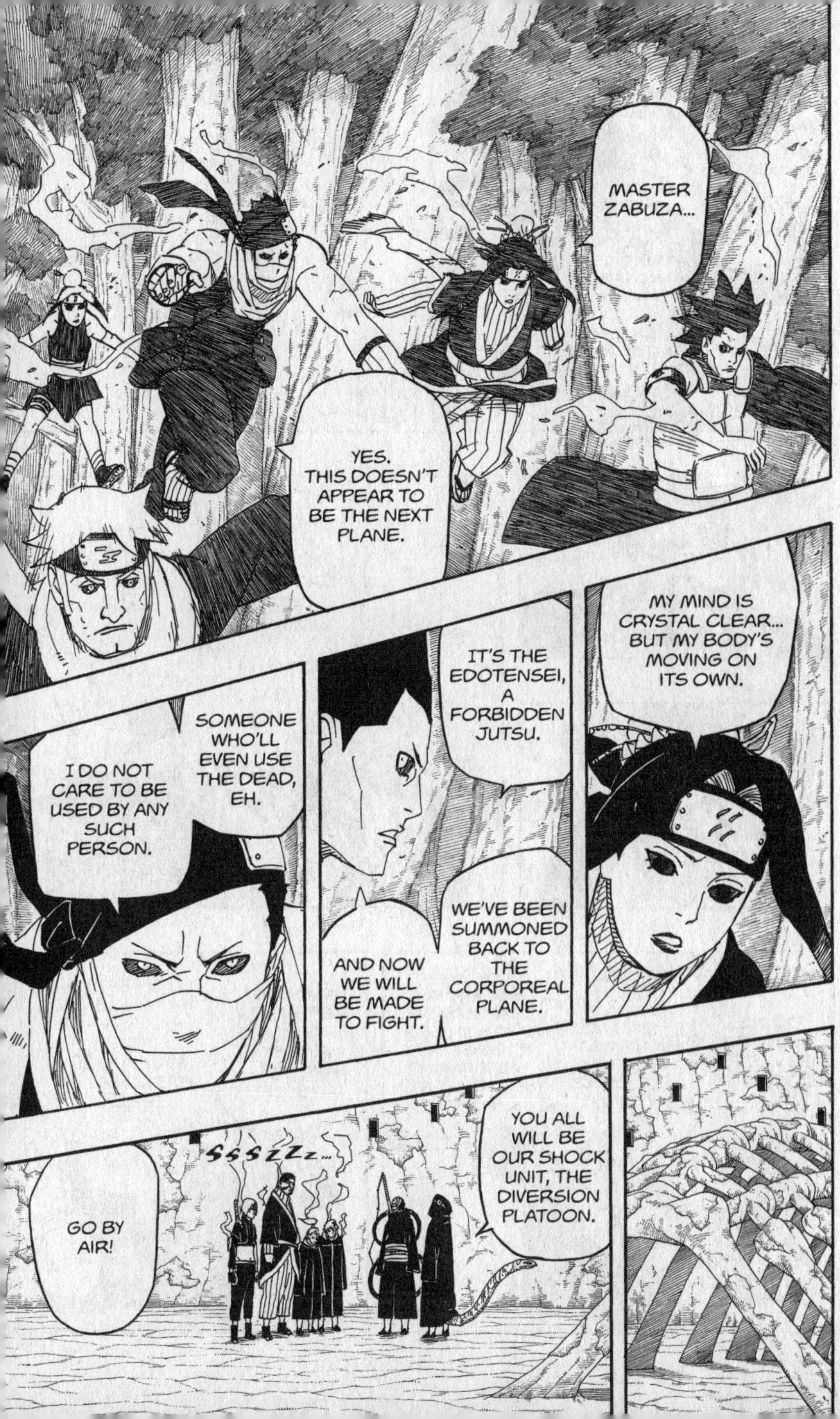
MASTER ZABUZA...
YES. THIS DOESN'T APPEAR TO BE THE NEXT PLANE.
MY MIND IS CRYSTAL CLEAR... BUT MY BODY'S MOVING ON ITS OWN.
IT'S THE EDOTENSEI, A FORBIDDEN JUTSU.
WE'VE BEEN SUMMONED BACK TO THE CORPOREAL PLANE.
AND NOW WE WILL BE MADE TO FIGHT.
SOMEONE WHO'LL EVEN USE THE DEAD, EH.
I DO NOT CARE TO BE USED BY ANY SUCH PERSON.
YOU ALL WILL BE OUR SHOCK UNIT, THE DIVERSION PLATOON.
SSSZZZ...
GO BY AIR!

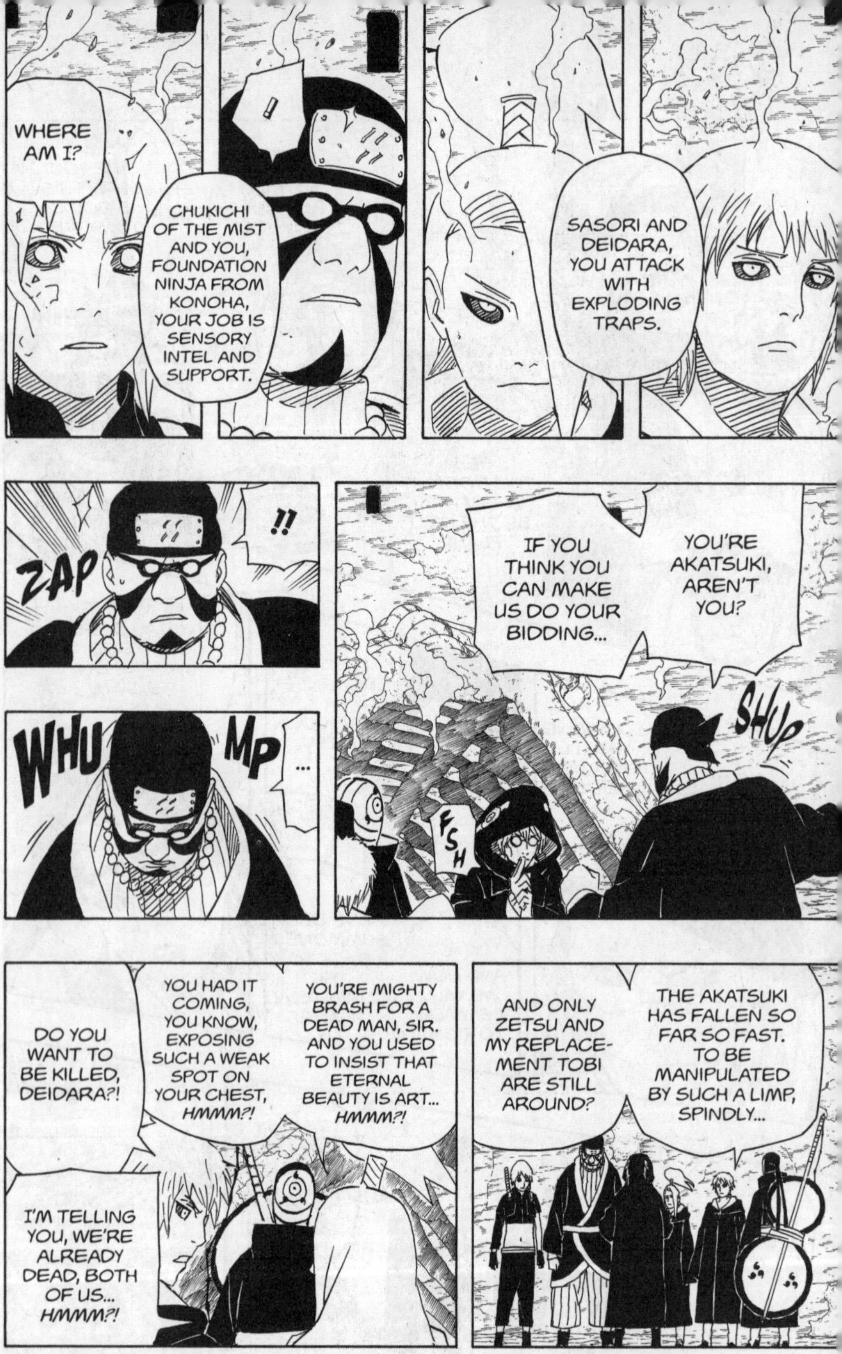
SASORI AND DEIDARA, YOU ATTACK WITH EXPLODING TRAPS.
!
CHUKICHI OF THE MIST AND YOU, FOUNDATION NINJA FROM KONOHA, YOUR JOB IS SENSORY INTEL AND SUPPORT.
WHERE AM I?
YOU'RE AKATSUKI, AREN'T YOU?
IF YOU THINK YOU CAN MAKE US DO YOUR BIDDING...
SHUP
FSH
!!
ZAP
WHUMP
...
THE AKATSUKI HAS FALLEN SO FAR SO FAST. TO BE MANIPULATED BY SUCH A LIMP, SPINDLY...
AND ONLY ZETSU AND MY REPLACEMENT TOBI ARE STILL AROUND?
YOU'RE MIGHTY BRASH FOR A DEAD MAN, SIR. AND YOU USED TO INSIST THAT ETERNAL BEAUTY IS ART... HMMM?!
YOU HAD IT COMING, YOU KNOW, EXPOSING SUCH A WEAK SPOT ON YOUR CHEST, HMMM?!
DO YOU WANT TO BE KILLED, DEIDARA?!
I'M TELLING YOU, WE'RE ALREADY DEAD, BOTH OF US... HMMM?!

READ THIS WAY

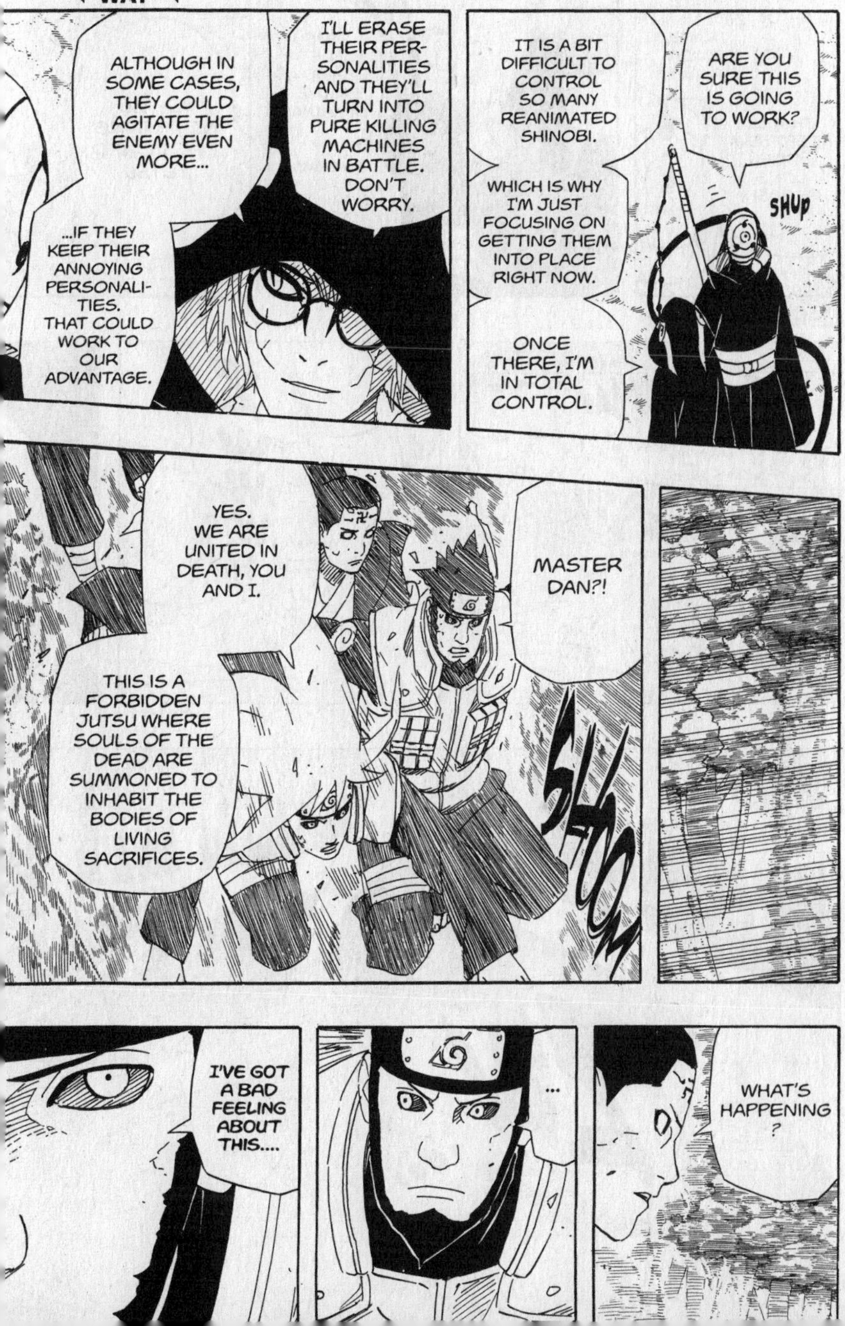
ARE YOU SURE THIS IS GOING TO WORK?
SHUP
IT IS A BIT DIFFICULT TO CONTROL SO MANY REANIMATED SHINOBI.
WHICH IS WHY I'M JUST FOCUSING ON GETTING THEM INTO PLACE RIGHT NOW.
ONCE THERE, I'M IN TOTAL CONTROL.
I'LL ERASE THEIR PERSONALITIES AND THEY'LL TURN INTO PURE KILLING MACHINES IN BATTLE. DON'T WORRY.
ALTHOUGH IN SOME CASES, THEY COULD AGITATE THE ENEMY EVEN MORE...
...IF THEY KEEP THEIR ANNOYING PERSONALITIES. THAT COULD WORK TO OUR ADVANTAGE.
MASTER DAN?!
SHOOM
YES. WE ARE UNITED IN DEATH, YOU AND I.
THIS IS A FORBIDDEN JUTSU WHERE SOULS OF THE DEAD ARE SUMMONED TO INHABIT THE BODIES OF LIVING SACRIFICES.
WHAT'S HAPPENING?
...
I'VE GOT A BAD FEELING ABOUT THIS....

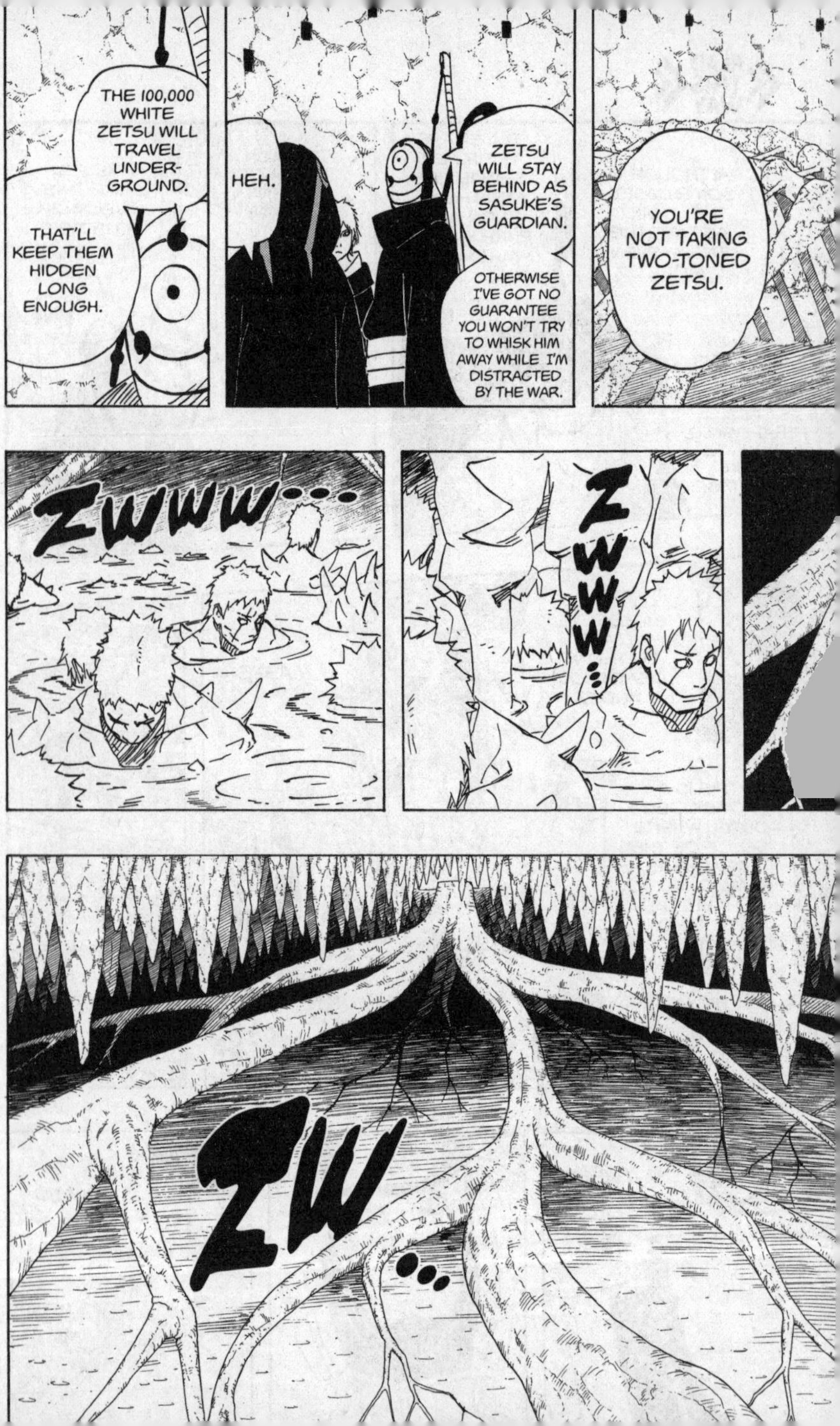
YOU'RE NOT TAKING TWO-TONED ZETSU.
ZETSU WILL STAY BEHIND AS SASUKE'S GUARDIAN.
HEH.
OTHERWISE I'VE GOT NO GUARANTEE YOU WON'T TRY TO WHISK HIM AWAY WHILE I'M DISTRACTED BY THE WAR.
THE 100,000 WHITE ZETSU WILL TRAVEL UNDER-GROUND.
THAT'LL KEEP THEM HIDDEN LONG ENOUGH.
ZWWWW...
ZWWWW...
ZW...

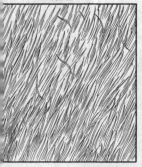

TIME FOR US TO HEAD OUT.

BUT FIRST...

FORGIVE US, CAPTAIN ANKO!! PLEASE BE SAFE!

SHOOM

?!

WHIRL

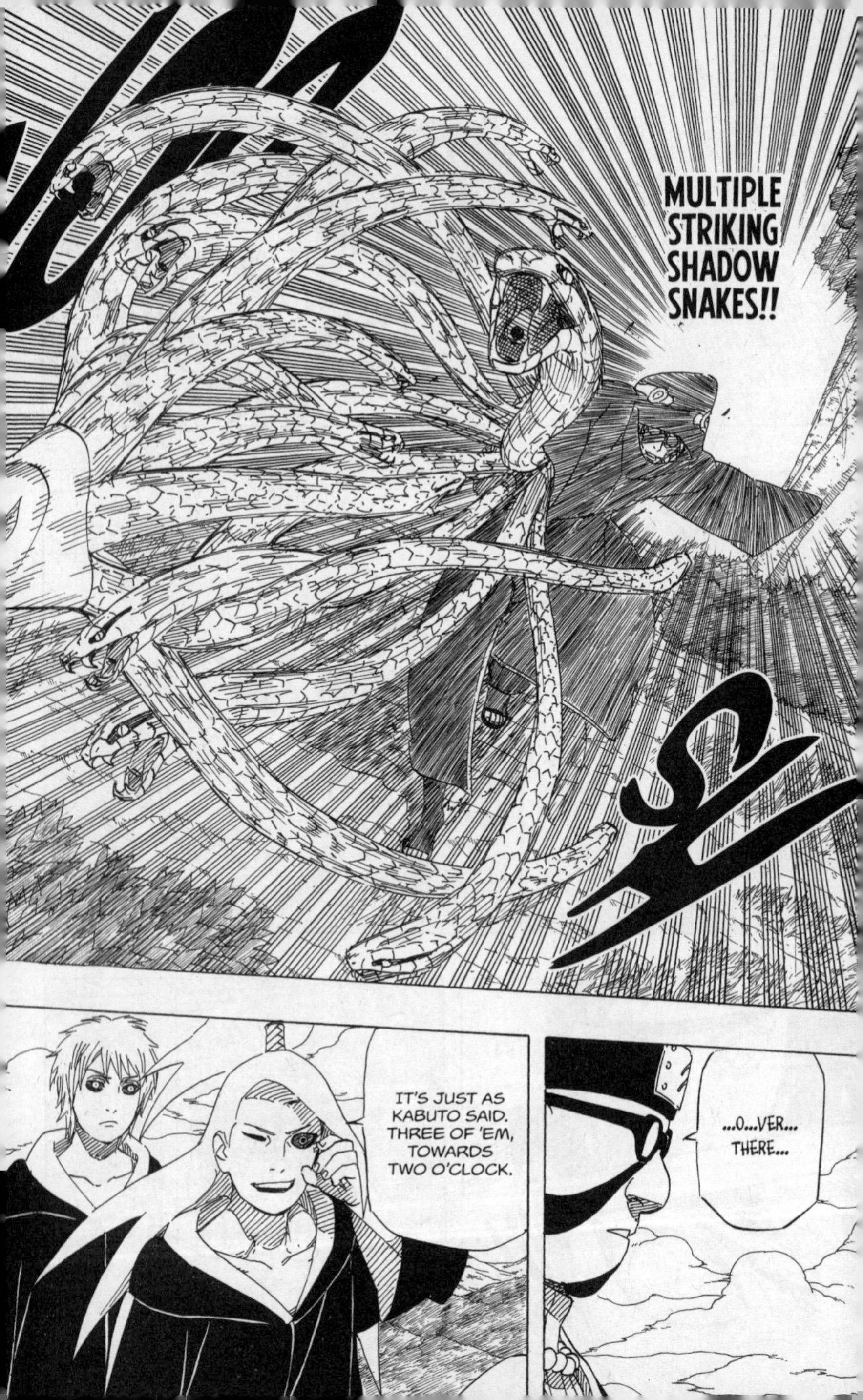
MULTIPLE STRIKING SHADOW SNAKES!!
...O...VER... THERE...
IT'S JUST AS KABUTO SAID. THREE OF 'EM, TOWARDS TWO O'CLOCK.

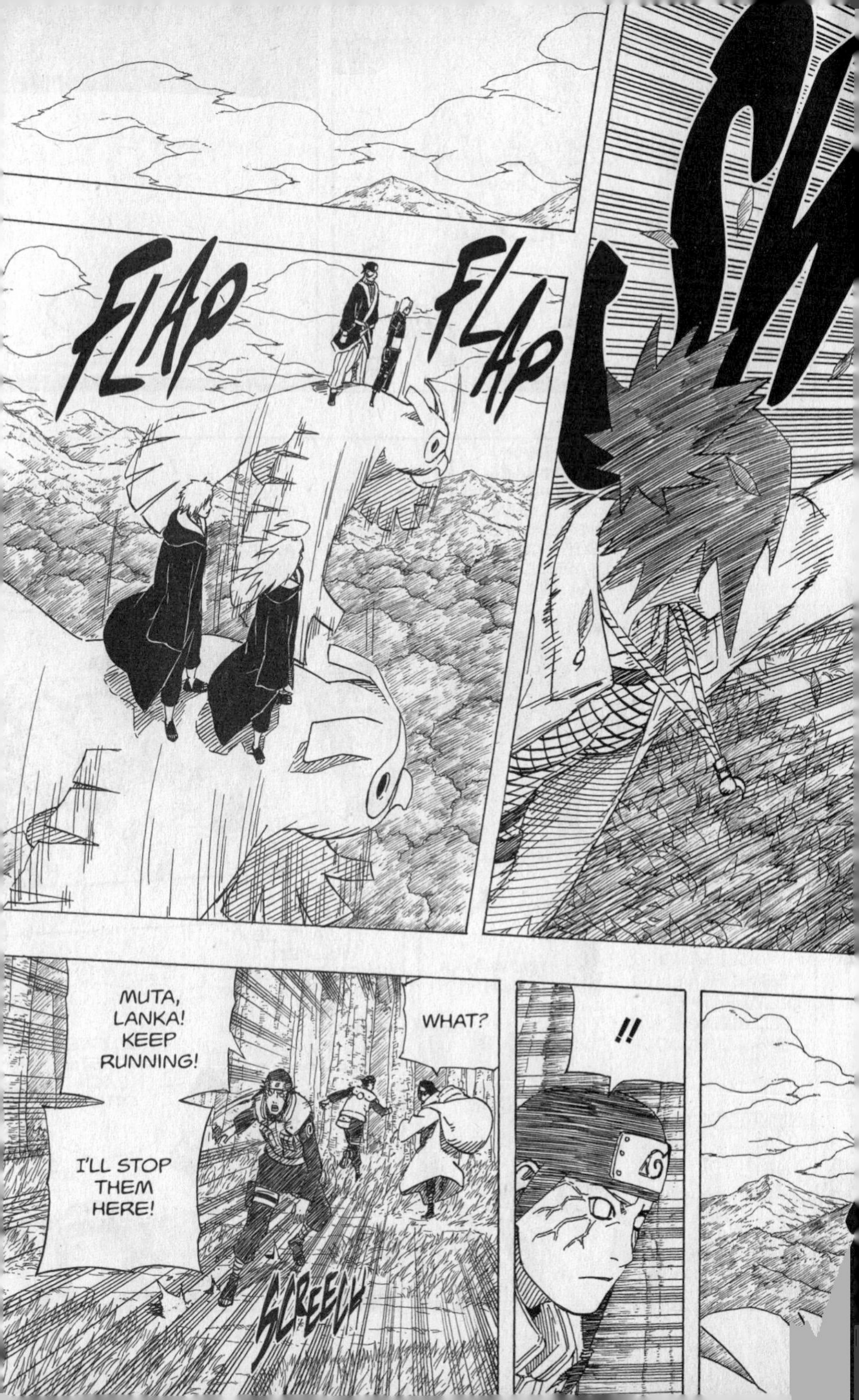
FLAP
FLAP
!!
WHAT?
MUTA, LANKA! KEEP RUNNING!
I'LL STOP THEM HERE!
SCREECH

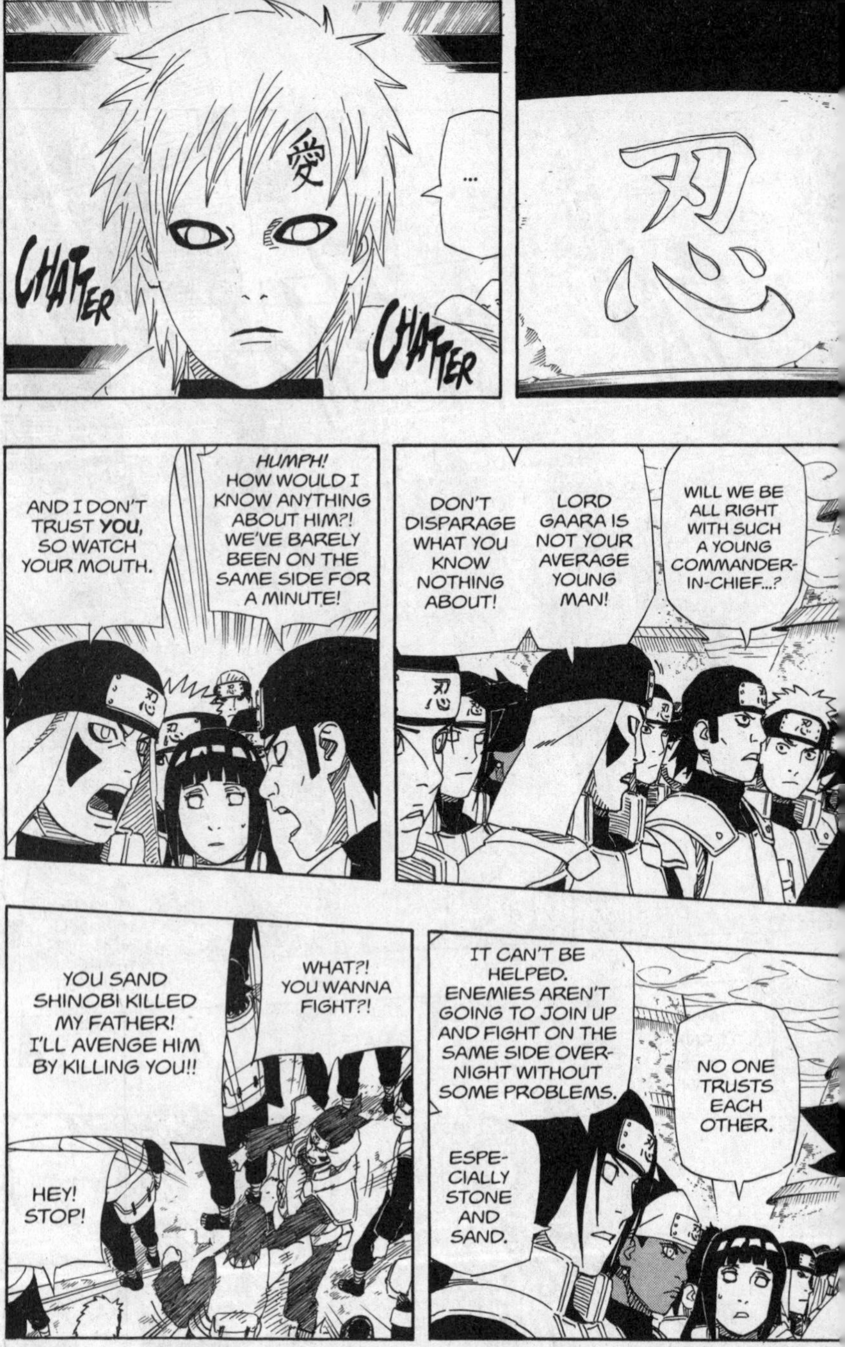
...
CHATTER
CHATTER
WILL WE BE ALL RIGHT WITH SUCH A YOUNG COMMANDER-IN-CHIEF...?
LORD GAARA IS NOT YOUR AVERAGE YOUNG MAN!
DON'T DISPARAGE WHAT YOU KNOW NOTHING ABOUT!
HUMPH! HOW WOULD I KNOW ANYTHING ABOUT HIM?! WE'VE BARELY BEEN ON THE SAME SIDE FOR A MINUTE!
AND I DON'T TRUST **YOU**, SO WATCH YOUR MOUTH.
NO ONE TRUSTS EACH OTHER.
IT CAN'T BE HELPED. ENEMIES AREN'T GOING TO JOIN UP AND FIGHT ON THE SAME SIDE OVER-NIGHT WITHOUT SOME PROBLEMS.
ESPE-CIALLY STONE AND SAND.
WHAT?! YOU WANNA FIGHT?!
YOU SAND SHINOBI KILLED MY FATHER! I'LL AVENGE HIM BY KILLING YOU!!
HEY! STOP!

READ THIS WAY

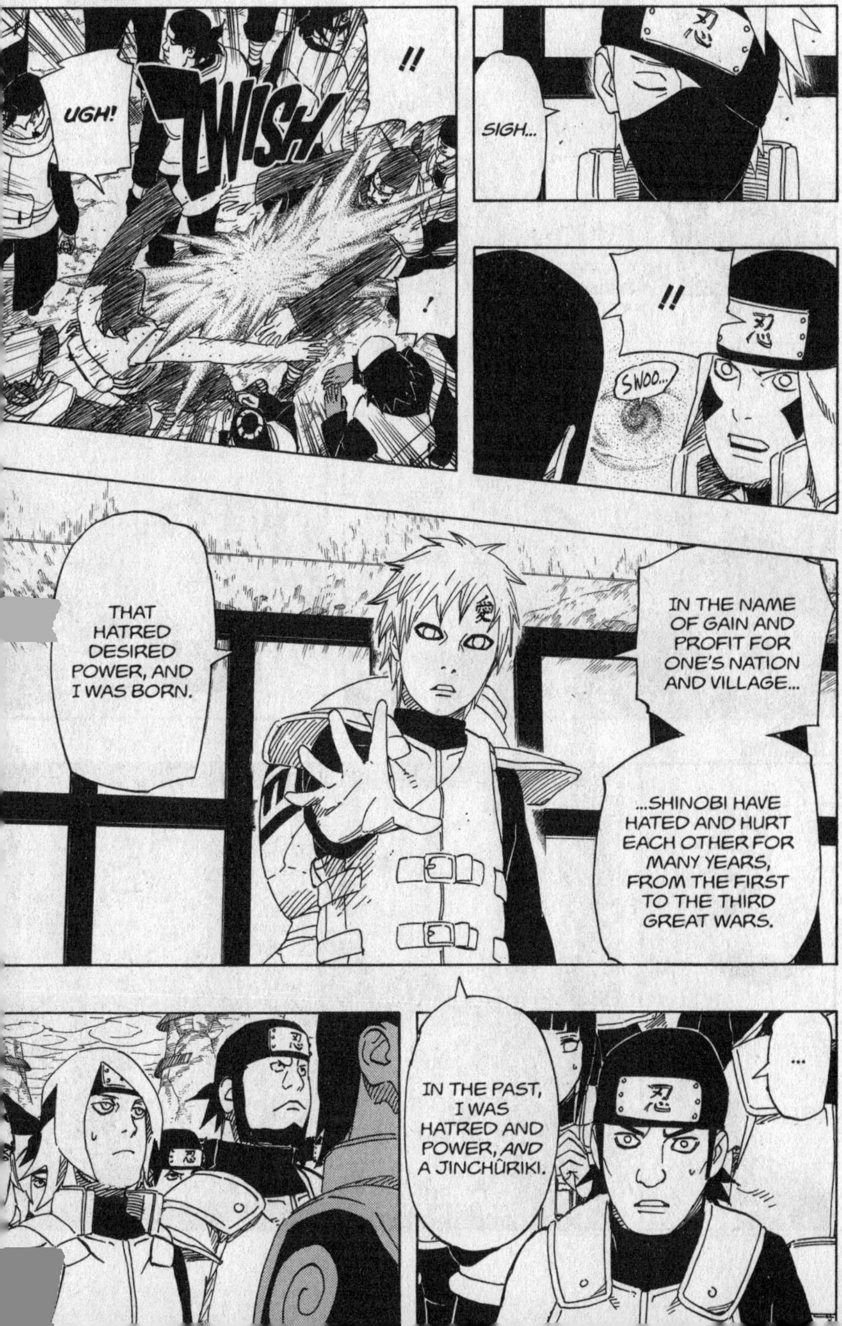
SIGH...
!!
SWOO...
!!
TWISH
UGH!
!
IN THE NAME OF GAIN AND PROFIT FOR ONE'S NATION AND VILLAGE...
...SHINOBI HAVE HATED AND HURT EACH OTHER FOR MANY YEARS, FROM THE FIRST TO THE THIRD GREAT WARS.
THAT HATRED DESIRED POWER, AND I WAS BORN.
...
IN THE PAST, I WAS HATRED AND POWER, AND A JINCHÛRIKI.

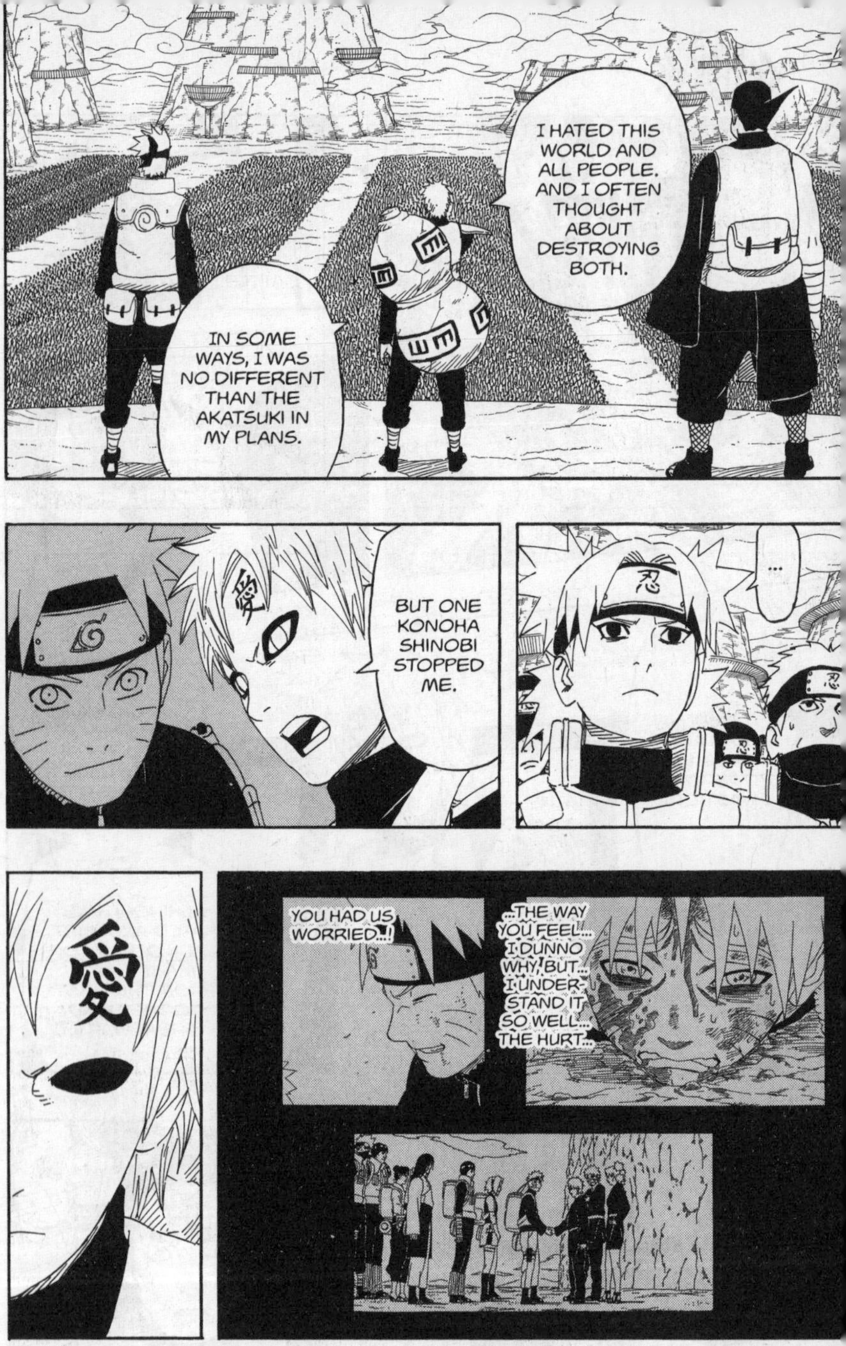

I HATED THIS WORLD AND ALL PEOPLE. AND I OFTEN THOUGHT ABOUT DESTROYING BOTH.
IN SOME WAYS, I WAS NO DIFFERENT THAN THE AKATSUKI IN MY PLANS.
...
BUT ONE KONOHA SHINOBI STOPPED ME.
...THE WAY YOU FEEL... I DUNNO WHY, BUT... I UNDER-STAND IT SO WELL... THE HURT...
YOU HAD US WORRIED...!

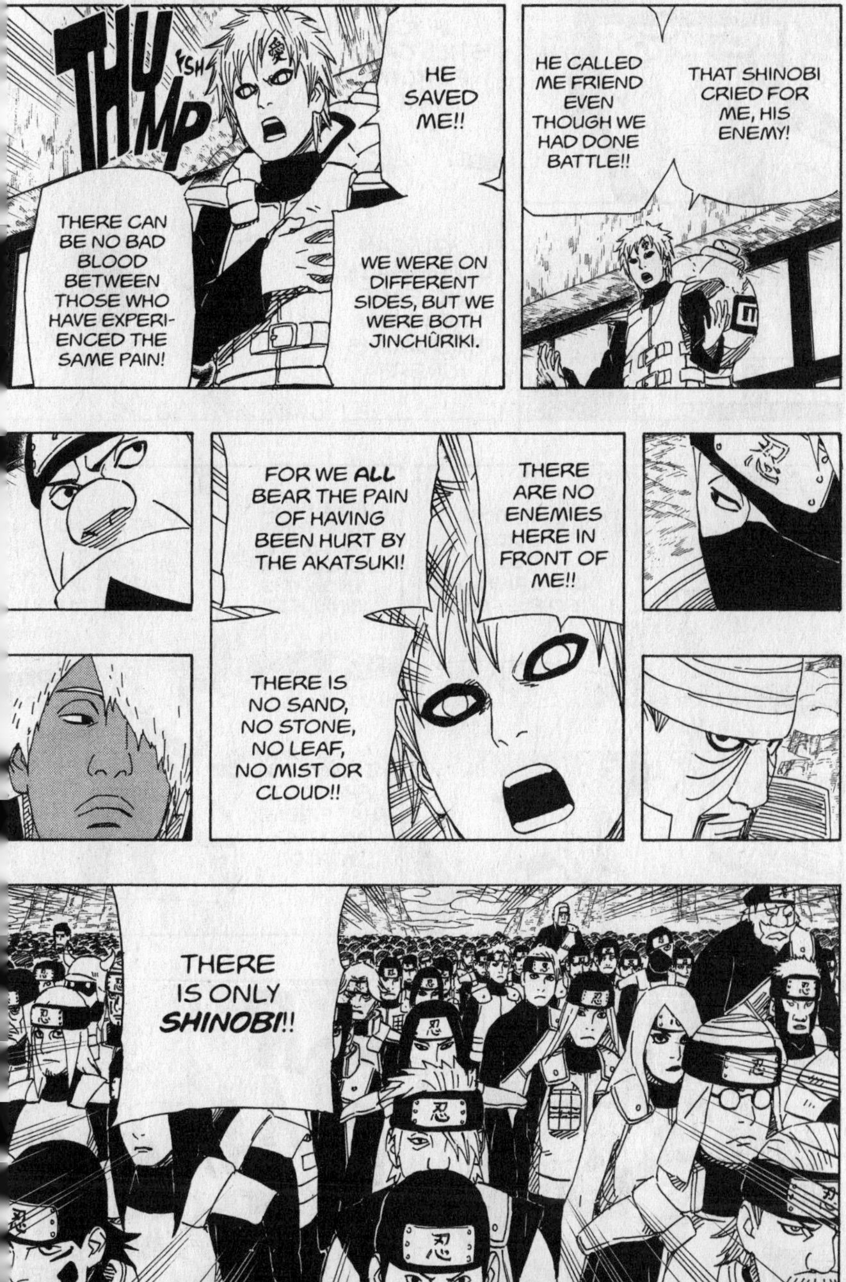
THAT SHINOBI CRIED FOR ME, HIS ENEMY!
HE CALLED ME FRIEND EVEN THOUGH WE HAD DONE BATTLE!!
HE SAVED ME!!
FSH
THUMP
WE WERE ON DIFFERENT SIDES, BUT WE WERE BOTH JINCHÛRIKI.
THERE CAN BE NO BAD BLOOD BETWEEN THOSE WHO HAVE EXPERIENCED THE SAME PAIN!
THERE ARE NO ENEMIES HERE IN FRONT OF ME!!
FOR WE **ALL** BEAR THE PAIN OF HAVING BEEN HURT BY THE AKATSUKI!
THERE IS NO SAND, NO STONE, NO LEAF, NO MIST OR CLOUD!!
THERE IS ONLY ***SHINOBI***!!

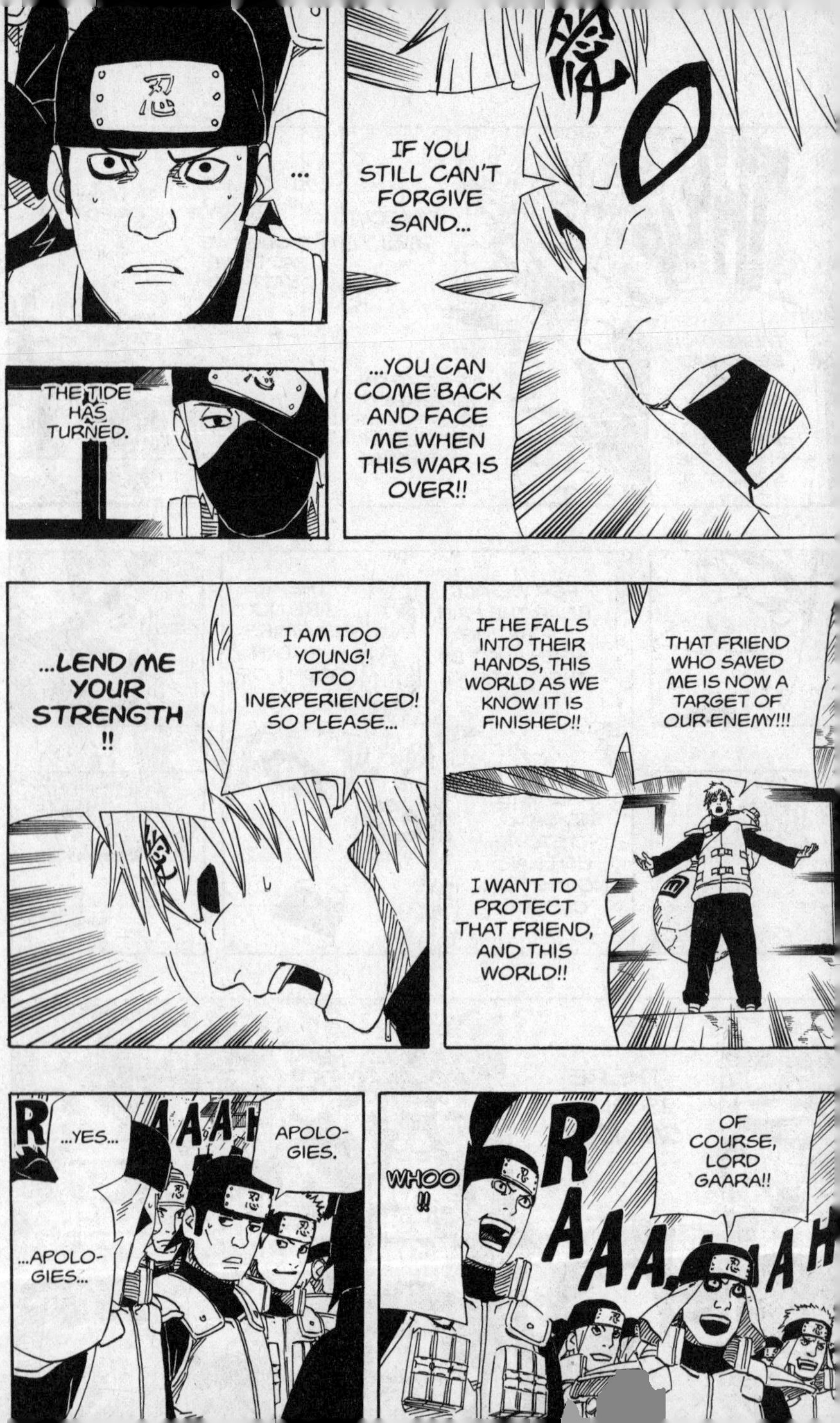
IF YOU STILL CAN'T FORGIVE SAND...
...YOU CAN COME BACK AND FACE ME WHEN THIS WAR IS OVER!!
...
THE TIDE HAS TURNED.
THAT FRIEND WHO SAVED ME IS NOW A TARGET OF OUR ENEMY!!!
IF HE FALLS INTO THEIR HANDS, THIS WORLD AS WE KNOW IT IS FINISHED!!
I WANT TO PROTECT THAT FRIEND, AND THIS WORLD!!
I AM TOO YOUNG! TOO INEXPERIENCED! SO PLEASE...
...LEND ME YOUR STRENGTH!!
OF COURSE, LORD GAARA!!
WHOO!!
RAAAAAAH
APOLOGIES.
...YES...
...APOLOGIES...
RAAAH

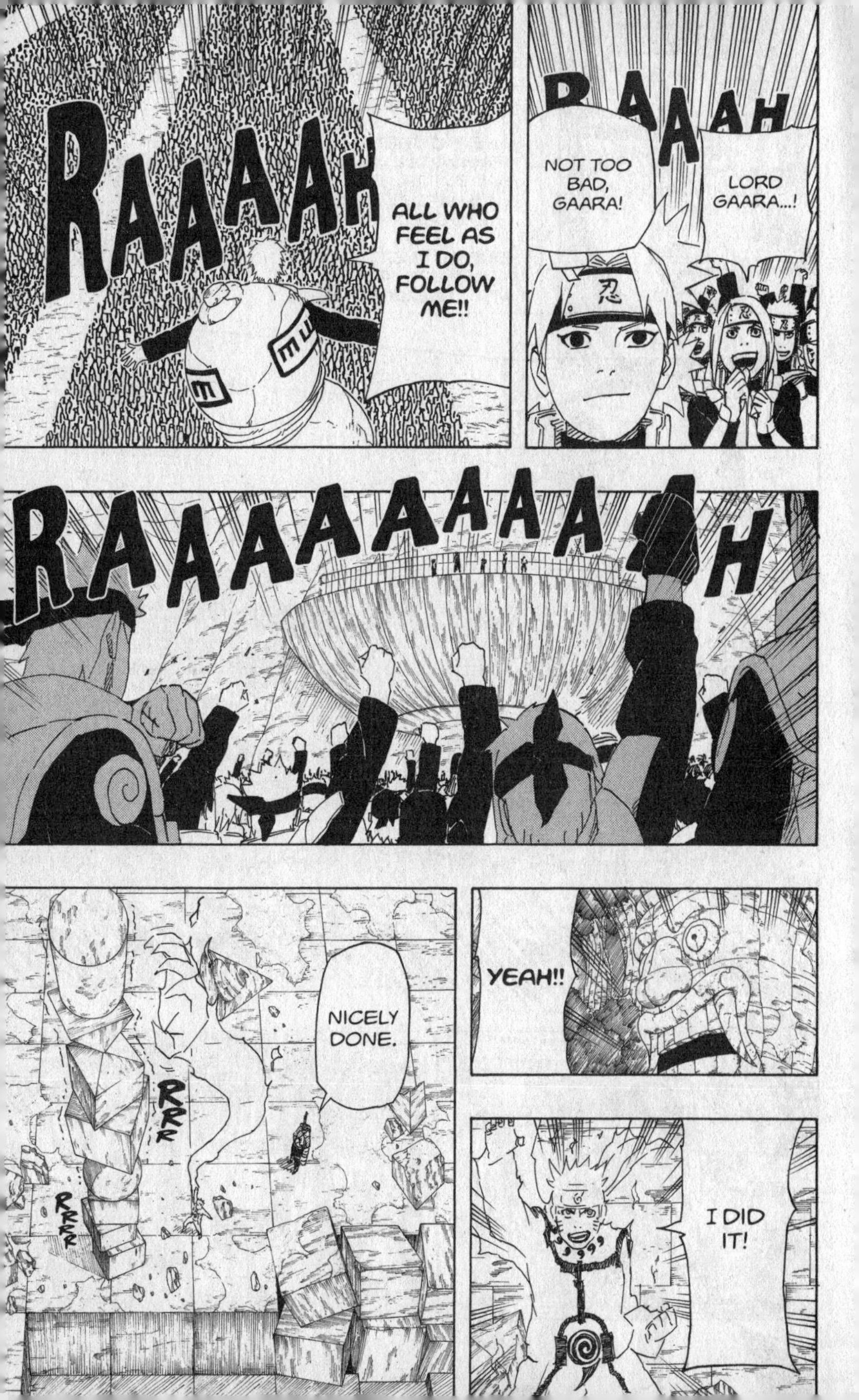
RAAAH
LORD GAARA...!
NOT TOO BAD, GAARA!
RAAAAH
ALL WHO FEEL AS I DO, FOLLOW ME!!
RAAAAAAAAH
YEAH!!
I DID IT!
NICELY DONE.
RRR
RRR

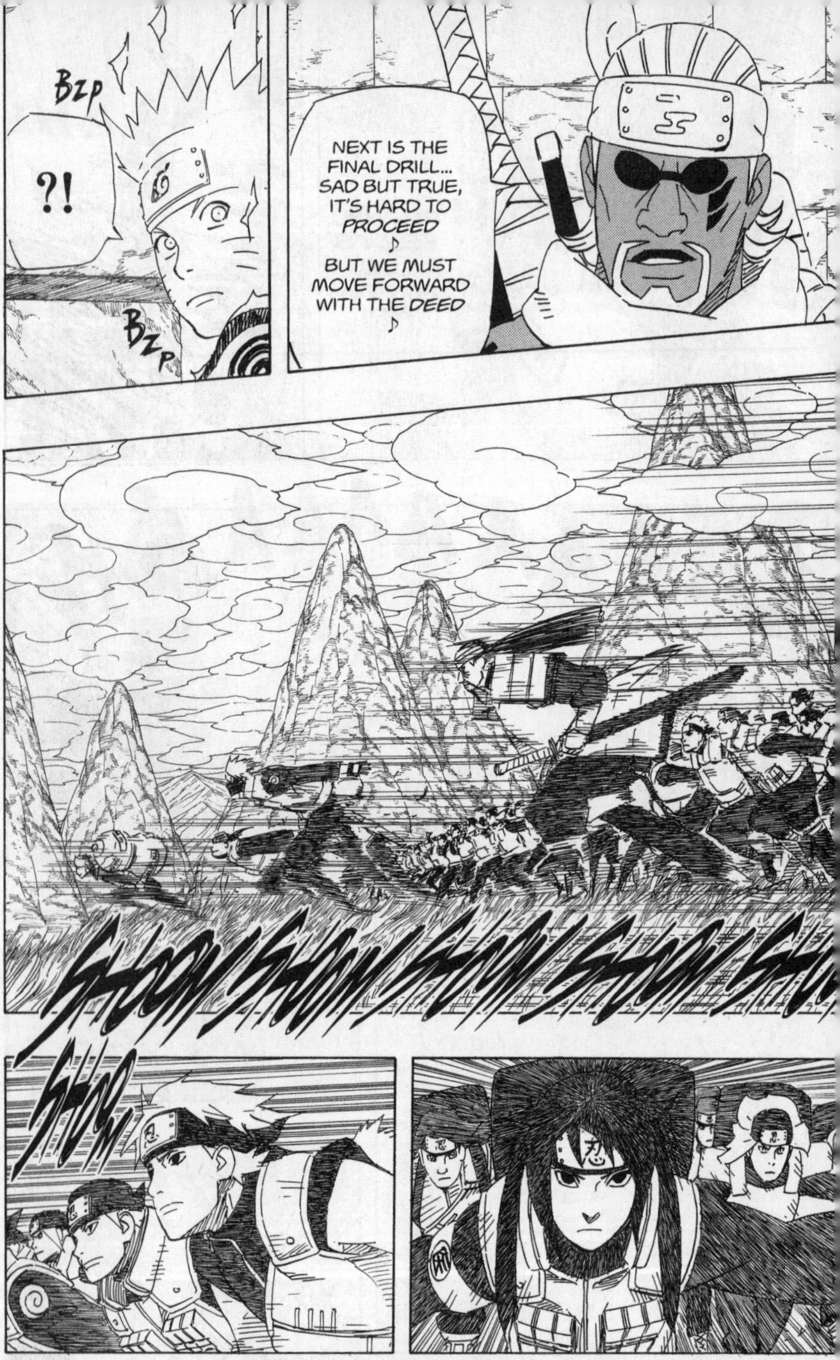
NEXT IS THE FINAL DRILL... SAD BUT TRUE, IT'S HARD TO *PROCEED* ♪ BUT WE MUST MOVE FORWARD WITH THE *DEED* ♪
BZP
?!
BZP

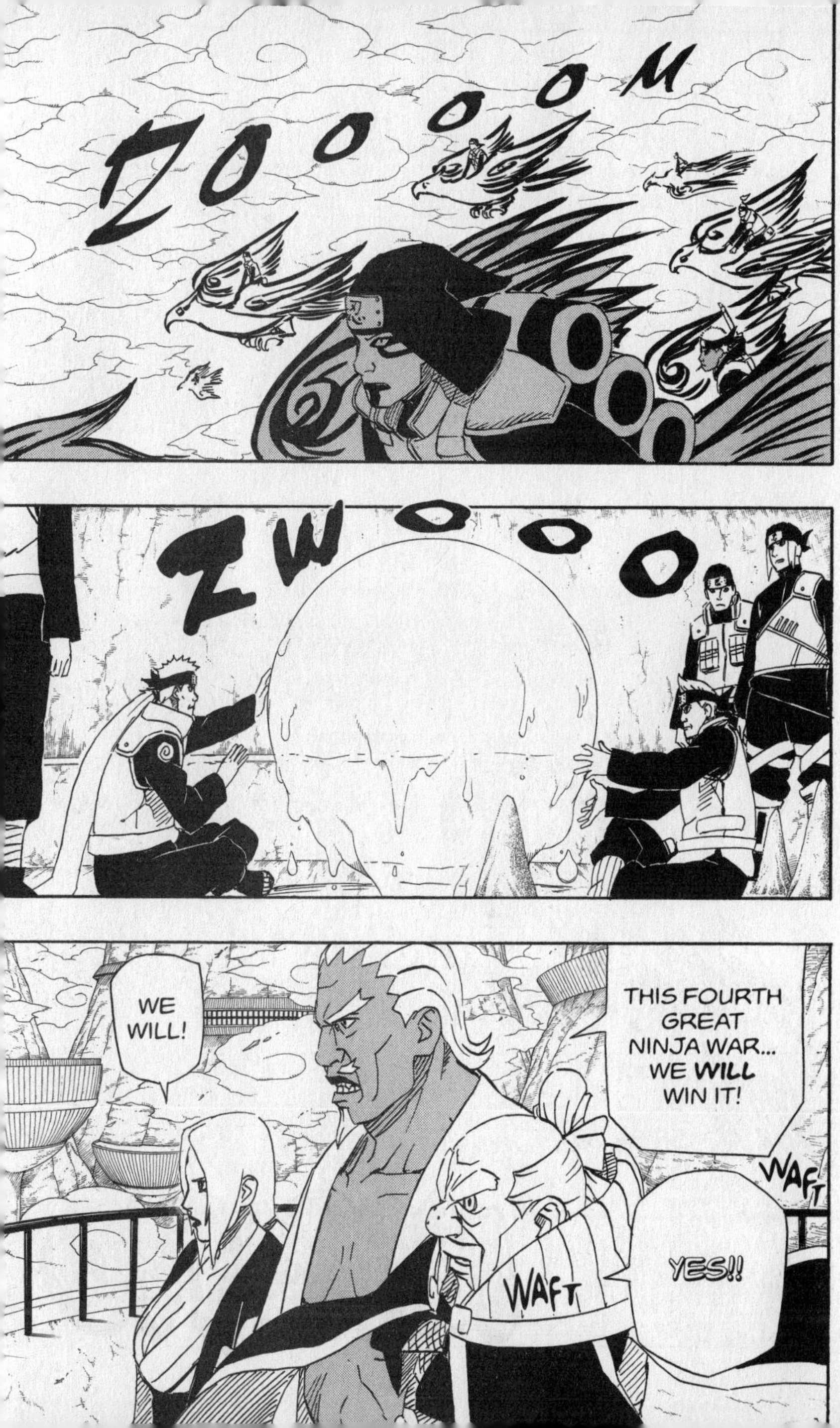
ZOOOOOM
ZWOOOO
THIS FOURTH GREAT NINJA WAR... WE **WILL** WIN IT!
WAFT
YES!!
WAFT
WE WILL!

NARUTO

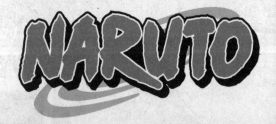

# Number 517: Omoi's War!!

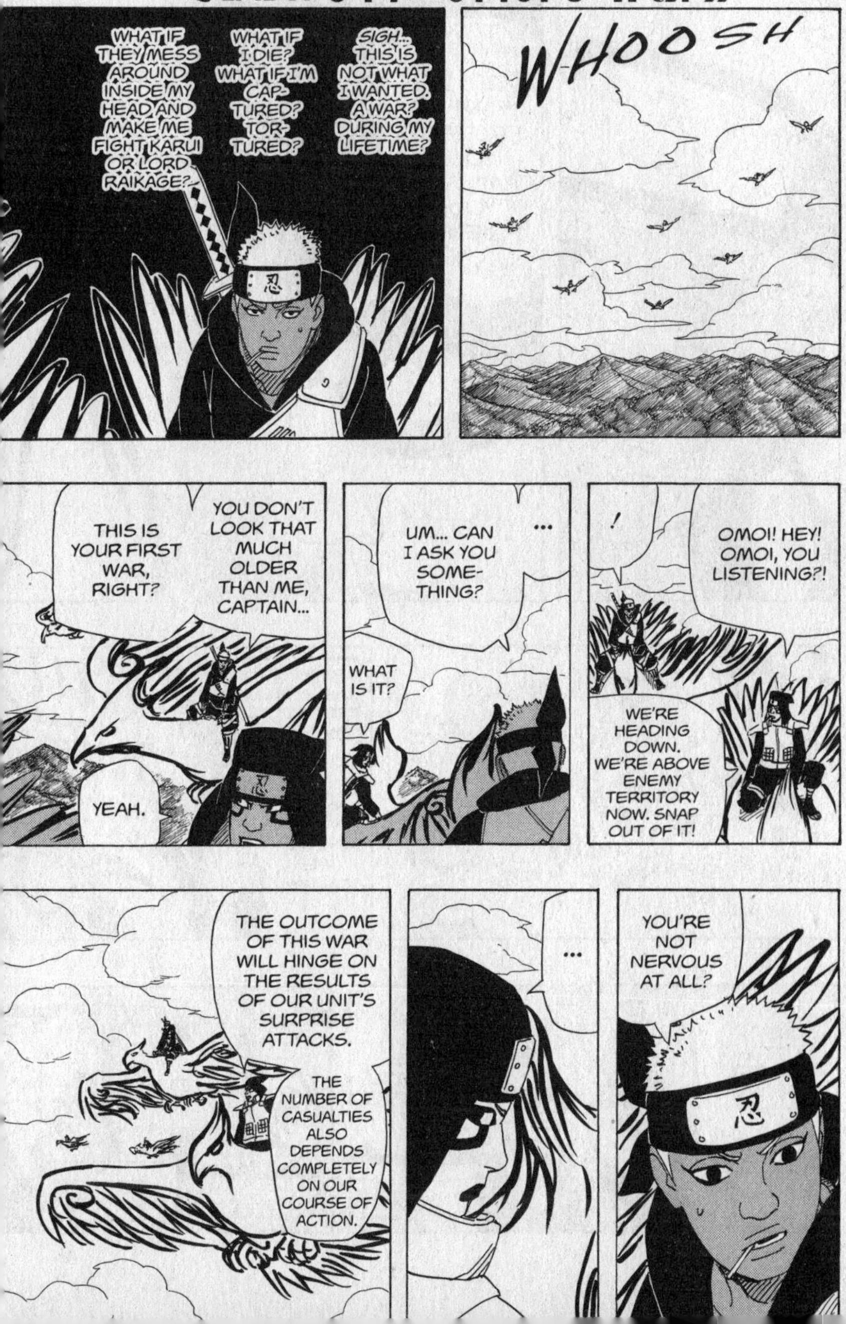
WHOOSH
SIGH... THIS IS NOT WHAT I WANTED. A WAR? DURING MY LIFETIME?
WHAT IF I DIE? WHAT IF I'M CAPTURED? TORTURED?
WHAT IF THEY MESS AROUND INSIDE MY HEAD AND MAKE ME FIGHT KARUI OR LORD RAIKAGE?
OMOI! HEY! OMOI, YOU LISTENING?!
!
WE'RE HEADING DOWN. WE'RE ABOVE ENEMY TERRITORY NOW. SNAP OUT OF IT!
...
UM... CAN I ASK YOU SOMETHING?
WHAT IS IT?
YOU DON'T LOOK THAT MUCH OLDER THAN ME, CAPTAIN...
THIS IS YOUR FIRST WAR, RIGHT?
YEAH.
YOU'RE NOT NERVOUS AT ALL?
...
THE OUTCOME OF THIS WAR WILL HINGE ON THE RESULTS OF OUR UNIT'S SURPRISE ATTACKS.
THE NUMBER OF CASUALTIES ALSO DEPENDS COMPLETELY ON OUR COURSE OF ACTION.

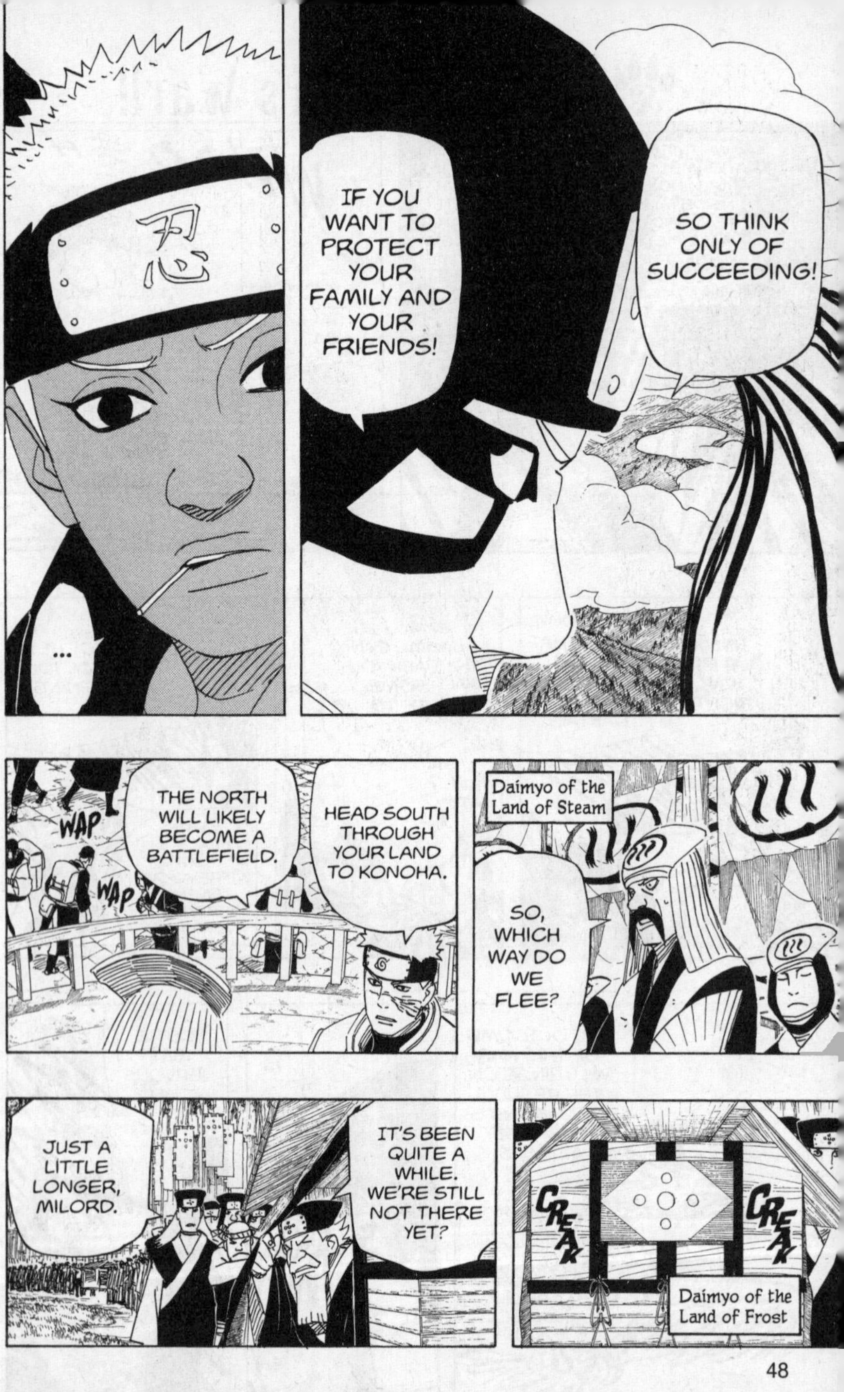
SO THINK ONLY OF SUCCEEDING!
IF YOU WANT TO PROTECT YOUR FAMILY AND YOUR FRIENDS!
...
Daimyo of the Land of Steam
SO, WHICH WAY DO WE FLEE?
HEAD SOUTH THROUGH YOUR LAND TO KONOHA.
THE NORTH WILL LIKELY BECOME A BATTLEFIELD.
WAP
WAP
CREAK
CREAK
Daimyo of the Land of Frost
IT'S BEEN QUITE A WHILE. WE'RE STILL NOT THERE YET?
JUST A LITTLE LONGER, MILORD.

READ THIS WAY

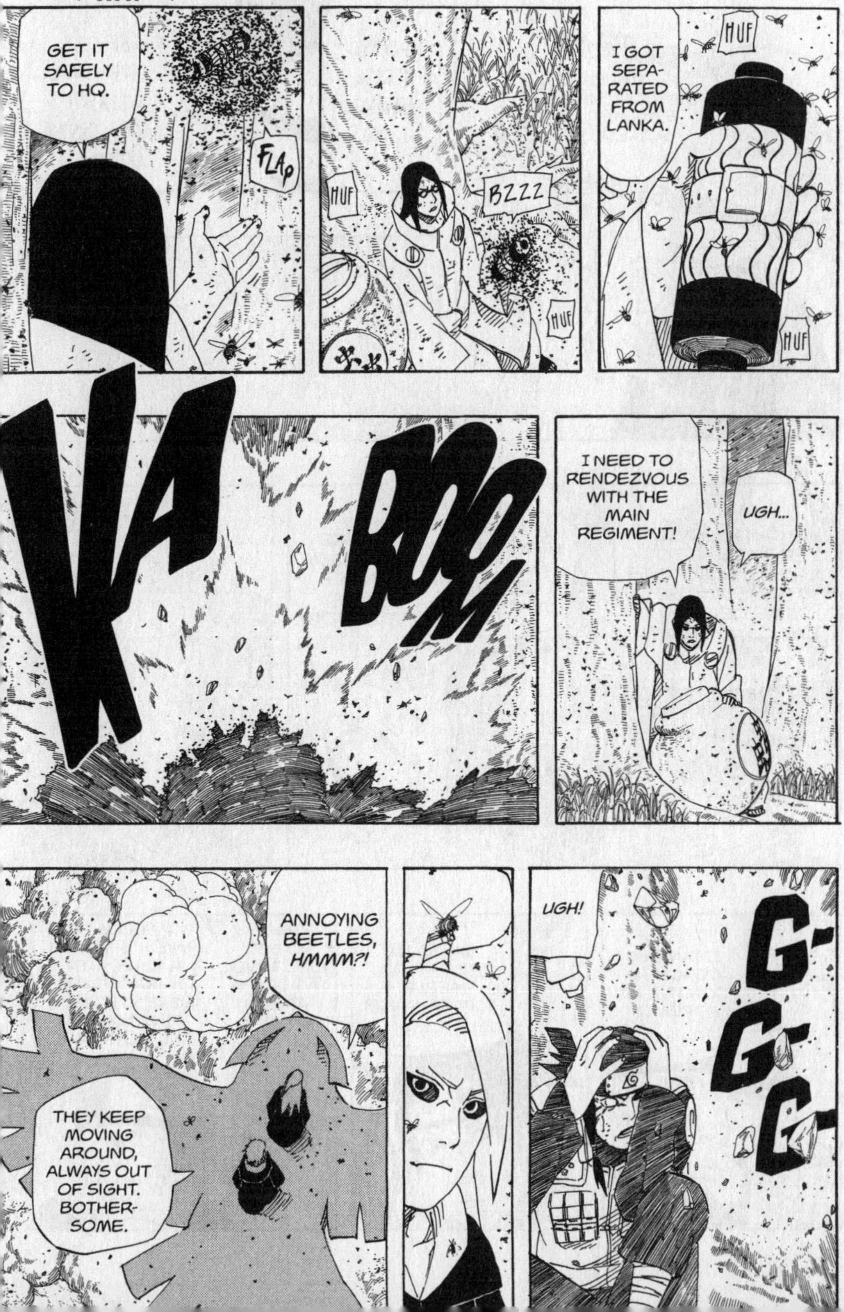
HUF
I GOT SEPA-RATED FROM LANKA.
HUF
HUF
BZZZ
HUF
GET IT SAFELY TO HQ.
FLAP
I NEED TO RENDEZVOUS WITH THE MAIN REGIMENT!
UGH...
KA
BOOM
UGH!
G-G-G
ANNOYING BEETLES, HMMM?!
THEY KEEP MOVING AROUND, ALWAYS OUT OF SIGHT. BOTHER-SOME.

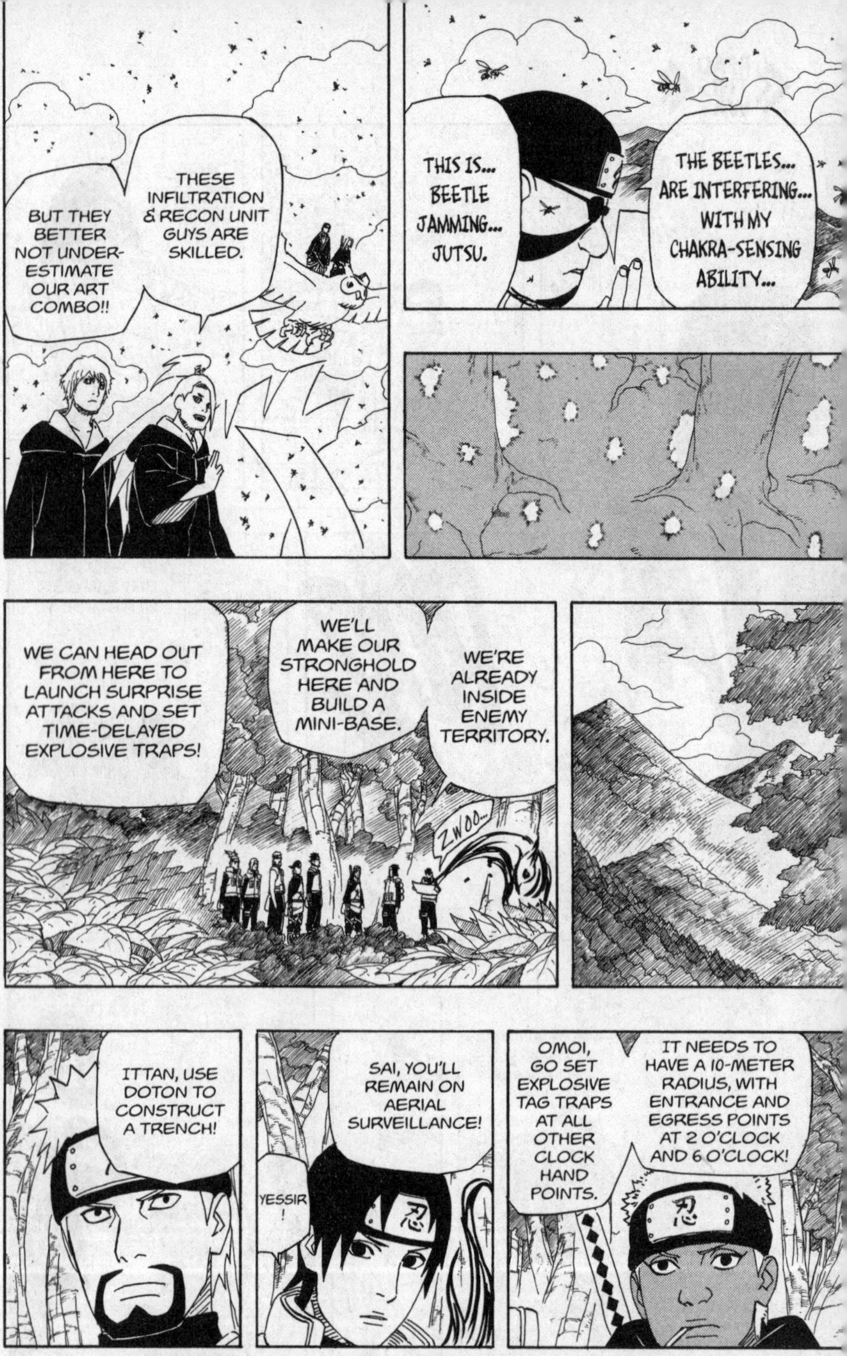
THE BEETLES... ARE INTERFERING... WITH MY CHAKRA-SENSING ABILITY...
THIS IS... BEETLE JAMMING... JUTSU.
THESE INFILTRATION & RECON UNIT GUYS ARE SKILLED.
BUT THEY BETTER NOT UNDER-ESTIMATE OUR ART COMBO!!
WE'RE ALREADY INSIDE ENEMY TERRITORY.
WE'LL MAKE OUR STRONGHOLD HERE AND BUILD A MINI-BASE.
WE CAN HEAD OUT FROM HERE TO LAUNCH SURPRISE ATTACKS AND SET TIME-DELAYED EXPLOSIVE TRAPS!
ZWOO...
IT NEEDS TO HAVE A 10-METER RADIUS, WITH ENTRANCE AND EGRESS POINTS AT 2 O'CLOCK AND 6 O'CLOCK!
OMOI, GO SET EXPLOSIVE TAG TRAPS AT ALL OTHER CLOCK HAND POINTS.
SAI, YOU'LL REMAIN ON AERIAL SURVEILLANCE!
YESSIR!
ITTAN, USE DOTON TO CONSTRUCT A TRENCH!

READ THIS WAY

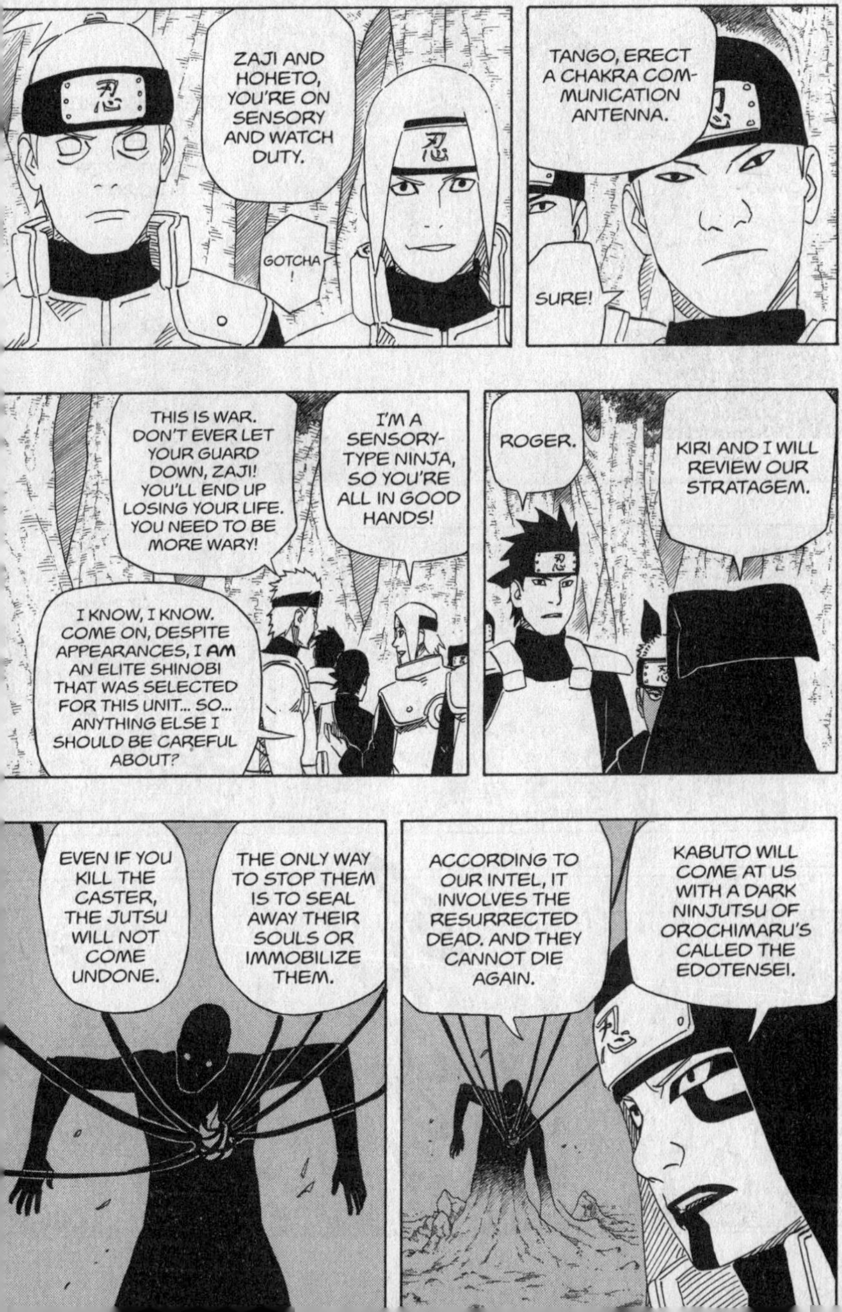
TANGO, ERECT A CHAKRA COMMUNICATION ANTENNA.
SURE!
ZAJI AND HOHETO, YOU'RE ON SENSORY AND WATCH DUTY.
GOTCHA!
KIRI AND I WILL REVIEW OUR STRATAGEM.
ROGER.
I'M A SENSORY-TYPE NINJA, SO YOU'RE ALL IN GOOD HANDS!
THIS IS WAR. DON'T EVER LET YOUR GUARD DOWN, ZAJI! YOU'LL END UP LOSING YOUR LIFE. YOU NEED TO BE MORE WARY!
I KNOW, I KNOW. COME ON, DESPITE APPEARANCES, I **AM** AN ELITE SHINOBI THAT WAS SELECTED FOR THIS UNIT... SO... ANYTHING ELSE I SHOULD BE CAREFUL ABOUT?
KABUTO WILL COME AT US WITH A DARK NINJUTSU OF OROCHIMARU'S CALLED THE EDOTENSEI.
ACCORDING TO OUR INTEL, IT INVOLVES THE RESURRECTED DEAD. AND THEY CANNOT DIE AGAIN.
THE ONLY WAY TO STOP THEM IS TO SEAL AWAY THEIR SOULS OR IMMOBILIZE THEM.
EVEN IF YOU KILL THE CASTER, THE JUTSU WILL NOT COME UNDONE.

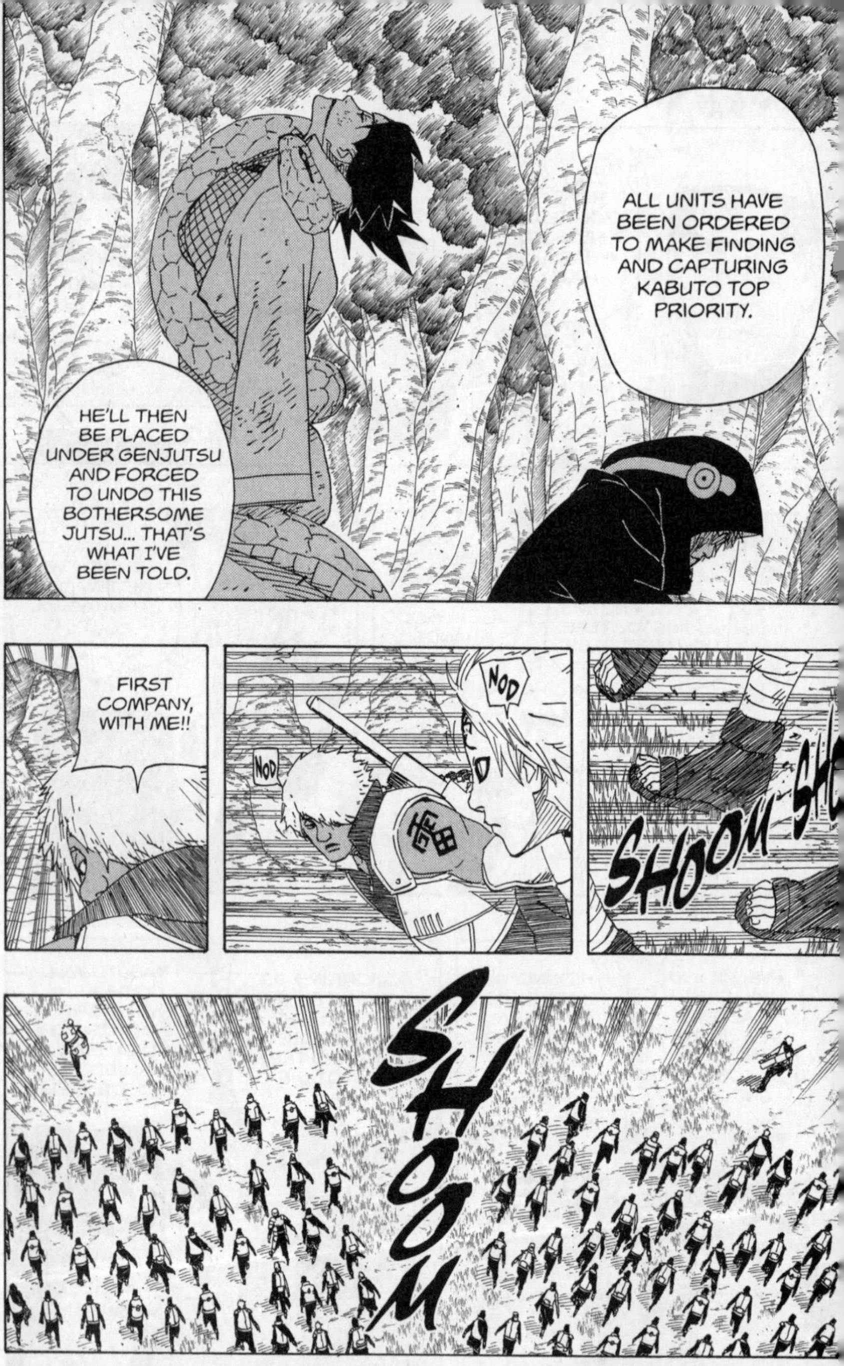
ALL UNITS HAVE BEEN ORDERED TO MAKE FINDING AND CAPTURING KABUTO TOP PRIORITY.
HE'LL THEN BE PLACED UNDER GENJUTSU AND FORCED TO UNDO THIS BOTHERSOME JUTSU... THAT'S WHAT I'VE BEEN TOLD.
SHOOM
NOD
NOD
FIRST COMPANY, WITH ME!!
SHOOM

READ THIS WAY

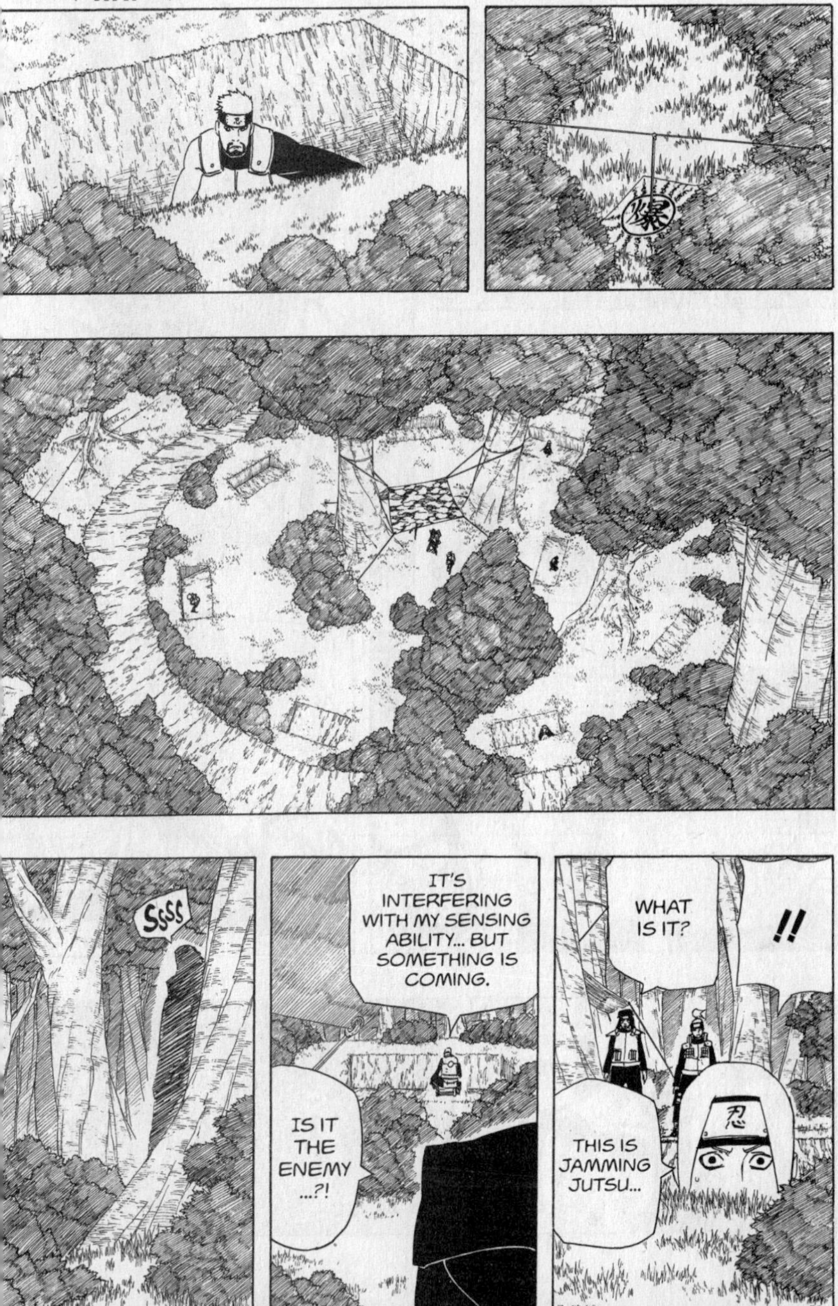
!!
WHAT IS IT?
THIS IS JAMMING JUTSU...
IT'S INTERFERING WITH MY SENSING ABILITY... BUT SOMETHING IS COMING.
IS IT THE ENEMY ...?!
SSSS

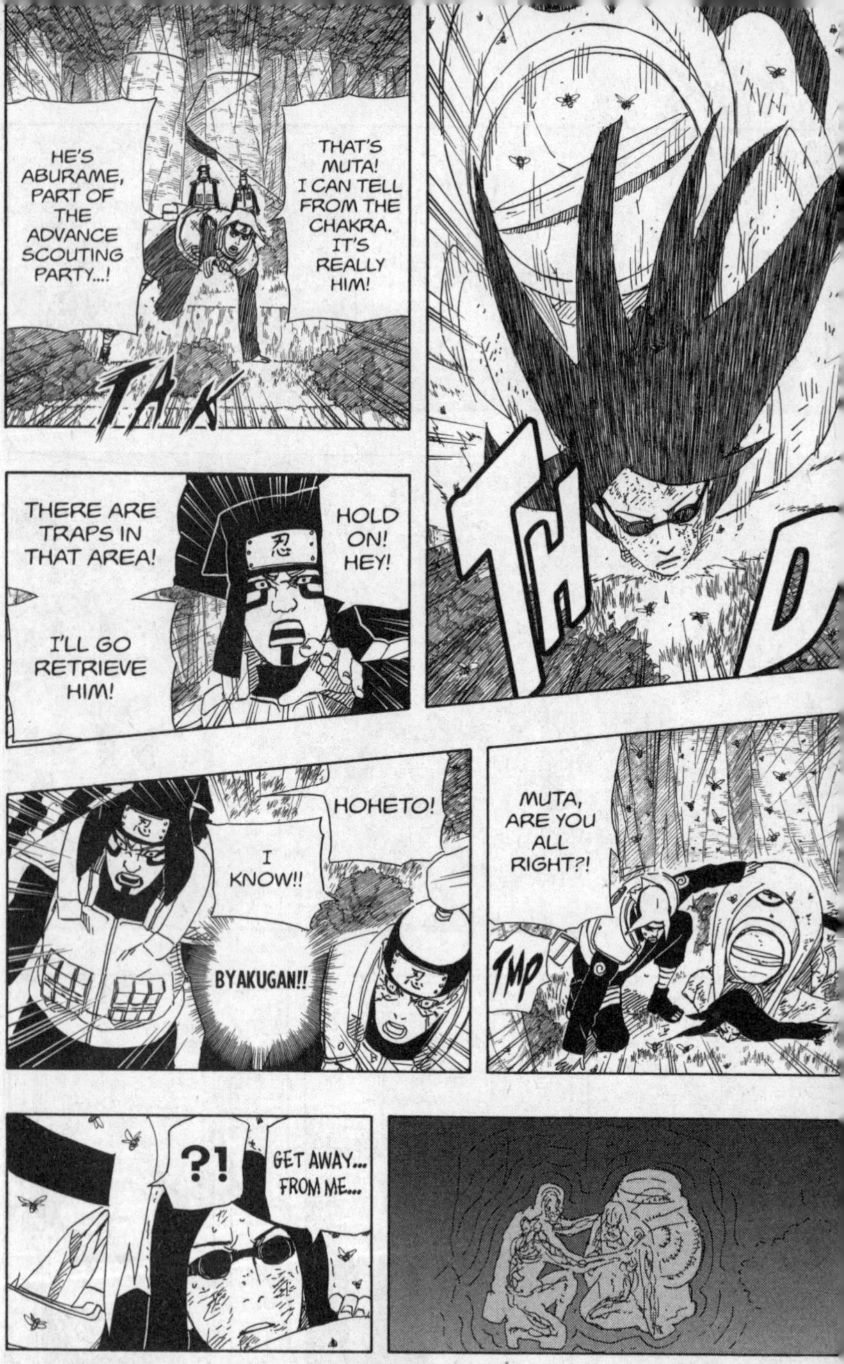
TH D
THAT'S MUTA! I CAN TELL FROM THE CHAKRA. IT'S REALLY HIM!
HE'S ABURAME, PART OF THE ADVANCE SCOUTING PARTY...!
TAK
HOLD ON! HEY!
THERE ARE TRAPS IN THAT AREA!
I'LL GO RETRIEVE HIM!
MUTA, ARE YOU ALL RIGHT?!
TMP
HOHETO!
I KNOW!!
BYAKUGAN!!
GET AWAY... FROM ME...
?!

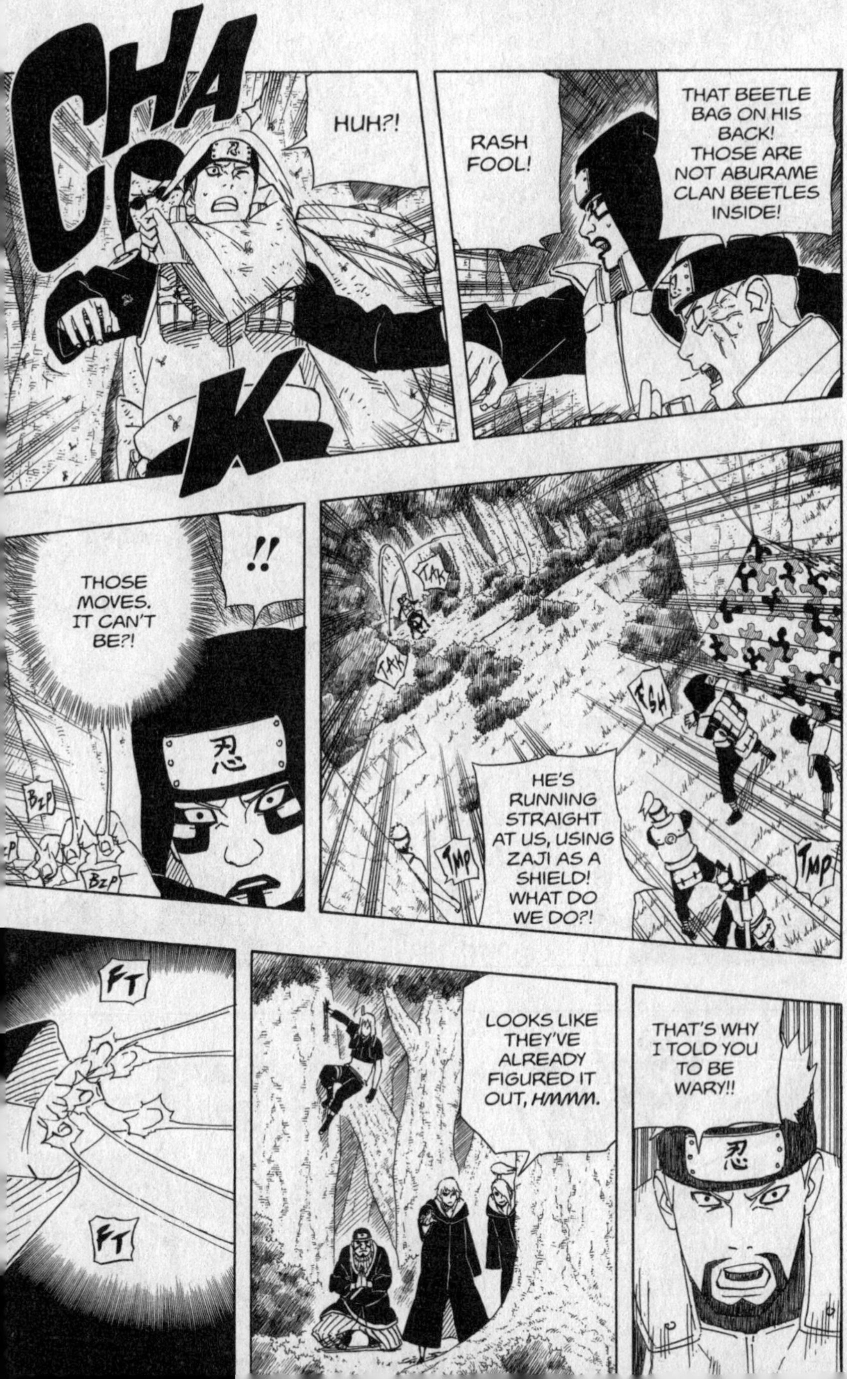
THAT BEETLE BAG ON HIS BACK! THOSE ARE NOT ABURAME CLAN BEETLES INSIDE!
RASH FOOL!
HUH?!
CHAK
TAK
TAK
FSH
TMP
HE'S RUNNING STRAIGHT AT US, USING ZAJI AS A SHIELD! WHAT DO WE DO?!
TMP
!!
THOSE MOVES. IT CAN'T BE?!
BZP
BZP
THAT'S WHY I TOLD YOU TO BE WARY!!
LOOKS LIKE THEY'VE ALREADY FIGURED IT OUT, *HMMM*.
FT
FT

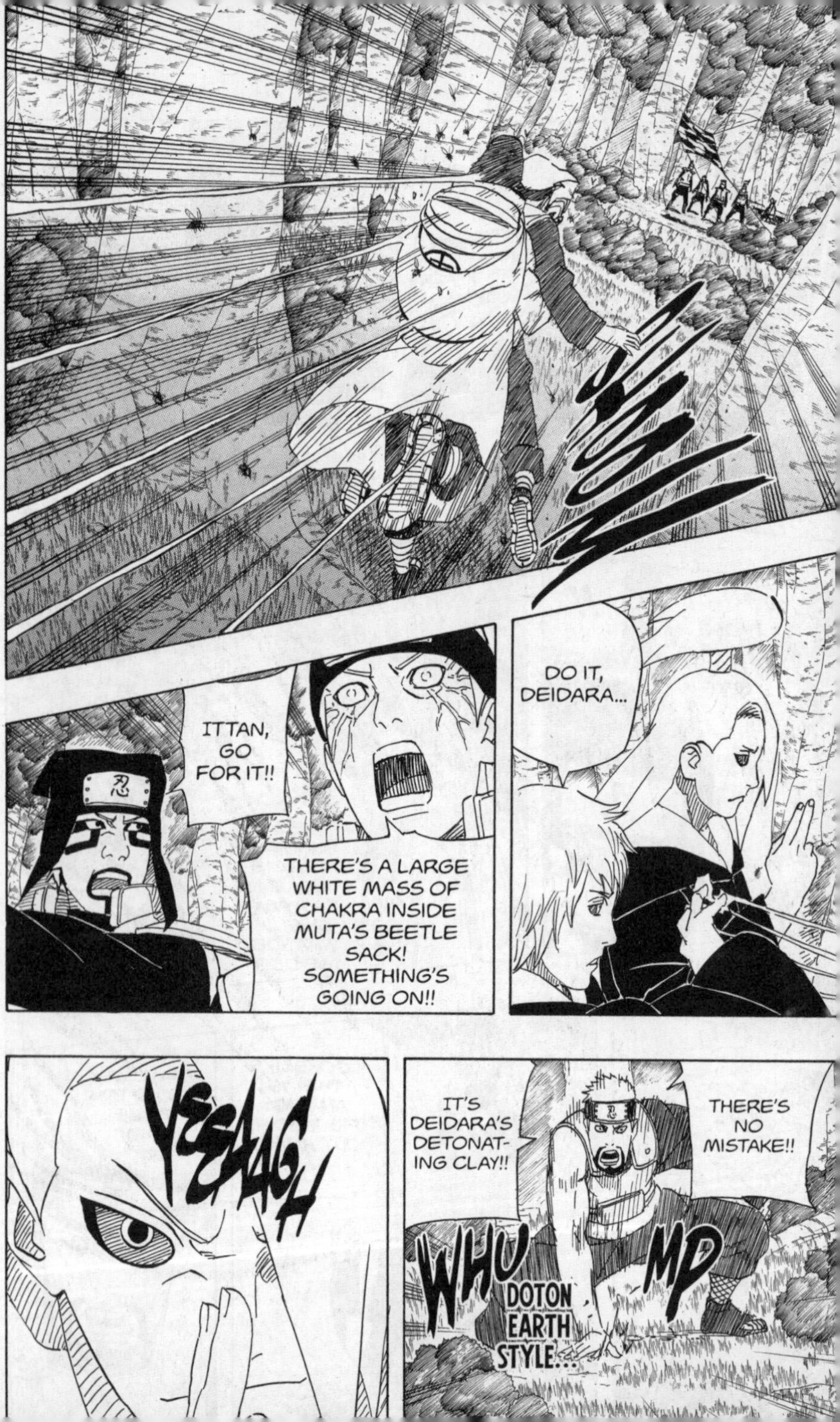
DO IT, DEIDARA...
ITTAN, GO FOR IT!!
THERE'S A LARGE WHITE MASS OF CHAKRA INSIDE MUTA'S BEETLE SACK! SOMETHING'S GOING ON!!
THERE'S NO MISTAKE!!
IT'S DEIDARA'S DETONATING CLAY!!
WHUMP
DOTON EARTH STYLE...
YEAAGH

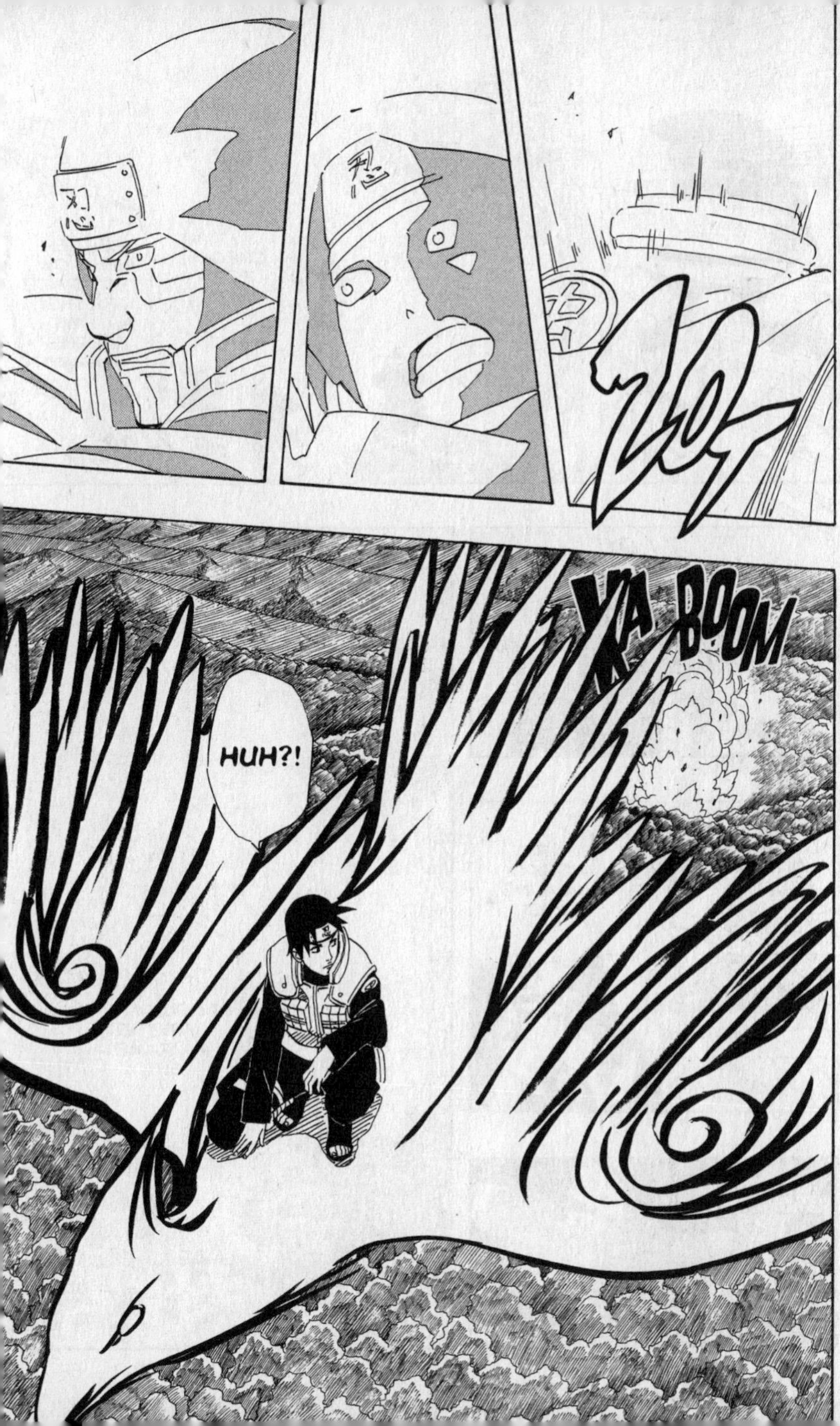
KA BOOM
HUH?!

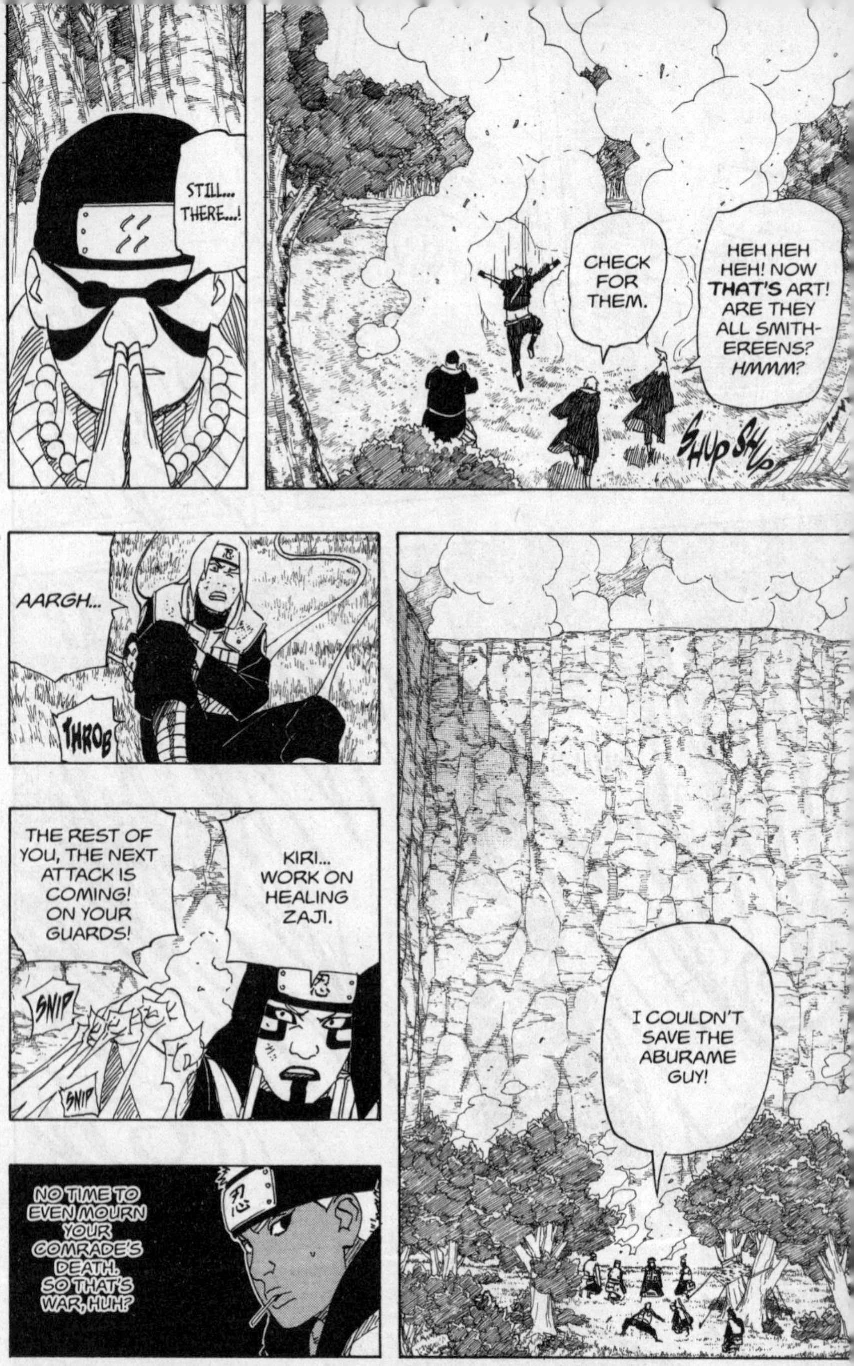
HEH HEH HEH! NOW THAT'S ART! ARE THEY ALL SMITHEREENS? HMMM?
CHECK FOR THEM.
SHUP SHUP
STILL... THERE...!
I COULDN'T SAVE THE ABURAME GUY!
AARGH...
THROB
KIRI... WORK ON HEALING ZAJI.
THE REST OF YOU, THE NEXT ATTACK IS COMING! ON YOUR GUARDS!
SNIP
SNIP
NO TIME TO EVEN MOURN YOUR COMRADE'S DEATH. SO THAT'S WAR, HUH?

READ THIS WAY

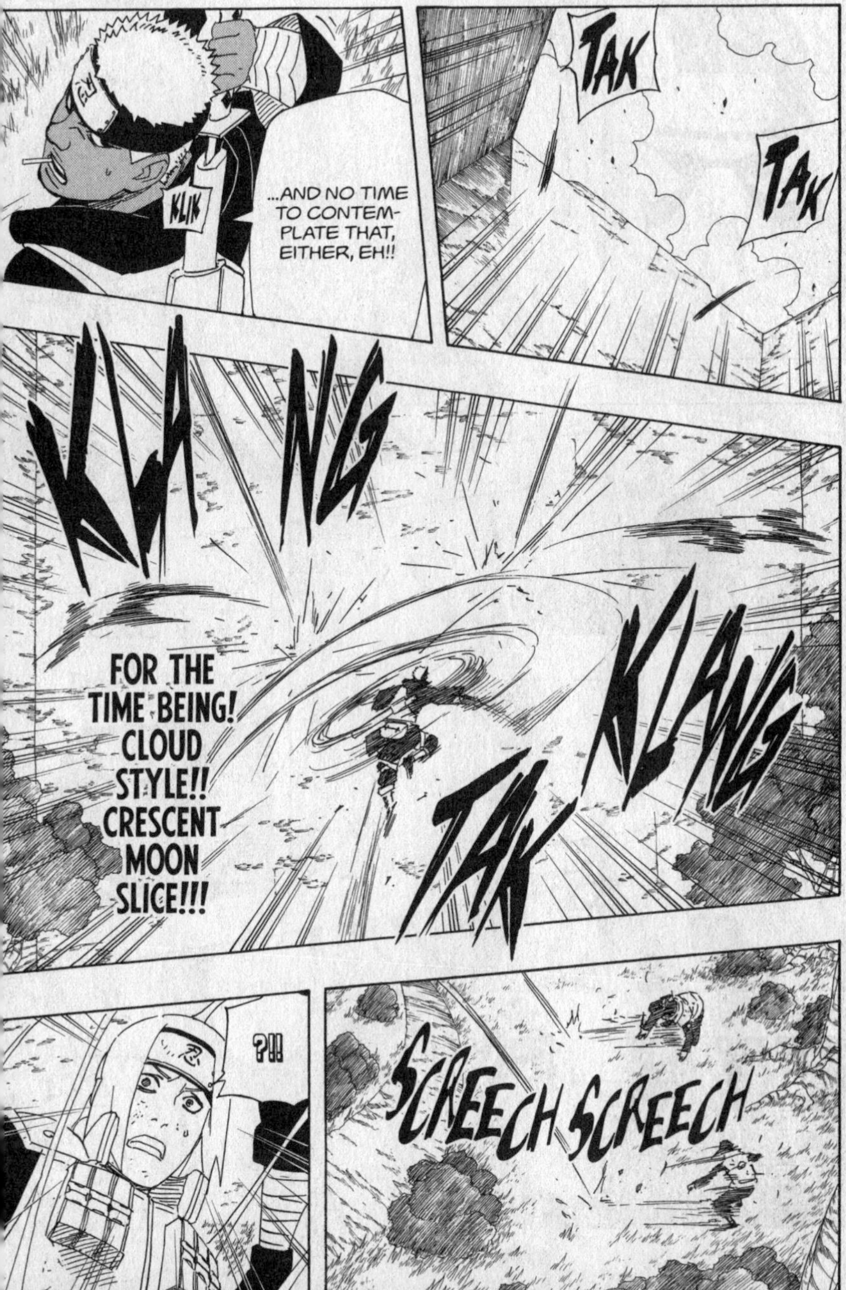
TAK
TAK
KLIK
...AND NO TIME TO CONTEMPLATE THAT, EITHER, EH!!
KLANG
KLANG
TAK
FOR THE TIME BEING! CLOUD STYLE!! CRESCENT MOON SLICE!!!
SCREECH SCREECH
?!!

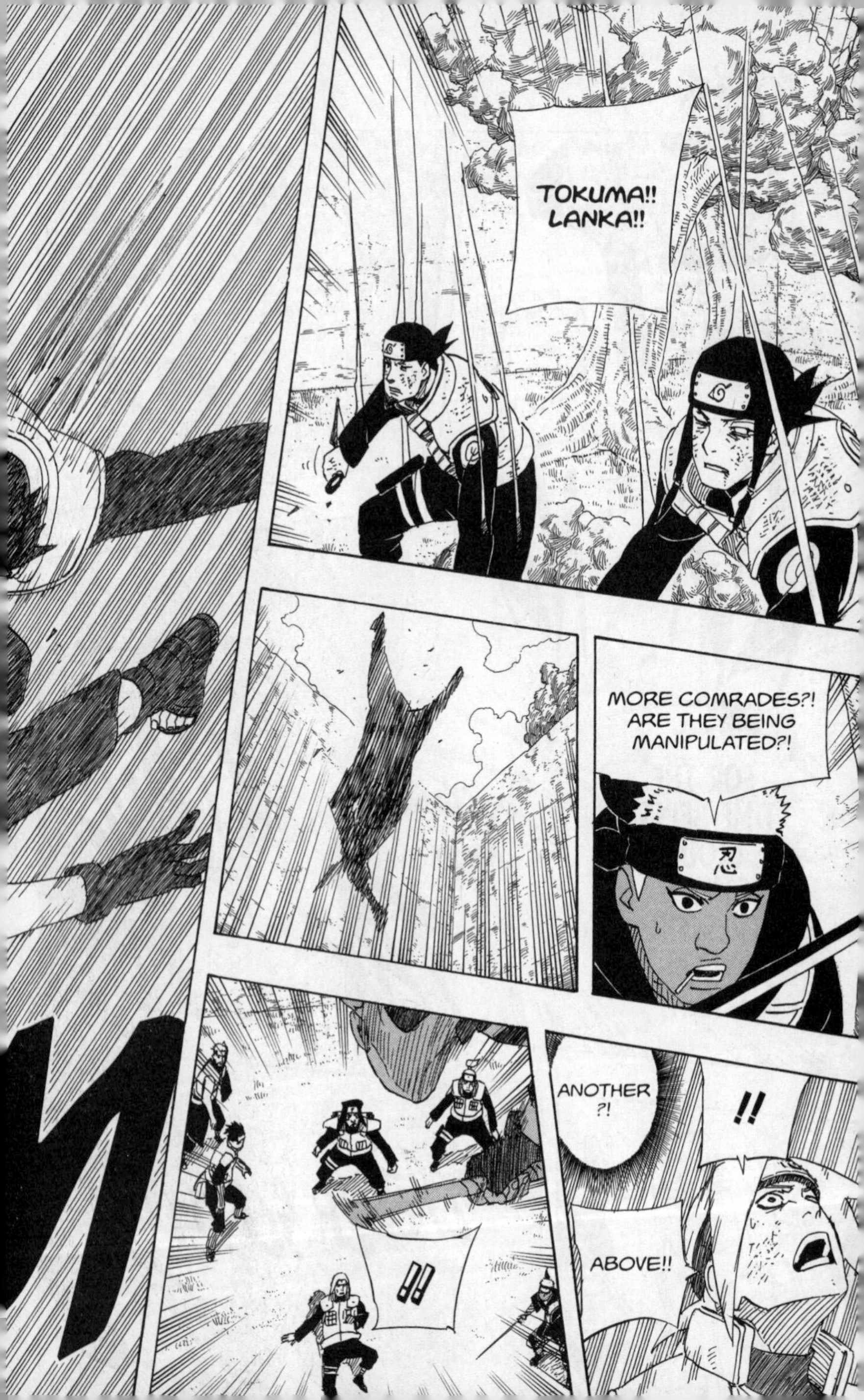
TOKUMA!! LANKA!!
MORE COMRADES?! ARE THEY BEING MANIPULATED?!
!!
ANOTHER ?!
ABOVE!!
!!

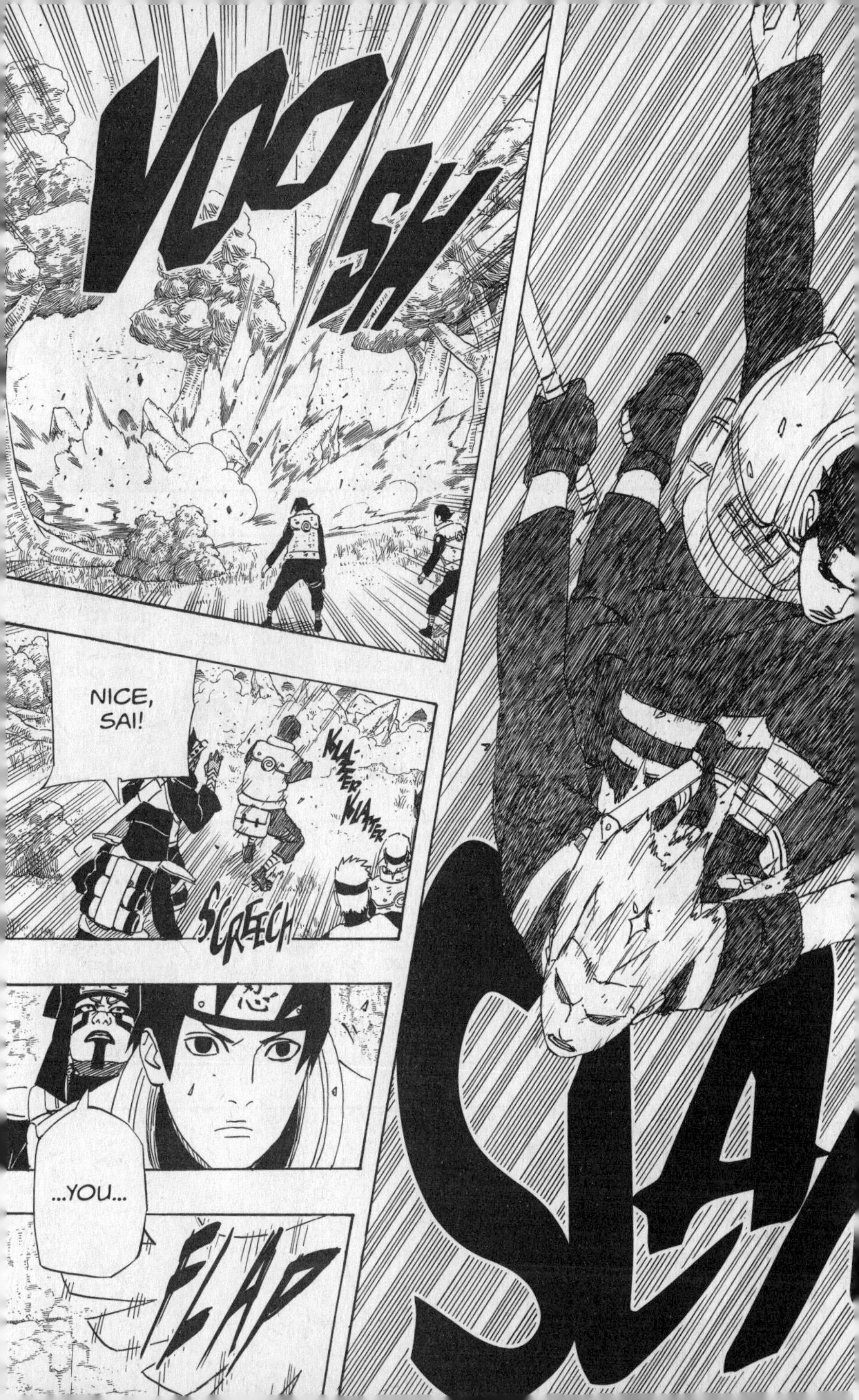
SLA
VOOSH
NICE, SAI!
KLATTER KLATTER
SCREECH
...YOU...
FLAP

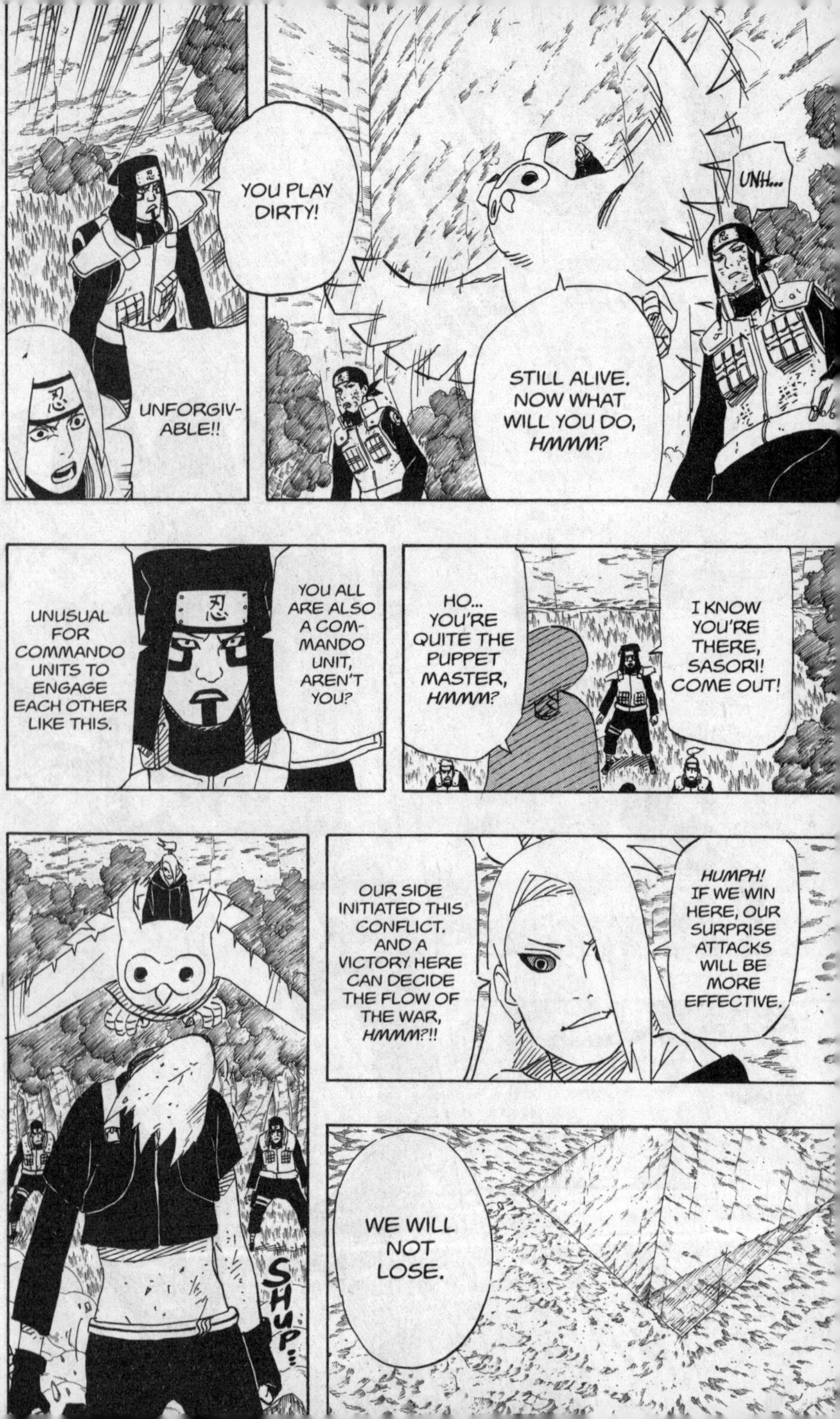
UNH...
STILL ALIVE. NOW WHAT WILL YOU DO, *HMMM?*
YOU PLAY DIRTY!
UNFORGIV-ABLE!!
I KNOW YOU'RE THERE, SASORI! COME OUT!
HO... YOU'RE QUITE THE PUPPET MASTER, *HMMM?*
YOU ALL ARE ALSO A COM-MANDO UNIT, AREN'T YOU?
UNUSUAL FOR COMMANDO UNITS TO ENGAGE EACH OTHER LIKE THIS.
*HUMPH!* IF WE WIN HERE, OUR SURPRISE ATTACKS WILL BE MORE EFFECTIVE.
OUR SIDE INITIATED THIS CONFLICT. AND A VICTORY HERE CAN DECIDE THE FLOW OF THE WAR, *HMMM?!!*
WE WILL NOT LOSE.
SHUP...

READ THIS WAY

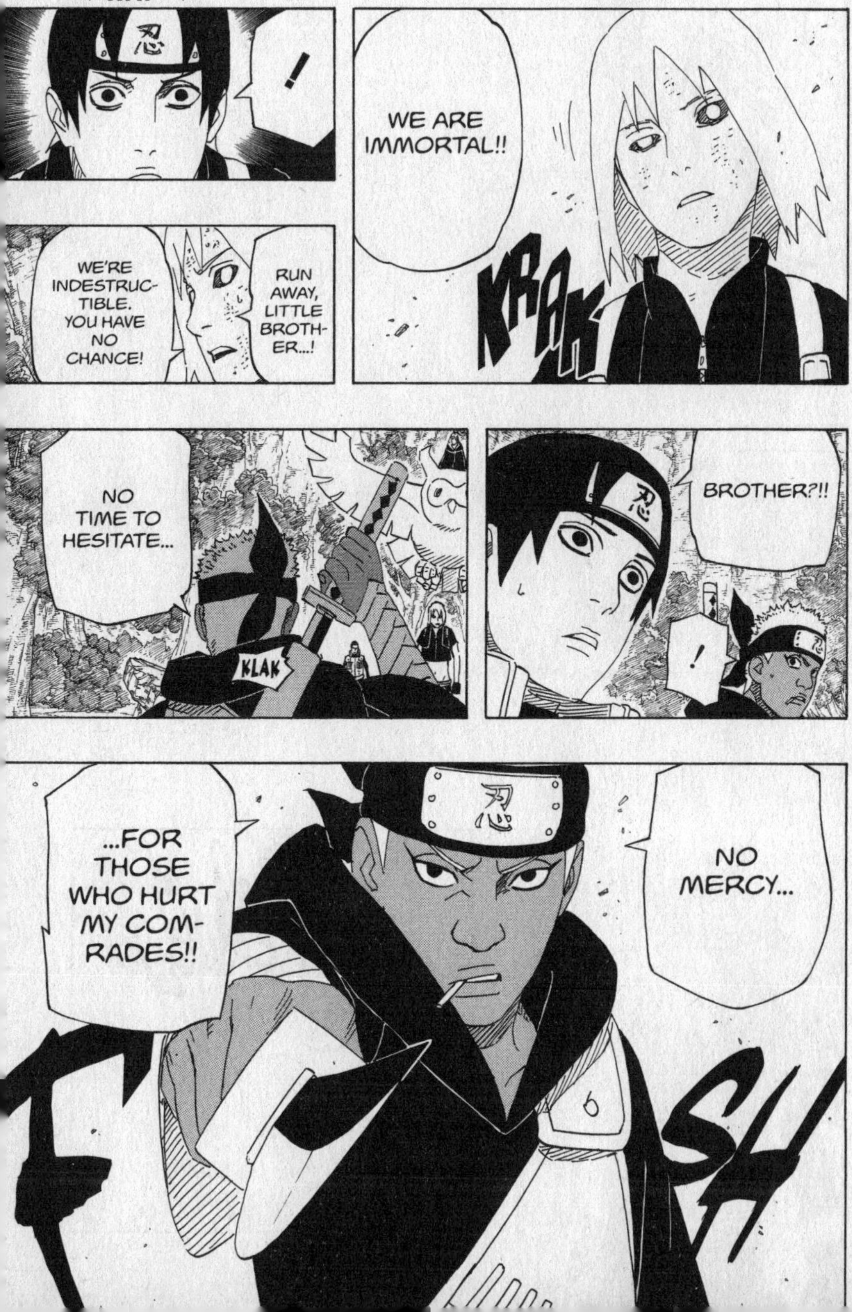
WE ARE IMMORTAL!!
KRAK
!
RUN AWAY, LITTLE BROTHER...!
WE'RE INDESTRUCTIBLE. YOU HAVE NO CHANCE!
BROTHER?!!
!
NO TIME TO HESITATE...
KLAK
NO MERCY...
...FOR THOSE WHO HURT MY COMRADES!!

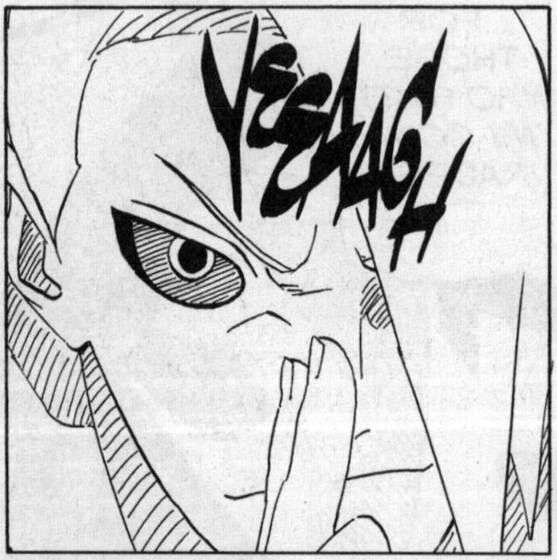
YEEAAGH

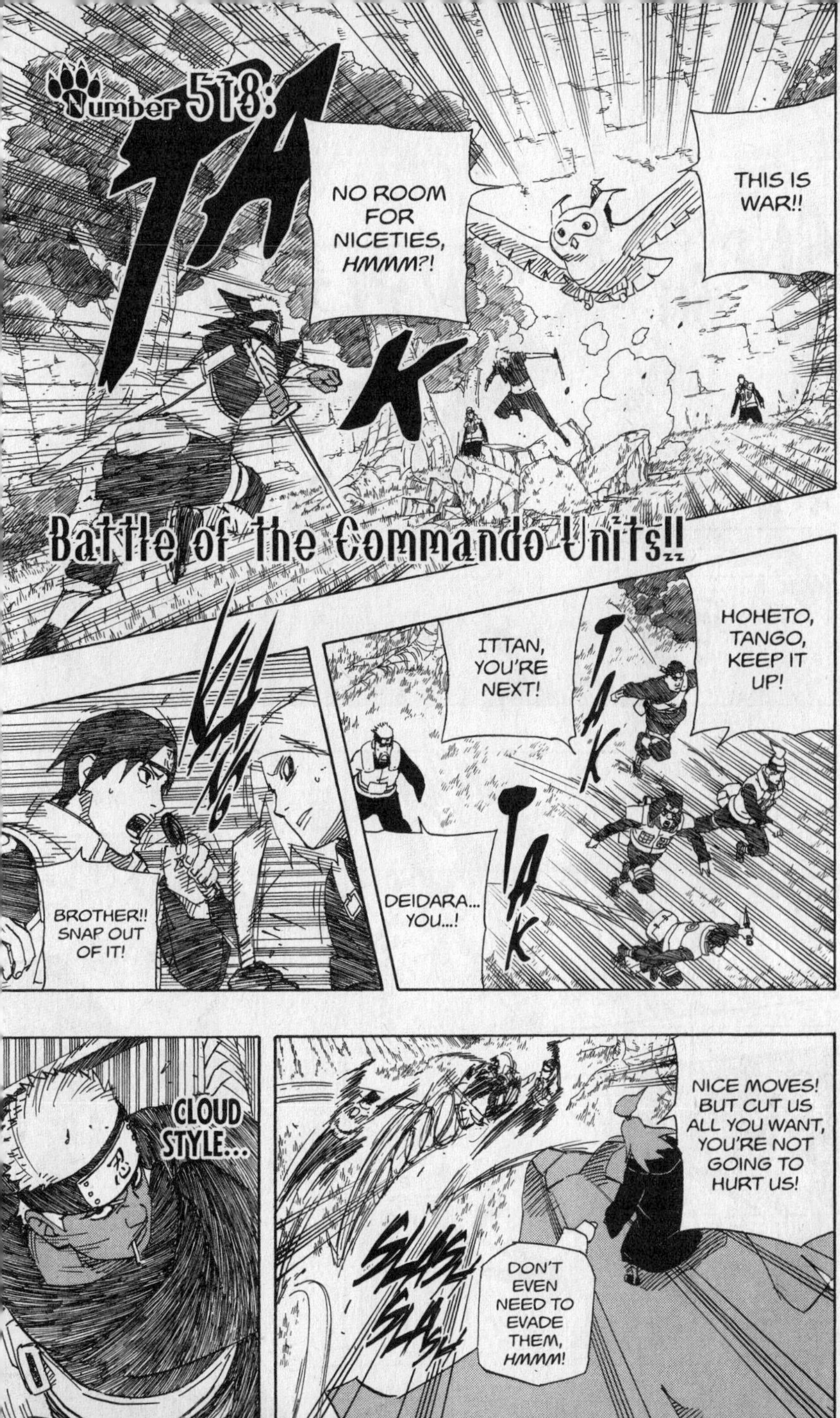
Number 518:
Battle of the Commando Units!!
TAK
THIS IS WAR!!
NO ROOM FOR NICETIES, HMMM?!
HOHETO, TANGO, KEEP IT UP!
ITTAN, YOU'RE NEXT!
TAK
TAK
DEIDARA... YOU...!
BROTHER!! SNAP OUT OF IT!
NICE MOVES! BUT CUT US ALL YOU WANT, YOU'RE NOT GOING TO HURT US!
SLASH
SLASH
DON'T EVEN NEED TO EVADE THEM, HMMM!
CLOUD STYLE...

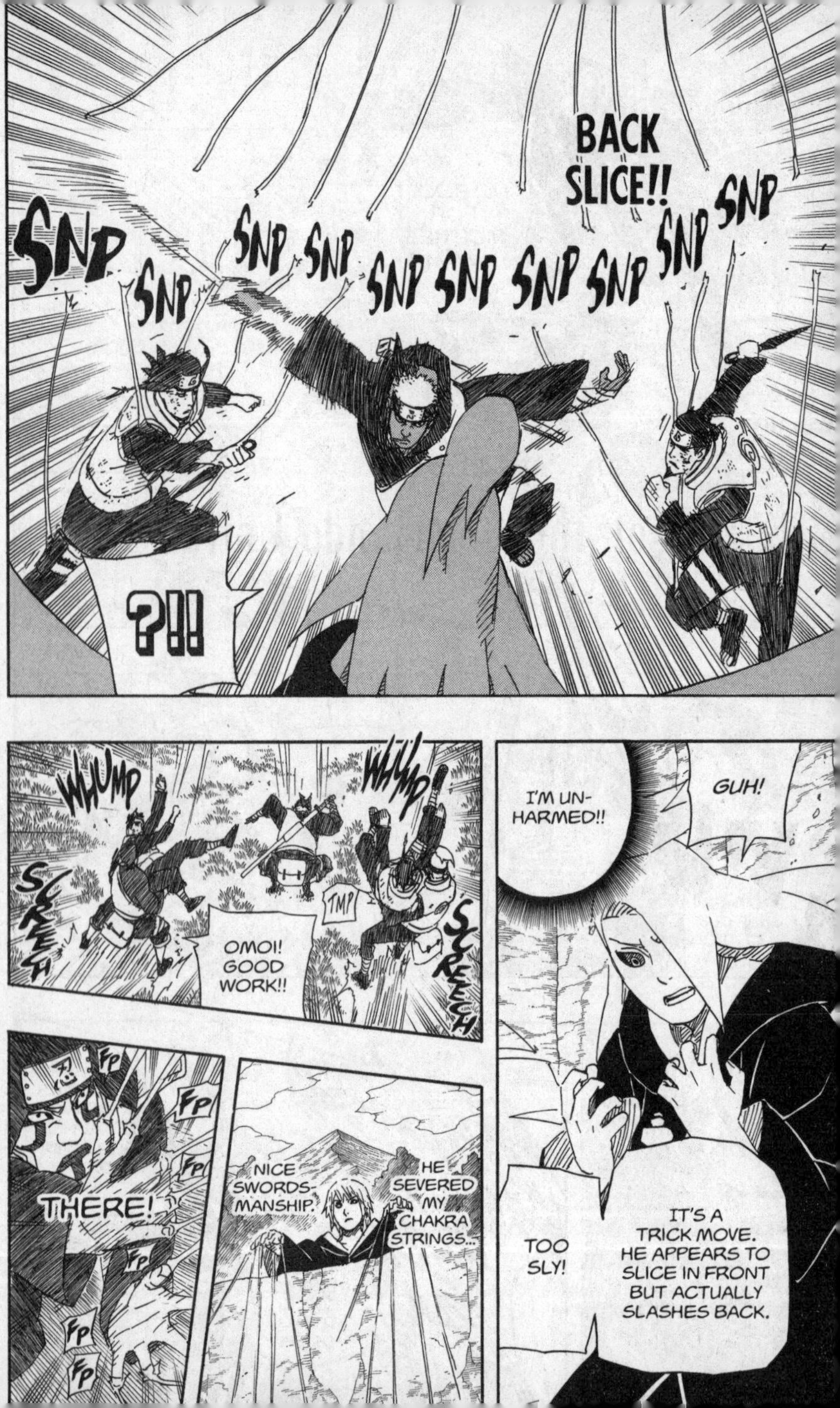

SNP
SNP
BACK SLICE!!
SNP SNP SNP SNP SNP SNP SNP SNP
SNP
SNP
?!!
GUH!
I'M UN-HARMED!!
IT'S A TRICK MOVE. HE APPEARS TO SLICE IN FRONT BUT ACTUALLY SLASHES BACK.
TOO SLY!
WHUMP
SCREECH
TMP
OMOI! GOOD WORK!!
WHUMP
SCREECH
HE SEVERED MY CHAKRA STRINGS...
NICE SWORDS-MANSHIP.
FP
FP
FP
THERE!
FP
FP
FP

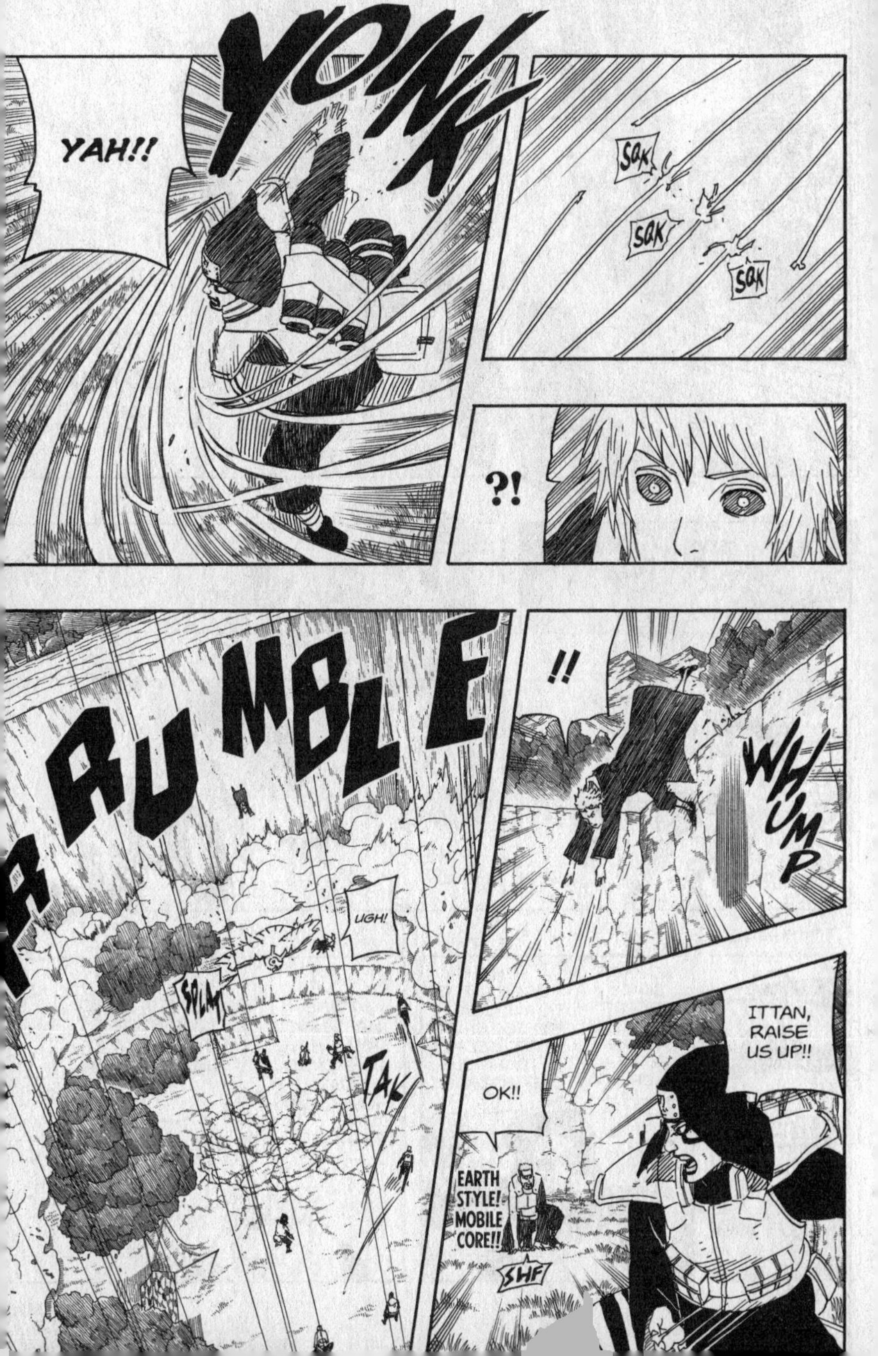
SQK
SQK
SQK
?!
YONK
YAH!!
!!
WHUMP
ITTAN, RAISE US UP!!
OK!!
EARTH STYLE! MOBILE CORE!!
SHF
RUMBLE
UGH!
TAK

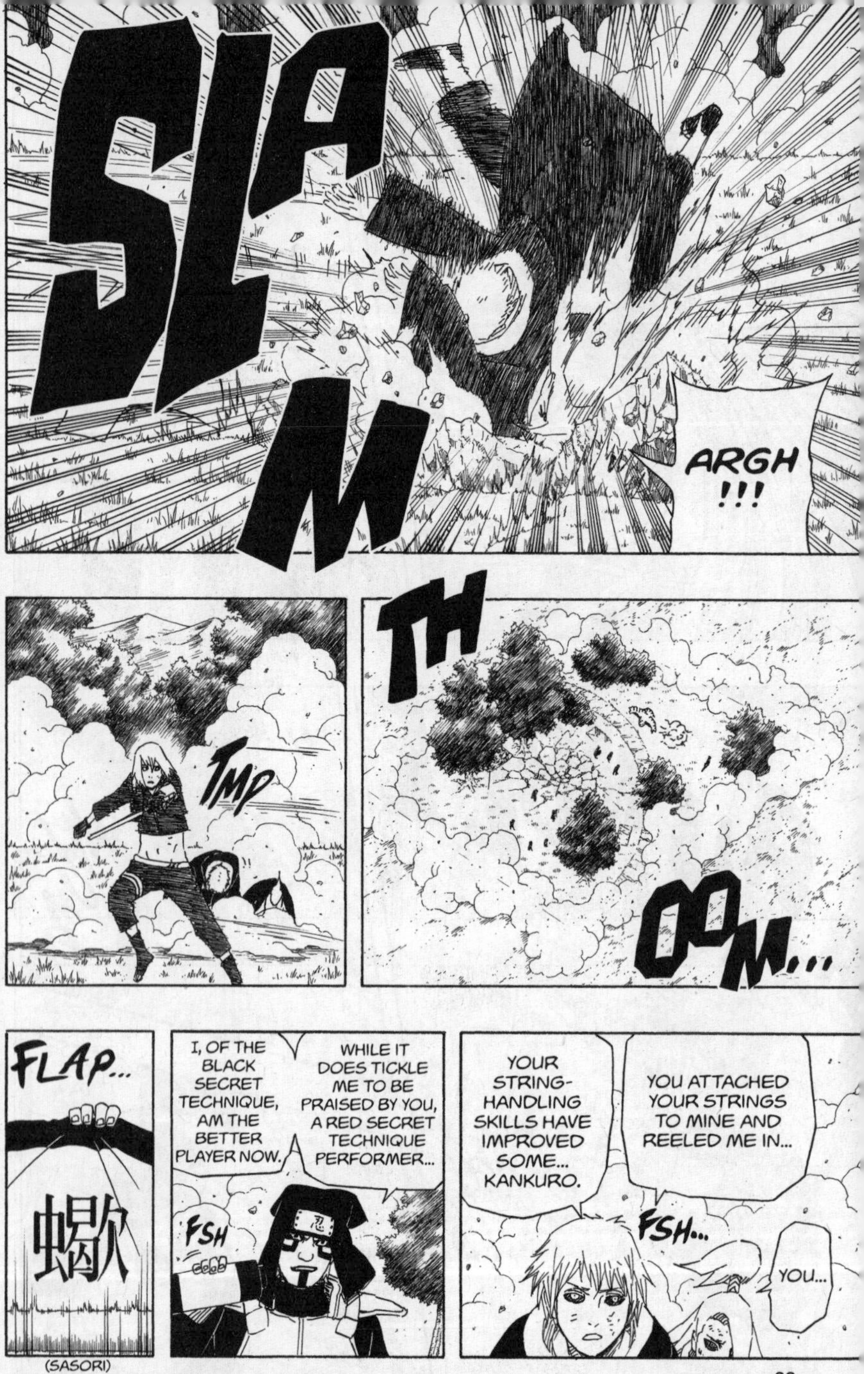
SLAM
ARGH!!!
THOOM...
TMP
YOU ATTACHED YOUR STRINGS TO MINE AND REELED ME IN...
YOUR STRING-HANDLING SKILLS HAVE IMPROVED SOME... KANKURO.
FSH...
YOU...
WHILE IT DOES TICKLE ME TO BE PRAISED BY YOU, A RED SECRET TECHNIQUE PERFORMER...
I, OF THE BLACK SECRET TECHNIQUE, AM THE BETTER PLAYER NOW.
FSH
FLAP...
蠍
(SASORI)

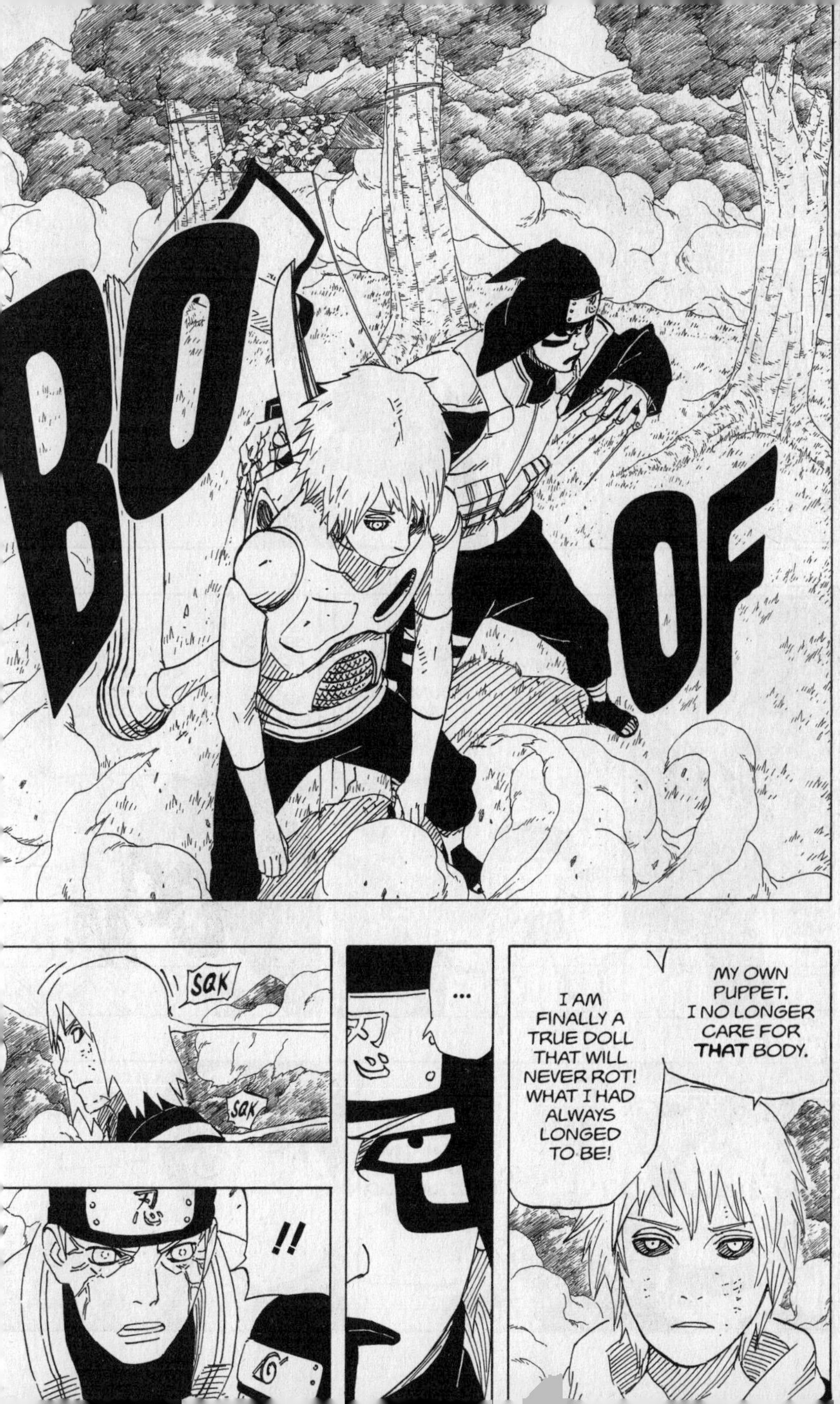
BOOF
MY OWN PUPPET. I NO LONGER CARE FOR THAT BODY.
I AM FINALLY A TRUE DOLL THAT WILL NEVER ROT! WHAT I HAD ALWAYS LONGED TO BE!
...
SQK
SQK
!!

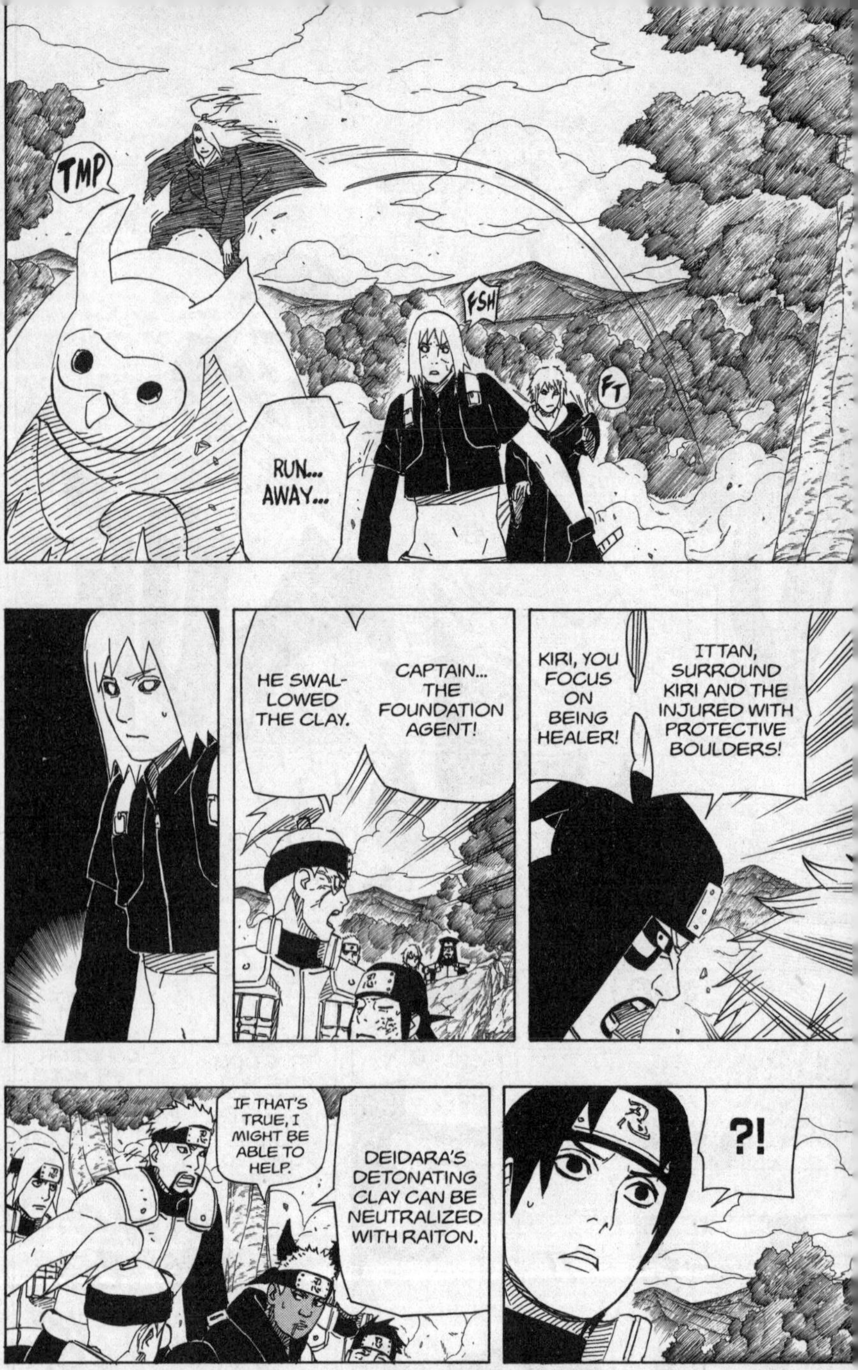
FSH
FT
TMP
RUN... AWAY...
ITTAN, SURROUND KIRI AND THE INJURED WITH PROTECTIVE BOULDERS!
KIRI, YOU FOCUS ON BEING HEALER!
CAPTAIN... THE FOUNDATION AGENT!
HE SWAL-LOWED THE CLAY.
?!
DEIDARA'S DETONATING CLAY CAN BE NEUTRALIZED WITH RAITON.
IF THAT'S TRUE, I MIGHT BE ABLE TO HELP.

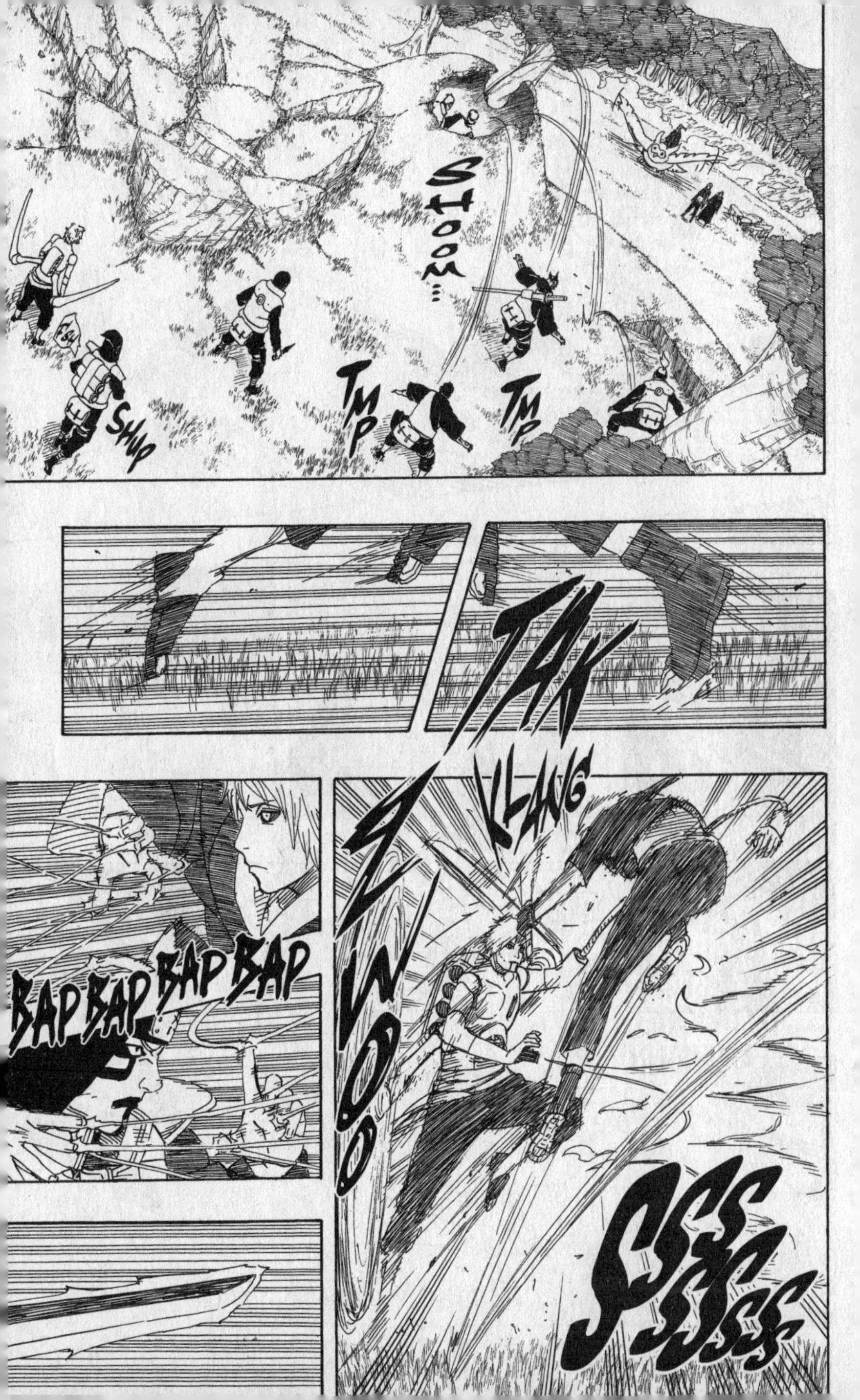
SHOOOM...
TMP
TMP
FSH
SHUP
TAK
KLANG
SWOOOO
BAP BAP BAP BAP
SSS

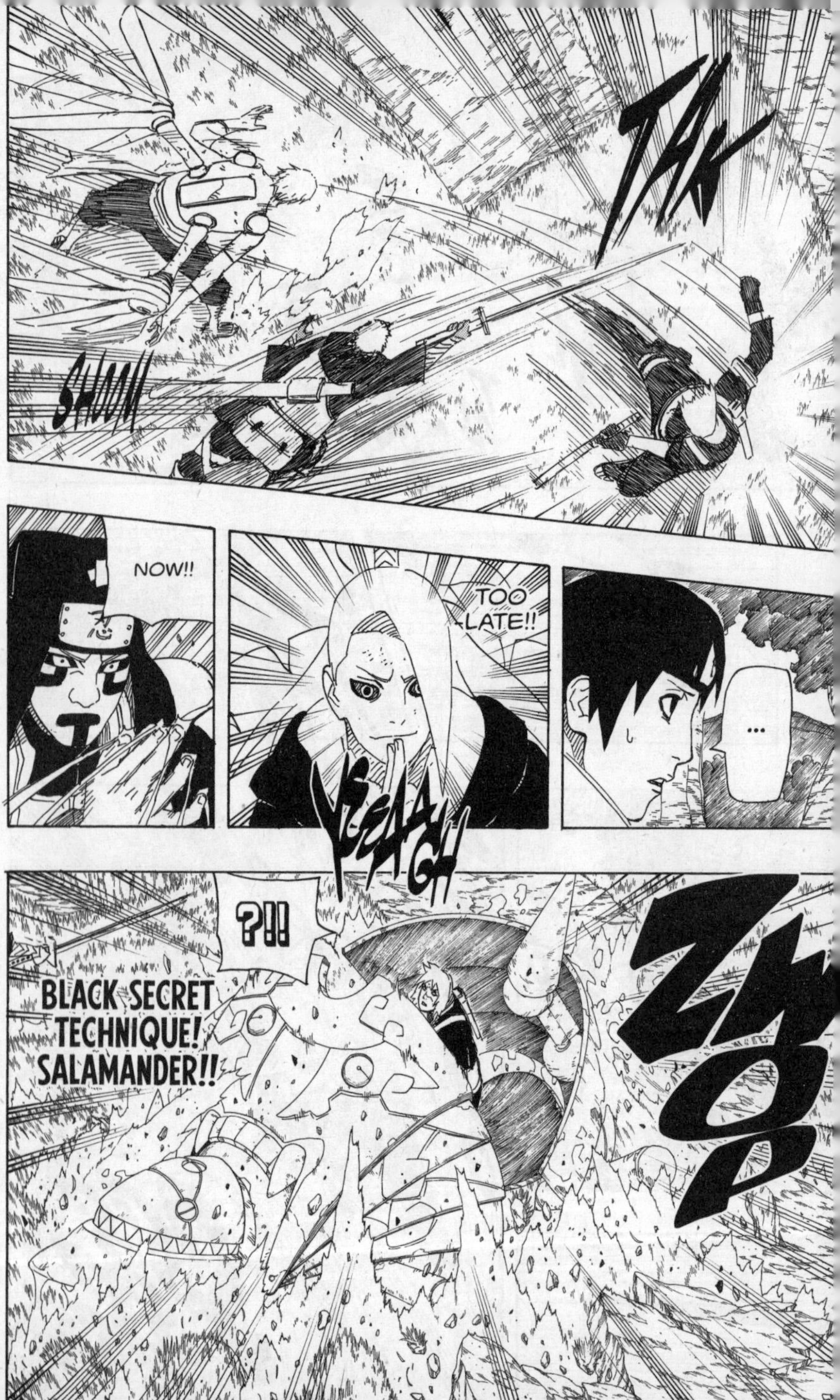
TAK
SHOOM
...
TOO LATE!!
YEAAGH
NOW!!
ZWOP
?!!
BLACK SECRET TECHNIQUE! SALAMANDER!!

READ THIS WAY

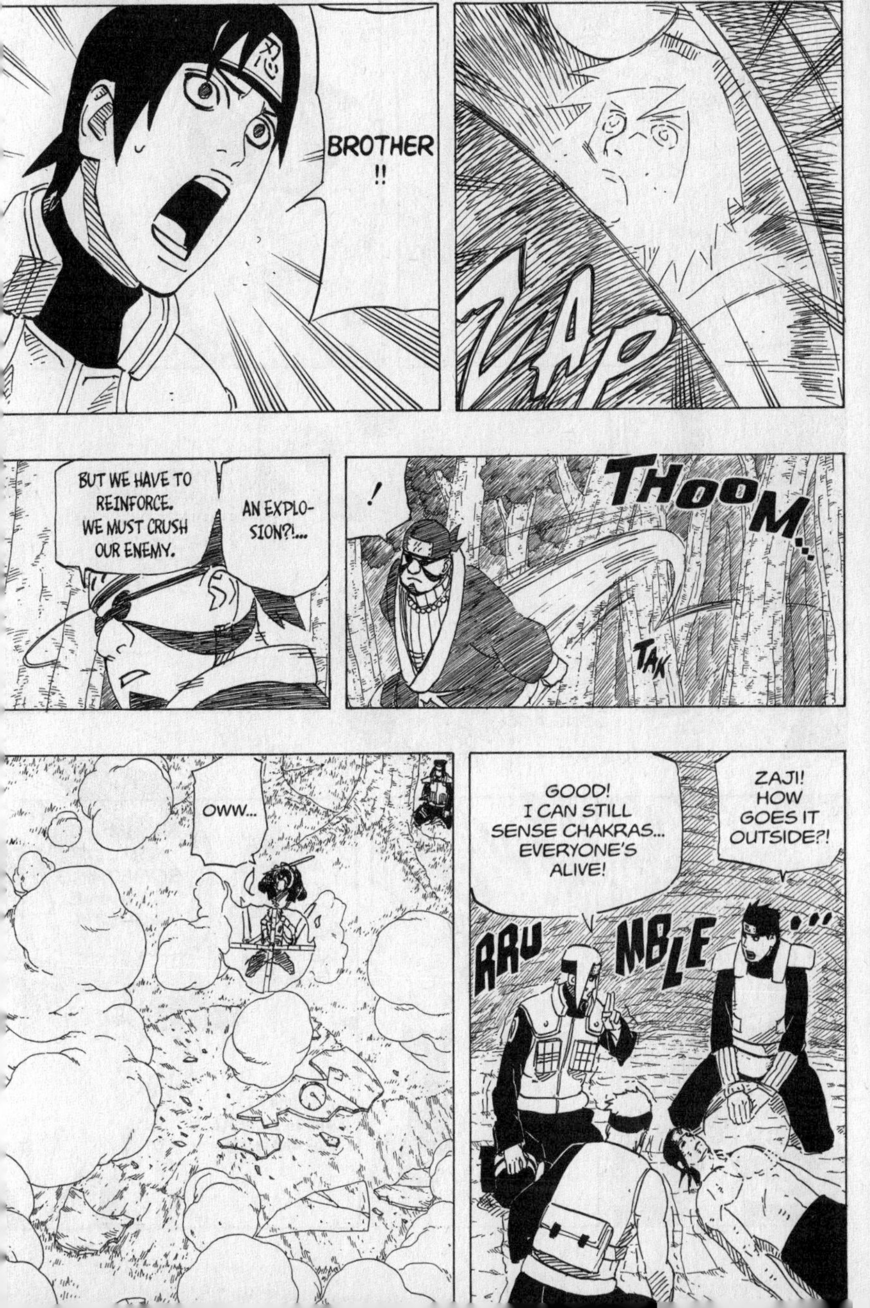
ZAP
BROTHER !!
THOOM...
!
TAK
AN EXPLO-SION?!...
BUT WE HAVE TO REINFORCE. WE MUST CRUSH OUR ENEMY.
ZAJI! HOW GOES IT OUTSIDE?!
GOOD! I CAN STILL SENSE CHAKRAS... EVERYONE'S ALIVE!
RRUMBLE...
OWW...

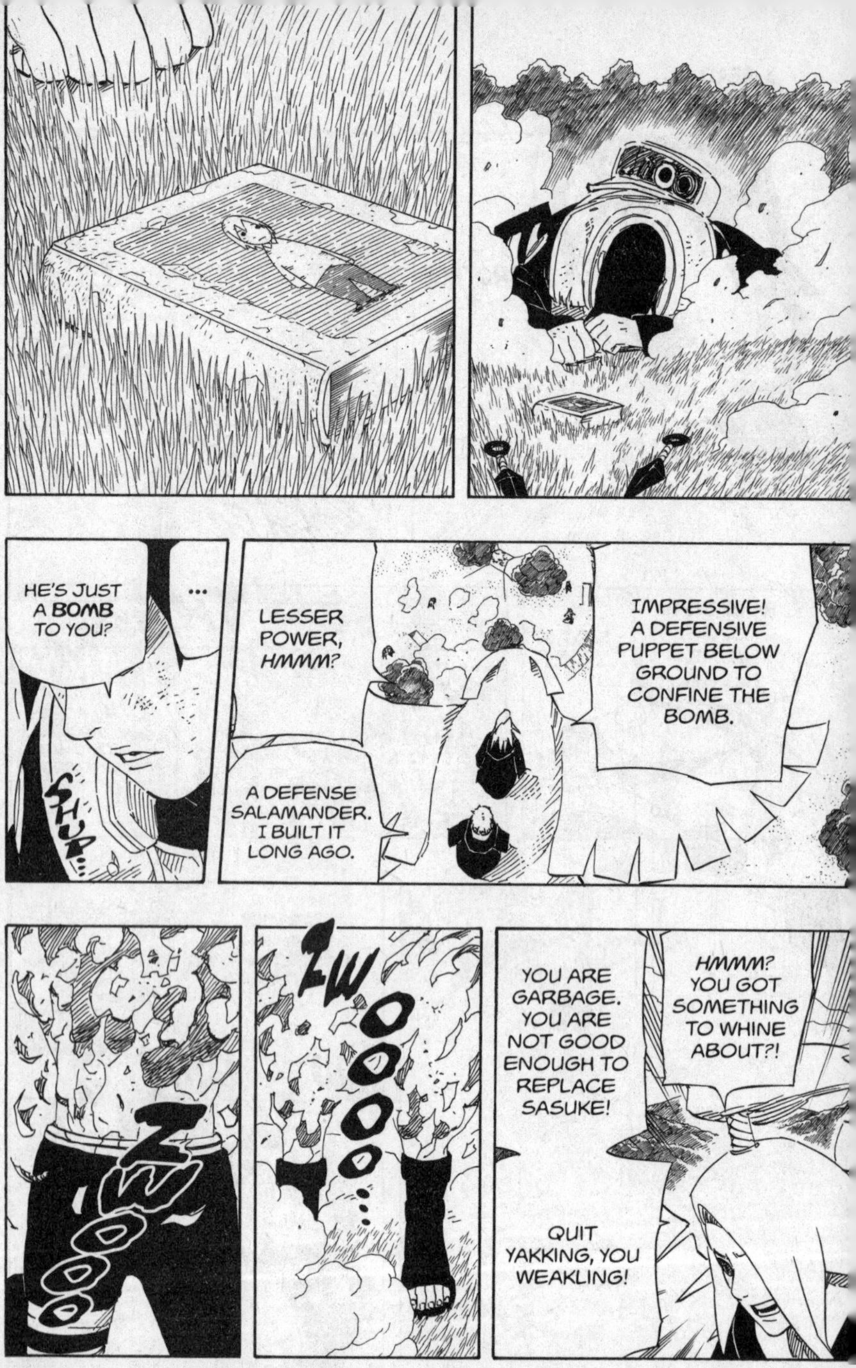
IMPRESSIVE! A DEFENSIVE PUPPET BELOW GROUND TO CONFINE THE BOMB.
LESSER POWER, *HMMM?*
A DEFENSE SALAMANDER. I BUILT IT LONG AGO.
...
HE'S JUST A **BOMB** TO YOU?
SHUP...
*HMMM?* YOU GOT SOMETHING TO WHINE ABOUT?!
YOU ARE GARBAGE. YOU ARE NOT GOOD ENOUGH TO REPLACE SASUKE!
QUIT YAKKING, YOU WEAKLING!
ZWOOOOO...
ZWOOOO

READ THIS WAY

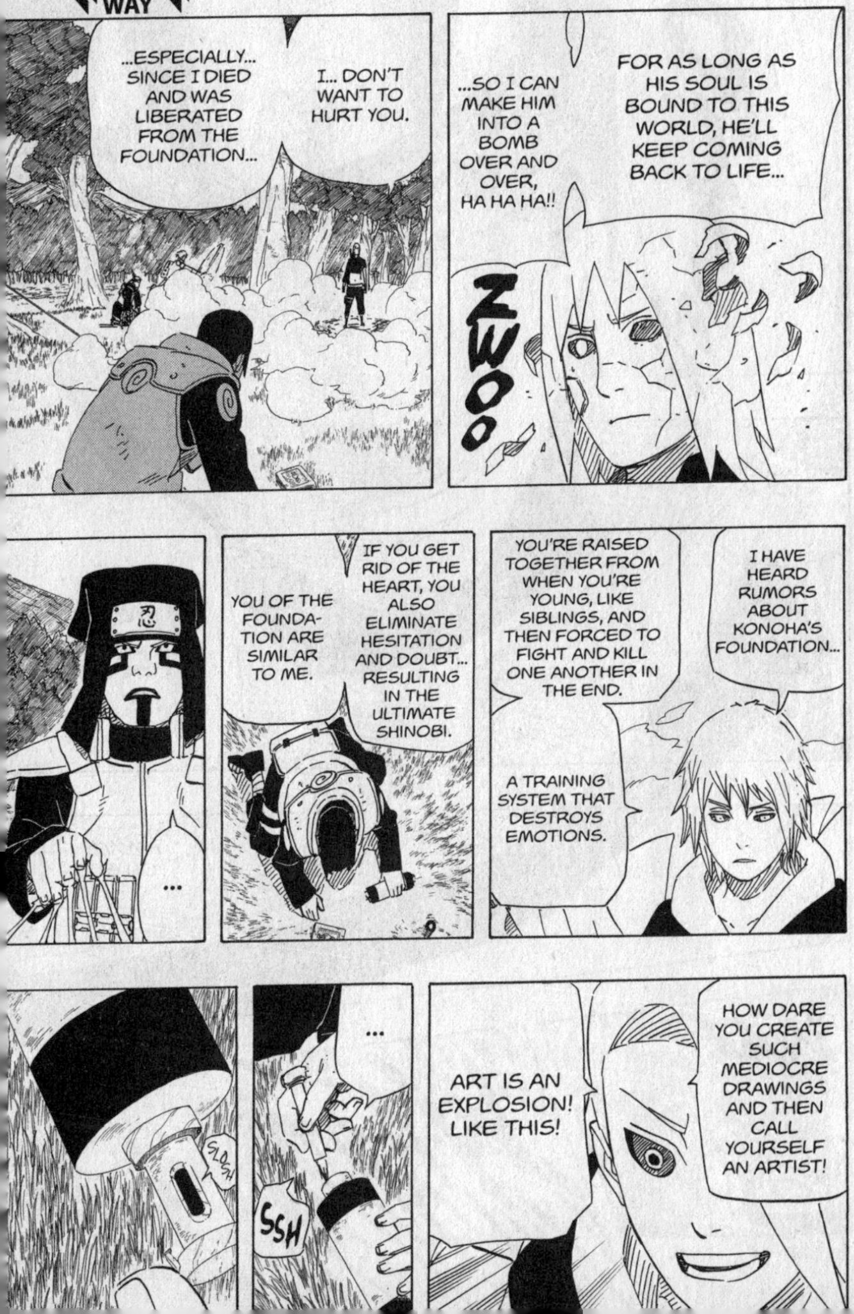
FOR AS LONG AS HIS SOUL IS BOUND TO THIS WORLD, HE'LL KEEP COMING BACK TO LIFE...
...SO I CAN MAKE HIM INTO A BOMB OVER AND OVER, HA HA HA!!
ZWOOO
I... DON'T WANT TO HURT YOU.
...ESPECIALLY... SINCE I DIED AND WAS LIBERATED FROM THE FOUNDATION...
I HAVE HEARD RUMORS ABOUT KONOHA'S FOUNDATION...
YOU'RE RAISED TOGETHER FROM WHEN YOU'RE YOUNG, LIKE SIBLINGS, AND THEN FORCED TO FIGHT AND KILL ONE ANOTHER IN THE END.
A TRAINING SYSTEM THAT DESTROYS EMOTIONS.
IF YOU GET RID OF THE HEART, YOU ALSO ELIMINATE HESITATION AND DOUBT... RESULTING IN THE ULTIMATE SHINOBI.
YOU OF THE FOUNDATION ARE SIMILAR TO ME.
...
HOW DARE YOU CREATE SUCH MEDIOCRE DRAWINGS AND THEN CALL YOURSELF AN ARTIST!
ART IS AN EXPLOSION! LIKE THIS!
...
SSH
SLOSH

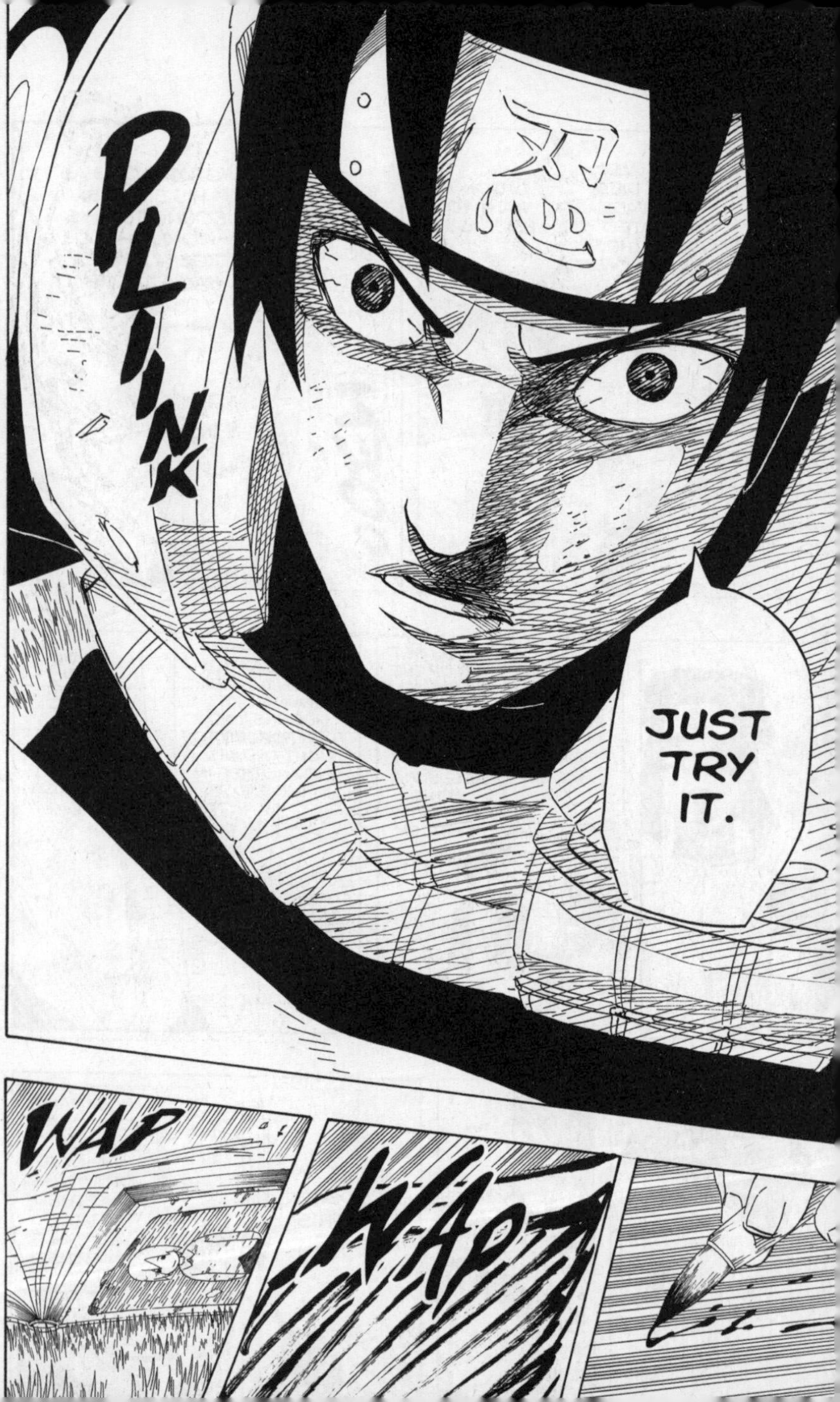
PLINK
JUST TRY IT.
WAP
WAP

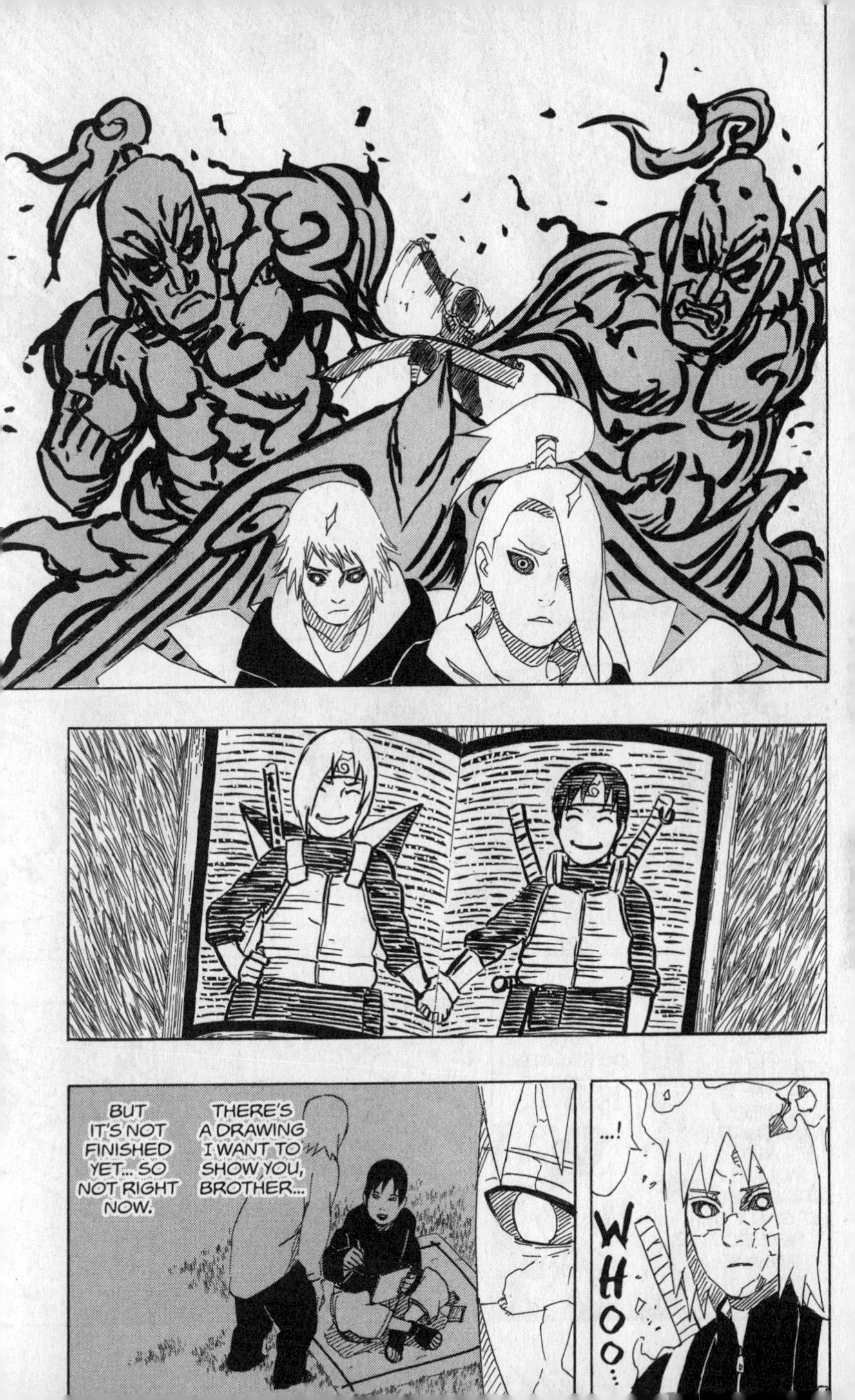
...!
WHOOO...
THERE'S A DRAWING I WANT TO SHOW YOU, BROTHER...
BUT IT'S NOT FINISHED YET... SO NOT RIGHT NOW.

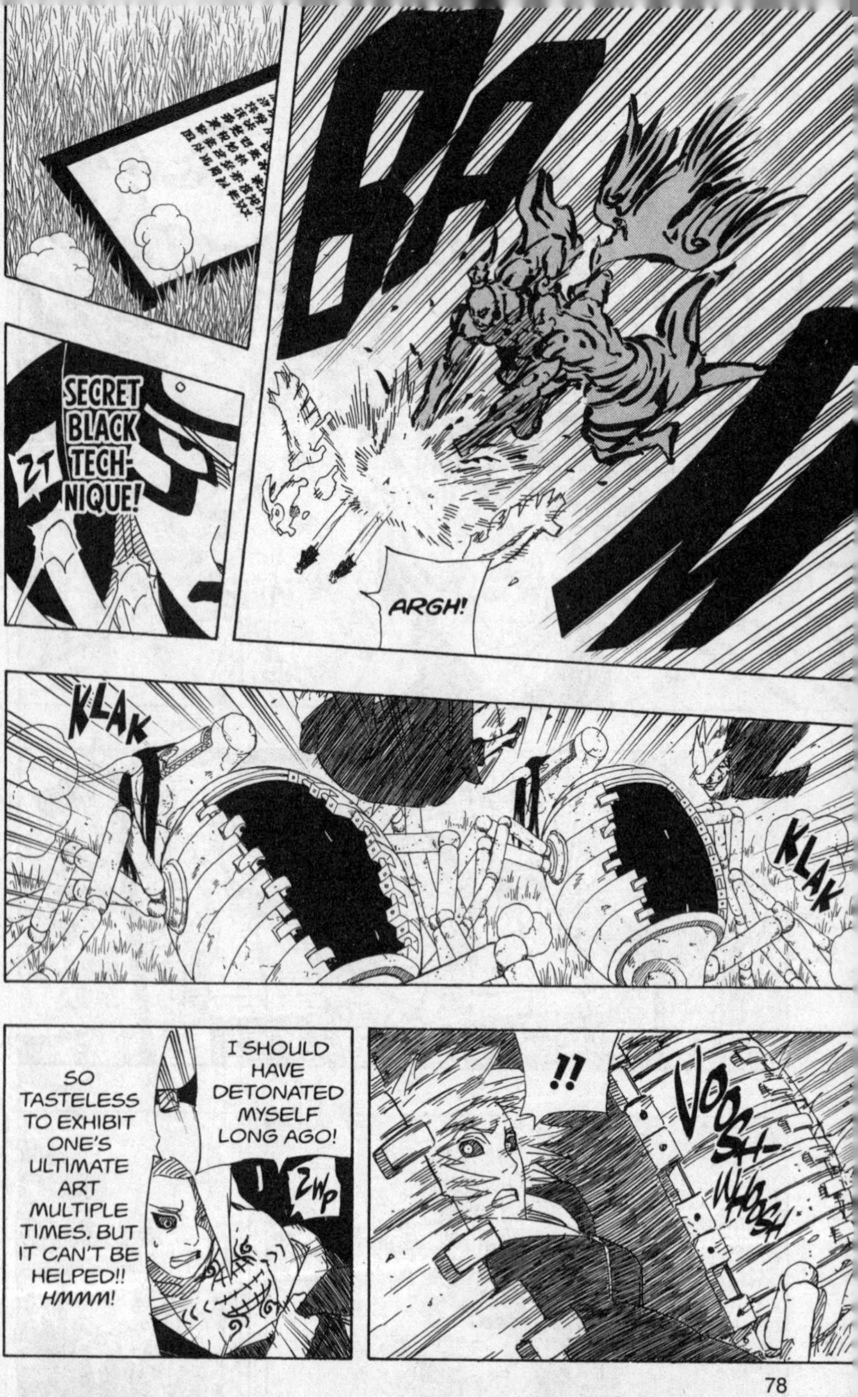
BAM
ARGH!
SECRET BLACK TECH-NIQUE!
ZT
KLAK
KLAK
!!
VOOSH
WHOOSH
I SHOULD HAVE DETONATED MYSELF LONG AGO!
SO TASTELESS TO EXHIBIT ONE'S ULTIMATE ART MULTIPLE TIMES. BUT IT CAN'T BE HELPED!! HMMM!
ZWP

READ THIS WAY

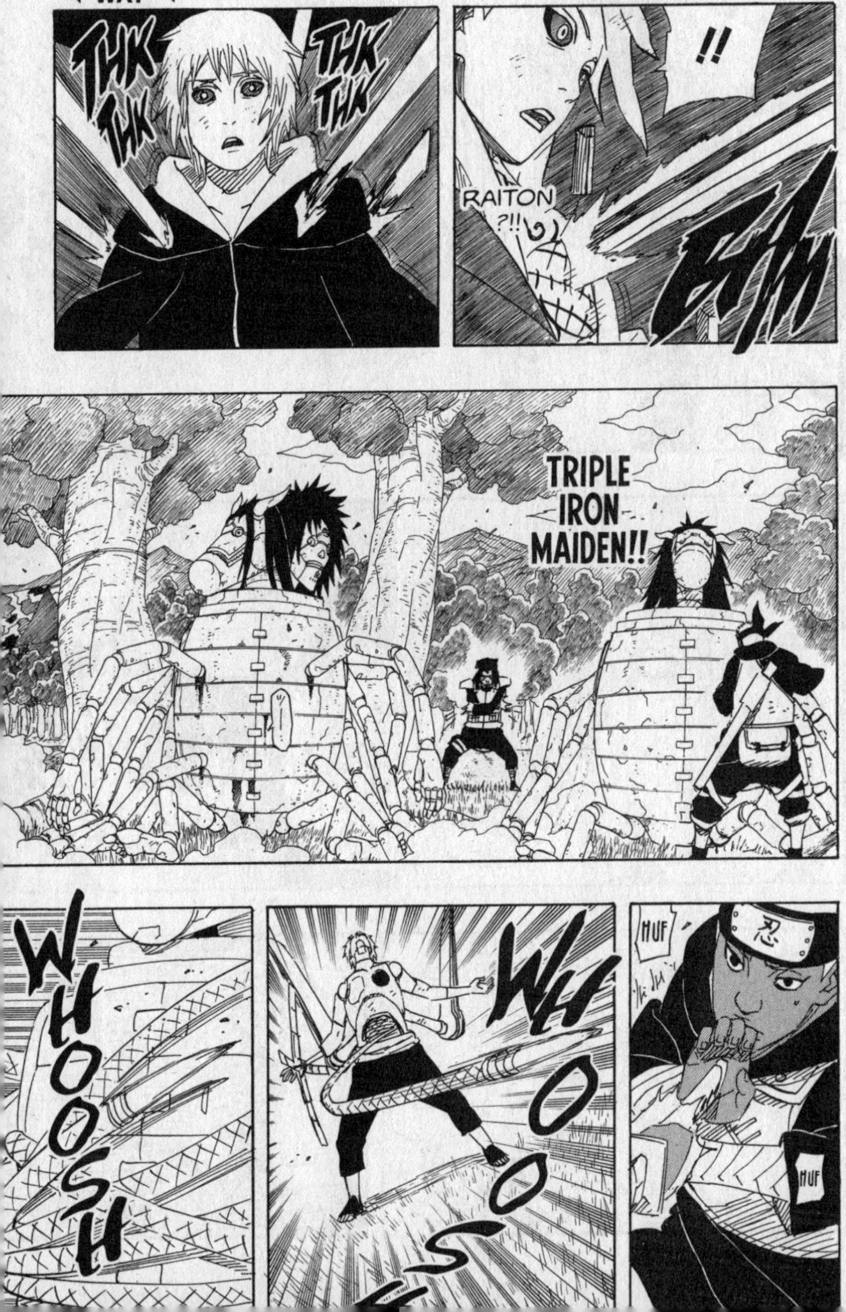
!!
RAITON ?!!
THK THK
THK THK
TRIPLE IRON MAIDEN!!
HUF
HUF
WHOOOSH
WHOOSH

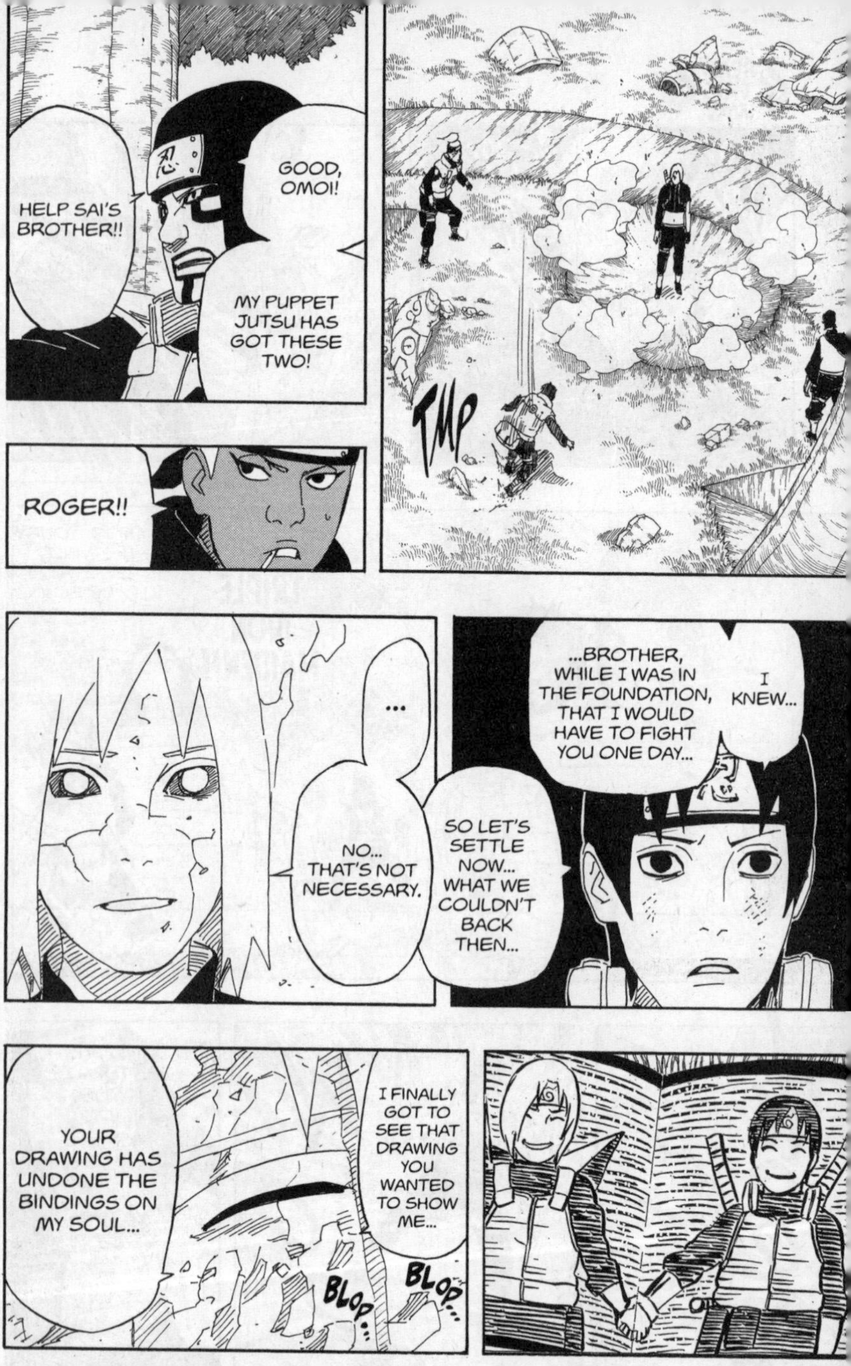
TMP
GOOD, OMOI!
MY PUPPET JUTSU HAS GOT THESE TWO!
HELP SAI'S BROTHER!!
ROGER!!
I KNEW...
...BROTHER, WHILE I WAS IN THE FOUNDATION, THAT I WOULD HAVE TO FIGHT YOU ONE DAY...
SO LET'S SETTLE NOW... WHAT WE COULDN'T BACK THEN...
...
NO... THAT'S NOT NECESSARY.
I FINALLY GOT TO SEE THAT DRAWING YOU WANTED TO SHOW ME...
BLOP...
BLOP...
YOUR DRAWING HAS UNDONE THE BINDINGS ON MY SOUL...

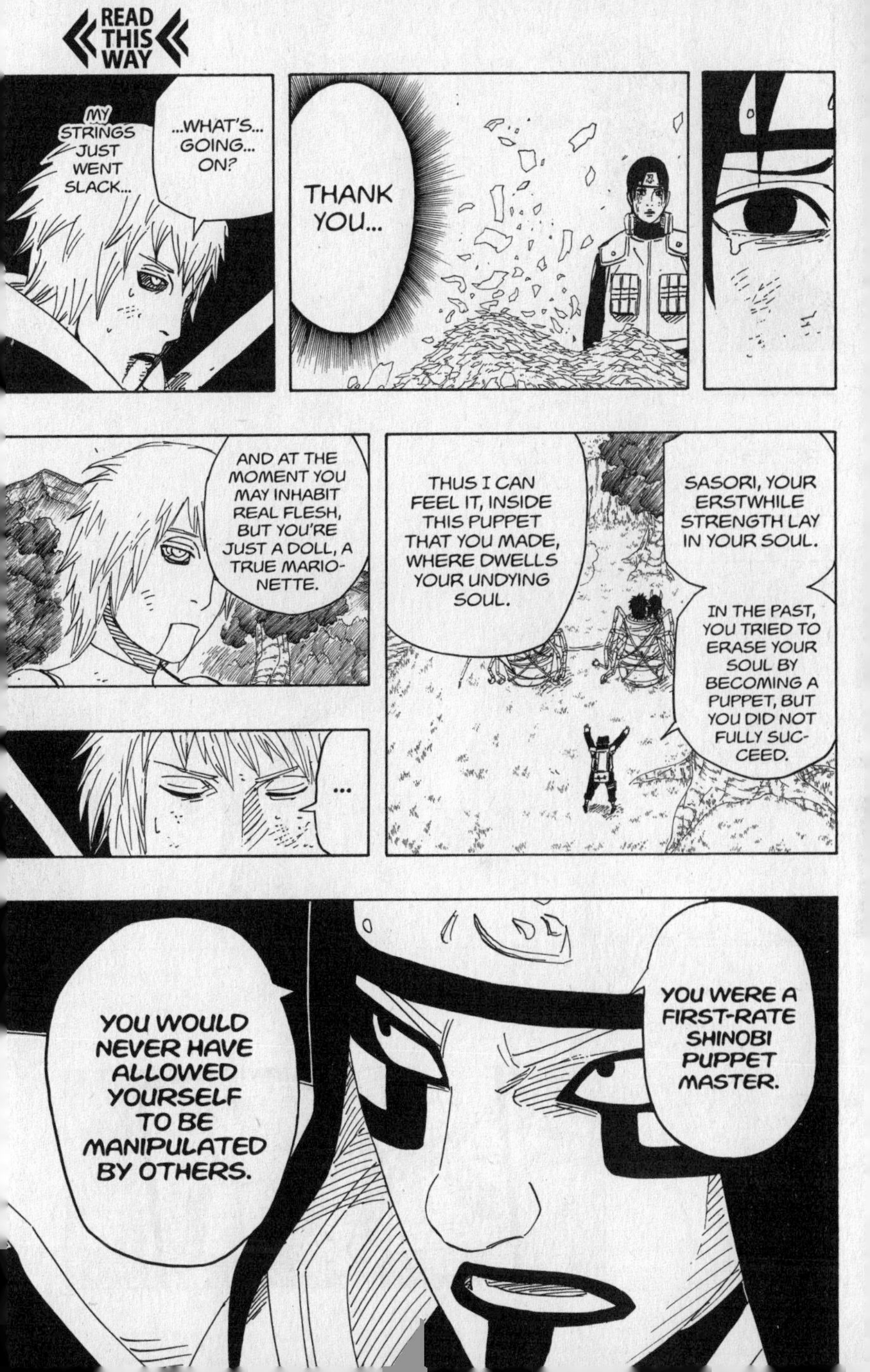
READ THIS WAY
...WHAT'S... GOING... ON?
MY STRINGS JUST WENT SLACK...
THANK YOU...
SASORI, YOUR ERSTWHILE STRENGTH LAY IN YOUR SOUL.
IN THE PAST, YOU TRIED TO ERASE YOUR SOUL BY BECOMING A PUPPET, BUT YOU DID NOT FULLY SUC-CEED.
THUS I CAN FEEL IT, INSIDE THIS PUPPET THAT YOU MADE, WHERE DWELLS YOUR UNDYING SOUL.
AND AT THE MOMENT YOU MAY INHABIT REAL FLESH, BUT YOU'RE JUST A DOLL, A TRUE MARIO-NETTE.
...
YOU WERE A FIRST-RATE SHINOBI PUPPET MASTER.
YOU WOULD NEVER HAVE ALLOWED YOURSELF TO BE MANIPULATED BY OTHERS.

# Number 519: The Biju Bomb

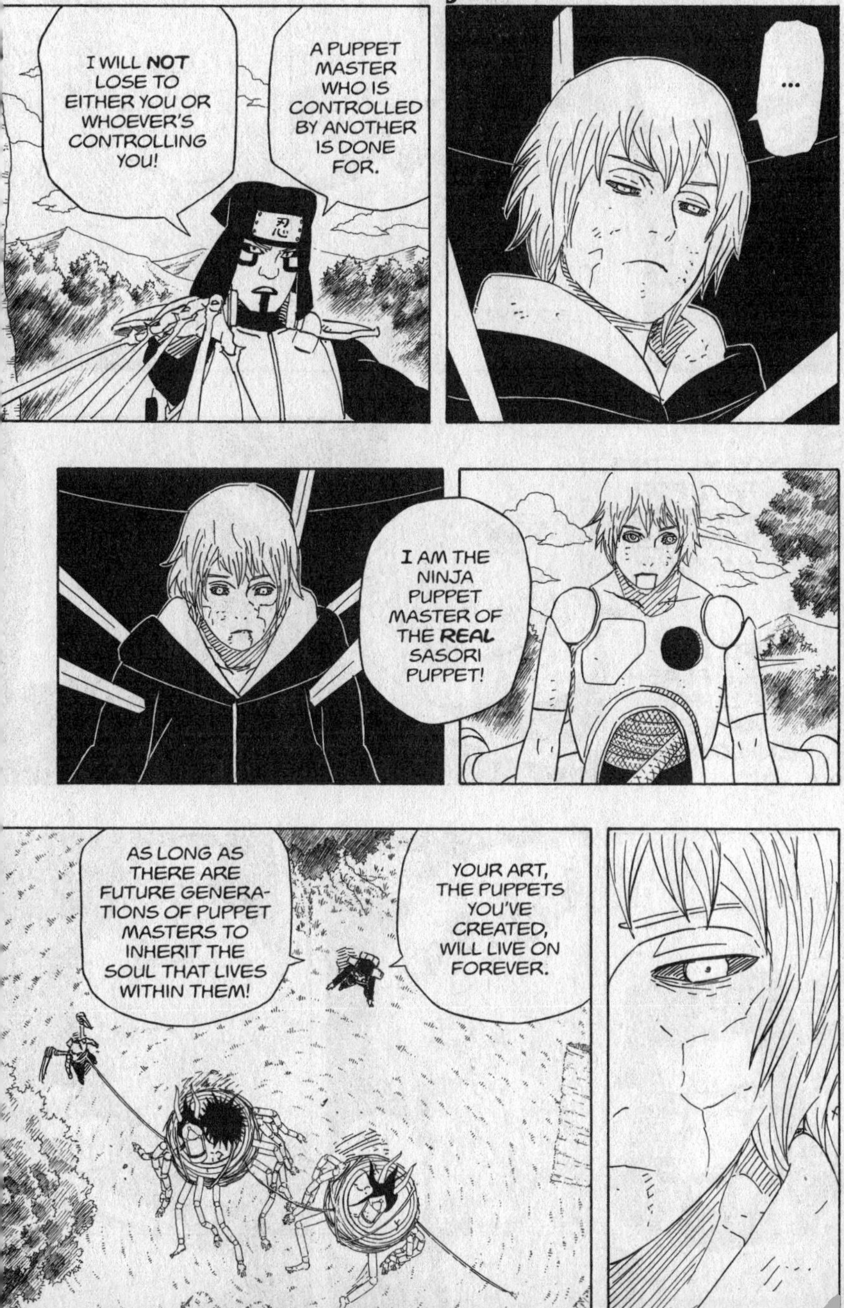
...
A PUPPET MASTER WHO IS CONTROLLED BY ANOTHER IS DONE FOR.
I WILL **NOT** LOSE TO EITHER YOU OR WHOEVER'S CONTROLLING YOU!
I AM THE NINJA PUPPET MASTER OF THE **REAL** SASORI PUPPET!
YOUR ART, THE PUPPETS YOU'VE CREATED, WILL LIVE ON FOREVER.
AS LONG AS THERE ARE FUTURE GENERATIONS OF PUPPET MASTERS TO INHERIT THE SOUL THAT LIVES WITHIN THEM!

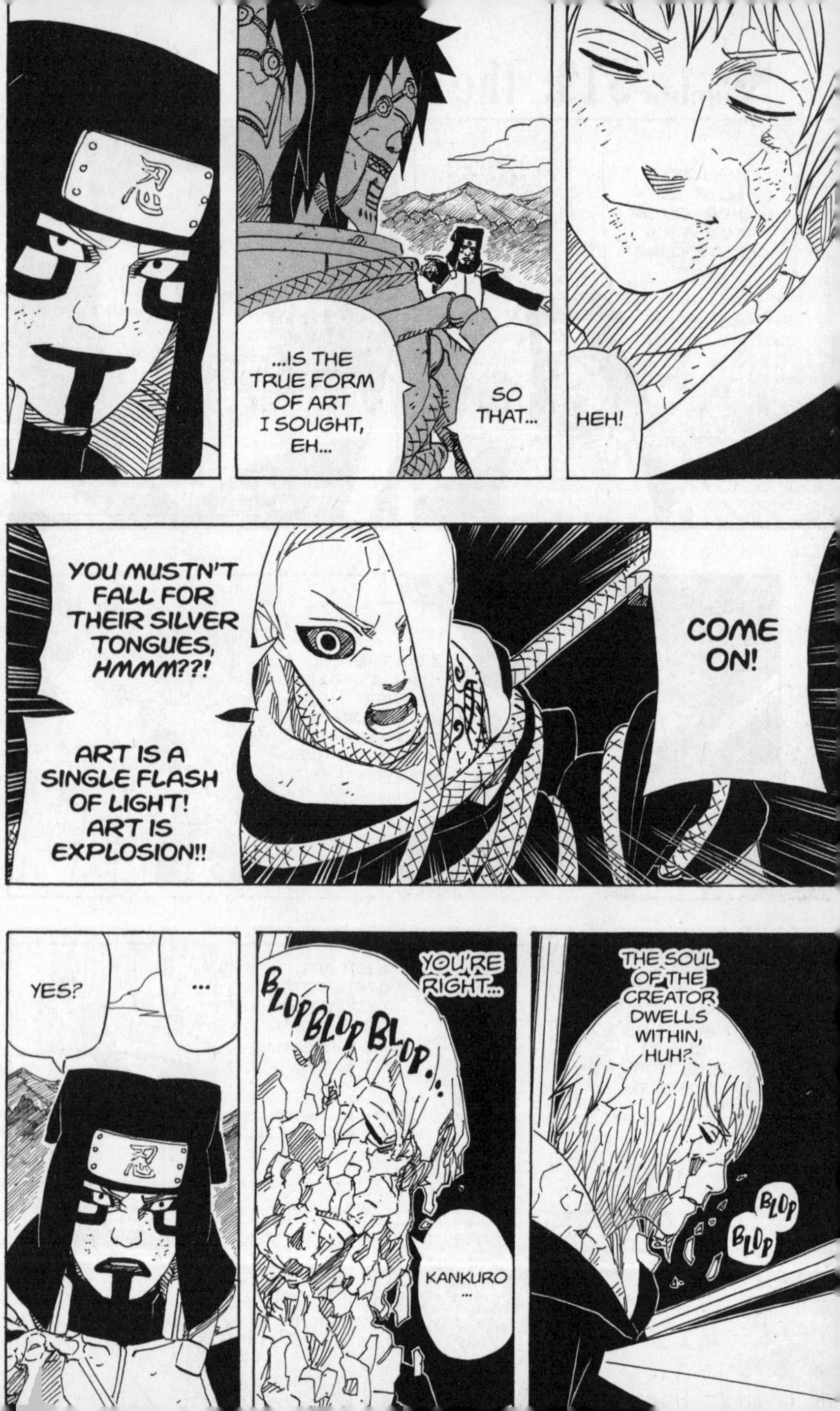
HEH!
SO THAT...
...IS THE TRUE FORM OF ART I SOUGHT, EH...
COME ON!
YOU MUSTN'T FALL FOR THEIR SILVER TONGUES, HMMM??!
ART IS A SINGLE FLASH OF LIGHT! ART IS EXPLOSION!!
THE SOUL OF THE CREATOR DWELLS WITHIN, HUH?
BLOP
BLOP
YOU'RE RIGHT...
BLOP BLOP BLOP...
KANKURO...
...
YES?

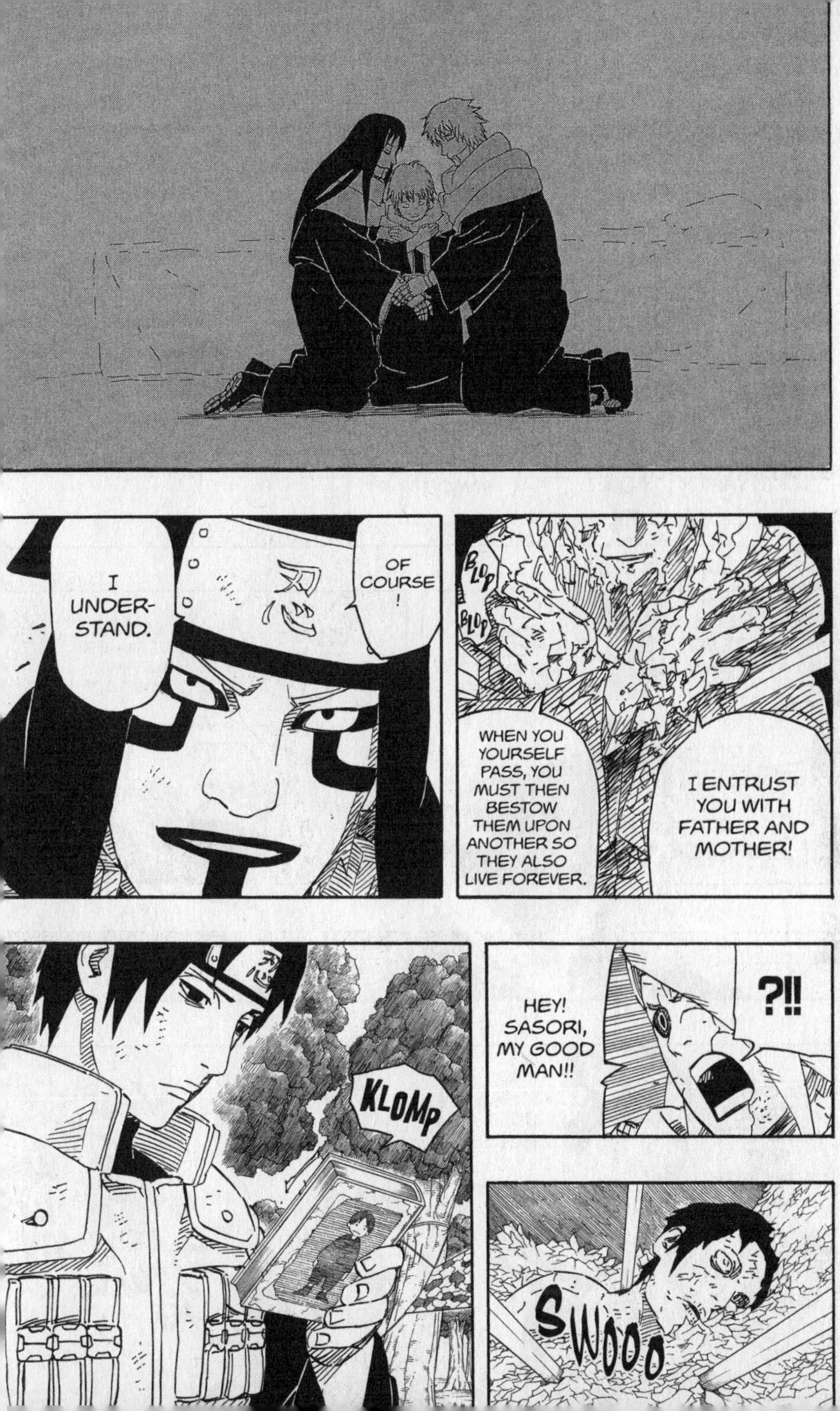
I ENTRUST YOU WITH FATHER AND MOTHER!
WHEN YOU YOURSELF PASS, YOU MUST THEN BESTOW THEM UPON ANOTHER SO THEY ALSO LIVE FOREVER.
BLOP
BLOP
OF COURSE!
I UNDERSTAND.
?!!
HEY! SASORI, MY GOOD MAN!!
SWOOO
KLOMP

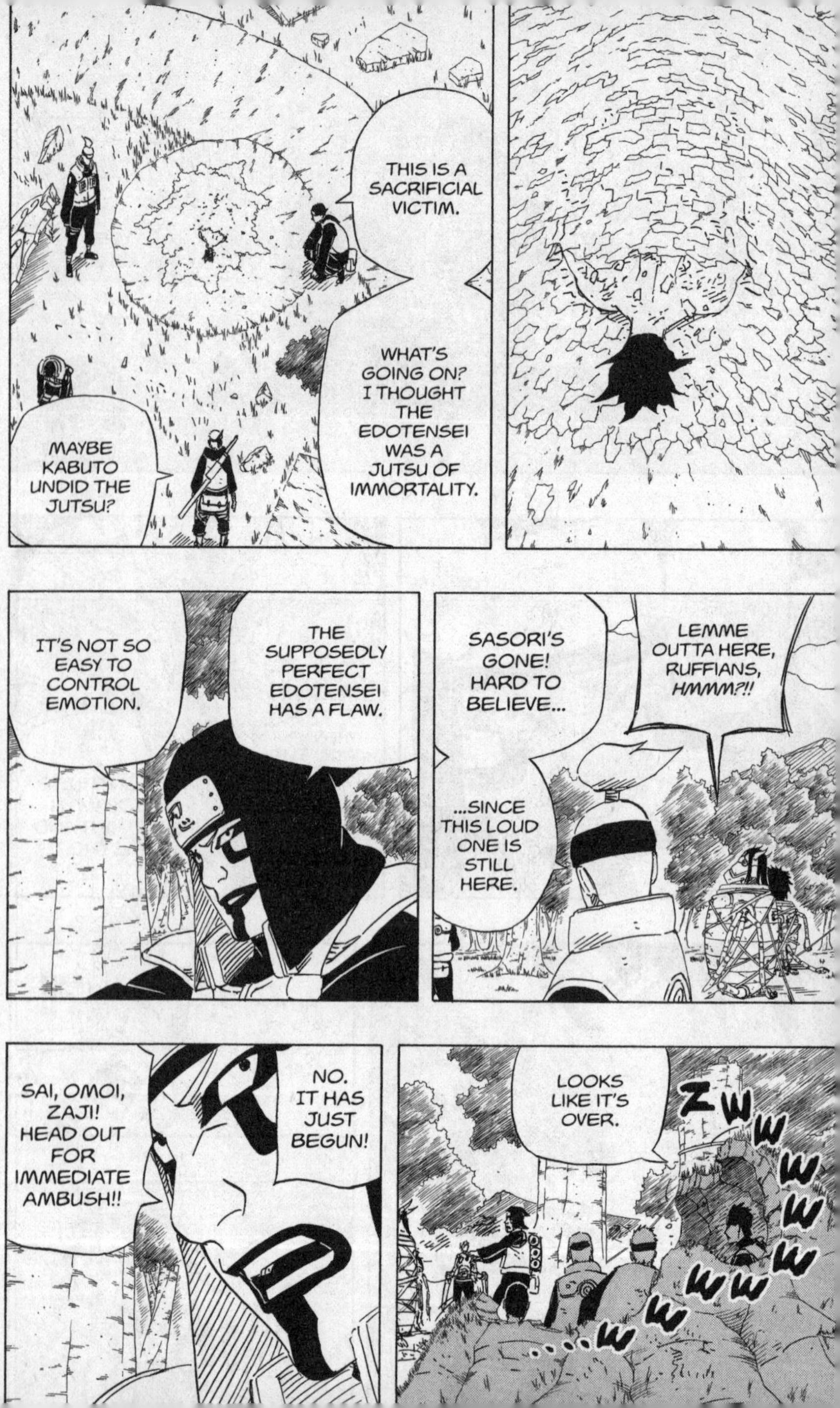
THIS IS A SACRIFICIAL VICTIM.
WHAT'S GOING ON? I THOUGHT THE EDOTENSEI WAS A JUTSU OF IMMORTALITY.
MAYBE KABUTO UNDID THE JUTSU?
LEMME OUTTA HERE, RUFFIANS, *HMMM?!!*
SASORI'S GONE! HARD TO BELIEVE...
...SINCE THIS LOUD ONE IS STILL HERE.
THE SUPPOSEDLY PERFECT EDOTENSEI HAS A FLAW.
IT'S NOT SO EASY TO CONTROL EMOTION.
LOOKS LIKE IT'S OVER.
ZWWWWW...W
NO. IT HAS JUST BEGUN!
SAI, OMOI, ZAJI! HEAD OUT FOR IMMEDIATE AMBUSH!!

READ THIS WAY

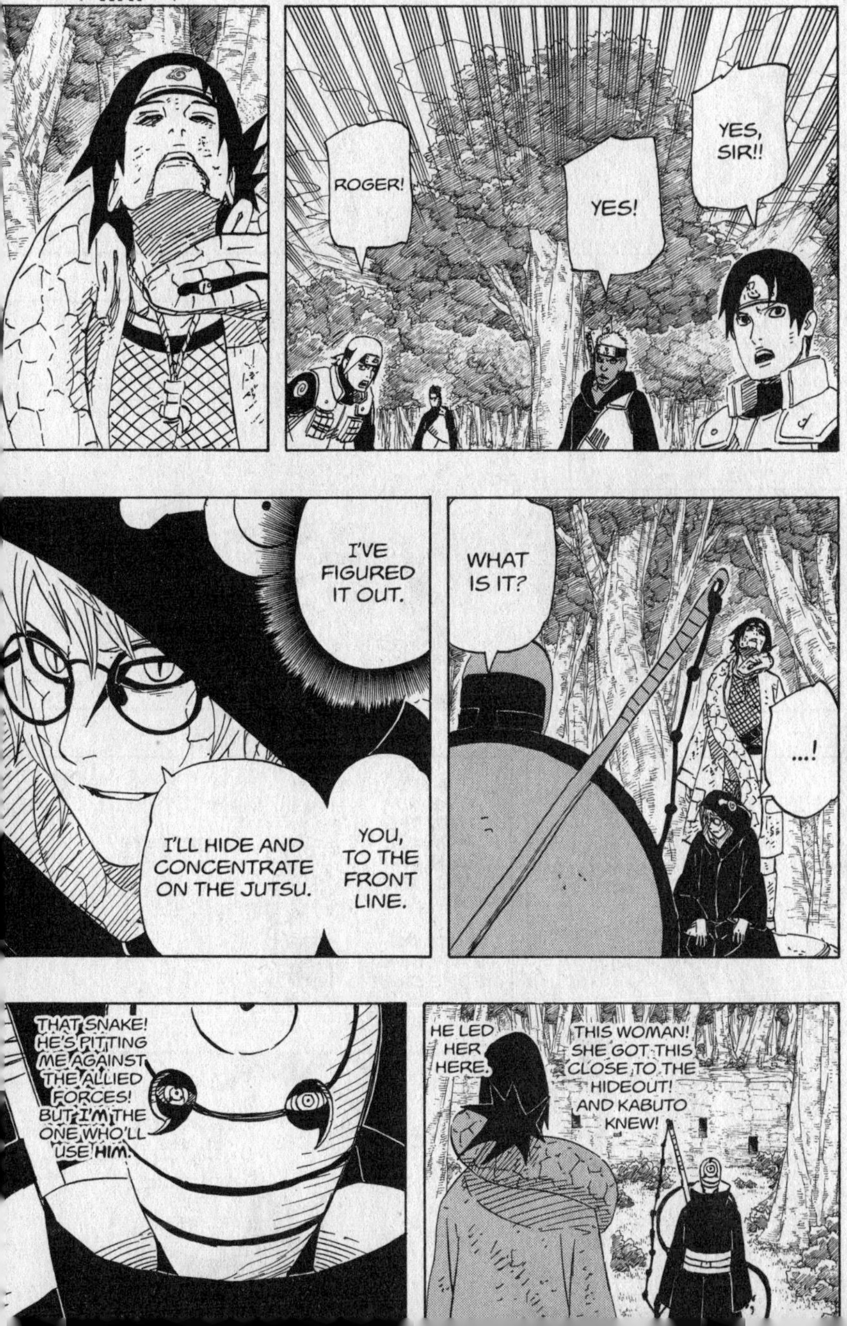
YES, SIR!!
YES!
ROGER!
WHAT IS IT?
...!
I'VE FIGURED IT OUT.
YOU, TO THE FRONT LINE.
I'LL HIDE AND CONCENTRATE ON THE JUTSU.
THIS WOMAN! SHE GOT THIS CLOSE TO THE HIDEOUT! AND KABUTO KNEW!
HE LED HER HERE.
THAT SNAKE! HE'S PITTING ME AGAINST THE ALLIED FORCES! BUT I'M THE ONE WHO'LL USE HIM.

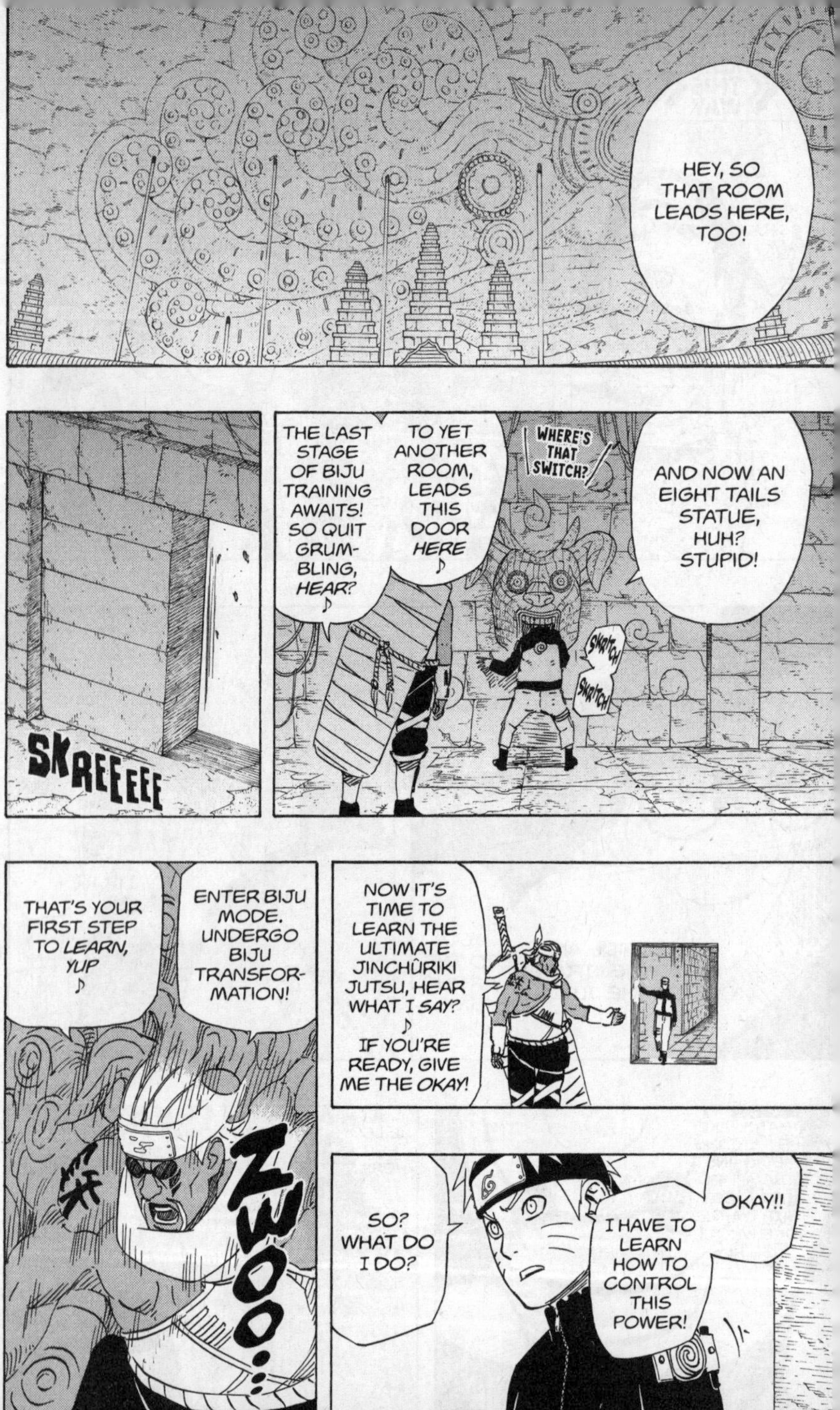
HEY, SO THAT ROOM LEADS HERE, TOO!
AND NOW AN EIGHT TAILS STATUE, HUH? STUPID!
WHERE'S THAT SWITCH?
TO YET ANOTHER ROOM, LEADS THIS DOOR *HERE* ♪
THE LAST STAGE OF BIJU TRAINING AWAITS! SO QUIT GRUM-BLING, *HEAR?* ♪
SKRITCH
SKRITCH
SKREEEEE
NOW IT'S TIME TO LEARN THE ULTIMATE JINCHÛRIKI JUTSU, HEAR WHAT I *SAY?* ♪ IF YOU'RE READY, GIVE ME THE *OKAY!*
OKAY!!
I HAVE TO LEARN HOW TO CONTROL THIS POWER!
SO? WHAT DO I DO?
ENTER BIJU MODE. UNDERGO BIJU TRANSFOR-MATION!
THAT'S YOUR FIRST STEP TO *LEARN, YUP* ♪
ZWOO...

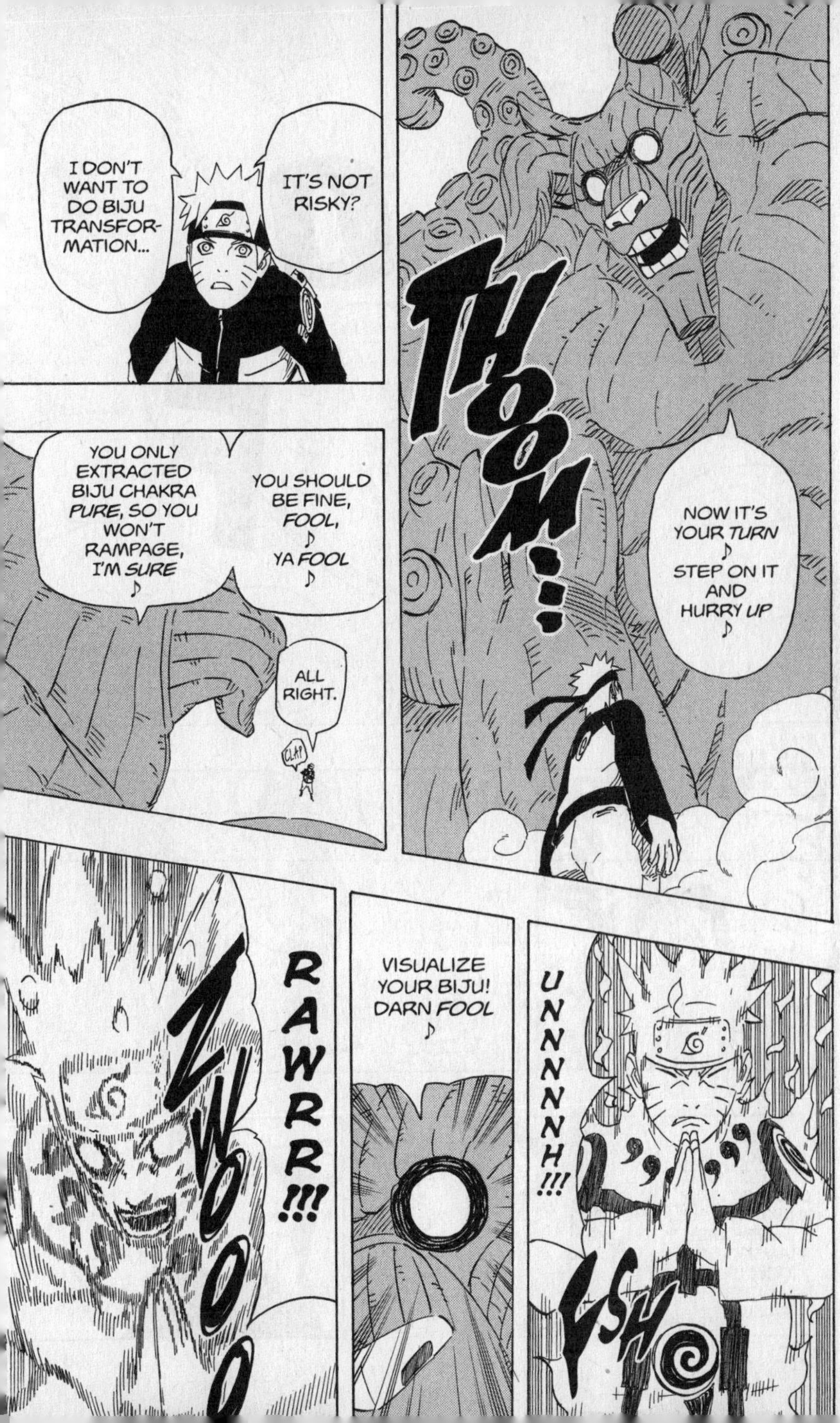
THOOM!!
NOW IT'S YOUR TURN ♪ STEP ON IT AND HURRY UP ♪
IT'S NOT RISKY?
I DON'T WANT TO DO BIJU TRANSFORMATION...
YOU SHOULD BE FINE, FOOL, ♪ YA FOOL ♪
YOU ONLY EXTRACTED BIJU CHAKRA PURE, SO YOU WON'T RAMPAGE, I'M SURE ♪
ALL RIGHT.
CLAP
UNNNNNH!!!
VISUALIZE YOUR BIJU! DARN FOOL ♪
RAWRR!!!

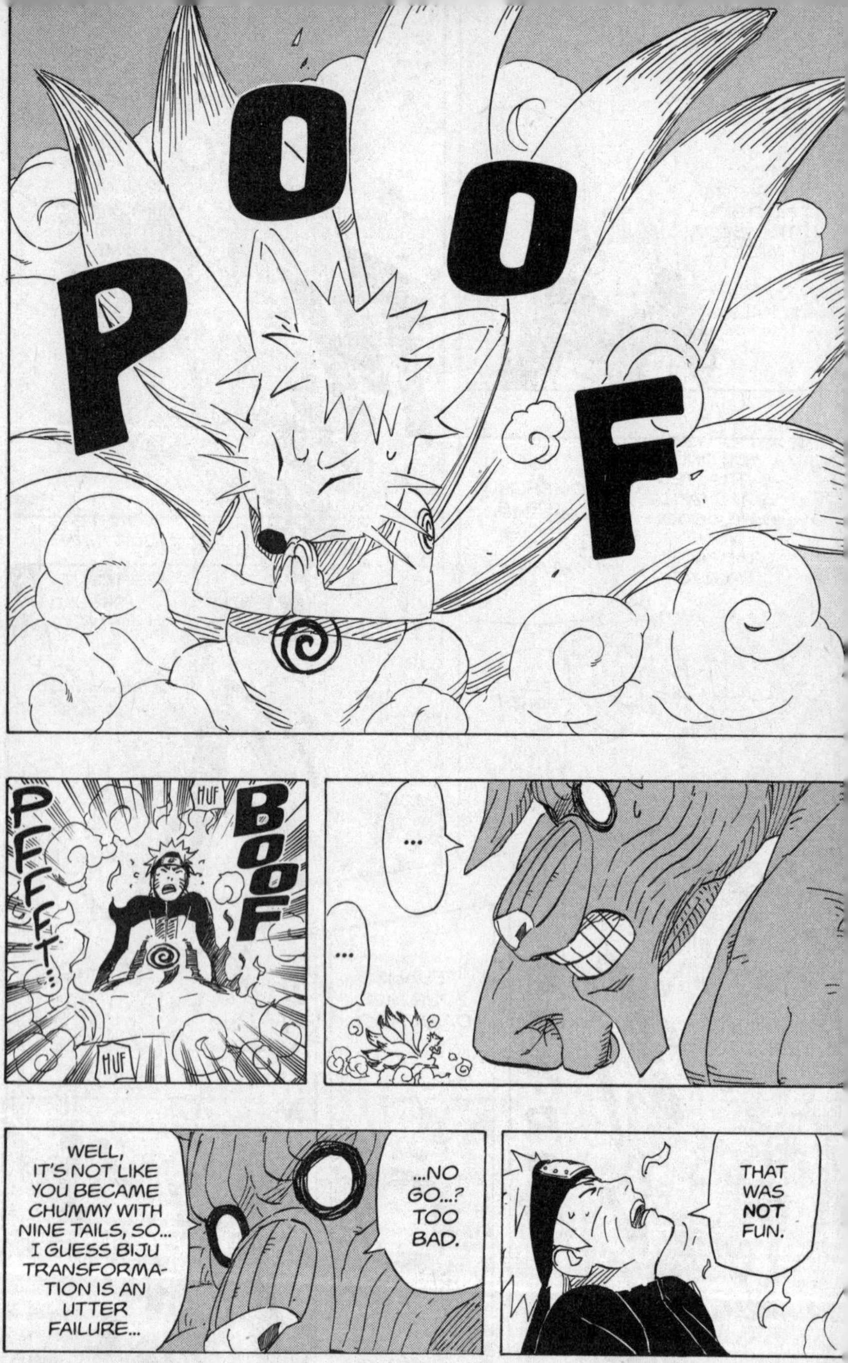
POOOF
...
...
HUF
BOOF
PFFFT...
HUF
THAT WAS **NOT** FUN.
...NO GO...? TOO BAD.
WELL, IT'S NOT LIKE YOU BECAME CHUMMY WITH NINE TAILS, SO... I GUESS BIJU TRANSFORMATION IS AN UTTER FAILURE...

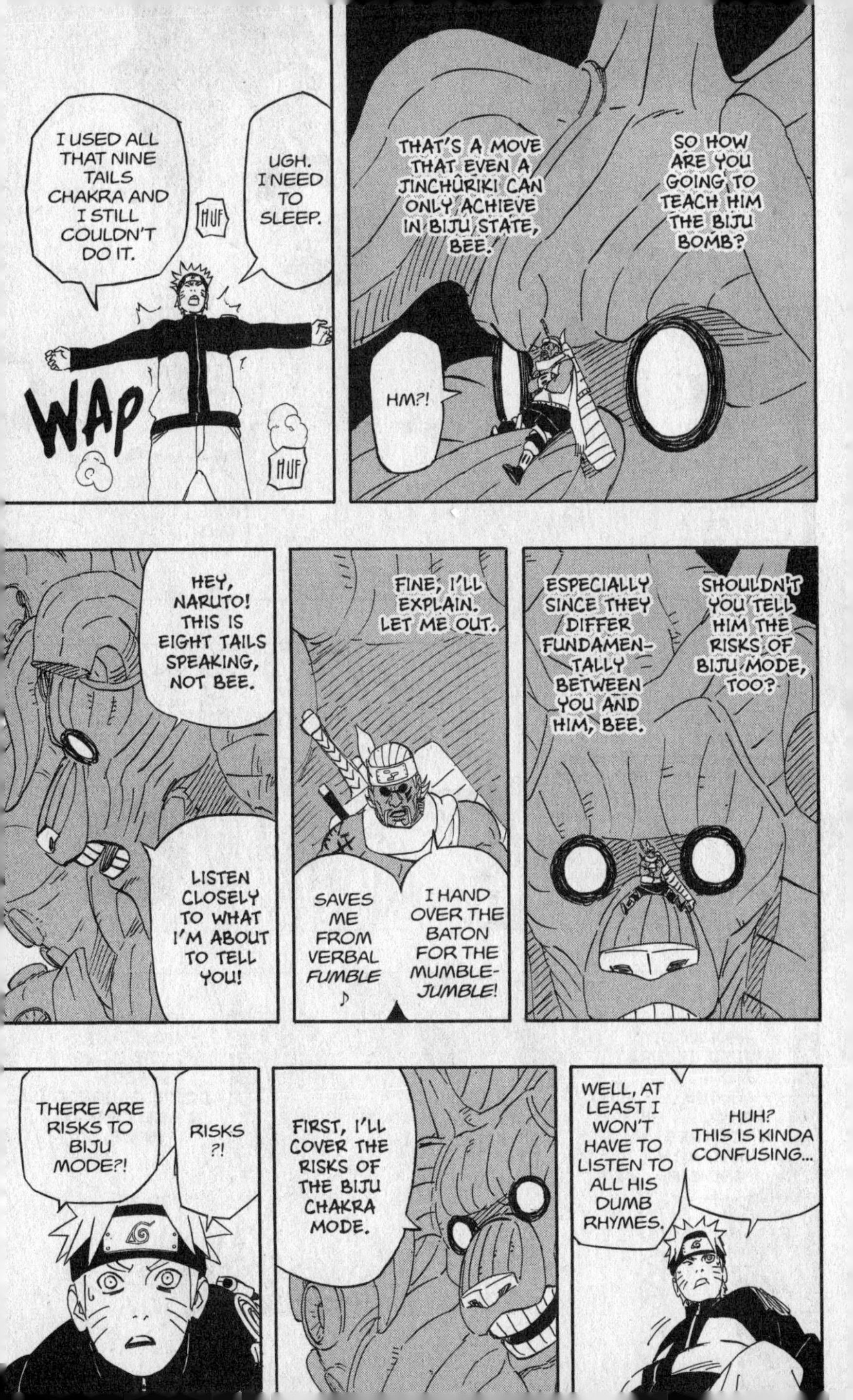
SO HOW ARE YOU GOING TO TEACH HIM THE BIJU BOMB?
THAT'S A MOVE THAT EVEN A JINCHÛRIKI CAN ONLY ACHIEVE IN BIJU STATE, BEE.
HM?!
UGH. I NEED TO SLEEP.
HUF
I USED ALL THAT NINE TAILS CHAKRA AND I STILL COULDN'T DO IT.
WAP
HUF
SHOULDN'T YOU TELL HIM THE RISKS OF BIJU MODE, TOO?
ESPECIALLY SINCE THEY DIFFER FUNDAMENTALLY BETWEEN YOU AND HIM, BEE.
FINE, I'LL EXPLAIN. LET ME OUT.
I HAND OVER THE BATON FOR THE MUMBLE-JUMBLE!
SAVES ME FROM VERBAL FUMBLE ♪
HEY, NARUTO! THIS IS EIGHT TAILS SPEAKING, NOT BEE.
LISTEN CLOSELY TO WHAT I'M ABOUT TO TELL YOU!
HUH? THIS IS KINDA CONFUSING...
WELL, AT LEAST I WON'T HAVE TO LISTEN TO ALL HIS DUMB RHYMES.
FIRST, I'LL COVER THE RISKS OF THE BIJU CHAKRA MODE.
RISKS?!
THERE ARE RISKS TO BIJU MODE?!

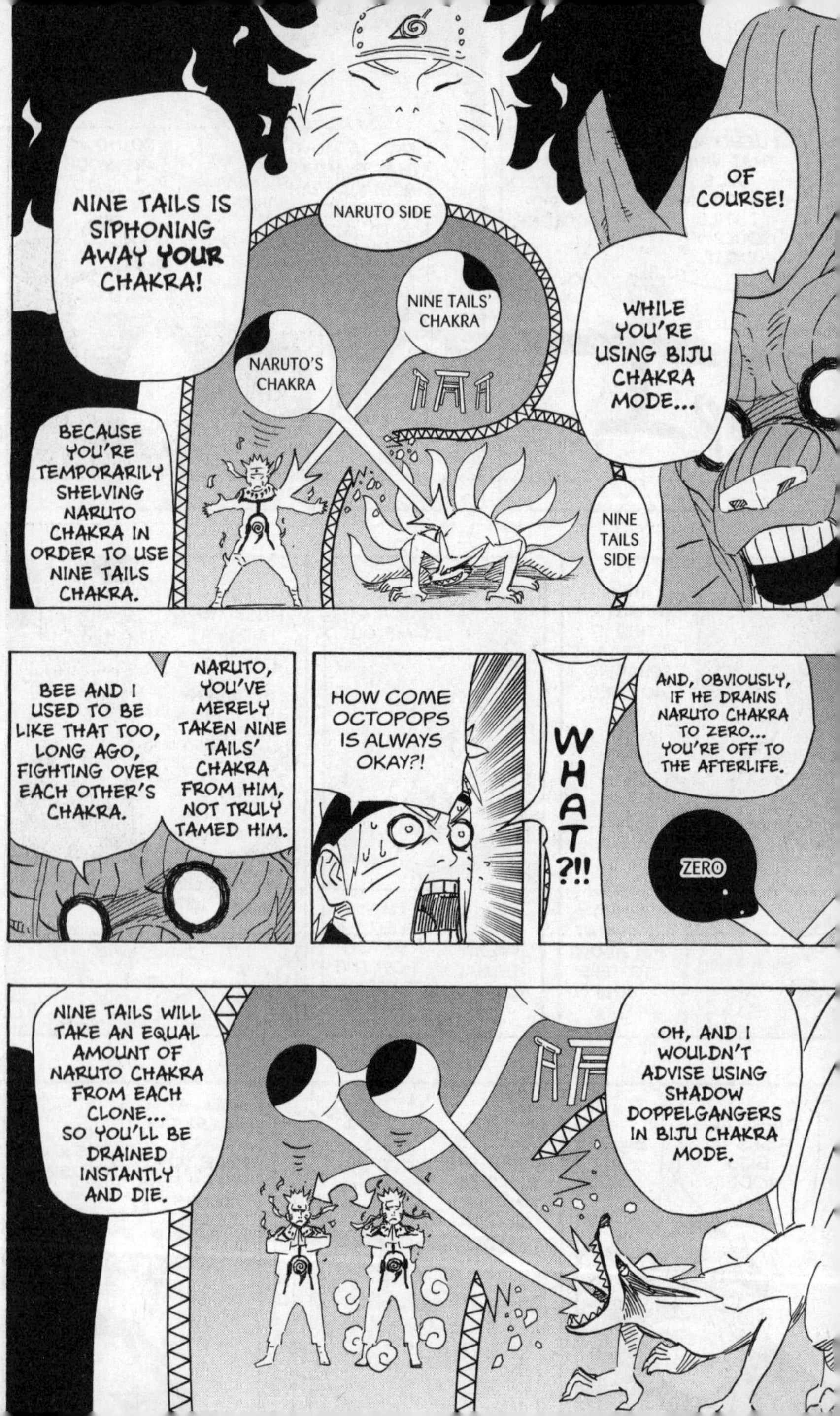
OF COURSE!
WHILE YOU'RE USING BIJU CHAKRA MODE...
NINE TAILS IS SIPHONING AWAY **YOUR** CHAKRA!
NARUTO SIDE
NINE TAILS' CHAKRA
NARUTO'S CHAKRA
NINE TAILS SIDE
BECAUSE YOU'RE TEMPORARILY SHELVING NARUTO CHAKRA IN ORDER TO USE NINE TAILS CHAKRA.
AND, OBVIOUSLY, IF HE DRAINS NARUTO CHAKRA TO ZERO... YOU'RE OFF TO THE AFTERLIFE.
ZERO
WHAT?!!
HOW COME OCTOPOPS IS ALWAYS OKAY?!
NARUTO, YOU'VE MERELY TAKEN NINE TAILS' CHAKRA FROM HIM, NOT TRULY TAMED HIM.
BEE AND I USED TO BE LIKE THAT TOO, LONG AGO, FIGHTING OVER EACH OTHER'S CHAKRA.
OH, AND I WOULDN'T ADVISE USING SHADOW DOPPELGANGERS IN BIJU CHAKRA MODE.
NINE TAILS WILL TAKE AN EQUAL AMOUNT OF NARUTO CHAKRA FROM EACH CLONE... SO YOU'LL BE DRAINED INSTANTLY AND DIE.

READ THIS WAY

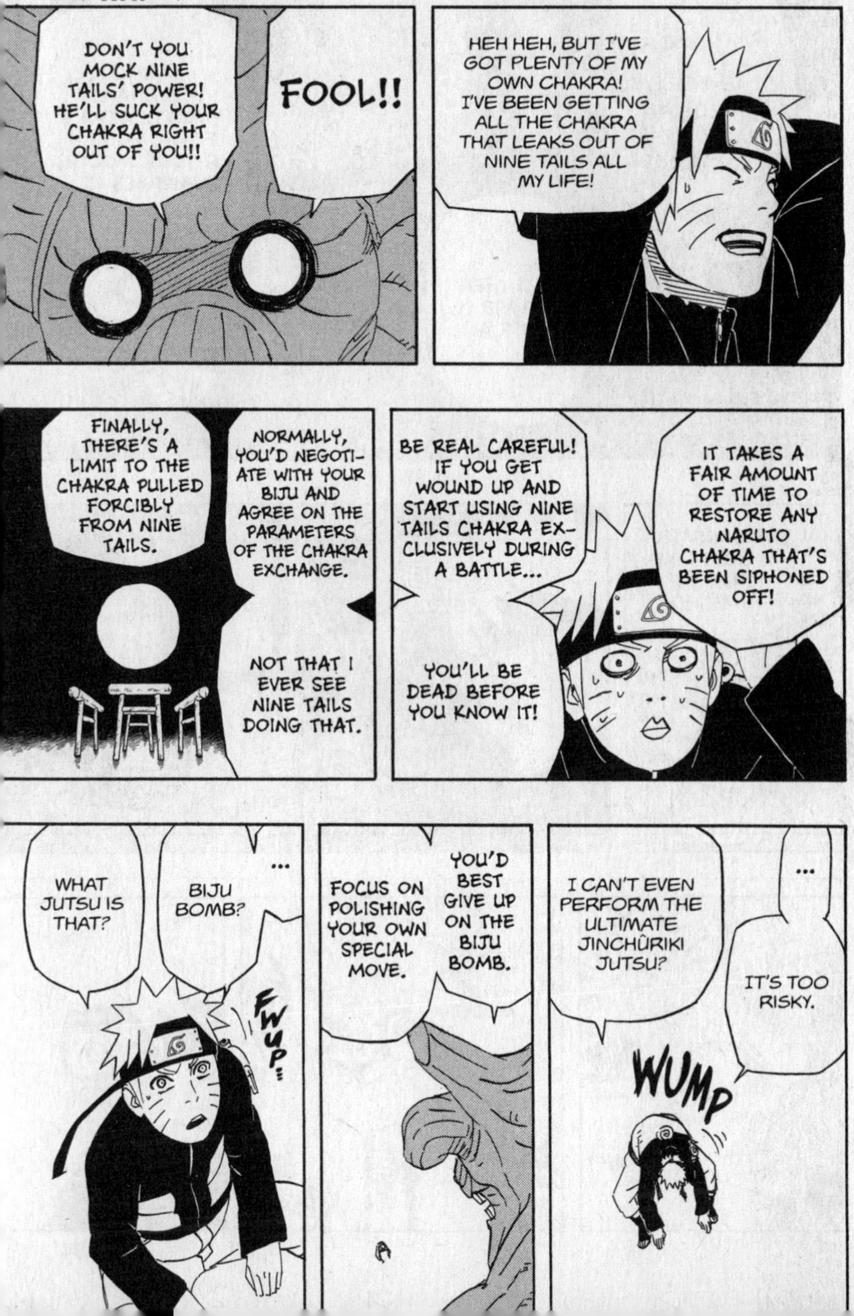
HEH HEH, BUT I'VE GOT PLENTY OF MY OWN CHAKRA! I'VE BEEN GETTING ALL THE CHAKRA THAT LEAKS OUT OF NINE TAILS ALL MY LIFE!
FOOL!!
DON'T YOU MOCK NINE TAILS' POWER! HE'LL SUCK YOUR CHAKRA RIGHT OUT OF YOU!!
IT TAKES A FAIR AMOUNT OF TIME TO RESTORE ANY NARUTO CHAKRA THAT'S BEEN SIPHONED OFF!
BE REAL CAREFUL! IF YOU GET WOUND UP AND START USING NINE TAILS CHAKRA EX-CLUSIVELY DURING A BATTLE...
YOU'LL BE DEAD BEFORE YOU KNOW IT!
NORMALLY, YOU'D NEGOTI-ATE WITH YOUR BIJU AND AGREE ON THE PARAMETERS OF THE CHAKRA EXCHANGE.
NOT THAT I EVER SEE NINE TAILS DOING THAT.
FINALLY, THERE'S A LIMIT TO THE CHAKRA PULLED FORCIBLY FROM NINE TAILS.
...
I CAN'T EVEN PERFORM THE ULTIMATE JINCHÛRIKI JUTSU?
IT'S TOO RISKY.
WUMP
YOU'D BEST GIVE UP ON THE BIJU BOMB.
FOCUS ON POLISHING YOUR OWN SPECIAL MOVE.
...
BIJU BOMB?
WHAT JUTSU IS THAT?
FWUP

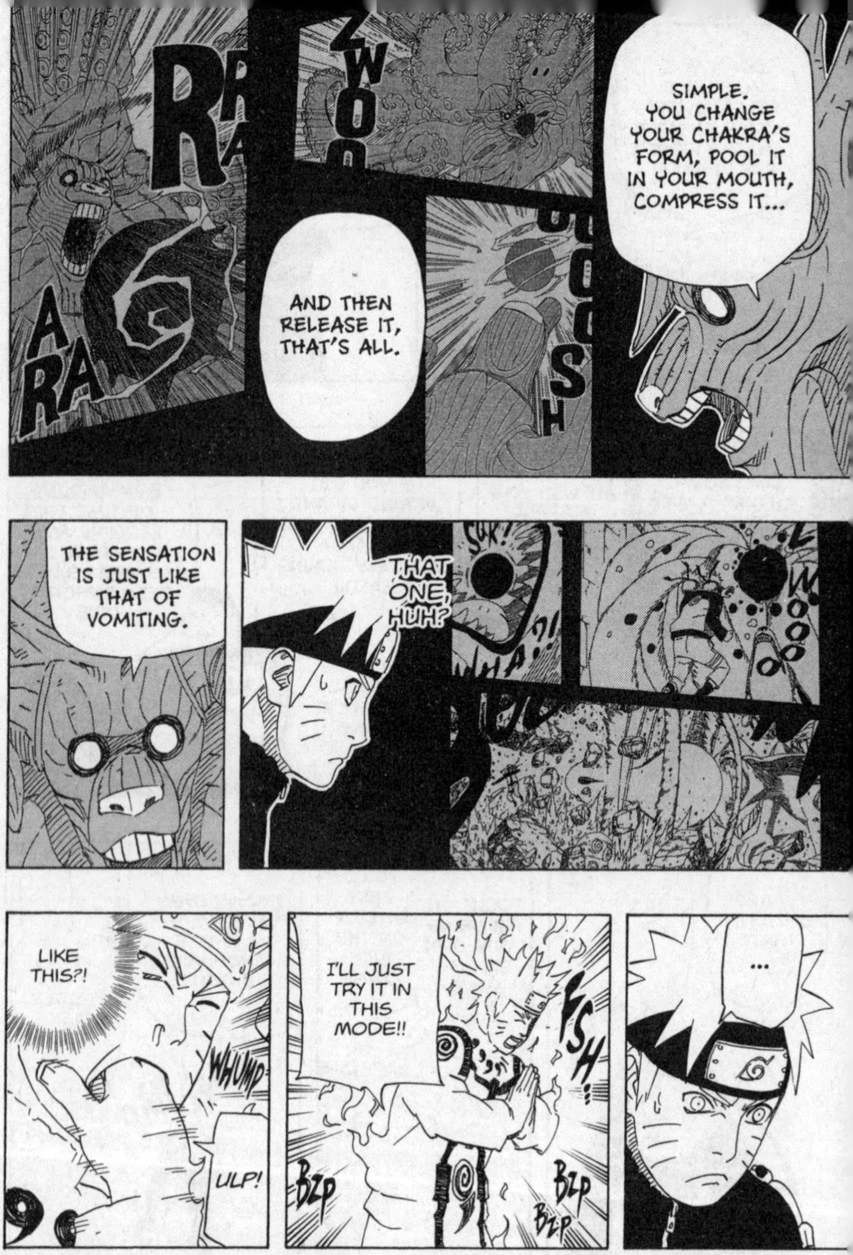
SIMPLE. YOU CHANGE YOUR CHAKRA'S FORM, POOL IT IN YOUR MOUTH, COMPRESS IT...
AND THEN RELEASE IT, THAT'S ALL.
THE SENSATION IS JUST LIKE THAT OF VOMITING.
THAT ONE, HUH?
...
I'LL JUST TRY IT IN THIS MODE!!
FSH!!
BZP
BZP
BZP
LIKE THIS?!
WHUMP
ULP!

READ THIS WAY

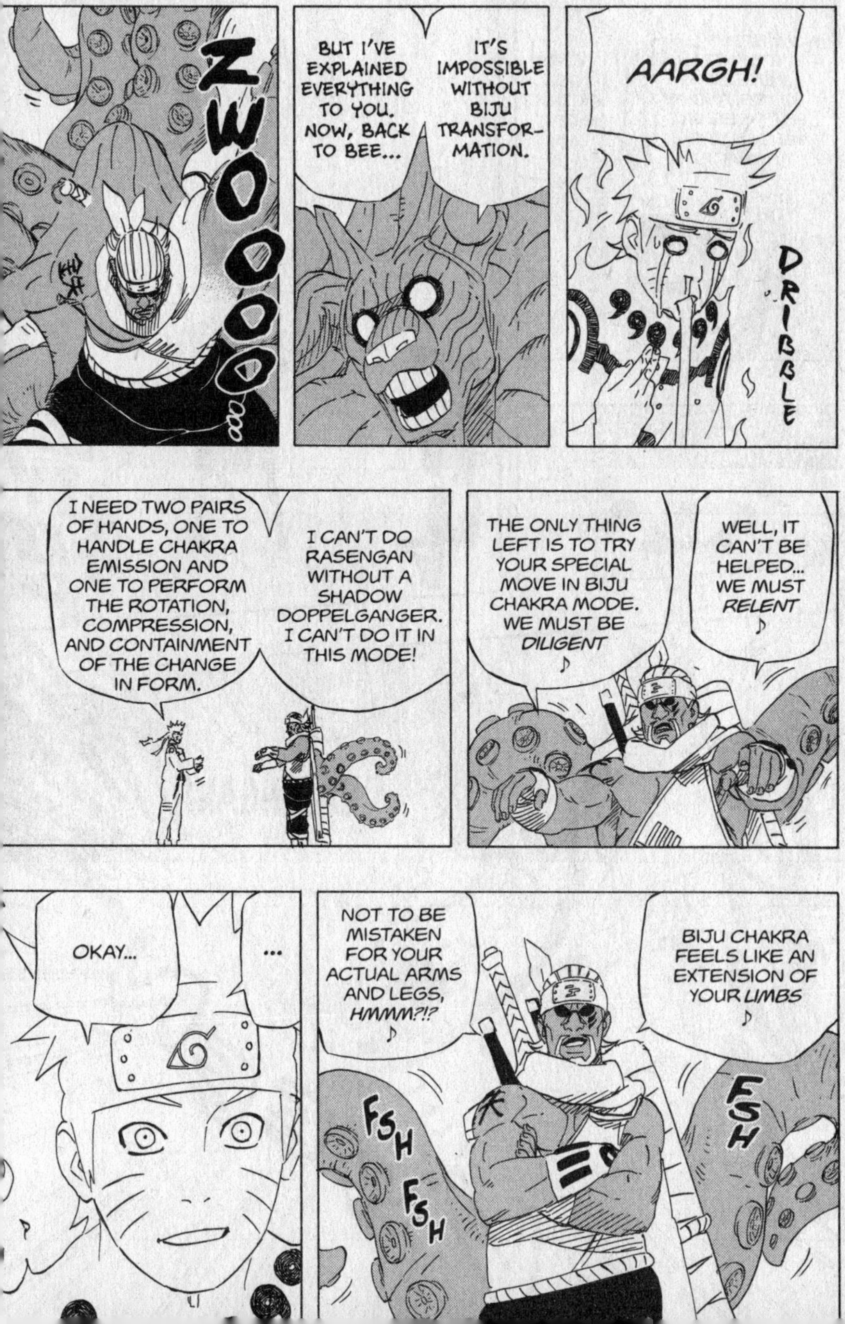
AARGH!
DRIBBLE
IT'S IMPOSSIBLE WITHOUT BIJU TRANSFORMATION.
BUT I'VE EXPLAINED EVERYTHING TO YOU. NOW, BACK TO BEE...
ZWOOOOO
WELL, IT CAN'T BE HELPED... WE MUST RELENT ♪
THE ONLY THING LEFT IS TO TRY YOUR SPECIAL MOVE IN BIJU CHAKRA MODE. WE MUST BE DILIGENT ♪
I CAN'T DO RASENGAN WITHOUT A SHADOW DOPPELGANGER. I CAN'T DO IT IN THIS MODE!
I NEED TWO PAIRS OF HANDS, ONE TO HANDLE CHAKRA EMISSION AND ONE TO PERFORM THE ROTATION, COMPRESSION, AND CONTAINMENT OF THE CHANGE IN FORM.
BIJU CHAKRA FEELS LIKE AN EXTENSION OF YOUR LIMBS ♪
NOT TO BE MISTAKEN FOR YOUR ACTUAL ARMS AND LEGS, HMMM?!? ♪
FSH
FSH
FSH
...
OKAY...

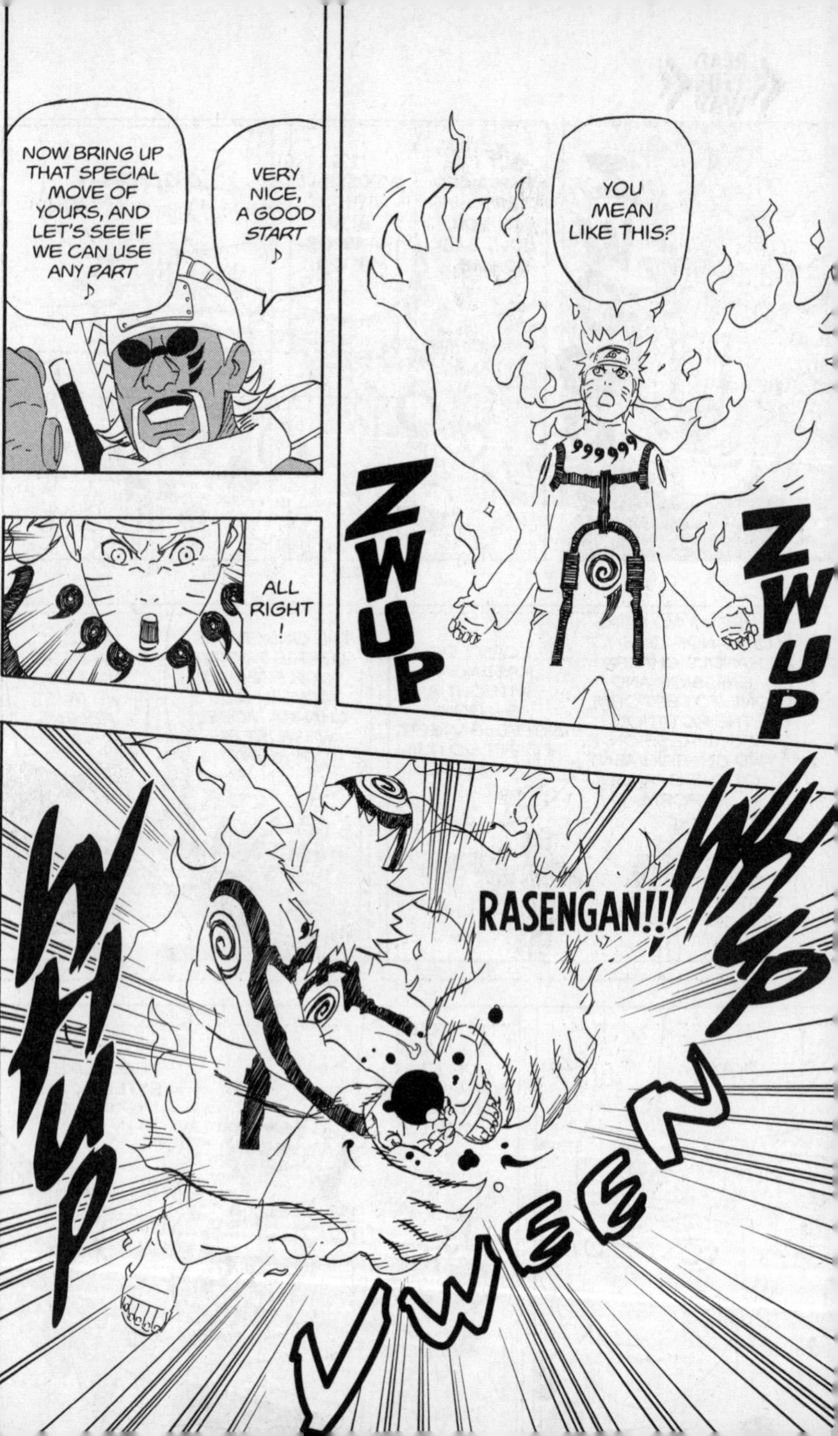
YOU MEAN LIKE THIS?
ZWUP
ZWUP
VERY NICE, A GOOD *START* ♪
NOW BRING UP THAT SPECIAL MOVE OF YOURS, AND LET'S SEE IF WE CAN USE ANY *PART* ♪
ALL RIGHT!
WHUP
RASENGAN!!
VWEEN
WHUP

READ THIS WAY

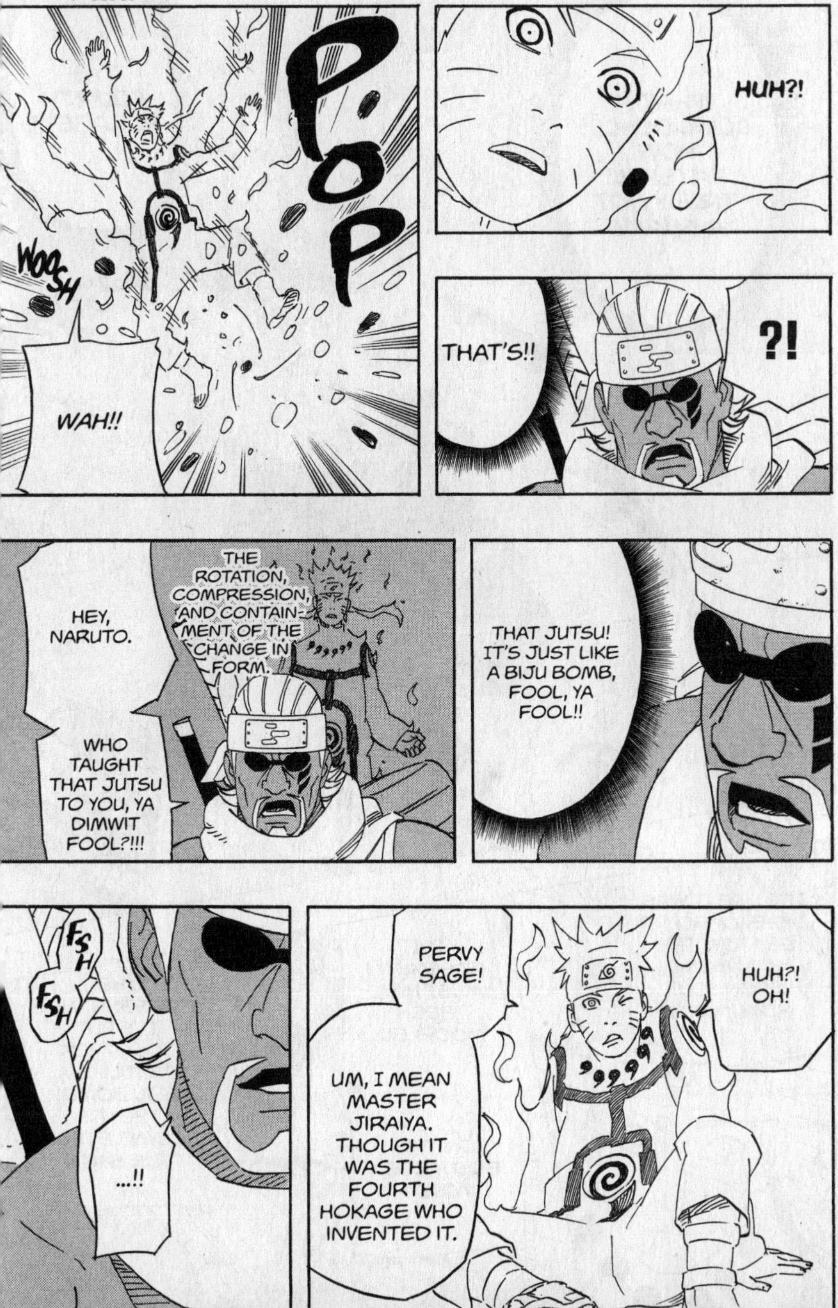

HUH?!
?!
THAT'S!!
POP
WOOSH
WAH!!
THAT JUTSU! IT'S JUST LIKE A BIJU BOMB, FOOL, YA FOOL!!
THE ROTATION, COMPRESSION, AND CONTAINMENT OF THE CHANGE IN FORM.
HEY, NARUTO.
WHO TAUGHT THAT JUTSU TO YOU, YA DIMWIT FOOL?!!!
HUH?! OH!
PERVY SAGE!
UM, I MEAN MASTER JIRAIYA. THOUGH IT WAS THE FOURTH HOKAGE WHO INVENTED IT.
FSH
FSH
...!!

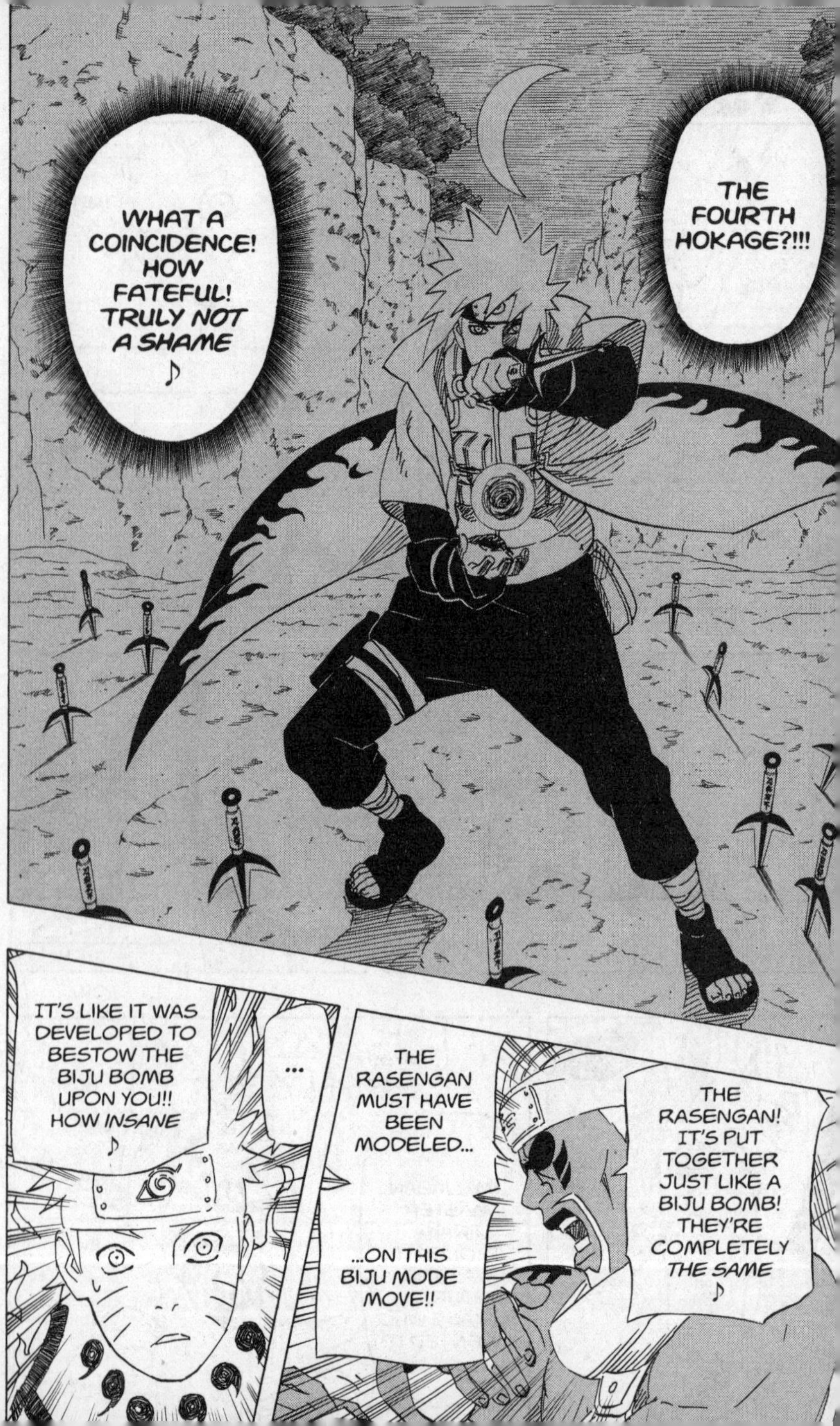
THE FOURTH HOKAGE?!!!
WHAT A COINCIDENCE! HOW FATEFUL! TRULY NOT A SHAME ♪
THE RASENGAN! IT'S PUT TOGETHER JUST LIKE A BIJU BOMB! THEY'RE COMPLETELY THE SAME ♪
THE RASENGAN MUST HAVE BEEN MODELED...
...ON THIS BIJU MODE MOVE!!
...
IT'S LIKE IT WAS DEVELOPED TO BESTOW THE BIJU BOMB UPON YOU!! HOW INSANE ♪

READ THIS WAY

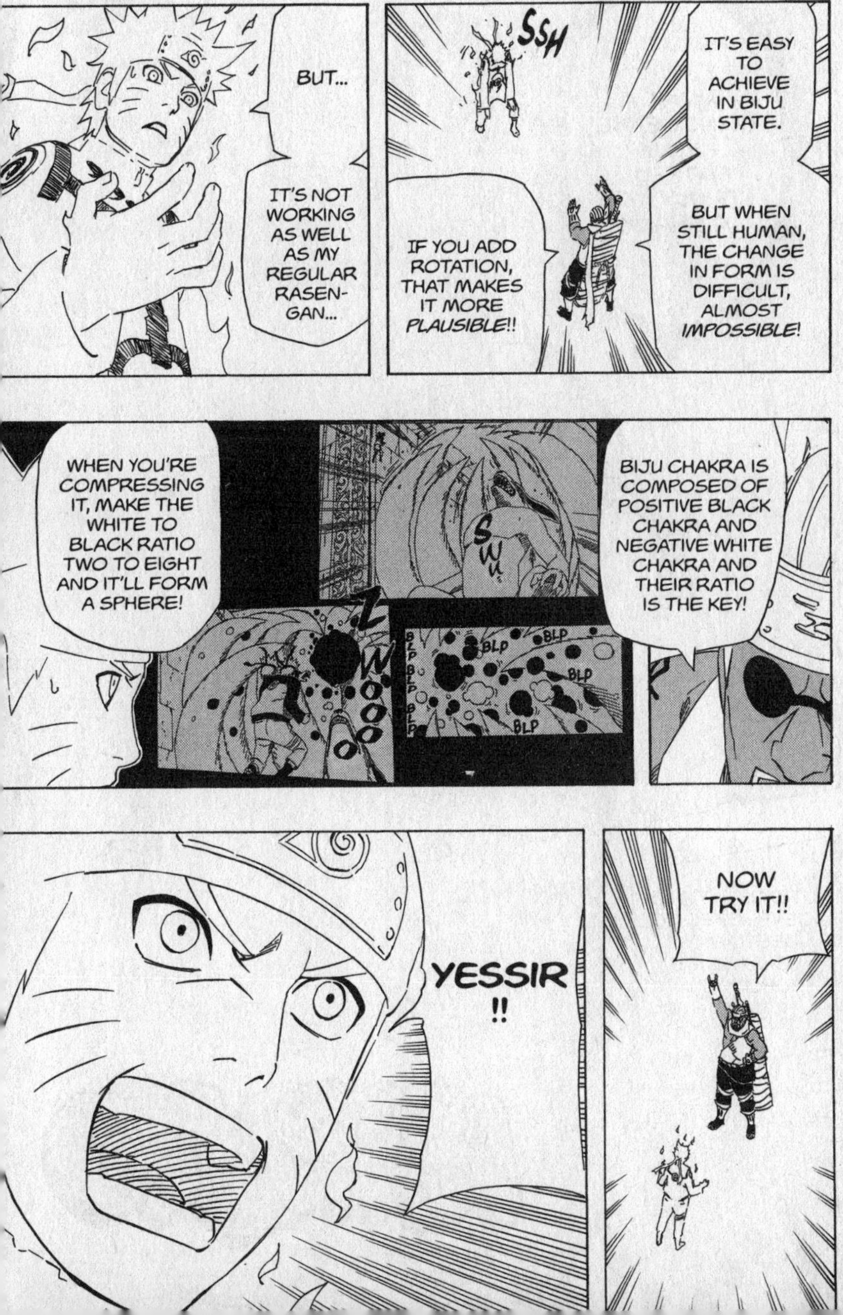

IT'S EASY TO ACHIEVE IN BIJU STATE.
BUT WHEN STILL HUMAN, THE CHANGE IN FORM IS DIFFICULT, ALMOST IMPOSSIBLE!
SSH
IF YOU ADD ROTATION, THAT MAKES IT MORE PLAUSIBLE!!
BUT...
IT'S NOT WORKING AS WELL AS MY REGULAR RASEN-GAN...
BIJU CHAKRA IS COMPOSED OF POSITIVE BLACK CHAKRA AND NEGATIVE WHITE CHAKRA AND THEIR RATIO IS THE KEY!
SWU
BLP BLP BLP BLP BLP BLP BLP BLP BLP
ZWOOOO
WHEN YOU'RE COMPRESSING IT, MAKE THE WHITE TO BLACK RATIO TWO TO EIGHT AND IT'LL FORM A SPHERE!
NOW TRY IT!!
YESSIR!!

NARUTO

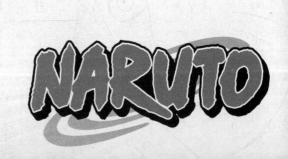

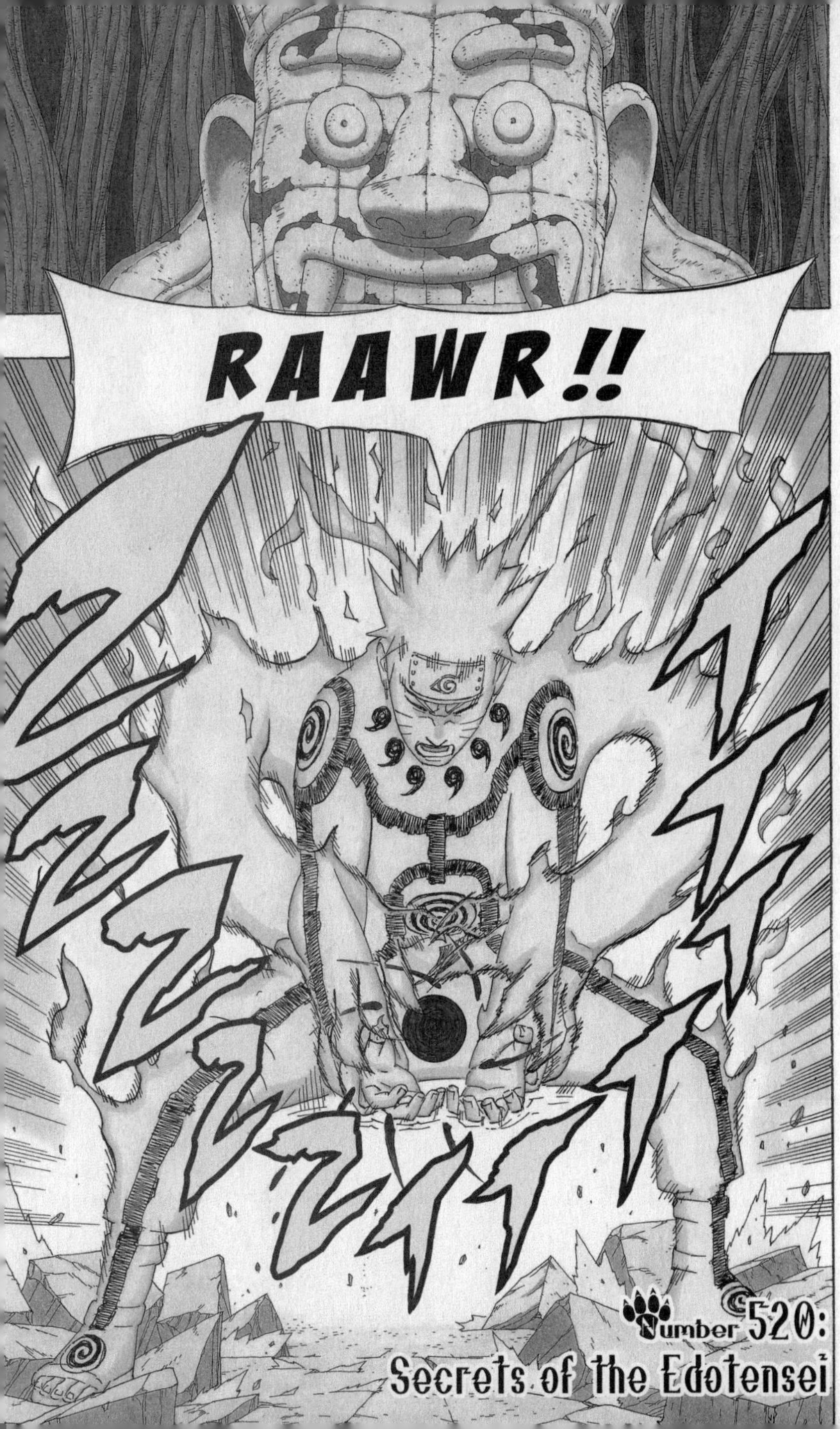
RAAWR!!
Number 520:
Secrets of the Edotensei

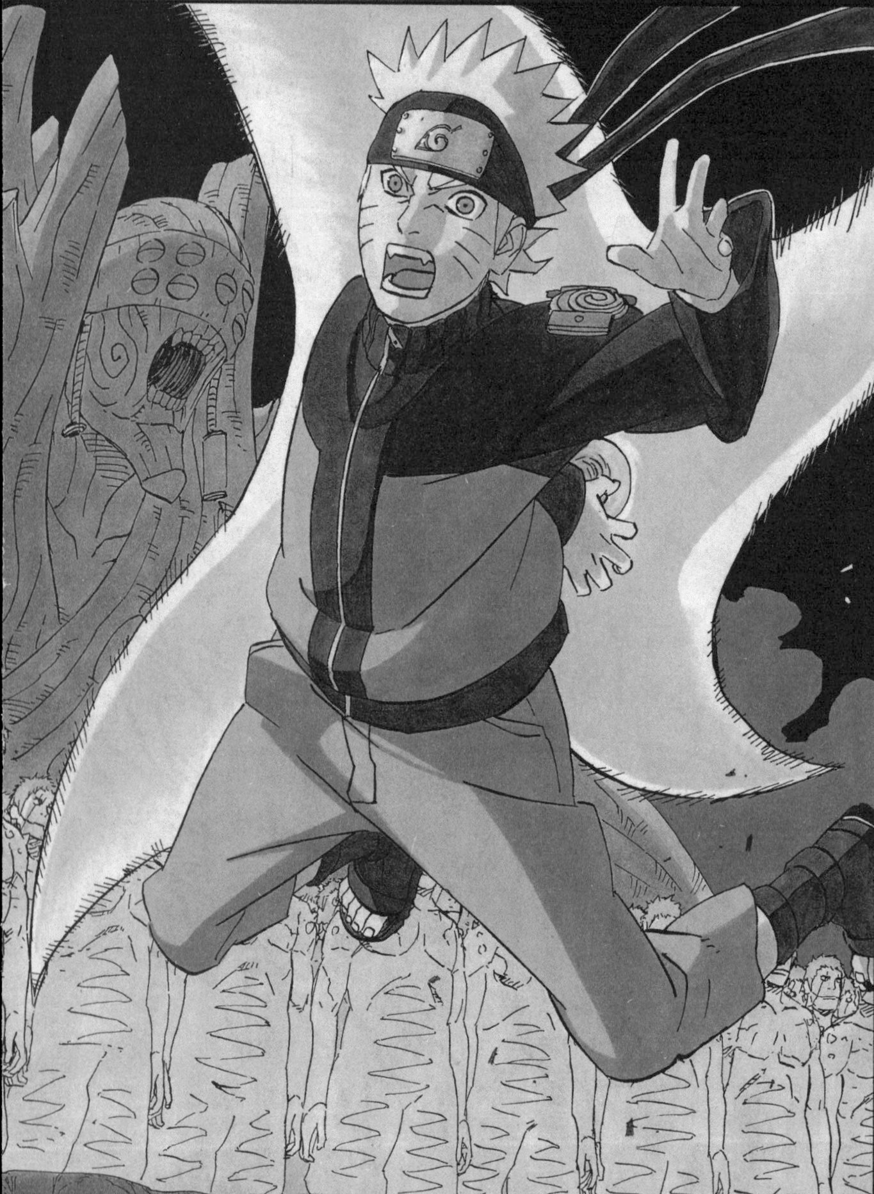

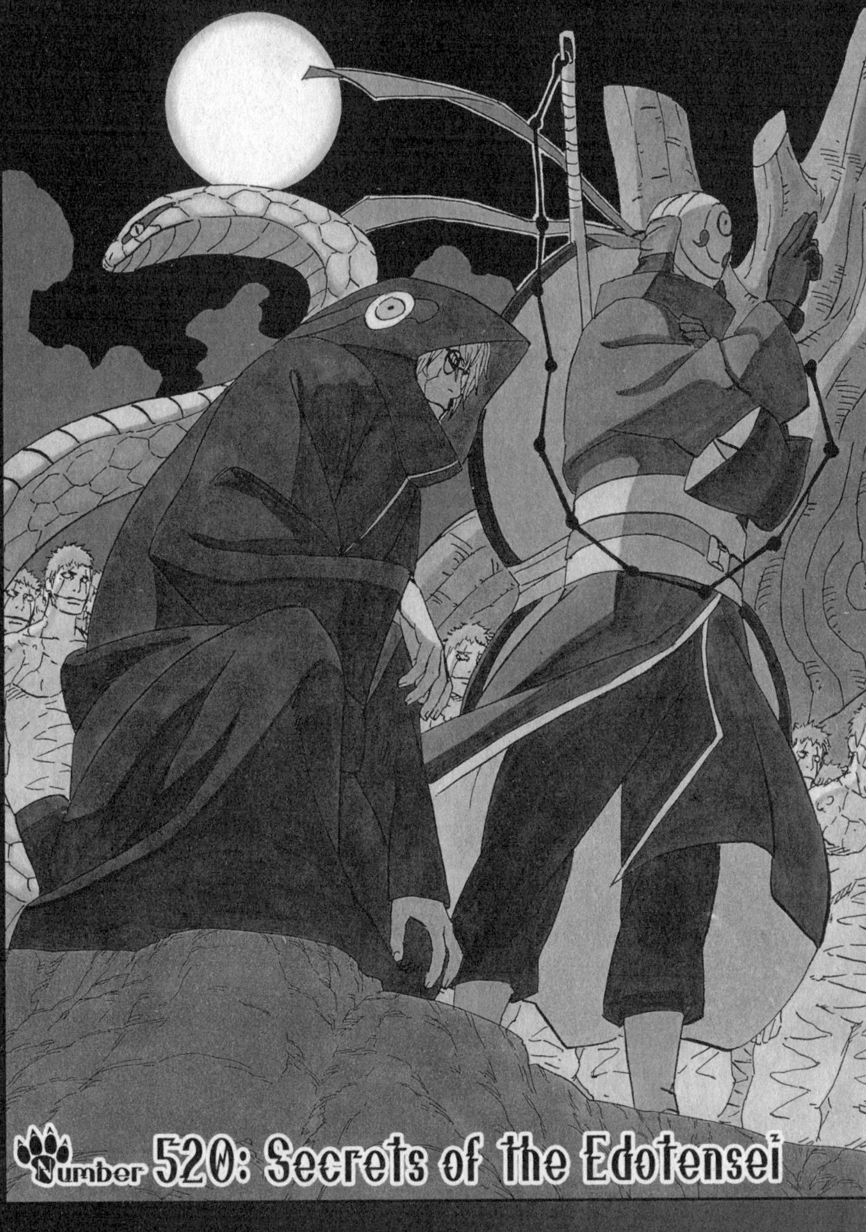

# Number 520: Secrets of the Edotensei

# NARUTO

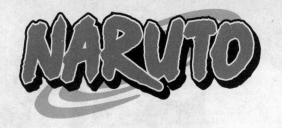

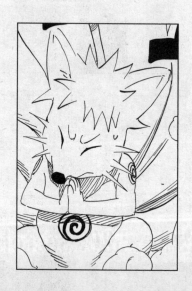

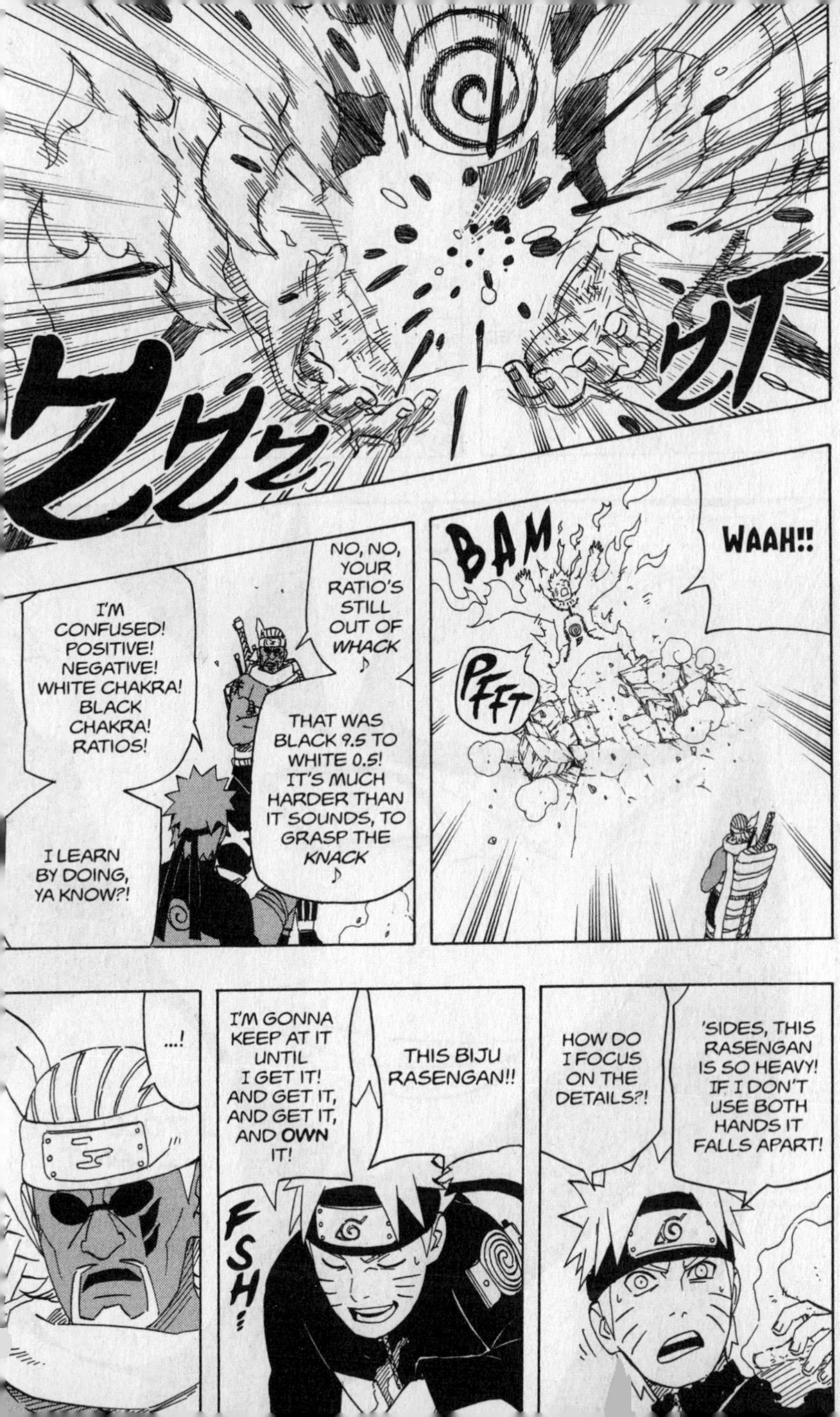
WAAH!!
BAM
PFFT
NO, NO, YOUR RATIO'S STILL OUT OF *WHACK* ♪
I'M CONFUSED! POSITIVE! NEGATIVE! WHITE CHAKRA! BLACK CHAKRA! RATIOS!
THAT WAS BLACK 9.5 TO WHITE 0.5! IT'S MUCH HARDER THAN IT SOUNDS, TO GRASP THE *KNACK* ♪
I LEARN BY DOING, YA KNOW?!
'SIDES, THIS RASENGAN IS SO HEAVY! IF I DON'T USE BOTH HANDS IT FALLS APART!
HOW DO I FOCUS ON THE DETAILS?!
I'M GONNA KEEP AT IT UNTIL I GET IT! AND GET IT, AND GET IT, AND **OWN** IT!
THIS BIJU RASENGAN!!
FSH!!
...!

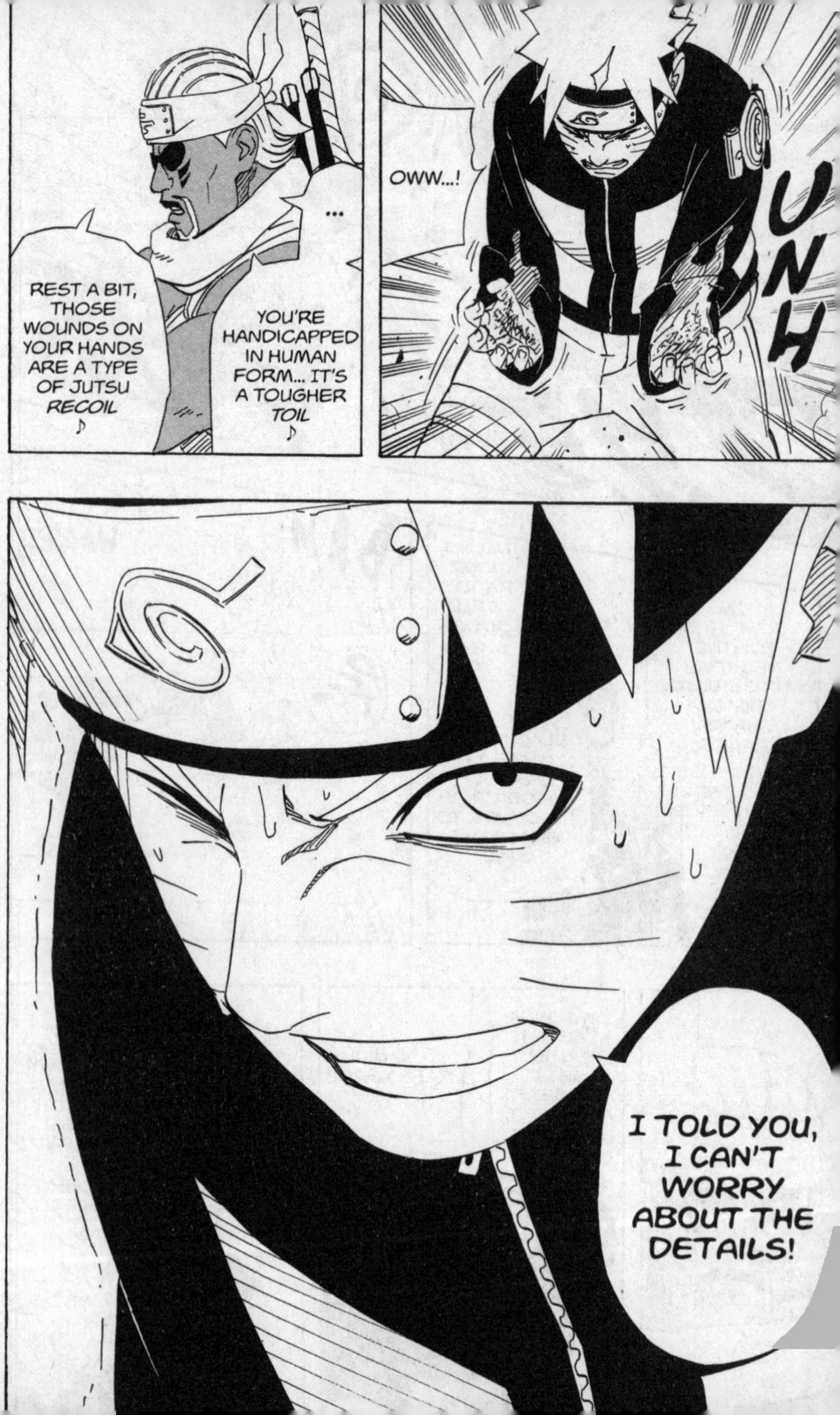
UNH
OWW...!
...
YOU'RE HANDICAPPED IN HUMAN FORM... IT'S A TOUGHER TOIL ♪
REST A BIT, THOSE WOUNDS ON YOUR HANDS ARE A TYPE OF JUTSU RECOIL ♪
I TOLD YOU, I CAN'T WORRY ABOUT THE DETAILS!

READ THIS WAY

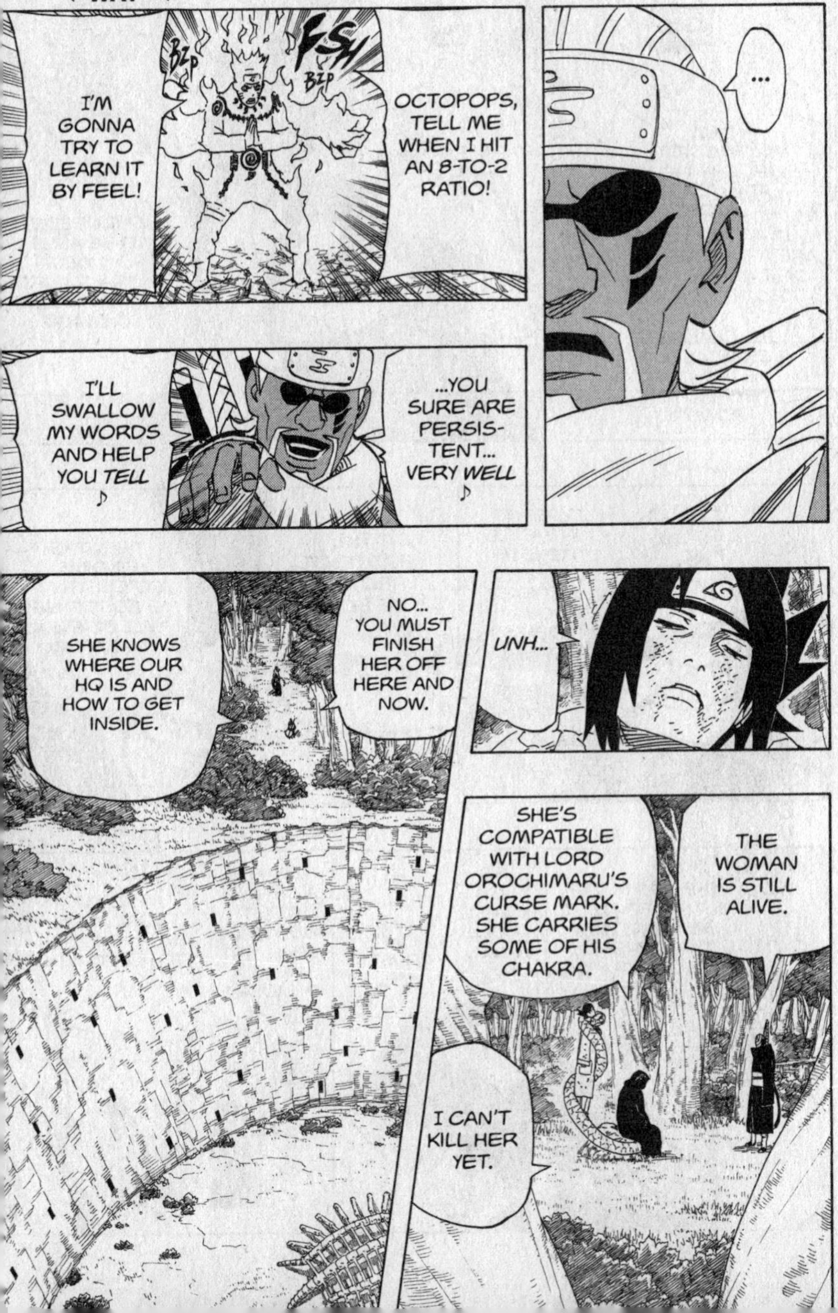
...
FSH
BZP
BZP
OCTOPOPS, TELL ME WHEN I HIT AN 8-TO-2 RATIO!
I'M GONNA TRY TO LEARN IT BY FEEL!
...YOU SURE ARE PERSISTENT... VERY *WELL* ♪
I'LL SWALLOW MY WORDS AND HELP YOU *TELL* ♪
*UNH...*
THE WOMAN IS STILL ALIVE.
SHE'S COMPATIBLE WITH LORD OROCHIMARU'S CURSE MARK. SHE CARRIES SOME OF HIS CHAKRA.
I CAN'T KILL HER YET.
NO... YOU MUST FINISH HER OFF HERE AND NOW.
SHE KNOWS WHERE OUR HQ IS AND HOW TO GET INSIDE.

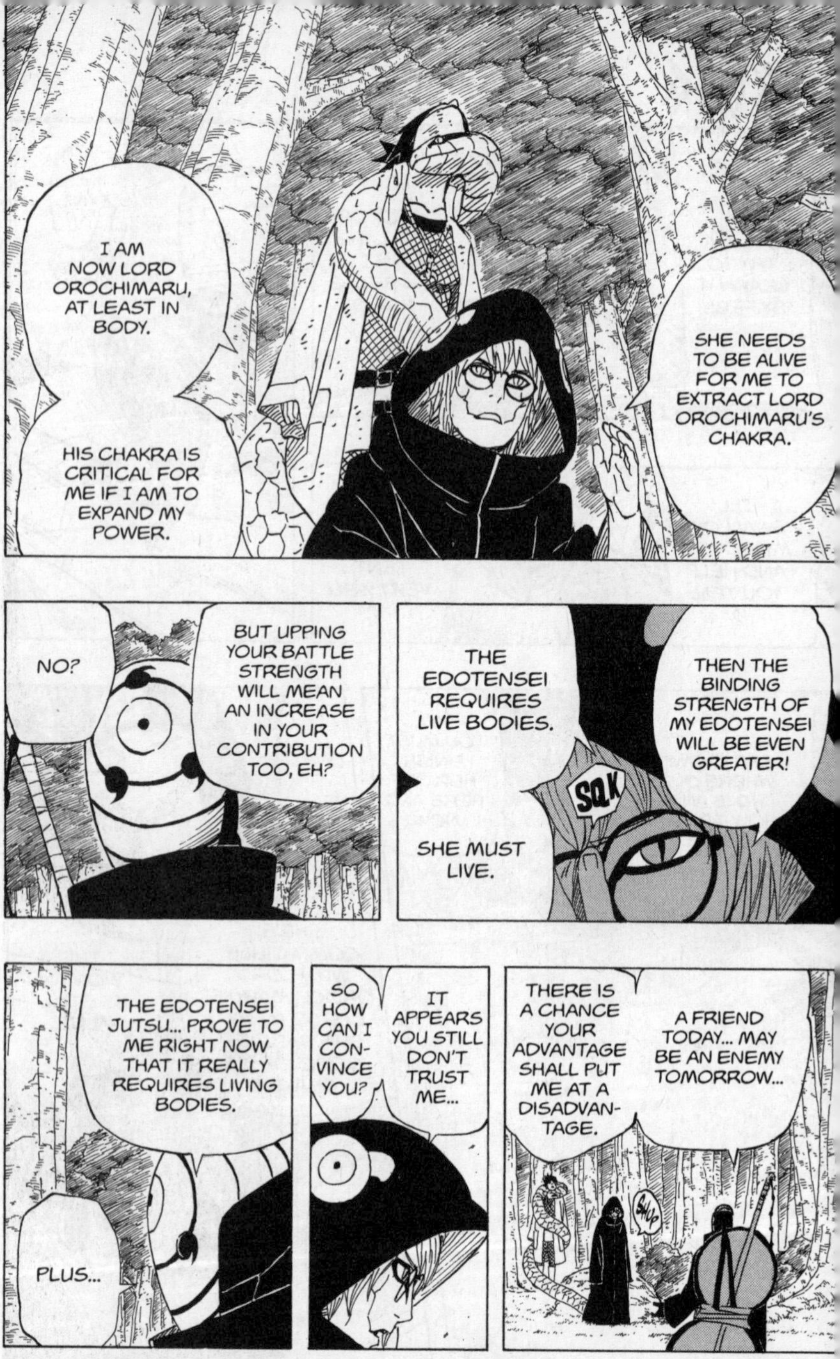

SHE NEEDS TO BE ALIVE FOR ME TO EXTRACT LORD OROCHIMARU'S CHAKRA.
I AM NOW LORD OROCHIMARU, AT LEAST IN BODY.
HIS CHAKRA IS CRITICAL FOR ME IF I AM TO EXPAND MY POWER.
THEN THE BINDING STRENGTH OF MY EDOTENSEI WILL BE EVEN GREATER!
THE EDOTENSEI REQUIRES LIVE BODIES.
SQK
SHE MUST LIVE.
BUT UPPING YOUR BATTLE STRENGTH WILL MEAN AN INCREASE IN YOUR CONTRIBUTION TOO, EH?
NO?
A FRIEND TODAY... MAY BE AN ENEMY TOMORROW...
THERE IS A CHANCE YOUR ADVANTAGE SHALL PUT ME AT A DISADVAN-TAGE.
IT APPEARS YOU STILL DON'T TRUST ME...
SO HOW CAN I CON-VINCE YOU?
THE EDOTENSEI JUTSU... PROVE TO ME RIGHT NOW THAT IT REALLY REQUIRES LIVING BODIES.
PLUS...

READ THIS WAY

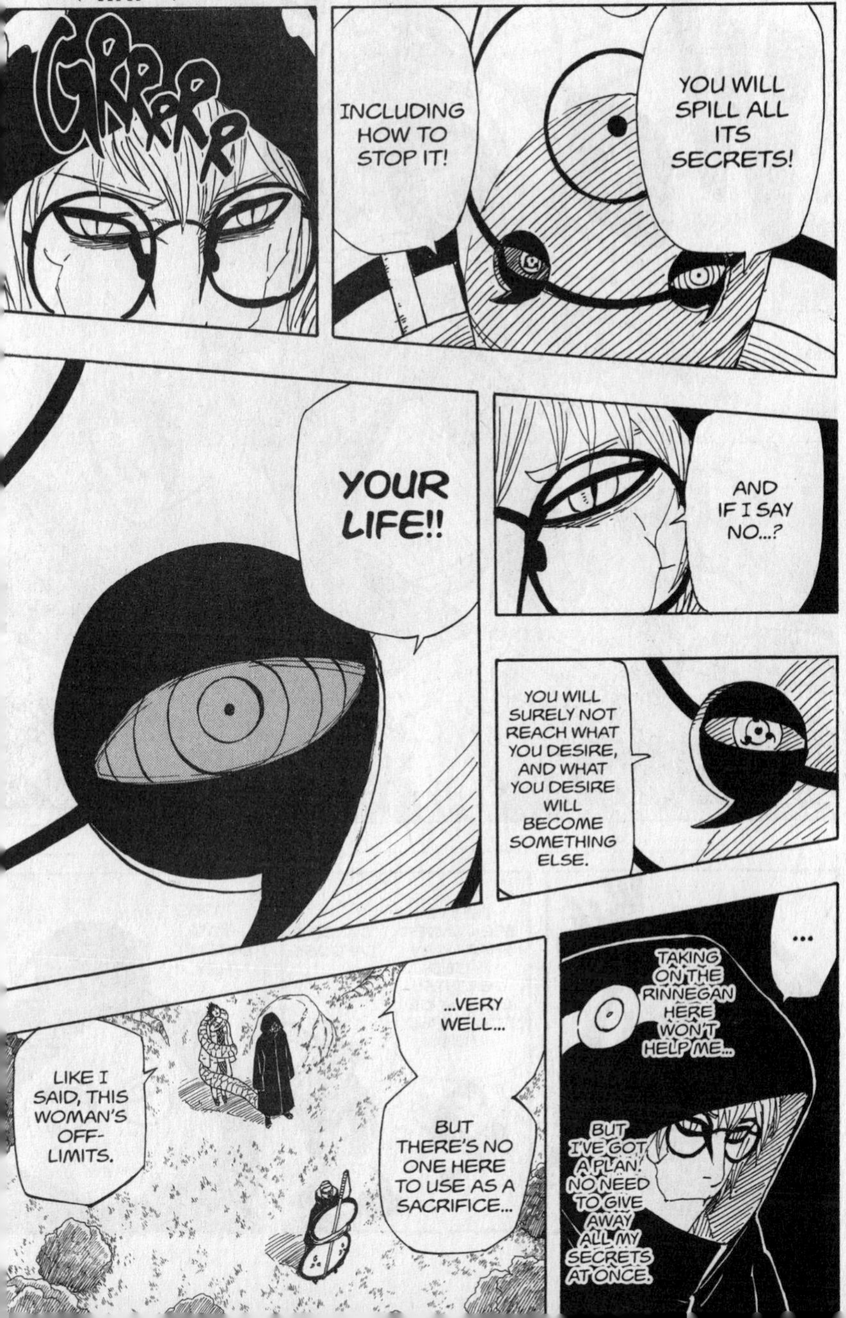
YOU WILL SPILL ALL ITS SECRETS!
INCLUDING HOW TO STOP IT!
GRRRRR
AND IF I SAY NO...?
YOU WILL SURELY NOT REACH WHAT YOU DESIRE, AND WHAT YOU DESIRE WILL BECOME SOMETHING ELSE.
YOUR LIFE!!
...
TAKING ON THE RINNEGAN HERE WON'T HELP ME...
BUT I'VE GOT A PLAN. NO NEED TO GIVE AWAY ALL MY SECRETS AT ONCE.
...VERY WELL...
BUT THERE'S NO ONE HERE TO USE AS A SACRIFICE...
LIKE I SAID, THIS WOMAN'S OFF-LIMITS.

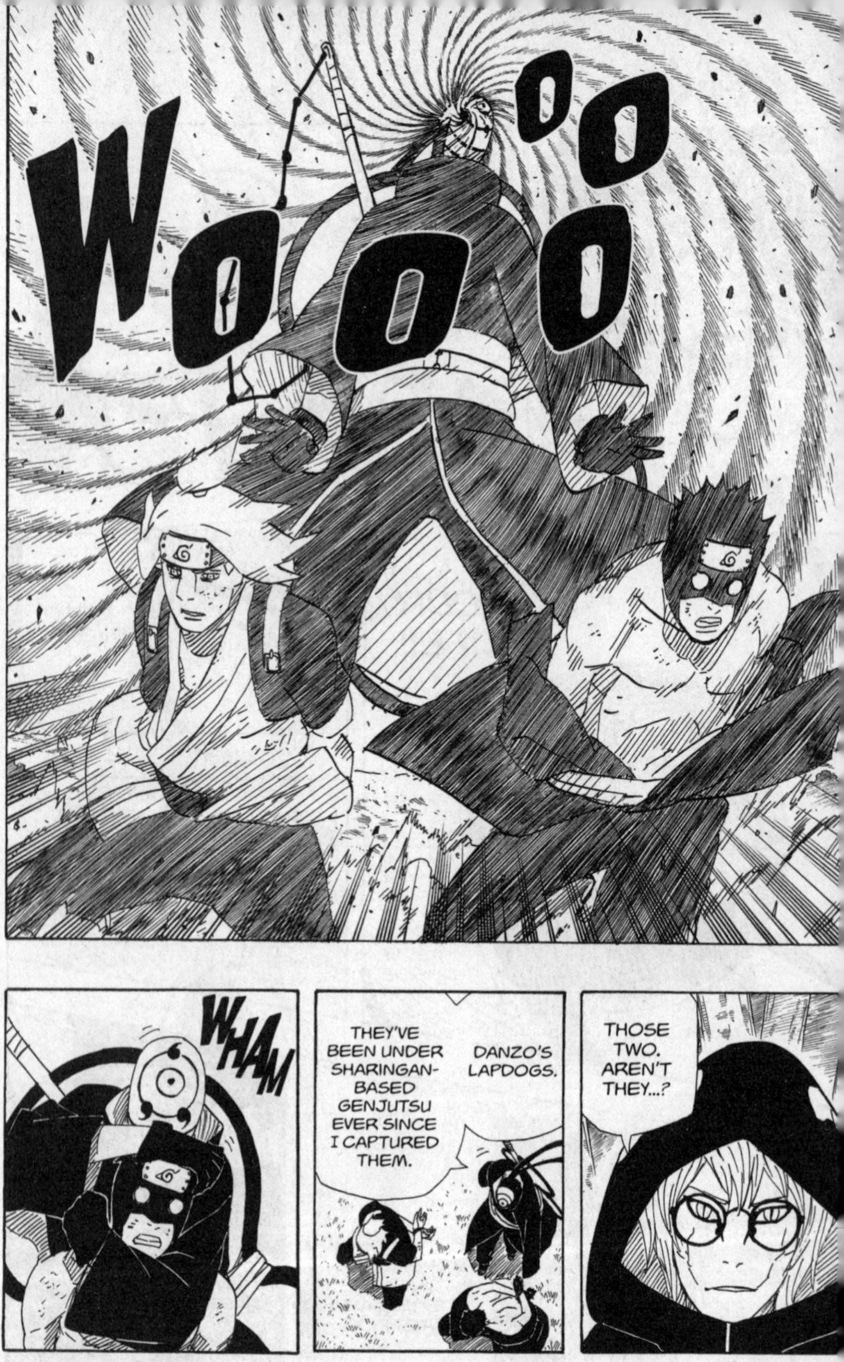
WOOOOOO
THOSE TWO. AREN'T THEY...?
DANZO'S LAPDOGS.
THEY'VE BEEN UNDER SHARINGAN-BASED GENJUTSU EVER SINCE I CAPTURED THEM.
WHAM

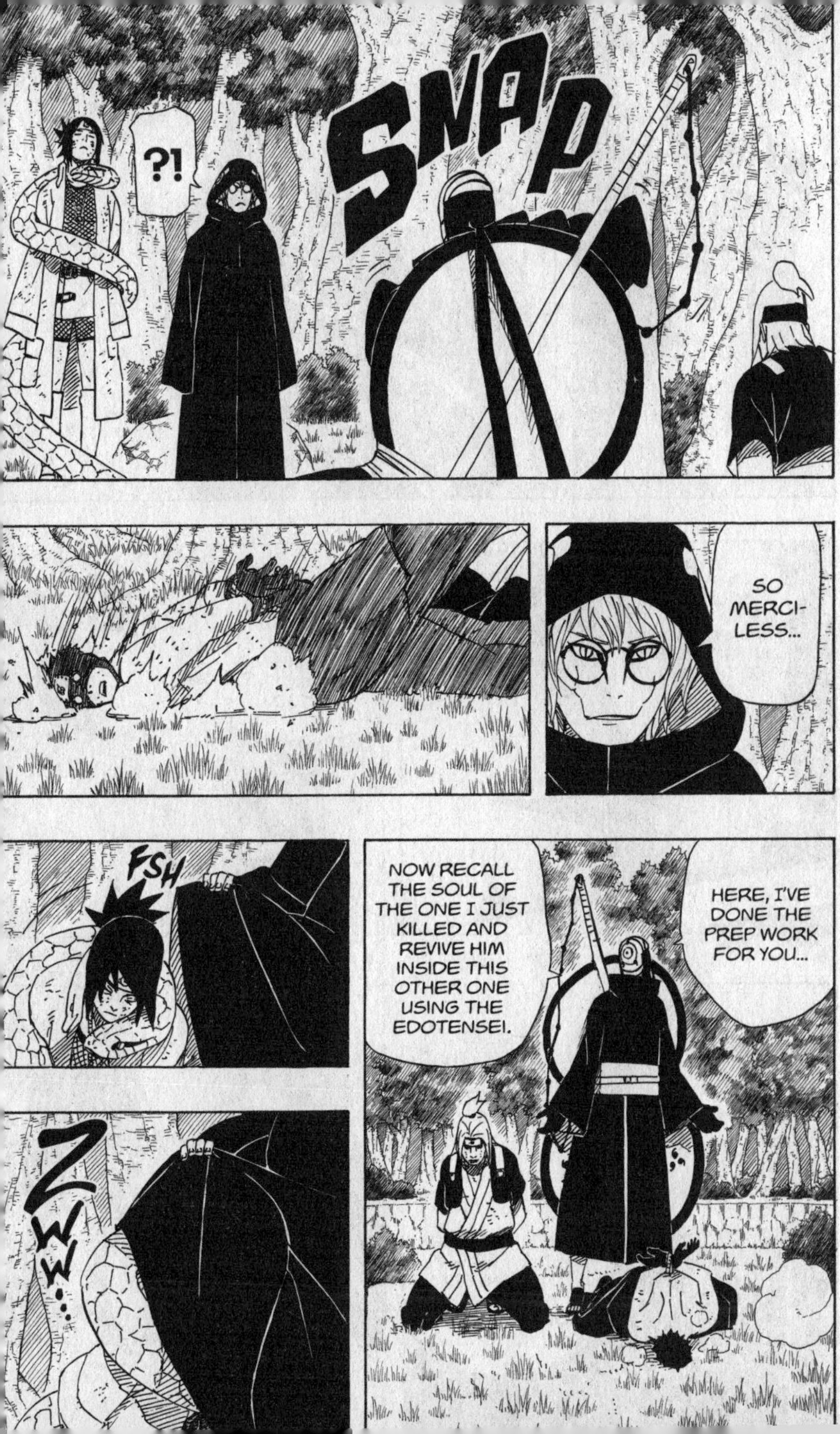
SNAP
?!
SO MERCI-LESS...
HERE, I'VE DONE THE PREP WORK FOR YOU...
NOW RECALL THE SOUL OF THE ONE I JUST KILLED AND REVIVE HIM INSIDE THIS OTHER ONE USING THE EDOTENSEI.
FSH
ZWW...

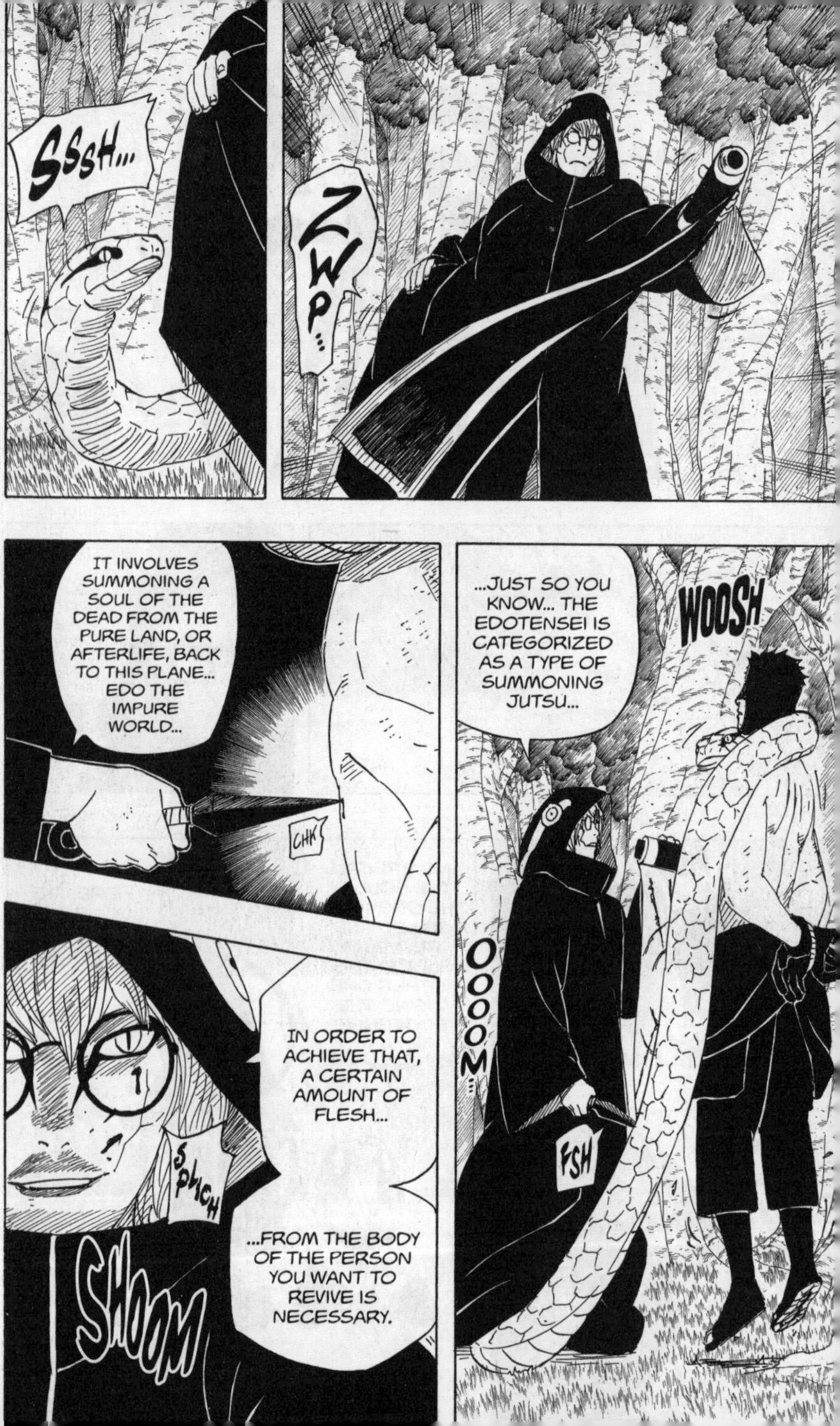
ZWP...
SSSH...
WOOSH
...JUST SO YOU KNOW... THE EDOTENSEI IS CATEGORIZED AS A TYPE OF SUMMONING JUTSU...
OOOOM...
FSH
IT INVOLVES SUMMONING A SOUL OF THE DEAD FROM THE PURE LAND, OR AFTERLIFE, BACK TO THIS PLANE... EDO THE IMPURE WORLD...
CHK
IN ORDER TO ACHIEVE THAT, A CERTAIN AMOUNT OF FLESH...
SPLICH
SHOOM
...FROM THE BODY OF THE PERSON YOU WANT TO REVIVE IS NECESSARY.

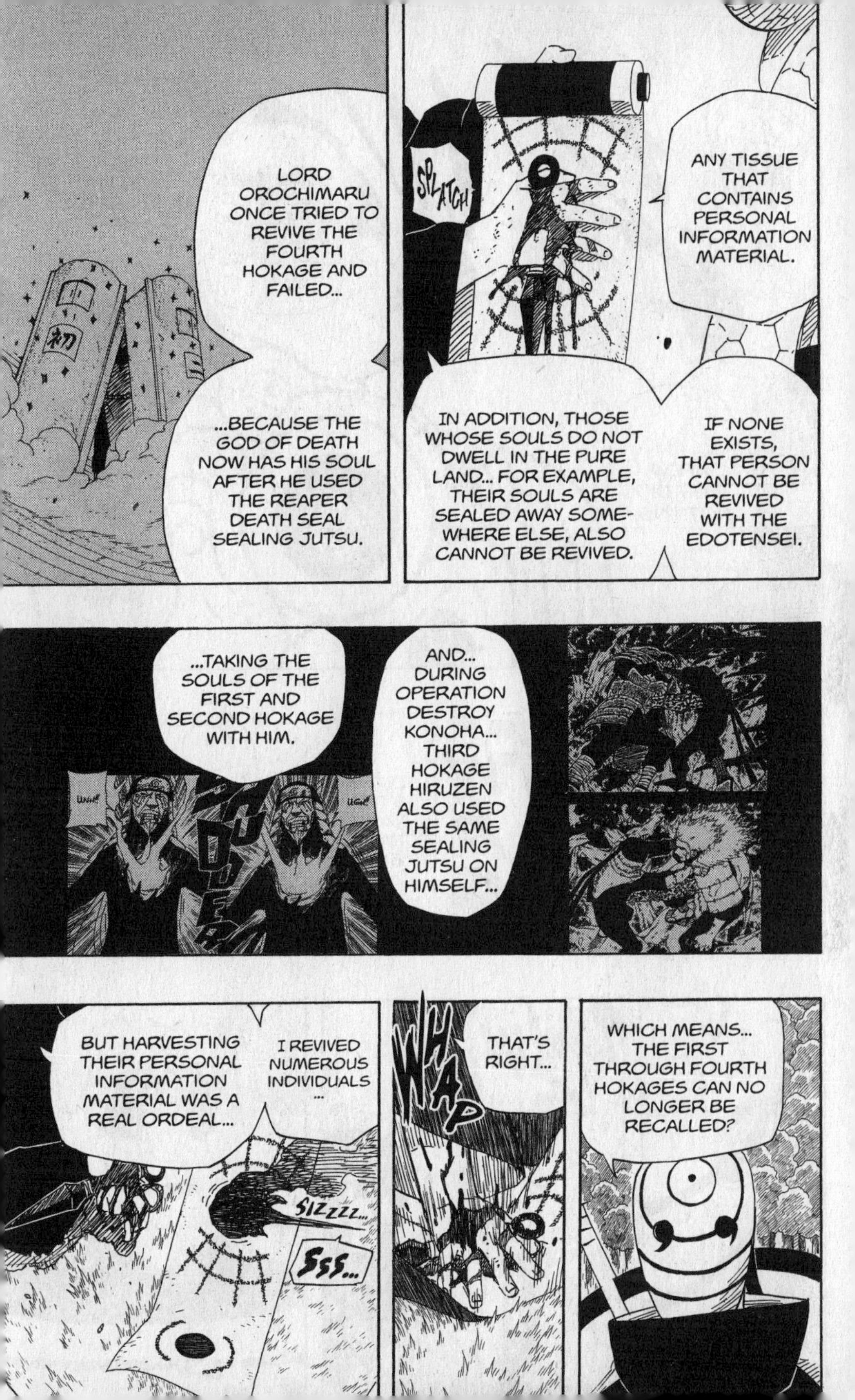
ANY TISSUE THAT CONTAINS PERSONAL INFORMATION MATERIAL.
SPLATCH
IF NONE EXISTS, THAT PERSON CANNOT BE REVIVED WITH THE EDOTENSEI.
IN ADDITION, THOSE WHOSE SOULS DO NOT DWELL IN THE PURE LAND... FOR EXAMPLE, THEIR SOULS ARE SEALED AWAY SOMEWHERE ELSE, ALSO CANNOT BE REVIVED.
LORD OROCHIMARU ONCE TRIED TO REVIVE THE FOURTH HOKAGE AND FAILED...
...BECAUSE THE GOD OF DEATH NOW HAS HIS SOUL AFTER HE USED THE REAPER DEATH SEAL SEALING JUTSU.
AND... DURING OPERATION DESTROY KONOHA... THIRD HOKAGE HIRUZEN ALSO USED THE SAME SEALING JUTSU ON HIMSELF...
...TAKING THE SOULS OF THE FIRST AND SECOND HOKAGE WITH HIM.
UGH!
UNH!
WHICH MEANS... THE FIRST THROUGH FOURTH HOKAGES CAN NO LONGER BE RECALLED?
WHAP
THAT'S RIGHT...
I REVIVED NUMEROUS INDIVIDUALS...
BUT HARVESTING THEIR PERSONAL INFORMATION MATERIAL WAS A REAL ORDEAL...
SIZZZZ...
SSS...

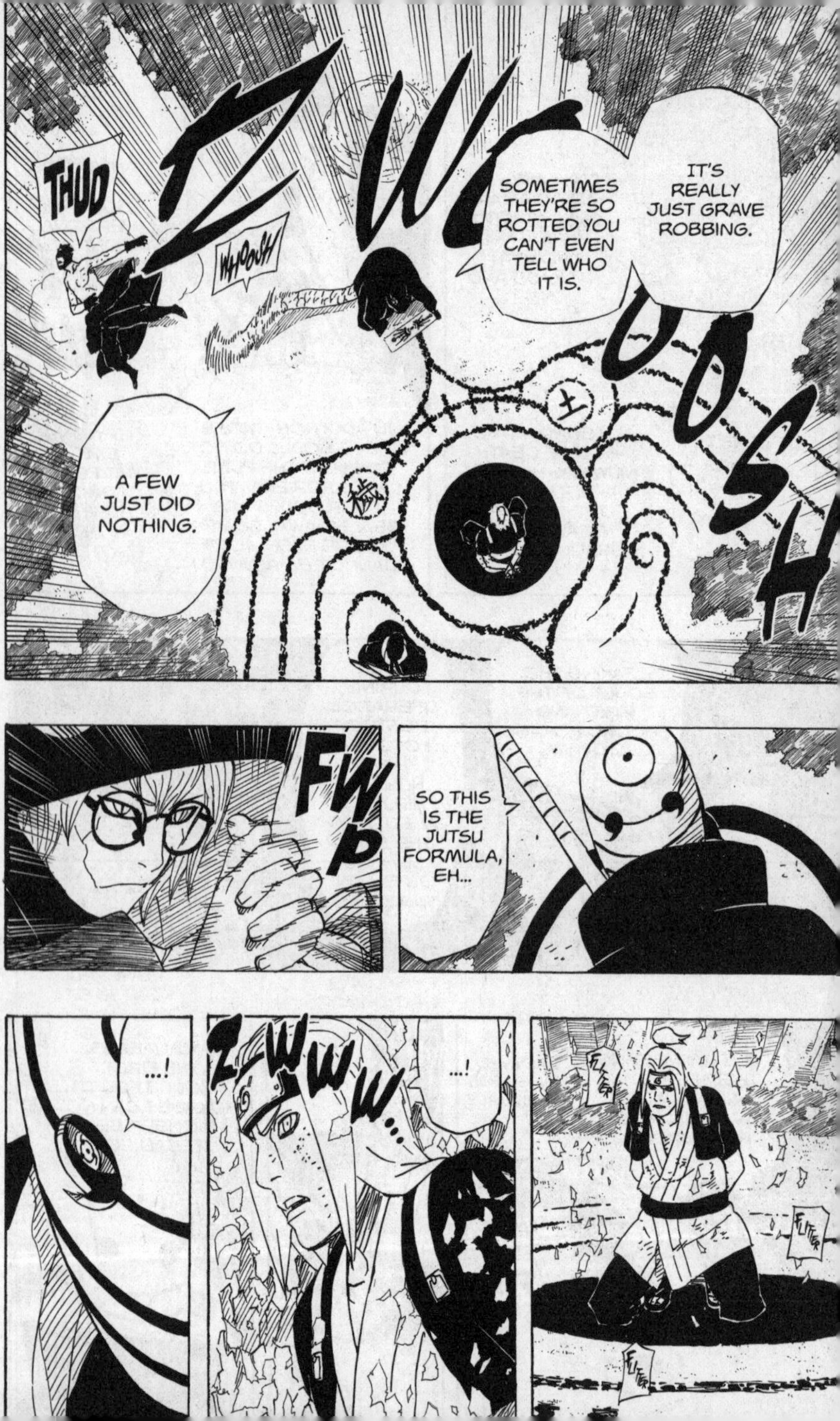
ZWOOOSH
IT'S REALLY JUST GRAVE ROBBING.
SOMETIMES THEY'RE SO ROTTED YOU CAN'T EVEN TELL WHO IT IS.
WHOOSH
THUD
A FEW JUST DID NOTHING.
SO THIS IS THE JUTSU FORMULA, EH...
FWP
FLITTER
FLITTER
FLITTER
...!
ZWWW...
...!

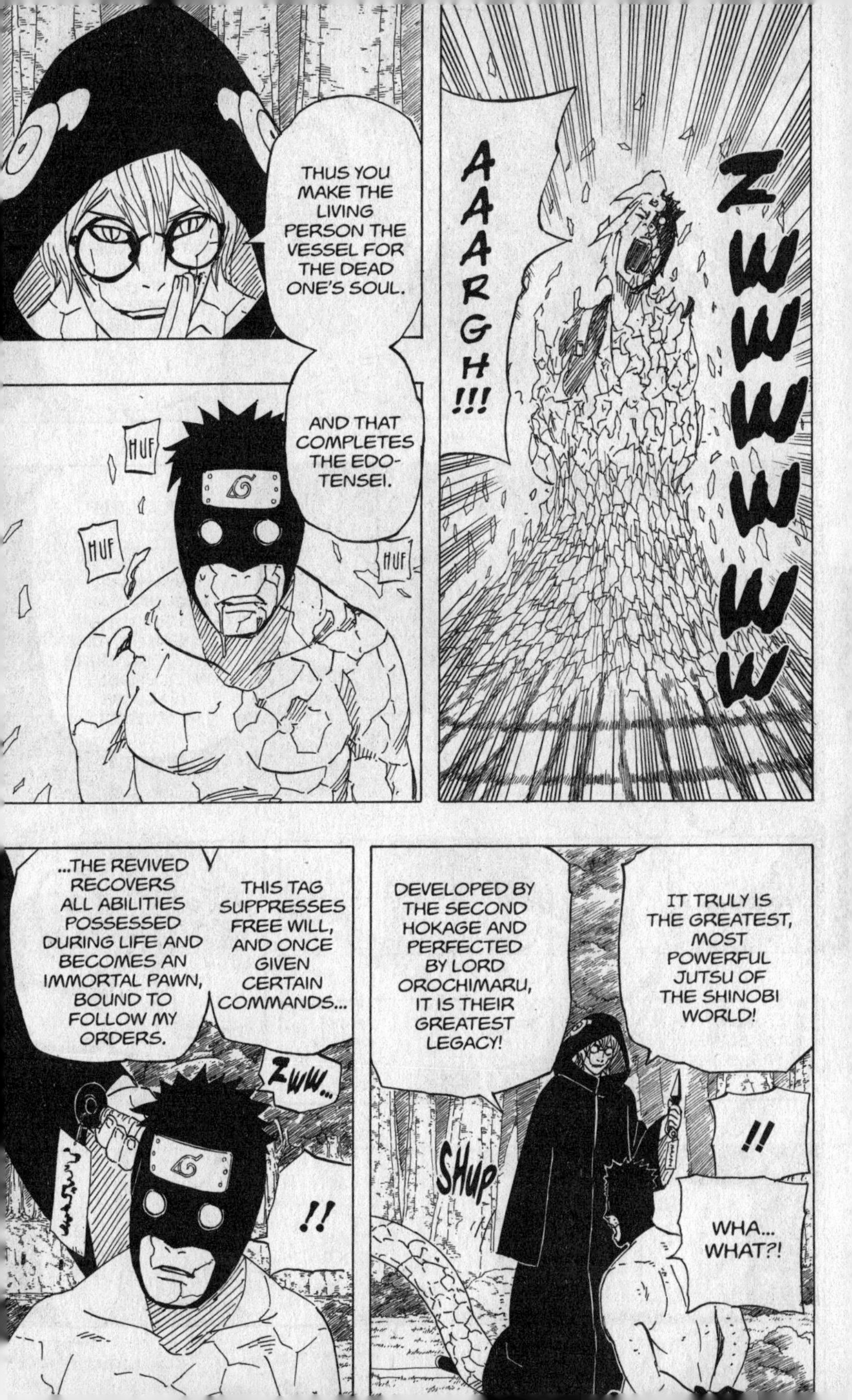
AAAARGH!!!
ZWWWWWW
THUS YOU MAKE THE LIVING PERSON THE VESSEL FOR THE DEAD ONE'S SOUL.
AND THAT COMPLETES THE EDO-TENSEI.
HUF
HUF
HUF
IT TRULY IS THE GREATEST, MOST POWERFUL JUTSU OF THE SHINOBI WORLD!
DEVELOPED BY THE SECOND HOKAGE AND PERFECTED BY LORD OROCHIMARU, IT IS THEIR GREATEST LEGACY!
!!
SHUP
WHA... WHAT?!
THIS TAG SUPPRESSES FREE WILL, AND ONCE GIVEN CERTAIN COMMANDS...
...THE REVIVED RECOVERS ALL ABILITIES POSSESSED DURING LIFE AND BECOMES AN IMMORTAL PAWN, BOUND TO FOLLOW MY ORDERS.
ZWW...
!!

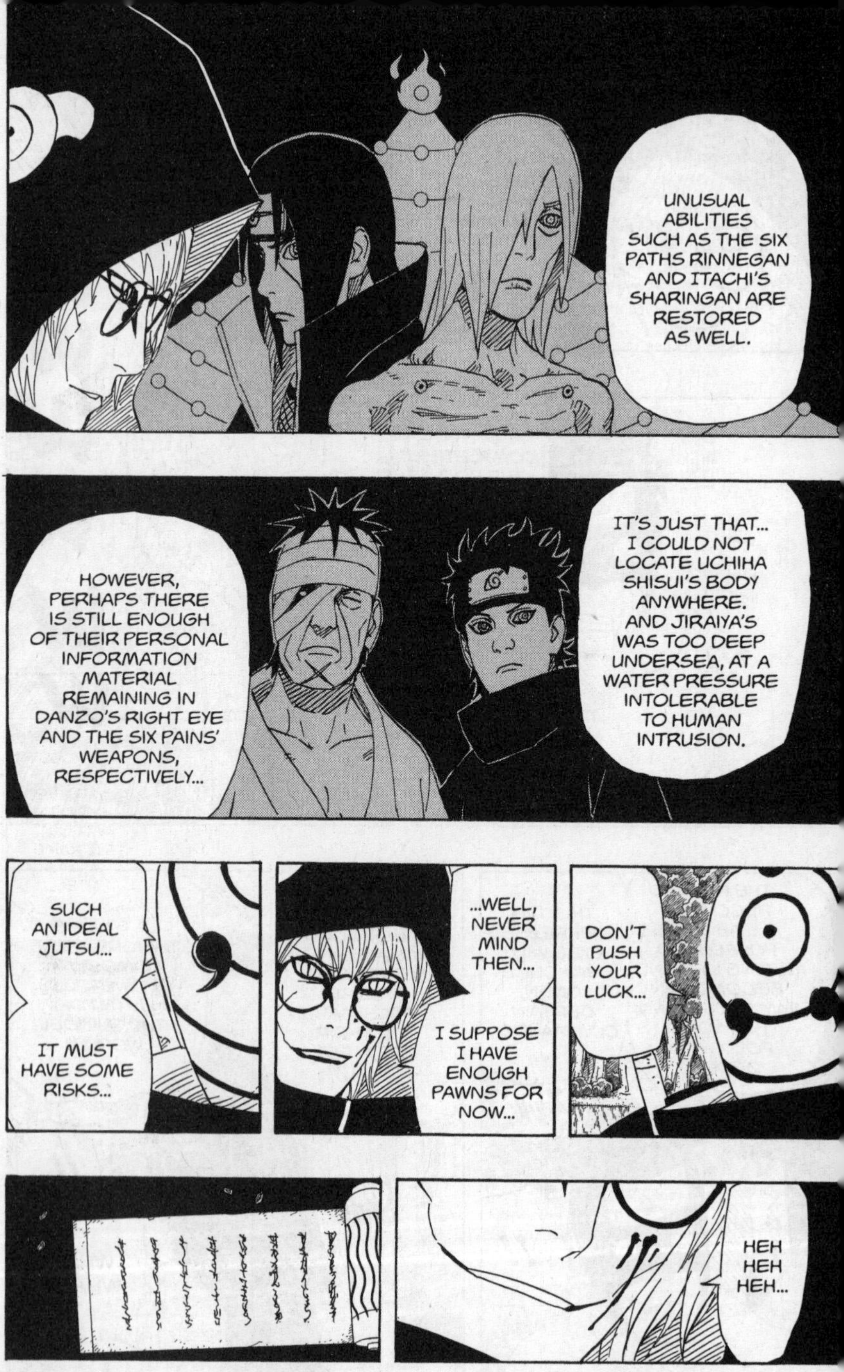
UNUSUAL ABILITIES SUCH AS THE SIX PATHS RINNEGAN AND ITACHI'S SHARINGAN ARE RESTORED AS WELL.
IT'S JUST THAT... I COULD NOT LOCATE UCHIHA SHISUI'S BODY ANYWHERE. AND JIRAIYA'S WAS TOO DEEP UNDERSEA, AT A WATER PRESSURE INTOLERABLE TO HUMAN INTRUSION.
HOWEVER, PERHAPS THERE IS STILL ENOUGH OF THEIR PERSONAL INFORMATION MATERIAL REMAINING IN DANZO'S RIGHT EYE AND THE SIX PAINS' WEAPONS, RESPECTIVELY...
DON'T PUSH YOUR LUCK...
...WELL, NEVER MIND THEN...
I SUPPOSE I HAVE ENOUGH PAWNS FOR NOW...
SUCH AN IDEAL JUTSU...
IT MUST HAVE SOME RISKS...
HEH HEH HEH...

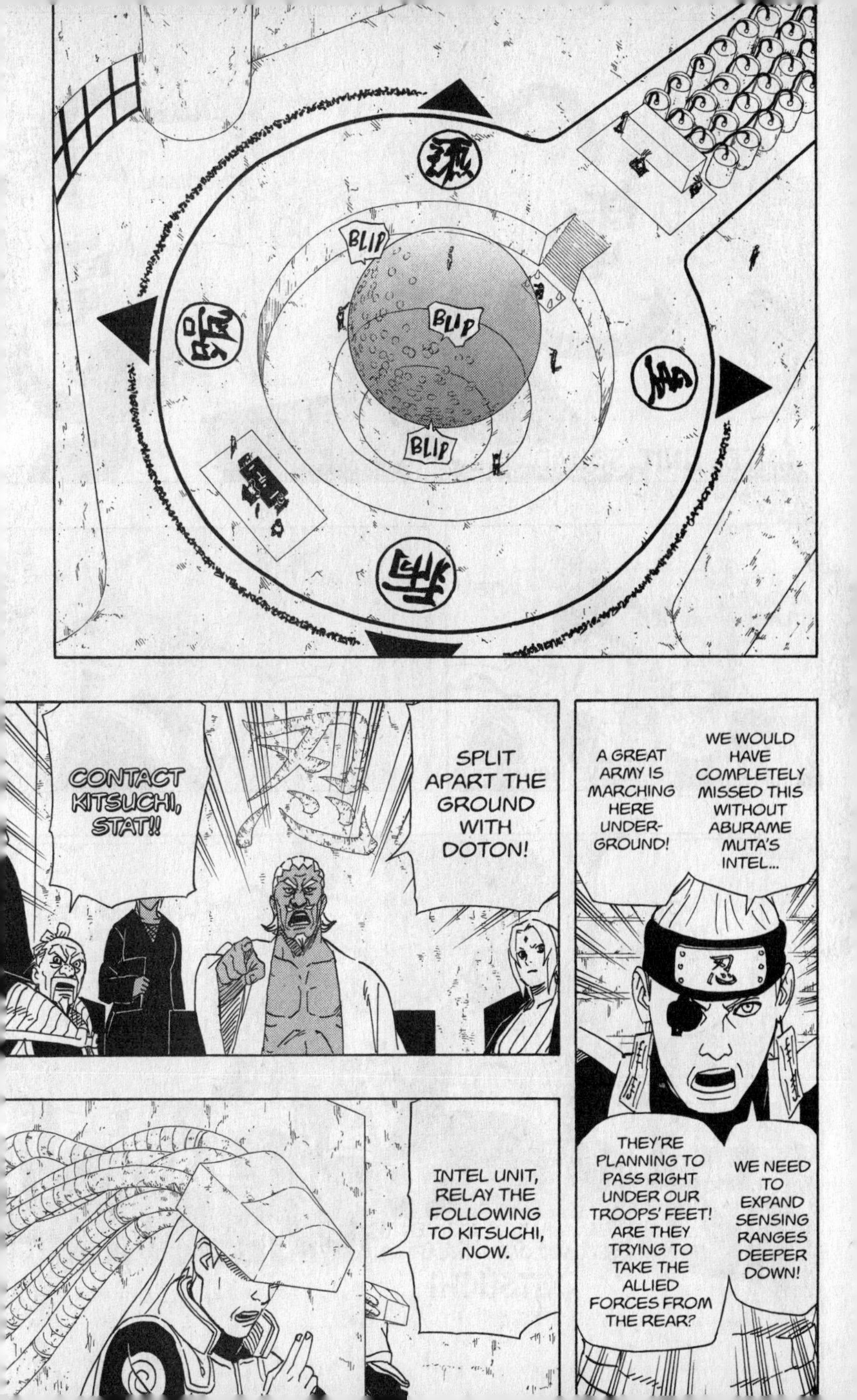
BLIP
BLIP
BLIP
WE WOULD HAVE COMPLETELY MISSED THIS WITHOUT ABURAME MUTA'S INTEL...
A GREAT ARMY IS MARCHING HERE UNDER-GROUND!
WE NEED TO EXPAND SENSING RANGES DEEPER DOWN!
THEY'RE PLANNING TO PASS RIGHT UNDER OUR TROOPS' FEET! ARE THEY TRYING TO TAKE THE ALLIED FORCES FROM THE REAR?
SPLIT APART THE GROUND WITH DOTON!
CONTACT KITSUCHI, STAT!!
INTEL UNIT, RELAY THE FOLLOWING TO KITSUCHI, NOW.

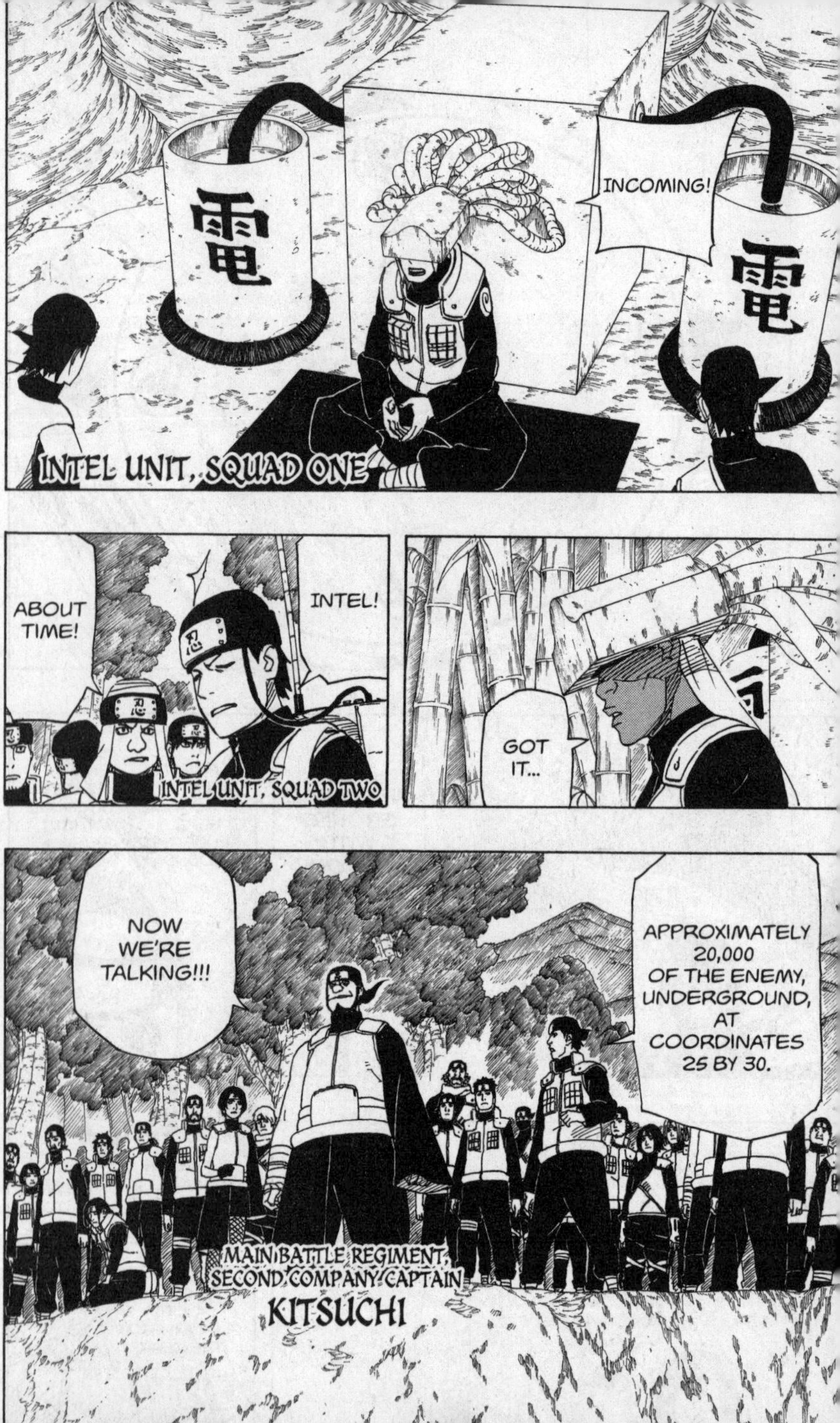
電
INCOMING!
電
INTEL UNIT, SQUAD ONE
GOT IT...
INTEL!
ABOUT TIME!
INTEL UNIT, SQUAD TWO
APPROXIMATELY 20,000 OF THE ENEMY, UNDERGROUND, AT COORDINATES 25 BY 30.
NOW WE'RE TALKING!!!
MAIN BATTLE REGIMENT, SECOND COMPANY CAPTAIN
KITSUCHI

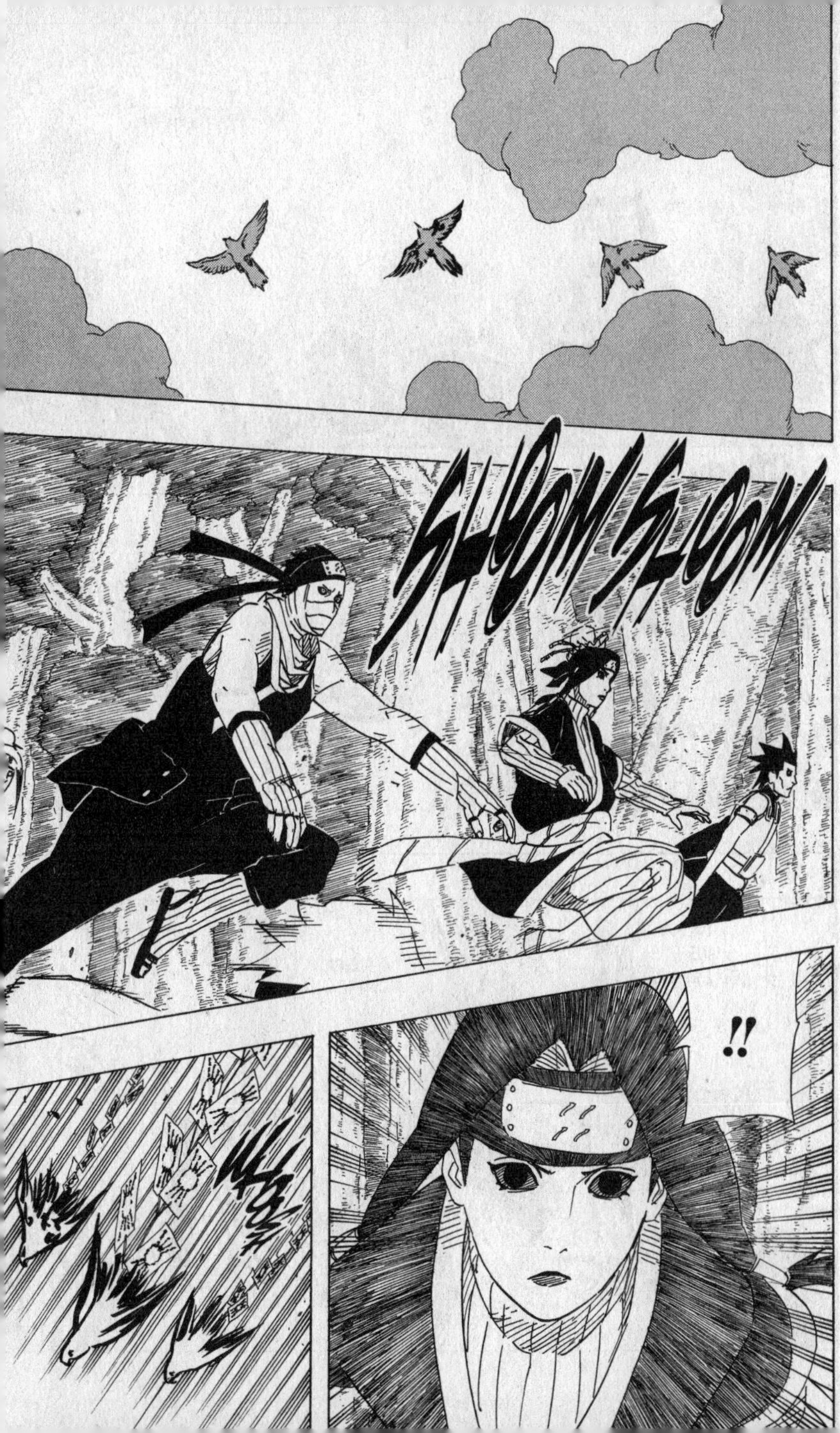
SHOOM SHOOM
!!

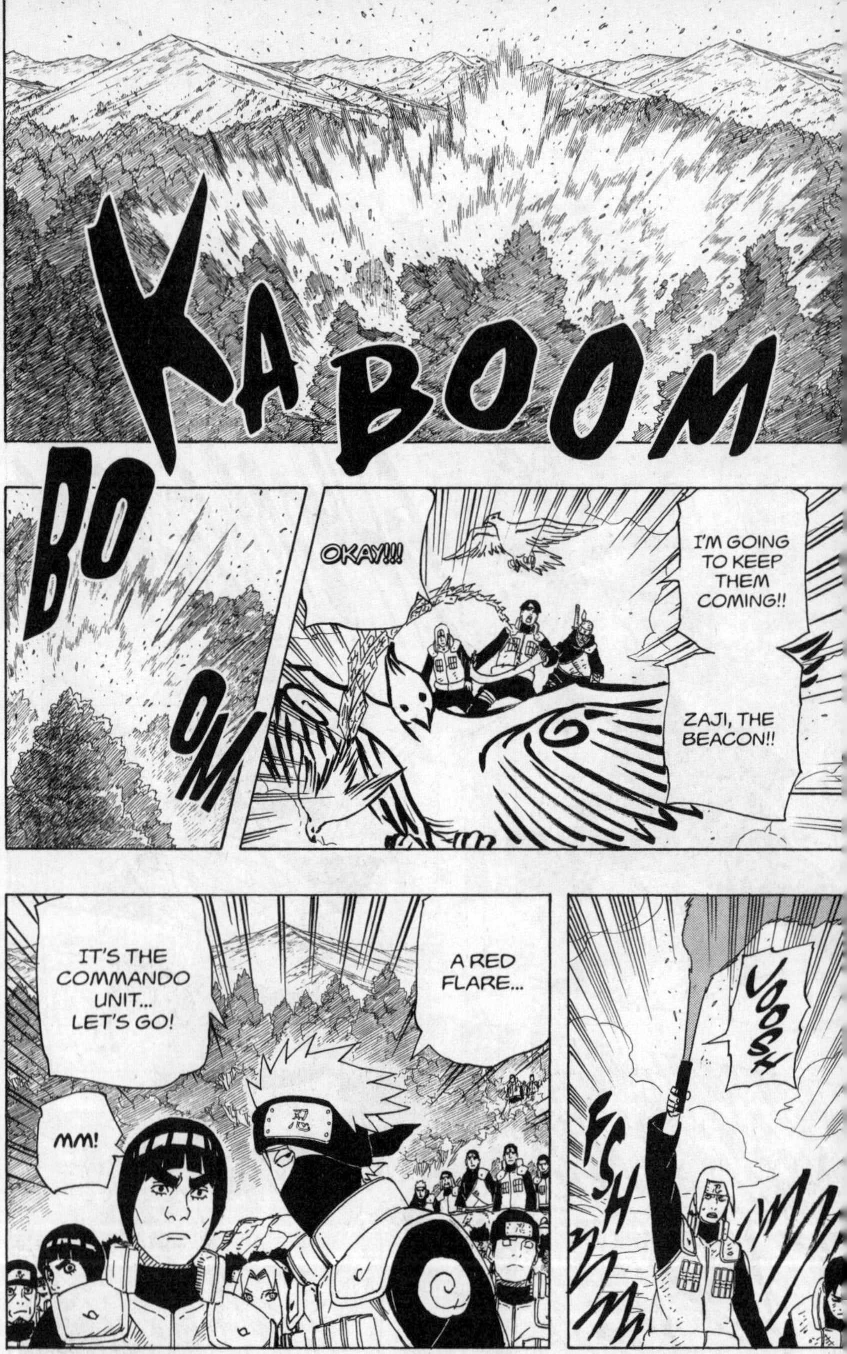
KABOOM
I'M GOING TO KEEP THEM COMING!!
ZAJI, THE BEACON!!
OKAY!!!
BOOOM
VOOOSH
FSH
A RED FLARE...
IT'S THE COMMANDO UNIT... LET'S GO!
MM!

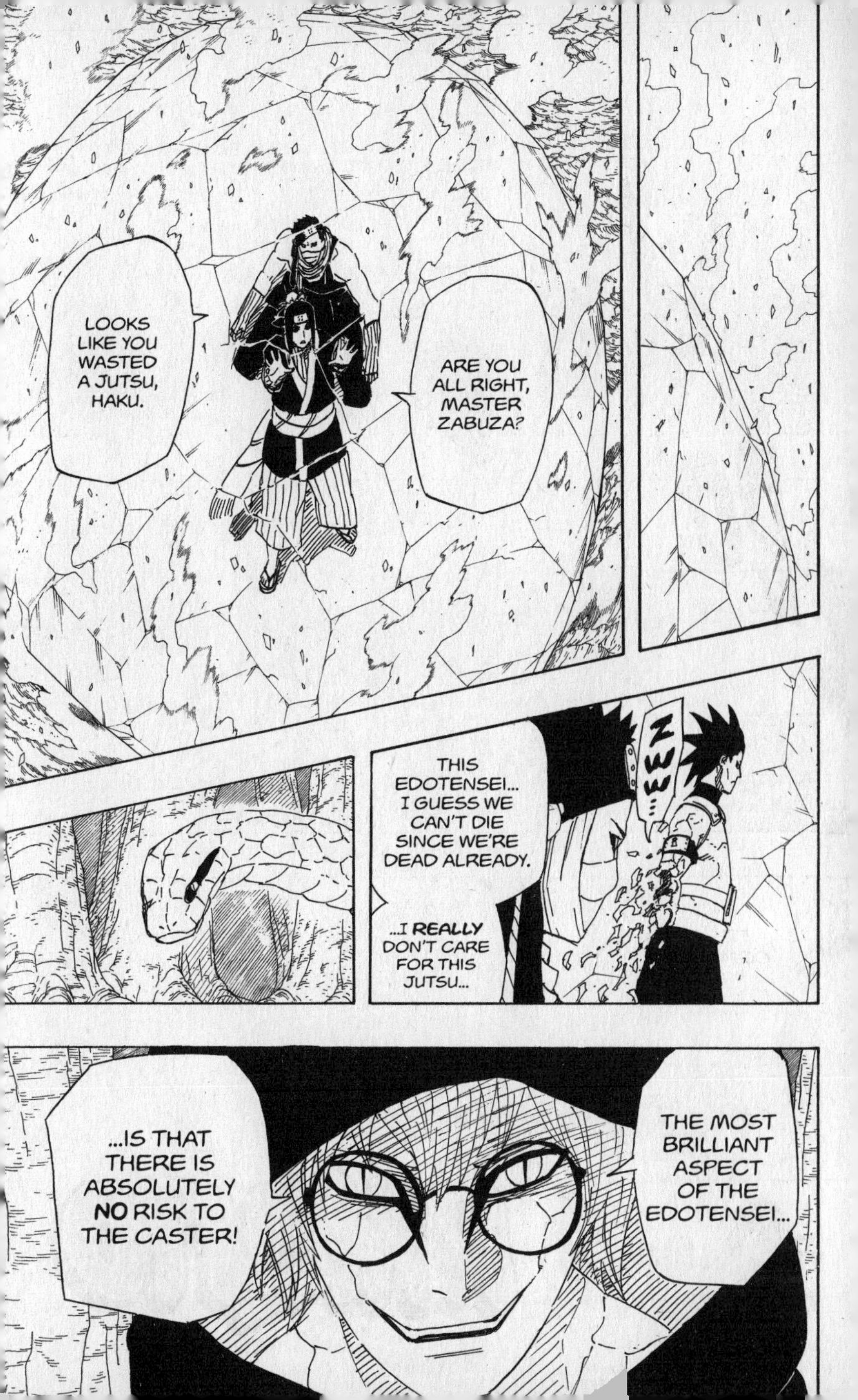
ARE YOU ALL RIGHT, MASTER ZABUZA?
LOOKS LIKE YOU WASTED A JUTSU, HAKU.
ZWW...
THIS EDOTENSEI... I GUESS WE CAN'T DIE SINCE WE'RE DEAD ALREADY.
...I **REALLY** DON'T CARE FOR THIS JUTSU...
THE MOST BRILLIANT ASPECT OF THE EDOTENSEI...
...IS THAT THERE IS ABSOLUTELY **NO** RISK TO THE CASTER!

NARUTO

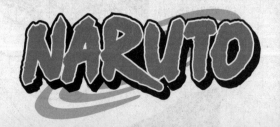

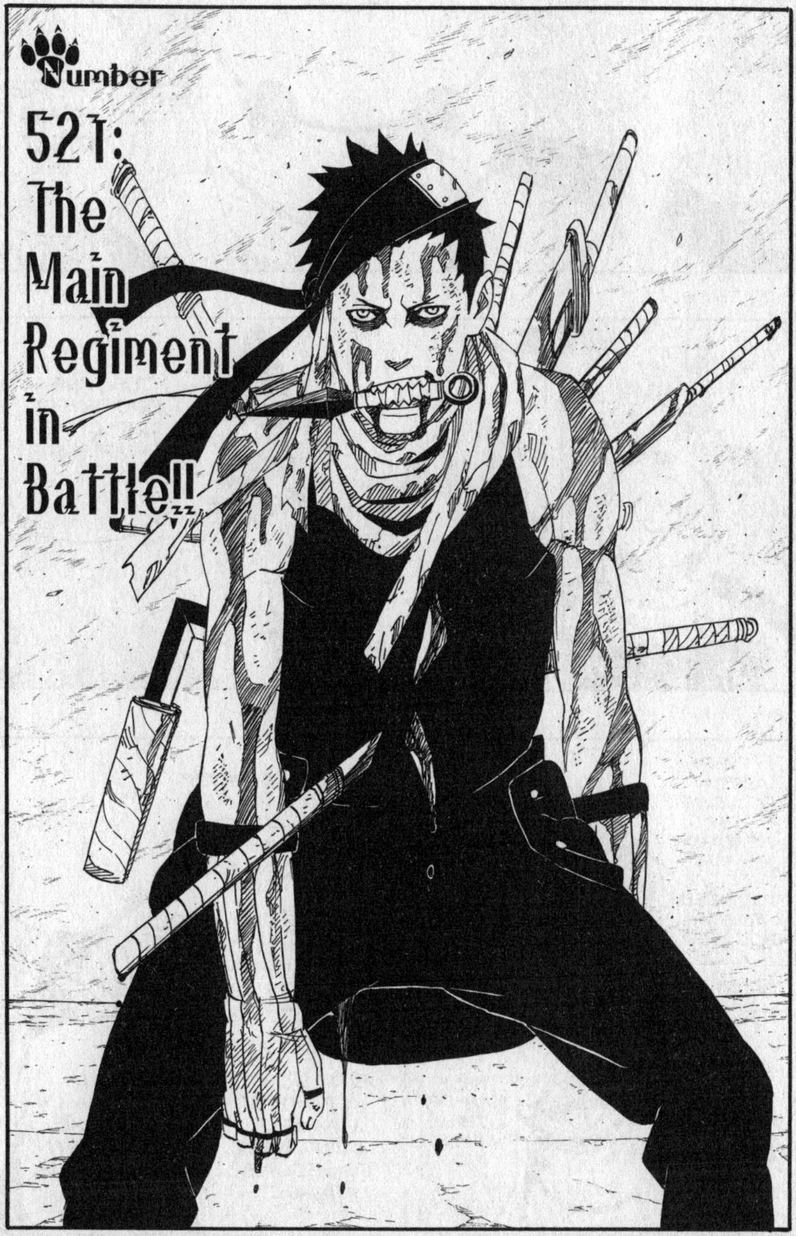
Number
521: The Main Regiment in Battle!!

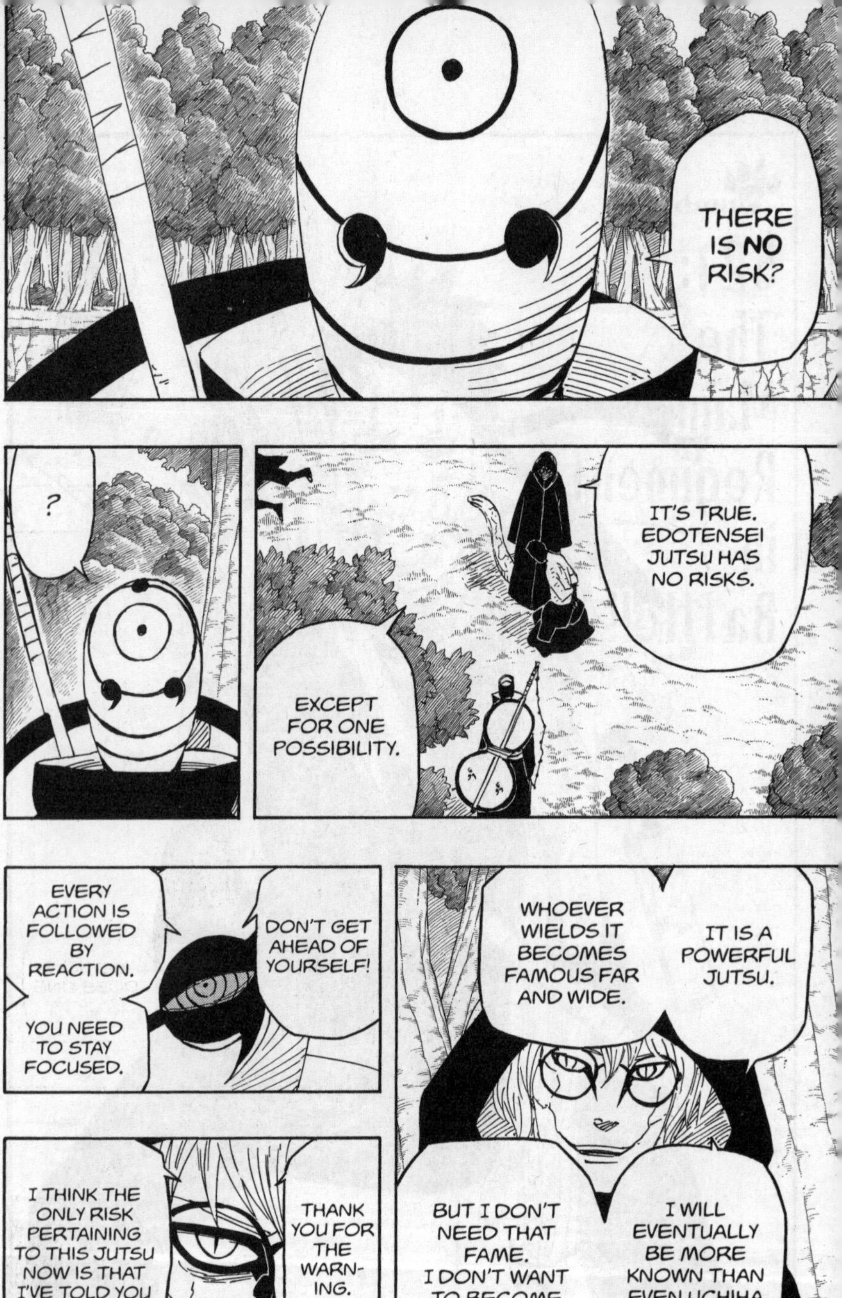
THERE IS NO RISK?
IT'S TRUE. EDOTENSEI JUTSU HAS NO RISKS.
EXCEPT FOR ONE POSSIBILITY.
?
IT IS A POWERFUL JUTSU.
WHOEVER WIELDS IT BECOMES FAMOUS FAR AND WIDE.
I WILL EVENTUALLY BE MORE KNOWN THAN EVEN UCHIHA MADARA.
BUT I DON'T NEED THAT FAME. I DON'T WANT TO BECOME A TARGET.
DON'T GET AHEAD OF YOURSELF!
EVERY ACTION IS FOLLOWED BY REACTION.
YOU NEED TO STAY FOCUSED.
THANK YOU FOR THE WARNING.
I THINK THE ONLY RISK PERTAINING TO THIS JUTSU NOW IS THAT I'VE TOLD YOU ABOUT IT.

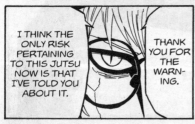

READ THIS WAY

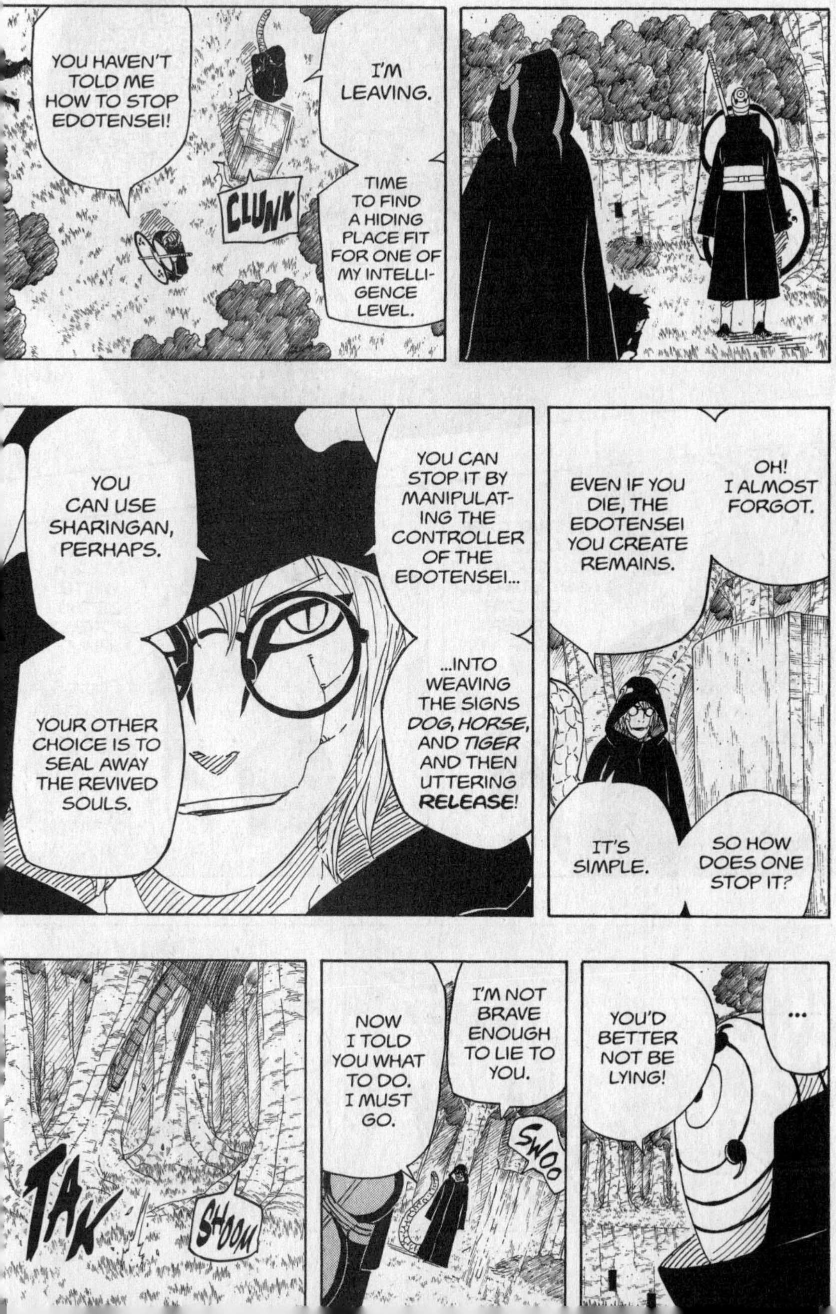
I'M LEAVING.
TIME TO FIND A HIDING PLACE FIT FOR ONE OF MY INTELLI-GENCE LEVEL.
YOU HAVEN'T TOLD ME HOW TO STOP EDOTENSEI!
CLUNK
OH! I ALMOST FORGOT.
EVEN IF YOU DIE, THE EDOTENSEI YOU CREATE REMAINS.
SO HOW DOES ONE STOP IT?
IT'S SIMPLE.
YOU CAN STOP IT BY MANIPULAT-ING THE CONTROLLER OF THE EDOTENSEI...
...INTO WEAVING THE SIGNS *DOG, HORSE,* AND *TIGER* AND THEN UTTERING **RELEASE**!
YOU CAN USE SHARINGAN, PERHAPS.
YOUR OTHER CHOICE IS TO SEAL AWAY THE REVIVED SOULS.
...
YOU'D BETTER NOT BE LYING!
I'M NOT BRAVE ENOUGH TO LIE TO YOU.
NOW I TOLD YOU WHAT TO DO. I MUST GO.
SWOO
SHOOM
TAK

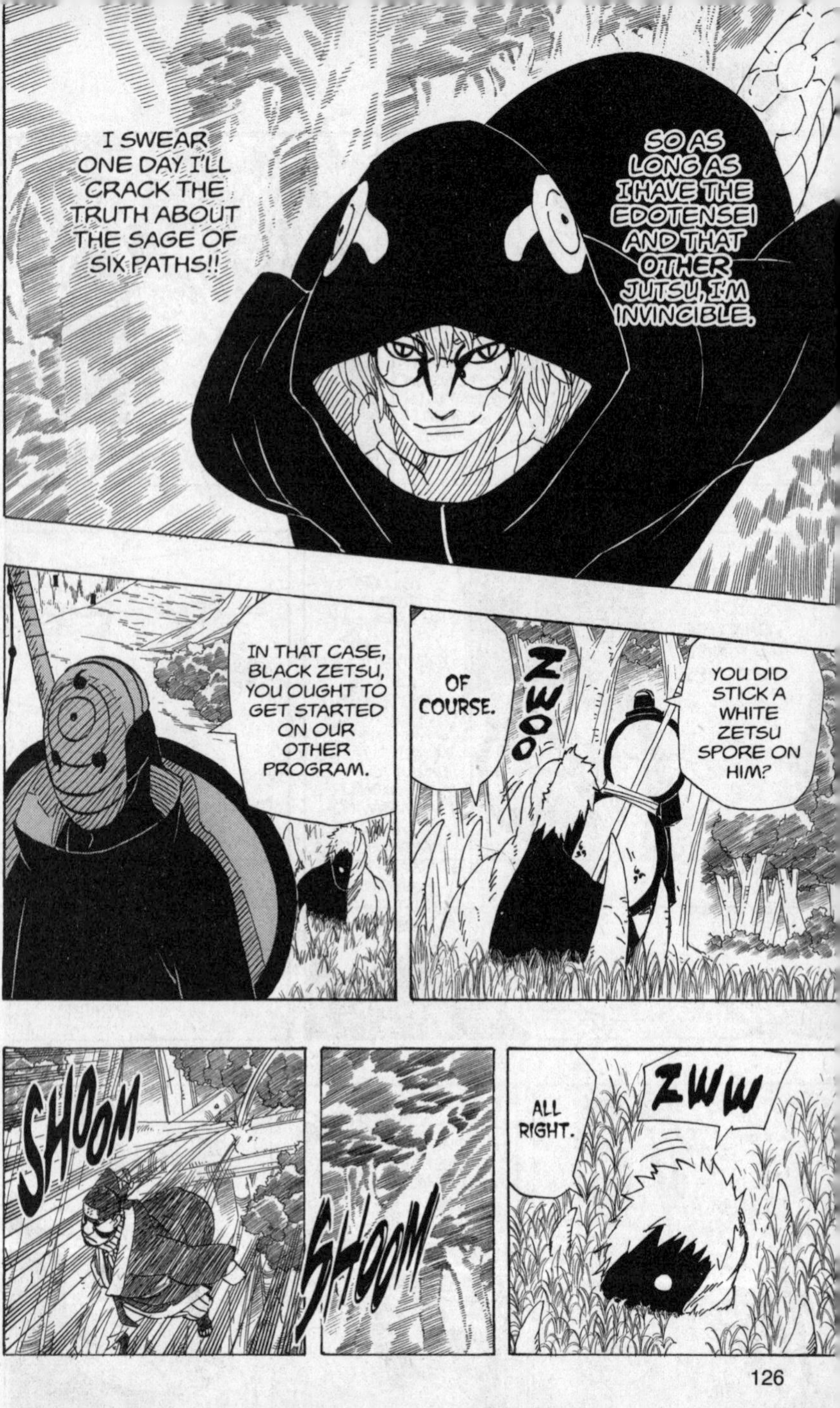
SO AS LONG AS I HAVE THE EDOTENSEI AND THAT OTHER JUTSU, I'M INVINCIBLE.
I SWEAR ONE DAY I'LL CRACK THE TRUTH ABOUT THE SAGE OF SIX PATHS!!
YOU DID STICK A WHITE ZETSU SPORE ON HIM?
ZWOOO
OF COURSE.
IN THAT CASE, BLACK ZETSU, YOU OUGHT TO GET STARTED ON OUR OTHER PROGRAM.
ZWW
ALL RIGHT.
SHOOM
SHOOM

READ THIS WAY

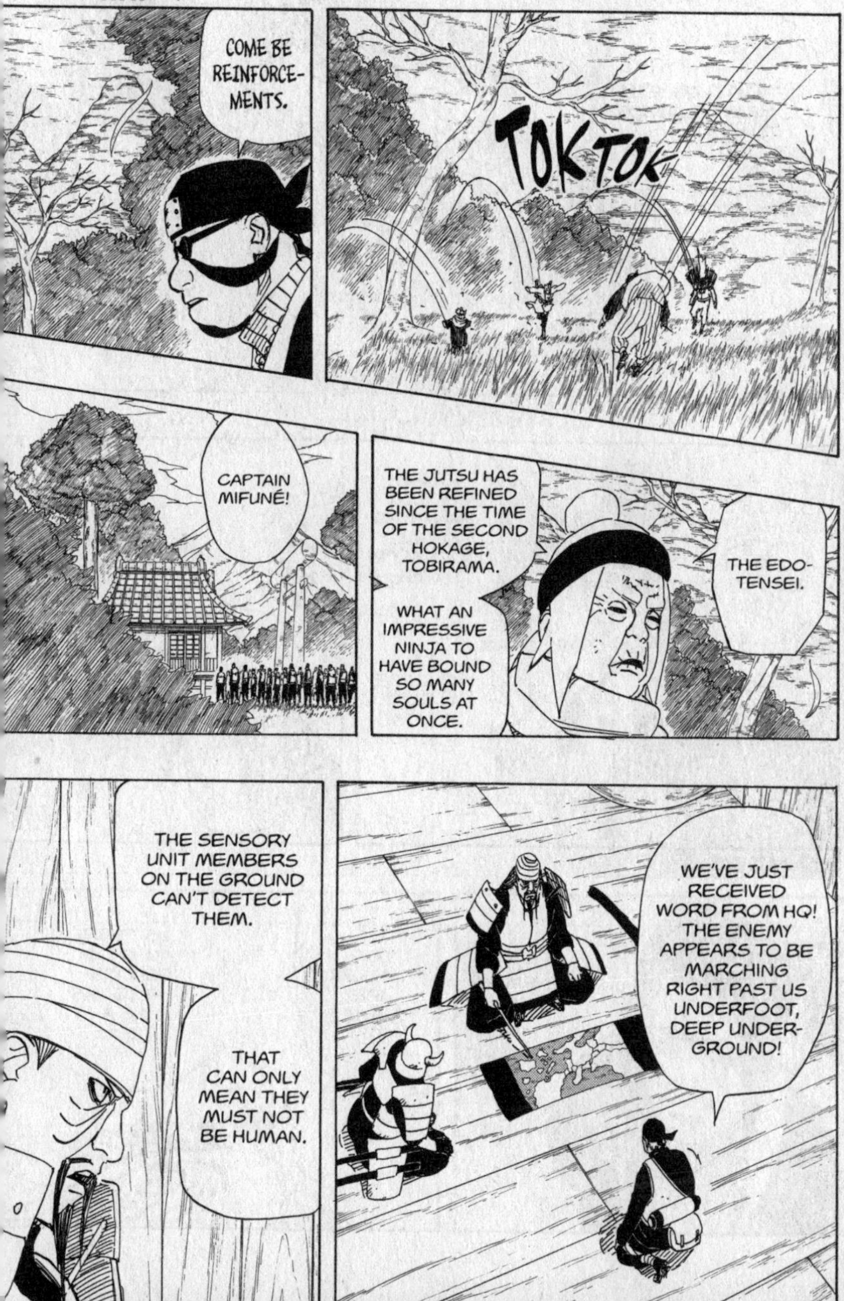
TOKTOK
COME BE REINFORCE-MENTS.
THE EDO-TENSEI.
THE JUTSU HAS BEEN REFINED SINCE THE TIME OF THE SECOND HOKAGE, TOBIRAMA.
WHAT AN IMPRESSIVE NINJA TO HAVE BOUND SO MANY SOULS AT ONCE.
CAPTAIN MIFUNÉ!
WE'VE JUST RECEIVED WORD FROM HQ! THE ENEMY APPEARS TO BE MARCHING RIGHT PAST US UNDERFOOT, DEEP UNDER-GROUND!
THE SENSORY UNIT MEMBERS ON THE GROUND CAN'T DETECT THEM.
THAT CAN ONLY MEAN THEY MUST NOT BE HUMAN.

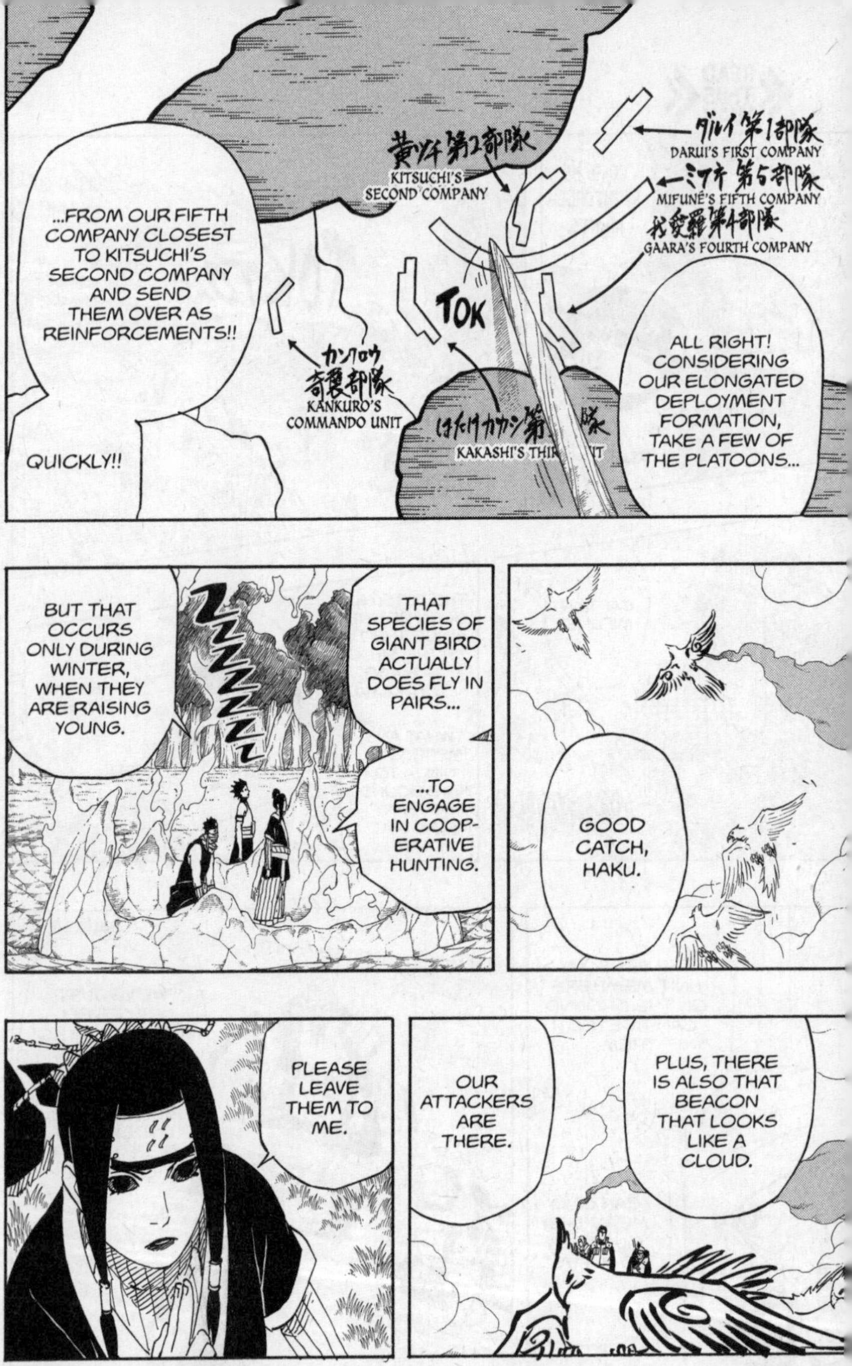
ダルイ第1部隊
DARUI'S FIRST COMPANY
ミフネ第5部隊
MIFUNÉ'S FIFTH COMPANY
我愛羅第4部隊
GAARA'S FOURTH COMPANY
黄ツチ第2部隊
KITSUCHI'S SECOND COMPANY
TOK
カンクロウ奇襲部隊
KANKURO'S COMMANDO UNIT
ALL RIGHT! CONSIDERING OUR ELONGATED DEPLOYMENT FORMATION, TAKE A FEW OF THE PLATOONS...
...FROM OUR FIFTH COMPANY CLOSEST TO KITSUCHI'S SECOND COMPANY AND SEND THEM OVER AS REINFORCEMENTS!!
QUICKLY!!
GOOD CATCH, HAKU.
THAT SPECIES OF GIANT BIRD ACTUALLY DOES FLY IN PAIRS...
...TO ENGAGE IN COOPERATIVE HUNTING.
BUT THAT OCCURS ONLY DURING WINTER, WHEN THEY ARE RAISING YOUNG.
PLUS, THERE IS ALSO THAT BEACON THAT LOOKS LIKE A CLOUD.
OUR ATTACKERS ARE THERE.
PLEASE LEAVE THEM TO ME.

READ THIS WAY

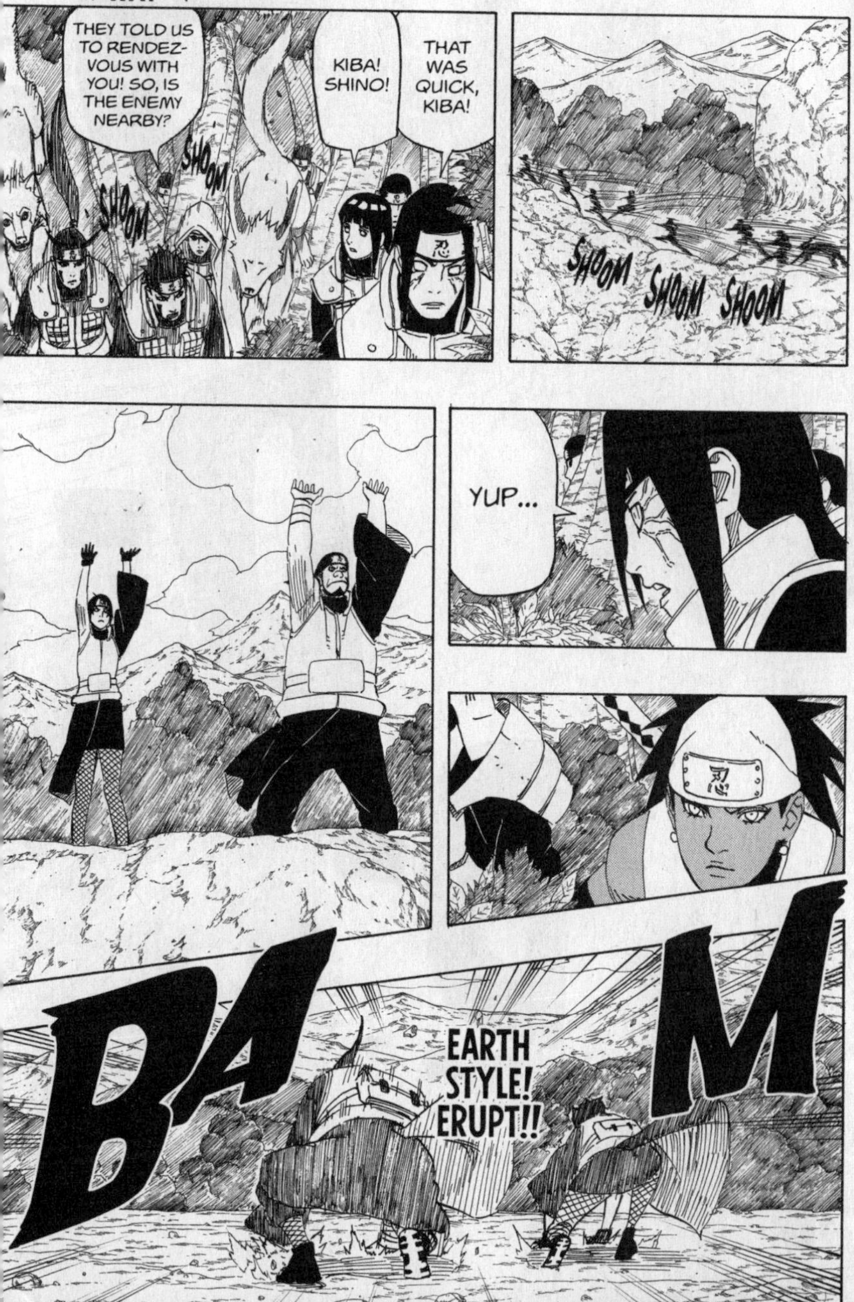
SHOOM SHOOM SHOOM
THAT WAS QUICK, KIBA!
KIBA! SHINO!
THEY TOLD US TO RENDEZ-VOUS WITH YOU! SO, IS THE ENEMY NEARBY?
SHOOM
SHOOM
YUP...
BAM
EARTH STYLE! ERUPT!!

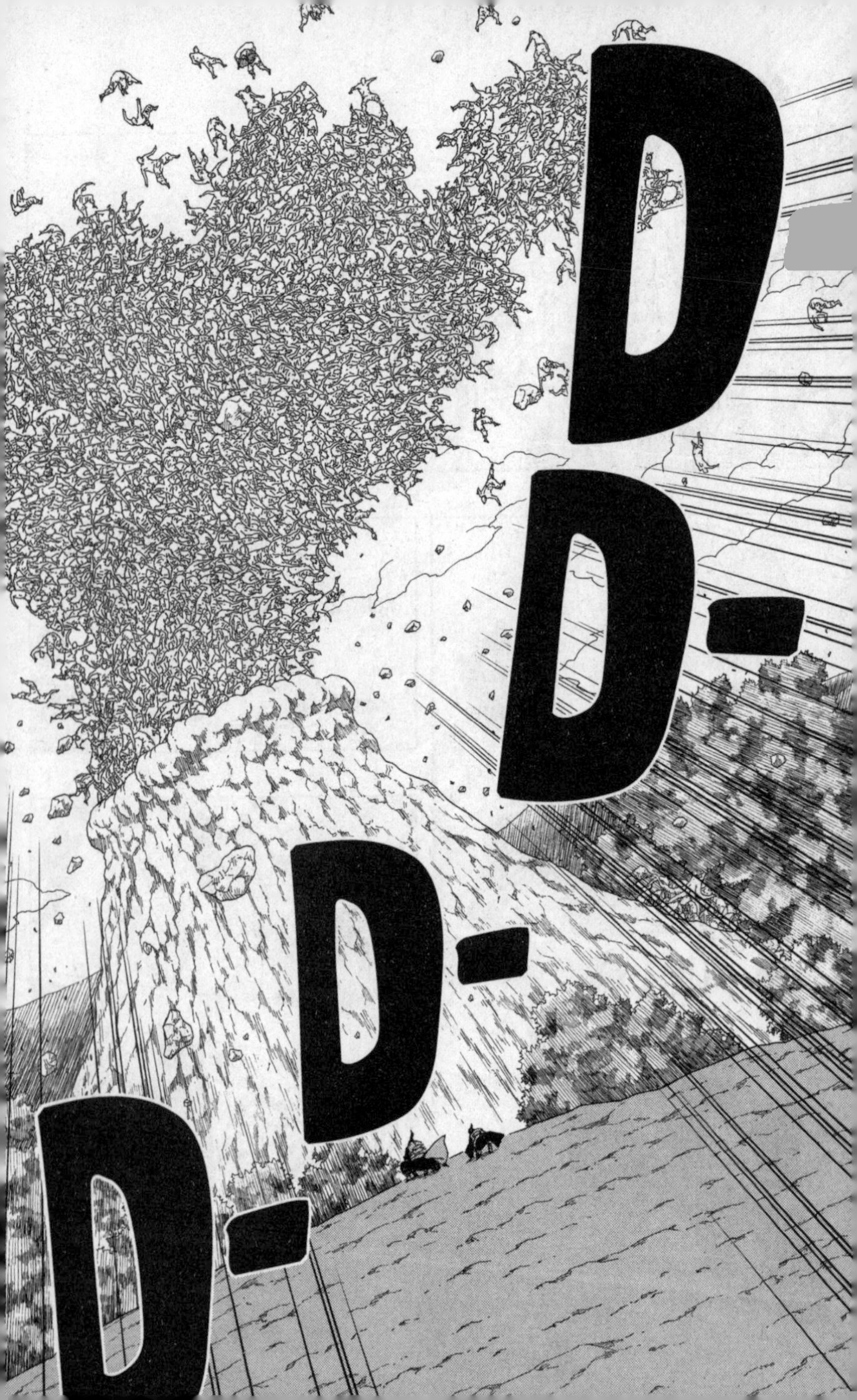
D-D-D-D

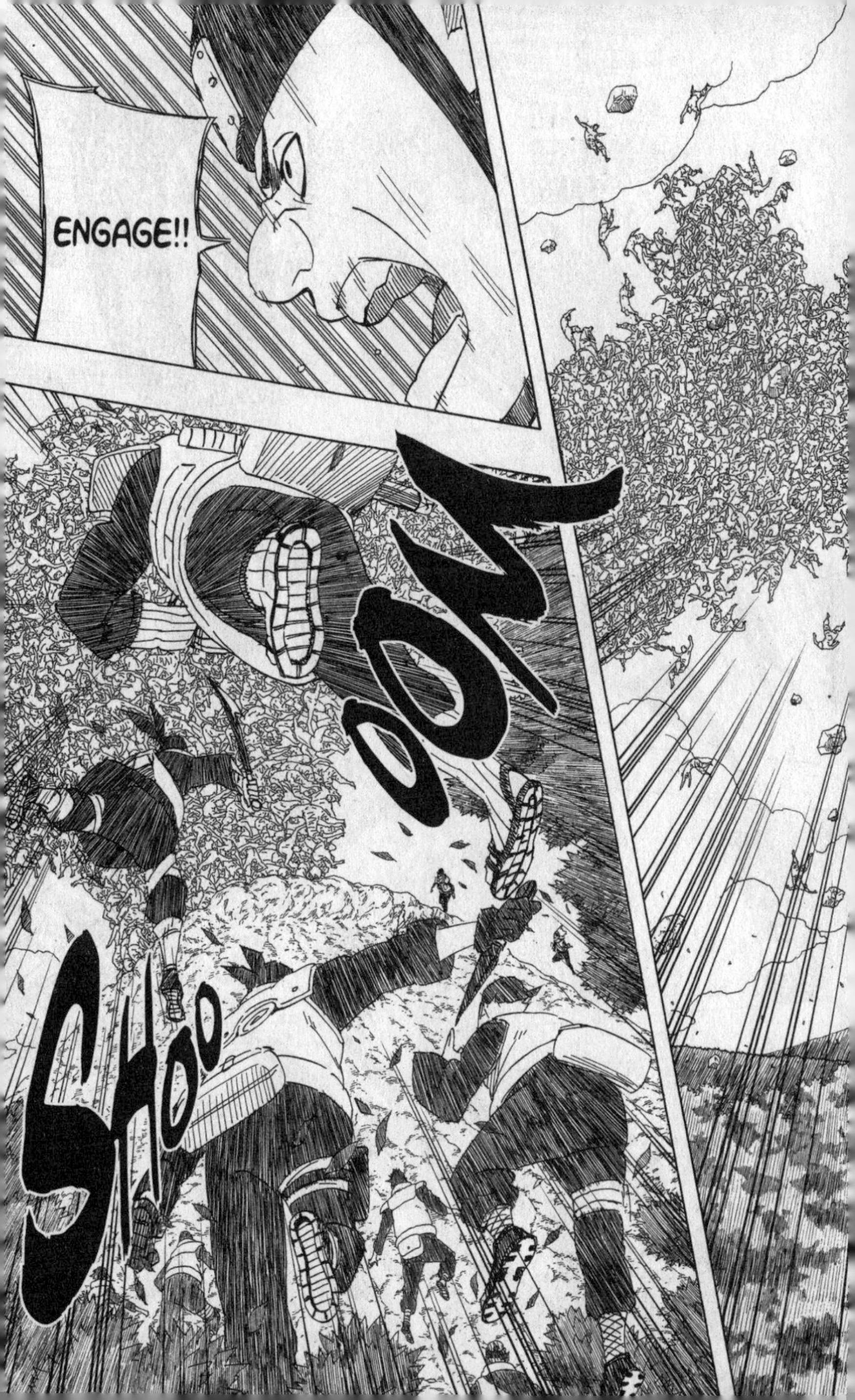
ENGAGE!!
VOOO
SHOO

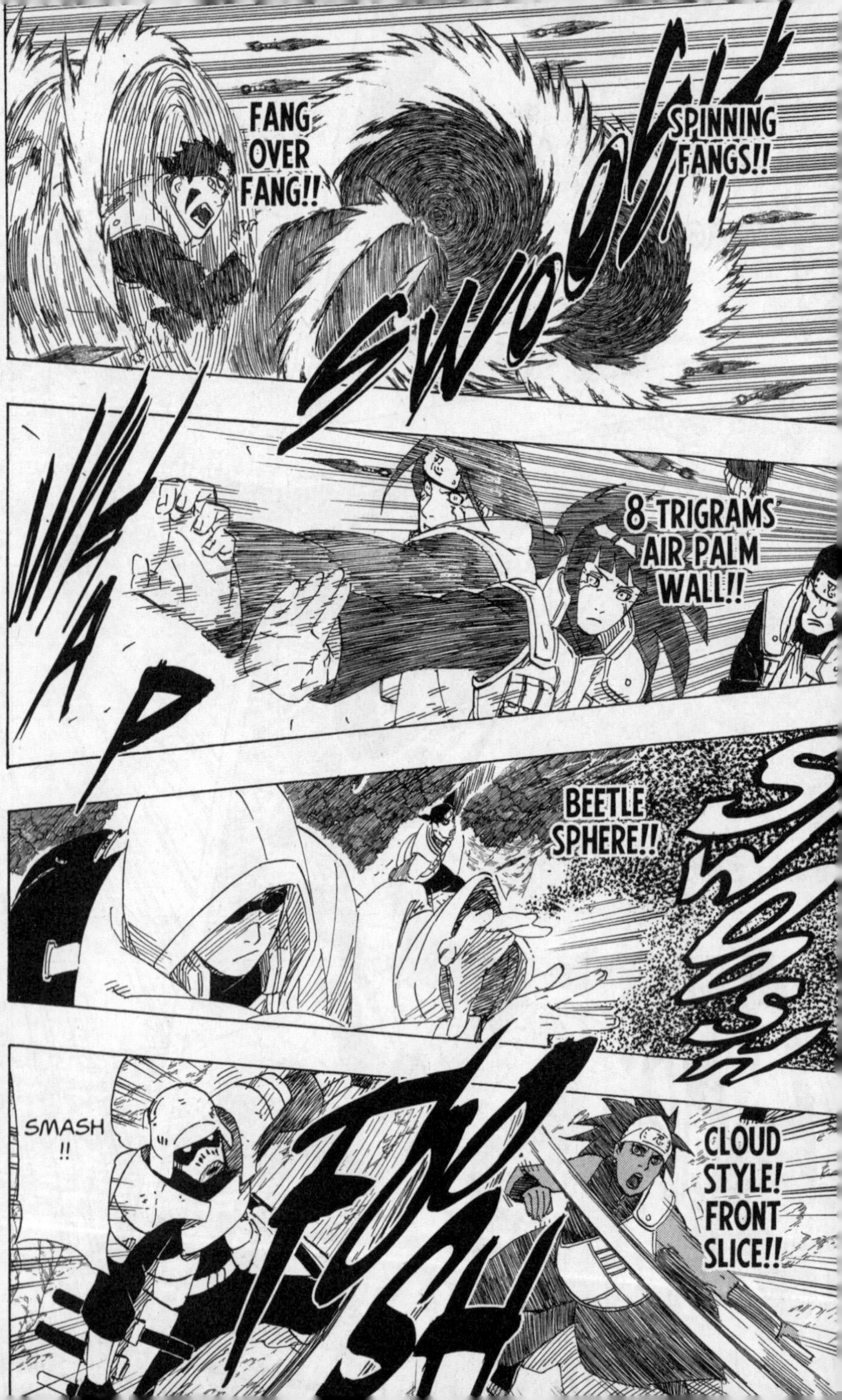
SPINNING FANGS!!
FANG OVER FANG!!
8 TRIGRAMS AIR PALM WALL!!
WHAP
SWOOSH
BEETLE SPHERE!!
CLOUD STYLE! FRONT SLICE!!
SMASH !!

THK-THK-THK-THK-THK-THK

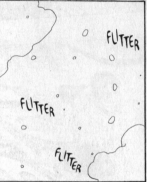

FLUTTER

FLUTTER

FLITTER

KABOOM

PLINK

PLINK

PLINK

COLD AIR?

!

SNOW?

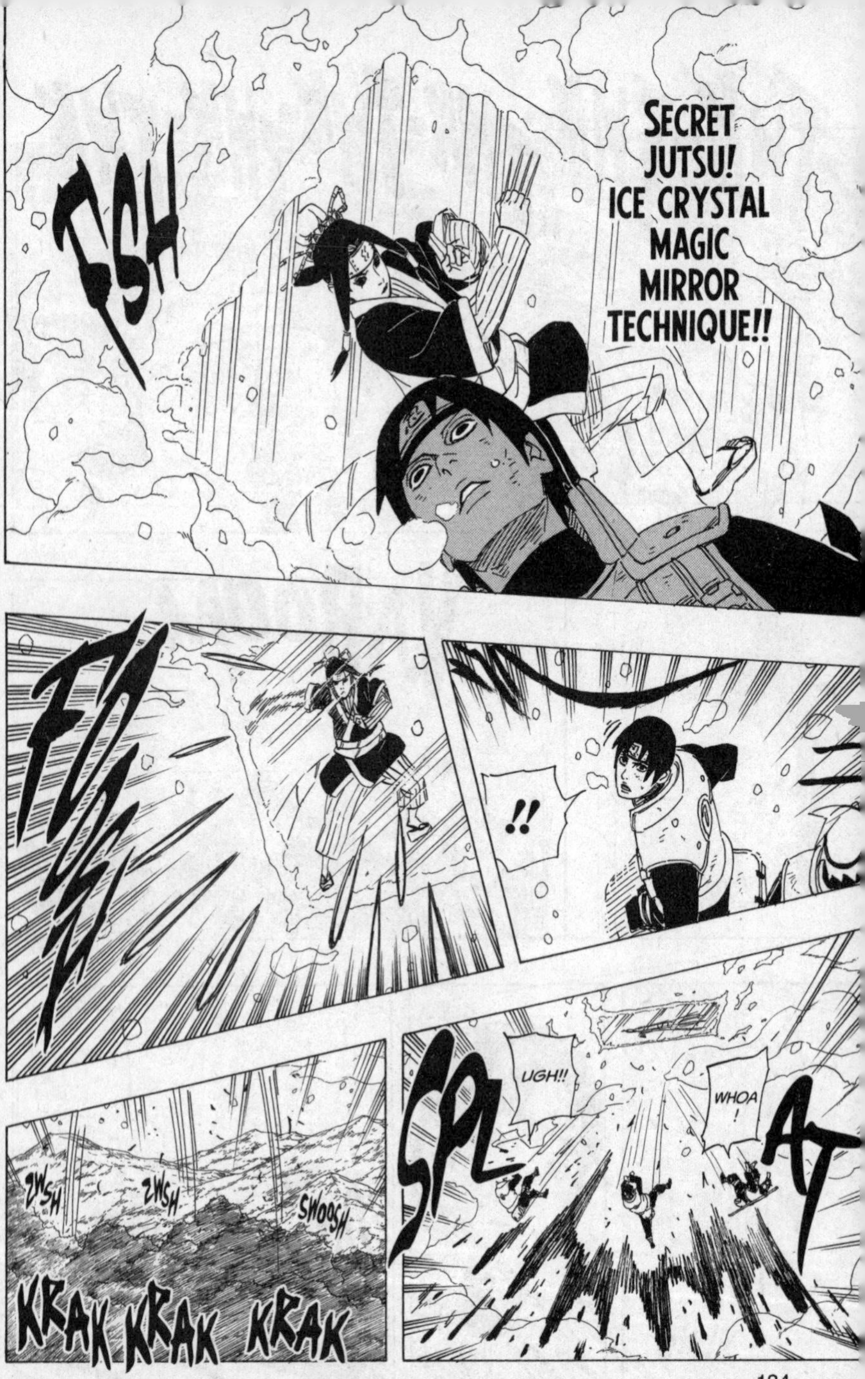
SECRET JUTSU! ICE CRYSTAL MAGIC MIRROR TECHNIQUE!!
FSH
!!
WHOA!
UGH!!
SPLAT
SWOOSH
ZWSH
ZWSH
KRAK KRAK KRAK

READ THIS WAY

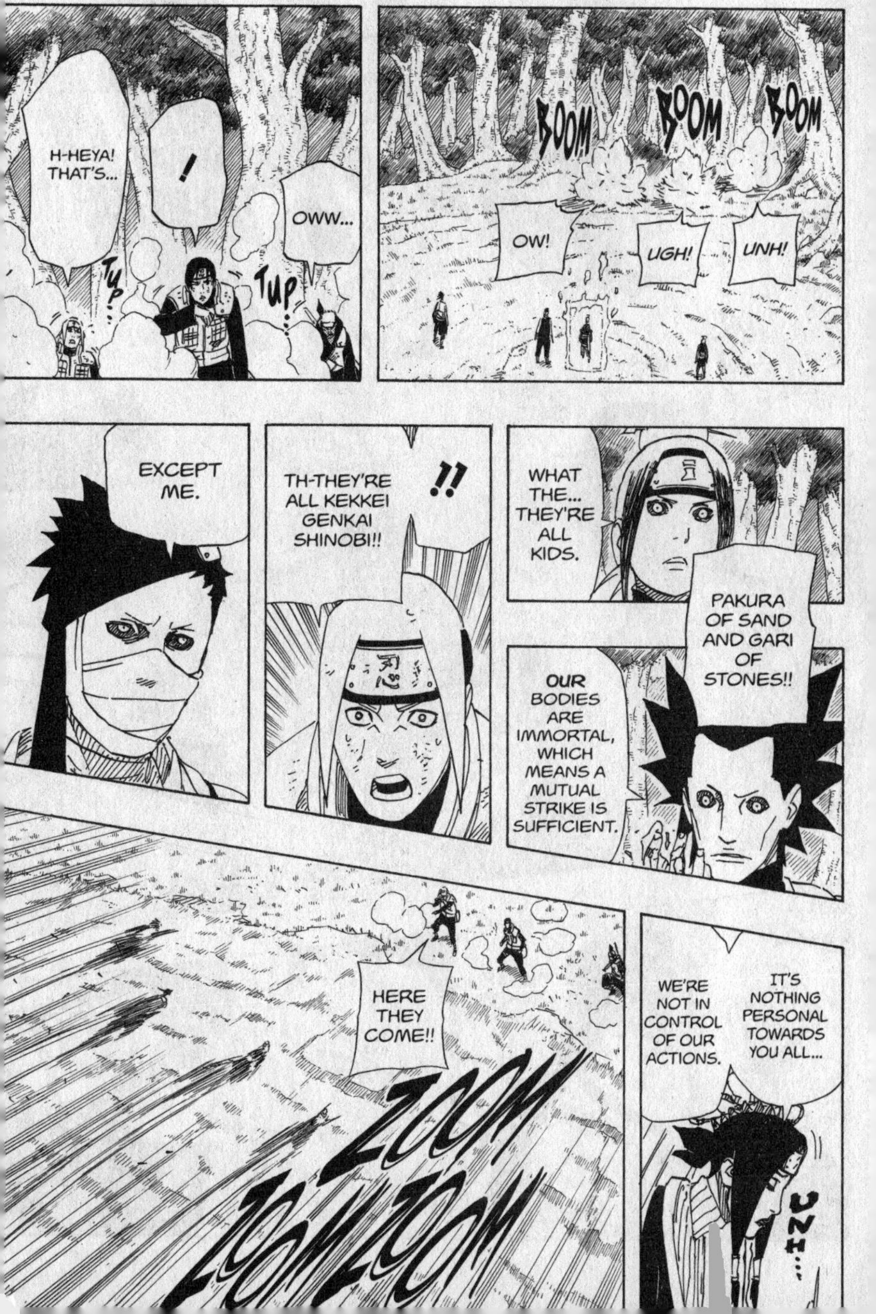

BOOM
BOOM
BOOM
OW!
UGH!
UNH!
OWW...
!
H-HEYA! THAT'S...
TUP
TUP
WHAT THE... THEY'RE ALL KIDS.
PAKURA OF SAND AND GARI OF STONES!!
OUR BODIES ARE IMMORTAL, WHICH MEANS A MUTUAL STRIKE IS SUFFICIENT.
TH-THEY'RE ALL KEKKEI GENKAI SHINOBI!!
!!
EXCEPT ME.
IT'S NOTHING PERSONAL TOWARDS YOU ALL...
WE'RE NOT IN CONTROL OF OUR ACTIONS.
UNH...
HERE THEY COME!!
ZOOM
ZOOM
ZOOM

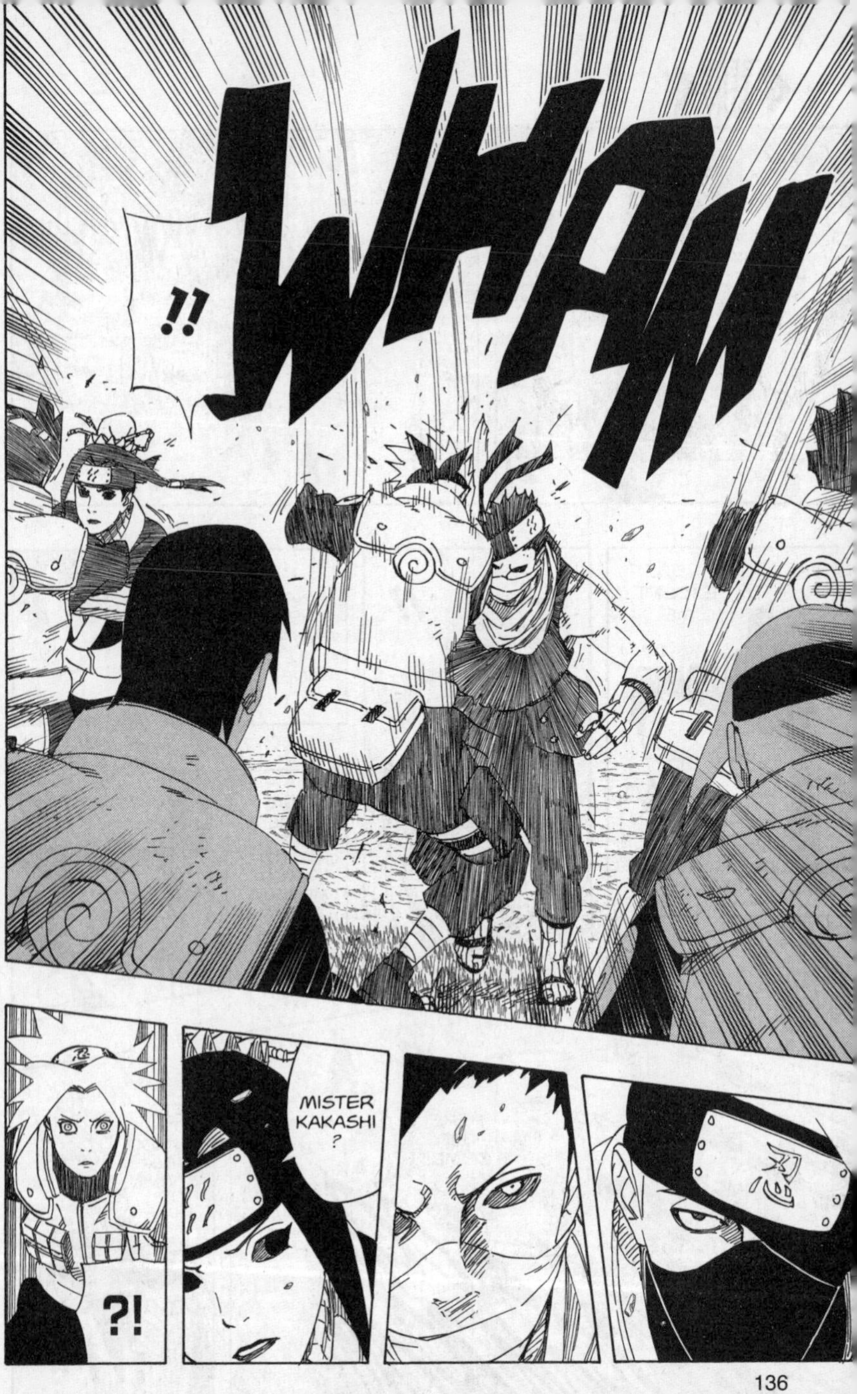
WHAM
!!
MISTER KAKASHI ?
?!

READ THIS WAY

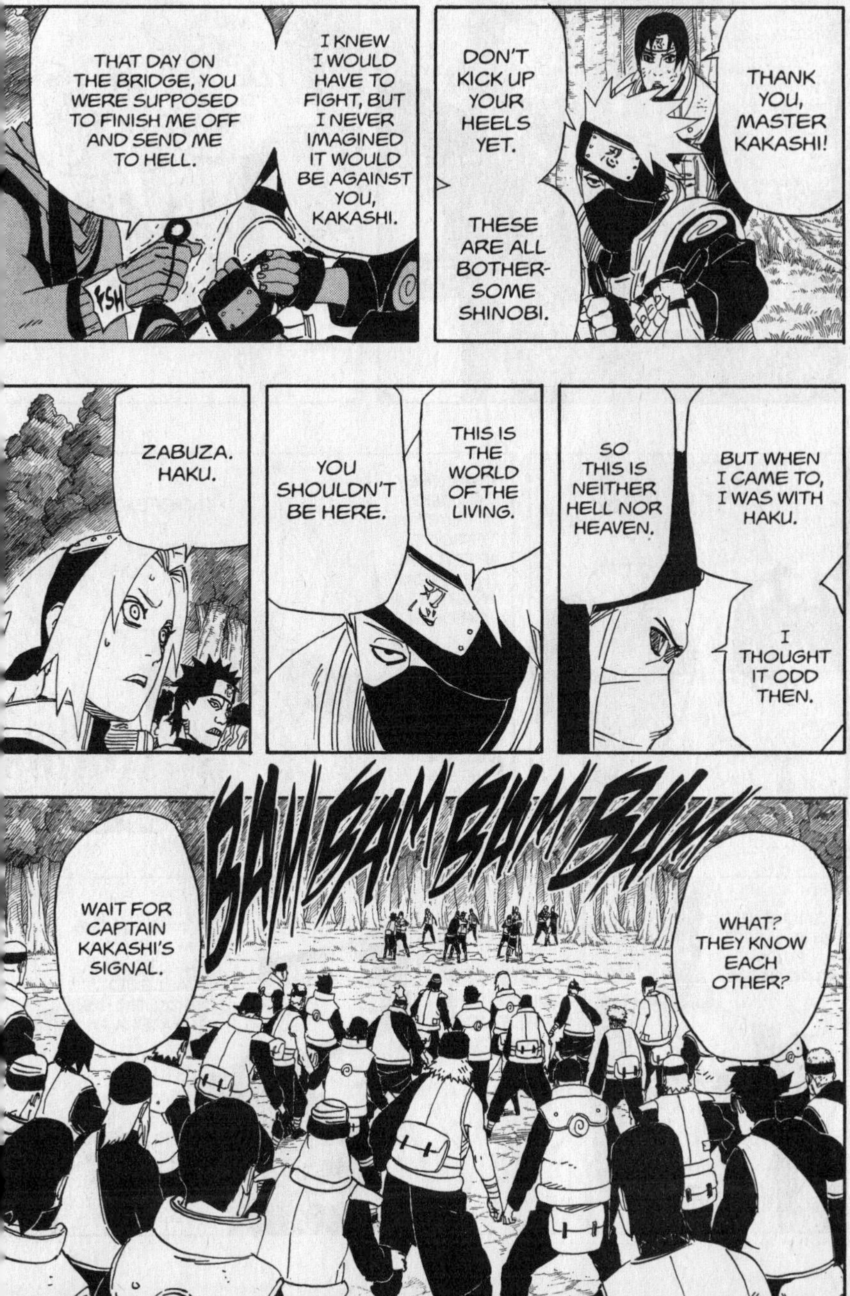
THANK YOU, MASTER KAKASHI!
DON'T KICK UP YOUR HEELS YET.
THESE ARE ALL BOTHER-SOME SHINOBI.
I KNEW I WOULD HAVE TO FIGHT, BUT I NEVER IMAGINED IT WOULD BE AGAINST YOU, KAKASHI.
THAT DAY ON THE BRIDGE, YOU WERE SUPPOSED TO FINISH ME OFF AND SEND ME TO HELL.
FSH
BUT WHEN I CAME TO, I WAS WITH HAKU.
SO THIS IS NEITHER HELL NOR HEAVEN.
I THOUGHT IT ODD THEN.
THIS IS THE WORLD OF THE LIVING.
YOU SHOULDN'T BE HERE.
ZABUZA. HAKU.
BAM BAM BAM BAM
WHAT? THEY KNOW EACH OTHER?
WAIT FOR CAPTAIN KAKASHI'S SIGNAL.

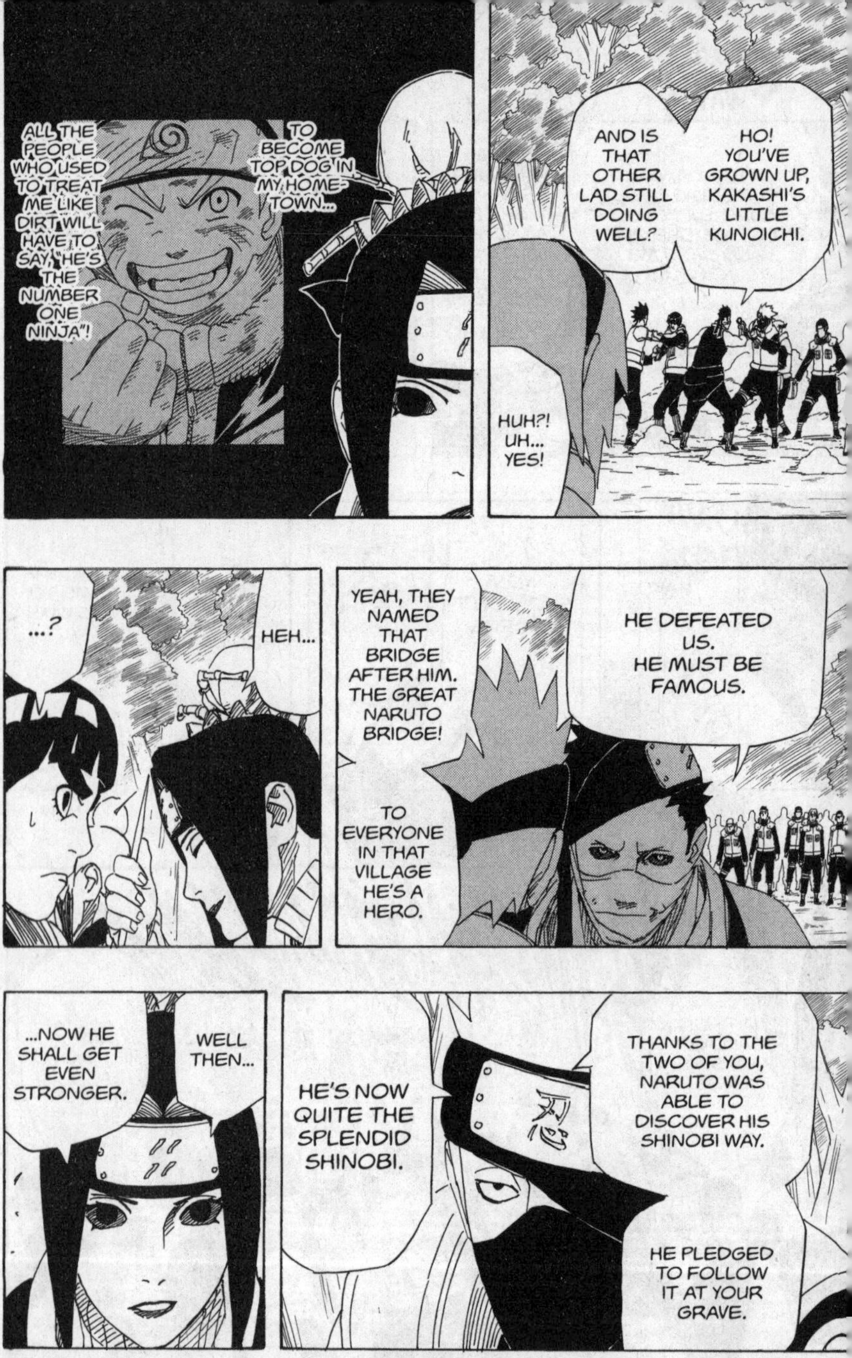
HO! YOU'VE GROWN UP, KAKASHI'S LITTLE KUNOICHI.
AND IS THAT OTHER LAD STILL DOING WELL?
HUH?! UH... YES!
TO BECOME TOP DOG IN MY HOME-TOWN...
ALL THE PEOPLE WHO USED TO TREAT ME LIKE DIRT WILL HAVE TO SAY, "HE'S THE NUMBER ONE NINJA"!
HE DEFEATED US. HE MUST BE FAMOUS.
YEAH, THEY NAMED THAT BRIDGE AFTER HIM. THE GREAT NARUTO BRIDGE!
TO EVERYONE IN THAT VILLAGE HE'S A HERO.
HEH...
...?
THANKS TO THE TWO OF YOU, NARUTO WAS ABLE TO DISCOVER HIS SHINOBI WAY.
HE PLEDGED TO FOLLOW IT AT YOUR GRAVE.
HE'S NOW QUITE THE SPLENDID SHINOBI.
WELL THEN...
...NOW HE SHALL GET EVEN STRONGER.

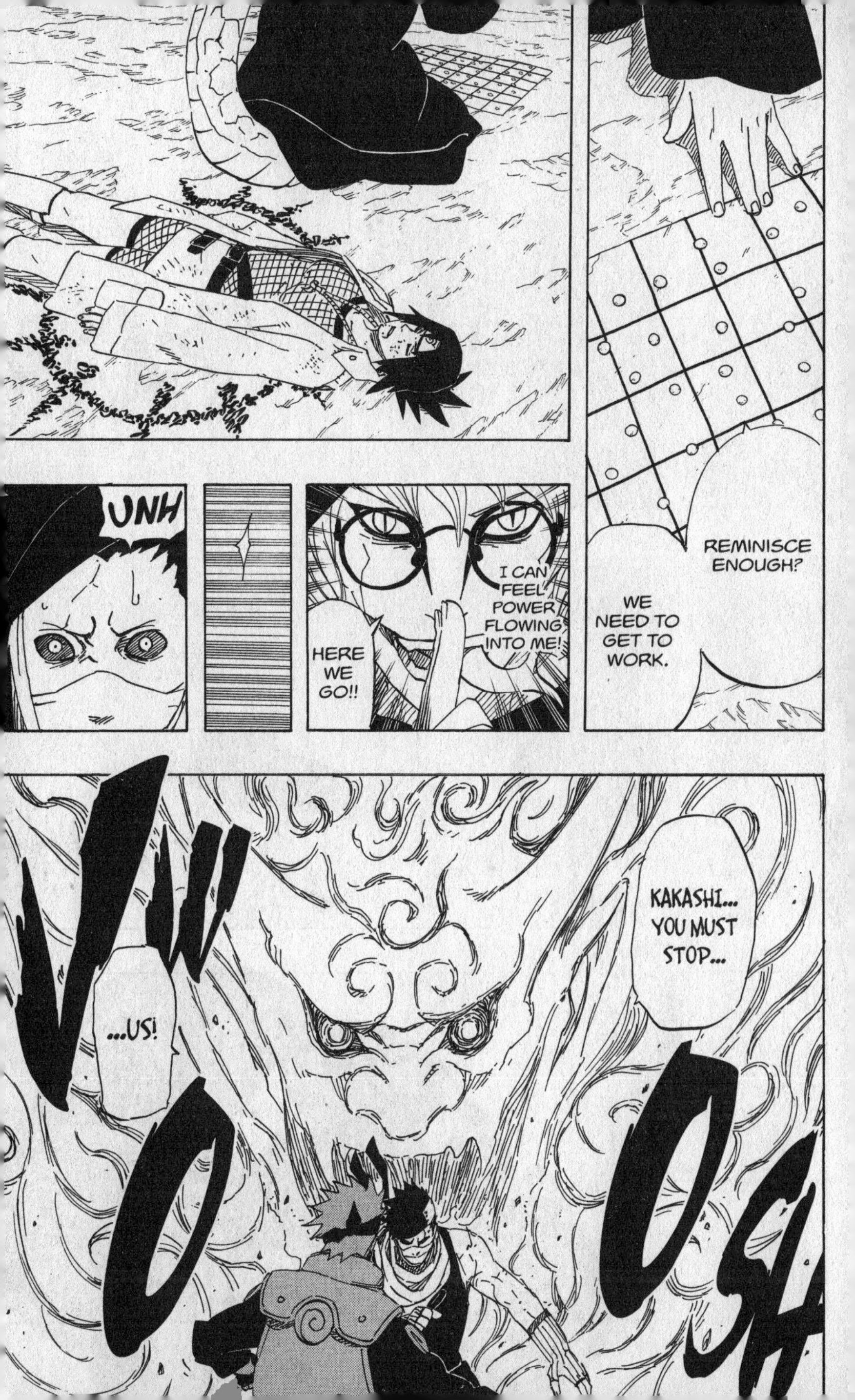
REMINISCE ENOUGH?
WE NEED TO GET TO WORK.
I CAN FEEL POWER FLOWING INTO ME!
HERE WE GO!!
UNH
KAKASHI... YOU MUST STOP...
...US!
VWOOSH

# Number 522: We Died.

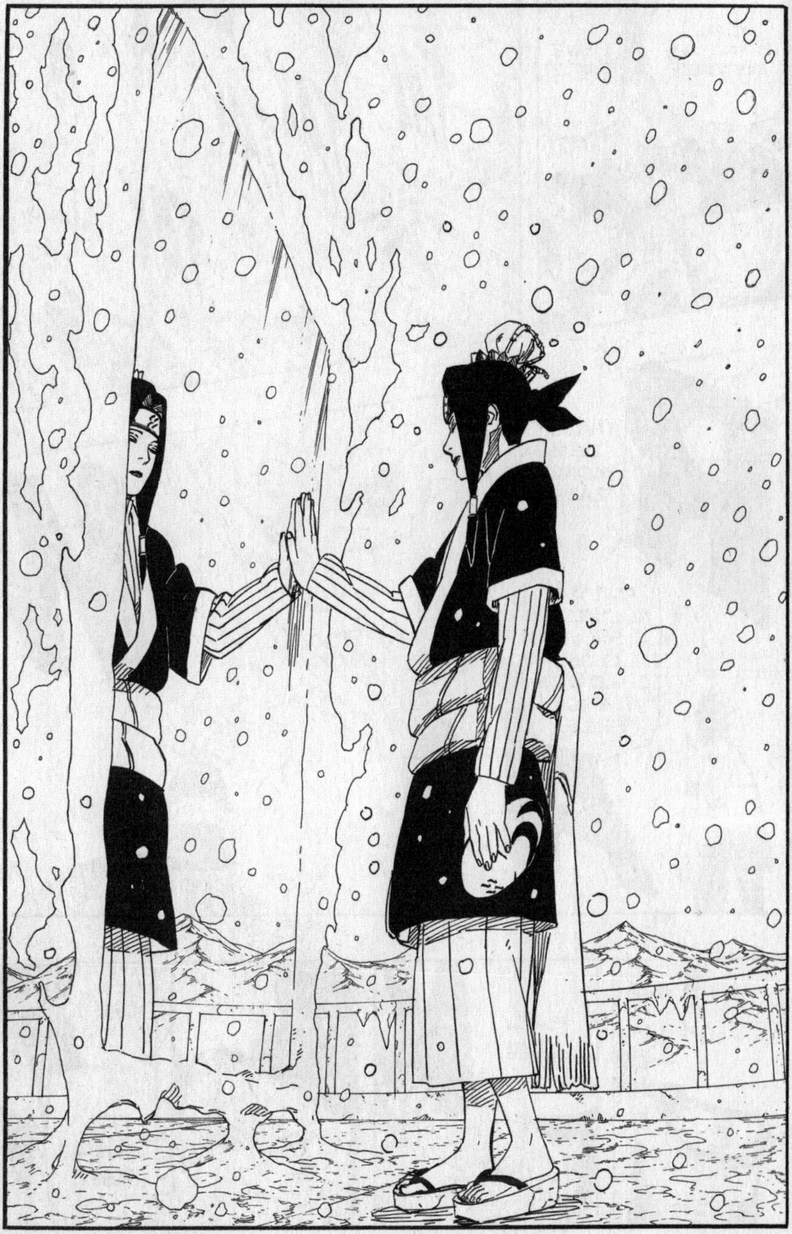

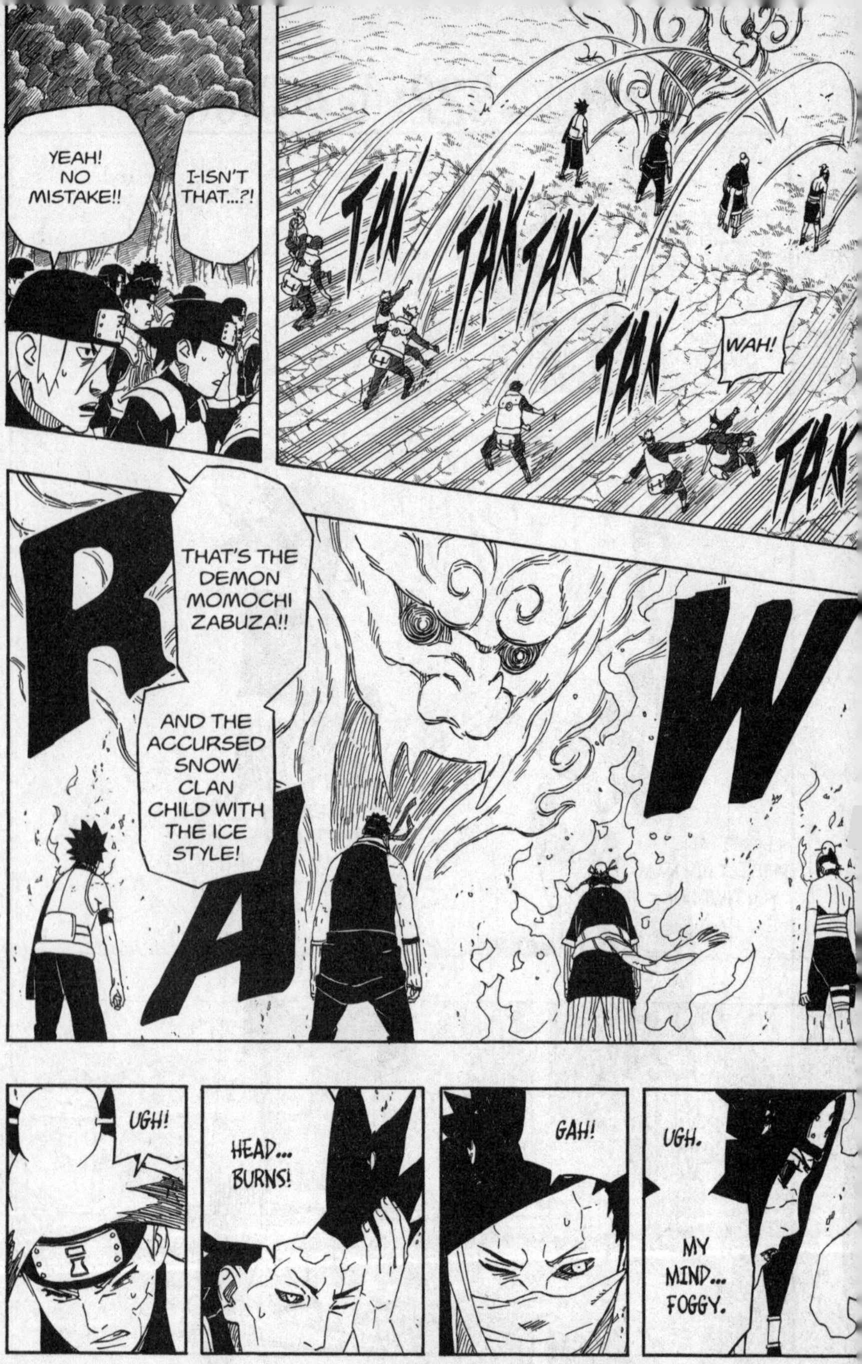
TAK
TAKTAK
WAH!
TAK
TAK
I-ISN'T THAT...?!
YEAH! NO MISTAKE!!
THAT'S THE DEMON MOMOCHI ZABUZA!!
AND THE ACCURSED SNOW CLAN CHILD WITH THE ICE STYLE!
RAW
UGH.
MY MIND... FOGGY.
GAH!
HEAD... BURNS!
UGH!

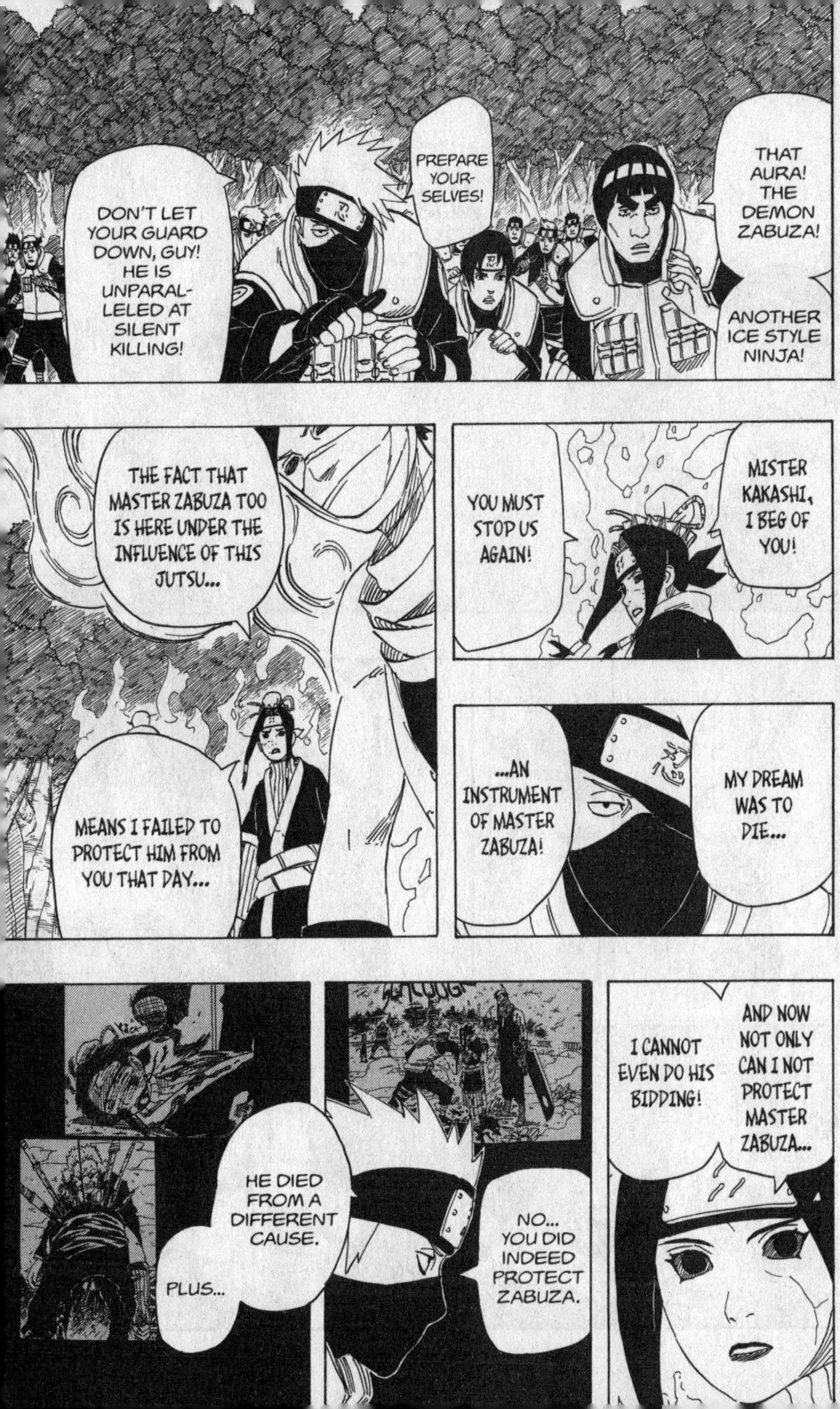
THAT AURA! THE DEMON ZABUZA!
ANOTHER ICE STYLE NINJA!
PREPARE YOUR-SELVES!
DON'T LET YOUR GUARD DOWN, GUY! HE IS UNPARAL-LELED AT SILENT KILLING!
MISTER KAKASHI, I BEG OF YOU!
YOU MUST STOP US AGAIN!
MY DREAM WAS TO DIE...
...AN INSTRUMENT OF MASTER ZABUZA!
THE FACT THAT MASTER ZABUZA TOO IS HERE UNDER THE INFLUENCE OF THIS JUTSU...
MEANS I FAILED TO PROTECT HIM FROM YOU THAT DAY...
AND NOW NOT ONLY CAN I NOT PROTECT MASTER ZABUZA...
I CANNOT EVEN DO HIS BIDDING!
NO... YOU DID INDEED PROTECT ZABUZA.
HE DIED FROM A DIFFERENT CAUSE.
PLUS...

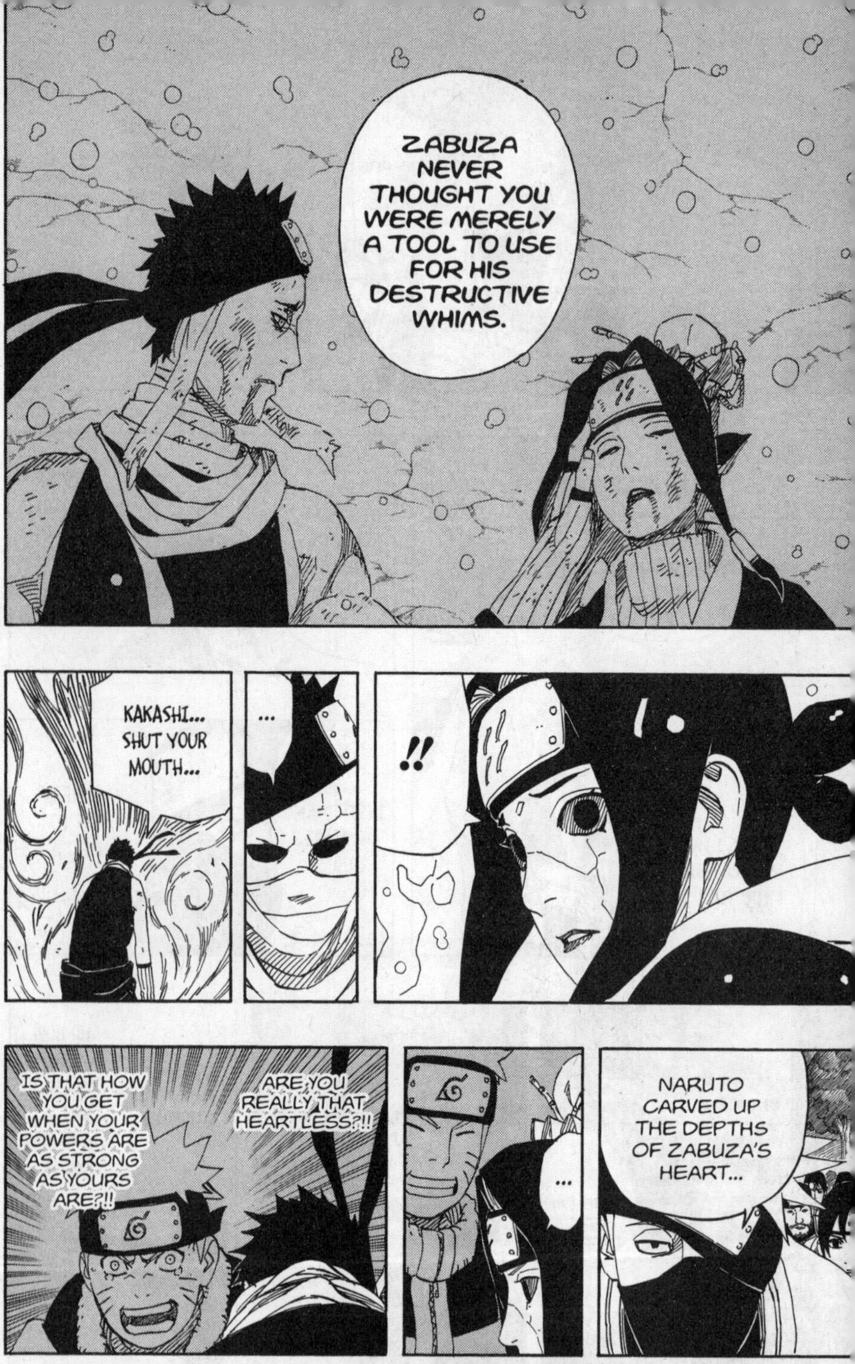
ZABUZA NEVER THOUGHT YOU WERE MERELY A TOOL TO USE FOR HIS DESTRUCTIVE WHIMS.
!!
...
KAKASHI... SHUT YOUR MOUTH...
NARUTO CARVED UP THE DEPTHS OF ZABUZA'S HEART...
...
ARE YOU REALLY THAT HEARTLESS?!!
IS THAT HOW YOU GET WHEN YOUR POWERS ARE AS STRONG AS YOURS ARE?!!

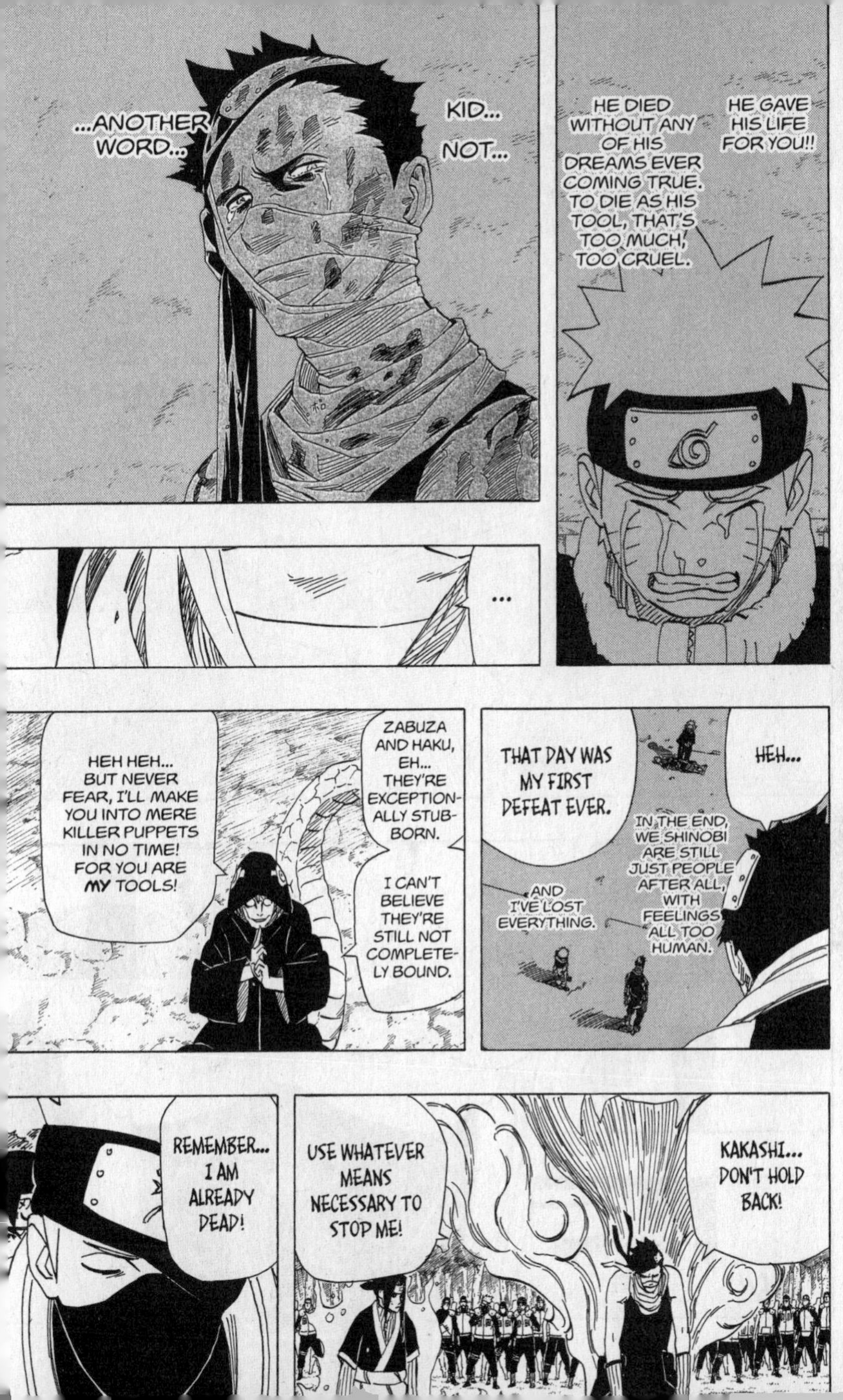
HE GAVE HIS LIFE FOR YOU!!
HE DIED WITHOUT ANY OF HIS DREAMS EVER COMING TRUE. TO DIE AS HIS TOOL, THAT'S TOO MUCH, TOO CRUEL.
KID... NOT...
...ANOTHER WORD...
...
HEH...
THAT DAY WAS MY FIRST DEFEAT EVER.
IN THE END, WE SHINOBI ARE STILL JUST PEOPLE AFTER ALL, WITH FEELINGS ALL TOO HUMAN.
AND I'VE LOST EVERYTHING.
ZABUZA AND HAKU, EH... THEY'RE EXCEPTION-ALLY STUB-BORN.
I CAN'T BELIEVE THEY'RE STILL NOT COMPLETE-LY BOUND.
HEH HEH... BUT NEVER FEAR, I'LL MAKE YOU INTO MERE KILLER PUPPETS IN NO TIME! FOR YOU ARE MY TOOLS!
KAKASHI... DON'T HOLD BACK!
USE WHATEVER MEANS NECESSARY TO STOP ME!
REMEMBER... I AM ALREADY DEAD!

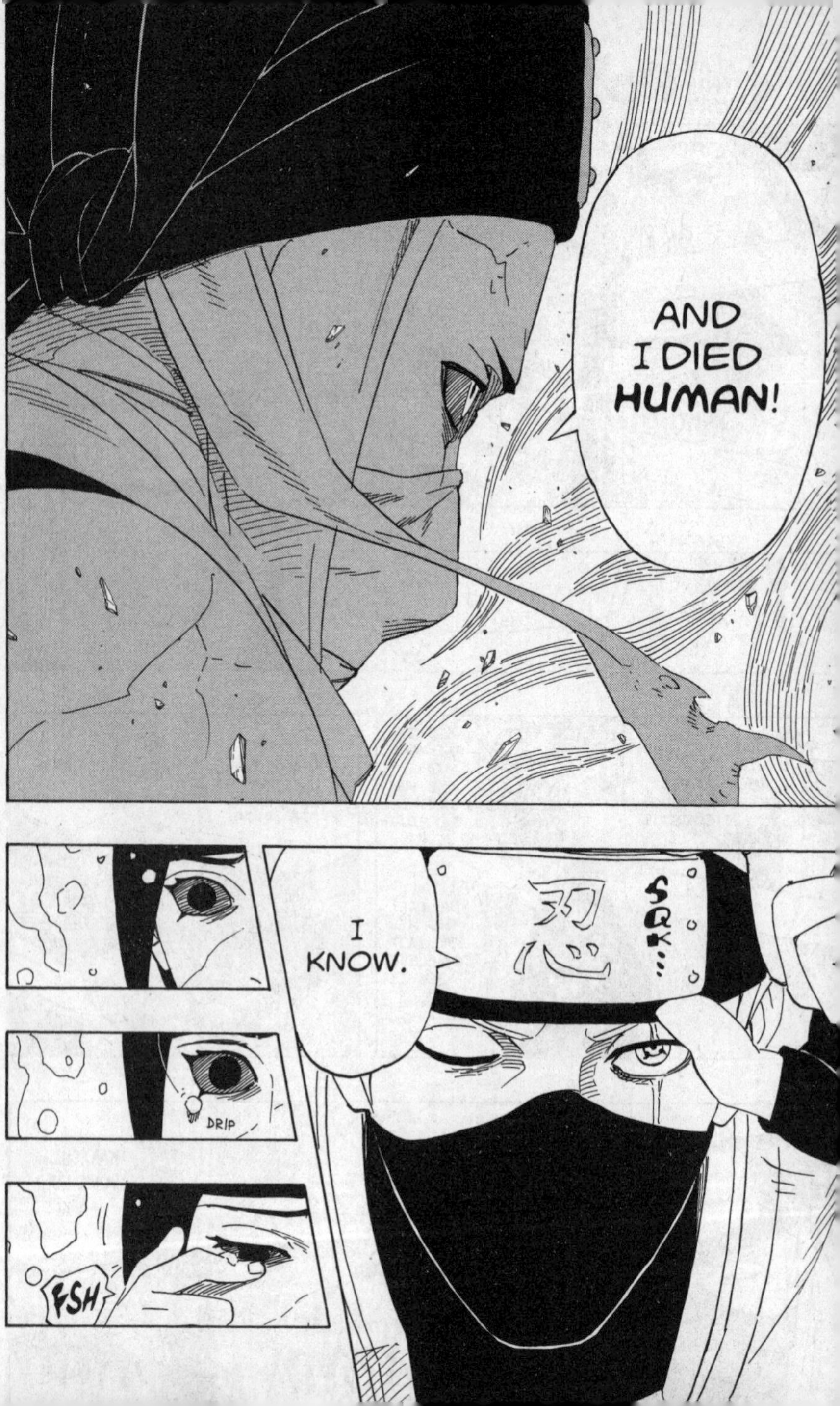
AND I DIED HUMAN!
SQK...
I KNOW.
DRIP
FSH

READ THIS WAY

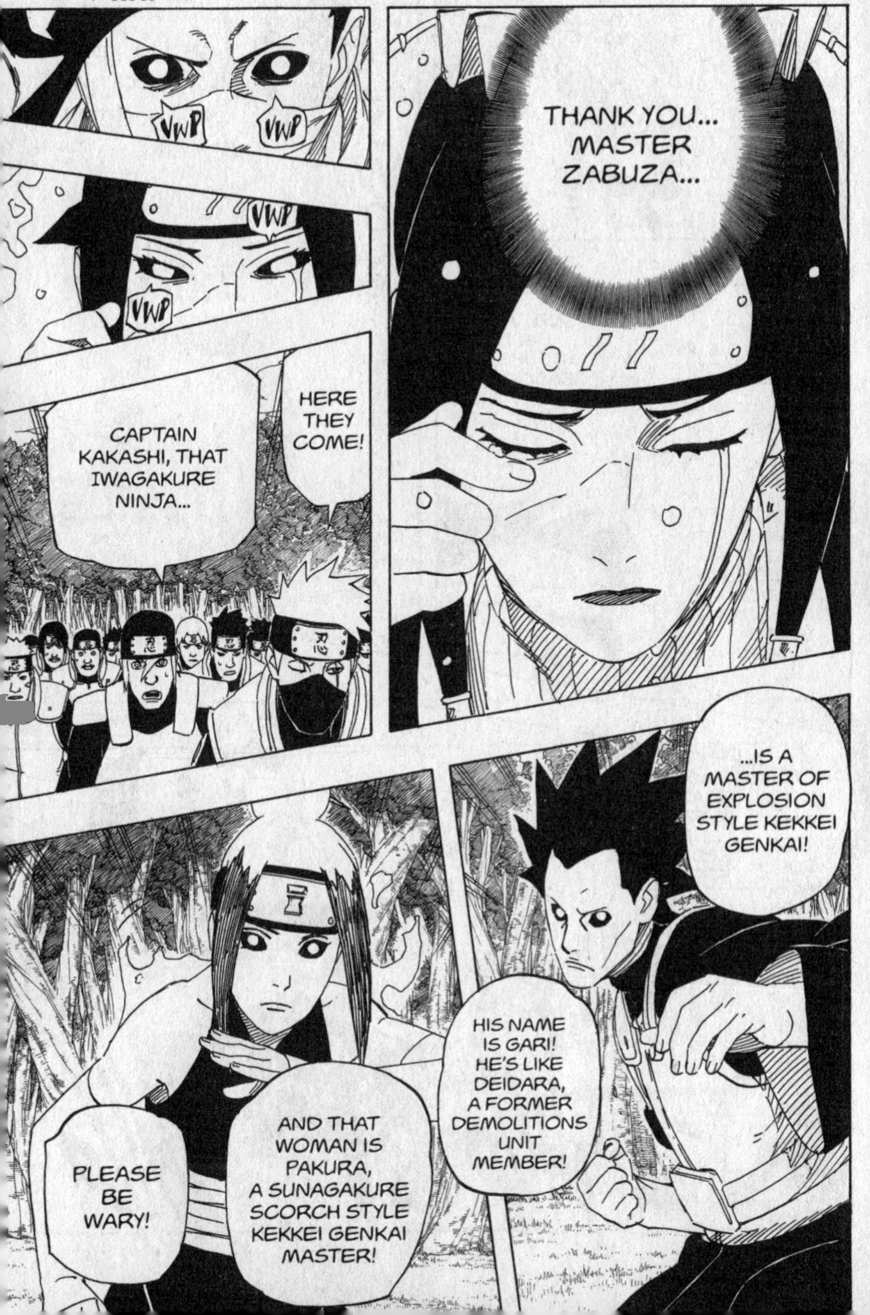
THANK YOU... MASTER ZABUZA...
VWP
VWP
VWP
VWP
HERE THEY COME!
CAPTAIN KAKASHI, THAT IWAGAKURE NINJA...
...IS A MASTER OF EXPLOSION STYLE KEKKEI GENKAI!
HIS NAME IS GARI! HE'S LIKE DEIDARA, A FORMER DEMOLITIONS UNIT MEMBER!
AND THAT WOMAN IS PAKURA, A SUNAGAKURE SCORCH STYLE KEKKEI GENKAI MASTER!
PLEASE BE WARY!

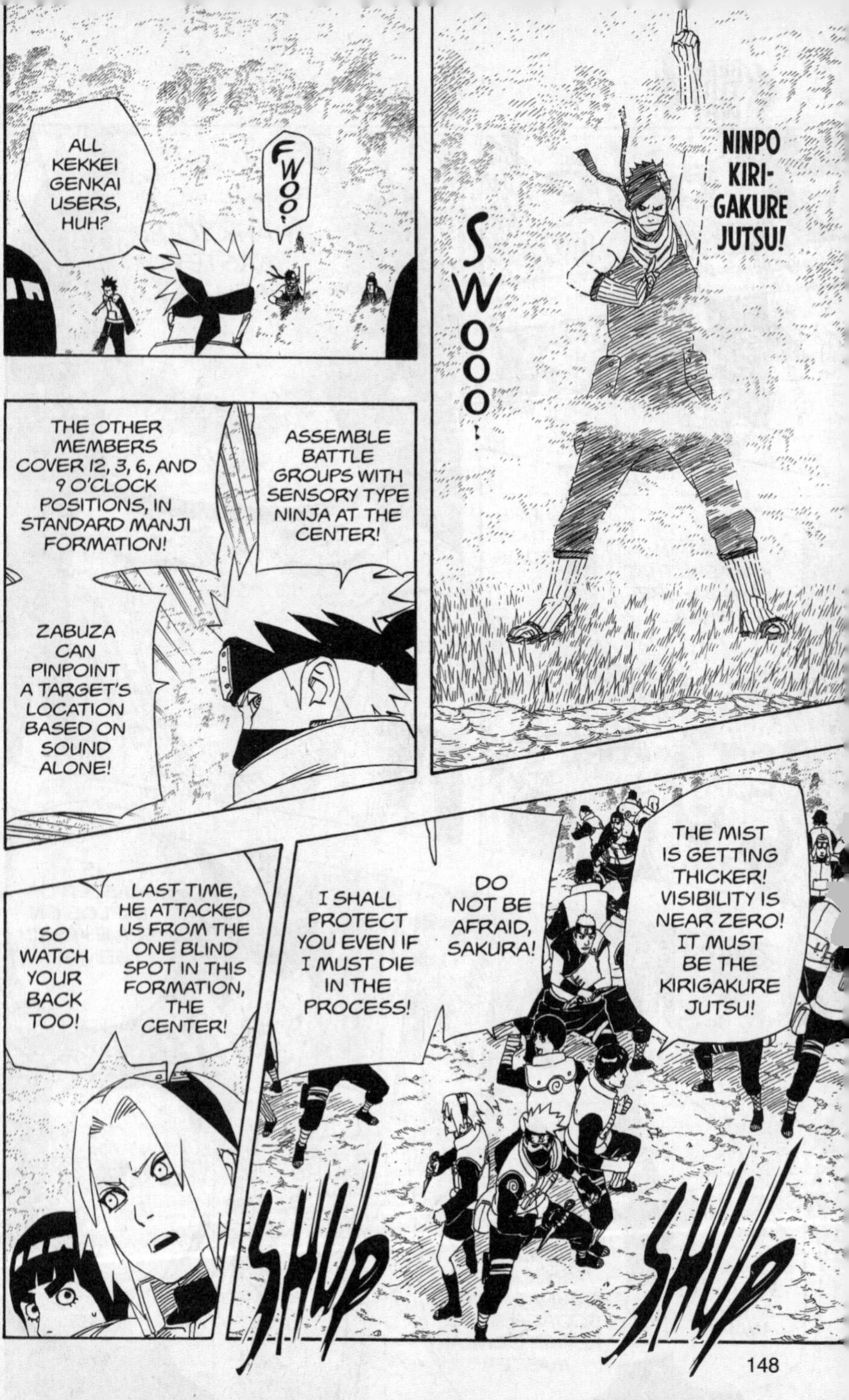
NINPO KIRIGAKURE JUTSU!
SWOOO!
FWOOO!
ALL KEKKEI GENKAI USERS, HUH?
ASSEMBLE BATTLE GROUPS WITH SENSORY TYPE NINJA AT THE CENTER!
THE OTHER MEMBERS COVER 12, 3, 6, AND 9 O'CLOCK POSITIONS, IN STANDARD MANJI FORMATION!
ZABUZA CAN PINPOINT A TARGET'S LOCATION BASED ON SOUND ALONE!
THE MIST IS GETTING THICKER! VISIBILITY IS NEAR ZERO! IT MUST BE THE KIRIGAKURE JUTSU!
DO NOT BE AFRAID, SAKURA!
I SHALL PROTECT YOU EVEN IF I MUST DIE IN THE PROCESS!
SHUP
SHUP
LAST TIME, HE ATTACKED US FROM THE ONE BLIND SPOT IN THIS FORMATION, THE CENTER!
SO WATCH YOUR BACK TOO!

READ THIS WAY

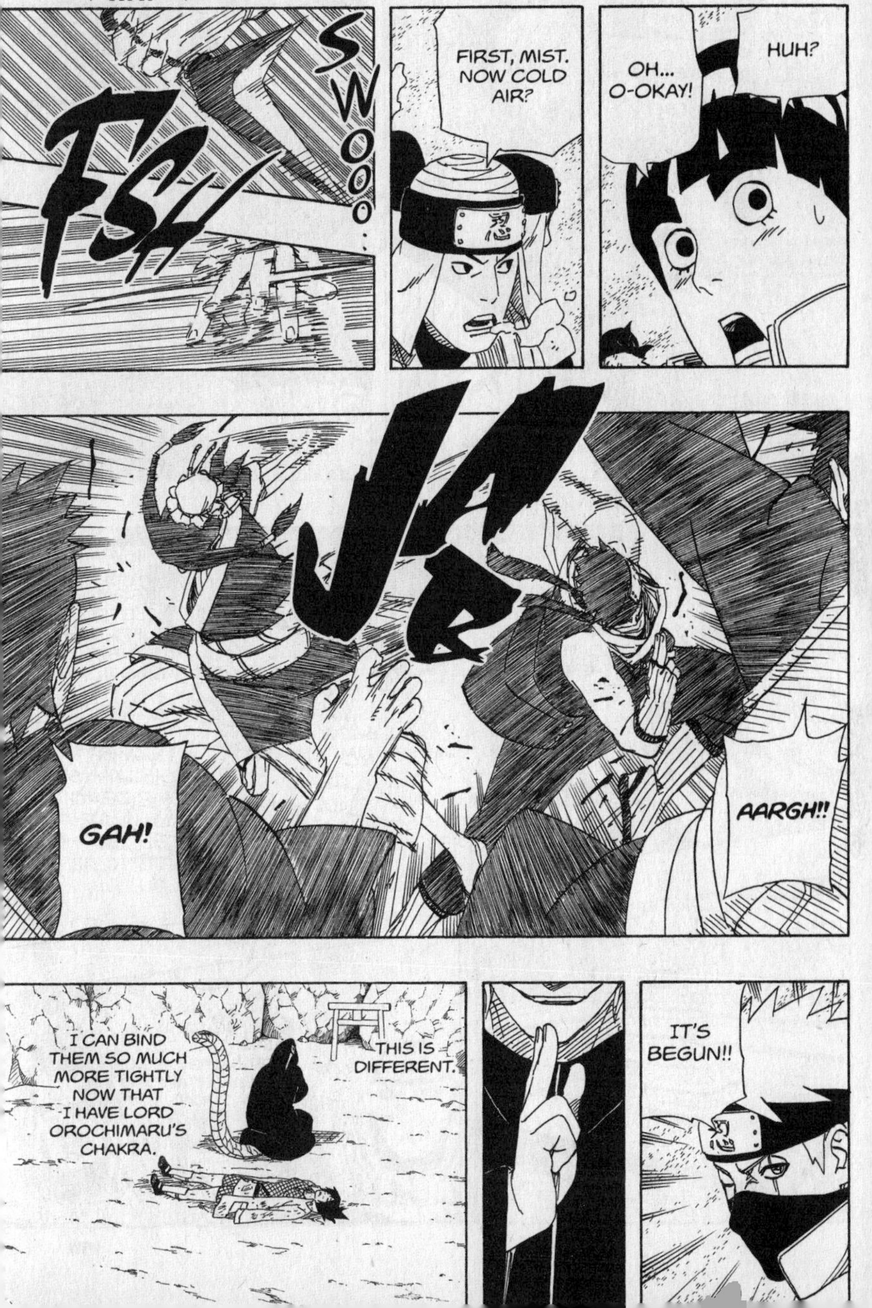
HUH?
OH... O-OKAY!
FIRST, MIST. NOW COLD AIR?
SWOOO...
FSH
AARGH!!
JAB
GAH!
IT'S BEGUN!!
THIS IS DIFFERENT.
I CAN BIND THEM SO MUCH MORE TIGHTLY NOW THAT I HAVE LORD OROCHIMARU'S CHAKRA.

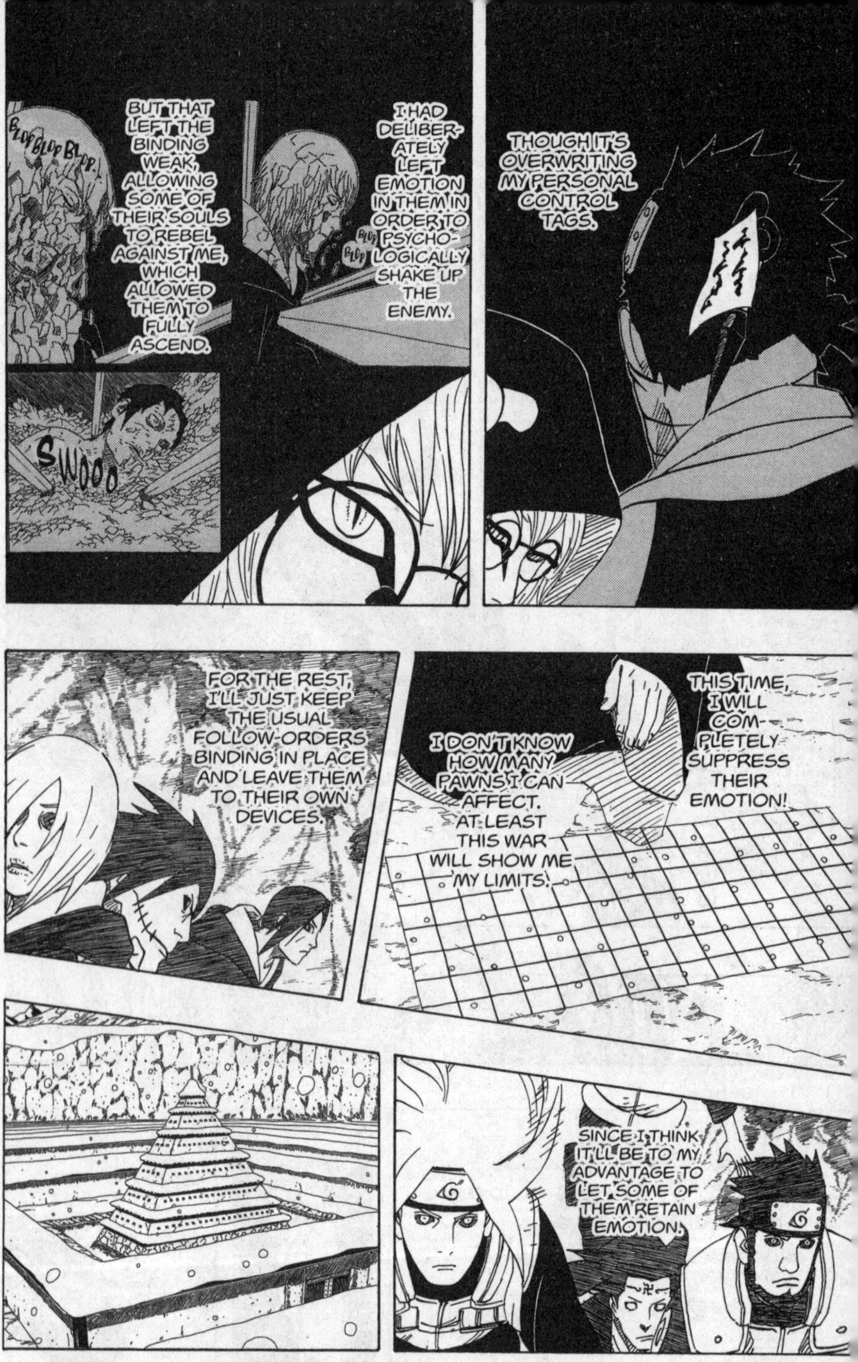
THOUGH IT'S OVERWRITING MY PERSONAL CONTROL TAGS.
I HAD DELIBER-ATELY LEFT EMOTION IN THEM IN ORDER TO PSYCHO-LOGICALLY SHAKE UP THE ENEMY.
BLOP BLOP
BLOP BLOP BLOP
BUT THAT LEFT THE BINDING WEAK, ALLOWING SOME OF THEIR SOULS TO REBEL AGAINST ME, WHICH ALLOWED THEM TO FULLY ASCEND.
SWOOO
THIS TIME, I WILL COM-PLETELY SUPPRESS THEIR EMOTION!
I DON'T KNOW HOW MANY PAWNS I CAN AFFECT. AT LEAST THIS WAR WILL SHOW ME MY LIMITS.
FOR THE REST, I'LL JUST KEEP THE USUAL FOLLOW-ORDERS BINDING IN PLACE AND LEAVE THEM TO THEIR OWN DEVICES.
SINCE I THINK IT'LL BE TO MY ADVANTAGE TO LET SOME OF THEM RETAIN EMOTION.

READ THIS WAY

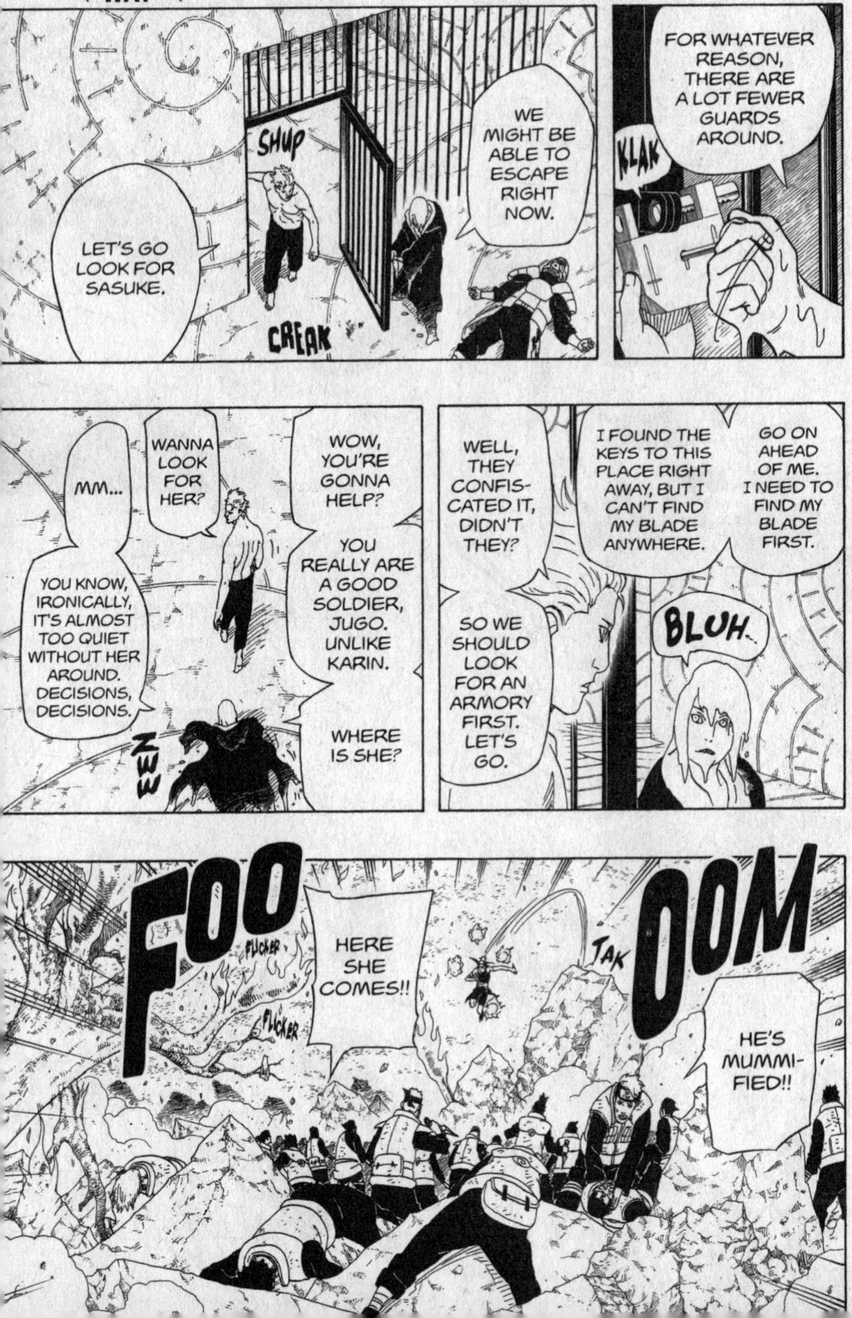
KLAK
FOR WHATEVER REASON, THERE ARE A LOT FEWER GUARDS AROUND.
WE MIGHT BE ABLE TO ESCAPE RIGHT NOW.
SHUP
CREAK
LET'S GO LOOK FOR SASUKE.
GO ON AHEAD OF ME. I NEED TO FIND MY BLADE FIRST.
I FOUND THE KEYS TO THIS PLACE RIGHT AWAY, BUT I CAN'T FIND MY BLADE ANYWHERE.
BLUH..
WELL, THEY CONFIS-CATED IT, DIDN'T THEY?
SO WE SHOULD LOOK FOR AN ARMORY FIRST. LET'S GO.
WOW, YOU'RE GONNA HELP?
YOU REALLY ARE A GOOD SOLDIER, JUGO. UNLIKE KARIN.
WHERE IS SHE?
WANNA LOOK FOR HER?
MM...
YOU KNOW, IRONICALLY, IT'S ALMOST TOO QUIET WITHOUT HER AROUND. DECISIONS, DECISIONS.
FOO
OOM
HE'S MUMMI-FIED!!
TAK
HERE SHE COMES!!
FLICKER
FLICKER

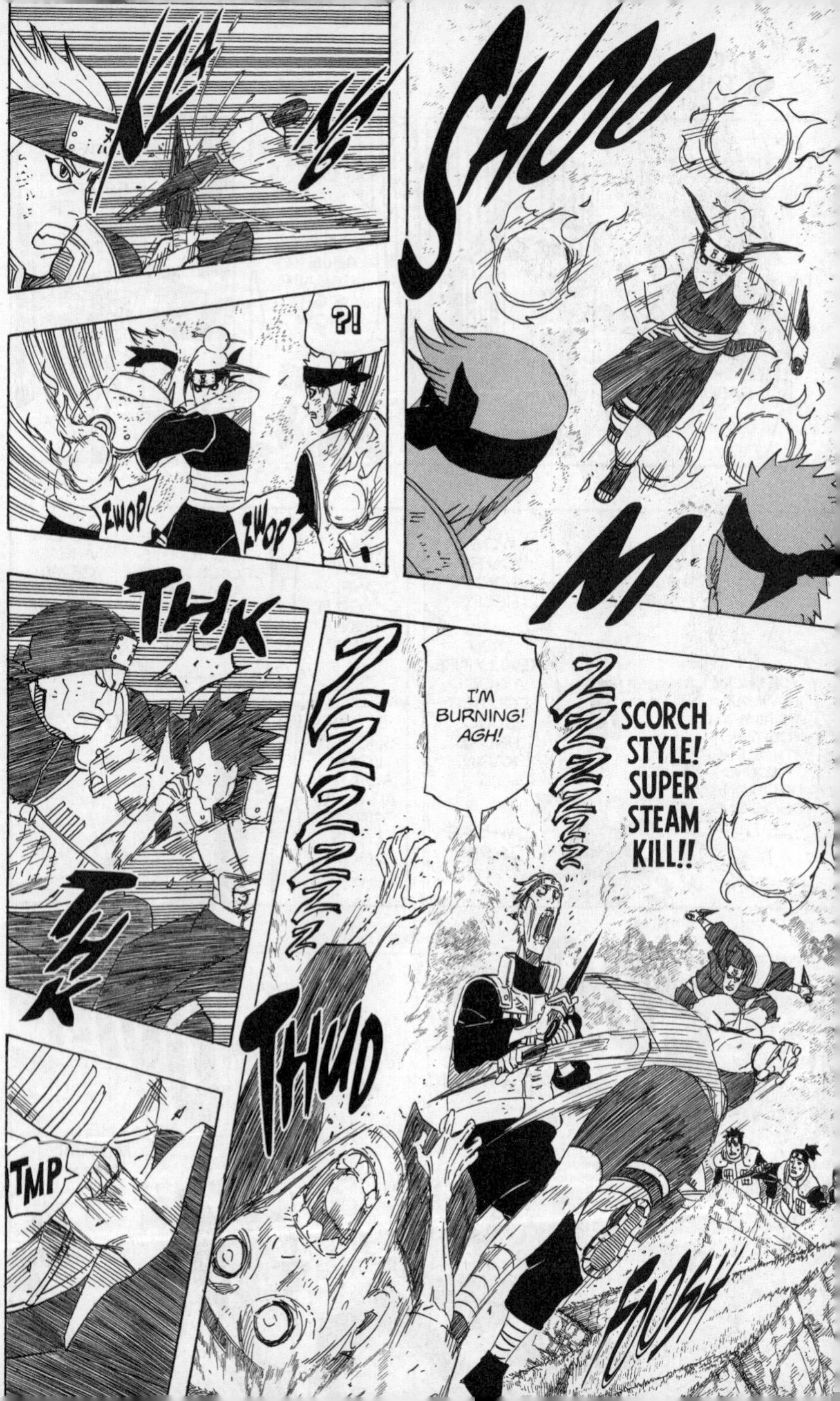
SHOOOM
KLA
NG
?!
ZWOP
ZWOP
SCORCH STYLE! SUPER STEAM KILL!!
I'M BURNING! AGH!
THK
THK
THUD
TMP

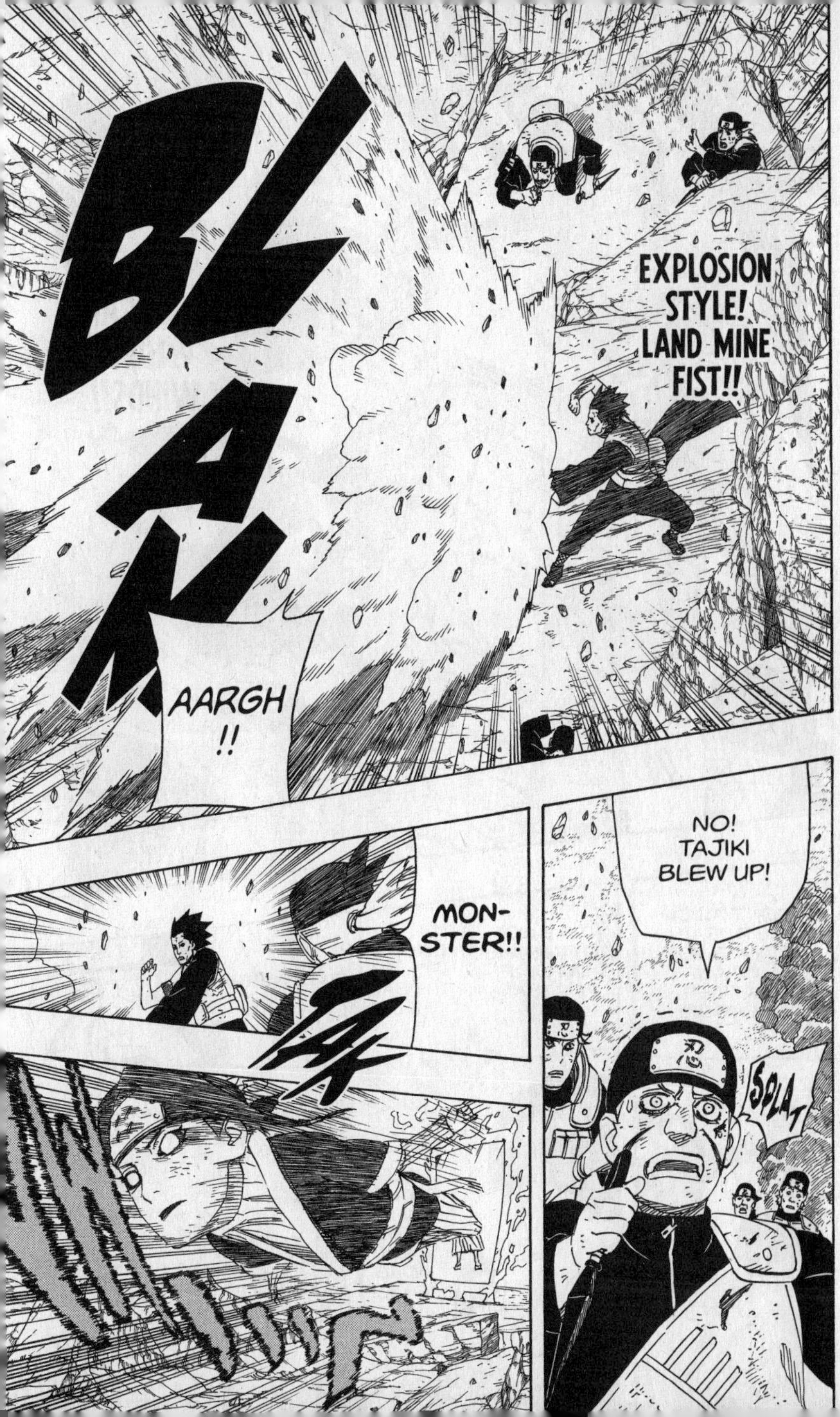
EXPLOSION STYLE! LAND MINE FIST!!
BLAM
AARGH!!
NO! TAJIKI BLEW UP!
SPLAT
MON-STER!!

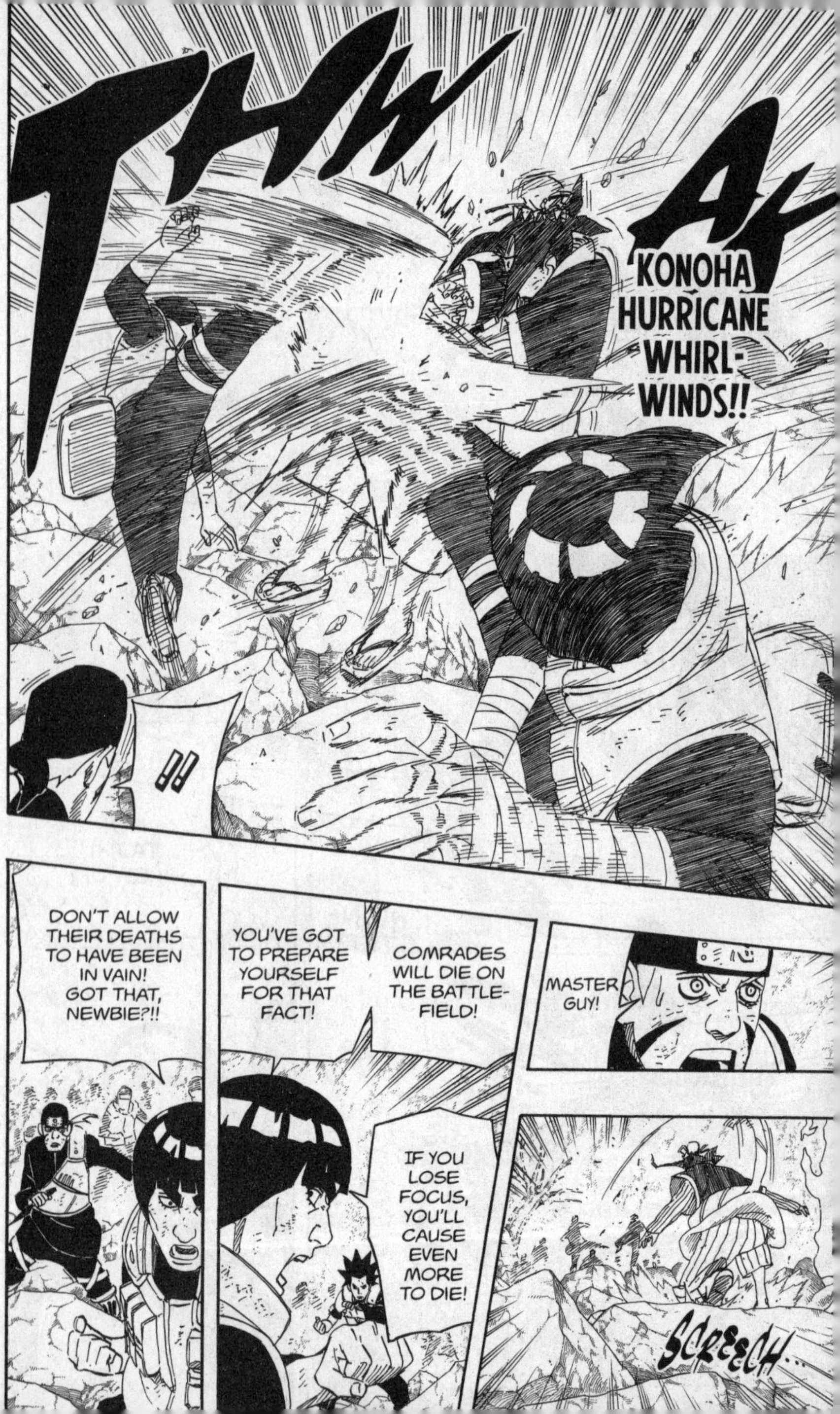
KONOHA HURRICANE WHIRL-WINDS!!
!!
MASTER GUY!
SCREECH...
COMRADES WILL DIE ON THE BATTLE-FIELD!
YOU'VE GOT TO PREPARE YOURSELF FOR THAT FACT!
IF YOU LOSE FOCUS, YOU'LL CAUSE EVEN MORE TO DIE!
DON'T ALLOW THEIR DEATHS TO HAVE BEEN IN VAIN! GOT THAT, NEWBIE?!!

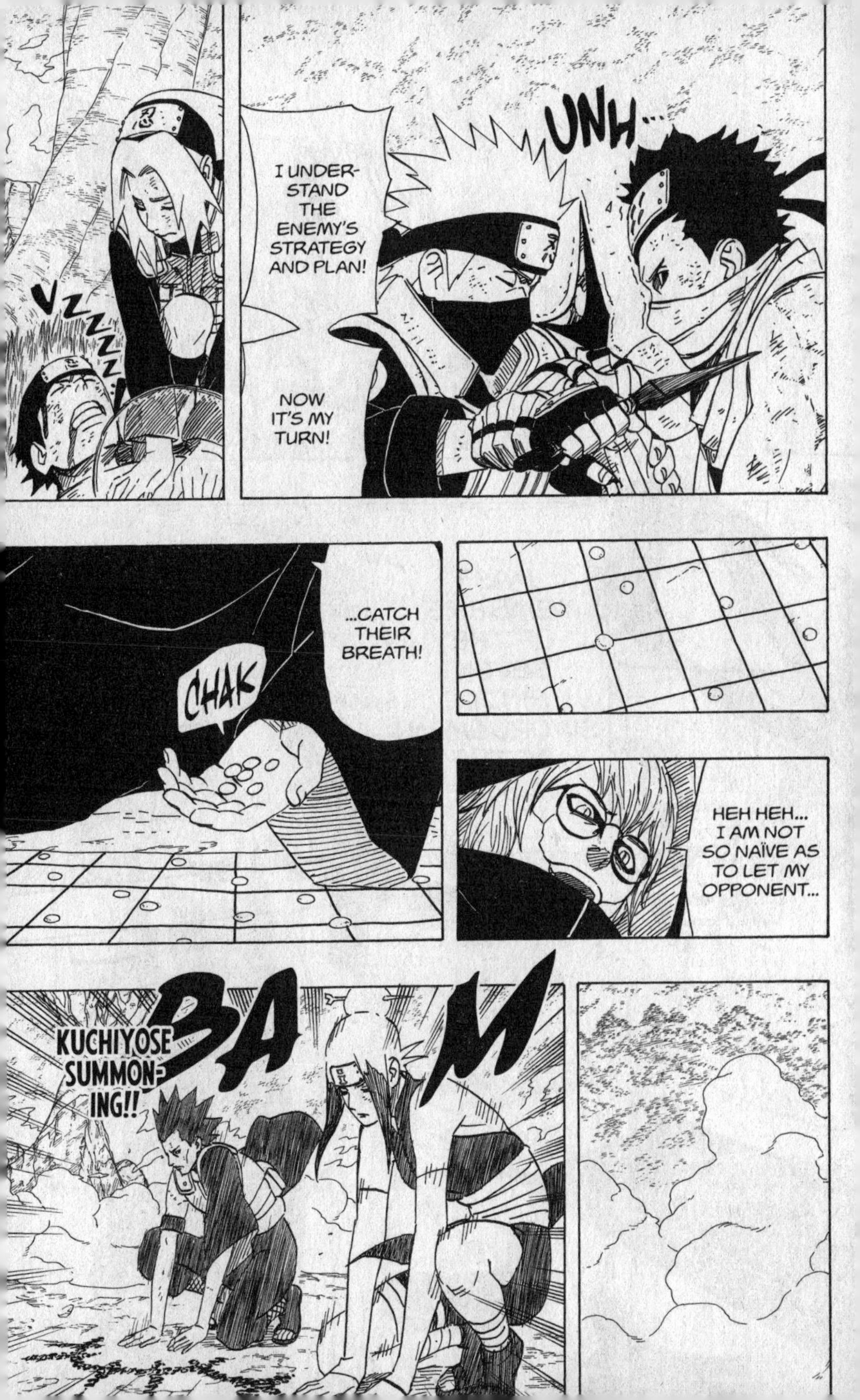
UNH...
I UNDERSTAND THE ENEMY'S STRATEGY AND PLAN!
NOW IT'S MY TURN!
ZZZZ
HEH HEH... I AM NOT SO NAÏVE AS TO LET MY OPPONENT...
CHAK
...CATCH THEIR BREATH!
BAM
KUCHIYOSE SUMMONING!!

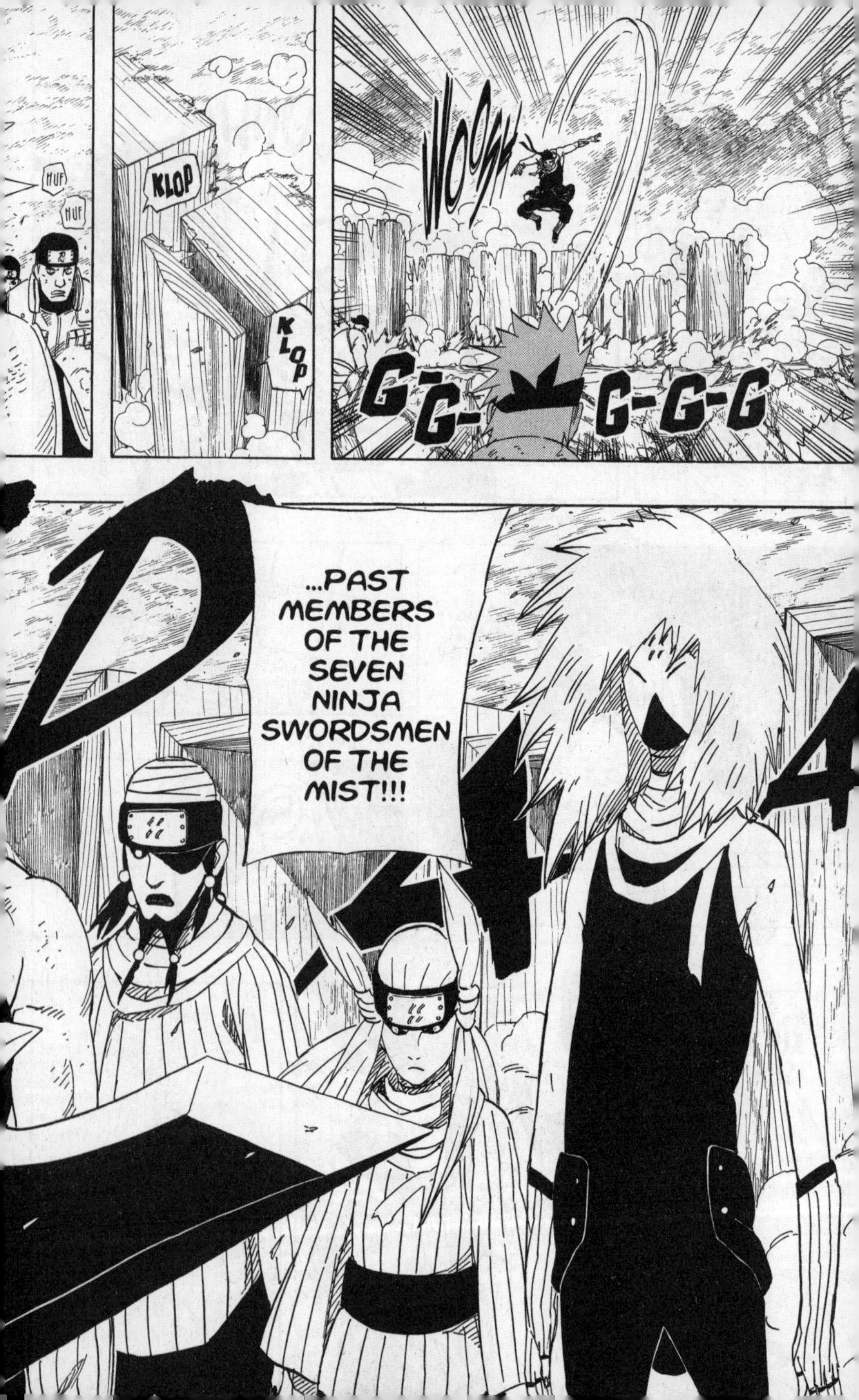
WOOSH
G-G-G-G-G
KLOP
KLOP
HUF
HUF
...PAST MEMBERS OF THE SEVEN NINJA SWORDSMEN OF THE MIST!!!

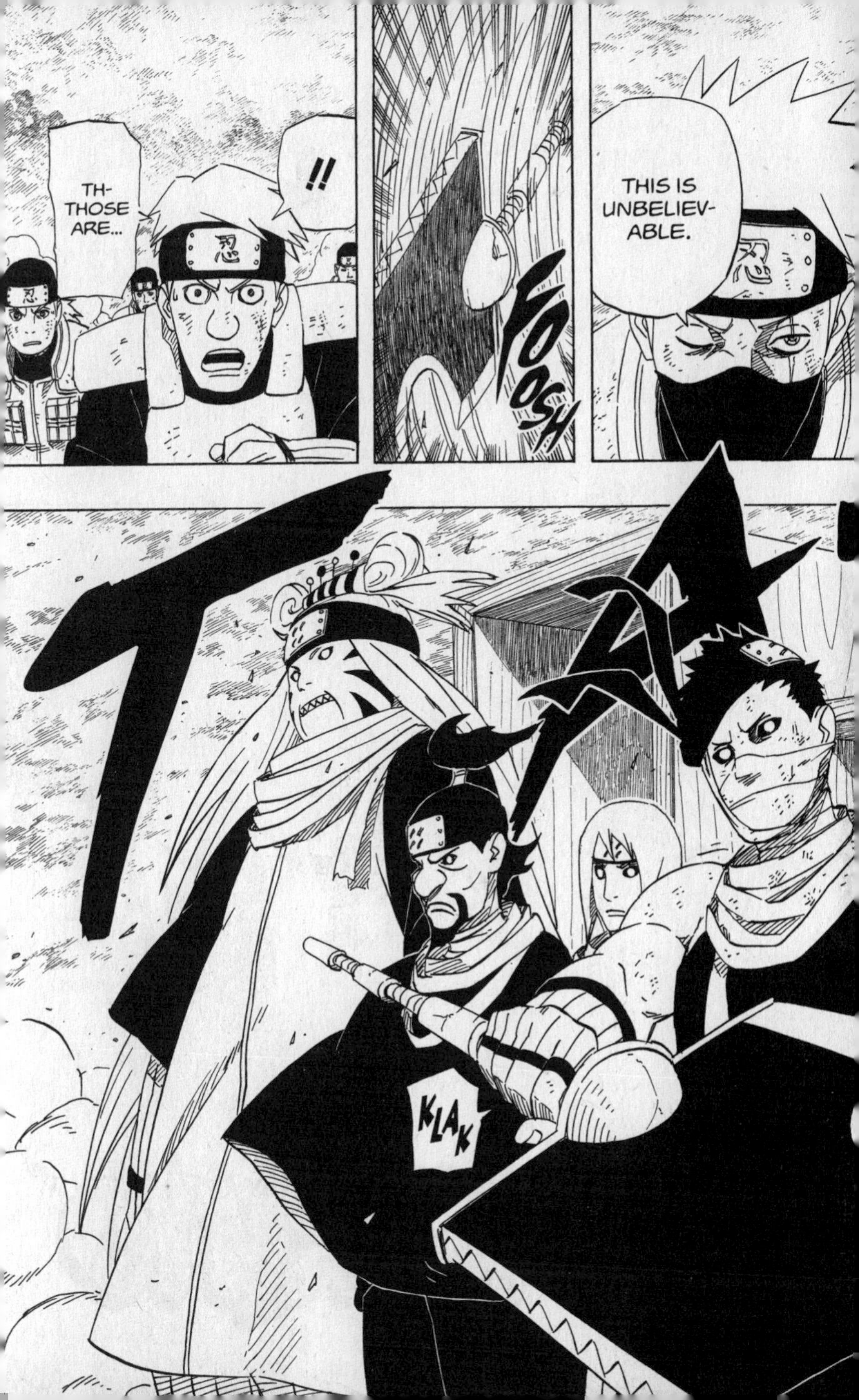
THIS IS UNBELIEV-ABLE.
FOOSH
!!
TH-THOSE ARE...
KLAK

NARUTO

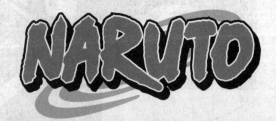

# Number 523: The Legendary Seven Swordsmen of the Mist!!

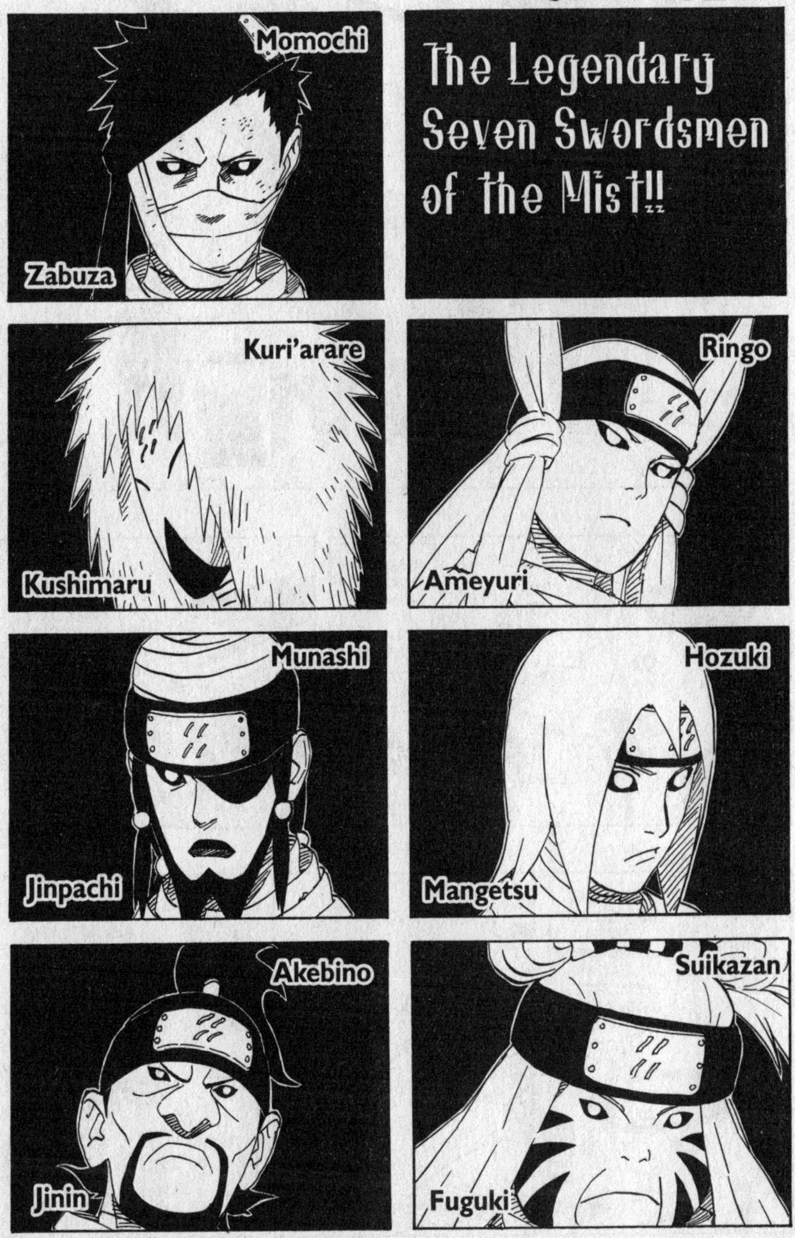
Momochi
Zabuza
Ringo
Ameyuri
Kuri'arare
Kushimaru
Hozuki
Mangetsu
Munashi
Jinpachi
Suikazan
Fuguki
Akebino
Jinin

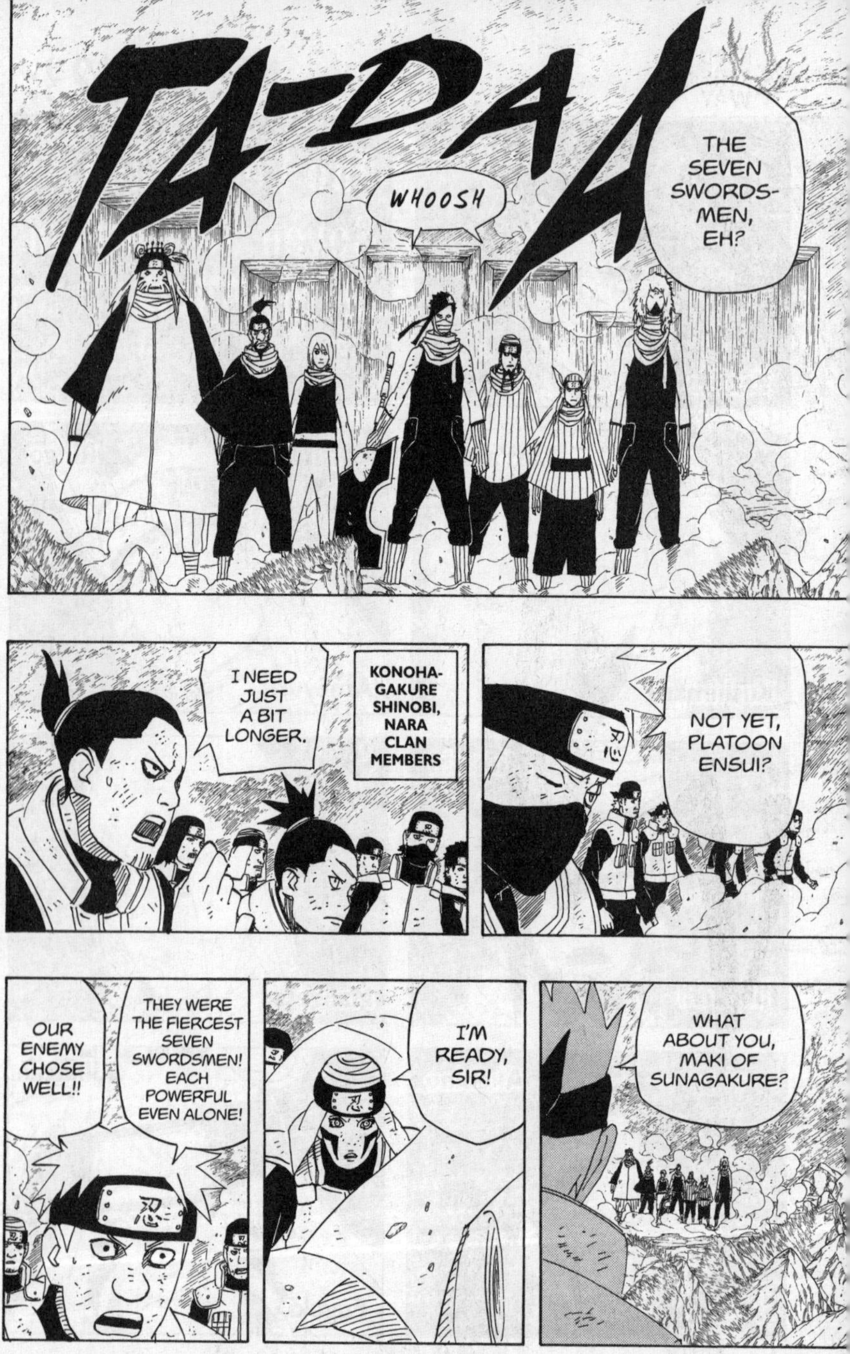
THE SEVEN SWORDS-MEN, EH?
TA-DAA
WHOOSH
NOT YET, PLATOON ENSUI?
KONOHAGAKURE SHINOBI, NARA CLAN MEMBERS
I NEED JUST A BIT LONGER.
WHAT ABOUT YOU, MAKI OF SUNAGAKURE?
I'M READY, SIR!
THEY WERE THE FIERCEST SEVEN SWORDSMEN! EACH POWERFUL EVEN ALONE!
OUR ENEMY CHOSE WELL!!

READ THIS WAY

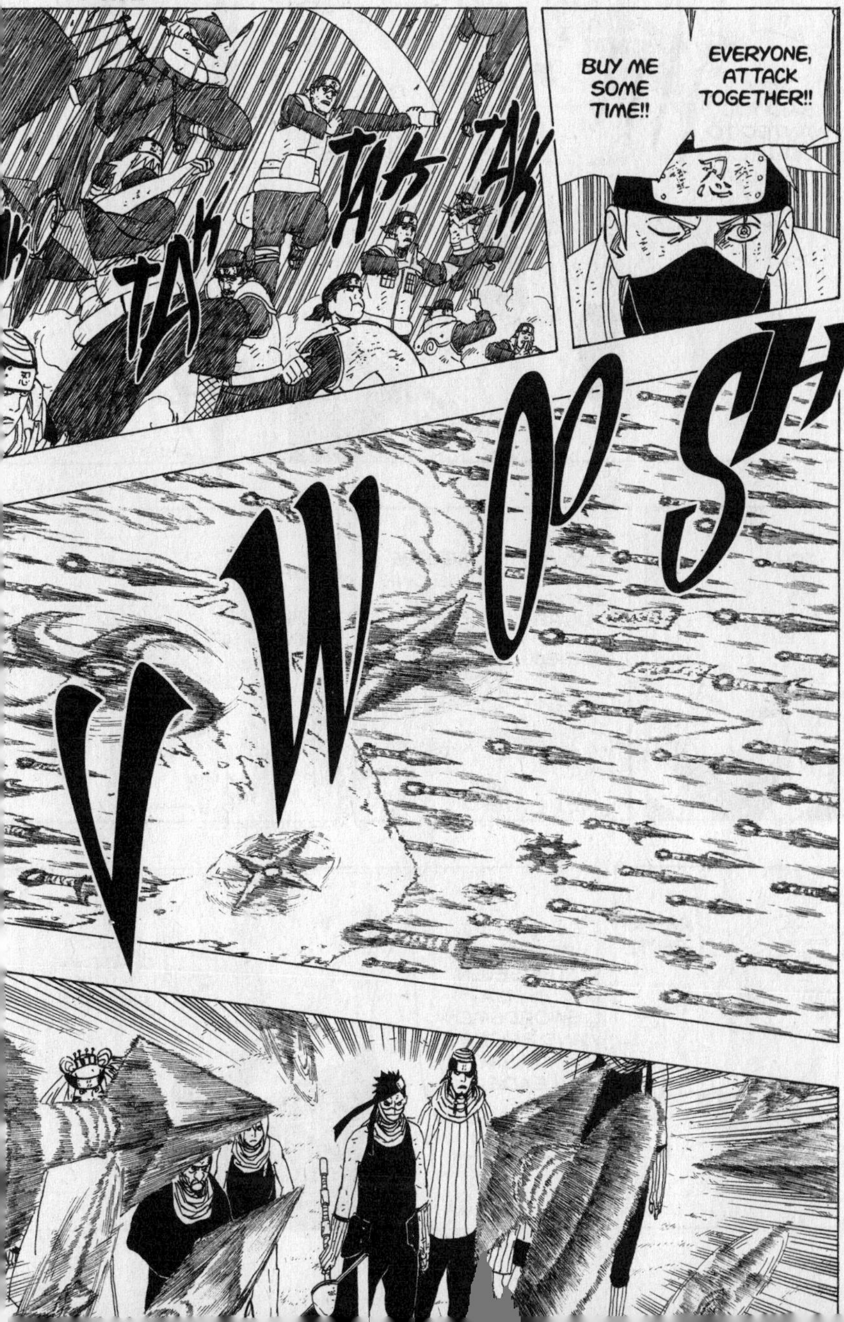
EVERYONE, ATTACK TOGETHER!!
BUY ME SOME TIME!!
TAK
TAK
TAK
VWOOSH

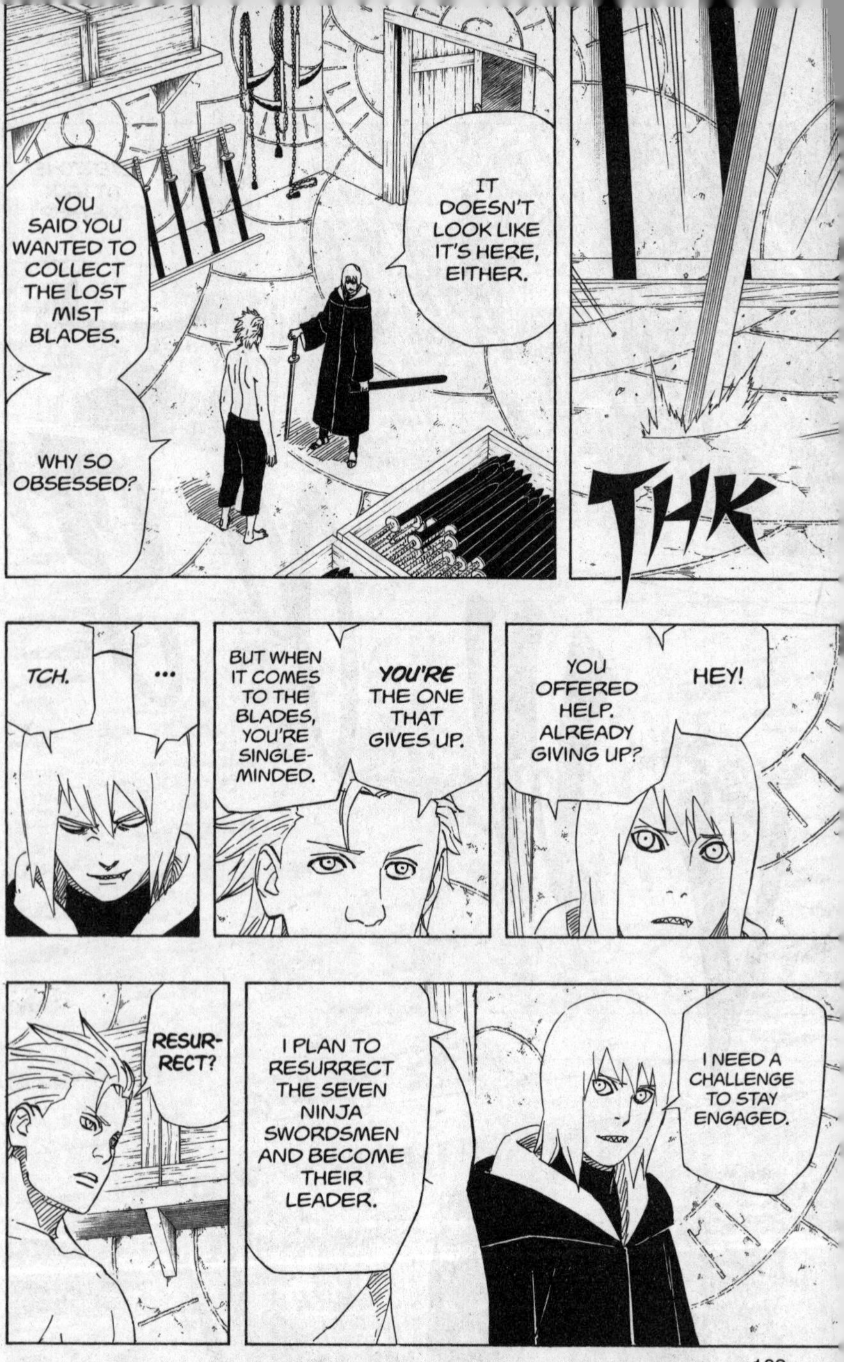
THK
IT DOESN'T LOOK LIKE IT'S HERE, EITHER.
YOU SAID YOU WANTED TO COLLECT THE LOST MIST BLADES.
WHY SO OBSESSED?
HEY!
YOU OFFERED HELP. ALREADY GIVING UP?
*YOU'RE* THE ONE THAT GIVES UP.
BUT WHEN IT COMES TO THE BLADES, YOU'RE SINGLE-MINDED.
...
TCH.
I NEED A CHALLENGE TO STAY ENGAGED.
I PLAN TO RESURRECT THE SEVEN NINJA SWORDSMEN AND BECOME THEIR LEADER.
RESURRECT?

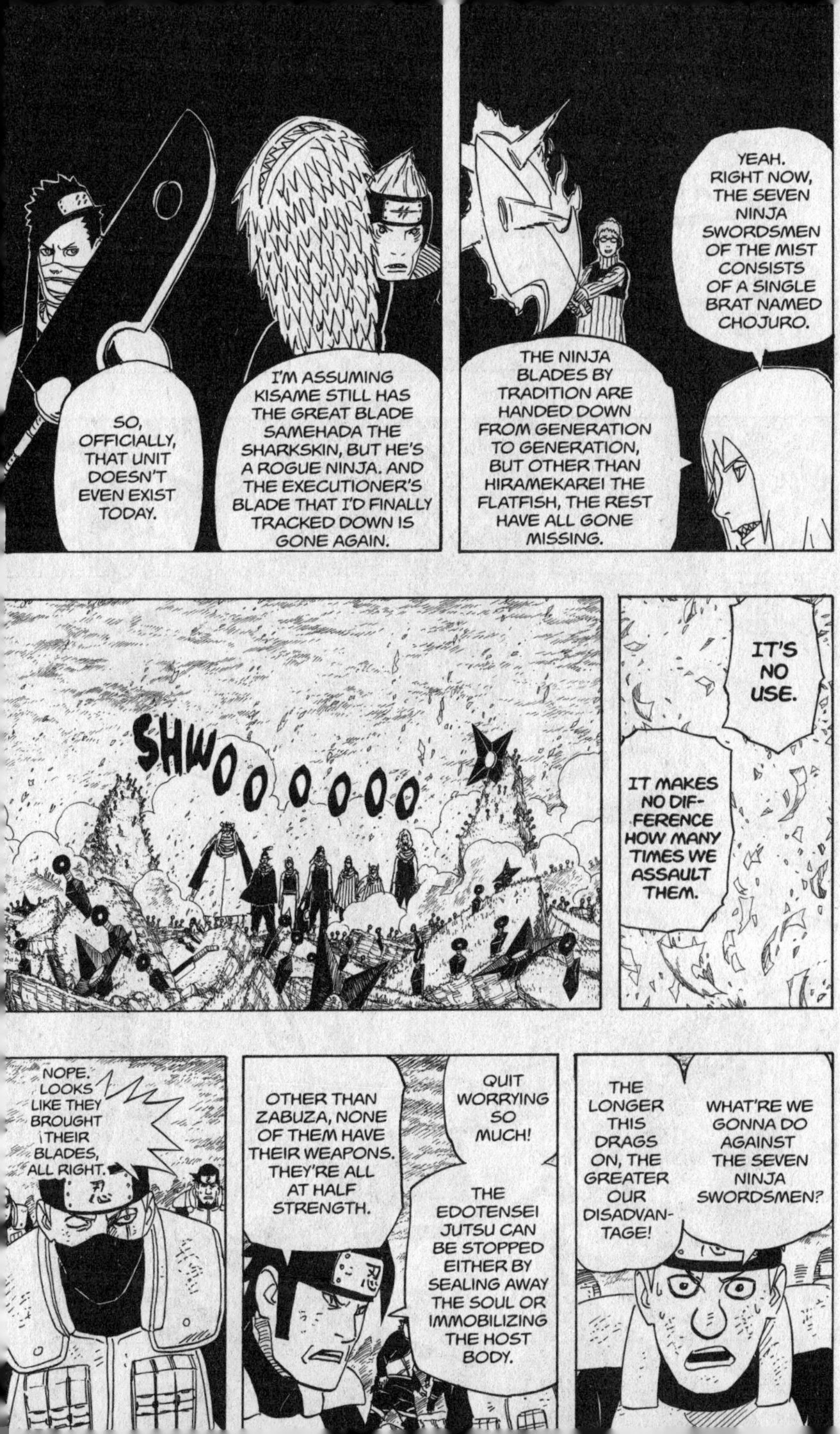
YEAH. RIGHT NOW, THE SEVEN NINJA SWORDSMEN OF THE MIST CONSISTS OF A SINGLE BRAT NAMED CHOJURO.
THE NINJA BLADES BY TRADITION ARE HANDED DOWN FROM GENERATION TO GENERATION, BUT OTHER THAN HIRAMEKAREI THE FLATFISH, THE REST HAVE ALL GONE MISSING.
I'M ASSUMING KISAME STILL HAS THE GREAT BLADE SAMEHADA THE SHARKSKIN, BUT HE'S A ROGUE NINJA. AND THE EXECUTIONER'S BLADE THAT I'D FINALLY TRACKED DOWN IS GONE AGAIN.
SO, OFFICIALLY, THAT UNIT DOESN'T EVEN EXIST TODAY.
IT'S NO USE.
IT MAKES NO DIFFERENCE HOW MANY TIMES WE ASSAULT THEM.
SHWOOOOOO
WHAT'RE WE GONNA DO AGAINST THE SEVEN NINJA SWORDSMEN?
THE LONGER THIS DRAGS ON, THE GREATER OUR DISADVANTAGE!
QUIT WORRYING SO MUCH!
THE EDOTENSEI JUTSU CAN BE STOPPED EITHER BY SEALING AWAY THE SOUL OR IMMOBILIZING THE HOST BODY.
OTHER THAN ZABUZA, NONE OF THEM HAVE THEIR WEAPONS. THEY'RE ALL AT HALF STRENGTH.
NOPE. LOOKS LIKE THEY BROUGHT THEIR BLADES, ALL RIGHT.

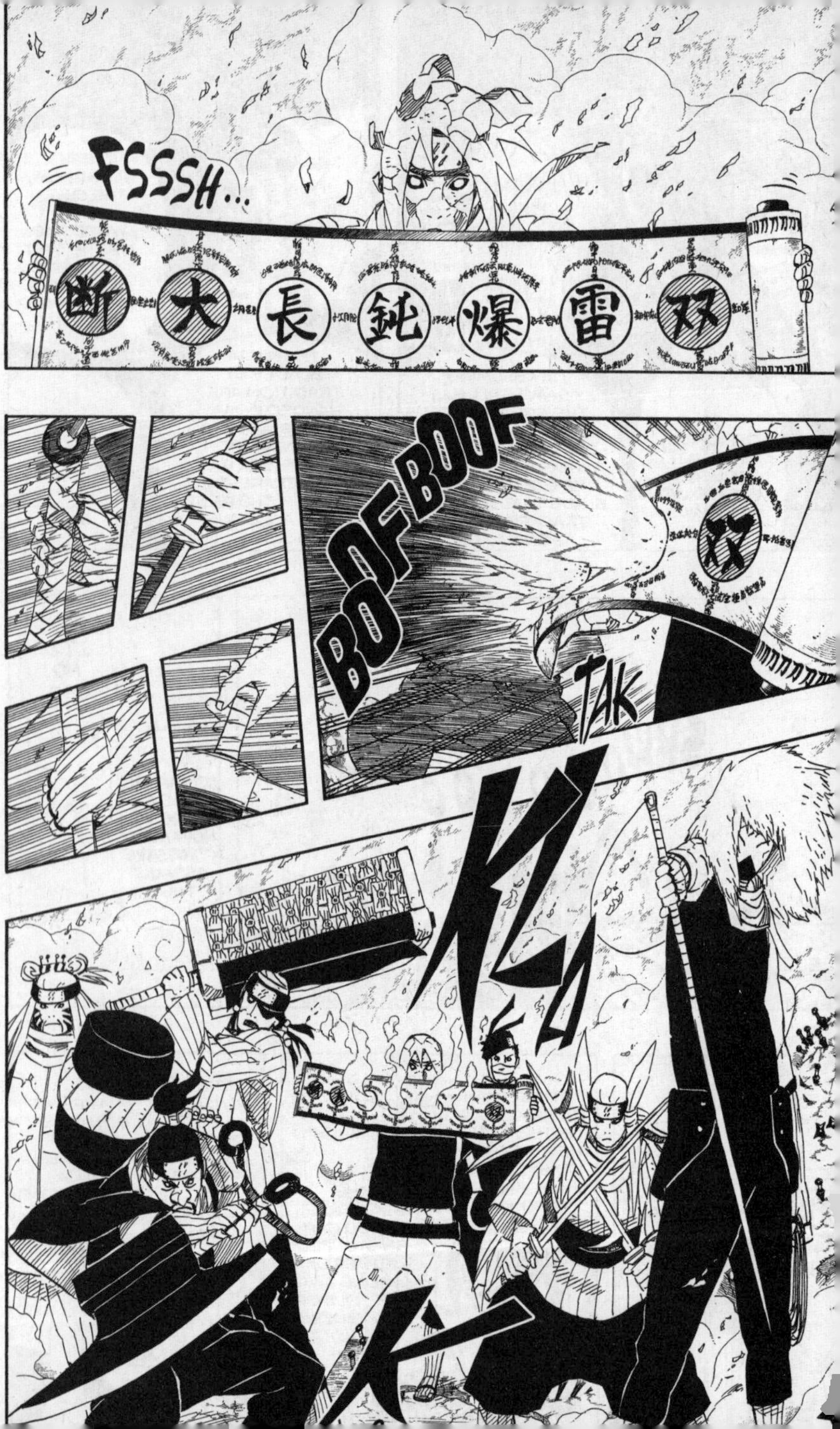
FSSSH...
断
大
長
鈍
爆
雷
双
BOOF BOOF
双
TAK
KLAK

READ THIS WAY

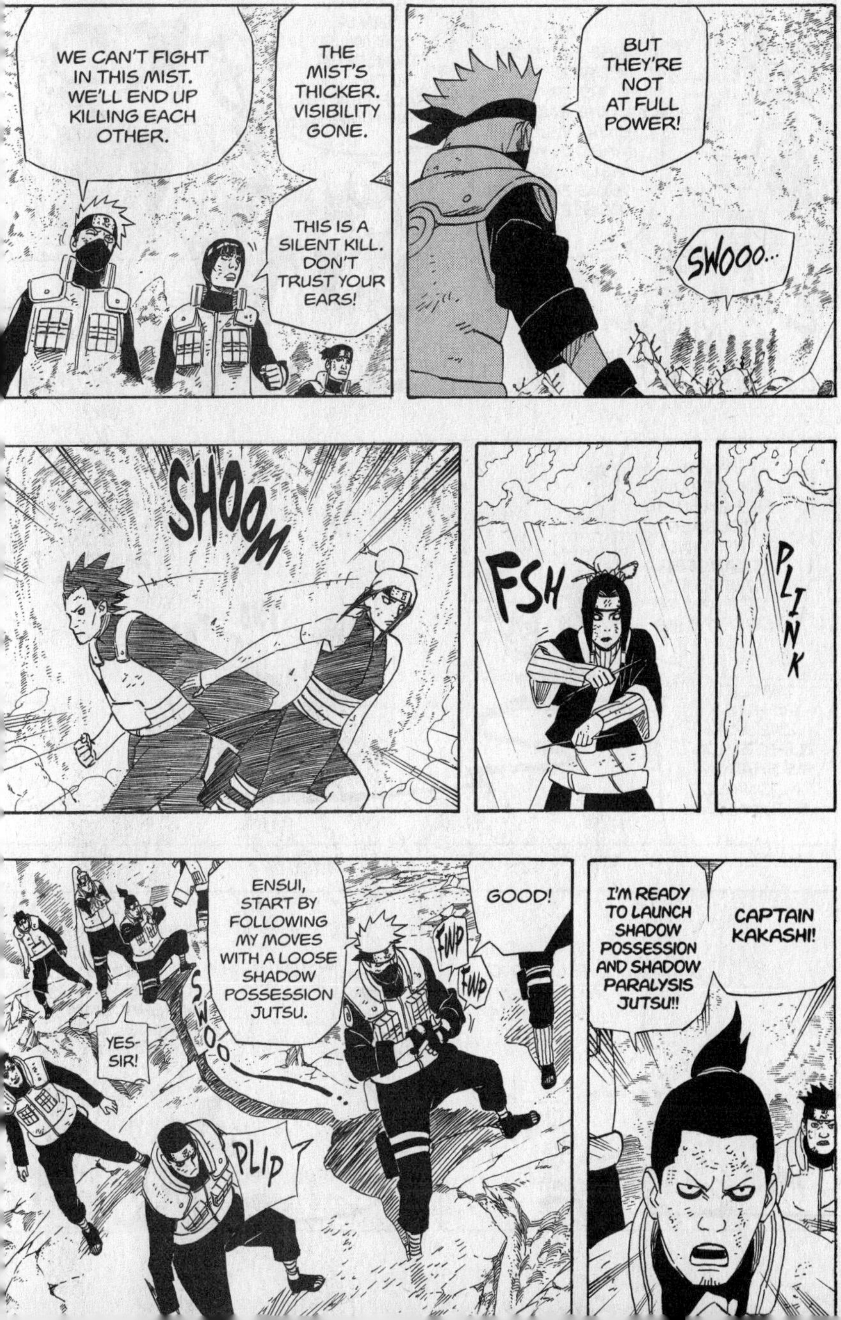
BUT THEY'RE NOT AT FULL POWER!
SWOOO...
THE MIST'S THICKER. VISIBILITY GONE.
WE CAN'T FIGHT IN THIS MIST. WE'LL END UP KILLING EACH OTHER.
THIS IS A SILENT KILL. DON'T TRUST YOUR EARS!
PLINK
FSH
SHOOM
CAPTAIN KAKASHI!
I'M READY TO LAUNCH SHADOW POSSESSION AND SHADOW PARALYSIS JUTSU!!
GOOD!
FWIP
FWIP
ENSUI, START BY FOLLOWING MY MOVES WITH A LOOSE SHADOW POSSESSION JUTSU.
SWOOO
YES SIR!
PLIP

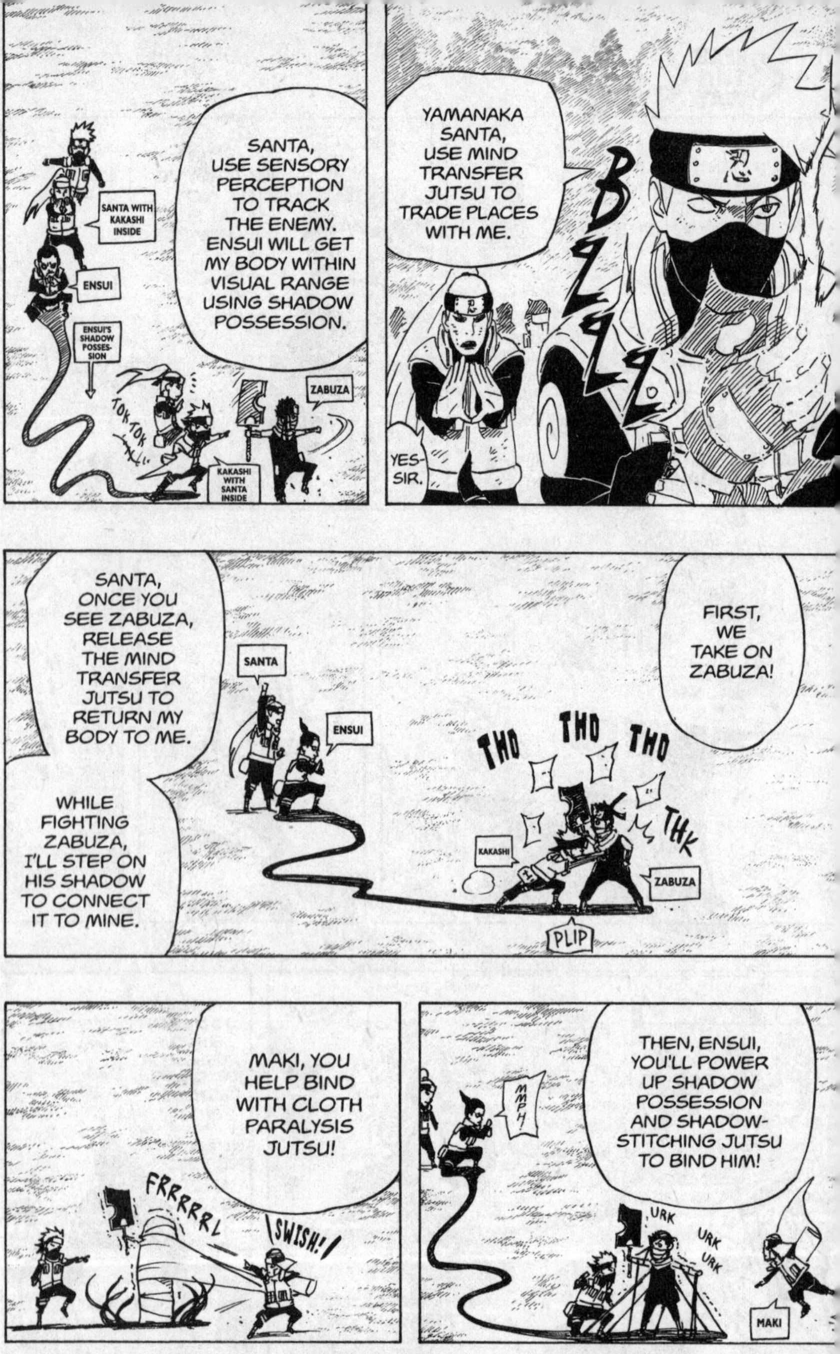
YAMANAKA SANTA, USE MIND TRANSFER JUTSU TO TRADE PLACES WITH ME.
YES-SIR.
SANTA, USE SENSORY PERCEPTION TO TRACK THE ENEMY. ENSUI WILL GET MY BODY WITHIN VISUAL RANGE USING SHADOW POSSESSION.
SANTA WITH KAKASHI INSIDE
ENSUI
ENSUI'S SHADOW POSSES-SION
ZABUZA
TOK TOK
KAKASHI WITH SANTA INSIDE
FIRST, WE TAKE ON ZABUZA!
SANTA, ONCE YOU SEE ZABUZA, RELEASE THE MIND TRANSFER JUTSU TO RETURN MY BODY TO ME.
WHILE FIGHTING ZABUZA, I'LL STEP ON HIS SHADOW TO CONNECT IT TO MINE.
SANTA
ENSUI
THD THD THD
THK
KAKASHI
ZABUZA
PLIP
THEN, ENSUI, YOU'LL POWER UP SHADOW POSSESSION AND SHADOW-STITCHING JUTSU TO BIND HIM!
MMPH!
URK URK URK
MAKI
MAKI, YOU HELP BIND WITH CLOTH PARALYSIS JUTSU!
FRRRRRL
SWISH!

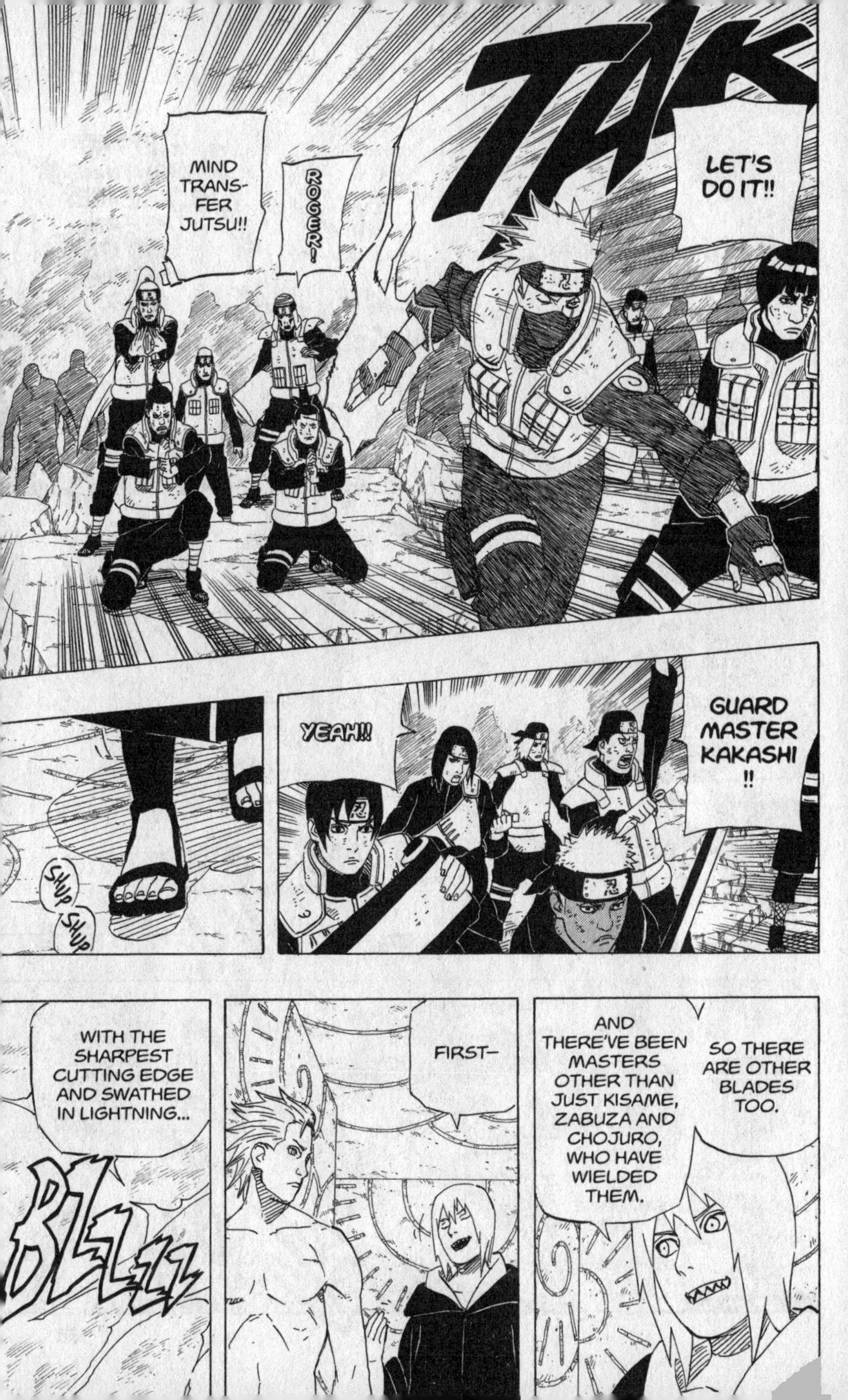
TAK
LET'S DO IT!!
ROGER!
MIND TRANSFER JUTSU!!
GUARD MASTER KAKASHI!!
YEAH!!
SHUP SHUP
SO THERE ARE OTHER BLADES TOO.
AND THERE'VE BEEN MASTERS OTHER THAN JUST KISAME, ZABUZA AND CHOJURO, WHO HAVE WIELDED THEM.
FIRST–
WITH THE SHARPEST CUTTING EDGE AND SWATHED IN LIGHTNING...

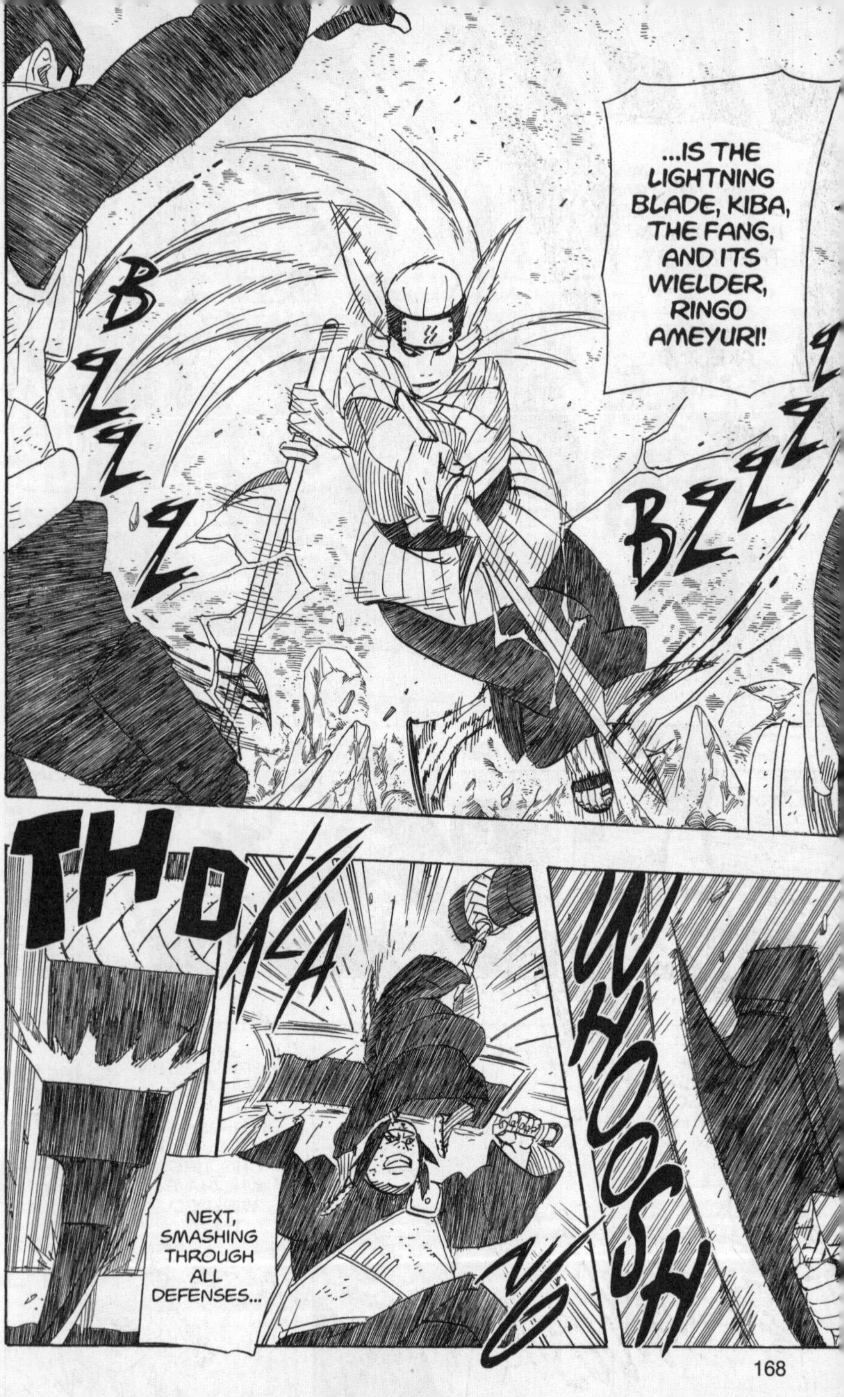

...IS THE LIGHTNING BLADE, KIBA, THE FANG, AND ITS WIELDER, RINGO AMEYURI!!
BZZZZ
BZZZZ
WHOOSH
KA
NEXT, SMASHING THROUGH ALL DEFENSES...
THD

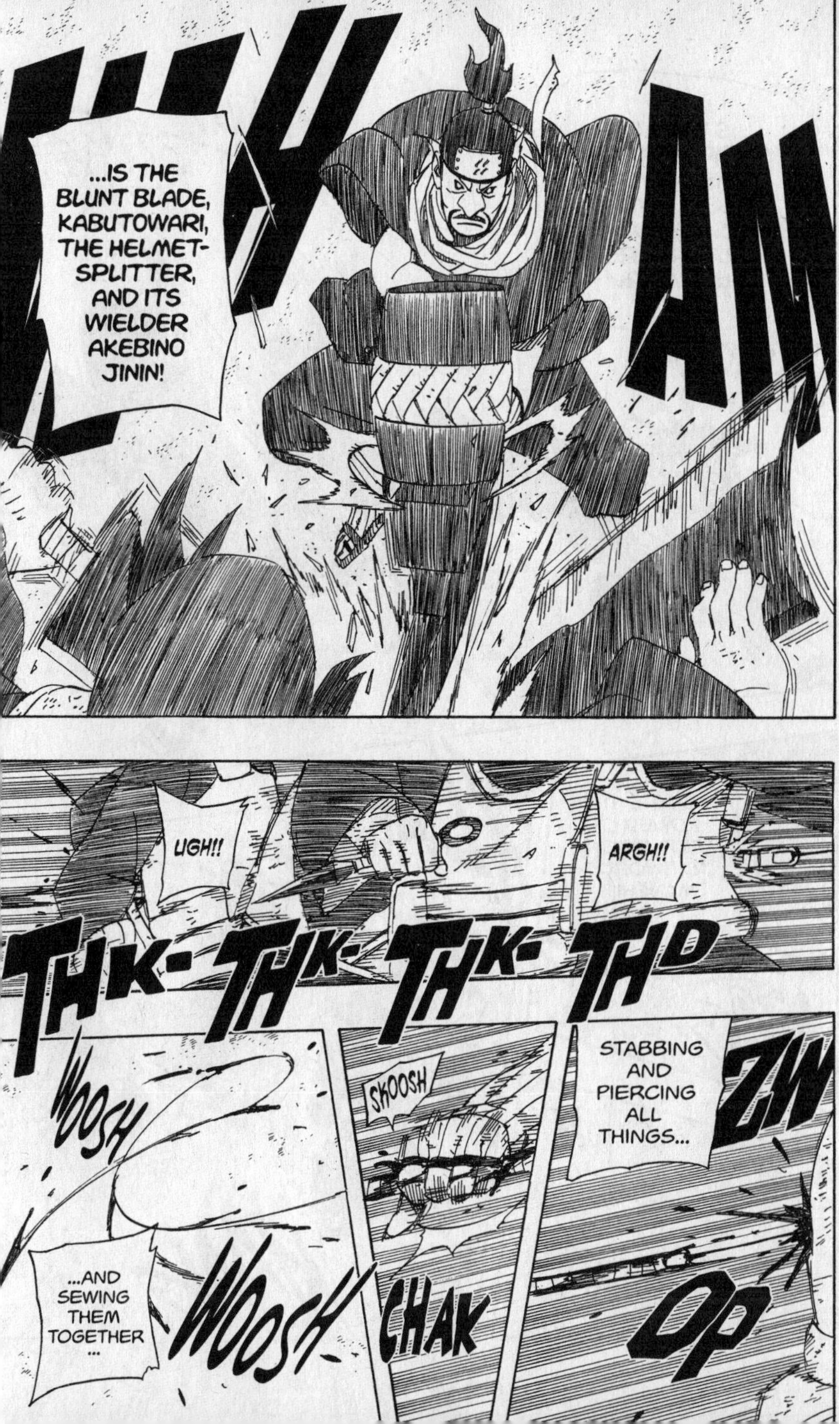
...IS THE BLUNT BLADE, KABUTOWARI, THE HELMET-SPLITTER, AND ITS WIELDER AKEBINO JININ!
ARGH!!
UGH!!
THK-THK-THK-THD
STABBING AND PIERCING ALL THINGS...
ZWOP
SKOOSH
CHAK
WOOSH
...AND SEWING THEM TOGETHER...
WOOSH

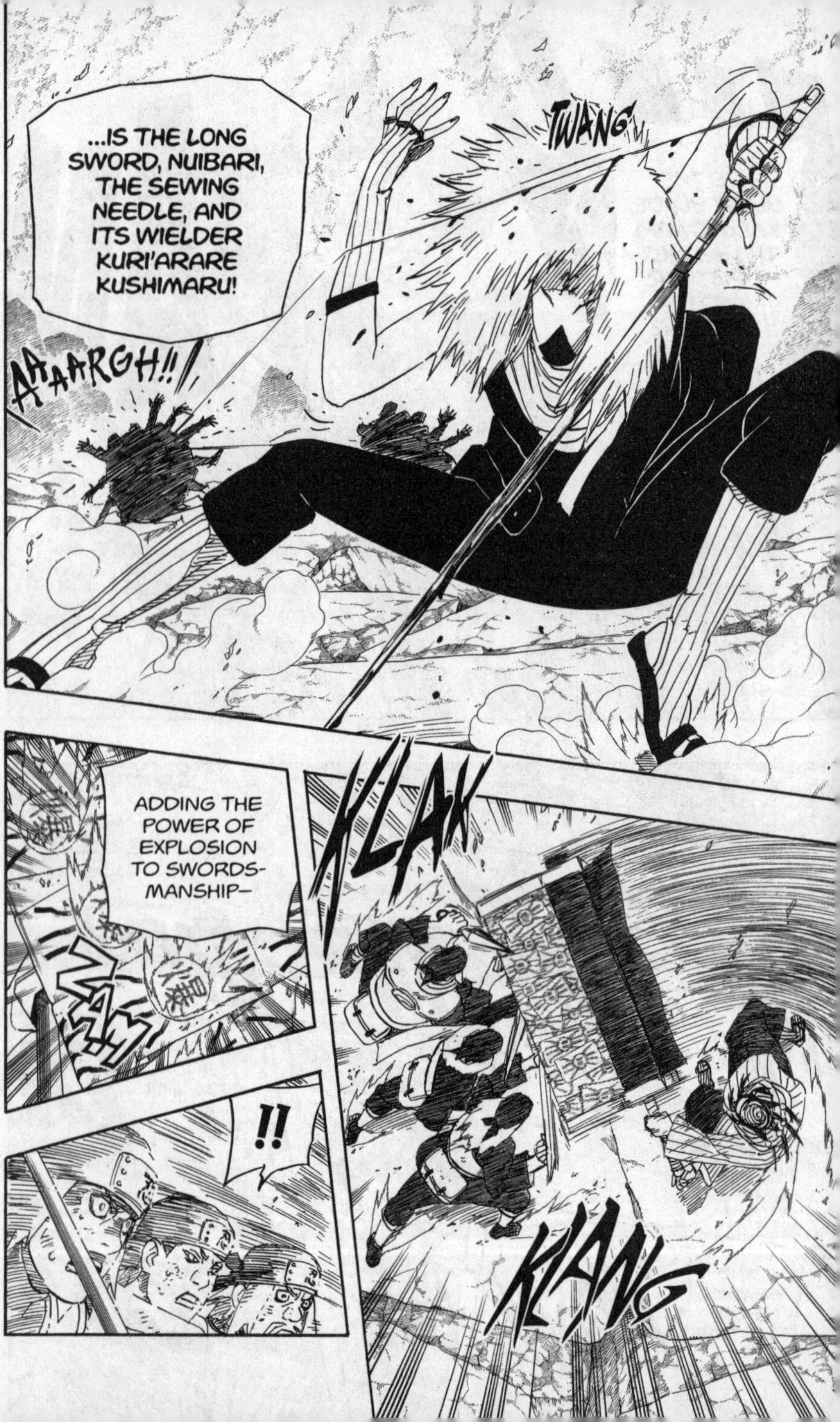

TWANG
...IS THE LONG SWORD, NUIBARI, THE SEWING NEEDLE, AND ITS WIELDER KURI'ARARE KUSHIMARU!
AAAARGH!!
KLAK
KLANG
ADDING THE POWER OF EXPLOSION TO SWORDS-MANSHIP–
ZAM
!!

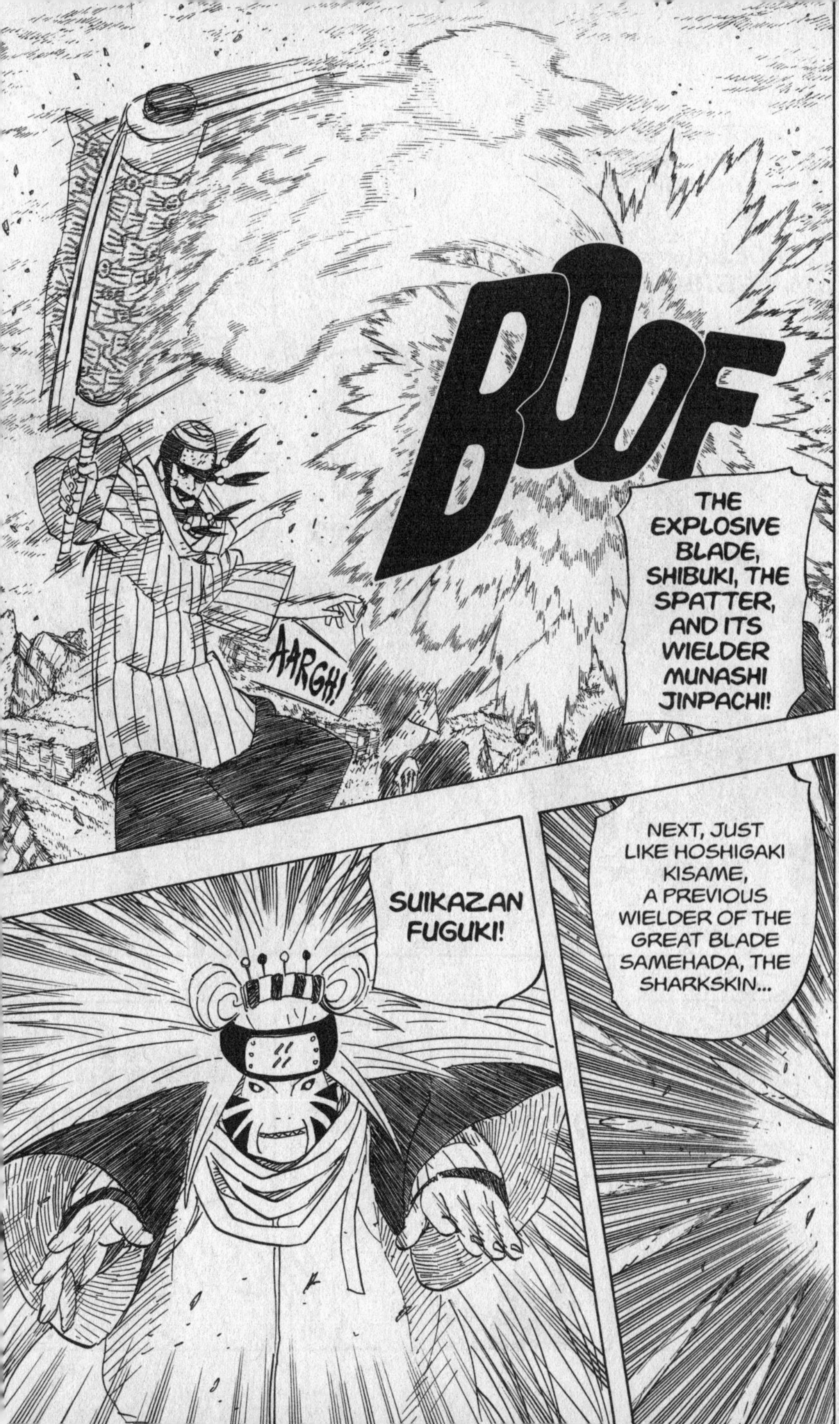
BOOF
THE EXPLOSIVE BLADE, SHIBUKI, THE SPATTER, AND ITS WIELDER MUNASHI JINPACHI!
AARGH!
NEXT, JUST LIKE HOSHIGAKI KISAME, A PREVIOUS WIELDER OF THE GREAT BLADE SAMEHADA, THE SHARKSKIN...
SUIKAZAN FUGUKI!

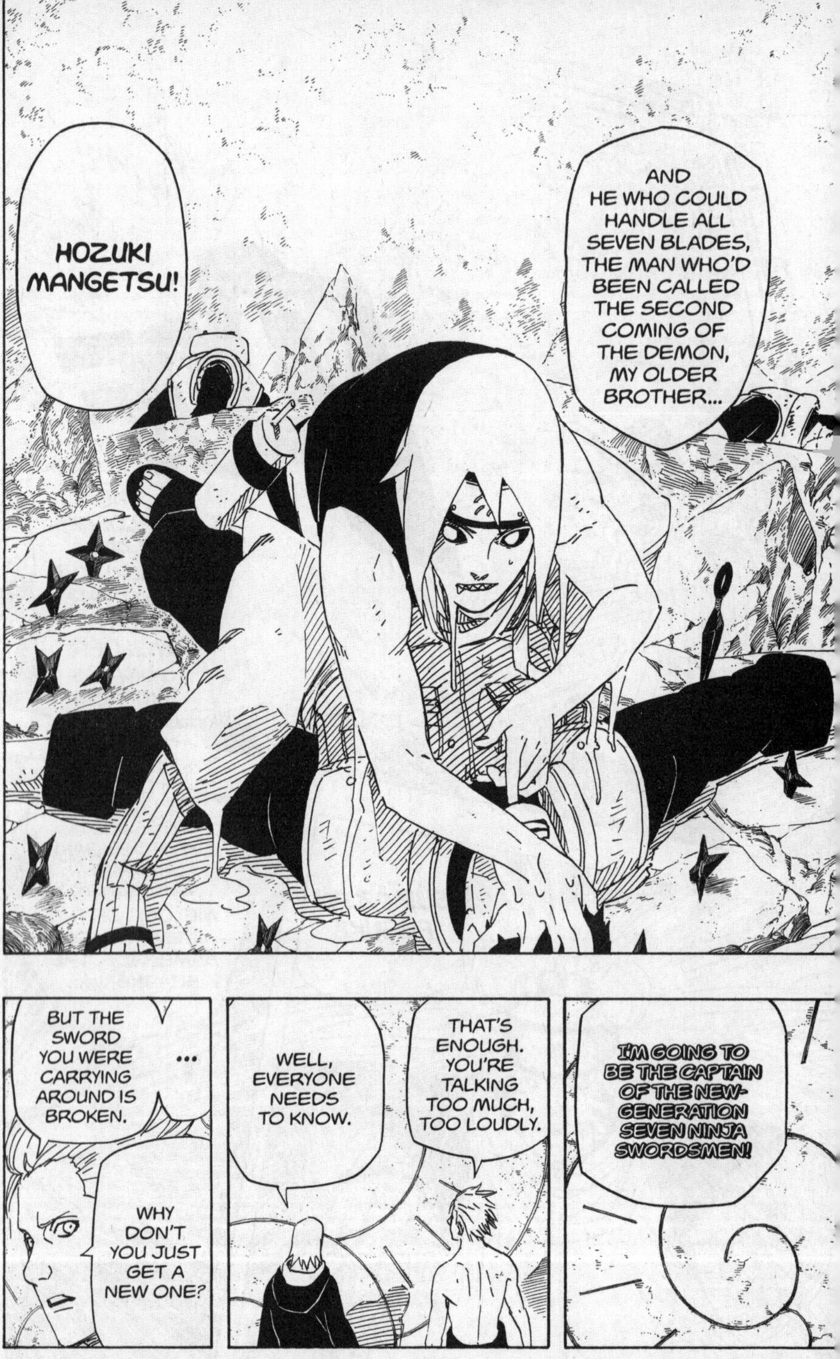
AND HE WHO COULD HANDLE ALL SEVEN BLADES, THE MAN WHO'D BEEN CALLED THE SECOND COMING OF THE DEMON, MY OLDER BROTHER...
HOZUKI MANGETSU!
I'M GOING TO BE THE CAPTAIN OF THE NEW-GENERATION SEVEN NINJA SWORDSMEN!
THAT'S ENOUGH. YOU'RE TALKING TOO MUCH, TOO LOUDLY.
WELL, EVERYONE NEEDS TO KNOW.
BUT THE SWORD YOU WERE CARRYING AROUND IS BROKEN.
...
WHY DON'T YOU JUST GET A NEW ONE?

READ THIS WAY

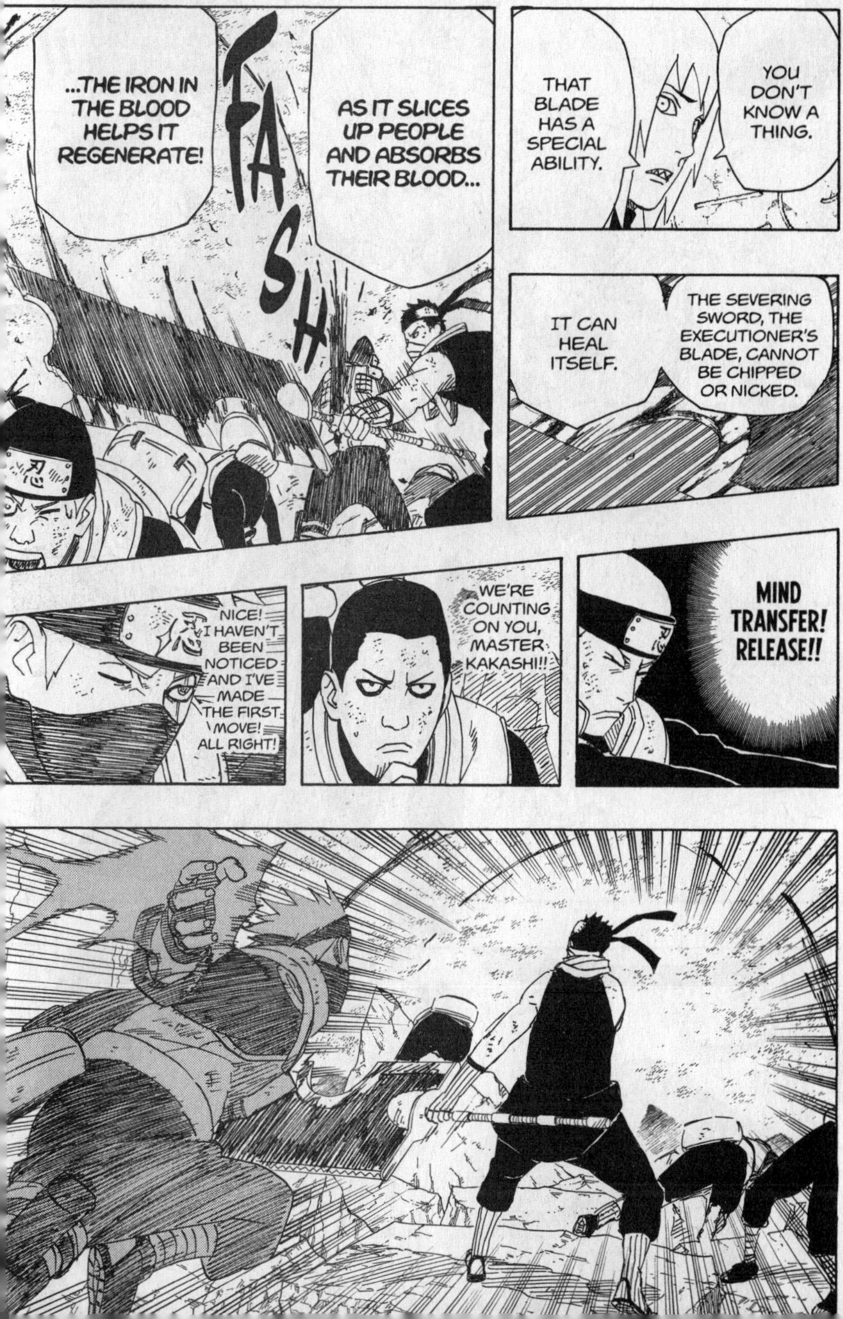
YOU DON'T KNOW A THING.
THAT BLADE HAS A SPECIAL ABILITY.
THE SEVERING SWORD, THE EXECUTIONER'S BLADE, CANNOT BE CHIPPED OR NICKED.
IT CAN HEAL ITSELF.
AS IT SLICES UP PEOPLE AND ABSORBS THEIR BLOOD...
FASH
...THE IRON IN THE BLOOD HELPS IT REGENERATE!
MIND TRANSFER! RELEASE!!
WE'RE COUNTING ON YOU, MASTER KAKASHI!!
NICE! I HAVEN'T BEEN NOTICED AND I'VE MADE THE FIRST MOVE! ALL RIGHT!

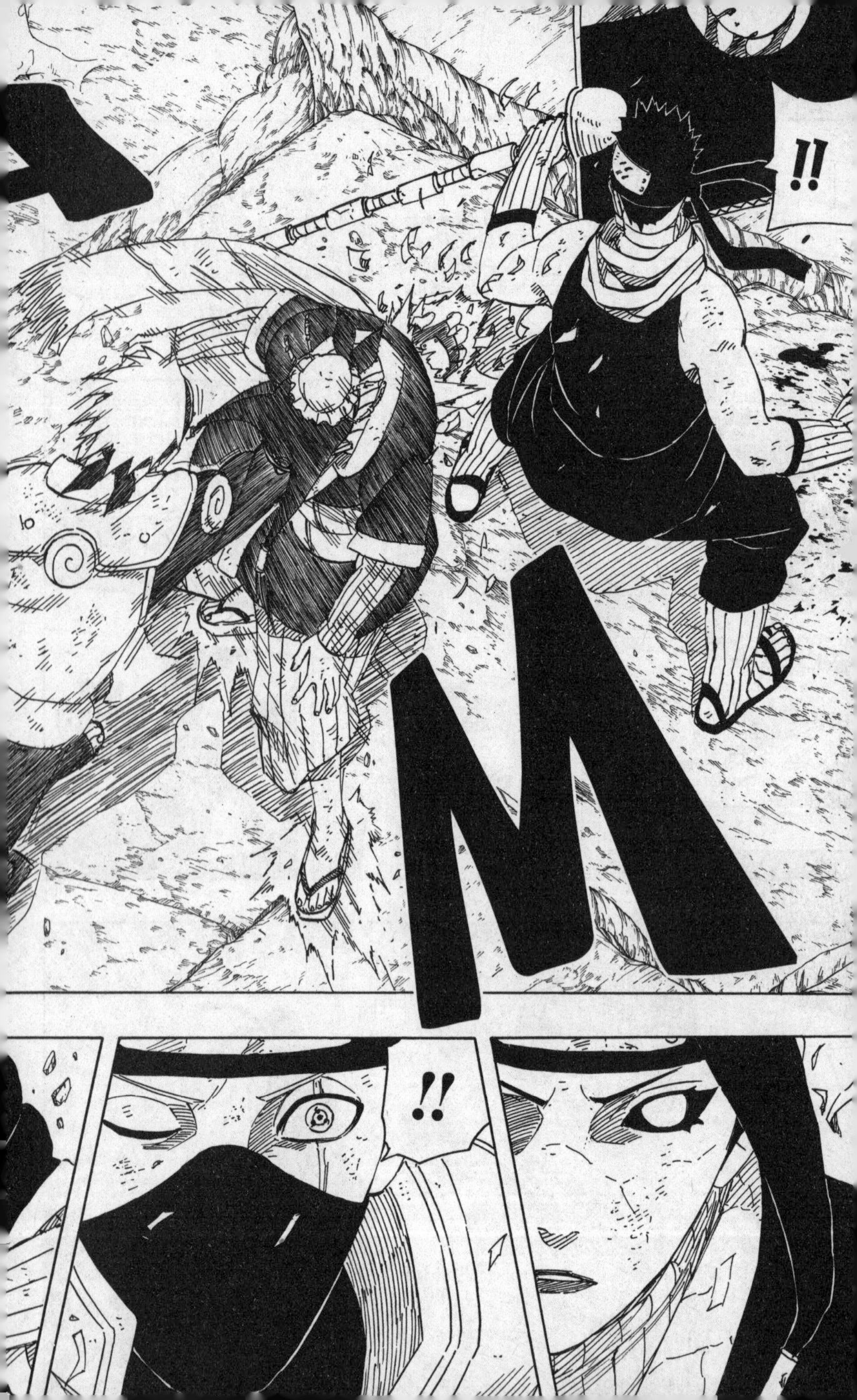
!!
M
!!

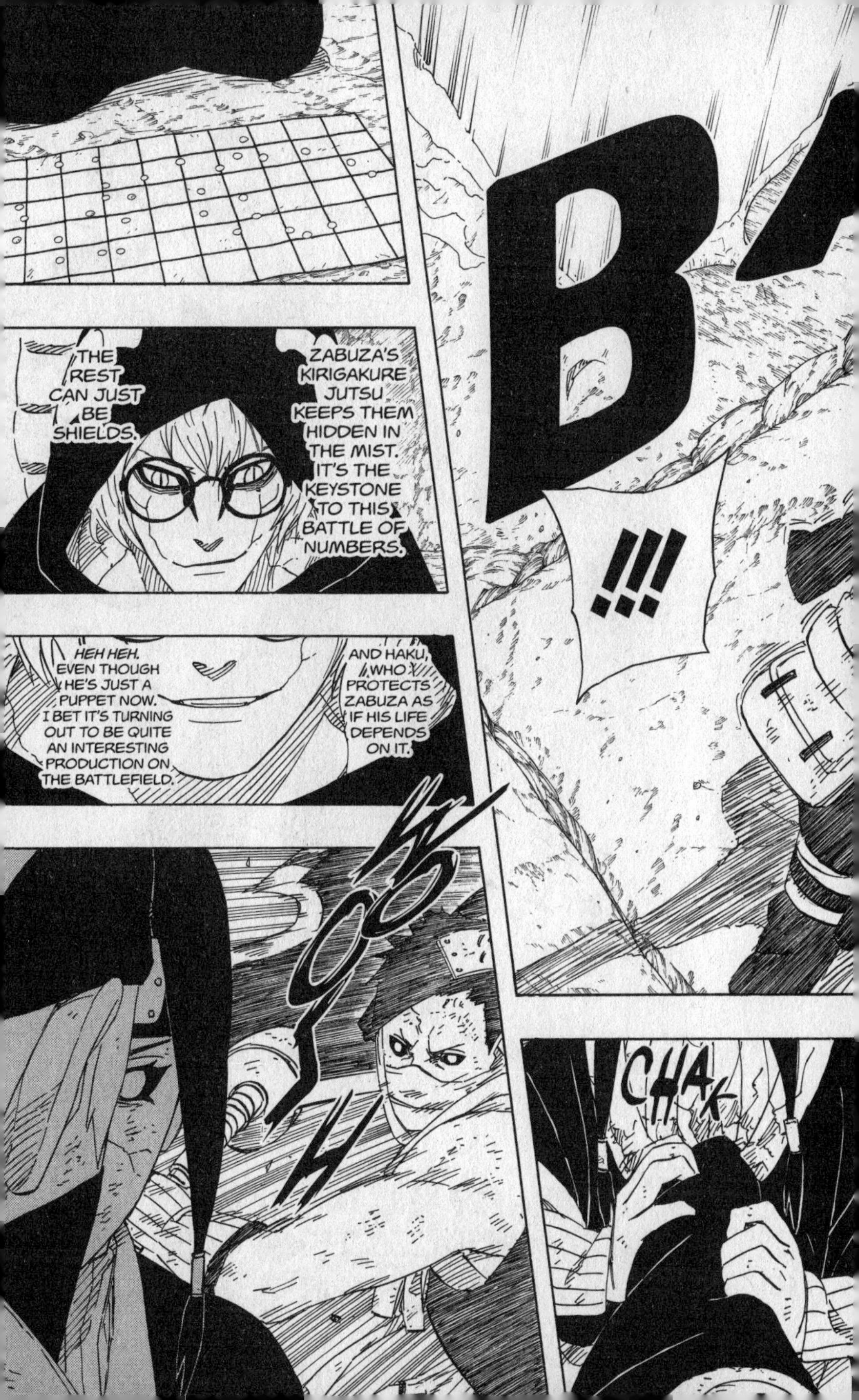

B
!!!!
ZABUZA'S KIRIGAKURE JUTSU KEEPS THEM HIDDEN IN THE MIST. IT'S THE KEYSTONE TO THIS BATTLE OF NUMBERS.
THE REST CAN JUST BE SHIELDS.
AND HAKU, WHO PROTECTS ZABUZA AS IF HIS LIFE DEPENDS ON IT.
HEH HEH. EVEN THOUGH HE'S JUST A PUPPET NOW. I BET IT'S TURNING OUT TO BE QUITE AN INTERESTING PRODUCTION ON THE BATTLEFIELD.
WHOOSH
CHAK

NARUTO

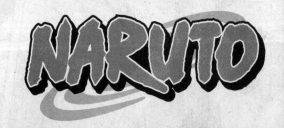

## Number 524: That Which Ought to Be Protected

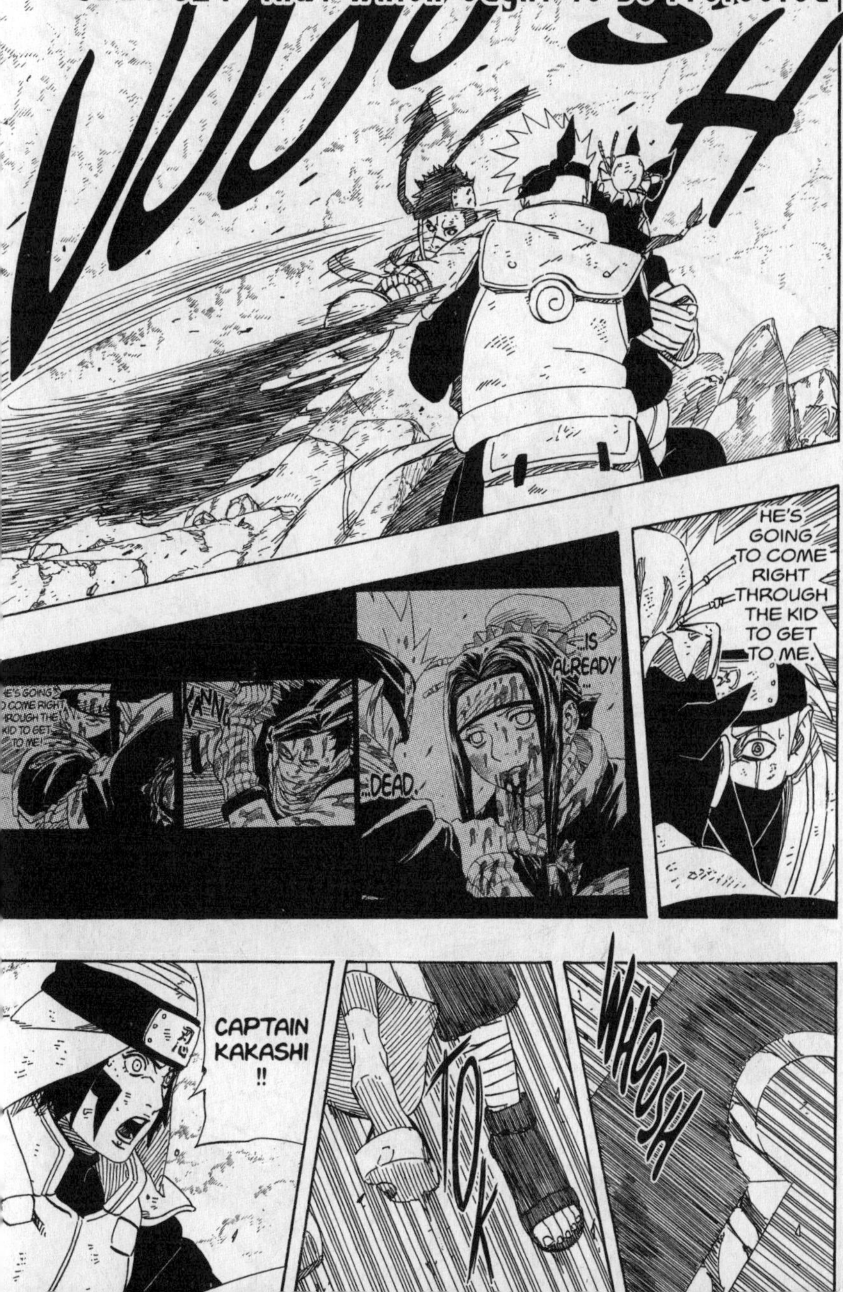
VOOOSH
HE'S GOING TO COME RIGHT THROUGH THE KID TO GET TO ME.
...IS ALREADY ...
...DEAD.
KANNG
E'S GOING O COME RIGHT KID TO GET TO ME!
WHOOSH
TOK
CAPTAIN KAKASHI !!

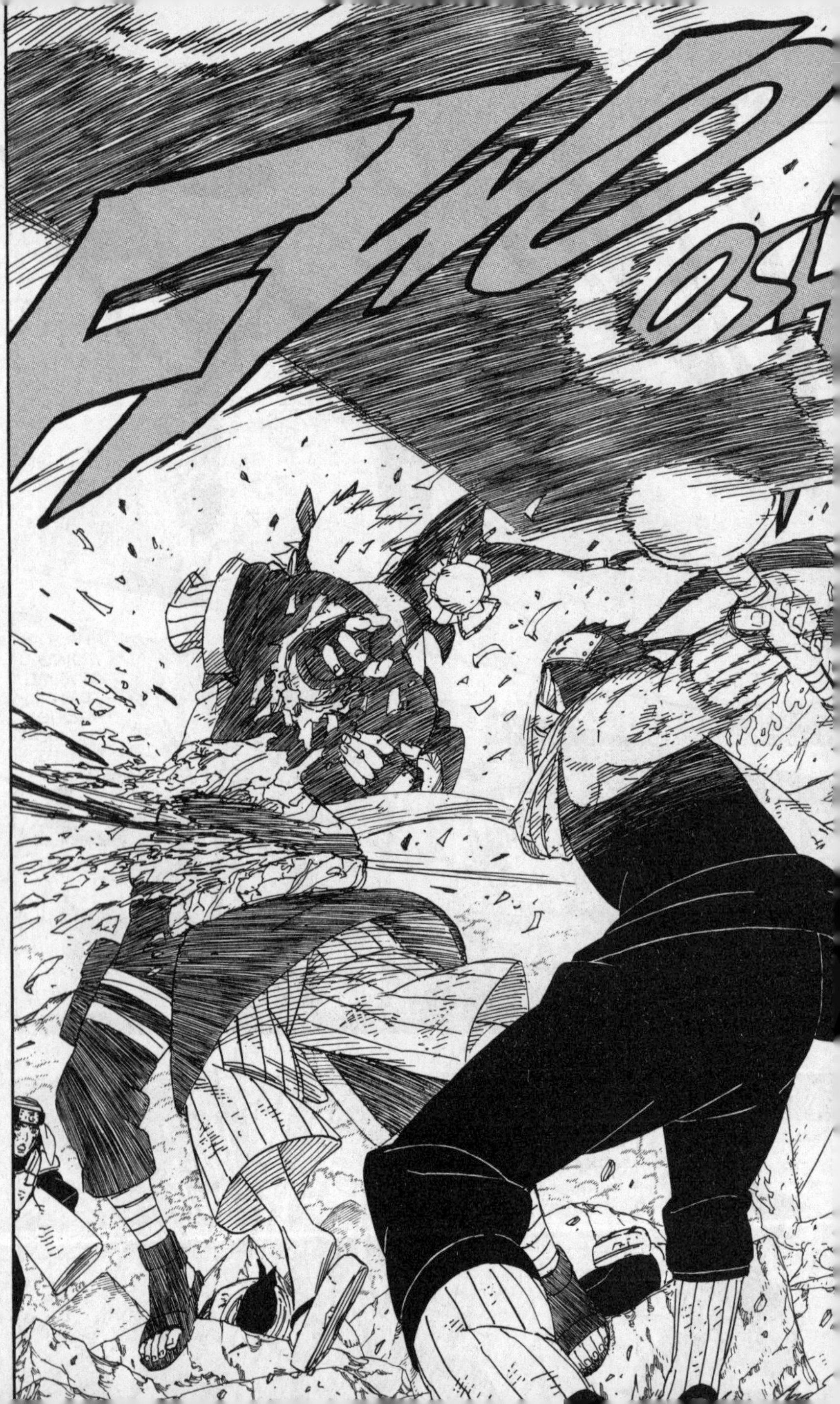

READ THIS WAY

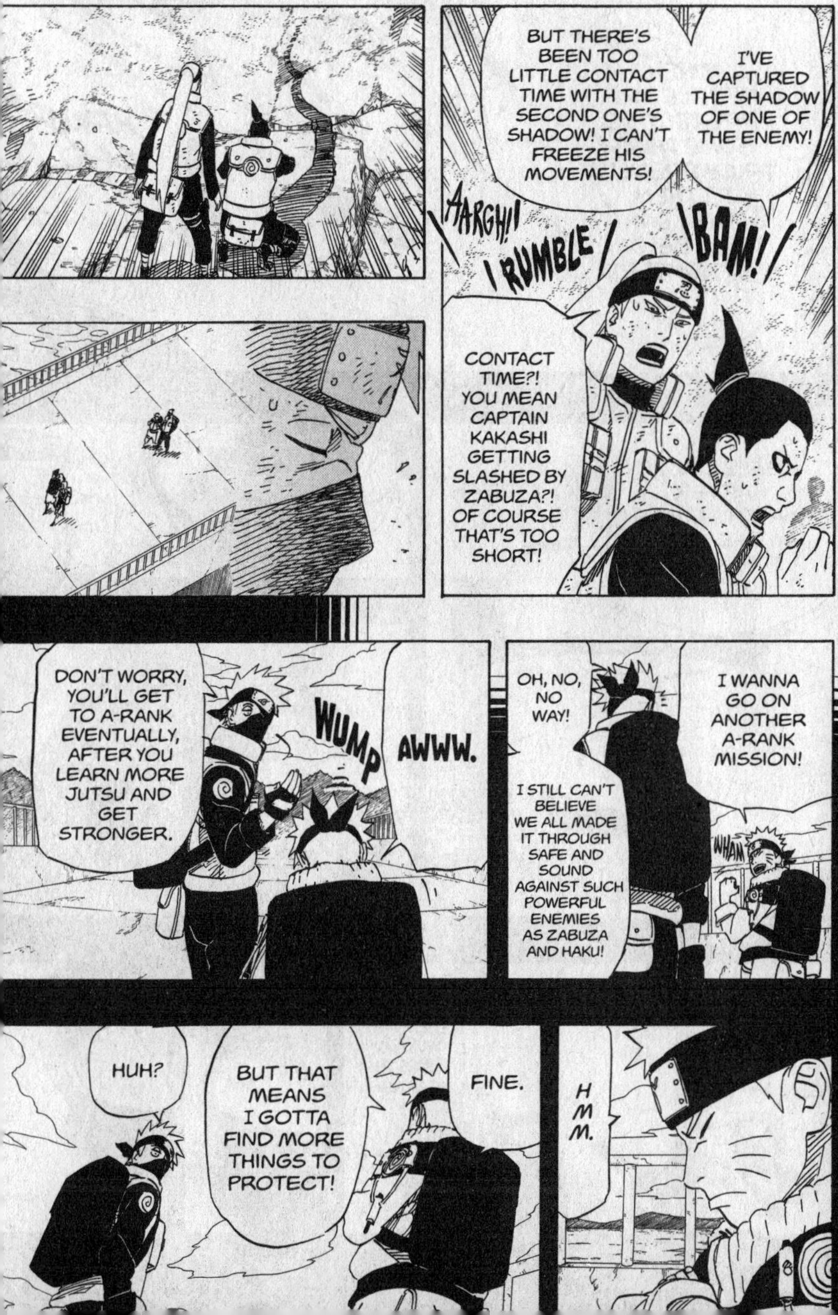
I'VE CAPTURED THE SHADOW OF ONE OF THE ENEMY!
BUT THERE'S BEEN TOO LITTLE CONTACT TIME WITH THE SECOND ONE'S SHADOW! I CAN'T FREEZE HIS MOVEMENTS!
BAM!
RUMBLE
AARGH!!
CONTACT TIME?! YOU MEAN CAPTAIN KAKASHI GETTING SLASHED BY ZABUZA?! OF COURSE THAT'S TOO SHORT!
I WANNA GO ON ANOTHER A-RANK MISSION!
OH, NO, NO WAY!
WHAM
I STILL CAN'T BELIEVE WE ALL MADE IT THROUGH SAFE AND SOUND AGAINST SUCH POWERFUL ENEMIES AS ZABUZA AND HAKU!
AWWW.
WUMP
DON'T WORRY, YOU'LL GET TO A-RANK EVENTUALLY, AFTER YOU LEARN MORE JUTSU AND GET STRONGER.
HMM.
FINE.
BUT THAT MEANS I GOTTA FIND MORE THINGS TO PROTECT!
HUH?

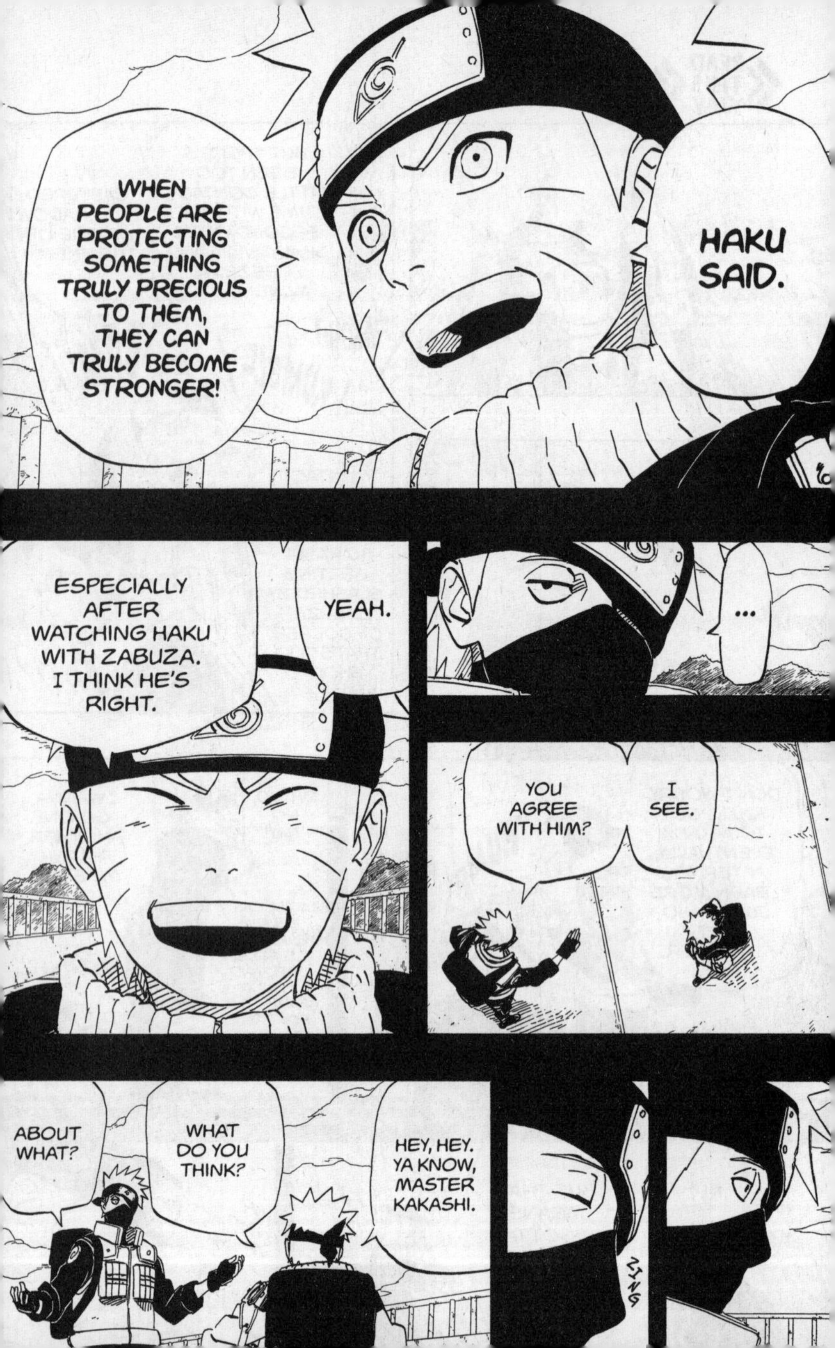
HAKU SAID.
WHEN PEOPLE ARE PROTECTING SOMETHING TRULY PRECIOUS TO THEM, THEY CAN TRULY BECOME STRONGER!
...
I SEE.
YOU AGREE WITH HIM?
YEAH.
ESPECIALLY AFTER WATCHING HAKU WITH ZABUZA. I THINK HE'S RIGHT.
ZING
HEY, HEY. YA KNOW, MASTER KAKASHI.
WHAT DO YOU THINK?
ABOUT WHAT?

READ THIS WAY

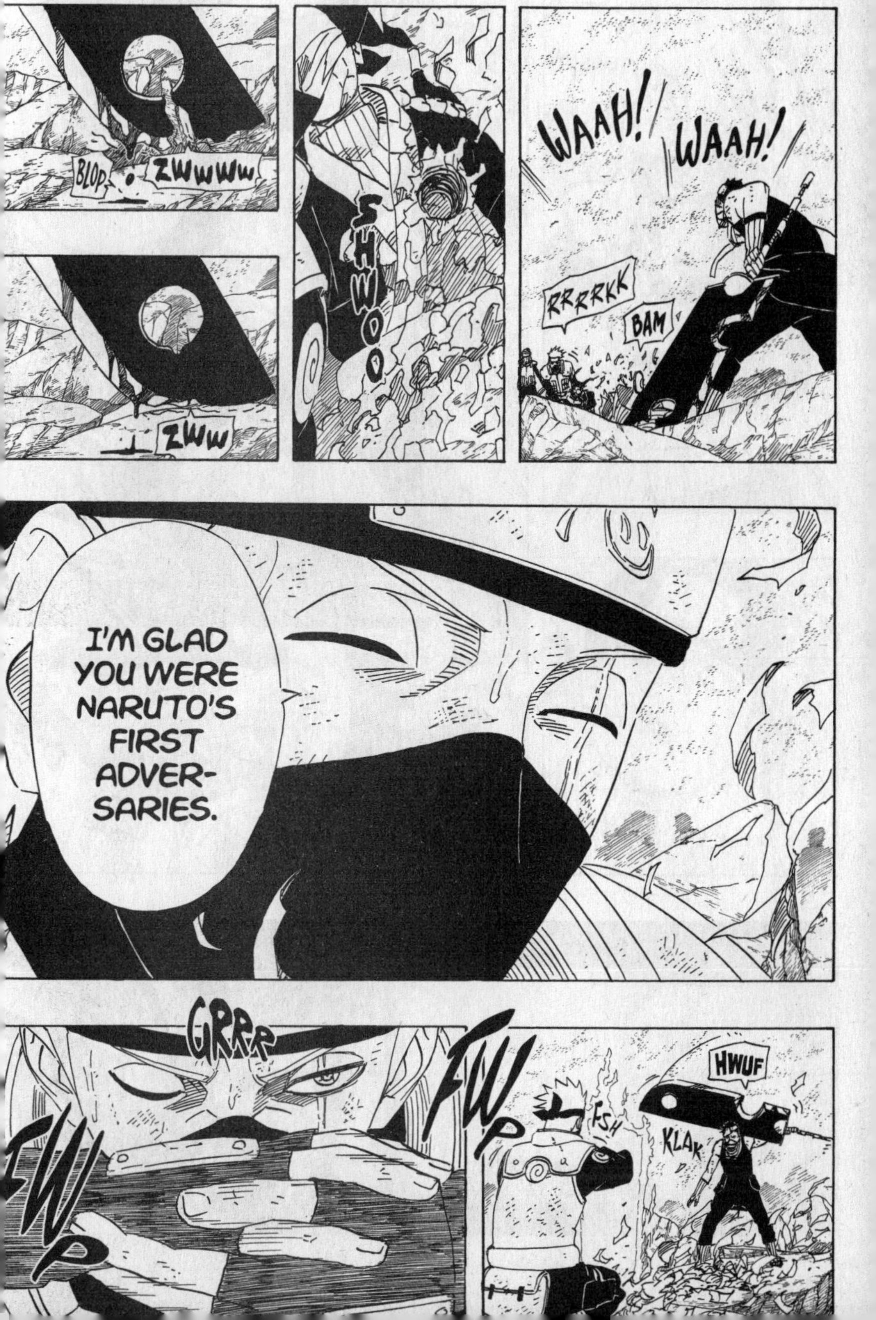

WAAH!
WAAH!
RRRRKK
BAM
SHWOOO
BLOP
ZWWWW
ZWW
I'M GLAD YOU WERE NARUTO'S FIRST ADVER-SARIES.
HWUF
KLAK
FSH
FWP
GRRR
FWP

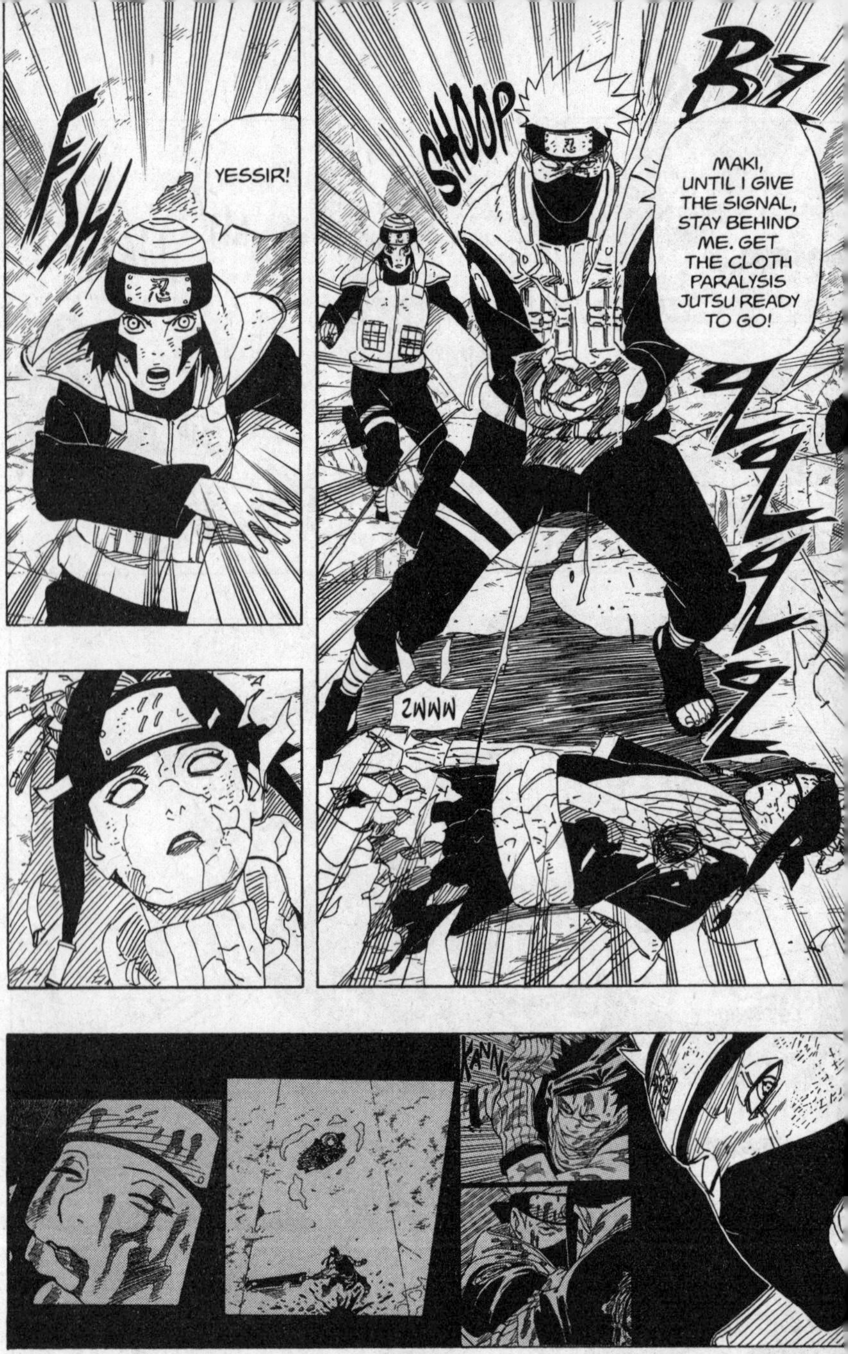
SHOOP
MAKI, UNTIL I GIVE THE SIGNAL, STAY BEHIND ME. GET THE CLOTH PARALYSIS JUTSU READY TO GO!
FSH
YESSIR!

READ THIS WAY

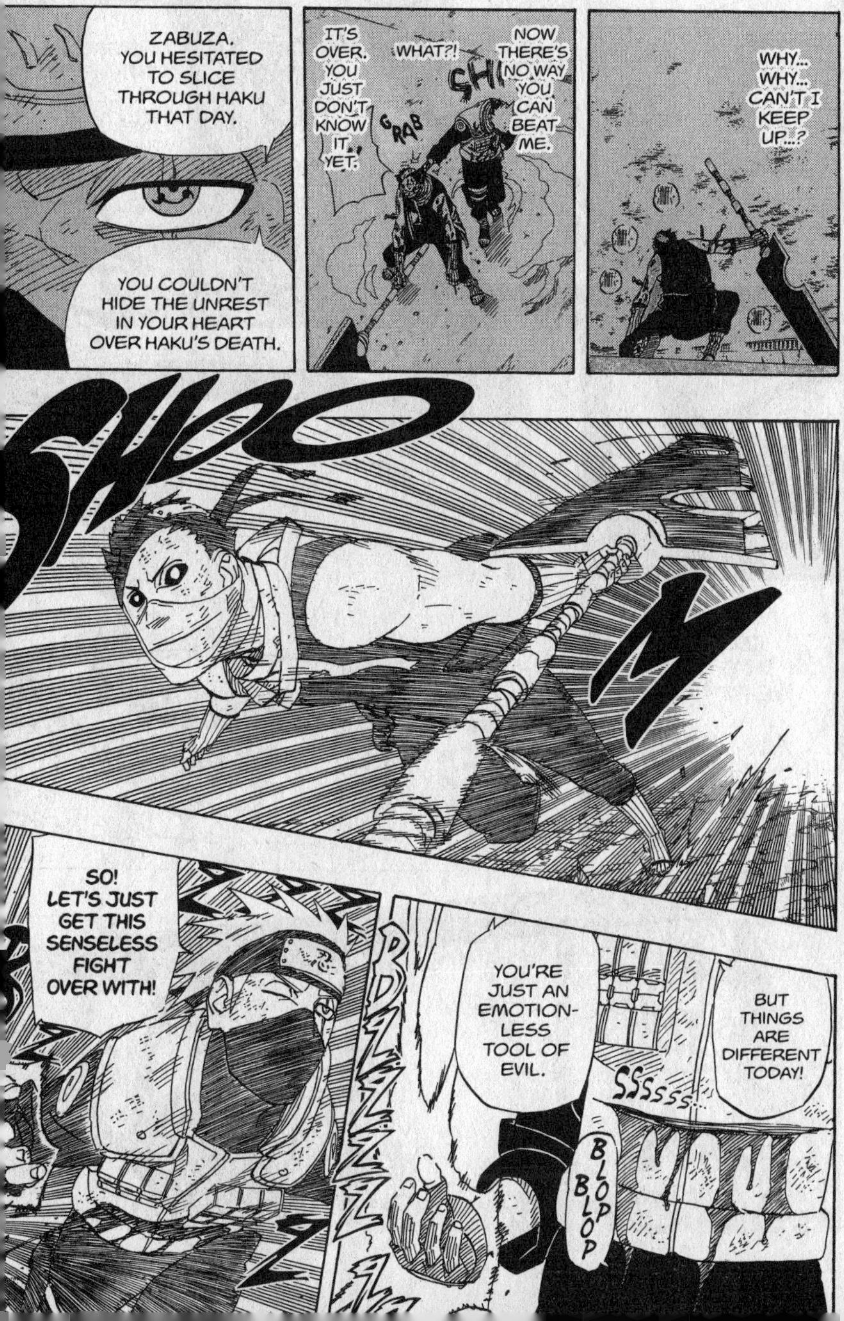
WHY... WHY... CAN'T I KEEP UP...?
NOW THERE'S NO WAY YOU CAN BEAT ME.
CHI
WHAT?!
IT'S OVER. YOU JUST DON'T KNOW IT YET.
GRAB
ZABUZA. YOU HESITATED TO SLICE THROUGH HAKU THAT DAY.
YOU COULDN'T HIDE THE UNREST IN YOUR HEART OVER HAKU'S DEATH.
SHOOM
BUT THINGS ARE DIFFERENT TODAY!
SSSSSS...
YOU'RE JUST AN EMOTION-LESS TOOL OF EVIL.
BLOP BLOP BLOP
SO! LET'S JUST GET THIS SENSELESS FIGHT OVER WITH!

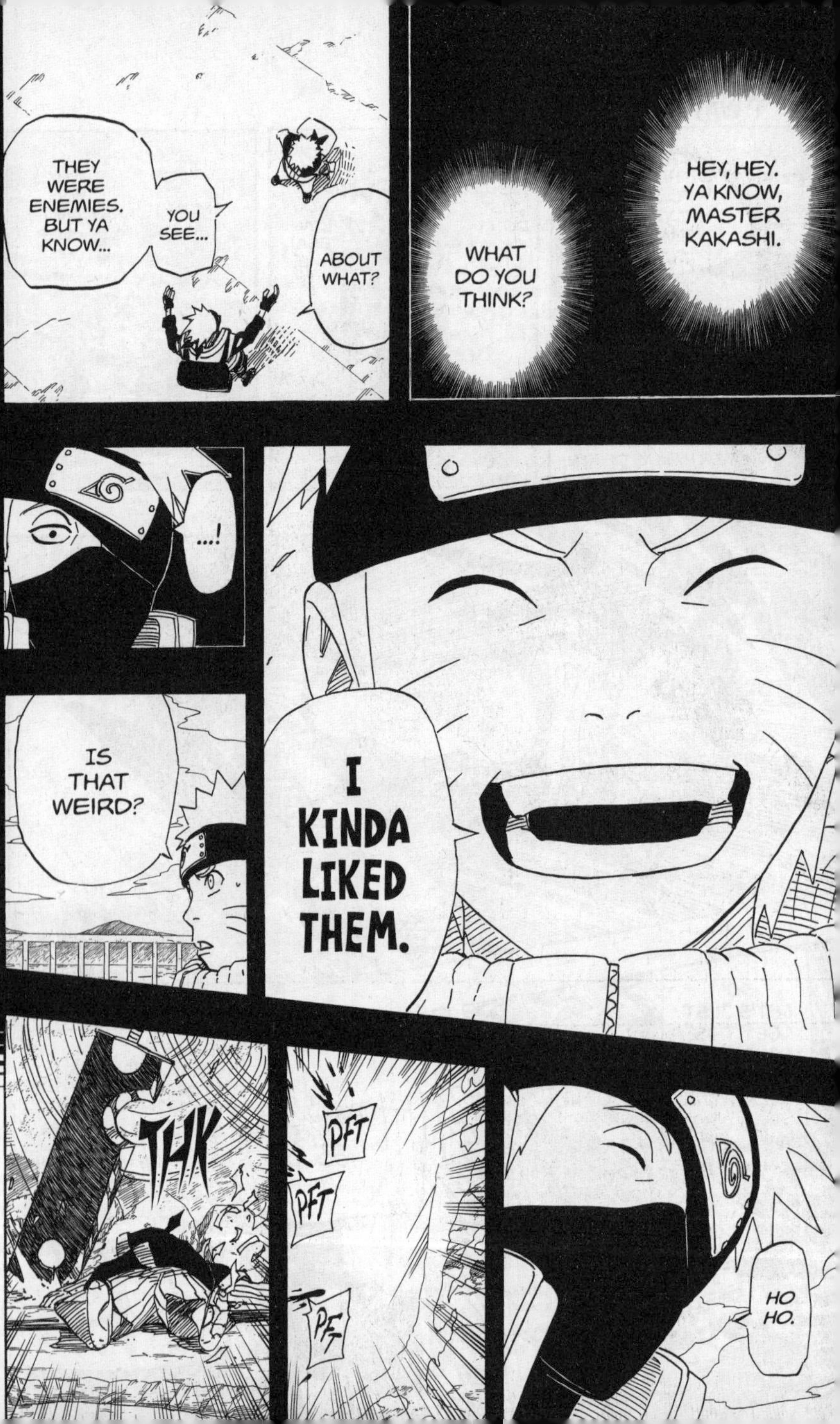
HEY, HEY. YA KNOW, MASTER KAKASHI.
WHAT DO YOU THINK?
ABOUT WHAT?
YOU SEE...
THEY WERE ENEMIES. BUT YA KNOW...
I KINDA LIKED THEM.
...!
IS THAT WEIRD?
HO HO.
PFT
PFT
PFT
THK

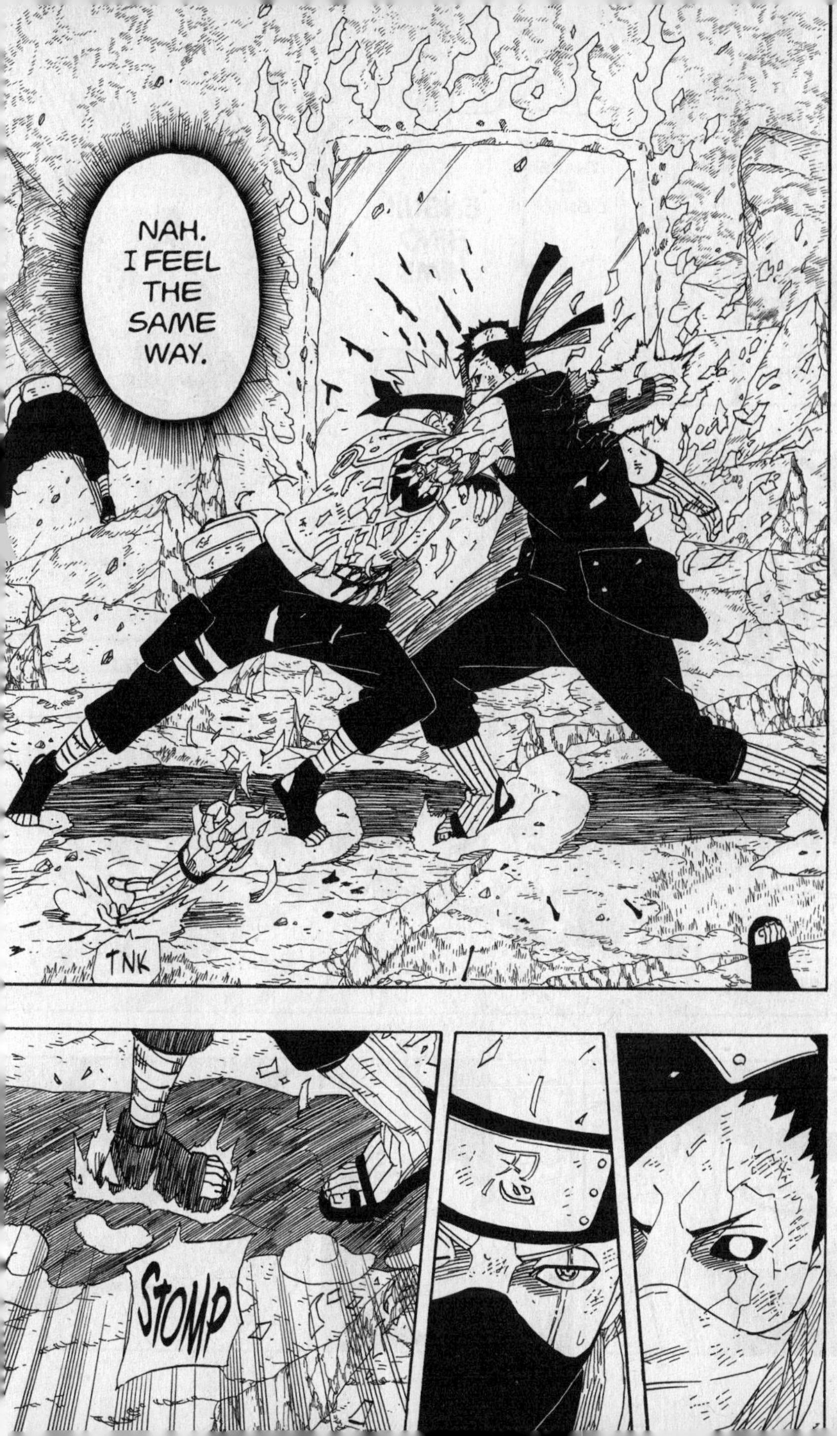
NAH. I FEEL THE SAME WAY.
TNK
STOMP

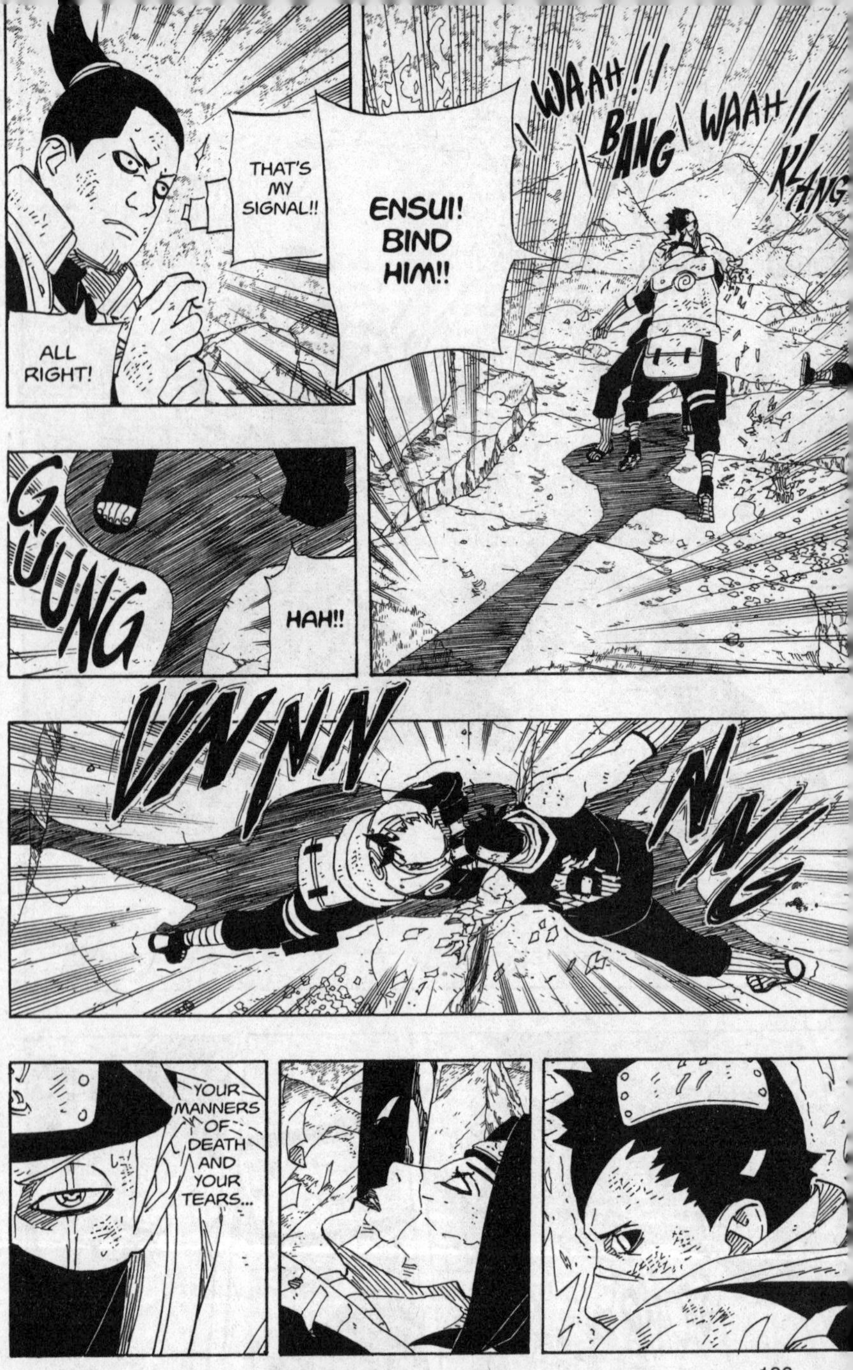
WAAH!!
BANG
WAAH!!
KLANG
ENSUI! BIND HIM!!
THAT'S MY SIGNAL!!
ALL RIGHT!
HAH!!
GUUNG
VWNN
NNG
YOUR MANNERS OF DEATH AND YOUR TEARS...

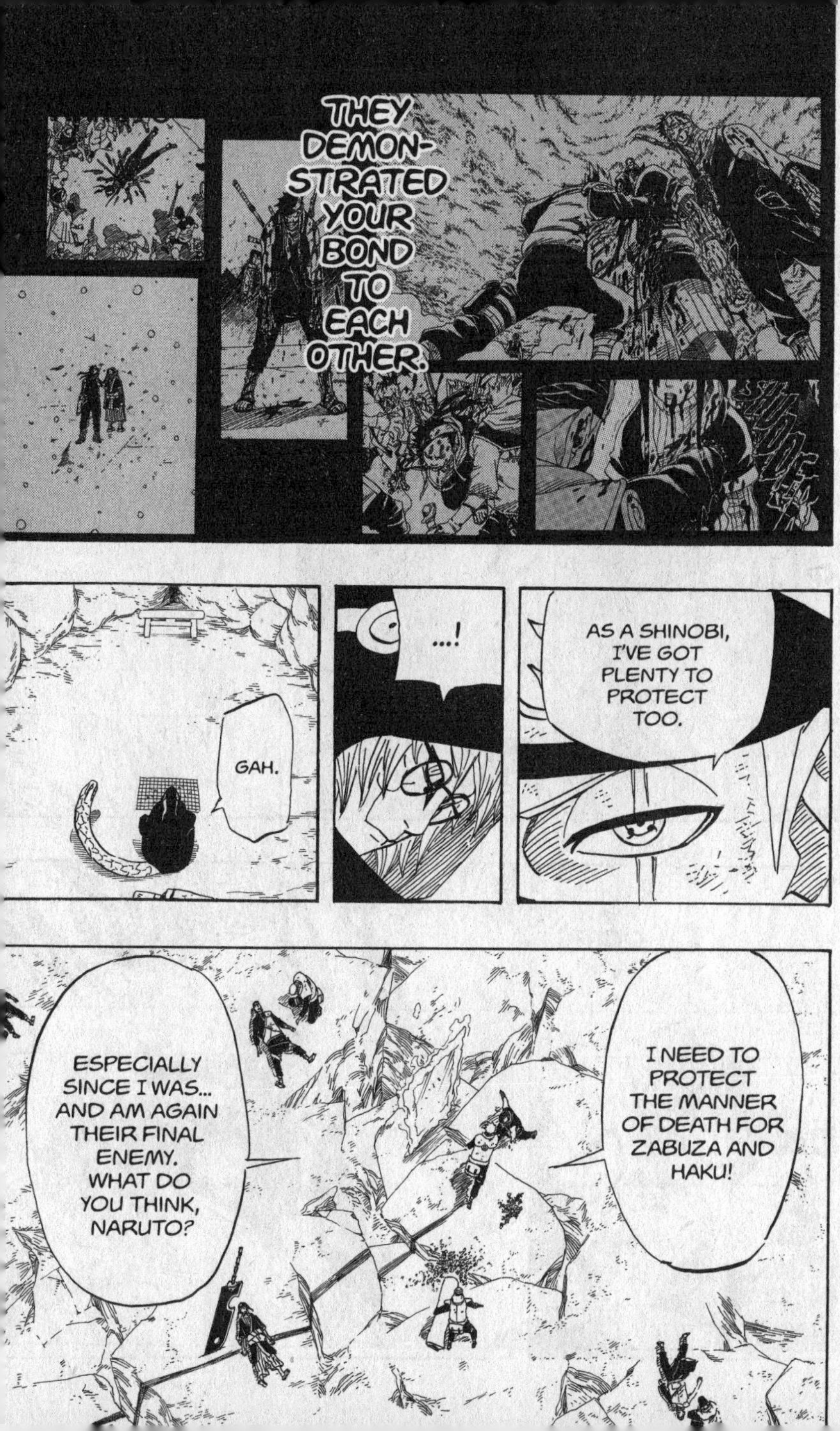
THEY DEMON-STRATED YOUR BOND TO EACH OTHER.
AS A SHINOBI, I'VE GOT PLENTY TO PROTECT TOO.
...!
GAH.
I NEED TO PROTECT THE MANNER OF DEATH FOR ZABUZA AND HAKU!
ESPECIALLY SINCE I WAS... AND AM AGAIN THEIR FINAL ENEMY. WHAT DO YOU THINK, NARUTO?

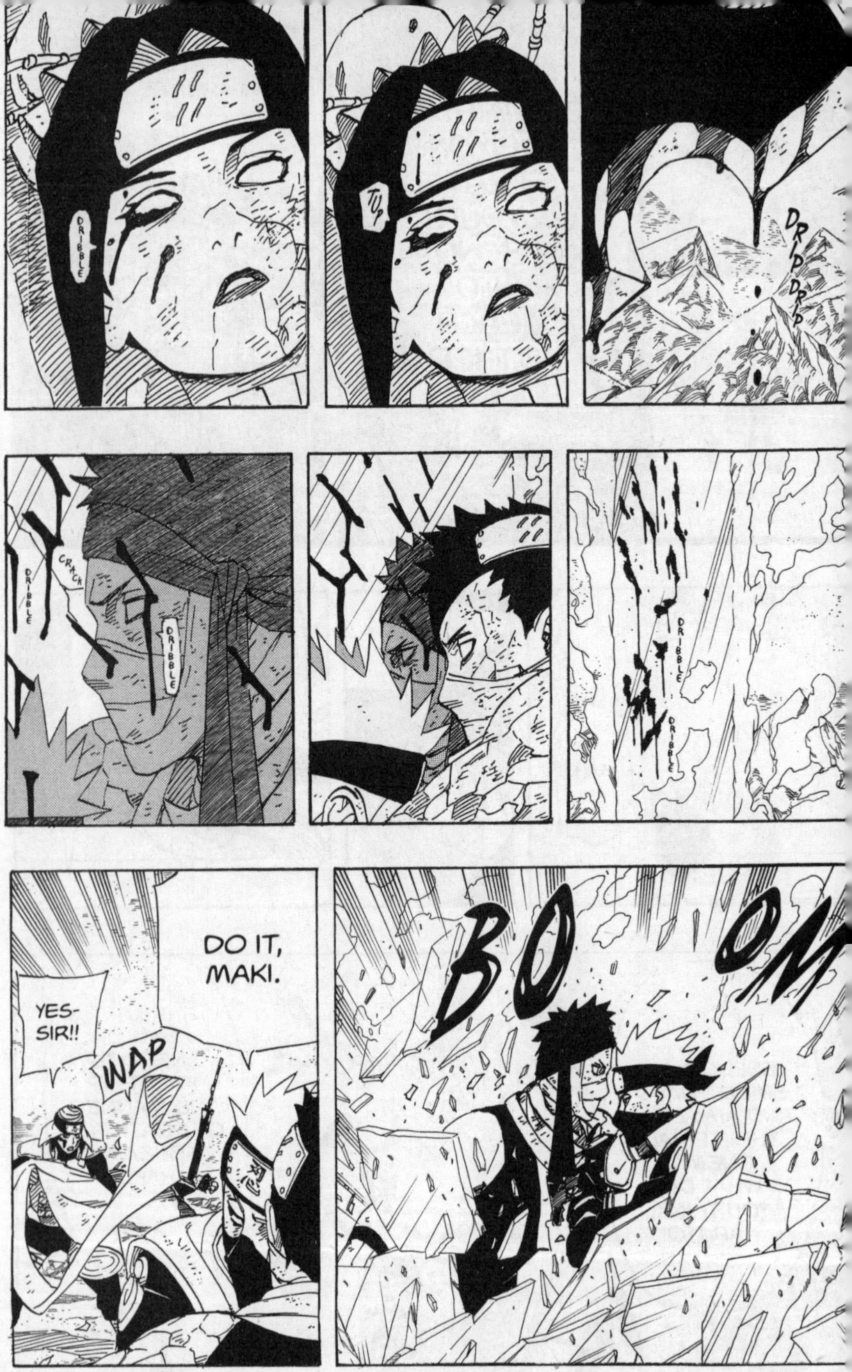
DRIP DRIP DRIP
DRIBBLE
DRIBBLE
DRIBBLE
CRACK
DRIBBLE
DRIBBLE
BOOM
DO IT, MAKI.
YES-SIR!!
WAP

READ THIS WAY

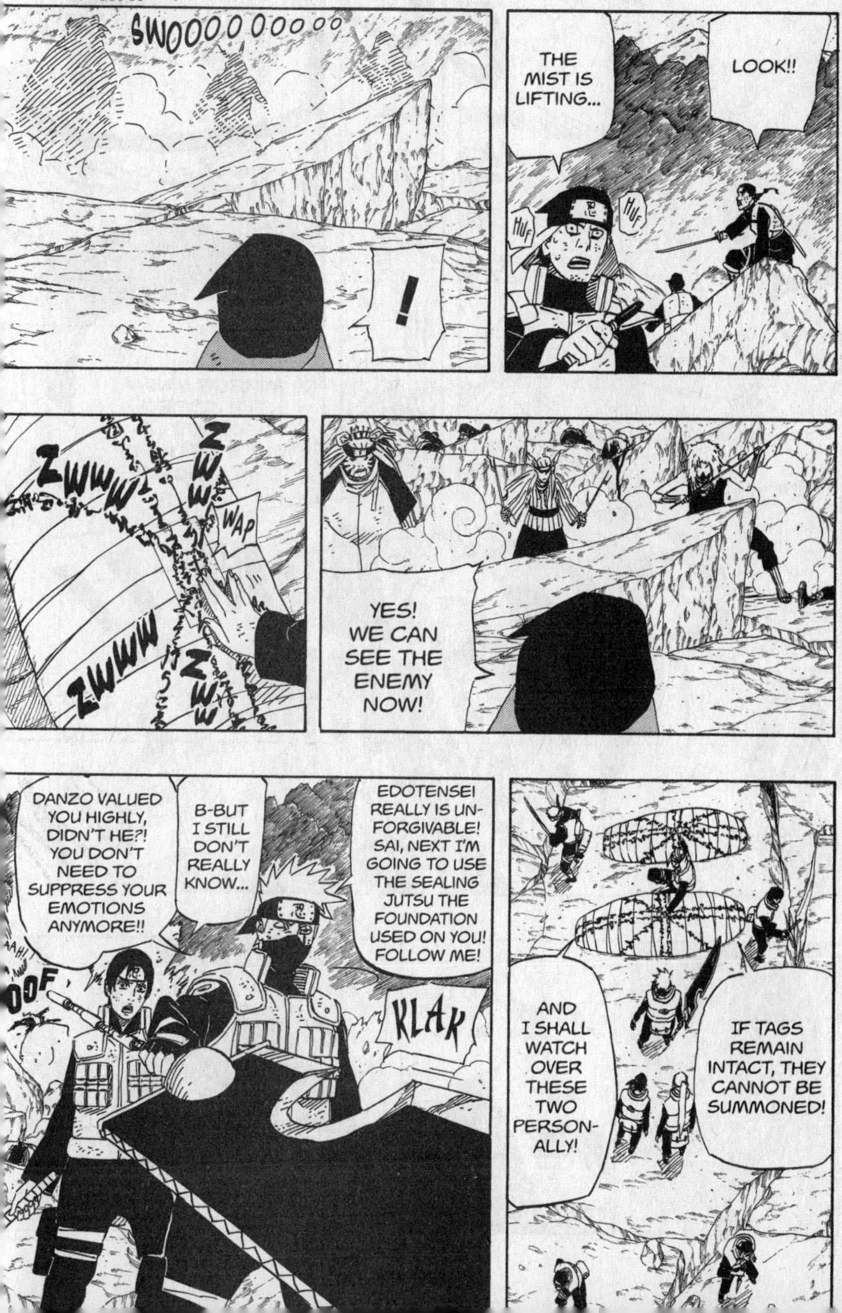
LOOK!!
THE MIST IS LIFTING...
HUF
HUF
SWOOOOOOOOO
!
YES! WE CAN SEE THE ENEMY NOW!
ZWWW
WAP
ZWWW
ZWWW
ZWWW
IF TAGS REMAIN INTACT, THEY CANNOT BE SUMMONED!
AND I SHALL WATCH OVER THESE TWO PERSONALLY!
EDOTENSEI REALLY IS UNFORGIVABLE! SAI, NEXT I'M GOING TO USE THE SEALING JUTSU THE FOUNDATION USED ON YOU! FOLLOW ME!
B-BUT I STILL DON'T REALLY KNOW...
DANZO VALUED YOU HIGHLY, DIDN'T HE?! YOU DON'T NEED TO SUPPRESS YOUR EMOTIONS ANYMORE!!
KLAK
AAH!
OOF

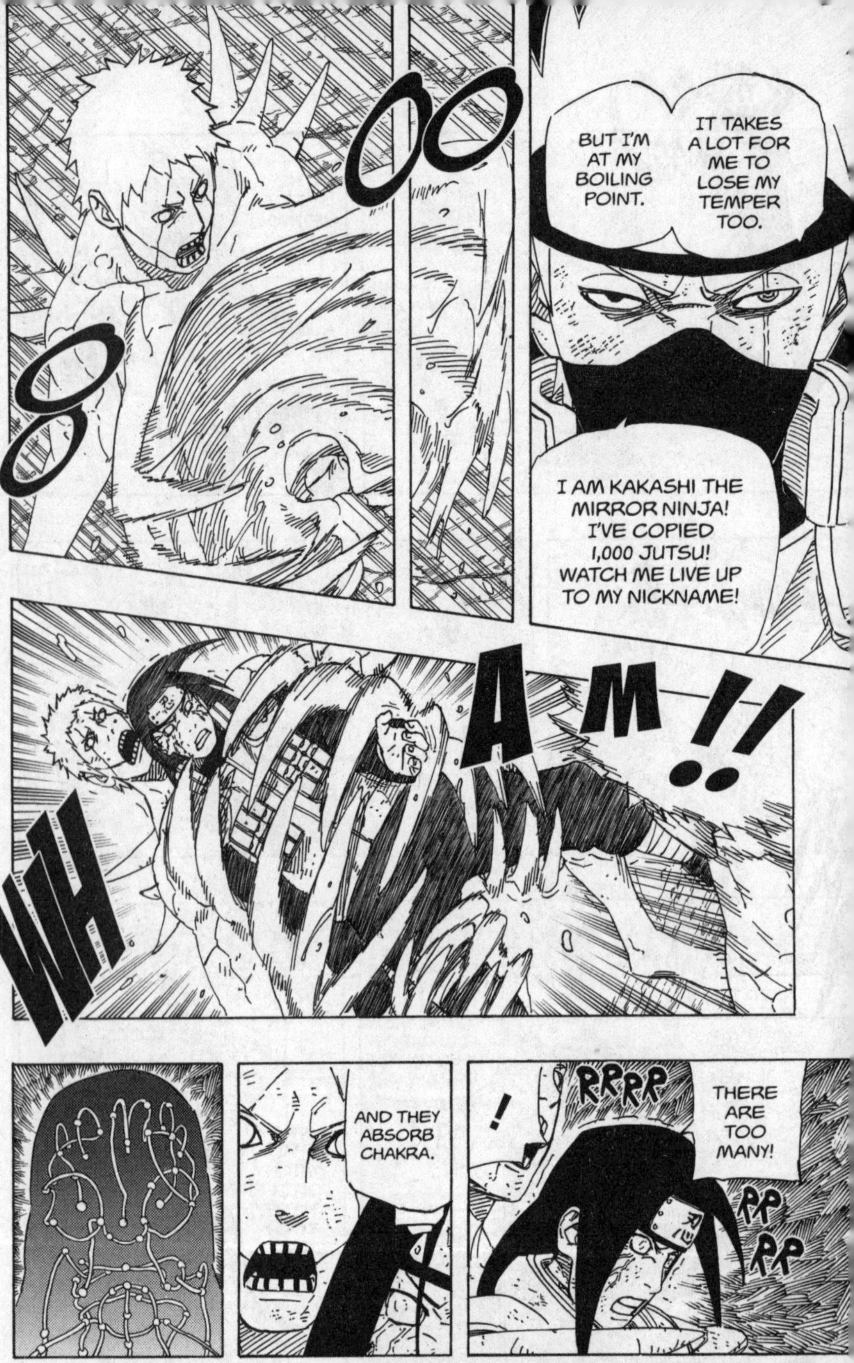

IT TAKES A LOT FOR ME TO LOSE MY TEMPER TOO.
BUT I'M AT MY BOILING POINT.
I AM KAKASHI THE MIRROR NINJA! I'VE COPIED 1,000 JUTSU! WATCH ME LIVE UP TO MY NICKNAME!
OO
O
WHAM!!
RRRR
THERE ARE TOO MANY!
!
RR RR
AND THEY ABSORB CHAKRA.

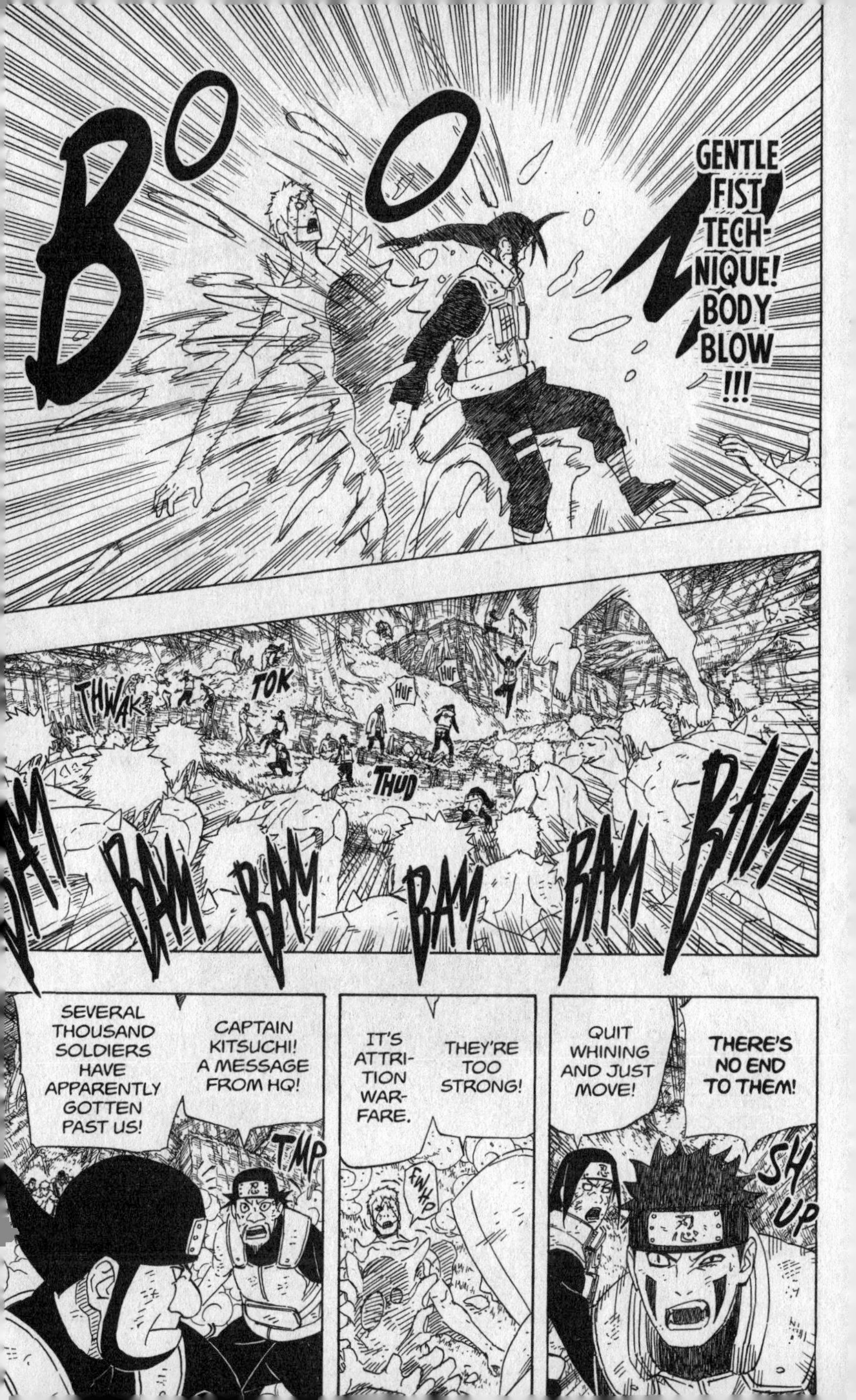
BOOOM
GENTLE FIST TECHNIQUE! BODY BLOW!!!
HUF
HUF
TOK
THWAK
THUD
BAM BAM BAM BAM BAM BAM
THERE'S NO END TO THEM!
QUIT WHINING AND JUST MOVE!
SHUP
THEY'RE TOO STRONG!
IT'S ATTRITION WARFARE.
CAPTAIN KITSUCHI! A MESSAGE FROM HQ!
SEVERAL THOUSAND SOLDIERS HAVE APPARENTLY GOTTEN PAST US!
TMP

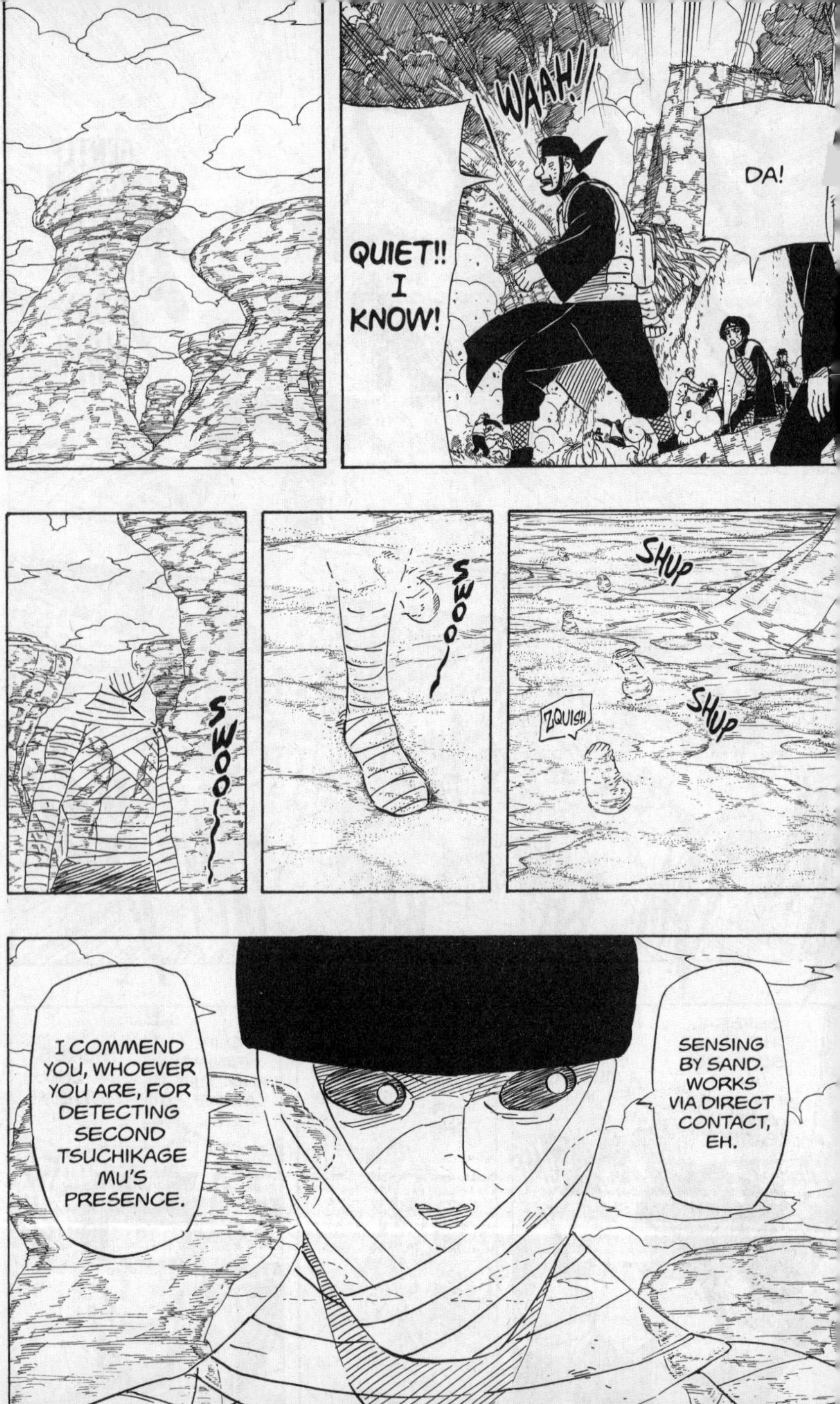
DA!
WAAH!!
QUIET!! I KNOW!
SHUP
ZQUISH
SHUP
SWOO...
SWOO...
SENSING BY SAND. WORKS VIA DIRECT CONTACT, EH.
I COMMEND YOU, WHOEVER YOU ARE, FOR DETECTING SECOND TSUCHIKAGE MU'S PRESENCE.

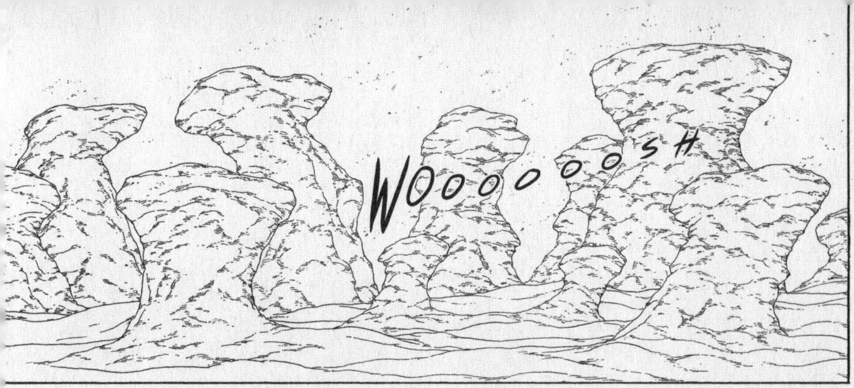
WOOOOOOOSH
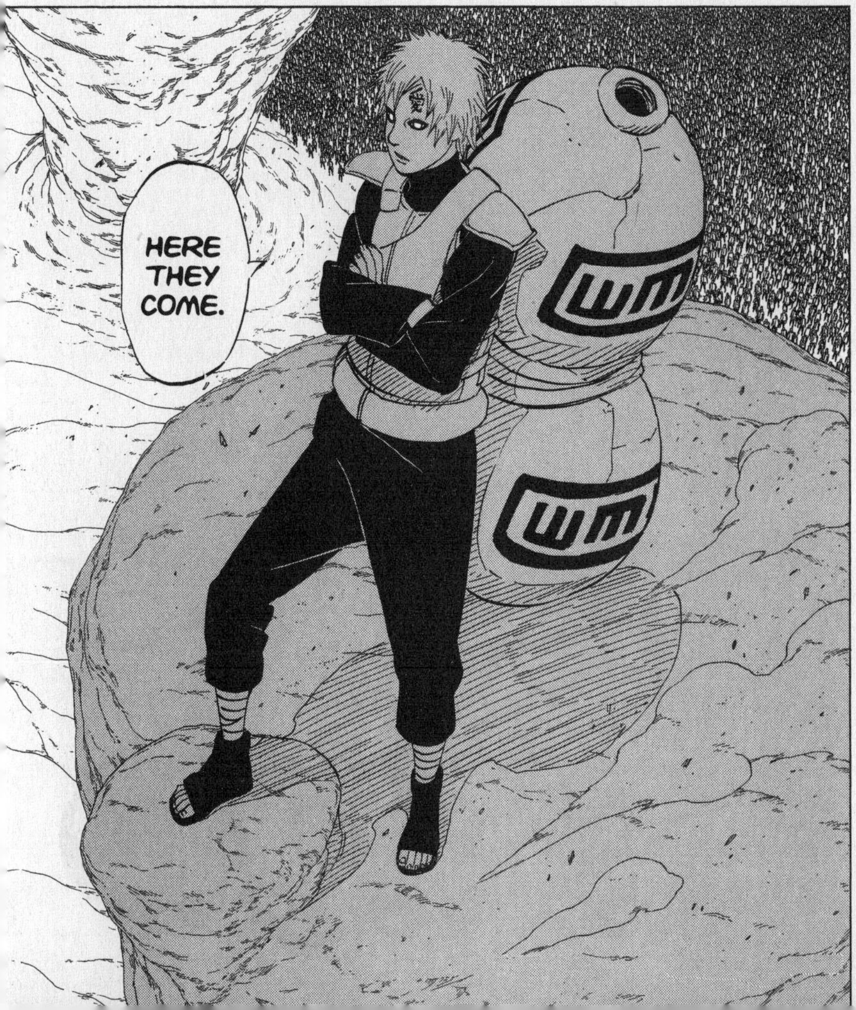
HERE THEY COME.

NARUTO

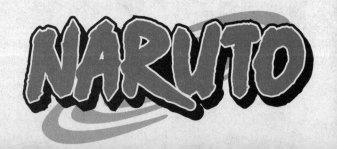

TOO MANY OLD FOGEYS...

岸本斉史

I'm always in a quandary over who to draw on the cover of each graphic novel volume... but I usually choose characters that were very prominent in the storylines within that volume. But lately they've all been unsightly old fogeys!!

—Masashi Kishimoto, 2011

NARUTO

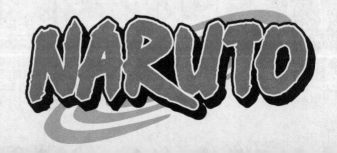

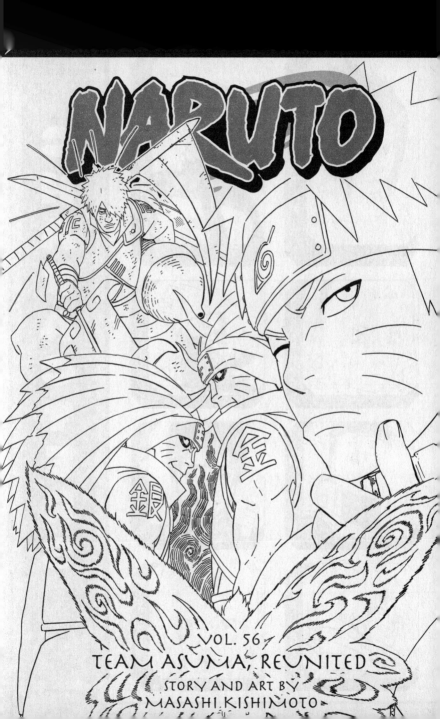

# NARUTO

VOL. 56
TEAM ASUMA, REUNITED
STORY AND ART BY
MASASHI KISHIMOTO

# CHARACTERS

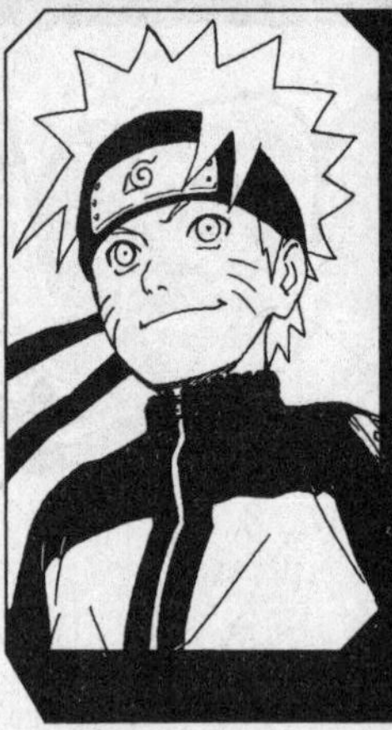

Naruto ナルト

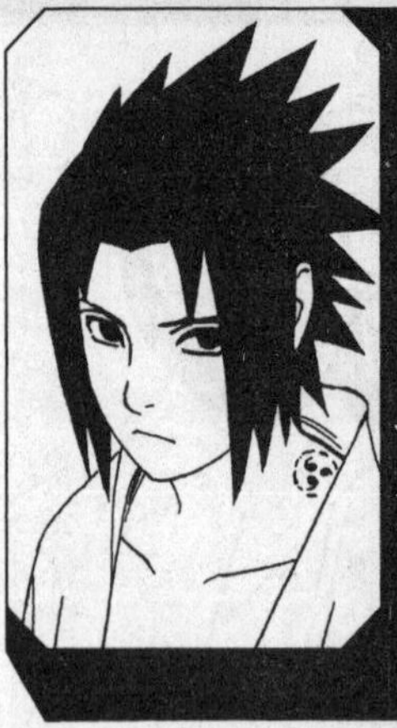

Sasuke サスケ

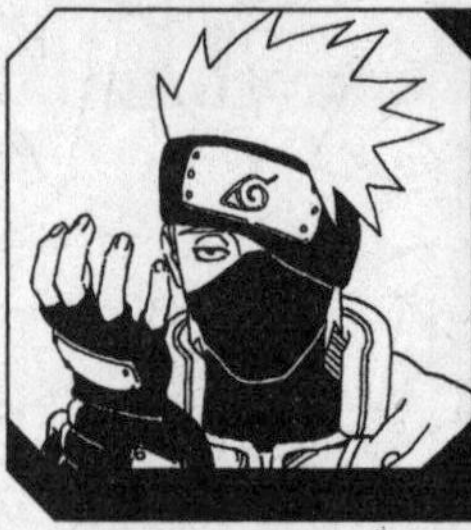

Kakashi カカシ

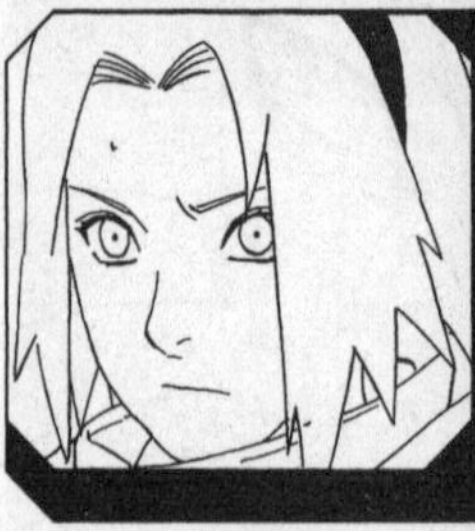

Sakura サクラ

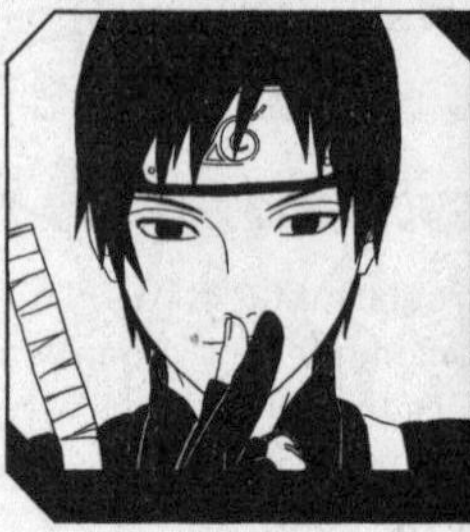

Sai サイ

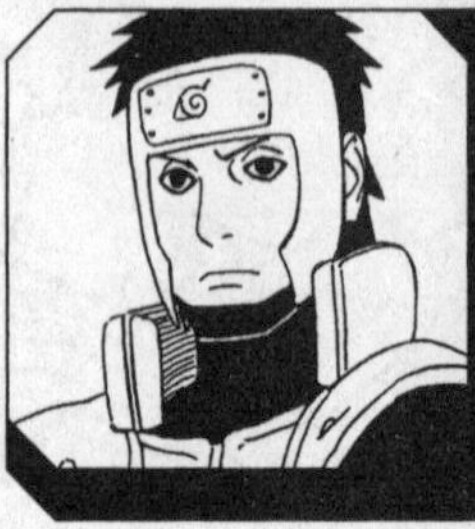

Yamato ヤマト

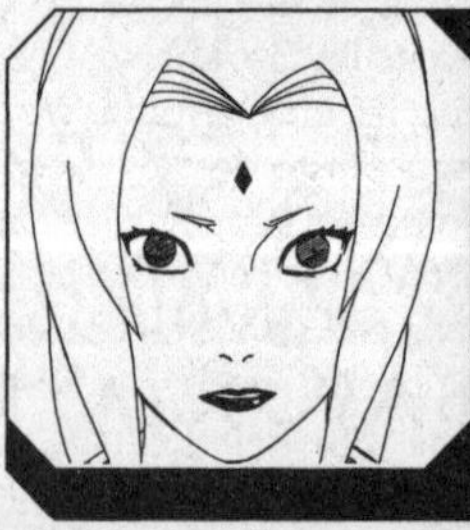

Tsunade 綱手

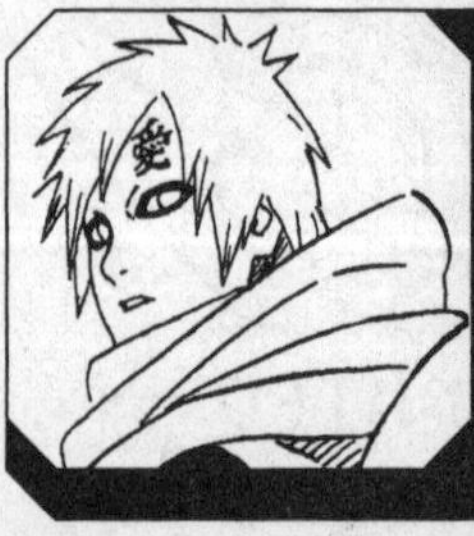

Gaara 我愛羅

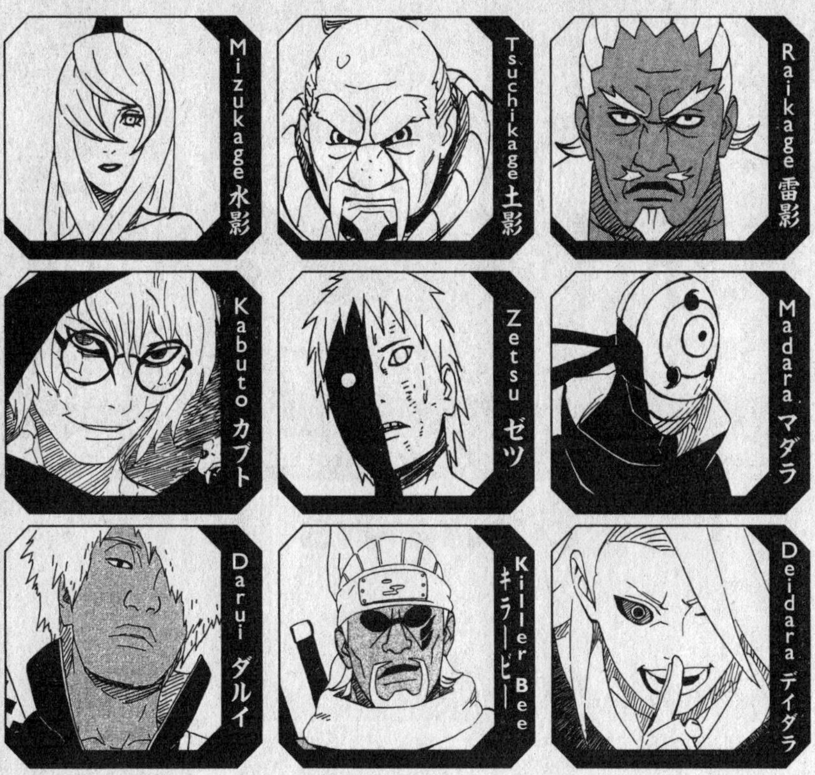
Raikage 雷影
Tsuchikage 土影
Mizukage 水影
Madara マダラ
Zetsu ゼツ
Kabuto カブト
Deidara デイダラ
Killer Bee キラービー
Darui ダルイ

## THE STORY SO FAR...

Naruto, the biggest troublemaker at the Ninja Academy in the Village of Konohagakure, finally becomes a ninja along with his classmates Sasuke and Sakura. They grow and mature through countless trials and battles. However, Sasuke, unable to give up his quest for vengeance, leaves Konohagakure to seek Orochimaru and his power…

Two years pass. Naruto grows up and engages in fierce battles against the Tailed Beast-targeting Akatsuki. Elsewhere, after winning the heroic battle against Itachi and learning his older brother's true intentions, Sasuke allies with the Akatsuki and sets out to destroy Konoha.

Upon Madara's declaration of war, the Five Kage put together an Allied Shinobi Force. The Fourth Great Ninja War against the Akatsuki begins. Naruto continues training, still sequestered from the battlefield, while the Allied Forces fight harsh battles against the heroes Kabuto has resurrected. And do additional enemies threaten the main regiment of the Allied Forces?!

# NARUTO

## VOL. 56
### TEAM ASUMA, REUNITED

# CONTENTS

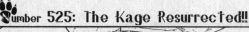

# Number 525: The Kage Resurrected!!

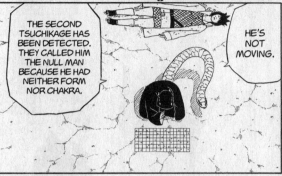

HISSSS
HE'S NOT MOVING.
THE SECOND TSUCHIKAGE HAS BEEN DETECTED. THEY CALLED HIM THE NULL MAN BECAUSE HE HAD NEITHER FORM NOR CHAKRA.
KLAK
THE BATTLE-FIELD SHOULD BE COMING TOGETHER NICELY. NOW BEGINS THE REAL FUN.
I THINK I'LL LET HIM DO HIS OWN THING AFTER THE KUCHIYOSE SUMMON-ING.
!!
URK
UNH
BOOF

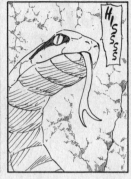

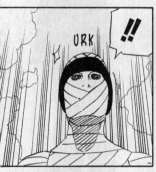

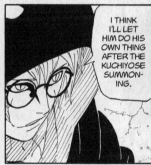

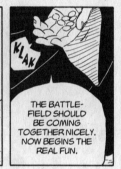

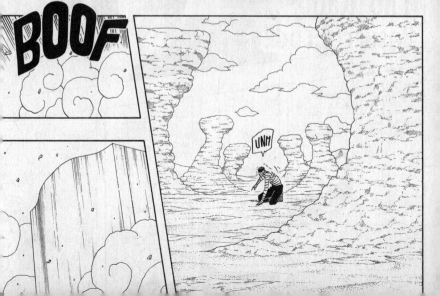

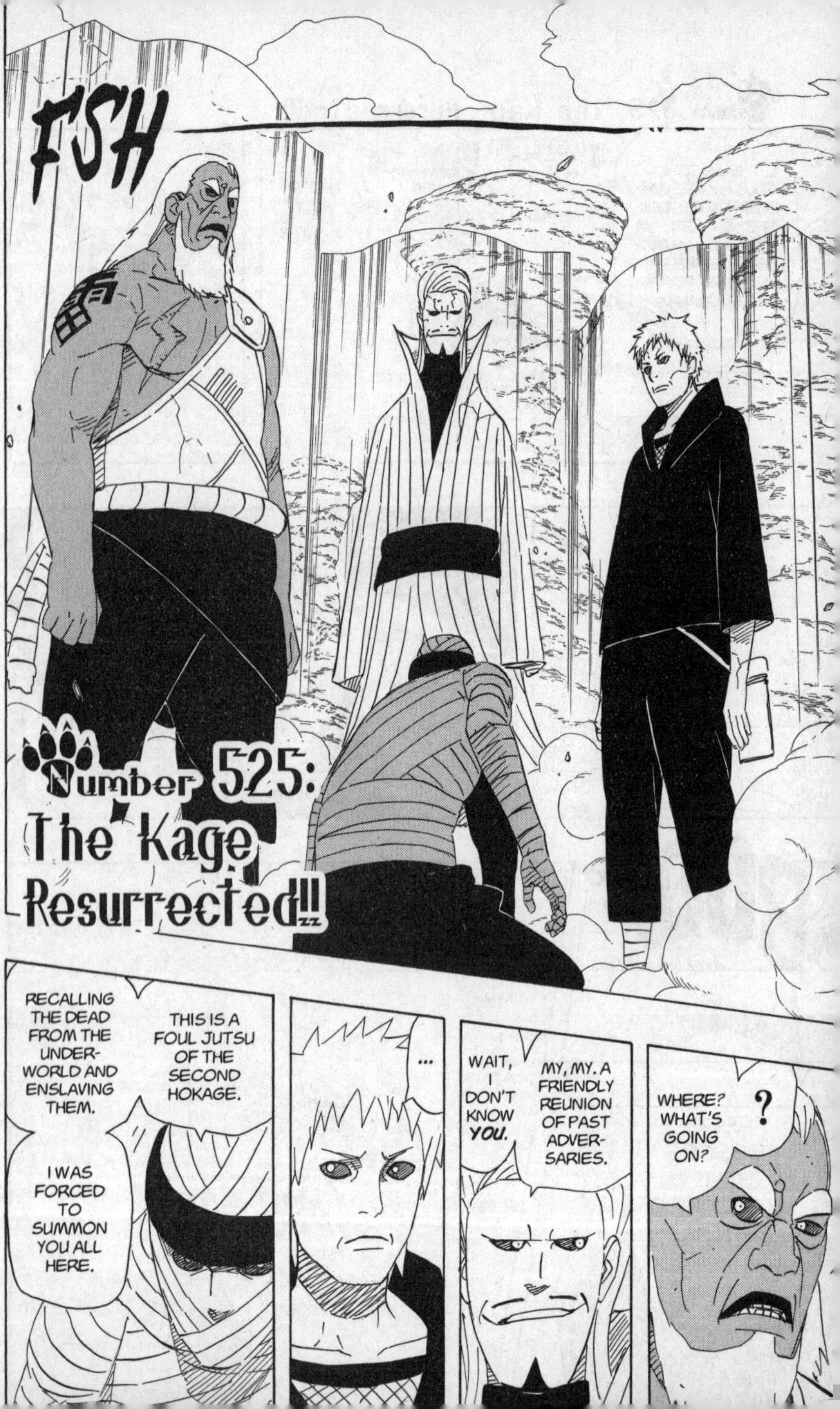
FSH
Number 525: The Kage Resurrected!!
?
WHERE? WHAT'S GOING ON?
MY, MY. A FRIENDLY REUNION OF PAST ADVER-SARIES.
WAIT, I DON'T KNOW YOU.
...
THIS IS A FOUL JUTSU OF THE SECOND HOKAGE.
RECALLING THE DEAD FROM THE UNDER-WORLD AND ENSLAVING THEM.
I WAS FORCED TO SUMMON YOU ALL HERE.

READ THIS WAY

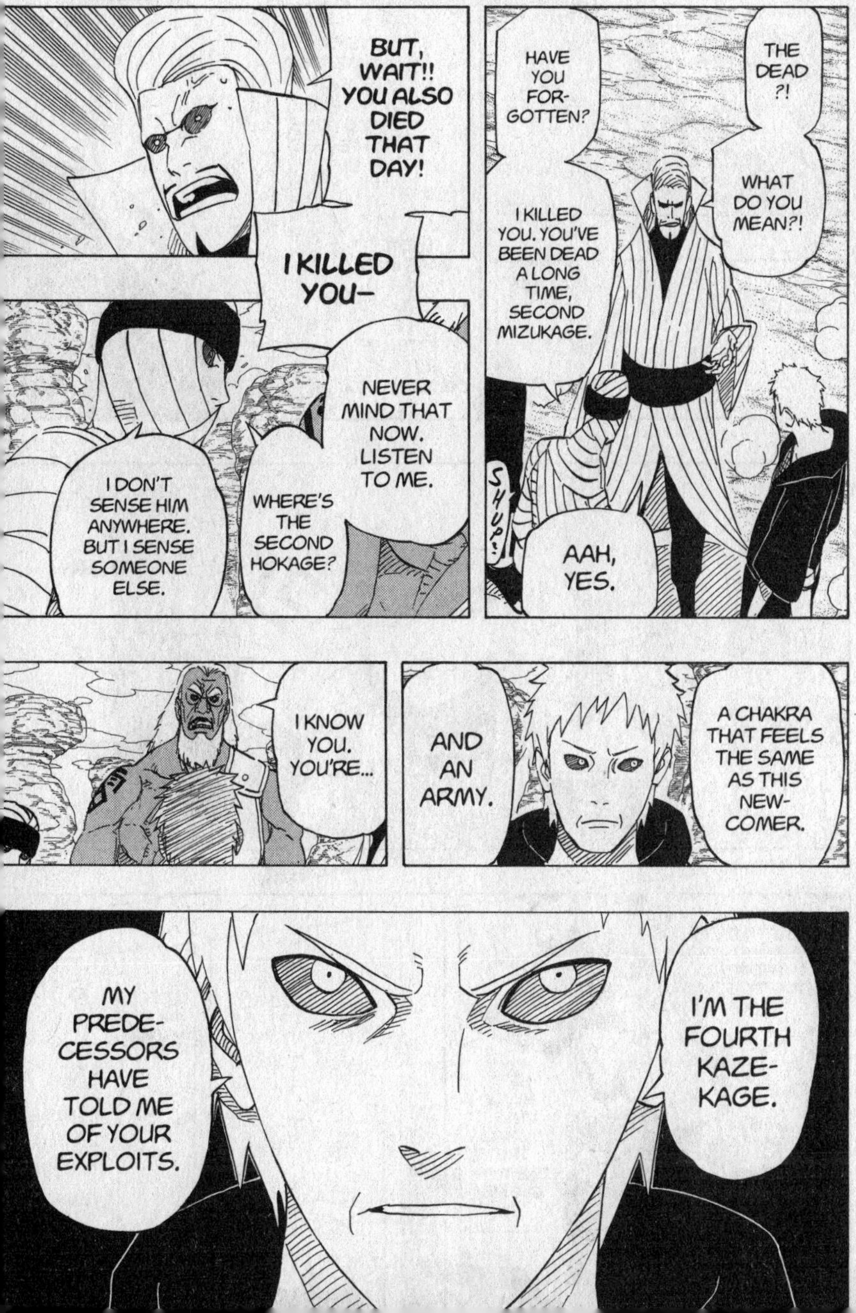
THE DEAD?!
WHAT DO YOU MEAN?!
HAVE YOU FOR-GOTTEN?
I KILLED YOU. YOU'VE BEEN DEAD A LONG TIME, SECOND MIZUKAGE.
SHUP!
AAH, YES.
BUT, WAIT!! YOU ALSO DIED THAT DAY!
I KILLED YOU-
NEVER MIND THAT NOW. LISTEN TO ME.
WHERE'S THE SECOND HOKAGE?
I DON'T SENSE HIM ANYWHERE. BUT I SENSE SOMEONE ELSE.
A CHAKRA THAT FEELS THE SAME AS THIS NEW-COMER.
AND AN ARMY.
I KNOW YOU. YOU'RE...
I'M THE FOURTH KAZE-KAGE.
MY PREDE-CESSORS HAVE TOLD ME OF YOUR EXPLOITS.

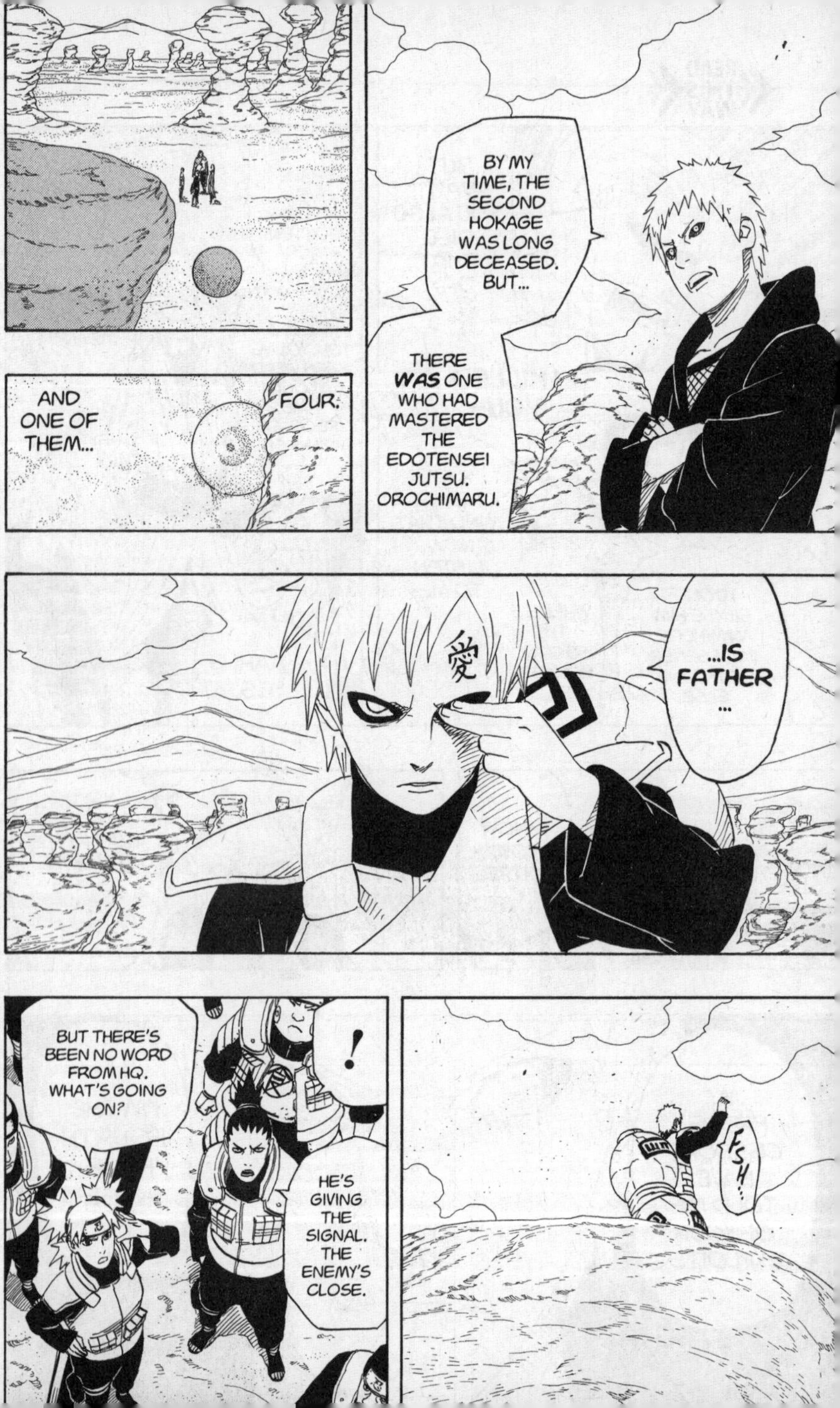
BY MY TIME, THE SECOND HOKAGE WAS LONG DECEASED. BUT...
THERE WAS ONE WHO HAD MASTERED THE EDOTENSEI JUTSU. OROCHIMARU.
FOUR.
AND ONE OF THEM...
...IS FATHER ...
FSH...
!
BUT THERE'S BEEN NO WORD FROM HQ. WHAT'S GOING ON?
HE'S GIVING THE SIGNAL. THE ENEMY'S CLOSE.

READ THIS WAY

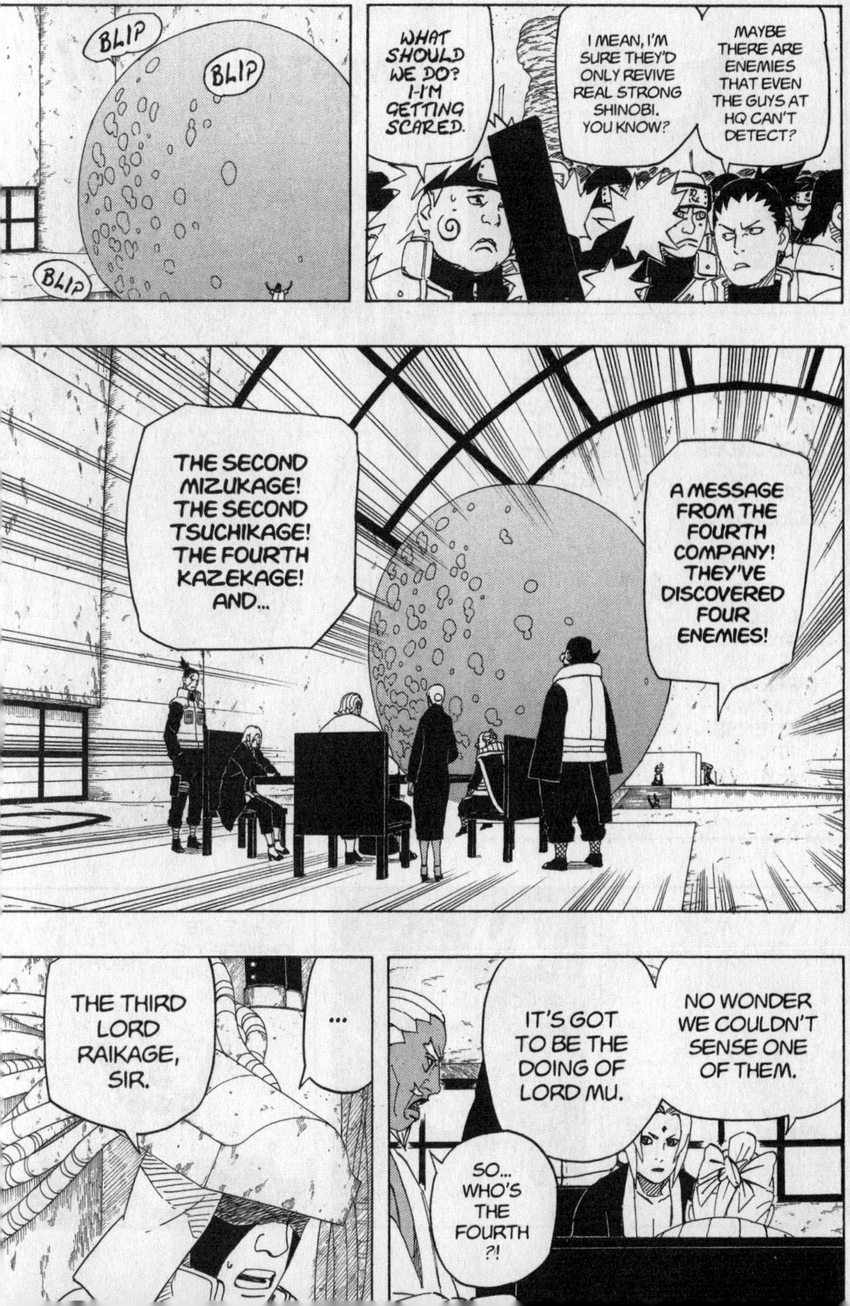
MAYBE THERE ARE ENEMIES THAT EVEN THE GUYS AT HQ CAN'T DETECT?
I MEAN, I'M SURE THEY'D ONLY REVIVE REAL STRONG SHINOBI. YOU KNOW?
WHAT SHOULD WE DO? I-I'M GETTING SCARED.
BLIP
BLIP
BLIP
A MESSAGE FROM THE FOURTH COMPANY! THEY'VE DISCOVERED FOUR ENEMIES!
THE SECOND MIZUKAGE! THE SECOND TSUCHIKAGE! THE FOURTH KAZEKAGE! AND...
NO WONDER WE COULDN'T SENSE ONE OF THEM.
IT'S GOT TO BE THE DOING OF LORD MU.
SO... WHO'S THE FOURTH ?!
...
THE THIRD LORD RAIKAGE, SIR.

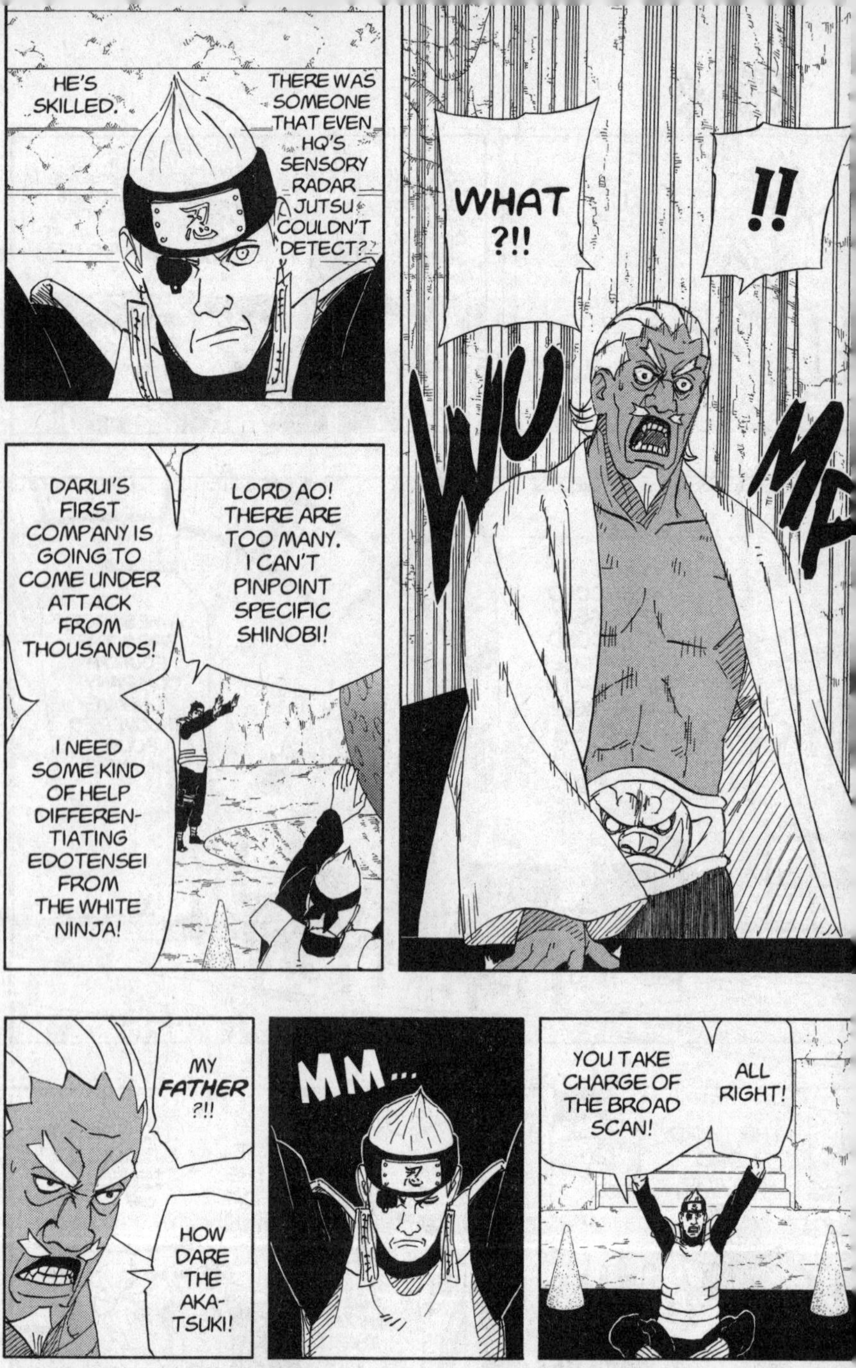
!!
WHAT ?!!
THERE WAS SOMEONE THAT EVEN HQ'S SENSORY RADAR JUTSU COULDN'T DETECT?
HE'S SKILLED.
LORD AO! THERE ARE TOO MANY. I CAN'T PINPOINT SPECIFIC SHINOBI!
DARUI'S FIRST COMPANY IS GOING TO COME UNDER ATTACK FROM THOUSANDS!
I NEED SOME KIND OF HELP DIFFEREN-TIATING EDOTENSEI FROM THE WHITE NINJA!
ALL RIGHT!
YOU TAKE CHARGE OF THE BROAD SCAN!
MM...
MY *FATHER*?!!
HOW DARE THE AKA-TSUKI!

READ THIS WAY

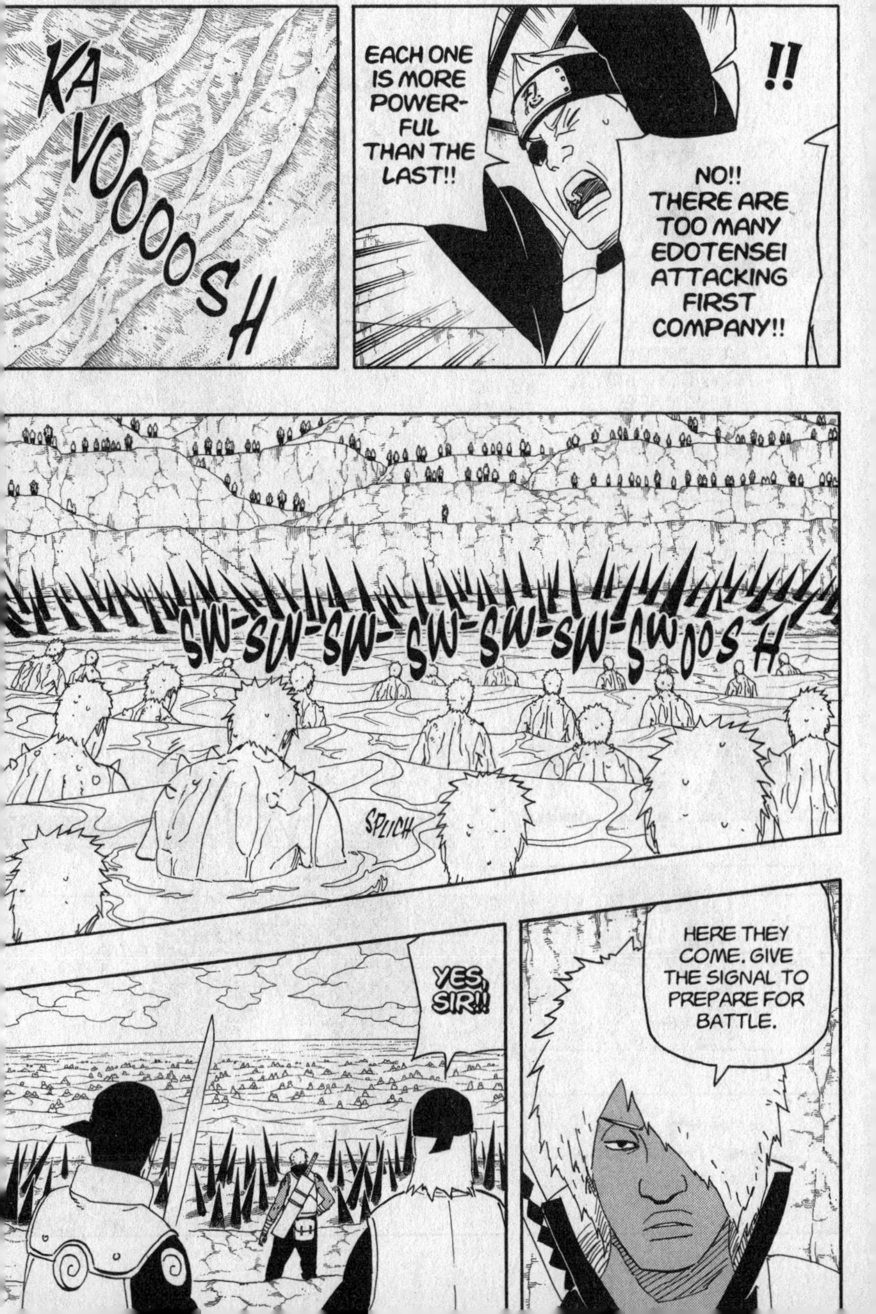
!!
NO!! THERE ARE TOO MANY EDOTENSEI ATTACKING FIRST COMPANY!!
EACH ONE IS MORE POWER-FUL THAN THE LAST!!
KA VOOOOSH
SW-SW-SW-SW-SW-SW-SWOOSH
SPLICH
HERE THEY COME. GIVE THE SIGNAL TO PREPARE FOR BATTLE.
YES, SIR!!

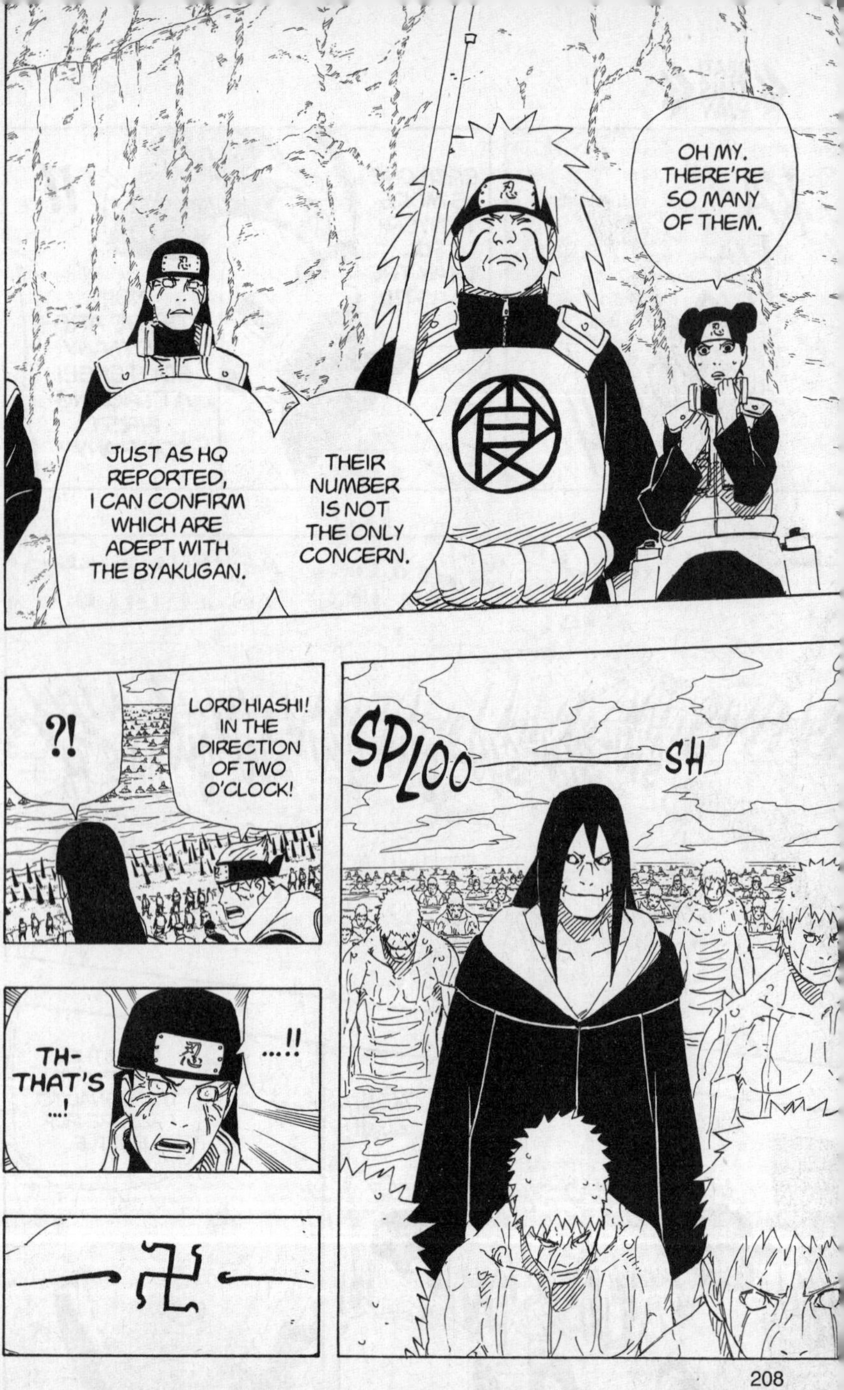
OH MY. THERE'RE SO MANY OF THEM.
THEIR NUMBER IS NOT THE ONLY CONCERN.
JUST AS HQ REPORTED, I CAN CONFIRM WHICH ARE ADEPT WITH THE BYAKUGAN.
SPLOO—SH
LORD HIASHI! IN THE DIRECTION OF TWO O'CLOCK!
?!
...!!
TH- THAT'S ...!

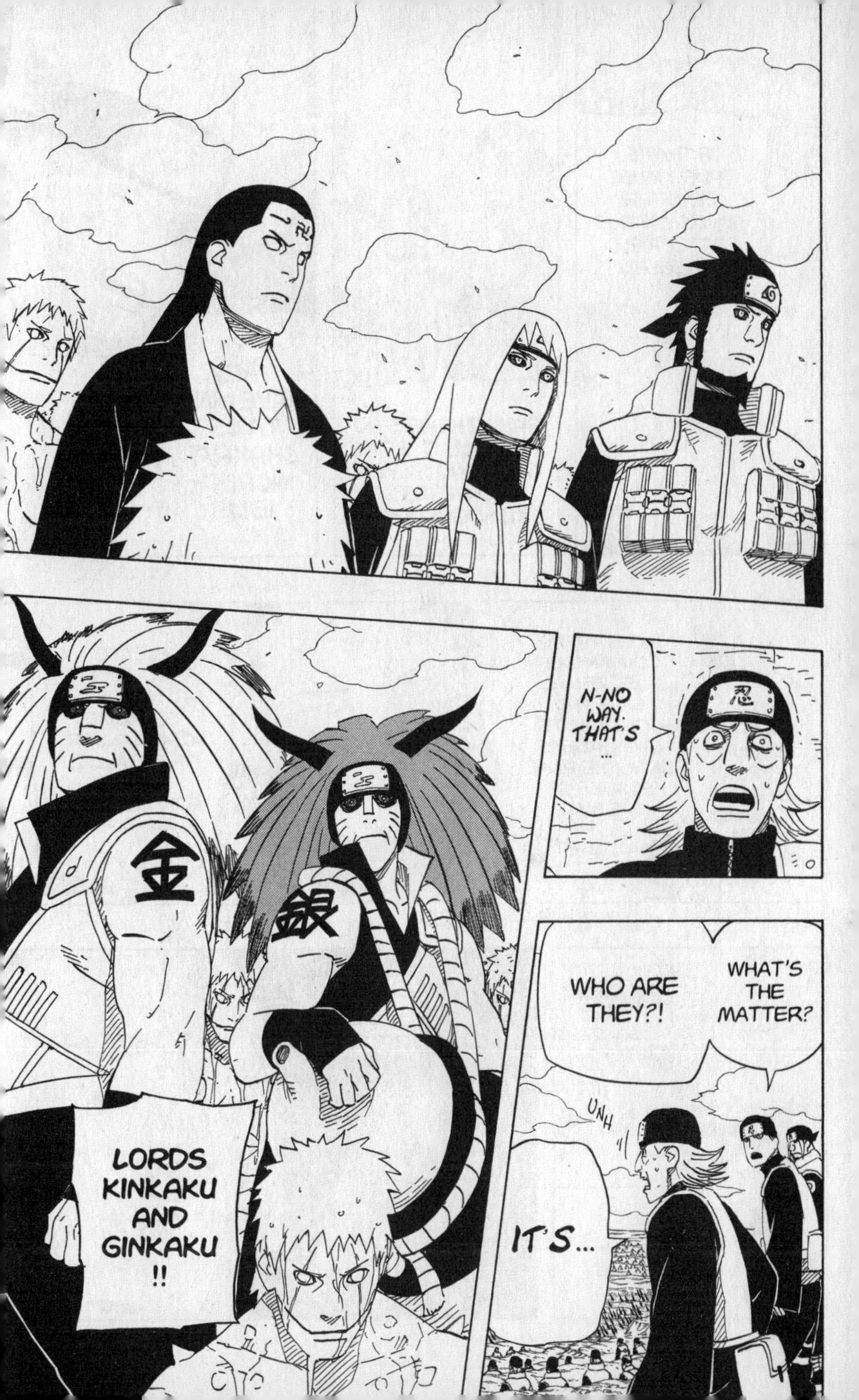
N-NO WAY. THAT'S ...
WHAT'S THE MATTER?
WHO ARE THEY?!
UNH
IT'S...
LORDS KINKAKU AND GINKAKU!!

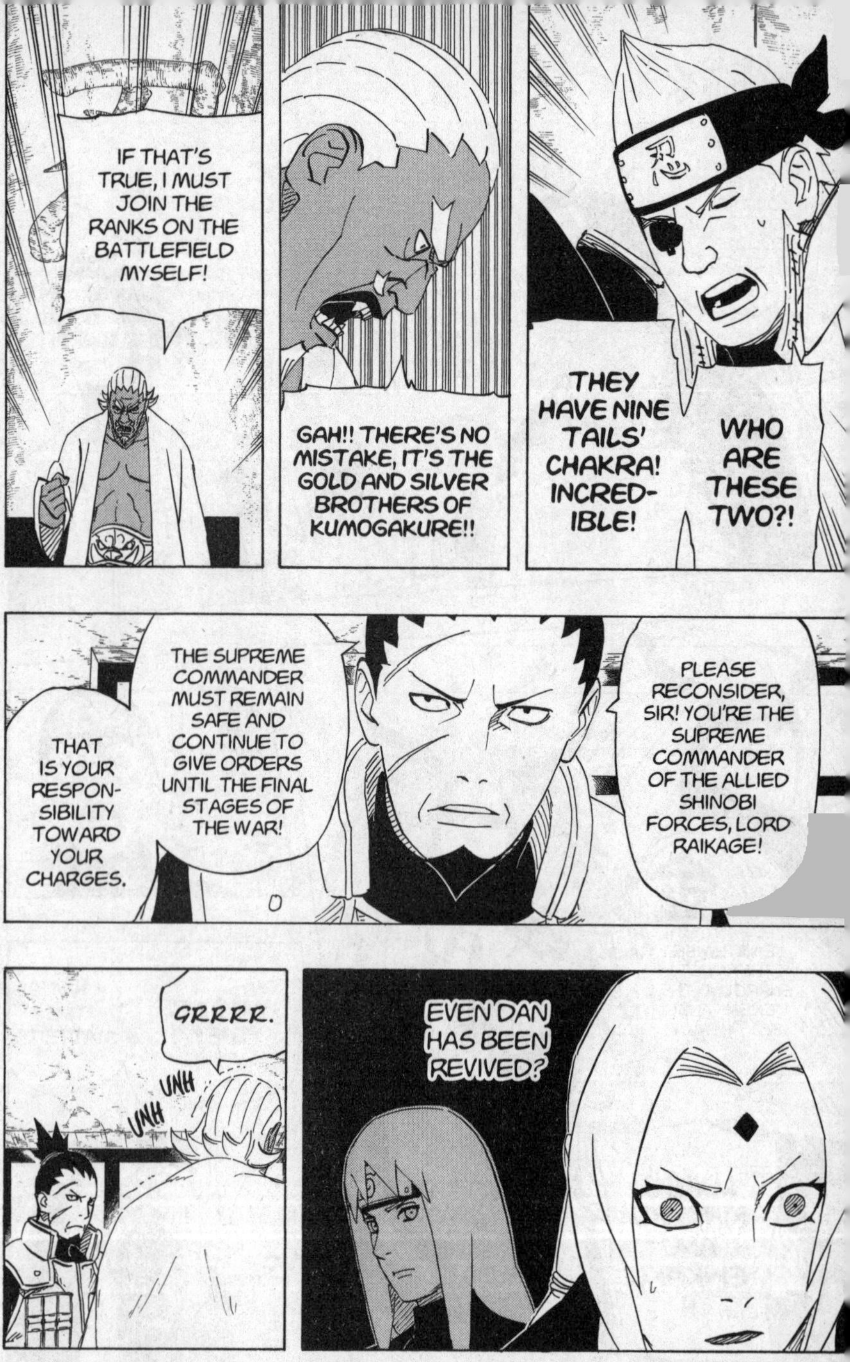
WHO ARE THESE TWO?!
THEY HAVE NINE TAILS' CHAKRA! INCREDIBLE!
GAH!! THERE'S NO MISTAKE, IT'S THE GOLD AND SILVER BROTHERS OF KUMOGAKURE!!
IF THAT'S TRUE, I MUST JOIN THE RANKS ON THE BATTLEFIELD MYSELF!
PLEASE RECONSIDER, SIR! YOU'RE THE SUPREME COMMANDER OF THE ALLIED SHINOBI FORCES, LORD RAIKAGE!
THE SUPREME COMMANDER MUST REMAIN SAFE AND CONTINUE TO GIVE ORDERS UNTIL THE FINAL STAGES OF THE WAR!
THAT IS YOUR RESPON-SIBILITY TOWARD YOUR CHARGES.
EVEN DAN HAS BEEN REVIVED?
GRRRR.
UNH
UNH

READ THIS WAY

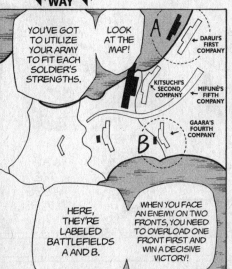

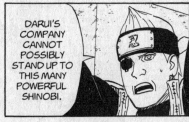

DARUI'S COMPANY CANNOT POSSIBLY STAND UP TO THIS MANY POWERFUL SHINOBI.
THE TIDE OF BATTLE CHANGES TOO QUICKLY.
FSH
I'VE GOT TO KEEP UP WITH MY STRATEGY ANALYSIS!
LOOK AT THE MAP!
YOU'VE GOT TO UTILIZE YOUR ARMY TO FIT EACH SOLDIER'S STRENGTHS.
A
DARUI'S FIRST COMPANY
KITSUCHI'S SECOND COMPANY
MIFUNÉ'S FIFTH COMPANY
GAARA'S FOURTH COMPANY
B
WHEN YOU FACE AN ENEMY ON TWO FRONTS, YOU NEED TO OVERLOAD ONE FRONT FIRST AND WIN A DECISIVE VICTORY!
HERE, THEY'RE LABELED BATTLEFIELDS A AND B.
IN OUR CASE, START WITH A!
CONCENTRATE FORCES AROUND DARUI'S FIRST COMPANY!
A
DARUI'S FIRST COMPANY
KITSUCHI'S SECOND COMPANY
MIFUNÉ'S FIFTH COMPANY
GAARA'S FOURTH COMPANY
B
MIFUNÉ'S FIFTH COMPANY NEEDS TO JOIN UP WITH FIRST COMPANY TO REINFORCE THE RANKS WHILE MAINTAINING THE BELT FORMATION.
KITSUCHI'S SECOND COMPANY NEEDS TO FAN OUT LENGTHWISE. THEY MUST SURROUND THE ENEMY AND BOX THEM IN.
SECOND COMPANY WILL BE STRETCHED THIN, BUT FIFTH COMPANY WILL BUTTRESS THEM.
A
DARUI'S FIRST COMPANY
KITSUCHI'S SECOND COMPANY
MIFUNÉ'S FIFTH COMPANY
GAARA'S FOURTH COMPANY
B
GAARA'S FOURTH COMPANY NEEDS TO RETREAT INTO A REVERSE L-FORMATION. THIS WILL LURE THE ENEMY FORWARD.

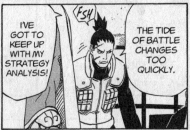

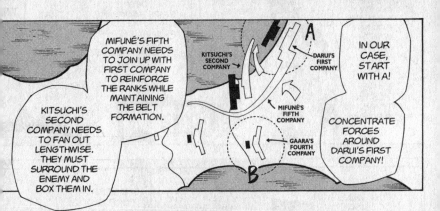

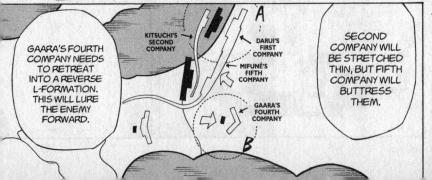

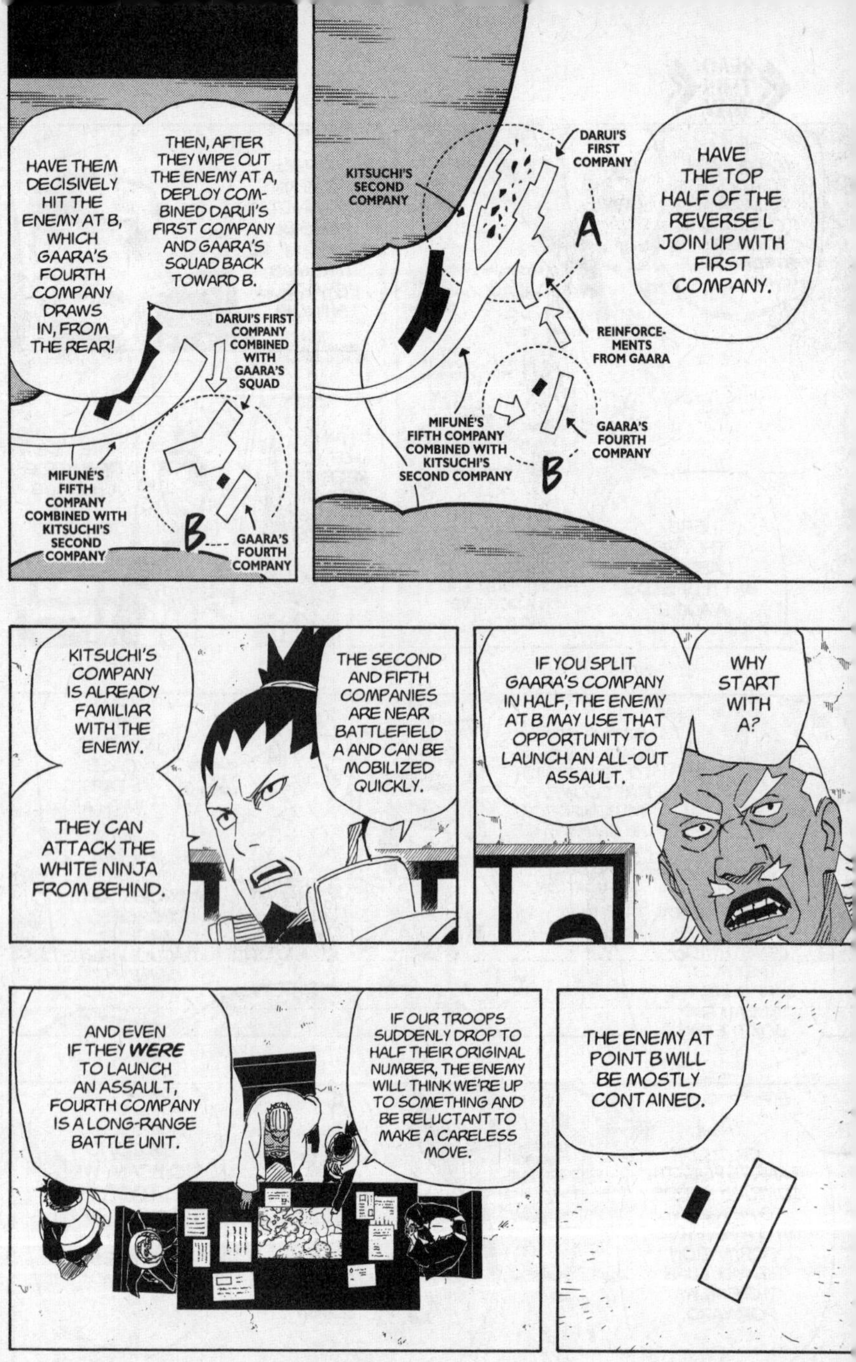
HAVE THE TOP HALF OF THE REVERSE L JOIN UP WITH FIRST COMPANY.
DARUI'S FIRST COMPANY
KITSUCHI'S SECOND COMPANY
A
REINFORCE-MENTS FROM GAARA
MIFUNÉ'S FIFTH COMPANY COMBINED WITH KITSUCHI'S SECOND COMPANY
GAARA'S FOURTH COMPANY
B
THEN, AFTER THEY WIPE OUT THE ENEMY AT A, DEPLOY COMBINED DARUI'S FIRST COMPANY AND GAARA'S SQUAD BACK TOWARD B.
HAVE THEM DECISIVELY HIT THE ENEMY AT B, WHICH GAARA'S FOURTH COMPANY DRAWS IN, FROM THE REAR!
DARUI'S FIRST COMPANY COMBINED WITH GAARA'S SQUAD
MIFUNÉ'S FIFTH COMPANY COMBINED WITH KITSUCHI'S SECOND COMPANY
B
GAARA'S FOURTH COMPANY
WHY START WITH A?
IF YOU SPLIT GAARA'S COMPANY IN HALF, THE ENEMY AT B MAY USE THAT OPPORTUNITY TO LAUNCH AN ALL-OUT ASSAULT.
THE SECOND AND FIFTH COMPANIES ARE NEAR BATTLEFIELD A AND CAN BE MOBILIZED QUICKLY.
KITSUCHI'S COMPANY IS ALREADY FAMILIAR WITH THE ENEMY.
THEY CAN ATTACK THE WHITE NINJA FROM BEHIND.
THE ENEMY AT POINT B WILL BE MOSTLY CONTAINED.
IF OUR TROOPS SUDDENLY DROP TO HALF THEIR ORIGINAL NUMBER, THE ENEMY WILL THINK WE'RE UP TO SOMETHING AND BE RELUCTANT TO MAKE A CARELESS MOVE.
AND EVEN IF THEY *WERE* TO LAUNCH AN ASSAULT, FOURTH COMPANY IS A LONG-RANGE BATTLE UNIT.

READ THIS WAY

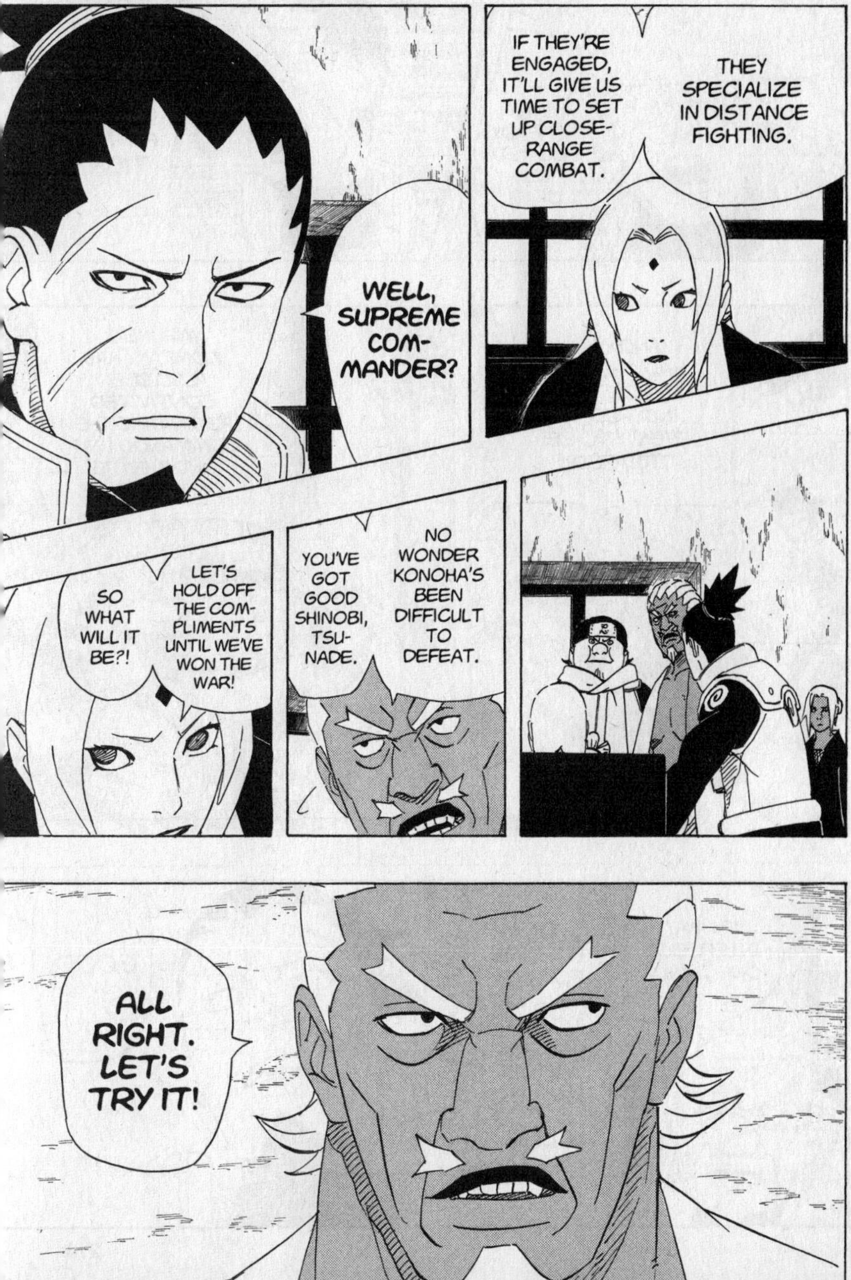
THEY SPECIALIZE IN DISTANCE FIGHTING.
IF THEY'RE ENGAGED, IT'LL GIVE US TIME TO SET UP CLOSE-RANGE COMBAT.
WELL, SUPREME COM-MANDER?
NO WONDER KONOHA'S BEEN DIFFICULT TO DEFEAT.
YOU'VE GOT GOOD SHINOBI, TSU-NADE.
LET'S HOLD OFF THE COM-PLIMENTS UNTIL WE'VE WON THE WAR!
SO WHAT WILL IT BE?!
ALL RIGHT. LET'S TRY IT!

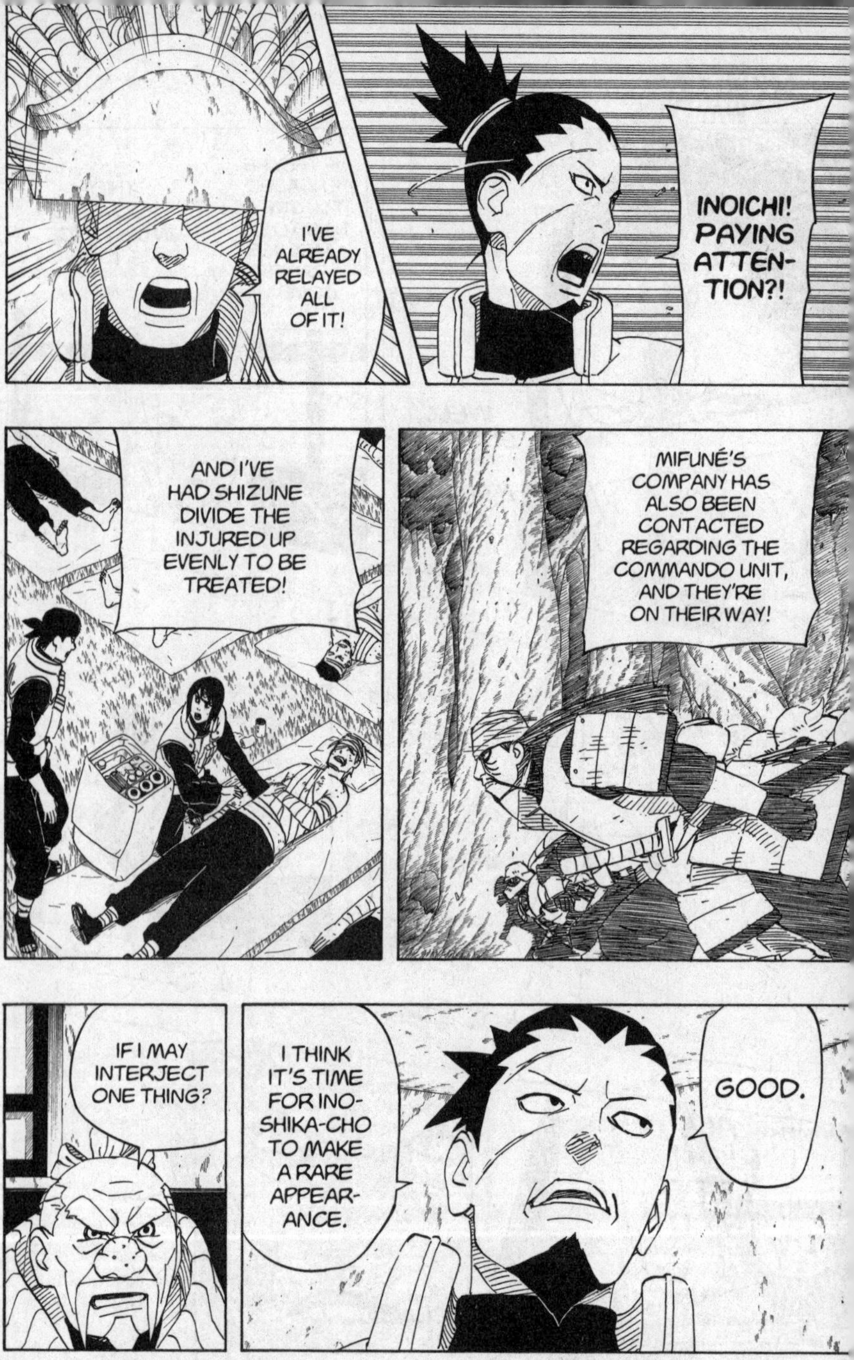
INOICHI! PAYING ATTEN-TION?!
I'VE ALREADY RELAYED ALL OF IT!
MIFUNÉ'S COMPANY HAS ALSO BEEN CONTACTED REGARDING THE COMMANDO UNIT, AND THEY'RE ON THEIR WAY!
AND I'VE HAD SHIZUNE DIVIDE THE INJURED UP EVENLY TO BE TREATED!
GOOD.
I THINK IT'S TIME FOR INO-SHIKA-CHO TO MAKE A RARE APPEAR-ANCE.
IF I MAY INTERJECT ONE THING?

READ THIS WAY

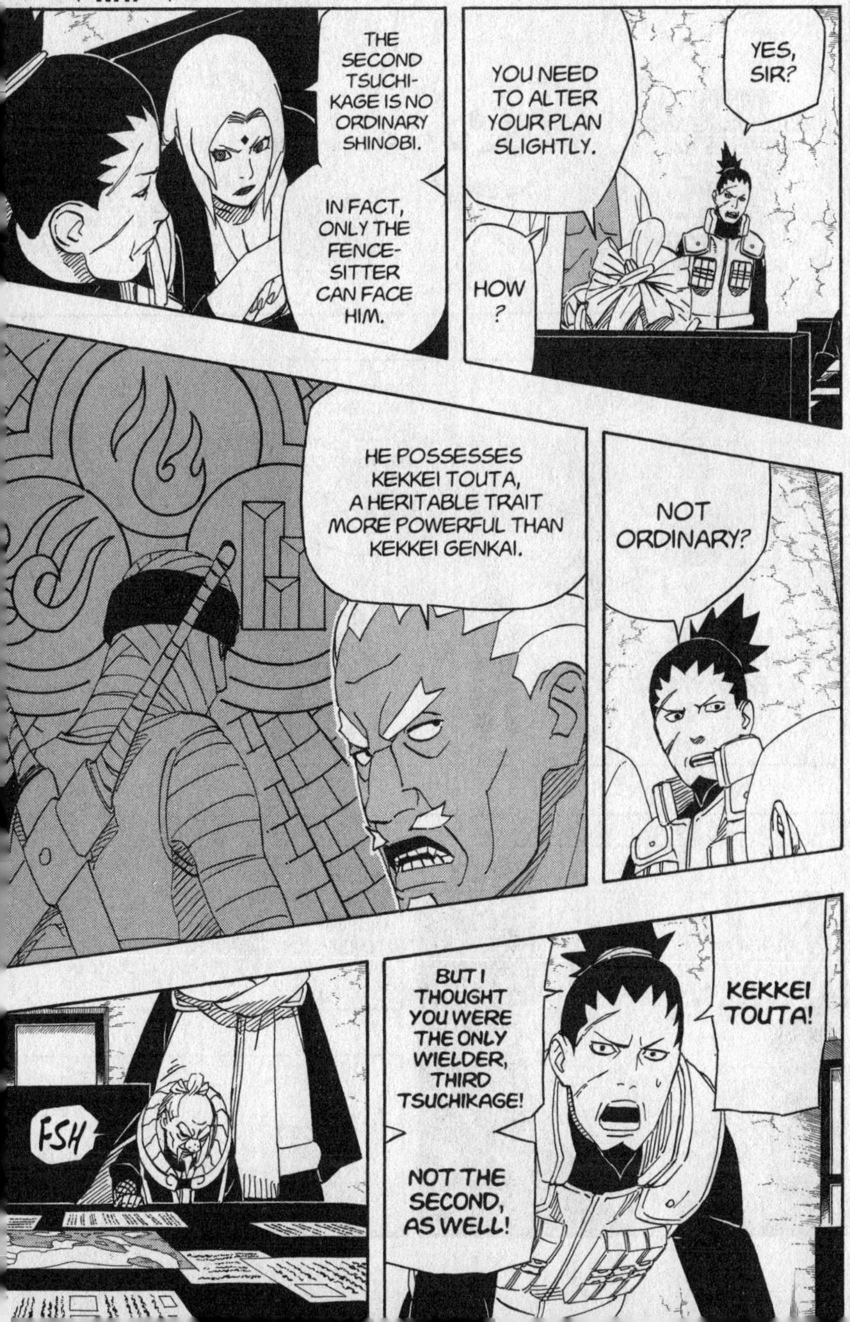
YES, SIR?
YOU NEED TO ALTER YOUR PLAN SLIGHTLY.
HOW?
THE SECOND TSUCHI-KAGE IS NO ORDINARY SHINOBI.
IN FACT, ONLY THE FENCE-SITTER CAN FACE HIM.
NOT ORDINARY?
HE POSSESSES KEKKEI TOUTA, A HERITABLE TRAIT MORE POWERFUL THAN KEKKEI GENKAI.
KEKKEI TOUTA!
BUT I THOUGHT YOU WERE THE ONLY WIELDER, THIRD TSUCHIKAGE!
NOT THE SECOND, AS WELL!
FSH

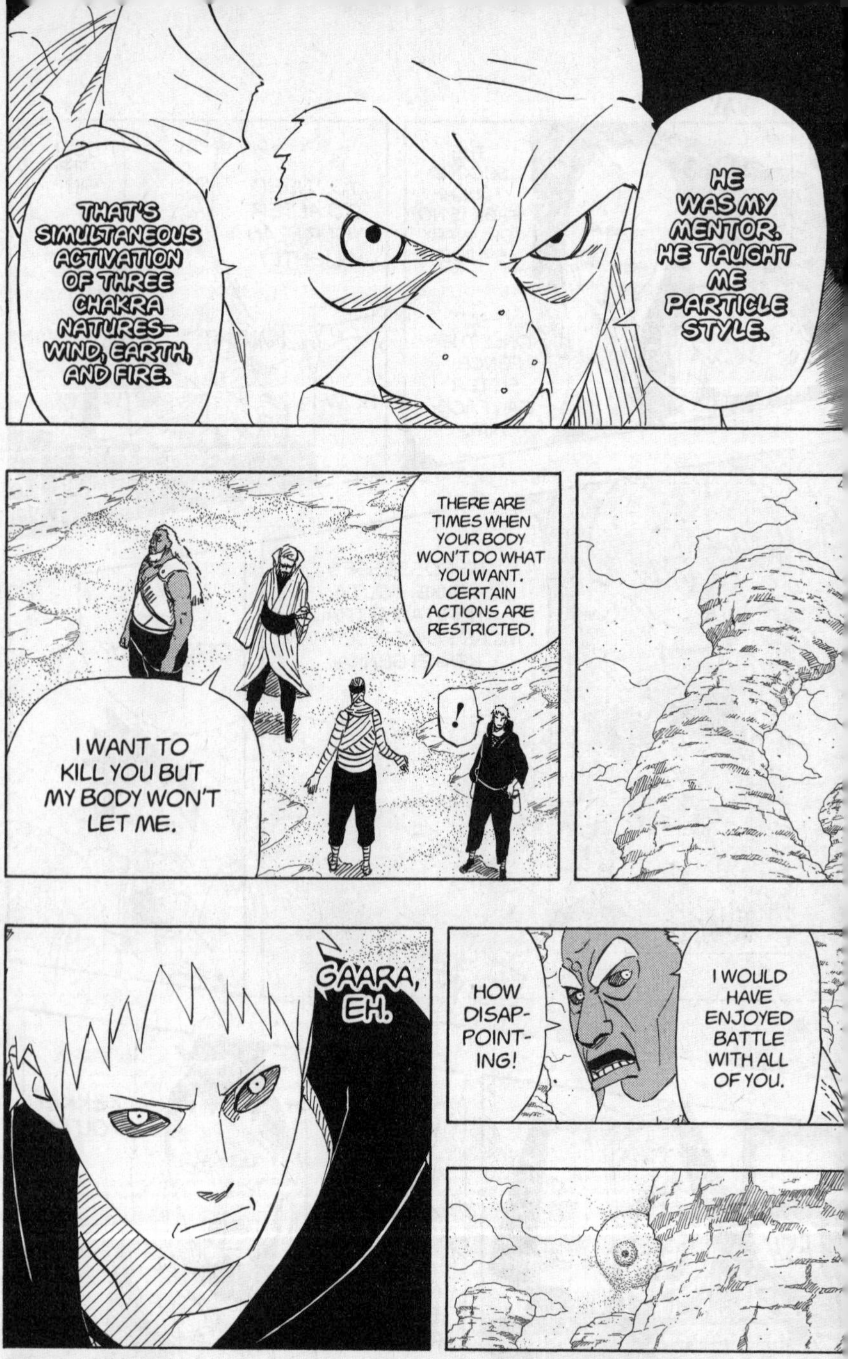
HE WAS MY MENTOR. HE TAUGHT ME PARTICLE STYLE.
THAT'S SIMULTANEOUS ACTIVATION OF THREE CHAKRA NATURES—WIND, EARTH, AND FIRE.
THERE ARE TIMES WHEN YOUR BODY WON'T DO WHAT YOU WANT. CERTAIN ACTIONS ARE RESTRICTED.
!
I WANT TO KILL YOU BUT MY BODY WON'T LET ME.
I WOULD HAVE ENJOYED BATTLE WITH ALL OF YOU.
HOW DISAPPOINTING!
GAARA, EH.

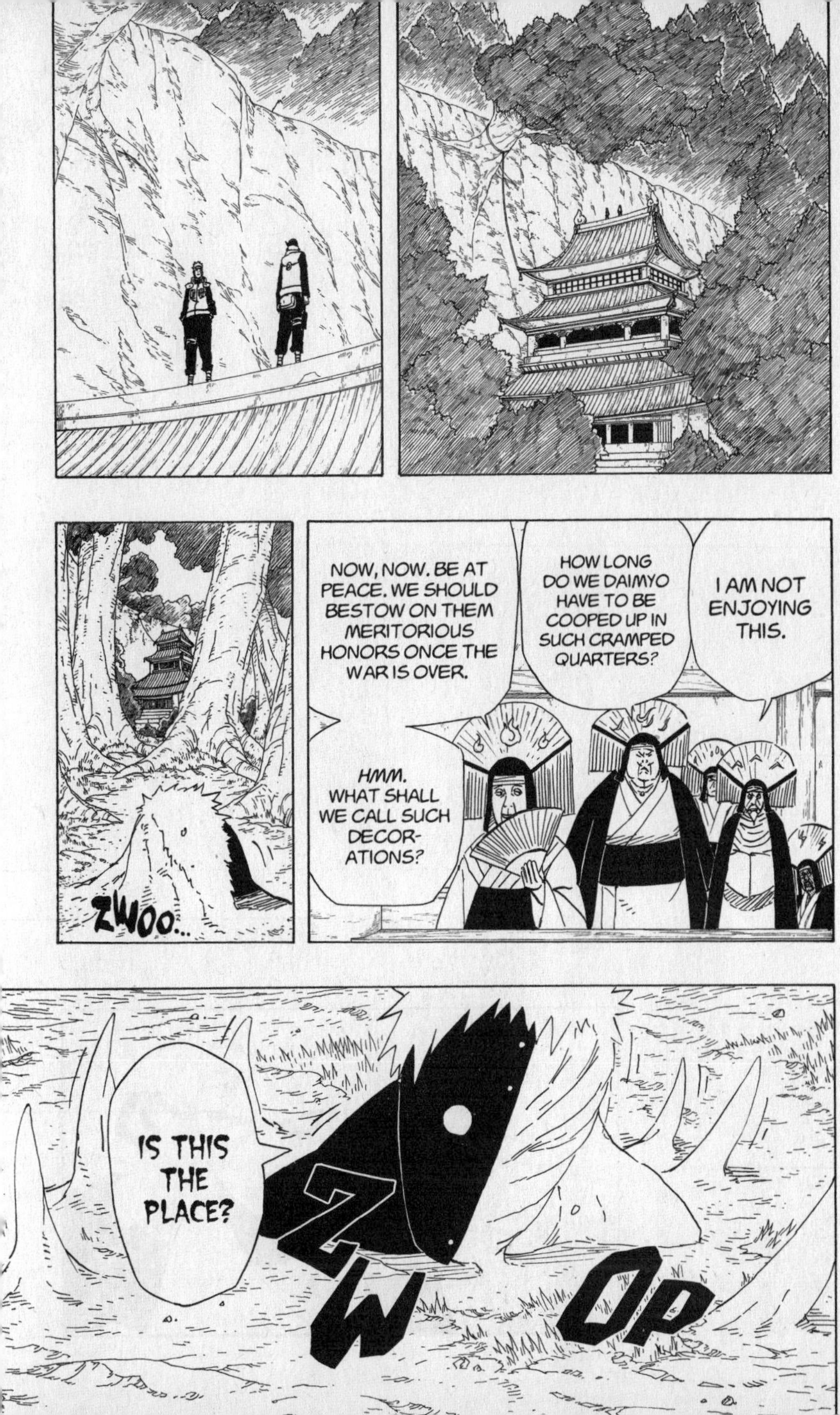
I AM NOT ENJOYING THIS.
HOW LONG DO WE DAIMYO HAVE TO BE COOPED UP IN SUCH CRAMPED QUARTERS?
NOW, NOW. BE AT PEACE. WE SHOULD BESTOW ON THEM MERITORIOUS HONORS ONCE THE WAR IS OVER.
HMM. WHAT SHALL WE CALL SUCH DECOR-ATIONS?
ZWOO...
ZWOOP
IS THIS THE PLACE?

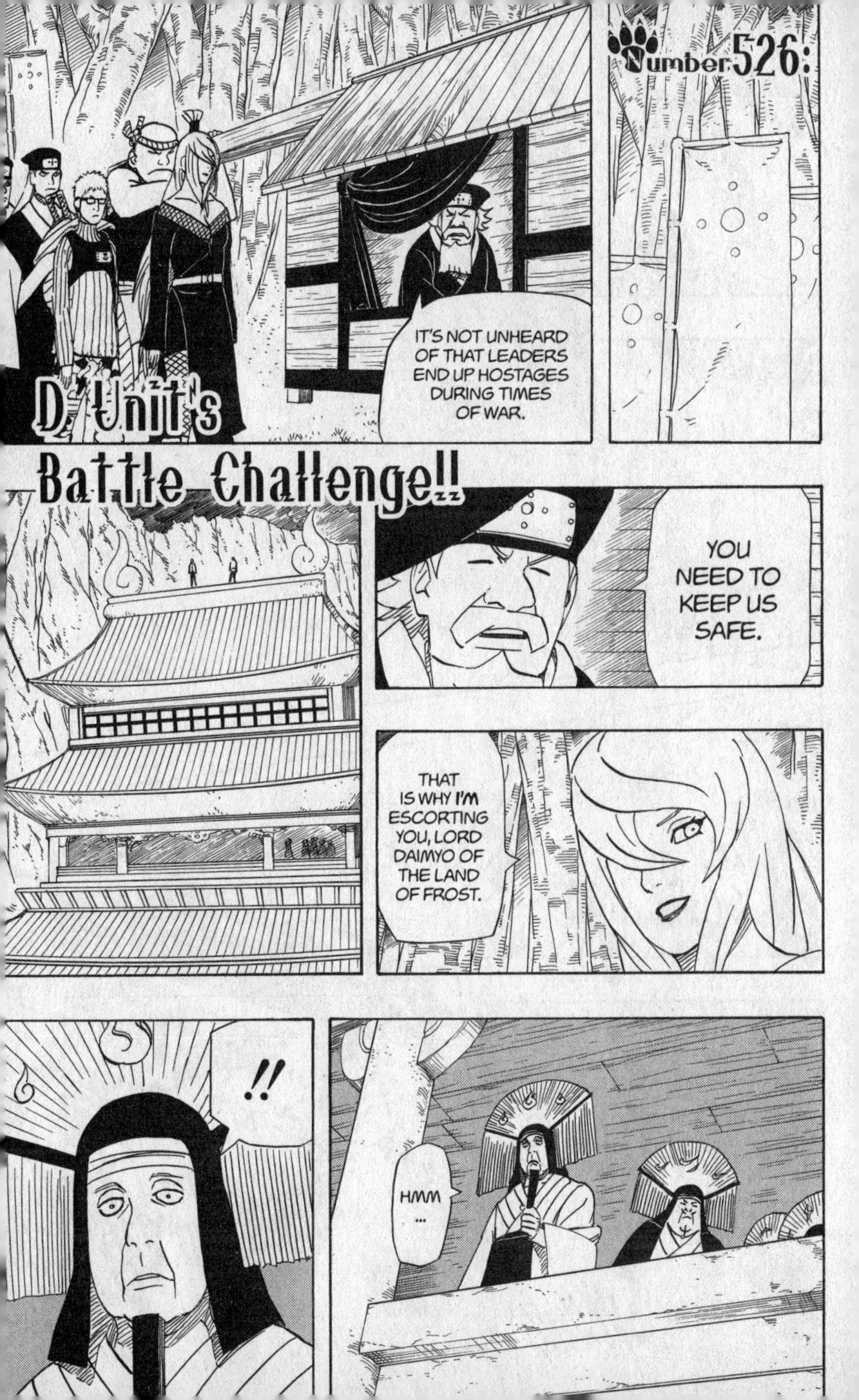
Number 526:
D Unit's Battle Challenge!!
IT'S NOT UNHEARD OF THAT LEADERS END UP HOSTAGES DURING TIMES OF WAR.
YOU NEED TO KEEP US SAFE.
THAT IS WHY I'M ESCORTING YOU, LORD DAIMYO OF THE LAND OF FROST.
HMM ...
!!

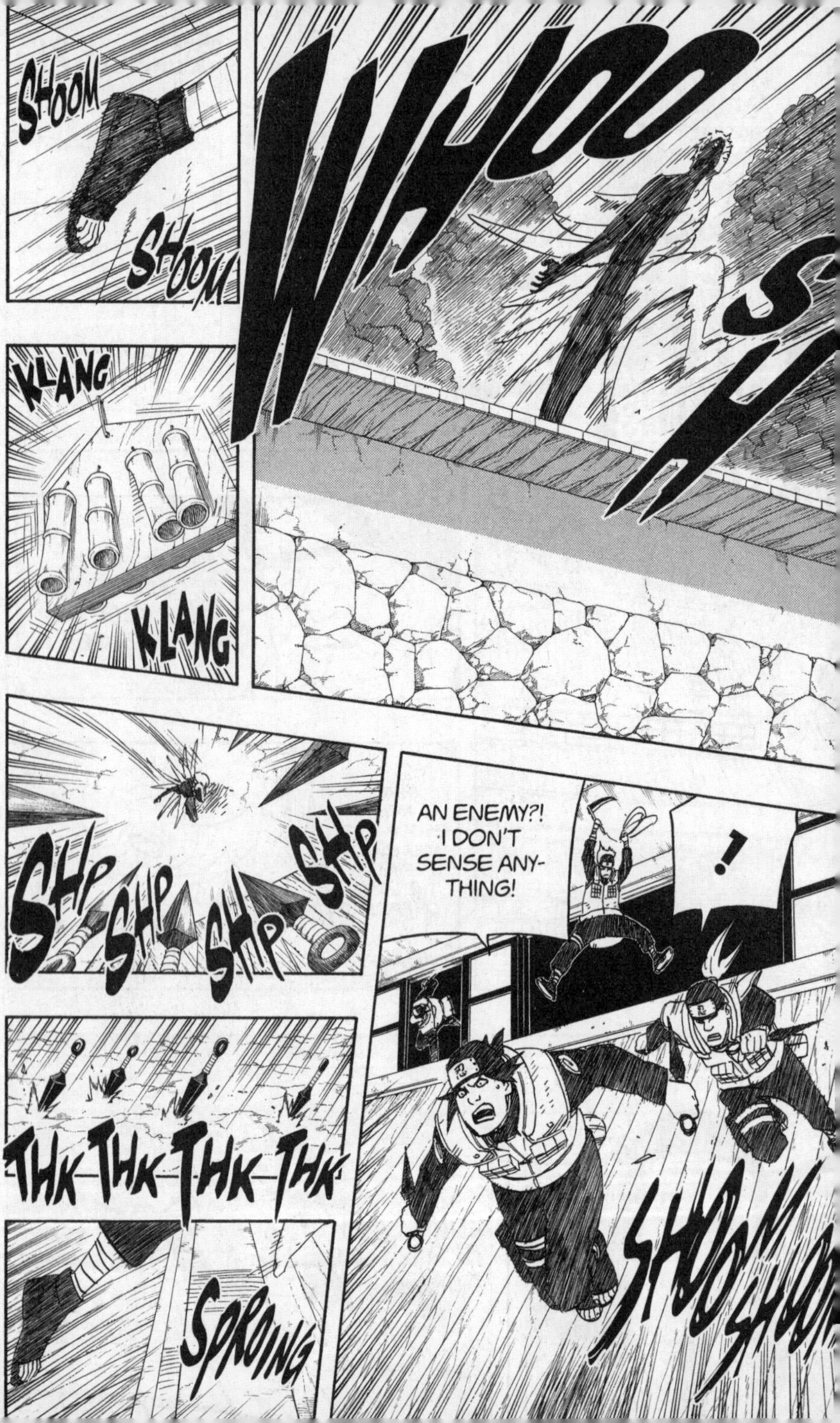
WHOOSH
SHOOM
SHOOM
KLANG
KLANG
AN ENEMY?! I DON'T SENSE ANYTHING!
!
SHOOM SHOOM
SHP SHP SHP SHP
THK THK THK THK
SPROING

READ THIS WAY

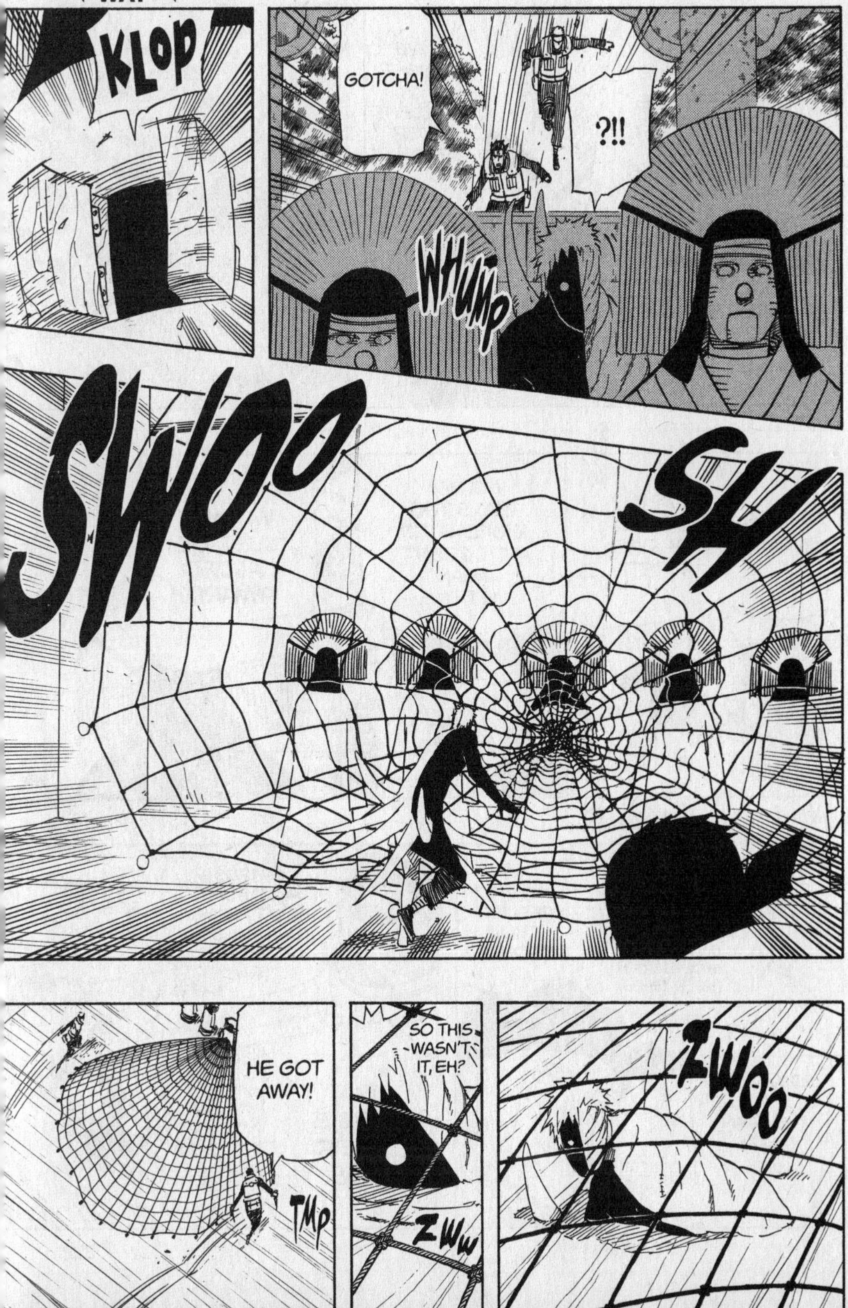

GOTCHA!
?!!
WHUMP
KLOP
SWOOSH
ZWOO
SO THIS WASN'T IT, EH?
ZWW
HE GOT AWAY!
TMP

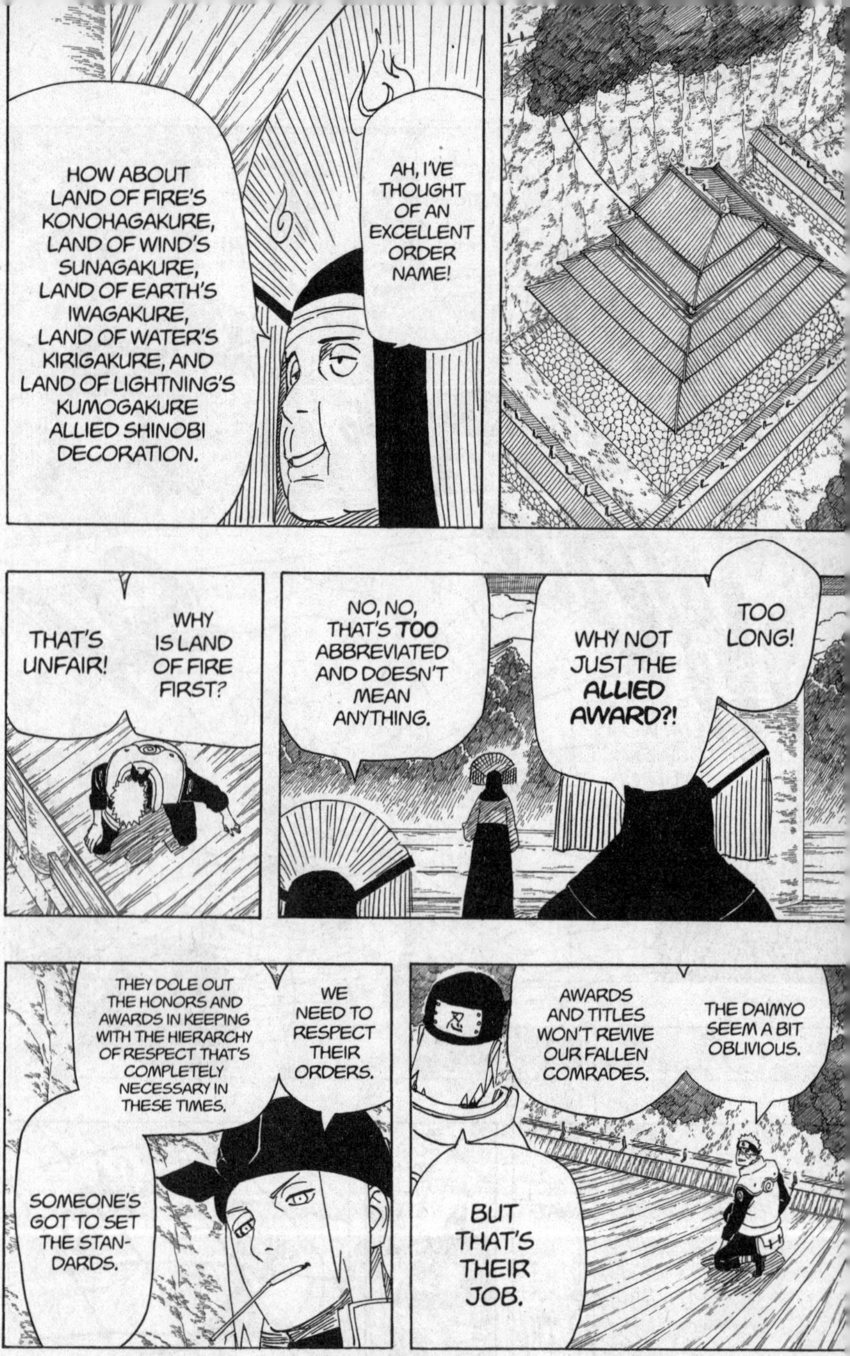
AH, I'VE THOUGHT OF AN EXCELLENT ORDER NAME!
HOW ABOUT LAND OF FIRE'S KONOHAGAKURE, LAND OF WIND'S SUNAGAKURE, LAND OF EARTH'S IWAGAKURE, LAND OF WATER'S KIRIGAKURE, AND LAND OF LIGHTNING'S KUMOGAKURE ALLIED SHINOBI DECORATION.
TOO LONG!
WHY NOT JUST THE **ALLIED AWARD**?!
NO, NO, THAT'S **TOO** ABBREVIATED AND DOESN'T MEAN ANYTHING.
WHY IS LAND OF FIRE FIRST?
THAT'S UNFAIR!
THE DAIMYO SEEM A BIT OBLIVIOUS.
AWARDS AND TITLES WON'T REVIVE OUR FALLEN COMRADES.
BUT THAT'S THEIR JOB.
WE NEED TO RESPECT THEIR ORDERS.
THEY DOLE OUT THE HONORS AND AWARDS IN KEEPING WITH THE HIERARCHY OF RESPECT THAT'S COMPLETELY NECESSARY IN THESE TIMES.
SOMEONE'S GOT TO SET THE STAN-DARDS.

READ THIS WAY

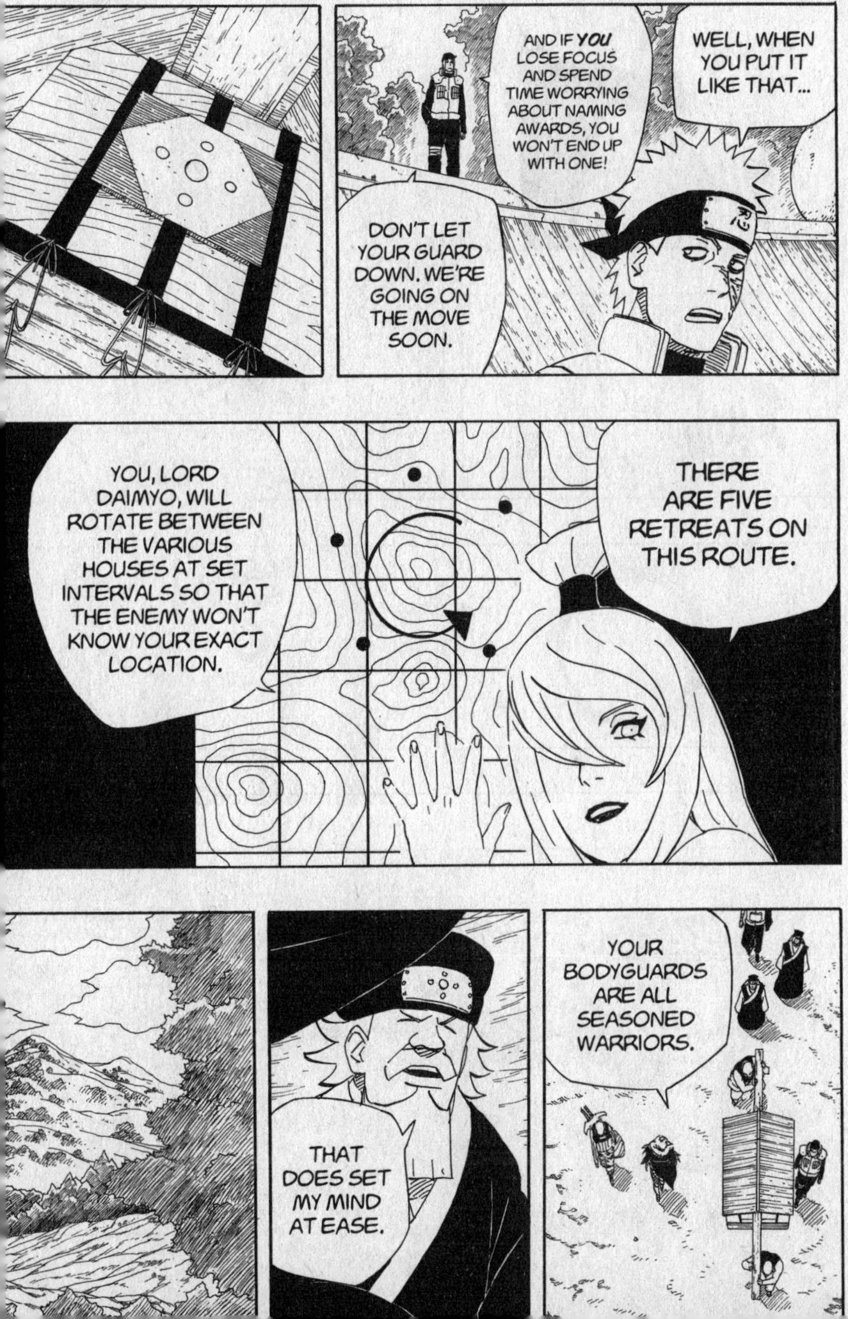
WELL, WHEN YOU PUT IT LIKE THAT...
AND IF *YOU* LOSE FOCUS AND SPEND TIME WORRYING ABOUT NAMING AWARDS, YOU WON'T END UP WITH ONE!
DON'T LET YOUR GUARD DOWN. WE'RE GOING ON THE MOVE SOON.
THERE ARE FIVE RETREATS ON THIS ROUTE.
YOU, LORD DAIMYO, WILL ROTATE BETWEEN THE VARIOUS HOUSES AT SET INTERVALS SO THAT THE ENEMY WON'T KNOW YOUR EXACT LOCATION.
YOUR BODYGUARDS ARE ALL SEASONED WARRIORS.
THAT DOES SET MY MIND AT EASE.

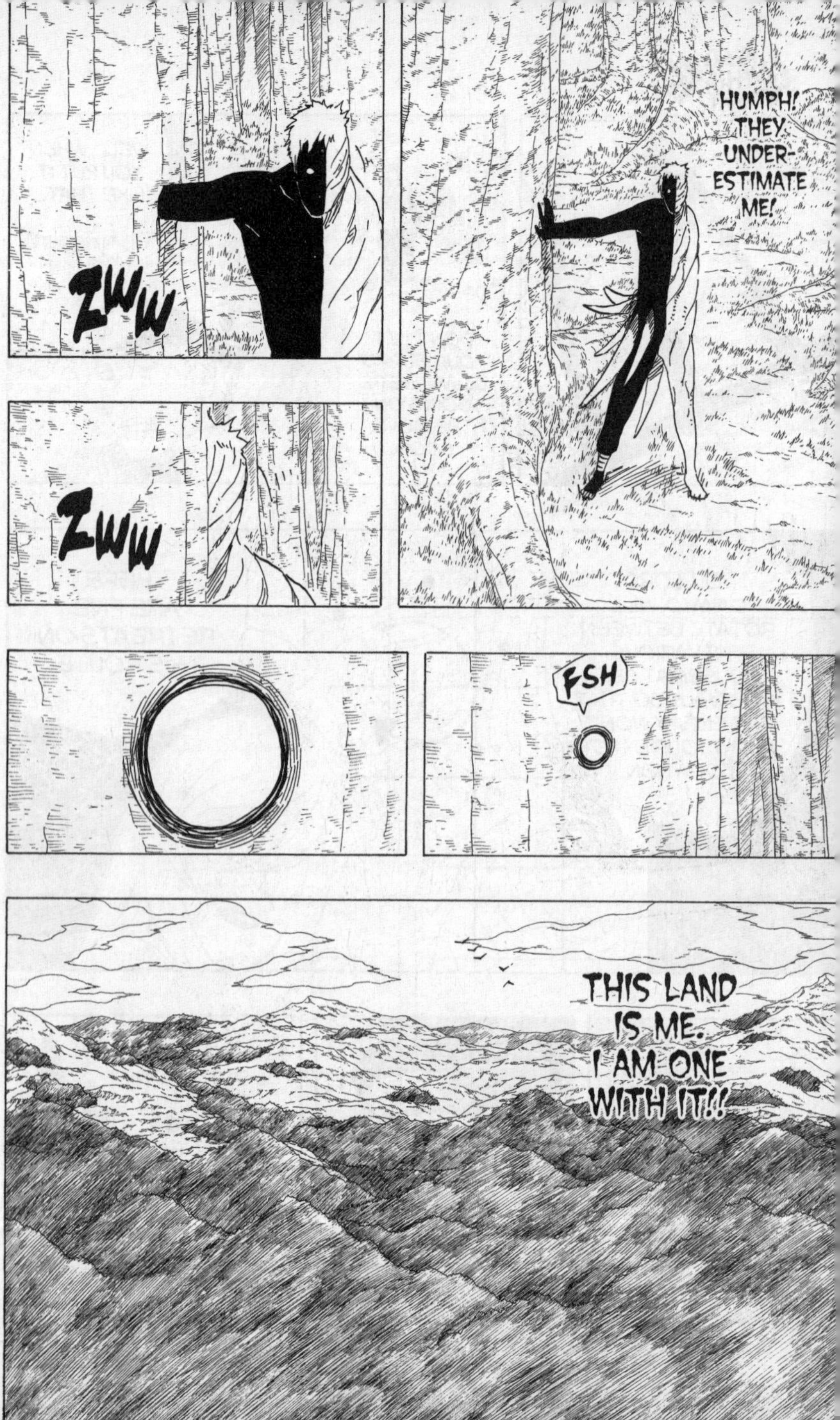
HUMPH! THEY UNDER-ESTIMATE ME!
ZWW
ZWW
FSH
THIS LAND IS ME. I AM ONE WITH IT!!

READ THIS WAY

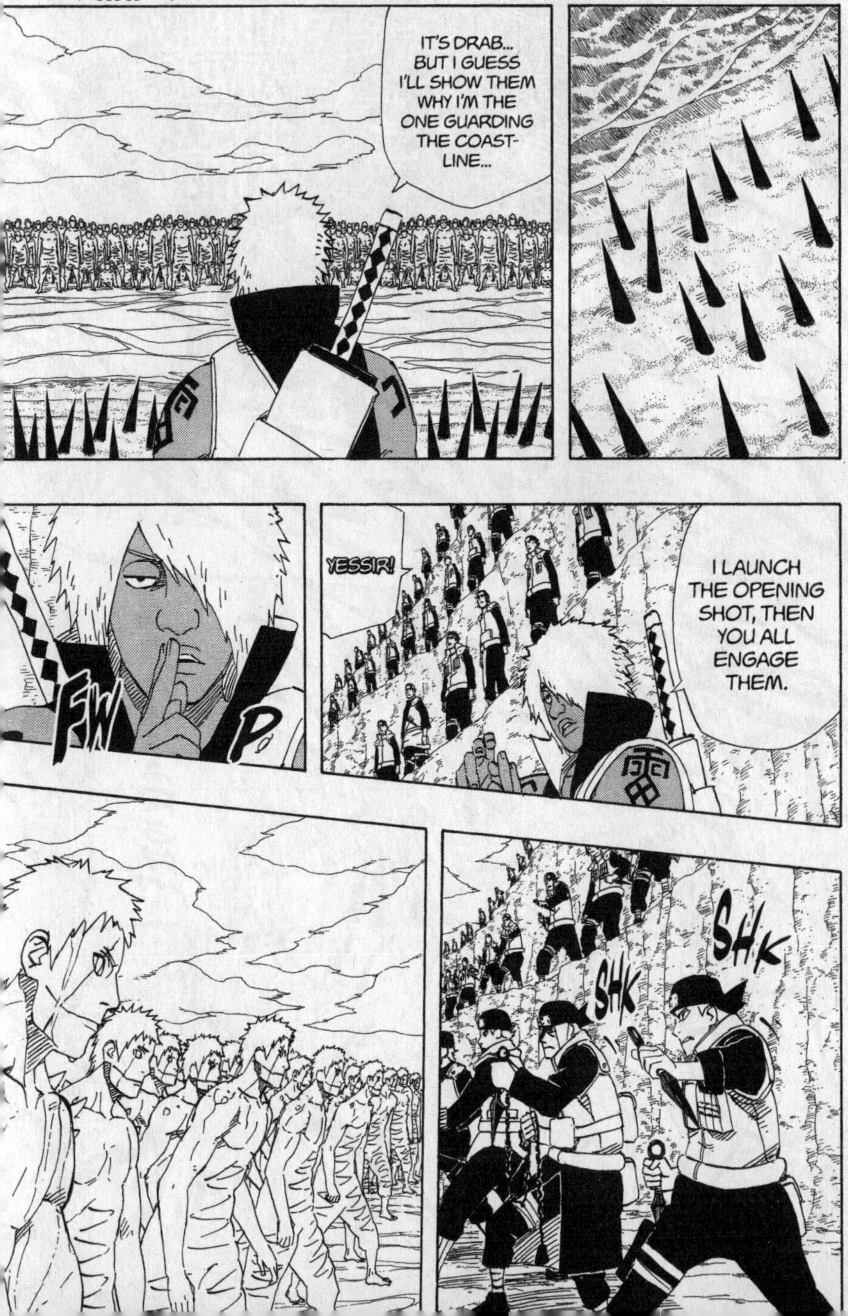
IT'S DRAB... BUT I GUESS I'LL SHOW THEM WHY I'M THE ONE GUARDING THE COAST-LINE...
I LAUNCH THE OPENING SHOT, THEN YOU ALL ENGAGE THEM.
YESSIR!
FWP
SHK
SHK

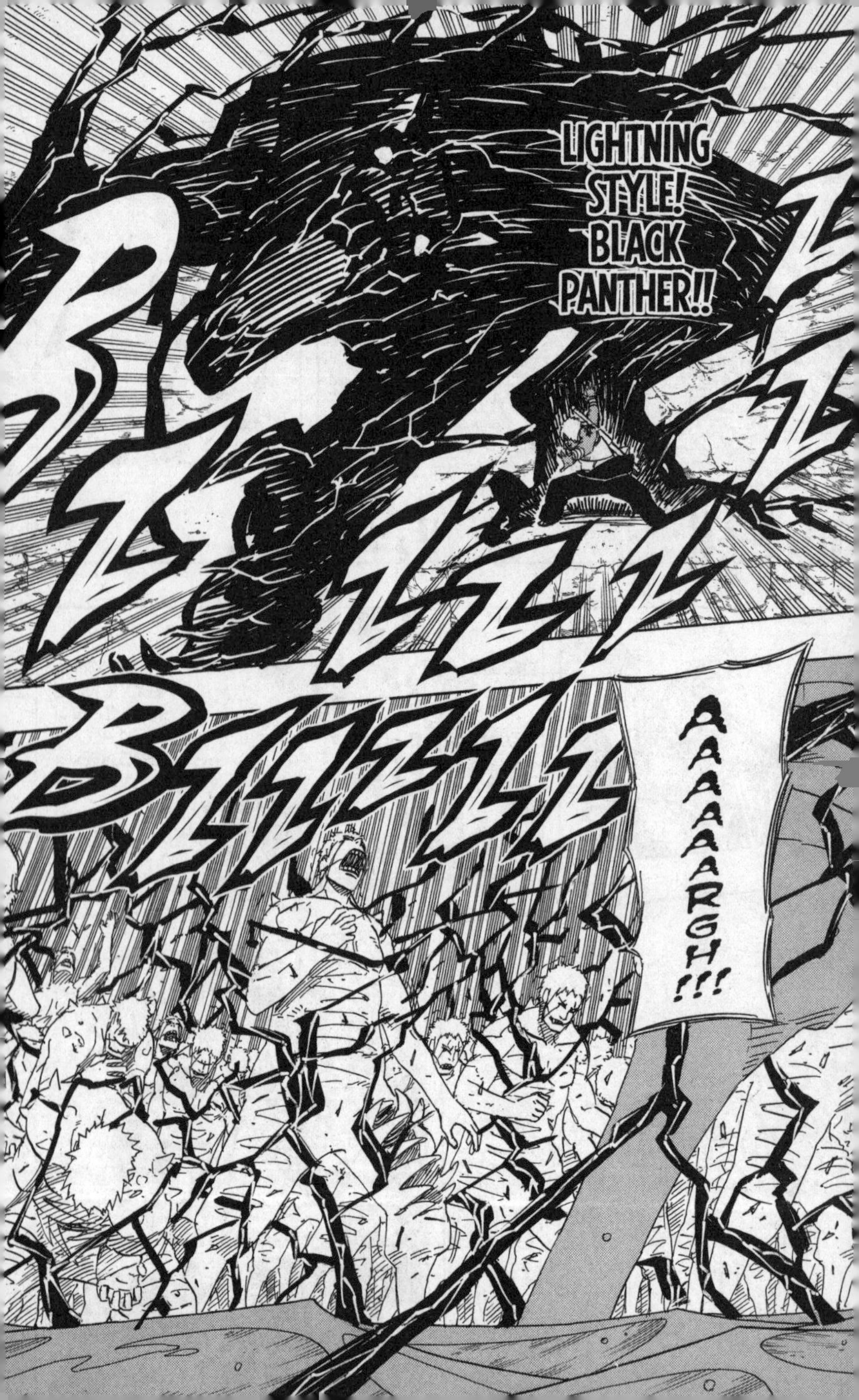
LIGHTNING STYLE! BLACK PANTHER!!
AAAAAARGH!!!

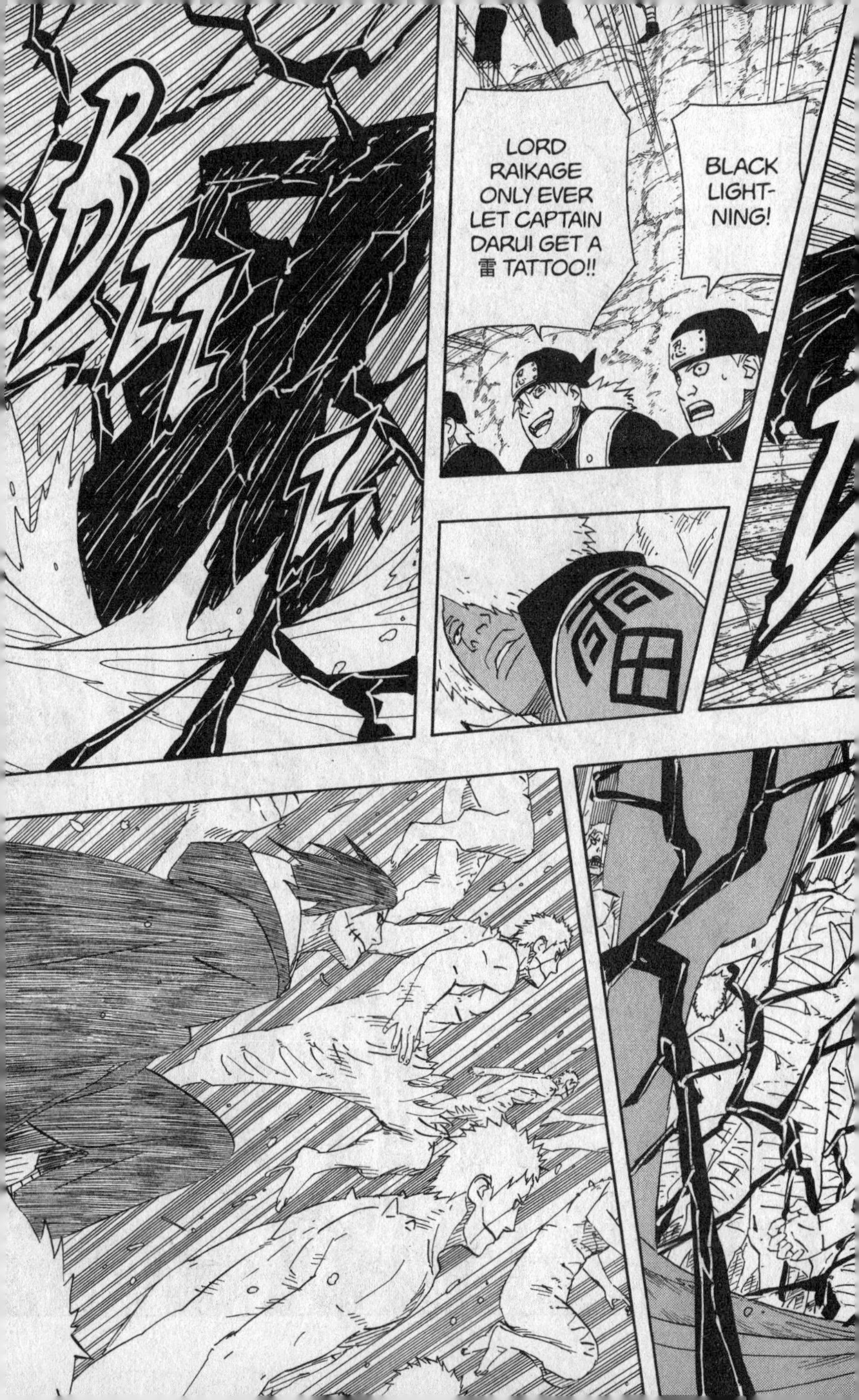

BLACK LIGHT-NING!
LORD RAIKAGE ONLY EVER LET CAPTAIN DARUI GET A 雷 TATTOO!!

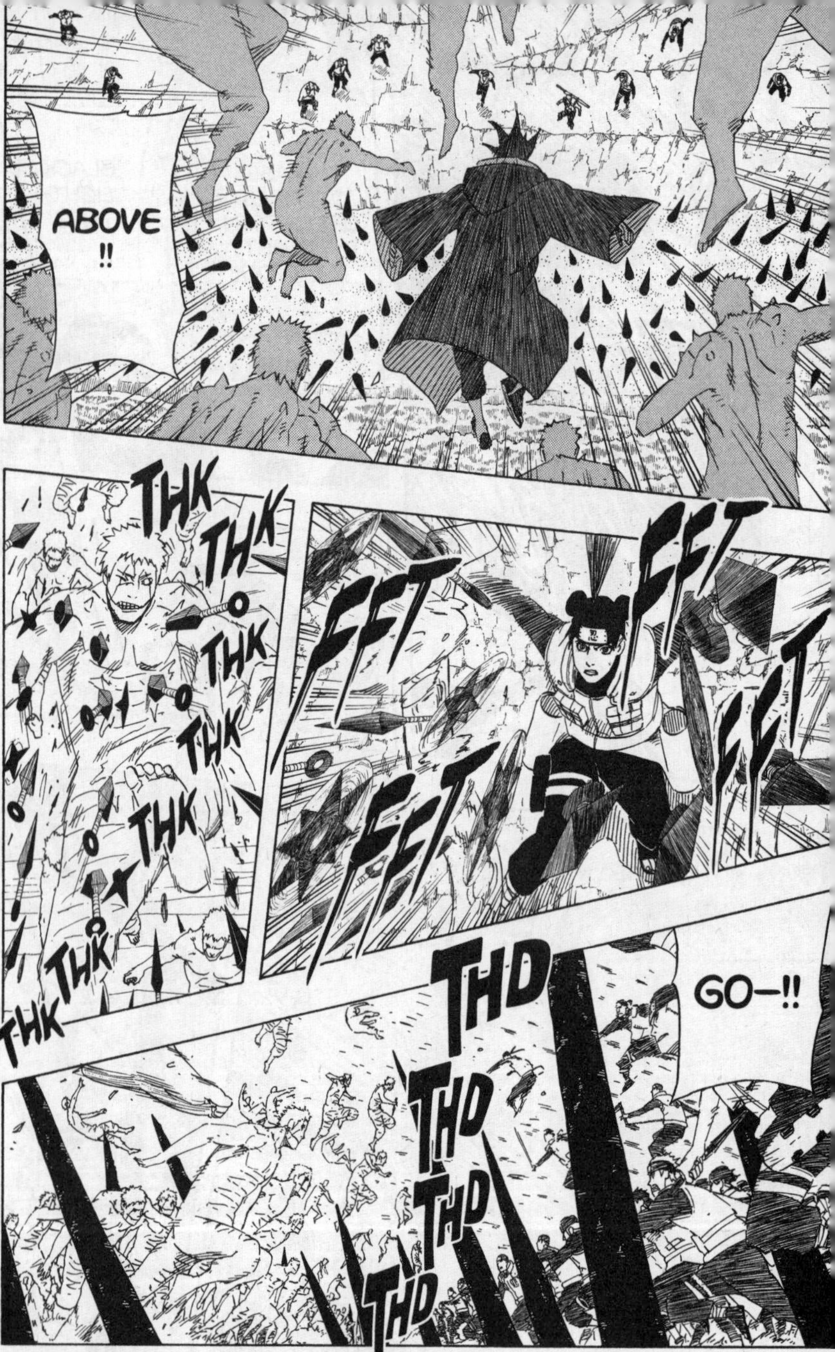

ABOVE !!
FFT
FFT
FFT
FFT
THK
THK
THK
THK
THK
THK
THK
GO-!!
THD
THD
THD
THD

READ THIS WAY

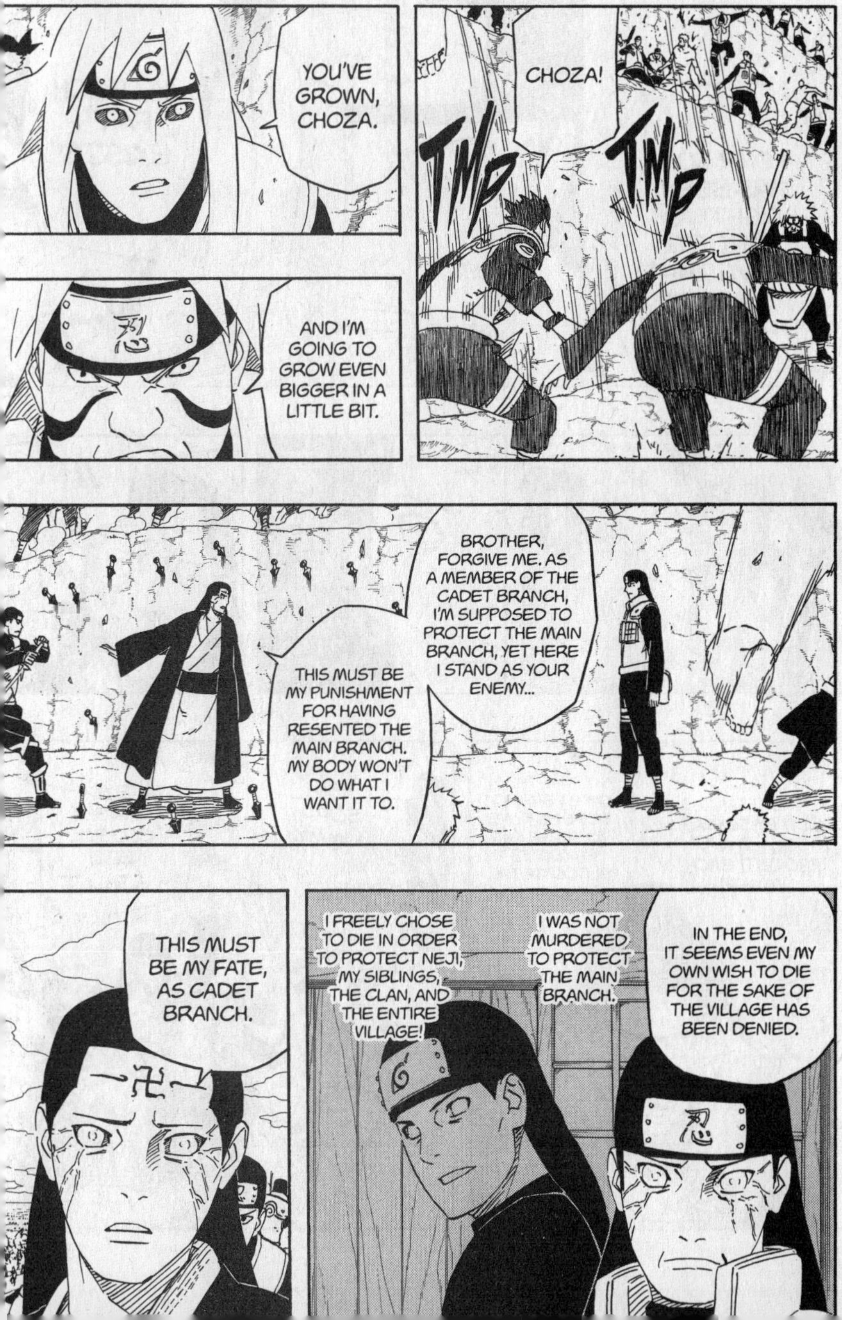
CHOZA!
TMP
TMP
YOU'VE GROWN, CHOZA.
AND I'M GOING TO GROW EVEN BIGGER IN A LITTLE BIT.
BROTHER, FORGIVE ME. AS A MEMBER OF THE CADET BRANCH, I'M SUPPOSED TO PROTECT THE MAIN BRANCH, YET HERE I STAND AS YOUR ENEMY...
THIS MUST BE MY PUNISHMENT FOR HAVING RESENTED THE MAIN BRANCH. MY BODY WON'T DO WHAT I WANT IT TO.
IN THE END, IT SEEMS EVEN MY OWN WISH TO DIE FOR THE SAKE OF THE VILLAGE HAS BEEN DENIED.
I WAS NOT MURDERED TO PROTECT THE MAIN BRANCH.
I FREELY CHOSE TO DIE IN ORDER TO PROTECT NEJI, MY SIBLINGS, THE CLAN, AND THE ENTIRE VILLAGE!
THIS MUST BE MY FATE, AS CADET BRANCH.

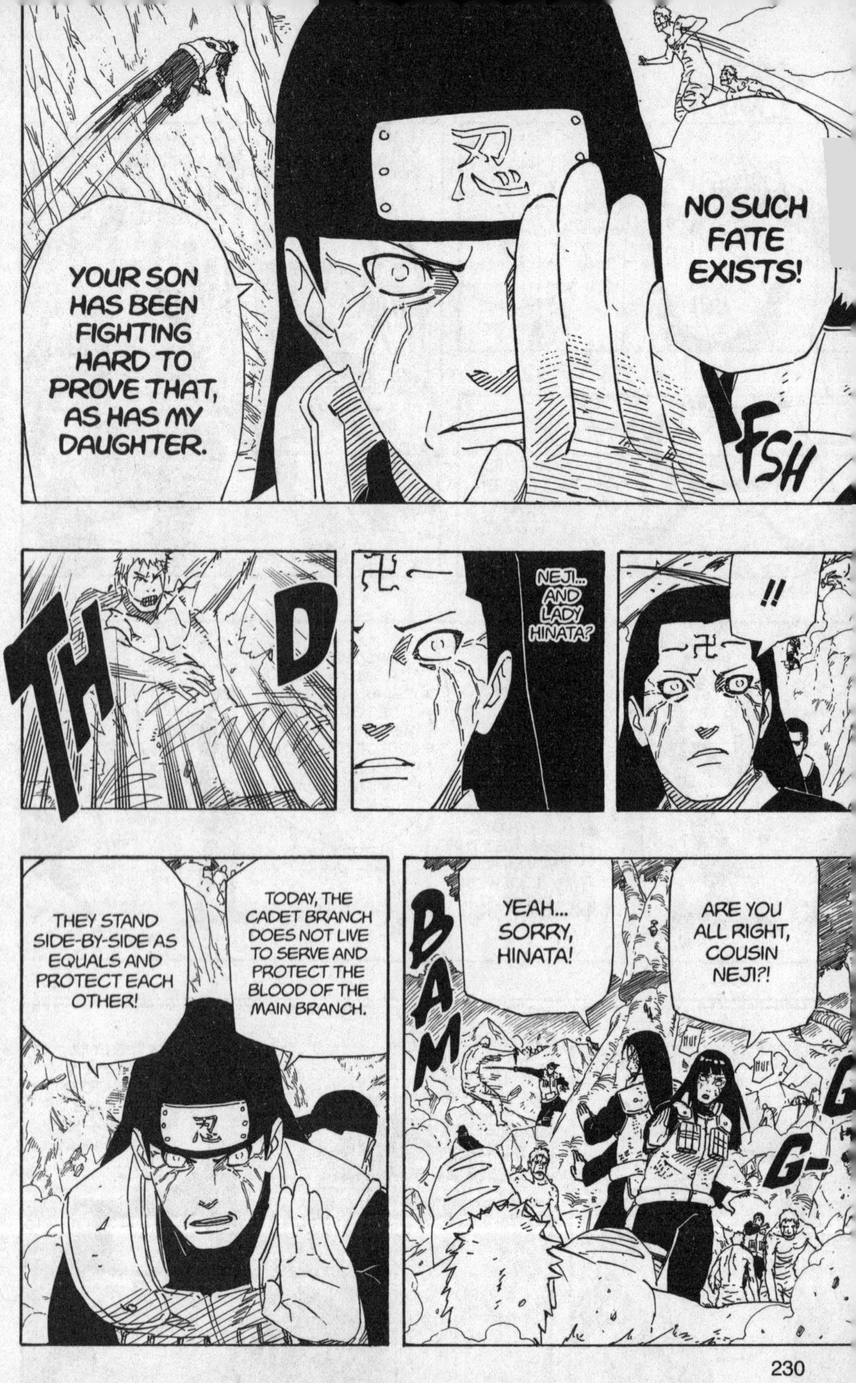
NO SUCH FATE EXISTS!
YOUR SON HAS BEEN FIGHTING HARD TO PROVE THAT, AS HAS MY DAUGHTER.
FSH
!!
NEJI... AND LADY HINATA?
THD
ARE YOU ALL RIGHT, COUSIN NEJI?!
G-
YEAH... SORRY, HINATA!
HUF
HUF
BAM
TODAY, THE CADET BRANCH DOES NOT LIVE TO SERVE AND PROTECT THE BLOOD OF THE MAIN BRANCH.
THEY STAND SIDE-BY-SIDE AS EQUALS AND PROTECT EACH OTHER!

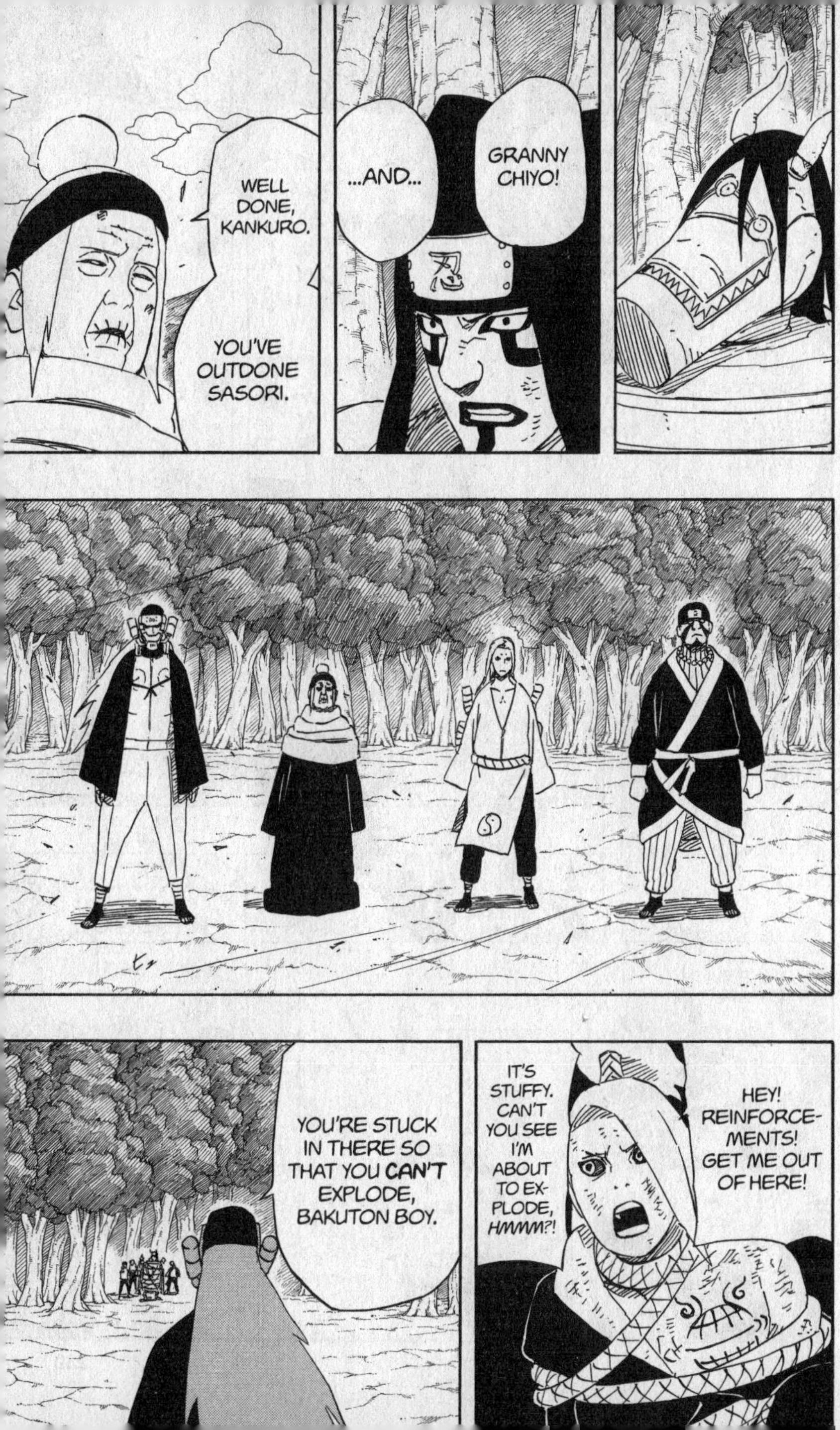

GRANNY CHIYO!
...AND...
WELL DONE, KANKURO.
YOU'VE OUTDONE SASORI.
HEY! REINFORCE-MENTS! GET ME OUT OF HERE!
IT'S STUFFY. CAN'T YOU SEE I'M ABOUT TO EX-PLODE, *HMMM?!*
YOU'RE STUCK IN THERE SO THAT YOU **CAN'T** EXPLODE, BAKUTON BOY.

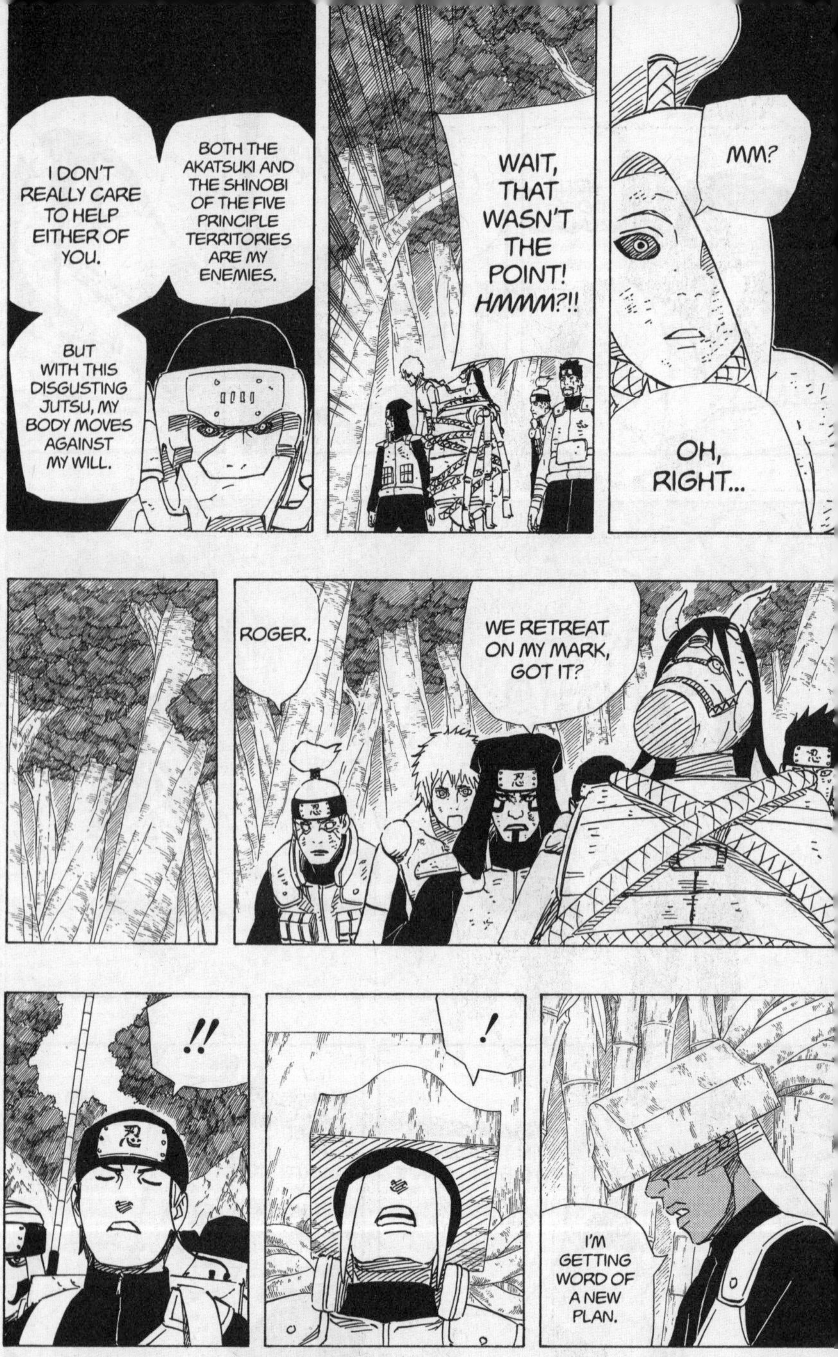
MM?
OH, RIGHT...
WAIT, THAT WASN'T THE POINT! *HMMM?!!*
BOTH THE AKATSUKI AND THE SHINOBI OF THE FIVE PRINCIPLE TERRITORIES ARE MY ENEMIES.
I DON'T REALLY CARE TO HELP EITHER OF YOU.
BUT WITH THIS DISGUSTING JUTSU, MY BODY MOVES AGAINST MY WILL.
WE RETREAT ON MY MARK, GOT IT?
ROGER.
I'M GETTING WORD OF A NEW PLAN.
!
!!

READ THIS WAY

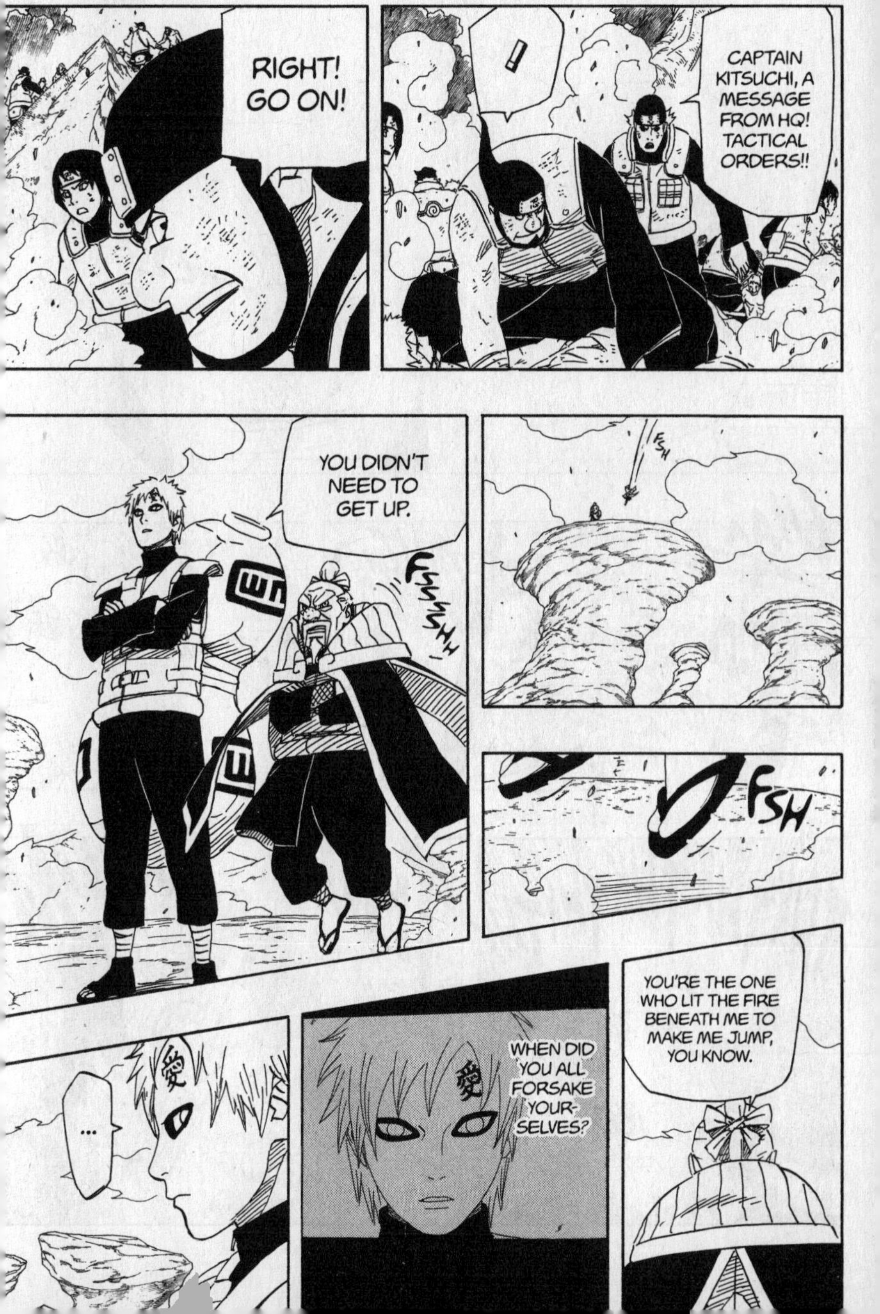
CAPTAIN KITSUCHI, A MESSAGE FROM HQ! TACTICAL ORDERS!!
!
RIGHT! GO ON!
FSH
FSH
YOU DIDN'T NEED TO GET UP.
FSSSHH
YOU'RE THE ONE WHO LIT THE FIRE BENEATH ME TO MAKE ME JUMP, YOU KNOW.
WHEN DID YOU ALL FORSAKE YOURSELVES?
...

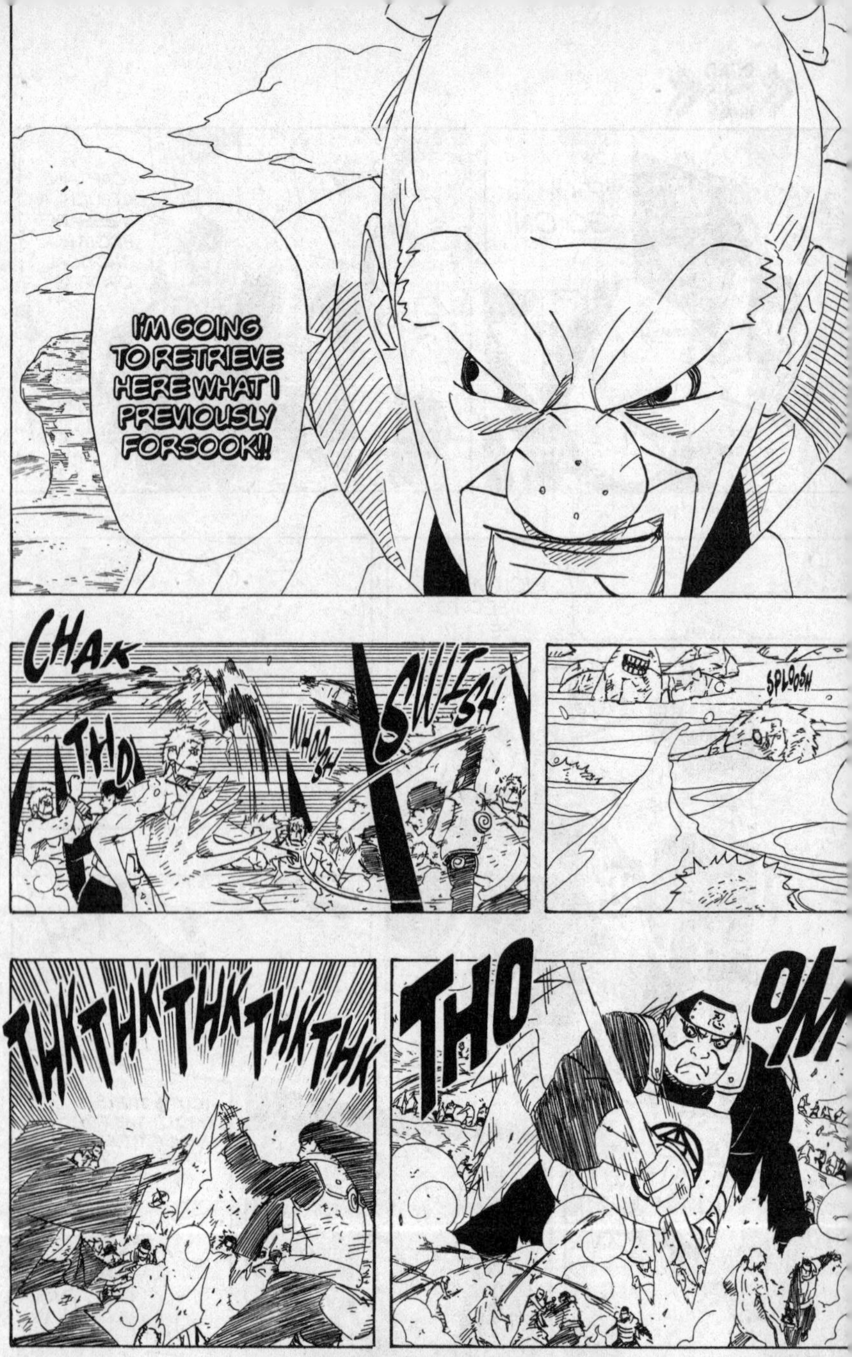
I'M GOING TO RETRIEVE HERE WHAT I PREVIOUSLY FORSOOK!!
SPLOOSH
CHAK
THD
WHOOSH
SWISH
THOOM
THKTHKTHKTHKTHK

READ THIS WAY

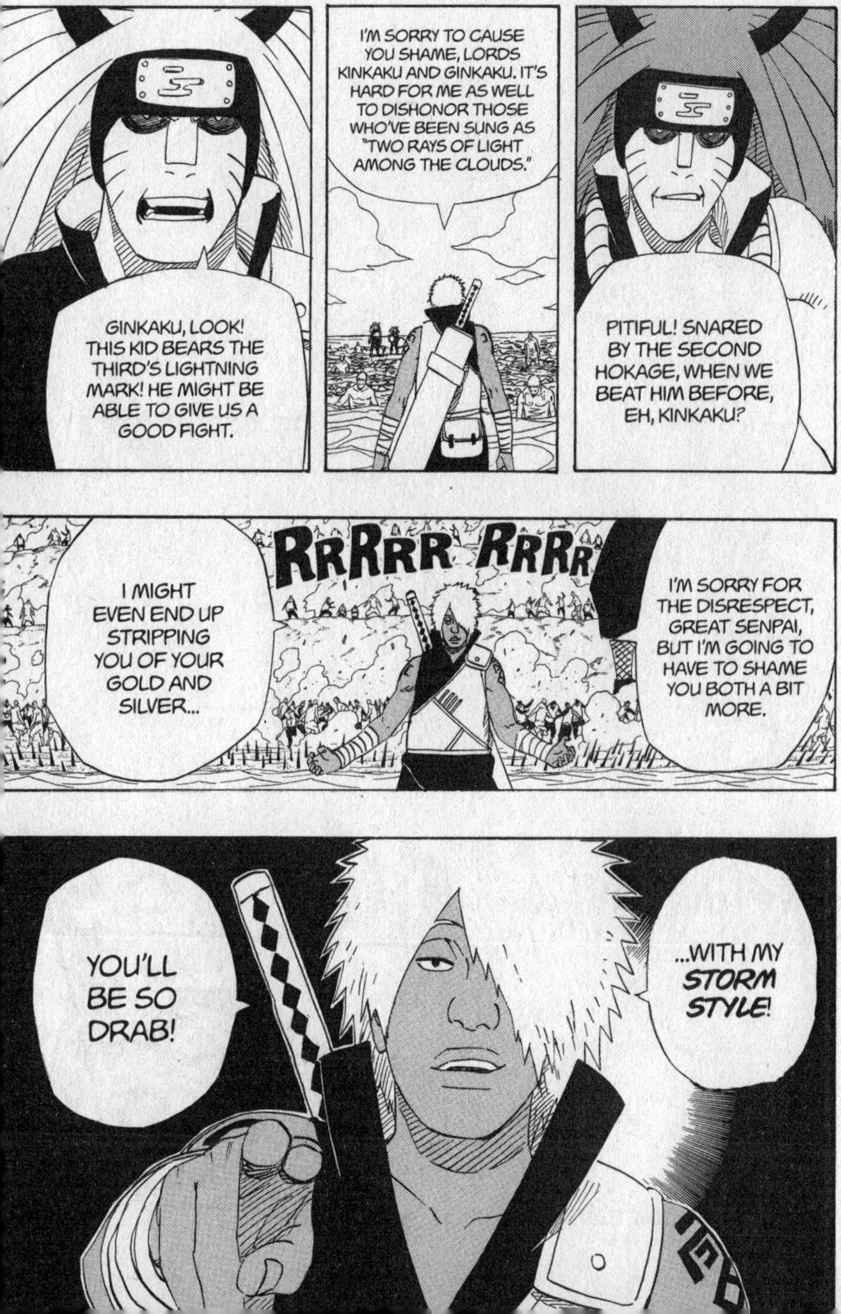
PITIFUL! SNARED BY THE SECOND HOKAGE, WHEN WE BEAT HIM BEFORE, EH, KINKAKU?
I'M SORRY TO CAUSE YOU SHAME, LORDS KINKAKU AND GINKAKU. IT'S HARD FOR ME AS WELL TO DISHONOR THOSE WHO'VE BEEN SUNG AS "TWO RAYS OF LIGHT AMONG THE CLOUDS."
GINKAKU, LOOK! THIS KID BEARS THE THIRD'S LIGHTNING MARK! HE MIGHT BE ABLE TO GIVE US A GOOD FIGHT.
I'M SORRY FOR THE DISRESPECT, GREAT SENPAI, BUT I'M GOING TO HAVE TO SHAME YOU BOTH A BIT MORE.
RRRRR RRRR
I MIGHT EVEN END UP STRIPPING YOU OF YOUR GOLD AND SILVER...
...WITH MY **STORM STYLE**!
YOU'LL BE SO DRAB!

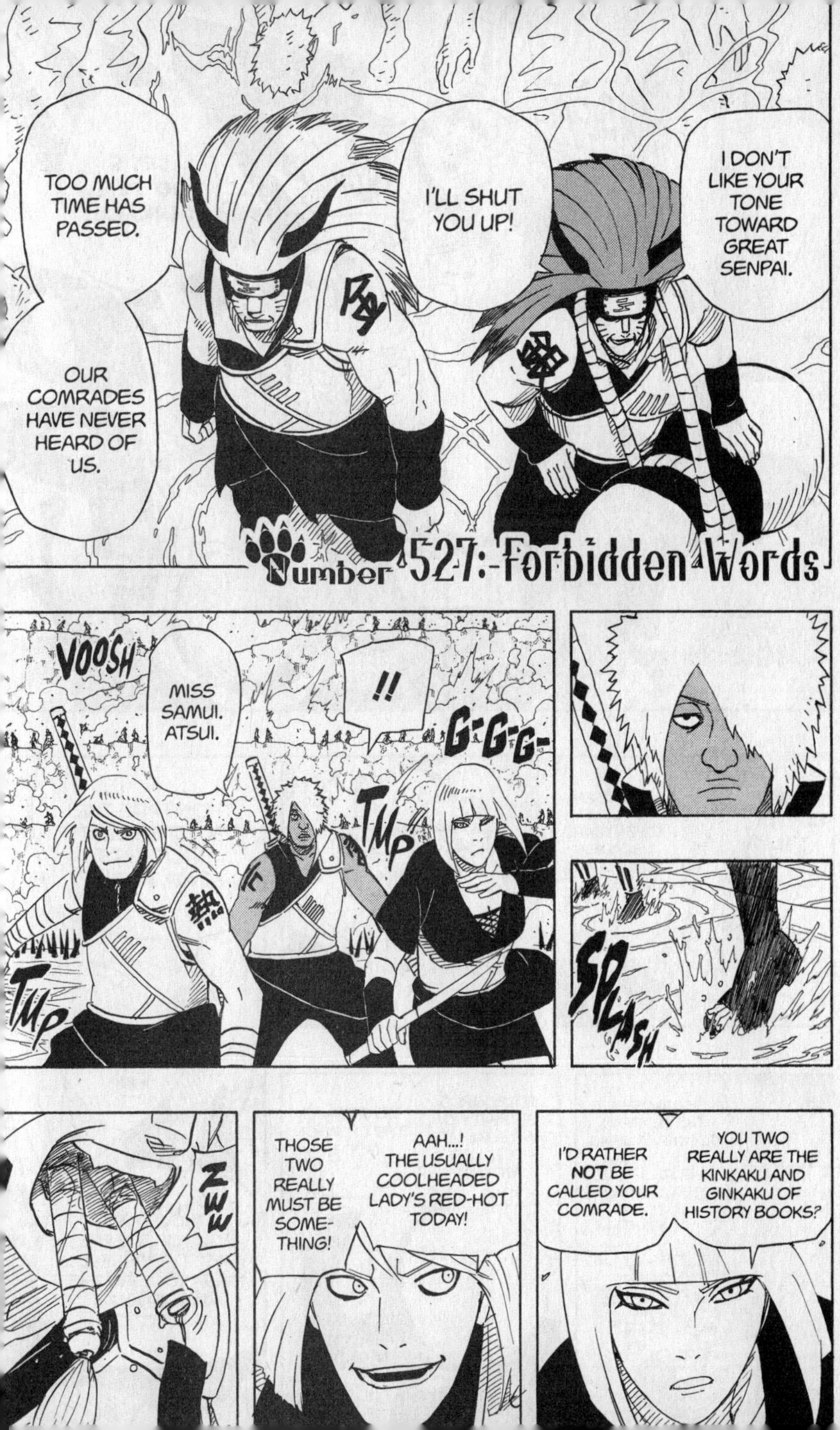
I DON'T LIKE YOUR TONE TOWARD GREAT SENPAI.
I'LL SHUT YOU UP!
TOO MUCH TIME HAS PASSED.
OUR COMRADES HAVE NEVER HEARD OF US.
Number 527: Forbidden Words
SPLASH
G-G-G-
!!
MISS SAMUI. ATSUI.
VOOSH
TMP
TMP
YOU TWO REALLY ARE THE KINKAKU AND GINKAKU OF HISTORY BOOKS?
I'D RATHER **NOT** BE CALLED YOUR COMRADE.
AAH...! THE USUALLY COOLHEADED LADY'S RED-HOT TODAY!
THOSE TWO REALLY MUST BE SOME-THING!
ZWW

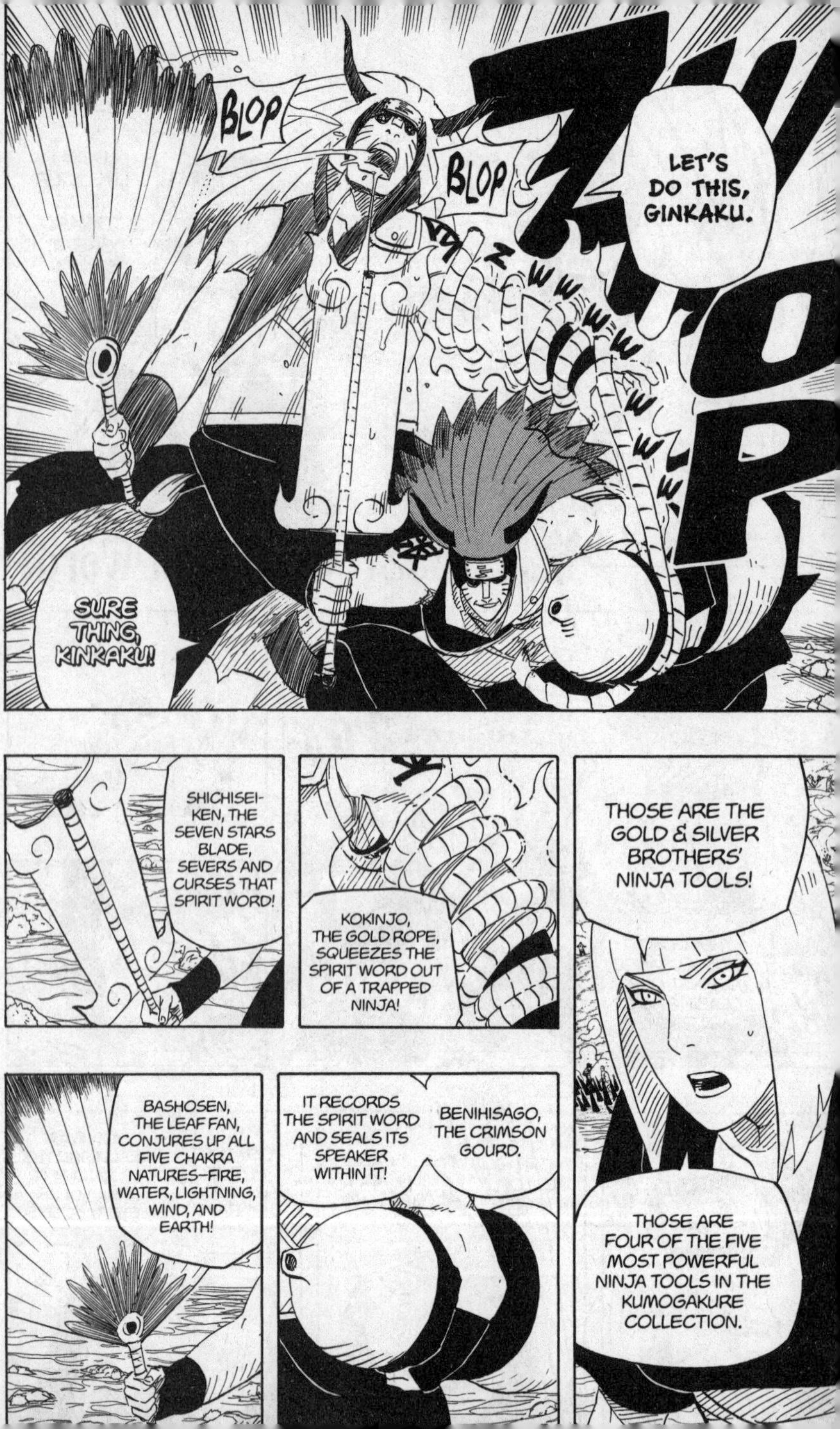
LET'S DO THIS, GINKAKU.
BLOP
BLOP
SURE THING, KINKAKU!
THOSE ARE THE GOLD & SILVER BROTHERS' NINJA TOOLS!
THOSE ARE FOUR OF THE FIVE MOST POWERFUL NINJA TOOLS IN THE KUMOGAKURE COLLECTION.
KOKINJO, THE GOLD ROPE, SQUEEZES THE SPIRIT WORD OUT OF A TRAPPED NINJA!
SHICHISEI-KEN, THE SEVEN STARS BLADE, SEVERS AND CURSES THAT SPIRIT WORD!
BENIHISAGO, THE CRIMSON GOURD.
IT RECORDS THE SPIRIT WORD AND SEALS ITS SPEAKER WITHIN IT!
BASHOSEN, THE LEAF FAN, CONJURES UP ALL FIVE CHAKRA NATURES--FIRE, WATER, LIGHTNING, WIND, AND EARTH!

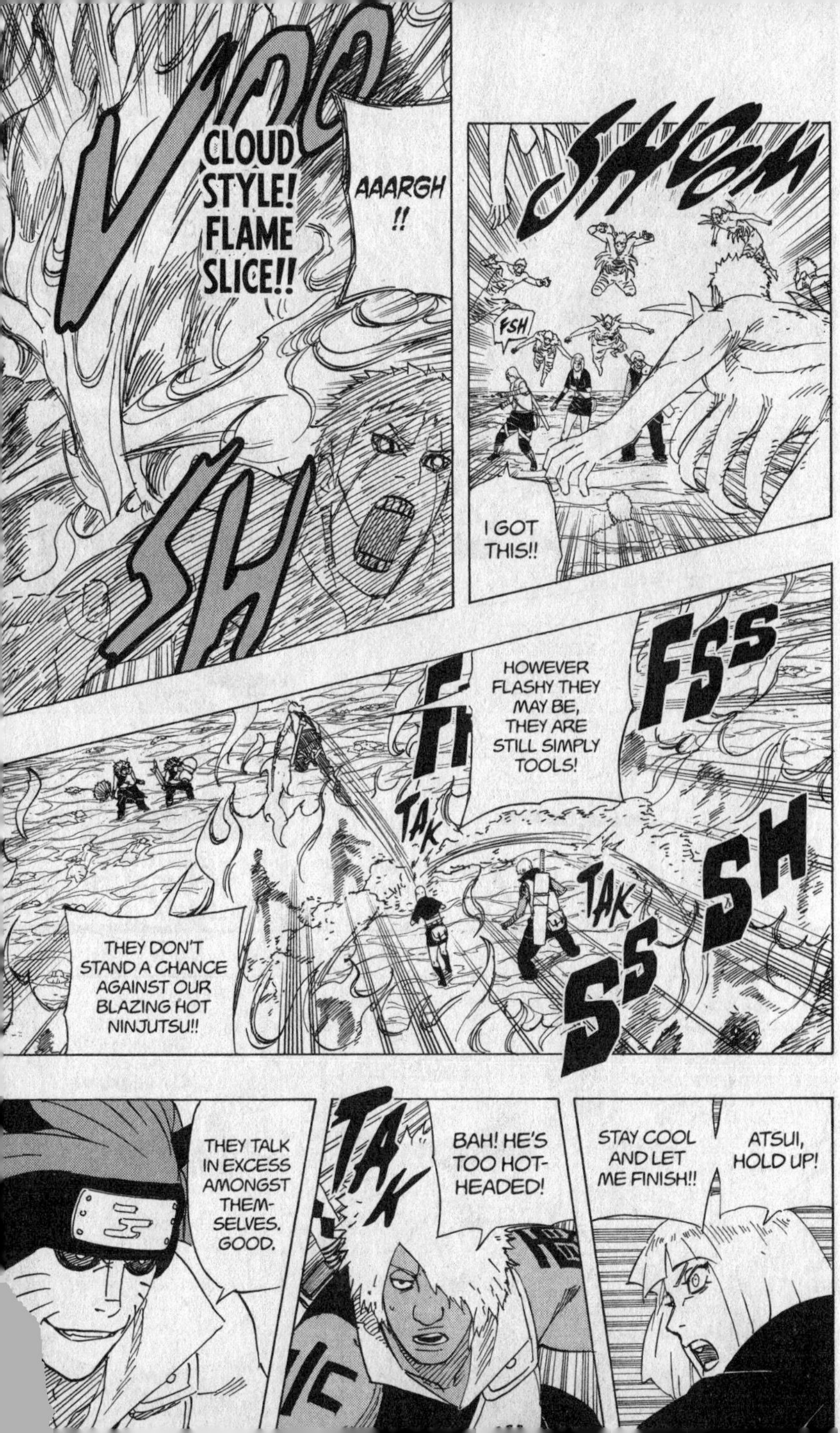
SHOOM
FSH
I GOT THIS!!
AAARGH!!
CLOUD STYLE! FLAME SLICE!!
SH
FSS
HOWEVER FLASHY THEY MAY BE, THEY ARE STILL SIMPLY TOOLS!
TAK
SH
TAK
SS
THEY DON'T STAND A CHANCE AGAINST OUR BLAZING HOT NINJUTSU!!
ATSUI, HOLD UP!
STAY COOL AND LET ME FINISH!!
BAH! HE'S TOO HOT-HEADED!
TAK
THEY TALK IN EXCESS AMONGST THEMSELVES. GOOD.

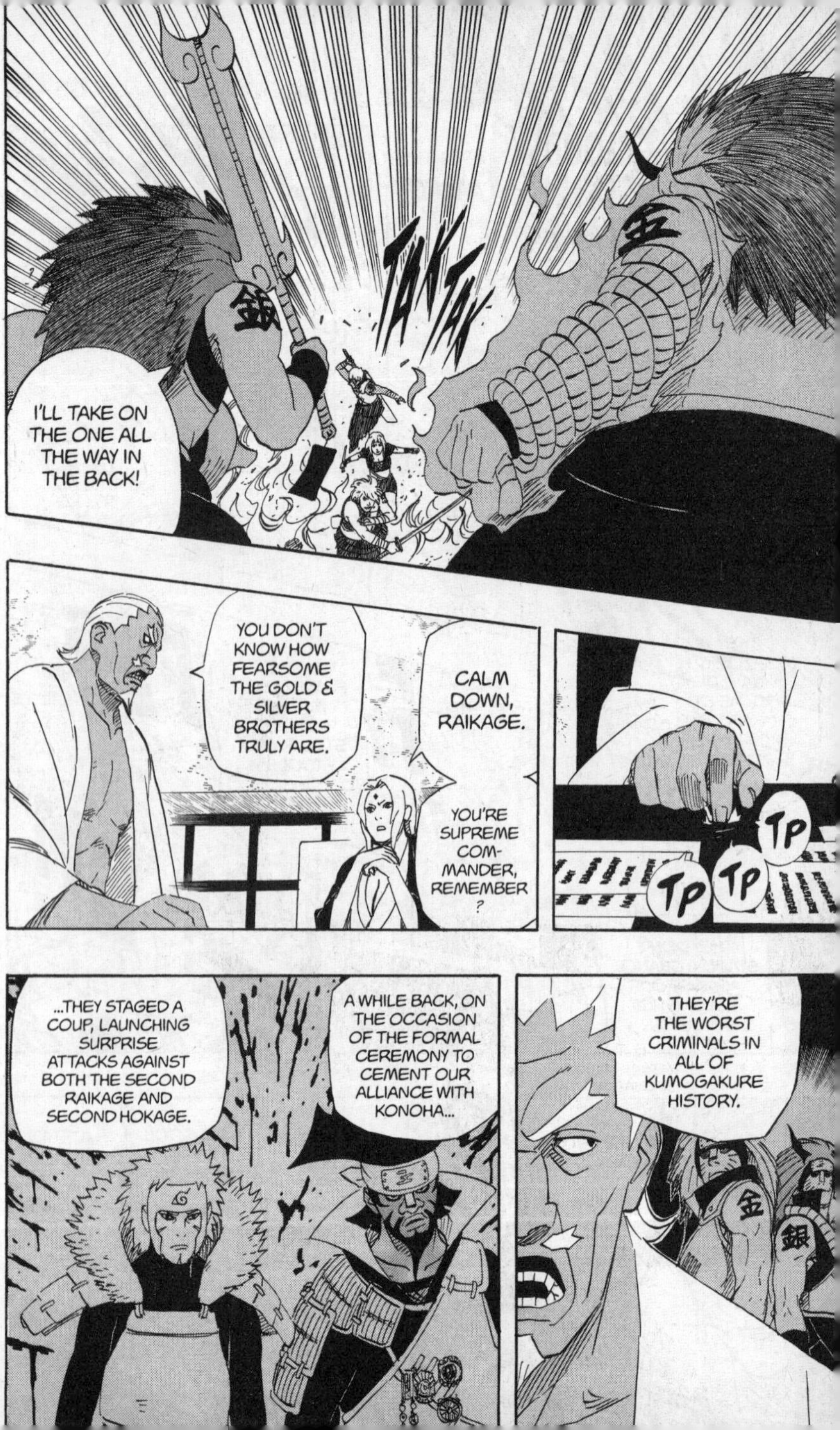

TAK TAK
I'LL TAKE ON THE ONE ALL THE WAY IN THE BACK!
Tp Tp Tp Tp
CALM DOWN, RAIKAGE.
YOU'RE SUPREME COM-MANDER, REMEMBER?
YOU DON'T KNOW HOW FEARSOME THE GOLD & SILVER BROTHERS TRULY ARE.
THEY'RE THE WORST CRIMINALS IN ALL OF KUMOGAKURE HISTORY.
A WHILE BACK, ON THE OCCASION OF THE FORMAL CEREMONY TO CEMENT OUR ALLIANCE WITH KONOHA...
...THEY STAGED A COUP, LAUNCHING SURPRISE ATTACKS AGAINST BOTH THE SECOND RAIKAGE AND SECOND HOKAGE.

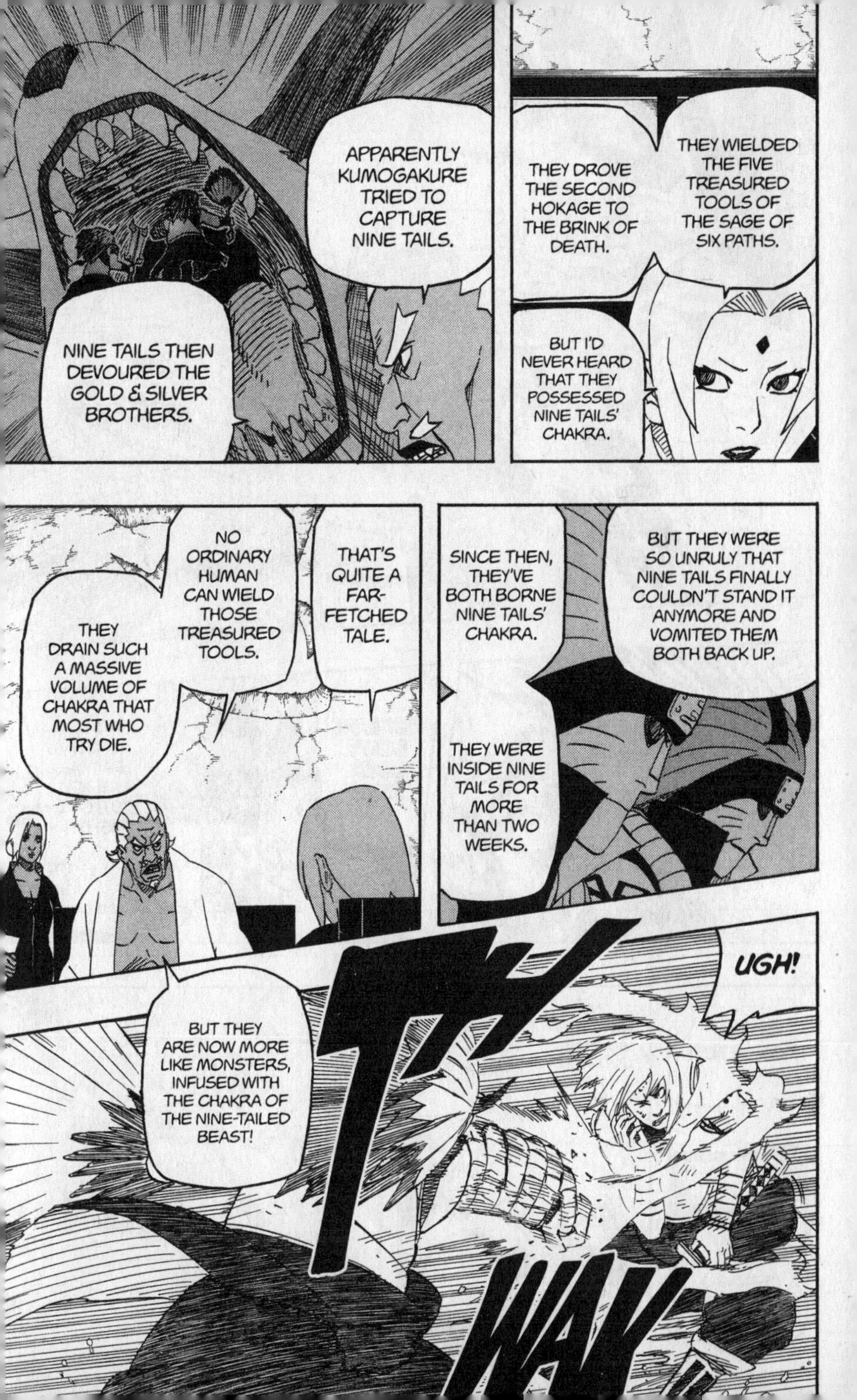
THEY WIELDED THE FIVE TREASURED TOOLS OF THE SAGE OF SIX PATHS.
THEY DROVE THE SECOND HOKAGE TO THE BRINK OF DEATH.
BUT I'D NEVER HEARD THAT THEY POSSESSED NINE TAILS' CHAKRA.
APPARENTLY KUMOGAKURE TRIED TO CAPTURE NINE TAILS.
NINE TAILS THEN DEVOURED THE GOLD & SILVER BROTHERS.
BUT THEY WERE SO UNRULY THAT NINE TAILS FINALLY COULDN'T STAND IT ANYMORE AND VOMITED THEM BOTH BACK UP.
SINCE THEN, THEY'VE BOTH BORNE NINE TAILS' CHAKRA.
THEY WERE INSIDE NINE TAILS FOR MORE THAN TWO WEEKS.
THAT'S QUITE A FAR-FETCHED TALE.
NO ORDINARY HUMAN CAN WIELD THOSE TREASURED TOOLS.
THEY DRAIN SUCH A MASSIVE VOLUME OF CHAKRA THAT MOST WHO TRY DIE.
UGH!
BUT THEY ARE NOW MORE LIKE MONSTERS, INFUSED WITH THE CHAKRA OF THE NINE-TAILED BEAST!
THWAK

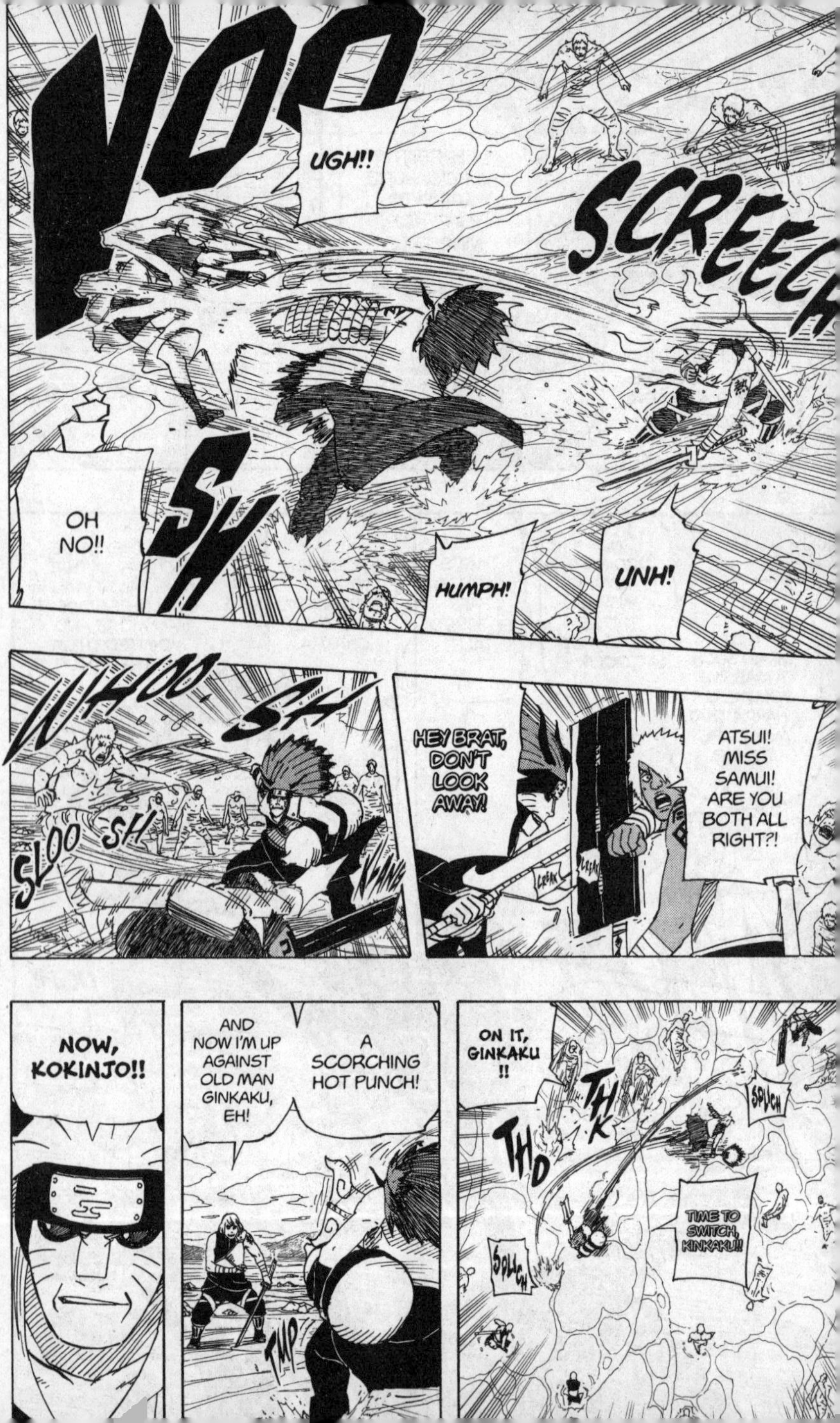
SCREECH
UGH!!
VOO
UNH!
HUMPH!
SH
OH NO!!
ATSUI! MISS SAMUI! ARE YOU BOTH ALL RIGHT?!
HEY BRAT, DON'T LOOK AWAY!
CREAK
CREAK
WHOO-SH
SLOO SH
ON IT, GINKAKU!!
SPLUCH
THK
THD
TIME TO SWITCH, KINKAKU!!
SPLUCH
A SCORCHING HOT PUNCH!
AND NOW I'M UP AGAINST OLD MAN GINKAKU, EH!
TMP
NOW, KOKINJO!!

READ THIS WAY

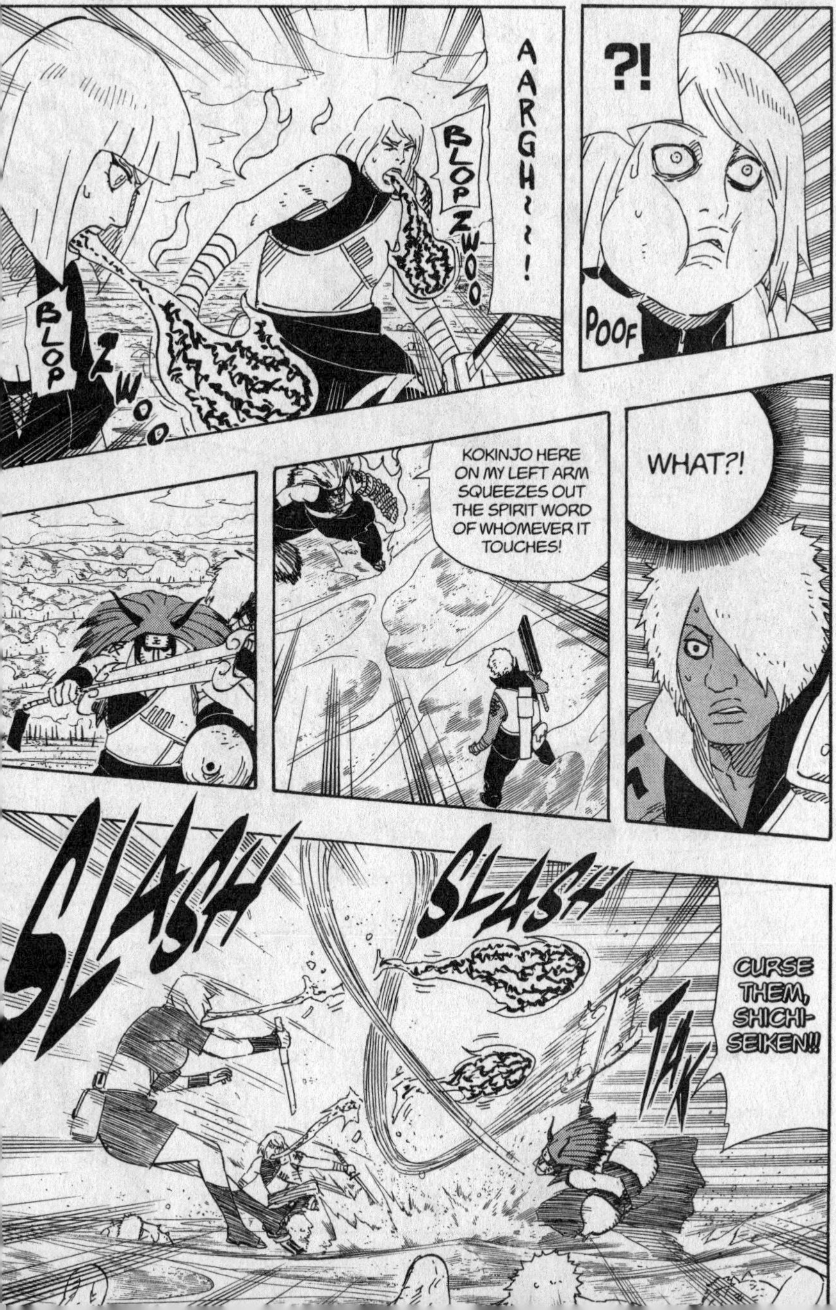
?!
POOF
AARGH~~!
BLOPZWOO
BLOP ZWOO
WHAT?!
KOKINJO HERE ON MY LEFT ARM SQUEEZES OUT THE SPIRIT WORD OF WHOMEVER IT TOUCHES!
CURSE THEM, SHICHI-SEIKEN!!
TAK
SLASH
SLASH

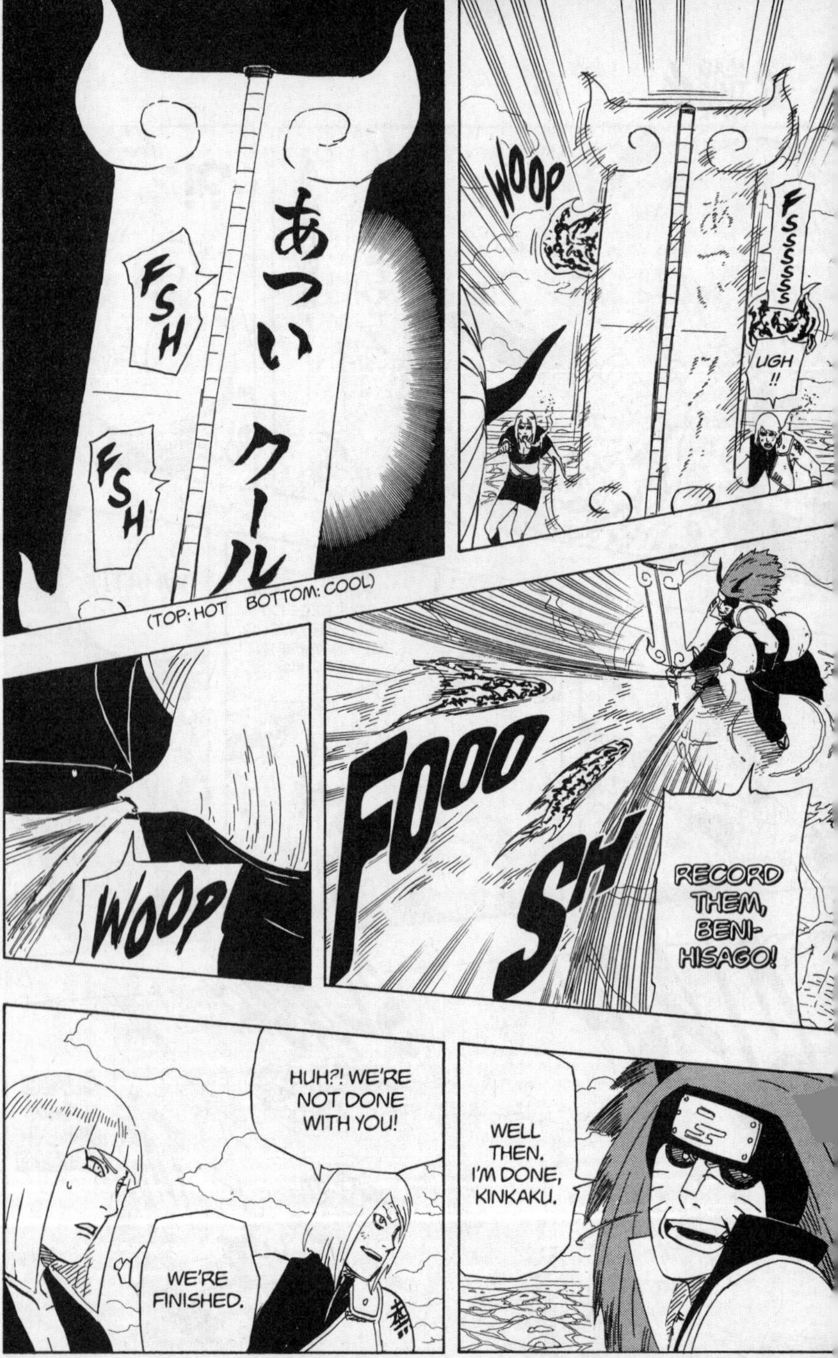
WOOP
FSSSSSS
UGH!!
あつい
クール
FSH
FSH
(TOP: HOT BOTTOM: COOL)
FOOOSH
RECORD THEM, BENI-HISAGO!
WOOP
WELL THEN. I'M DONE, KINKAKU.
HUH?! WE'RE NOT DONE WITH YOU!
WE'RE FINISHED.

READ THIS WAY

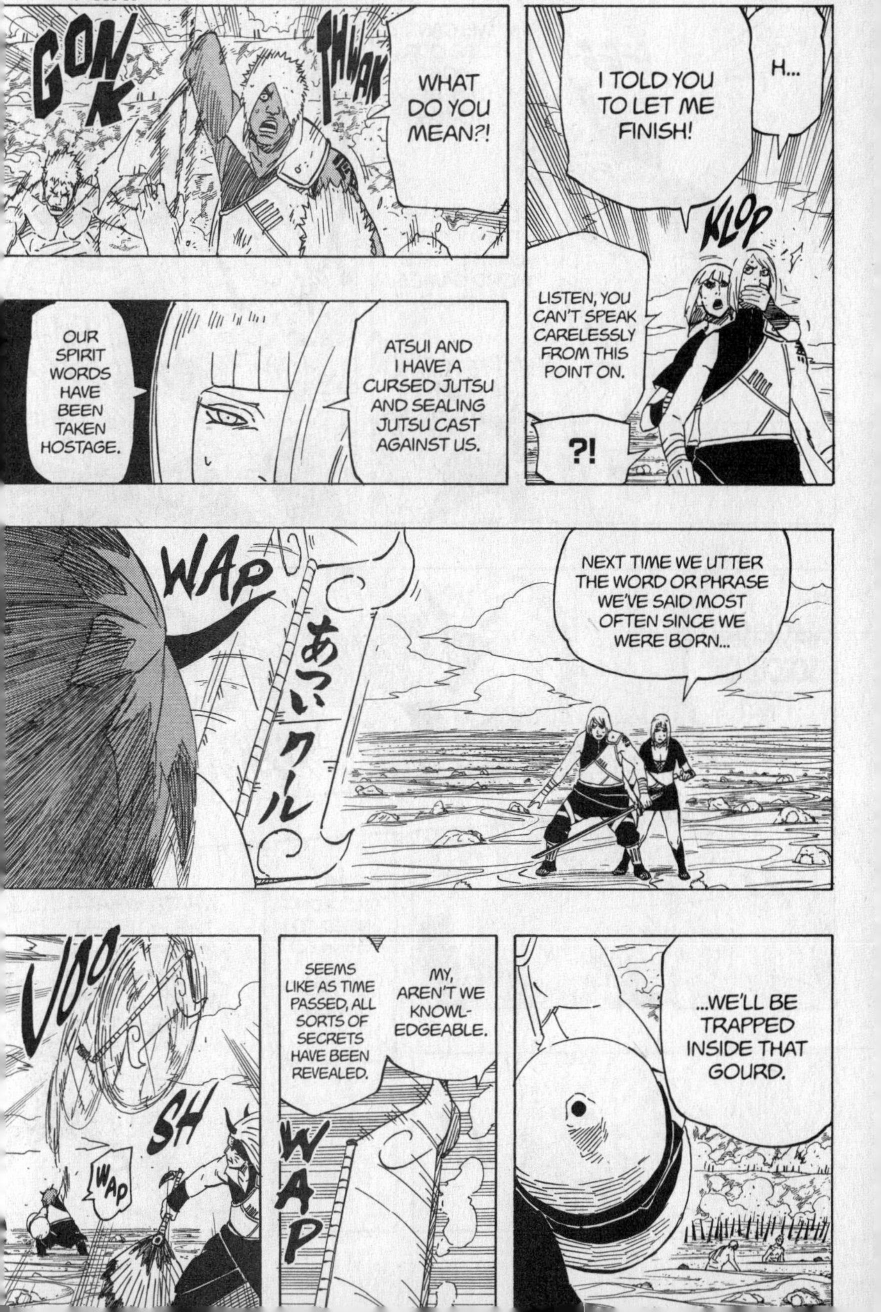
H...
I TOLD YOU TO LET ME FINISH!
KLOP
LISTEN, YOU CAN'T SPEAK CARELESSLY FROM THIS POINT ON.
?!
WHAT DO YOU MEAN?!
THWAK
GONK
ATSUI AND I HAVE A CURSED JUTSU AND SEALING JUTSU CAST AGAINST US.
OUR SPIRIT WORDS HAVE BEEN TAKEN HOSTAGE.
NEXT TIME WE UTTER THE WORD OR PHRASE WE'VE SAID MOST OFTEN SINCE WE WERE BORN...
あついクル
WAP
...WE'LL BE TRAPPED INSIDE THAT GOURD.
MY, AREN'T WE KNOWL-EDGEABLE.
SEEMS LIKE AS TIME PASSED, ALL SORTS OF SECRETS HAVE BEEN REVEALED.
WAP
JOO
SH
WAP

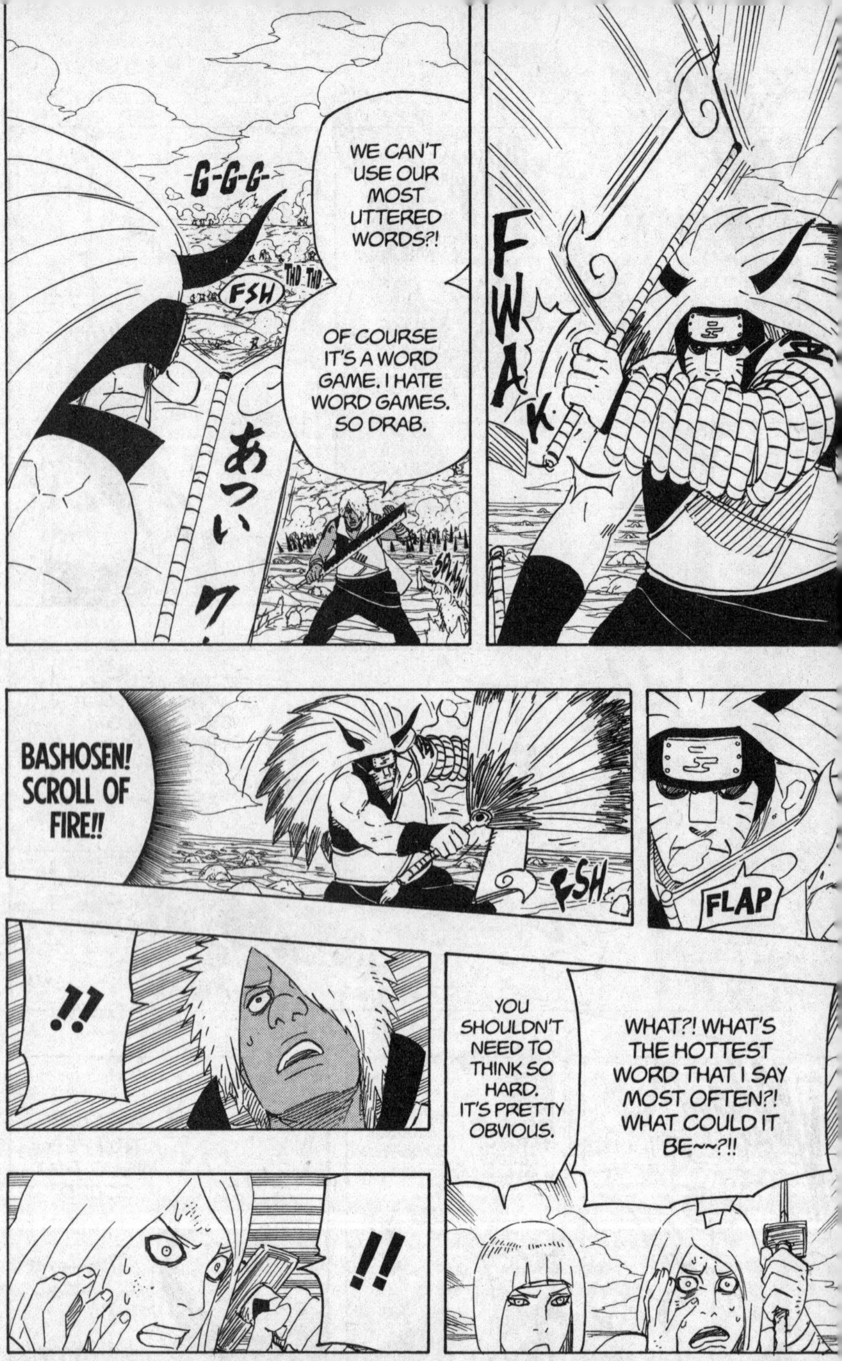
F W A K
WE CAN'T USE OUR MOST UTTERED WORDS?!
G-G-G-
THD THD
FSH
OF COURSE IT'S A WORD GAME. I HATE WORD GAMES. SO DRAB.
あつい
SPLASH
FLAP
BASHOSEN! SCROLL OF FIRE!!
FSH
WHAT?! WHAT'S THE HOTTEST WORD THAT I SAY MOST OFTEN?! WHAT COULD IT BE~~?!!
YOU SHOULDN'T NEED TO THINK SO HARD. IT'S PRETTY OBVIOUS.
!!
!!

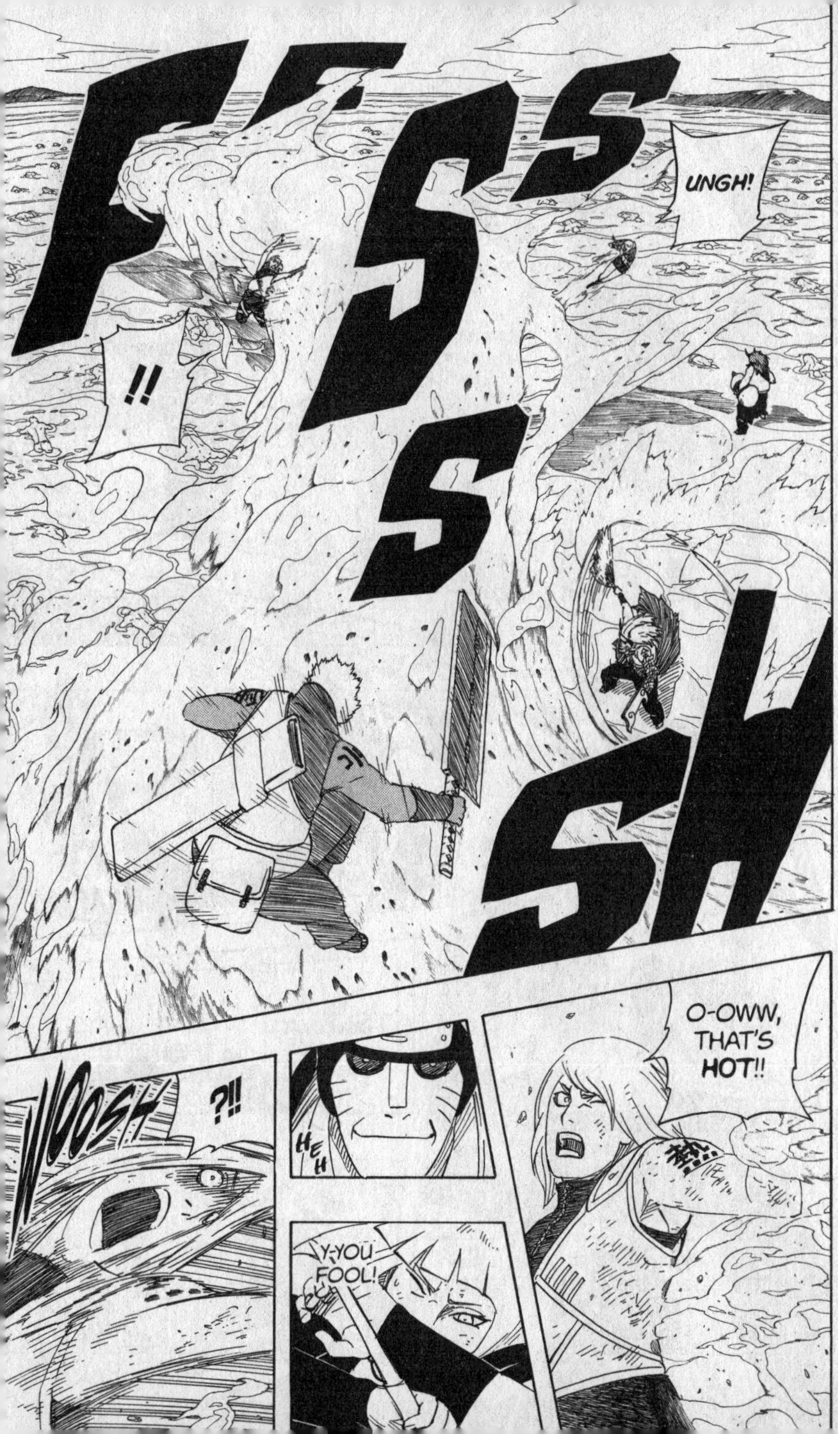
UNGH!
!!
FSSSSSH
O-OWW, THAT'S HOT!!
HEH
Y-YOU FOOL!
WHOOSH
?!!

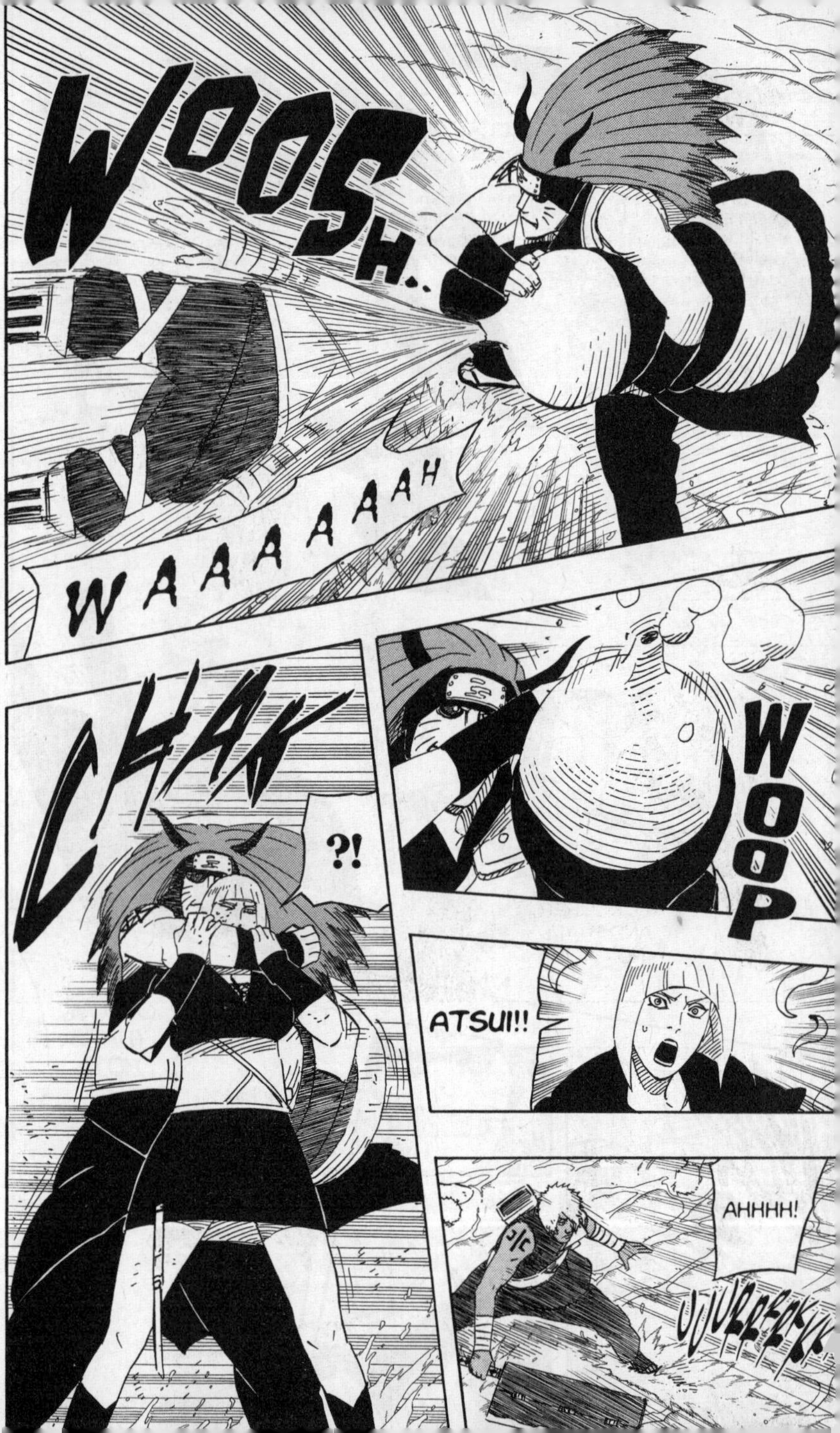
WOOSH..
WAAAAAAAH
WOOP
ATSUI!!!
AHHHH!
CHAK
?!

READ THIS WAY

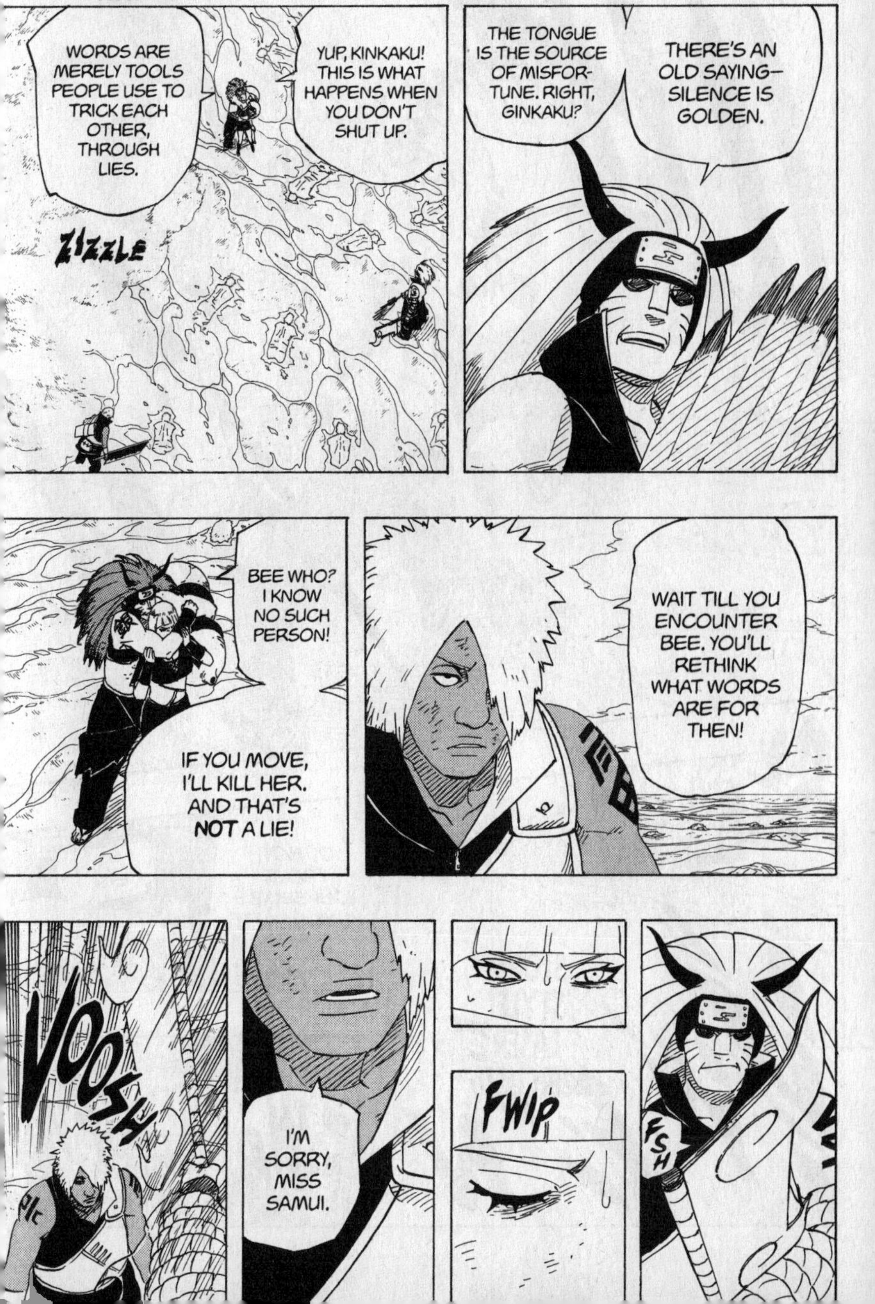
THERE'S AN OLD SAYING— SILENCE IS GOLDEN.
THE TONGUE IS THE SOURCE OF MISFOR-TUNE. RIGHT, GINKAKU?
YUP, KINKAKU! THIS IS WHAT HAPPENS WHEN YOU DON'T SHUT UP.
WORDS ARE MERELY TOOLS PEOPLE USE TO TRICK EACH OTHER, THROUGH LIES.
ZIZZLE
WAIT TILL YOU ENCOUNTER BEE. YOU'LL RETHINK WHAT WORDS ARE FOR THEN!
BEE WHO? I KNOW NO SUCH PERSON!
IF YOU MOVE, I'LL KILL HER. AND THAT'S NOT A LIE!
FSH
FWIP
I'M SORRY, MISS SAMUI.
VOOSH

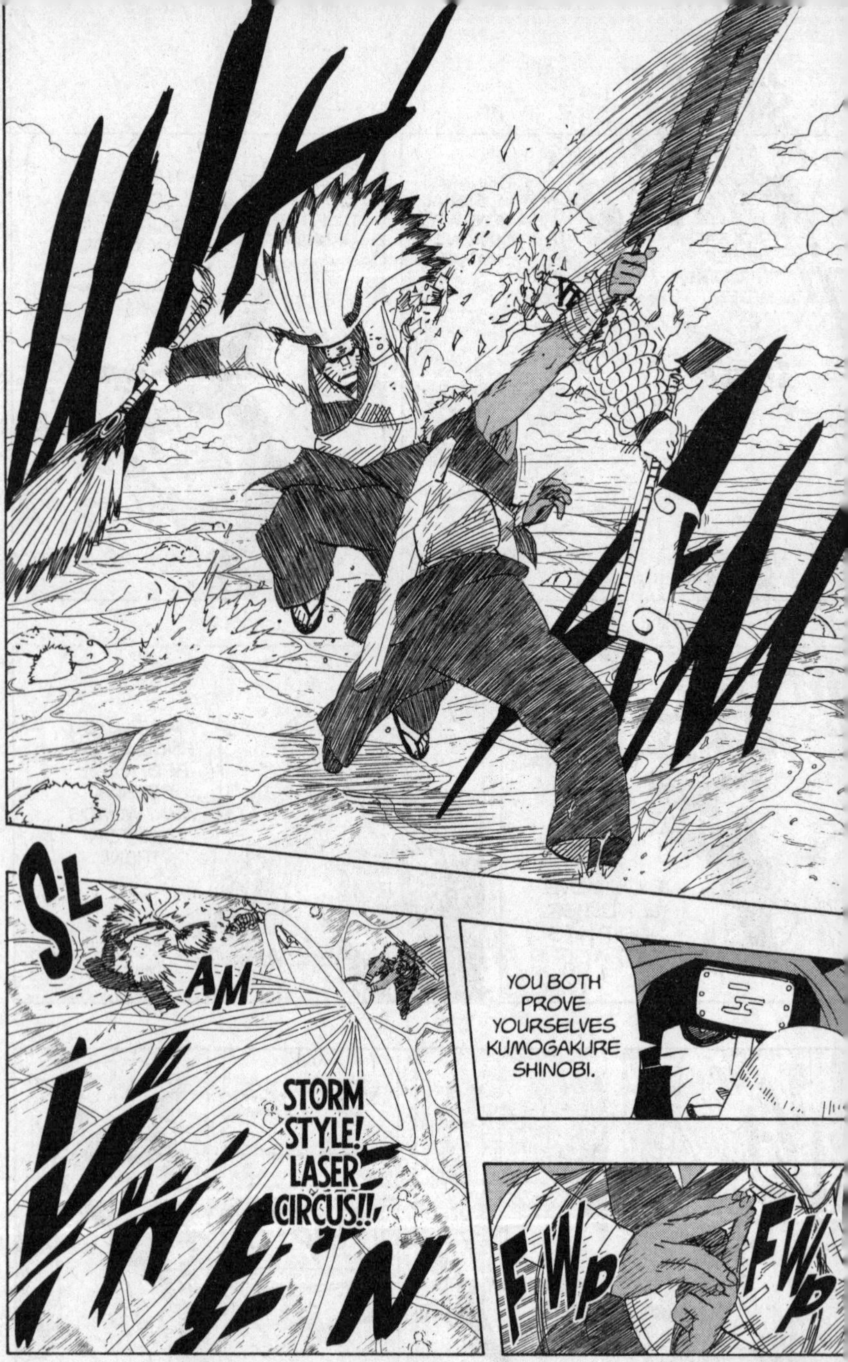

YOU BOTH PROVE YOURSELVES KUMOGAKURE SHINOBI.
FWP
FWP
SLAM
STORM STYLE! LASER CIRCUS!!

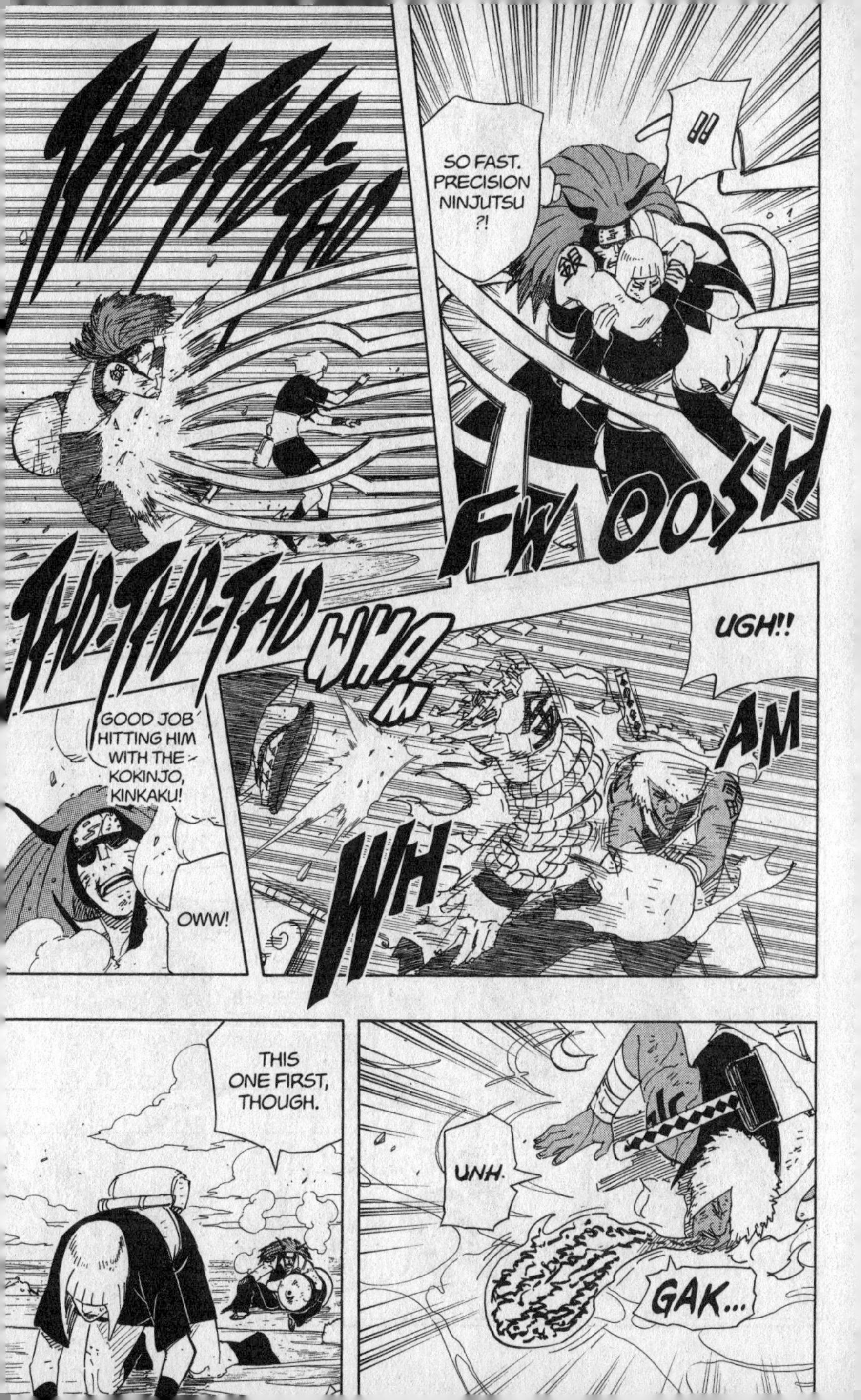
!!
SO FAST. PRECISION NINJUTSU ?!
FWOOSH
THD-THD-THD
UGH!!
WHAM
GOOD JOB HITTING HIM WITH THE KOKINJO, KINKAKU!
OWW!
UNH.
GAK...
THIS ONE FIRST, THOUGH.

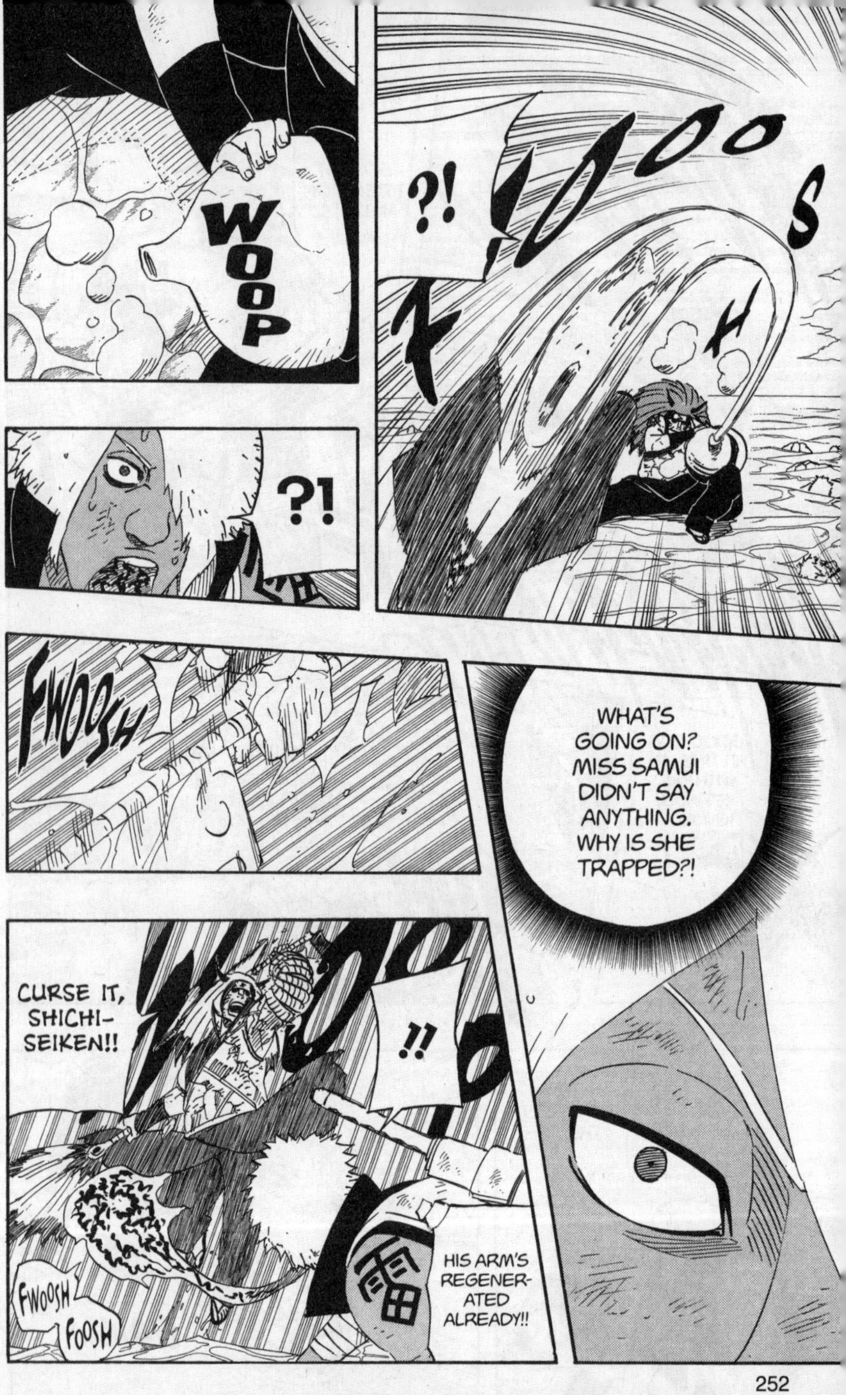
?!
WOOP
?!
FWOOSH
WHAT'S GOING ON? MISS SAMUI DIDN'T SAY ANYTHING. WHY IS SHE TRAPPED?!
CURSE IT, SHICHI-SEIKEN!!
!!
HIS ARM'S REGENER-ATED ALREADY!!
FWOOSH
FOOSH

READ THIS WAY

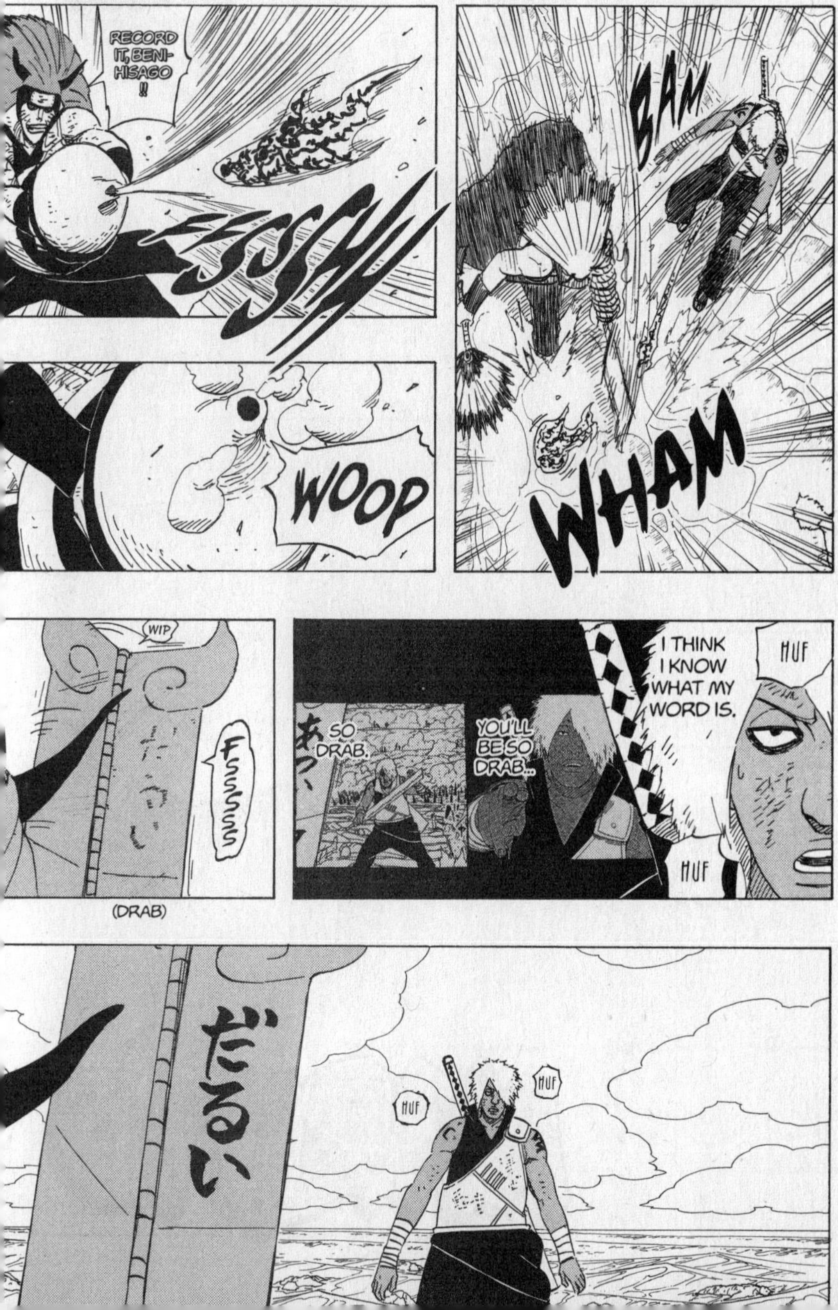
BAM
WHAM
RECORD IT, BENI-HISAGO!!
FSSSH
WOOP
HUF
I THINK I KNOW WHAT MY WORD IS.
YOU'LL BE SO DRAB...
SO DRAB.
あっ、
HUF
WIP
FSSSSS
だるい
HUF
HUF
(DRAB)

NARUTO

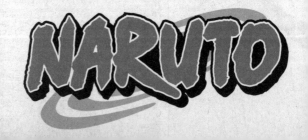

# Number 528: Transcendent Drab

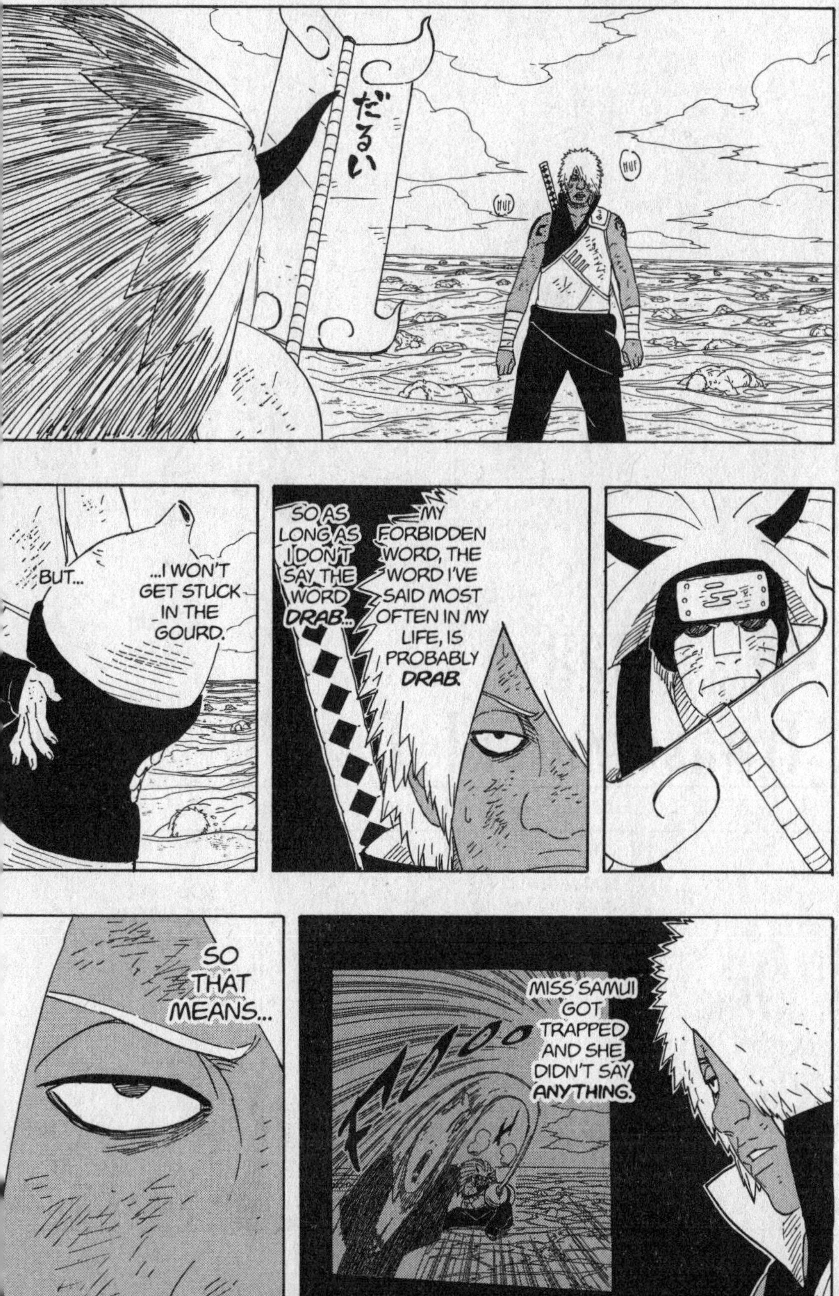
だるい
HUF
HUF
MY FORBIDDEN WORD, THE WORD I'VE SAID MOST OFTEN IN MY LIFE, IS PROBABLY DRAB.
SO AS LONG AS I DON'T SAY THE WORD DRAB...
...I WON'T GET STUCK IN THE GOURD.
BUT...
MISS SAMUI GOT TRAPPED AND SHE DIDN'T SAY ANYTHING.
SO THAT MEANS...

# Number 528: Transcendent Drab

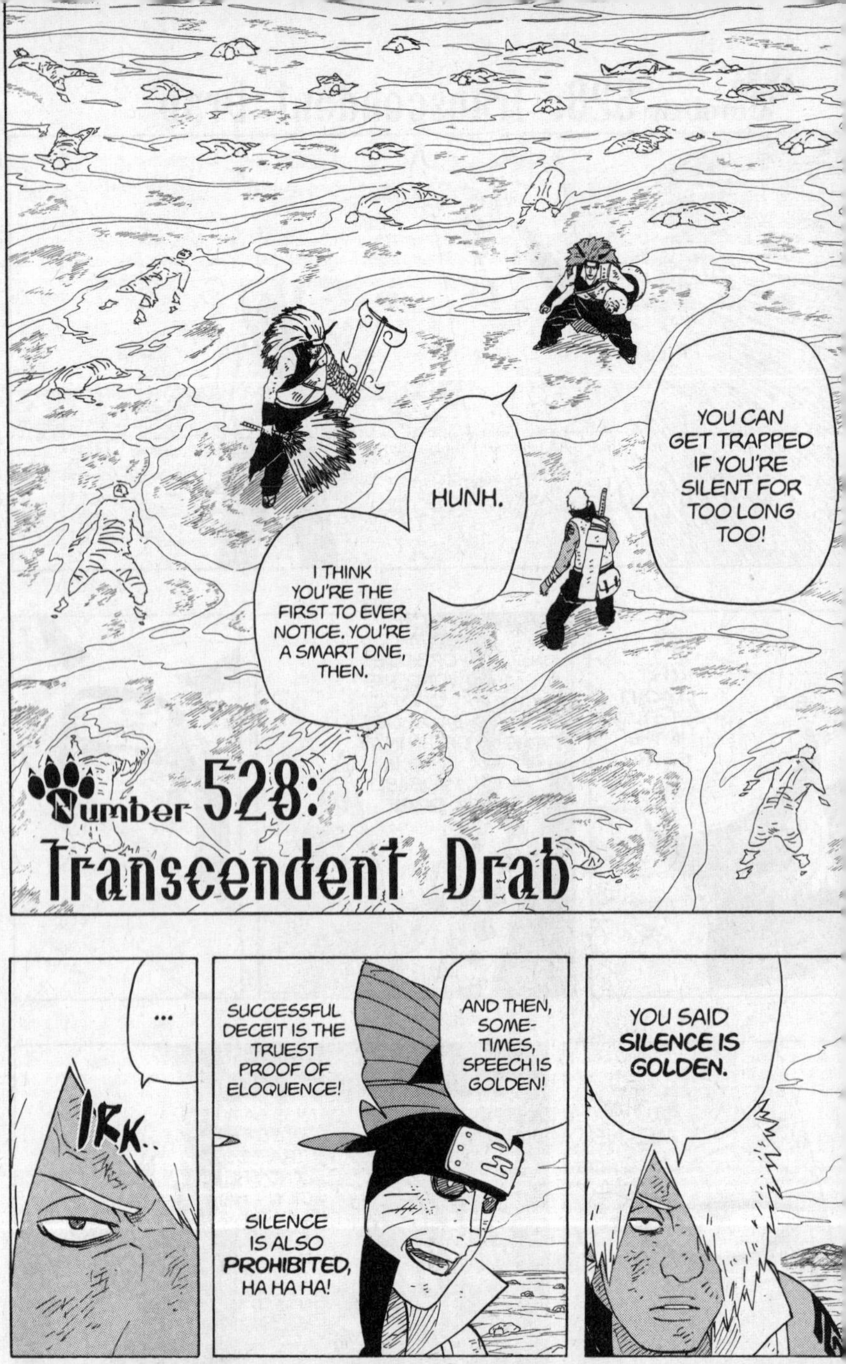
YOU CAN GET TRAPPED IF YOU'RE SILENT FOR TOO LONG TOO!
HUNH.
I THINK YOU'RE THE FIRST TO EVER NOTICE. YOU'RE A SMART ONE, THEN.
YOU SAID **SILENCE IS GOLDEN.**
AND THEN, SOME-TIMES, SPEECH IS GOLDEN!
SUCCESSFUL DECEIT IS THE TRUEST PROOF OF ELOQUENCE!
SILENCE IS ALSO **PROHIBITED,** HA HA HA!
...
IRK..

READ THIS WAY

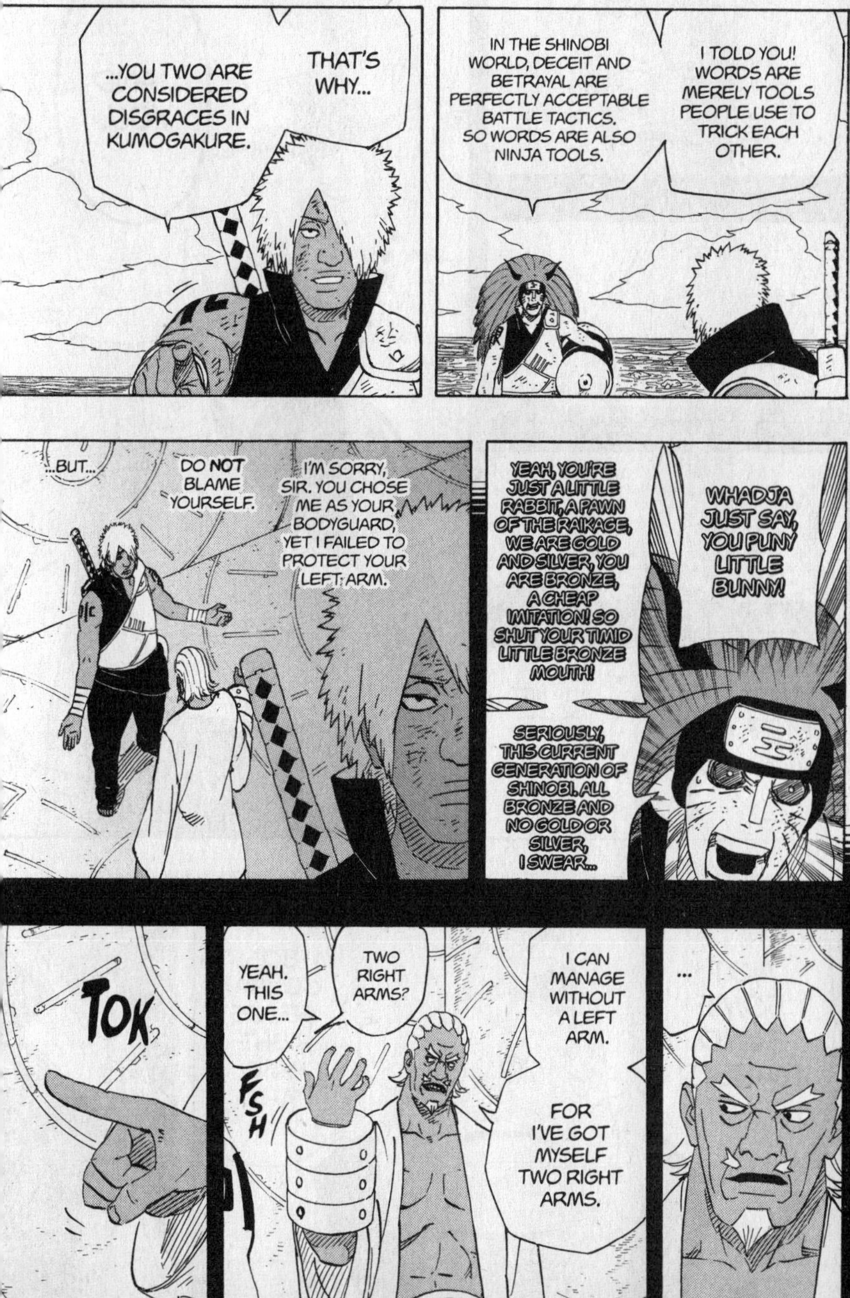
I TOLD YOU! WORDS ARE MERELY TOOLS PEOPLE USE TO TRICK EACH OTHER.
IN THE SHINOBI WORLD, DECEIT AND BETRAYAL ARE PERFECTLY ACCEPTABLE BATTLE TACTICS. SO WORDS ARE ALSO NINJA TOOLS.
THAT'S WHY...
...YOU TWO ARE CONSIDERED DISGRACES IN KUMOGAKURE.
WHADJA JUST SAY, YOU PUNY LITTLE BUNNY!
YEAH, YOU'RE JUST A LITTLE RABBIT, A PAWN OF THE RAIKAGE, WE ARE GOLD AND SILVER, YOU ARE BRONZE, A CHEAP IMITATION! SO SHUT YOUR TIMID LITTLE BRONZE MOUTH!
SERIOUSLY, THIS CURRENT GENERATION OF SHINOBI. ALL BRONZE AND NO GOLD OR SILVER, I SWEAR...
I'M SORRY, SIR. YOU CHOSE ME AS YOUR BODYGUARD, YET I FAILED TO PROTECT YOUR LEFT ARM.
DO NOT BLAME YOURSELF.
...BUT...
...
I CAN MANAGE WITHOUT A LEFT ARM.
FOR I'VE GOT MYSELF TWO RIGHT ARMS.
TWO RIGHT ARMS?
YEAH. THIS ONE...
FSH
TOK

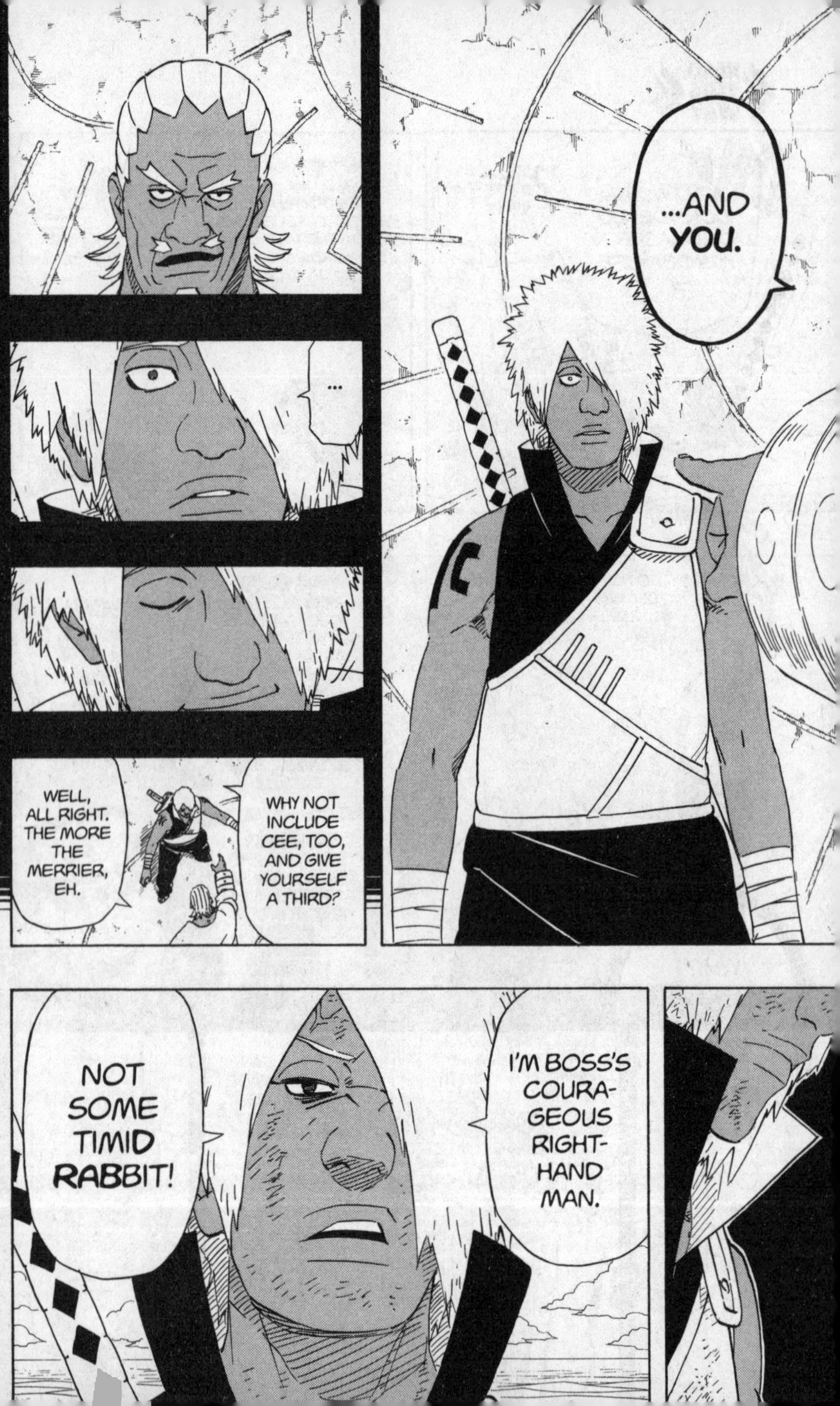
...AND YOU.
...
WHY NOT INCLUDE CEE, TOO, AND GIVE YOURSELF A THIRD?
WELL, ALL RIGHT. THE MORE THE MERRIER, EH.
I'M BOSS'S COURAGEOUS RIGHT-HAND MAN.
NOT SOME TIMID RABBIT!

READ THIS WAY

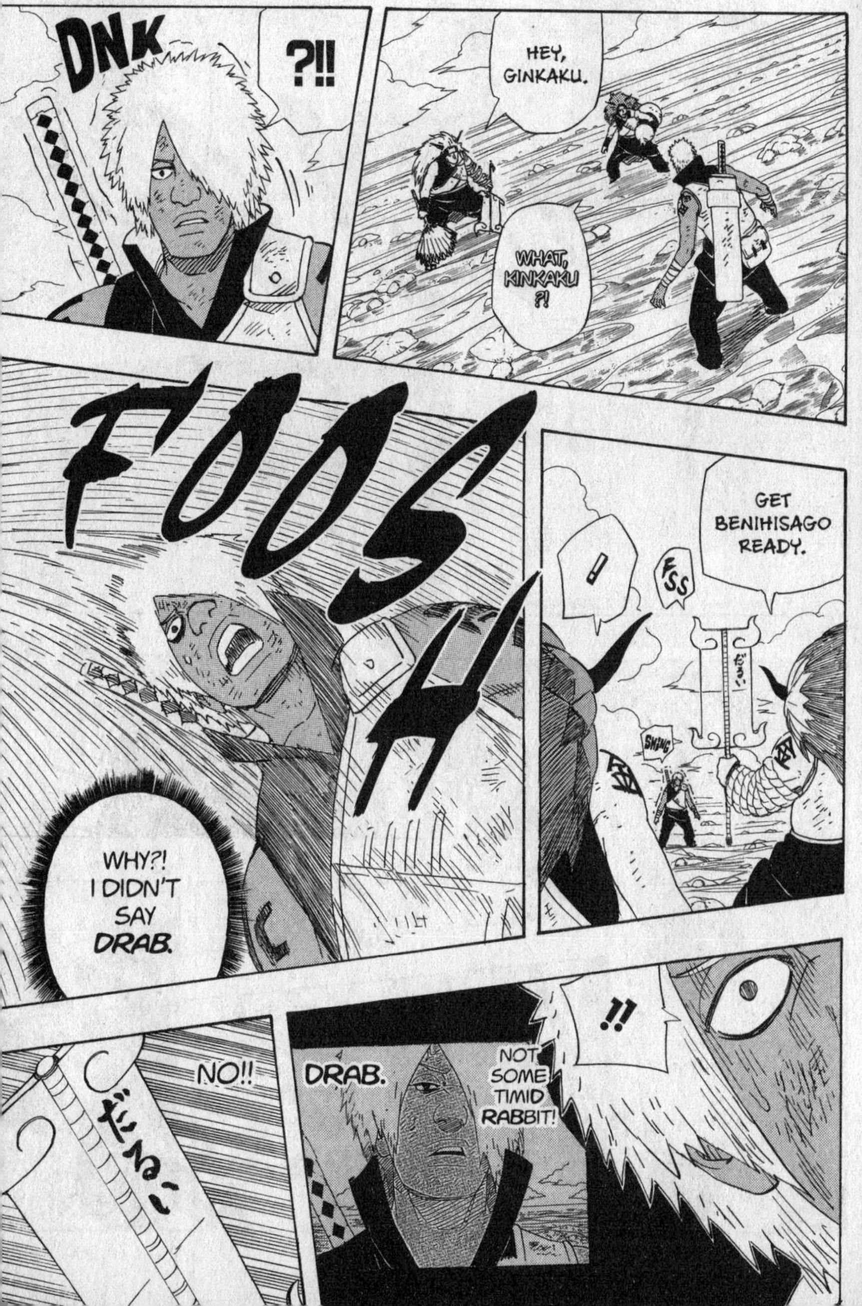
HEY, GINKAKU.
WHAT, KINKAKU?!
DNK
?!!
GET BENIHISAGO READY.
FSS
!
SHING
FOOSH
WHY?! I DIDN'T SAY DRAB.
!!
NOT SOME TIMID RABBIT!
DRAB.
NO!!

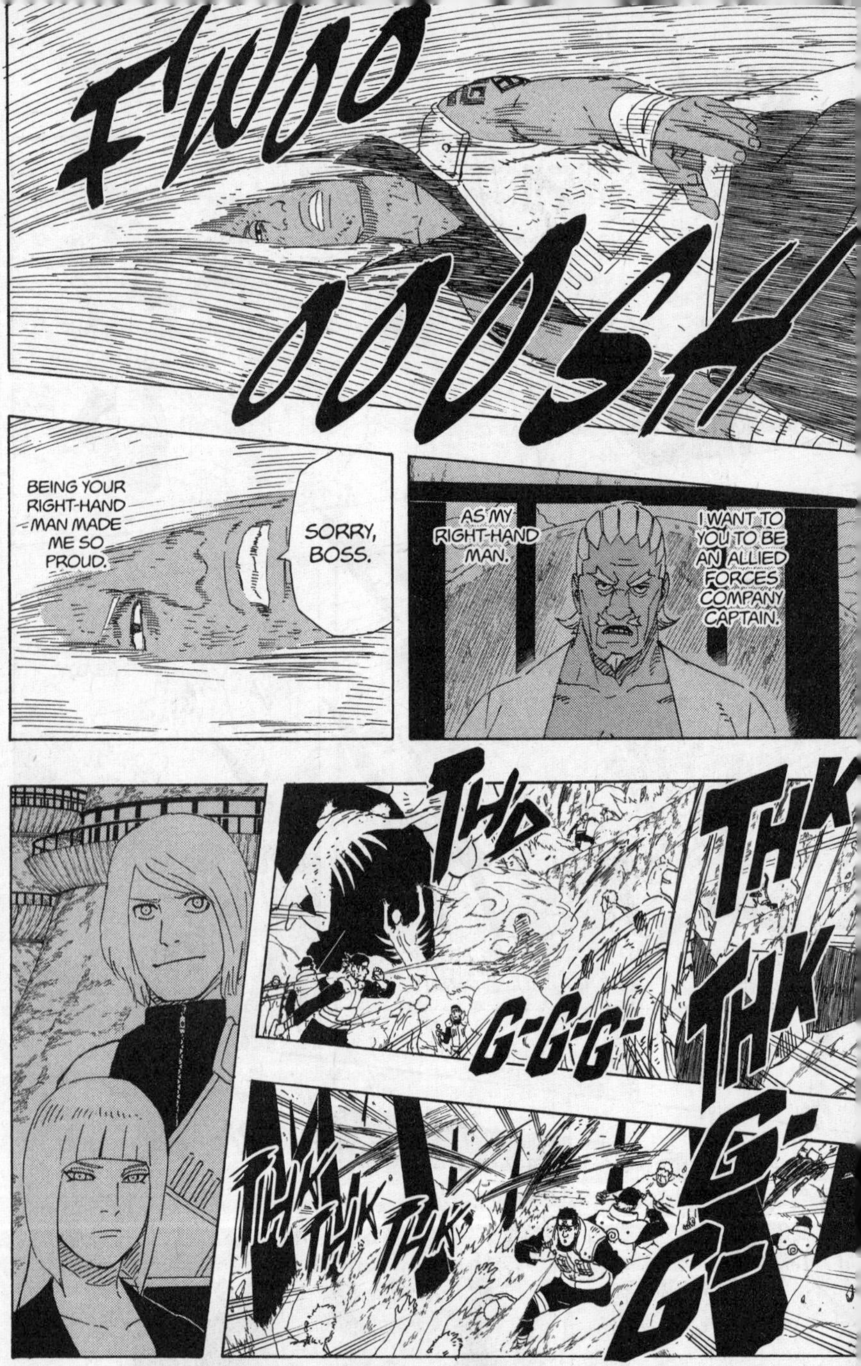
FWOO
OOOSH
I WANT TO YOU TO BE AN ALLIED FORCES COMPANY CAPTAIN.
AS MY RIGHT-HAND MAN.
SORRY, BOSS.
BEING YOUR RIGHT-HAND MAN MADE ME SO PROUD.
THK THK
THD
G-G-G-
G- G-
THK THK THK

READ THIS WAY

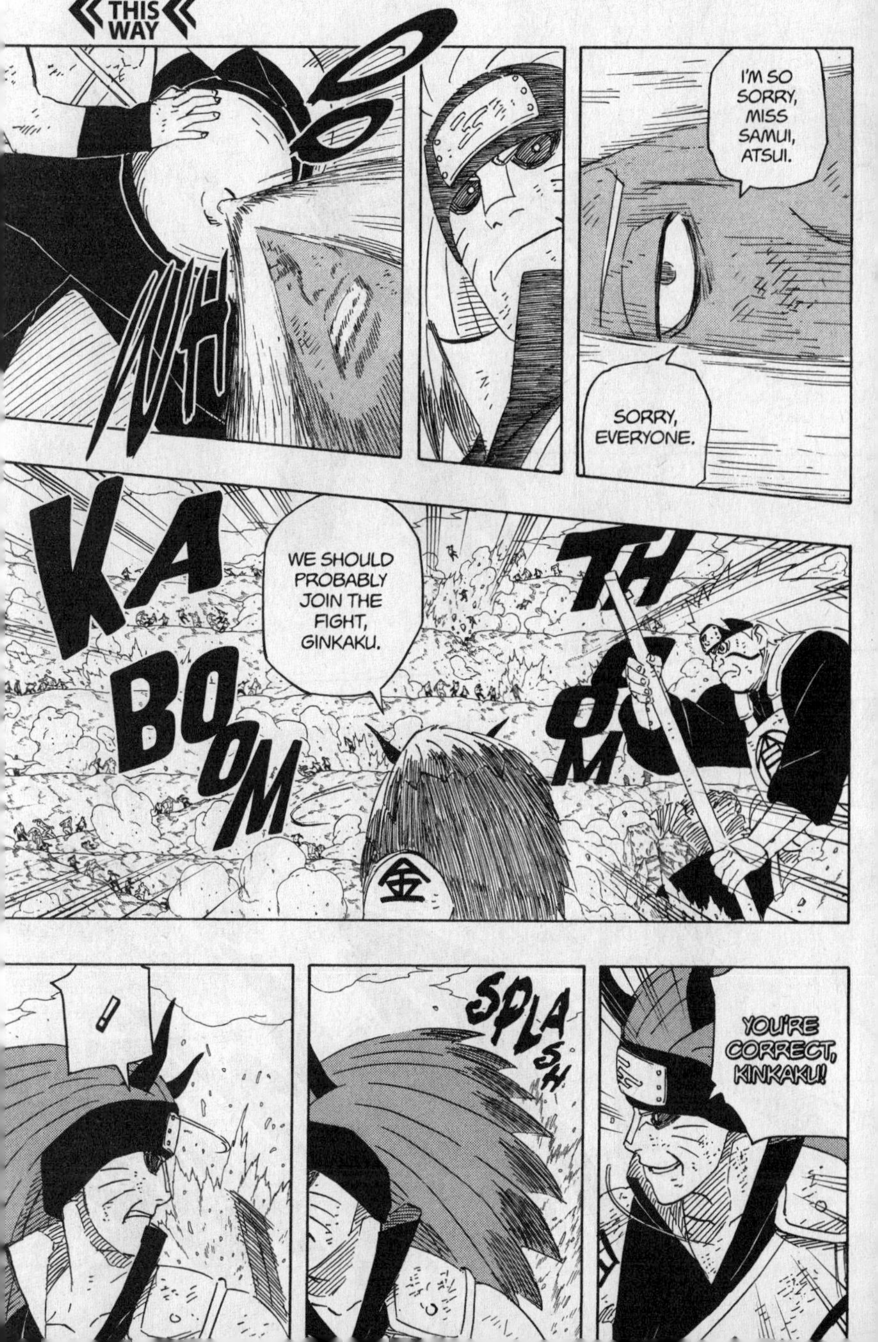
I'M SO SORRY, MISS SAMUI, ATSUI.
SORRY, EVERYONE.
WHOOSH
THOOM
WE SHOULD PROBABLY JOIN THE FIGHT, GINKAKU.
KABOOM
YOU'RE CORRECT, KINKAKU!
SPLASH
!

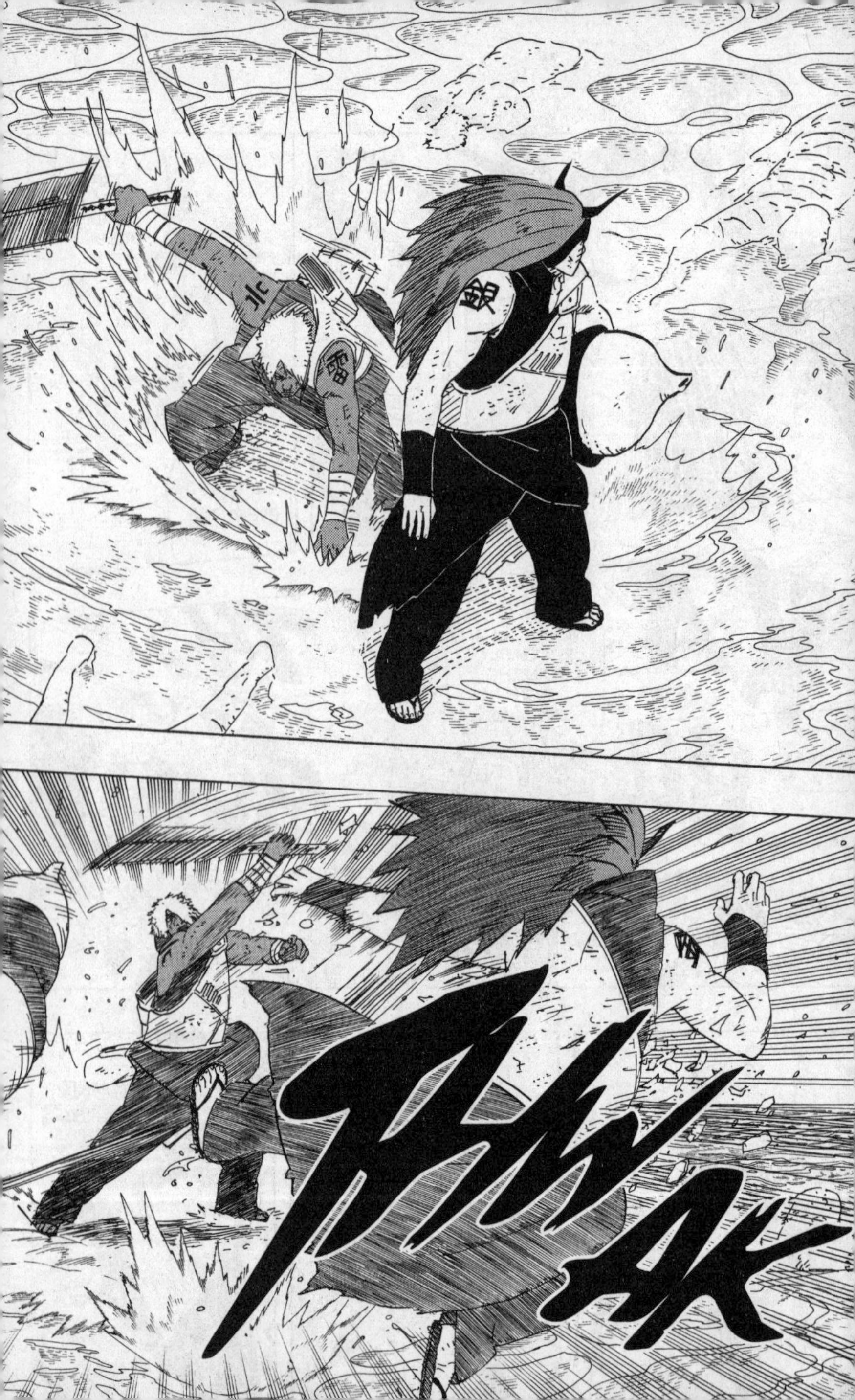
THWAK

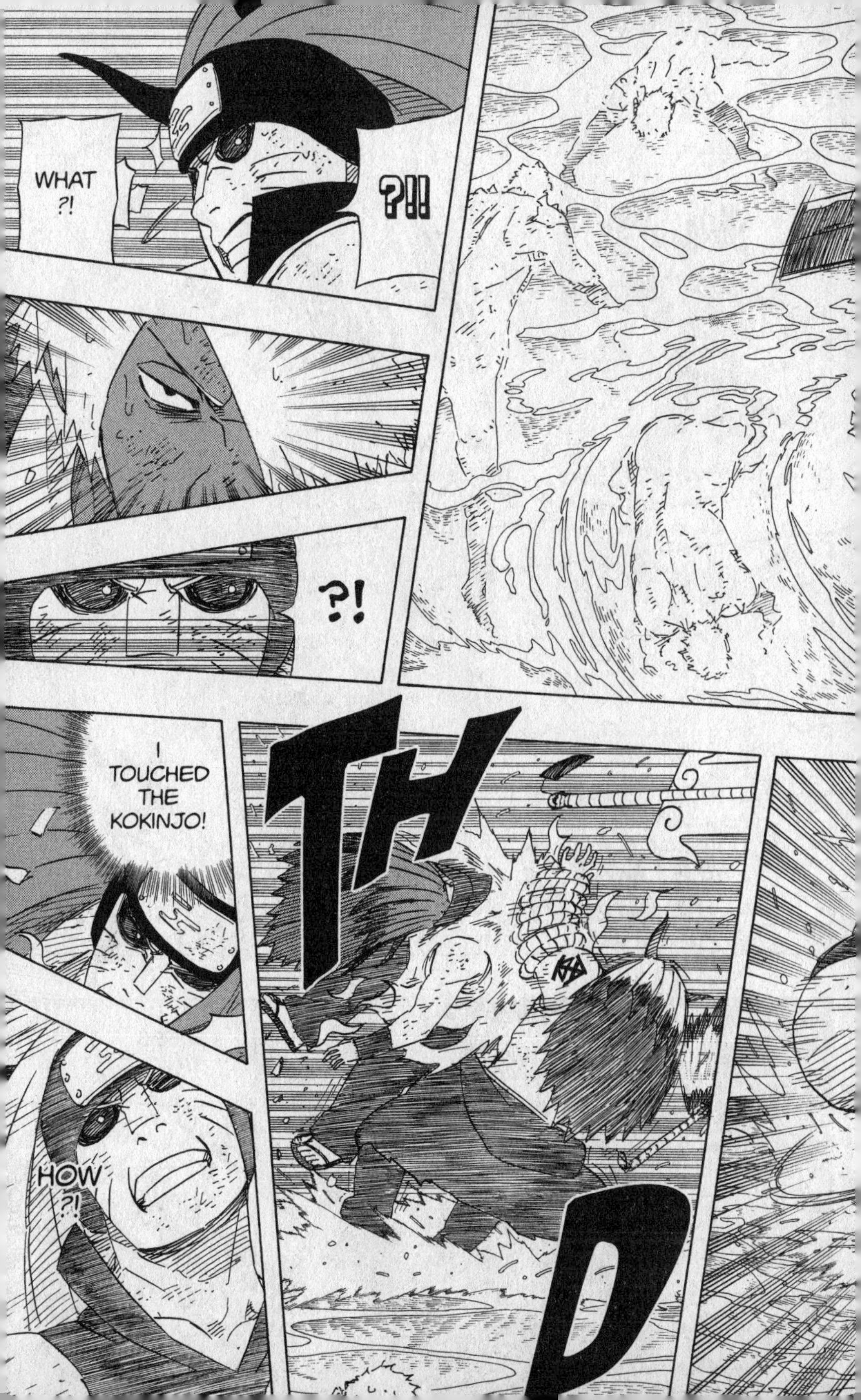
?!!
WHAT ?!
?!
TH
D
I TOUCHED THE KOKINJO!
HOW ?!

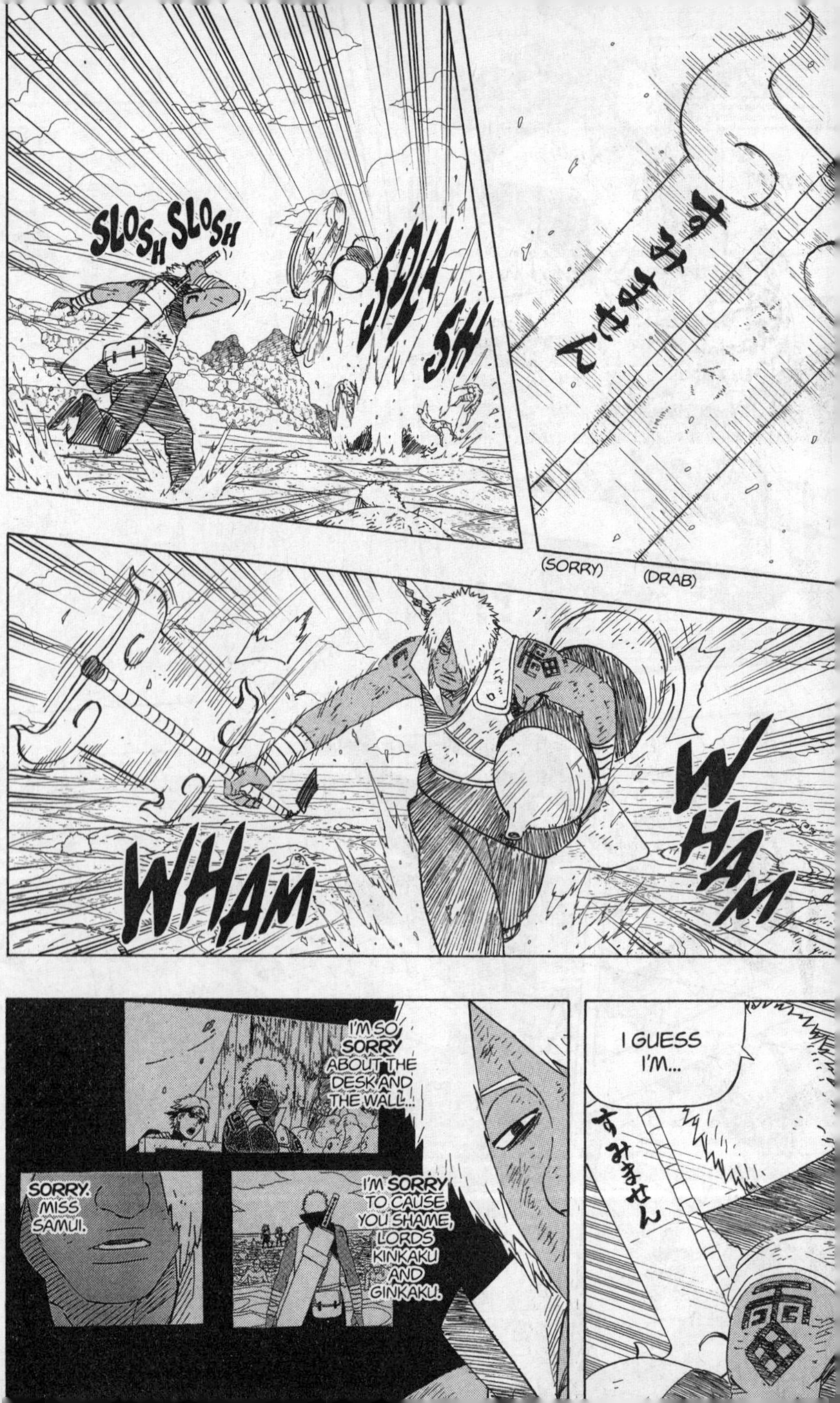
すみません
(SORRY)
(DRAB)
SLOSH SLOSH
SPLASH
WHAM
WHAM
I GUESS I'M...
すみません
I'M SO SORRY ABOUT THE DESK AND THE WALL...
I'M SORRY TO CAUSE YOU SHAME, LORDS KINKAKU AND GINKAKU.
SORRY. MISS SAMUI.

READ THIS WAY

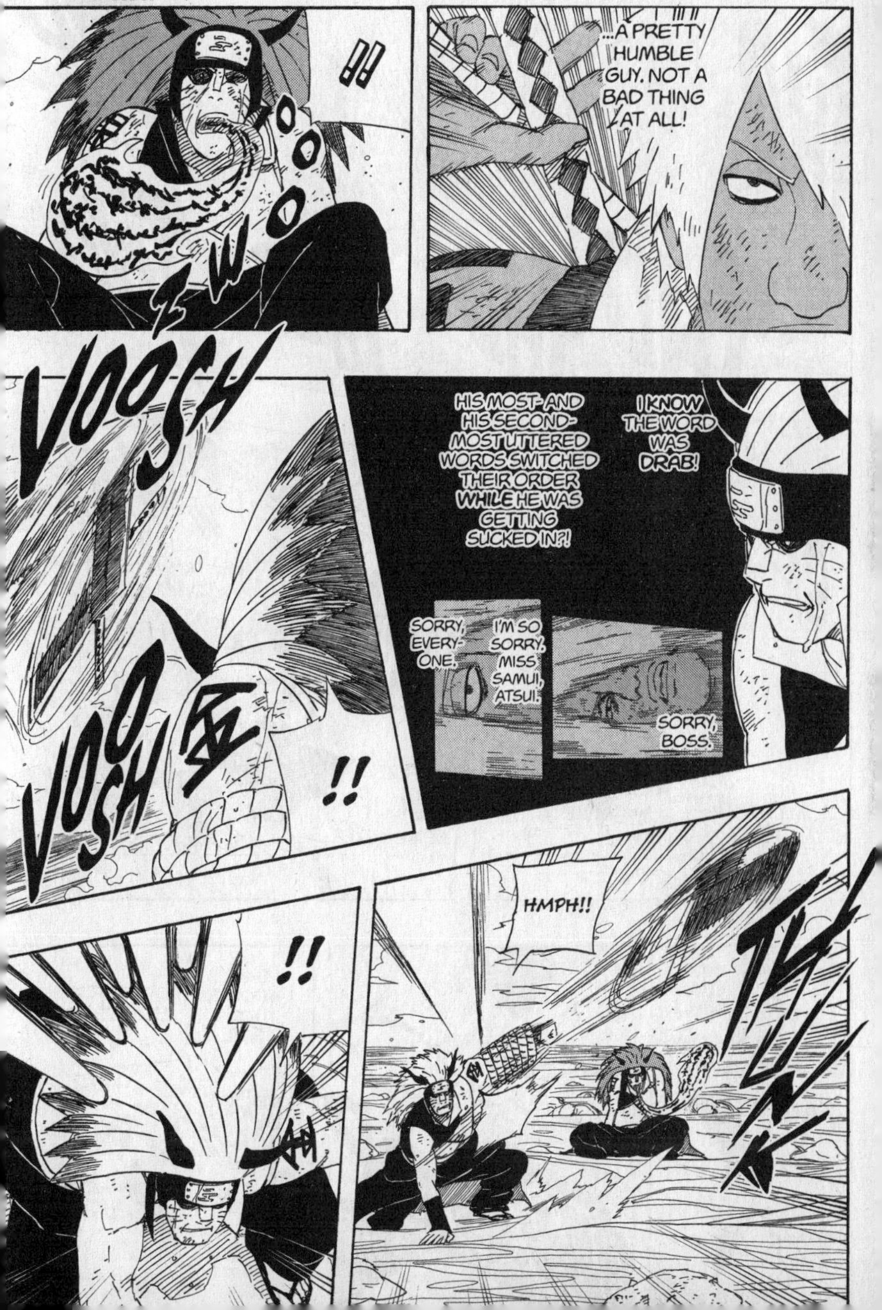
...A PRETTY HUMBLE GUY. NOT A BAD THING AT ALL!
!!
I KNOW THE WORD WAS DRAB!
HIS MOST- AND HIS SECOND-MOST UTTERED WORDS SWITCHED THEIR ORDER WHILE HE WAS GETTING SUCKED IN?!
SORRY, BOSS.
I'M SO SORRY. MISS SAMUI, ATSUI.
SORRY, EVERY-ONE.
VOOSH
VOOSH
!!
HMPH!!
!!

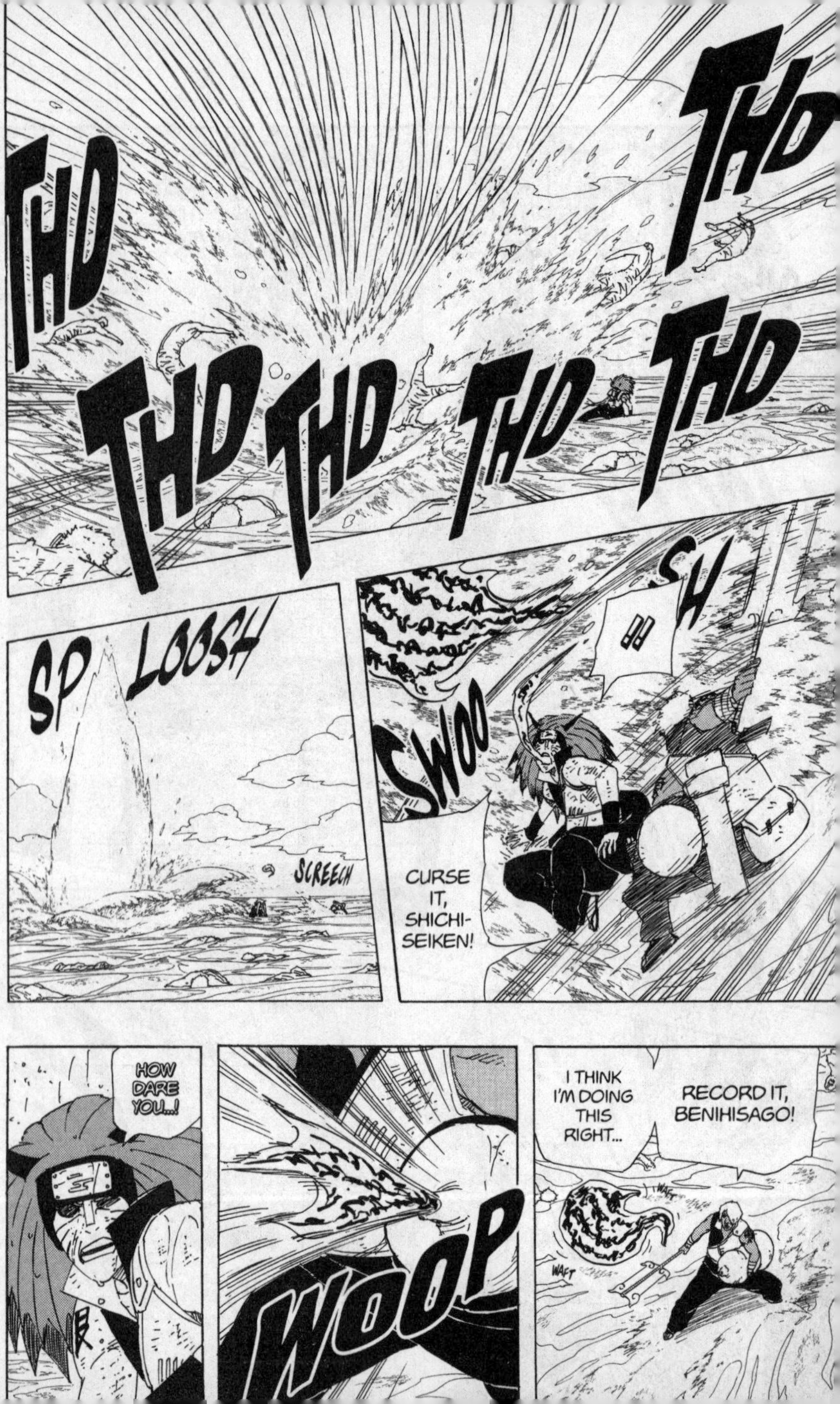
THD
THD
THD
THD
THD
THD
SH
SWOO
CURSE IT, SHICHI-SEIKEN!
SP LOOSH
SCREECH
RECORD IT, BENIHISAGO!
I THINK I'M DOING THIS RIGHT...
WAFT
WAFT
WOOP
HOW DARE YOU...!

READ THIS WAY

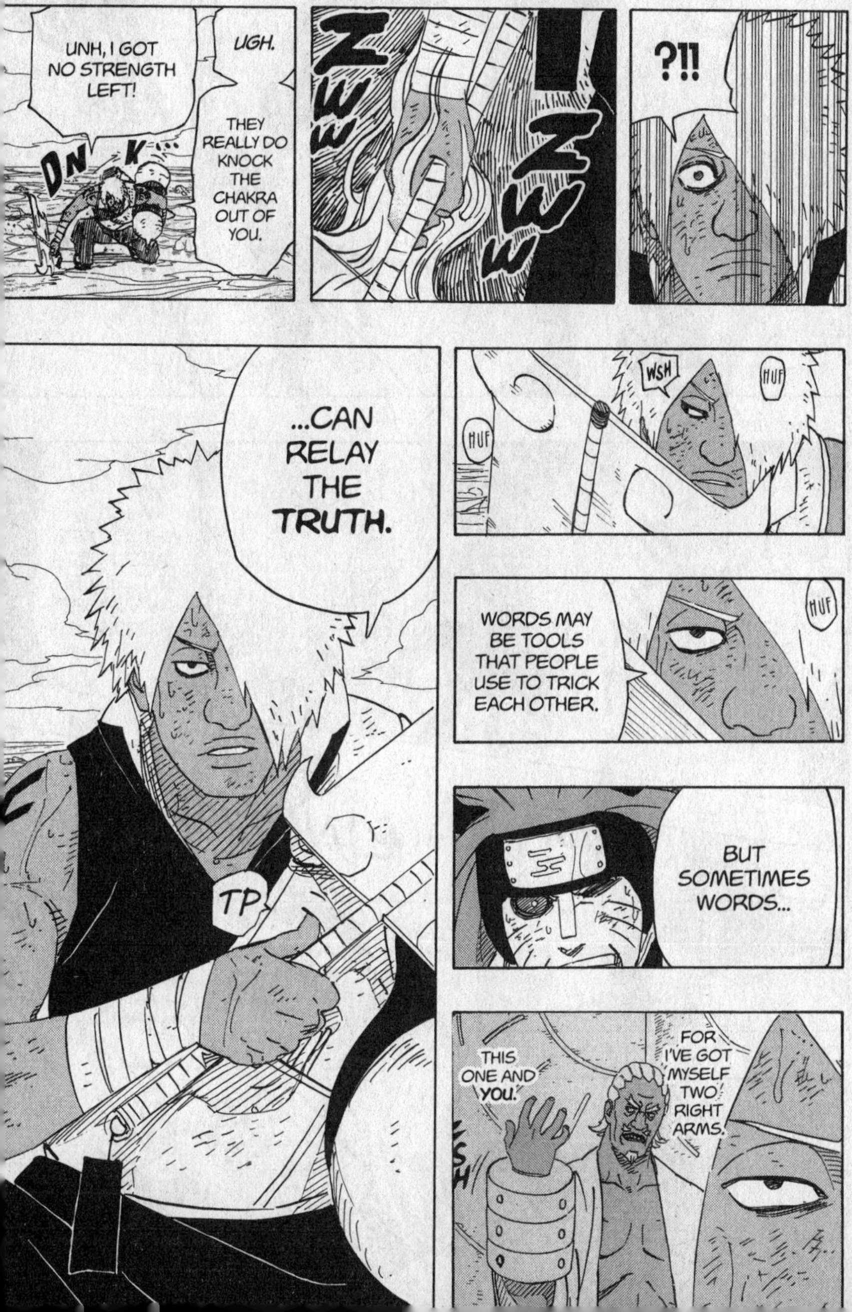
?!!
UGH.
THEY REALLY DO KNOCK THE CHAKRA OUT OF YOU.
UNH, I GOT NO STRENGTH LEFT!
WSH
HUF
HUF
WORDS MAY BE TOOLS THAT PEOPLE USE TO TRICK EACH OTHER.
HUF
BUT SOMETIMES WORDS...
FOR I'VE GOT MYSELF TWO RIGHT ARMS.
THIS ONE AND YOU.
...CAN RELAY THE TRUTH.
TP

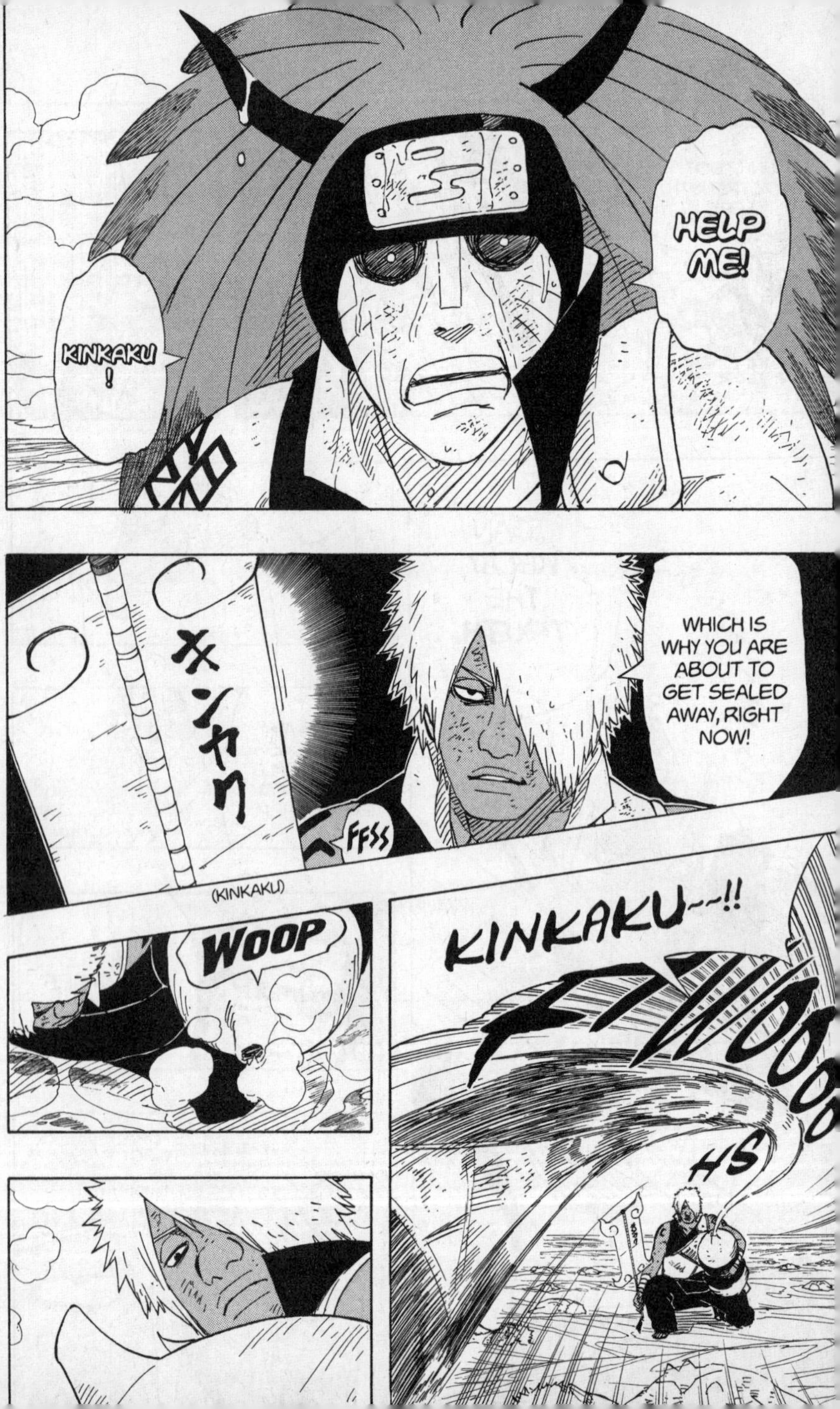
HELP ME!
KINKAKU!
WHICH IS WHY YOU ARE ABOUT TO GET SEALED AWAY, RIGHT NOW!
キンカク
FFSS
(KINKAKU)
KINKAKU~~!!
FWOOOO
HS
WOOP

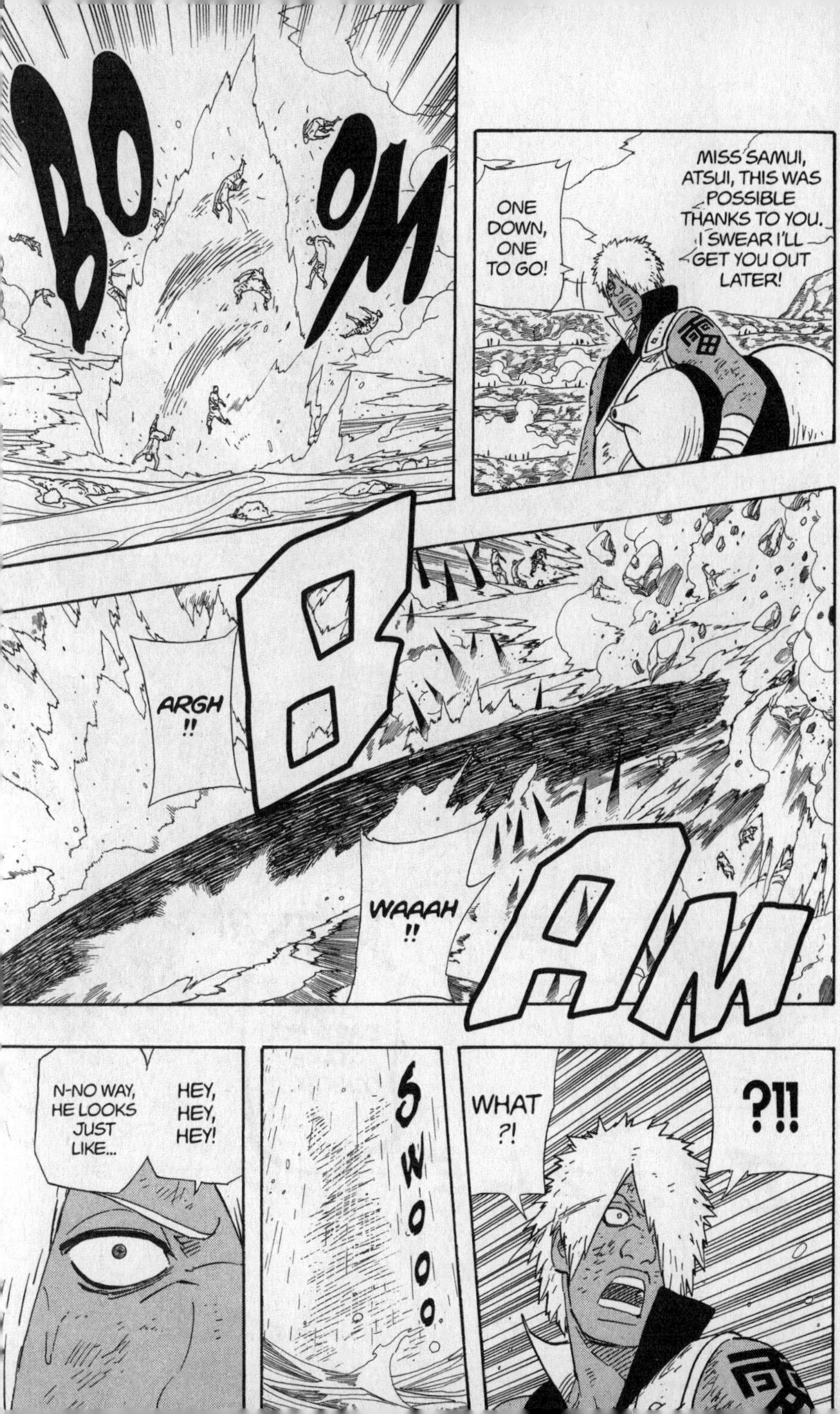
BOOM
MISS SAMUI, ATSUI, THIS WAS POSSIBLE THANKS TO YOU. I SWEAR I'LL GET YOU OUT LATER!
ONE DOWN, ONE TO GO!
BAM
ARGH !!
WAAAH !!
?!!
WHAT ?!
SWOOO
HEY, HEY, HEY!
N-NO WAY, HE LOOKS JUST LIKE...

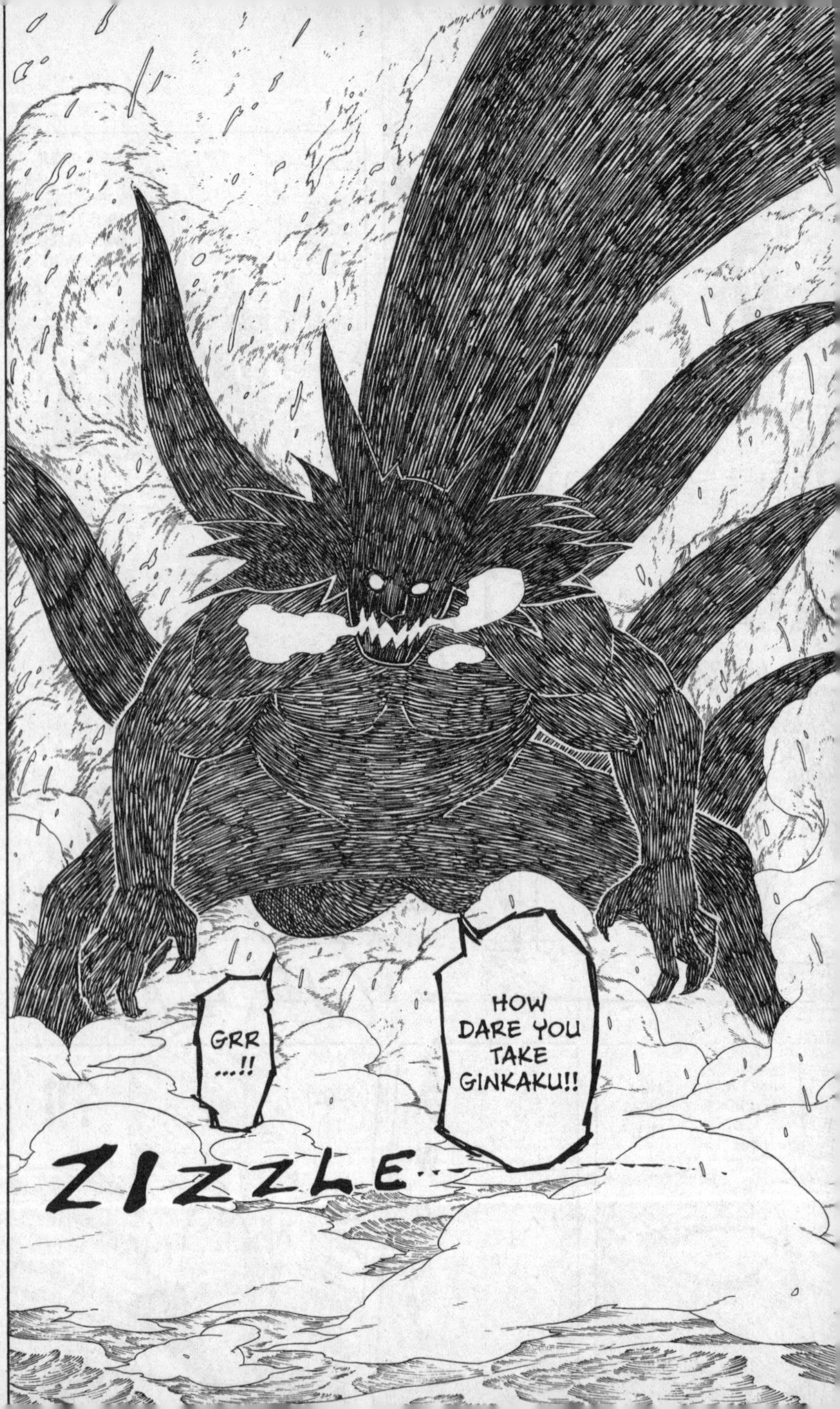
HOW DARE YOU TAKE GINKAKU!!
GRR ...!!
ZIZZLE...

READ THIS WAY

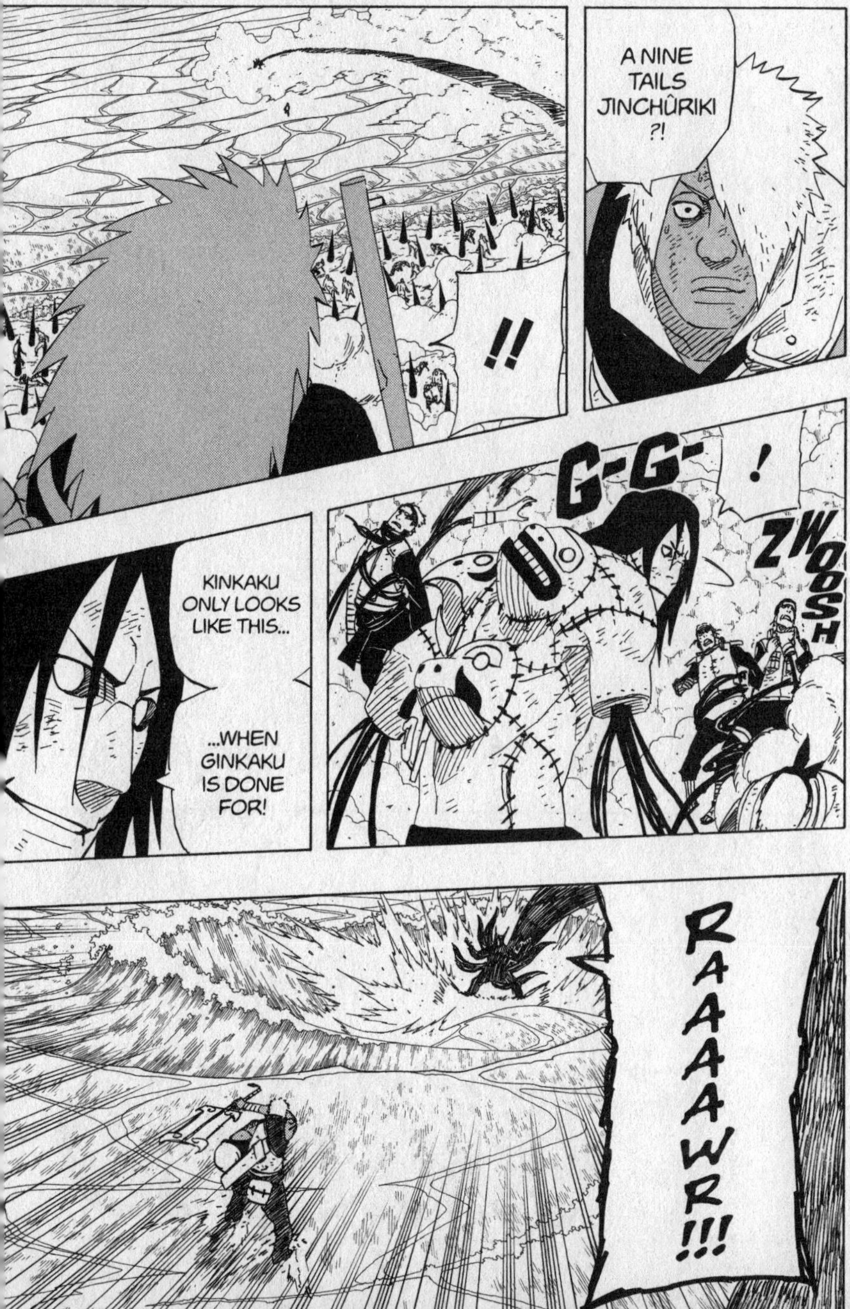
A NINE TAILS JINCHÛRIKI ?!
!!
G-G- !
ZWOOSH
KINKAKU ONLY LOOKS LIKE THIS...
...WHEN GINKAKU IS DONE FOR!
RAAAAWR!!!

NARUTO

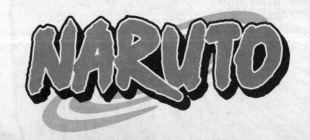

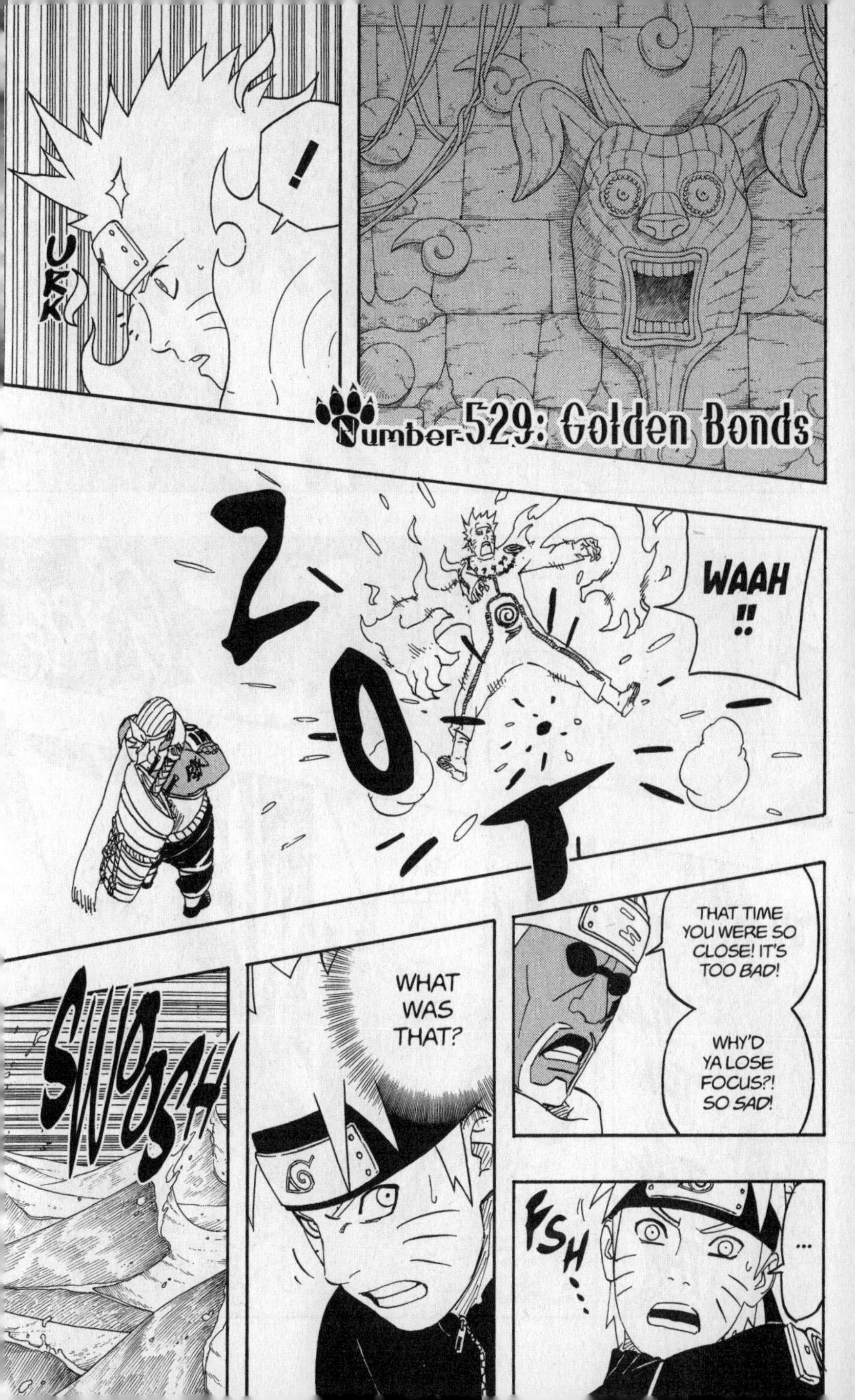
Number 529: Golden Bonds
!
URK
WAAH!!
ZOT
THAT TIME YOU WERE SO CLOSE! IT'S TOO BAD!
WHY'D YA LOSE FOCUS?! SO SAD!
FSH
...
WHAT WAS THAT?
SWOOSH

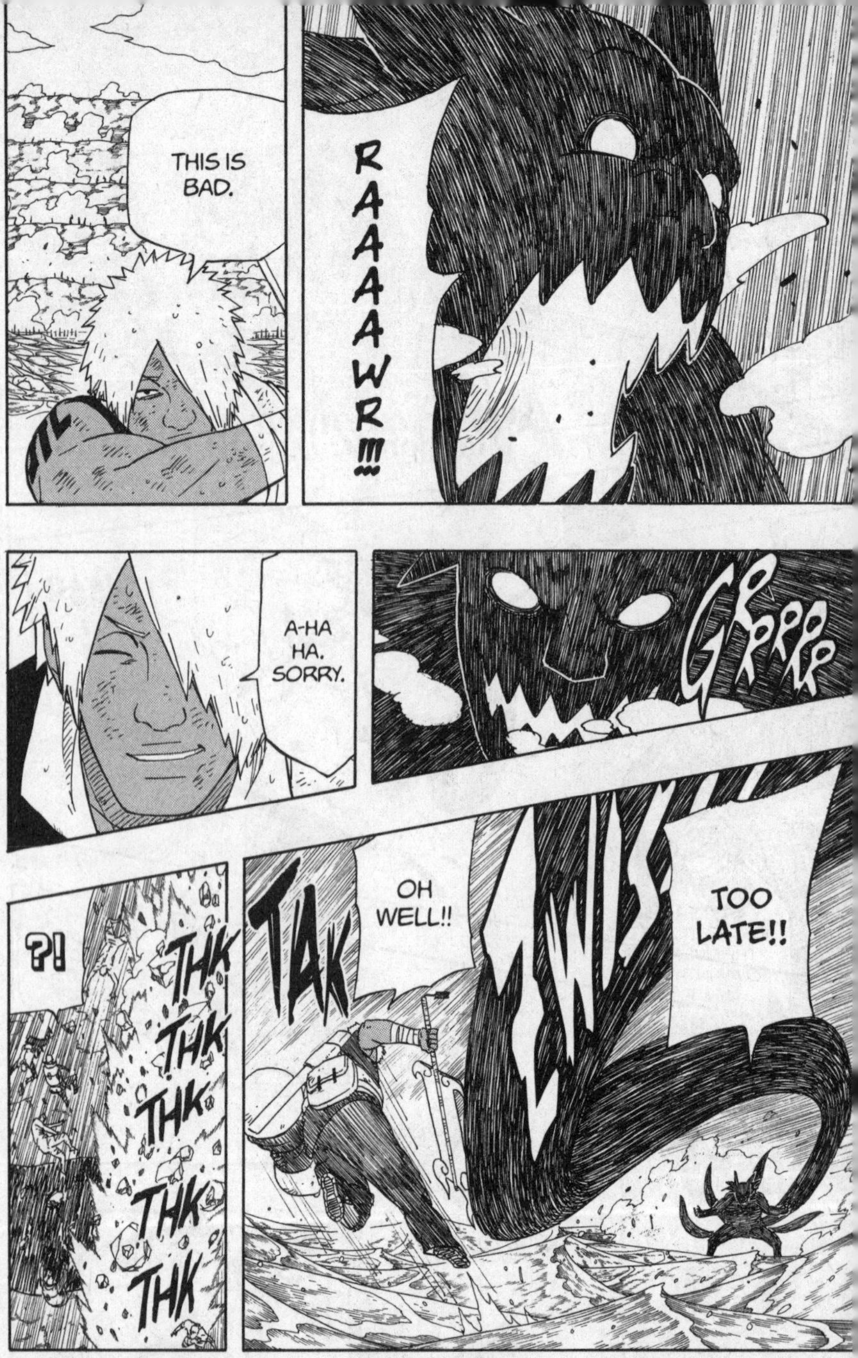
RAAAAAWR!!!
THIS IS BAD.
GRRRR
A-HA HA. SORRY.
TOO LATE!!
OH WELL!!
TAK
?!
THK
THK
THK
THK
THK

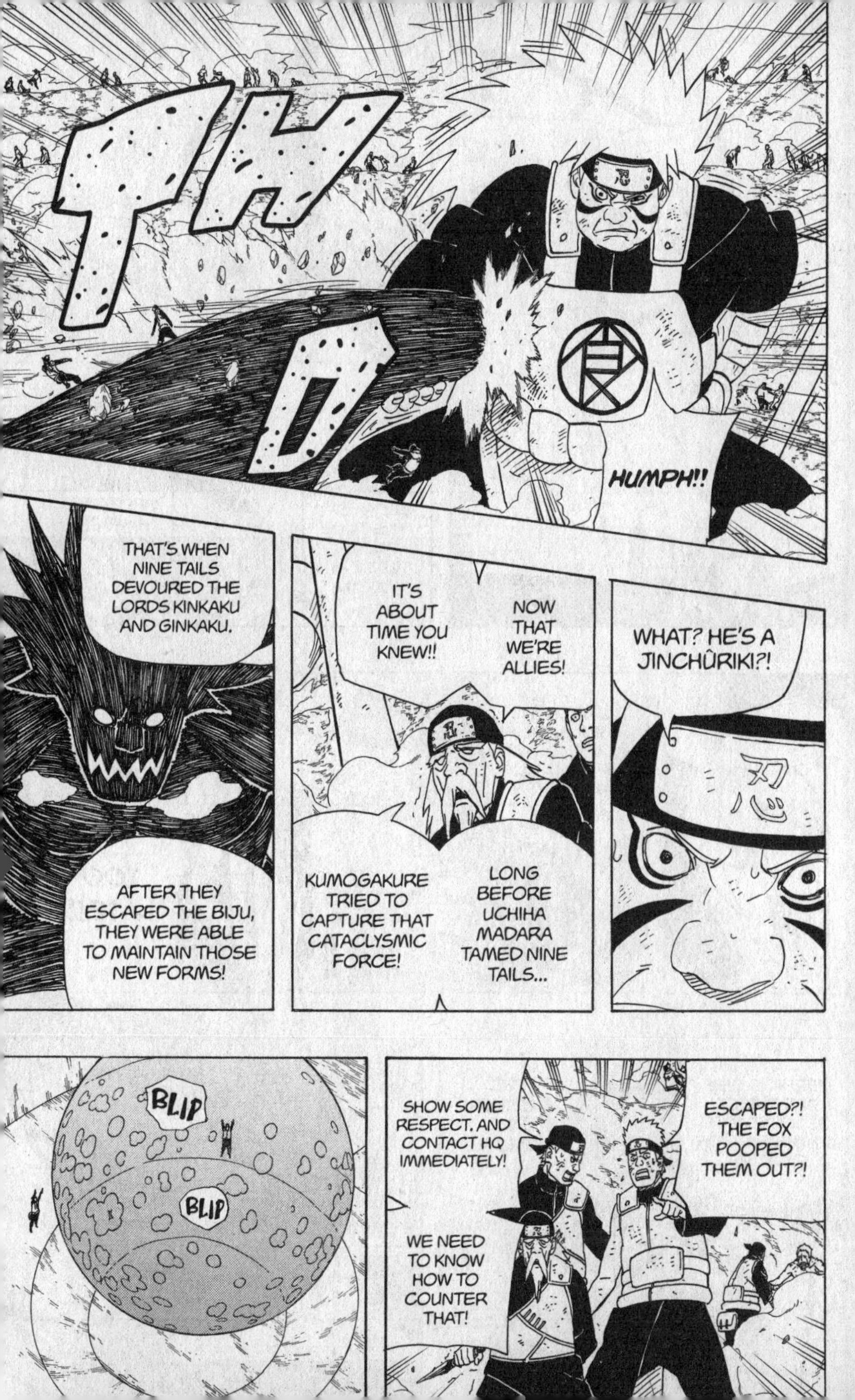
HUMPH!!
WHAT? HE'S A JINCHÛRIKI?!
NOW THAT WE'RE ALLIES!
IT'S ABOUT TIME YOU KNEW!!
LONG BEFORE UCHIHA MADARA TAMED NINE TAILS...
KUMOGAKURE TRIED TO CAPTURE THAT CATACLYSMIC FORCE!
THAT'S WHEN NINE TAILS DEVOURED THE LORDS KINKAKU AND GINKAKU.
AFTER THEY ESCAPED THE BIJU, THEY WERE ABLE TO MAINTAIN THOSE NEW FORMS!
ESCAPED?! THE FOX POOPED THEM OUT?!
SHOW SOME RESPECT. AND CONTACT HQ IMMEDIATELY!
WE NEED TO KNOW HOW TO COUNTER THAT!
BLIP
BLIP

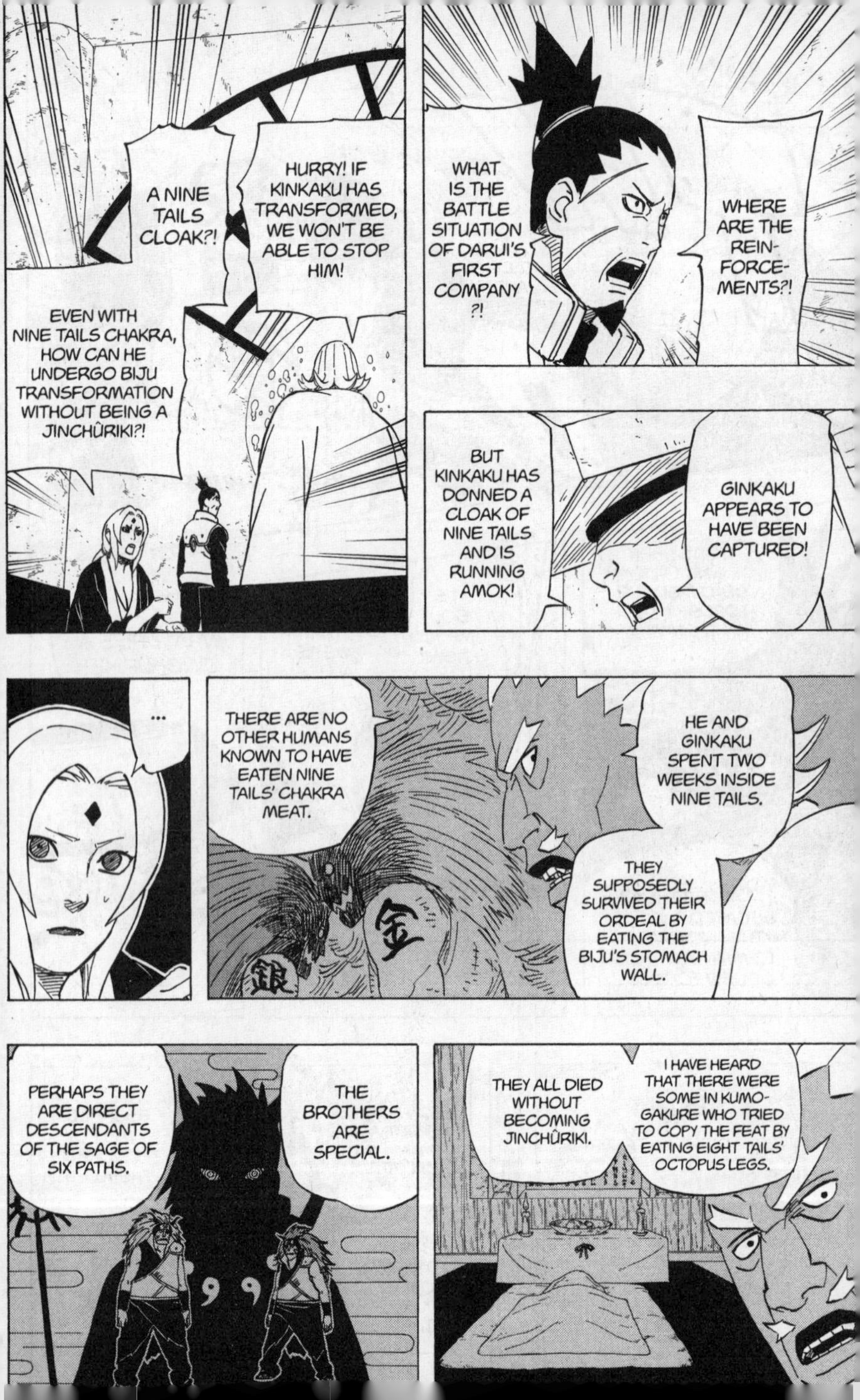
WHERE ARE THE REIN-FORCEMENTS?!
WHAT IS THE BATTLE SITUATION OF DARUI'S FIRST COMPANY ?!
GINKAKU APPEARS TO HAVE BEEN CAPTURED!
BUT KINKAKU HAS DONNED A CLOAK OF NINE TAILS AND IS RUNNING AMOK!
HURRY! IF KINKAKU HAS TRANSFORMED, WE WON'T BE ABLE TO STOP HIM!
A NINE TAILS CLOAK?!
EVEN WITH NINE TAILS CHAKRA, HOW CAN HE UNDERGO BIJU TRANSFORMATION WITHOUT BEING A JINCHÛRIKI?!
HE AND GINKAKU SPENT TWO WEEKS INSIDE NINE TAILS.
THEY SUPPOSEDLY SURVIVED THEIR ORDEAL BY EATING THE BIJU'S STOMACH WALL.
THERE ARE NO OTHER HUMANS KNOWN TO HAVE EATEN NINE TAILS' CHAKRA MEAT.
...
I HAVE HEARD THAT THERE WERE SOME IN KUMO-GAKURE WHO TRIED TO COPY THE FEAT BY EATING EIGHT TAILS' OCTOPUS LEGS.
THEY ALL DIED WITHOUT BECOMING JINCHÛRIKI.
THE BROTHERS ARE SPECIAL.
PERHAPS THEY ARE DIRECT DESCENDANTS OF THE SAGE OF SIX PATHS.

READ THIS WAY

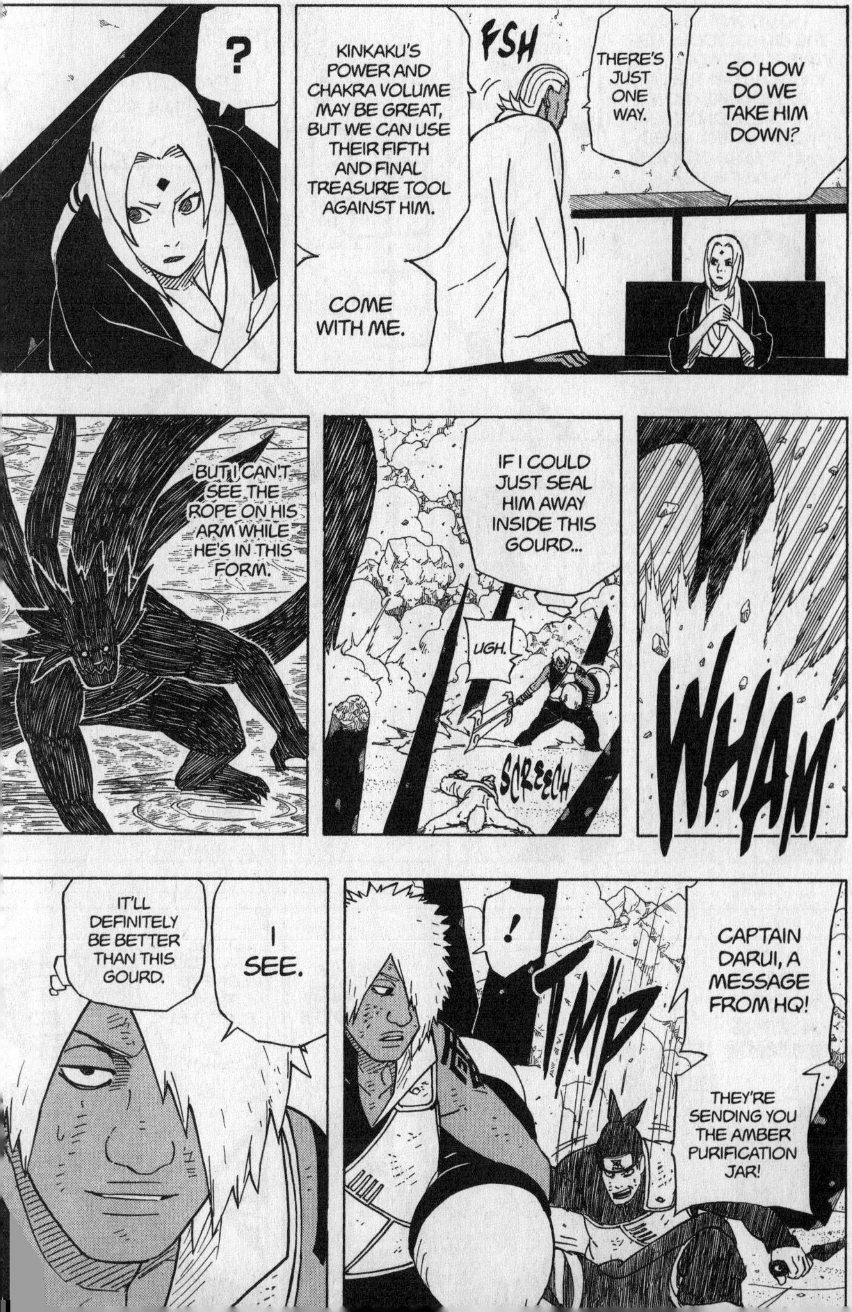
SO HOW DO WE TAKE HIM DOWN?
THERE'S JUST ONE WAY.
FSH
KINKAKU'S POWER AND CHAKRA VOLUME MAY BE GREAT, BUT WE CAN USE THEIR FIFTH AND FINAL TREASURE TOOL AGAINST HIM.
COME WITH ME.
?
WHAM
IF I COULD JUST SEAL HIM AWAY INSIDE THIS GOURD...
UGH.
SCREECH
BUT I CAN'T SEE THE ROPE ON HIS ARM WHILE HE'S IN THIS FORM.
CAPTAIN DARUI, A MESSAGE FROM HQ!
TMP
!
THEY'RE SENDING YOU THE AMBER PURIFICATION JAR!
I SEE.
IT'LL DEFINITELY BE BETTER THAN THIS GOURD.

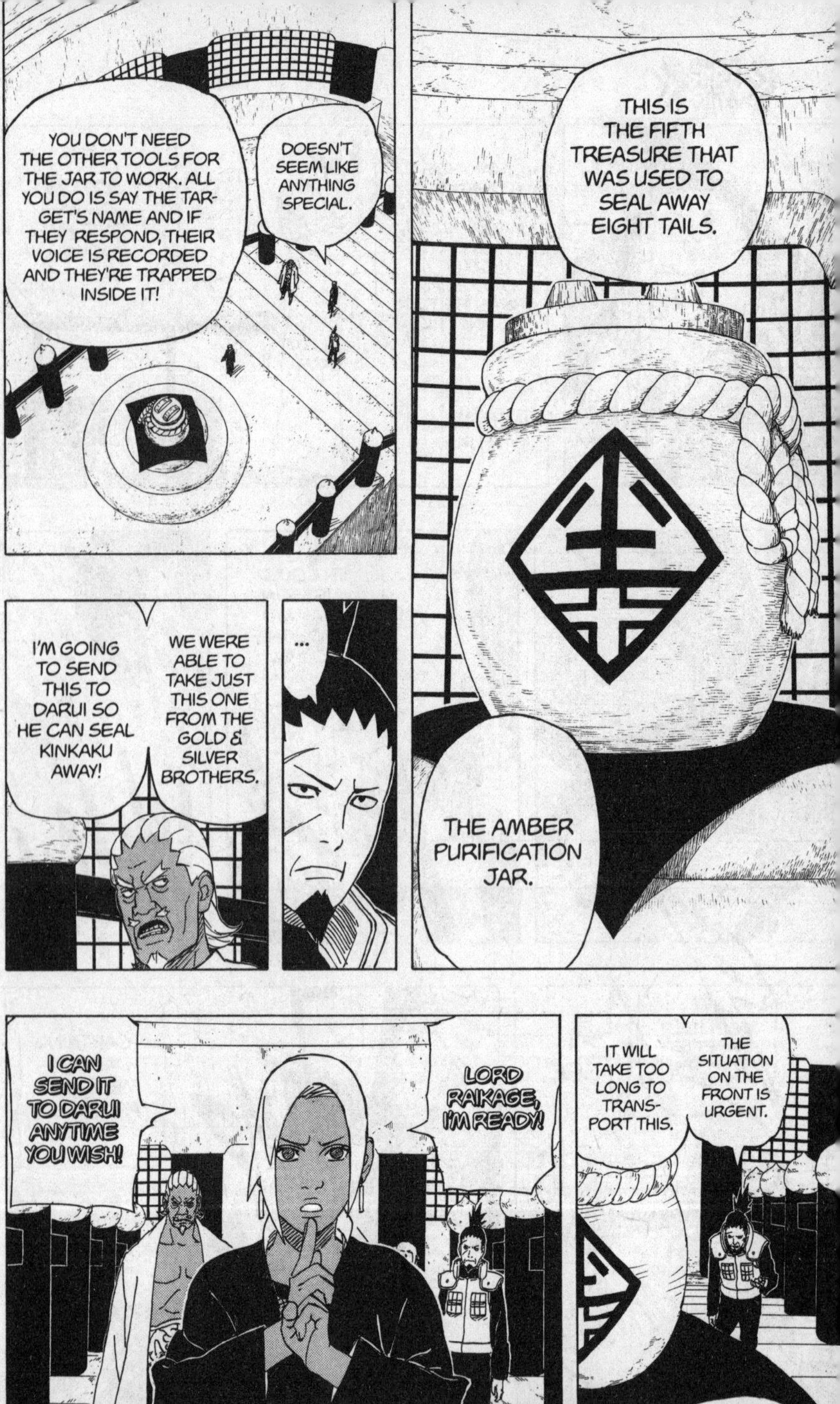

THIS IS THE FIFTH TREASURE THAT WAS USED TO SEAL AWAY EIGHT TAILS.
THE AMBER PURIFICATION JAR.
DOESN'T SEEM LIKE ANYTHING SPECIAL.
YOU DON'T NEED THE OTHER TOOLS FOR THE JAR TO WORK. ALL YOU DO IS SAY THE TARGET'S NAME AND IF THEY RESPOND, THEIR VOICE IS RECORDED AND THEY'RE TRAPPED INSIDE IT!
...
WE WERE ABLE TO TAKE JUST THIS ONE FROM THE GOLD & SILVER BROTHERS.
I'M GOING TO SEND THIS TO DARUI SO HE CAN SEAL KINKAKU AWAY!
THE SITUATION ON THE FRONT IS URGENT.
IT WILL TAKE TOO LONG TO TRANSPORT THIS.
LORD RAIKAGE, I'M READY!
I CAN SEND IT TO DARUI ANYTIME YOU WISH!

READ THIS WAY

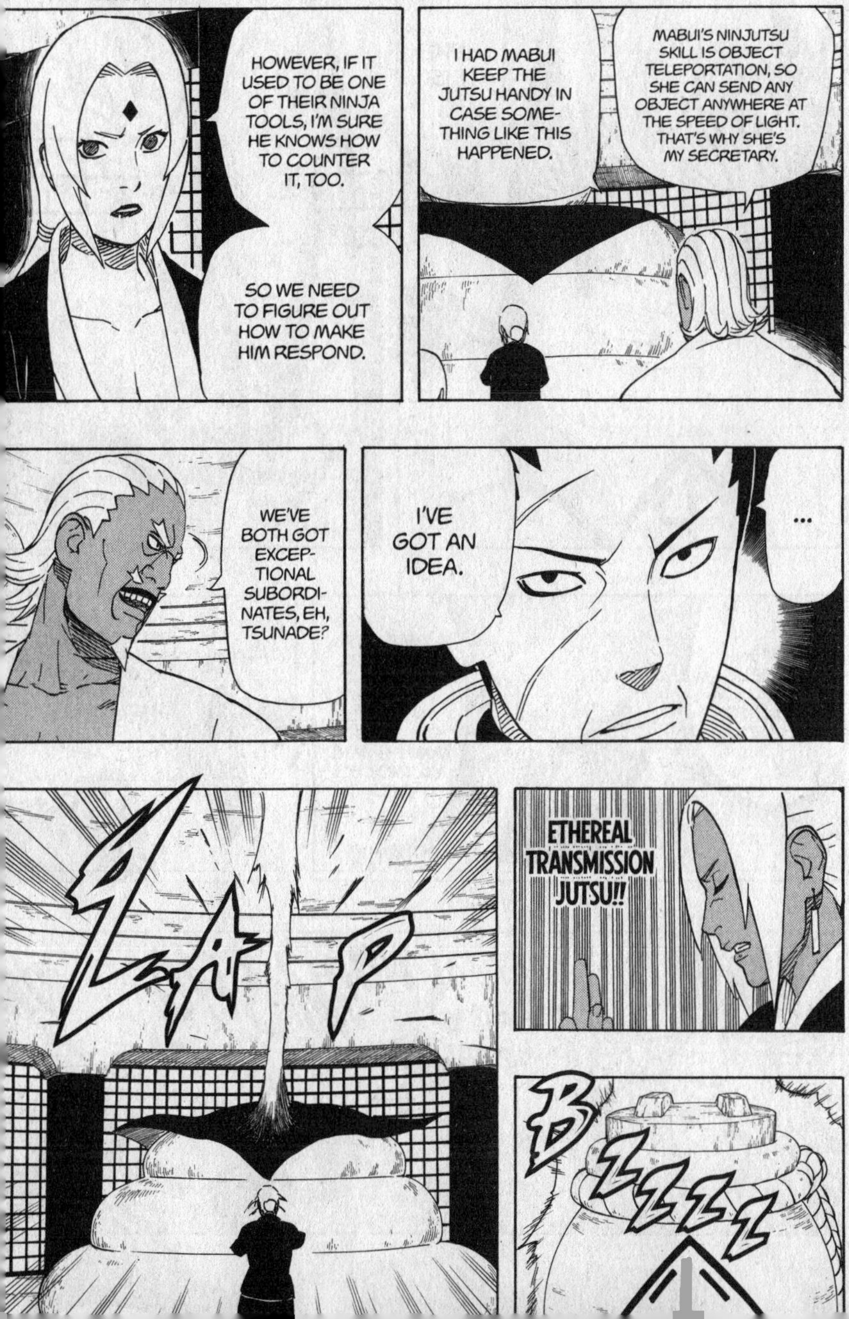
MABUI'S NINJUTSU SKILL IS OBJECT TELEPORTATION, SO SHE CAN SEND ANY OBJECT ANYWHERE AT THE SPEED OF LIGHT. THAT'S WHY SHE'S MY SECRETARY.
I HAD MABUI KEEP THE JUTSU HANDY IN CASE SOME-THING LIKE THIS HAPPENED.
HOWEVER, IF IT USED TO BE ONE OF THEIR NINJA TOOLS, I'M SURE HE KNOWS HOW TO COUNTER IT, TOO.
SO WE NEED TO FIGURE OUT HOW TO MAKE HIM RESPOND.
...
I'VE GOT AN IDEA.
WE'VE BOTH GOT EXCEP-TIONAL SUBORDI-NATES, EH, TSUNADE?
ETHEREAL TRANSMISSION JUTSU!!
BZZZZZ
ZAP

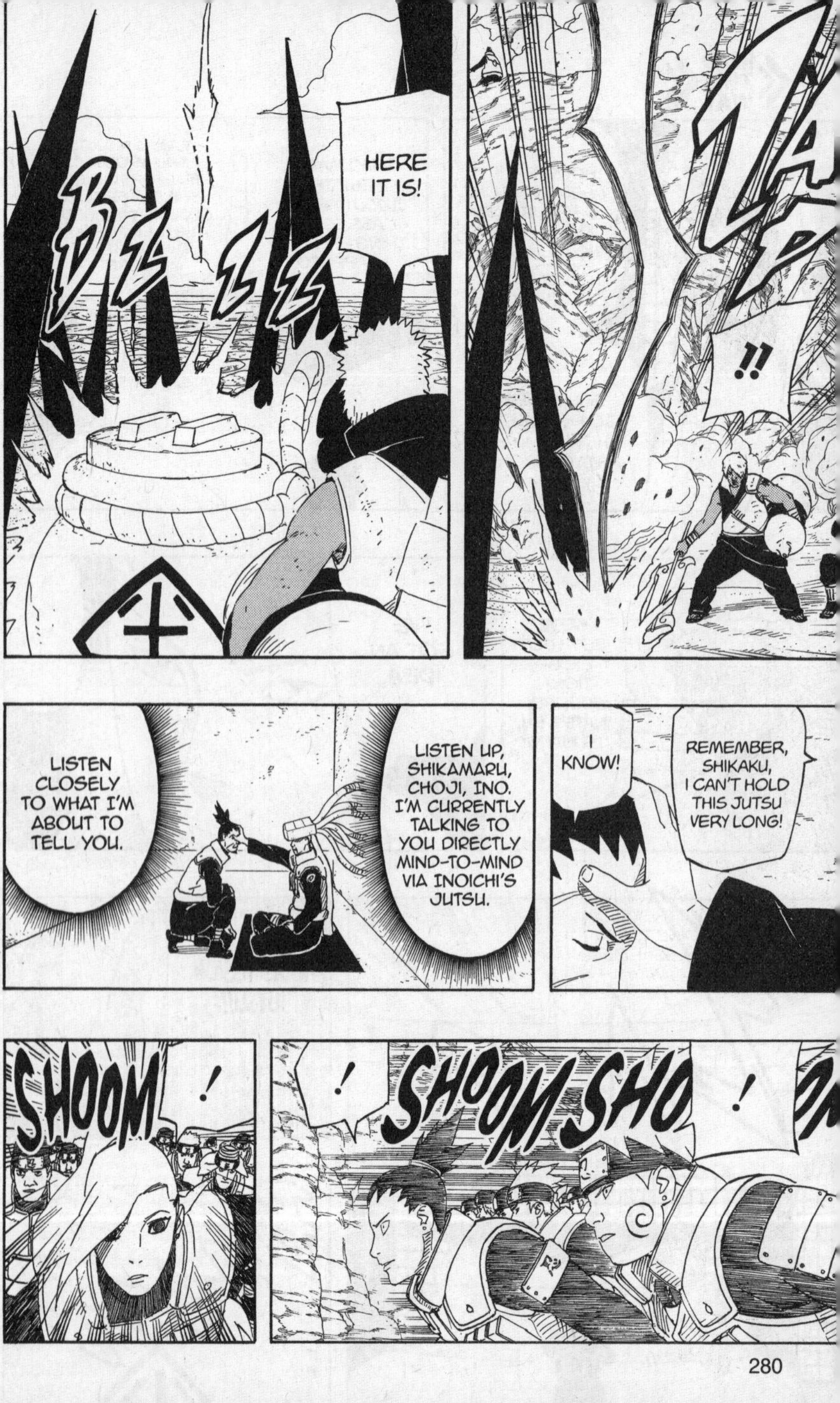
!!
BZZZ
HERE IT IS!
REMEMBER, SHIKAKU, I CAN'T HOLD THIS JUTSU VERY LONG!
I KNOW!
LISTEN UP, SHIKAMARU, CHOJI, INO. I'M CURRENTLY TALKING TO YOU DIRECTLY MIND-TO-MIND VIA INOICHI'S JUTSU.
LISTEN CLOSELY TO WHAT I'M ABOUT TO TELL YOU.
!
SHOOM
!
SHOOM
!

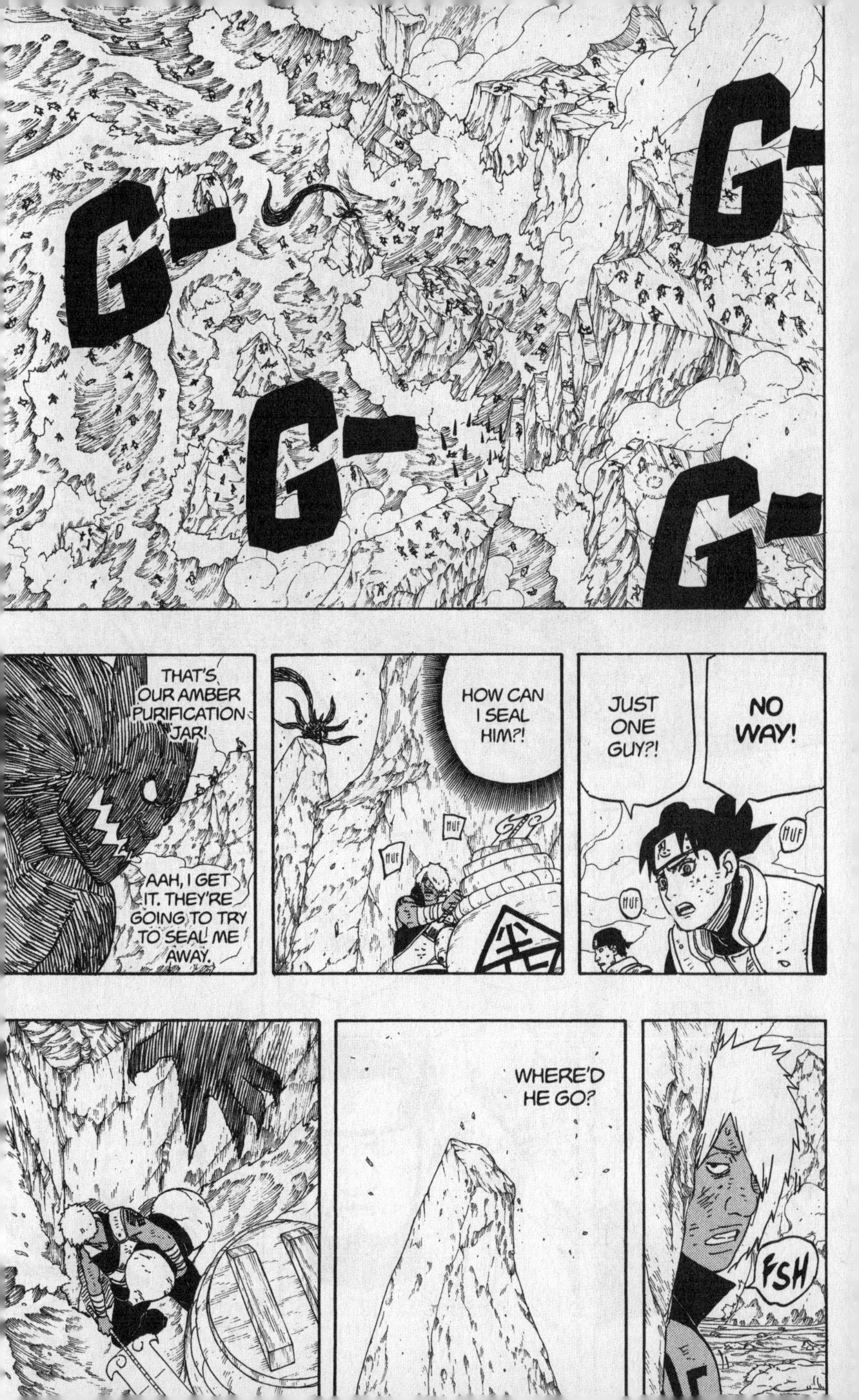
G-
G-
G-
G-
NO WAY!
JUST ONE GUY?!
HUF
HUF
HOW CAN I SEAL HIM?!
HUF
HUF
THAT'S OUR AMBER PURIFICATION JAR!
AAH, I GET IT. THEY'RE GOING TO TRY TO SEAL ME AWAY.
FSH
WHERE'D HE GO?

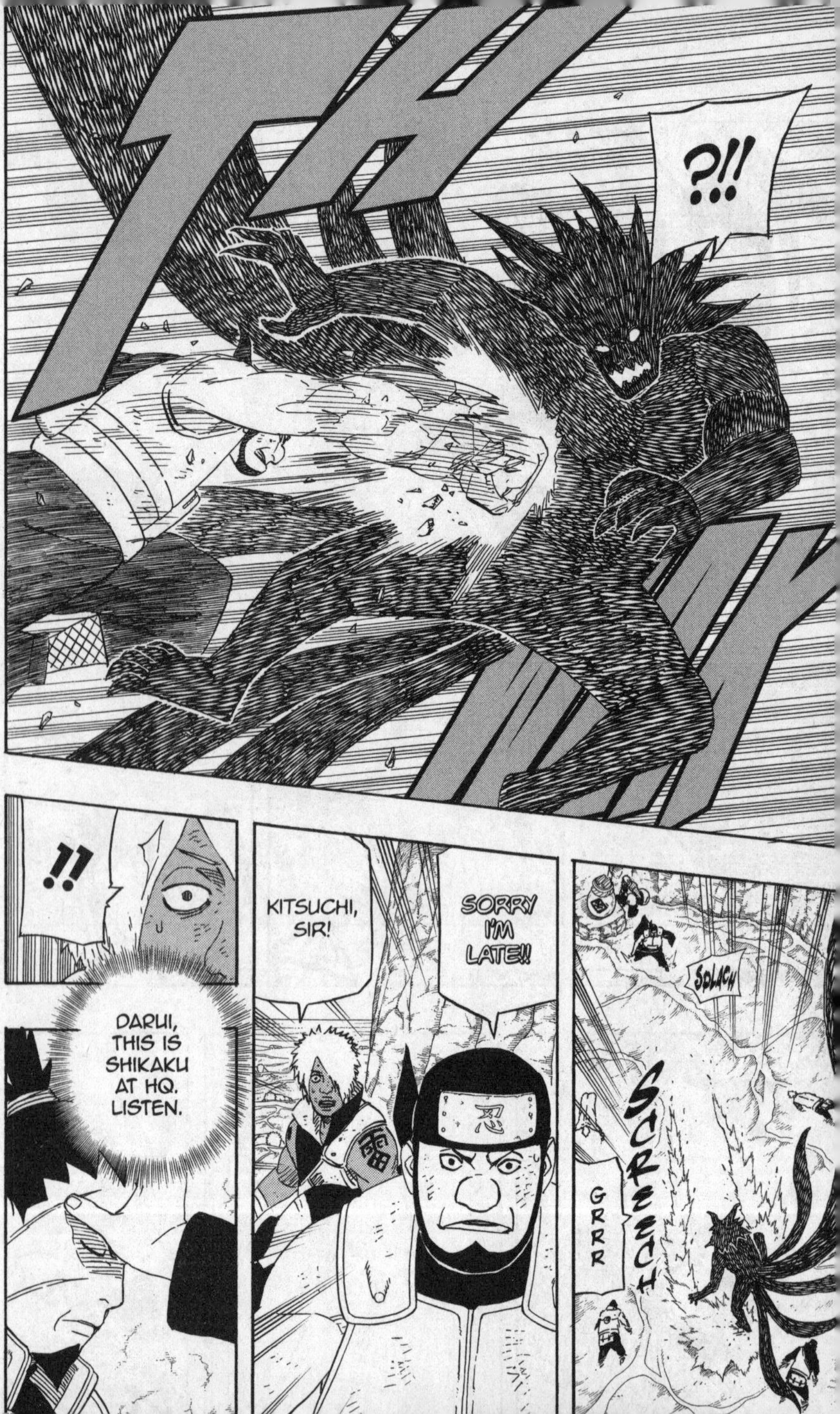
?!!
SPLACH
SCREECH
GRRR
SORRY I'M LATE!!
KITSUCHI, SIR!
!!
DARUI, THIS IS SHIKAKU AT HQ. LISTEN.

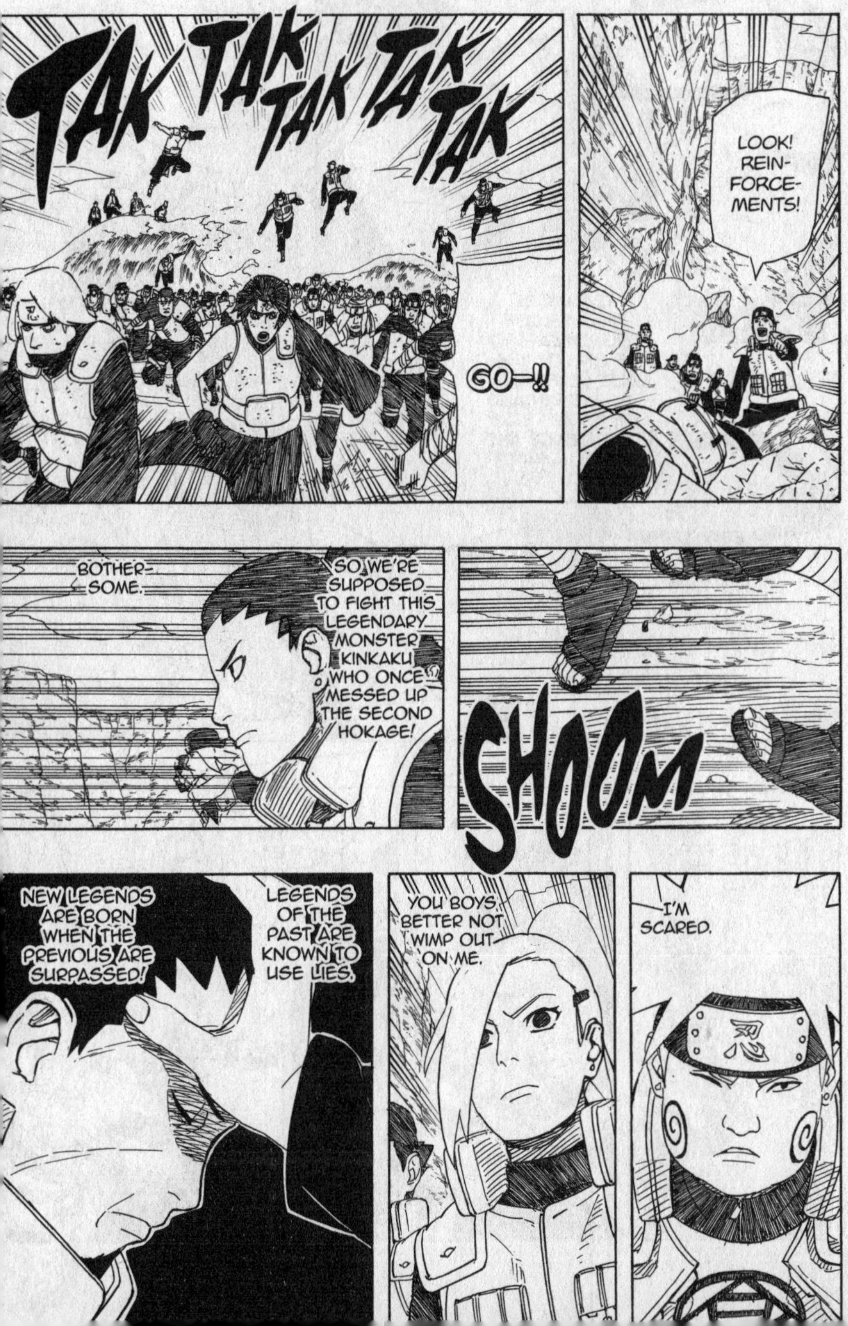
LOOK! REIN-FORCEMENTS!
TAK TAK TAK TAK TAK TAK
GO—!!
SHOOM
SO WE'RE SUPPOSED TO FIGHT THIS LEGENDARY MONSTER KINKAKU WHO ONCE MESSED UP THE SECOND HOKAGE!
BOTHER-SOME.
I'M SCARED.
YOU BOYS BETTER NOT WIMP OUT ON ME.
LEGENDS OF THE PAST ARE KNOWN TO USE LIES.
NEW LEGENDS ARE BORN WHEN THE PREVIOUS ARE SURPASSED!

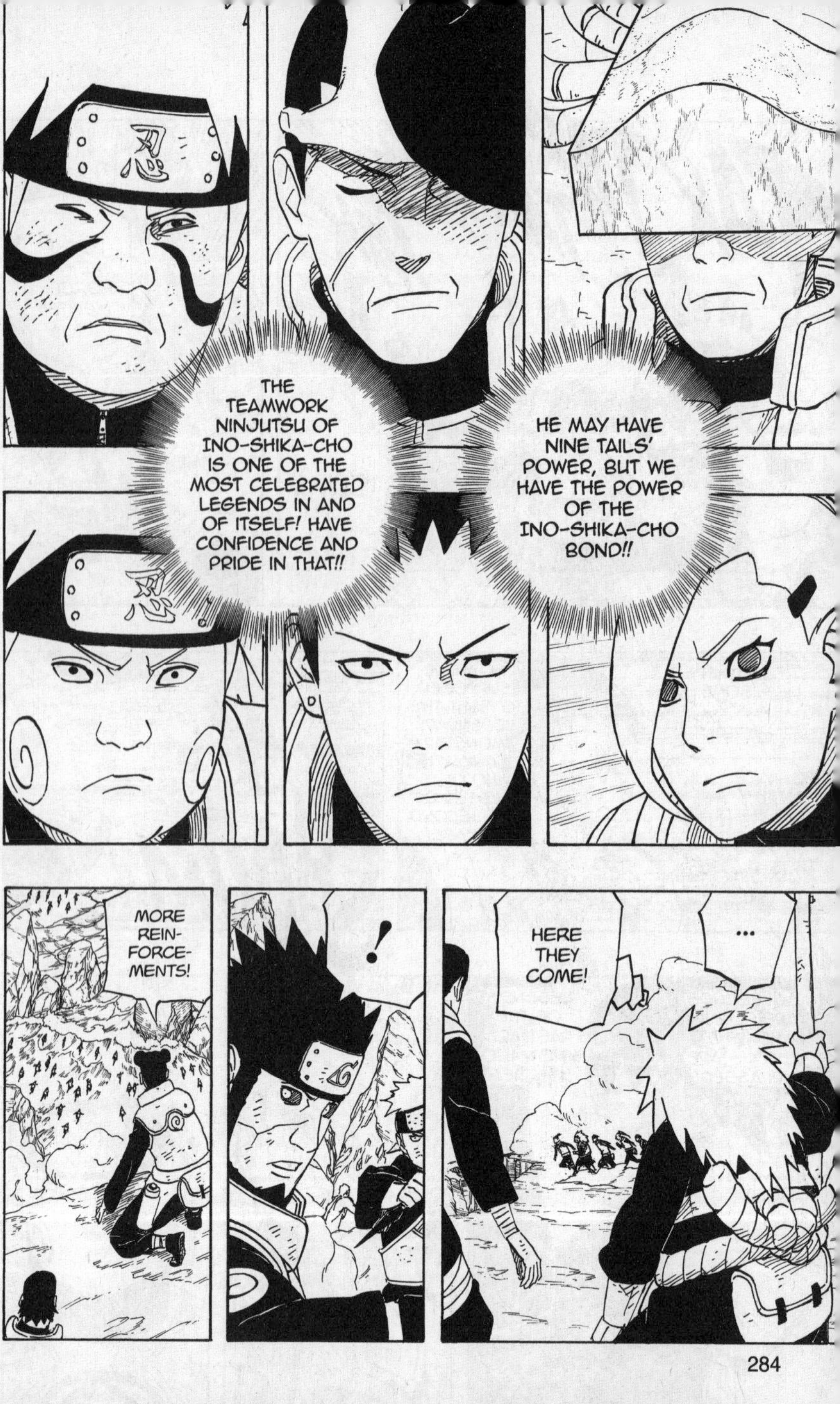
HE MAY HAVE NINE TAILS' POWER, BUT WE HAVE THE POWER OF THE INO-SHIKA-CHO BOND!!
THE TEAMWORK NINJUTSU OF INO-SHIKA-CHO IS ONE OF THE MOST CELEBRATED LEGENDS IN AND OF ITSELF! HAVE CONFIDENCE AND PRIDE IN THAT!!
...
HERE THEY COME!
!
MORE REIN-FORCE-MENTS!

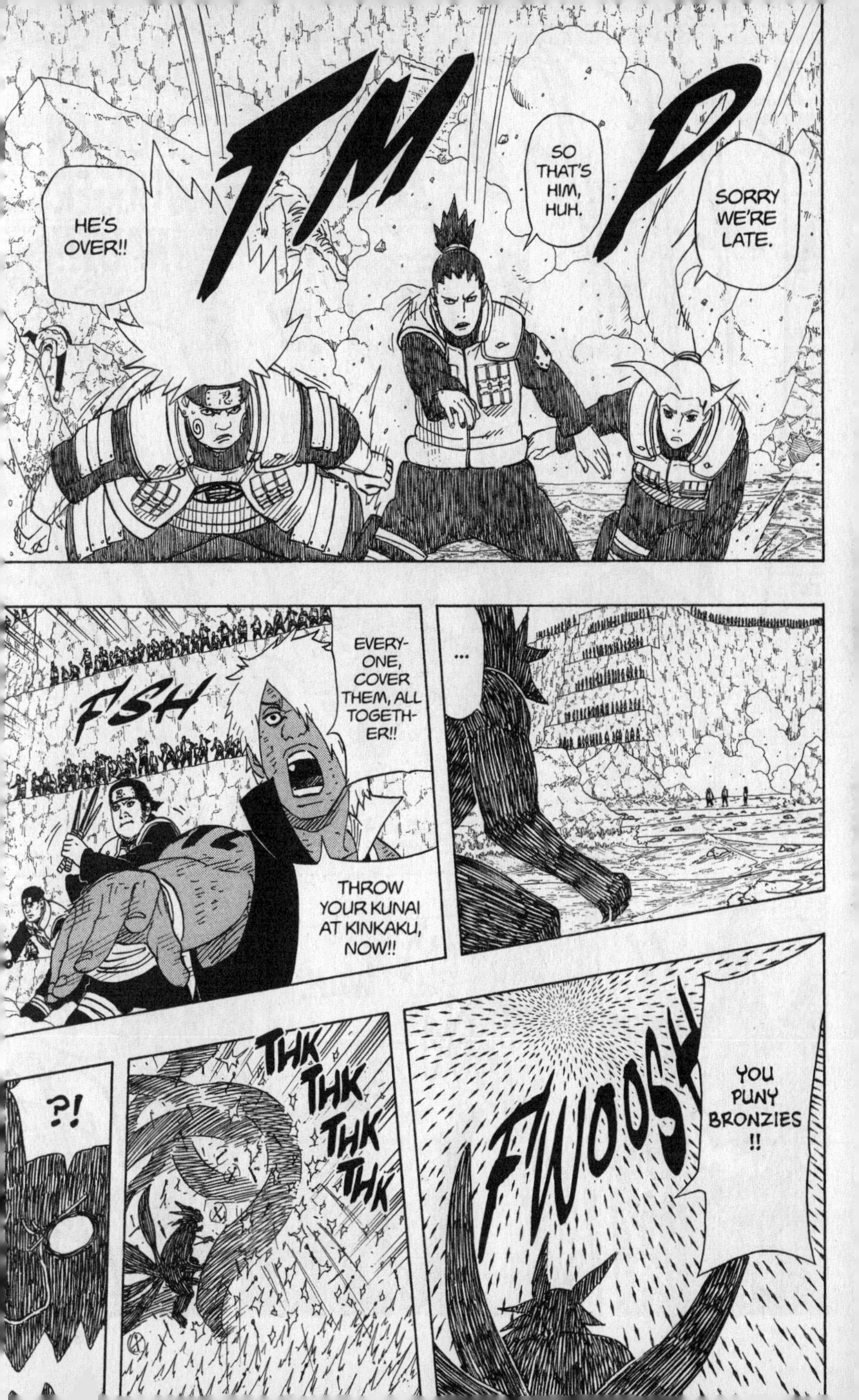
SORRY WE'RE LATE.
SO THAT'S HIM, HUH.
TMP
HE'S OVER!!
...
EVERY-ONE, COVER THEM, ALL TOGETH-ER!!
FSH
THROW YOUR KUNAI AT KINKAKU, NOW!!
YOU PUNY BRONZIES!!
FWOOSH
THK THK THK THK
?!

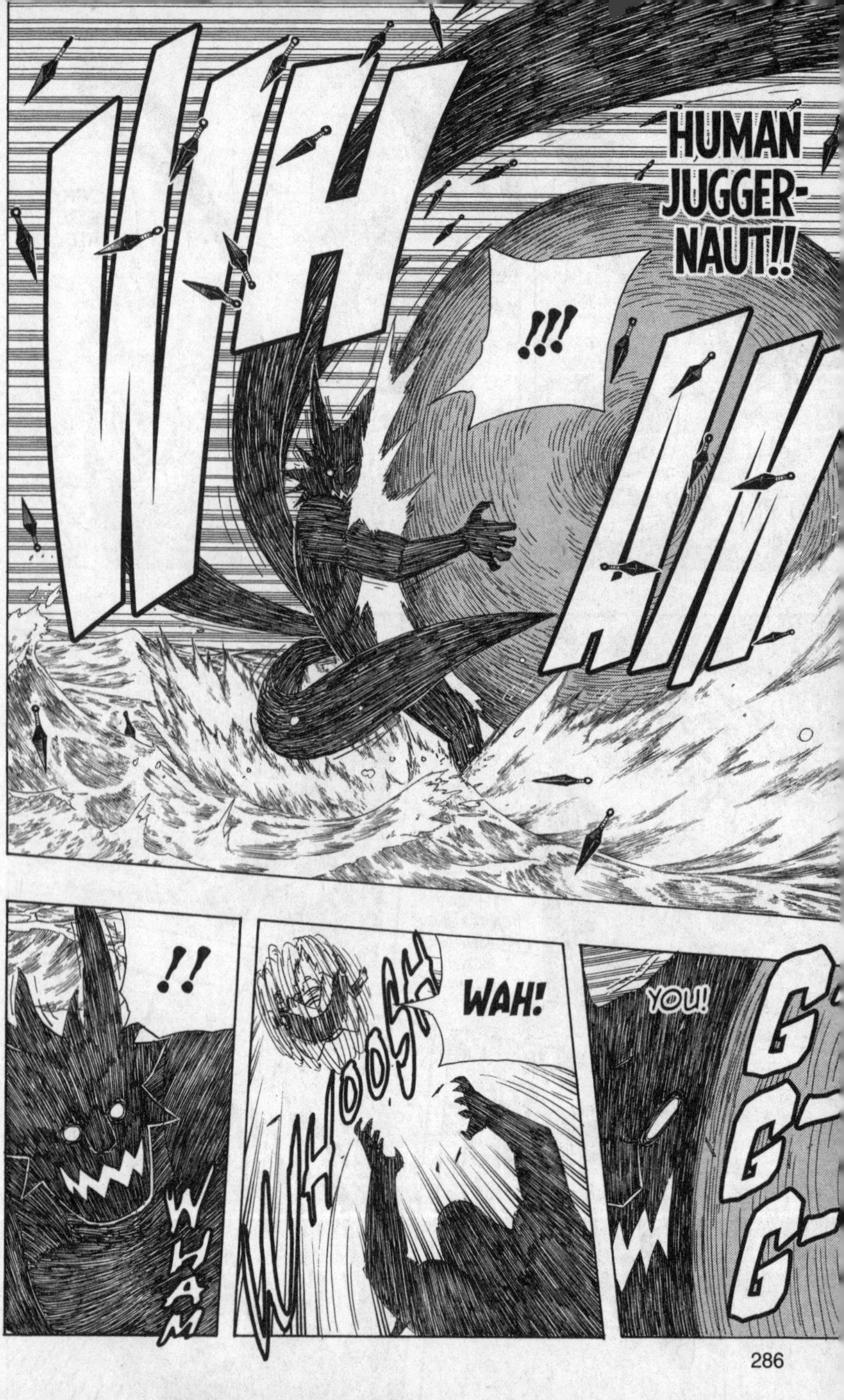
HUMAN JUGGER-NAUT!!
!!!
WAH
YOU!
G- G- G-
WAH!
WHOOSH
!!
WHAM

READ THIS WAY

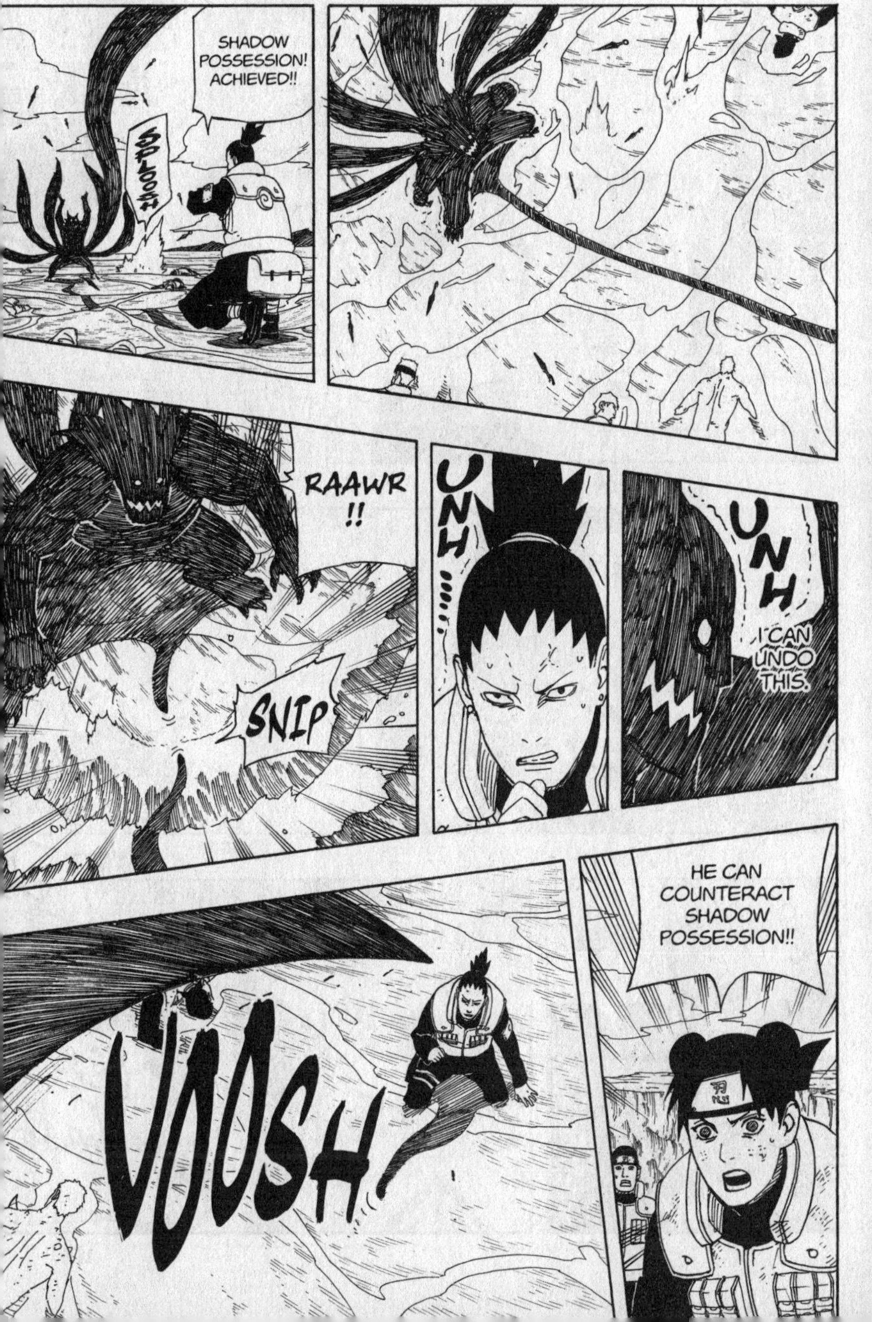

SHADOW POSSESSION! ACHIEVED!!
SPLOOSH
UNH
I CAN UNDO THIS.
UNH.....
RAAWR !!
SNIP
HE CAN COUNTERACT SHADOW POSSESSION!!
VOOSH

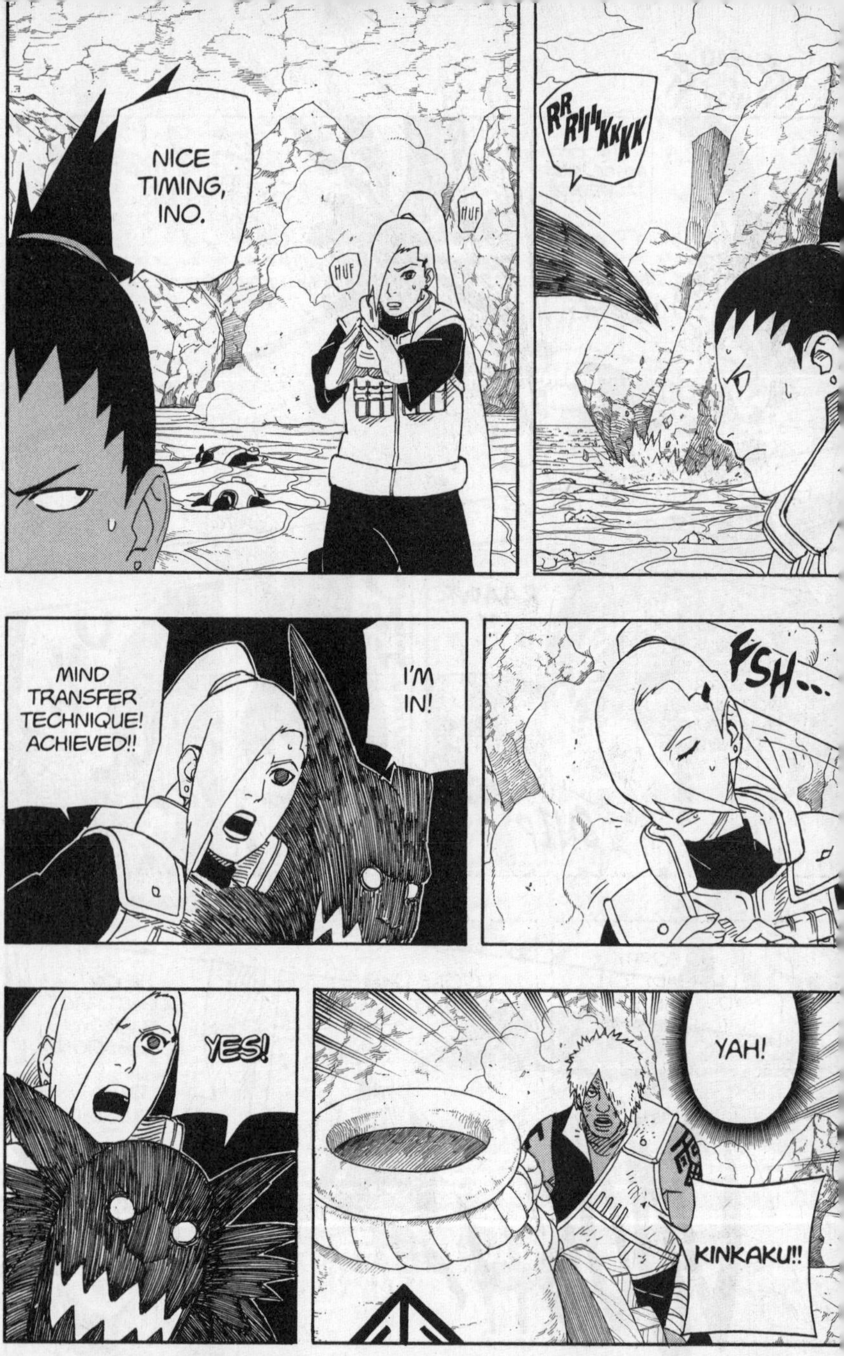
RRRIIIKKKK
NICE TIMING, INO.
HUF
HUF
FSH...
I'M IN!
MIND TRANSFER TECHNIQUE! ACHIEVED!!
YAH!
KINKAKU!!
YES!

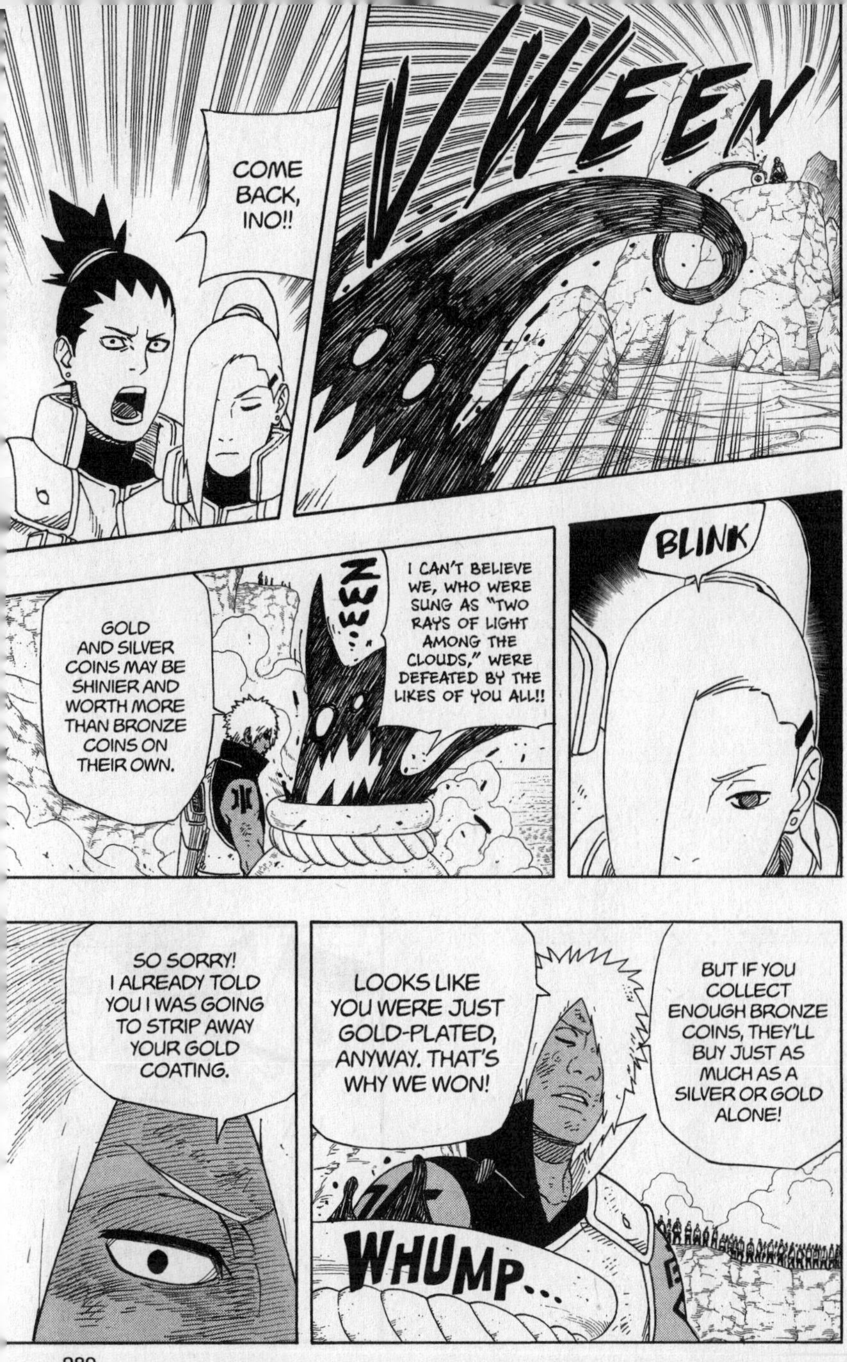
VWEEN
COME BACK, INO!!
BLINK
I CAN'T BELIEVE WE, WHO WERE SUNG AS "TWO RAYS OF LIGHT AMONG THE CLOUDS," WERE DEFEATED BY THE LIKES OF YOU ALL!!
ZWEEN...
GOLD AND SILVER COINS MAY BE SHINIER AND WORTH MORE THAN BRONZE COINS ON THEIR OWN.
BUT IF YOU COLLECT ENOUGH BRONZE COINS, THEY'LL BUY JUST AS MUCH AS A SILVER OR GOLD ALONE!
LOOKS LIKE YOU WERE JUST GOLD-PLATED, ANYWAY. THAT'S WHY WE WON!
WHUMP...
SO SORRY! I ALREADY TOLD YOU I WAS GOING TO STRIP AWAY YOUR GOLD COATING.

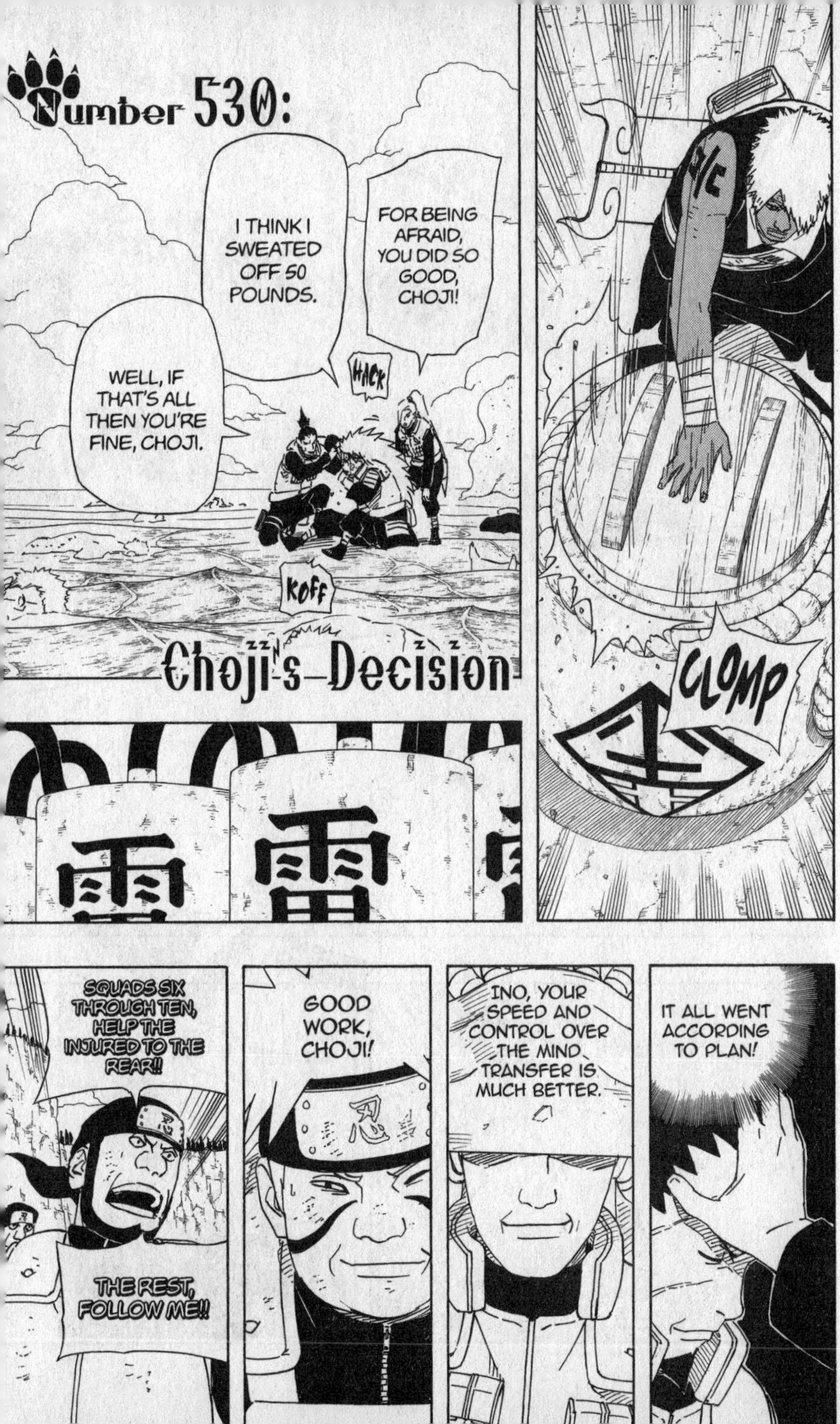

CLOMP
Number 530:
FOR BEING AFRAID, YOU DID SO GOOD, CHOJI!
I THINK I SWEATED OFF 50 POUNDS.
HACK
WELL, IF THAT'S ALL THEN YOU'RE FINE, CHOJI.
KOFF
Choji's Decision
IT ALL WENT ACCORDING TO PLAN!
INO, YOUR SPEED AND CONTROL OVER THE MIND TRANSFER IS MUCH BETTER.
GOOD WORK, CHOJI!
SQUADS SIX THROUGH TEN, HELP THE INJURED TO THE REAR!!
THE REST, FOLLOW ME!!

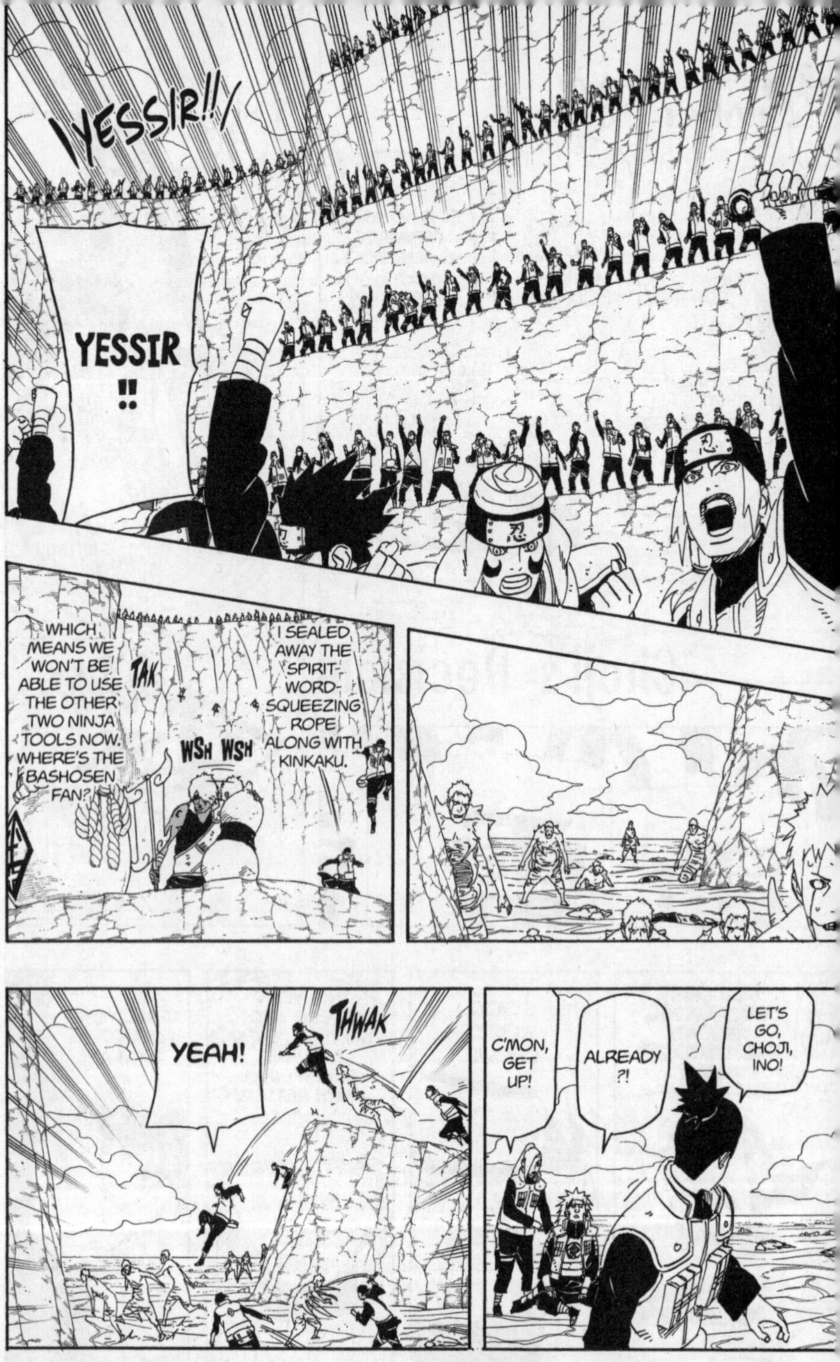
YESSIR!!
YESSIR!!
I SEALED AWAY THE SPIRIT-WORD-SQUEEZING ROPE ALONG WITH KINKAKU.
WHICH MEANS WE WON'T BE ABLE TO USE THE OTHER TWO NINJA TOOLS NOW. WHERE'S THE BASHOSEN FAN?!
TAK
WSH WSH
LET'S GO, CHOJI, INO!
ALREADY?!
C'MON, GET UP!
THWAK
YEAH!

READ THIS WAY

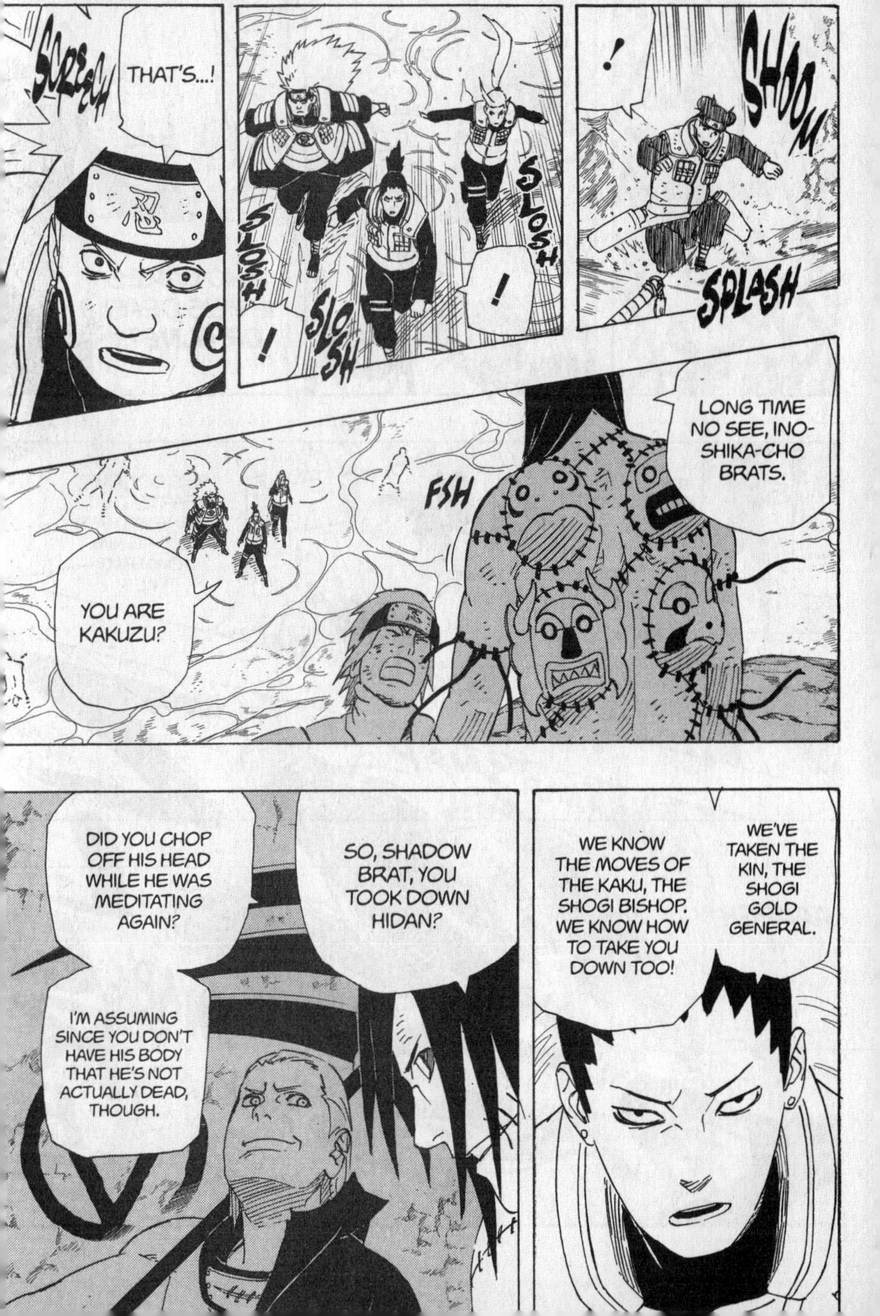
!
SHOOM
SPLASH
SLOSH
!
!
SLOSH
SLOSH
SCREECH
THAT'S...!
LONG TIME NO SEE, INO-SHIKA-CHO BRATS.
FSH
YOU ARE KAKUZU?
WE'VE TAKEN THE KIN, THE SHOGI GOLD GENERAL.
WE KNOW THE MOVES OF THE KAKU, THE SHOGI BISHOP. WE KNOW HOW TO TAKE YOU DOWN TOO!
SO, SHADOW BRAT, YOU TOOK DOWN HIDAN?
DID YOU CHOP OFF HIS HEAD WHILE HE WAS MEDITATING AGAIN?
I'M ASSUMING SINCE YOU DON'T HAVE HIS BODY THAT HE'S NOT ACTUALLY DEAD, THOUGH.

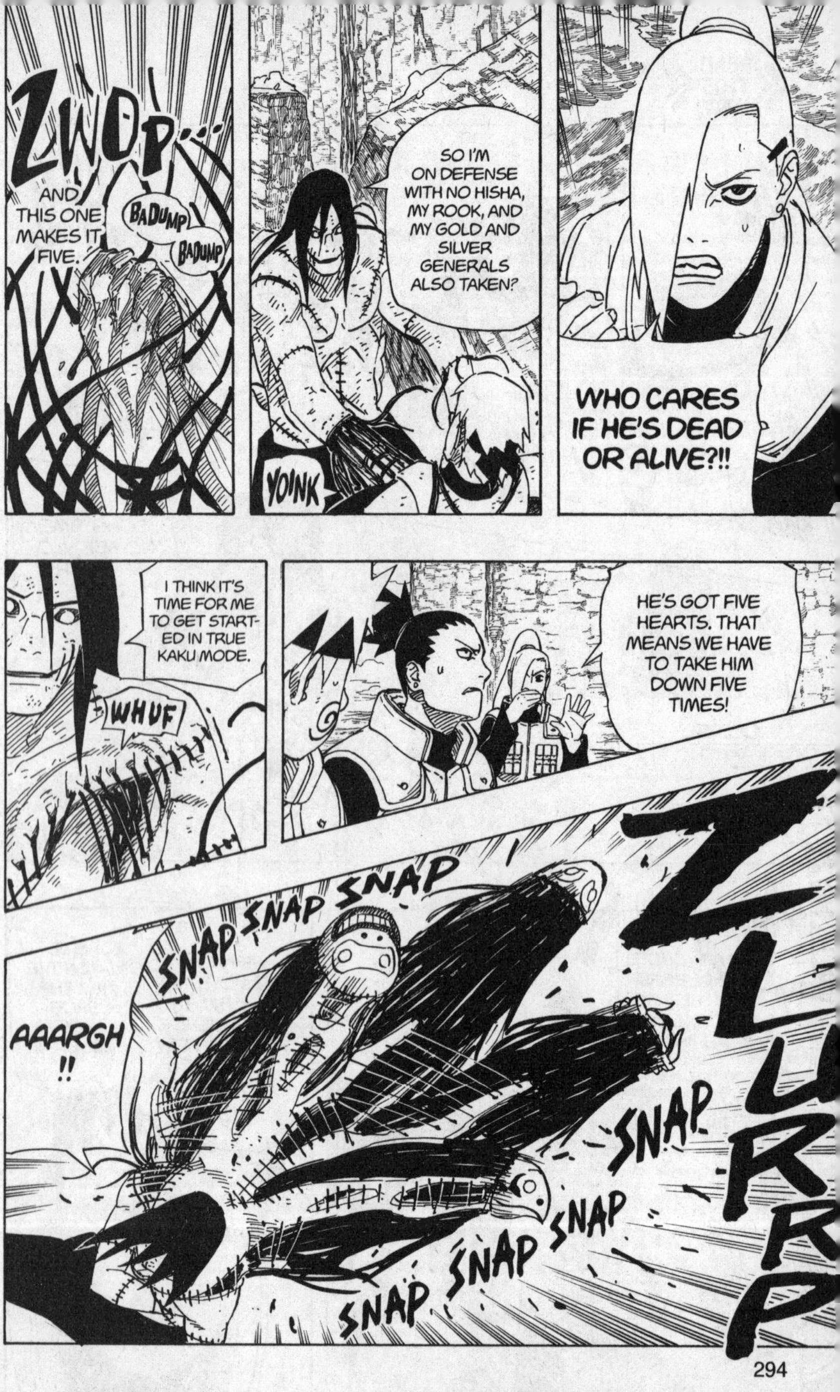
WHO CARES IF HE'S DEAD OR ALIVE?!!
SO I'M ON DEFENSE WITH NO HISHA, MY ROOK, AND MY GOLD AND SILVER GENERALS ALSO TAKEN?
YOINK
ZWOP...
AND THIS ONE MAKES IT FIVE.
BADUMP
BADUMP
HE'S GOT FIVE HEARTS. THAT MEANS WE HAVE TO TAKE HIM DOWN FIVE TIMES!
I THINK IT'S TIME FOR ME TO GET START-ED IN TRUE KAKU MODE.
WHUF
ZLURP
SNAP SNAP SNAP SNAP
SNAP
SNAP SNAP SNAP
AAARGH!!

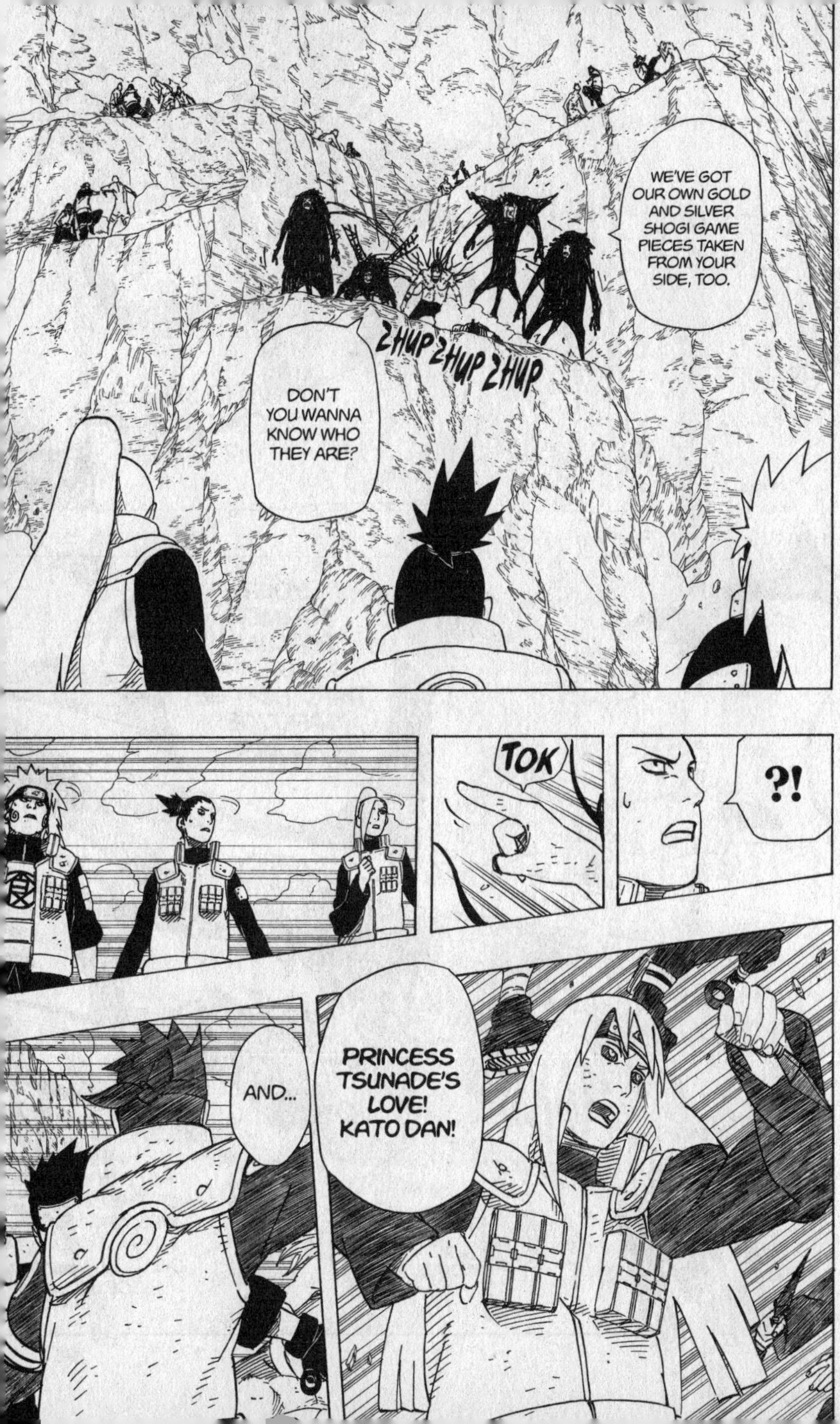
WE'VE GOT OUR OWN GOLD AND SILVER SHOGI GAME PIECES TAKEN FROM YOUR SIDE, TOO.
ZHUP ZHUP ZHUP
DON'T YOU WANNA KNOW WHO THEY ARE?
?!
TOK
PRINCESS TSUNADE'S LOVE! KATO DAN!
AND...

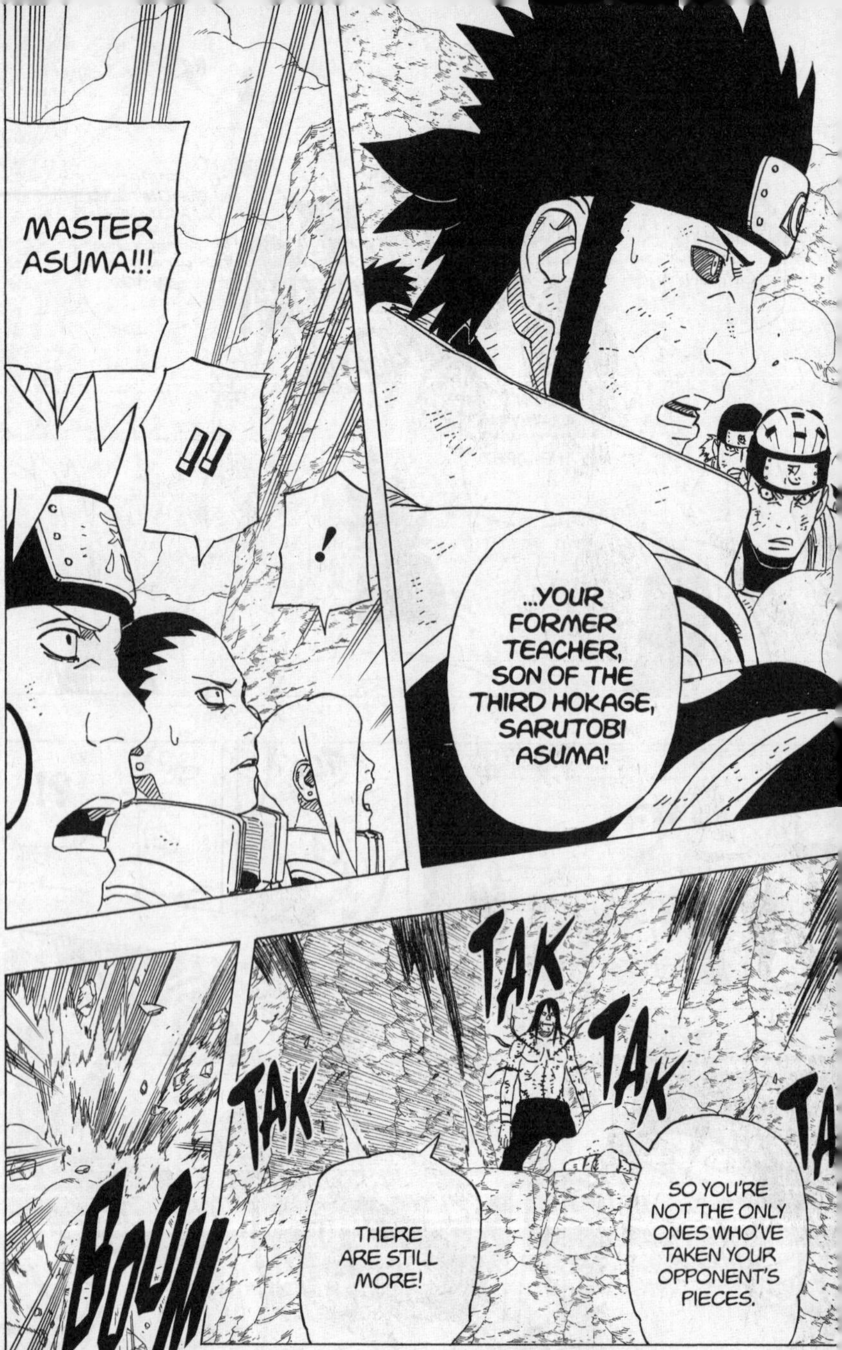
...YOUR FORMER TEACHER, SON OF THE THIRD HOKAGE, SARUTOBI ASUMA!
MASTER ASUMA!!!
!!
!
TAK
TAK
SO YOU'RE NOT THE ONLY ONES WHO'VE TAKEN YOUR OPPONENT'S PIECES.
THERE ARE STILL MORE!
TAK
BOOM

READ THIS WAY

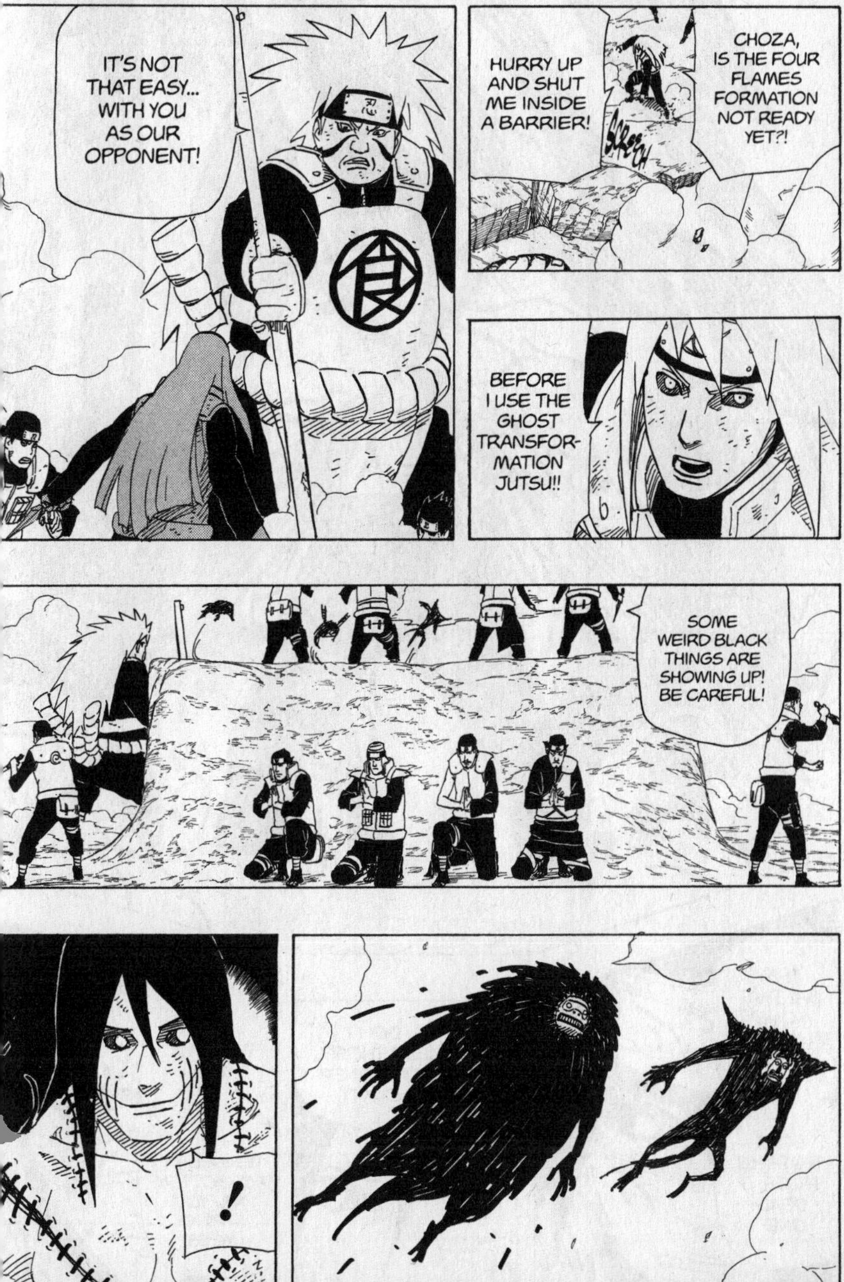
CHOZA, IS THE FOUR FLAMES FORMATION NOT READY YET?!
SCREECH
HURRY UP AND SHUT ME INSIDE A BARRIER!
BEFORE I USE THE GHOST TRANSFORMATION JUTSU!!
IT'S NOT THAT EASY... WITH YOU AS OUR OPPONENT!
SOME WEIRD BLACK THINGS ARE SHOWING UP! BE CAREFUL!
!

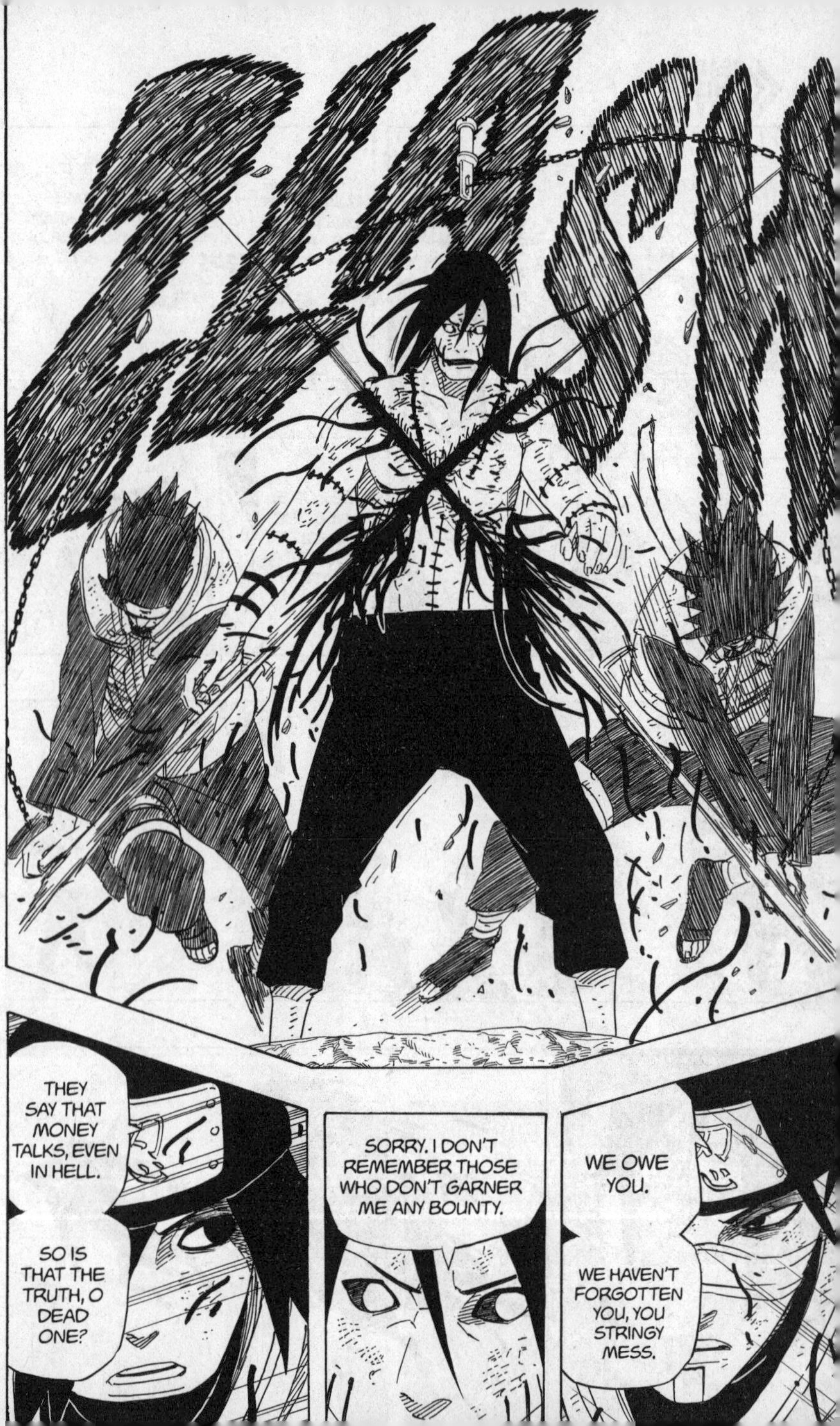
WE OWE YOU.
WE HAVEN'T FORGOTTEN YOU, YOU STRINGY MESS.
SORRY. I DON'T REMEMBER THOSE WHO DON'T GARNER ME ANY BOUNTY.
THEY SAY THAT MONEY TALKS, EVEN IN HELL.
SO IS THAT THE TRUTH, O DEAD ONE?

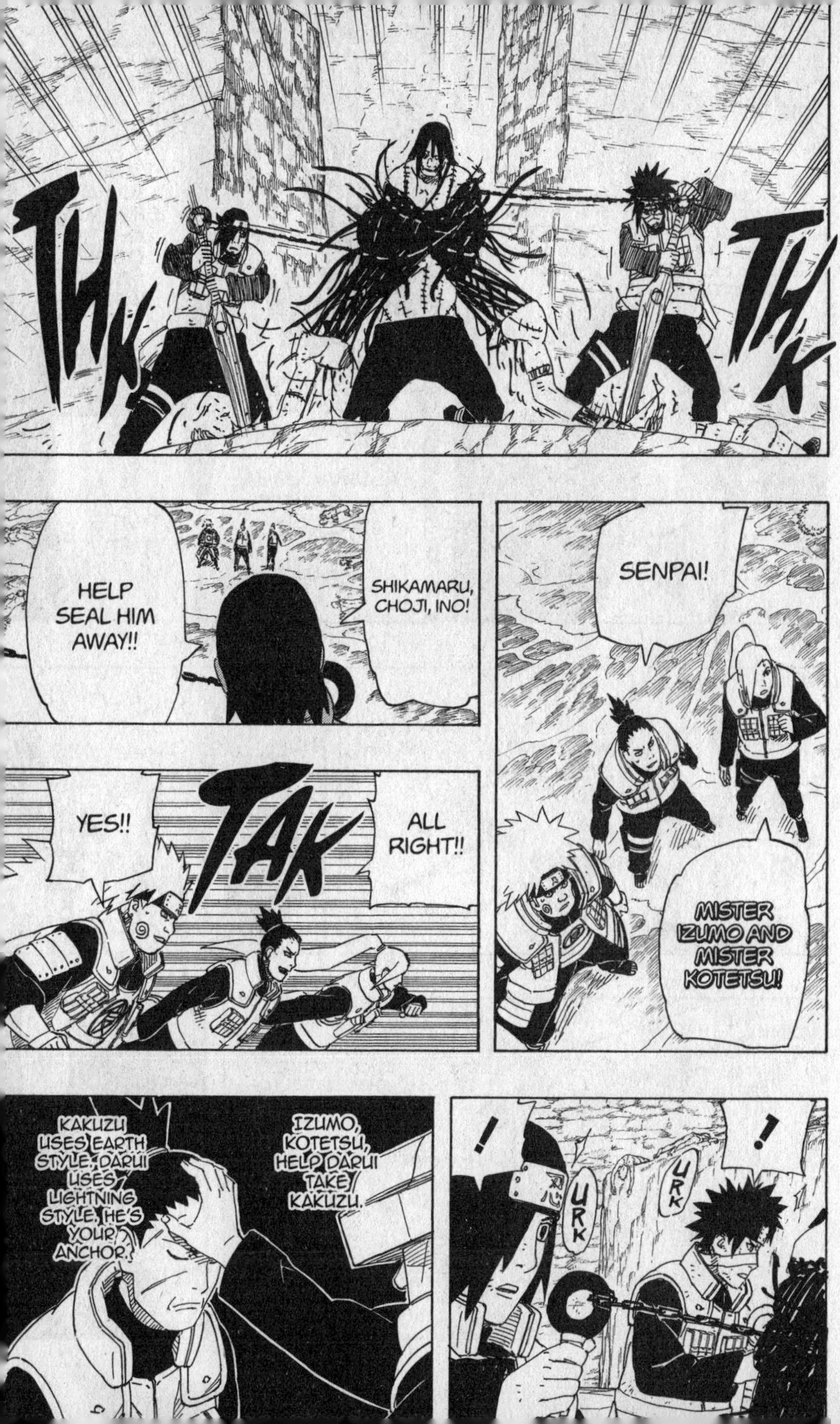
THK
THK
SENPAI!
MISTER IZUMO AND MISTER KOTETSU!
SHIKAMARU, CHOJI, INO!
HELP SEAL HIM AWAY!!
ALL RIGHT!!
TAK
YES!!
!
URK
!
URK
IZUMO, KOTETSU, HELP DARUI TAKE KAKUZU.
KAKUZU USES EARTH STYLE, DARUI USES LIGHTNING STYLE, HE'S YOUR ANCHOR.

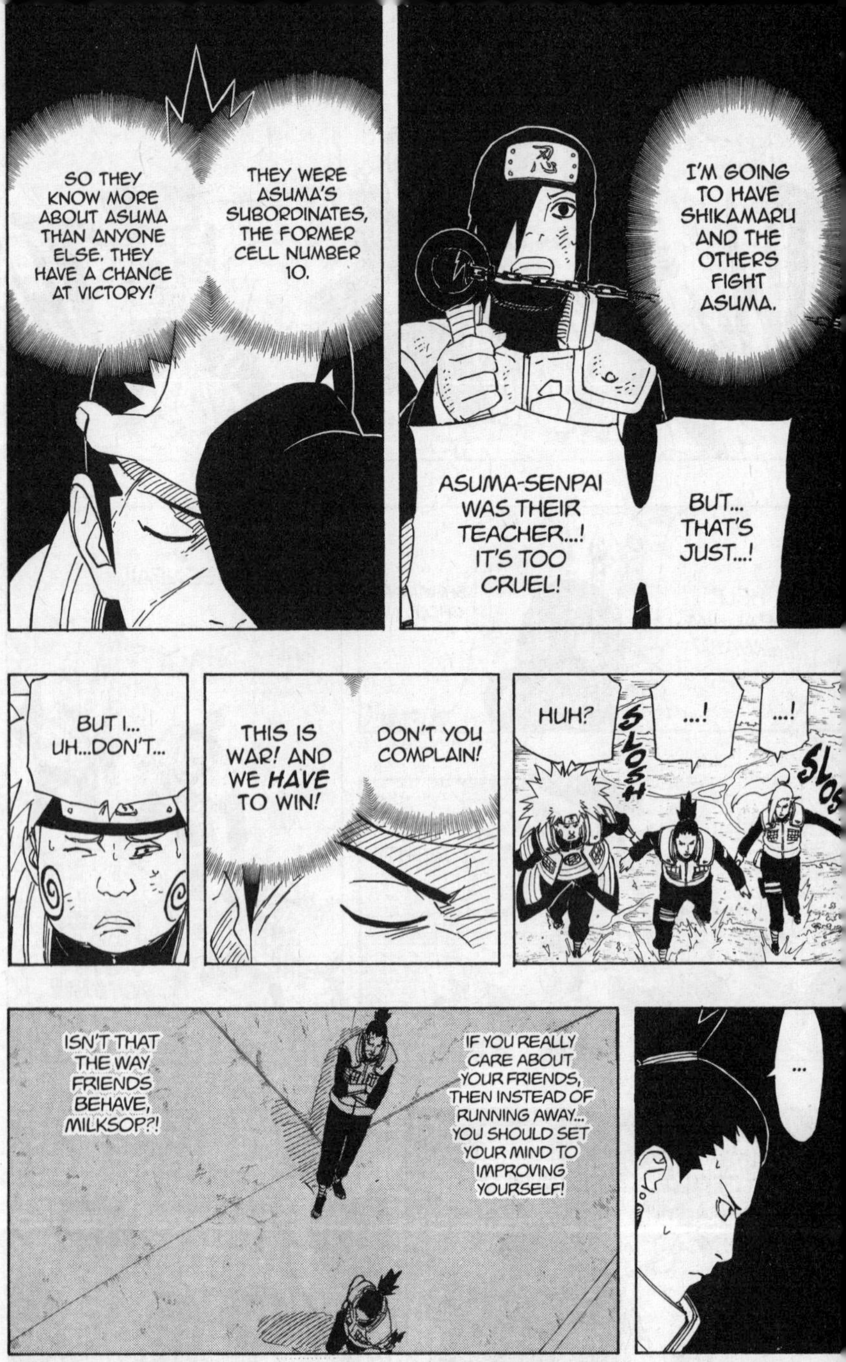
I'M GOING TO HAVE SHIKAMARU AND THE OTHERS FIGHT ASUMA.
BUT... THAT'S JUST...!
ASUMA-SENPAI WAS THEIR TEACHER...! IT'S TOO CRUEL!
THEY WERE ASUMA'S SUBORDINATES, THE FORMER CELL NUMBER 10.
SO THEY KNOW MORE ABOUT ASUMA THAN ANYONE ELSE. THEY HAVE A CHANCE AT VICTORY!
...!
SLOS
...!
SLOSH
HUH?
DON'T YOU COMPLAIN!
THIS IS WAR! AND WE *HAVE* TO WIN!
BUT I... UH...DON'T...
...
IF YOU REALLY CARE ABOUT YOUR FRIENDS, THEN INSTEAD OF RUNNING AWAY... YOU SHOULD SET YOUR MIND TO IMPROVING YOURSELF!
ISN'T THAT THE WAY FRIENDS BEHAVE, MILKSOP?!

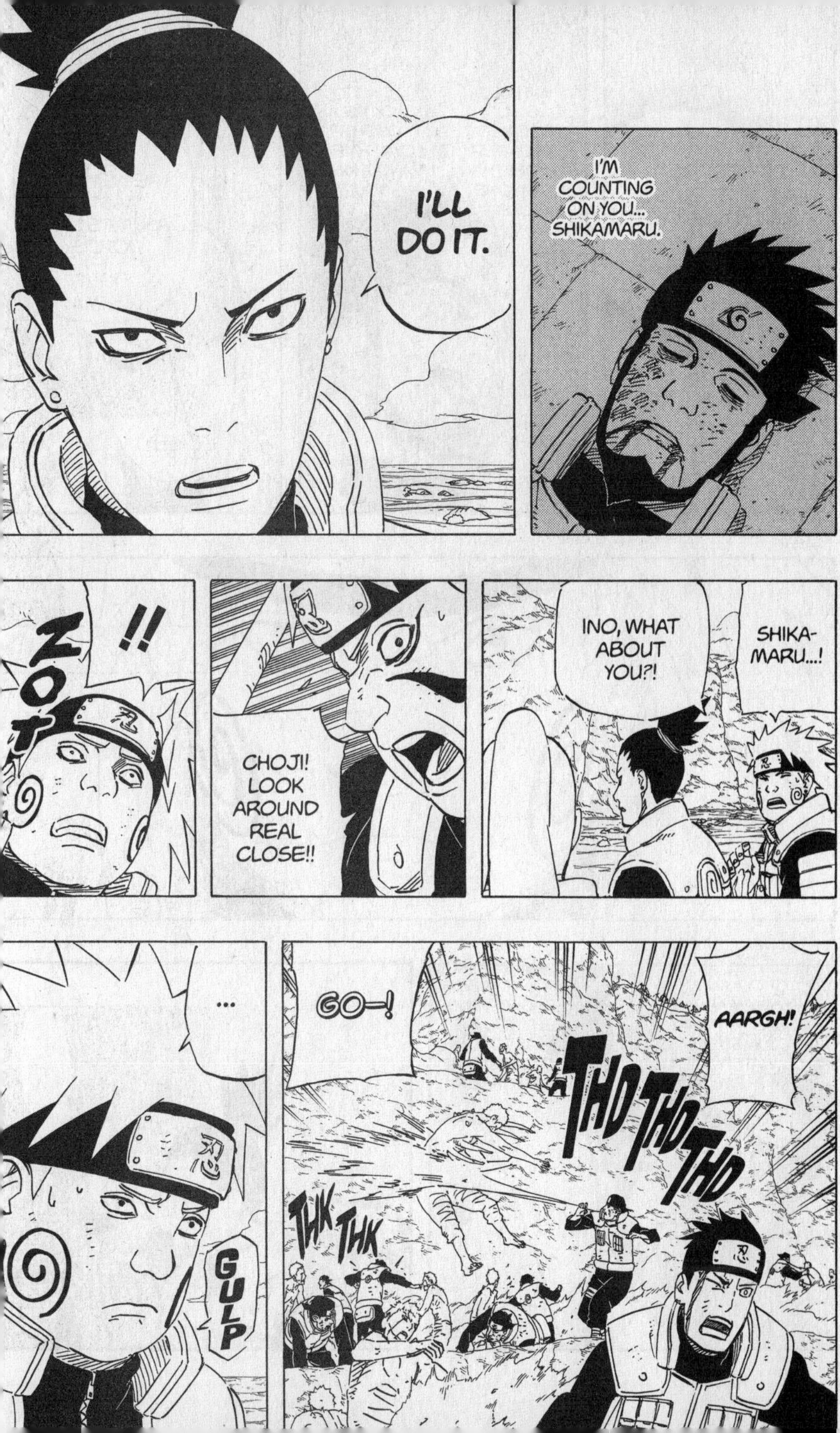
I'M COUNTING ON YOU... SHIKAMARU.
I'LL DO IT.
SHIKA-MARU...!
INO, WHAT ABOUT YOU?!
CHOJI! LOOK AROUND REAL CLOSE!!
!!
ZOT
AARGH!
THD THD THD
GO—!
THK THK
...
GULP

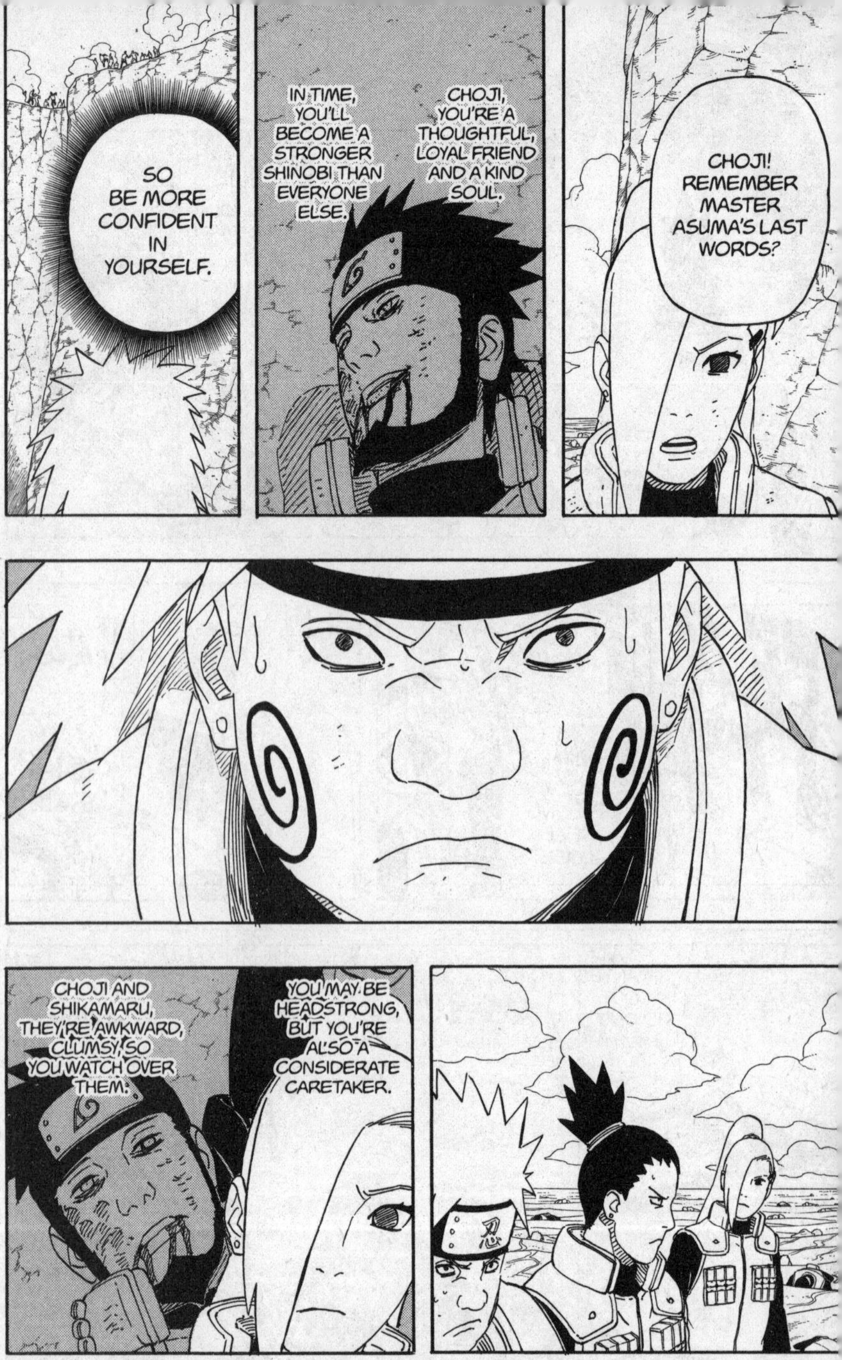
CHOJI! REMEMBER MASTER ASUMA'S LAST WORDS?
CHOJI, YOU'RE A THOUGHTFUL, LOYAL FRIEND AND A KIND SOUL.
IN TIME, YOU'LL BECOME A STRONGER SHINOBI THAN EVERYONE ELSE.
SO BE MORE CONFIDENT IN YOURSELF.
YOU MAY BE HEADSTRONG, BUT YOU'RE ALSO A CONSIDERATE CARETAKER.
CHOJI AND SHIKAMARU, THEY'RE AWKWARD, CLUMSY, SO YOU WATCH OVER THEM.

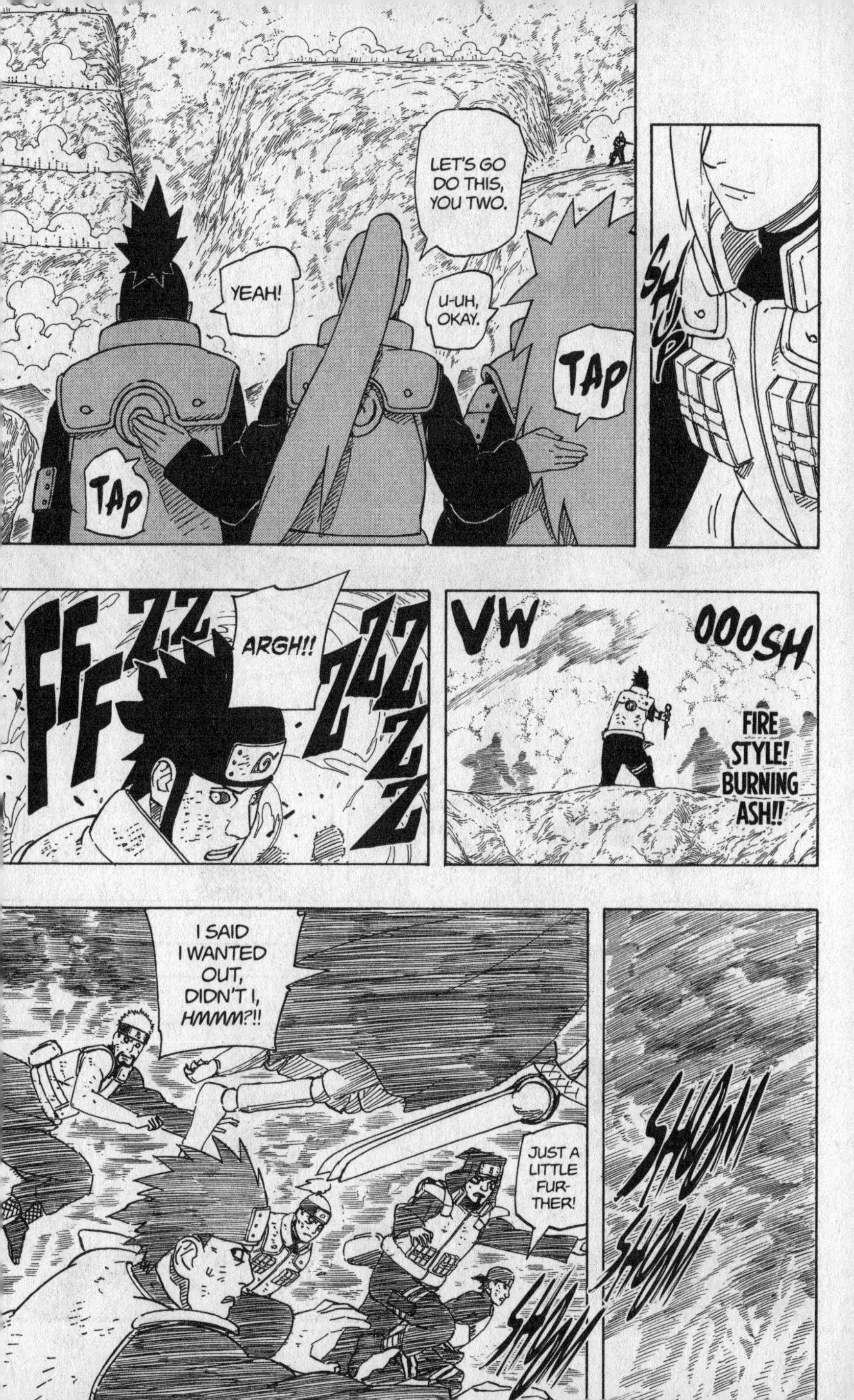
SHUP
LET'S GO DO THIS, YOU TWO.
TAP
U-UH, OKAY.
YEAH!
TAP
OOOSH
VW
FIRE STYLE! BURNING ASH!!
ZZZZ
ARGH!!
ZZ
FFF
SHUNN
SHUNN
SHUNN
JUST A LITTLE FUR-THER!
I SAID I WANTED OUT, DIDN'T I, HMMM?!!

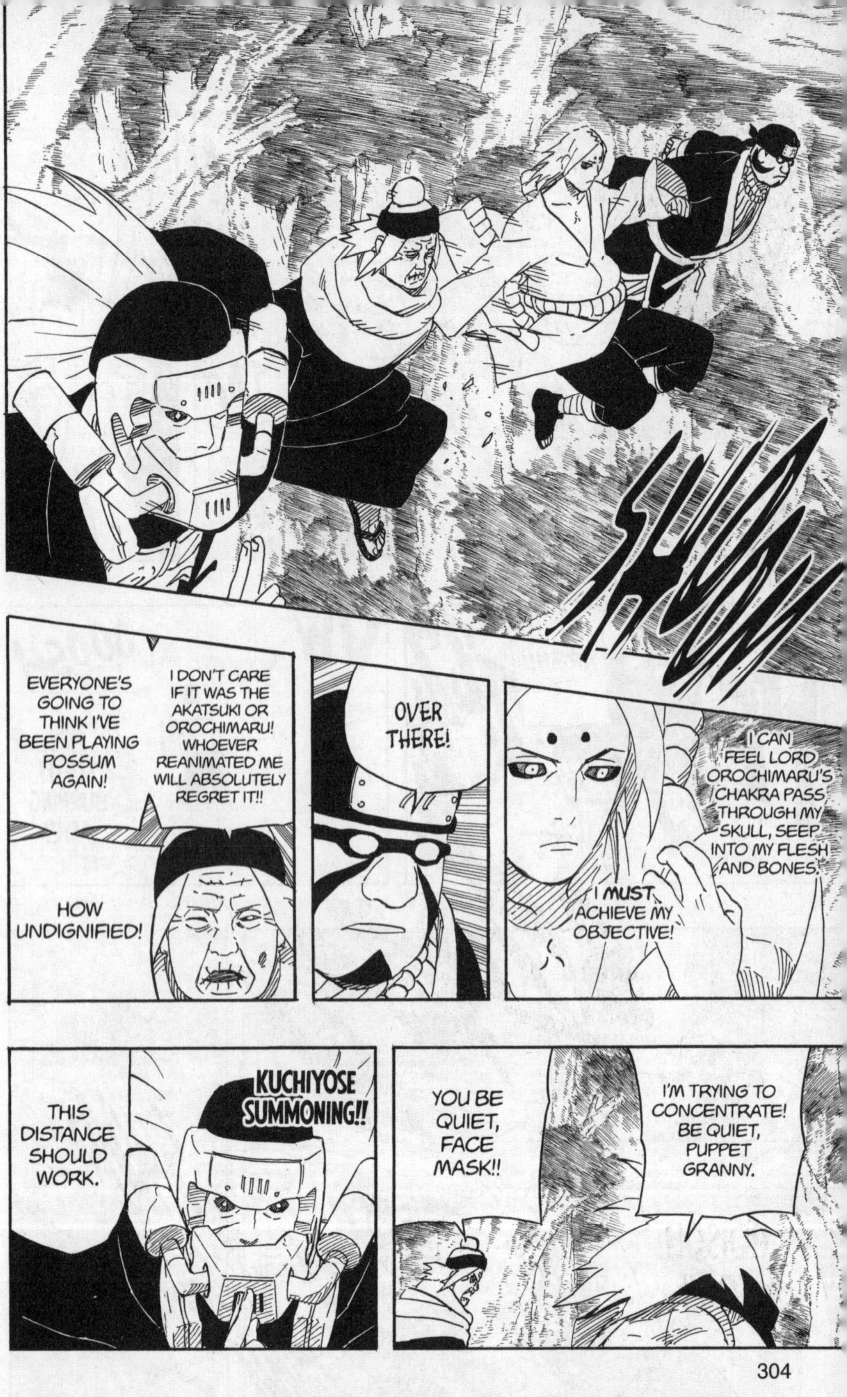
SHUUN
I CAN FEEL LORD OROCHIMARU'S CHAKRA PASS THROUGH MY SKULL, SEEP INTO MY FLESH AND BONES.
I MUST ACHIEVE MY OBJECTIVE!
OVER THERE!
I DON'T CARE IF IT WAS THE AKATSUKI OR OROCHIMARU! WHOEVER REANIMATED ME WILL ABSOLUTELY REGRET IT!!
EVERYONE'S GOING TO THINK I'VE BEEN PLAYING POSSUM AGAIN!
HOW UNDIGNIFIED!
I'M TRYING TO CONCENTRATE! BE QUIET, PUPPET GRANNY.
YOU BE QUIET, FACE MASK!!
KUCHIYOSE SUMMONING!!
THIS DISTANCE SHOULD WORK.

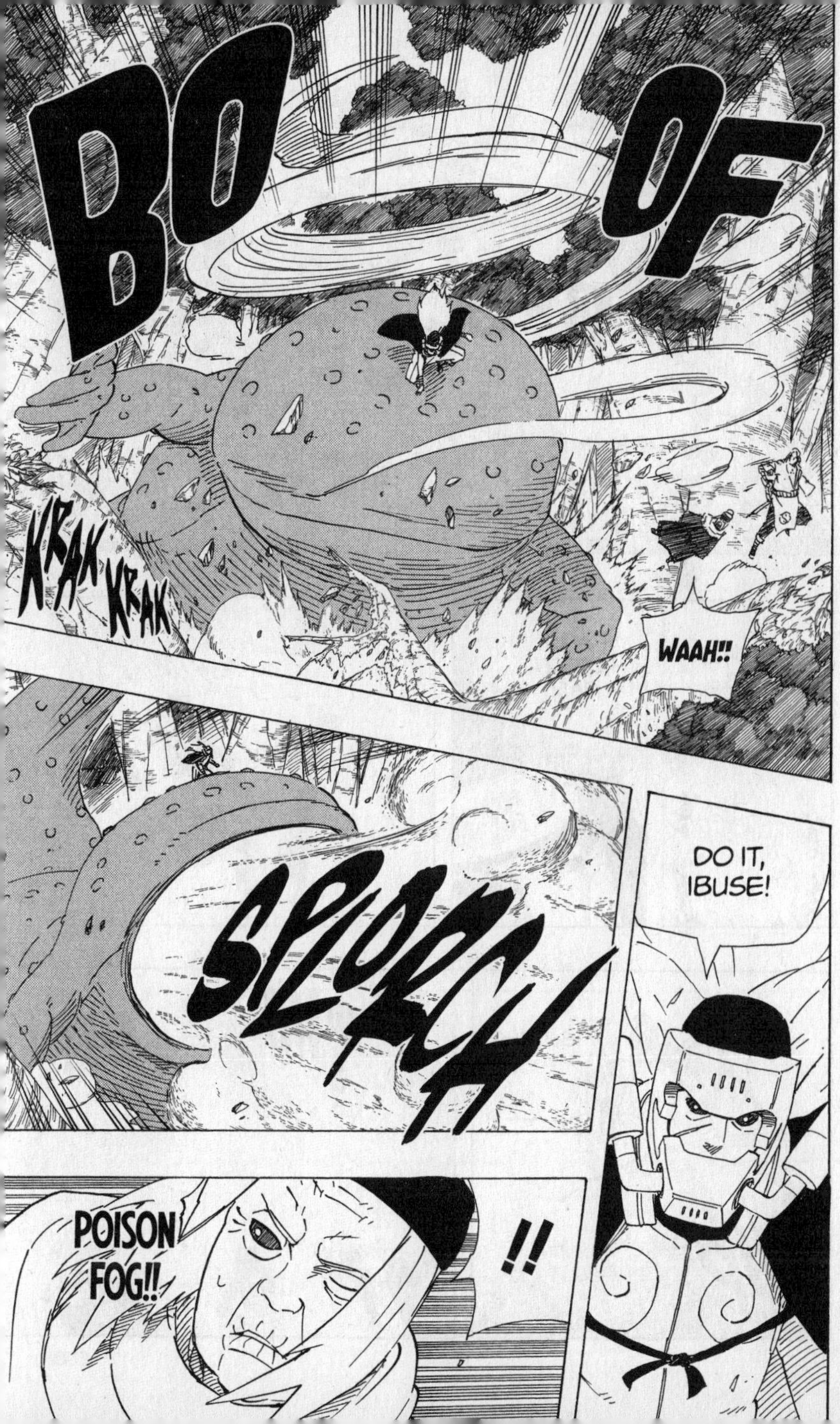
BOOF
KRAK KRAK
WAAH!!
DO IT, IBUSE!
SPLOOCH
!!
POISON FOG!!

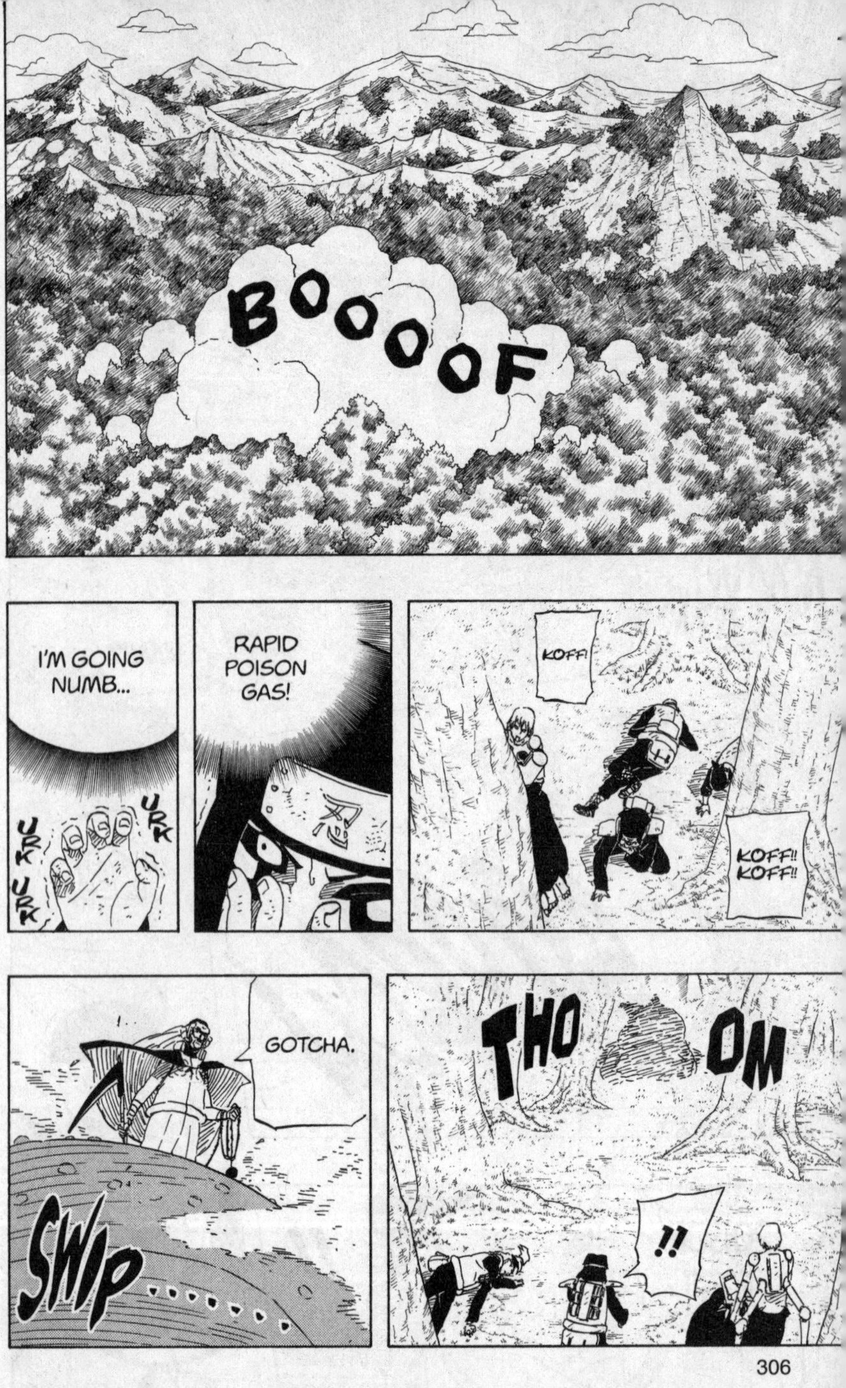
BOOOOF
KOFF!
KOFF!! KOFF!!
RAPID POISON GAS!
I'M GOING NUMB...
URK URK
URK URK
THO OM
!!
GOTCHA.
SWIP

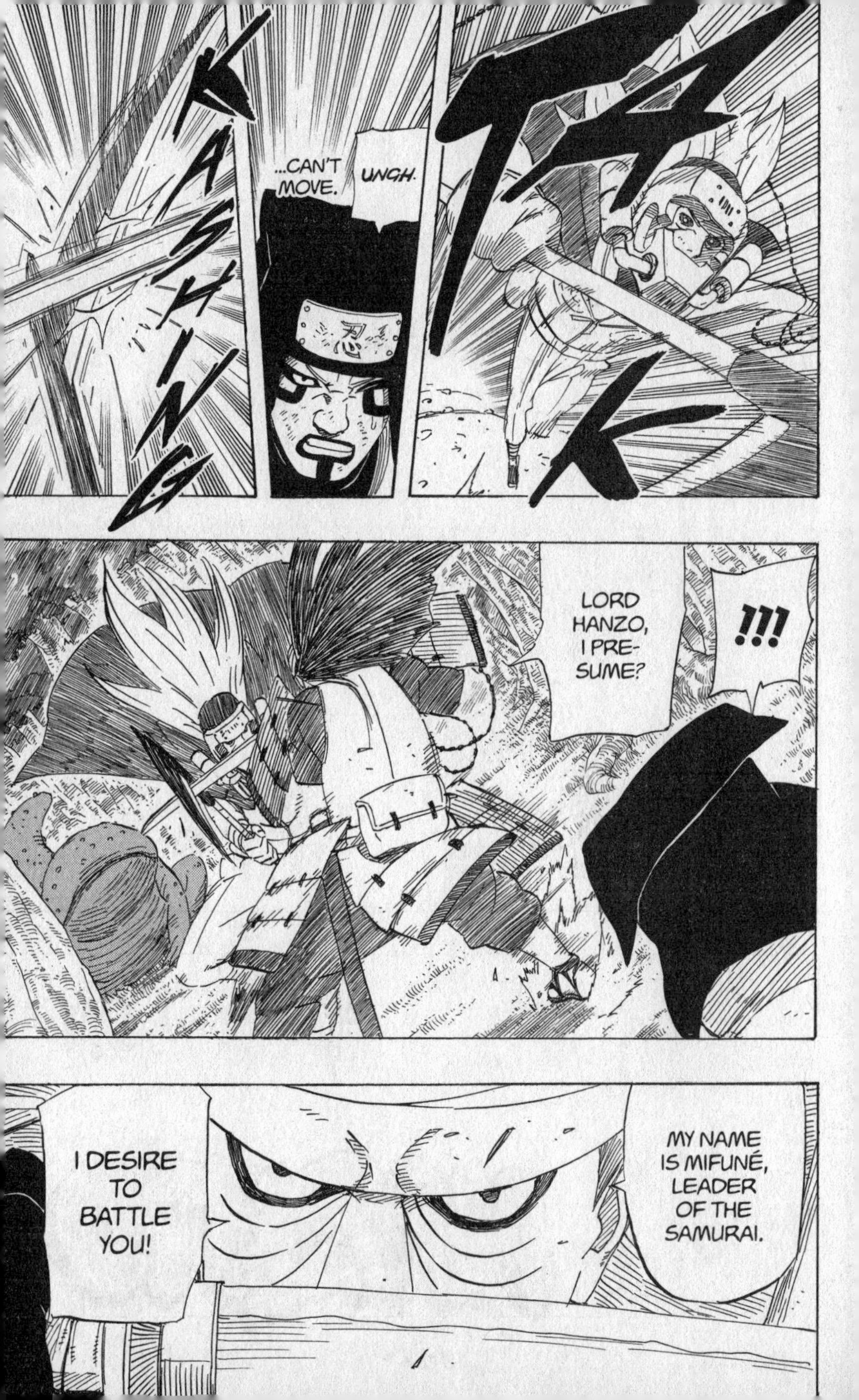

TAK
UNGH.
...CAN'T MOVE.
KASHING
!!!
LORD HANZO, I PRESUME?
MY NAME IS MIFUNÉ, LEADER OF THE SAMURAI.
I DESIRE TO BATTLE YOU!

NARUTO

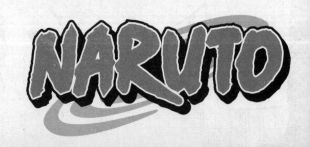

# Number 531: Team Asuma, Reunited!

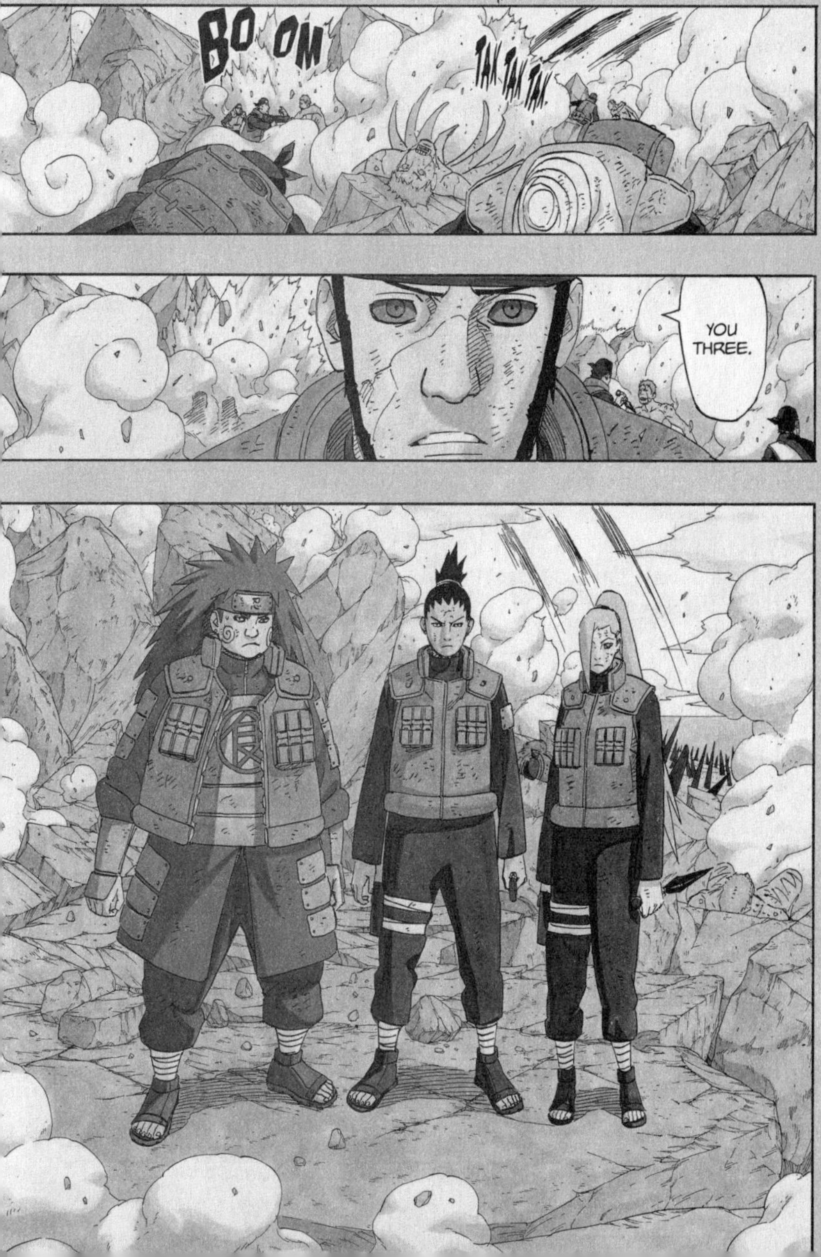
TAK TAK TAK
BOOM
YOU THREE.

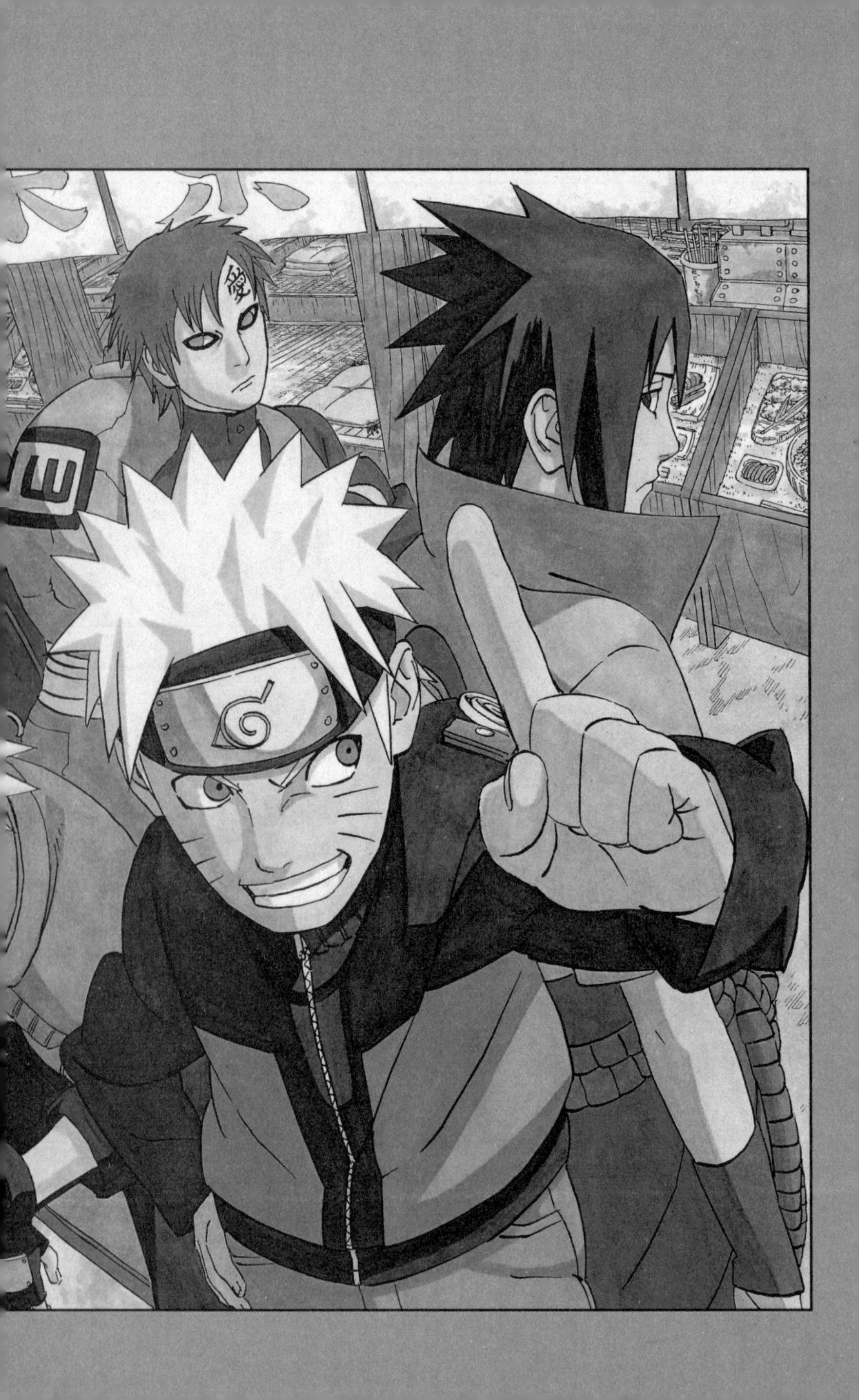

# Number 531: Team Asuma, Reunited!

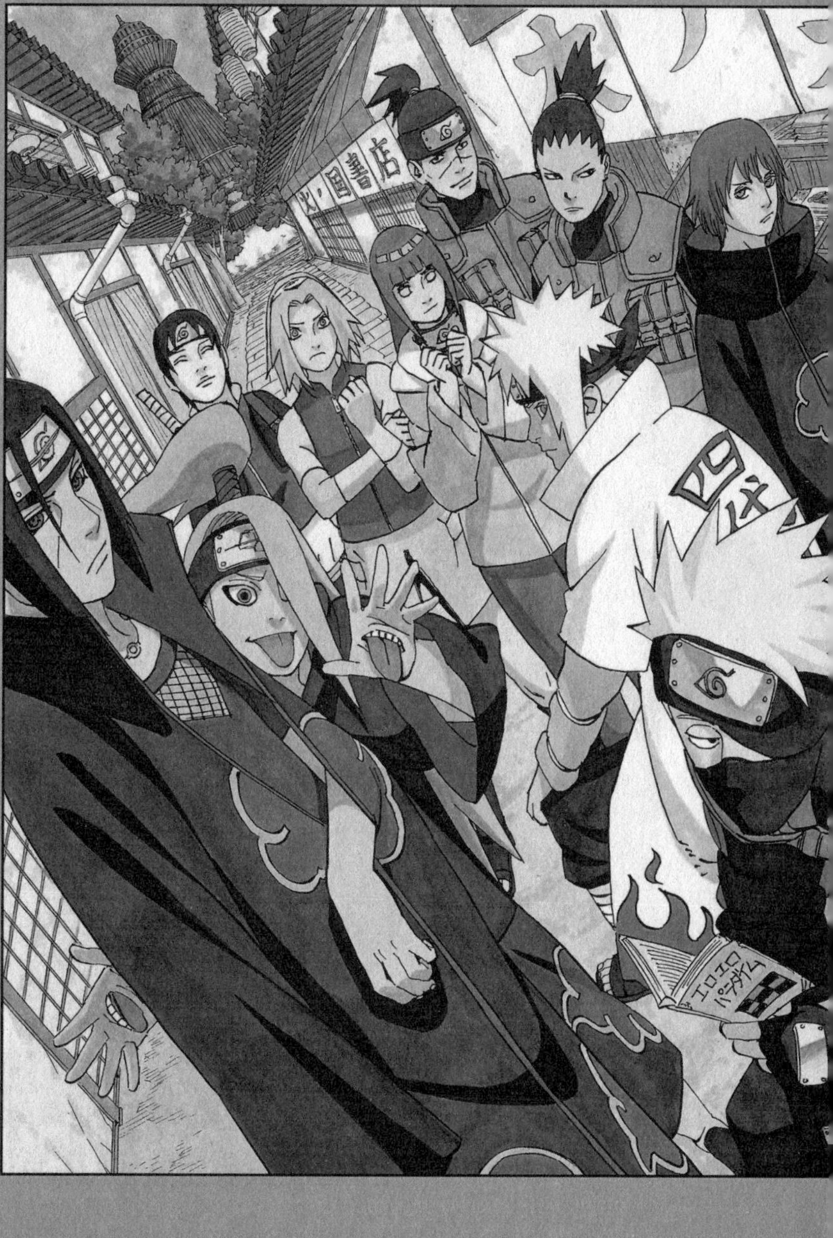

NARUTO

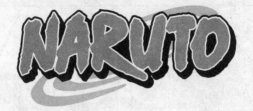

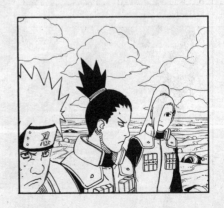

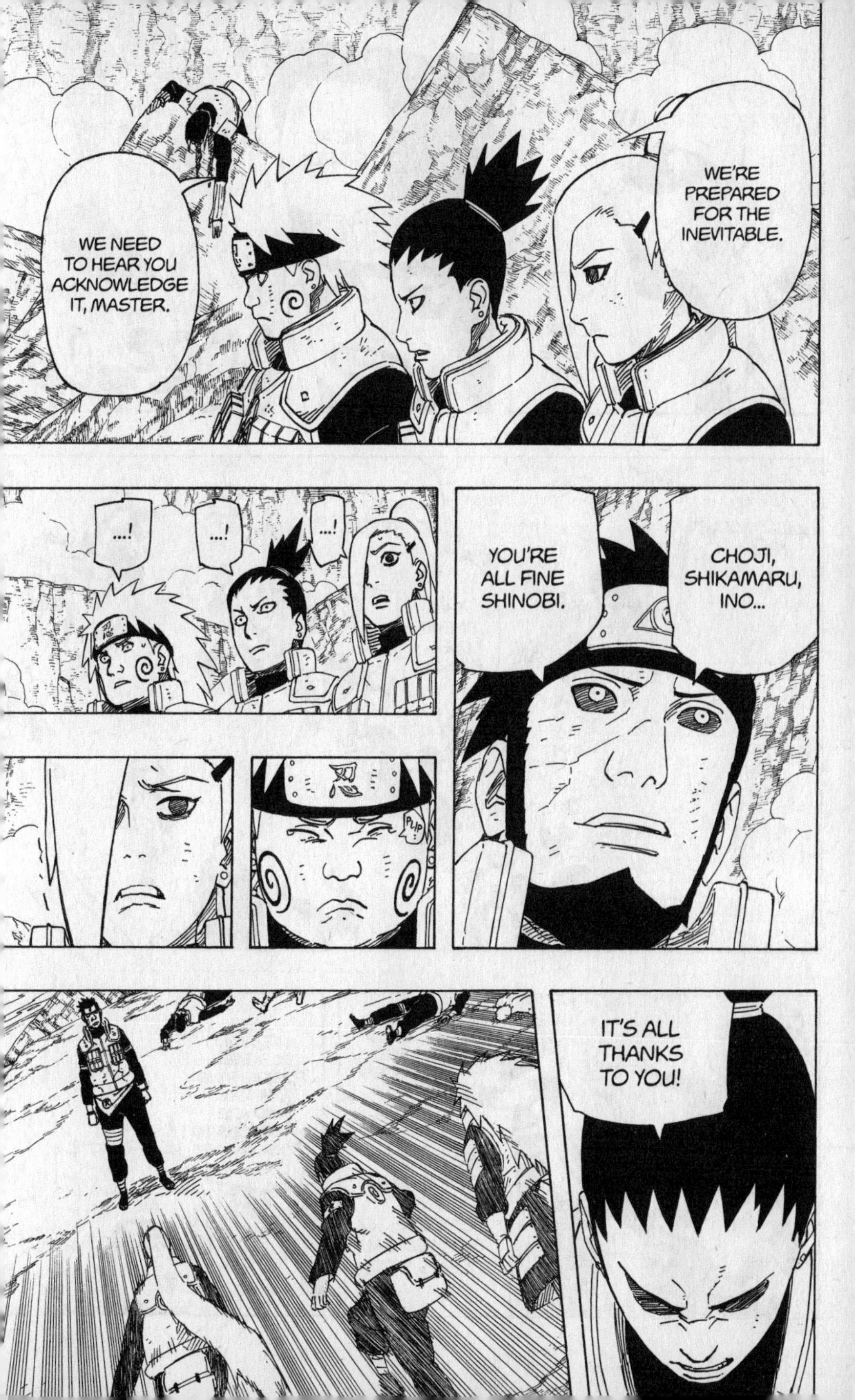
WE'RE PREPARED FOR THE INEVITABLE.
WE NEED TO HEAR YOU ACKNOWLEDGE IT, MASTER.
CHOJI, SHIKAMARU, INO...
YOU'RE ALL FINE SHINOBI.
...!
...!
...!
PLIP
IT'S ALL THANKS TO YOU!

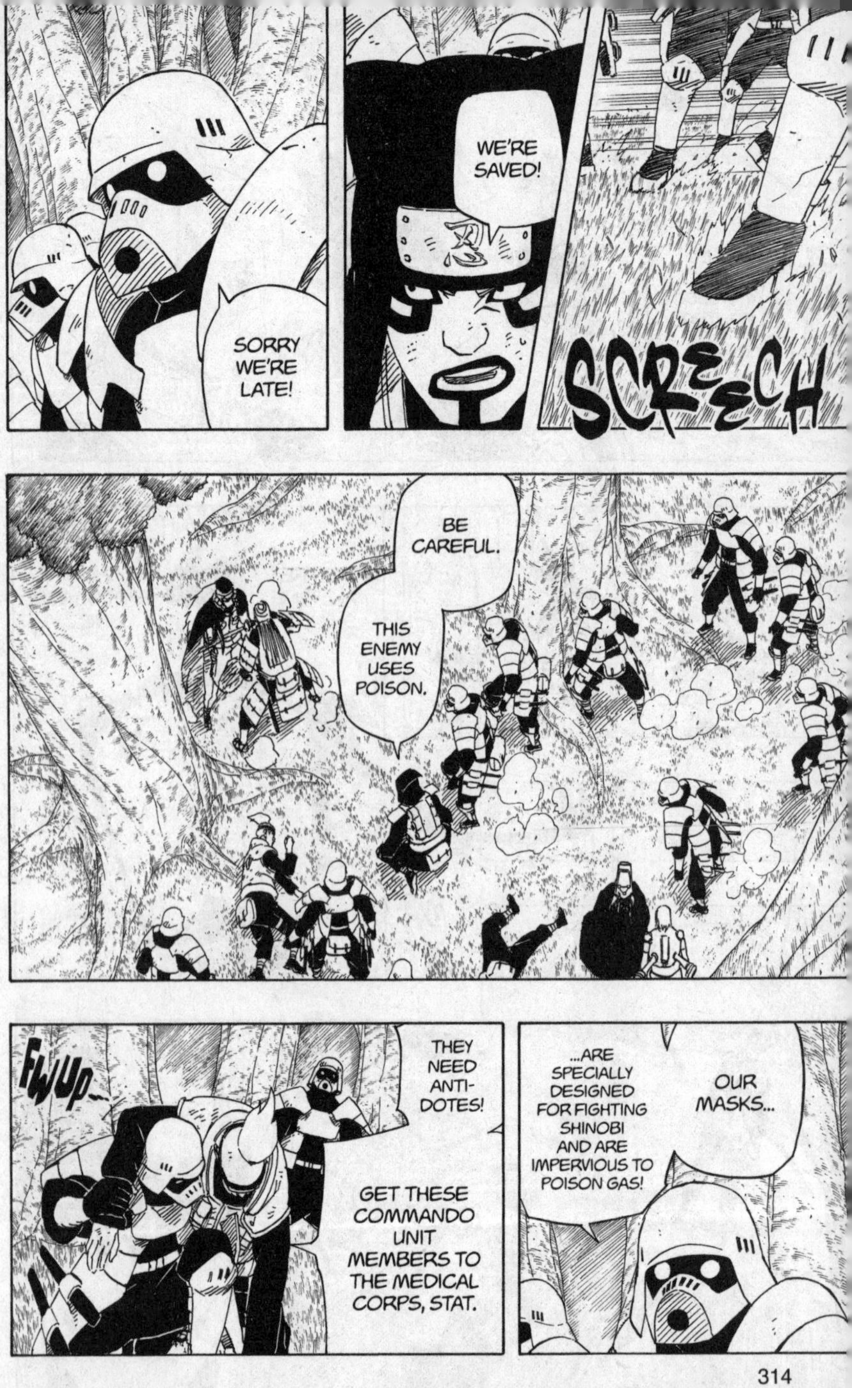
SCREECH
WE'RE SAVED!
SORRY WE'RE LATE!
BE CAREFUL.
THIS ENEMY USES POISON.
OUR MASKS...
...ARE SPECIALLY DESIGNED FOR FIGHTING SHINOBI AND ARE IMPERVIOUS TO POISON GAS!
THEY NEED ANTI-DOTES!
FWUP
GET THESE COMMANDO UNIT MEMBERS TO THE MEDICAL CORPS, STAT.

READ THIS WAY

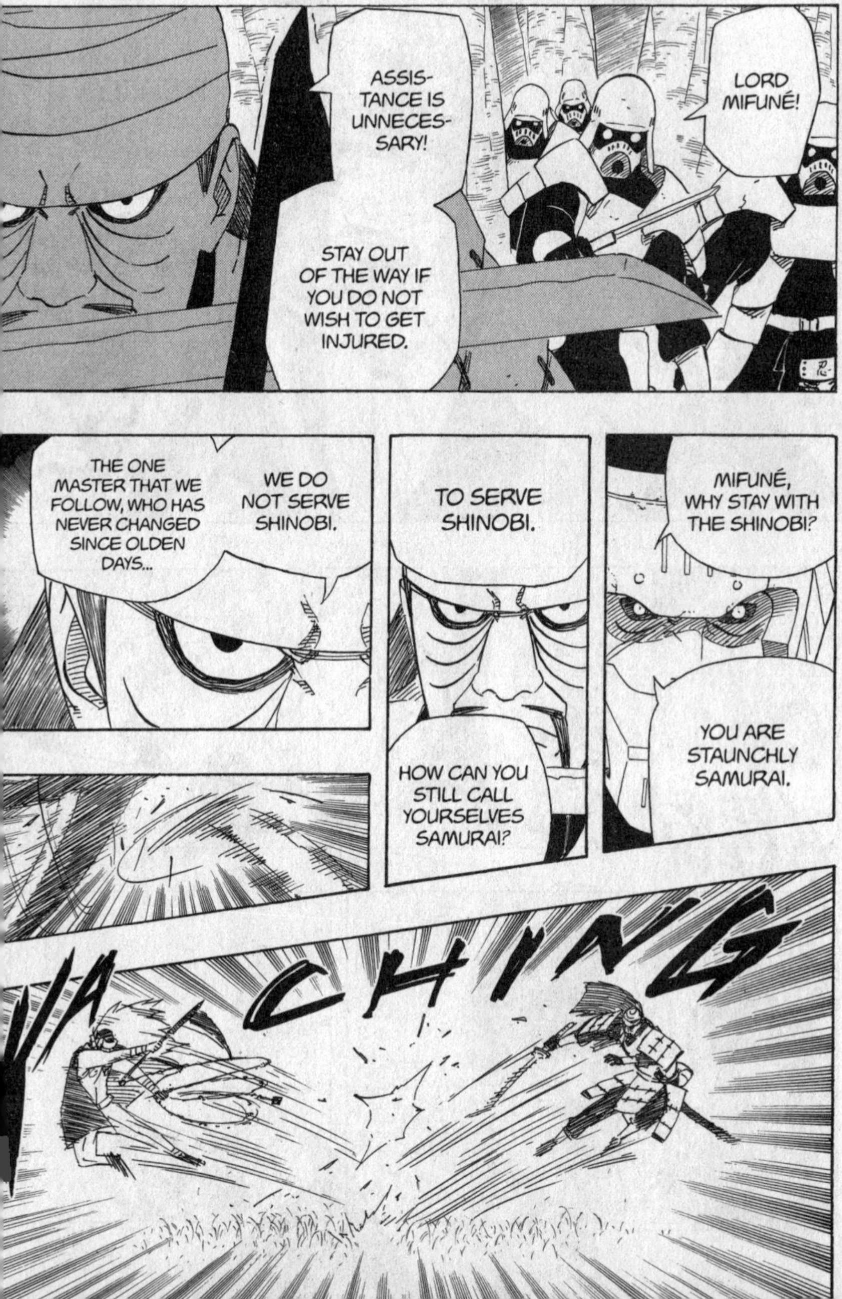
LORD MIFUNÉ!
ASSIS-TANCE IS UNNECES-SARY!
STAY OUT OF THE WAY IF YOU DO NOT WISH TO GET INJURED.
MIFUNÉ, WHY STAY WITH THE SHINOBI?
YOU ARE STAUNCHLY SAMURAI.
HOW CAN YOU STILL CALL YOURSELVES SAMURAI?
TO SERVE SHINOBI.
WE DO NOT SERVE SHINOBI.
THE ONE MASTER THAT WE FOLLOW, WHO HAS NEVER CHANGED SINCE OLDEN DAYS...
CHING

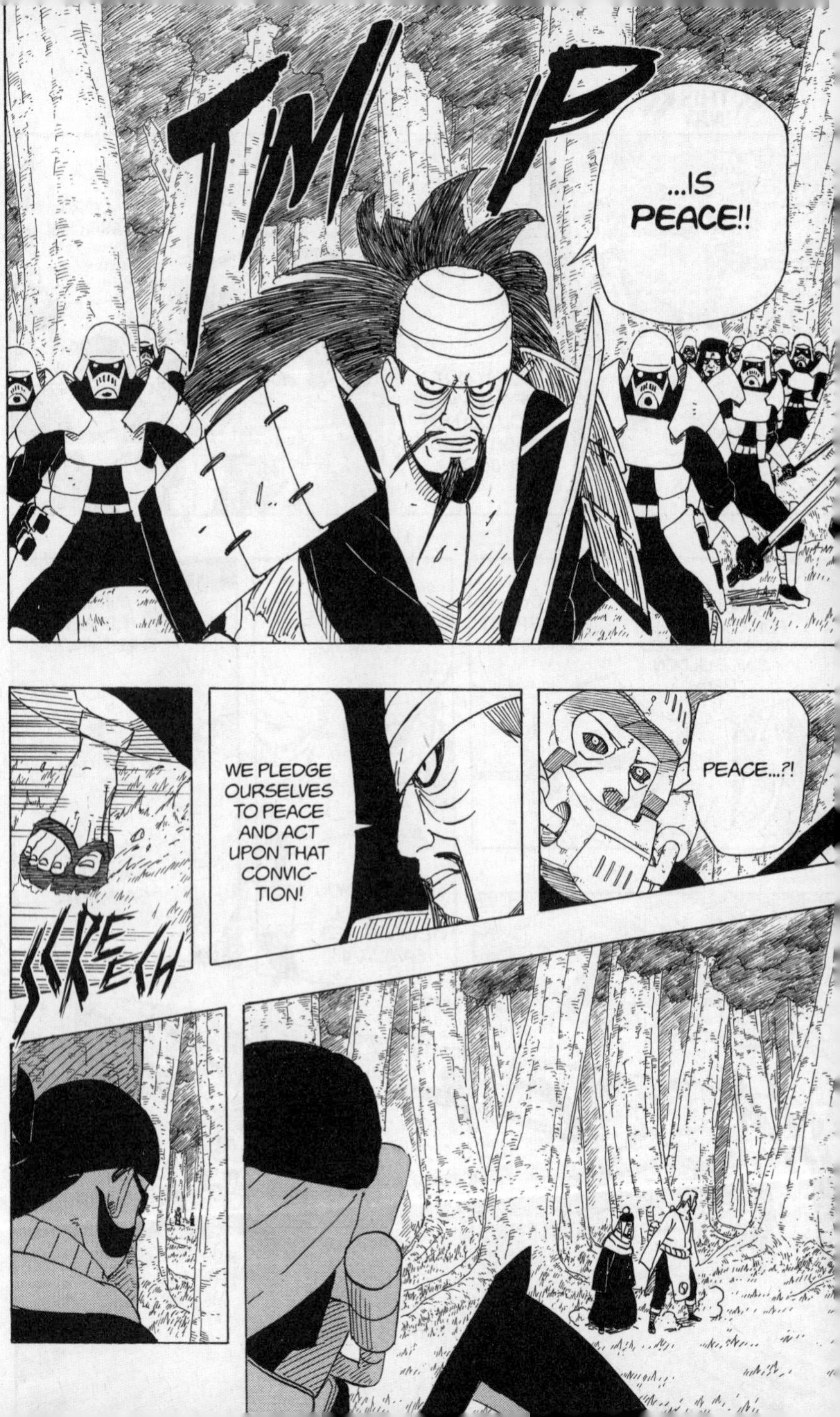
TMP
...IS PEACE!!
PEACE...?!
WE PLEDGE OURSELVES TO PEACE AND ACT UPON THAT CONVIC-TION!
SCREECH

READ THIS WAY

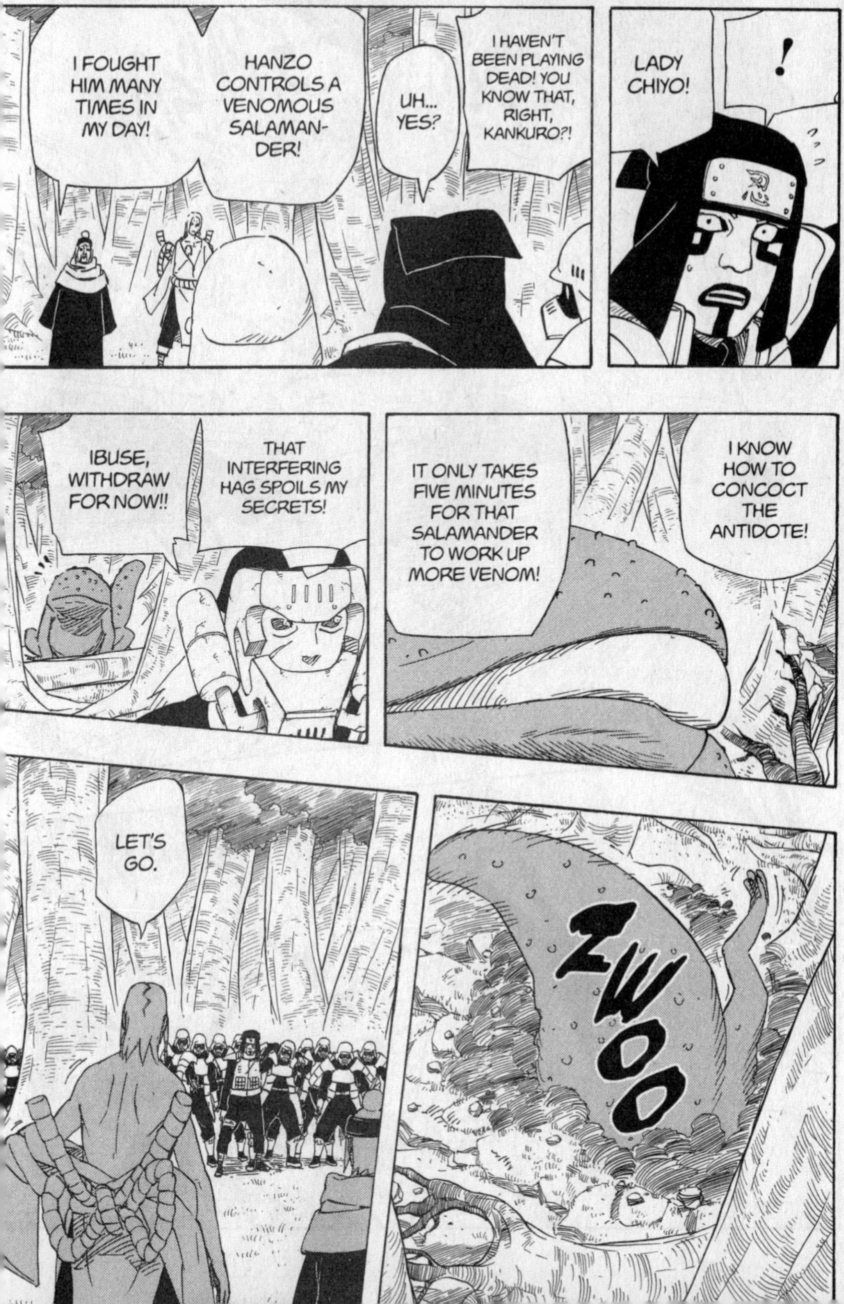
!
LADY CHIYO!
I HAVEN'T BEEN PLAYING DEAD! YOU KNOW THAT, RIGHT, KANKURO?!
UH... YES?
HANZO CONTROLS A VENOMOUS SALAMANDER!
I FOUGHT HIM MANY TIMES IN MY DAY!
I KNOW HOW TO CONCOCT THE ANTIDOTE!
IT ONLY TAKES FIVE MINUTES FOR THAT SALAMANDER TO WORK UP MORE VENOM!
THAT INTERFERING HAG SPOILS MY SECRETS!
IBUSE, WITHDRAW FOR NOW!!
ZWOO
LET'S GO.

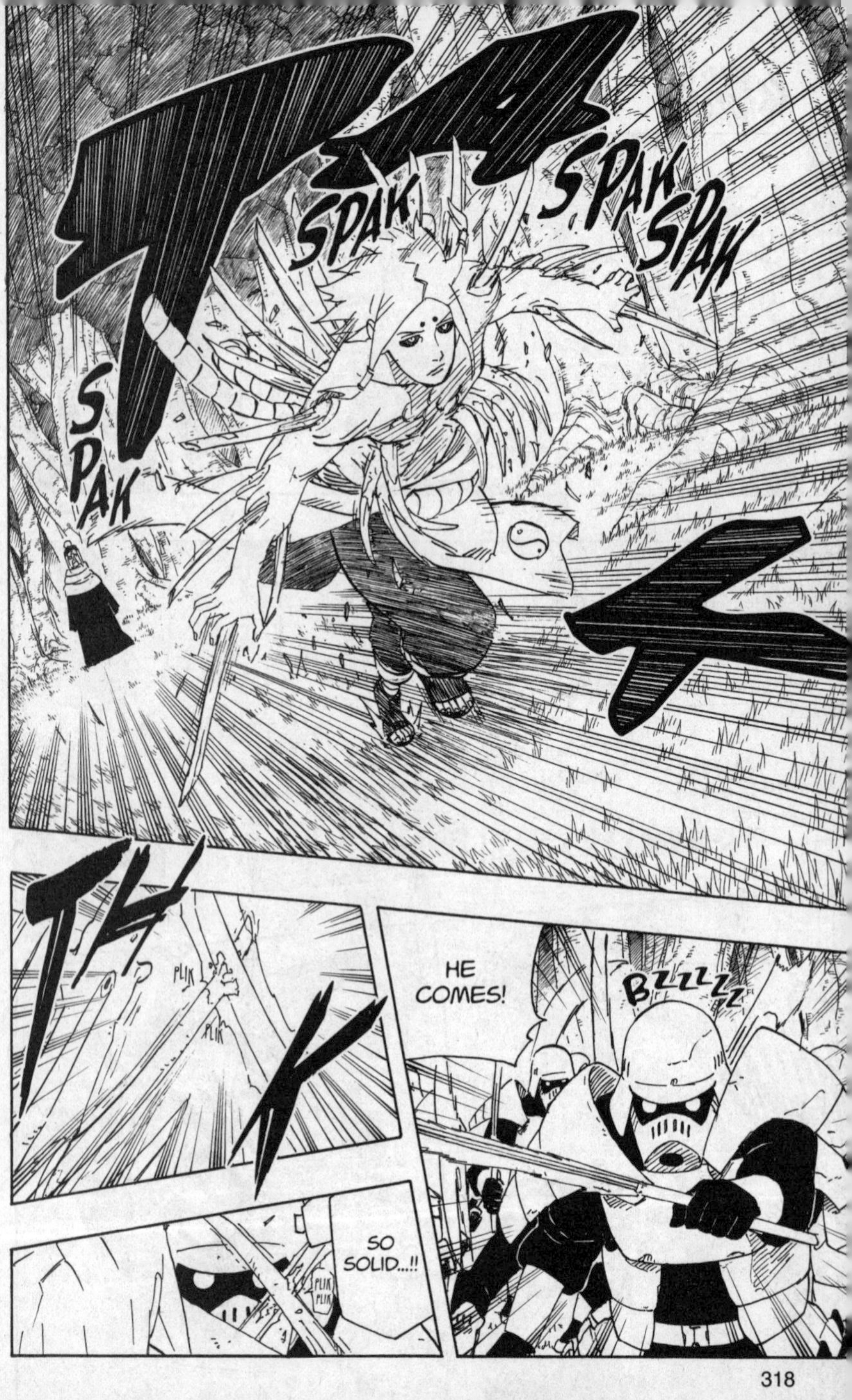
SPAK
SPAK
SPAK
SPAK
HE COMES!
BZZZZZ
PLIK
PLIK
SO SOLID...!!
PLIK PLIK

READ THIS WAY

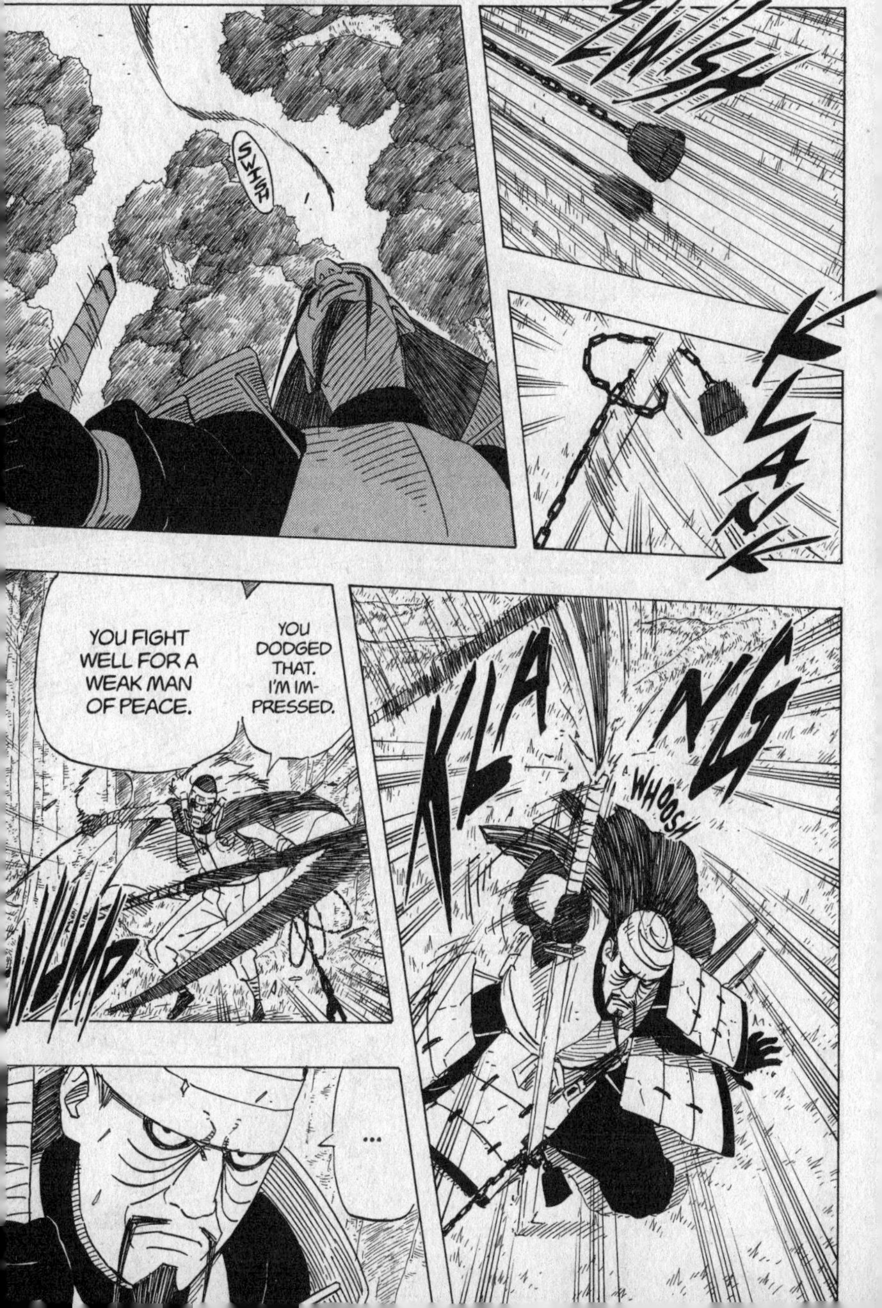
SWISH
KLANNK
SWISH
KLANG
WHOOSH
YOU DODGED THAT. I'M IM-PRESSED.
YOU FIGHT WELL FOR A WEAK MAN OF PEACE.
...

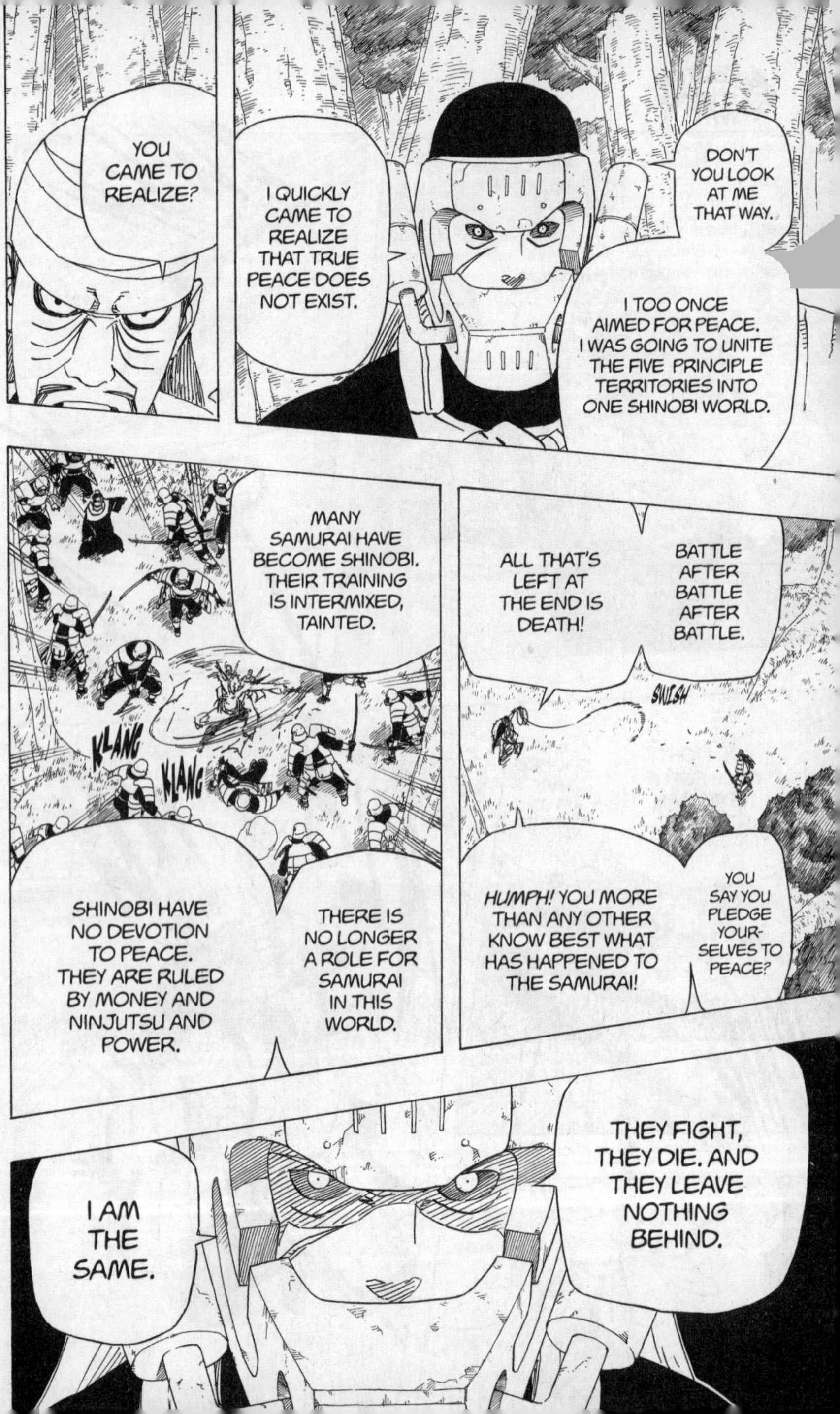
DON'T YOU LOOK AT ME THAT WAY.
I TOO ONCE AIMED FOR PEACE. I WAS GOING TO UNITE THE FIVE PRINCIPLE TERRITORIES INTO ONE SHINOBI WORLD.
I QUICKLY CAME TO REALIZE THAT TRUE PEACE DOES NOT EXIST.
YOU CAME TO REALIZE?
BATTLE AFTER BATTLE AFTER BATTLE.
ALL THAT'S LEFT AT THE END IS DEATH!
SWISH
YOU SAY YOU PLEDGE YOUR-SELVES TO PEACE?
*HUMPH!* YOU MORE THAN ANY OTHER KNOW BEST WHAT HAS HAPPENED TO THE SAMURAI!
MANY SAMURAI HAVE BECOME SHINOBI. THEIR TRAINING IS INTERMIXED, TAINTED.
KLANG
KLANG
THERE IS NO LONGER A ROLE FOR SAMURAI IN THIS WORLD.
SHINOBI HAVE NO DEVOTION TO PEACE. THEY ARE RULED BY MONEY AND NINJUTSU AND POWER.
THEY FIGHT, THEY DIE. AND THEY LEAVE NOTHING BEHIND.
I AM THE SAME.

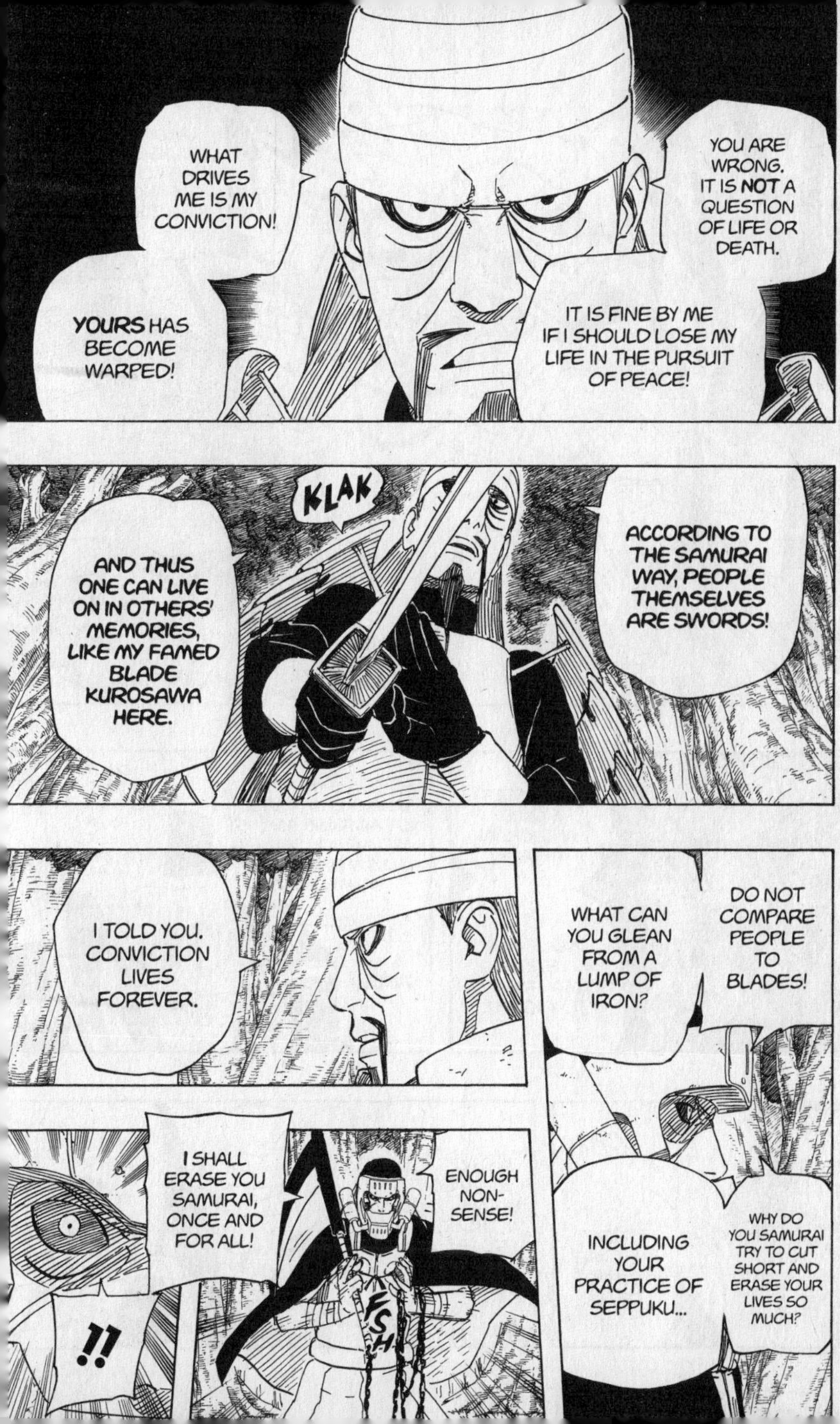
YOU ARE WRONG. IT IS **NOT** A QUESTION OF LIFE OR DEATH.
IT IS FINE BY ME IF I SHOULD LOSE MY LIFE IN THE PURSUIT OF PEACE!
WHAT DRIVES ME IS MY CONVICTION!
**YOURS** HAS BECOME WARPED!
ACCORDING TO THE SAMURAI WAY, PEOPLE THEMSELVES ARE SWORDS!
KLAK
AND THUS ONE CAN LIVE ON IN OTHERS' MEMORIES, LIKE MY FAMED BLADE KUROSAWA HERE.
DO NOT COMPARE PEOPLE TO BLADES!
WHAT CAN YOU GLEAN FROM A LUMP OF IRON?
WHY DO YOU SAMURAI TRY TO CUT SHORT AND ERASE YOUR LIVES SO MUCH?
INCLUDING YOUR PRACTICE OF SEPPUKU...
I TOLD YOU. CONVICTION LIVES FOREVER.
ENOUGH NON-SENSE!
I SHALL ERASE YOU SAMURAI, ONCE AND FOR ALL!
FSH
!!

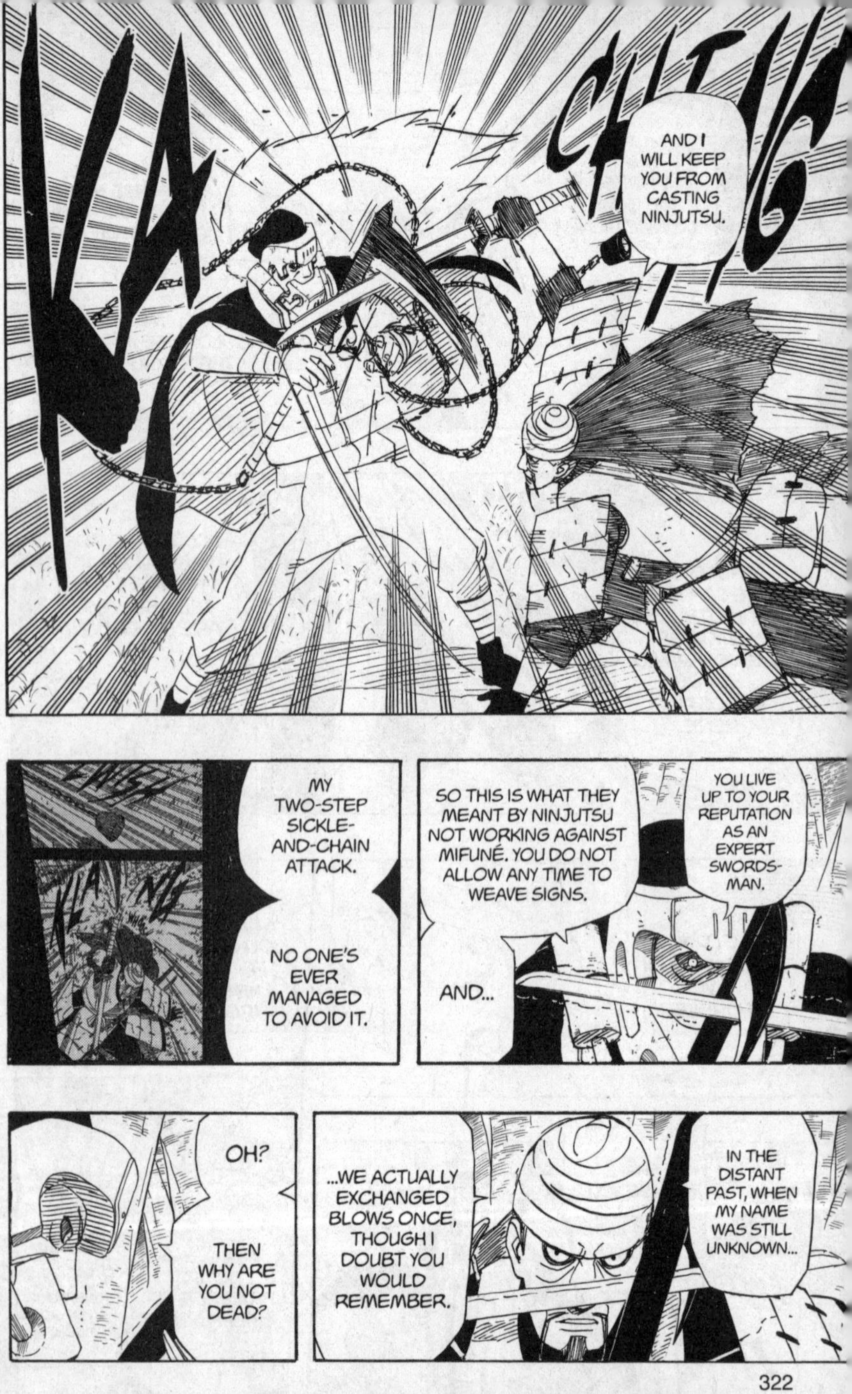
KA
AND I WILL KEEP YOU FROM CASTING NINJUTSU.
YOU LIVE UP TO YOUR REPUTATION AS AN EXPERT SWORDS-MAN.
SO THIS IS WHAT THEY MEANT BY NINJUTSU NOT WORKING AGAINST MIFUNÉ. YOU DO NOT ALLOW ANY TIME TO WEAVE SIGNS.
AND...
MY TWO-STEP SICKLE-AND-CHAIN ATTACK.
NO ONE'S EVER MANAGED TO AVOID IT.
IN THE DISTANT PAST, WHEN MY NAME WAS STILL UNKNOWN...
...WE ACTUALLY EXCHANGED BLOWS ONCE, THOUGH I DOUBT YOU WOULD REMEMBER.
OH?
THEN WHY ARE YOU NOT DEAD?

READ THIS WAY

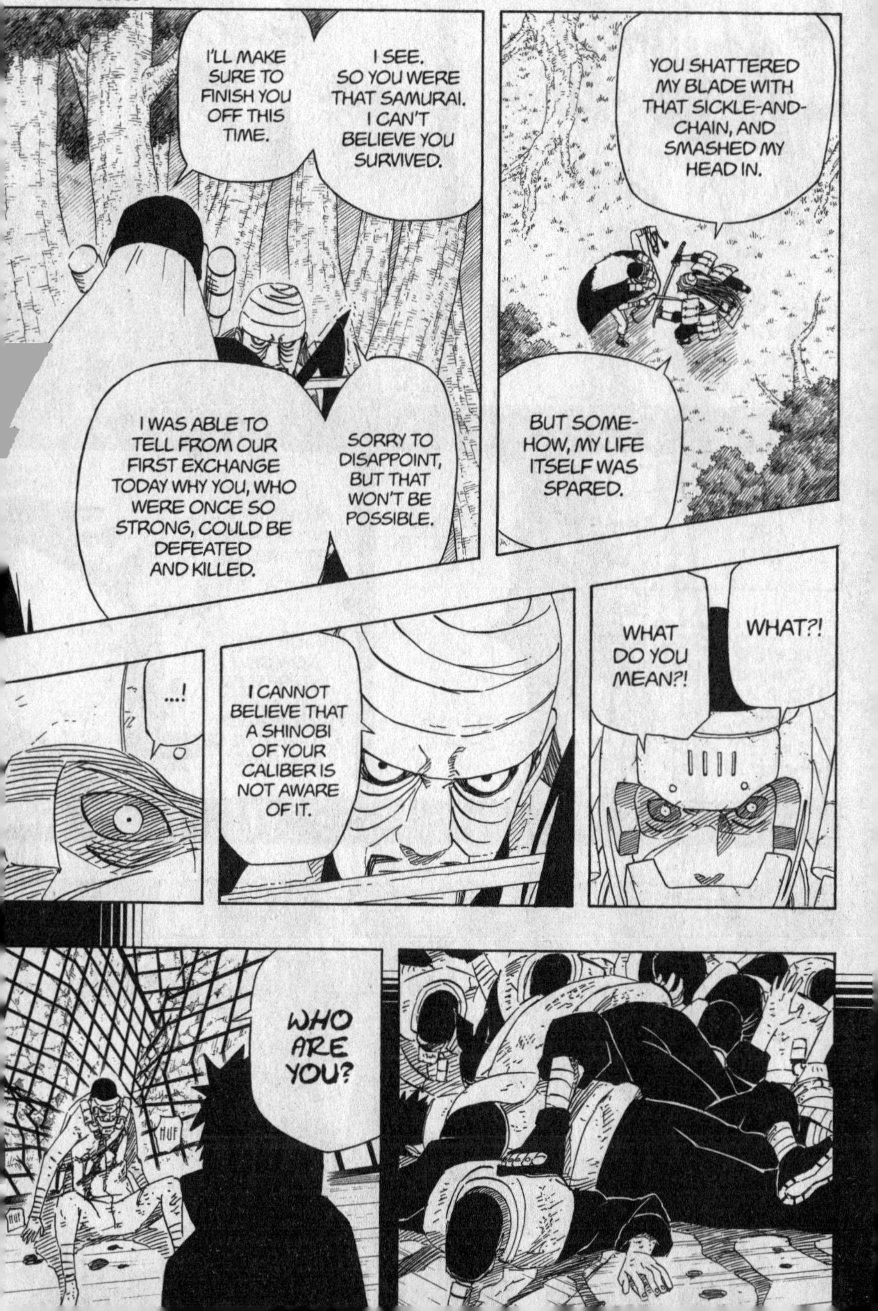
YOU SHATTERED MY BLADE WITH THAT SICKLE-AND-CHAIN, AND SMASHED MY HEAD IN.
BUT SOME-HOW, MY LIFE ITSELF WAS SPARED.
I SEE. SO YOU WERE THAT SAMURAI. I CAN'T BELIEVE YOU SURVIVED.
I'LL MAKE SURE TO FINISH YOU OFF THIS TIME.
SORRY TO DISAPPOINT, BUT THAT WON'T BE POSSIBLE.
I WAS ABLE TO TELL FROM OUR FIRST EXCHANGE TODAY WHY YOU, WHO WERE ONCE SO STRONG, COULD BE DEFEATED AND KILLED.
WHAT?!
WHAT DO YOU MEAN?!
I CANNOT BELIEVE THAT A SHINOBI OF YOUR CALIBER IS NOT AWARE OF IT.
...!
WHO ARE YOU?

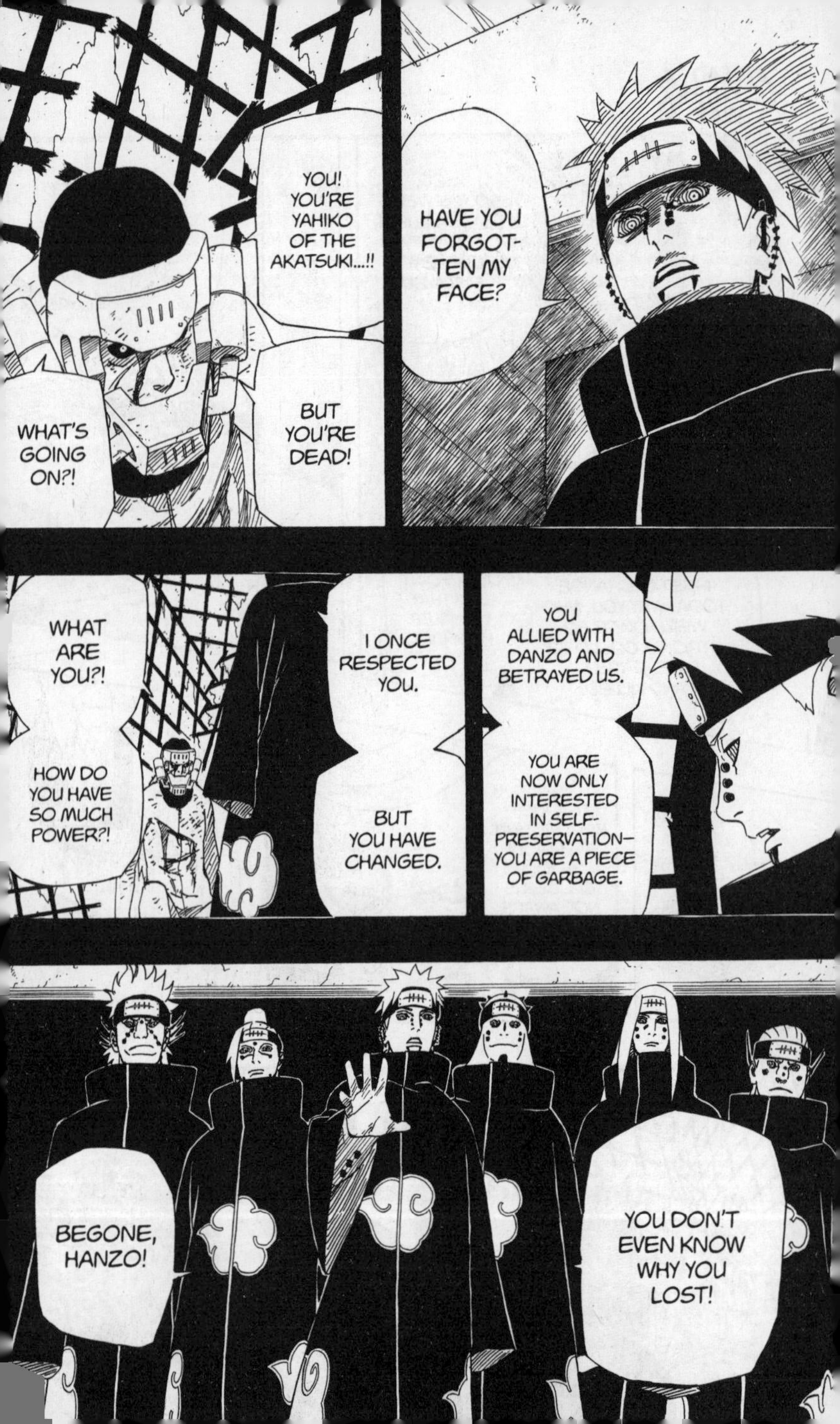
HAVE YOU FORGOTTEN MY FACE?
YOU! YOU'RE YAHIKO OF THE AKATSUKI...!!
BUT YOU'RE DEAD!
WHAT'S GOING ON?!
YOU ALLIED WITH DANZO AND BETRAYED US.
YOU ARE NOW ONLY INTERESTED IN SELF-PRESERVATION— YOU ARE A PIECE OF GARBAGE.
I ONCE RESPECTED YOU.
BUT YOU HAVE CHANGED.
WHAT ARE YOU?!
HOW DO YOU HAVE SO MUCH POWER?!
YOU DON'T EVEN KNOW WHY YOU LOST!
BEGONE, HANZO!

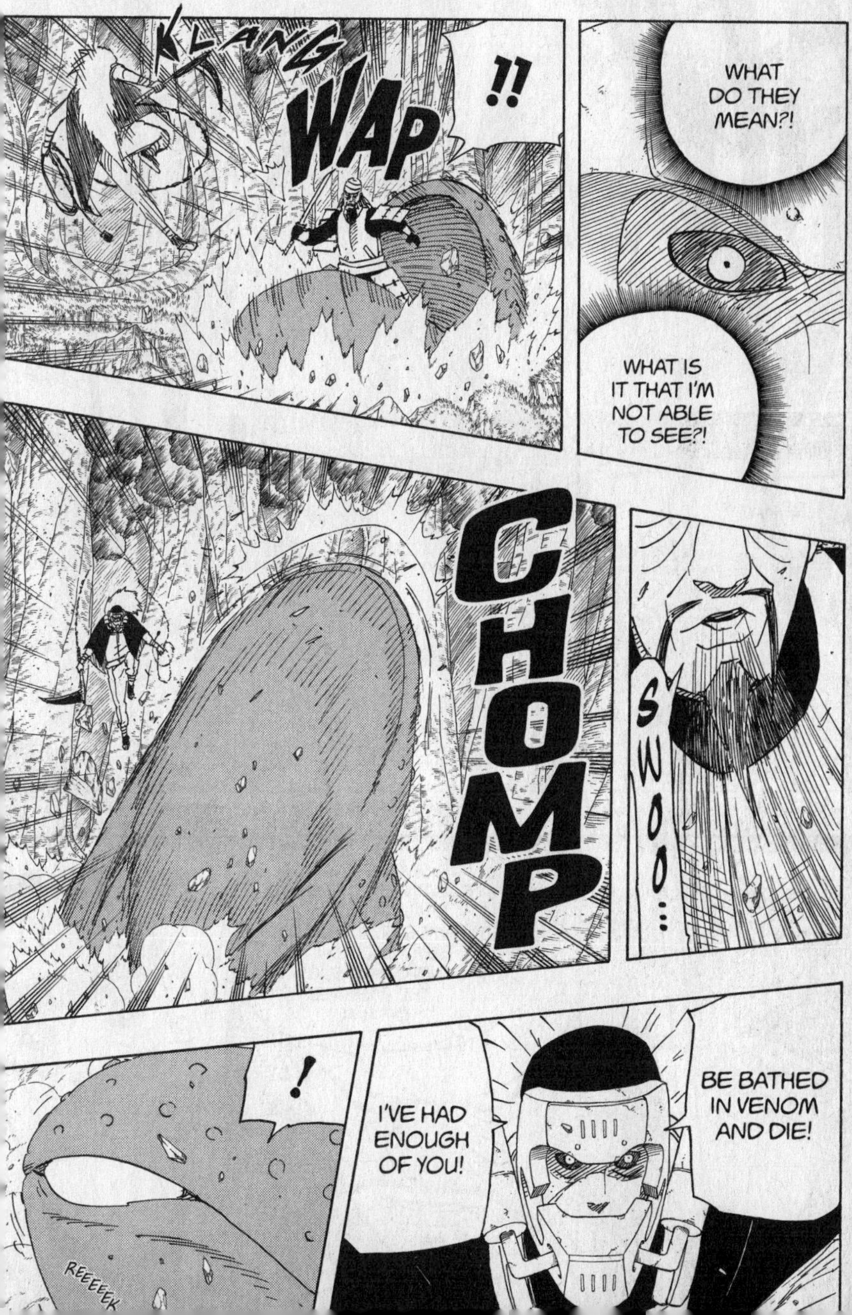
WHAT DO THEY MEAN?!
WHAT IS IT THAT I'M NOT ABLE TO SEE?!
KLANG
WAP
!!
SWOO...
CHOMP
BE BATHED IN VENOM AND DIE!
I'VE HAD ENOUGH OF YOU!
!
REEEEEK

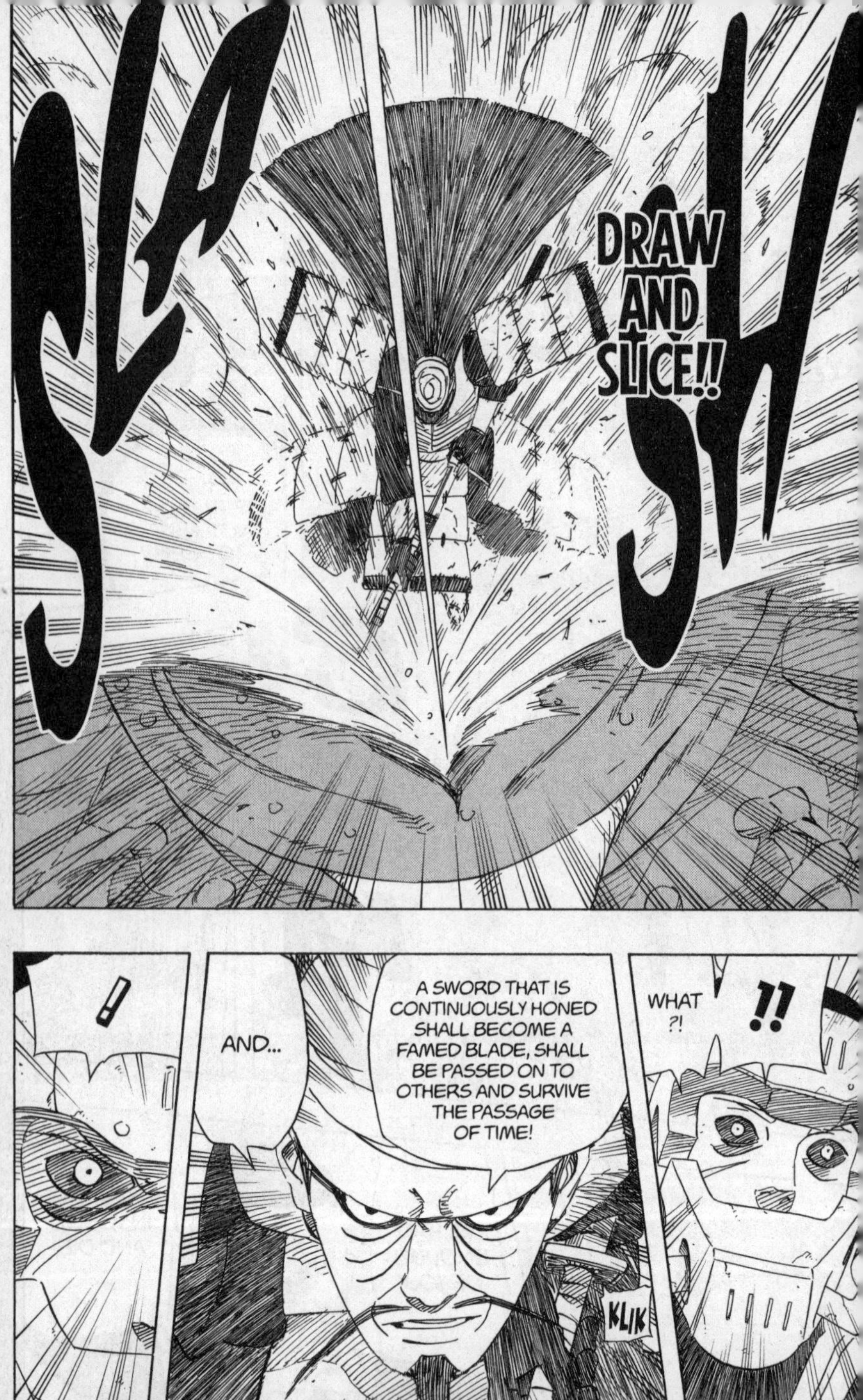
SLASH
DRAW AND SLICE!!
WHAT ?!
!!
A SWORD THAT IS CONTINUOUSLY HONED SHALL BECOME A FAMED BLADE, SHALL BE PASSED ON TO OTHERS AND SURVIVE THE PASSAGE OF TIME!
AND...
KLIK
!

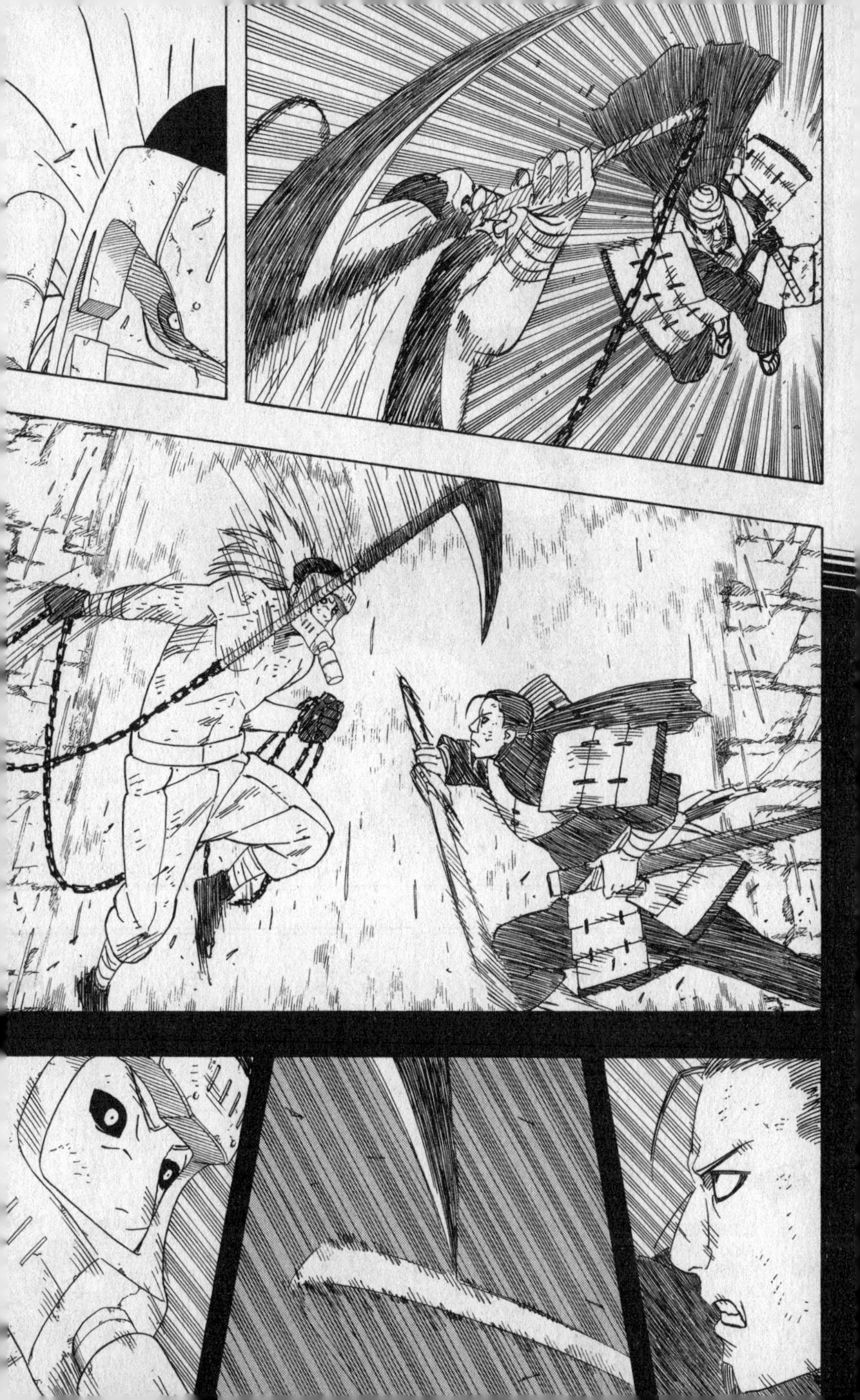

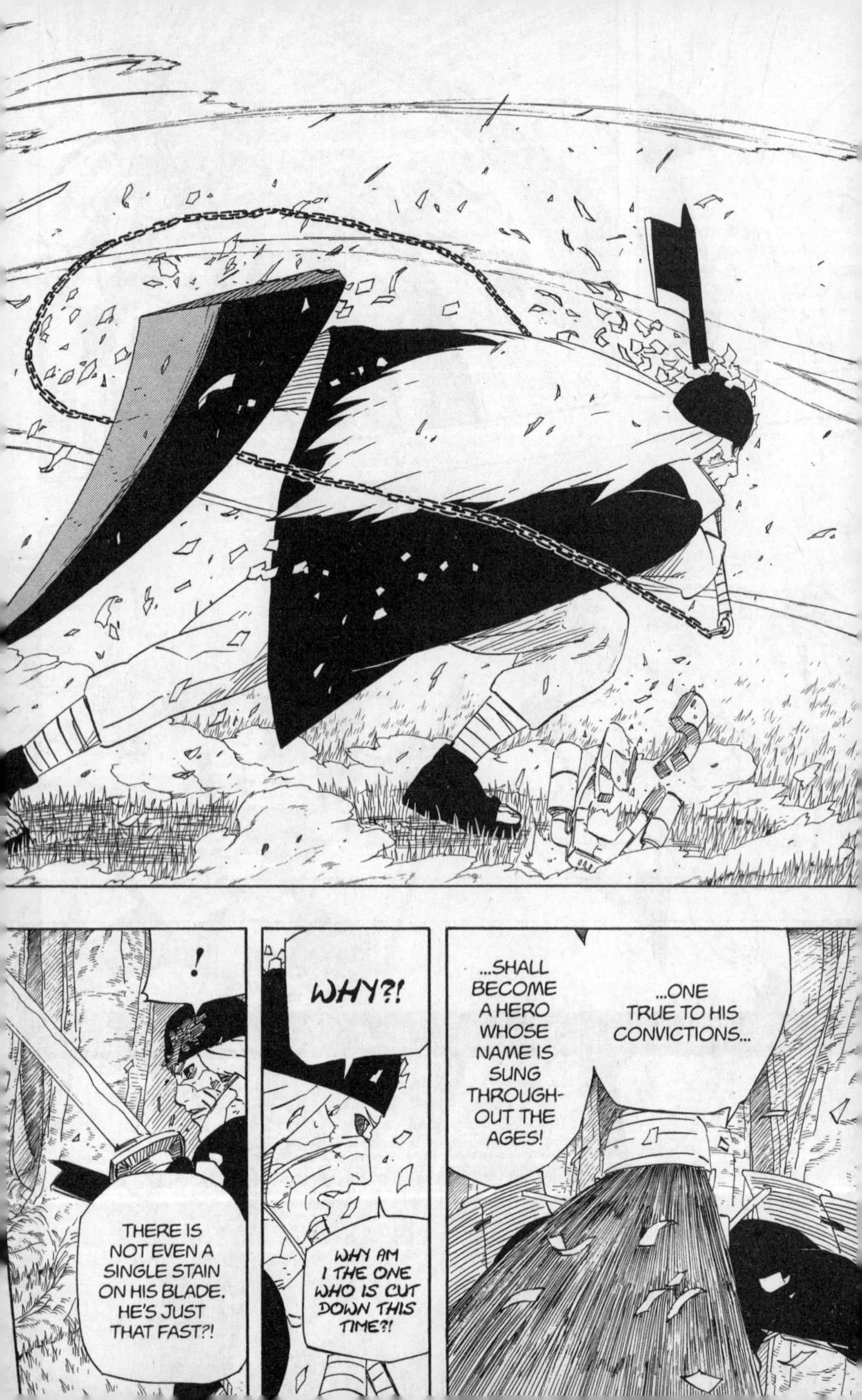
...ONE TRUE TO HIS CONVICTIONS...
...SHALL BECOME A HERO WHOSE NAME IS SUNG THROUGH-OUT THE AGES!
WHY?!
WHY AM I THE ONE WHO IS CUT DOWN THIS TIME?!
!
THERE IS NOT EVEN A SINGLE STAIN ON HIS BLADE. HE'S JUST THAT FAST?!

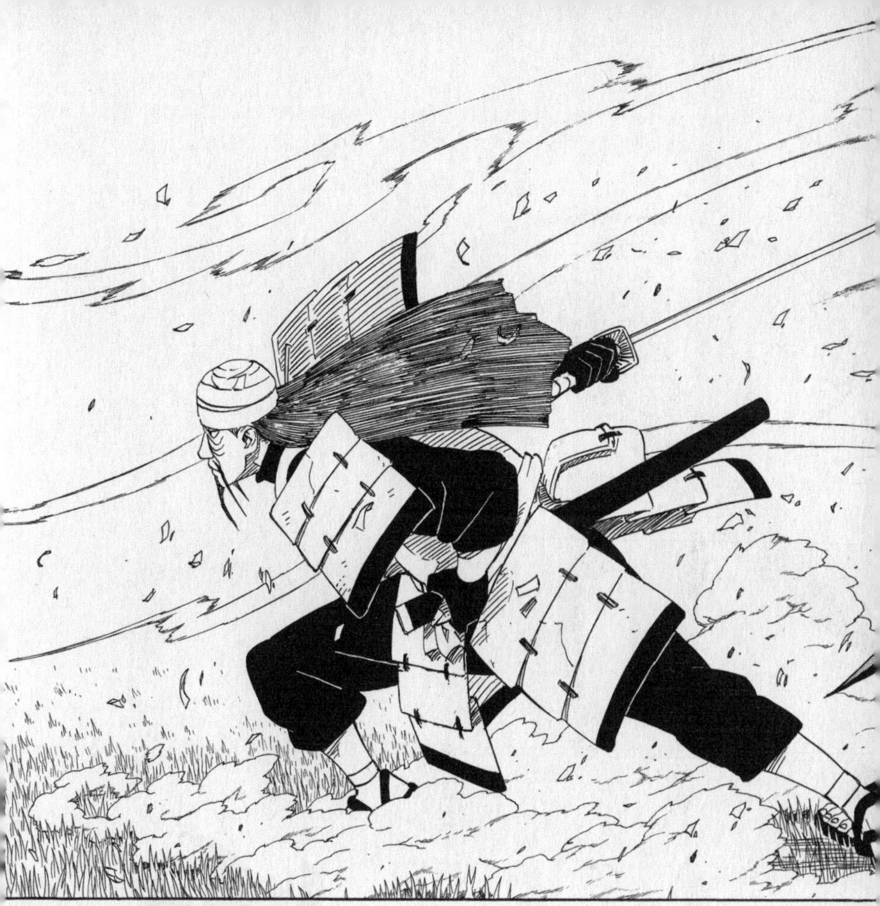

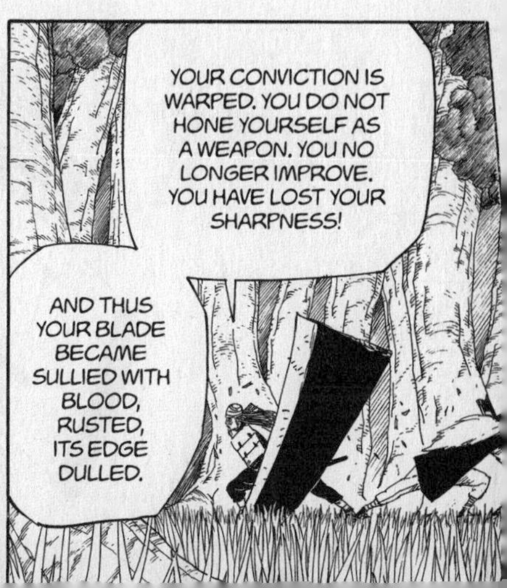
YOUR CONVICTION IS WARPED. YOU DO NOT HONE YOURSELF AS A WEAPON. YOU NO LONGER IMPROVE. YOU HAVE LOST YOUR SHARPNESS!
AND THUS YOUR BLADE BECAME SULLIED WITH BLOOD, RUSTED, ITS EDGE DULLED.

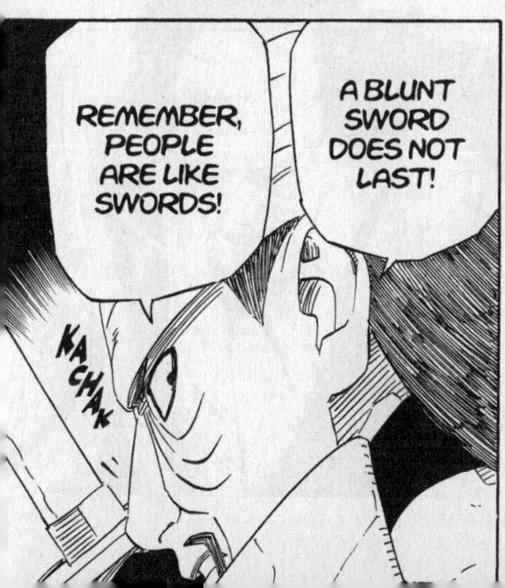
REMEMBER, PEOPLE ARE LIKE SWORDS!
A BLUNT SWORD DOES NOT LAST!
KACHAK

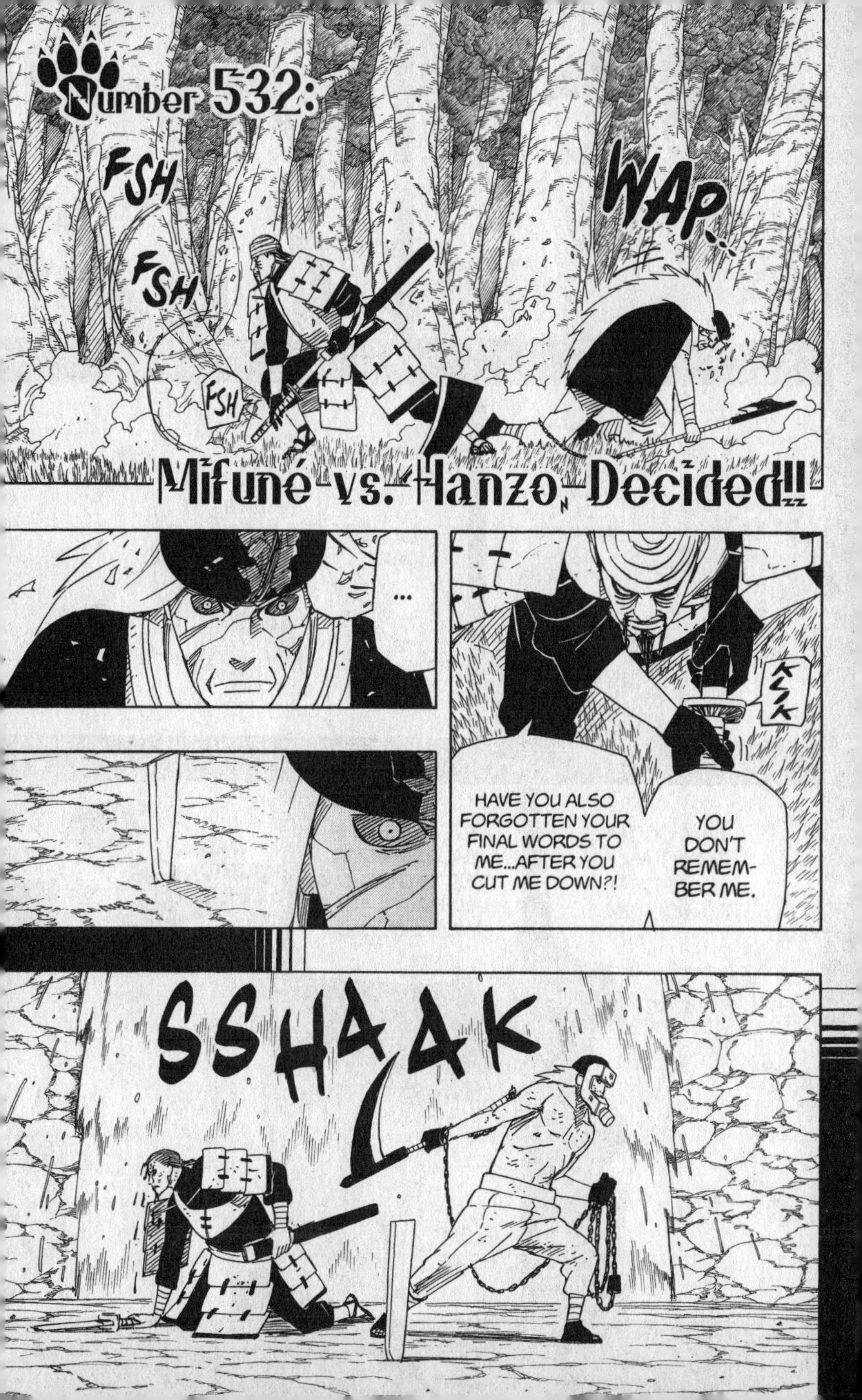
Number 532:
Mifuné vs. Hanzo, Decided!!
WAP
FSH
FSH
FSH
KLIK
YOU DON'T REMEM-BER ME.
HAVE YOU ALSO FORGOTTEN YOUR FINAL WORDS TO ME...AFTER YOU CUT ME DOWN?!
...
SSHAAK

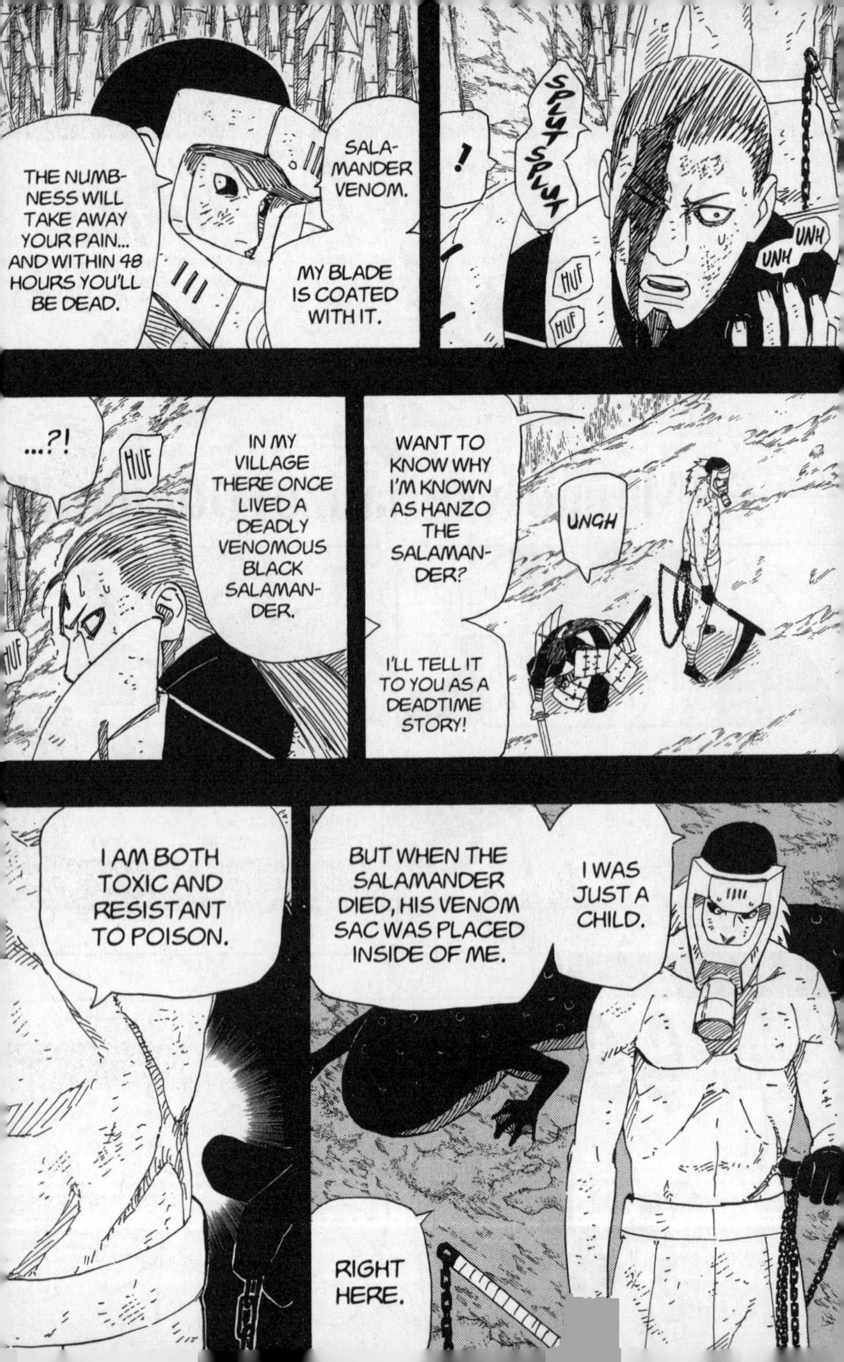
UNH
UNH
SPLUT SPLUT
!
HUF
HUF
SALAMANDER VENOM.
MY BLADE IS COATED WITH IT.
THE NUMBNESS WILL TAKE AWAY YOUR PAIN... AND WITHIN 48 HOURS YOU'LL BE DEAD.
WANT TO KNOW WHY I'M KNOWN AS HANZO THE SALAMANDER?
UNGH
I'LL TELL IT TO YOU AS A DEADTIME STORY!
IN MY VILLAGE THERE ONCE LIVED A DEADLY VENOMOUS BLACK SALAMANDER.
HUF
...?!
HUF
I WAS JUST A CHILD.
BUT WHEN THE SALAMANDER DIED, HIS VENOM SAC WAS PLACED INSIDE OF ME.
RIGHT HERE.
I AM BOTH TOXIC AND RESISTANT TO POISON.

READ THIS WAY

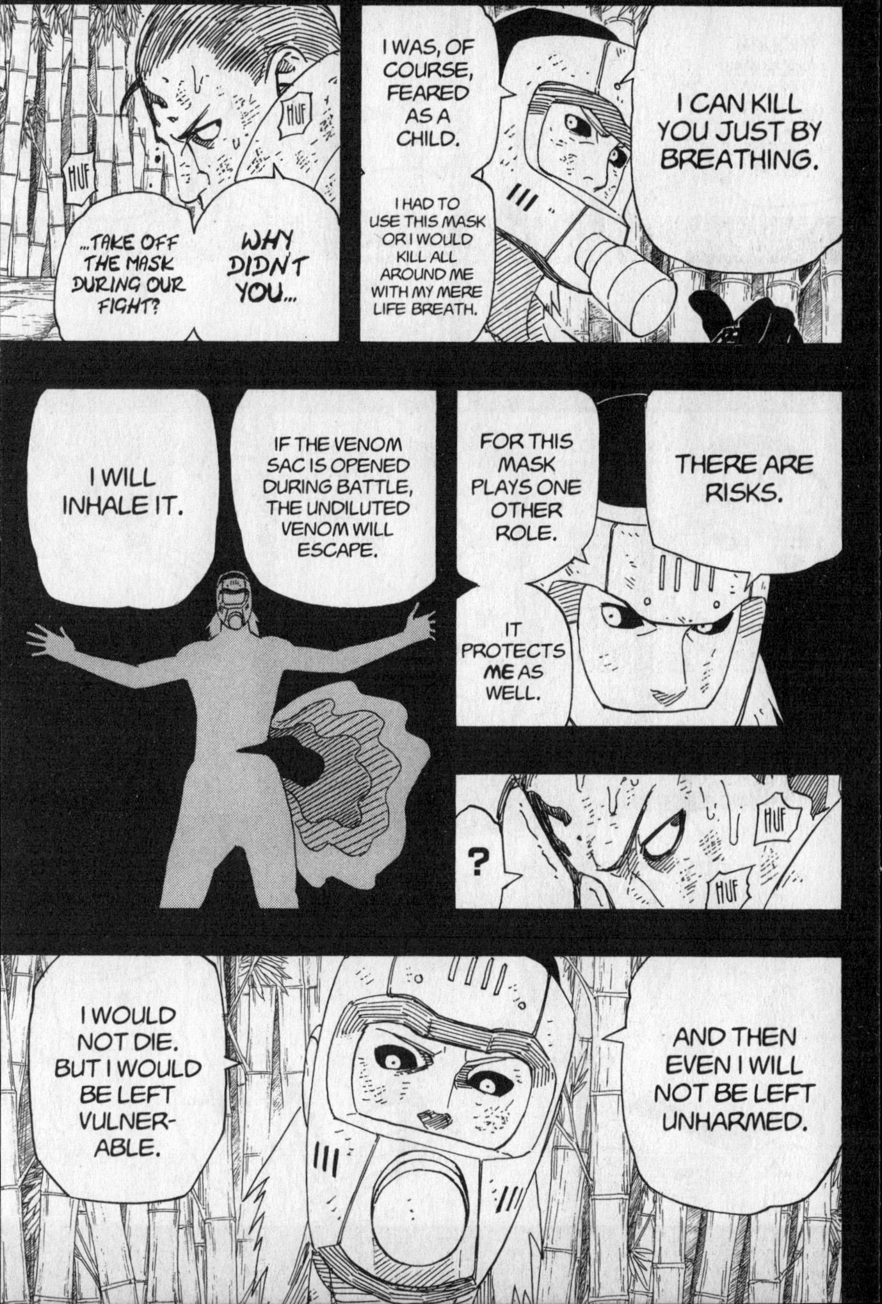
I CAN KILL YOU JUST BY BREATHING.
I WAS, OF COURSE, FEARED AS A CHILD.
I HAD TO USE THIS MASK OR I WOULD KILL ALL AROUND ME WITH MY MERE LIFE BREATH.
HUF
HUF
WHY DIDN'T YOU...
...TAKE OFF THE MASK DURING OUR FIGHT?
THERE ARE RISKS.
FOR THIS MASK PLAYS ONE OTHER ROLE.
IT PROTECTS ME AS WELL.
HUF
HUF
?
IF THE VENOM SAC IS OPENED DURING BATTLE, THE UNDILUTED VENOM WILL ESCAPE.
I WILL INHALE IT.
AND THEN EVEN I WILL NOT BE LEFT UNHARMED.
I WOULD NOT DIE. BUT I WOULD BE LEFT VULNERABLE.

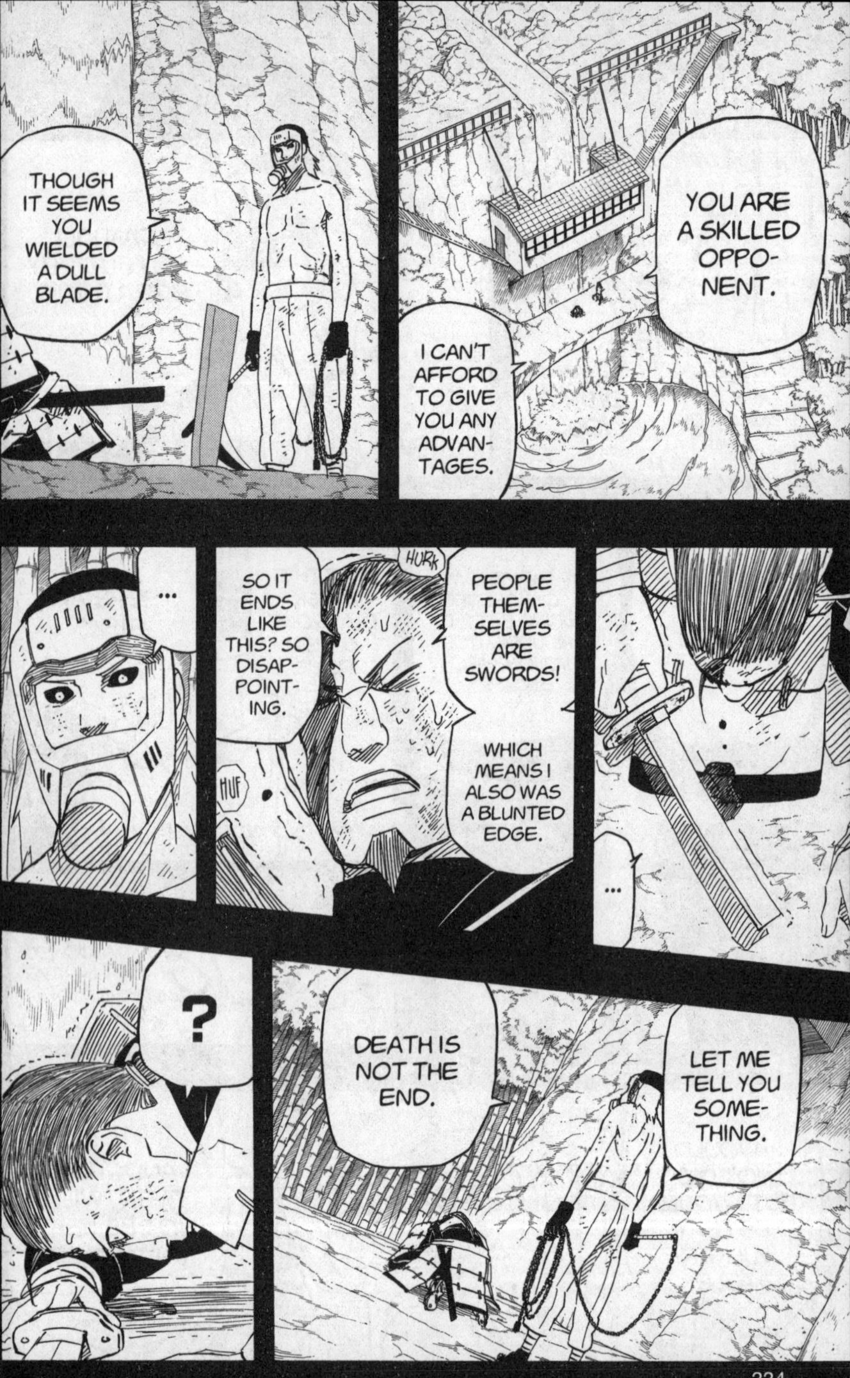
YOU ARE A SKILLED OPPO-NENT.
I CAN'T AFFORD TO GIVE YOU ANY ADVAN-TAGES.
THOUGH IT SEEMS YOU WIELDED A DULL BLADE.
...
HURK
PEOPLE THEM-SELVES ARE SWORDS!
WHICH MEANS I ALSO WAS A BLUNTED EDGE.
SO IT ENDS LIKE THIS? SO DISAP-POINT-ING.
HUF
...
LET ME TELL YOU SOME-THING.
DEATH IS NOT THE END.
?

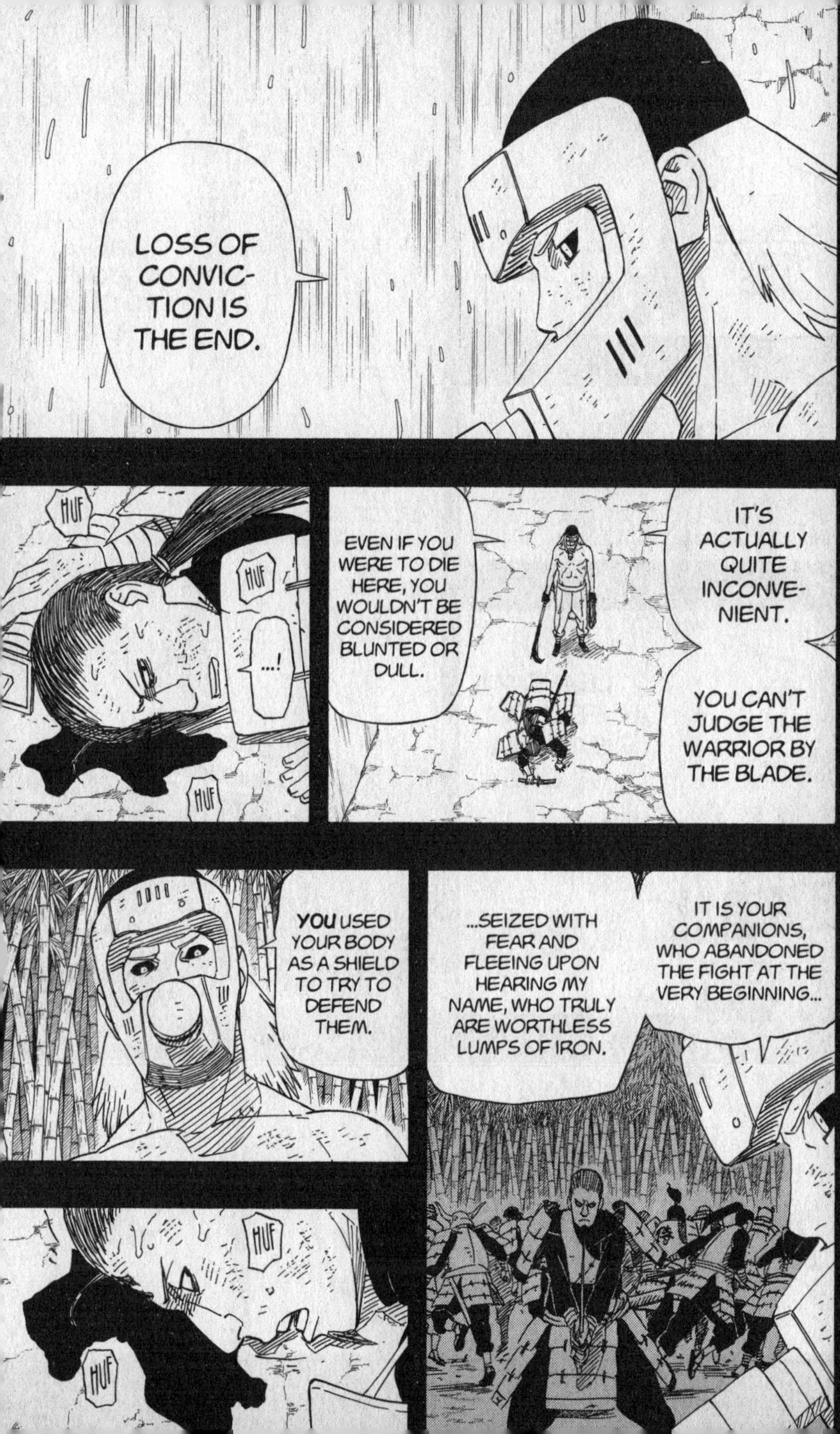
LOSS OF CONVICTION IS THE END.
IT'S ACTUALLY QUITE INCONVENIENT.
YOU CAN'T JUDGE THE WARRIOR BY THE BLADE.
EVEN IF YOU WERE TO DIE HERE, YOU WOULDN'T BE CONSIDERED BLUNTED OR DULL.
HUF
HUF
...!
HUF
IT IS YOUR COMPANIONS, WHO ABANDONED THE FIGHT AT THE VERY BEGINNING...
...SEIZED WITH FEAR AND FLEEING UPON HEARING MY NAME, WHO TRULY ARE WORTHLESS LUMPS OF IRON.
**YOU** USED YOUR BODY AS A SHIELD TO TRY TO DEFEND THEM.
HUF
HUF

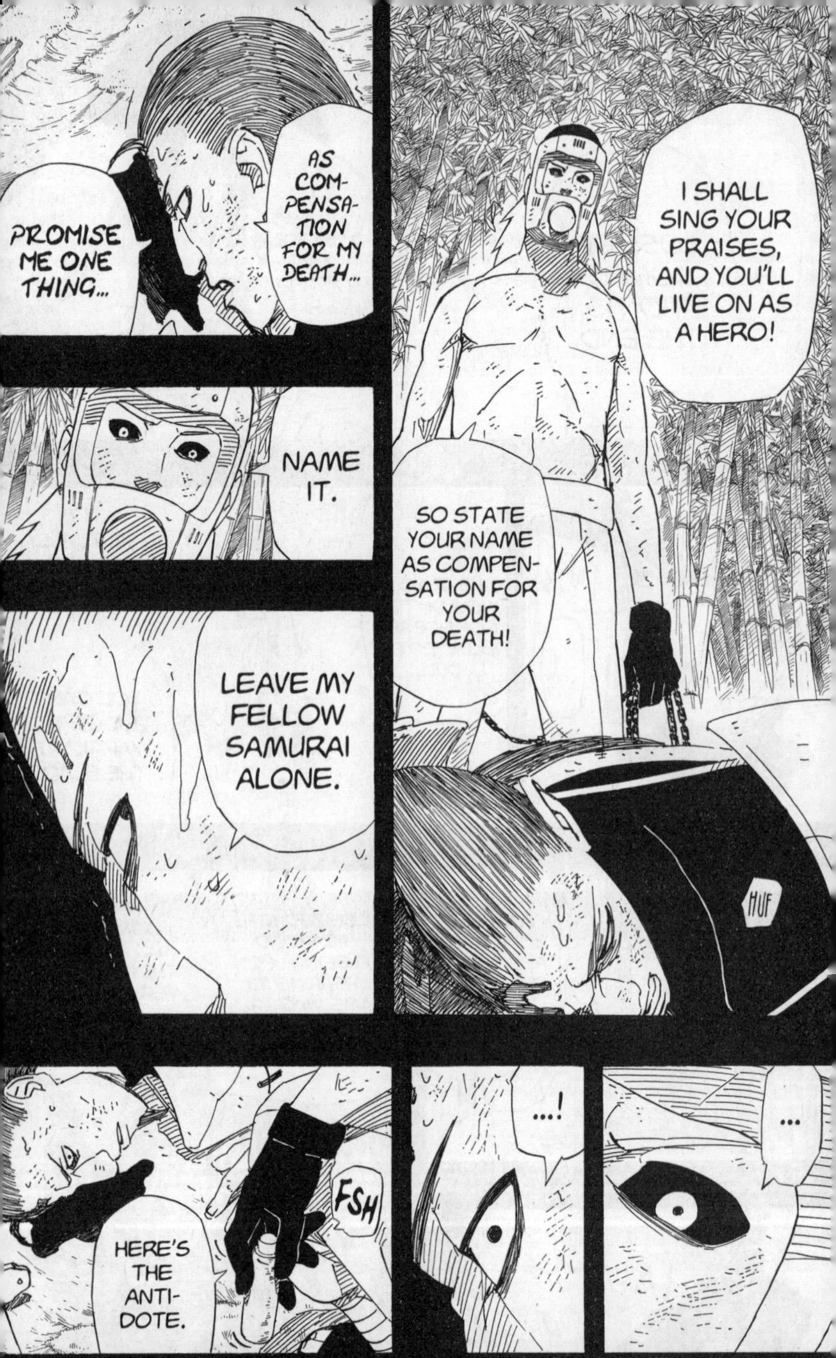
I SHALL SING YOUR PRAISES, AND YOU'LL LIVE ON AS A HERO!
SO STATE YOUR NAME AS COMPENSATION FOR YOUR DEATH!
HUF
AS COMPENSATION FOR MY DEATH...
PROMISE ME ONE THING...
NAME IT.
LEAVE MY FELLOW SAMURAI ALONE.
...
...!
FSH
HERE'S THE ANTIDOTE.

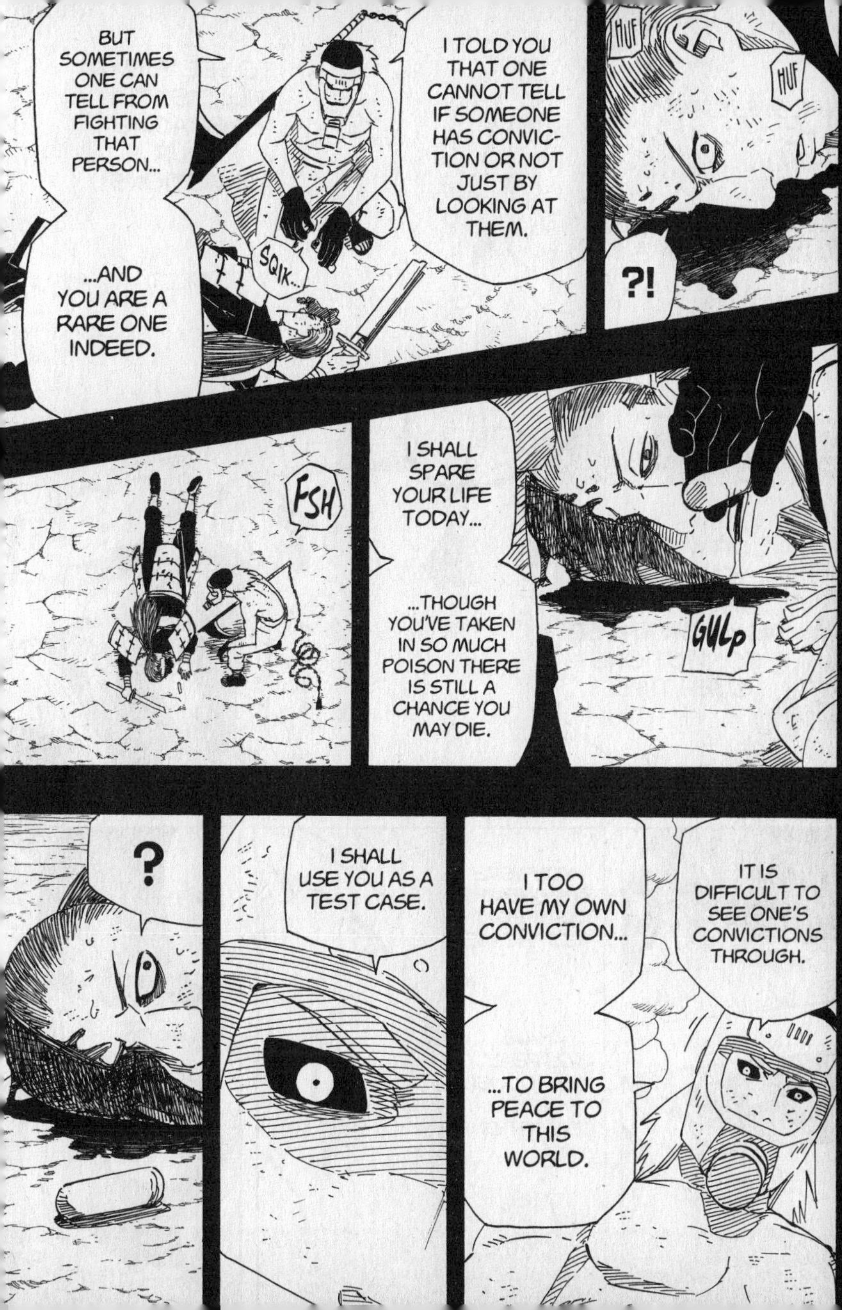
HUF
HUF
?!
I TOLD YOU THAT ONE CANNOT TELL IF SOMEONE HAS CONVICTION OR NOT JUST BY LOOKING AT THEM.
BUT SOMETIMES ONE CAN TELL FROM FIGHTING THAT PERSON...
SQIK...
...AND YOU ARE A RARE ONE INDEED.
I SHALL SPARE YOUR LIFE TODAY...
...THOUGH YOU'VE TAKEN IN SO MUCH POISON THERE IS STILL A CHANCE YOU MAY DIE.
GULp
FSH
IT IS DIFFICULT TO SEE ONE'S CONVICTIONS THROUGH.
I TOO HAVE MY OWN CONVICTION...
...TO BRING PEACE TO THIS WORLD.
I SHALL USE YOU AS A TEST CASE.
?

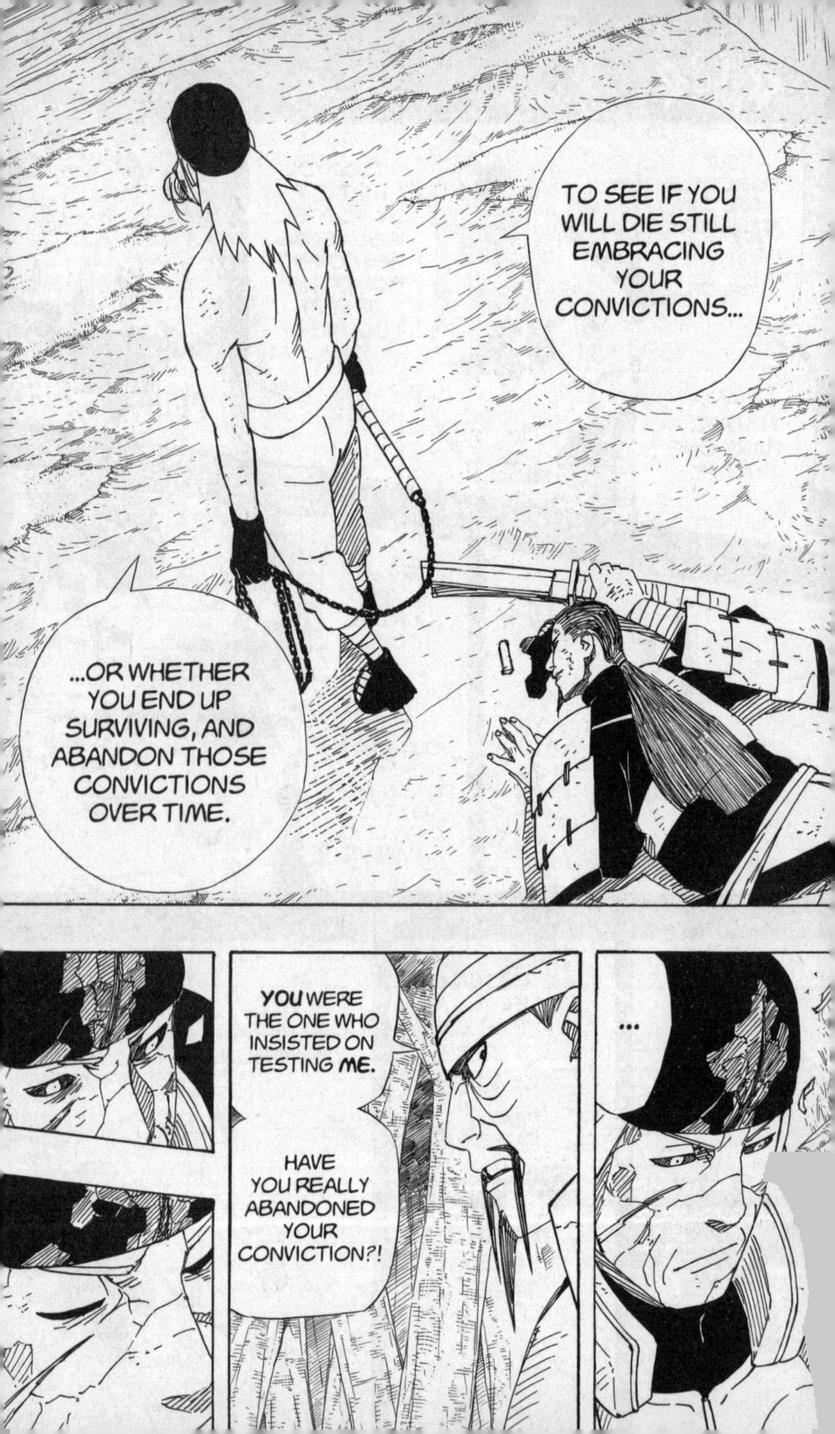
TO SEE IF YOU WILL DIE STILL EMBRACING YOUR CONVICTIONS...
...OR WHETHER YOU END UP SURVIVING, AND ABANDON THOSE CONVICTIONS OVER TIME.
...
YOU WERE THE ONE WHO INSISTED ON TESTING ME.
HAVE YOU REALLY ABANDONED YOUR CONVICTION?!

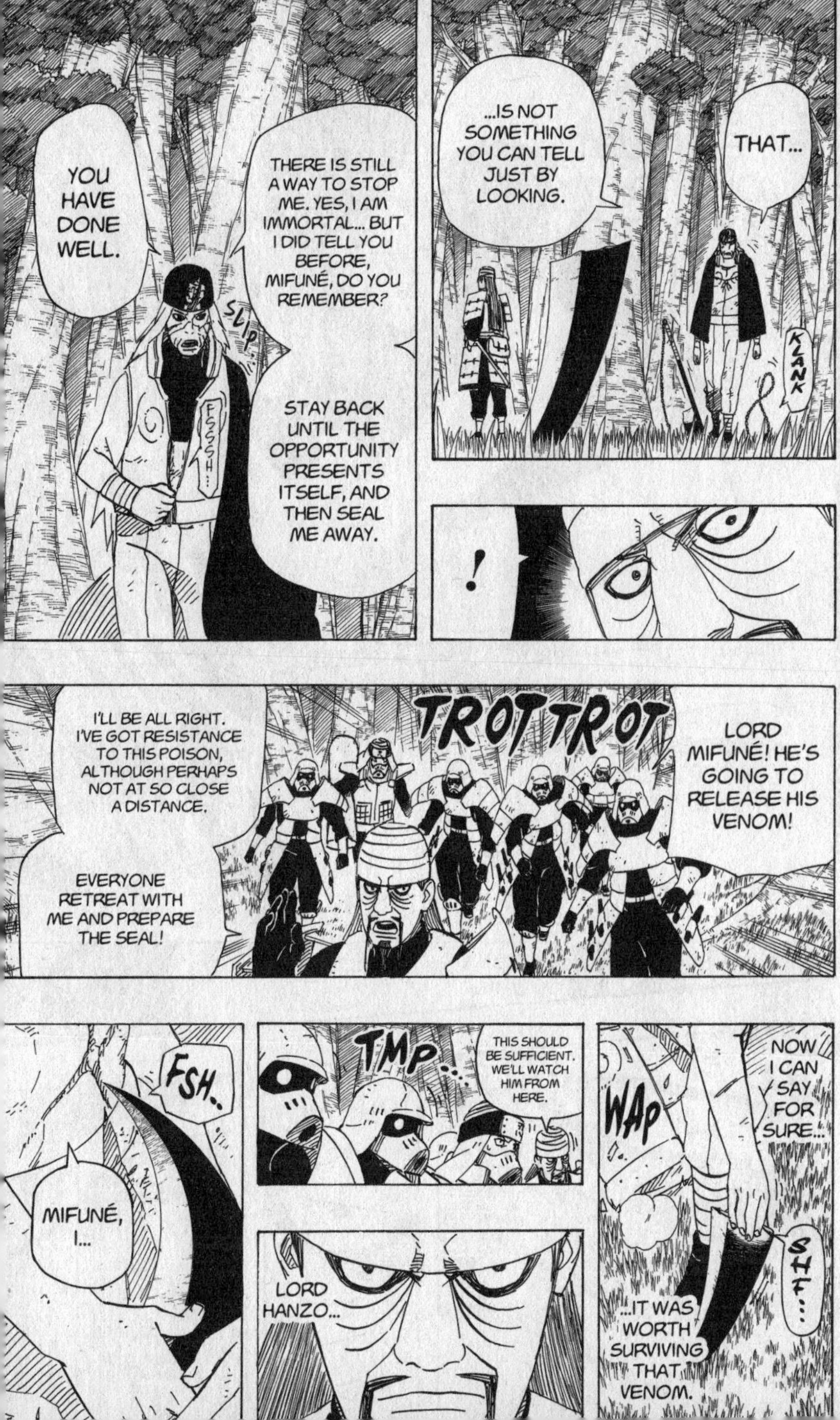
THAT...
...IS NOT SOMETHING YOU CAN TELL JUST BY LOOKING.
KLANK
!
THERE IS STILL A WAY TO STOP ME. YES, I AM IMMORTAL... BUT I DID TELL YOU BEFORE, MIFUNÉ, DO YOU REMEMBER?
STAY BACK UNTIL THE OPPORTUNITY PRESENTS ITSELF, AND THEN SEAL ME AWAY.
SLIP.
YOU HAVE DONE WELL.
FSSSH...
LORD MIFUNÉ! HE'S GOING TO RELEASE HIS VENOM!
TROT TROT
I'LL BE ALL RIGHT. I'VE GOT RESISTANCE TO THIS POISON, ALTHOUGH PERHAPS NOT AT SO CLOSE A DISTANCE.
EVERYONE RETREAT WITH ME AND PREPARE THE SEAL!
NOW I CAN SAY FOR SURE...
WAP
SHF...
...IT WAS WORTH SURVIVING THAT VENOM.
THIS SHOULD BE SUFFICIENT. WE'LL WATCH HIM FROM HERE.
TMP...
LORD HANZO...
FSH..
MIFUNÉ, I...

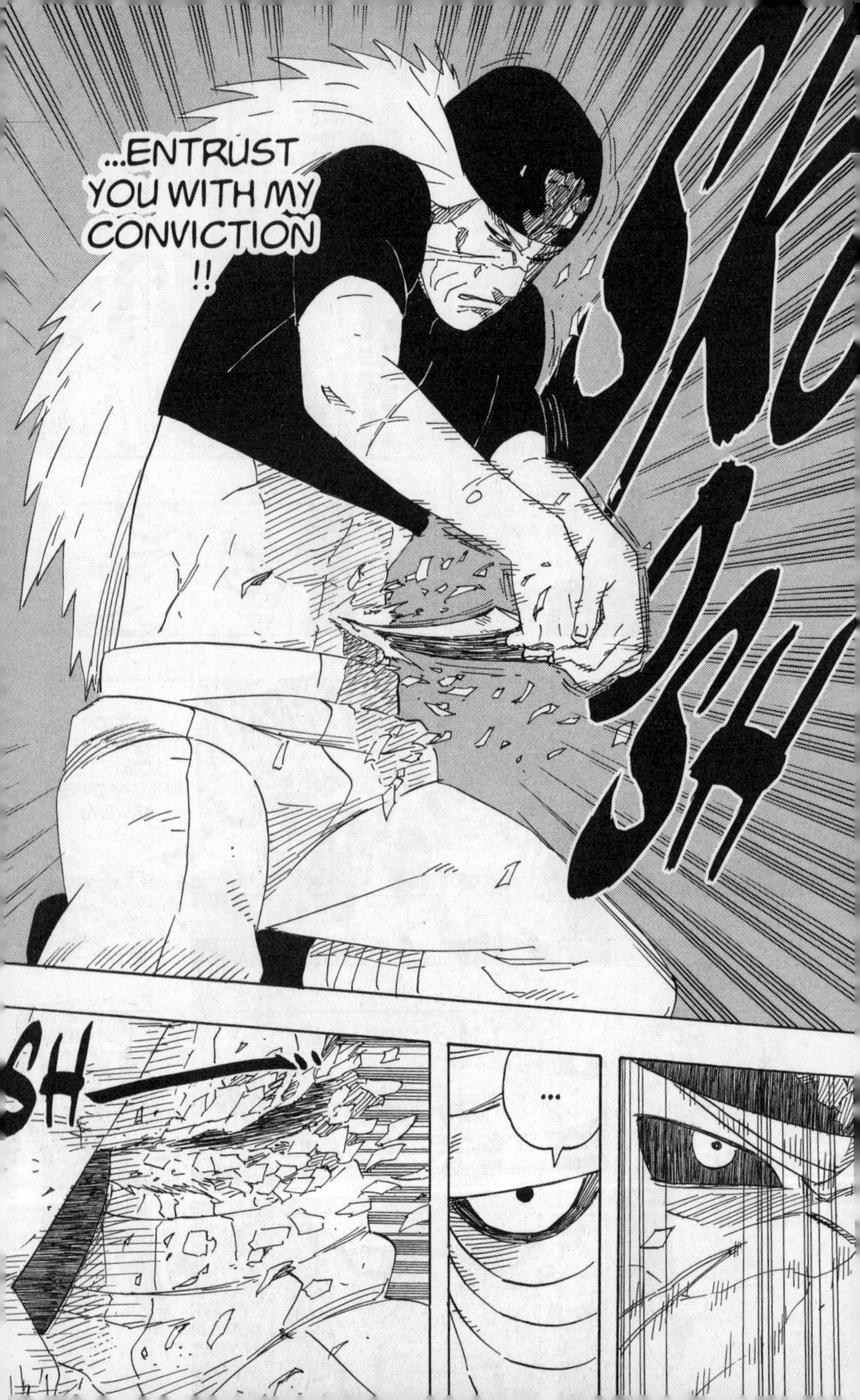
...ENTRUST YOU WITH MY CONVICTION !!
SHSH
...
SH—

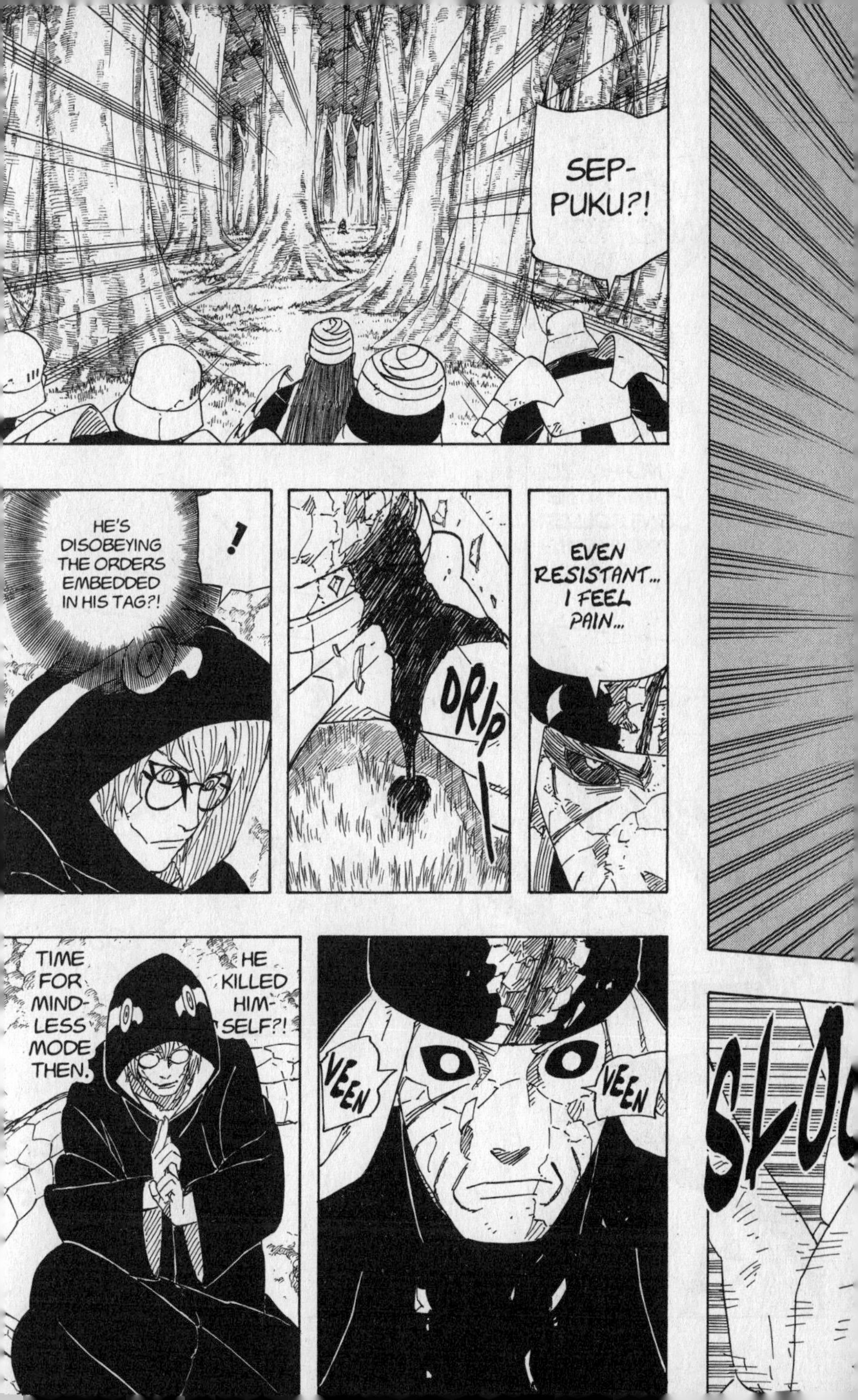
SLO
SEP-PUKU?!
EVEN RESISTANT... I FEEL PAIN...
DRIP
!
HE'S DISOBEYING THE ORDERS EMBEDDED IN HIS TAG?!
VEEN
VEEN
HE KILLED HIM-SELF?!
TIME FOR MIND-LESS MODE THEN.

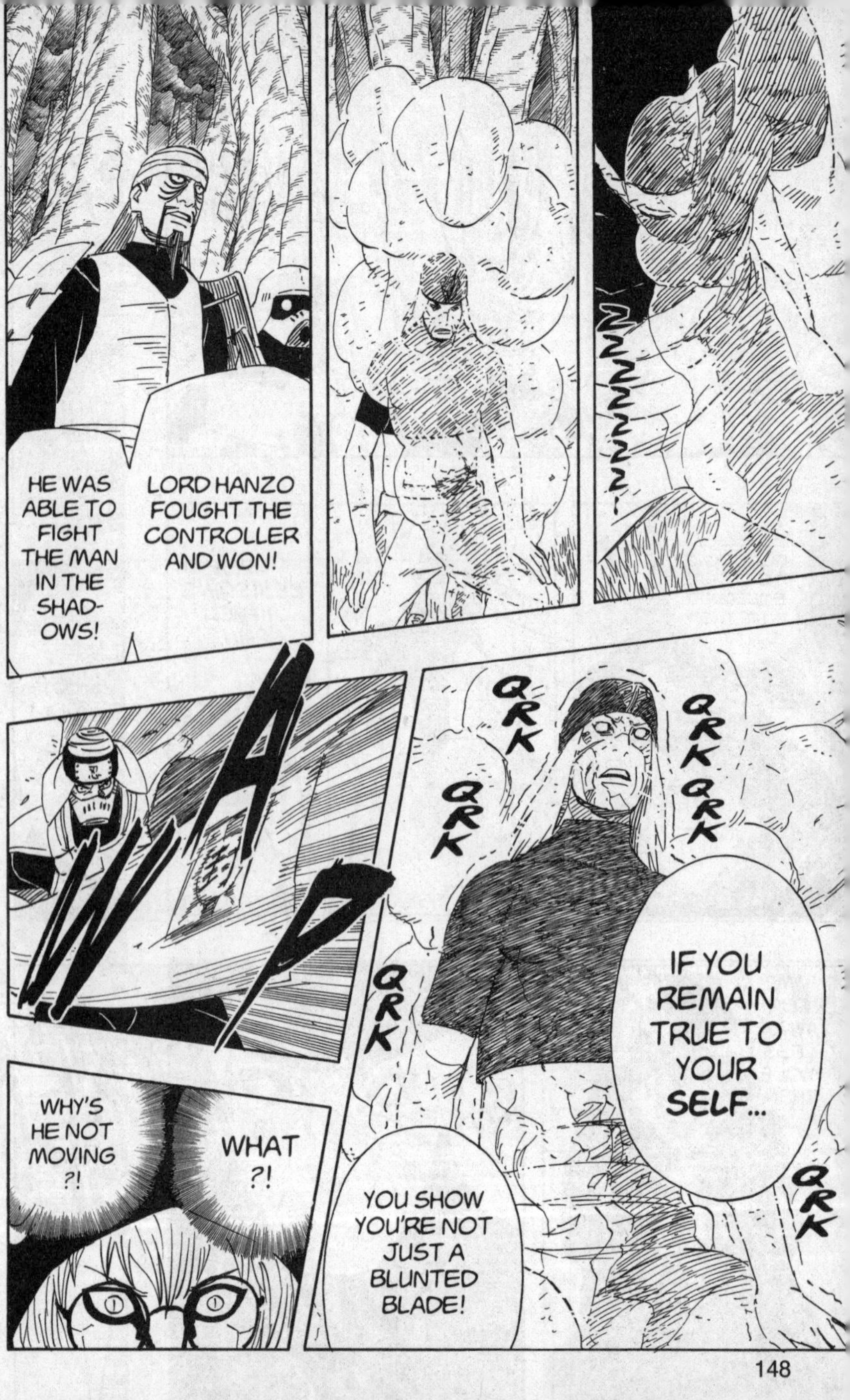
ZZZZZZZ-
LORD HANZO FOUGHT THE CONTROLLER AND WON!
HE WAS ABLE TO FIGHT THE MAN IN THE SHADOWS!
QRK
QRK
QRK QRK
QRK
IF YOU REMAIN TRUE TO YOUR SELF...
YOU SHOW YOU'RE NOT JUST A BLUNTED BLADE!
QRK
WHAP
WHAT ?!
WHY'S HE NOT MOVING ?!

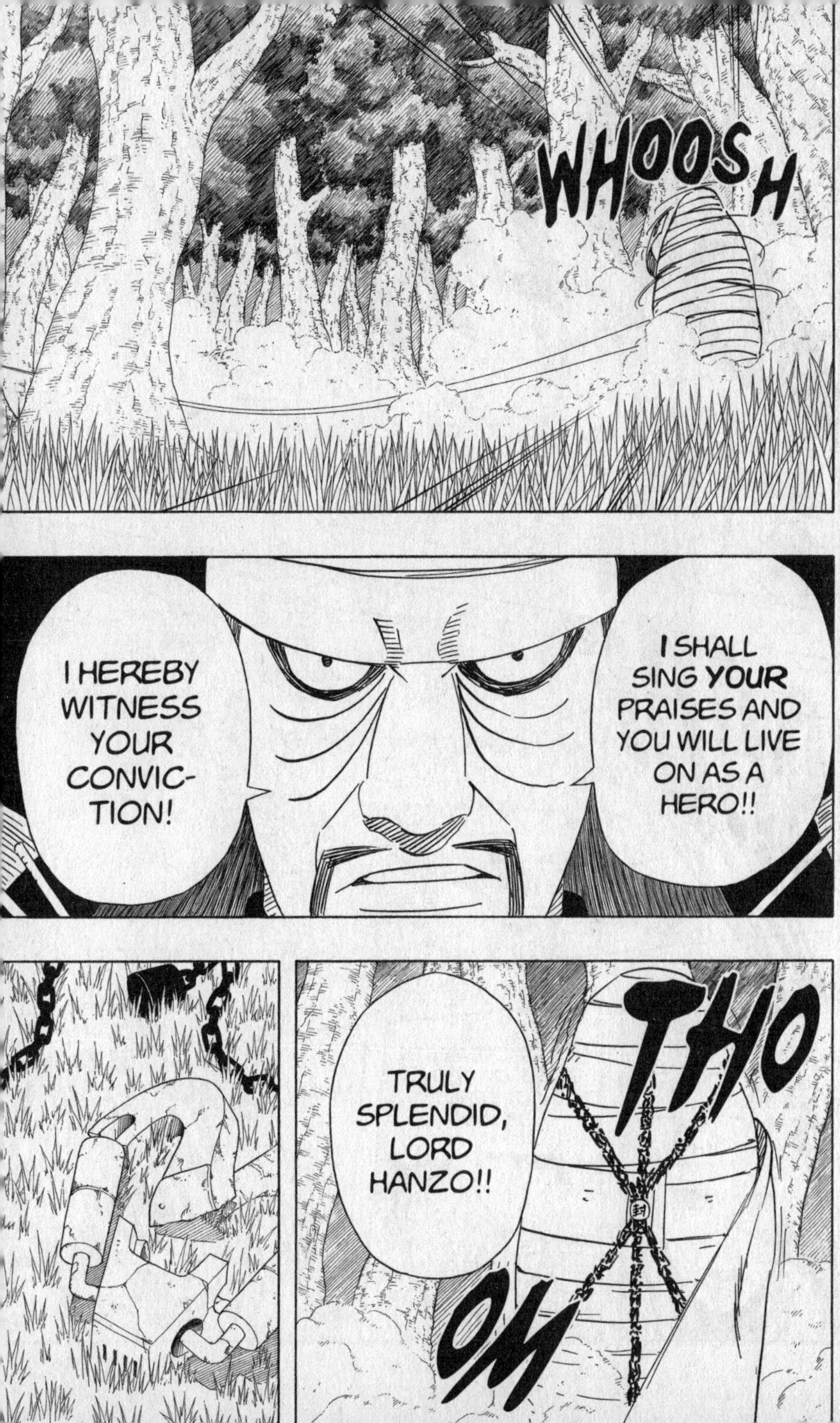
WHOOSH
I SHALL SING YOUR PRAISES AND YOU WILL LIVE ON AS A HERO!!
I HEREBY WITNESS YOUR CONVIC-TION!
THOOM
TRULY SPLENDID, LORD HANZO!!

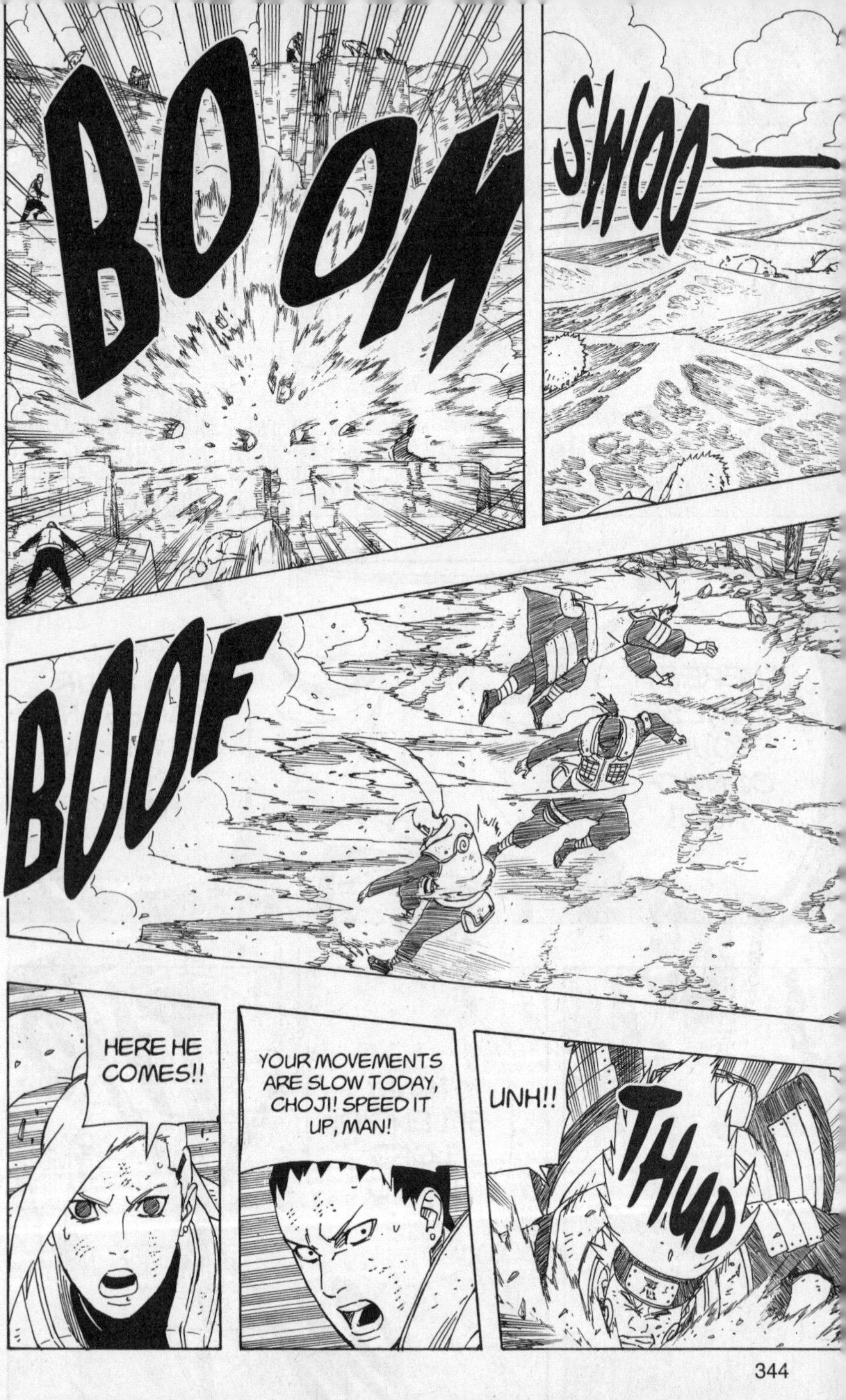
SHOOO—
BOOM
BOOF
THUD
UNH!!
YOUR MOVEMENTS ARE SLOW TODAY, CHOJI! SPEED IT UP, MAN!
HERE HE COMES!!

READ THIS WAY

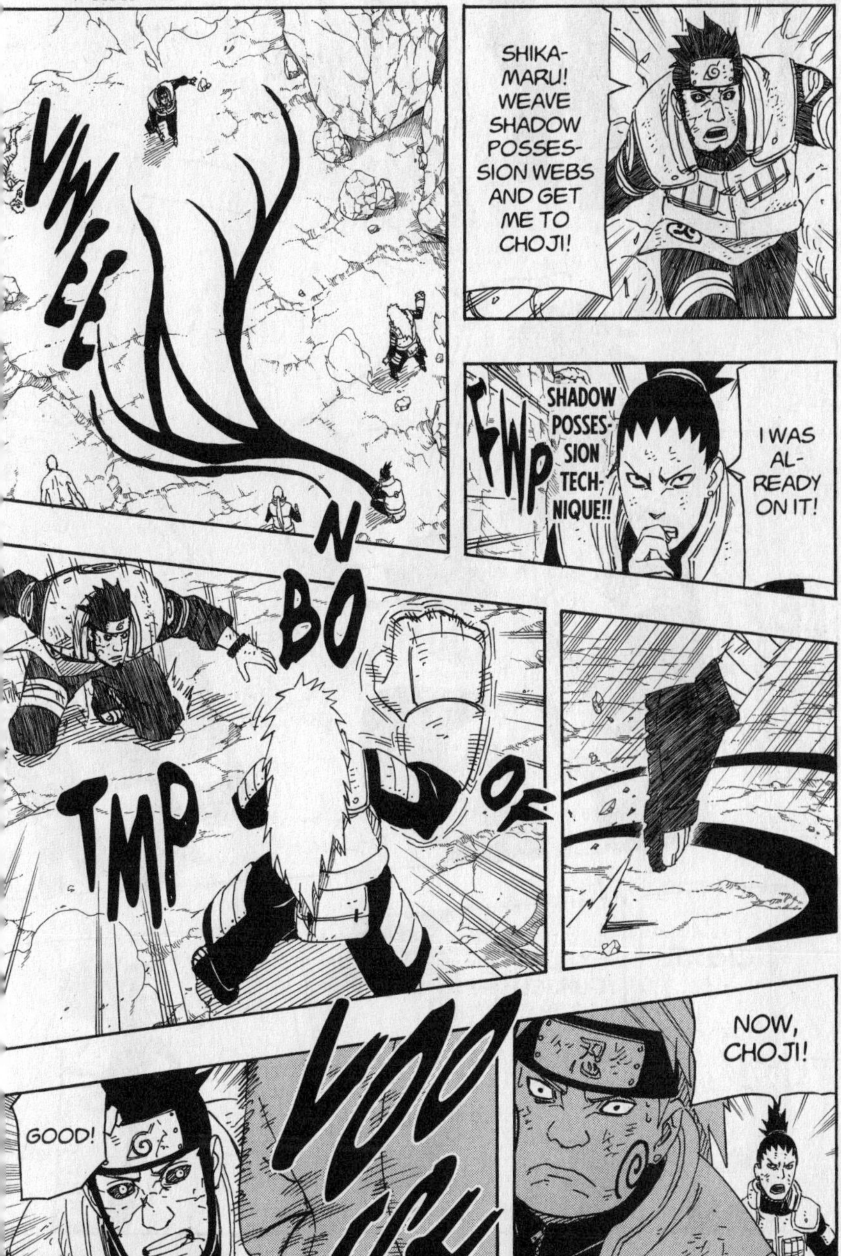
SHIKA-MARU! WEAVE SHADOW POSSES-SION WEBS AND GET ME TO CHOJI!
I WAS AL-READY ON IT!
SHADOW POSSES-SION TECH-NIQUE!!
FWP
VWEEE
N
BO
OF
TMP
NOW, CHOJI!
VOOOSH
GOOD!

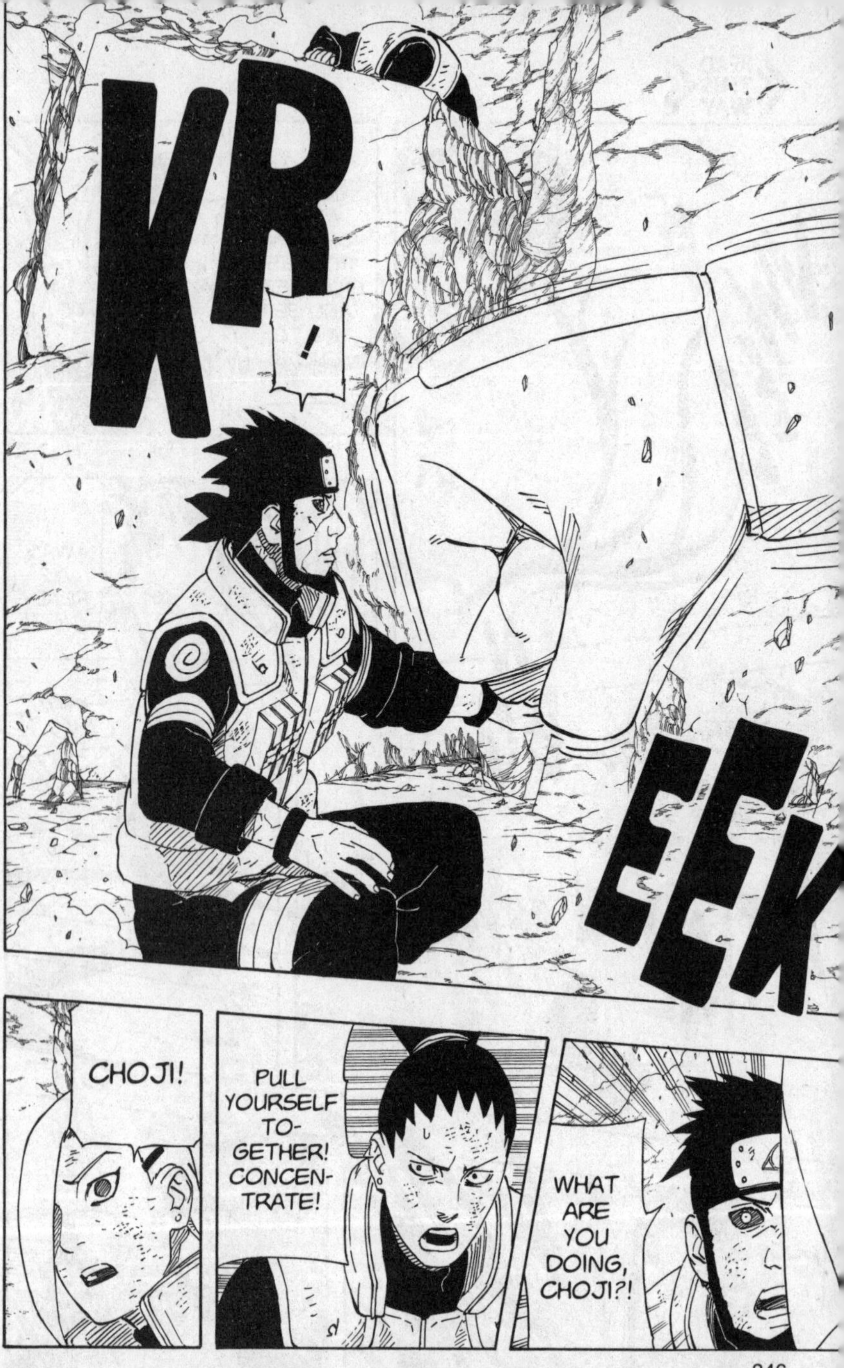
KR
!
EEK
WHAT ARE YOU DOING, CHOJI?!
PULL YOURSELF TO-GETHER! CONCEN-TRATE!
CHOJI!

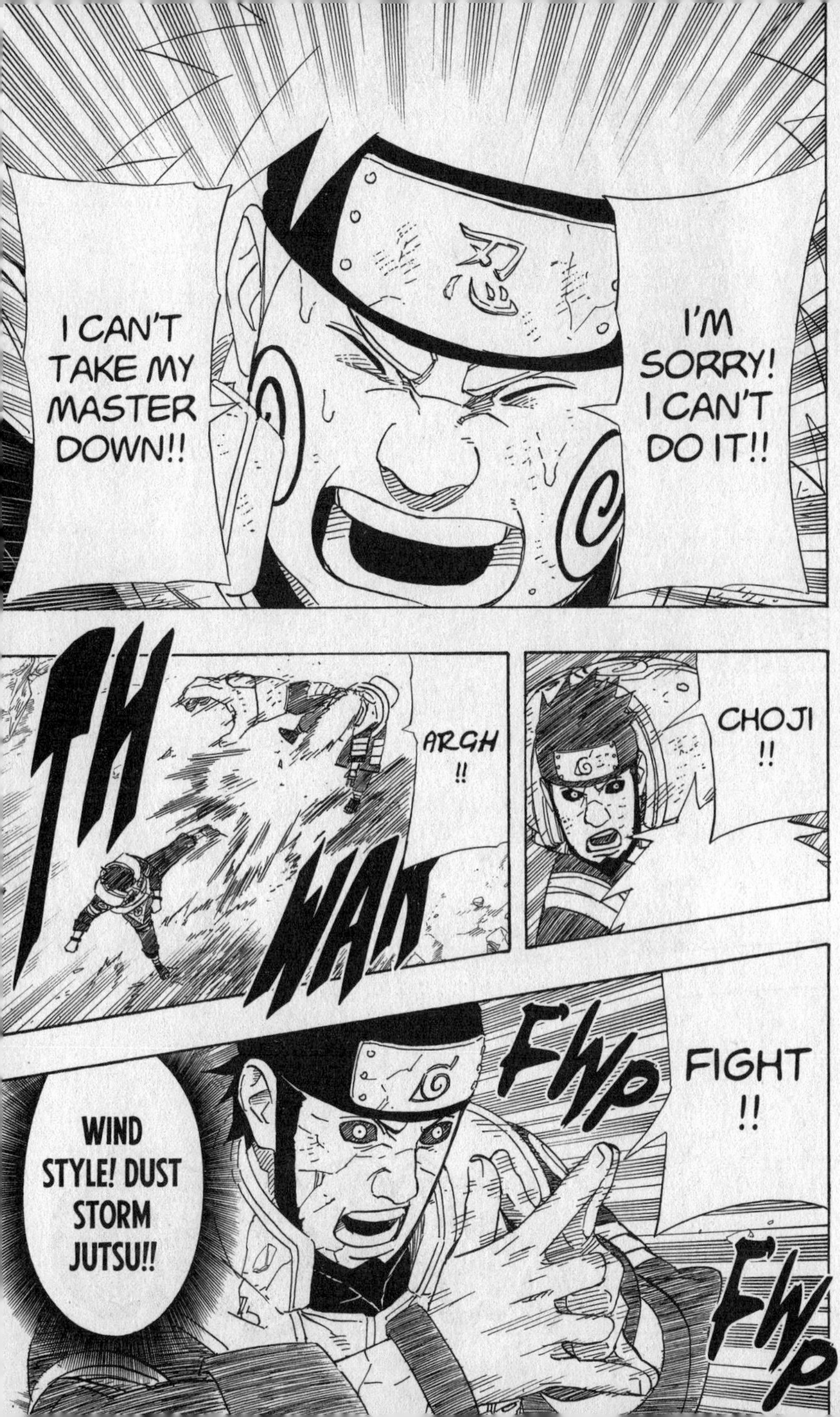
I'M SORRY! I CAN'T DO IT!!
I CAN'T TAKE MY MASTER DOWN!!
CHOJI !!
ARGH !!
THWAK
FIGHT !!
FWP
WIND STYLE! DUST STORM JUTSU!!
FWP

NARUTO

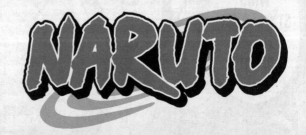

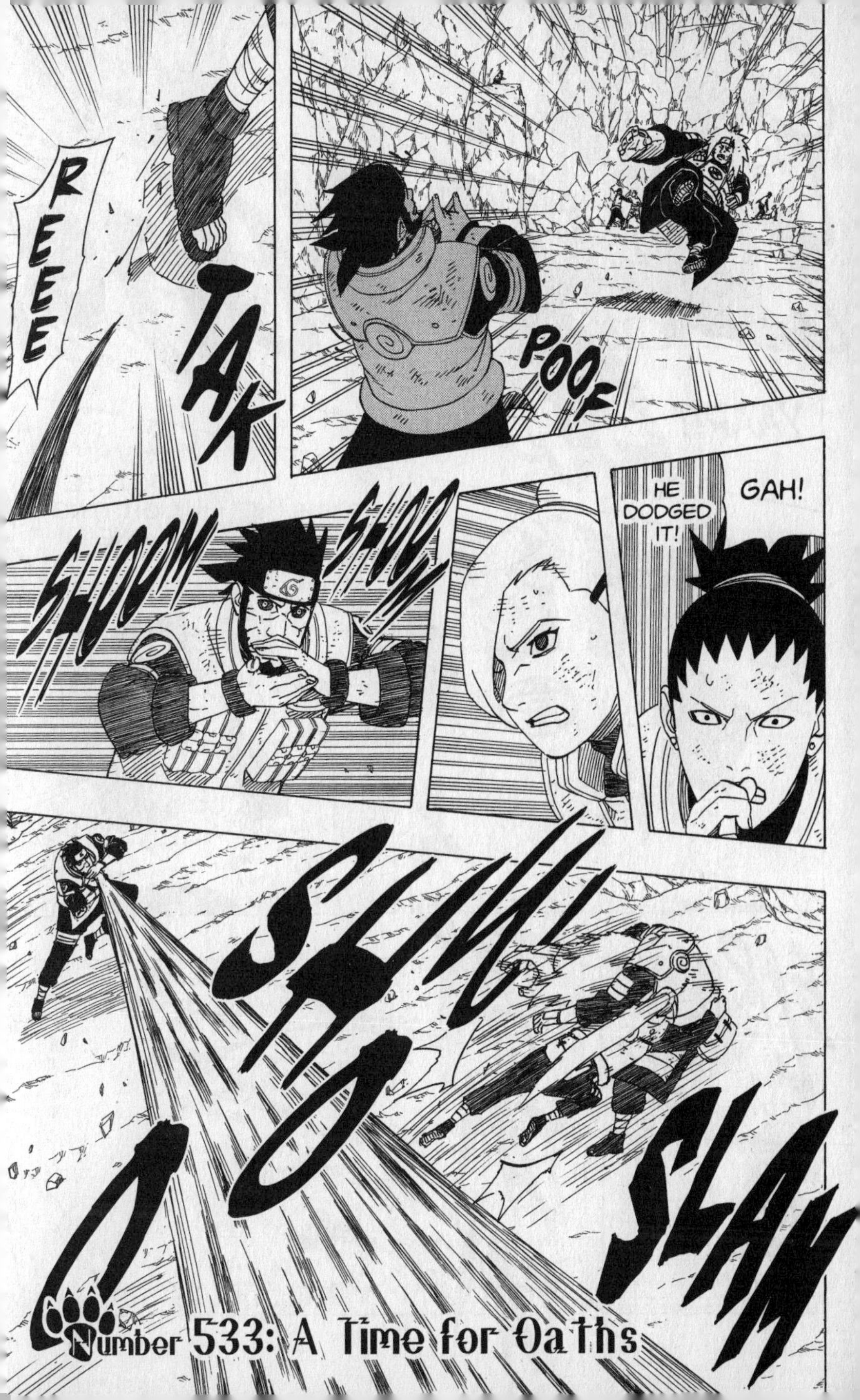
POOF
REEEE
TAK
GAH!
HE DODGED IT!
SHOOM
SHOOM
SLAM

## Number 533: A Time for Oaths

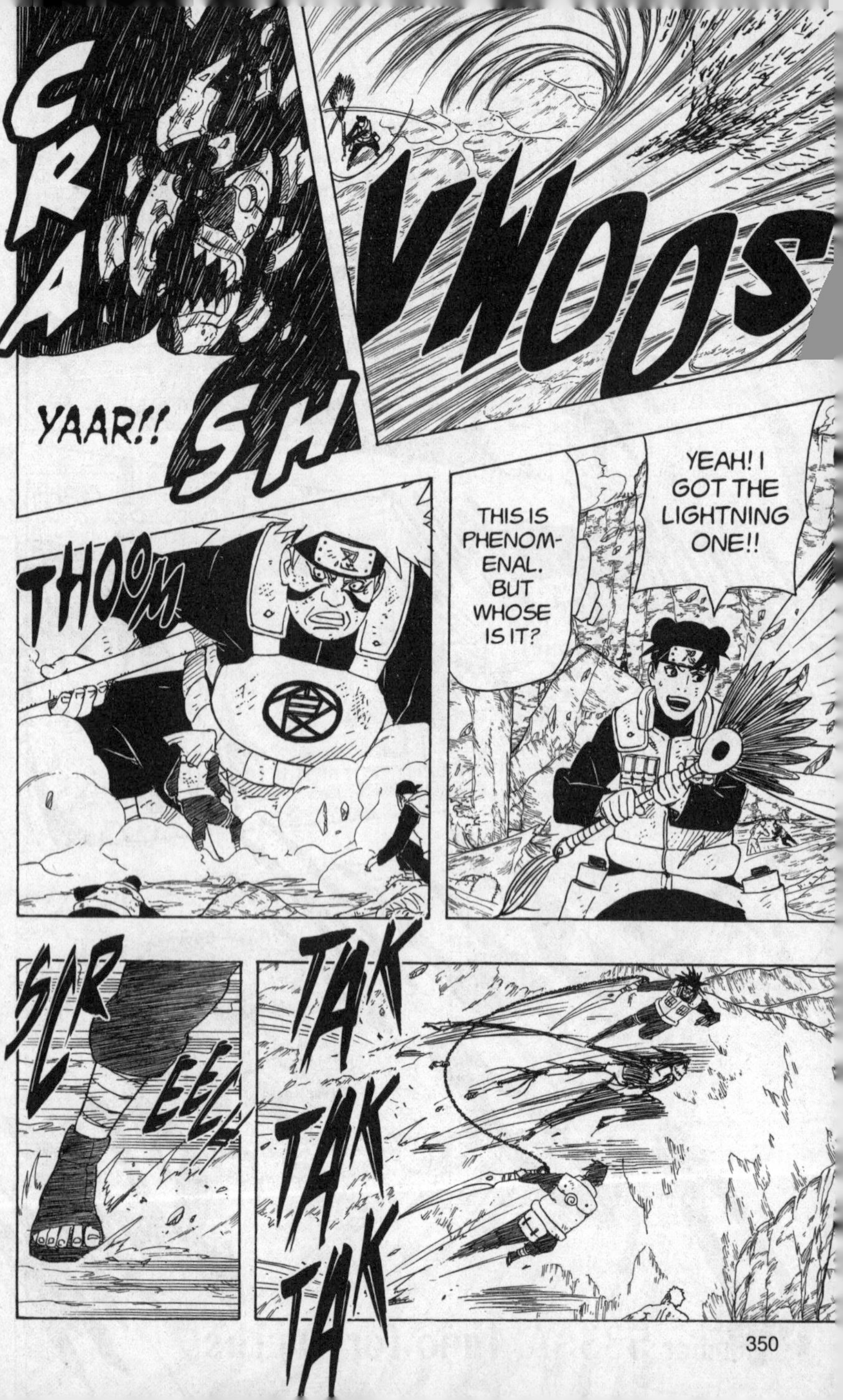
WHOOS
CRA
SH
YAAR!!
YEAH!! I GOT THE LIGHTNING ONE!!
THIS IS PHENOM-ENAL. BUT WHOSE IS IT?
THOOM
TAK TAK TAK TAK
SCREEE

READ THIS WAY

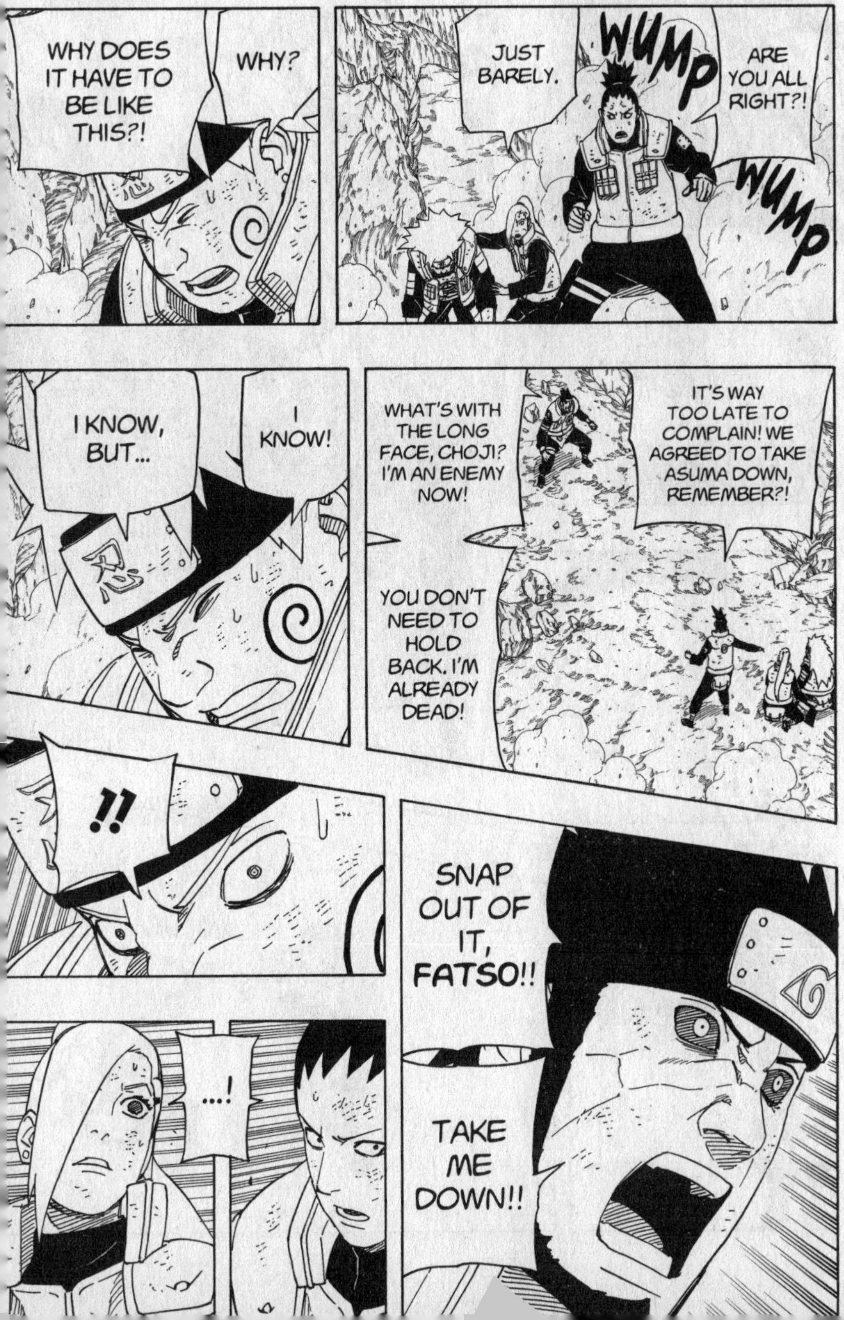
ARE YOU ALL RIGHT?!
WUMP
JUST BARELY.
WUMP
WHY?
WHY DOES IT HAVE TO BE LIKE THIS?!
IT'S WAY TOO LATE TO COMPLAIN! WE AGREED TO TAKE ASUMA DOWN, REMEMBER?!
WHAT'S WITH THE LONG FACE, CHOJI? I'M AN ENEMY NOW!
YOU DON'T NEED TO HOLD BACK. I'M ALREADY DEAD!
I KNOW!
I KNOW, BUT...
SNAP OUT OF IT, FATSO!!
TAKE ME DOWN!!
!!
...!

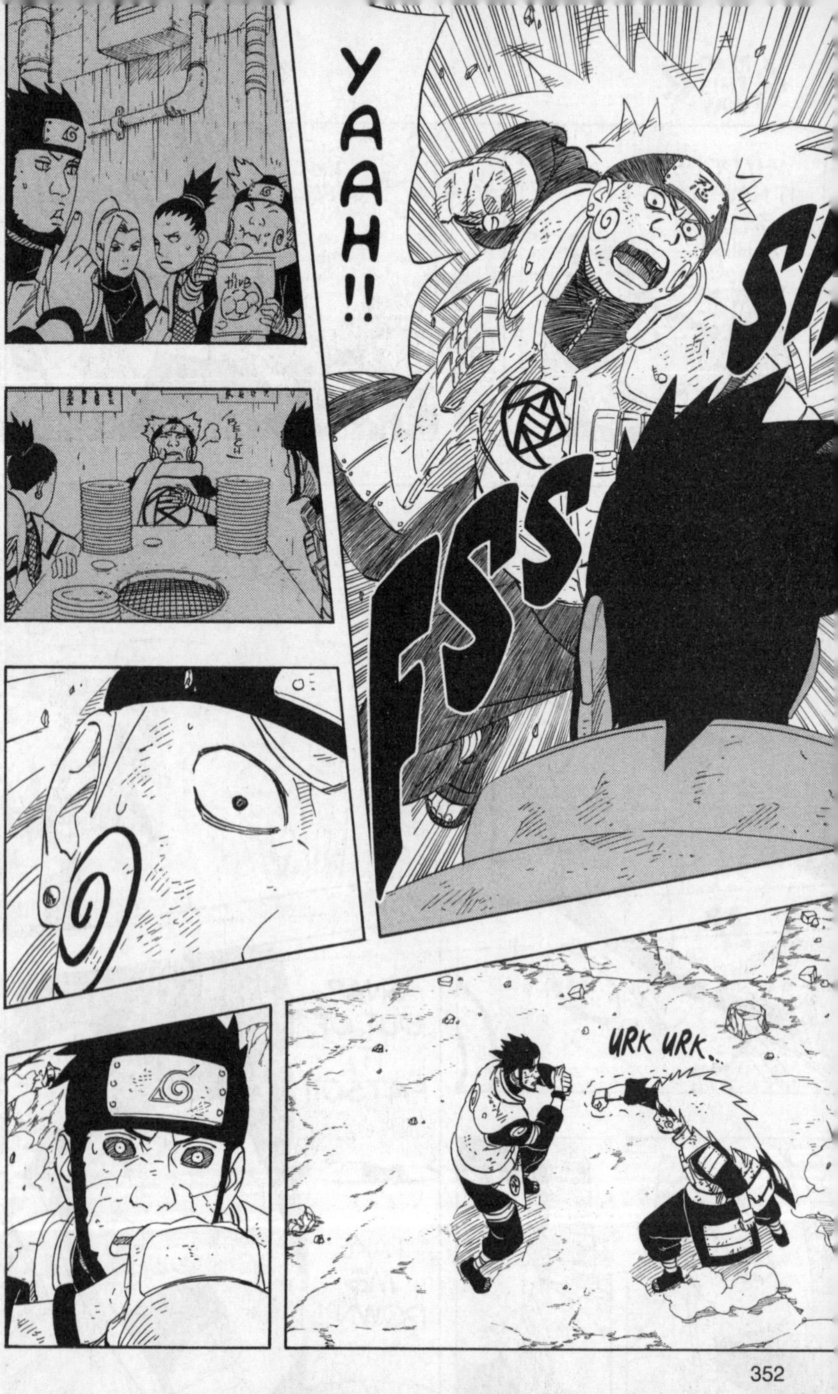
YAAH!!
FSS
BELCH
URK URK...

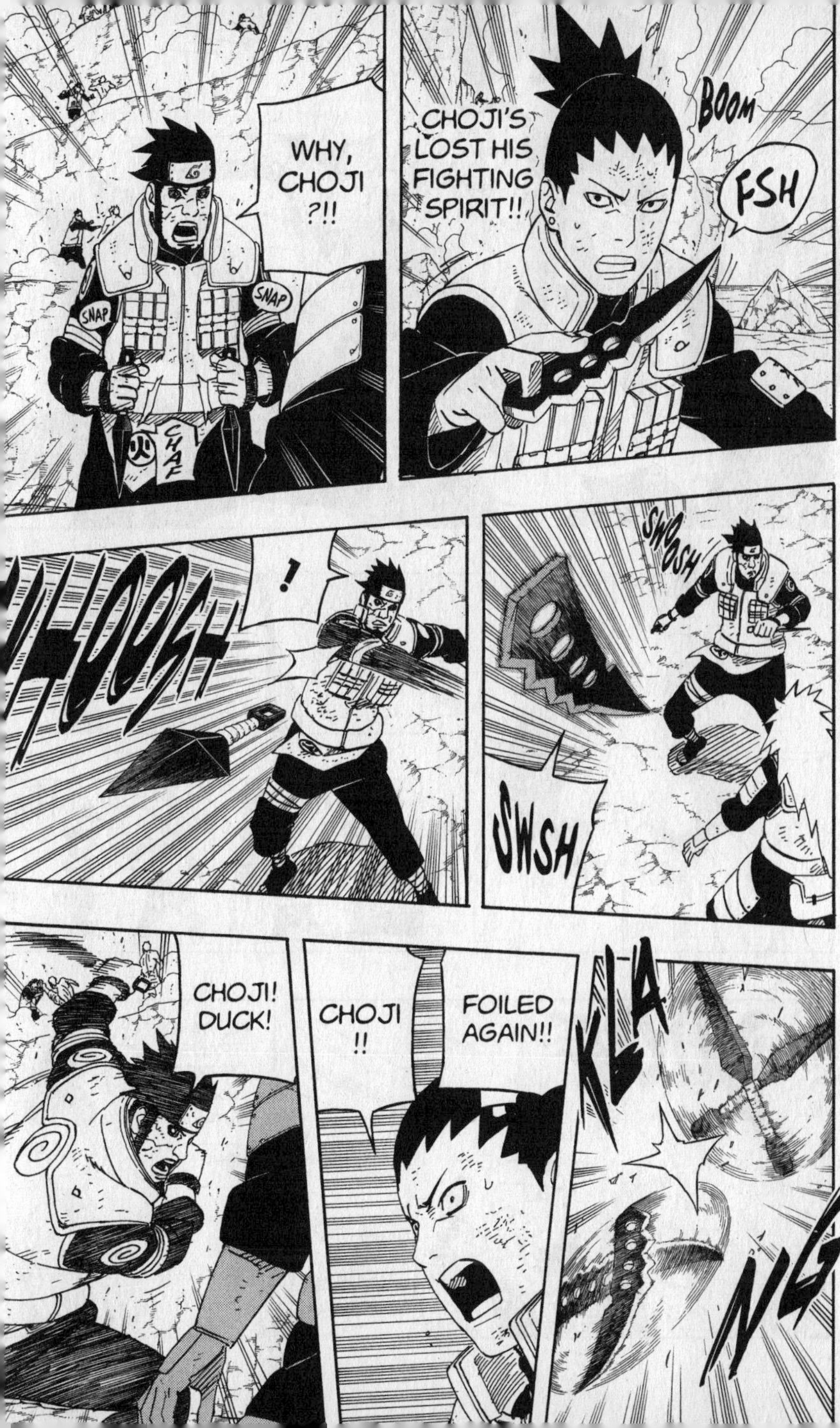
BOOM
CHOJI'S LOST HIS FIGHTING SPIRIT!!
FSH
WHY, CHOJI ?!!
SNAP
SNAP
CHAF
SWOOSH
SWSH
!
KLANG
FOILED AGAIN!!
CHOJI !!
CHOJI! DUCK!

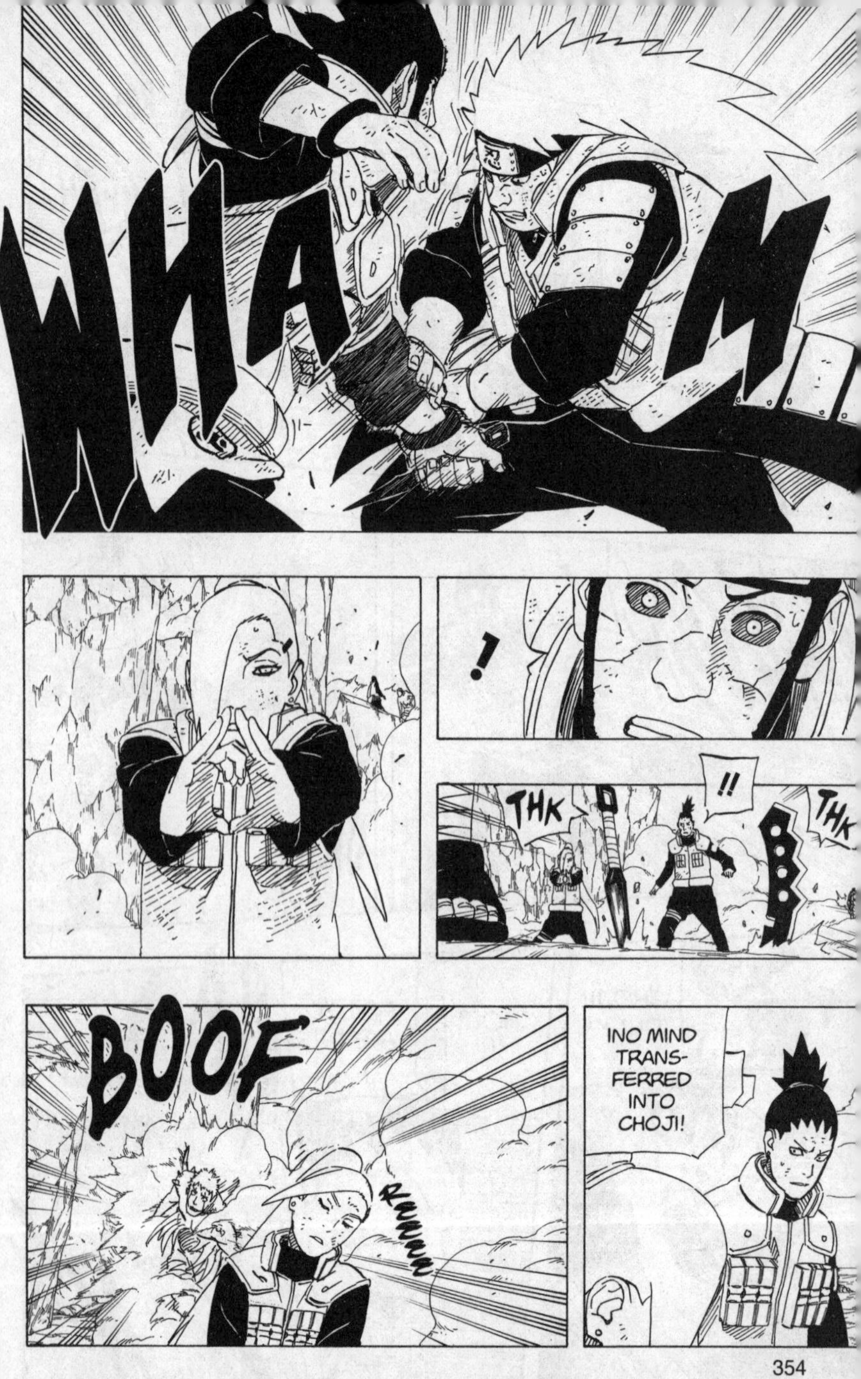
WHAM
!
THK
!!
THK
INO MIND TRANS-FERRED INTO CHOJI!
BOOF

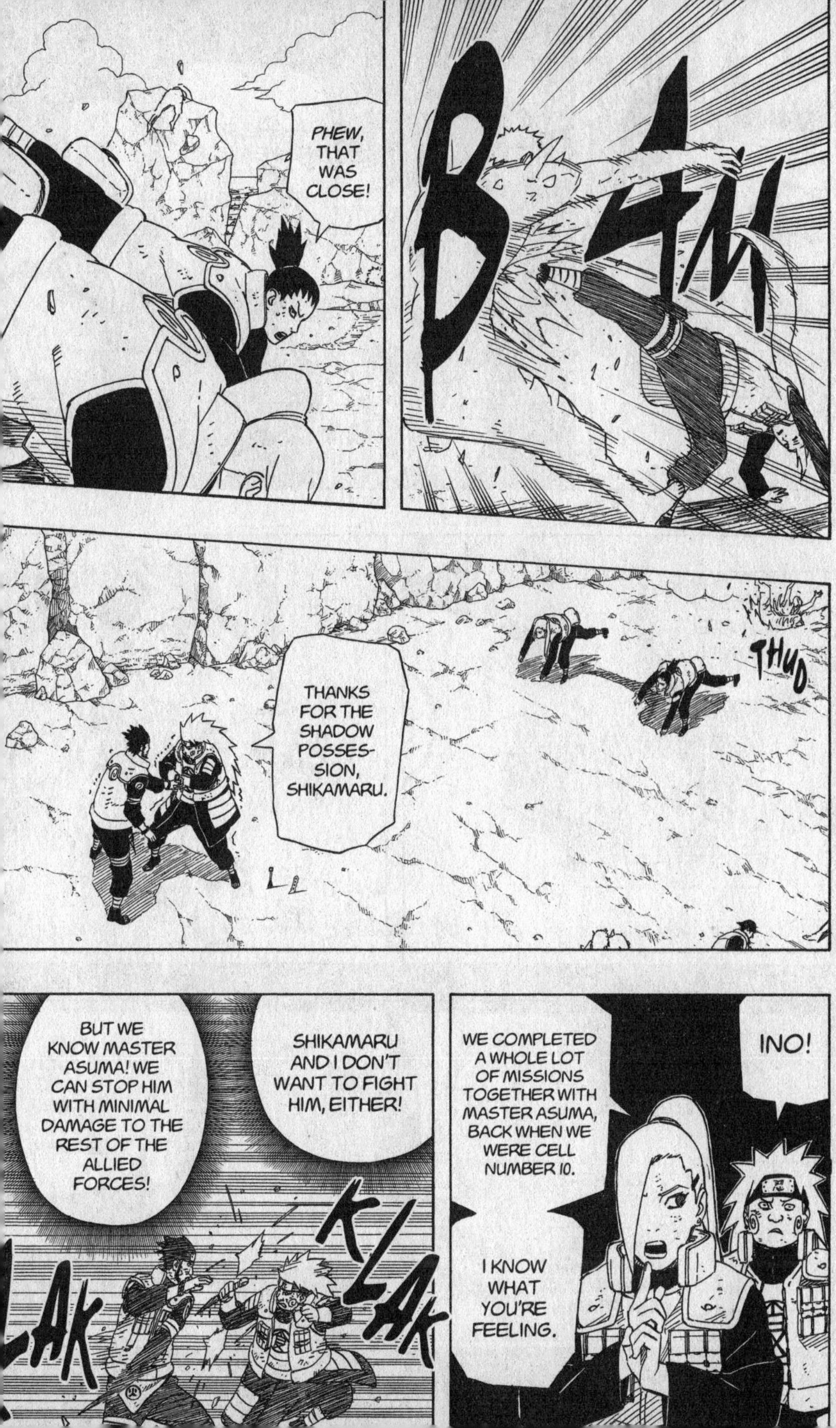
BAM
PHEW, THAT WAS CLOSE!
THUD
THANKS FOR THE SHADOW POSSES-SION, SHIKAMARU.
INO!
WE COMPLETED A WHOLE LOT OF MISSIONS TOGETHER WITH MASTER ASUMA, BACK WHEN WE WERE CELL NUMBER 10.
I KNOW WHAT YOU'RE FEELING.
SHIKAMARU AND I DON'T WANT TO FIGHT HIM, EITHER!
BUT WE KNOW MASTER ASUMA! WE CAN STOP HIM WITH MINIMAL DAMAGE TO THE REST OF THE ALLIED FORCES!
KLAK
KLAK
KLAK

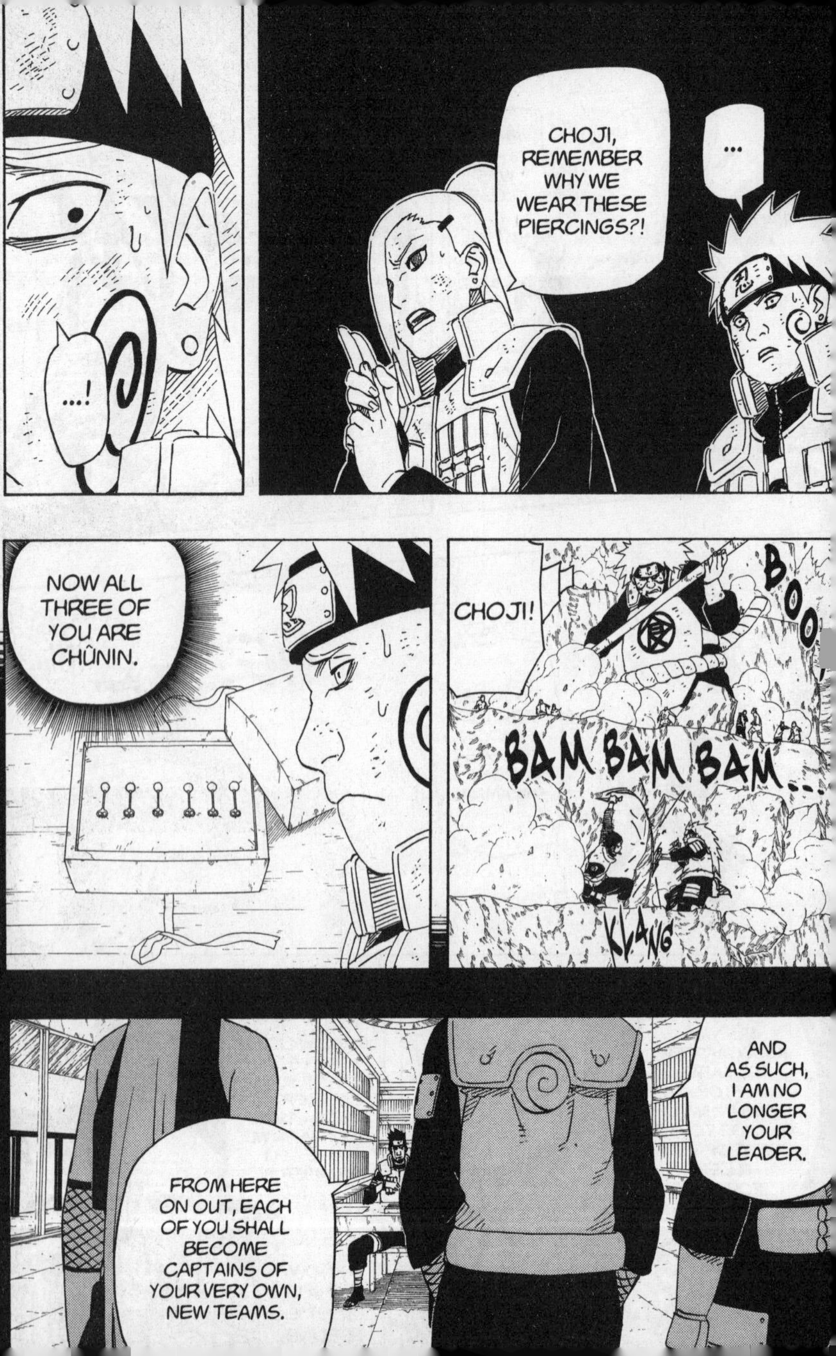
...
CHOJI, REMEMBER WHY WE WEAR THESE PIERCINGS?!
...!
CHOJI!
BOOM
BAM BAM BAM...
KLANG
NOW ALL THREE OF YOU ARE CHŪNIN.
AND AS SUCH, I AM NO LONGER YOUR LEADER.
FROM HERE ON OUT, EACH OF YOU SHALL BECOME CAPTAINS OF YOUR VERY OWN, NEW TEAMS.

READ THIS WAY

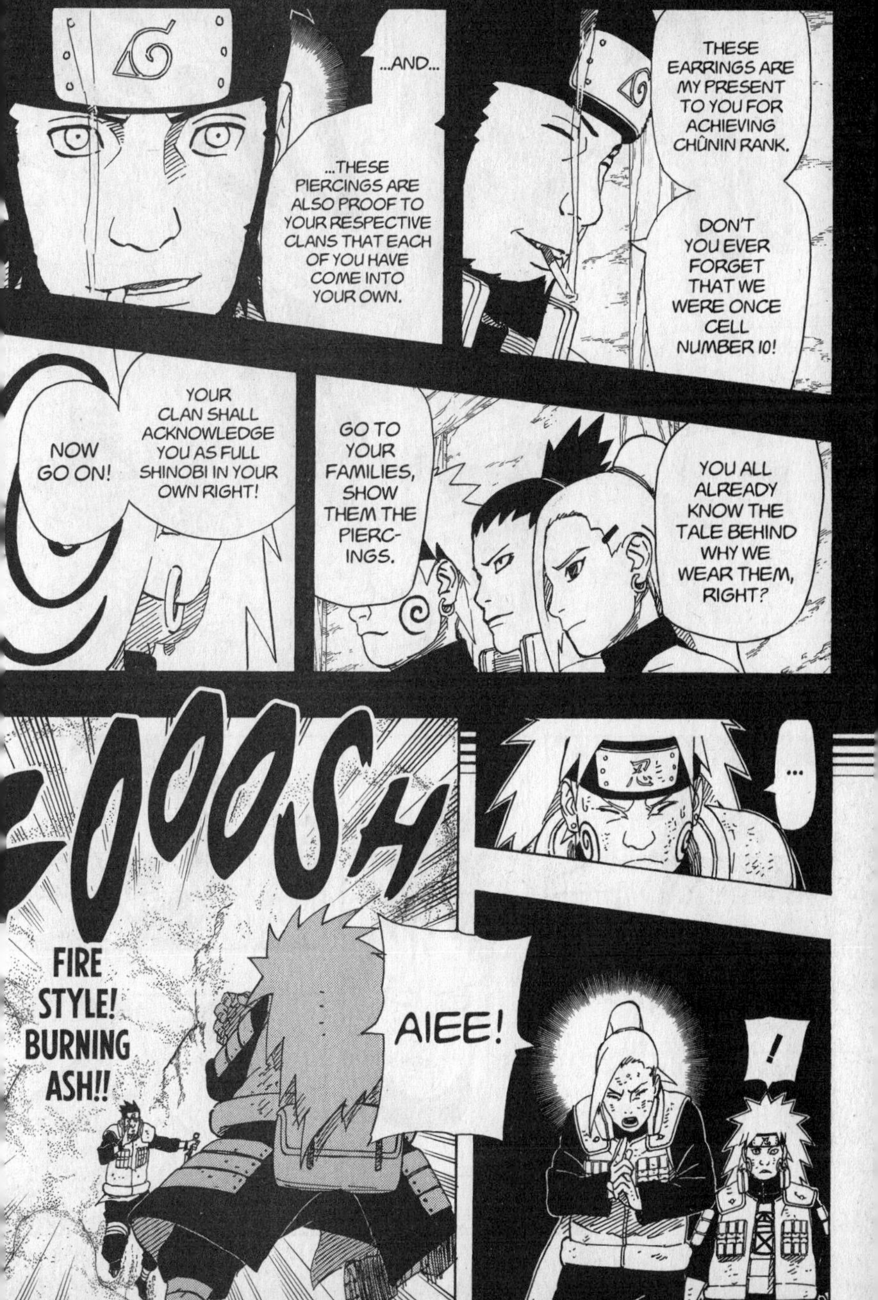

THESE EARRINGS ARE MY PRESENT TO YOU FOR ACHIEVING CHŪNIN RANK.
DON'T YOU EVER FORGET THAT WE WERE ONCE CELL NUMBER 10!
...AND...
...THESE PIERCINGS ARE ALSO PROOF TO YOUR RESPECTIVE CLANS THAT EACH OF YOU HAVE COME INTO YOUR OWN.
YOU ALL ALREADY KNOW THE TALE BEHIND WHY WE WEAR THEM, RIGHT?
GO TO YOUR FAMILIES, SHOW THEM THE PIERC-INGS.
YOUR CLAN SHALL ACKNOWLEDGE YOU AS FULL SHINOBI IN YOUR OWN RIGHT!
NOW GO ON!
...
!
OOOSH
AIEE!
FIRE STYLE! BURNING ASH!!

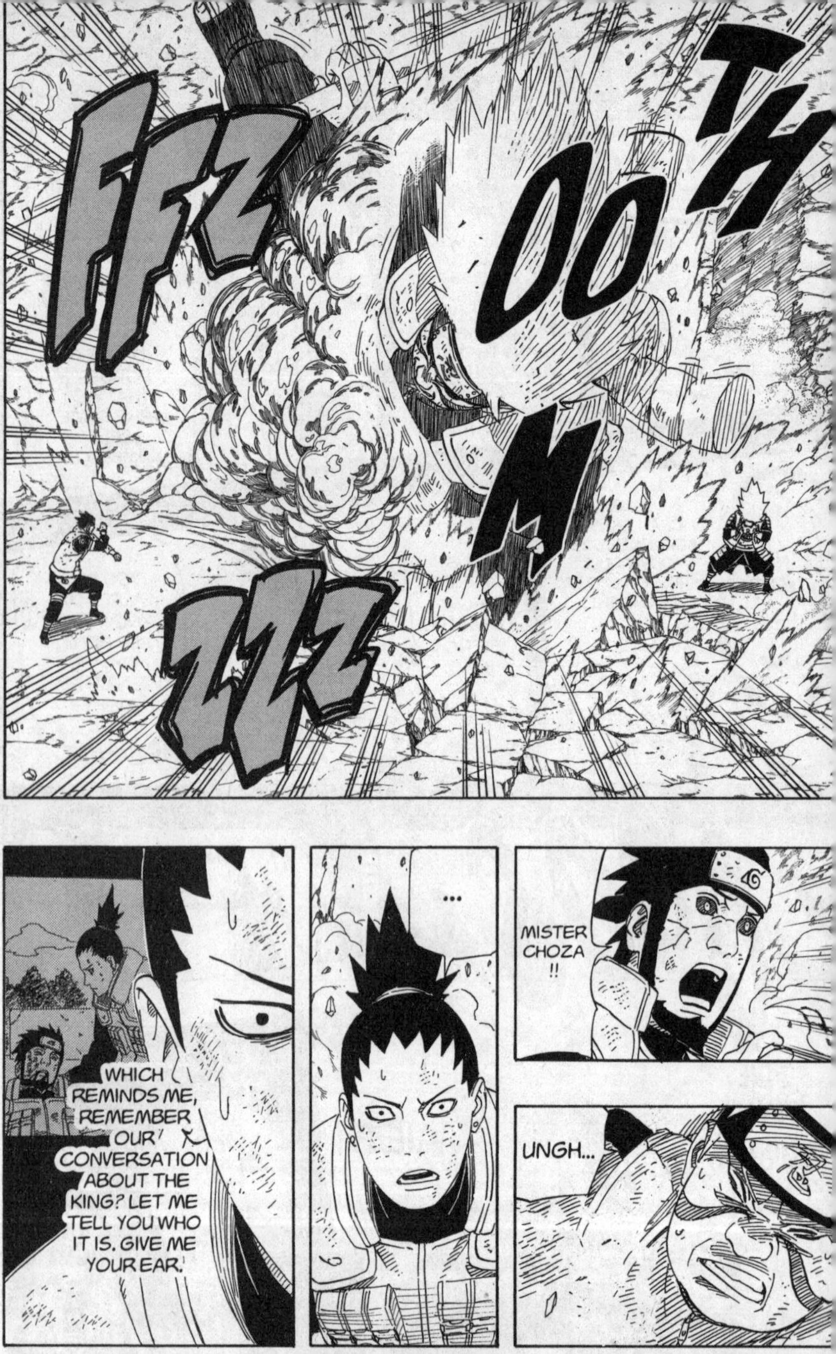
THOOM
MISTER CHOZA!!
UNGH...
...
WHICH REMINDS ME, REMEMBER OUR CONVERSATION ABOUT THE KING? LET ME TELL YOU WHO IT IS. GIVE ME YOUR EAR.

READ THIS WAY

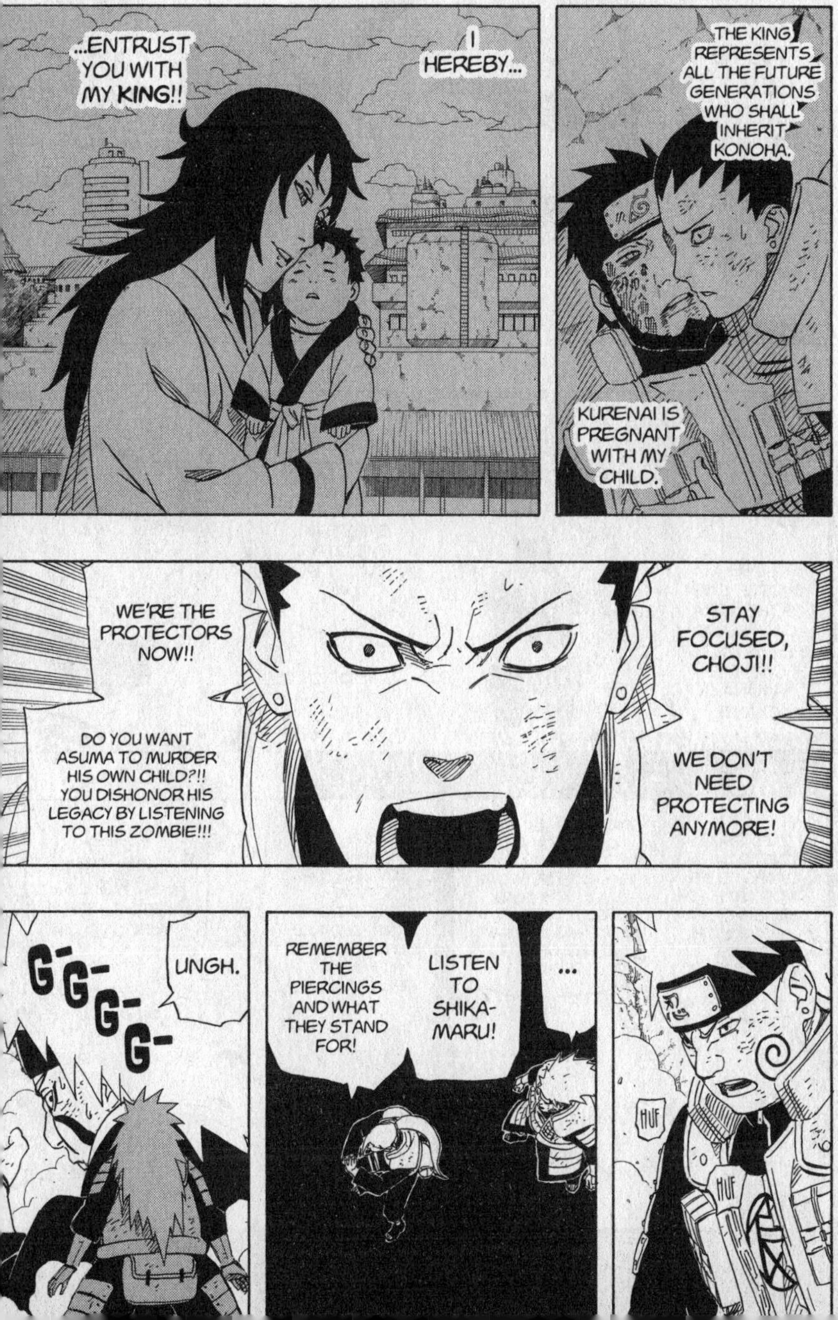

THE KING REPRESENTS ALL THE FUTURE GENERATIONS WHO SHALL INHERIT KONOHA.
KURENAI IS PREGNANT WITH MY CHILD.
I HEREBY...
...ENTRUST YOU WITH MY KING!!
STAY FOCUSED, CHOJI!!
WE DON'T NEED PROTECTING ANYMORE!
WE'RE THE PROTECTORS NOW!!
DO YOU WANT ASUMA TO MURDER HIS OWN CHILD?!! YOU DISHONOR HIS LEGACY BY LISTENING TO THIS ZOMBIE!!!
HUF
HUF
...
LISTEN TO SHIKA-MARU!
REMEMBER THE PIERCINGS AND WHAT THEY STAND FOR!
UNGH.
G-G-G-G-

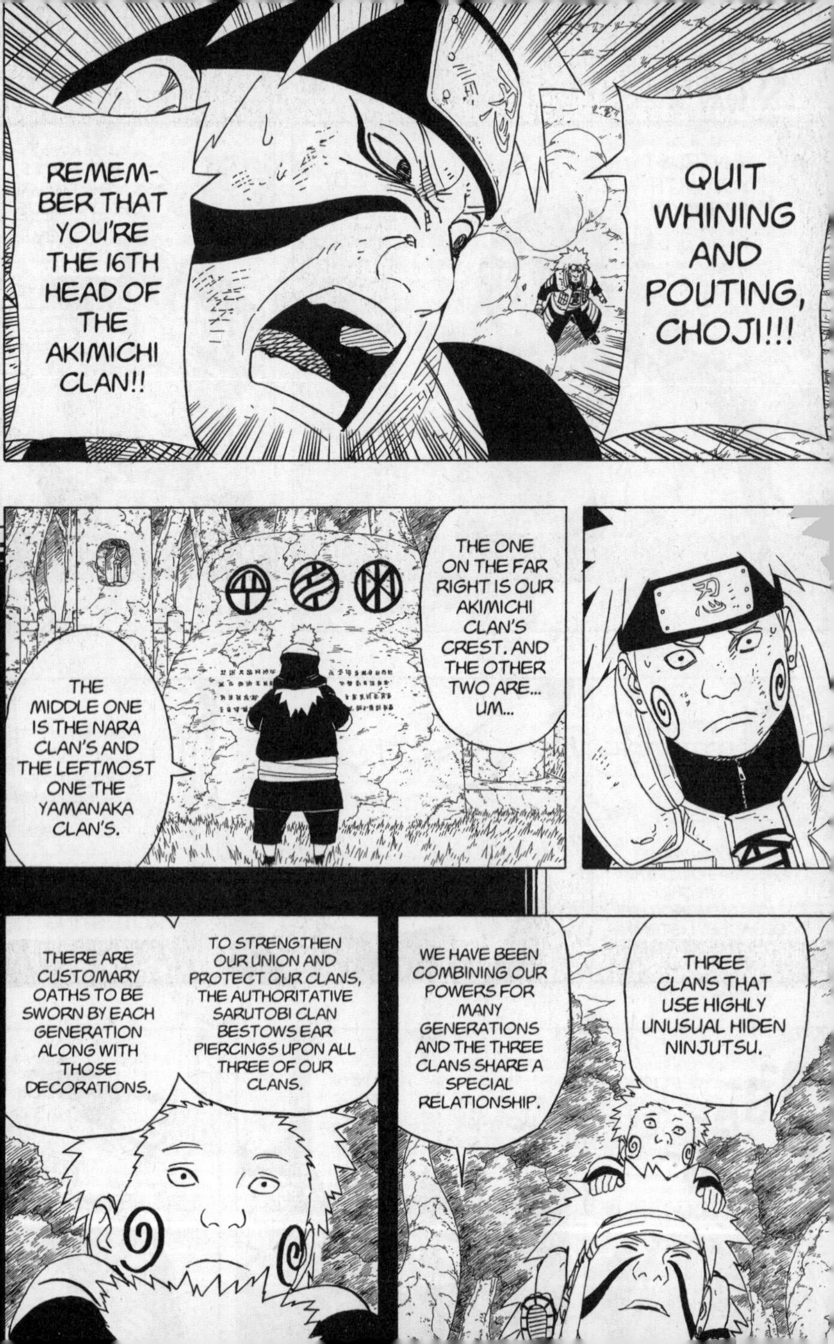
QUIT WHINING AND POUTING, CHOJI!!!
REMEMBER THAT YOU'RE THE 16TH HEAD OF THE AKIMICHI CLAN!!
THE ONE ON THE FAR RIGHT IS OUR AKIMICHI CLAN'S CREST. AND THE OTHER TWO ARE... UM...
THE MIDDLE ONE IS THE NARA CLAN'S AND THE LEFTMOST ONE THE YAMANAKA CLAN'S.
THREE CLANS THAT USE HIGHLY UNUSUAL HIDEN NINJUTSU.
WE HAVE BEEN COMBINING OUR POWERS FOR MANY GENERATIONS AND THE THREE CLANS SHARE A SPECIAL RELATIONSHIP.
TO STRENGTHEN OUR UNION AND PROTECT OUR CLANS, THE AUTHORITATIVE SARUTOBI CLAN BESTOWS EAR PIERCINGS UPON ALL THREE OF OUR CLANS.
THERE ARE CUSTOMARY OATHS TO BE SWORN BY EACH GENERATION ALONG WITH THOSE DECORATIONS.

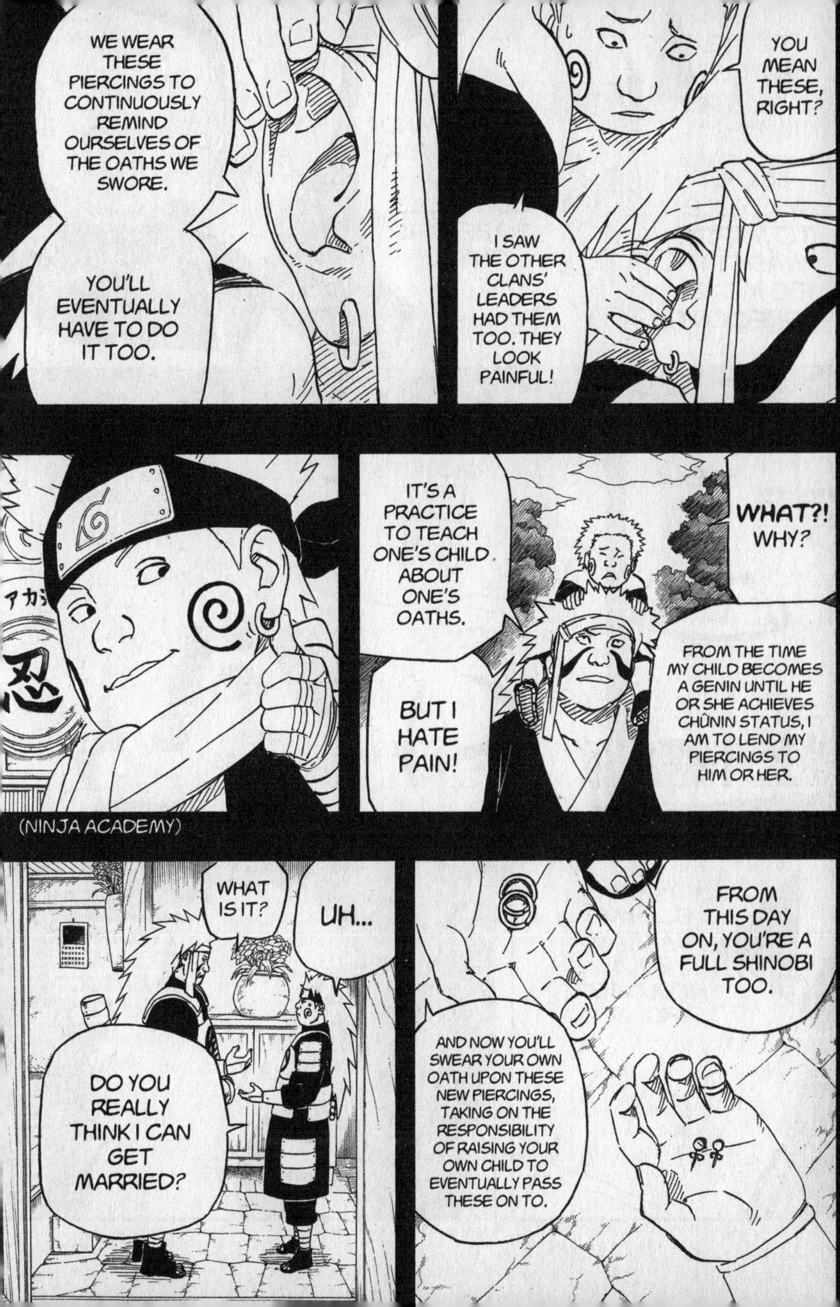
YOU MEAN THESE, RIGHT?
I SAW THE OTHER CLANS' LEADERS HAD THEM TOO. THEY LOOK PAINFUL!
WE WEAR THESE PIERCINGS TO CONTINUOUSLY REMIND OURSELVES OF THE OATHS WE SWORE.
YOU'LL EVENTUALLY HAVE TO DO IT TOO.
WHAT?! WHY?
IT'S A PRACTICE TO TEACH ONE'S CHILD ABOUT ONE'S OATHS.
FROM THE TIME MY CHILD BECOMES A GENIN UNTIL HE OR SHE ACHIEVES CHÛNIN STATUS, I AM TO LEND MY PIERCINGS TO HIM OR HER.
BUT I HATE PAIN!
忍
FROM THIS DAY ON, YOU'RE A FULL SHINOBI TOO.
AND NOW YOU'LL SWEAR YOUR OWN OATH UPON THESE NEW PIERCINGS, TAKING ON THE RESPONSIBILITY OF RAISING YOUR OWN CHILD TO EVENTUALLY PASS THESE ON TO.
(NINJA ACADEMY)
UH...
WHAT IS IT?
DO YOU REALLY THINK I CAN GET MARRIED?

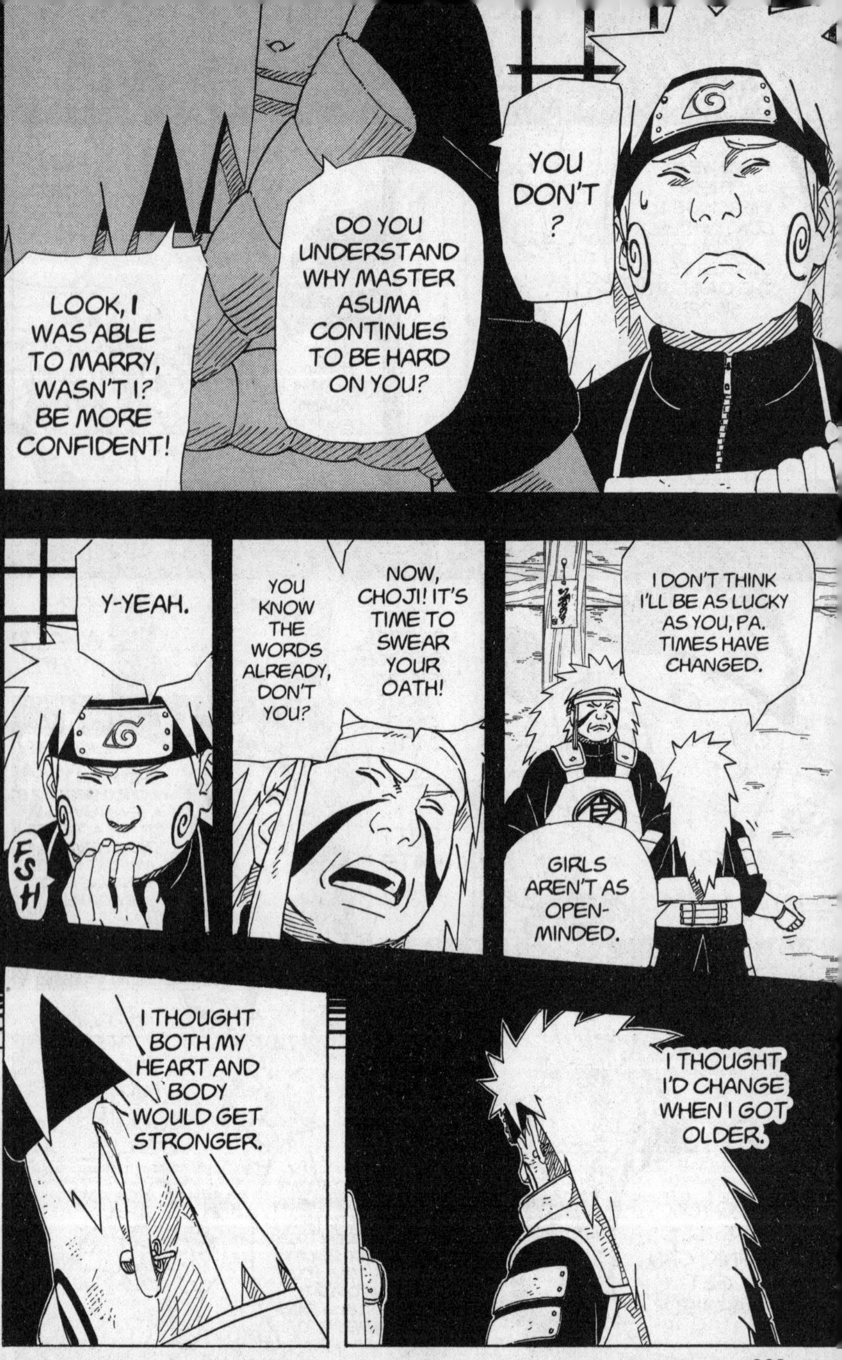
YOU DON'T ?
DO YOU UNDERSTAND WHY MASTER ASUMA CONTINUES TO BE HARD ON YOU?
LOOK, I WAS ABLE TO MARRY, WASN'T I? BE MORE CONFIDENT!
I DON'T THINK I'LL BE AS LUCKY AS YOU, PA. TIMES HAVE CHANGED.
GIRLS AREN'T AS OPEN-MINDED.
NOW, CHOJI! IT'S TIME TO SWEAR YOUR OATH!
YOU KNOW THE WORDS ALREADY, DON'T YOU?
Y-YEAH.
FSH
I THOUGHT I'D CHANGE WHEN I GOT OLDER.
I THOUGHT BOTH MY HEART AND BODY WOULD GET STRONGER.

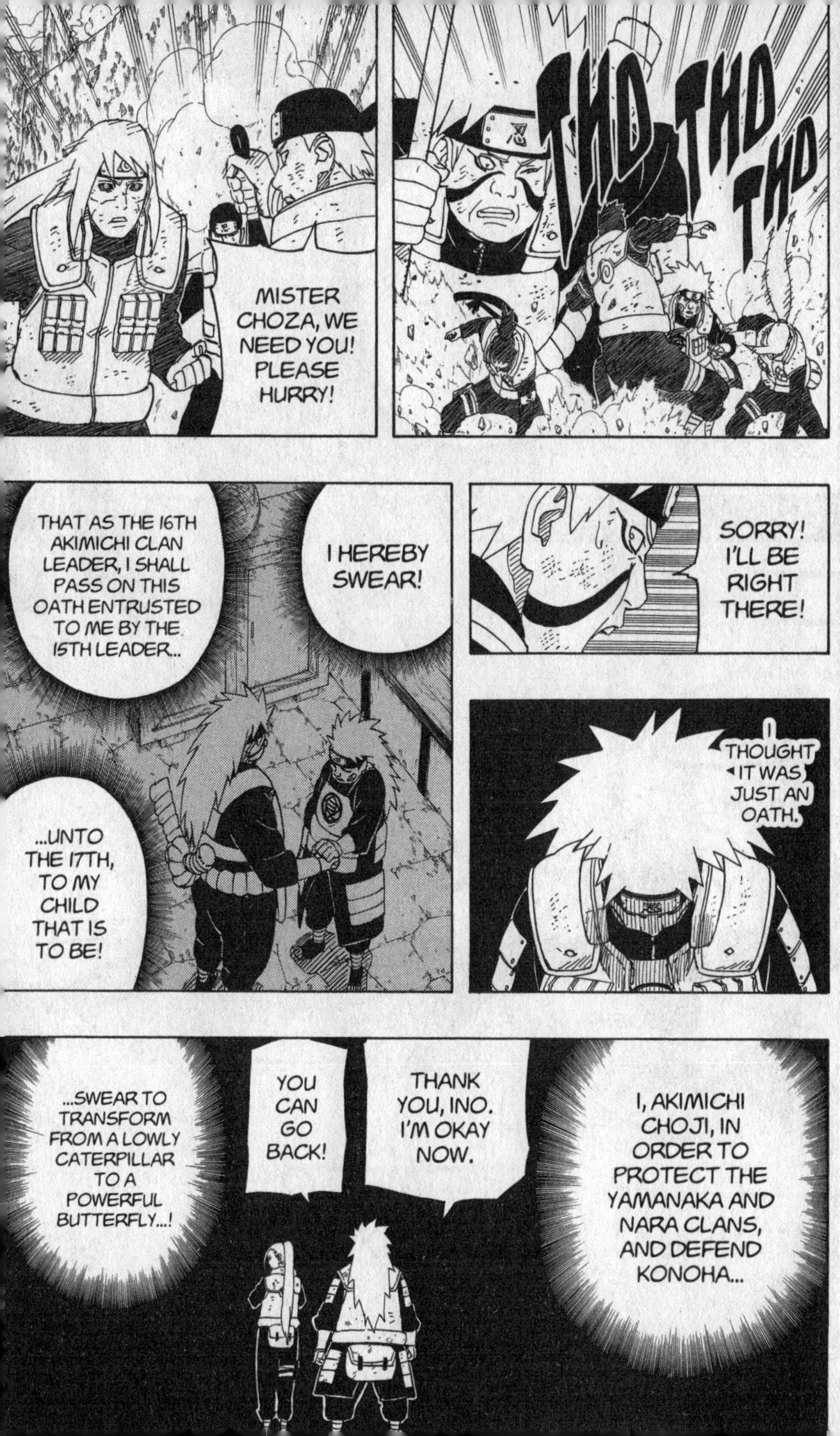
THD THD THD
MISTER CHOZA, WE NEED YOU! PLEASE HURRY!
SORRY! I'LL BE RIGHT THERE!
I THOUGHT IT WAS JUST AN OATH.
I HEREBY SWEAR!
THAT AS THE 16TH AKIMICHI CLAN LEADER, I SHALL PASS ON THIS OATH ENTRUSTED TO ME BY THE 15TH LEADER...
...UNTO THE 17TH, TO MY CHILD THAT IS TO BE!
I, AKIMICHI CHOJI, IN ORDER TO PROTECT THE YAMANAKA AND NARA CLANS, AND DEFEND KONOHA...
THANK YOU, INO. I'M OKAY NOW.
YOU CAN GO BACK!
...SWEAR TO TRANSFORM FROM A LOWLY CATERPILLAR TO A POWERFUL BUTTERFLY...!

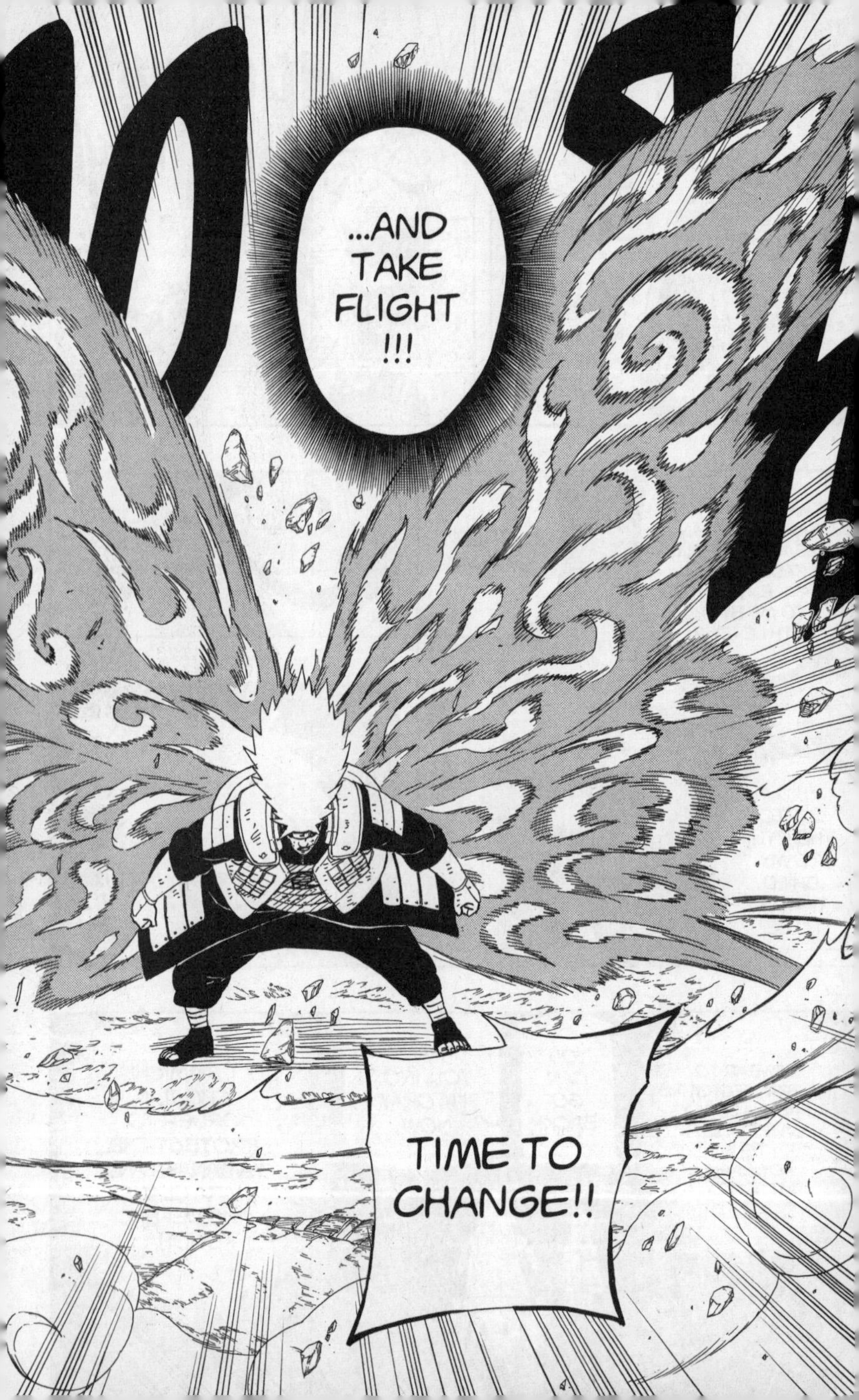
...AND TAKE FLIGHT !!!
TIME TO CHANGE!!

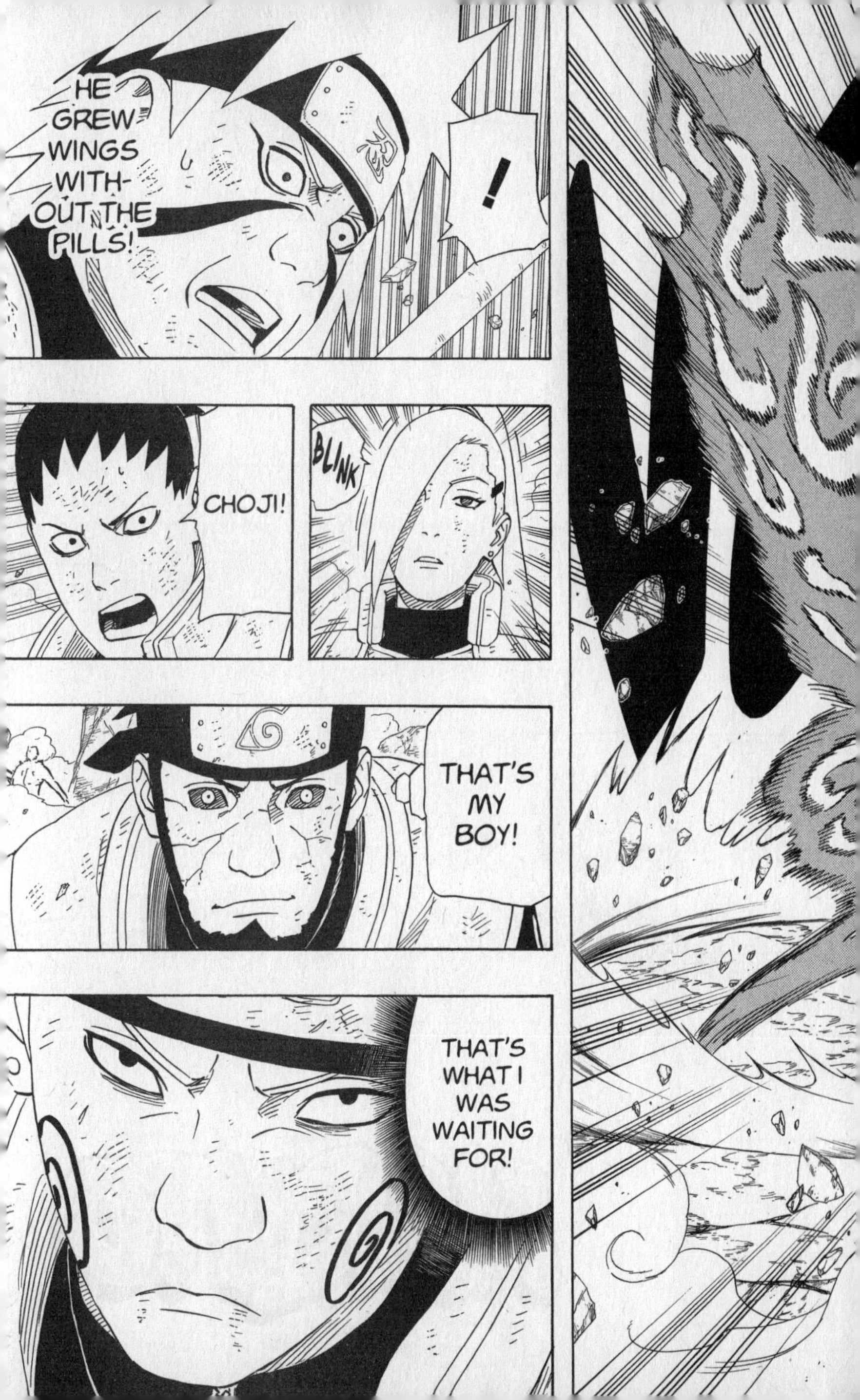
!
HE GREW WINGS WITH-OUT THE PILLS!
BLINK
CHOJI!
THAT'S MY BOY!
THAT'S WHAT I WAS WAITING FOR!

NARUTO

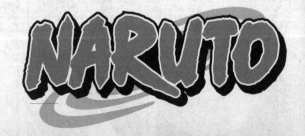

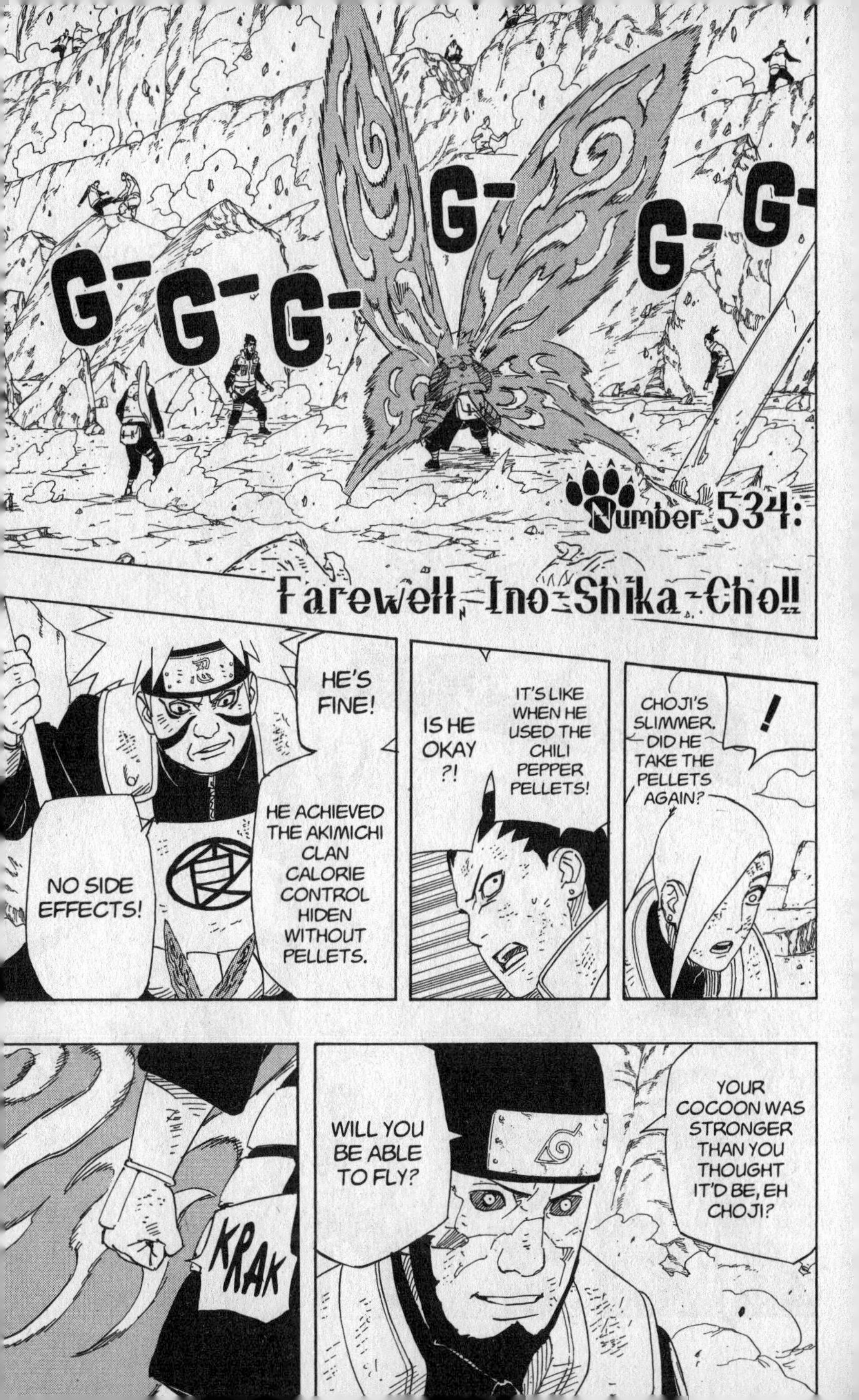
G-G-G-G-G-G-
Number 534:
Farewell, Ino-Shika-Cho!!
!
CHOJI'S SLIMMER. DID HE TAKE THE PELLETS AGAIN?
IT'S LIKE WHEN HE USED THE CHILI PEPPER PELLETS!
IS HE OKAY ?!
HE'S FINE!
HE ACHIEVED THE AKIMICHI CLAN CALORIE CONTROL HIDEN WITHOUT PELLETS.
NO SIDE EFFECTS!
YOUR COCOON WAS STRONGER THAN YOU THOUGHT IT'D BE, EH CHOJI?
WILL YOU BE ABLE TO FLY?
KRAK

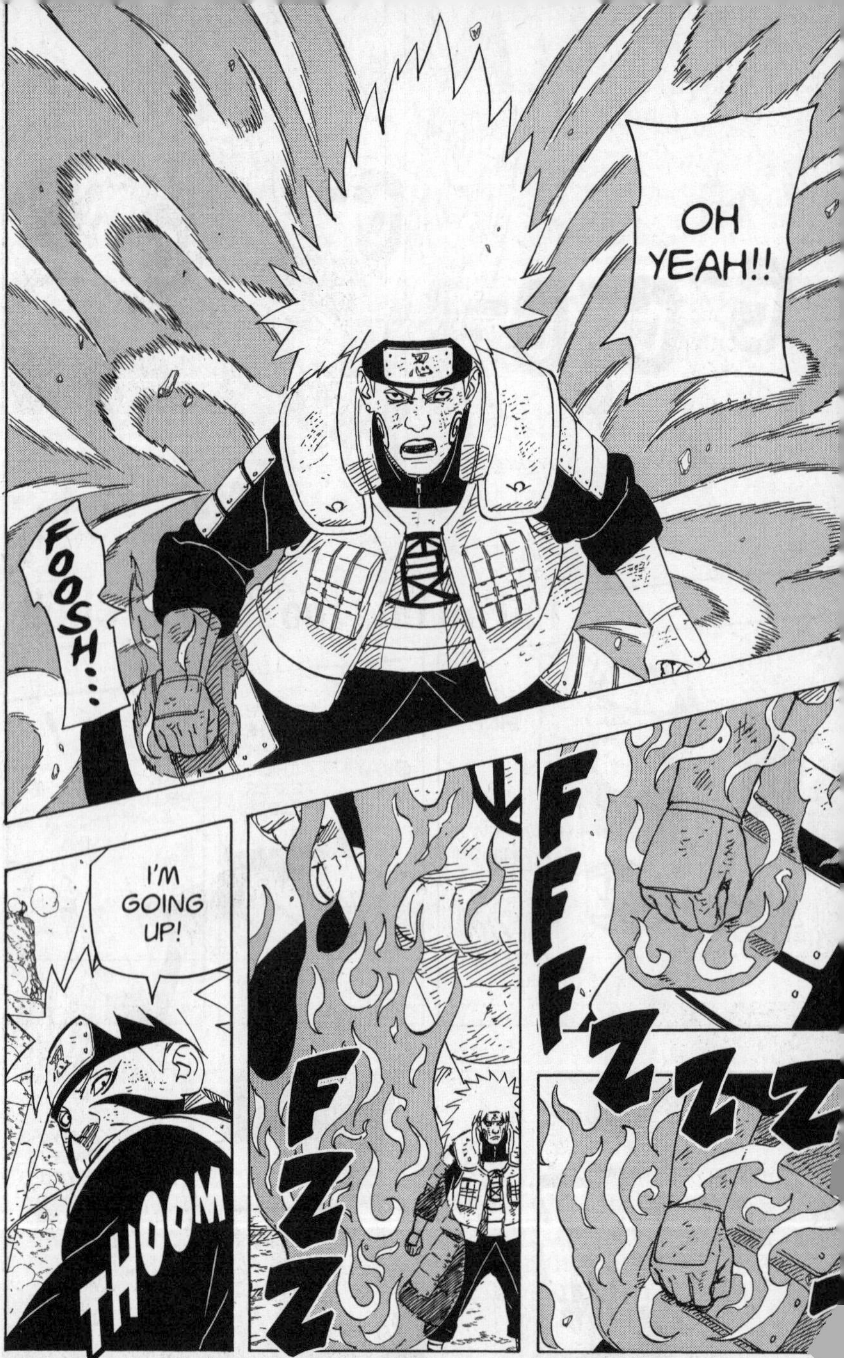
OH YEAH!!
FOOSH...
FFFFZZZZ
FZZZ
I'M GOING UP!
THOOM

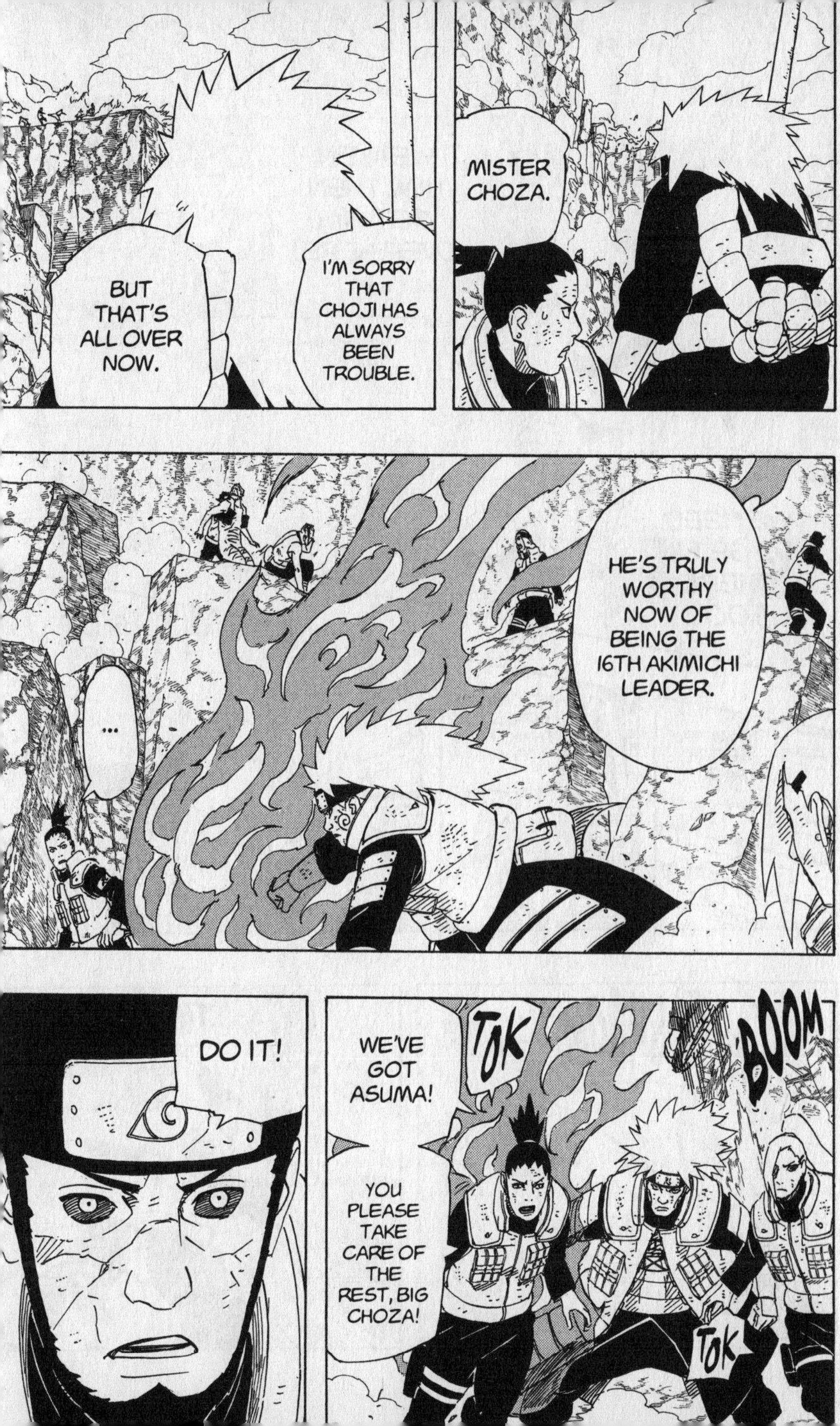
MISTER CHOZA.
I'M SORRY THAT CHOJI HAS ALWAYS BEEN TROUBLE.
BUT THAT'S ALL OVER NOW.
HE'S TRULY WORTHY NOW OF BEING THE 16TH AKIMICHI LEADER.
...
BOOM
TOK
WE'VE GOT ASUMA!
YOU PLEASE TAKE CARE OF THE REST, BIG CHOZA!
TOK
DO IT!

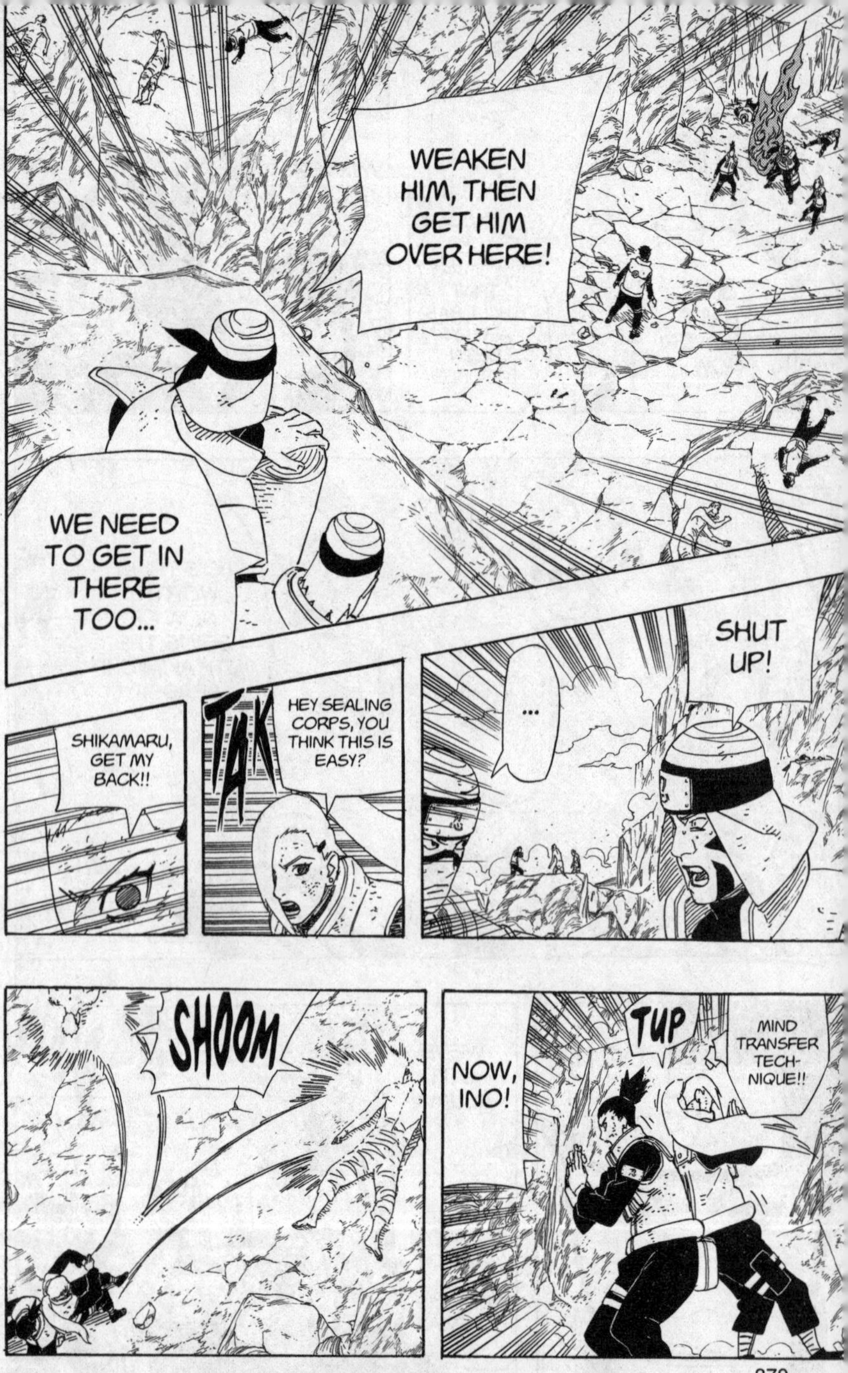
WEAKEN HIM, THEN GET HIM OVER HERE!
WE NEED TO GET IN THERE TOO...
SHUT UP!
...
TAK
HEY SEALING CORPS, YOU THINK THIS IS EASY?
SHIKAMARU, GET MY BACK!!
MIND TRANSFER TECH-NIQUE!!
TUP
NOW, INO!
SHOOM

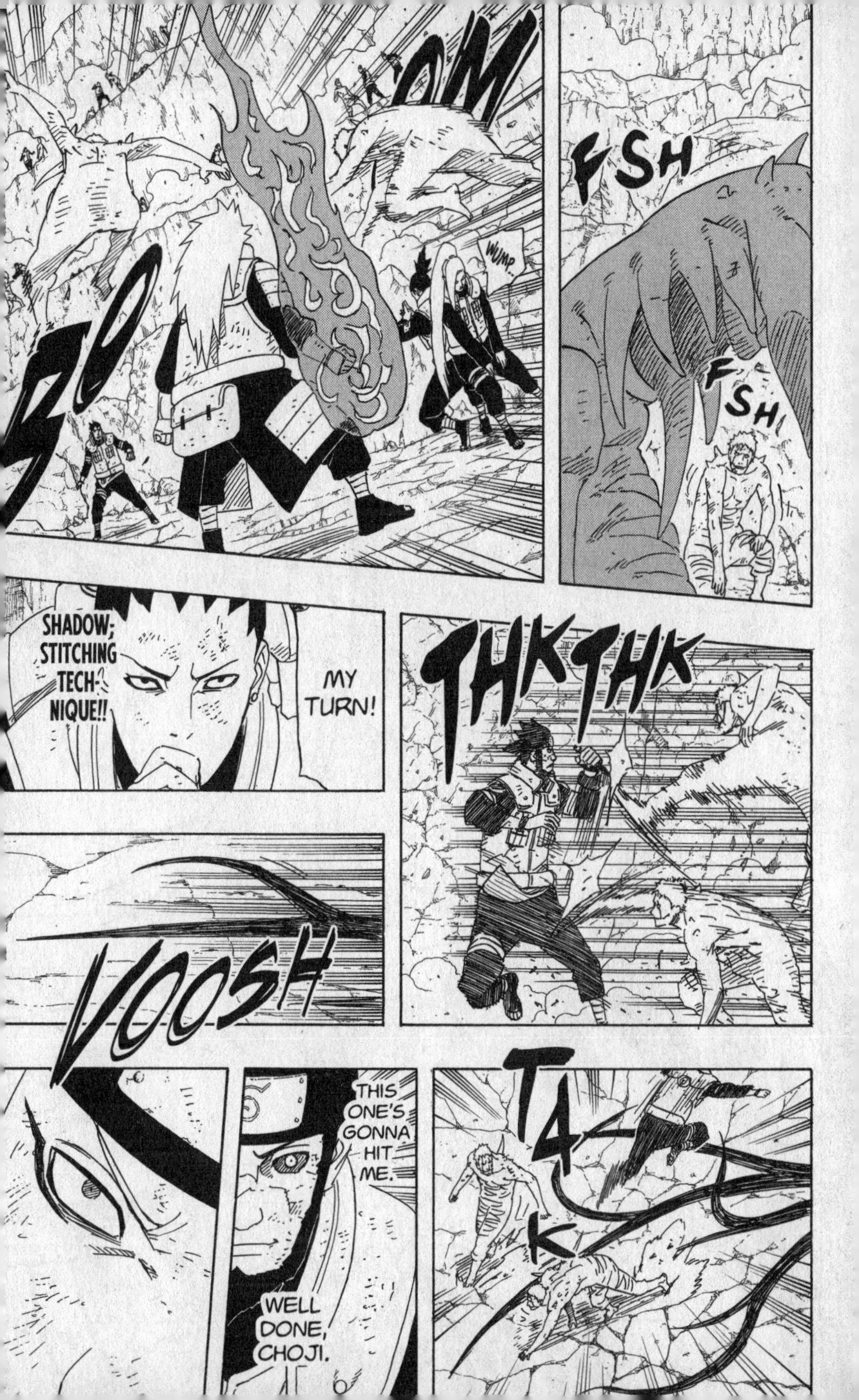
FSH
FSH
WUMP
THKTHK
MY TURN!
SHADOW; STITCHING TECH-NIQUE!!
VOOSH
TA
K
THIS ONE'S GONNA HIT ME.
WELL DONE, CHOJI.

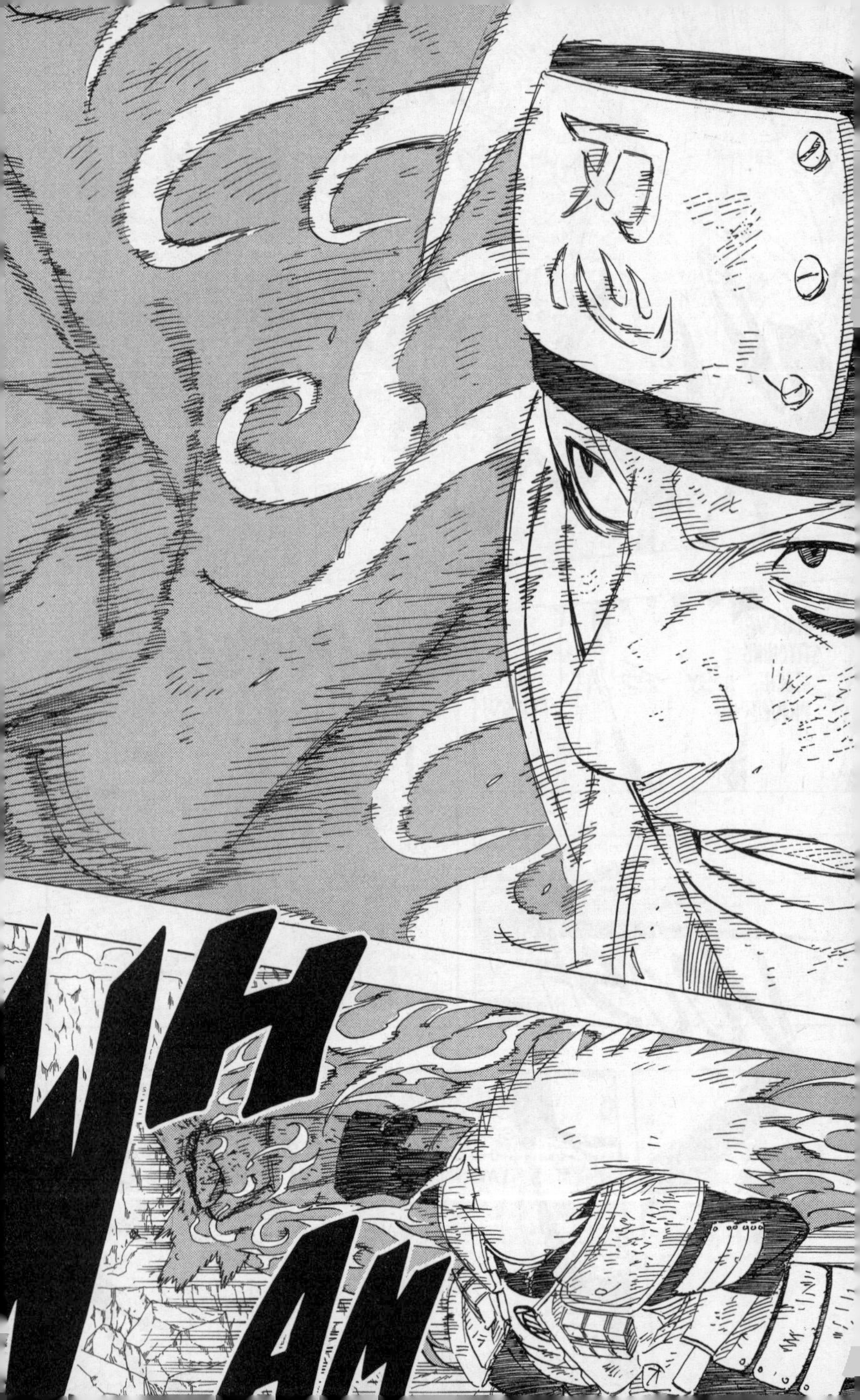
WHAM

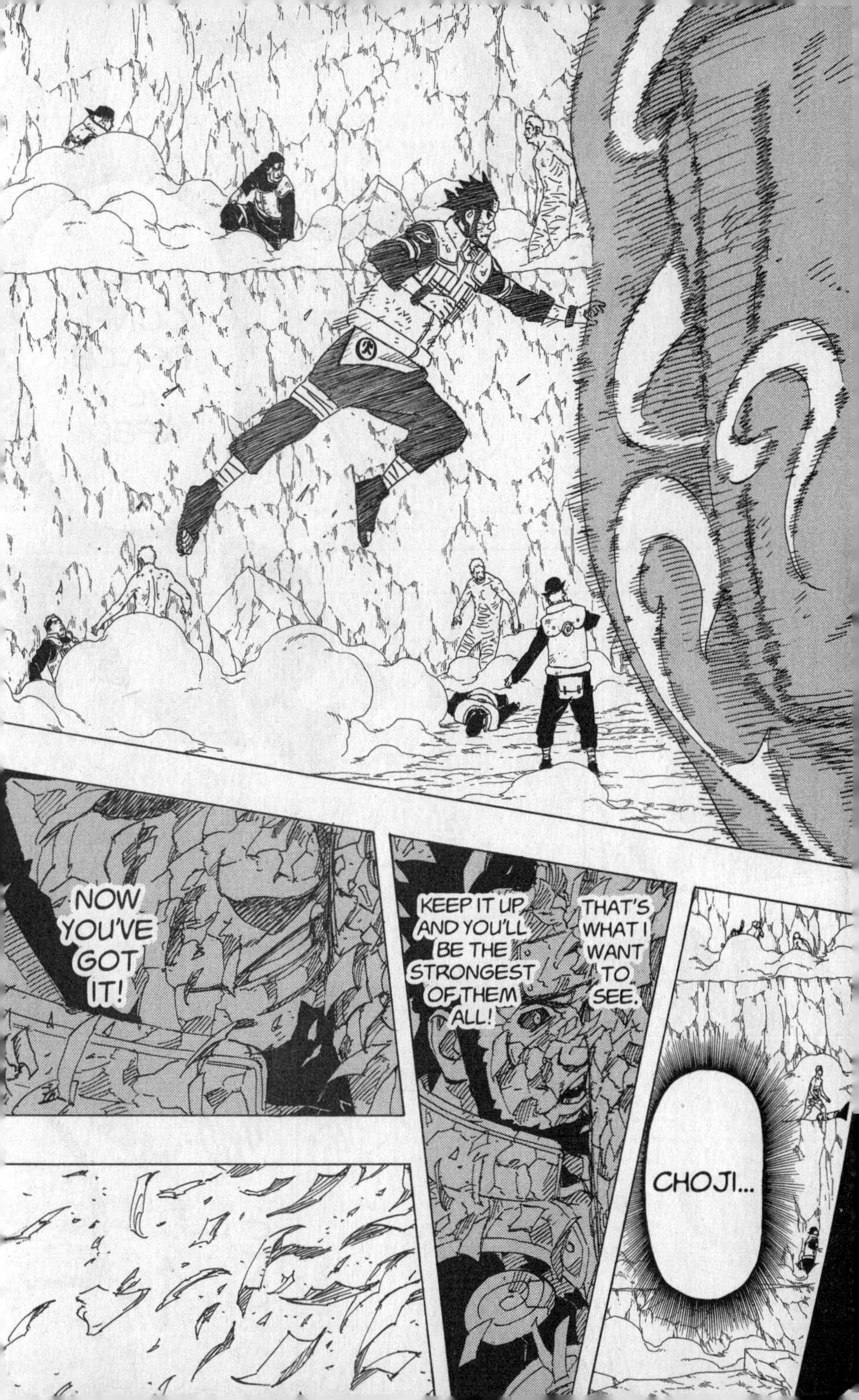
CHOJI...
THAT'S WHAT I WANT TO SEE.
KEEP IT UP AND YOU'LL BE THE STRONGEST OF THEM ALL!
NOW YOU'VE GOT IT!

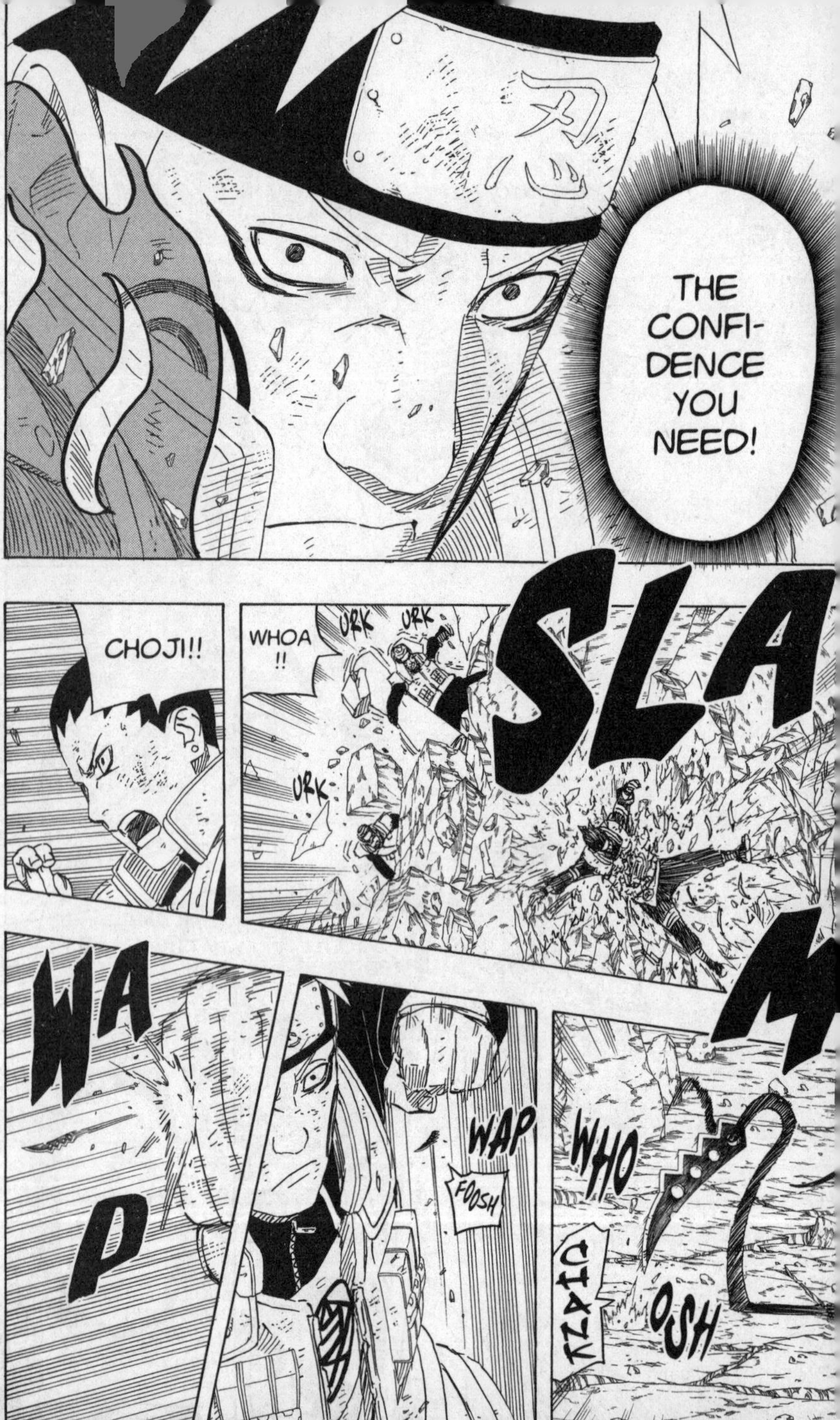
THE CONFIDENCE YOU NEED!
SLAM
URK
URK
WHOA!!
URK
CHOJI!!
WHOOSH
WAP
FOOSH
WAP

READ THIS WAY

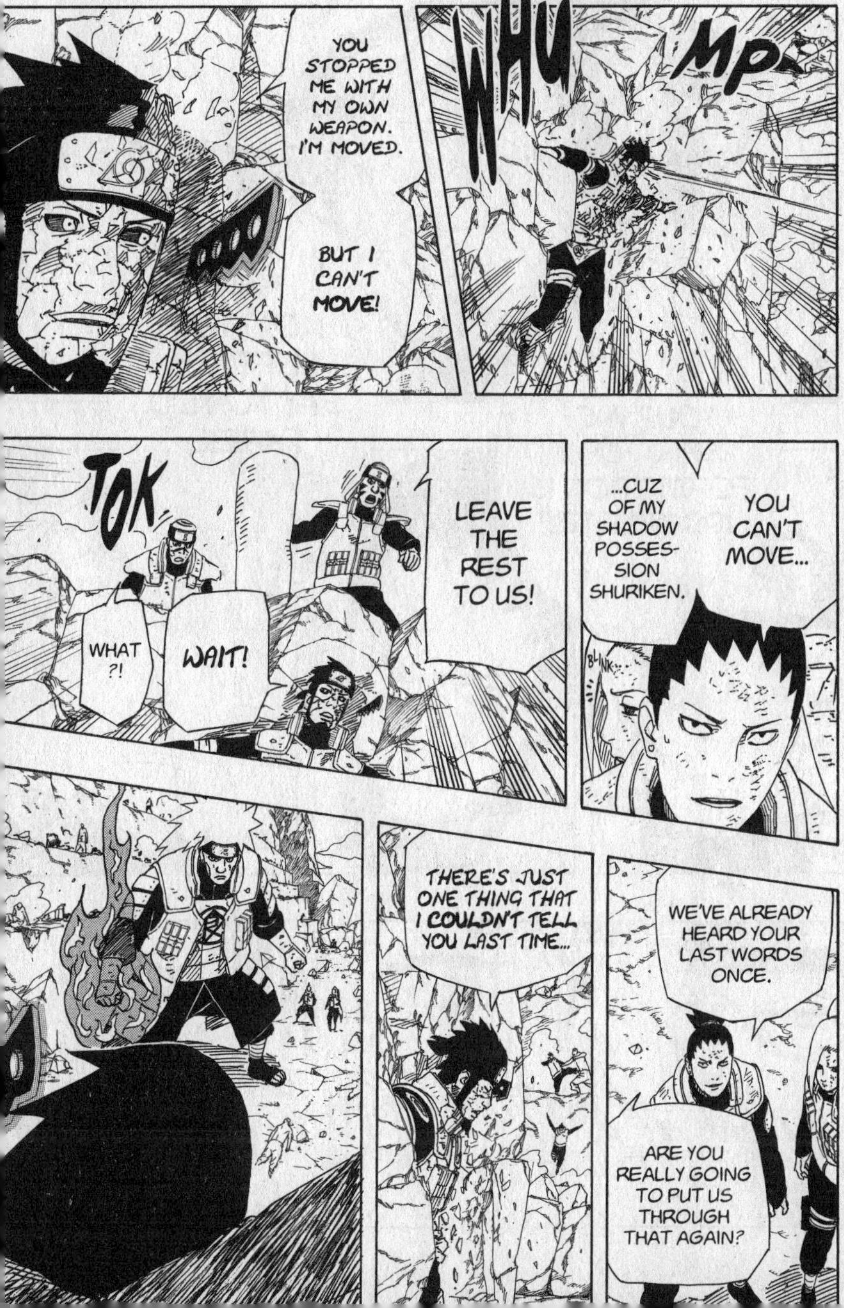
WHUMP
YOU STOPPED ME WITH MY OWN WEAPON. I'M MOVED.
BUT I CAN'T **MOVE!**
YOU CAN'T MOVE...
...CUZ OF MY SHADOW POSSESSION SHURIKEN.
BLINK
LEAVE THE REST TO US!
WAIT!
WHAT?!
TOK
WE'VE ALREADY HEARD YOUR LAST WORDS ONCE.
ARE YOU REALLY GOING TO PUT US THROUGH THAT AGAIN?
THERE'S JUST ONE THING THAT I **COULDN'T** TELL YOU LAST TIME...

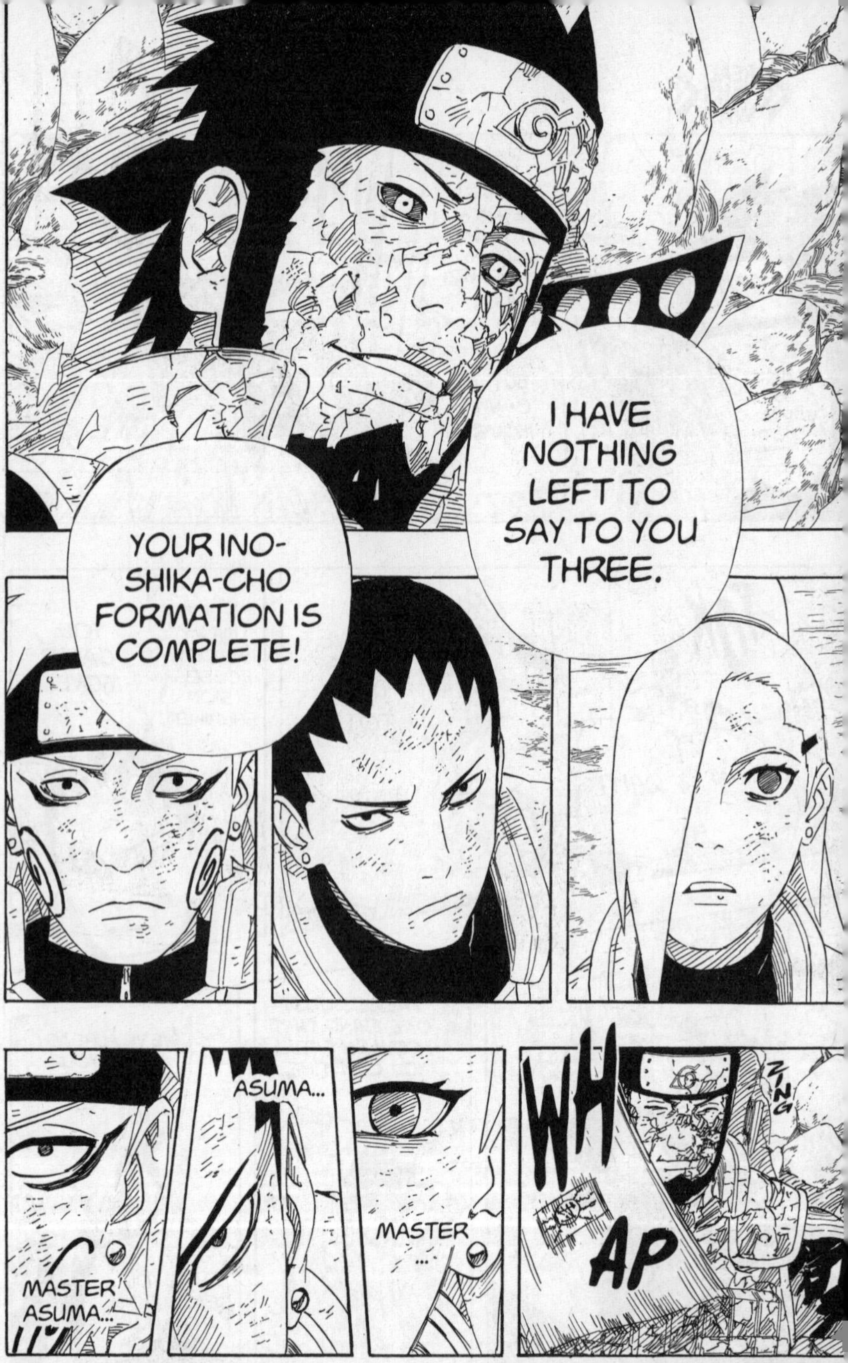
I HAVE NOTHING LEFT TO SAY TO YOU THREE.
YOUR INO-SHIKA-CHO FORMATION IS COMPLETE!
WHAP
ZING
MASTER ...
ASUMA...
MASTER ASUMA...

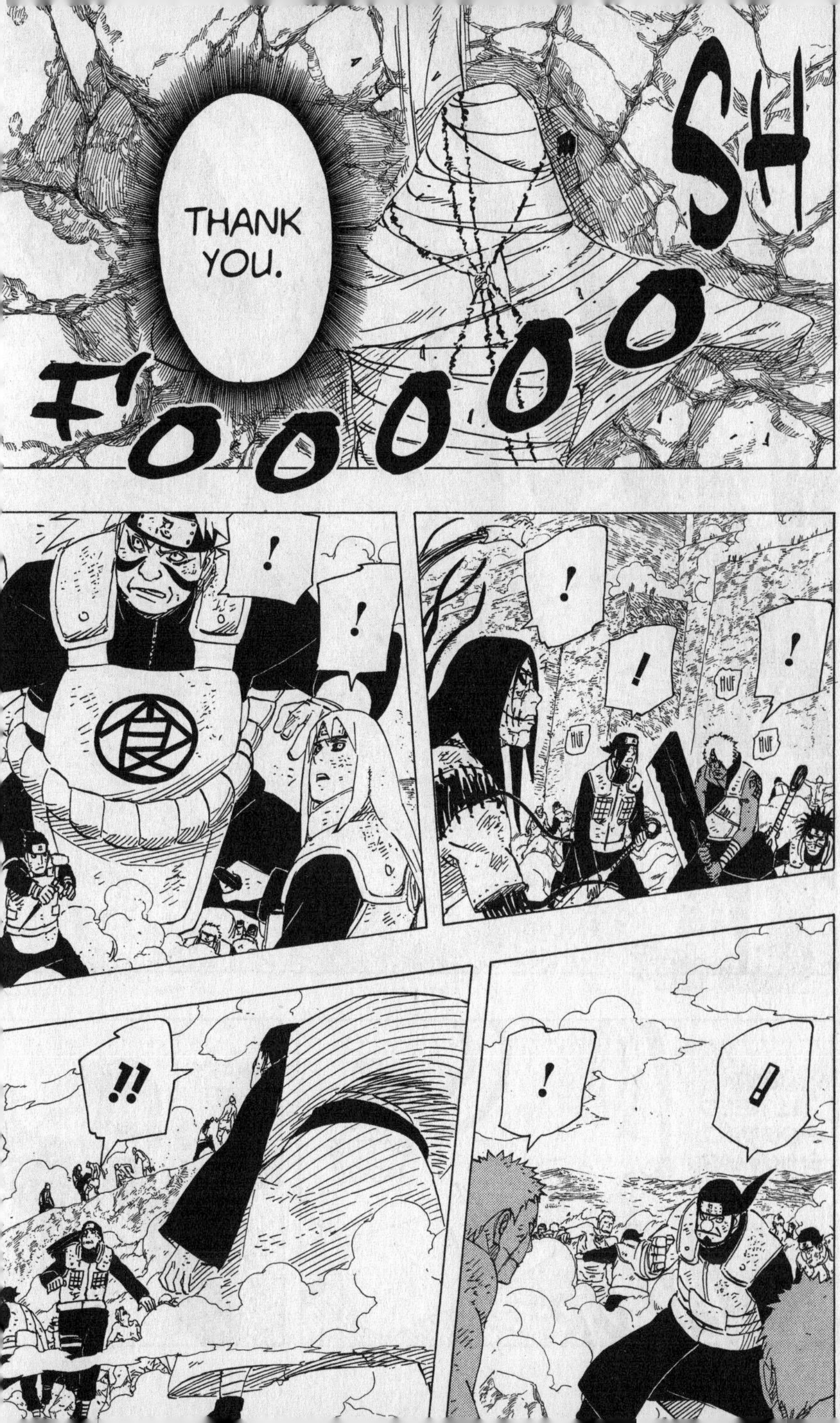
THANK YOU.
F'OOOOOSH
!
!
!
!
HUF
HUF
HUF
!
!
!
!
!!

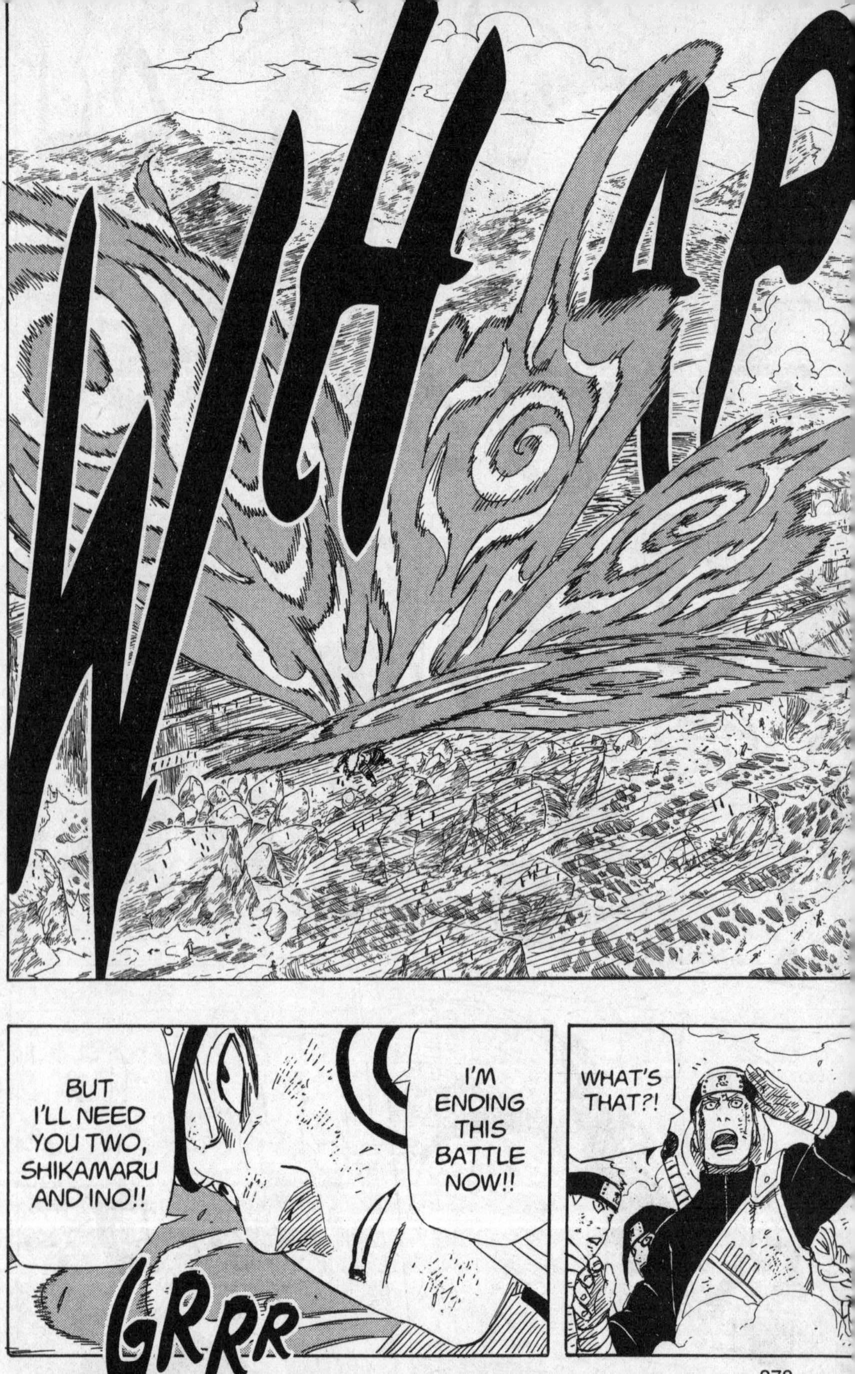
WHAP
WHAT'S THAT?!
I'M ENDING THIS BATTLE NOW!!
BUT I'LL NEED YOU TWO, SHIKAMARU AND INO!!
GRRR

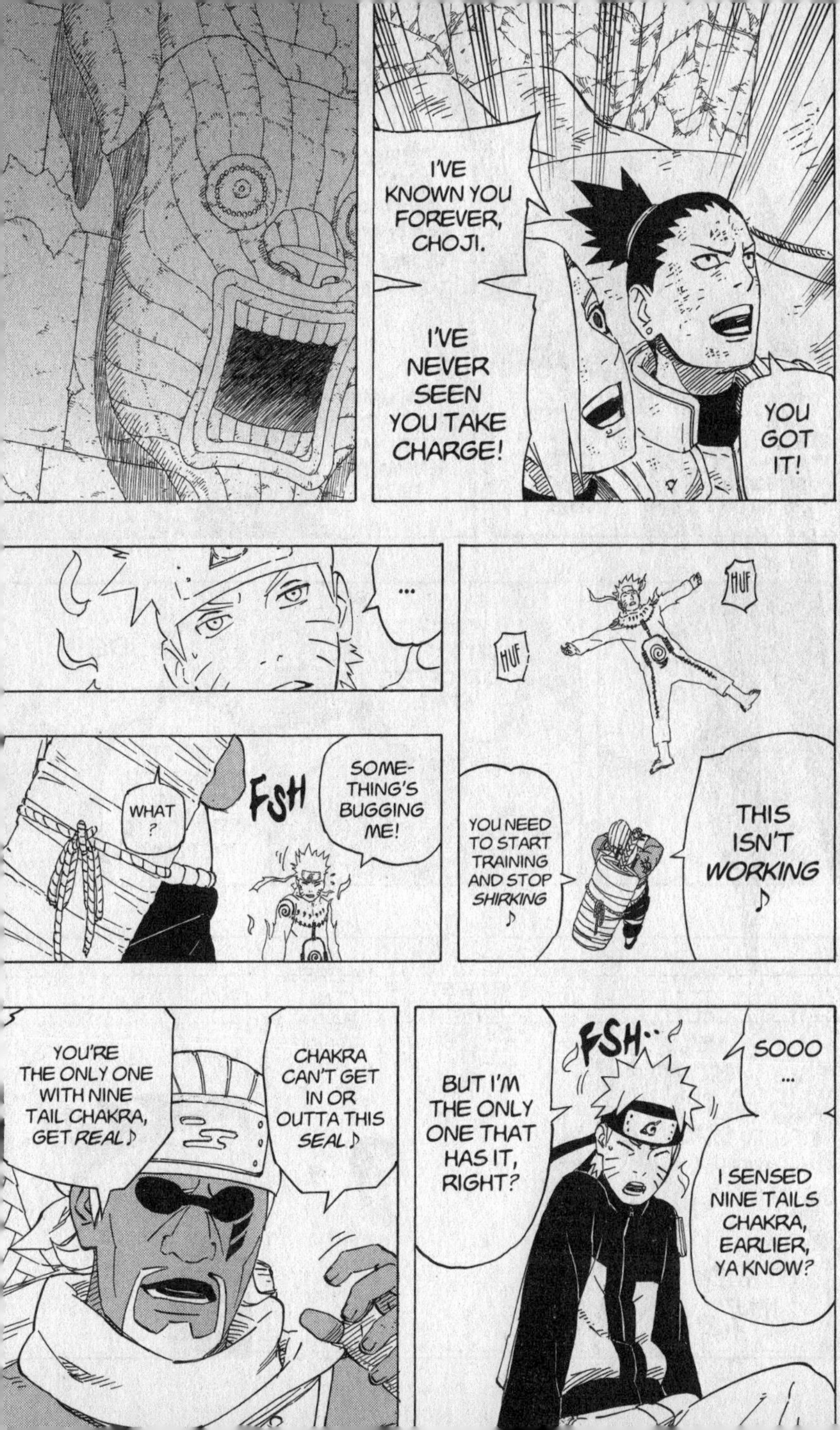
I'VE KNOWN YOU FOREVER, CHOJI.
I'VE NEVER SEEN YOU TAKE CHARGE!
YOU GOT IT!
HUF
HUF
THIS ISN'T *WORKING* ♪
YOU NEED TO START TRAINING AND STOP *SHIRKING* ♪
...
SOME-THING'S BUGGING ME!
FSH
WHAT ?
SOOO ...
I SENSED NINE TAILS CHAKRA, EARLIER, YA KNOW?
FSH
BUT I'M THE ONLY ONE THAT HAS IT, RIGHT?
CHAKRA CAN'T GET IN OR OUTTA THIS *SEAL* ♪
YOU'RE THE ONLY ONE WITH NINE TAIL CHAKRA, GET *REAL* ♪

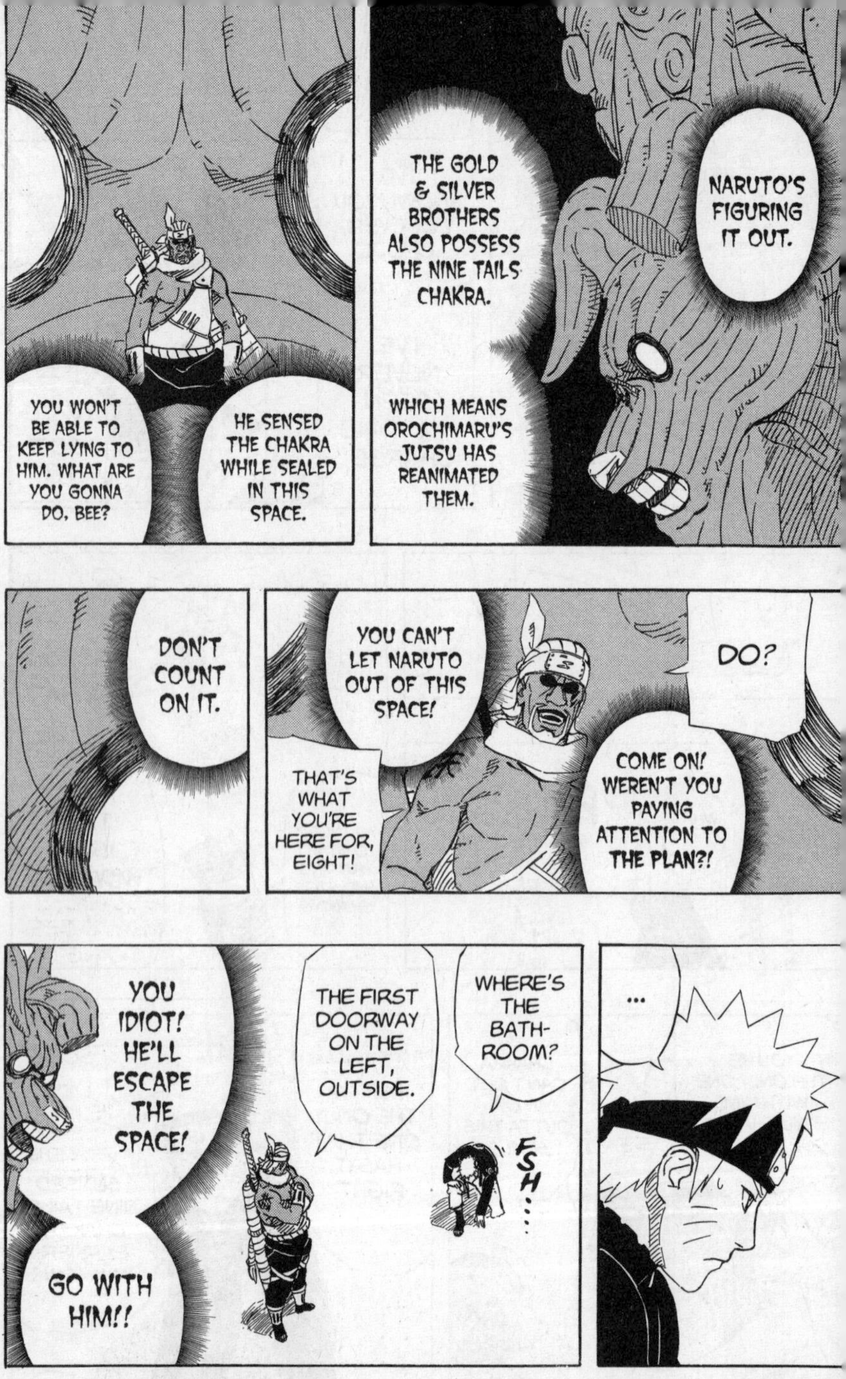
NARUTO'S FIGURING IT OUT.
THE GOLD & SILVER BROTHERS ALSO POSSESS THE NINE TAILS CHAKRA.
WHICH MEANS OROCHIMARU'S JUTSU HAS REANIMATED THEM.
HE SENSED THE CHAKRA WHILE SEALED IN THIS SPACE.
YOU WON'T BE ABLE TO KEEP LYING TO HIM. WHAT ARE YOU GONNA DO, BEE?
DO?
COME ON! WEREN'T YOU PAYING ATTENTION TO THE PLAN?!
YOU CAN'T LET NARUTO OUT OF THIS SPACE!
THAT'S WHAT YOU'RE HERE FOR, EIGHT!
DON'T COUNT ON IT.
...
WHERE'S THE BATH-ROOM?
THE FIRST DOORWAY ON THE LEFT, OUTSIDE.
FSH...
YOU IDIOT! HE'LL ESCAPE THE SPACE!
GO WITH HIM!!

READ THIS WAY

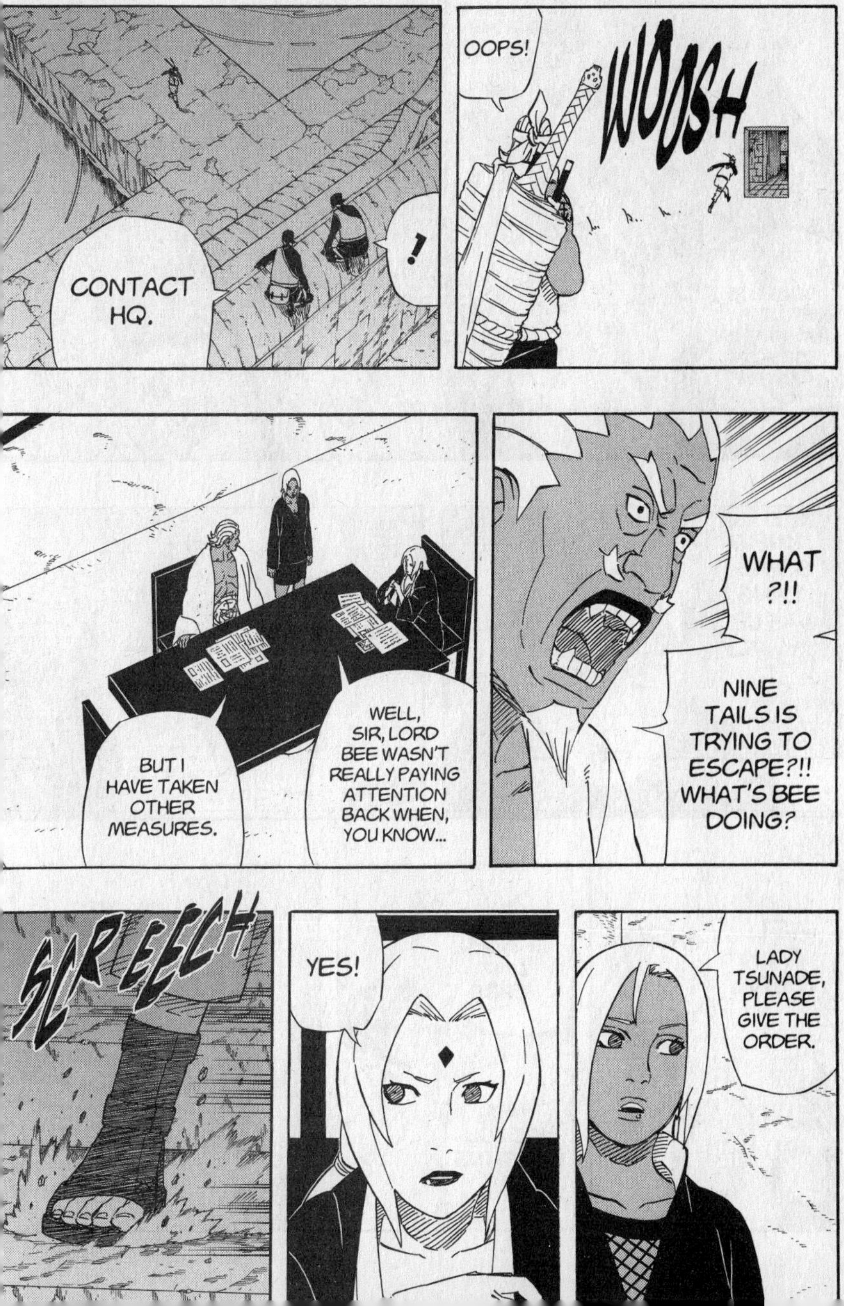
OOPS!
WOOSH
!
CONTACT HQ.
WHAT?!!
NINE TAILS IS TRYING TO ESCAPE?!! WHAT'S BEE DOING?
WELL, SIR, LORD BEE WASN'T REALLY PAYING ATTENTION BACK WHEN, YOU KNOW...
BUT I HAVE TAKEN OTHER MEASURES.
LADY TSUNADE, PLEASE GIVE THE ORDER.
YES!
SCREECH

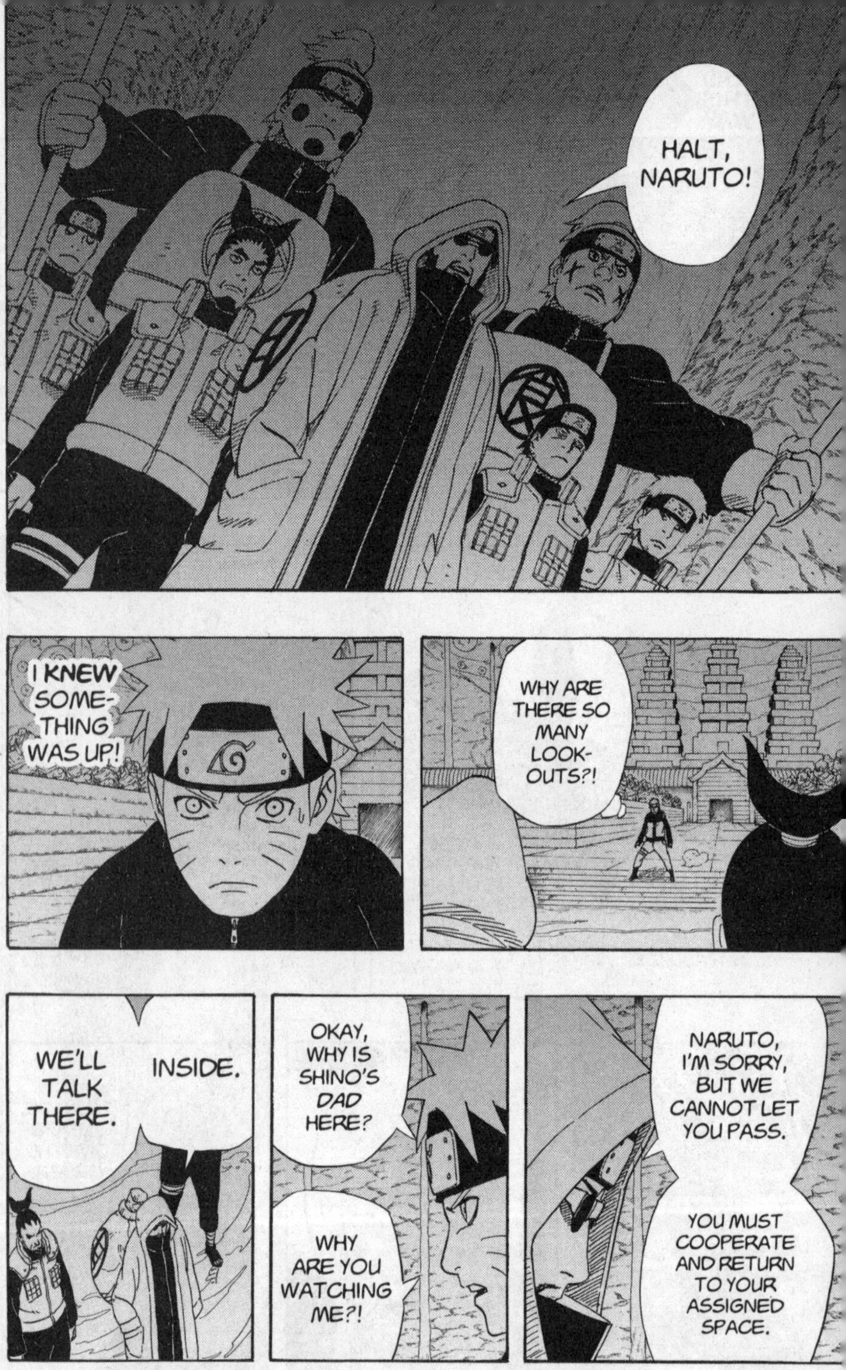
HALT, NARUTO!
WHY ARE THERE SO MANY LOOK-OUTS?!
I KNEW SOME-THING WAS UP!
NARUTO, I'M SORRY, BUT WE CANNOT LET YOU PASS.
YOU MUST COOPERATE AND RETURN TO YOUR ASSIGNED SPACE.
OKAY, WHY IS SHINO'S *DAD* HERE?
WHY ARE YOU WATCHING *ME*?!
INSIDE.
WE'LL TALK THERE.

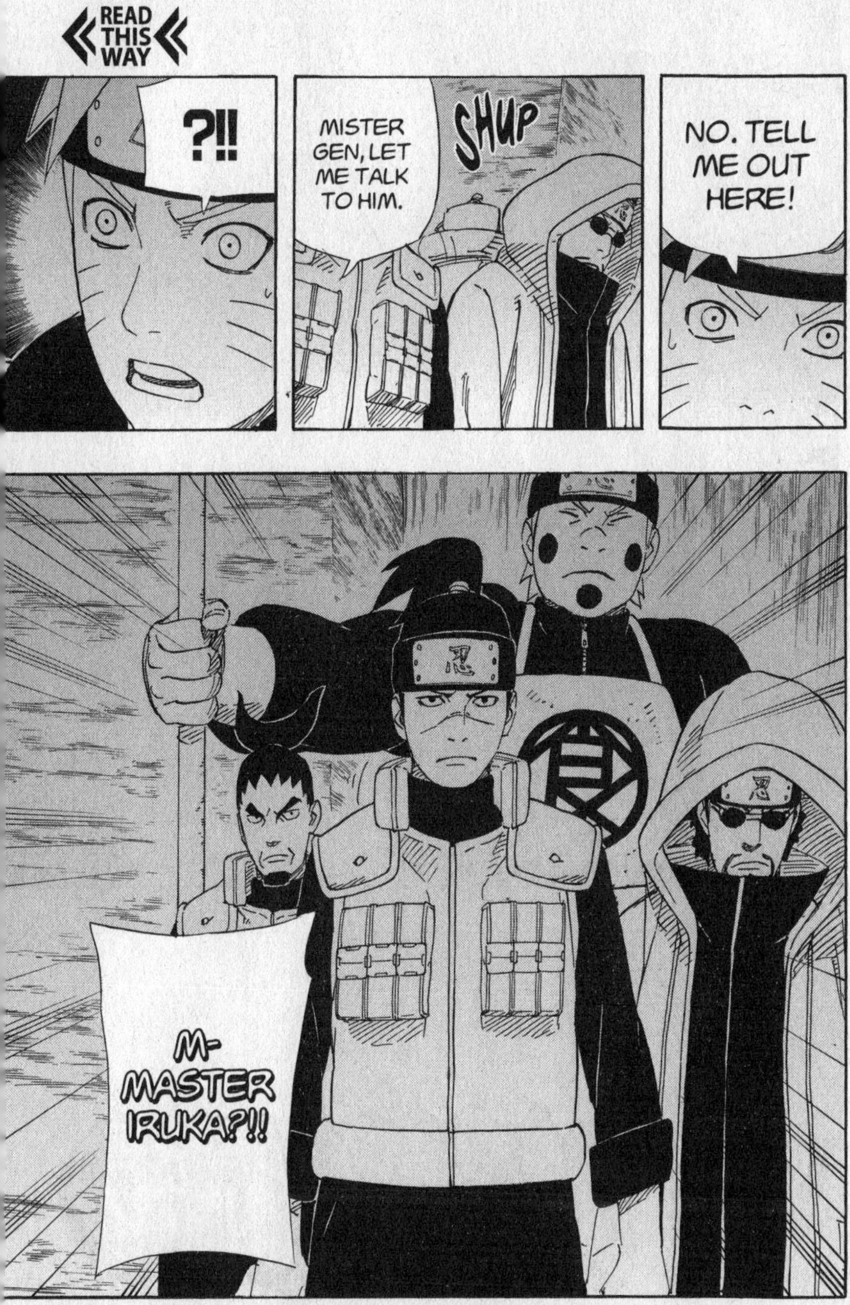
READ THIS WAY
NO. TELL ME OUT HERE!
SHUP
MISTER GEN, LET ME TALK TO HIM.
?!!
M-MASTER IRUKA?!!

NARUTO

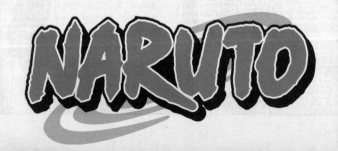

SPOTLIGHT!! HERE! OVER HERE!!

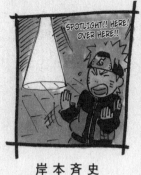

岸本斉史

Main character Naruto finally returns to center stage in this volume! I'm so glad to be able to draw the titular character again! I was told by someone that this was "a manga where the main character ~~isn't very involved~~ is used quite stingily," but he'll be really active from here on out!! ...I think! ...Er... Hmm, I wonder... I don't really know about the future... Well...

—Masashi Kishimoto, 2011

ラーメン一楽
一楽

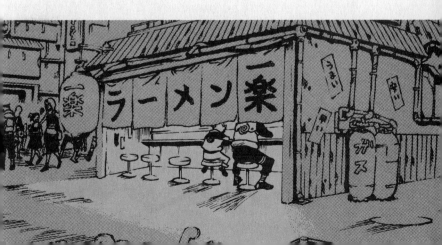

NARUTO

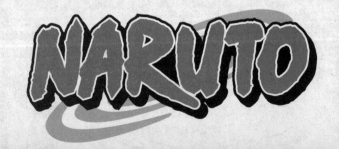

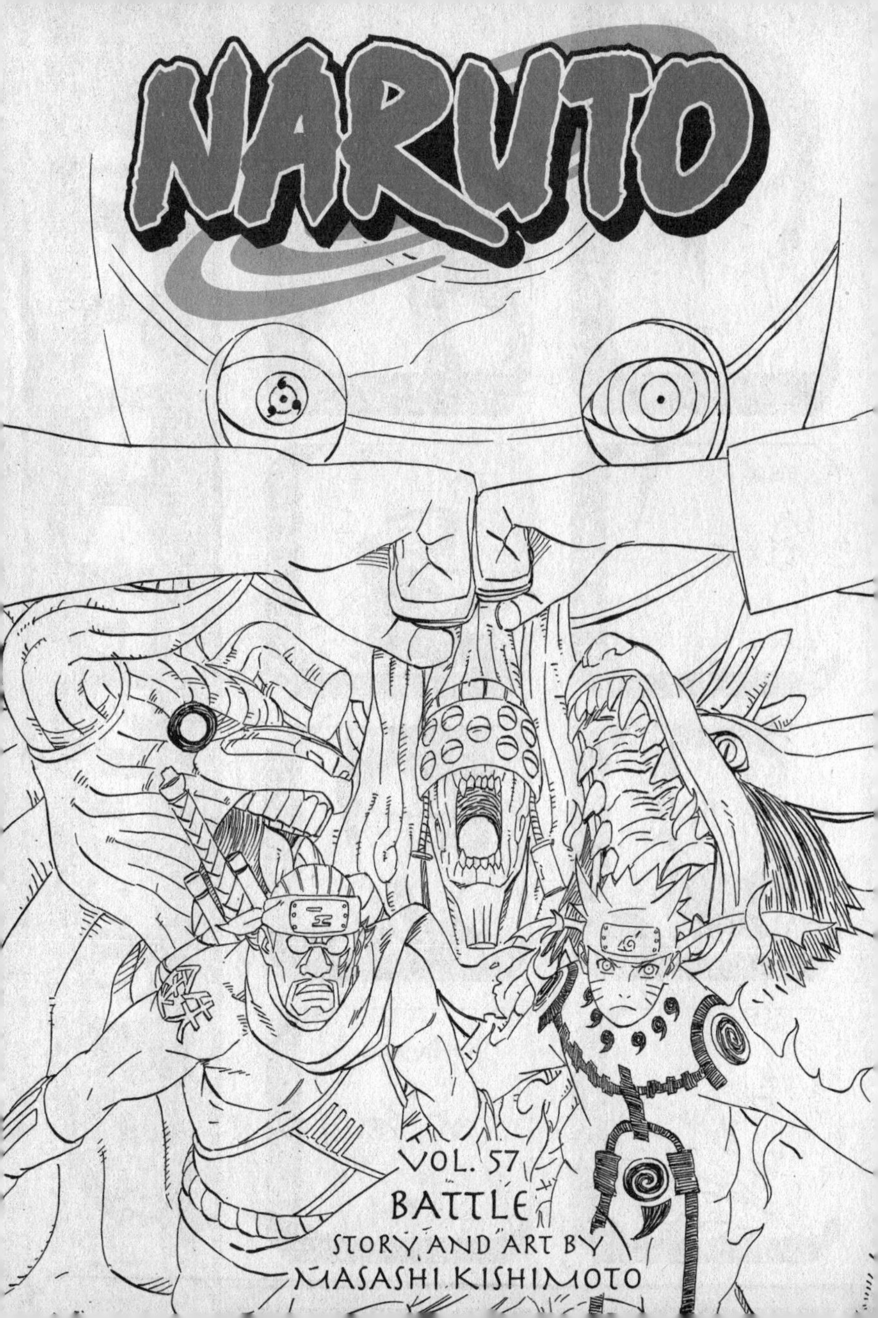
NARUTO
VOL. 57
BATTLE
STORY AND ART BY
MASASHI KISHIMOTO

# CHARACTERS

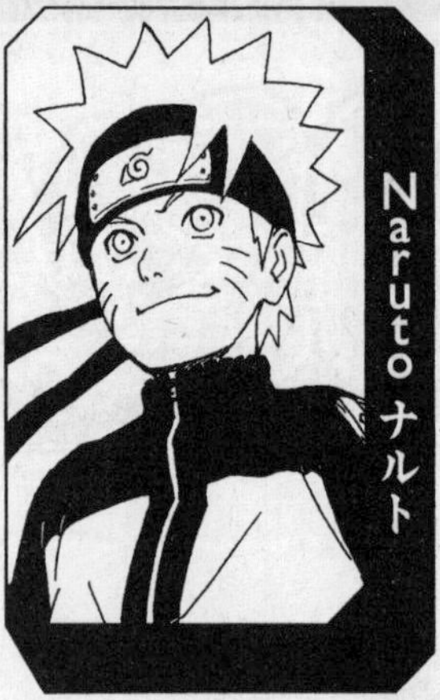

Naruto ナルト

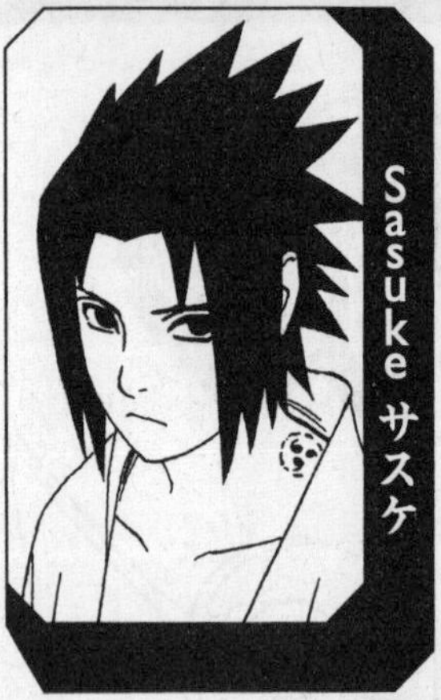

Sasuke サスケ

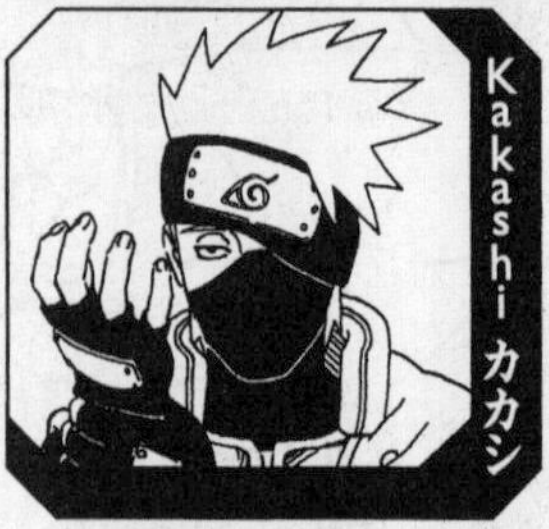

Kakashi カカシ

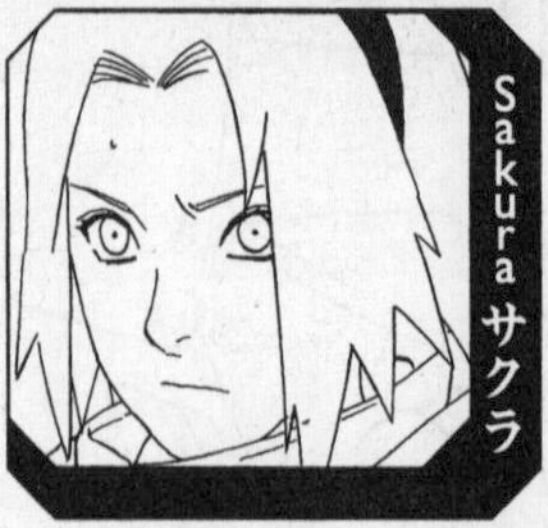

Sakura サクラ

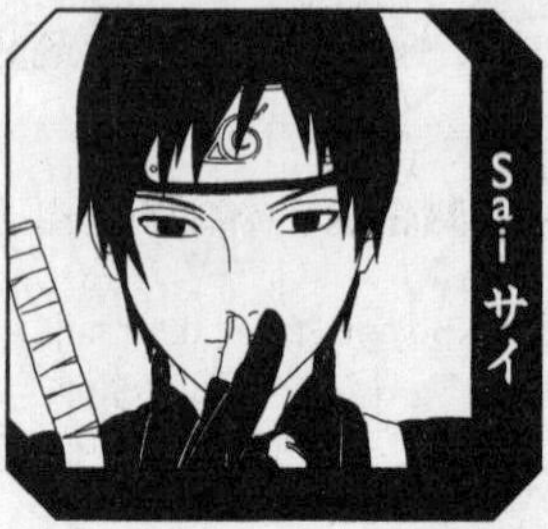

Sai サイ

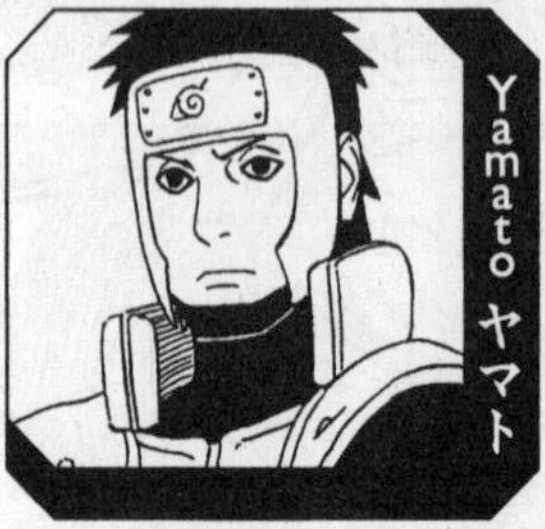

Yamato ヤマト

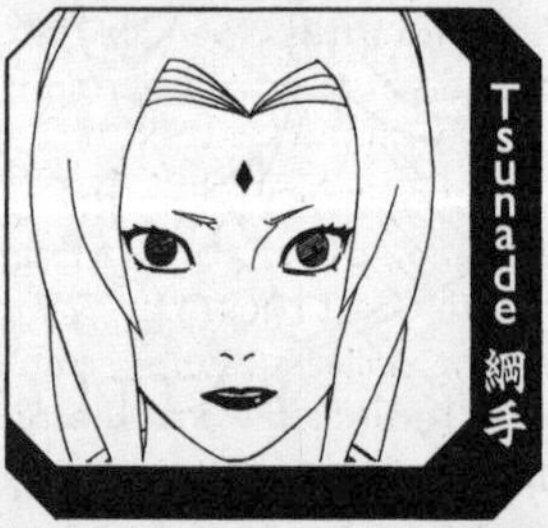

Tsunade 綱手

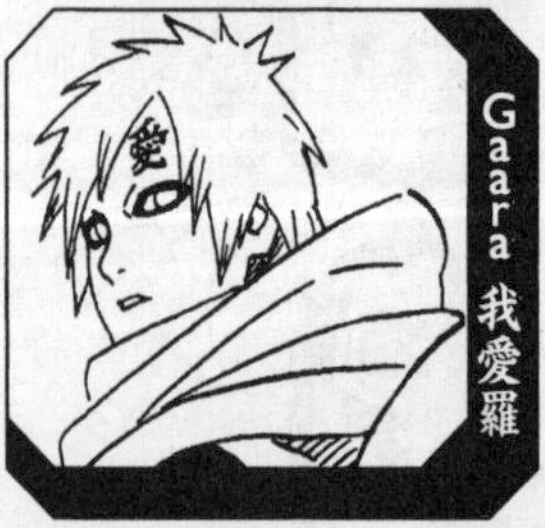

Gaara 我愛羅

Mizukage 水影

Tsuchikage 土影

Raikage 雷影

Kabuto カブト

Zetsu ゼツ

Madara マダラ

Iruka イルカ

Darui ダルイ

Killer Bee キラービー

# THE STORY SO FAR...

Naruto, the biggest troublemaker at the Ninja Academy in the Village of Konohagakure, finally becomes a ninja along with his classmates Sasuke and Sakura. They grow and mature through countless trials and battles. However, Sasuke, unable to give up his quest for vengeance, leaves Konohagakure to seek Orochimaru and his power…

As two years pass, Naruto battles the Tailed Beast-targeting Akatsuki organization while Sasuke triumphs over his murderous brother, Itachi. But new intel sets Sasuke, now aligned with the Akatsuki, on a new mission of revenge, this time against the village of Konoha itself.

Upon Madara's declaration of war, the Five Kage put together an Allied Shinobi Force. The Fourth Great Ninja War against the Akatsuki begins. Naruto continues training, still sequestered from the battlefield, while the Allied Forces fight harsh battles against the heroes Kabuto has resurrected. And do additional enemies threaten the main regiment of the Allied Forces?!

# NARUTO

## VOL. 57
## BATTLE

## CONTENTS

# Number 535: Iruka's Impact

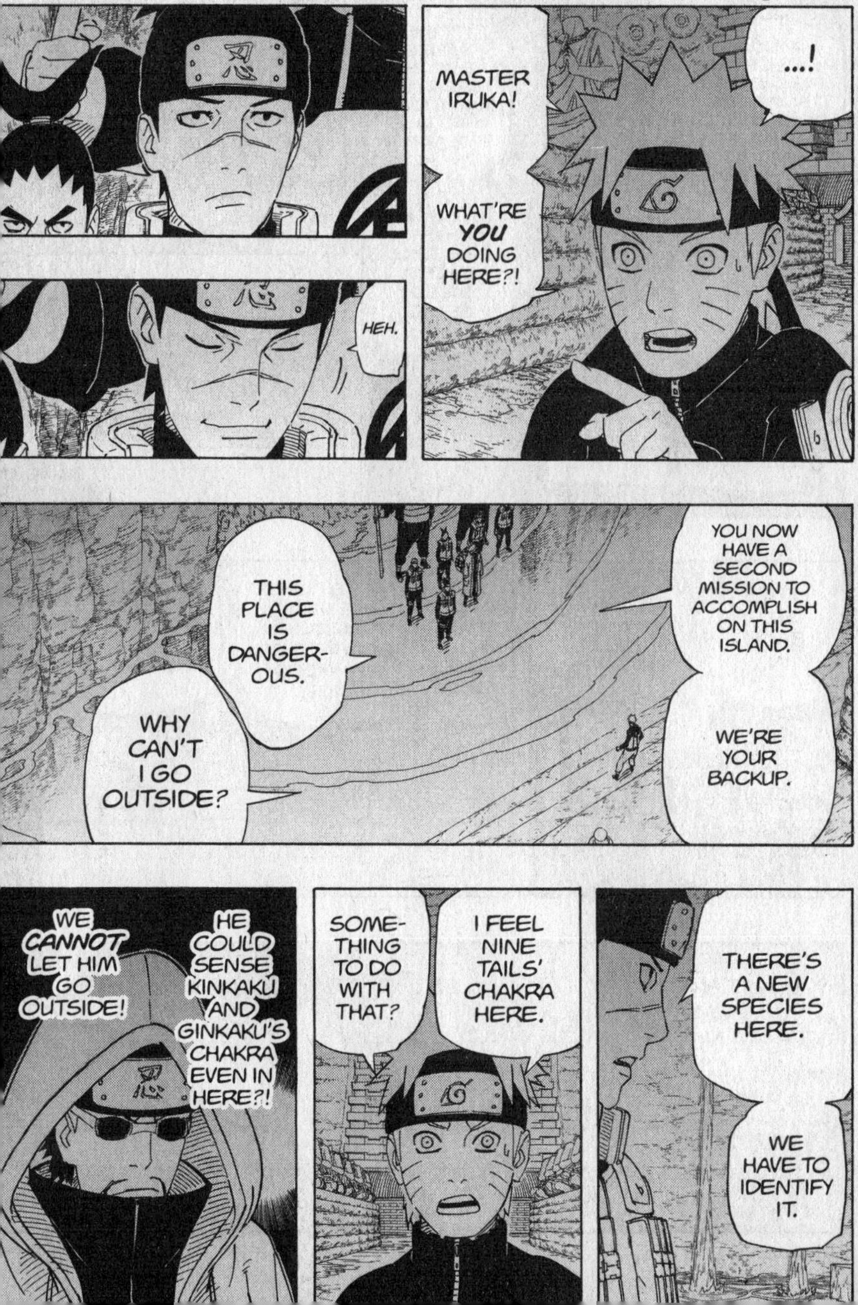
...!
MASTER IRUKA!
WHAT'RE YOU DOING HERE?!
HEH.
YOU NOW HAVE A SECOND MISSION TO ACCOMPLISH ON THIS ISLAND.
WE'RE YOUR BACKUP.
THIS PLACE IS DANGER-OUS.
WHY CAN'T I GO OUTSIDE?
THERE'S A NEW SPECIES HERE.
WE HAVE TO IDENTIFY IT.
I FEEL NINE TAILS' CHAKRA HERE.
SOME-THING TO DO WITH THAT?
HE COULD SENSE KINKAKU AND GINKAKU'S CHAKRA EVEN IN HERE?!
WE CANNOT LET HIM GO OUTSIDE!

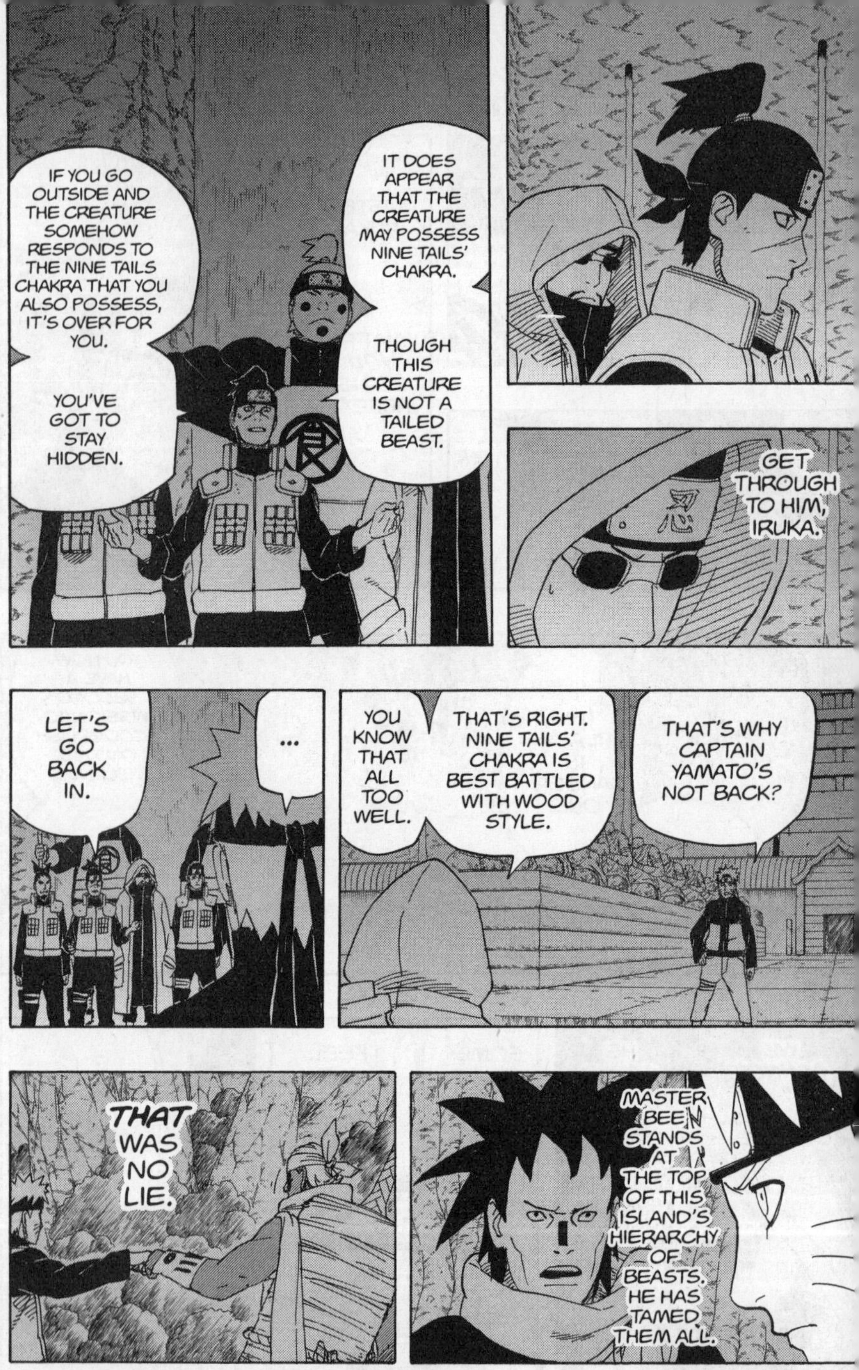
GET THROUGH TO HIM, IRUKA.
IT DOES APPEAR THAT THE CREATURE MAY POSSESS NINE TAILS' CHAKRA.
THOUGH THIS CREATURE IS NOT A TAILED BEAST.
IF YOU GO OUTSIDE AND THE CREATURE SOMEHOW RESPONDS TO THE NINE TAILS CHAKRA THAT YOU ALSO POSSESS, IT'S OVER FOR YOU.
YOU'VE GOT TO STAY HIDDEN.
THAT'S WHY CAPTAIN YAMATO'S NOT BACK?
THAT'S RIGHT. NINE TAILS' CHAKRA IS BEST BATTLED WITH WOOD STYLE.
YOU KNOW THAT ALL TOO WELL.
...
LET'S GO BACK IN.
MASTER BEE STANDS AT THE TOP OF THIS ISLAND'S HIERARCHY OF BEASTS. HE HAS TAMED THEM ALL.
THAT WAS NO LIE.

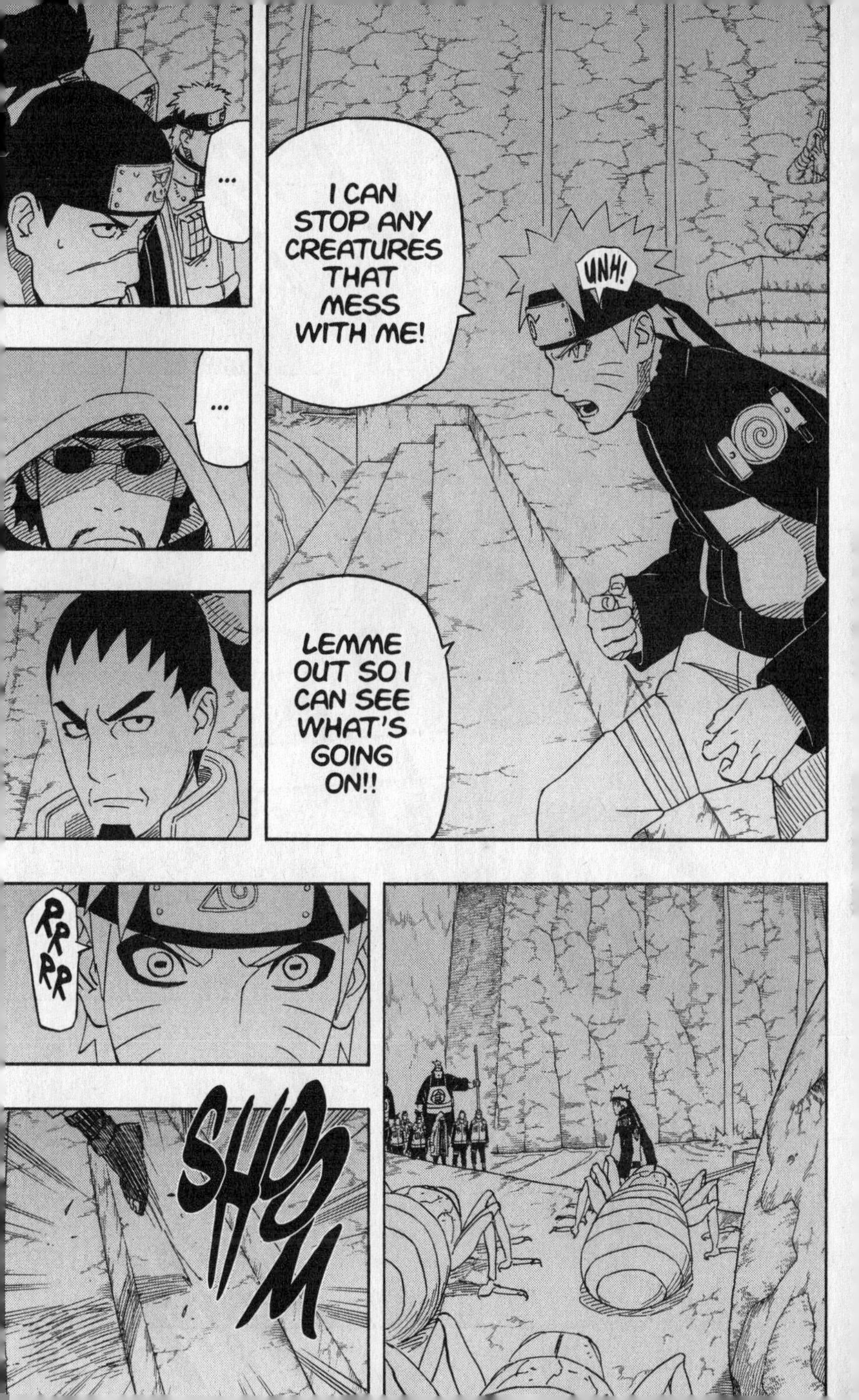

I CAN STOP ANY CREATURES THAT MESS WITH ME!
UNH!
LEMME OUT SO I CAN SEE WHAT'S GOING ON!!
...
...
RRRR
SHOOM

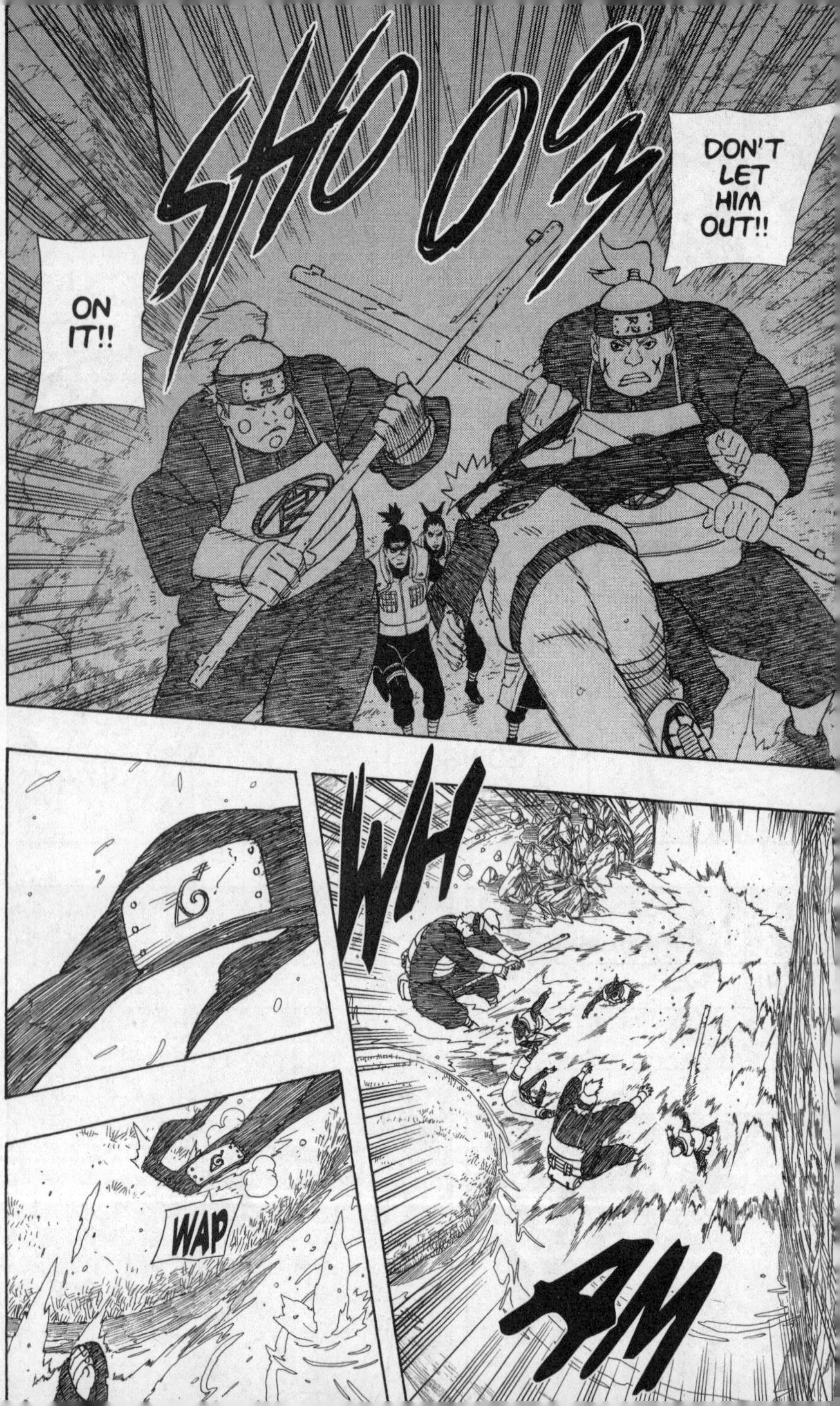
DON'T LET HIM OUT!!
SHOOG
ON IT!!
WH
AM
WAP

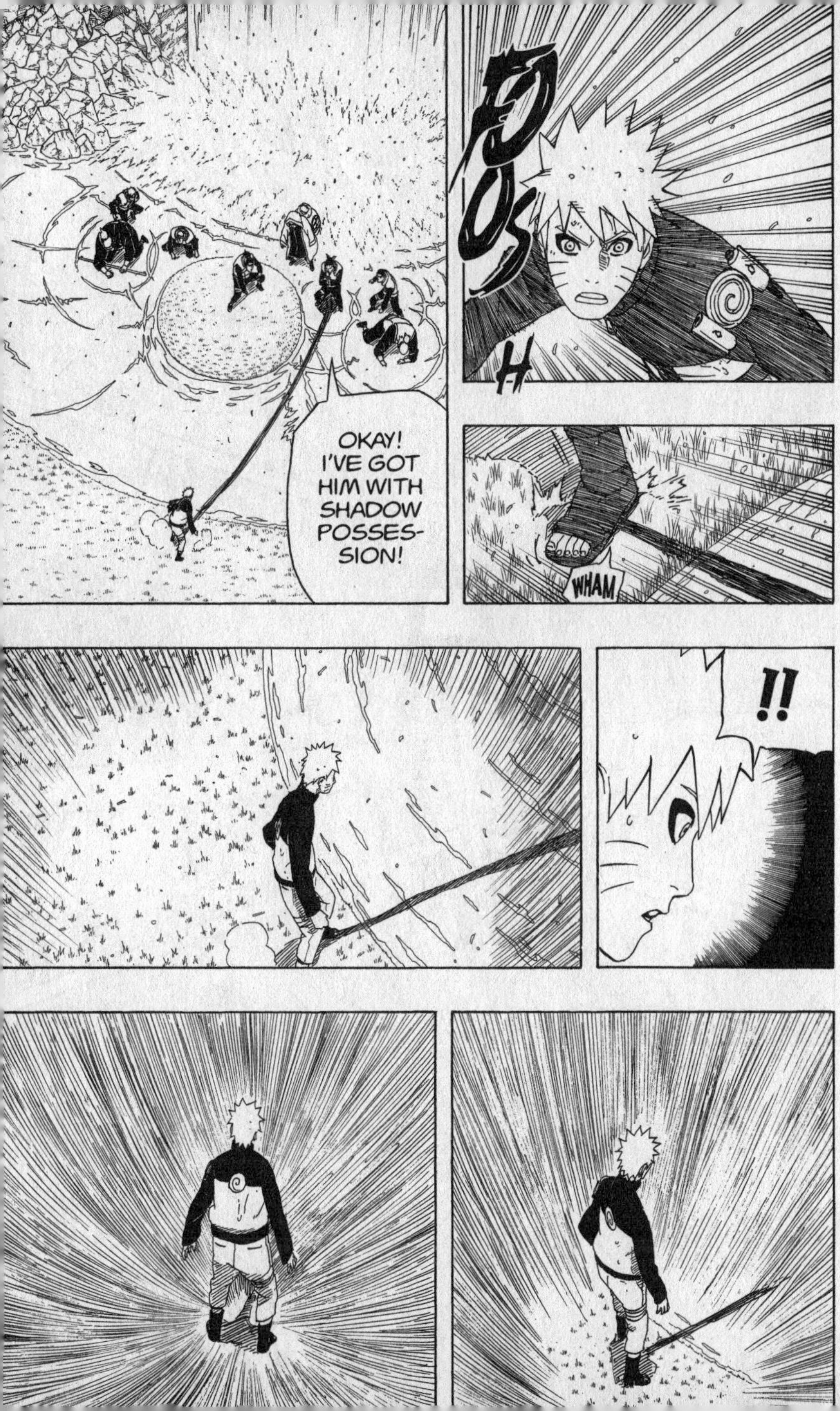
FOOSH
WHAM
OKAY! I'VE GOT HIM WITH SHADOW POSSESSION!
!!

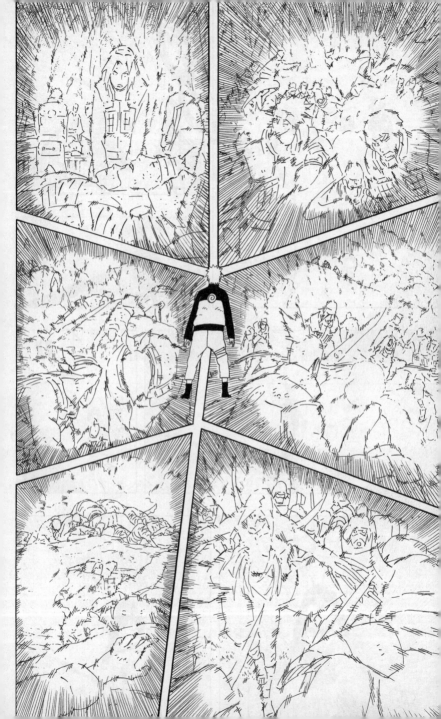

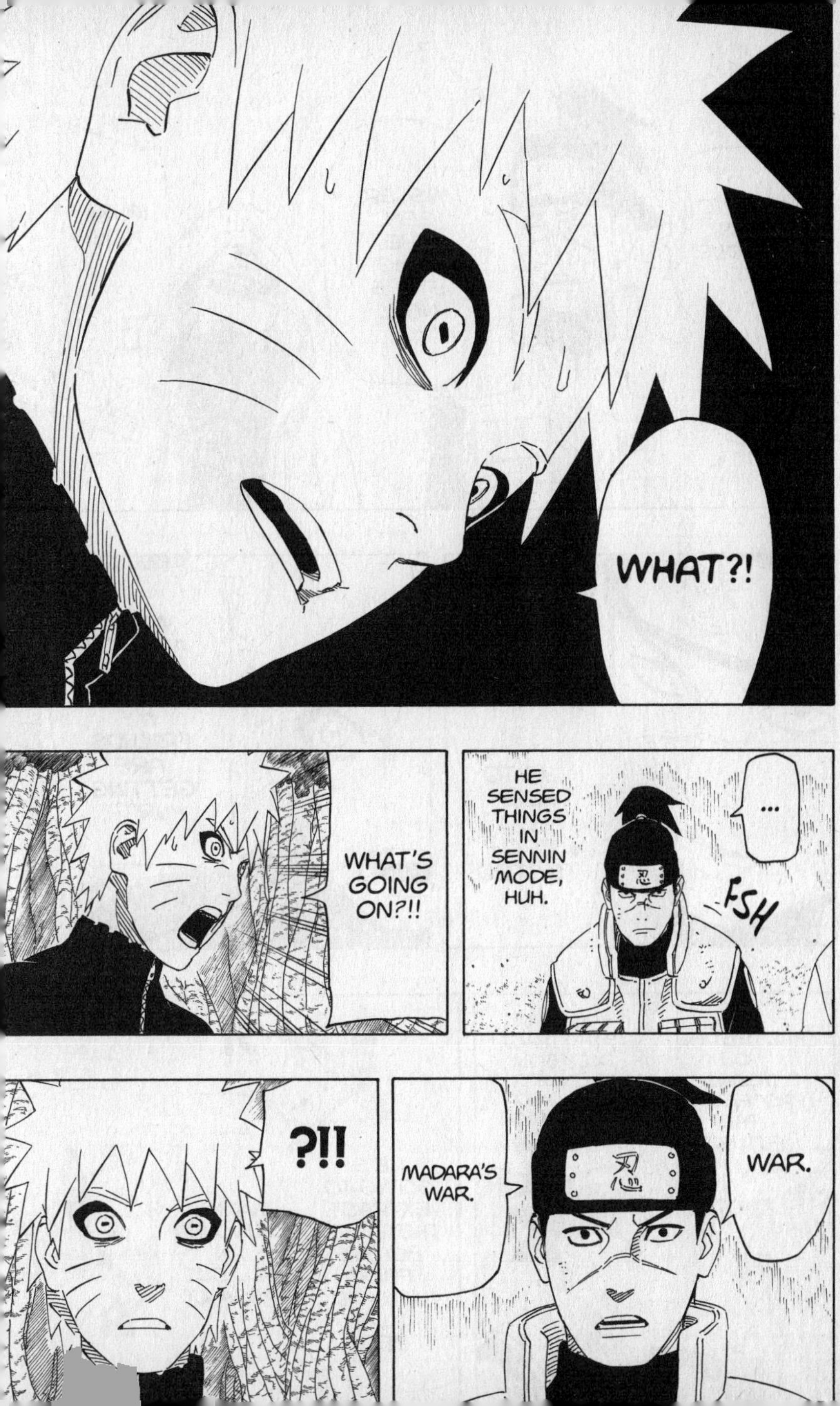
WHAT?!
...
HE SENSED THINGS IN SENNIN MODE, HUH.
FSH
WHAT'S GOING ON?!!
WAR.
MADARA'S WAR.
?!!

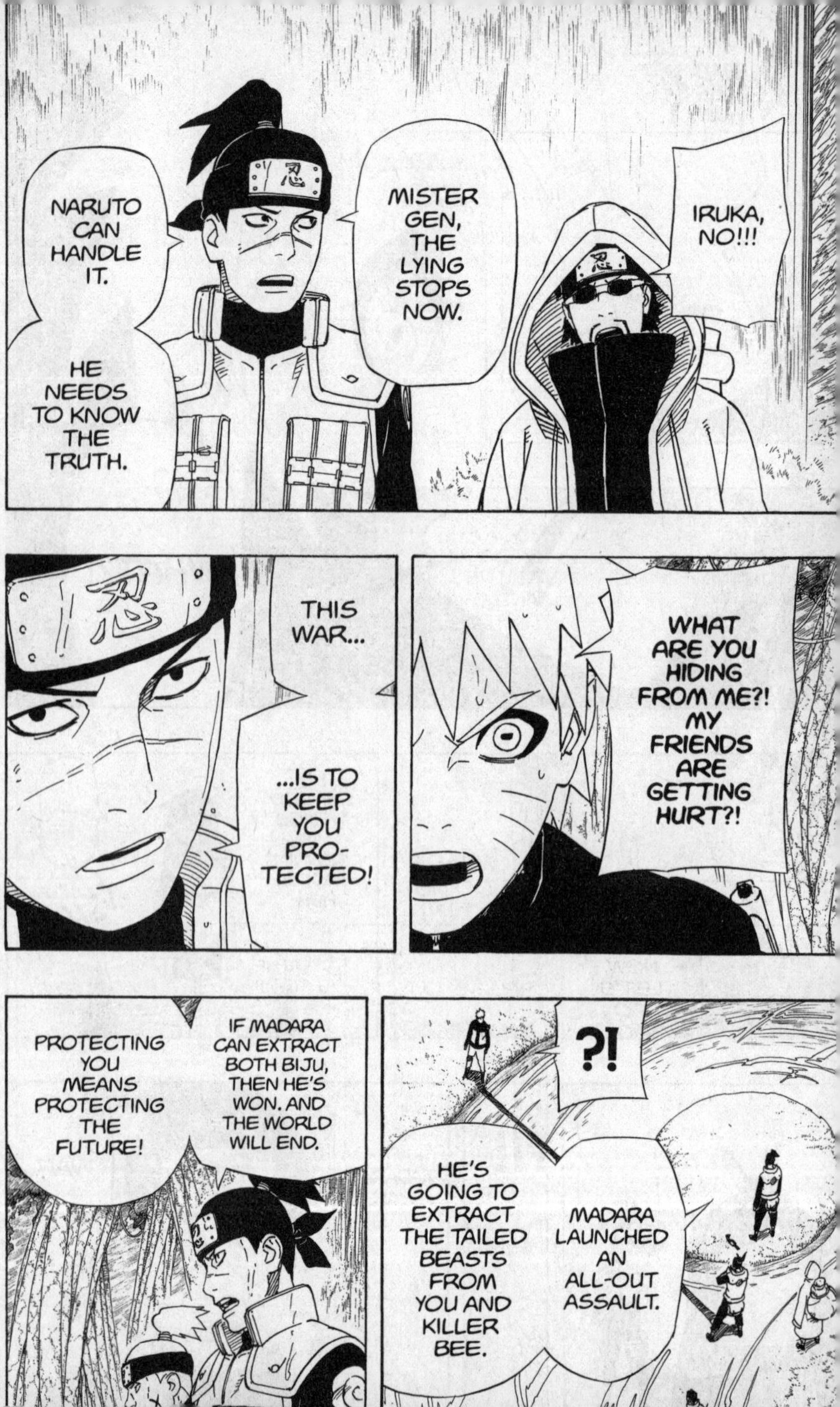
IRUKA, NO!!!
MISTER GEN, THE LYING STOPS NOW.
NARUTO CAN HANDLE IT.
HE NEEDS TO KNOW THE TRUTH.
WHAT ARE YOU HIDING FROM ME?! MY FRIENDS ARE GETTING HURT?!
THIS WAR...
...IS TO KEEP YOU PRO-TECTED!
?!
MADARA LAUNCHED AN ALL-OUT ASSAULT.
HE'S GOING TO EXTRACT THE TAILED BEASTS FROM YOU AND KILLER BEE.
IF MADARA CAN EXTRACT BOTH BIJU, THEN HE'S WON. AND THE WORLD WILL END.
PROTECTING YOU MEANS PROTECTING THE FUTURE!

READ THIS WAY

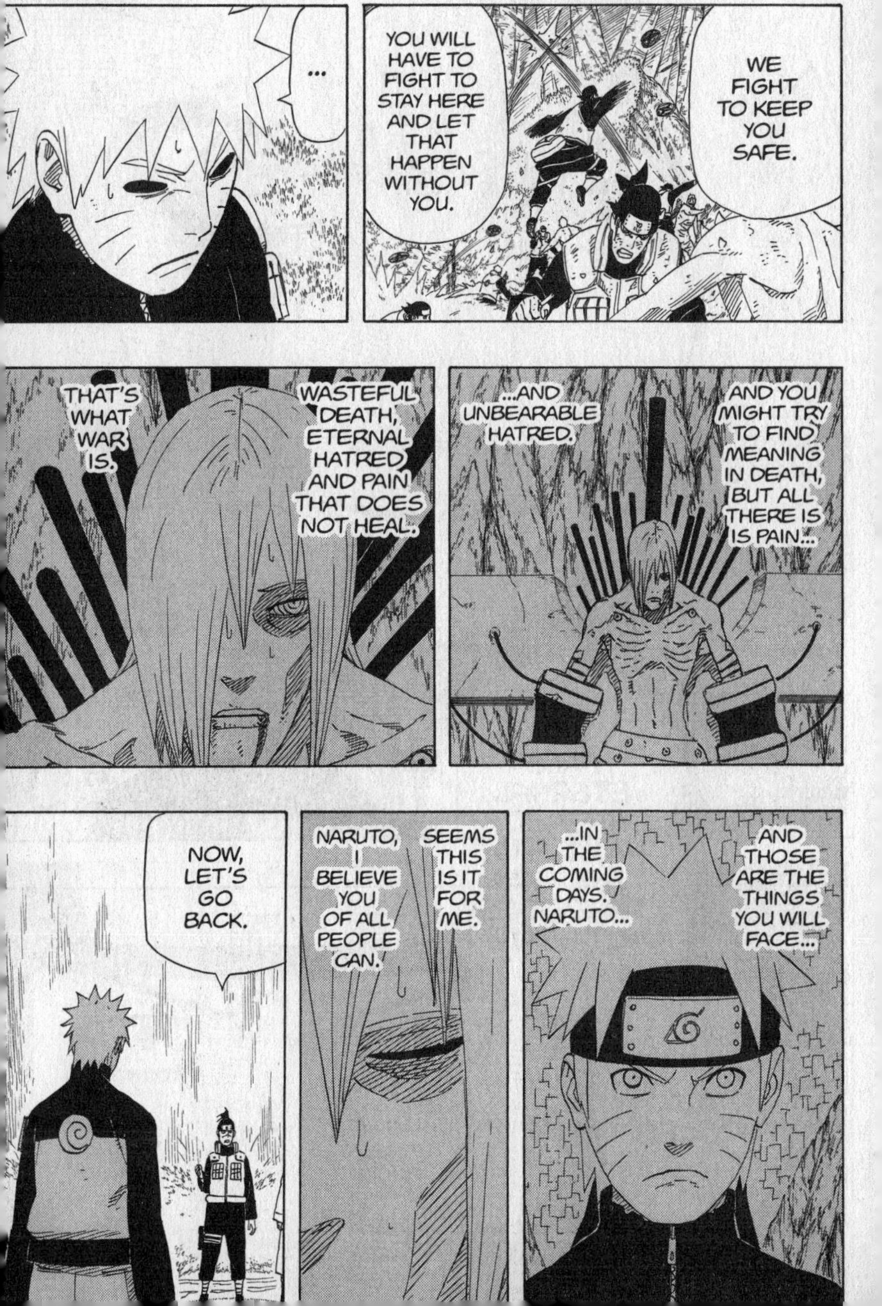
WE FIGHT TO KEEP YOU SAFE.
YOU WILL HAVE TO FIGHT TO STAY HERE AND LET THAT HAPPEN WITHOUT YOU.
...
AND YOU MIGHT TRY TO FIND MEANING IN DEATH, BUT ALL THERE IS IS PAIN...
...AND UNBEARABLE HATRED.
WASTEFUL DEATH, ETERNAL HATRED AND PAIN THAT DOES NOT HEAL.
THAT'S WHAT WAR IS.
AND THOSE ARE THE THINGS YOU WILL FACE...
...IN THE COMING DAYS. NARUTO...
SEEMS THIS IS IT FOR ME.
NARUTO, I BELIEVE YOU OF ALL PEOPLE CAN.
NOW, LET'S GO BACK.

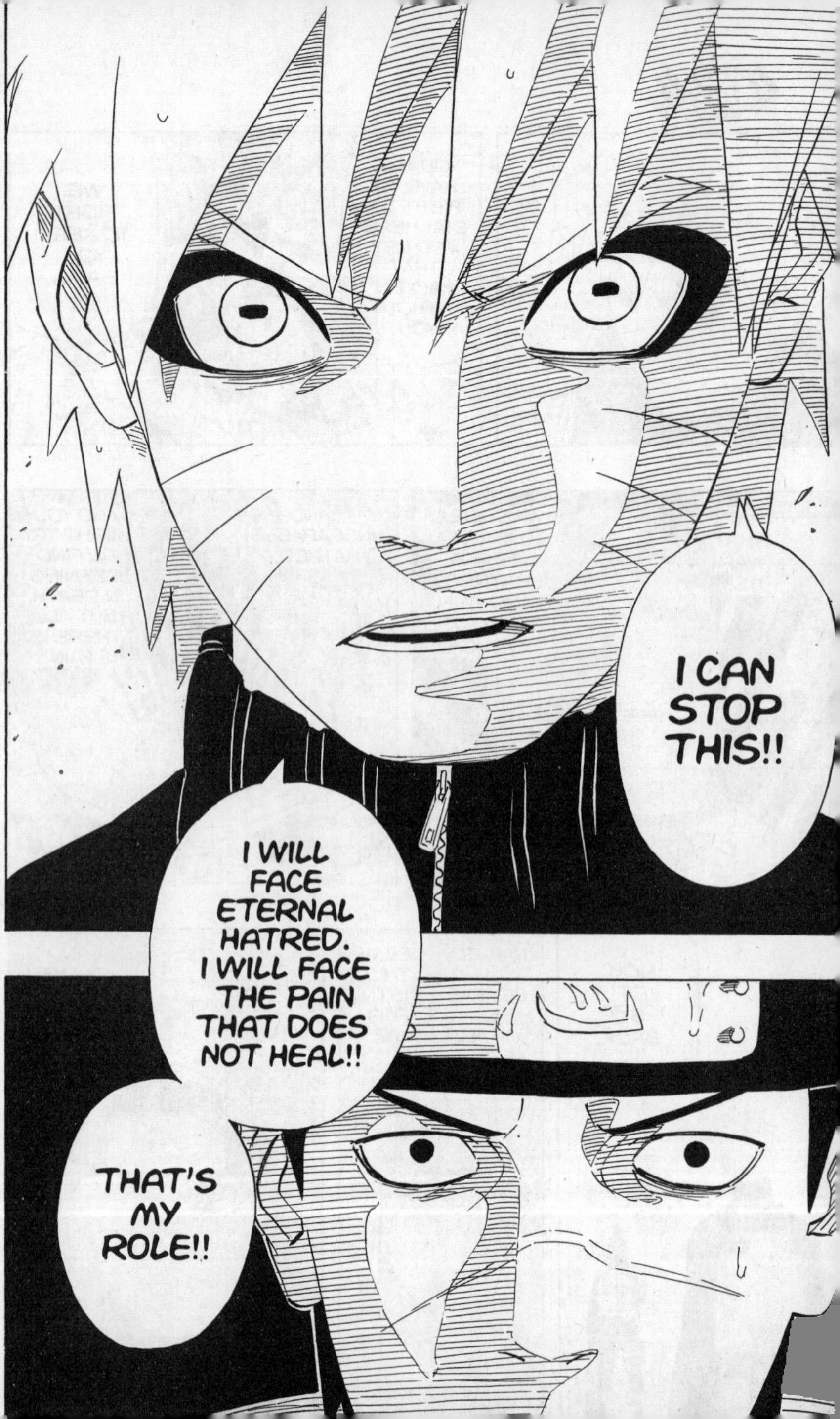
I CAN STOP THIS!!
I WILL FACE ETERNAL HATRED. I WILL FACE THE PAIN THAT DOES NOT HEAL!!
THAT'S MY ROLE!!

READ THIS WAY

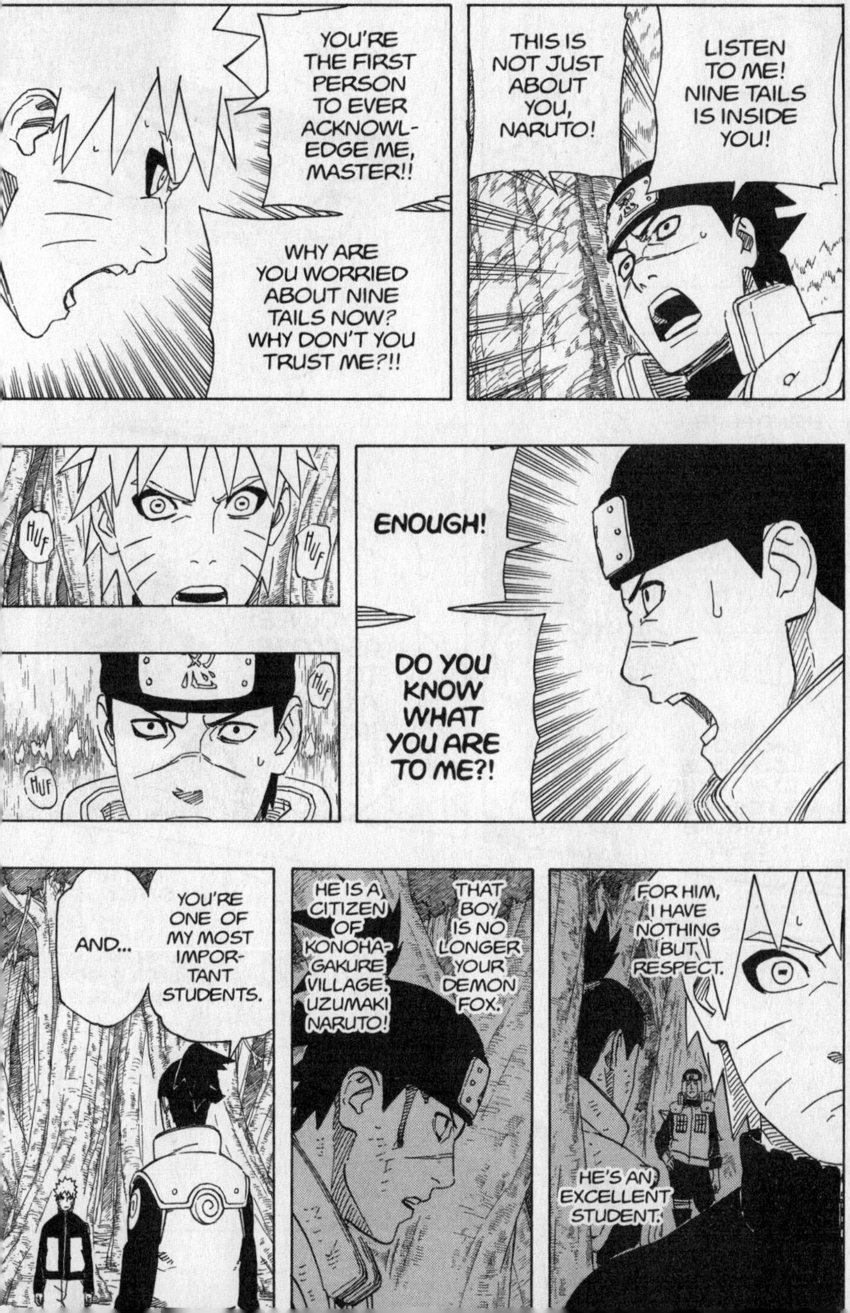
LISTEN TO ME! NINE TAILS IS INSIDE YOU!
THIS IS NOT JUST ABOUT YOU, NARUTO!
YOU'RE THE FIRST PERSON TO EVER ACKNOWL-EDGE ME, MASTER!!
WHY ARE YOU WORRIED ABOUT NINE TAILS NOW? WHY DON'T YOU TRUST ME?!!
ENOUGH!
DO YOU KNOW WHAT YOU ARE TO ME?!
HUF
HUF
HUF
HUF
FOR HIM, I HAVE NOTHING BUT RESPECT.
HE'S AN EXCELLENT STUDENT.
THAT BOY IS NO LONGER YOUR DEMON FOX.
HE IS A CITIZEN OF KONOHA-GAKURE VILLAGE. UZUMAKI NARUTO!
YOU'RE ONE OF MY MOST IMPOR-TANT STUDENTS.
AND...

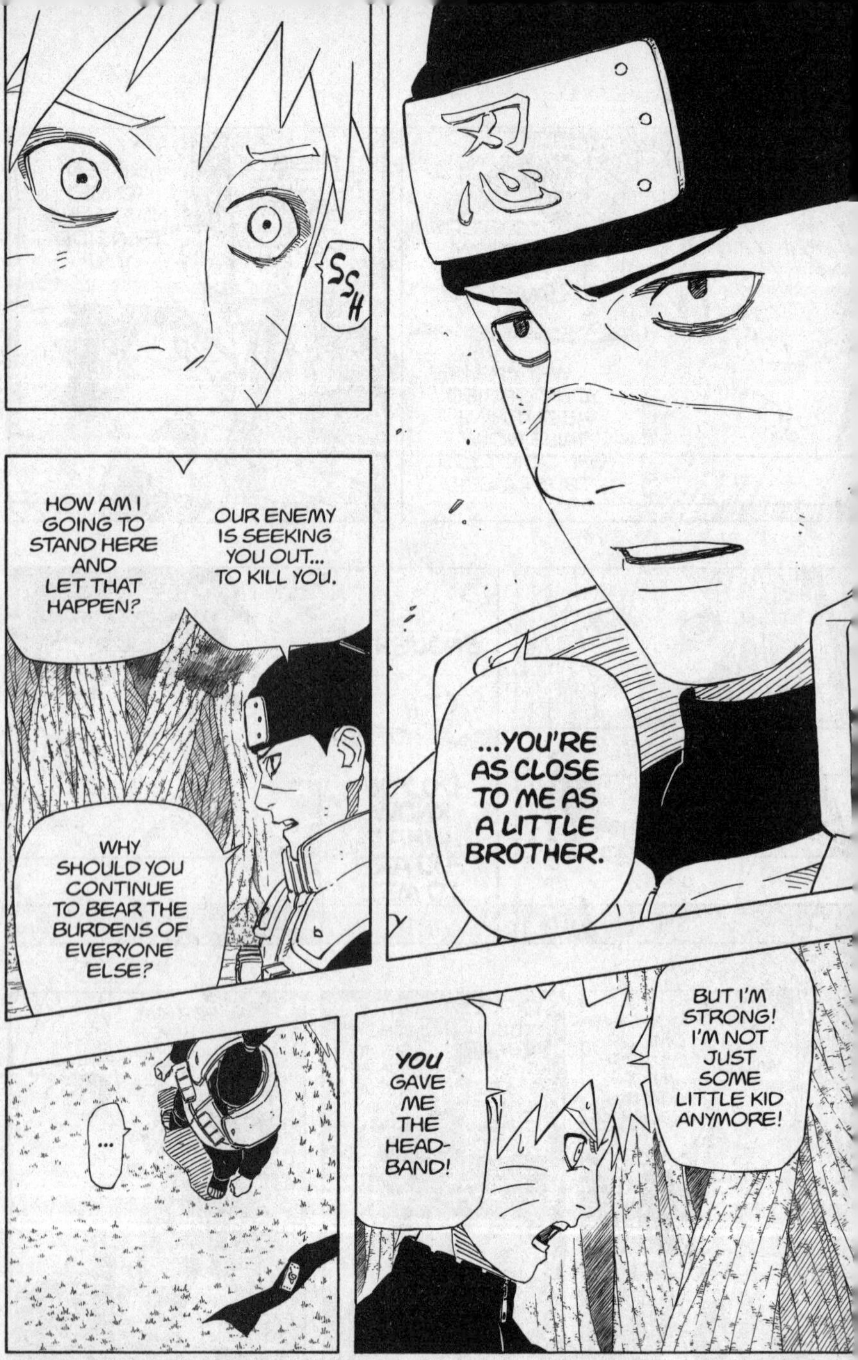
...YOU'RE AS CLOSE TO ME AS A LITTLE BROTHER.
SSH
OUR ENEMY IS SEEKING YOU OUT... TO KILL YOU.
HOW AM I GOING TO STAND HERE AND LET THAT HAPPEN?
WHY SHOULD YOU CONTINUE TO BEAR THE BURDENS OF EVERYONE ELSE?
BUT I'M STRONG! I'M NOT JUST SOME LITTLE KID ANYMORE!
YOU GAVE ME THE HEAD-BAND!
...

READ THIS WAY

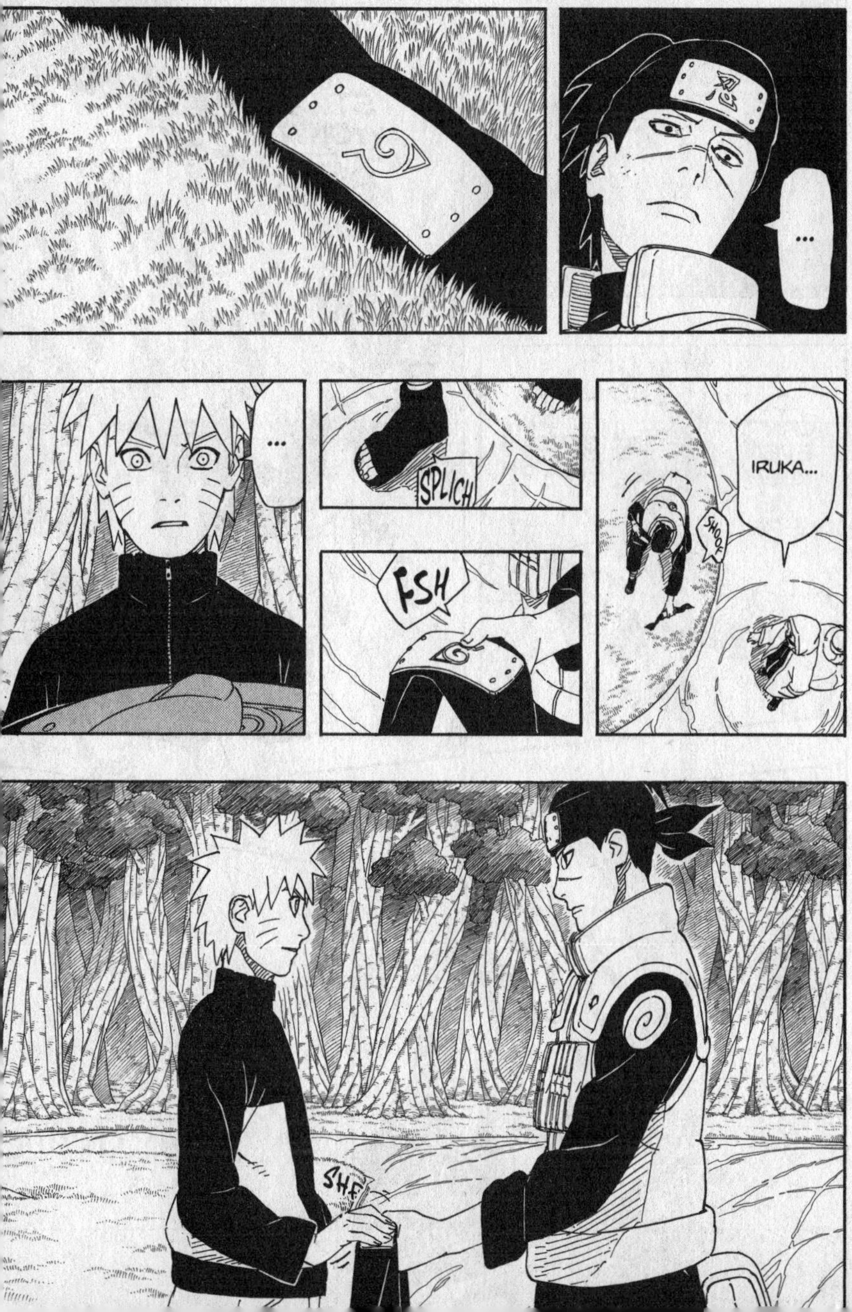
...
IRUKA...
SHOOF
SPLICH
FSH
...
SHF

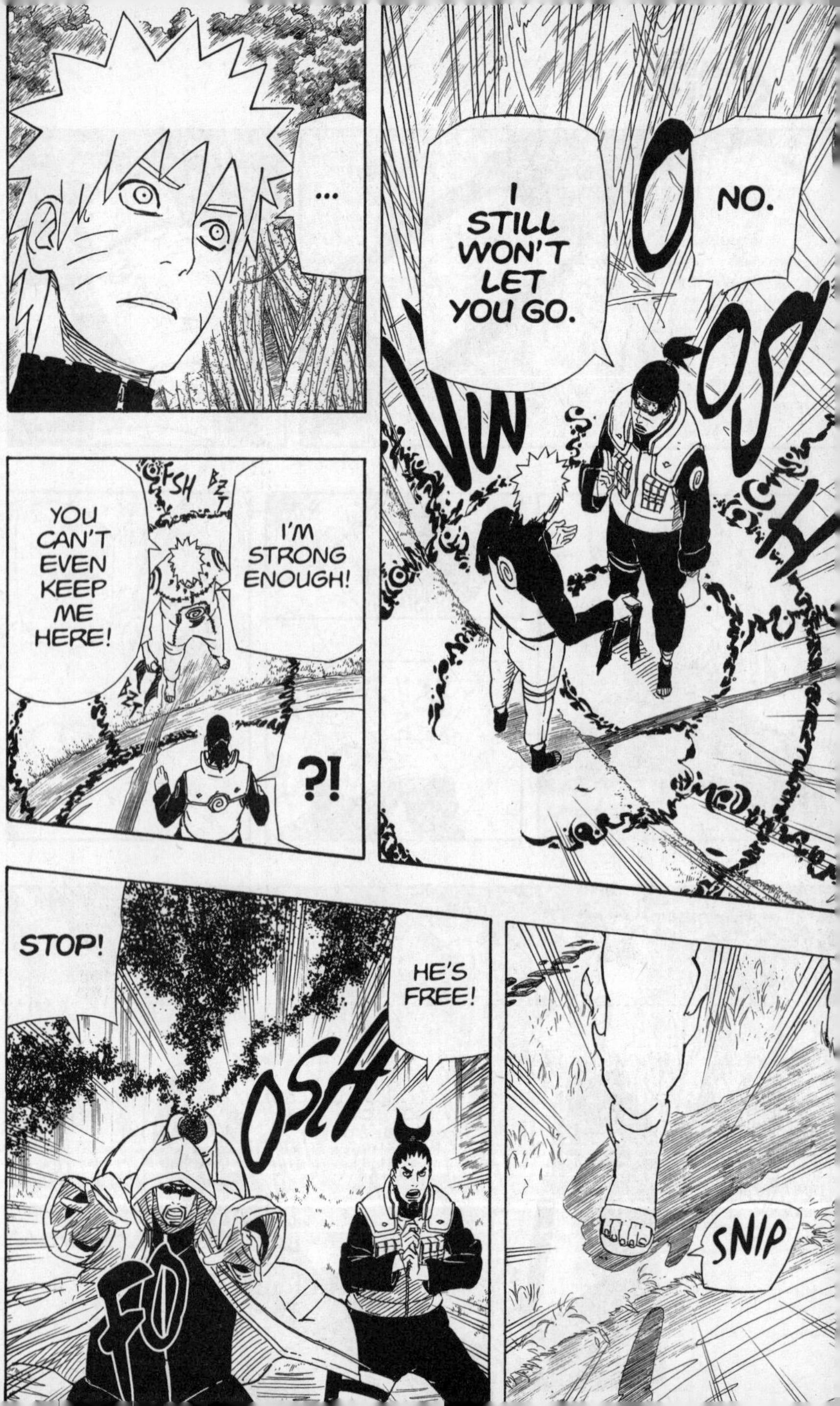
NO.
I STILL WON'T LET YOU GO.
VWOOSH
...
FSH
BZT
I'M STRONG ENOUGH!
YOU CAN'T EVEN KEEP ME HERE!
BZT
?!
SNIP
HE'S FREE!
OSH
STOP!

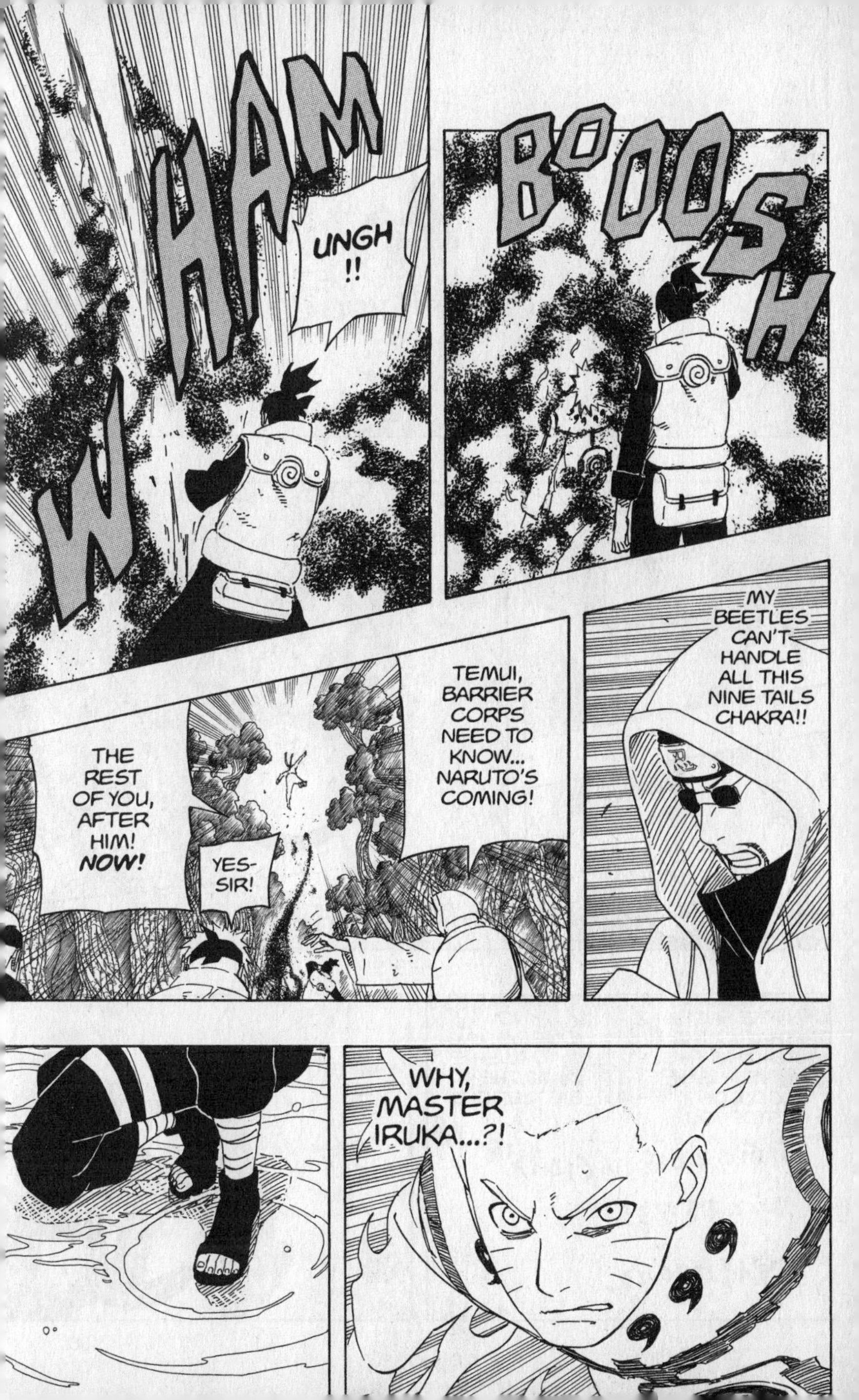
BOOOSH
WHAM
UNGH!!
MY BEETLES CAN'T HANDLE ALL THIS NINE TAILS CHAKRA!!
TEMUI, BARRIER CORPS NEED TO KNOW... NARUTO'S COMING!
THE REST OF YOU, AFTER HIM! NOW!
YES-SIR!
WHY, MASTER IRUKA...?!

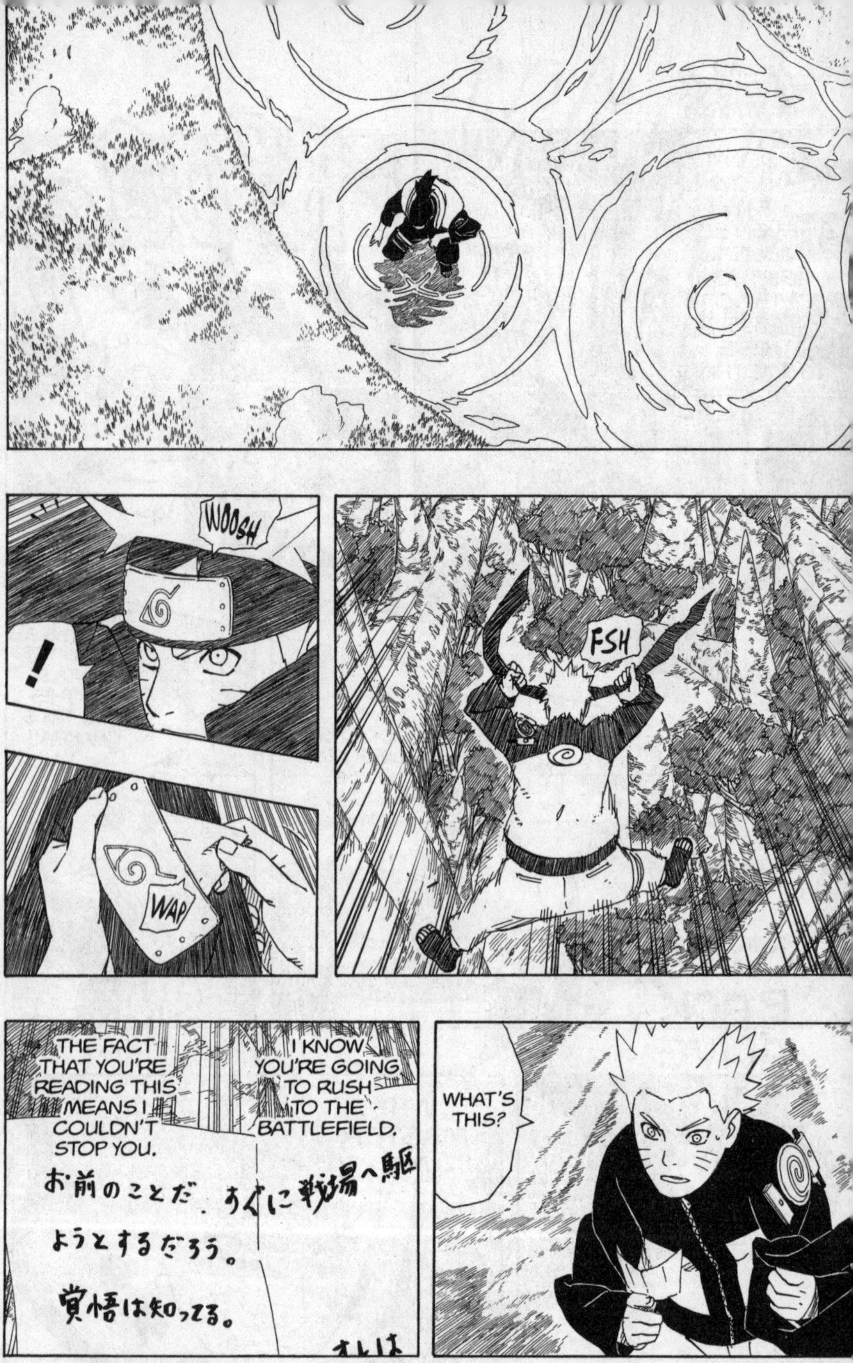
FSH
WOOSH
!
WAP
WHAT'S THIS?
I KNOW YOU'RE GOING TO RUSH TO THE BATTLEFIELD.
THE FACT THAT YOU'RE READING THIS MEANS I COULDN'T STOP YOU.
お前のことだ．すぐに戦場へ駆
ようとするだろう。
覚悟は知ってる。
オレは

READ THIS WAY

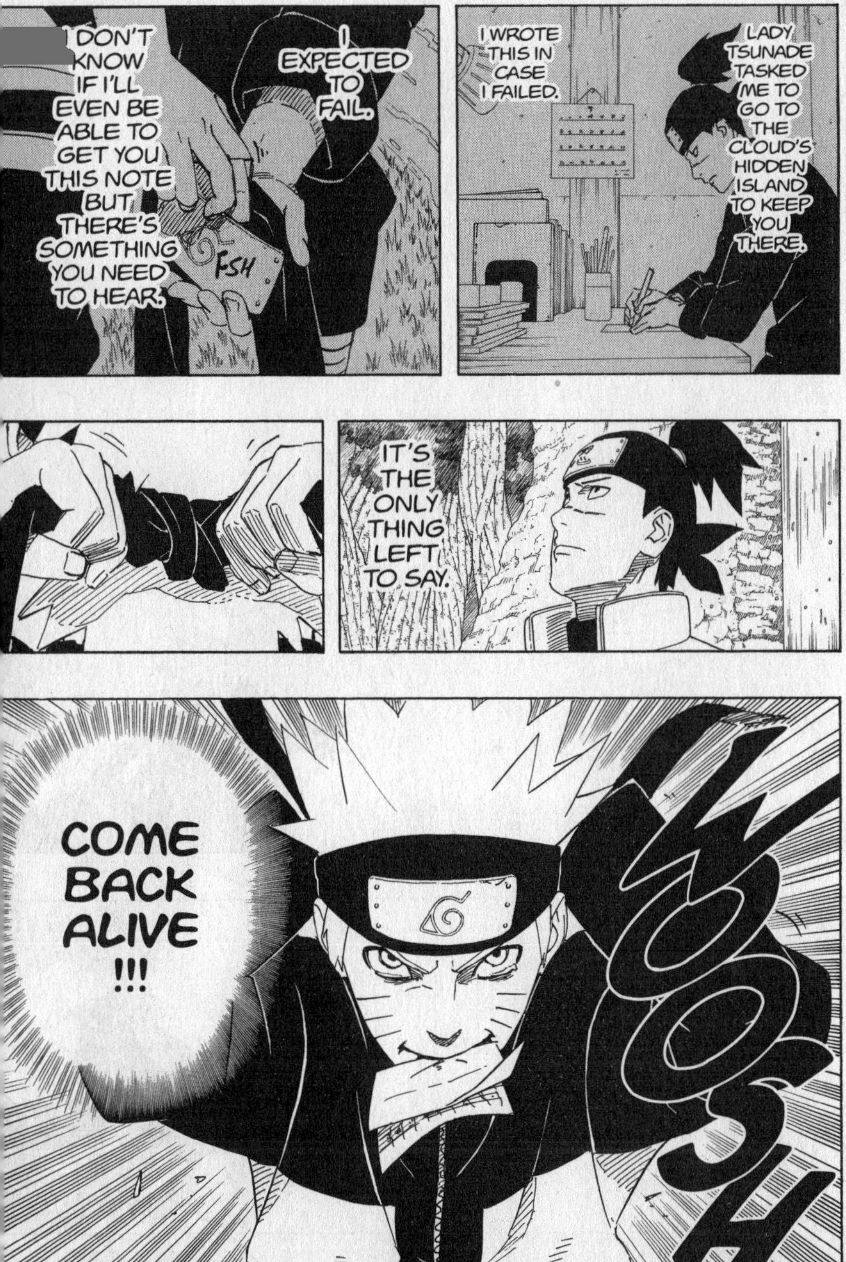

LADY TSUNADE TASKED ME TO GO TO THE CLOUD'S HIDDEN ISLAND TO KEEP YOU THERE.
I WROTE THIS IN CASE I FAILED.
I EXPECTED TO FAIL.
I DON'T KNOW IF I'LL EVEN BE ABLE TO GET YOU THIS NOTE BUT THERE'S SOMETHING YOU NEED TO HEAR.
FSH
IT'S THE ONLY THING LEFT TO SAY.
WHOOSH
COME BACK ALIVE !!!

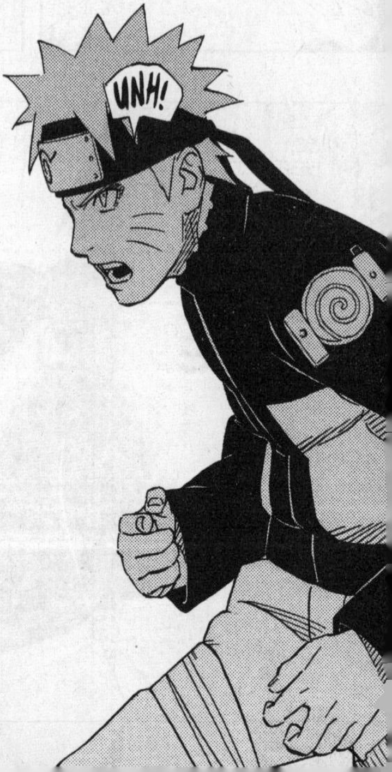
UNH!

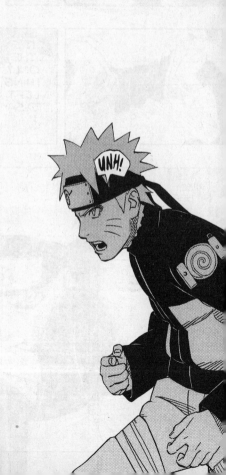

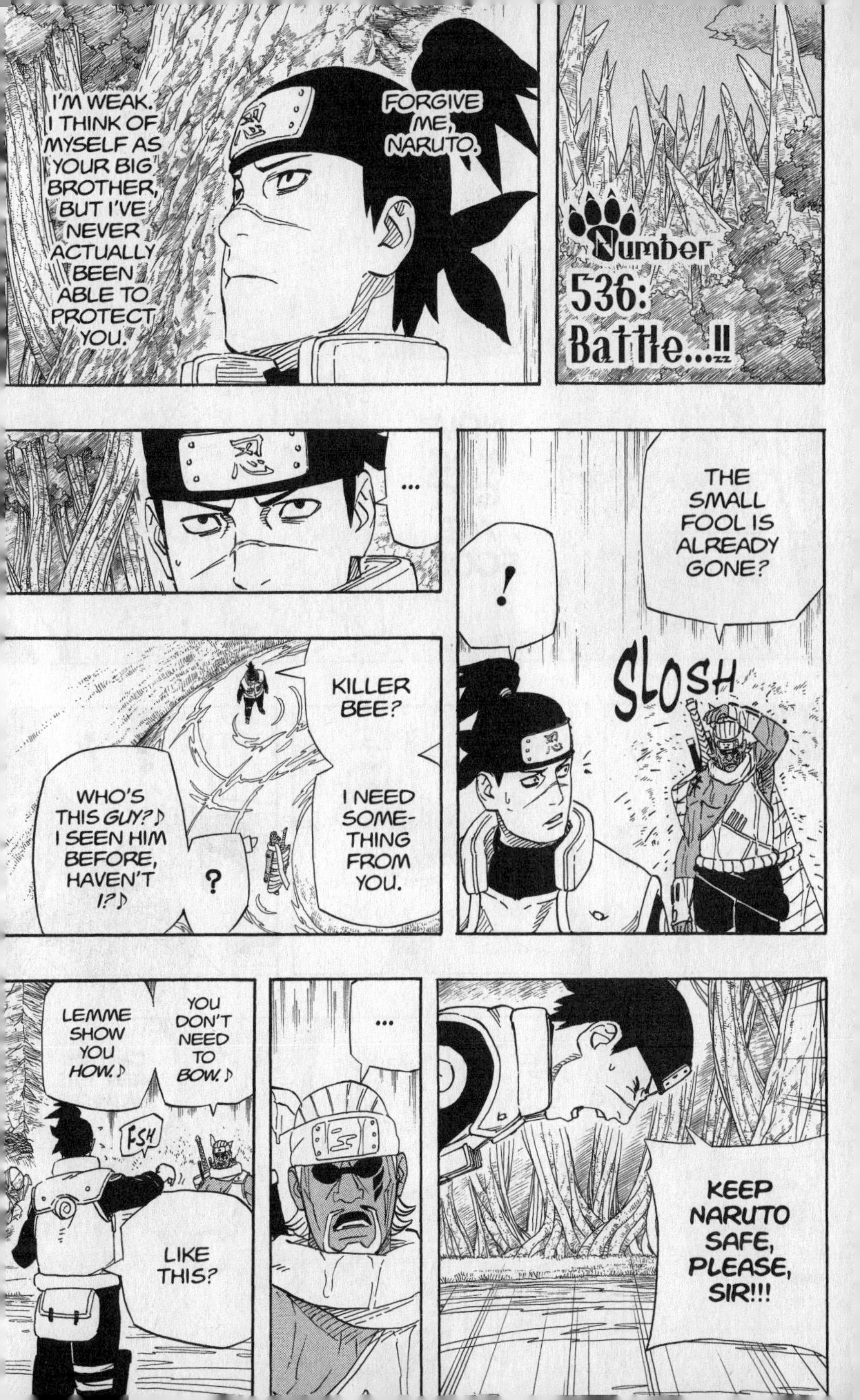
Number 536: Battle...!!
FORGIVE ME, NARUTO.
I'M WEAK. I THINK OF MYSELF AS YOUR BIG BROTHER, BUT I'VE NEVER ACTUALLY BEEN ABLE TO PROTECT YOU.
THE SMALL FOOL IS ALREADY GONE?
!
SLOSH
...
KILLER BEE?
I NEED SOMETHING FROM YOU.
WHO'S THIS GUY?♪ I SEEN HIM BEFORE, HAVEN'T I?♪
?
KEEP NARUTO SAFE, PLEASE, SIR!!!
...
YOU DON'T NEED TO BOW.♪
LEMME SHOW YOU HOW.♪
FSH
LIKE THIS?

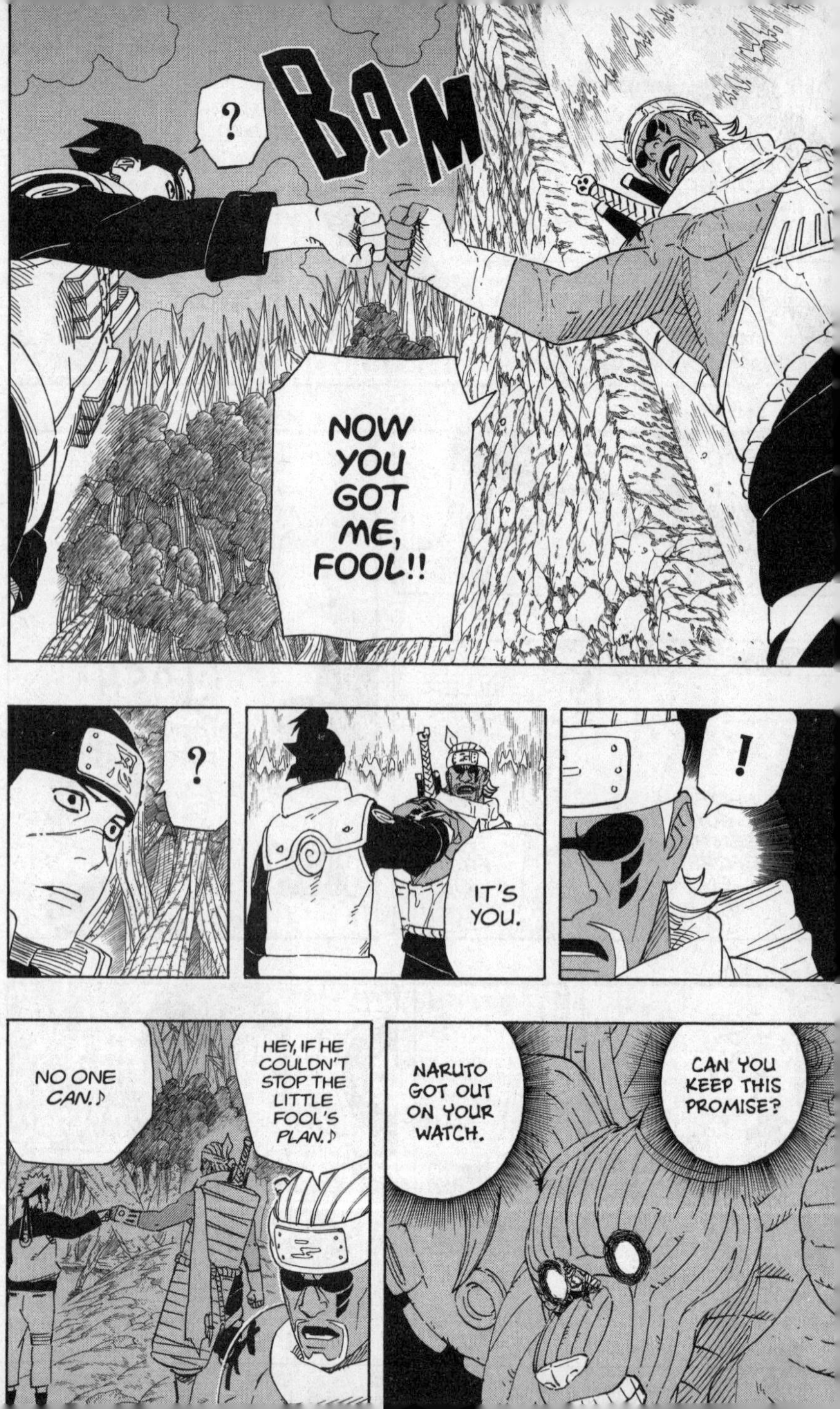
BAM
?
NOW YOU GOT ME, FOOL!!
!
IT'S YOU.
?
CAN YOU KEEP THIS PROMISE?
NARUTO GOT OUT ON YOUR WATCH.
HEY, IF HE COULDN'T STOP THE LITTLE FOOL'S PLAN.♪
NO ONE CAN.♪

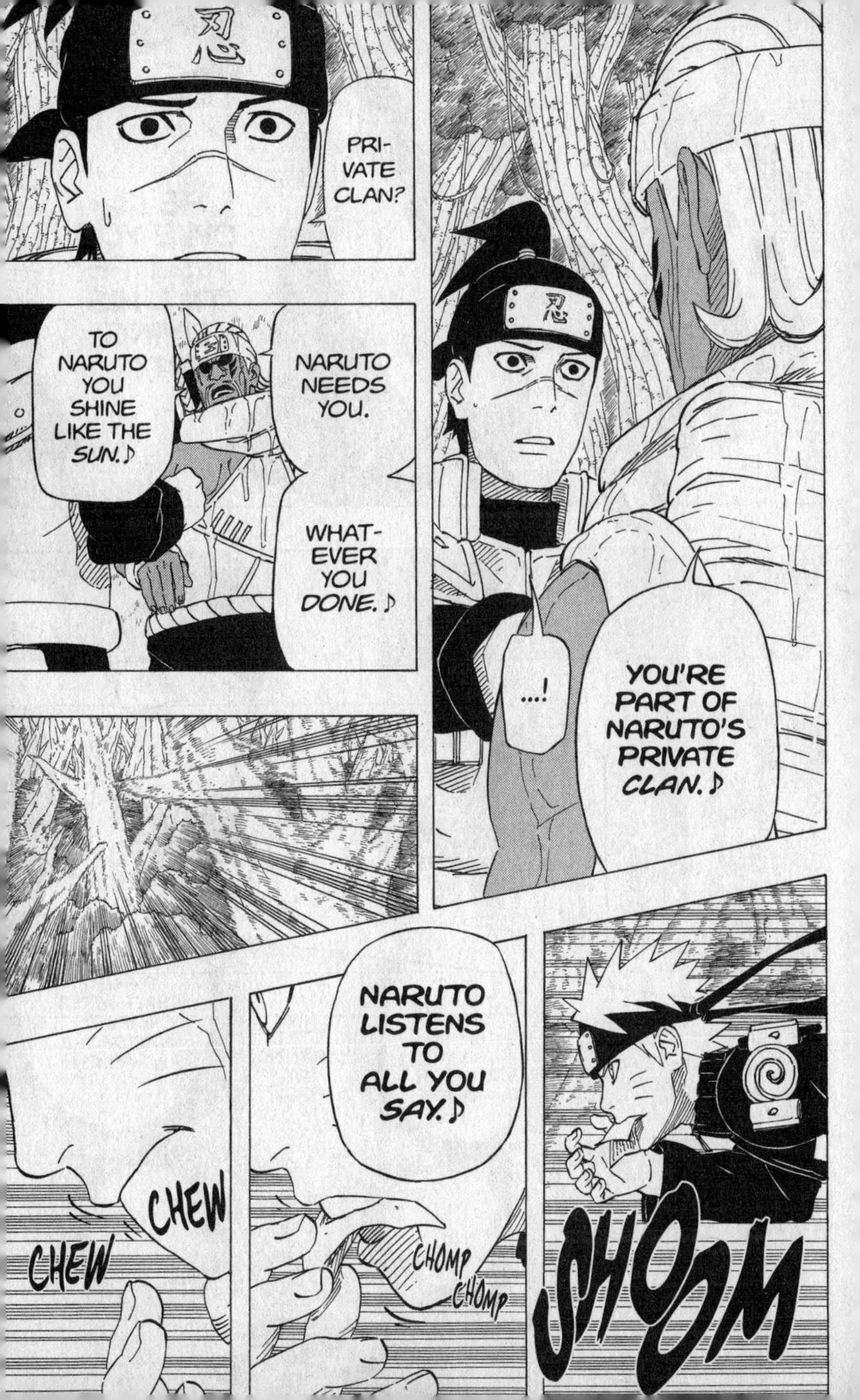

YOU'RE PART OF NARUTO'S PRIVATE CLAN.♪
...!
PRIVATE CLAN?
NARUTO NEEDS YOU.
WHATEVER YOU DONE.♪
TO NARUTO YOU SHINE LIKE THE SUN.♪
SHOOM
NARUTO LISTENS TO ALL YOU SAY.♪
CHOMP CHOMP
CHEW
CHEW

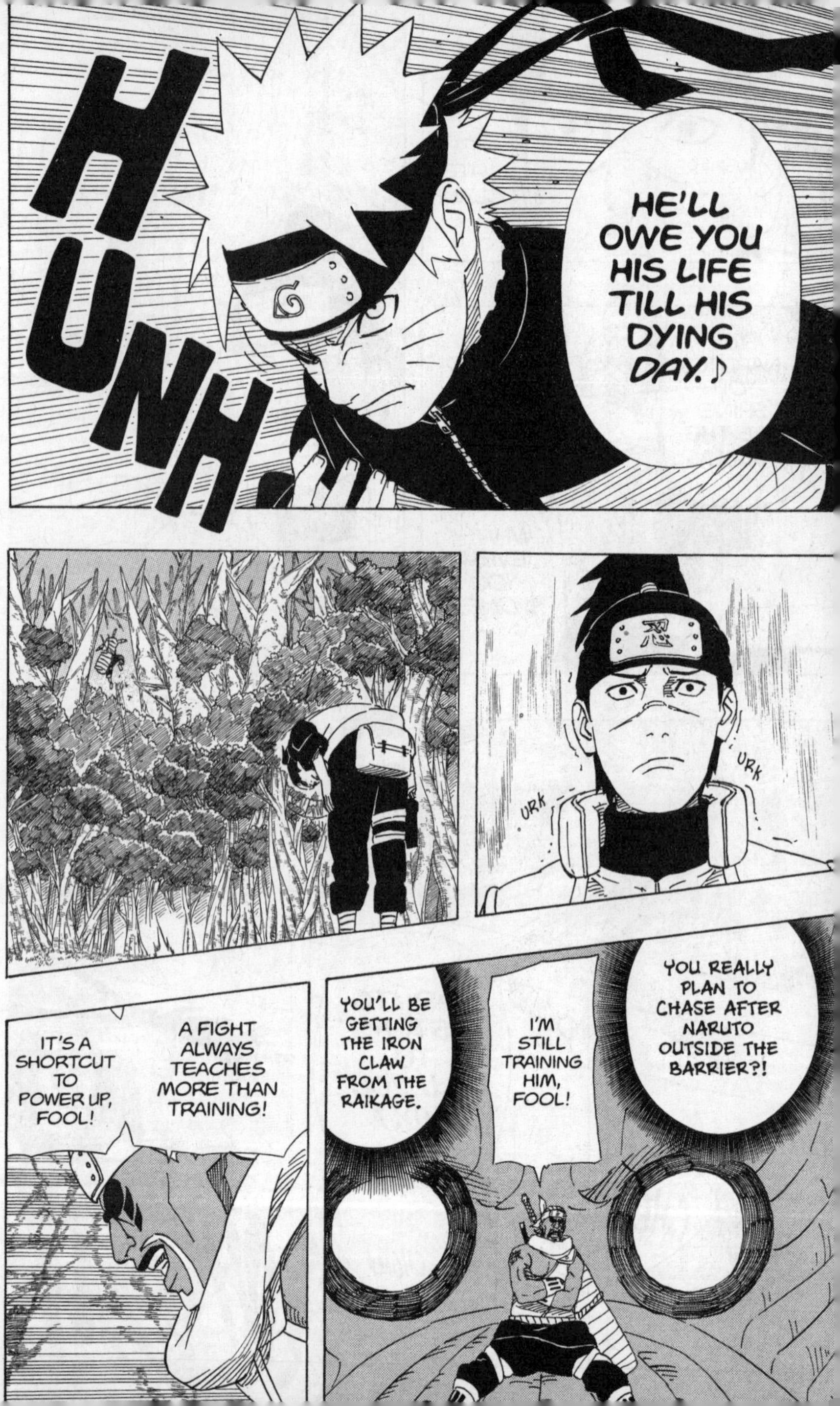
HE'LL OWE YOU HIS LIFE TILL HIS DYING DAY.♪
HUNH...
URK
URK
YOU REALLY PLAN TO CHASE AFTER NARUTO OUTSIDE THE BARRIER?!
I'M STILL TRAINING HIM, FOOL!
YOU'LL BE GETTING THE IRON CLAW FROM THE RAIKAGE.
A FIGHT ALWAYS TEACHES MORE THAN TRAINING!
IT'S A SHORTCUT TO POWER UP, FOOL!

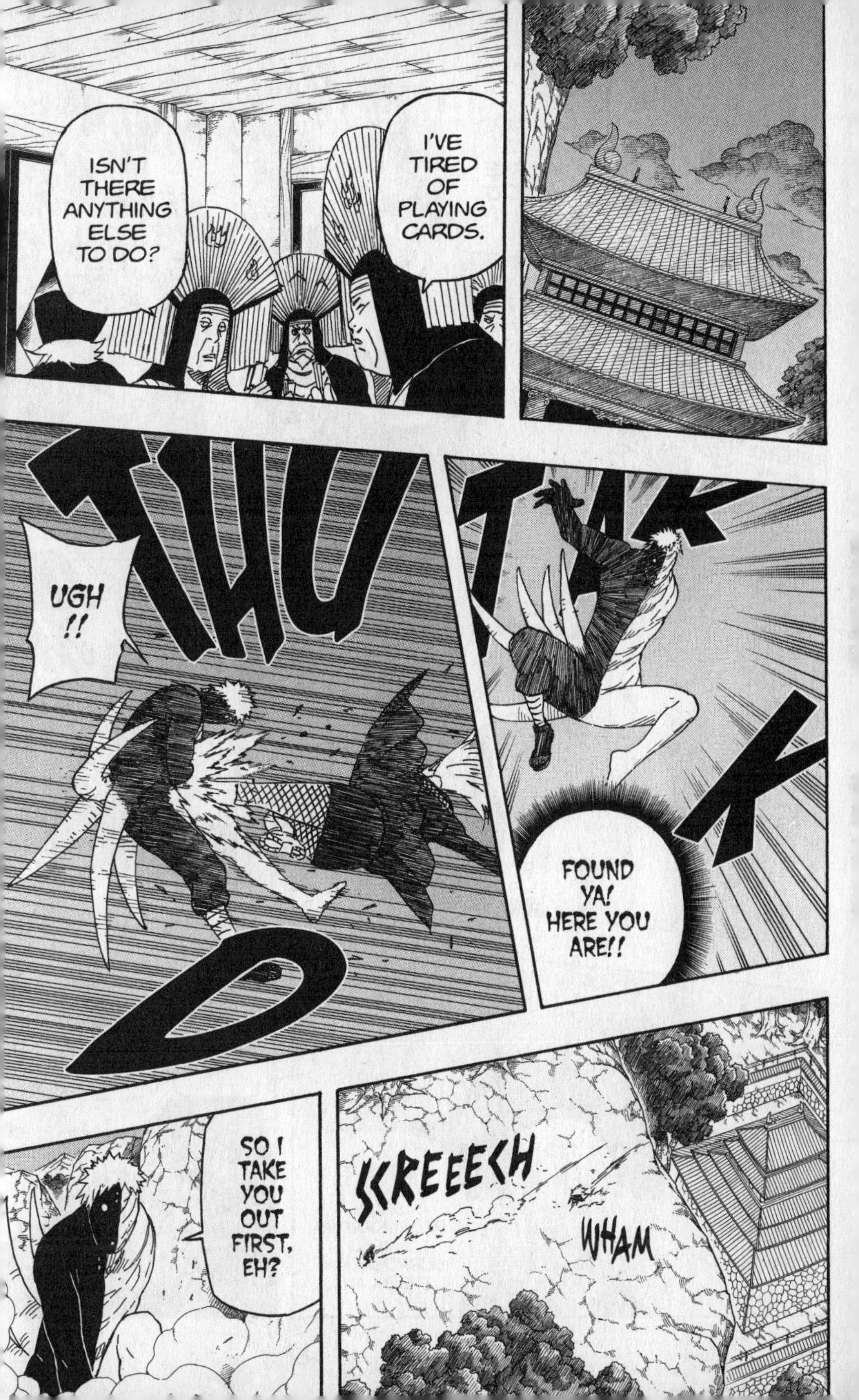

I'VE TIRED OF PLAYING CARDS.
ISN'T THERE ANYTHING ELSE TO DO?
TAKK
FOUND YA! HERE YOU ARE!!
THUD
UGH!!
SCREEECH
WHAM
SO I TAKE YOU OUT FIRST, EH?

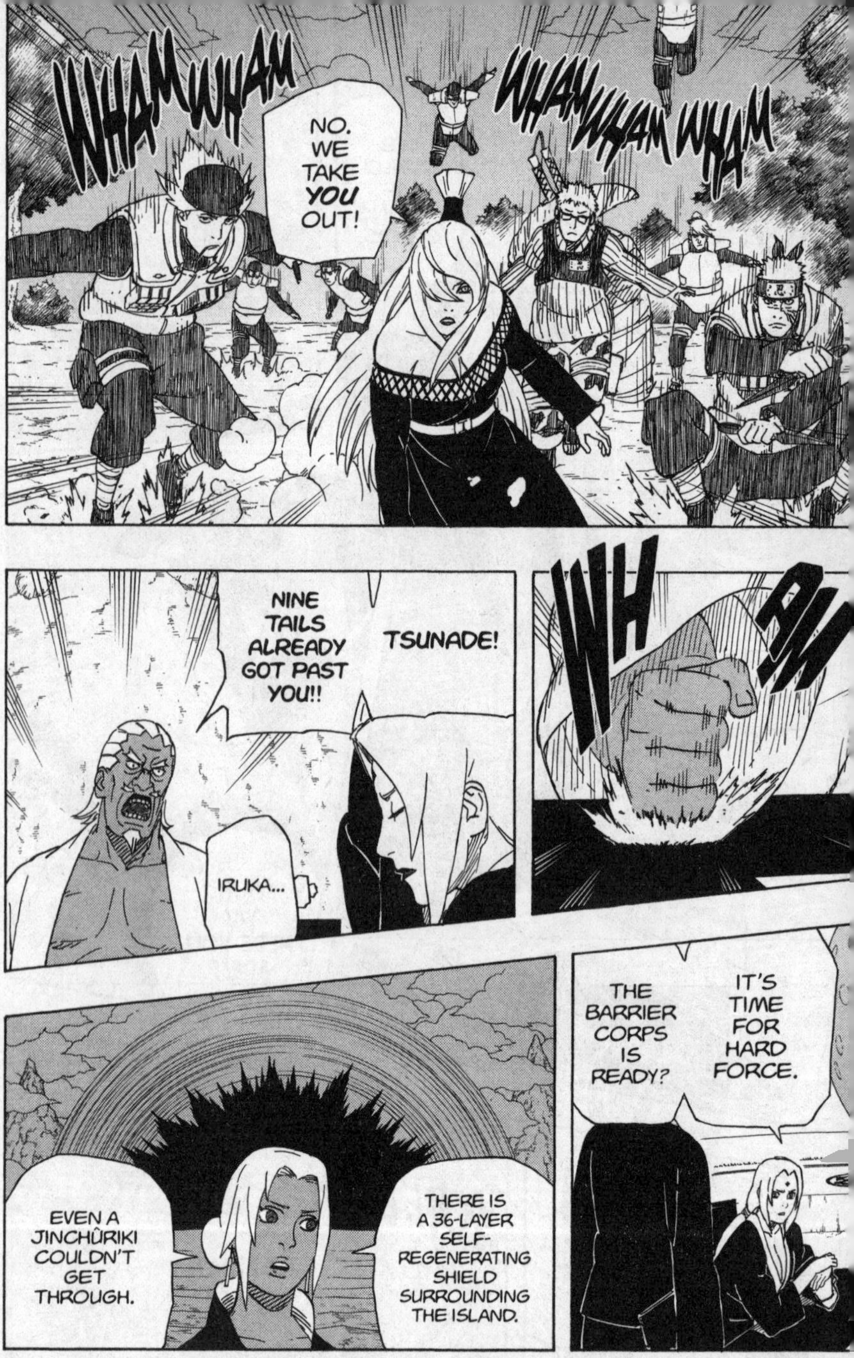
WHAMWHAMWHAM
NO. WE TAKE YOU OUT!
WHAMWHAM
WHAM
TSUNADE!
NINE TAILS ALREADY GOT PAST YOU!!
IRUKA...
IT'S TIME FOR HARD FORCE.
THE BARRIER CORPS IS READY?
THERE IS A 36-LAYER SELF-REGENERATING SHIELD SURROUNDING THE ISLAND.
EVEN A JINCHŪRIKI COULDN'T GET THROUGH.

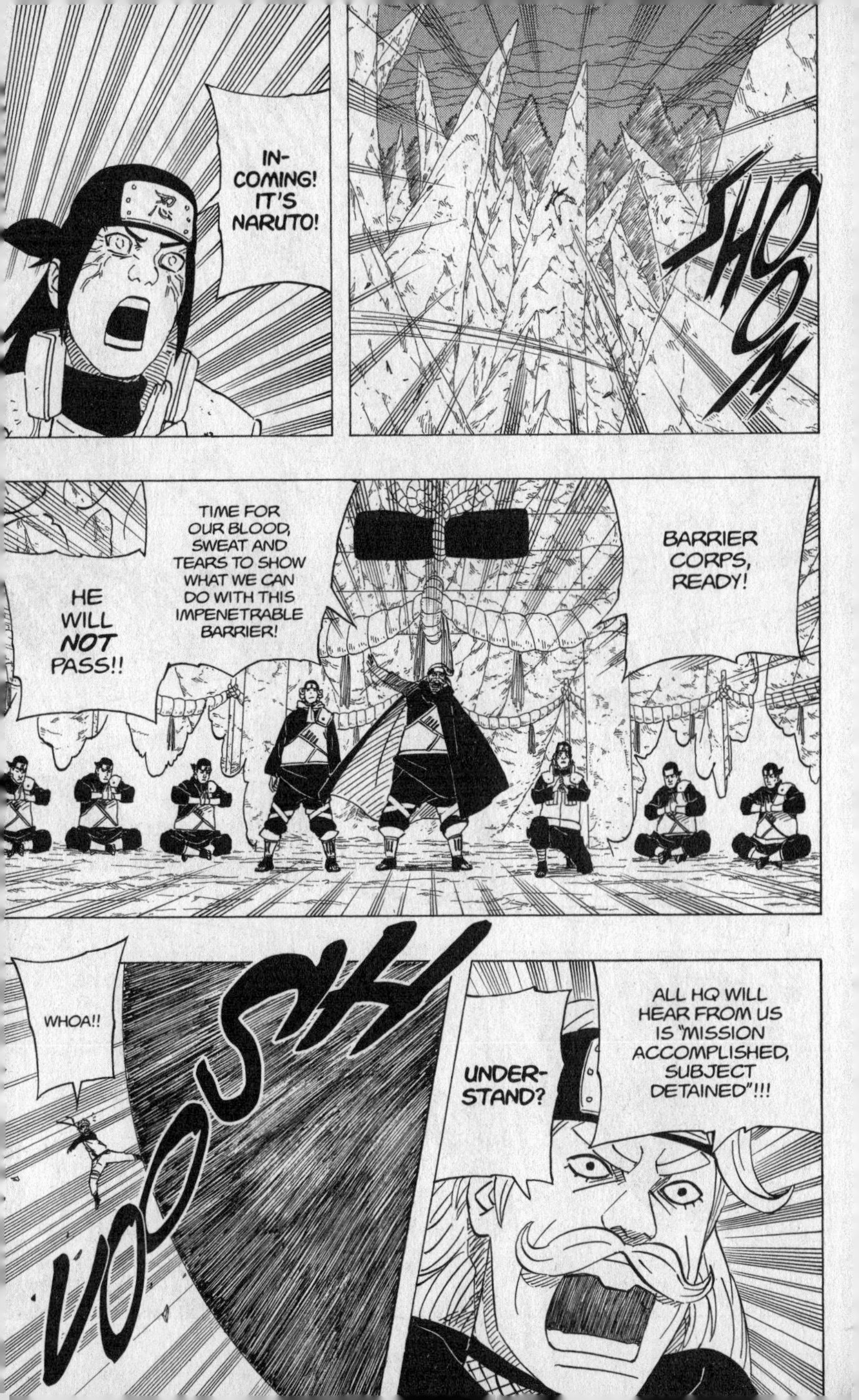
SHOOM
IN-COMING! IT'S NARUTO!
BARRIER CORPS, READY!
TIME FOR OUR BLOOD, SWEAT AND TEARS TO SHOW WHAT WE CAN DO WITH THIS IMPENETRABLE BARRIER!
HE WILL NOT PASS!!
ALL HQ WILL HEAR FROM US IS "MISSION ACCOMPLISHED, SUBJECT DETAINED"!!!
UNDER-STAND?
WHOA!!
VOOSH

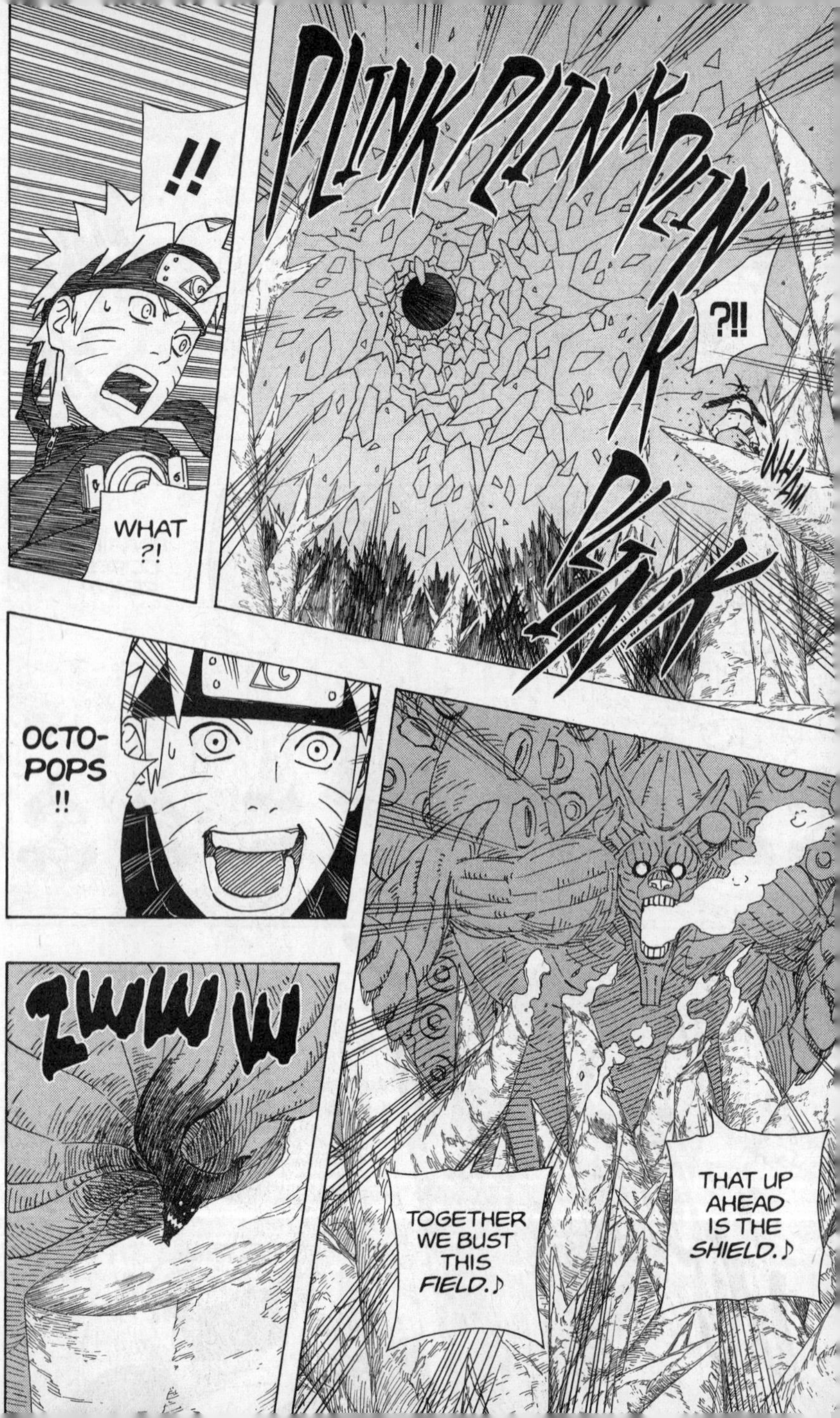
PLINK PLINK PLINK PLINK
?!!
WHAM
!!
WHAT ?!
THAT UP AHEAD IS THE SHIELD.♪
TOGETHER WE BUST THIS FIELD.♪
OCTO-POPS !!
ZWWW

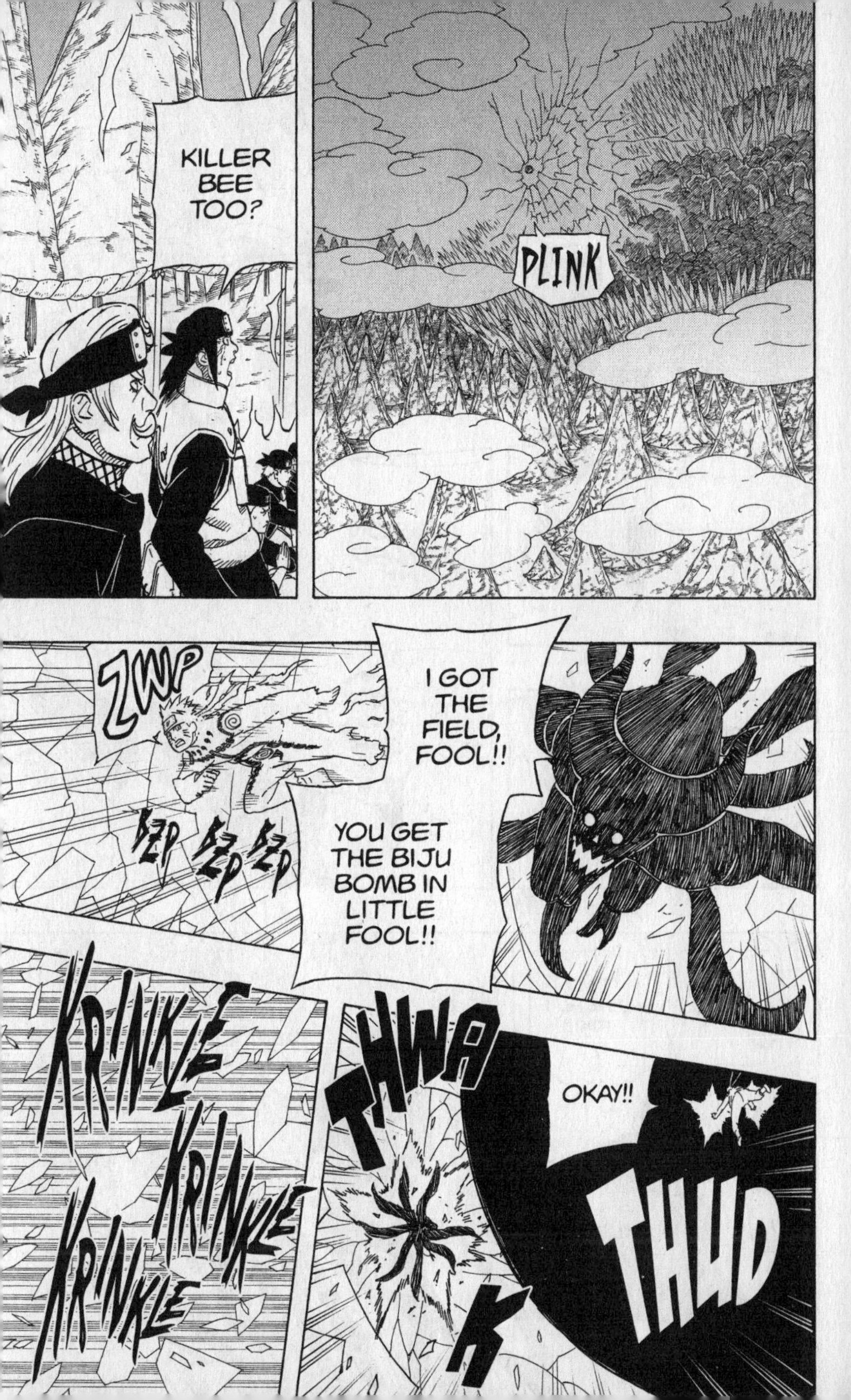
PLINK
KILLER BEE TOO?
I GOT THE FIELD, FOOL!!
YOU GET THE BIJU BOMB IN LITTLE FOOL!!
ZWP
BZP BZP BZP
OKAY!!
THUD
THWAK
KRINKLE KRINKLE KRINKLE

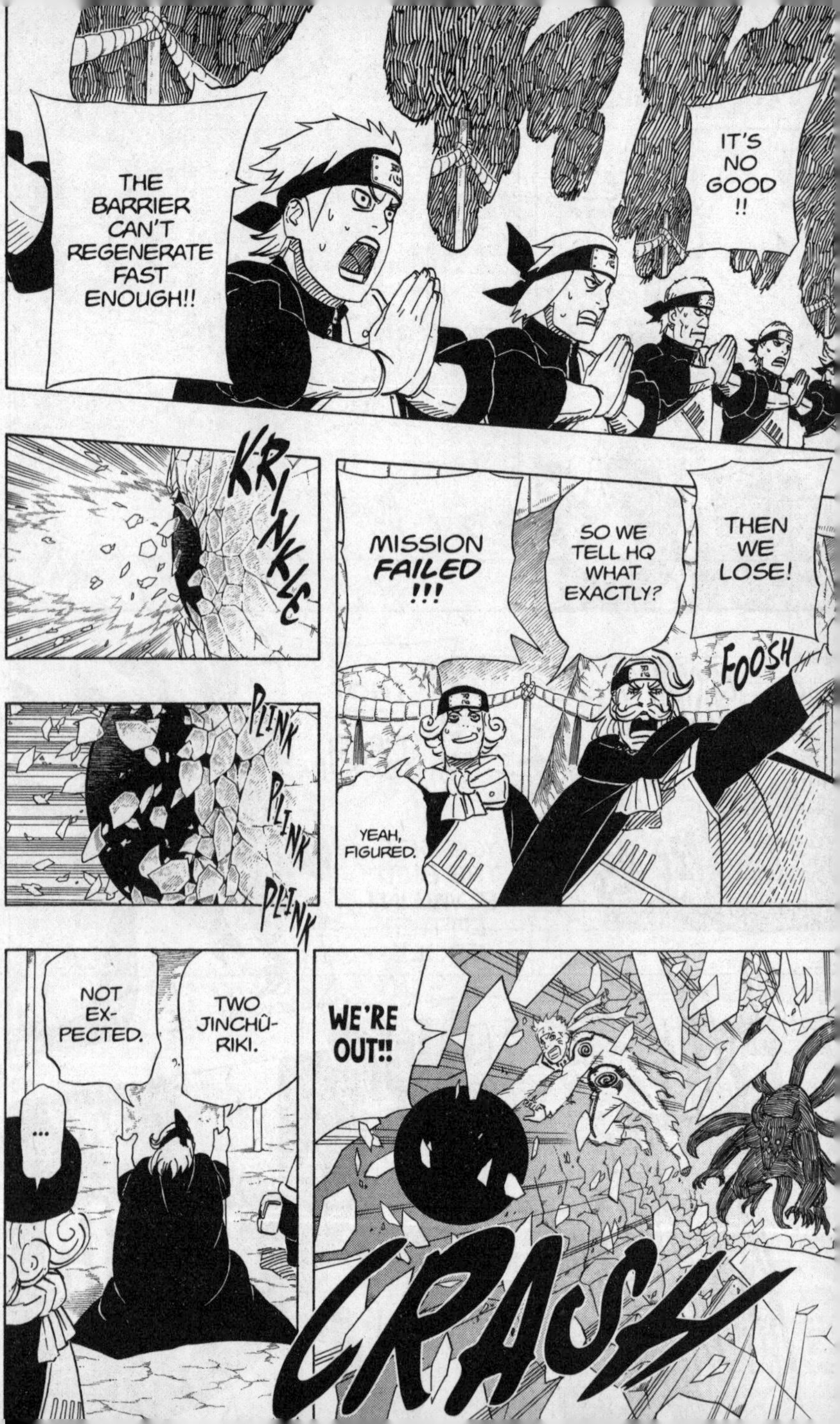
IT'S NO GOOD !!
THE BARRIER CAN'T REGENERATE FAST ENOUGH!!
THEN WE LOSE!
SO WE TELL HQ WHAT EXACTLY?
MISSION FAILED !!!
FOOSH
YEAH, FIGURED.
KRINKLE
PLINK
PLINK
PLINK
WE'RE OUT!!
CRASH
TWO JINCHÛ-RIKI.
NOT EX-PECTED.
...

READ THIS WAY

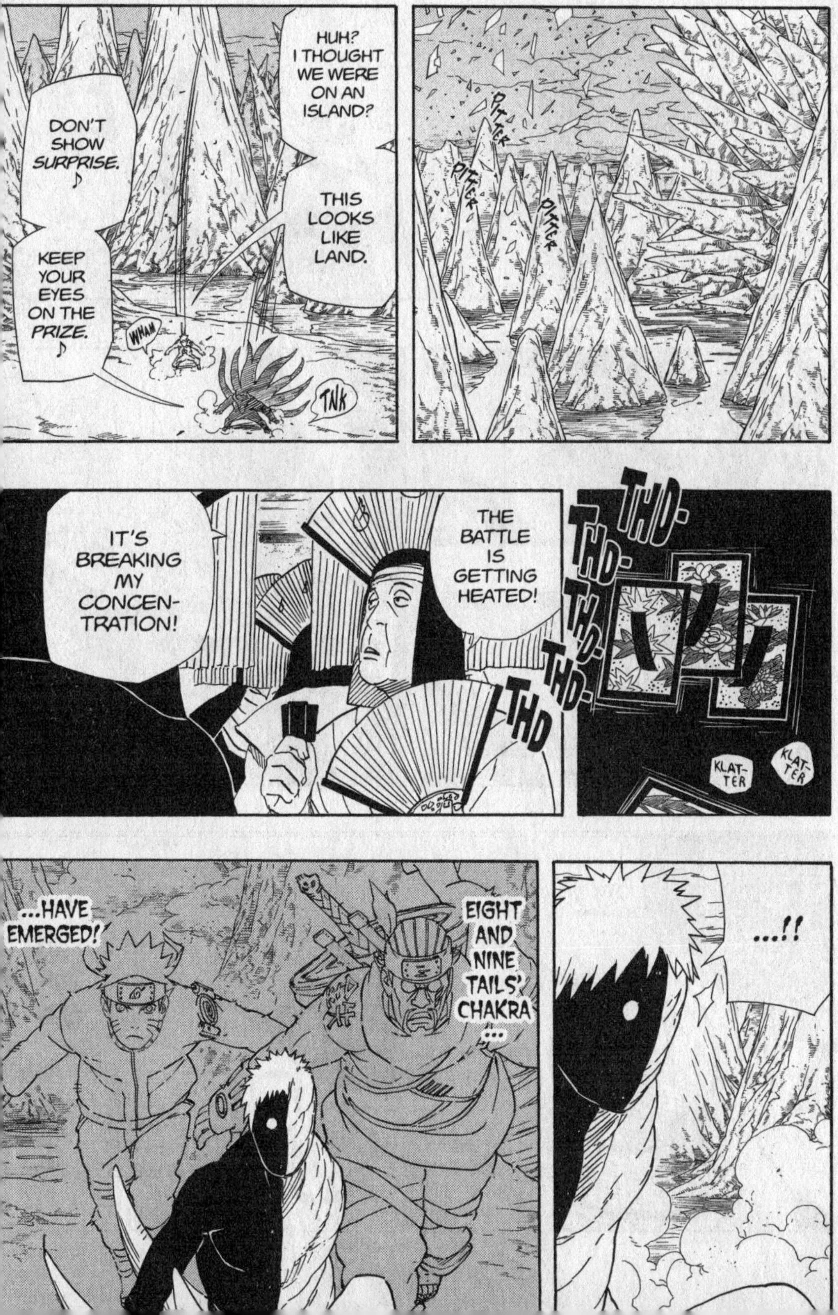
PITTER
PITTER
PITTER
HUH? I THOUGHT WE WERE ON AN ISLAND?
THIS LOOKS LIKE LAND.
DON'T SHOW SURPRISE. ♪
KEEP YOUR EYES ON THE PRIZE. ♪
WHAM
TNK
THD- THD- THD- THD- THD
KLATTER
KLATTER
THE BATTLE IS GETTING HEATED!
IT'S BREAKING MY CONCENTRATION!
...!!
EIGHT AND NINE TAILS' CHAKRA...
...HAVE EMERGED!

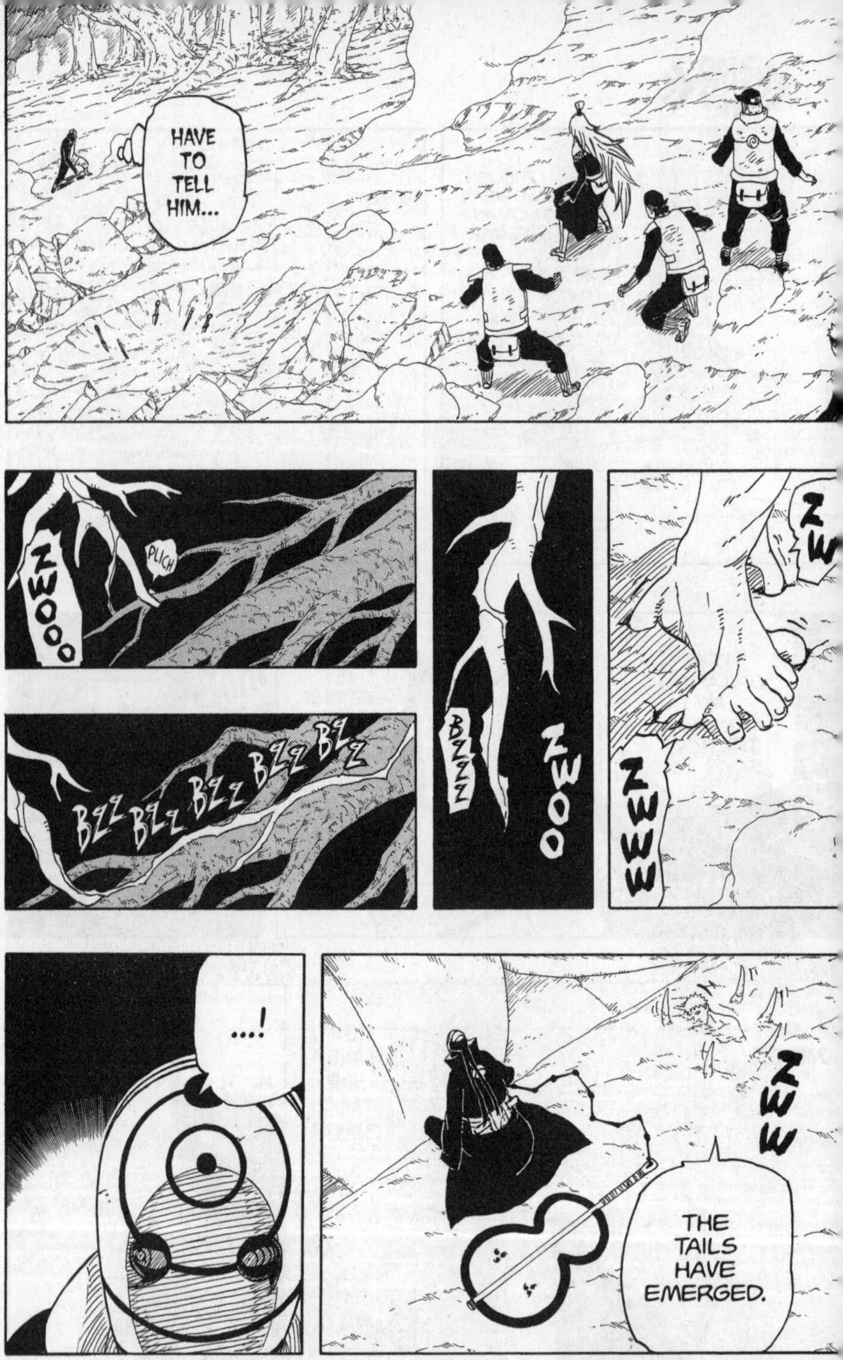
HAVE TO TELL HIM...
ZW
ZWWW
ZWOO
BZZZZ
ZWOOO
PLICH
BZZ BZZ BZZ BZZ BZZ BZZ
ZWW
THE TAILS HAVE EMERGED.
...!

READ THIS WAY

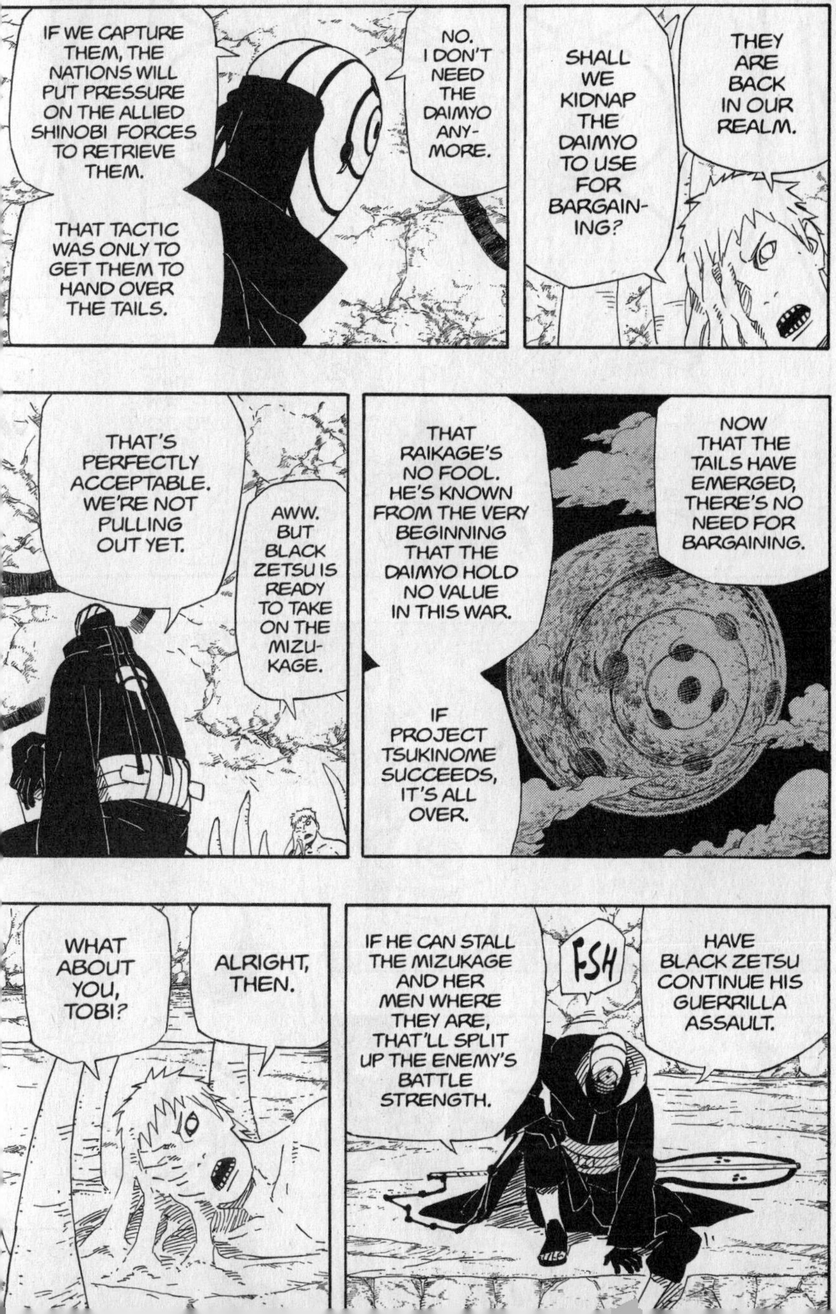
THEY ARE BACK IN OUR REALM.
SHALL WE KIDNAP THE DAIMYO TO USE FOR BARGAINING?
NO. I DON'T NEED THE DAIMYO ANYMORE.
IF WE CAPTURE THEM, THE NATIONS WILL PUT PRESSURE ON THE ALLIED SHINOBI FORCES TO RETRIEVE THEM.
THAT TACTIC WAS ONLY TO GET THEM TO HAND OVER THE TAILS.
NOW THAT THE TAILS HAVE EMERGED, THERE'S NO NEED FOR BARGAINING.
THAT RAIKAGE'S NO FOOL. HE'S KNOWN FROM THE VERY BEGINNING THAT THE DAIMYO HOLD NO VALUE IN THIS WAR.
IF PROJECT TSUKINOME SUCCEEDS, IT'S ALL OVER.
AWW. BUT BLACK ZETSU IS READY TO TAKE ON THE MIZUKAGE.
THAT'S PERFECTLY ACCEPTABLE. WE'RE NOT PULLING OUT YET.
HAVE BLACK ZETSU CONTINUE HIS GUERRILLA ASSAULT.
FSH
IF HE CAN STALL THE MIZUKAGE AND HER MEN WHERE THEY ARE, THAT'LL SPLIT UP THE ENEMY'S BATTLE STRENGTH.
ALRIGHT, THEN.
WHAT ABOUT YOU, TOBI?

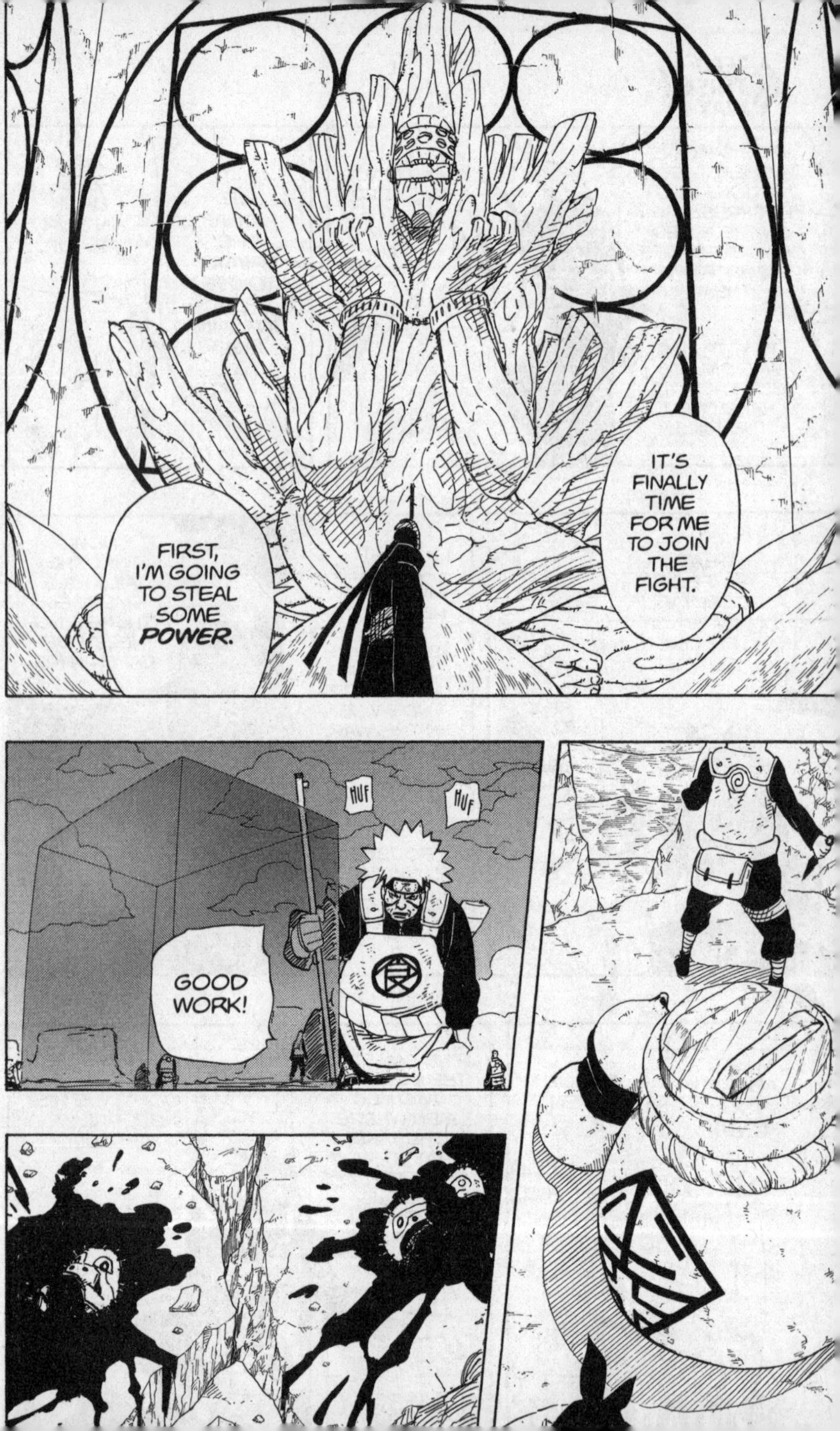
IT'S FINALLY TIME FOR ME TO JOIN THE FIGHT.
FIRST, I'M GOING TO STEAL SOME POWER.
HUF
HUF
GOOD WORK!

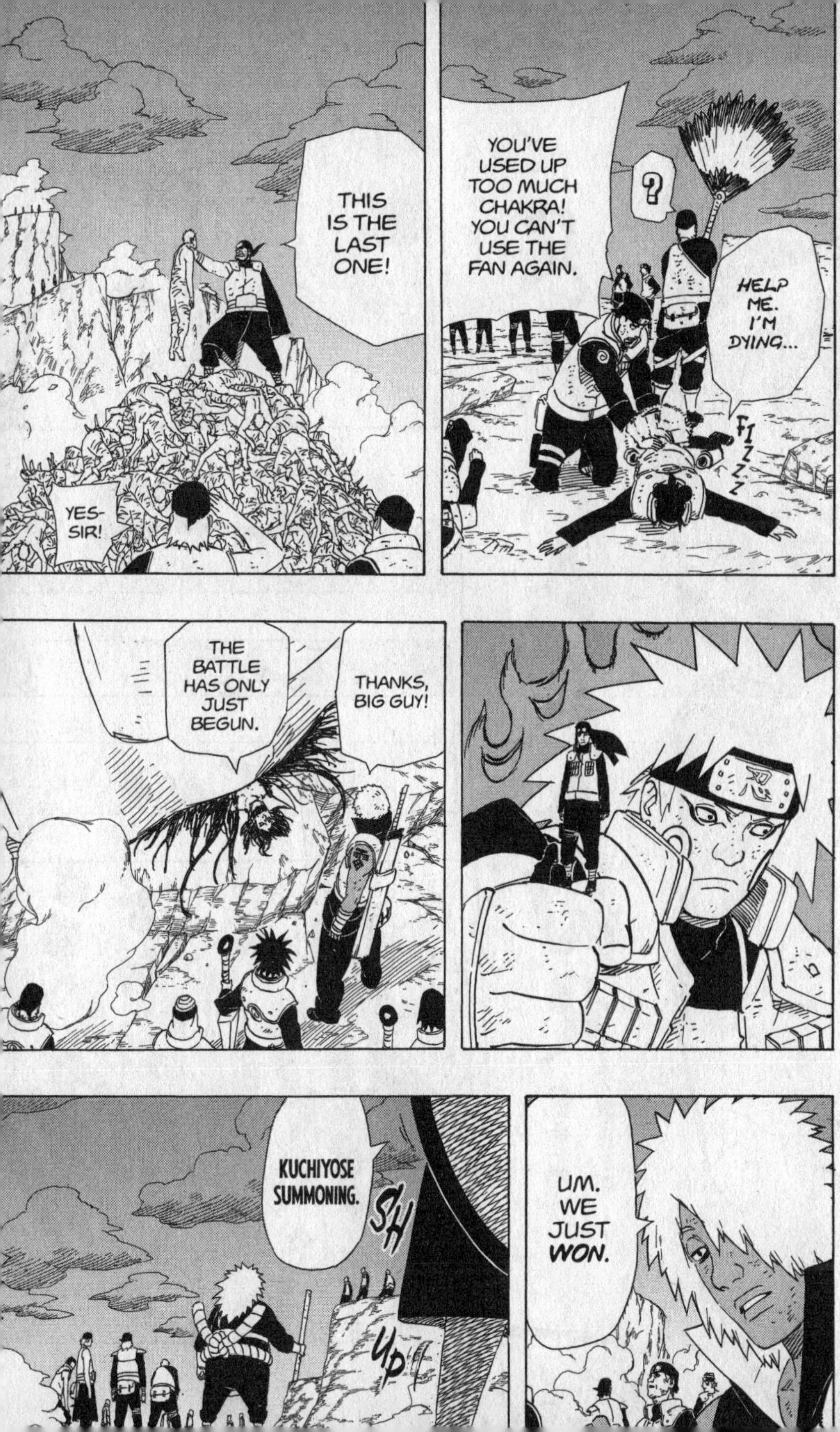
YOU'VE USED UP TOO MUCH CHAKRA! YOU CAN'T USE THE FAN AGAIN.
?
HELP ME. I'M DYING...
FIZZZZ
THIS IS THE LAST ONE!
YES-SIR!
THANKS, BIG GUY!
THE BATTLE HAS ONLY JUST BEGUN.
UM. WE JUST WON.
KUCHIYOSE SUMMONING.
SHUP

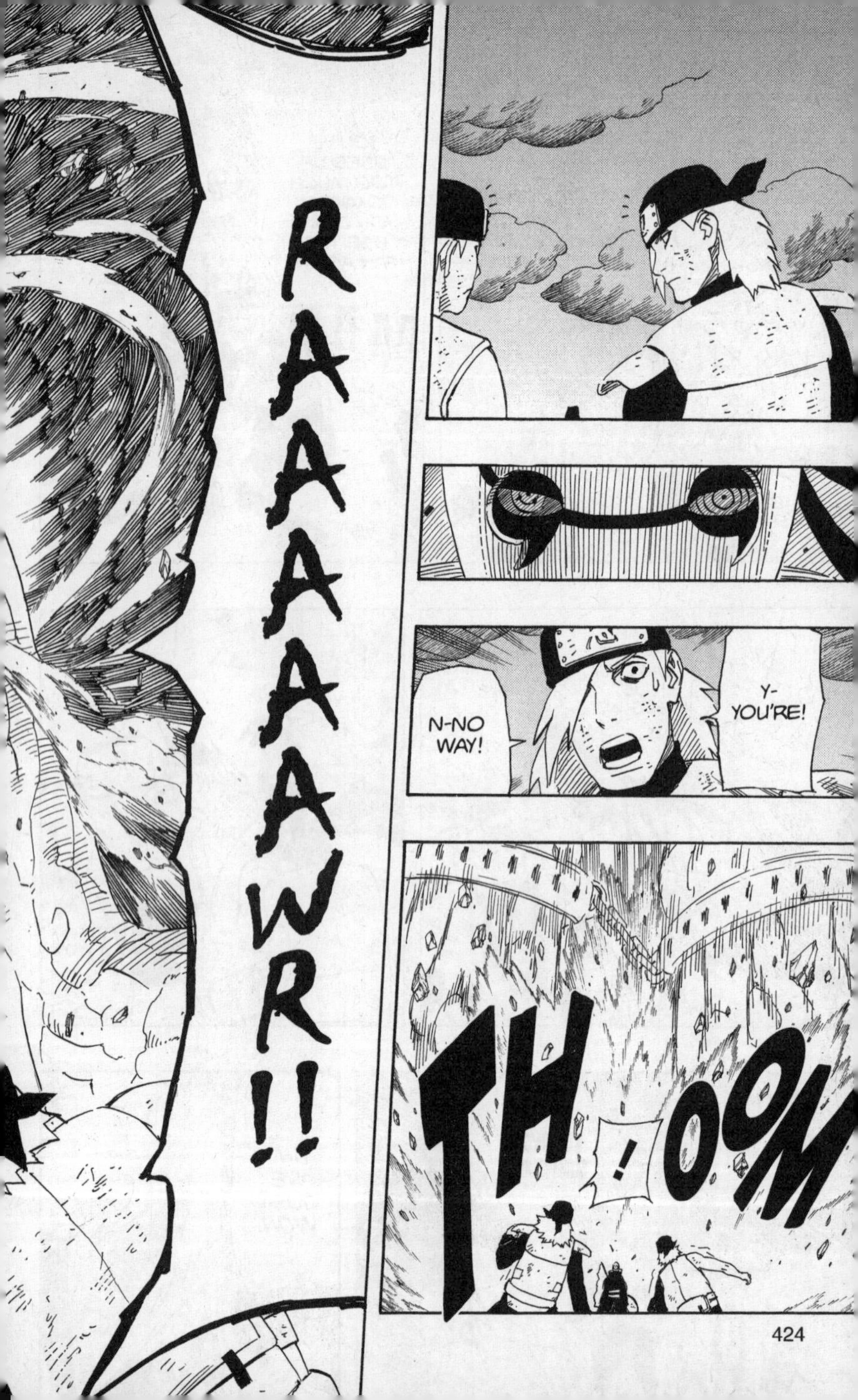
Y- YOU'RE!
N-NO WAY!
THOOM
!
RAAAAAWR!!

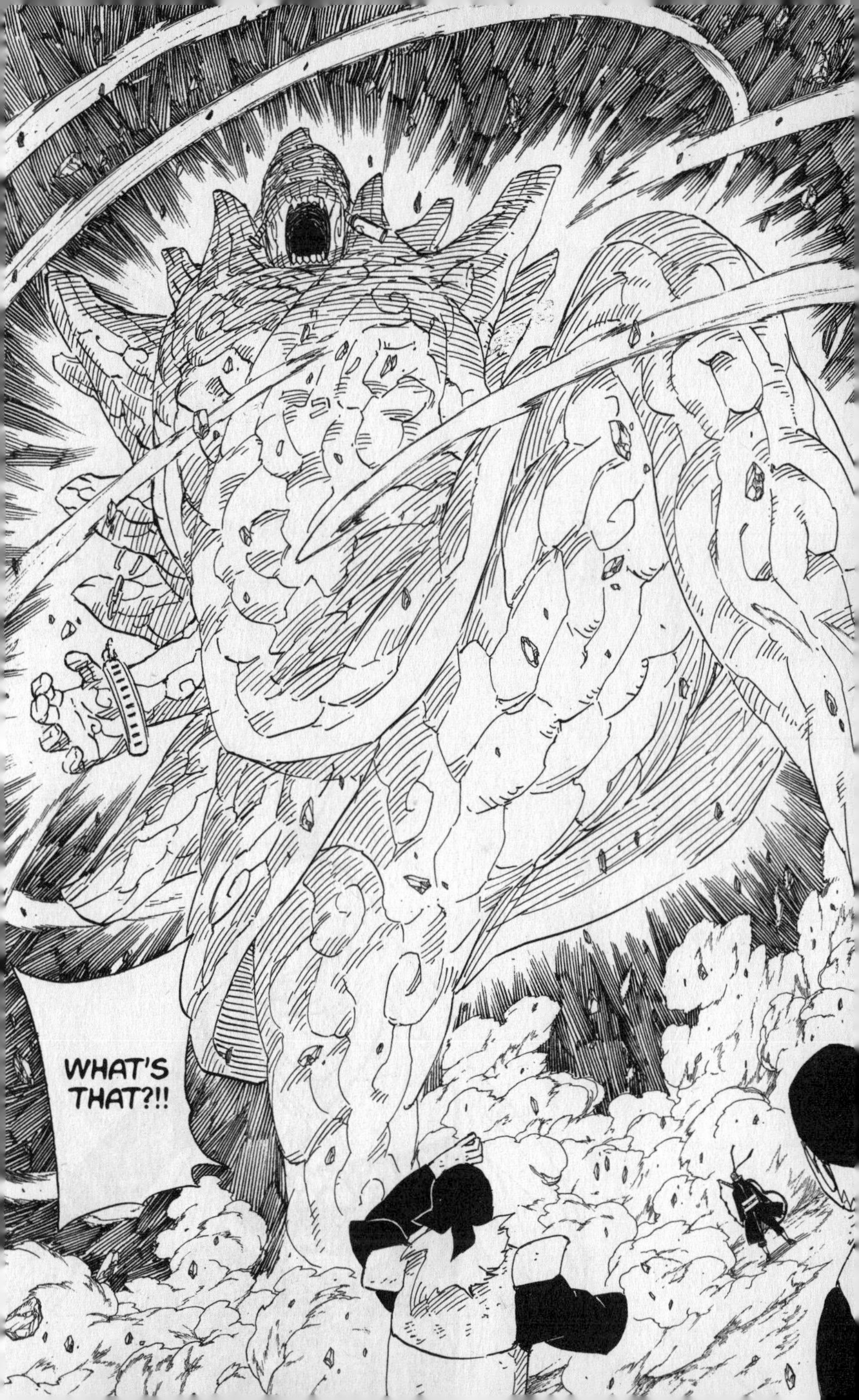
WHAT'S THAT?!!

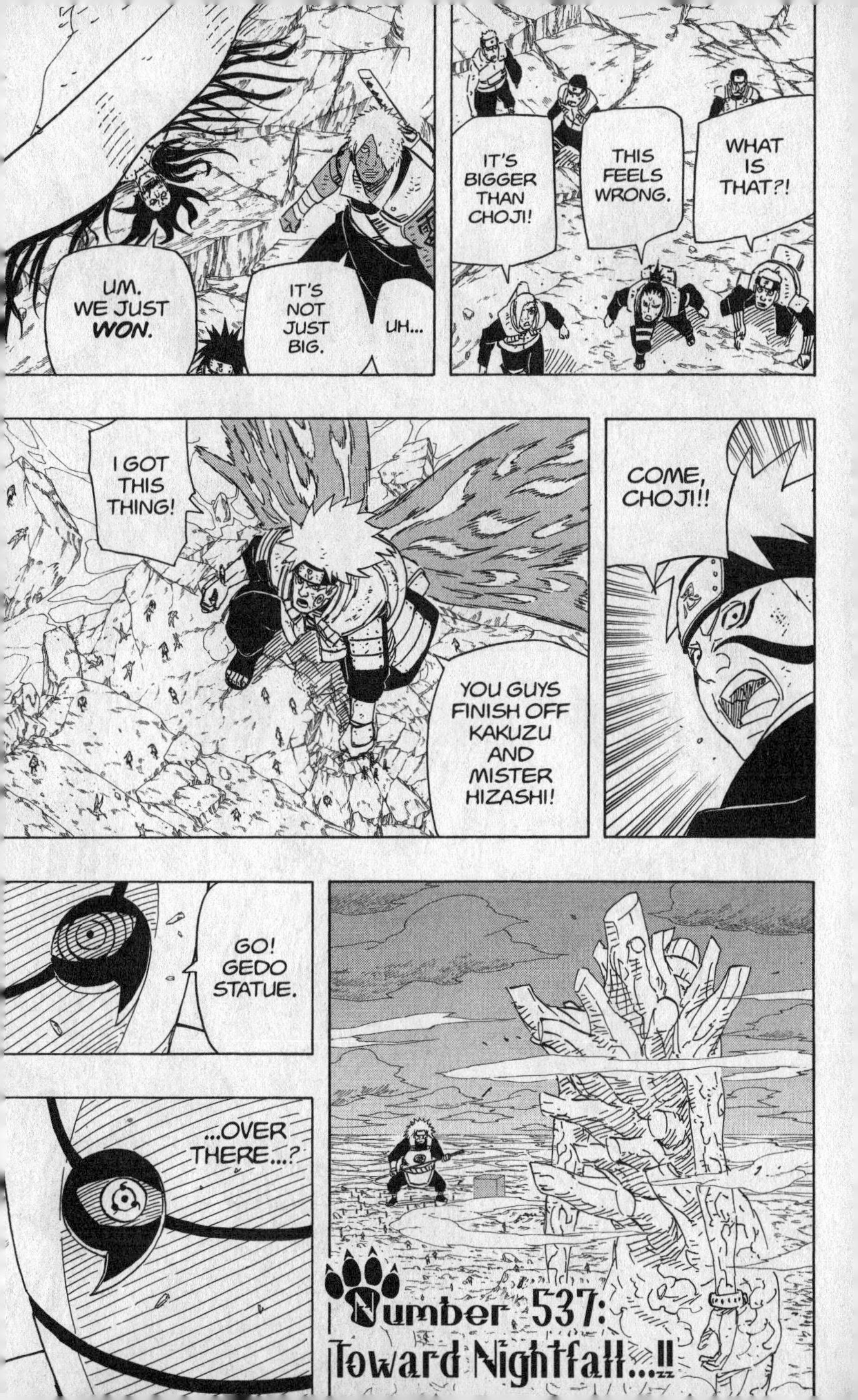
WHAT IS THAT?!
THIS FEELS WRONG.
IT'S BIGGER THAN CHOJI!
UH...
IT'S NOT JUST BIG.
UM. WE JUST **WON**.
COME, CHOJI!!
I GOT THIS THING!
YOU GUYS FINISH OFF KAKUZU AND MISTER HIZASHI!
Number 537: Toward Nightfall...!!
GO! GEDO STATUE.
...OVER THERE...?

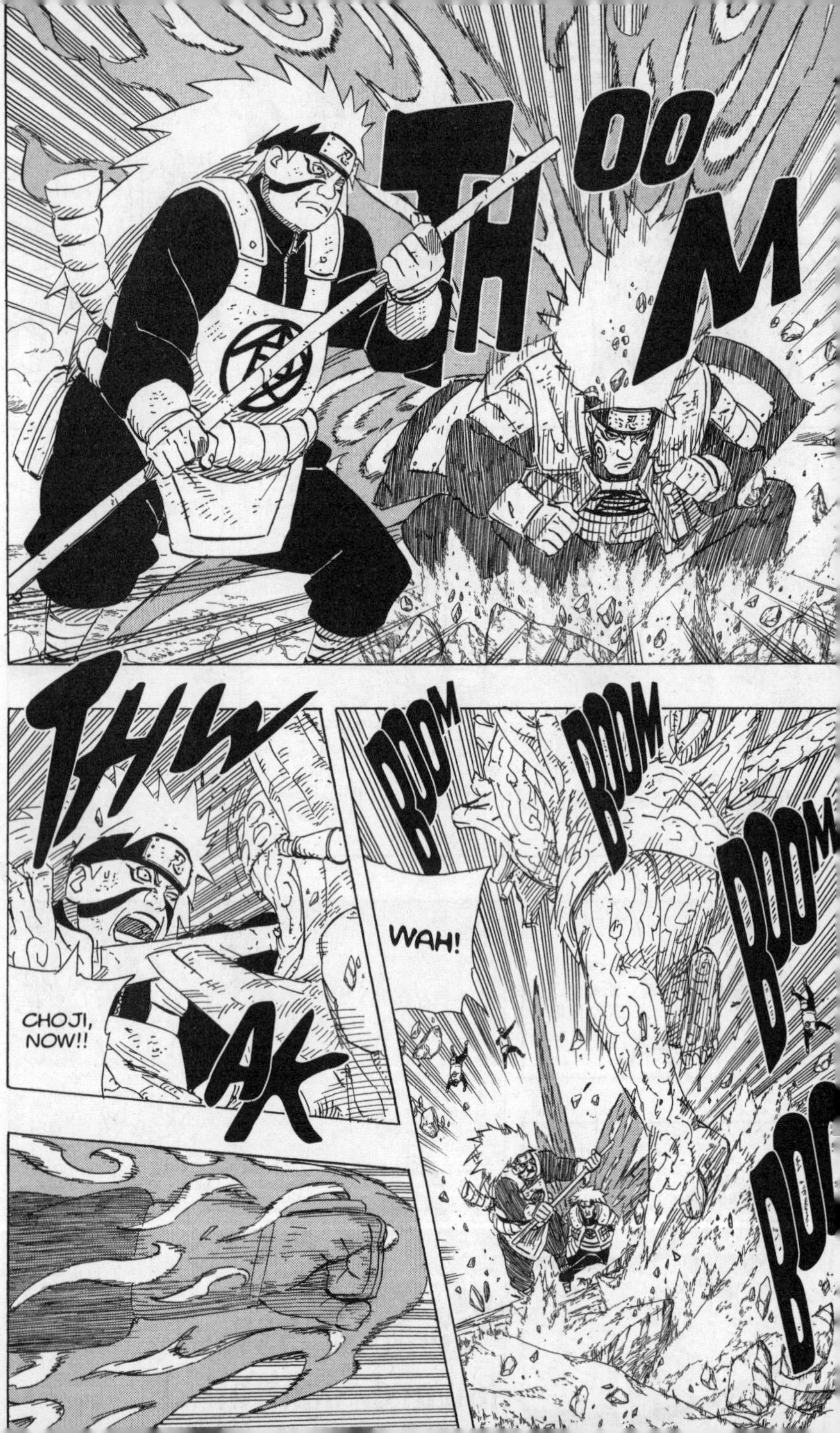
THOOM
BOOM
BOOM
BOOM
WAH!
THWAK
CHOJI, NOW!!

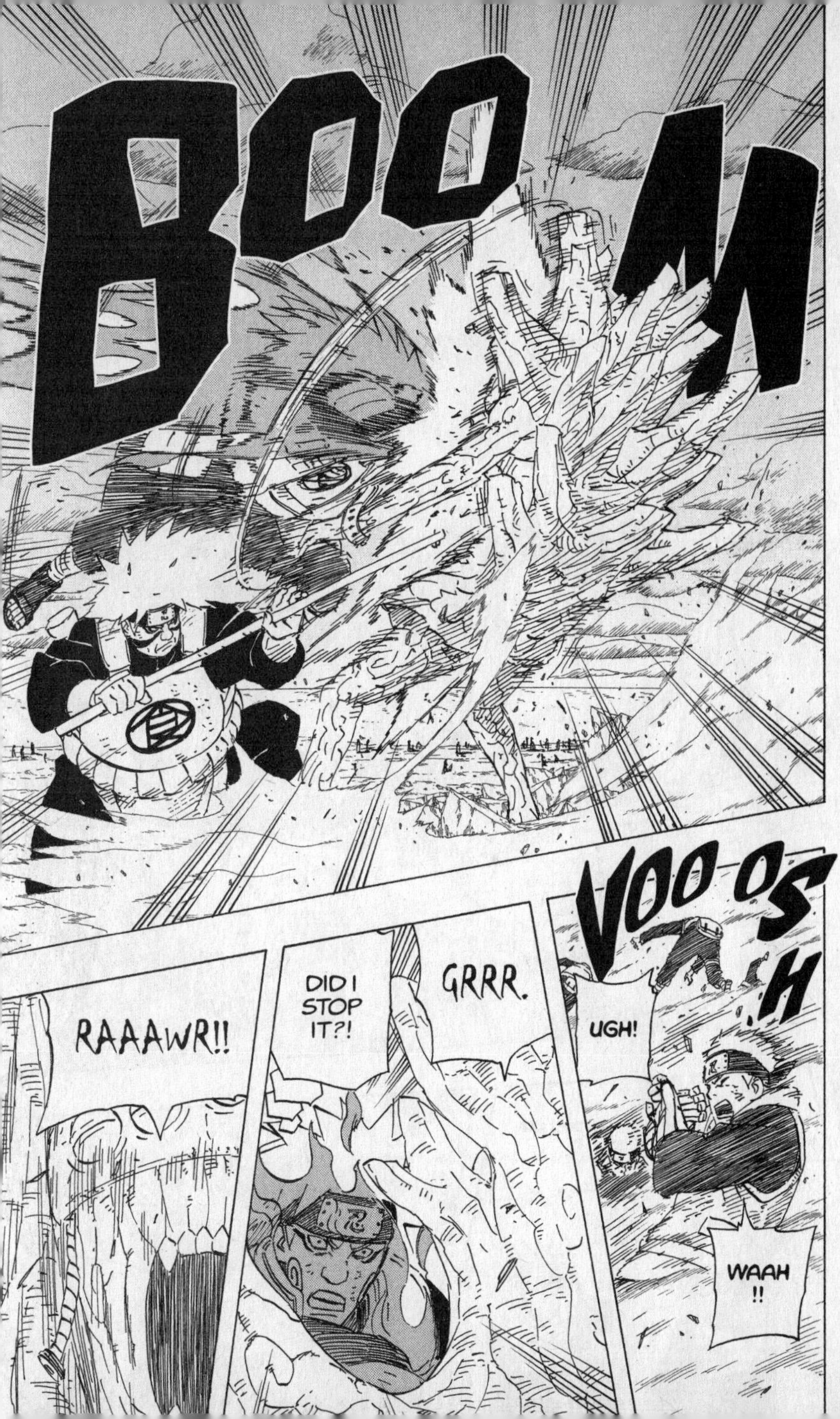
BOOM
VOOOSH
UGH!
WAAH!!
GRRR.
DID I STOP IT?!
RAAAWR!!

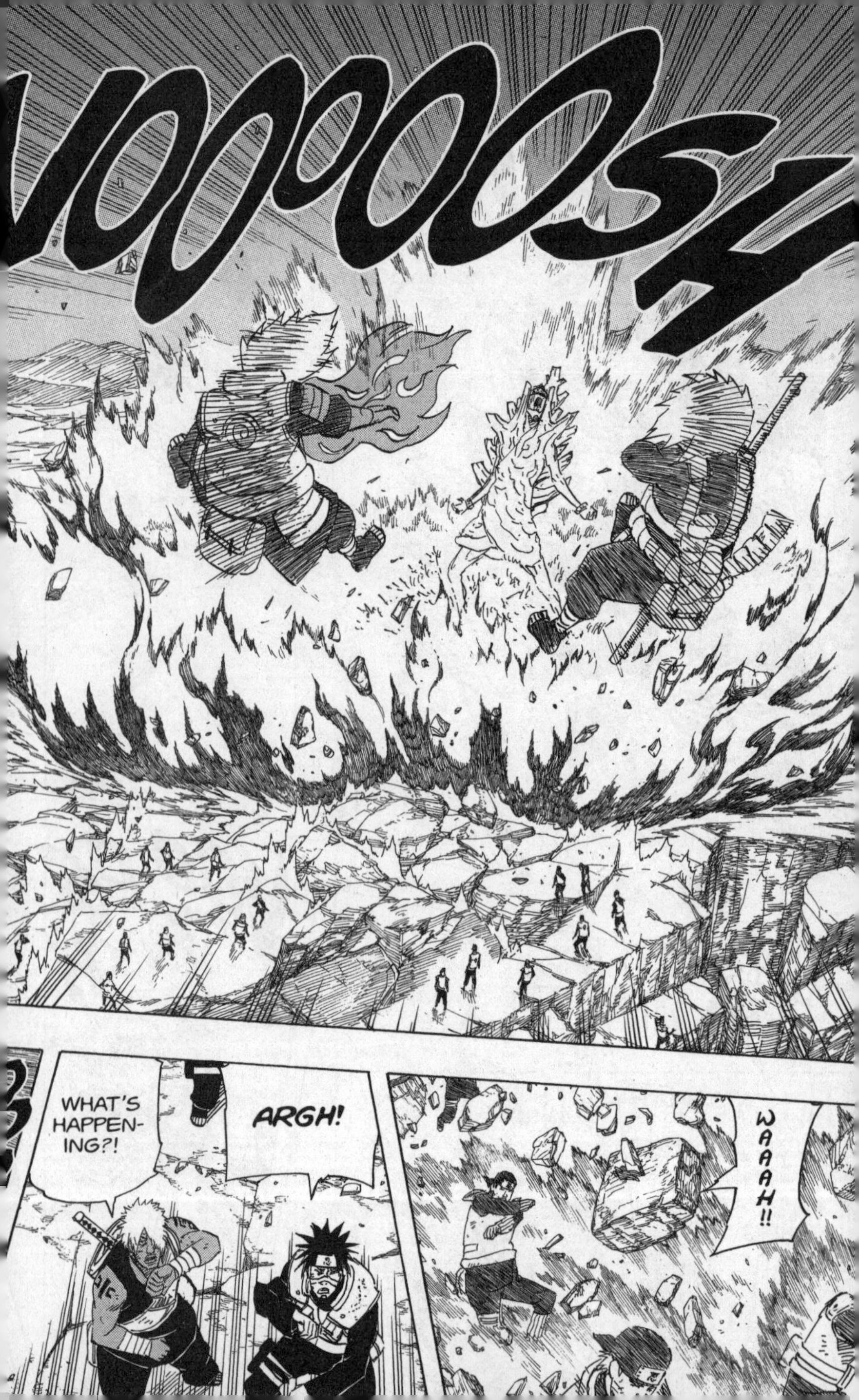
WAAAAH!!
ARGH!
WHAT'S HAPPENING?!

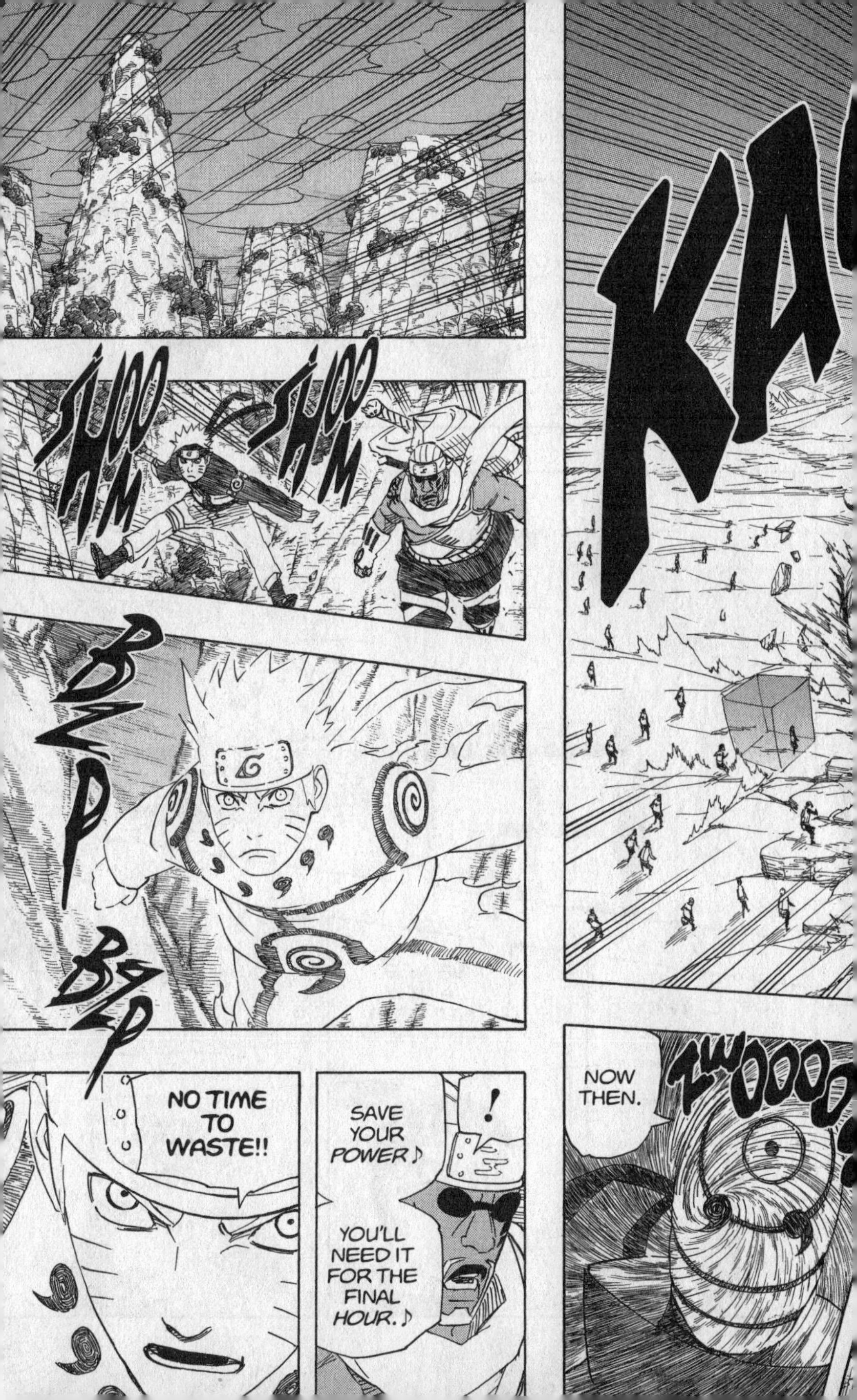
KA
SHOOM
SHOOM
BZZP
BZZP
NOW THEN.
ZWOOOO
!
SAVE YOUR POWER♪
YOU'LL NEED IT FOR THE FINAL HOUR.♪
NO TIME TO WASTE!!

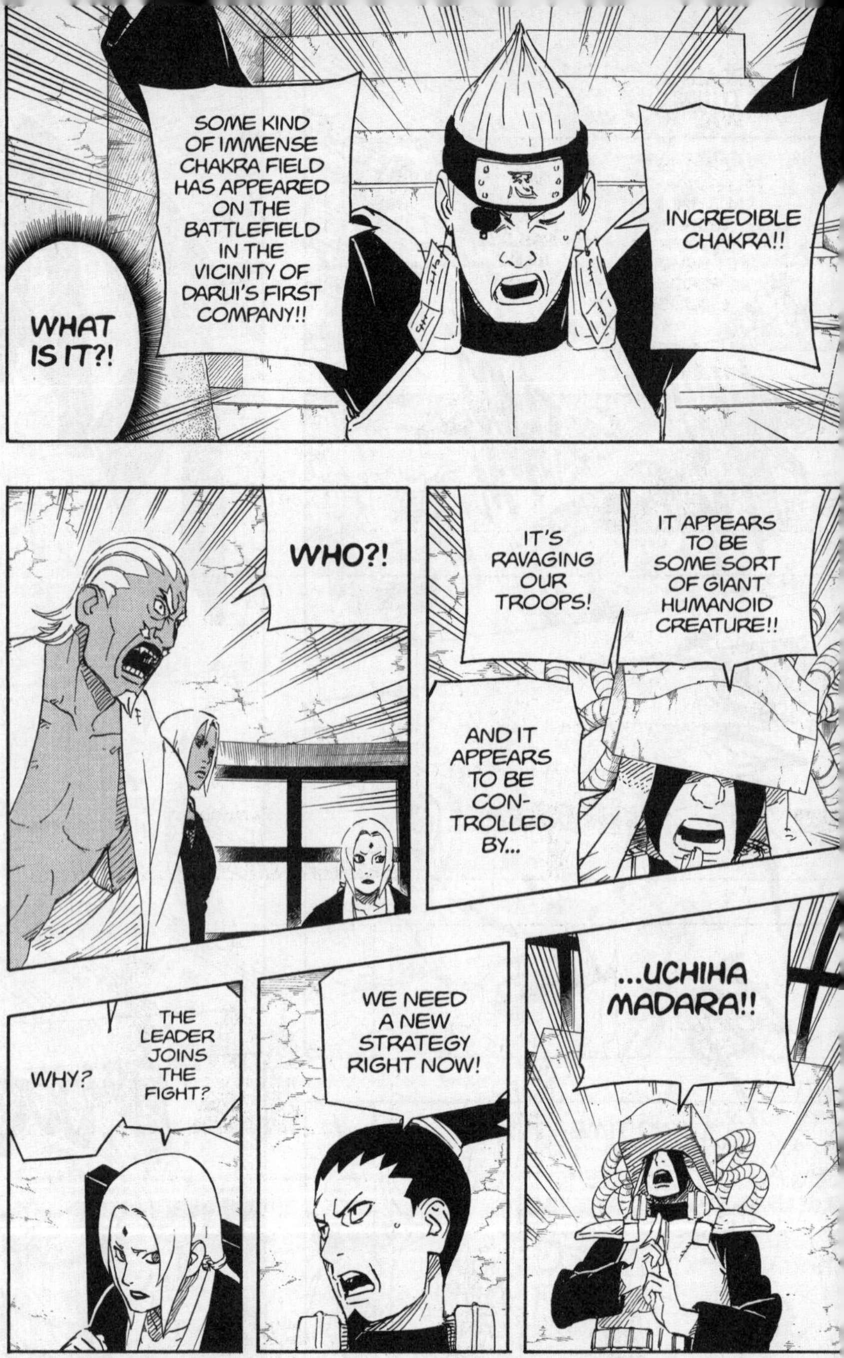
INCREDIBLE CHAKRA!!
SOME KIND OF IMMENSE CHAKRA FIELD HAS APPEARED ON THE BATTLEFIELD IN THE VICINITY OF DARUI'S FIRST COMPANY!!
WHAT IS IT?!
IT APPEARS TO BE SOME SORT OF GIANT HUMANOID CREATURE!!
IT'S RAVAGING OUR TROOPS!
AND IT APPEARS TO BE CON-TROLLED BY...
WHO?!
...UCHIHA MADARA!!
WE NEED A NEW STRATEGY RIGHT NOW!
THE LEADER JOINS THE FIGHT?
WHY?

READ THIS WAY

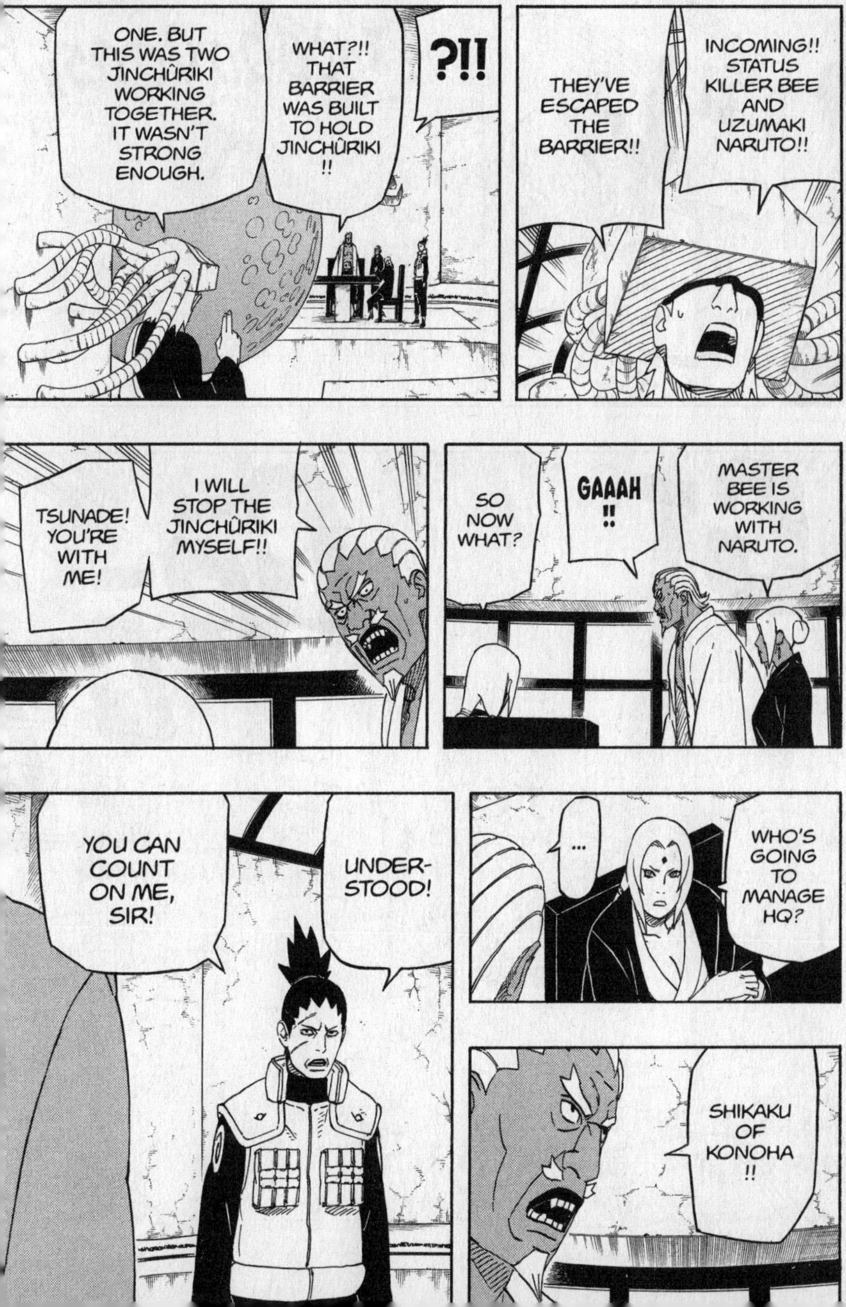
INCOMING!! STATUS KILLER BEE AND UZUMAKI NARUTO!!
THEY'VE ESCAPED THE BARRIER!!
?!!
WHAT?!! THAT BARRIER WAS BUILT TO HOLD JINCHÛRIKI !!
ONE. BUT THIS WAS TWO JINCHÛRIKI WORKING TOGETHER. IT WASN'T STRONG ENOUGH.
MASTER BEE IS WORKING WITH NARUTO.
GAAAH !!
SO NOW WHAT?
I WILL STOP THE JINCHÛRIKI MYSELF!!
TSUNADE! YOU'RE WITH ME!
WHO'S GOING TO MANAGE HQ?
...
SHIKAKU OF KONOHA !!
UNDER-STOOD!
YOU CAN COUNT ON ME, SIR!

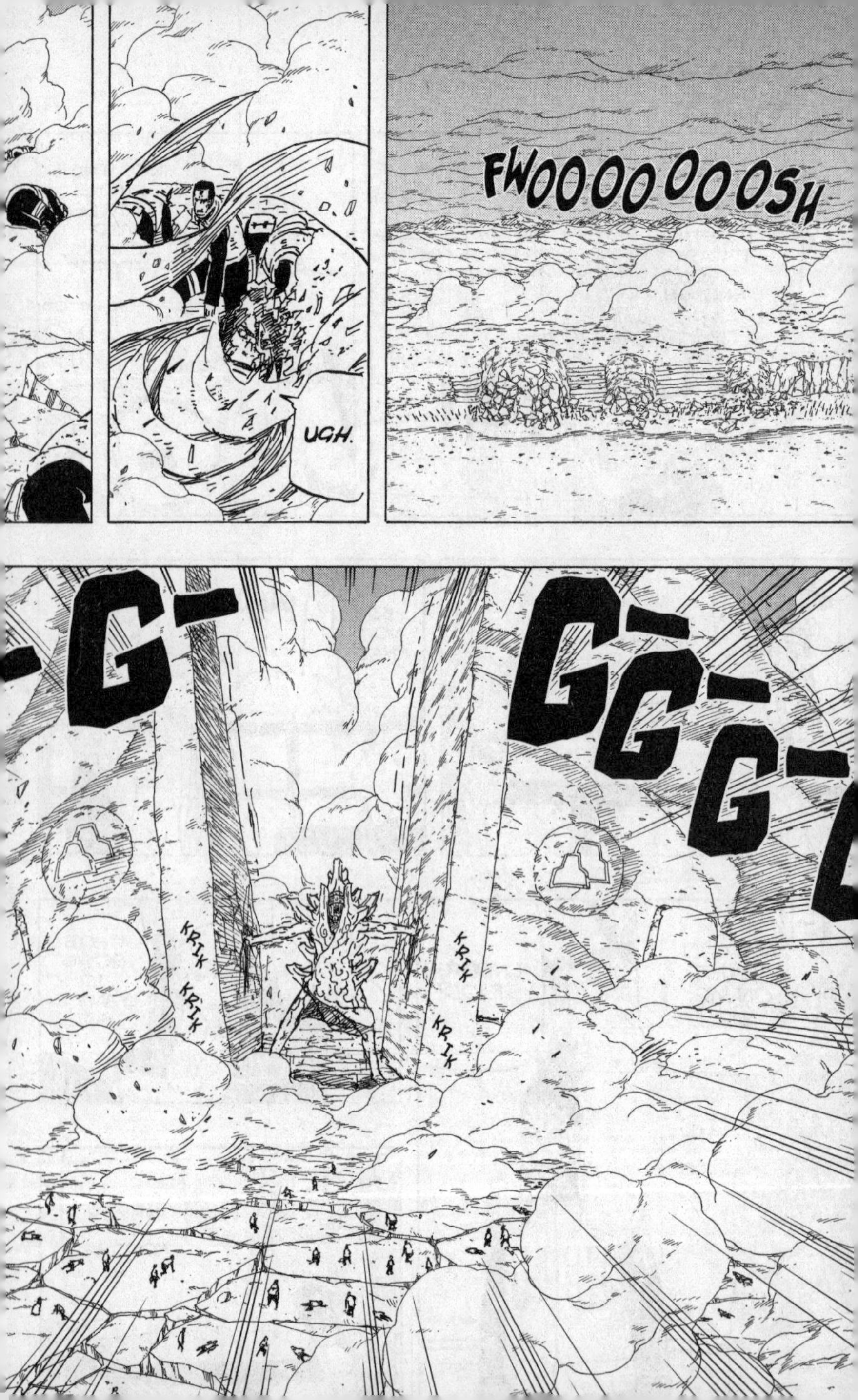
FWOOOOOOOSH
UGH.
G-G-G-
KRIK KRIK
KRIK KRIK
-G-

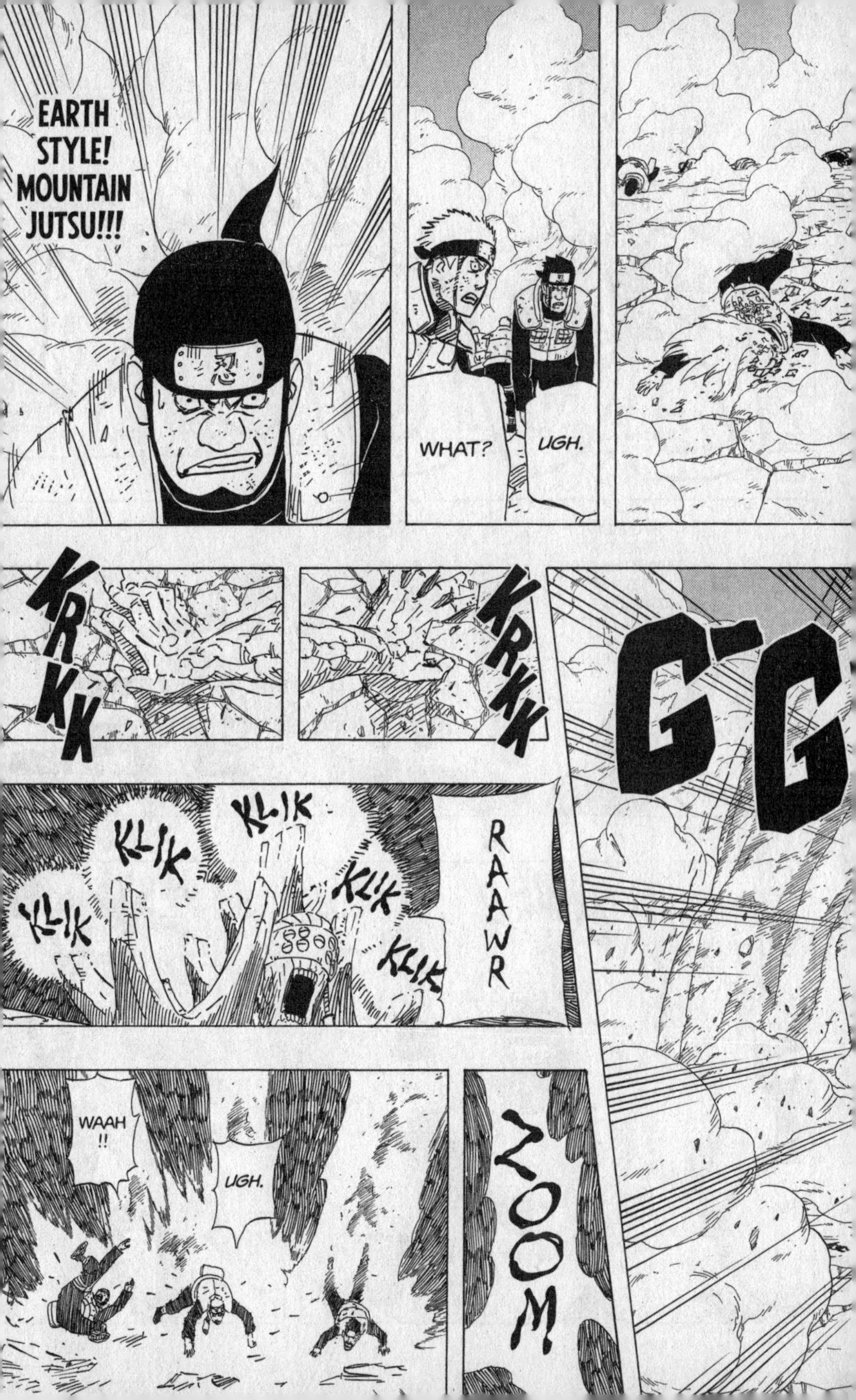

UGH.
WHAT?
EARTH STYLE! MOUNTAIN JUTSU!!!
G-G
KRKK
KRKK
RAAWR
KLIK
KLIK
KLIK
KLIK
KLIK
ZOOM!
UGH.
WAAH!!

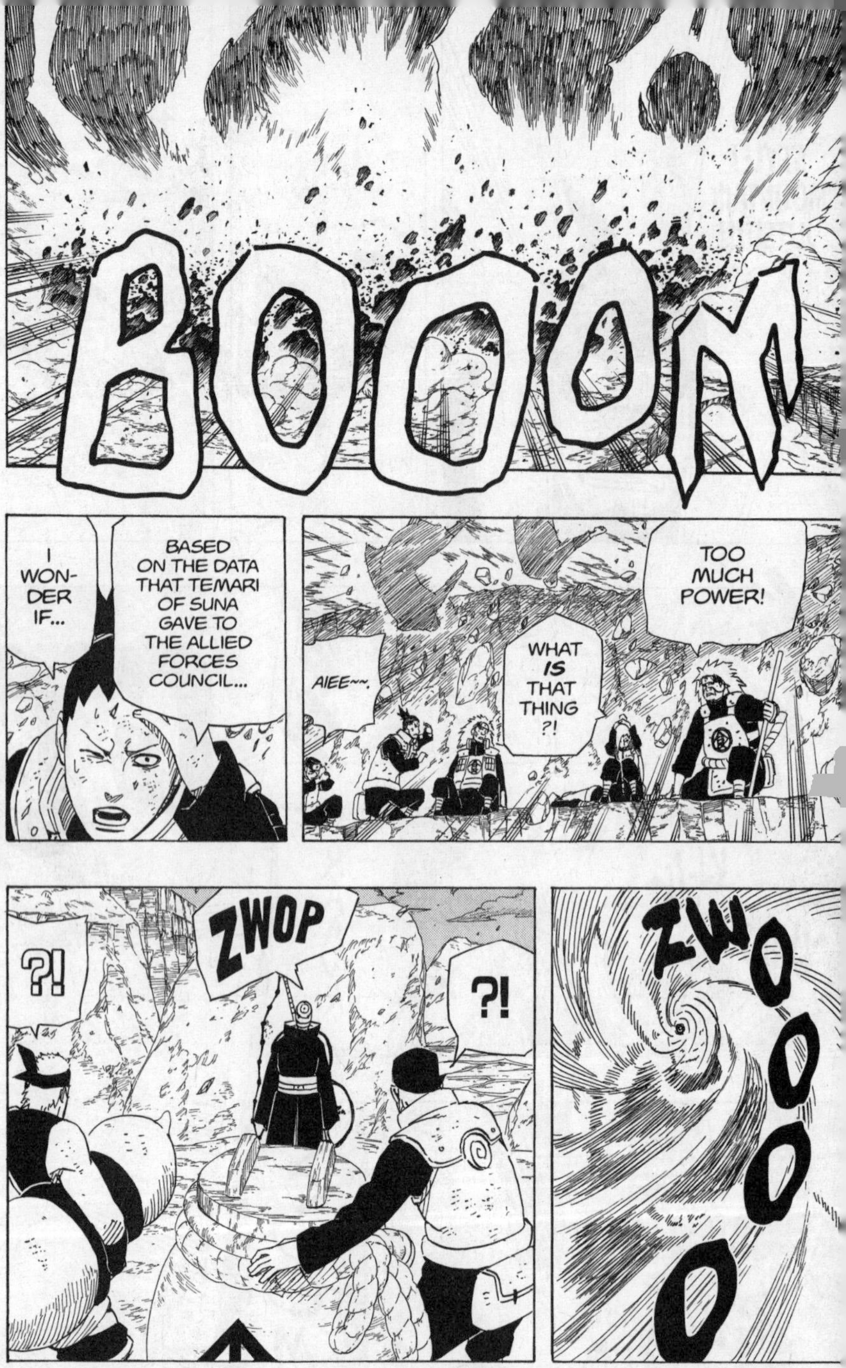
BOOOM
TOO MUCH POWER!
WHAT *IS* THAT THING?!
AIEE~~.
BASED ON THE DATA THAT TEMARI OF SUNA GAVE TO THE ALLIED FORCES COUNCIL...
I WONDER IF...
ZWOOOOOO
?!
ZWOP
?!

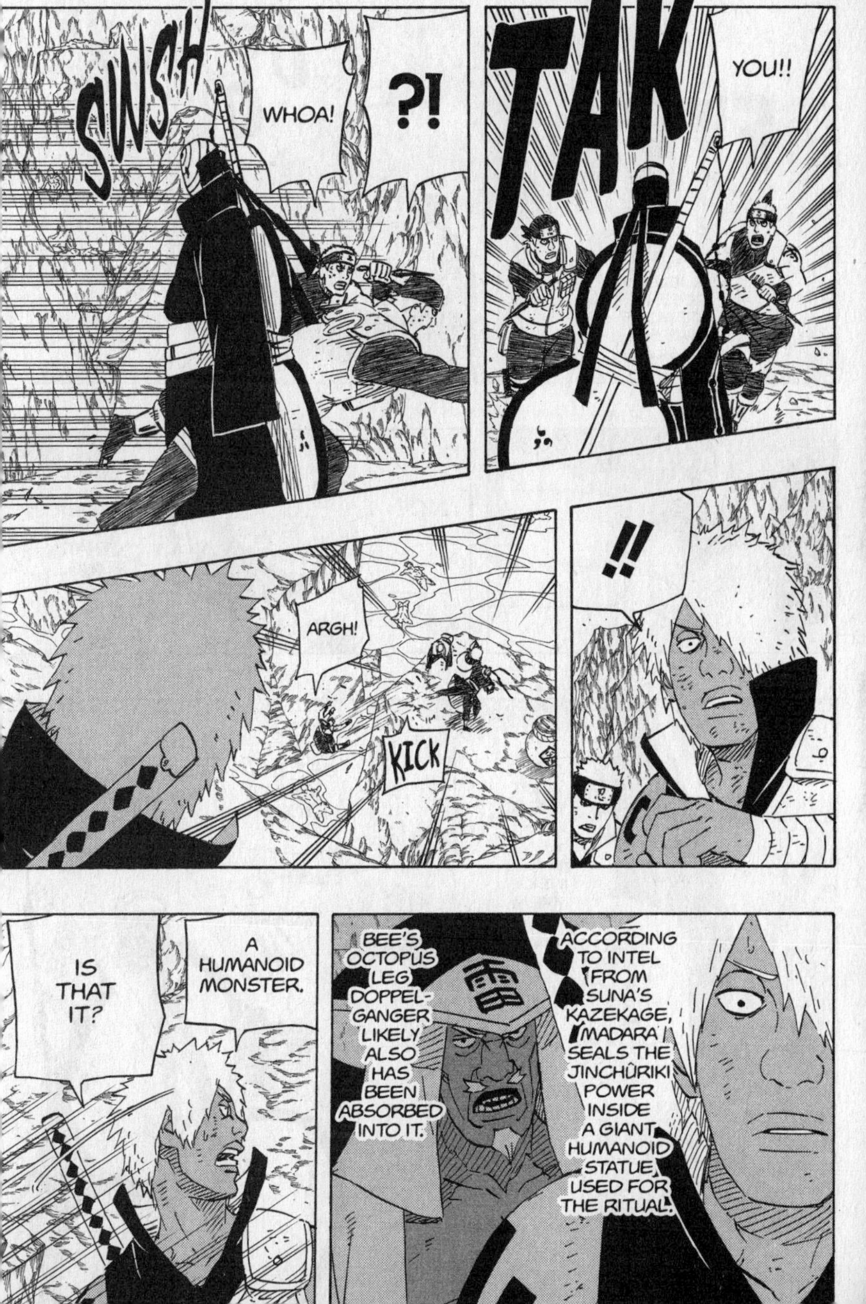
TAK
YOU!!
SWISH
?!
WHOA!
!!
ARGH!
KICK
ACCORDING TO INTEL FROM SUNA'S KAZEKAGE, MADARA SEALS THE JINCHÛRIKI POWER INSIDE A GIANT HUMANOID STATUE USED FOR THE RITUAL.
BEE'S OCTOPUS LEG DOPPELGANGER LIKELY ALSO HAS BEEN ABSORBED INTO IT.
A HUMANOID MONSTER.
IS THAT IT?

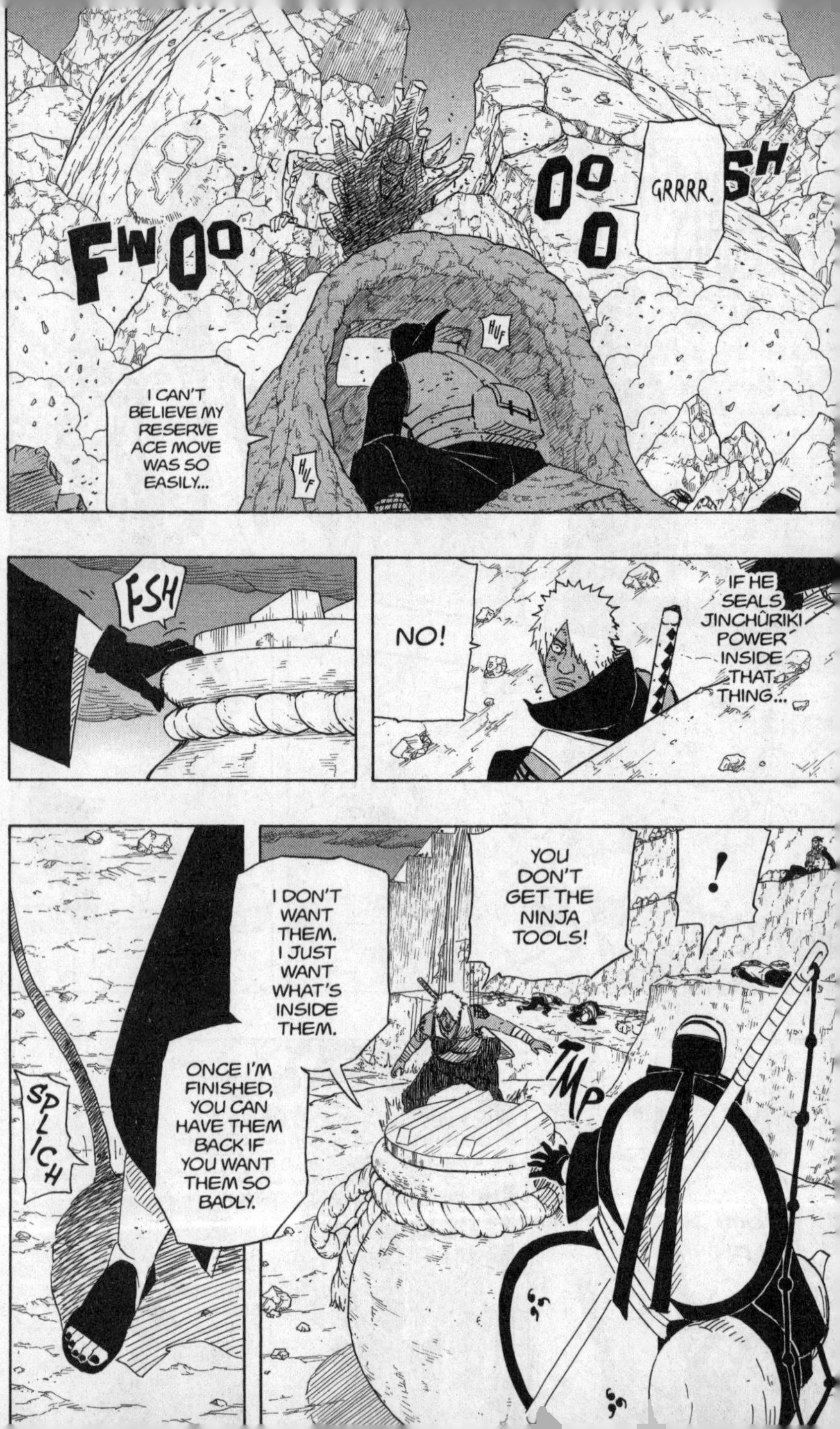
GRRRR.
FWOO OOO SH
HUF
I CAN'T BELIEVE MY RESERVE ACE MOVE WAS SO EASILY...
HUF
IF HE SEALS JINCHÛRIKI POWER INSIDE THAT THING...
NO!
FSH
!
YOU DON'T GET THE NINJA TOOLS!
TMP
I DON'T WANT THEM. I JUST WANT WHAT'S INSIDE THEM.
ONCE I'M FINISHED, YOU CAN HAVE THEM BACK IF YOU WANT THEM SO BADLY.
SPLICH

READ THIS WAY

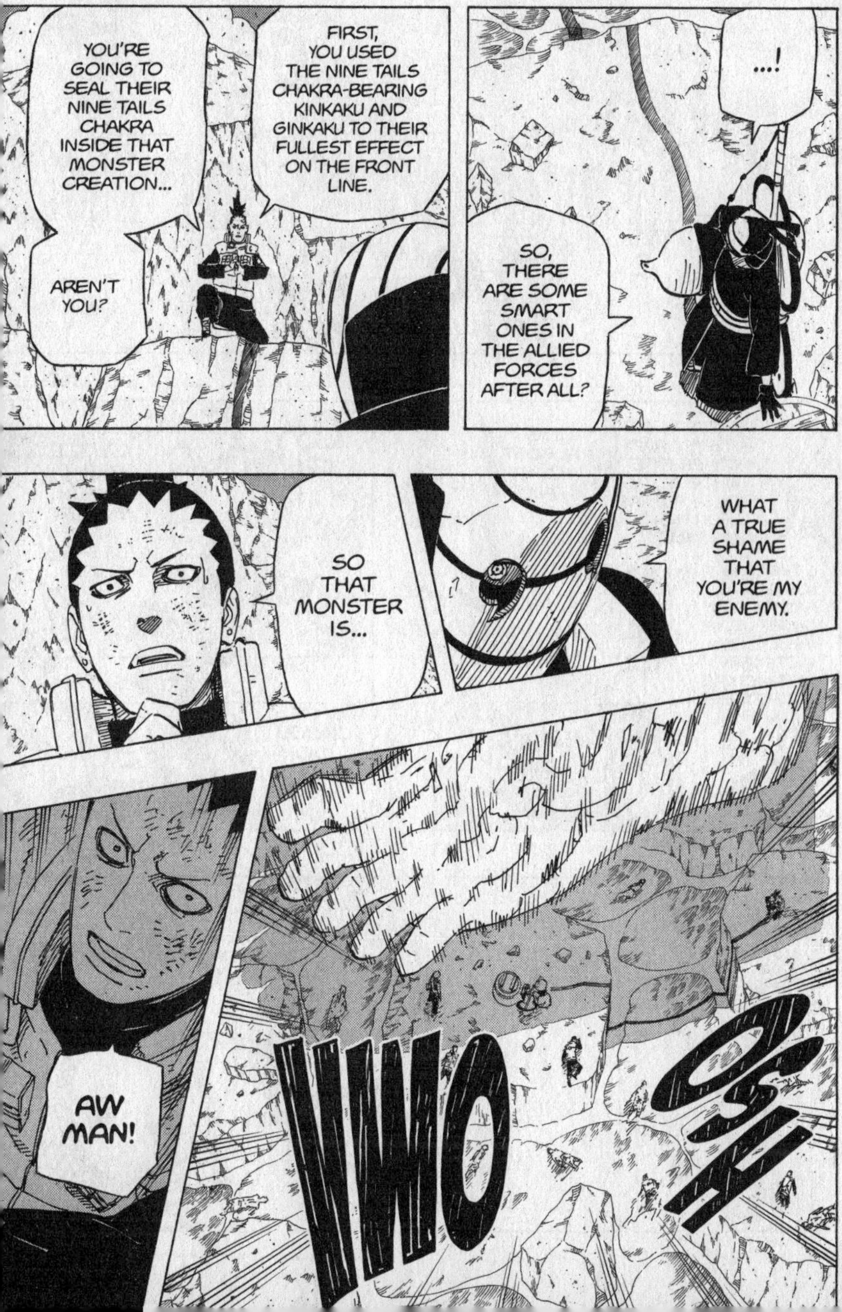
...!
SO, THERE ARE SOME SMART ONES IN THE ALLIED FORCES AFTER ALL?
FIRST, YOU USED THE NINE TAILS CHAKRA-BEARING KINKAKU AND GINKAKU TO THEIR FULLEST EFFECT ON THE FRONT LINE.
YOU'RE GOING TO SEAL THEIR NINE TAILS CHAKRA INSIDE THAT MONSTER CREATION...
AREN'T YOU?
WHAT A TRUE SHAME THAT YOU'RE MY ENEMY.
SO THAT MONSTER IS...
WHOOSH
AW MAN!

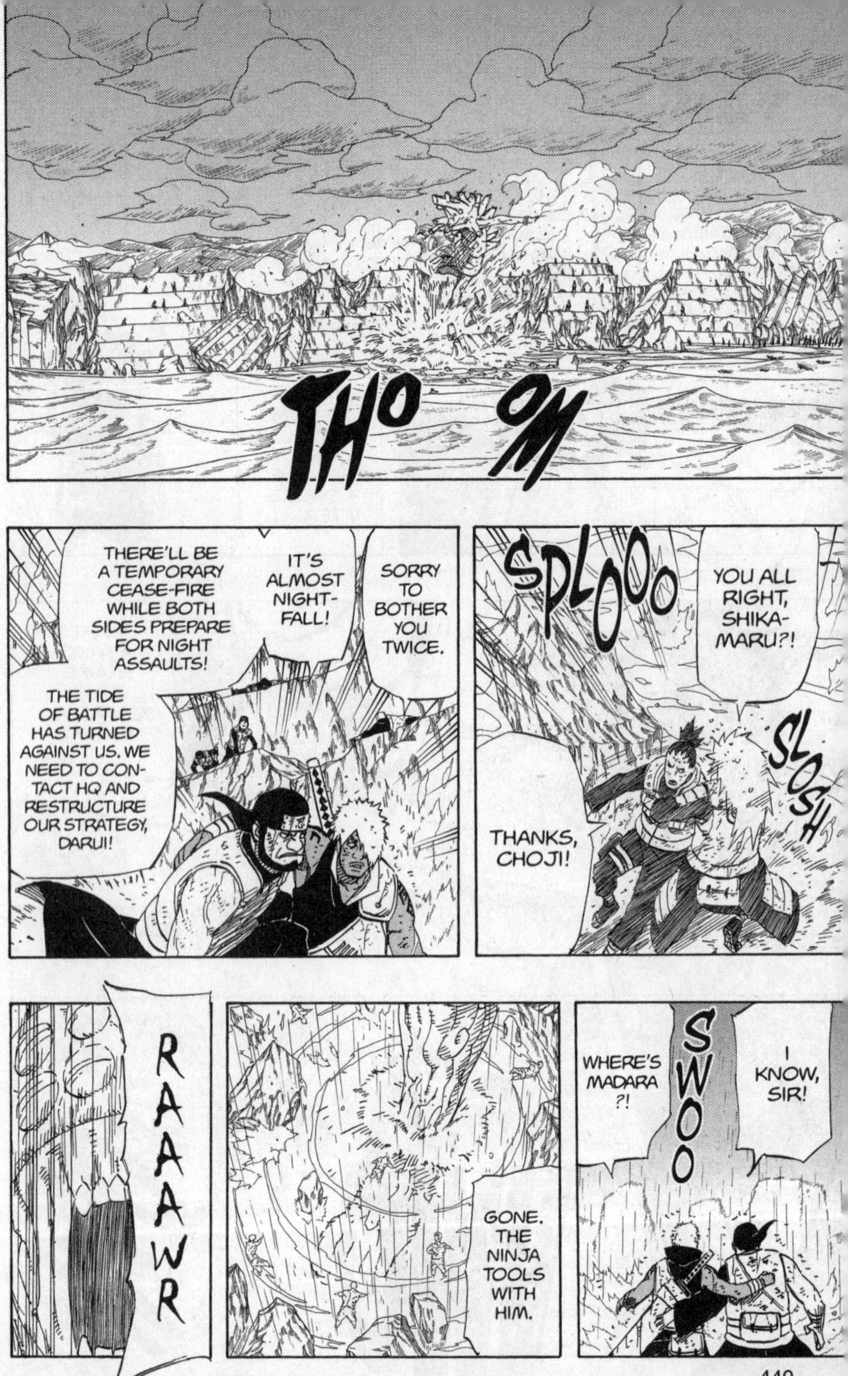
THOOM
SPLOOO
YOU ALL RIGHT, SHIKAMARU?!
SLOSH
THANKS, CHOJI!
SORRY TO BOTHER YOU TWICE.
IT'S ALMOST NIGHTFALL!
THERE'LL BE A TEMPORARY CEASE-FIRE WHILE BOTH SIDES PREPARE FOR NIGHT ASSAULTS!
THE TIDE OF BATTLE HAS TURNED AGAINST US. WE NEED TO CONTACT HQ AND RESTRUCTURE OUR STRATEGY, DARUI!
I KNOW, SIR!
SWOOO
WHERE'S MADARA?!
GONE. THE NINJA TOOLS WITH HIM.
RAAAWR

THEY'RE RETREAT-ING?

?!

**BO OF**

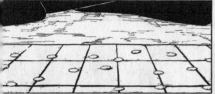

MADARA MUST HAVE KINKAKU AND GINKAKU.

WITH ONLY A SINGLE TENTACLE'S WORTH OF EIGHT TAILS' CHAKRA.

HE'S LOSING PATIENCE.

I WILL NOT LOSE THIS WAR.

I'VE PREPARED FAR TOO LONG.

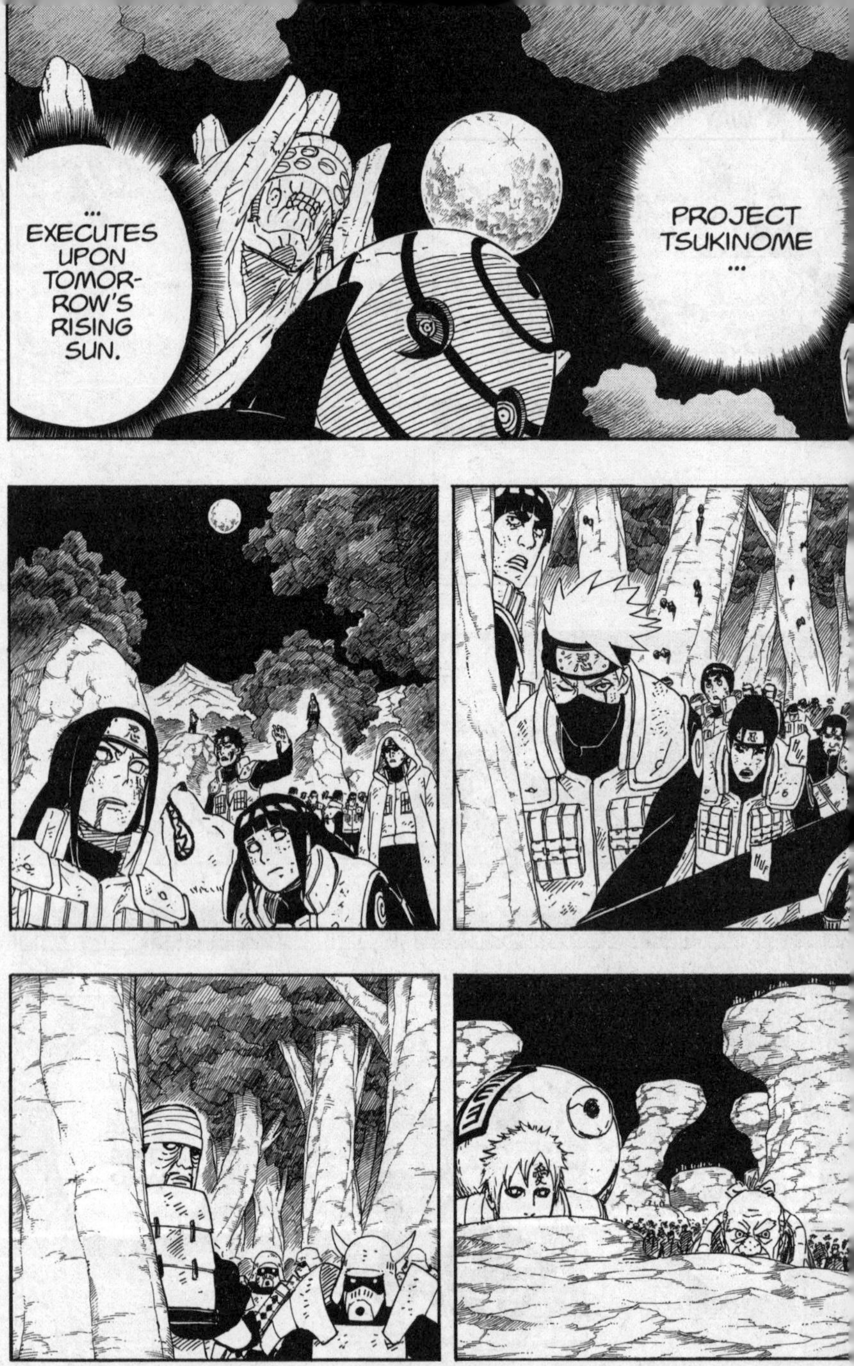
PROJECT TSUKINOME ...
... EXECUTES UPON TOMORROW'S RISING SUN.

READ THIS WAY

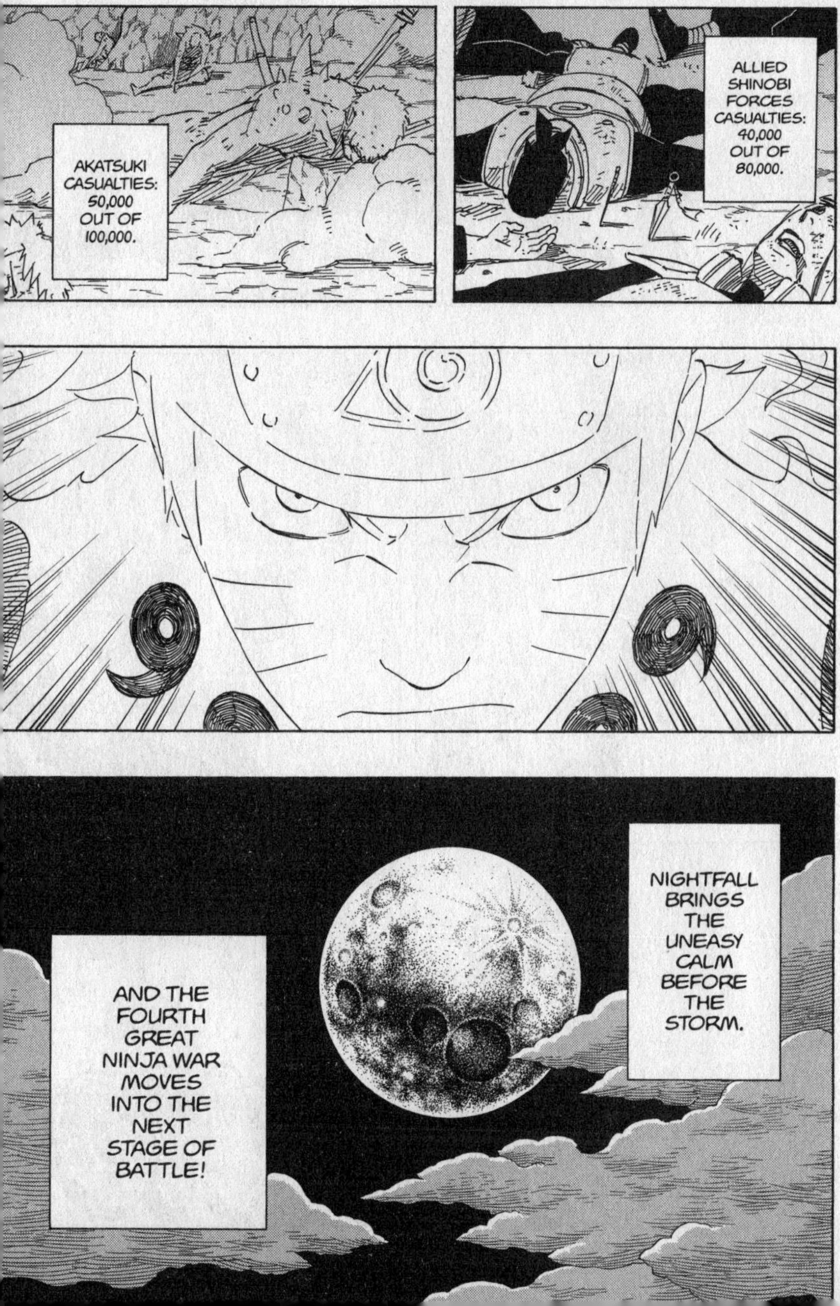
ALLIED SHINOBI FORCES CASUALTIES: 40,000 OUT OF 80,000.
AKATSUKI CASUALTIES: 50,000 OUT OF 100,000.
NIGHTFALL BRINGS THE UNEASY CALM BEFORE THE STORM.
AND THE FOURTH GREAT NINJA WAR MOVES INTO THE NEXT STAGE OF BATTLE!

NARUTO

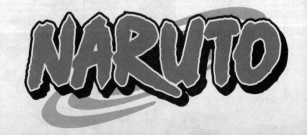

# Number 538: Cross-Examination

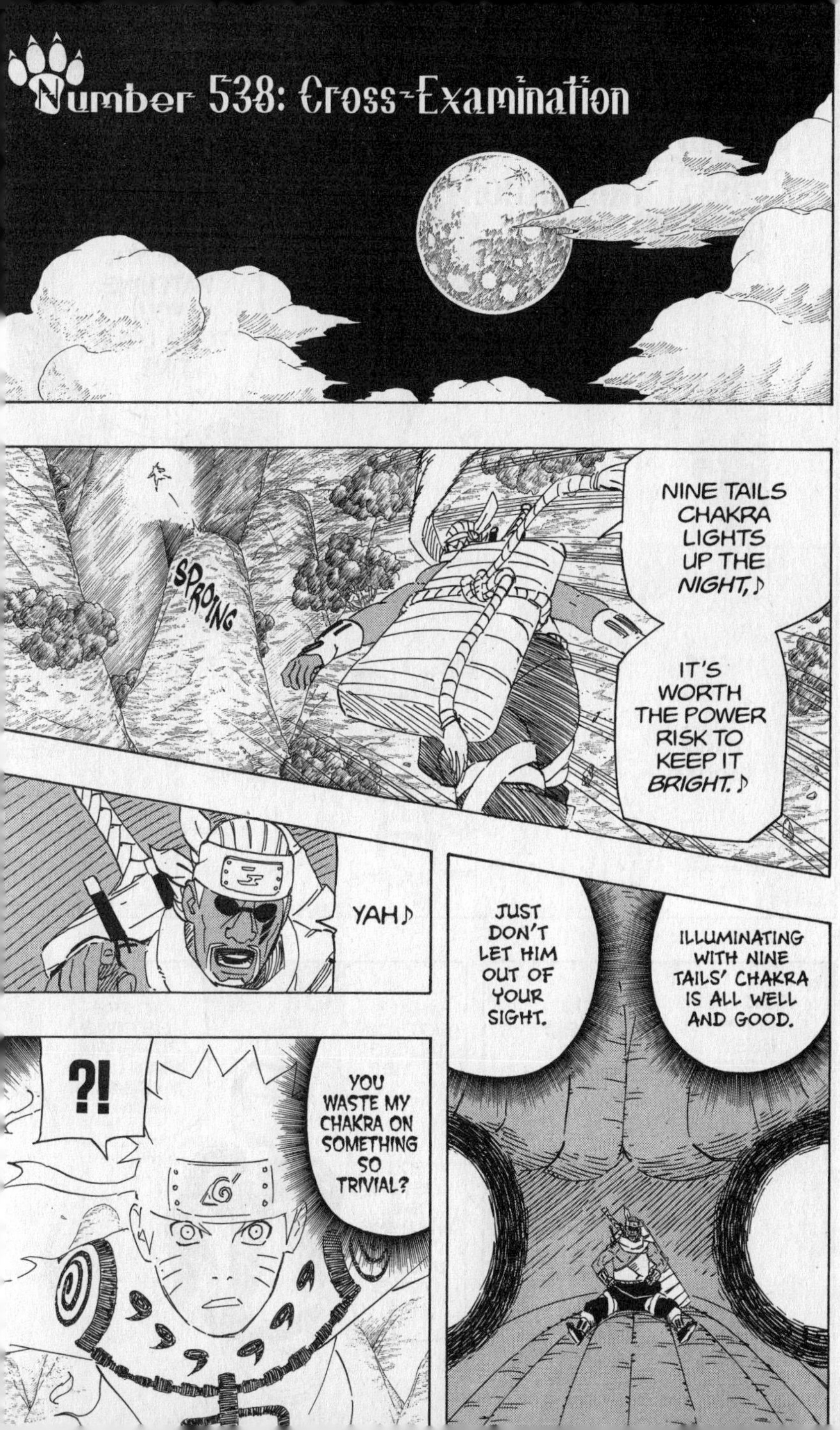
NINE TAILS CHAKRA LIGHTS UP THE NIGHT,♪
IT'S WORTH THE POWER RISK TO KEEP IT BRIGHT.♪
SPROING
ILLUMINATING WITH NINE TAILS' CHAKRA IS ALL WELL AND GOOD.
JUST DON'T LET HIM OUT OF YOUR SIGHT.
YAH♪
YOU WASTE MY CHAKRA ON SOMETHING SO TRIVIAL?
?!

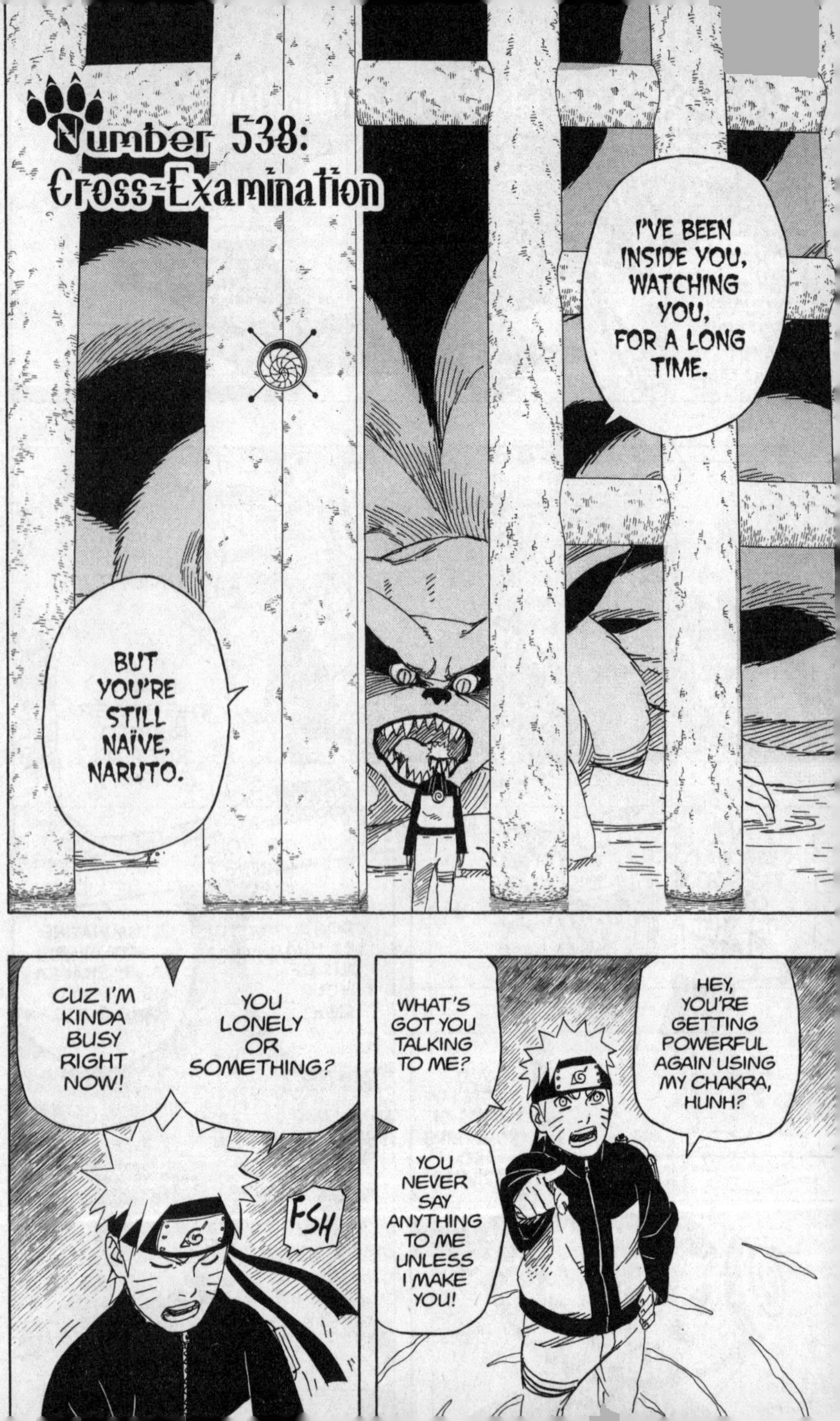
Number 538: Cross-Examination
I'VE BEEN INSIDE YOU, WATCHING YOU, FOR A LONG TIME.
BUT YOU'RE STILL NAÏVE, NARUTO.
HEY, YOU'RE GETTING POWERFUL AGAIN USING MY CHAKRA, HUNH?
WHAT'S GOT YOU TALKING TO ME?
YOU NEVER SAY ANYTHING TO ME UNLESS I MAKE YOU!
YOU LONELY OR SOMETHING?
CUZ I'M KINDA BUSY RIGHT NOW!
FSH

READ THIS WAY

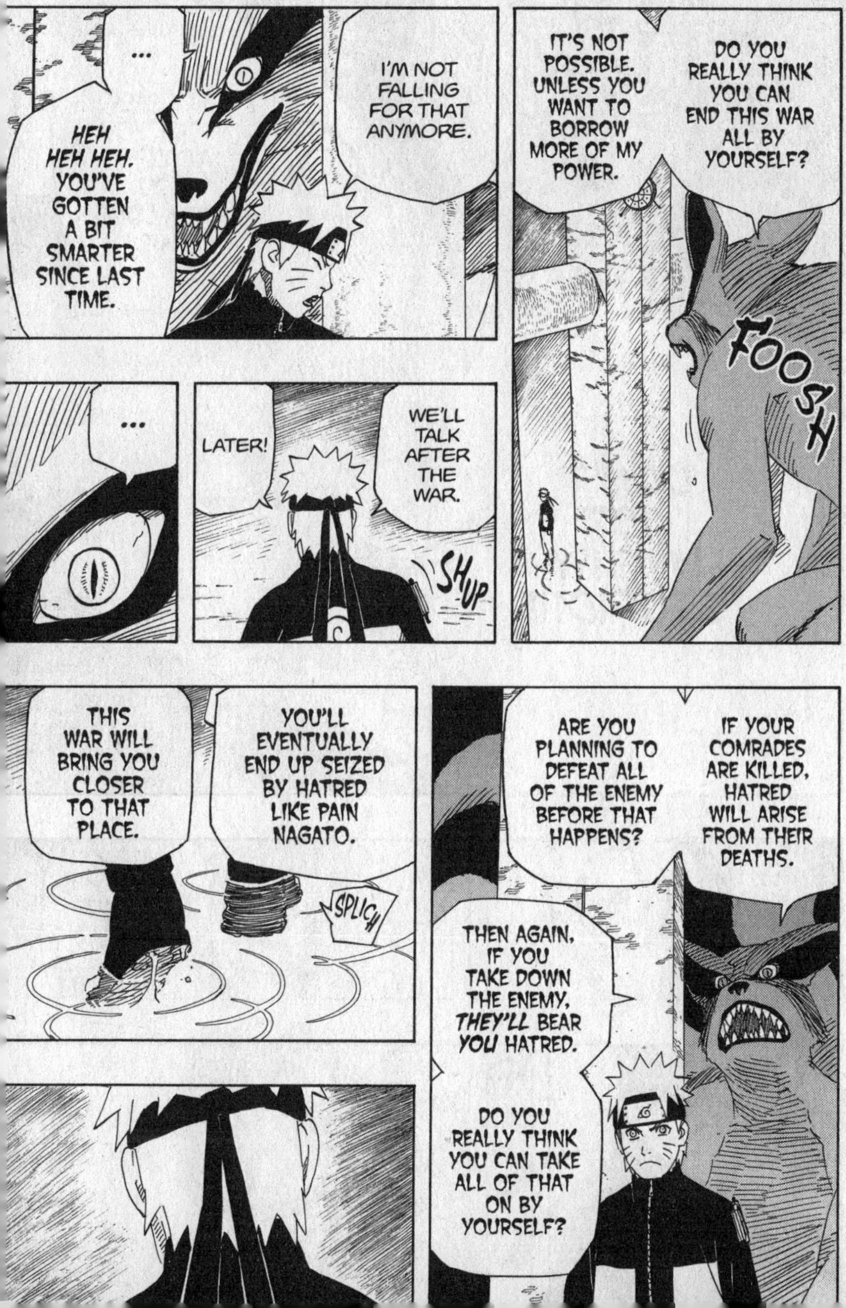
DO YOU REALLY THINK YOU CAN END THIS WAR ALL BY YOURSELF?
IT'S NOT POSSIBLE. UNLESS YOU WANT TO BORROW MORE OF MY POWER.
FOOSH
I'M NOT FALLING FOR THAT ANYMORE.
...
HEH HEH HEH. YOU'VE GOTTEN A BIT SMARTER SINCE LAST TIME.
WE'LL TALK AFTER THE WAR.
LATER!
SHUP
...
IF YOUR COMRADES ARE KILLED, HATRED WILL ARISE FROM THEIR DEATHS.
ARE YOU PLANNING TO DEFEAT ALL OF THE ENEMY BEFORE THAT HAPPENS?
THEN AGAIN, IF YOU TAKE DOWN THE ENEMY, *THEY'LL* BEAR *YOU* HATRED.
DO YOU REALLY THINK YOU CAN TAKE ALL OF THAT ON BY YOURSELF?
YOU'LL EVENTUALLY END UP SEIZED BY HATRED LIKE PAIN NAGATO.
THIS WAR WILL BRING YOU CLOSER TO THAT PLACE.
SPLICH

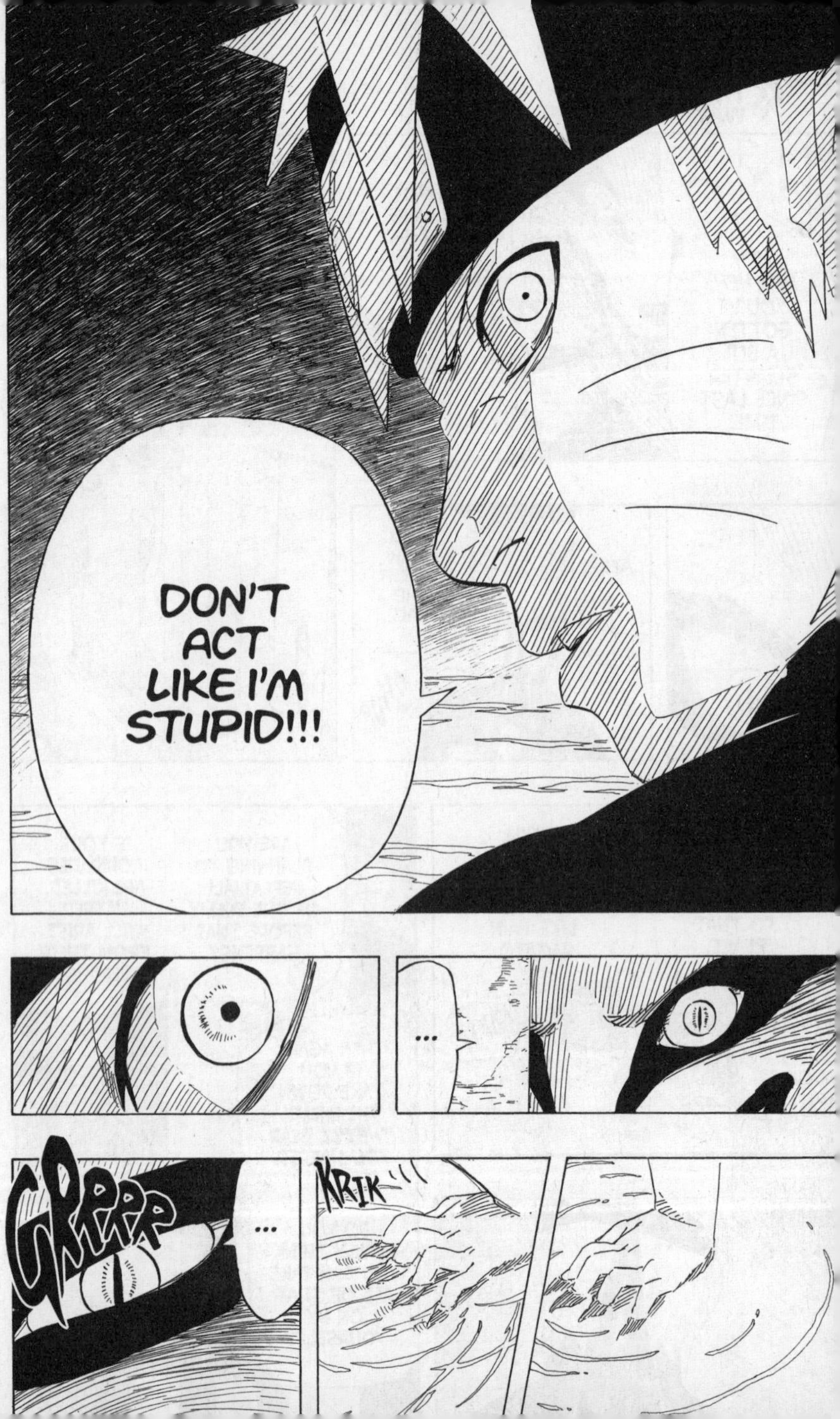
DON'T ACT LIKE I'M STUPID!!!
...
KRIK
...
GRRRR

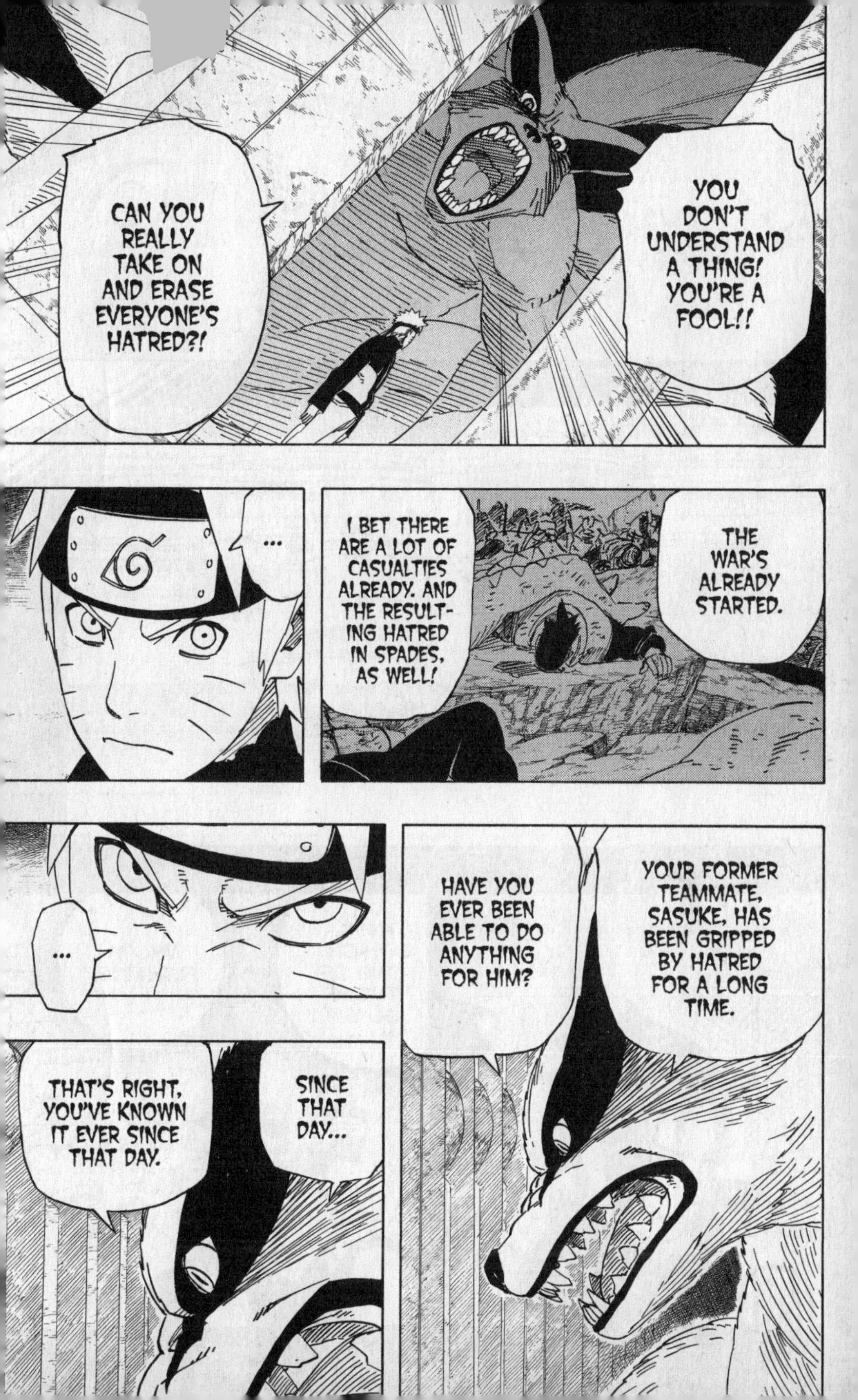
YOU DON'T UNDERSTAND A THING! YOU'RE A FOOL!!
CAN YOU REALLY TAKE ON AND ERASE EVERYONE'S HATRED?!
THE WAR'S ALREADY STARTED.
I BET THERE ARE A LOT OF CASUALTIES ALREADY. AND THE RESULTING HATRED IN SPADES, AS WELL!
...
YOUR FORMER TEAMMATE, SASUKE, HAS BEEN GRIPPED BY HATRED FOR A LONG TIME.
HAVE YOU EVER BEEN ABLE TO DO ANYTHING FOR HIM?
...
SINCE THAT DAY...
THAT'S RIGHT, YOU'VE KNOWN IT EVER SINCE THAT DAY.

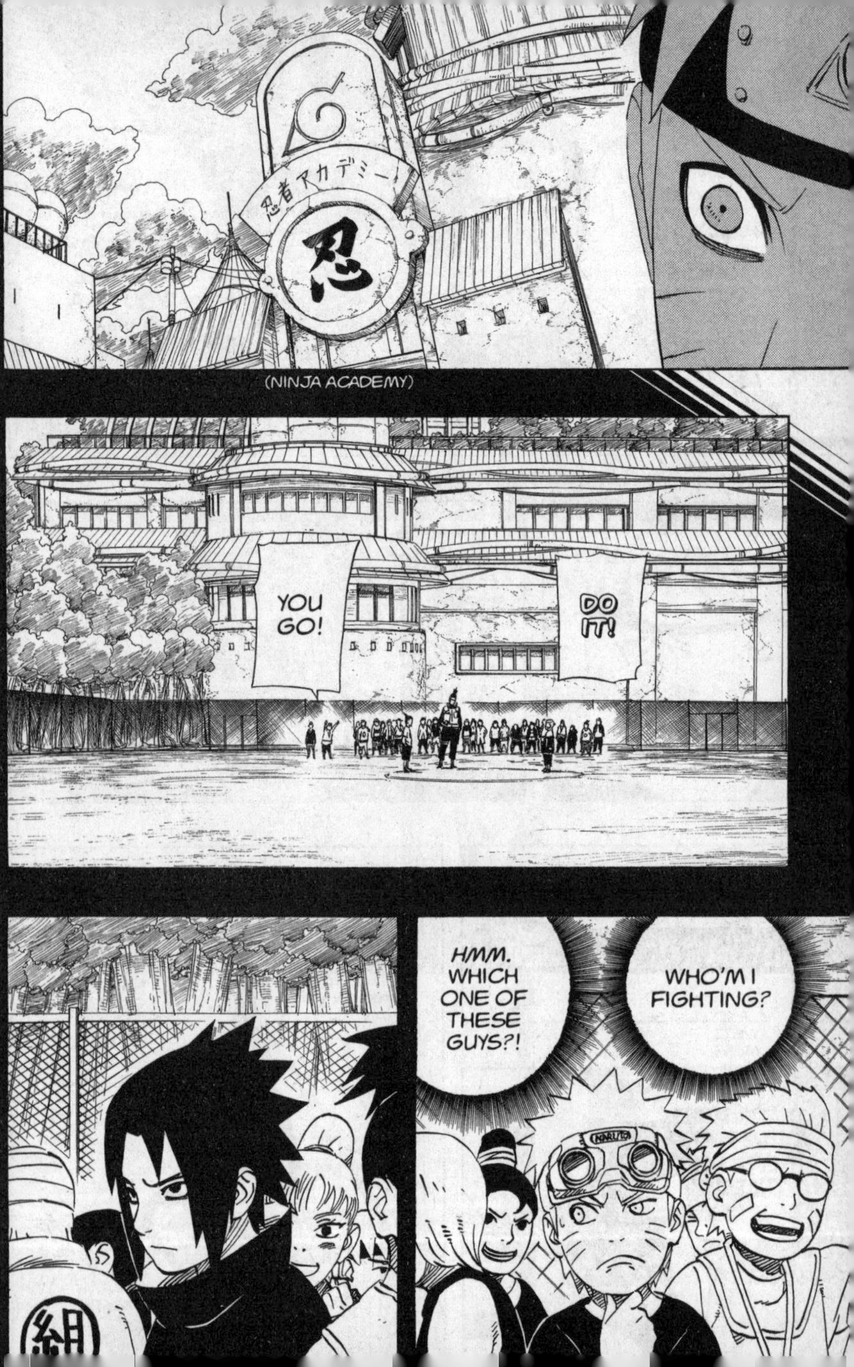
忍者アカデミー
忍
(NINJA ACADEMY)
DO IT!
YOU GO!
WHO'M I FIGHTING?
HMM. WHICH ONE OF THESE GUYS?!

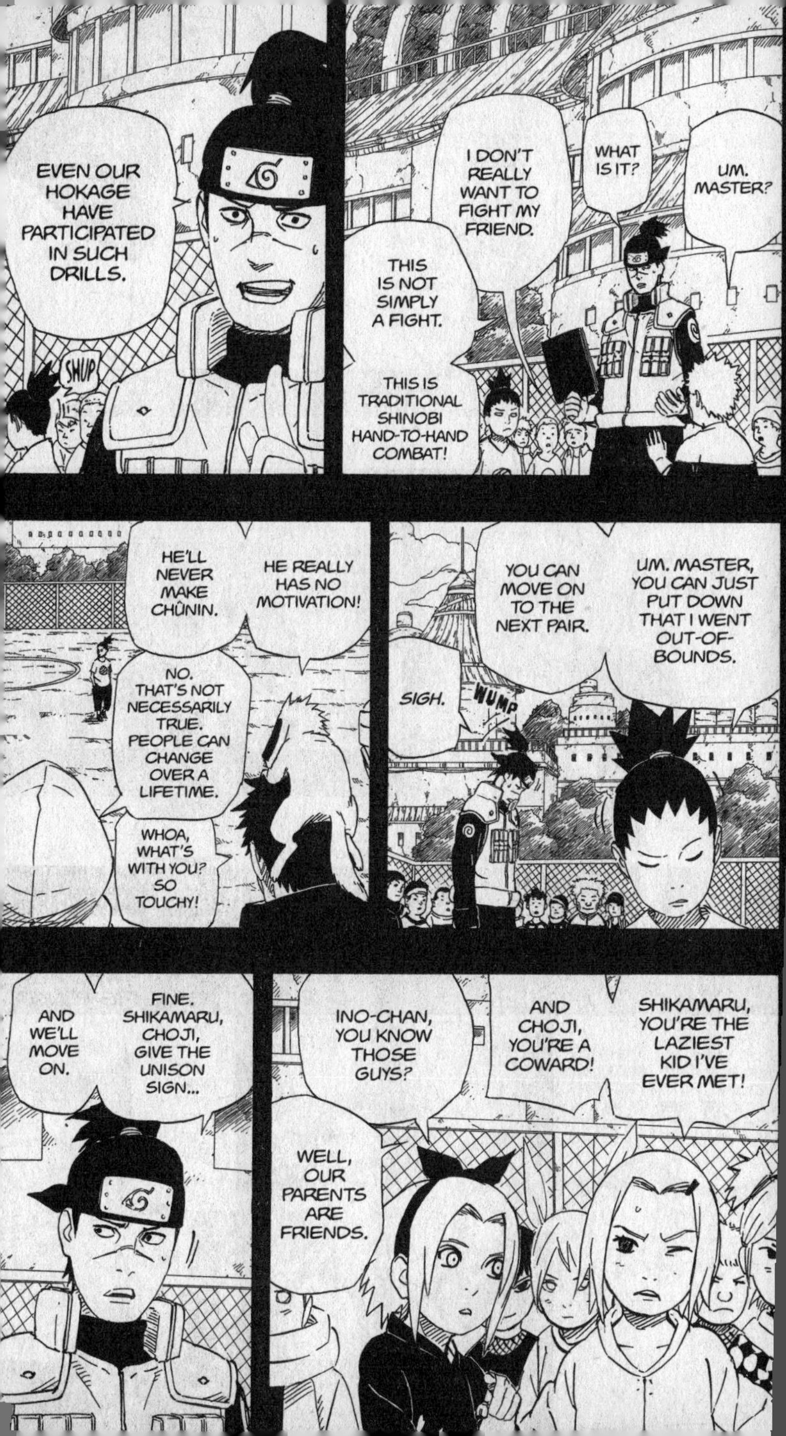
UM. MASTER?
WHAT IS IT?
I DON'T REALLY WANT TO FIGHT MY FRIEND.
THIS IS NOT SIMPLY A FIGHT.
THIS IS TRADITIONAL SHINOBI HAND-TO-HAND COMBAT!
EVEN OUR HOKAGE HAVE PARTICIPATED IN SUCH DRILLS.
SHUP
UM. MASTER, YOU CAN JUST PUT DOWN THAT I WENT OUT-OF-BOUNDS.
YOU CAN MOVE ON TO THE NEXT PAIR.
SIGH.
WUMP
HE REALLY HAS NO MOTIVATION!
HE'LL NEVER MAKE CHÛNIN.
NO. THAT'S NOT NECESSARILY TRUE. PEOPLE CAN CHANGE OVER A LIFETIME.
WHOA, WHAT'S WITH YOU? SO TOUCHY!
SHIKAMARU, YOU'RE THE LAZIEST KID I'VE EVER MET!
AND CHOJI, YOU'RE A COWARD!
INO-CHAN, YOU KNOW THOSE GUYS?
WELL, OUR PARENTS ARE FRIENDS.
FINE. SHIKAMARU, CHOJI, GIVE THE UNISON SIGN...
AND WE'LL MOVE ON.

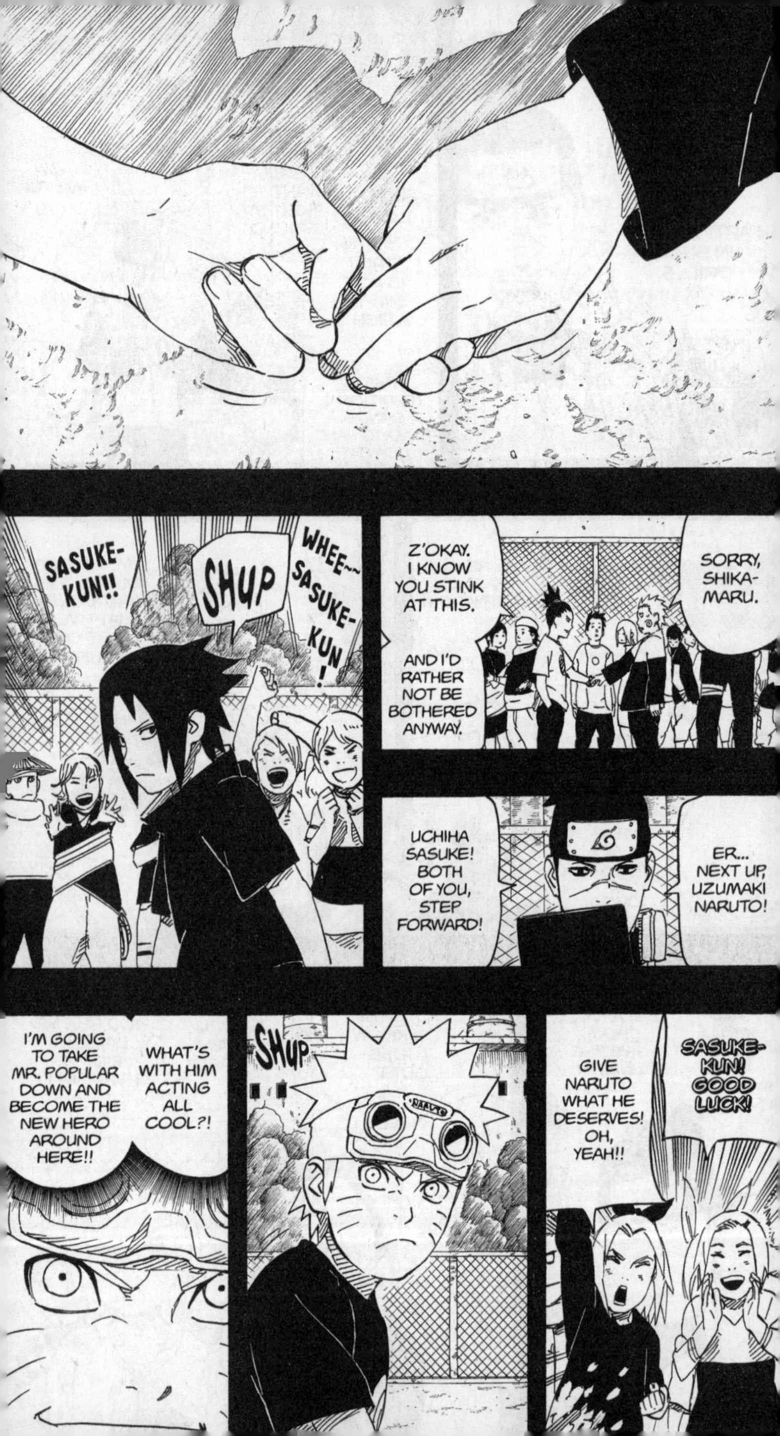
SORRY, SHIKA-MARU.
Z'OKAY. I KNOW YOU STINK AT THIS.
AND I'D RATHER NOT BE BOTHERED ANYWAY.
ER... NEXT UP, UZUMAKI NARUTO!
UCHIHA SASUKE! BOTH OF YOU, STEP FORWARD!
WHEE~~ SASUKE-KUN!
SHUP
SASUKE-KUN!!
SASUKE-KUN! GOOD LUCK!
GIVE NARUTO WHAT HE DESERVES! OH, YEAH!!
SHUP
WHAT'S WITH HIM ACTING ALL COOL?!
I'M GOING TO TAKE MR. POPULAR DOWN AND BECOME THE NEW HERO AROUND HERE!!

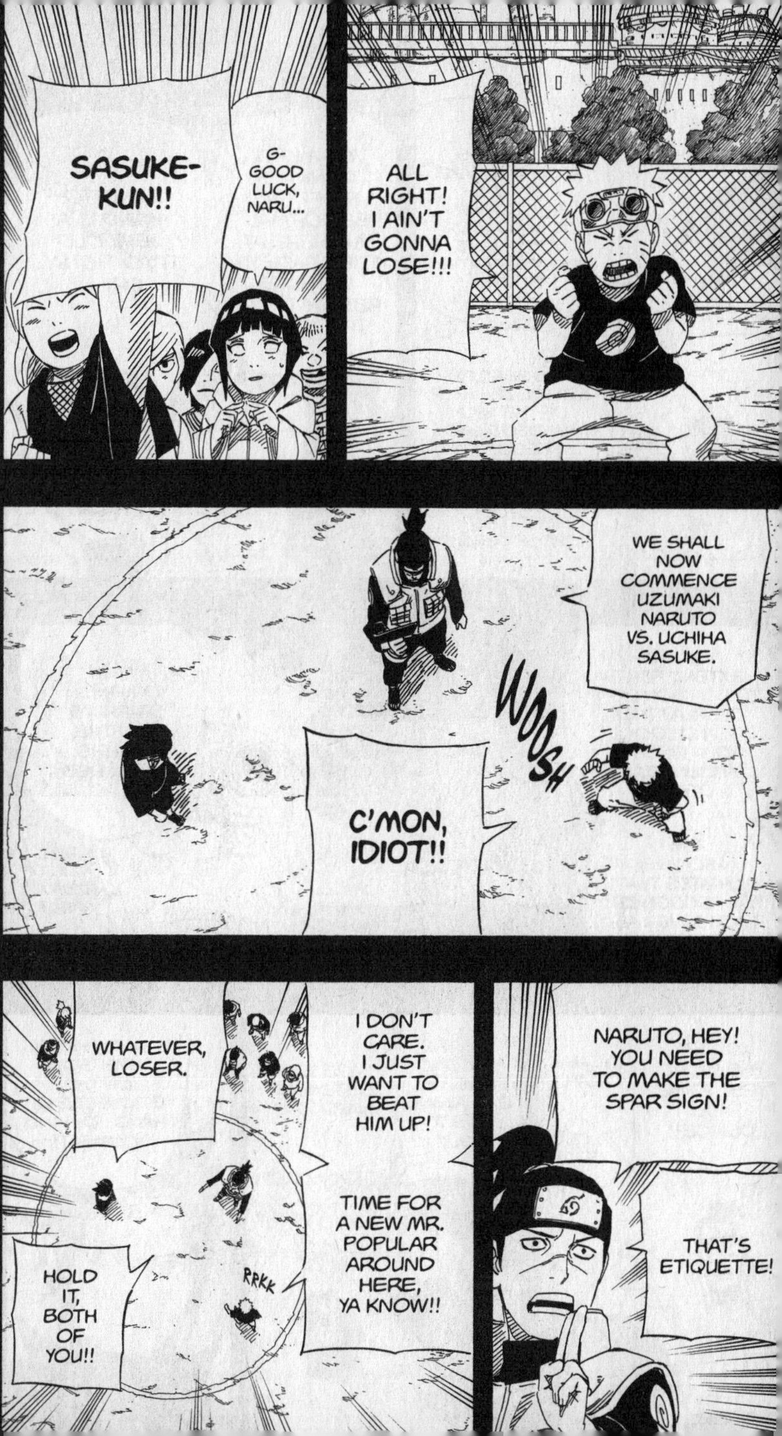
ALL RIGHT! I AIN'T GONNA LOSE!!!
G-GOOD LUCK, NARU...
SASUKE-KUN!!
WE SHALL NOW COMMENCE UZUMAKI NARUTO VS. UCHIHA SASUKE.
WOOSH
C'MON, IDIOT!!
NARUTO, HEY! YOU NEED TO MAKE THE SPAR SIGN!
THAT'S ETIQUETTE!
I DON'T CARE. I JUST WANT TO BEAT HIM UP!
WHATEVER, LOSER.
TIME FOR A NEW MR. POPULAR AROUND HERE, YA KNOW!!
RRKK
HOLD IT, BOTH OF YOU!!

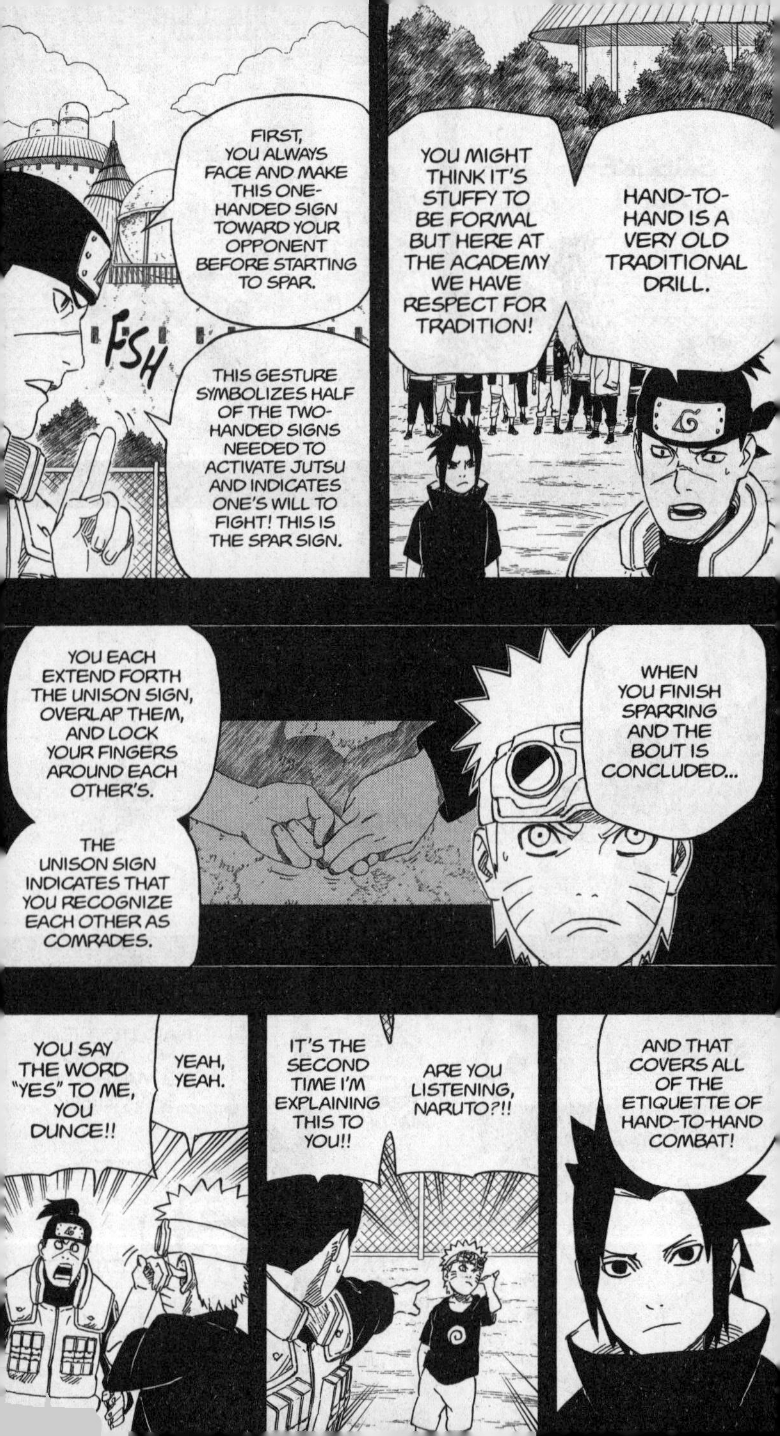
HAND-TO-HAND IS A VERY OLD TRADITIONAL DRILL.
YOU MIGHT THINK IT'S STUFFY TO BE FORMAL BUT HERE AT THE ACADEMY WE HAVE RESPECT FOR TRADITION!
FIRST, YOU ALWAYS FACE AND MAKE THIS ONE-HANDED SIGN TOWARD YOUR OPPONENT BEFORE STARTING TO SPAR.
FSH
THIS GESTURE SYMBOLIZES HALF OF THE TWO-HANDED SIGNS NEEDED TO ACTIVATE JUTSU AND INDICATES ONE'S WILL TO FIGHT! THIS IS THE SPAR SIGN.
WHEN YOU FINISH SPARRING AND THE BOUT IS CONCLUDED...
YOU EACH EXTEND FORTH THE UNISON SIGN, OVERLAP THEM, AND LOCK YOUR FINGERS AROUND EACH OTHER'S.
THE UNISON SIGN INDICATES THAT YOU RECOGNIZE EACH OTHER AS COMRADES.
AND THAT COVERS ALL OF THE ETIQUETTE OF HAND-TO-HAND COMBAT!
ARE YOU LISTENING, NARUTO?!!
IT'S THE SECOND TIME I'M EXPLAINING THIS TO YOU!!
YEAH, YEAH.
YOU SAY THE WORD "YES" TO ME, YOU DUNCE!!

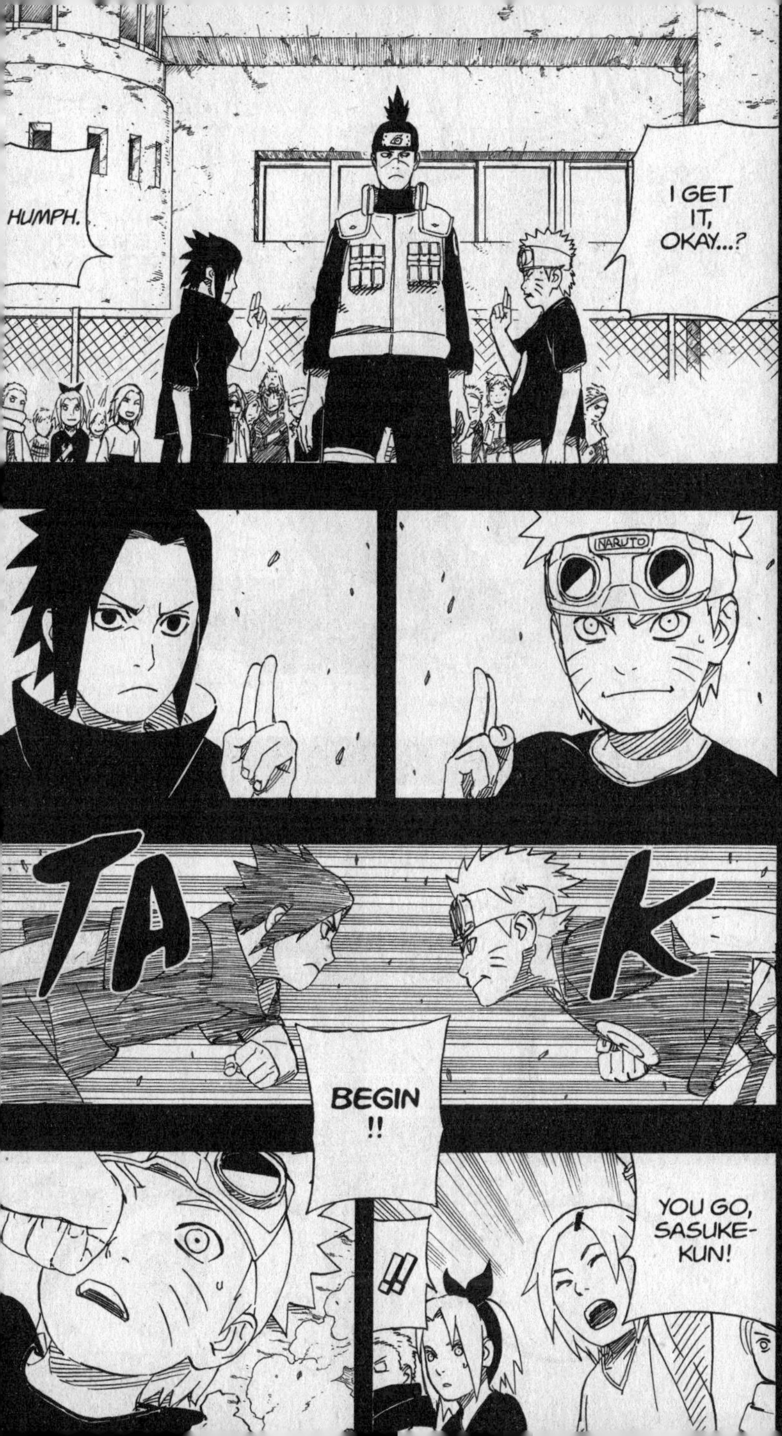
I GET IT, OKAY...?
HUMPH.
TAK
BEGIN!!
YOU GO, SASUKE-KUN!
!!

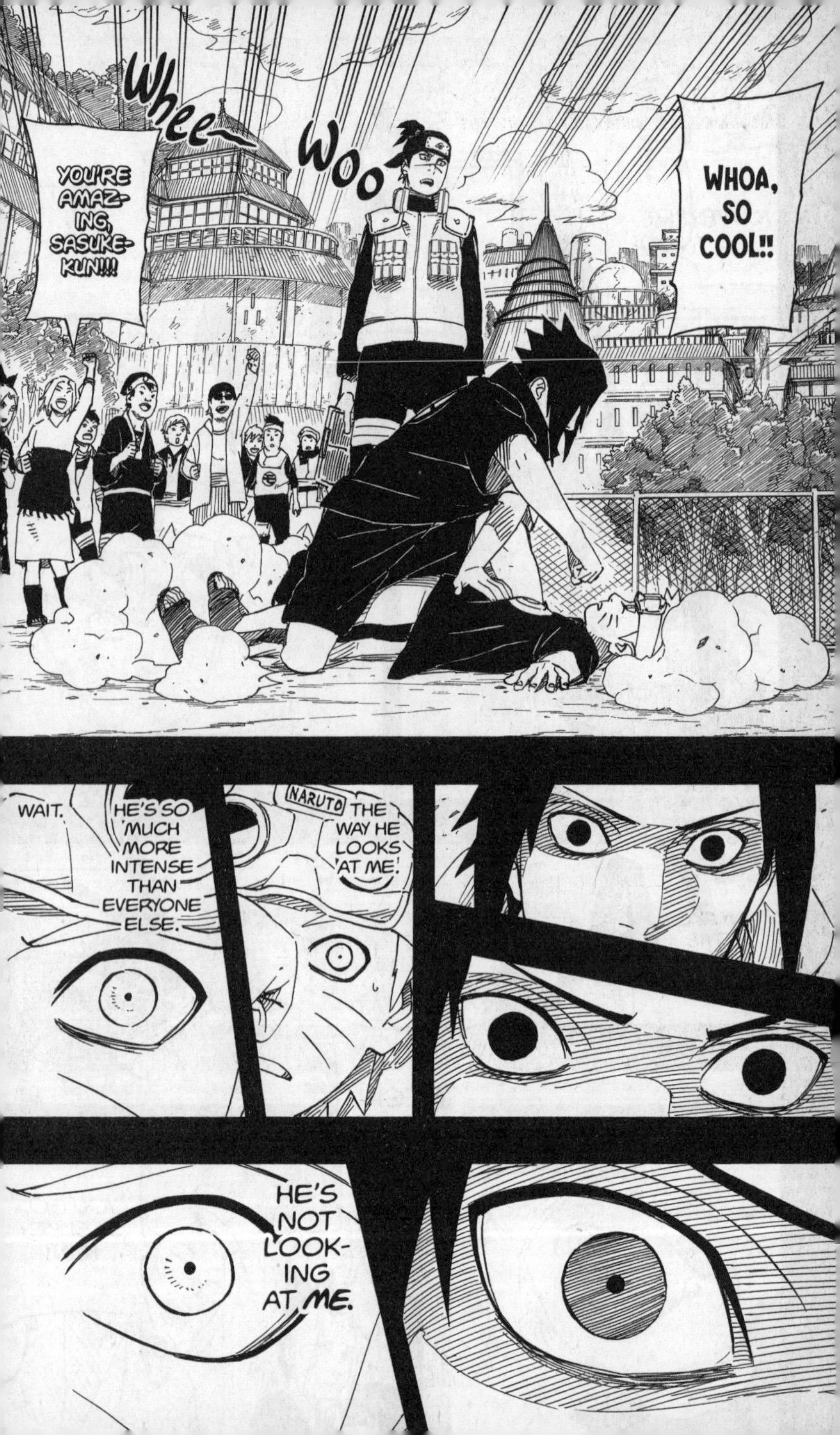
WHOA, SO COOL!!
Whee— Woo
YOU'RE AMAZING, SASUKE-KUN!!!
NARUTO
THE WAY HE LOOKS AT ME.
HE'S SO MUCH MORE INTENSE THAN EVERYONE ELSE.
WAIT.
HE'S NOT LOOKING AT ME.

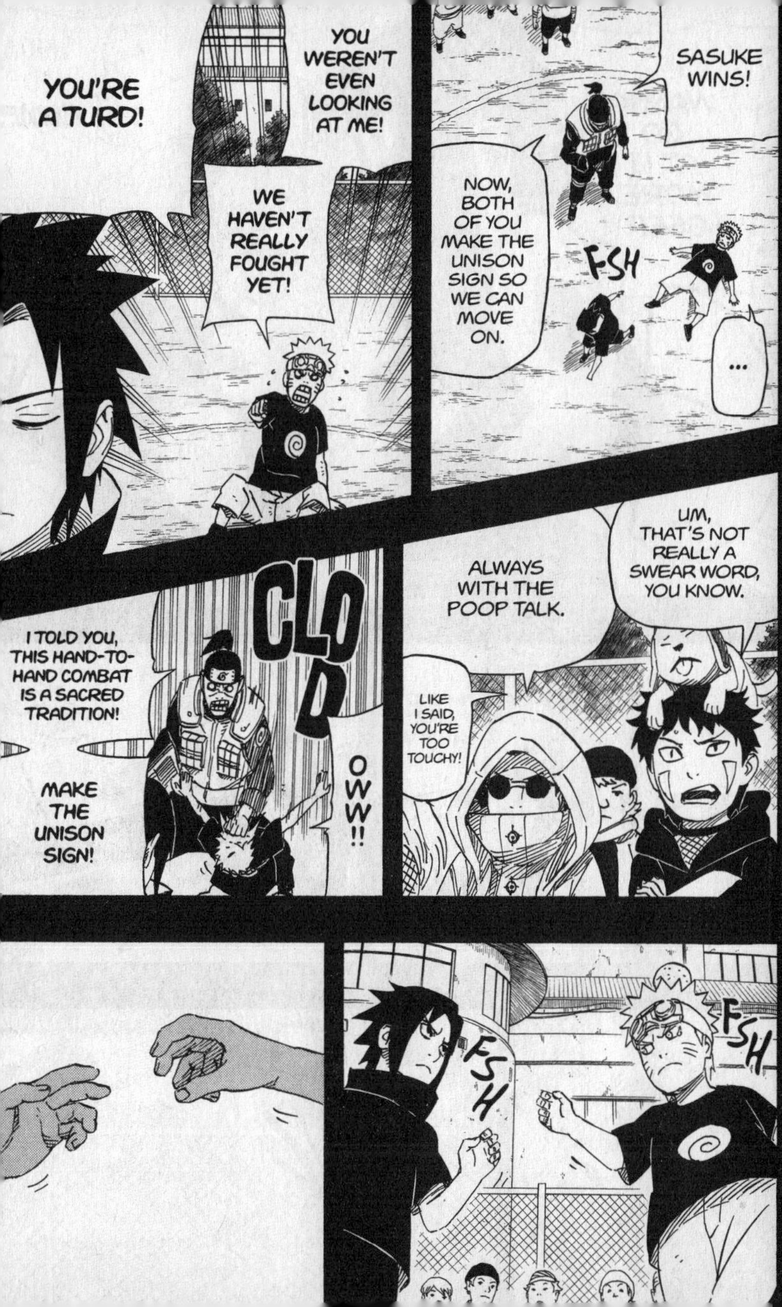
SASUKE WINS!
NOW, BOTH OF YOU MAKE THE UNISON SIGN SO WE CAN MOVE ON.
FSH
...
YOU WEREN'T EVEN LOOKING AT ME!
YOU'RE A TURD!
WE HAVEN'T REALLY FOUGHT YET!
UM, THAT'S NOT REALLY A SWEAR WORD, YOU KNOW.
ALWAYS WITH THE POOP TALK.
LIKE I SAID, YOU'RE TOO TOUCHY!
CLOD
OWW!!
I TOLD YOU, THIS HAND-TO-HAND COMBAT IS A SACRED TRADITION!
MAKE THE UNISON SIGN!
FSH
FSH

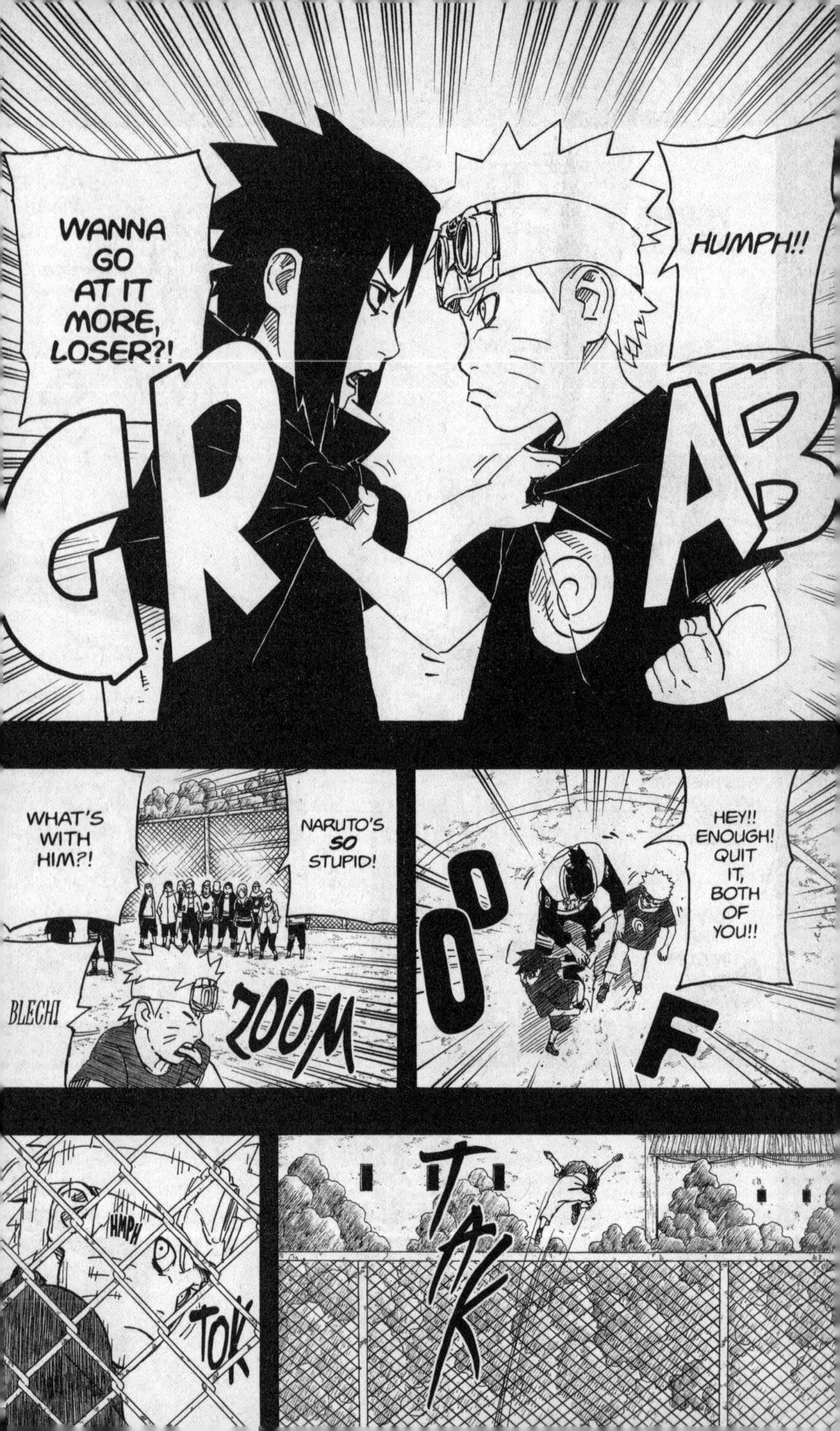
HUMPH!!
WANNA GO AT IT MORE, LOSER?!
GRAB
HEY!! ENOUGH! QUIT IT, BOTH OF YOU!!
OOF
NARUTO'S SO STUPID!
WHAT'S WITH HIM?!
ZOOM
BLECH!
TAK
HMPH
TOK

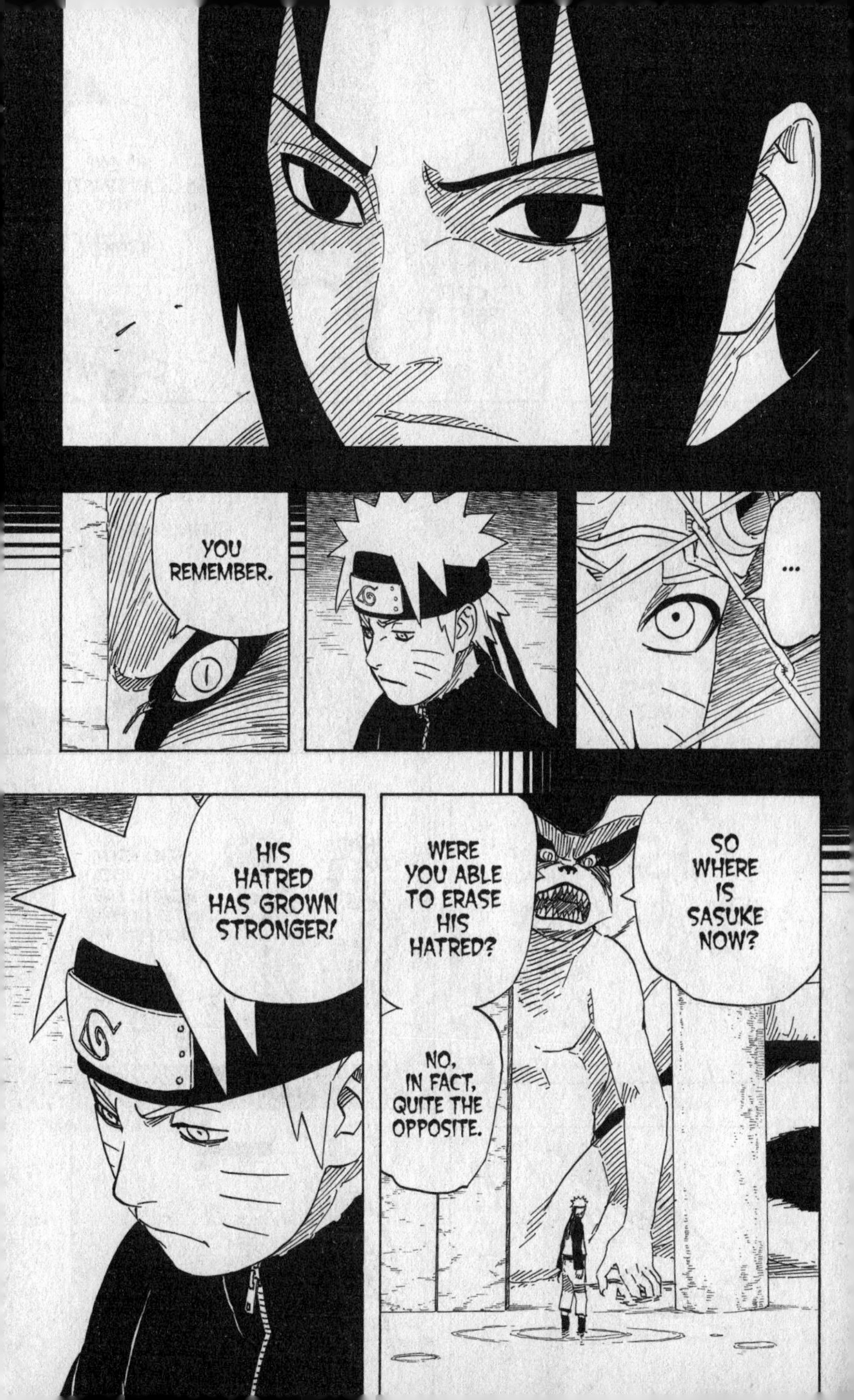
...
YOU REMEMBER.
SO WHERE IS SASUKE NOW?
WERE YOU ABLE TO ERASE HIS HATRED?
NO, IN FACT, QUITE THE OPPOSITE.
HIS HATRED HAS GROWN STRONGER!

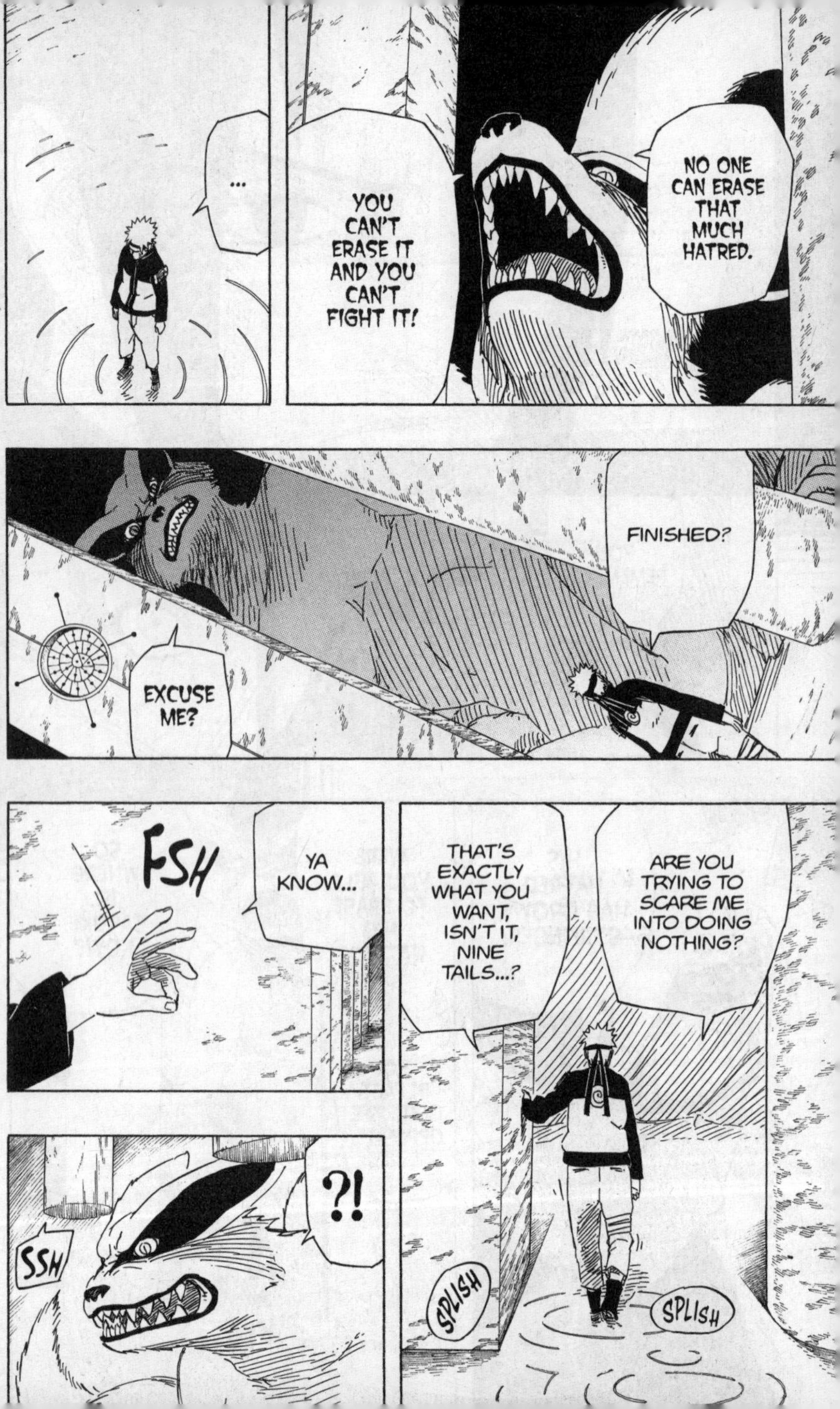
NO ONE CAN ERASE THAT MUCH HATRED.
YOU CAN'T ERASE IT AND YOU CAN'T FIGHT IT!
...
FINISHED?
EXCUSE ME?
ARE YOU TRYING TO SCARE ME INTO DOING NOTHING?
THAT'S EXACTLY WHAT YOU WANT, ISN'T IT, NINE TAILS...?
SPLISH
SPLISH
YA KNOW...
FSH
?!
SSH

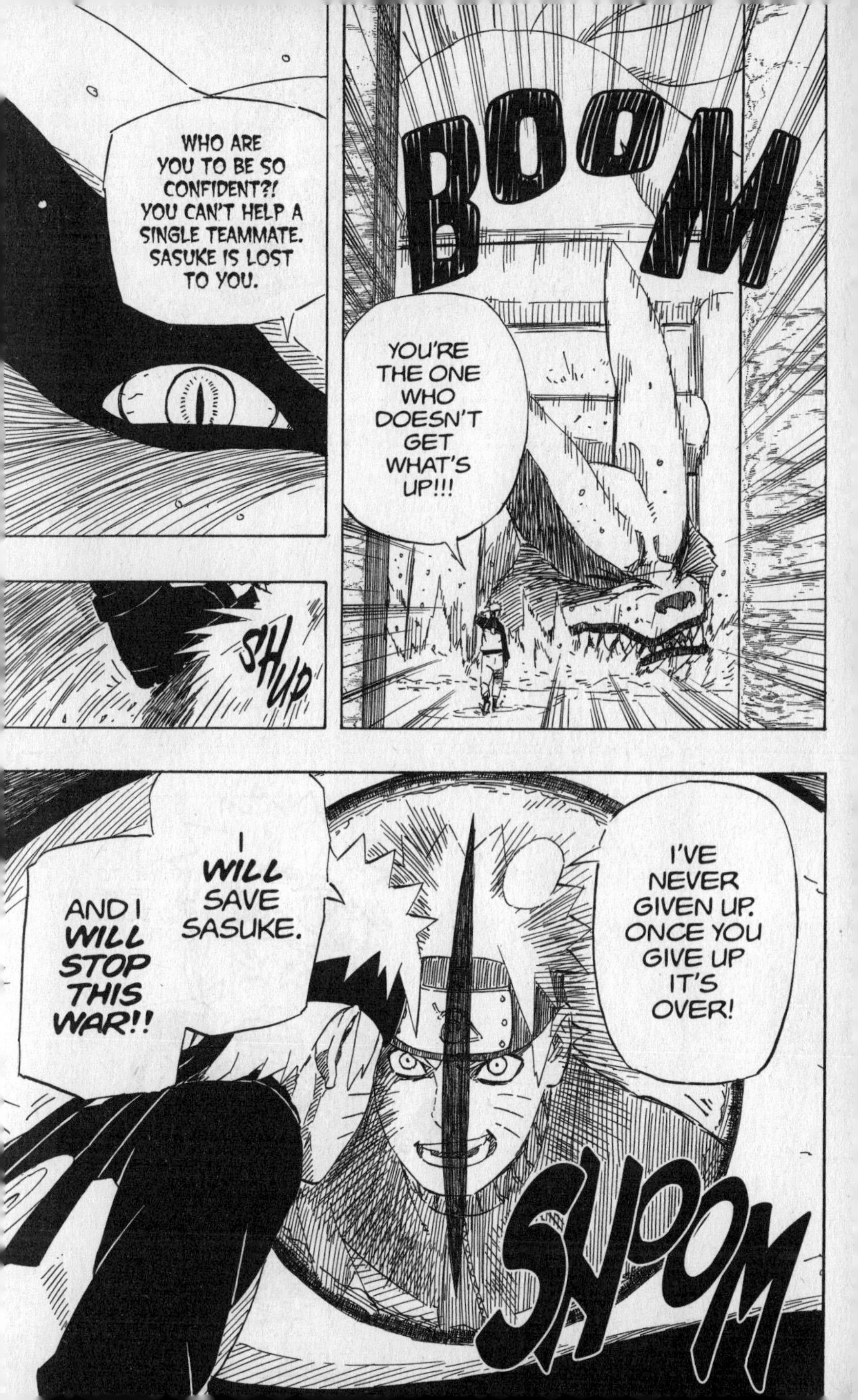
BOOM
YOU'RE THE ONE WHO DOESN'T GET WHAT'S UP!!!
WHO ARE YOU TO BE SO CONFIDENT?! YOU CAN'T HELP A SINGLE TEAMMATE. SASUKE IS LOST TO YOU.
SHUP
I'VE NEVER GIVEN UP. ONCE YOU GIVE UP IT'S OVER!
I WILL SAVE SASUKE.
AND I WILL STOP THIS WAR!!
SVOOM

# Number 539: Blood Night...!!

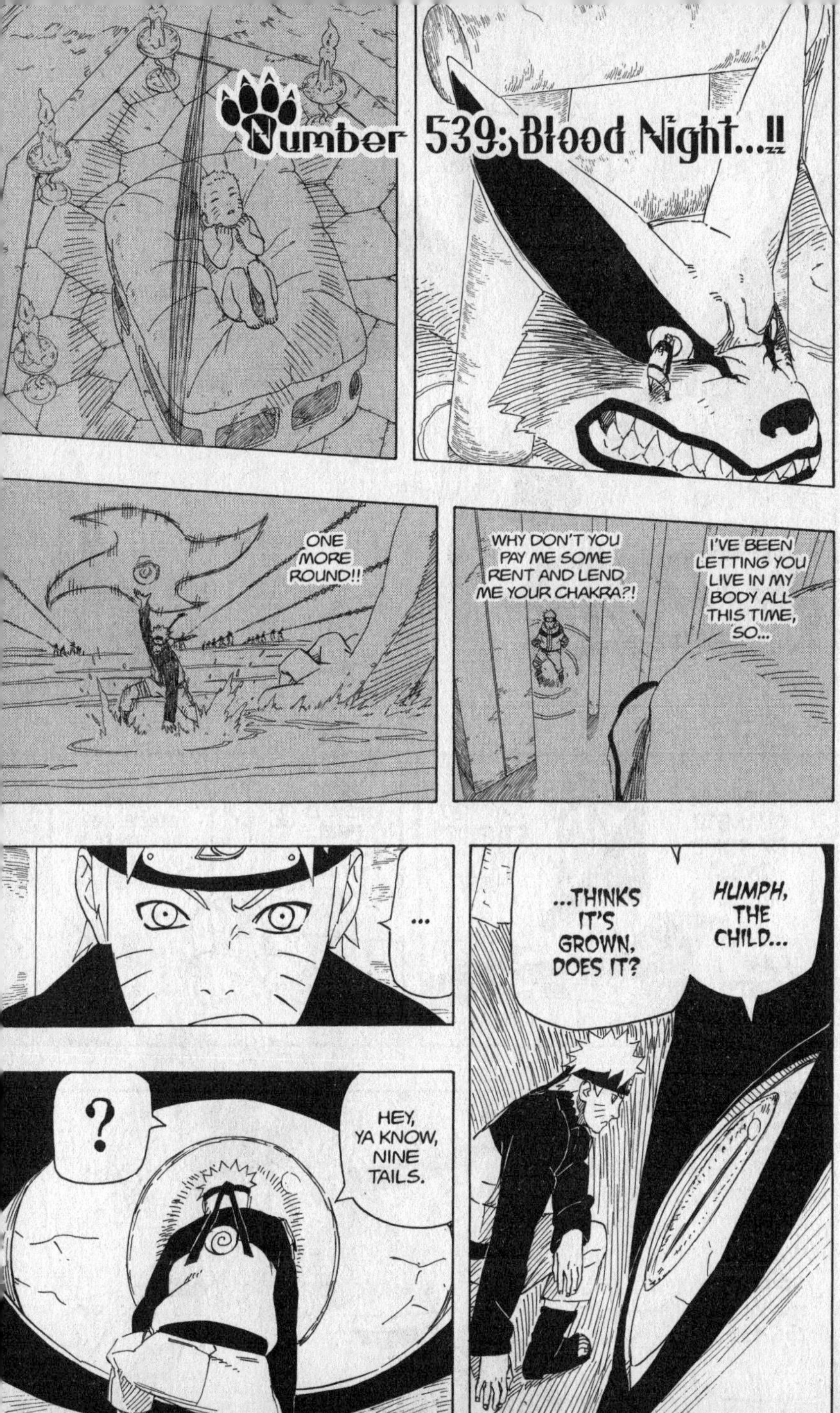
I'VE BEEN LETTING YOU LIVE IN MY BODY ALL THIS TIME, SO...
WHY DON'T YOU PAY ME SOME RENT AND LEND ME YOUR CHAKRA?!
ONE MORE ROUND!!
HUMPH, THE CHILD...
...THINKS IT'S GROWN, DOES IT?
...
HEY, YA KNOW, NINE TAILS.
?

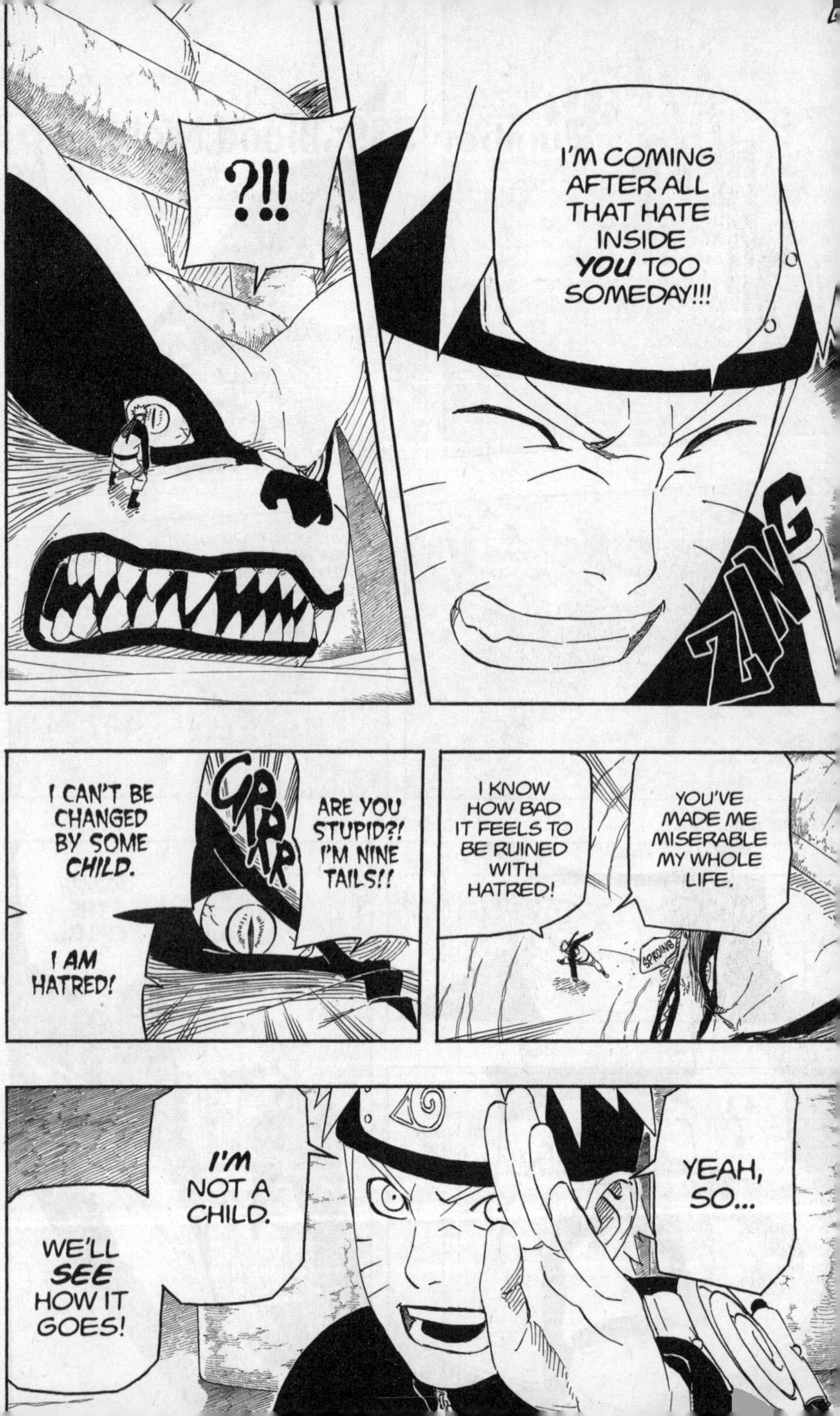
I'M COMING AFTER ALL THAT HATE INSIDE *YOU* TOO SOMEDAY!!!
ZING
?!!
YOU'VE MADE ME MISERABLE MY WHOLE LIFE.
I KNOW HOW BAD IT FEELS TO BE RUINED WITH HATRED!
SPROING
ARE YOU STUPID?! I'M NINE TAILS!!
GRRR
I CAN'T BE CHANGED BY SOME *CHILD.*
I *AM* HATRED!
YEAH, SO...
*I'M* NOT A CHILD.
WE'LL *SEE* HOW IT GOES!

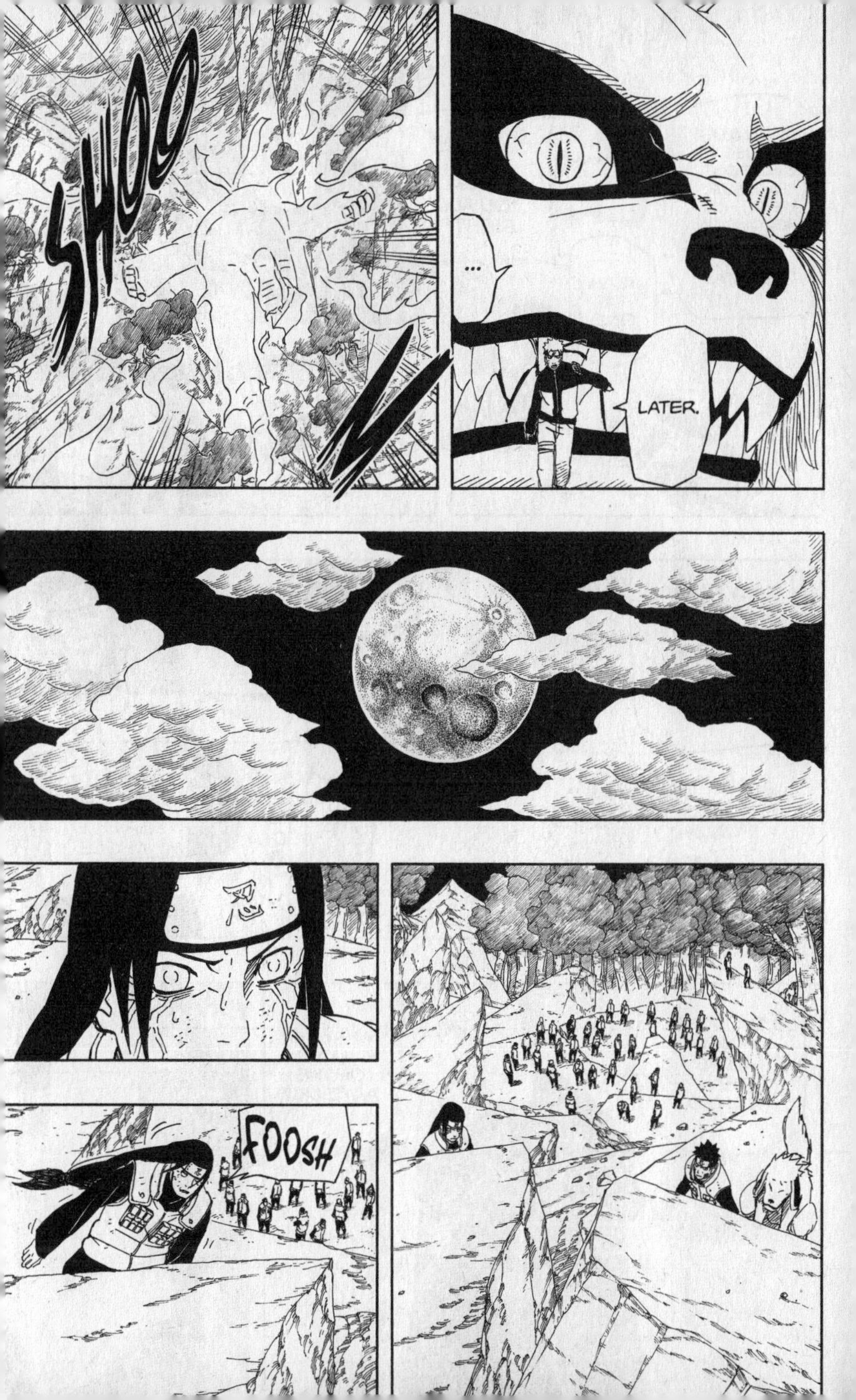
...
LATER.
SHOO
FOOSH

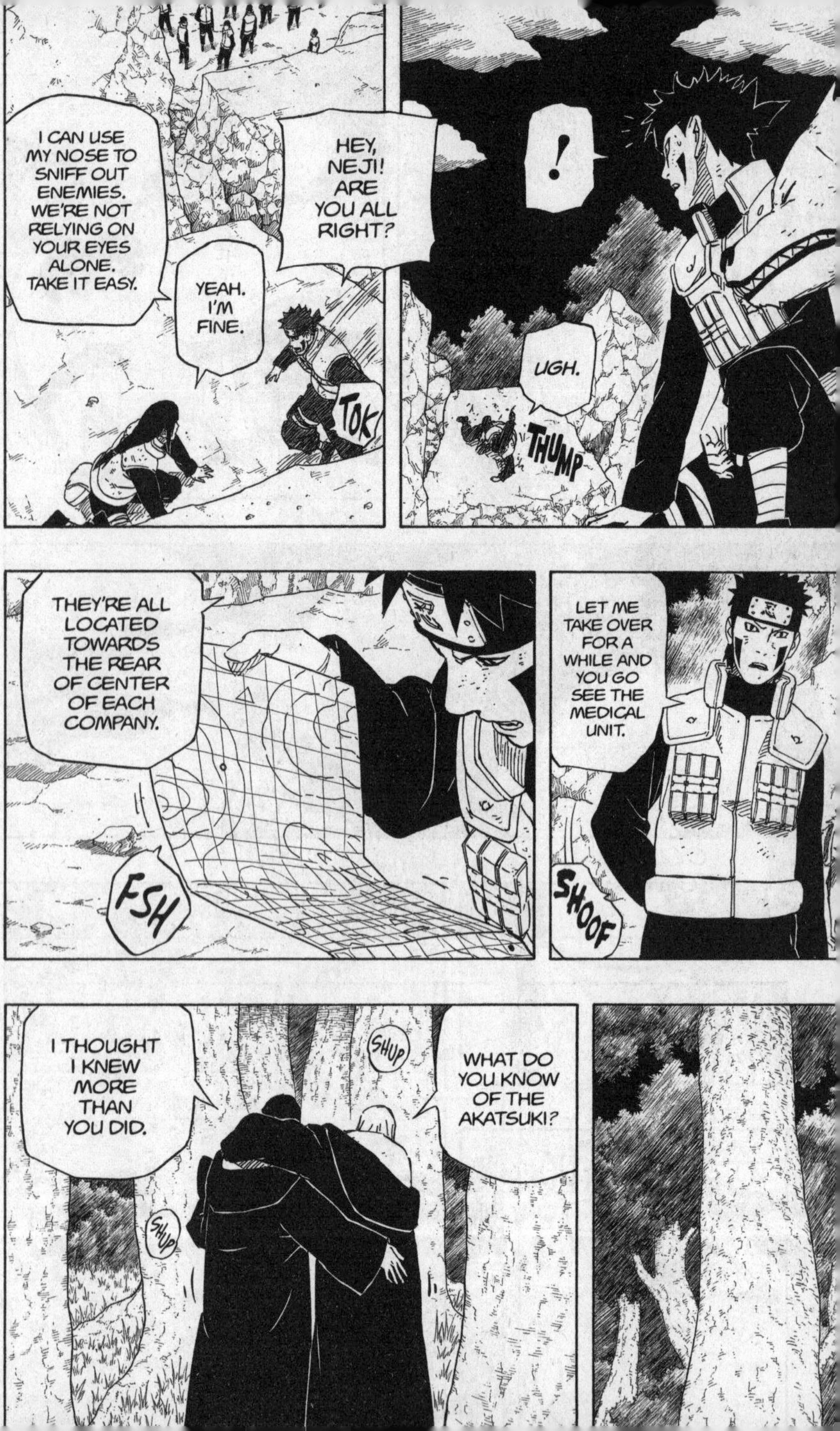
!
UGH.
THUMP
HEY, NEJI! ARE YOU ALL RIGHT?
I CAN USE MY NOSE TO SNIFF OUT ENEMIES. WE'RE NOT RELYING ON YOUR EYES ALONE. TAKE IT EASY.
YEAH. I'M FINE.
TOK
LET ME TAKE OVER FOR A WHILE AND YOU GO SEE THE MEDICAL UNIT.
SHOOF
THEY'RE ALL LOCATED TOWARDS THE REAR OF CENTER OF EACH COMPANY.
FSH
SHUP
WHAT DO YOU KNOW OF THE AKATSUKI?
I THOUGHT I KNEW MORE THAN YOU DID.
SHUP

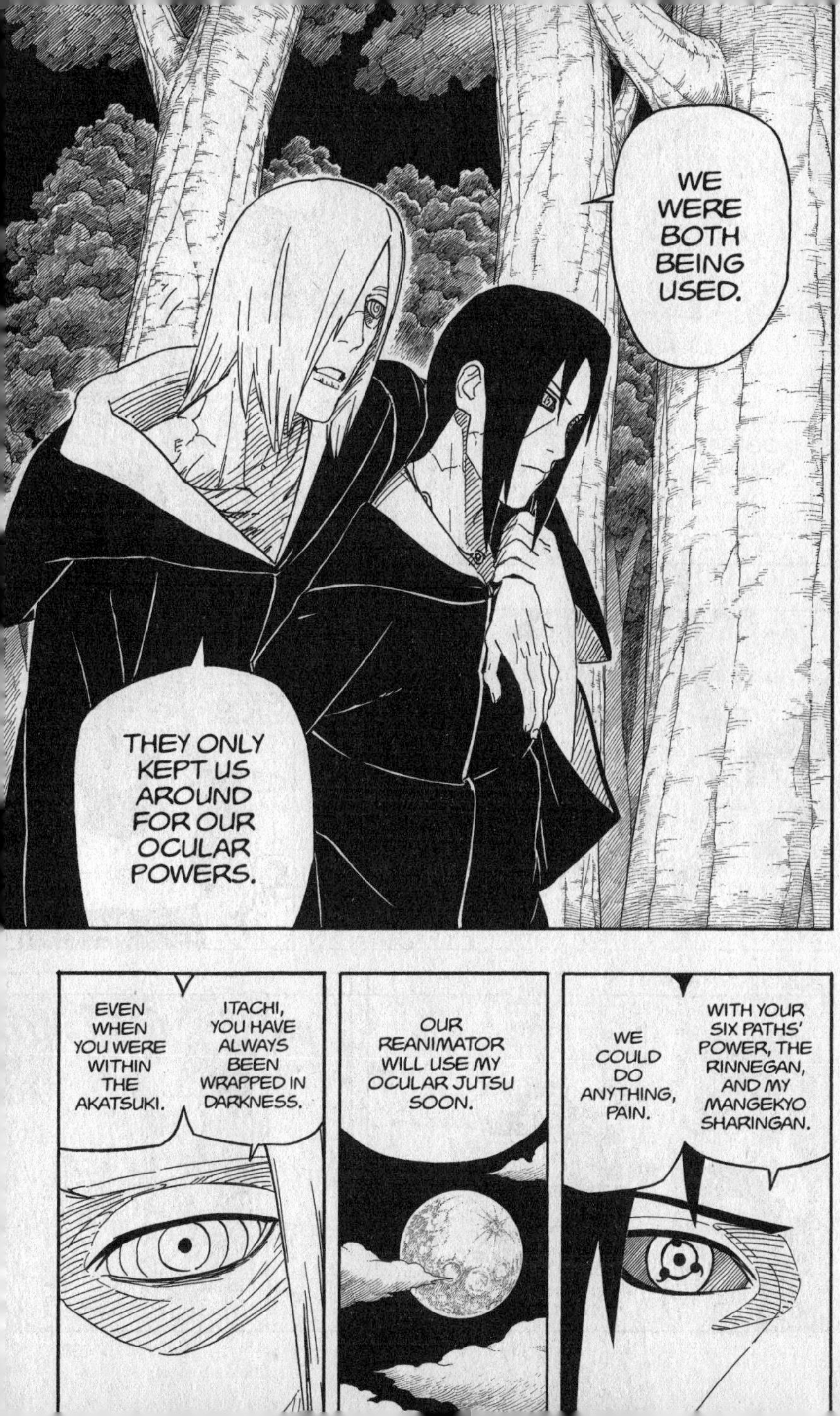
WE WERE BOTH BEING USED.
THEY ONLY KEPT US AROUND FOR OUR OCULAR POWERS.
WITH YOUR SIX PATHS' POWER, THE RINNEGAN, AND MY MANGEKYO SHARINGAN.
WE COULD DO ANYTHING, PAIN.
OUR REANIMATOR WILL USE MY OCULAR JUTSU SOON.
ITACHI, YOU HAVE ALWAYS BEEN WRAPPED IN DARKNESS.
EVEN WHEN YOU WERE WITHIN THE AKATSUKI.

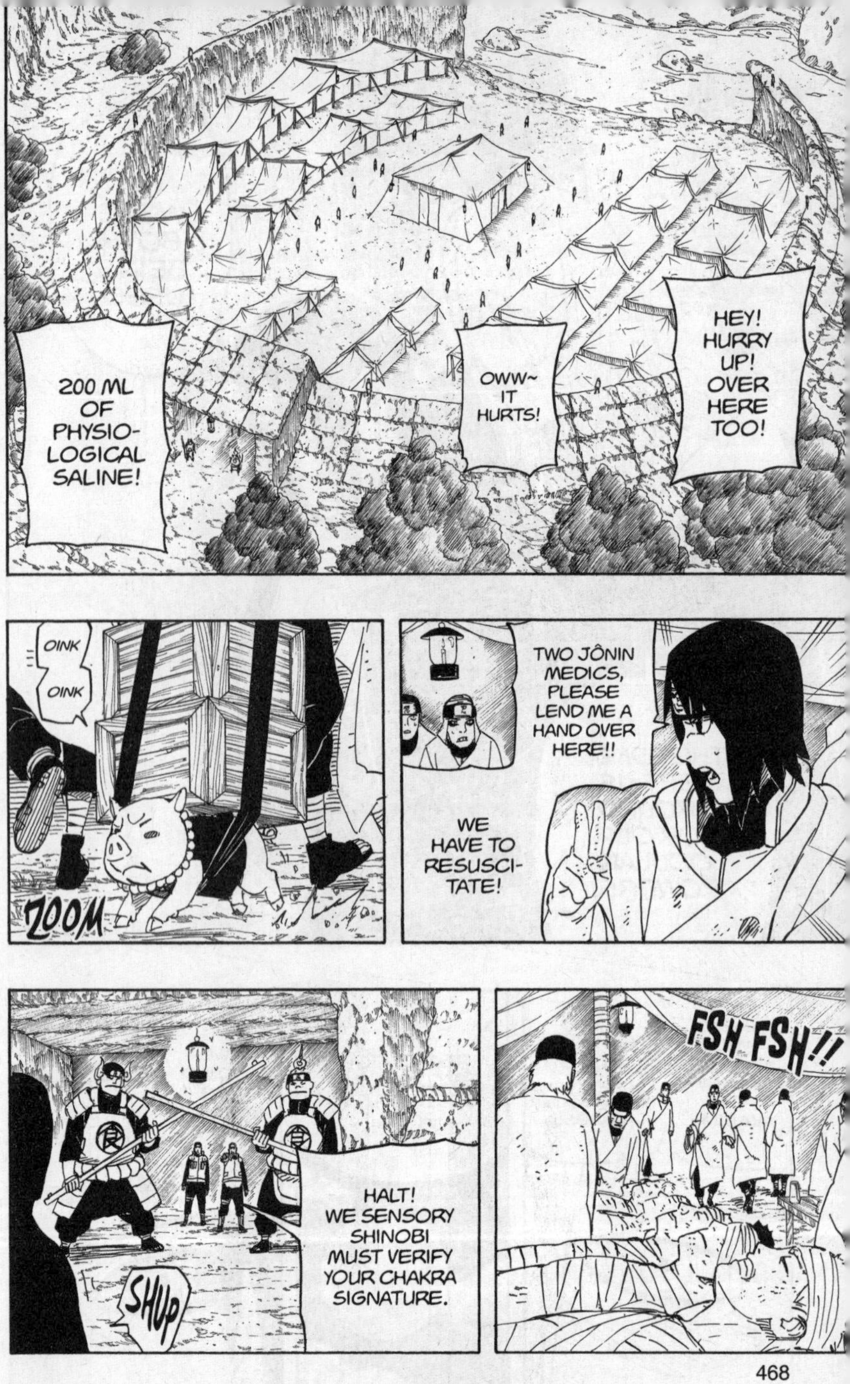
HEY! HURRY UP! OVER HERE TOO!
OWW~ IT HURTS!
200 ML OF PHYSIO-LOGICAL SALINE!
TWO JÔNIN MEDICS, PLEASE LEND ME A HAND OVER HERE!!
WE HAVE TO RESUSCI-TATE!
OINK
OINK
ZOOM
FSH FSH!!
HALT! WE SENSORY SHINOBI MUST VERIFY YOUR CHAKRA SIGNATURE.
SHUP

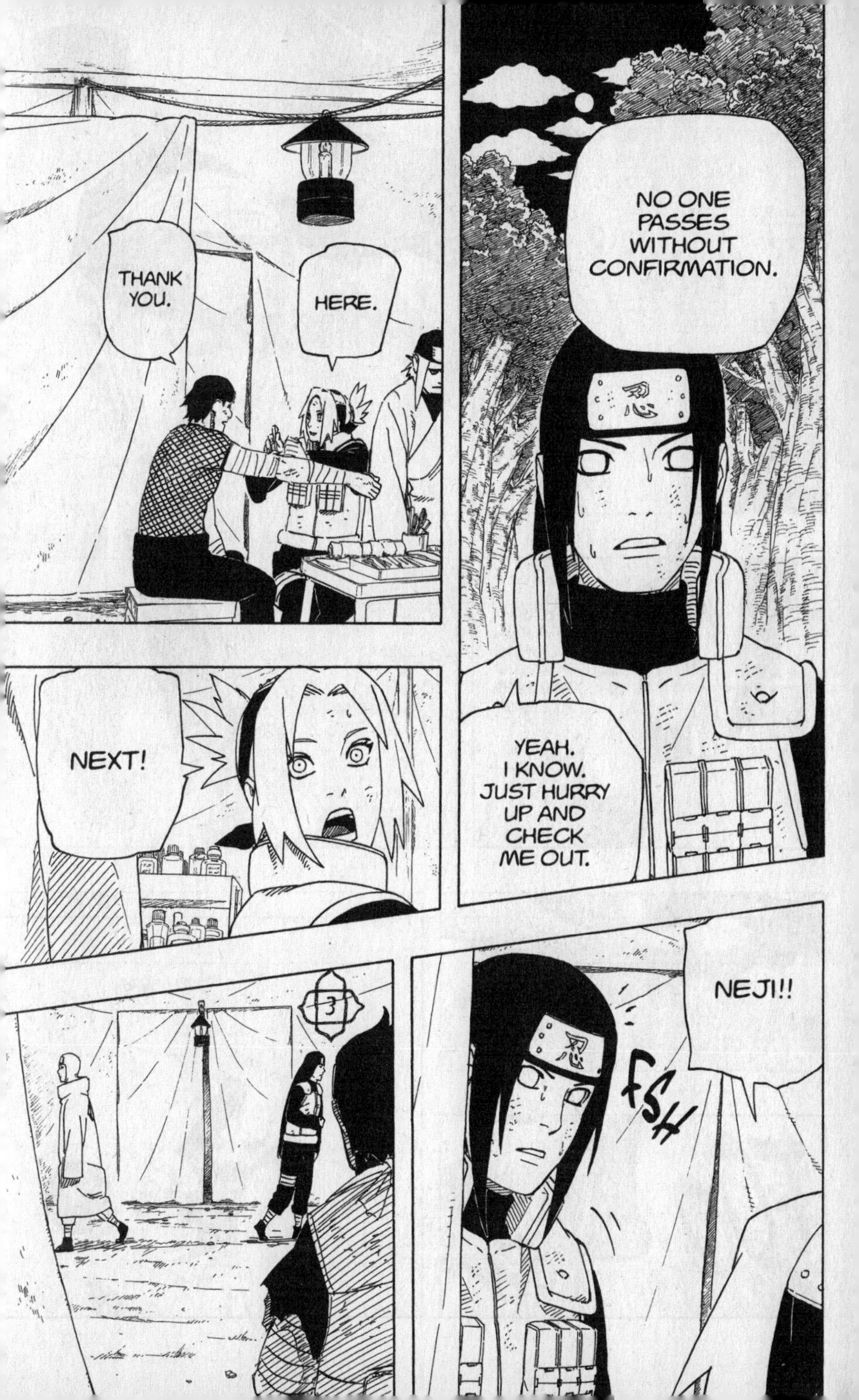
NO ONE PASSES WITHOUT CONFIRMATION.
YEAH. I KNOW. JUST HURRY UP AND CHECK ME OUT.
HERE.
THANK YOU.
NEXT!
NEJI!!
FSH
3

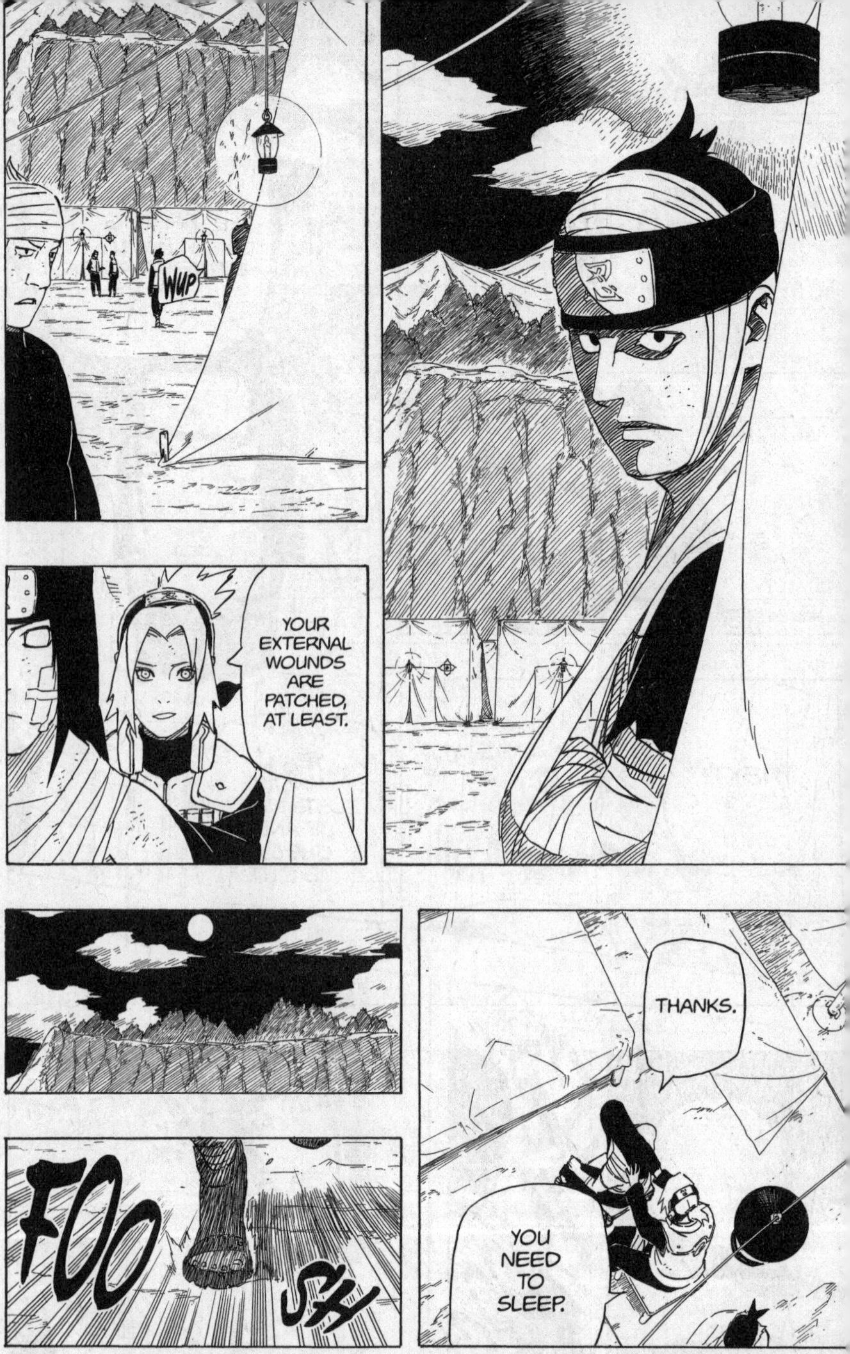
WUP
YOUR EXTERNAL WOUNDS ARE PATCHED, AT LEAST.
THANKS.
YOU NEED TO SLEEP.
FOOSH

READ THIS WAY

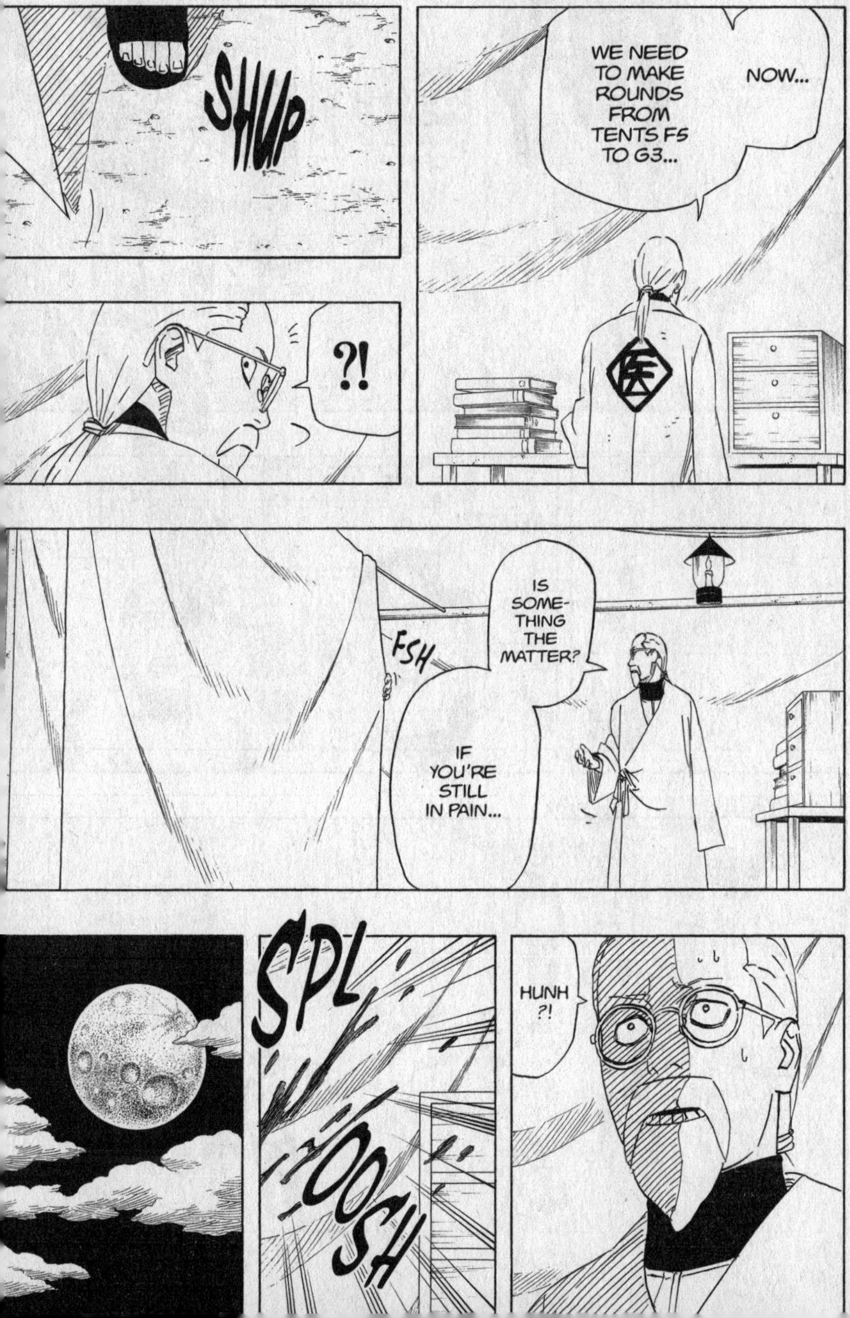
NOW...
WE NEED TO MAKE ROUNDS FROM TENTS F5 TO G3...
SHUP
?!
IS SOMETHING THE MATTER?
FSH
IF YOU'RE STILL IN PAIN...
HUNH ?!
SPL
OOSH

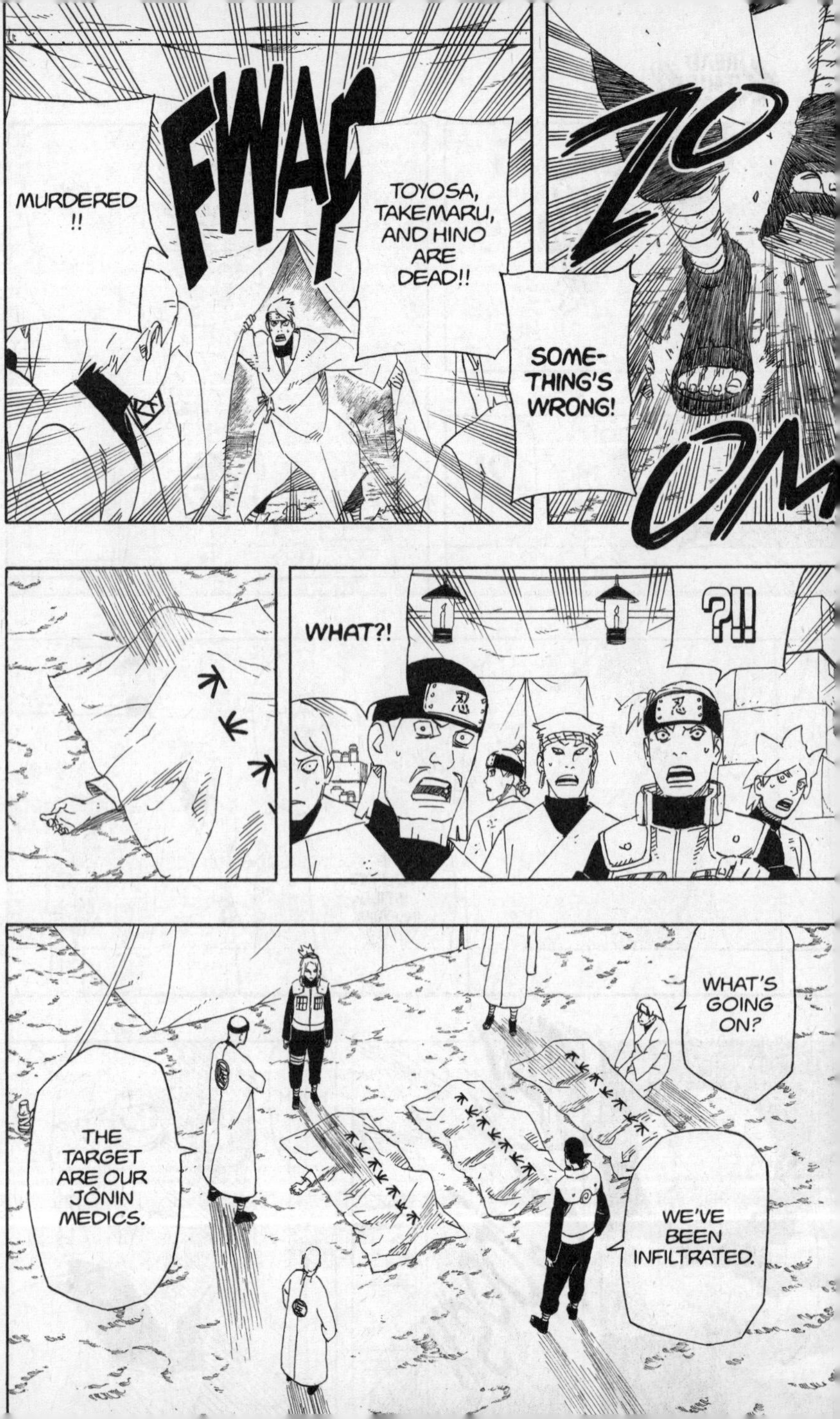
ZOOM
SOMETHING'S WRONG!
TOYOSA, TAKEMARU, AND HINO ARE DEAD!!
FWAP
MURDERED!!
?!!
WHAT?!
WHAT'S GOING ON?
WE'VE BEEN INFILTRATED.
THE TARGET ARE OUR JÔNIN MEDICS.

READ THIS WAY

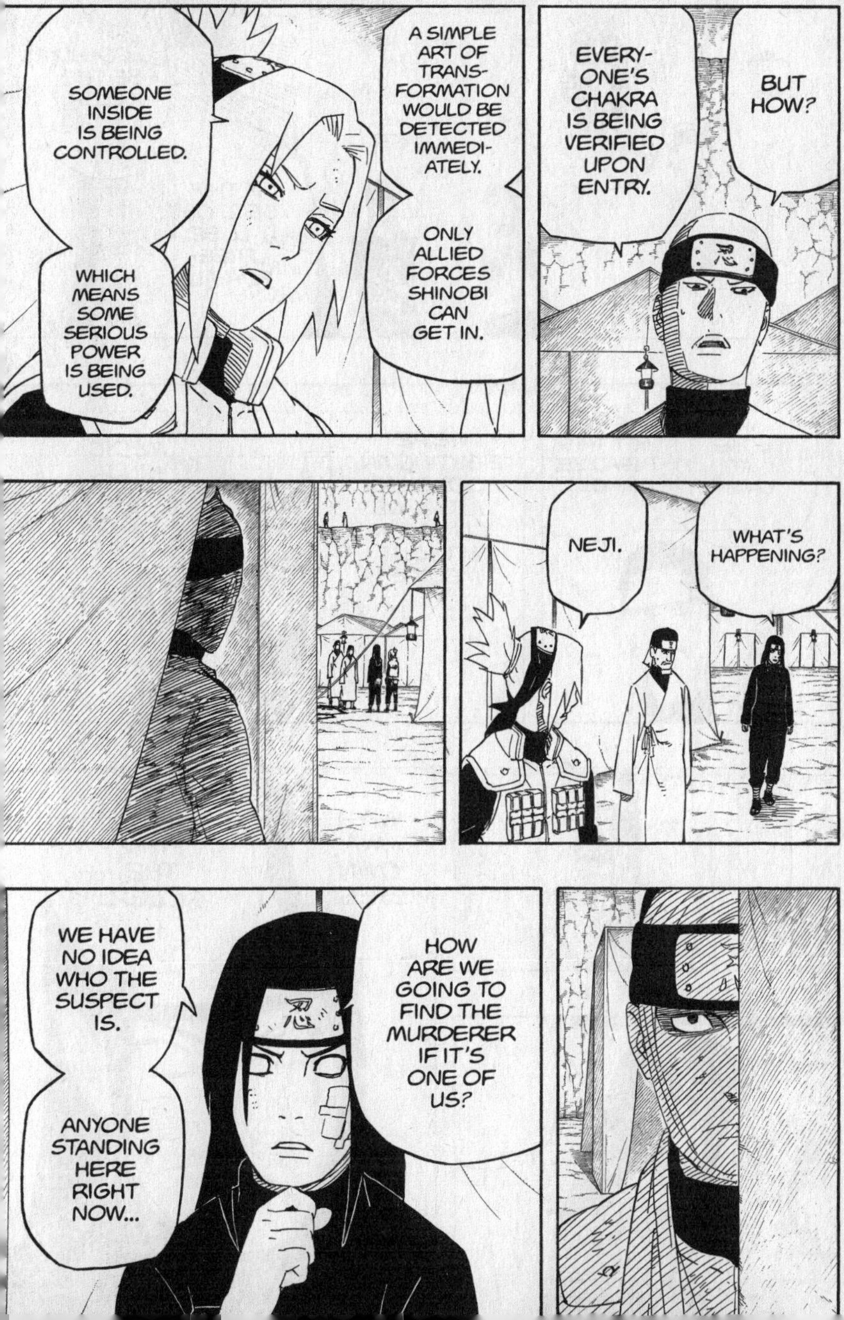
BUT HOW?
EVERY-ONE'S CHAKRA IS BEING VERIFIED UPON ENTRY.
A SIMPLE ART OF TRANS-FORMATION WOULD BE DETECTED IMMEDI-ATELY.
ONLY ALLIED FORCES SHINOBI CAN GET IN.
SOMEONE INSIDE IS BEING CONTROLLED.
WHICH MEANS SOME SERIOUS POWER IS BEING USED.
WHAT'S HAPPENING?
NEJI.
HOW ARE WE GOING TO FIND THE MURDERER IF IT'S ONE OF US?
WE HAVE NO IDEA WHO THE SUSPECT IS.
ANYONE STANDING HERE RIGHT NOW...

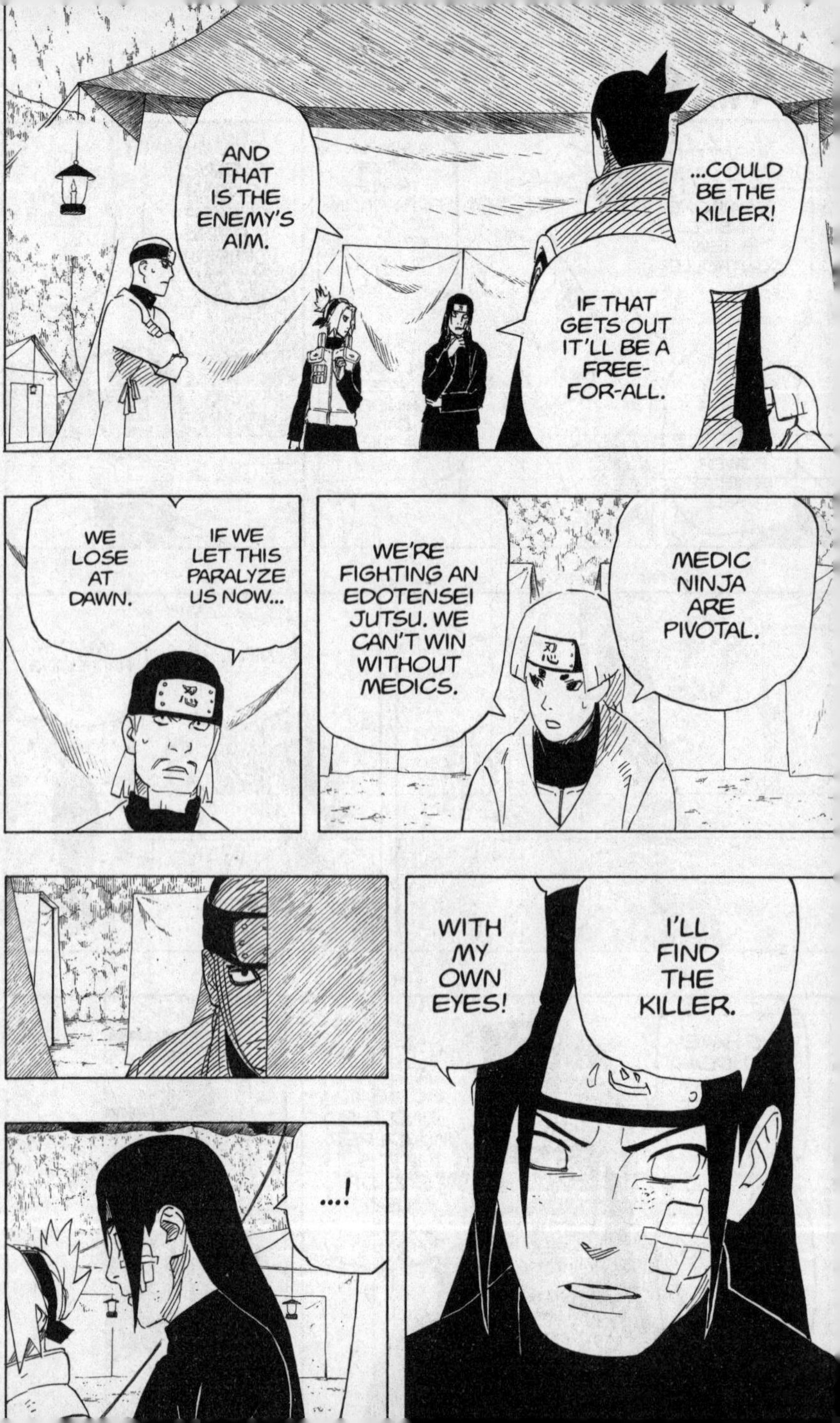
...COULD BE THE KILLER!
IF THAT GETS OUT IT'LL BE A FREE-FOR-ALL.
AND THAT IS THE ENEMY'S AIM.
MEDIC NINJA ARE PIVOTAL.
WE'RE FIGHTING AN EDOTENSEI JUTSU. WE CAN'T WIN WITHOUT MEDICS.
IF WE LET THIS PARALYZE US NOW...
WE LOSE AT DAWN.
I'LL FIND THE KILLER.
WITH MY OWN EYES!
...!

READ THIS WAY

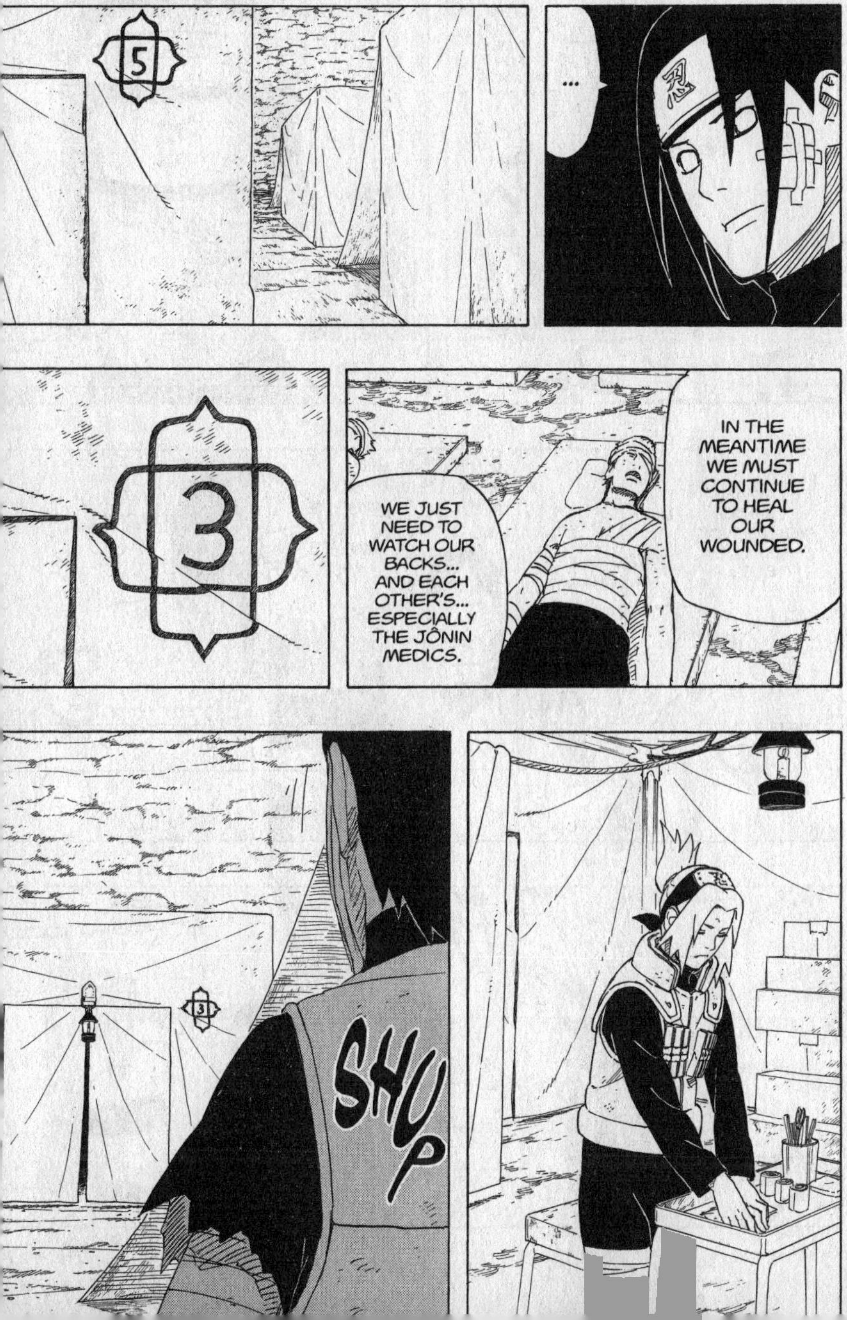
...
5
IN THE MEANTIME WE MUST CONTINUE TO HEAL OUR WOUNDED.
WE JUST NEED TO WATCH OUR BACKS... AND EACH OTHER'S... ESPECIALLY THE JÔNIN MEDICS.
3
3
SHUP

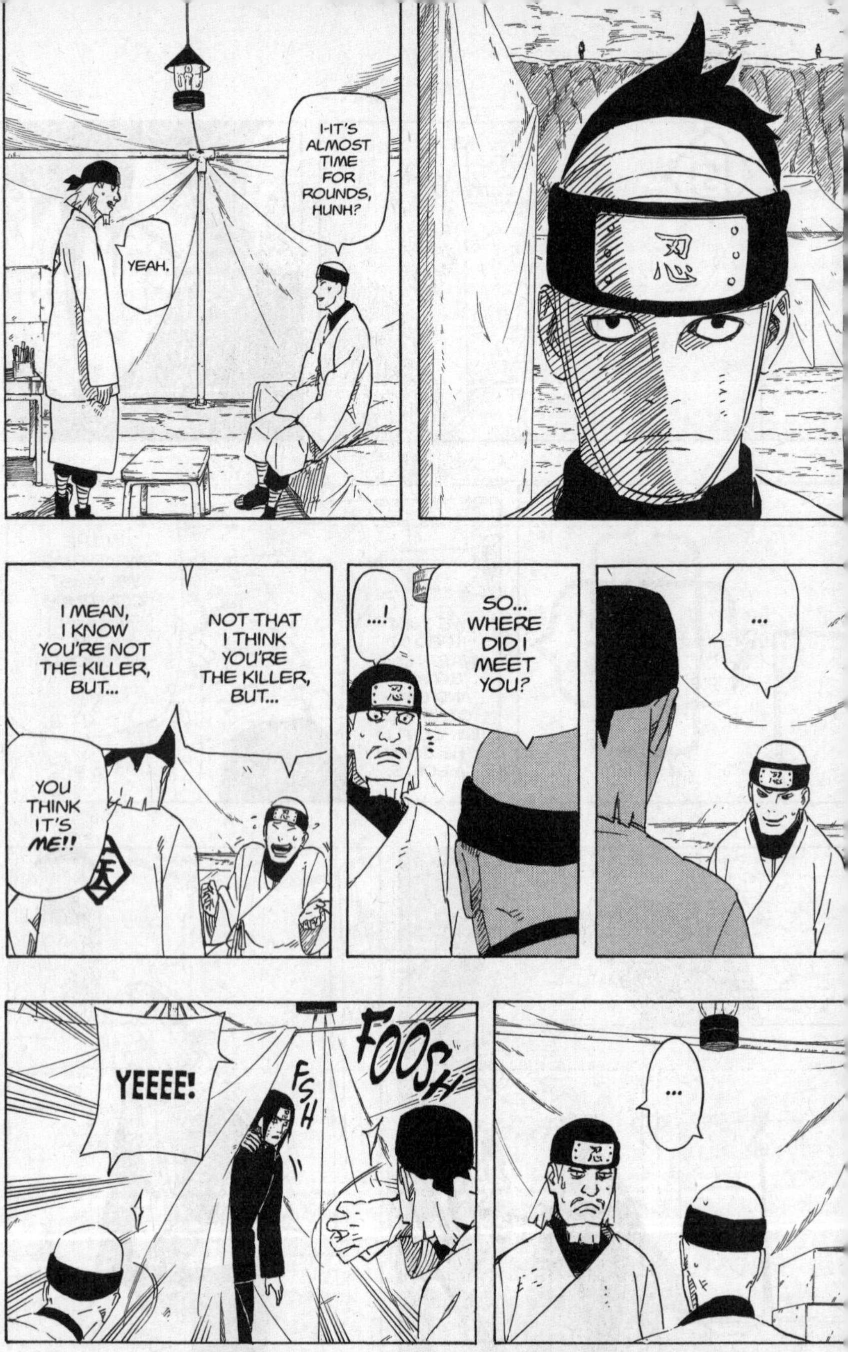
I-IT'S ALMOST TIME FOR ROUNDS, HUNH?
YEAH.
...
SO... WHERE DID I MEET YOU?
...!
NOT THAT I THINK YOU'RE THE KILLER, BUT...
I MEAN, I KNOW YOU'RE NOT THE KILLER, BUT...
YOU THINK IT'S *ME!!*
...
FOOSH
FSH
YEEEE!

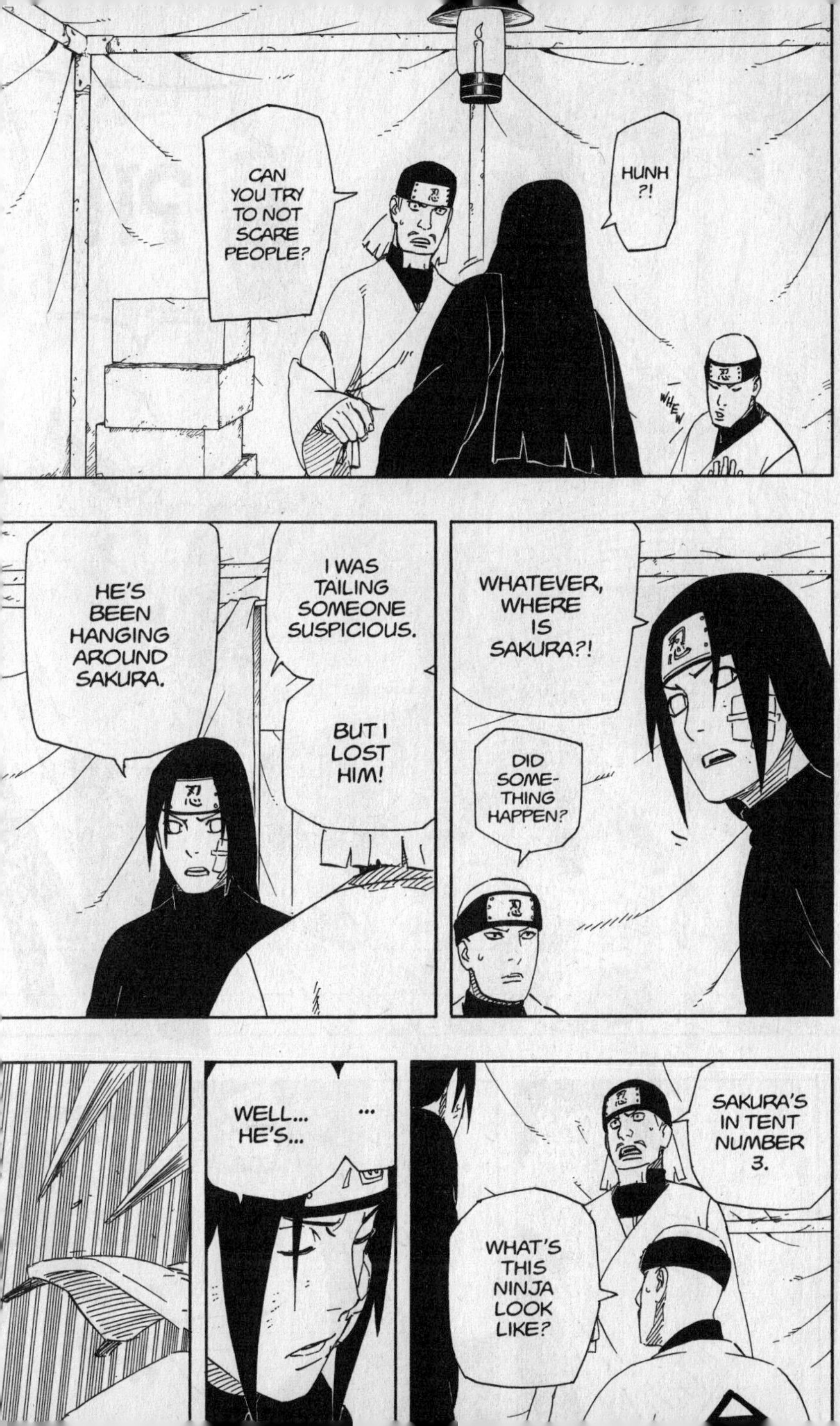
HUNH ?!
CAN YOU TRY TO NOT SCARE PEOPLE?
WHEW
WHATEVER, WHERE IS SAKURA?!
DID SOMETHING HAPPEN?
I WAS TAILING SOMEONE SUSPICIOUS.
BUT I LOST HIM!
HE'S BEEN HANGING AROUND SAKURA.
SAKURA'S IN TENT NUMBER 3.
WHAT'S THIS NINJA LOOK LIKE?
...
WELL... HE'S...

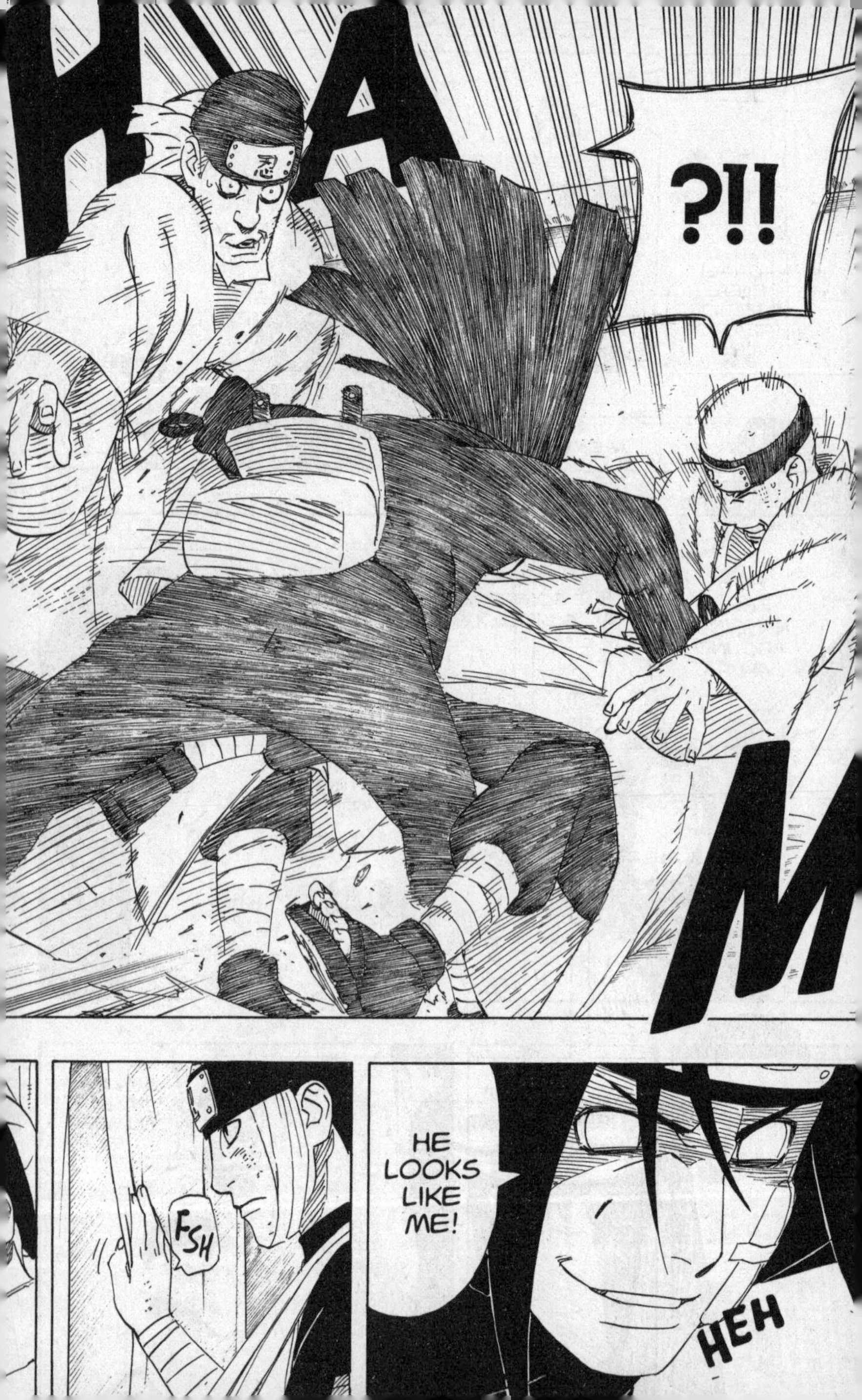
?!!
HAM
HE LOOKS LIKE ME!
HEH
FSH

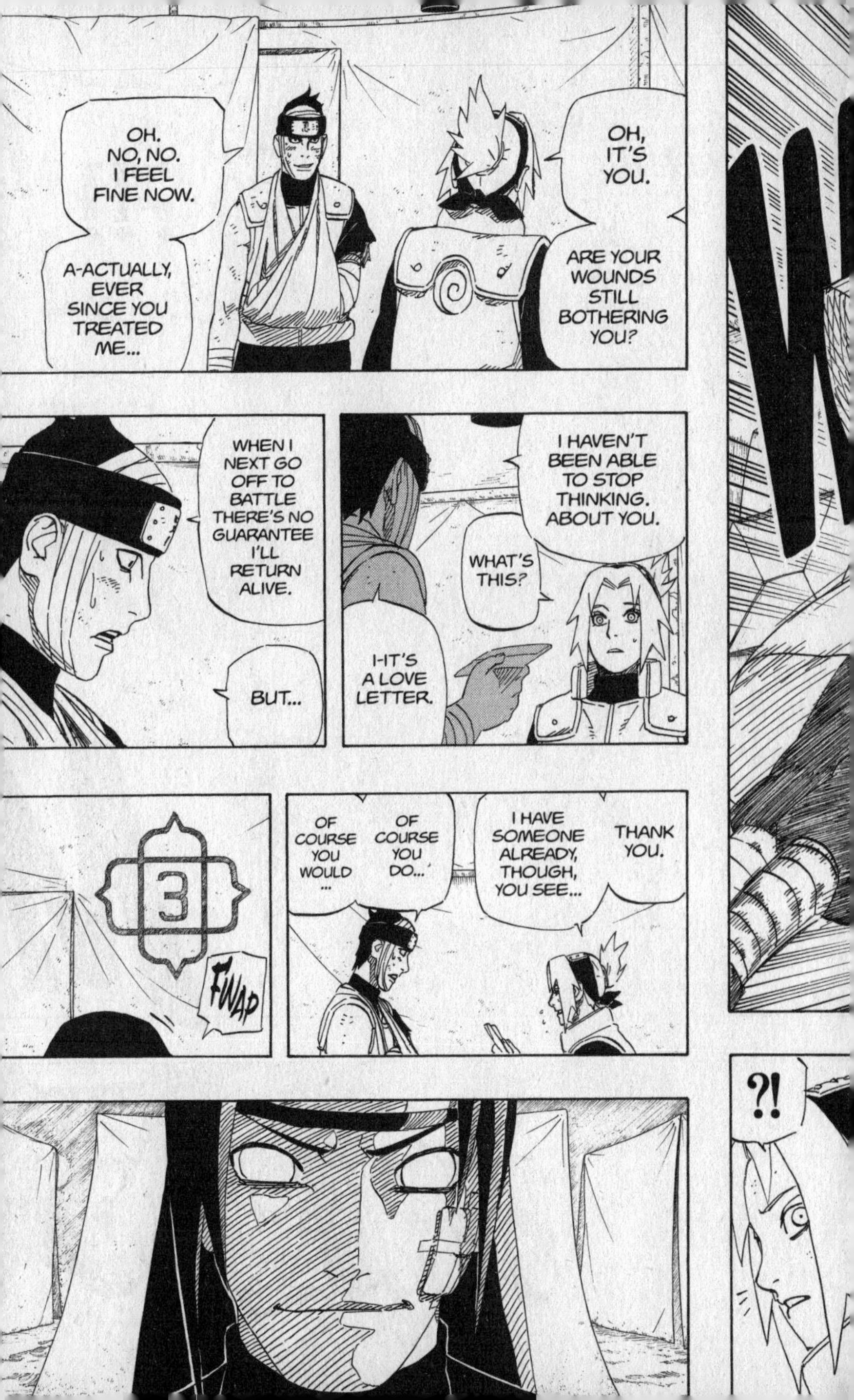
?!
OH, IT'S YOU.
ARE YOUR WOUNDS STILL BOTHERING YOU?
OH. NO, NO. I FEEL FINE NOW.
A-ACTUALLY, EVER SINCE YOU TREATED ME...
I HAVEN'T BEEN ABLE TO STOP THINKING. ABOUT YOU.
WHAT'S THIS?
I-IT'S A LOVE LETTER.
WHEN I NEXT GO OFF TO BATTLE THERE'S NO GUARANTEE I'LL RETURN ALIVE.
BUT...
THANK YOU.
I HAVE SOMEONE ALREADY, THOUGH, YOU SEE...
OF COURSE YOU DO...
OF COURSE YOU WOULD ...
3
FWAP

NARUTO

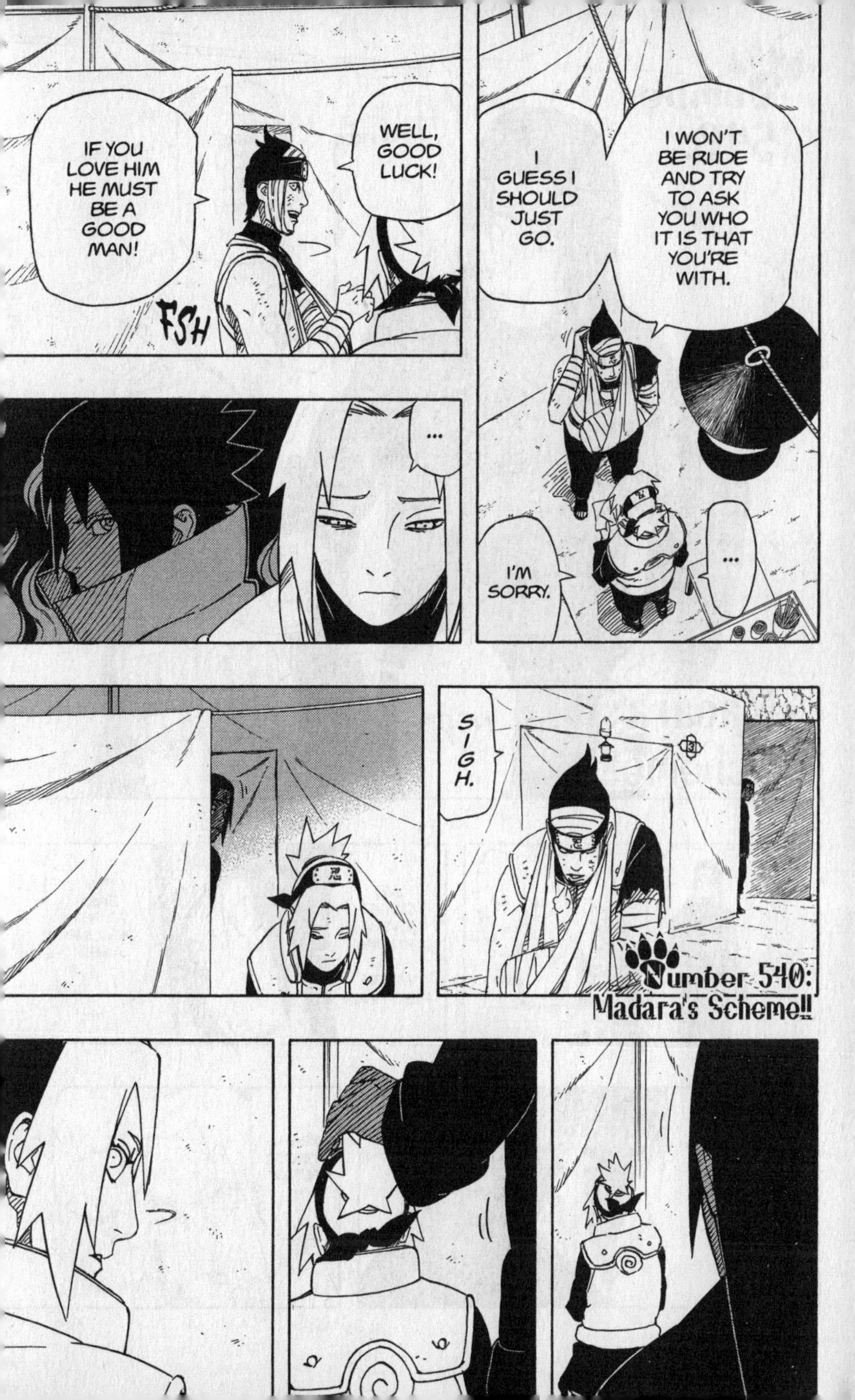
I WON'T BE RUDE AND TRY TO ASK YOU WHO IT IS THAT YOU'RE WITH.
I GUESS I SHOULD JUST GO.
...
I'M SORRY.
WELL, GOOD LUCK!
IF YOU LOVE HIM HE MUST BE A GOOD MAN!
FSH
...
SIGH.
Number 540: Madara's Scheme!!

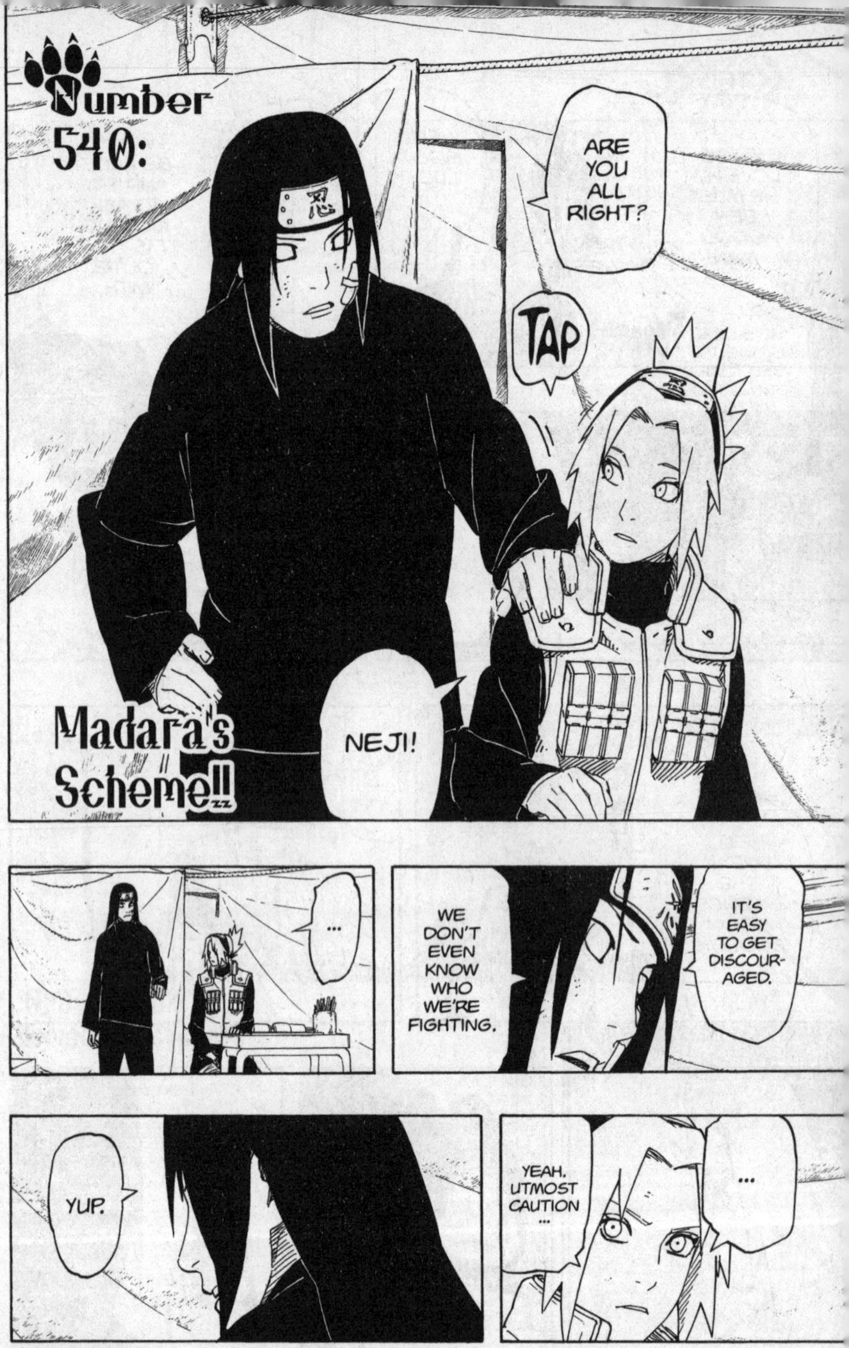
Number 540:
Madara's Scheme!!
ARE YOU ALL RIGHT?
TAP
NEJI!
IT'S EASY TO GET DISCOURAGED.
WE DON'T EVEN KNOW WHO WE'RE FIGHTING.
...
...
YEAH. UTMOST CAUTION ...
YUP.

READ THIS WAY

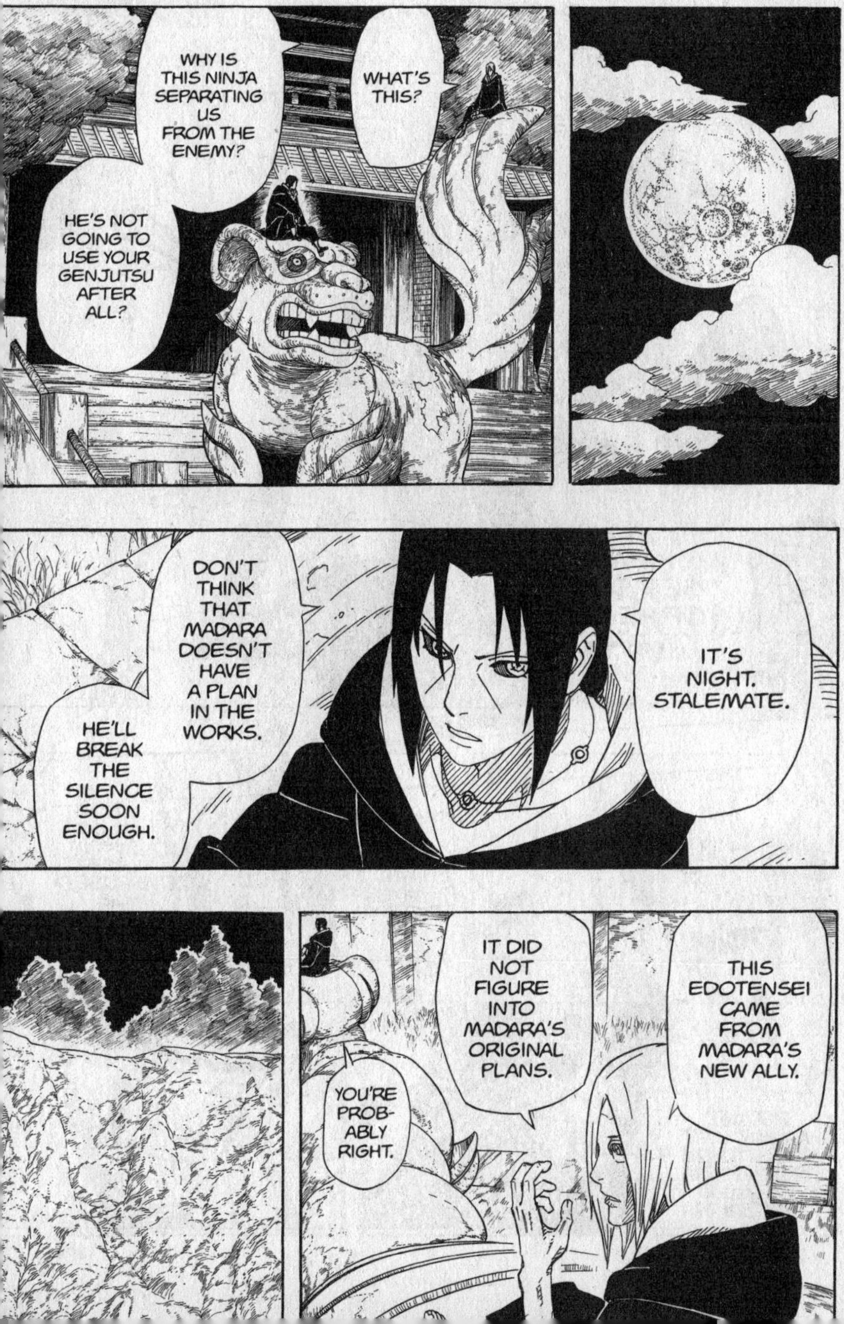
WHAT'S THIS?
WHY IS THIS NINJA SEPARATING US FROM THE ENEMY?
HE'S NOT GOING TO USE YOUR GENJUTSU AFTER ALL?
IT'S NIGHT. STALEMATE.
DON'T THINK THAT MADARA DOESN'T HAVE A PLAN IN THE WORKS.
HE'LL BREAK THE SILENCE SOON ENOUGH.
THIS EDOTENSEI CAME FROM MADARA'S NEW ALLY.
IT DID NOT FIGURE INTO MADARA'S ORIGINAL PLANS.
YOU'RE PROB-ABLY RIGHT.

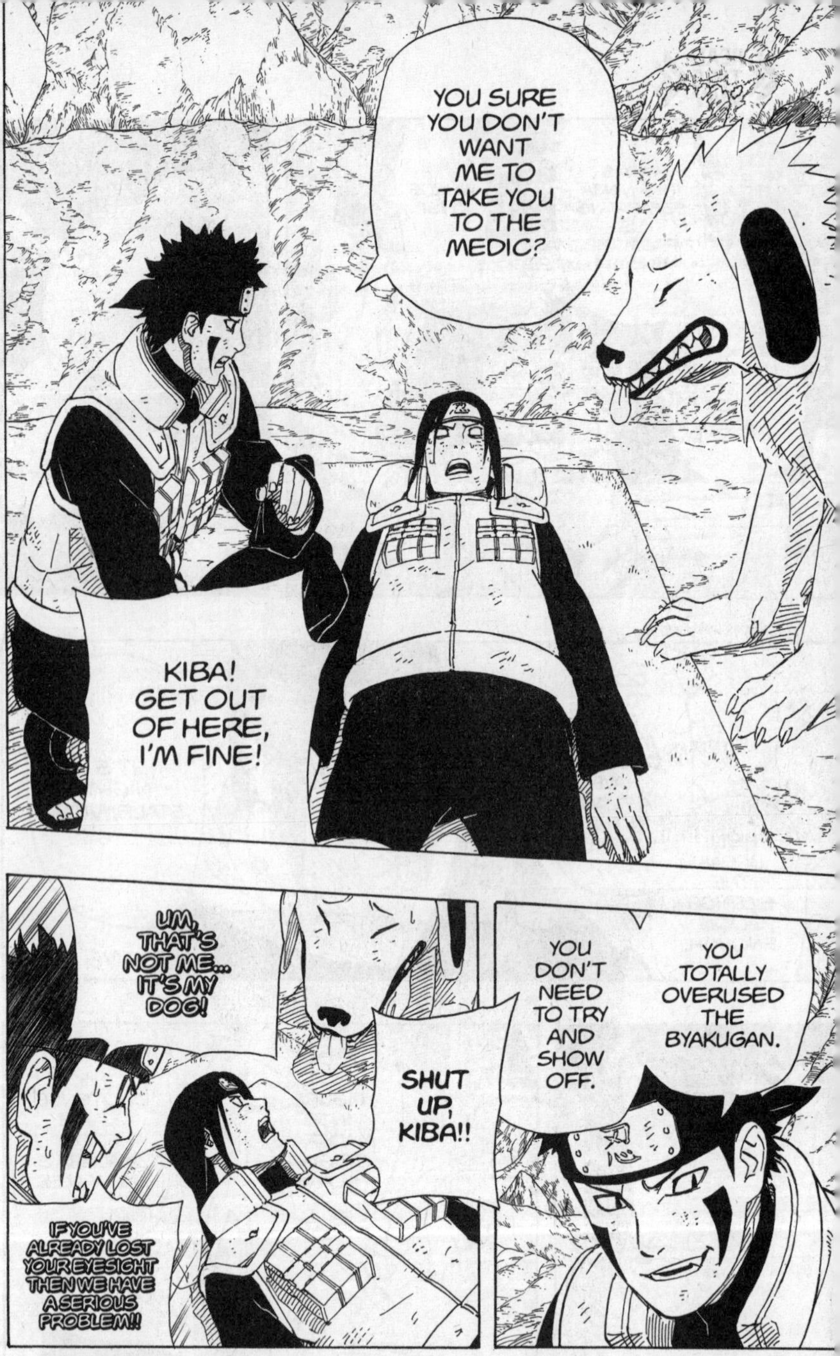
YOU SURE YOU DON'T WANT ME TO TAKE YOU TO THE MEDIC?
KIBA! GET OUT OF HERE, I'M FINE!
YOU TOTALLY OVERUSED THE BYAKUGAN.
YOU DON'T NEED TO TRY AND SHOW OFF.
SHUT UP, KIBA!!
UM, THAT'S NOT ME... IT'S MY DOG!
IF YOU'VE ALREADY LOST YOUR EYESIGHT THEN WE HAVE A SERIOUS PROBLEM!!

READ THIS WAY

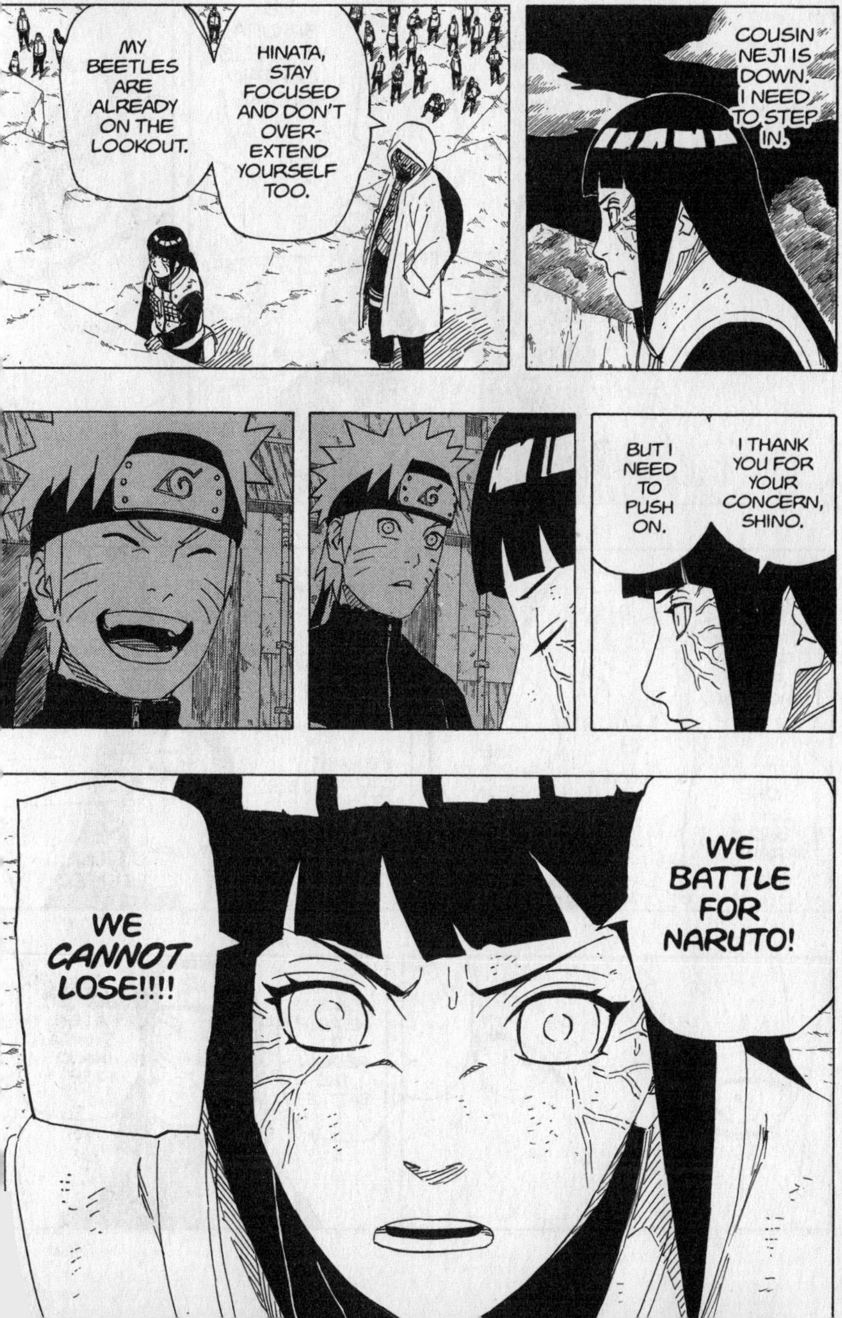
COUSIN NEJI IS DOWN. I NEED TO STEP IN.
HINATA, STAY FOCUSED AND DON'T OVER-EXTEND YOURSELF TOO.
MY BEETLES ARE ALREADY ON THE LOOKOUT.
I THANK YOU FOR YOUR CONCERN, SHINO.
BUT I NEED TO PUSH ON.
WE BATTLE FOR NARUTO!
WE CANNOT LOSE!!!!

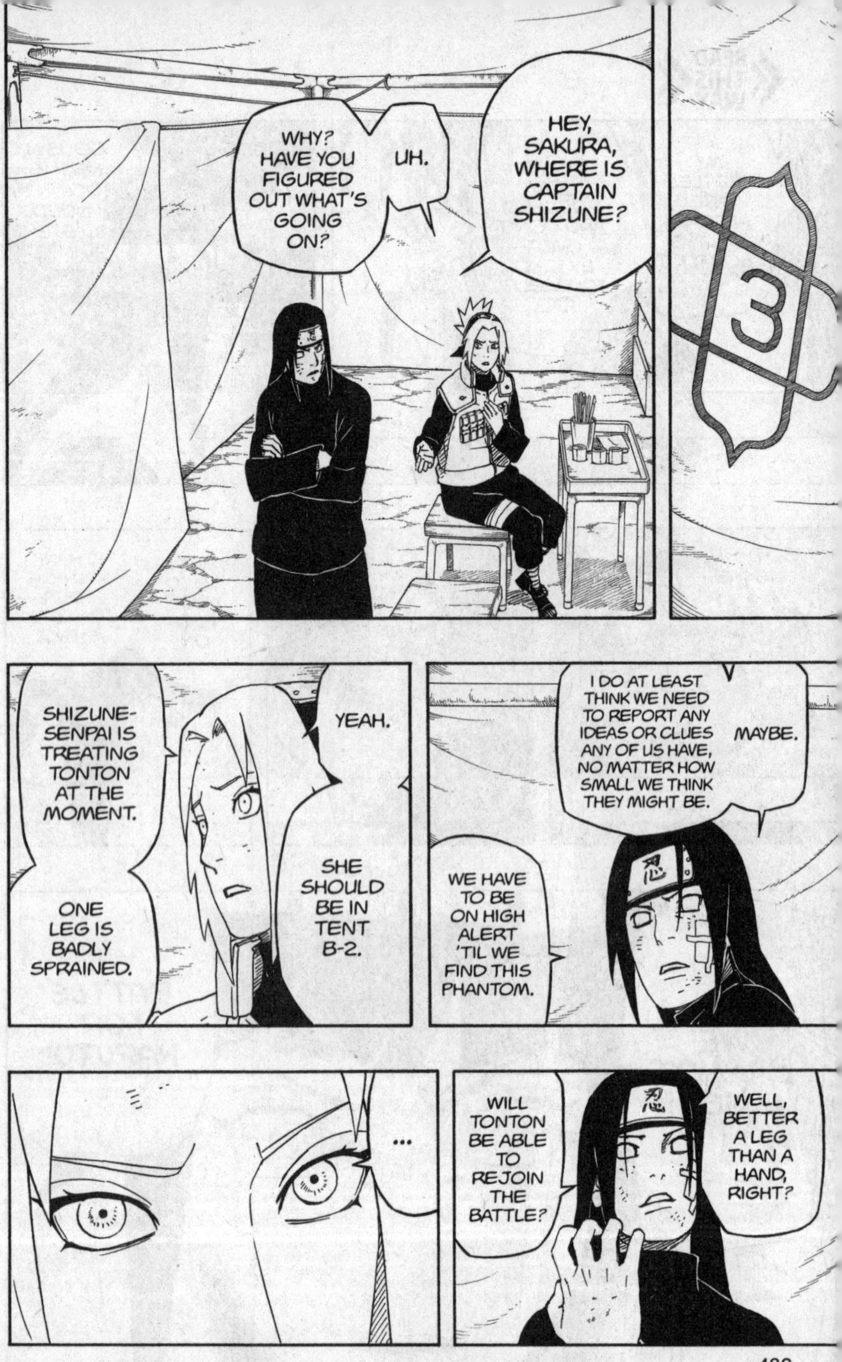
HEY, SAKURA, WHERE IS CAPTAIN SHIZUNE?
UH.
WHY? HAVE YOU FIGURED OUT WHAT'S GOING ON?
MAYBE.
I DO AT LEAST THINK WE NEED TO REPORT ANY IDEAS OR CLUES ANY OF US HAVE, NO MATTER HOW SMALL WE THINK THEY MIGHT BE.
WE HAVE TO BE ON HIGH ALERT 'TIL WE FIND THIS PHANTOM.
YEAH.
SHIZUNE-SENPAI IS TREATING TONTON AT THE MOMENT.
SHE SHOULD BE IN TENT B-2.
ONE LEG IS BADLY SPRAINED.
WELL, BETTER A LEG THAN A HAND, RIGHT?
WILL TONTON BE ABLE TO REJOIN THE BATTLE?
...

READ THIS WAY

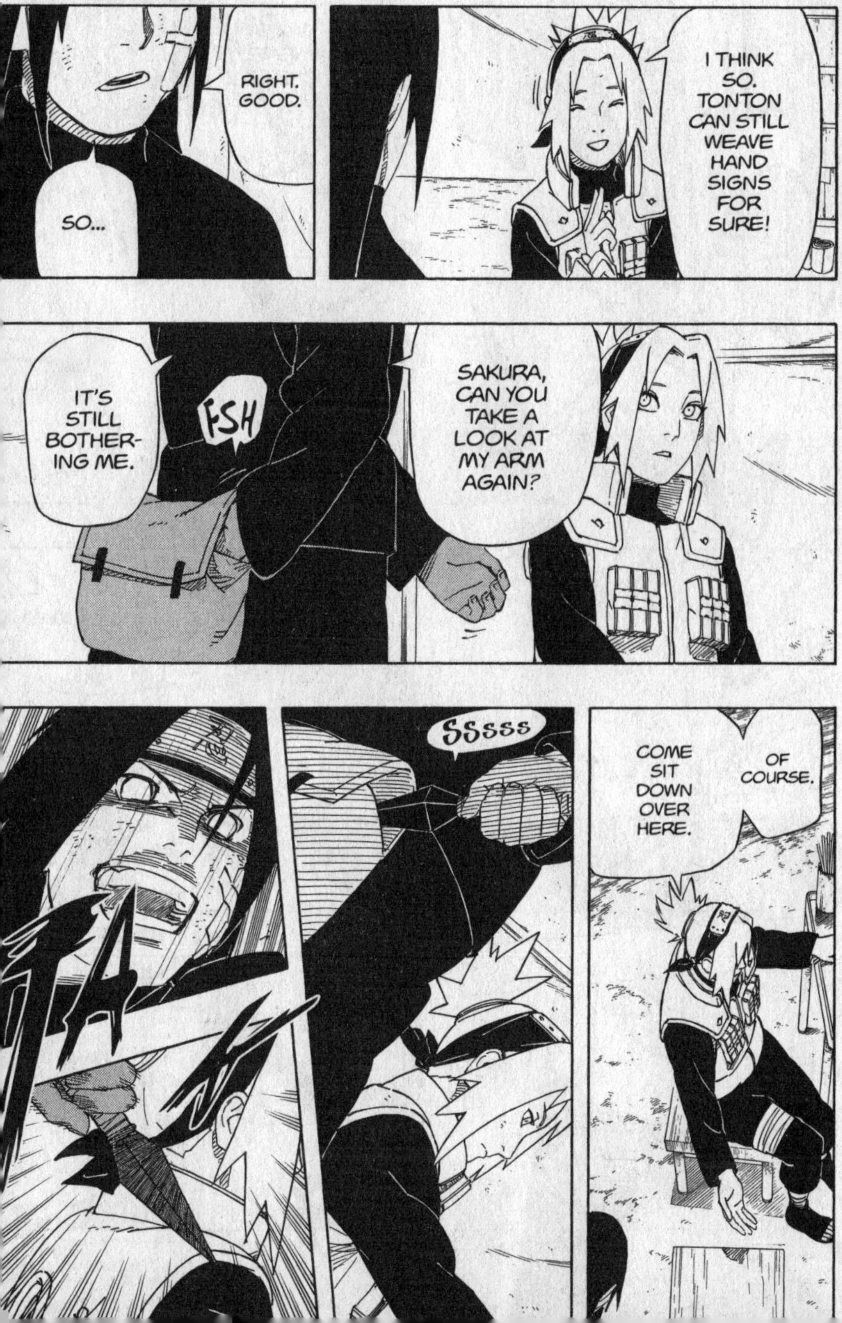
I THINK SO. TONTON CAN STILL WEAVE HAND SIGNS FOR SURE!
RIGHT. GOOD.
SO...
SAKURA, CAN YOU TAKE A LOOK AT MY ARM AGAIN?
IT'S STILL BOTHERING ME.
FSH
OF COURSE.
COME SIT DOWN OVER HERE.
SSSSS

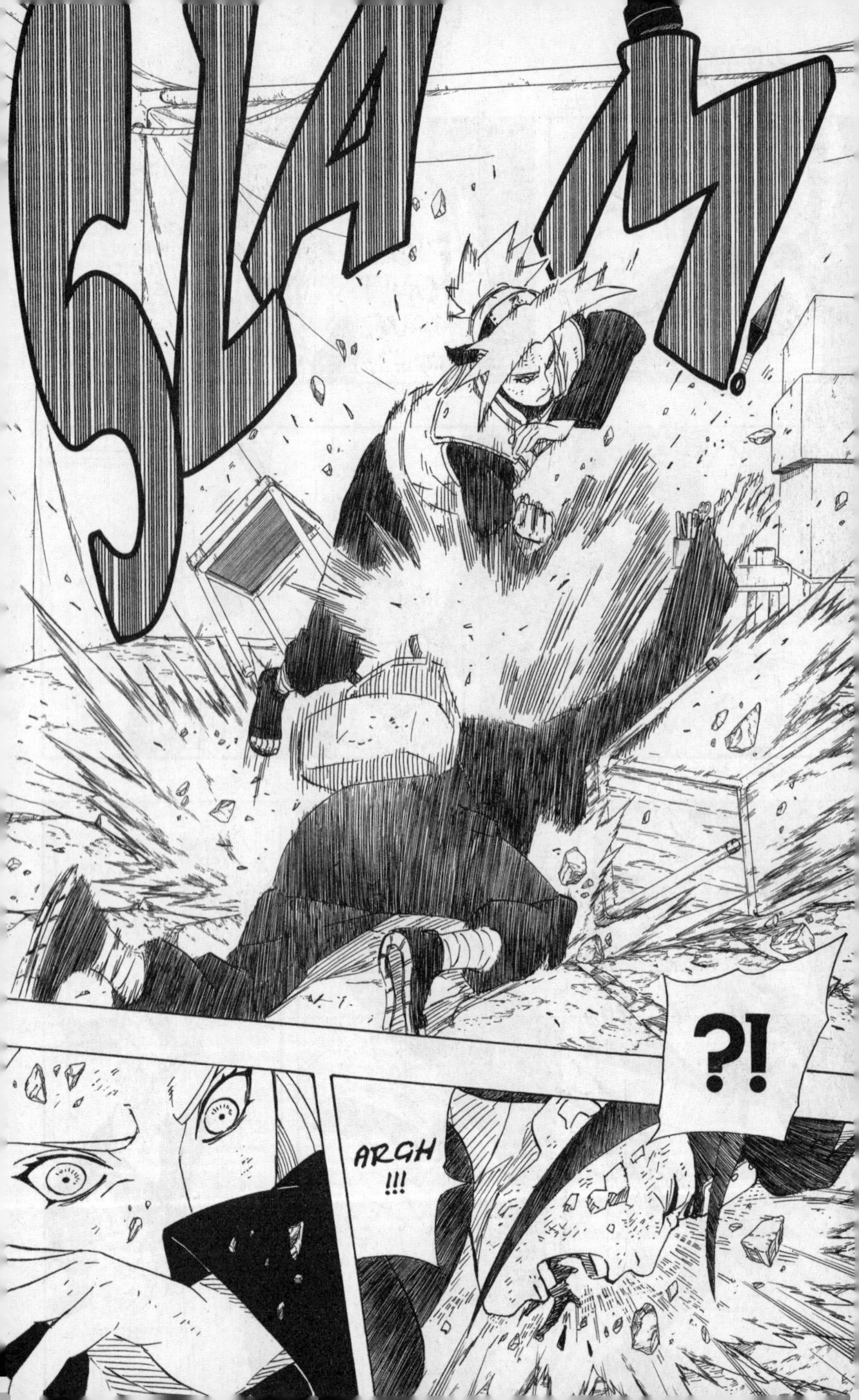
SLAM!
?!
ARGH !!!

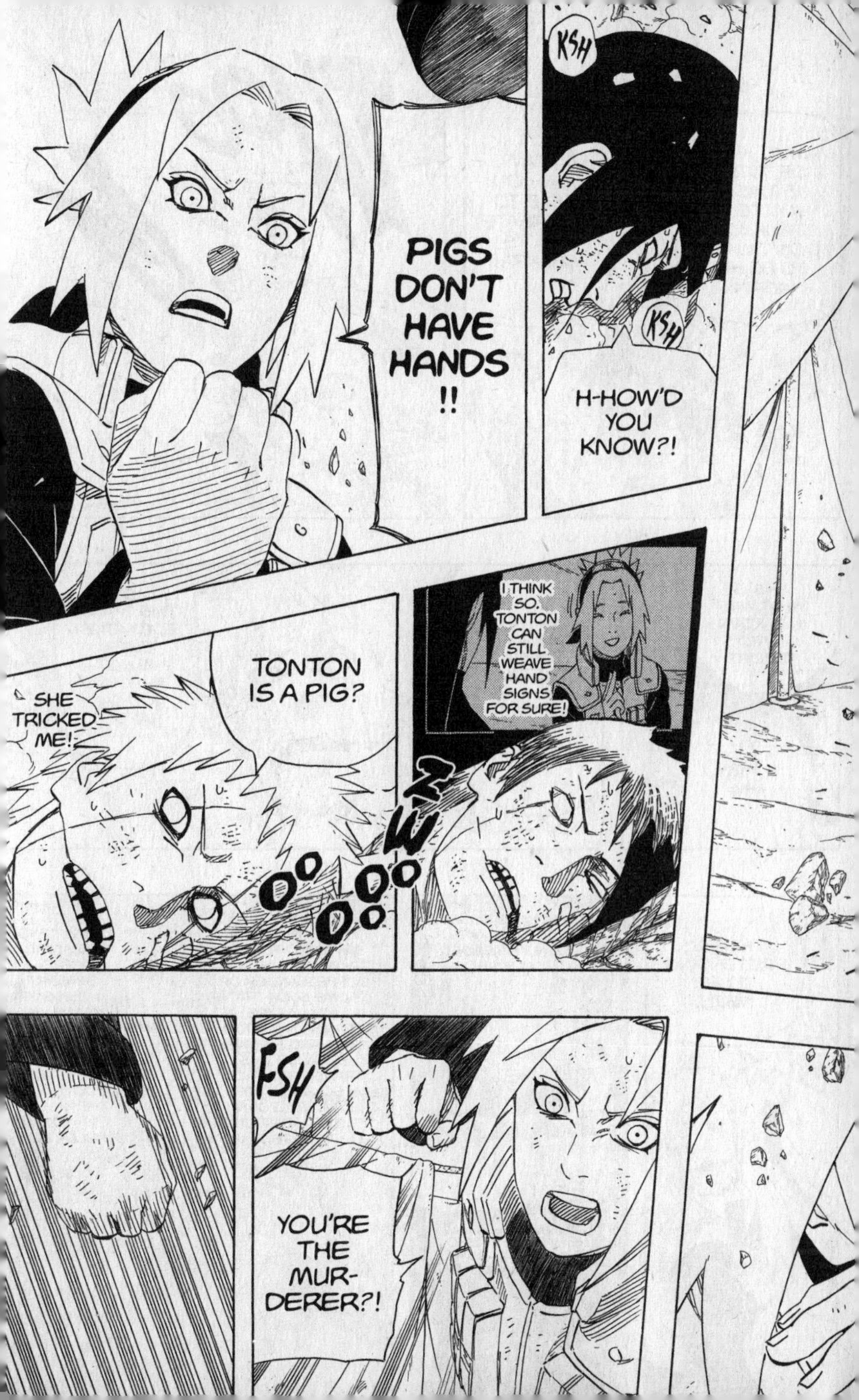
KSH
KSH
H-HOW'D YOU KNOW?!
PIGS DON'T HAVE HANDS !!
I THINK SO. TONTON CAN STILL WEAVE HAND SIGNS FOR SURE!
ZWOOO
TONTON IS A PIG?
SHE TRICKED ME!
FSH
YOU'RE THE MUR-DERER?!

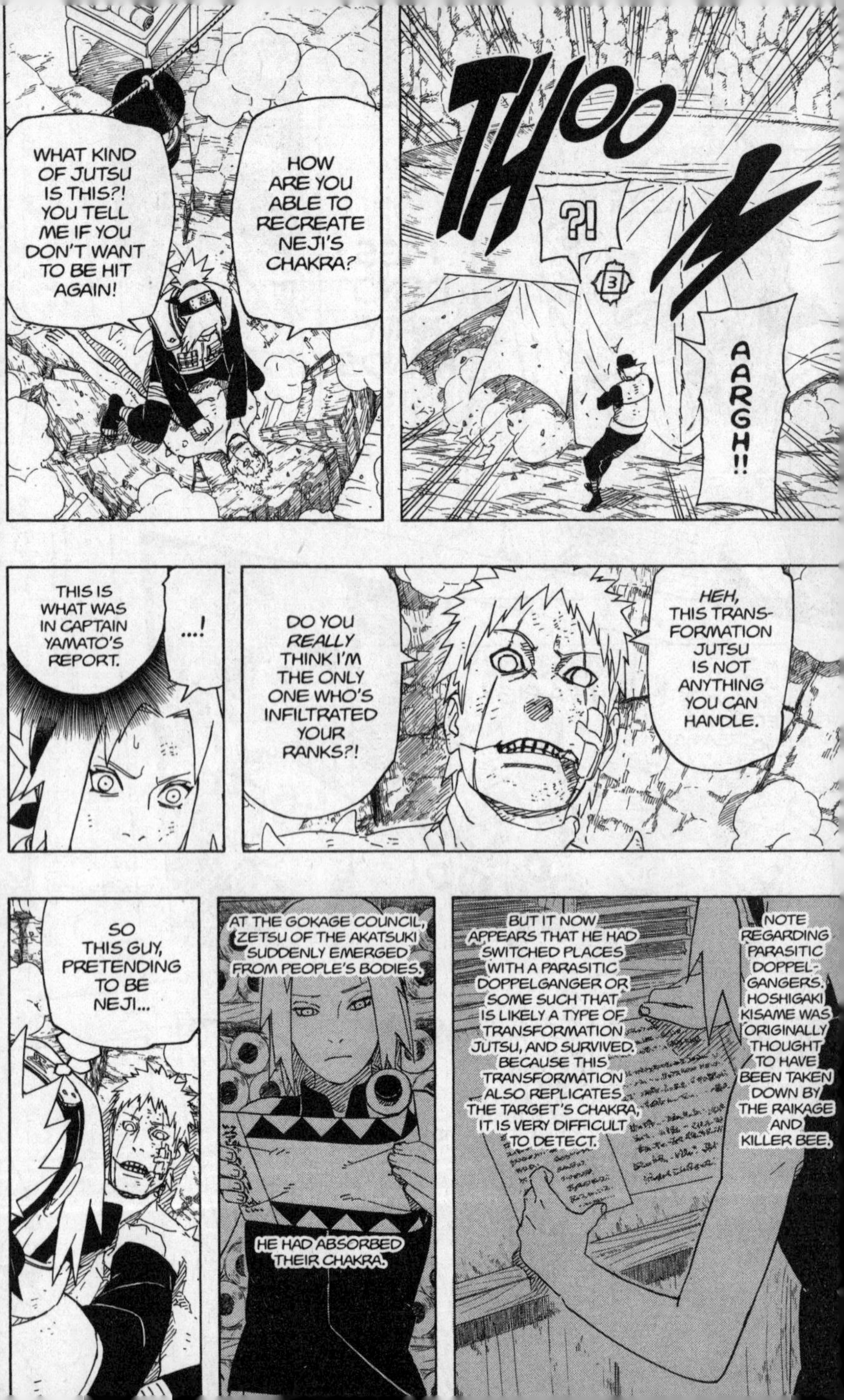
THOOM
?!
AARGH!!
HOW ARE YOU ABLE TO RECREATE NEJI'S CHAKRA?
WHAT KIND OF JUTSU IS THIS?! YOU TELL ME IF YOU DON'T WANT TO BE HIT AGAIN!
HEH, THIS TRANS-FORMATION JUTSU IS NOT ANYTHING YOU CAN HANDLE.
DO YOU *REALLY* THINK I'M THE ONLY ONE WHO'S INFILTRATED YOUR RANKS?!
...!
THIS IS WHAT WAS IN CAPTAIN YAMATO'S REPORT.
NOTE REGARDING PARASITIC DOPPEL-GANGERS. HOSHIGAKI KISAME WAS ORIGINALLY THOUGHT TO HAVE BEEN TAKEN DOWN BY THE RAIKAGE AND KILLER BEE.
BUT IT NOW APPEARS THAT HE HAD SWITCHED PLACES WITH A PARASITIC DOPPELGANGER OR SOME SUCH THAT IS LIKELY A TYPE OF TRANSFORMATION JUTSU, AND SURVIVED. BECAUSE THIS TRANSFORMATION ALSO REPLICATES THE TARGET'S CHAKRA, IT IS VERY DIFFICULT TO DETECT.
AT THE GOKAGE COUNCIL, ZETSU OF THE AKATSUKI SUDDENLY EMERGED FROM PEOPLE'S BODIES.
HE HAD ABSORBED THEIR CHAKRA.
SO THIS GUY, PRETENDING TO BE NEJI...

READ THIS WAY

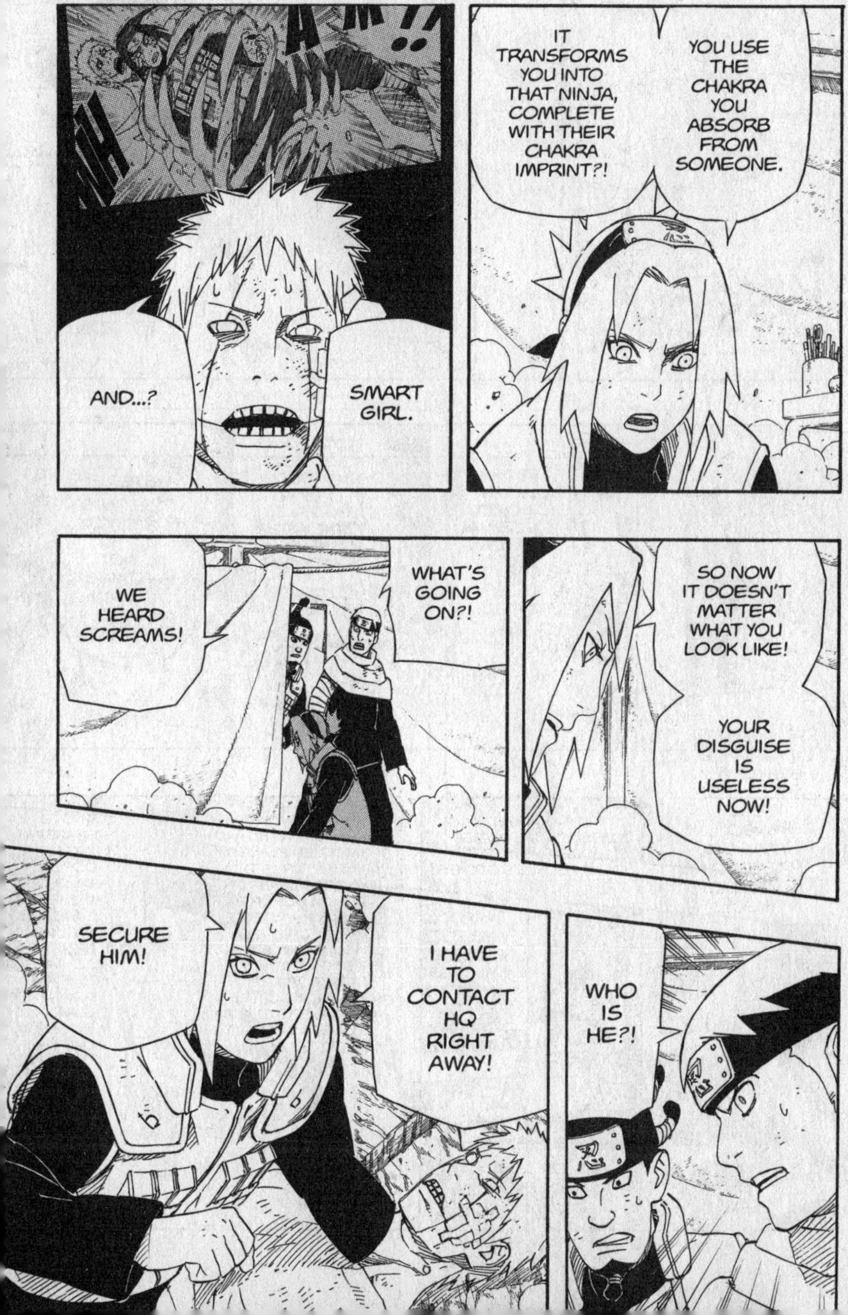
YOU USE THE CHAKRA YOU ABSORB FROM SOMEONE.
IT TRANSFORMS YOU INTO THAT NINJA, COMPLETE WITH THEIR CHAKRA IMPRINT?!
SMART GIRL.
AND...?
SO NOW IT DOESN'T MATTER WHAT YOU LOOK LIKE!
YOUR DISGUISE IS USELESS NOW!
WHAT'S GOING ON?!
WE HEARD SCREAMS!
WHO IS HE?!
I HAVE TO CONTACT HQ RIGHT AWAY!
SECURE HIM!

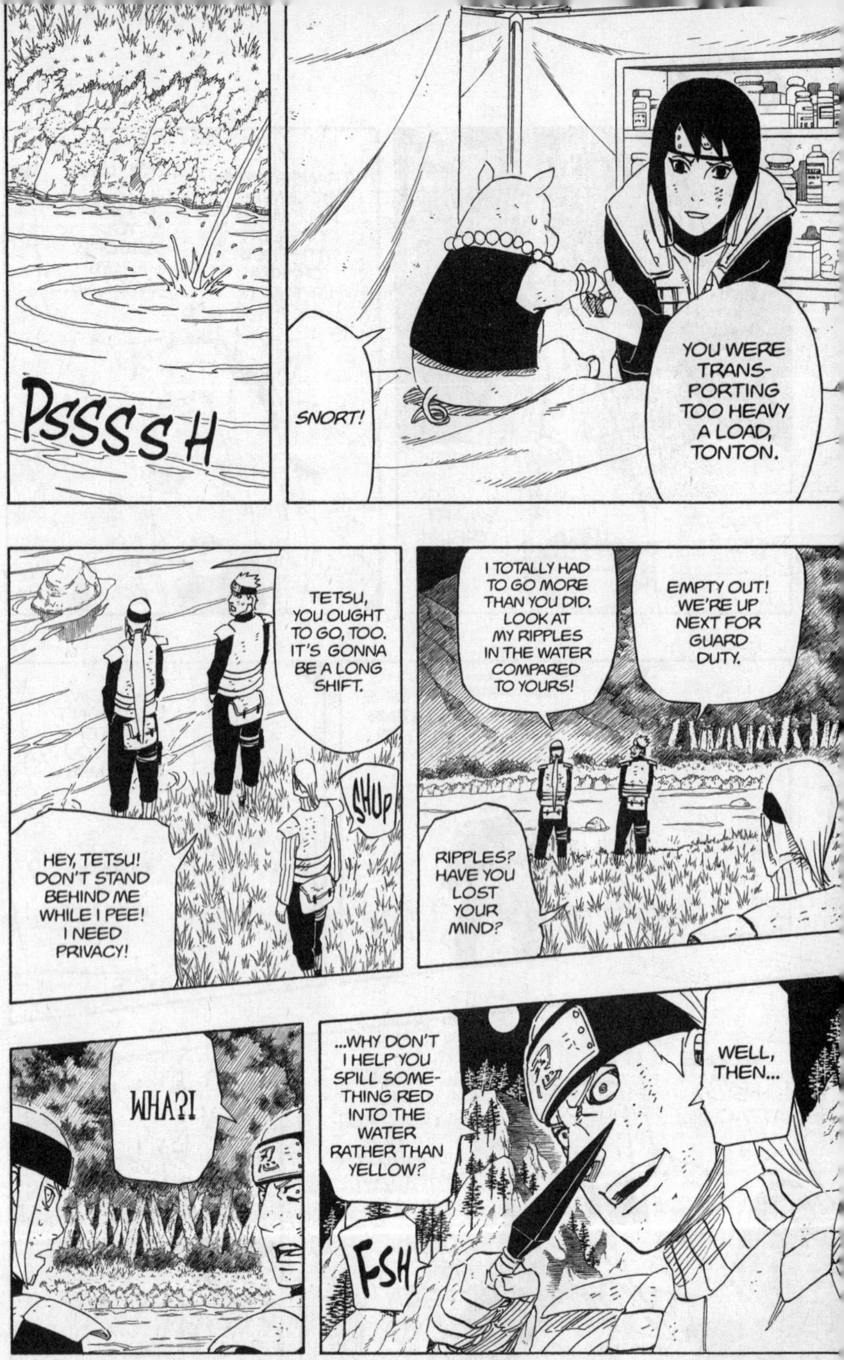
YOU WERE TRANSPORTING TOO HEAVY A LOAD, TONTON.
SNORT!
PSSSSH
EMPTY OUT! WE'RE UP NEXT FOR GUARD DUTY.
I TOTALLY HAD TO GO MORE THAN YOU DID. LOOK AT MY RIPPLES IN THE WATER COMPARED TO YOURS!
RIPPLES? HAVE YOU LOST YOUR MIND?
TETSU, YOU OUGHT TO GO, TOO. IT'S GONNA BE A LONG SHIFT.
SHUP
HEY, TETSU! DON'T STAND BEHIND ME WHILE I PEE! I NEED PRIVACY!
WELL, THEN...
...WHY DON'T I HELP YOU SPILL SOMETHING RED INTO THE WATER RATHER THAN YELLOW?
FSH
WHA?!

READ THIS WAY

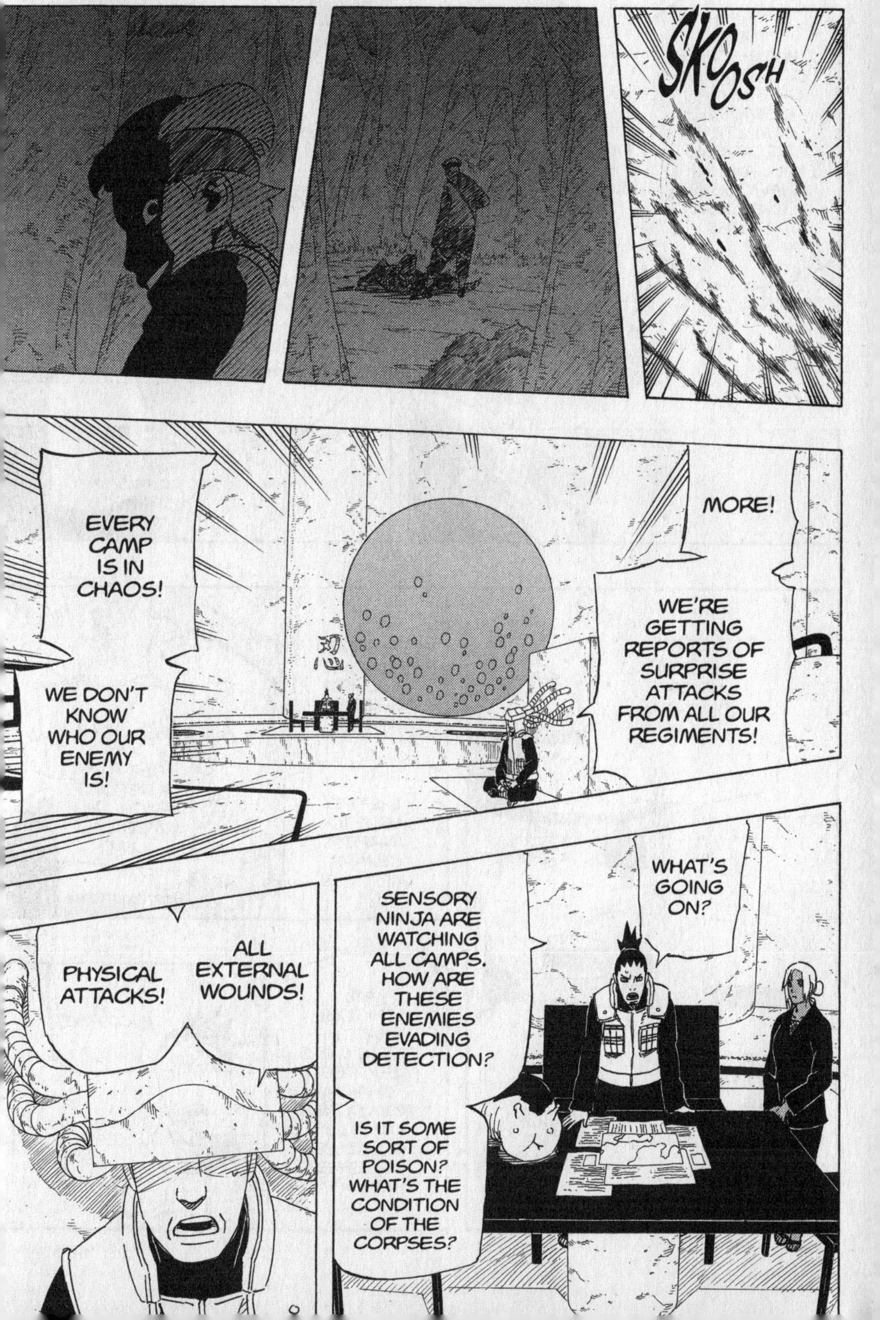
SKOOSH
MORE!
WE'RE GETTING REPORTS OF SURPRISE ATTACKS FROM ALL OUR REGIMENTS!
EVERY CAMP IS IN CHAOS!
WE DON'T KNOW WHO OUR ENEMY IS!
WHAT'S GOING ON?
SENSORY NINJA ARE WATCHING ALL CAMPS. HOW ARE THESE ENEMIES EVADING DETECTION?
IS IT SOME SORT OF POISON? WHAT'S THE CONDITION OF THE CORPSES?
ALL EXTERNAL WOUNDS!
PHYSICAL ATTACKS!

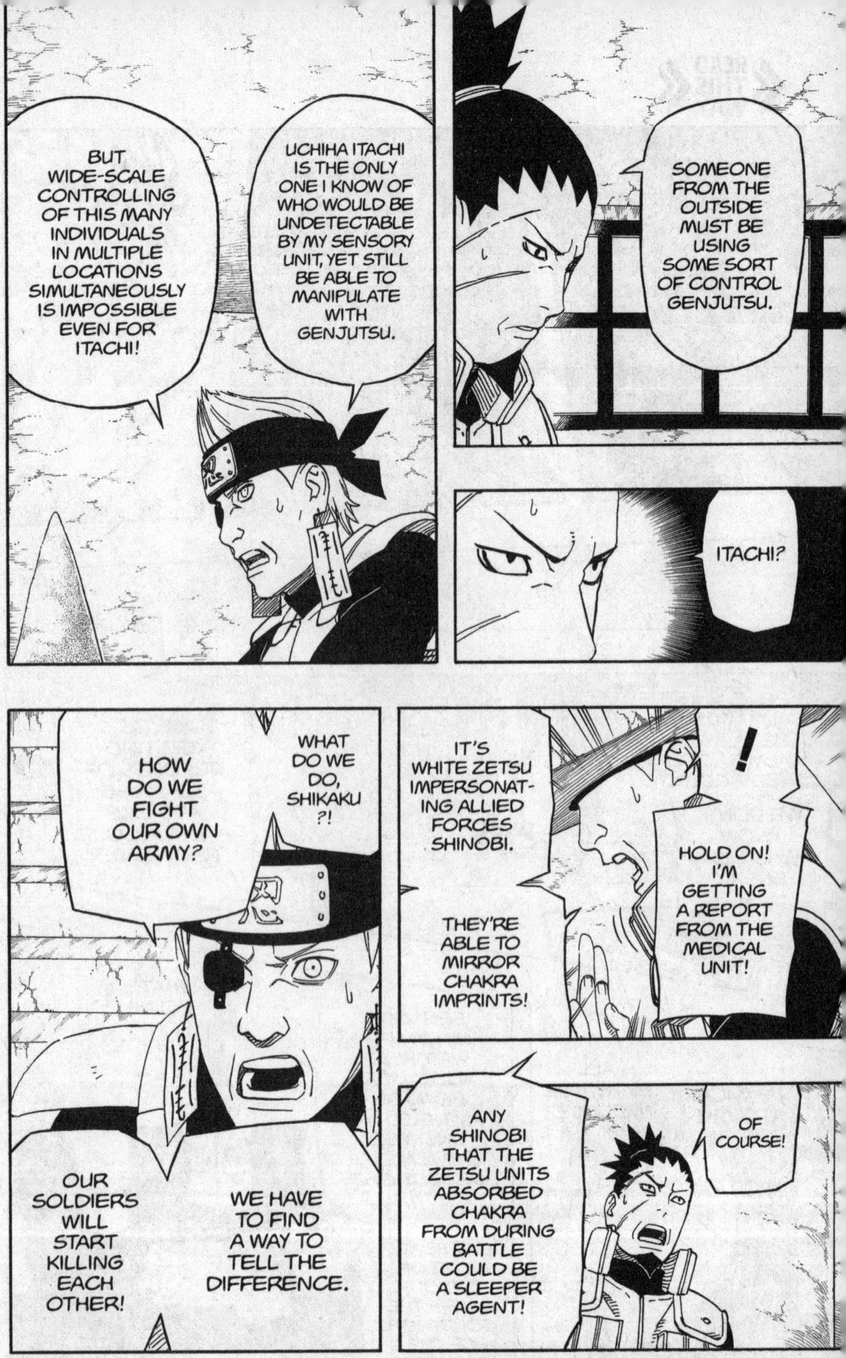

SOMEONE FROM THE OUTSIDE MUST BE USING SOME SORT OF CONTROL GENJUTSU.
ITACHI?
UCHIHA ITACHI IS THE ONLY ONE I KNOW OF WHO WOULD BE UNDETECTABLE BY MY SENSORY UNIT, YET STILL BE ABLE TO MANIPULATE WITH GENJUTSU.
BUT WIDE-SCALE CONTROLLING OF THIS MANY INDIVIDUALS IN MULTIPLE LOCATIONS SIMULTANEOUSLY IS IMPOSSIBLE EVEN FOR ITACHI!
!
HOLD ON! I'M GETTING A REPORT FROM THE MEDICAL UNIT!
IT'S WHITE ZETSU IMPERSONATING ALLIED FORCES SHINOBI.
THEY'RE ABLE TO MIRROR CHAKRA IMPRINTS!
OF COURSE!
ANY SHINOBI THAT THE ZETSU UNITS ABSORBED CHAKRA FROM DURING BATTLE COULD BE A SLEEPER AGENT!
WHAT DO WE DO, SHIKAKU?!
HOW DO WE FIGHT OUR OWN ARMY?
WE HAVE TO FIND A WAY TO TELL THE DIFFERENCE.
OUR SOLDIERS WILL START KILLING EACH OTHER!

READ THIS WAY

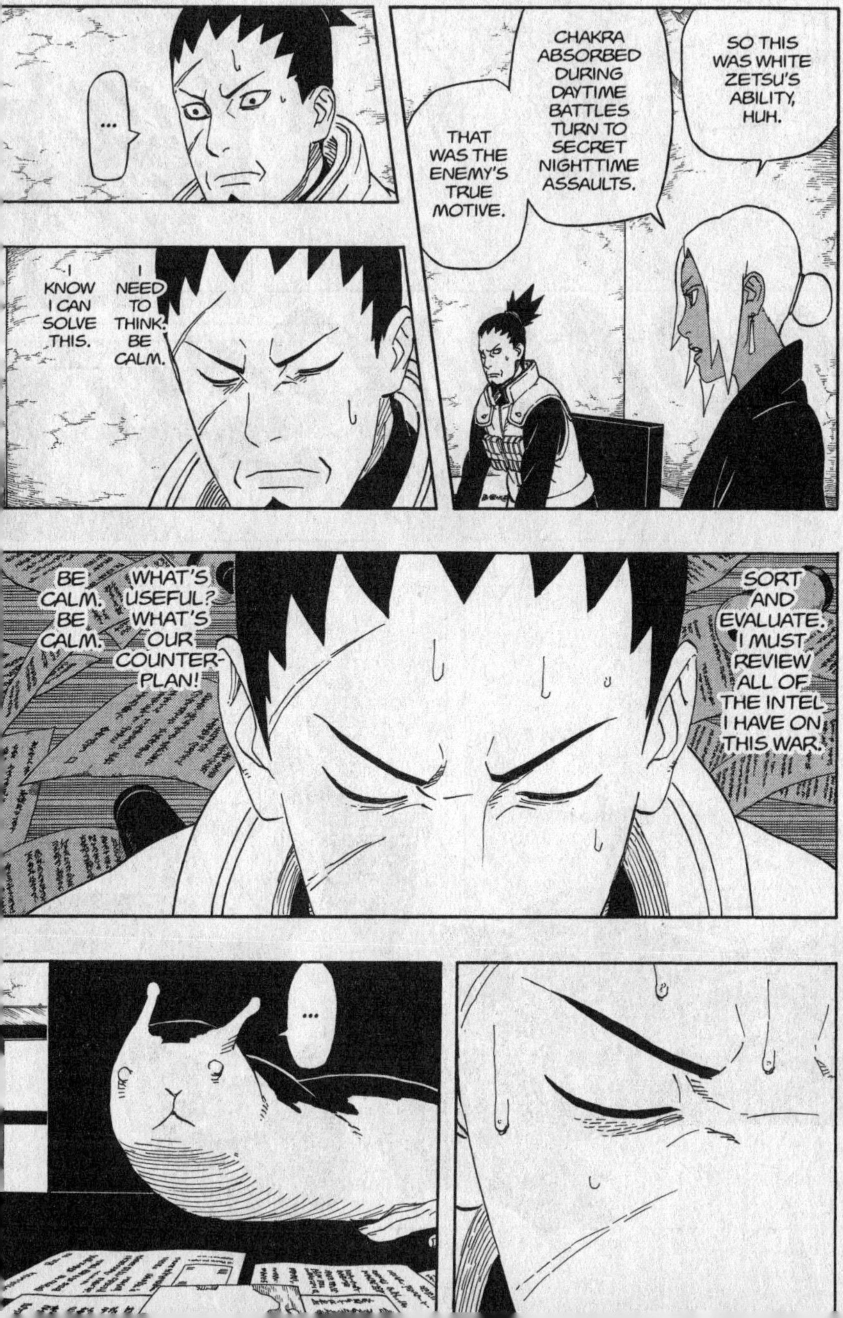
SO THIS WAS WHITE ZETSU'S ABILITY, HUH.
CHAKRA ABSORBED DURING DAYTIME BATTLES TURN TO SECRET NIGHTTIME ASSAULTS.
THAT WAS THE ENEMY'S TRUE MOTIVE.
...
I NEED TO THINK. BE CALM.
I KNOW I CAN SOLVE THIS.
SORT AND EVALUATE. I MUST REVIEW ALL OF THE INTEL I HAVE ON THIS WAR.
WHAT'S USEFUL? WHAT'S OUR COUNTER-PLAN!
BE CALM. BE CALM.
...

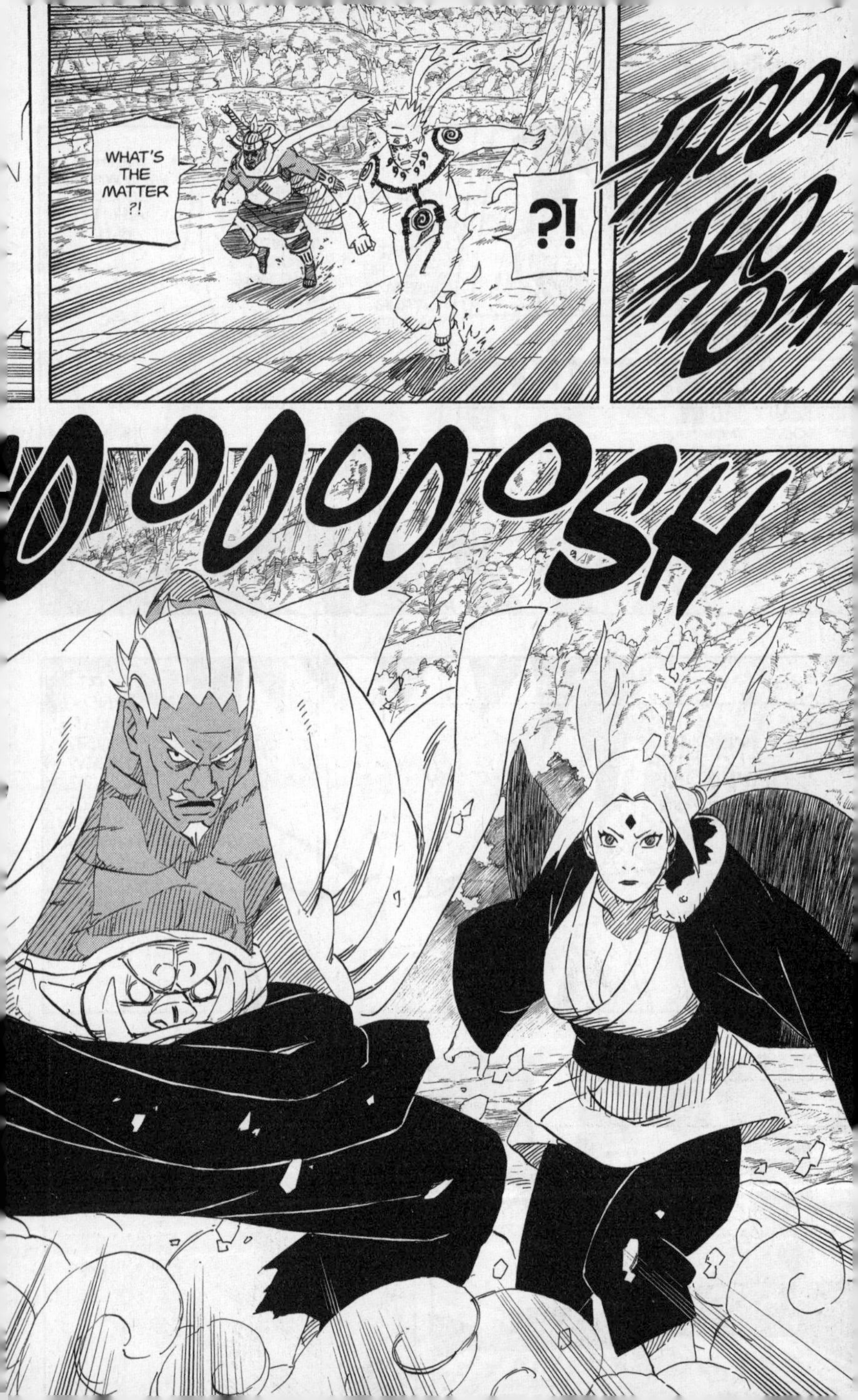
?!
WHAT'S THE MATTER ?!
OOOOOOSH

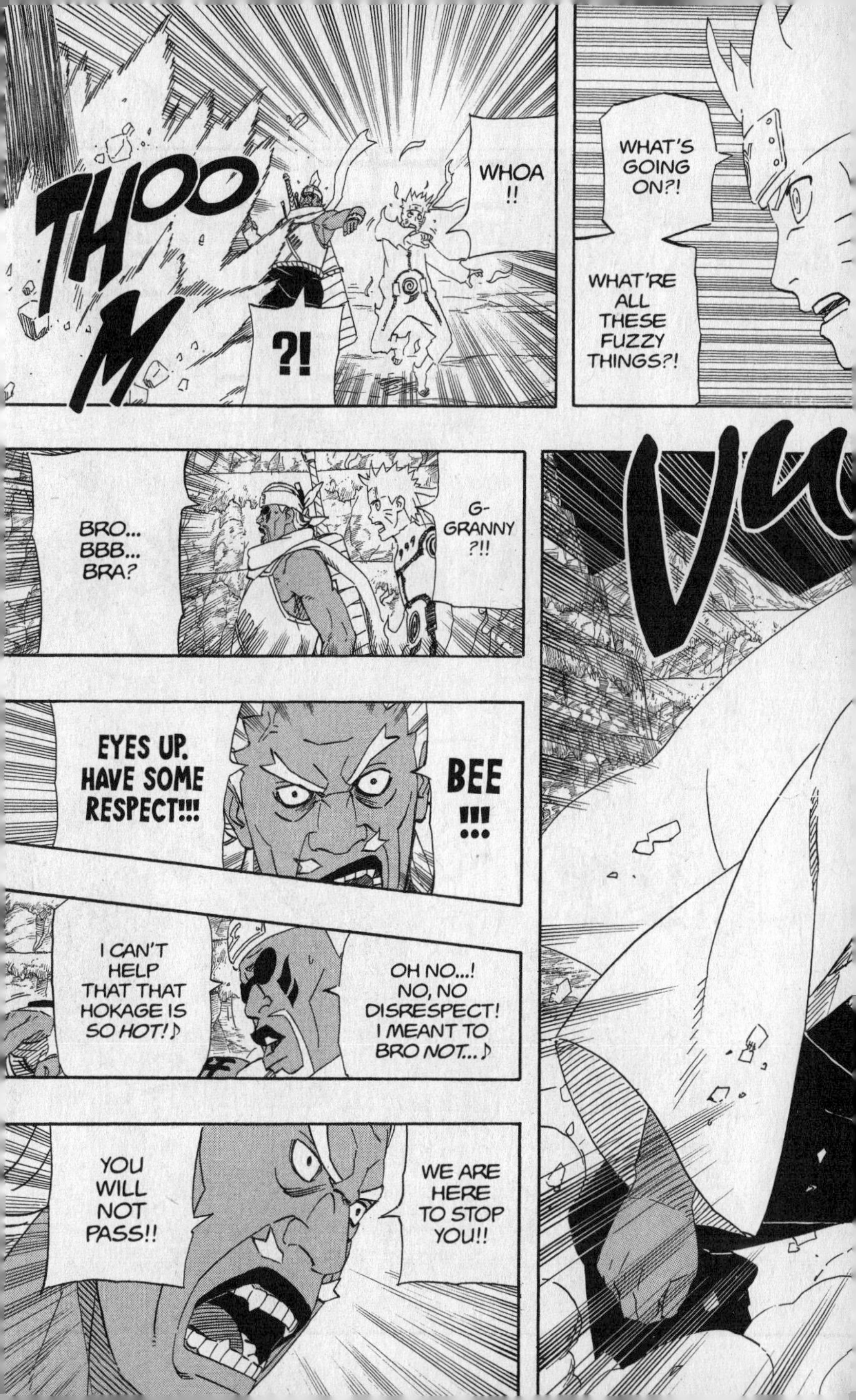
WHAT'S GOING ON?!
WHAT'RE ALL THESE FUZZY THINGS?!
WHOA !!
?!
THOOM
G-GRANNY ?!!
BRO... BBB... BRA?
BEE !!!
EYES UP. HAVE SOME RESPECT!!!
OH NO...! NO, NO DISRESPECT! I MEANT TO BRO NOT...♪
I CAN'T HELP THAT THAT HOKAGE IS SO HOT!♪
WE ARE HERE TO STOP YOU!!
YOU WILL NOT PASS!!

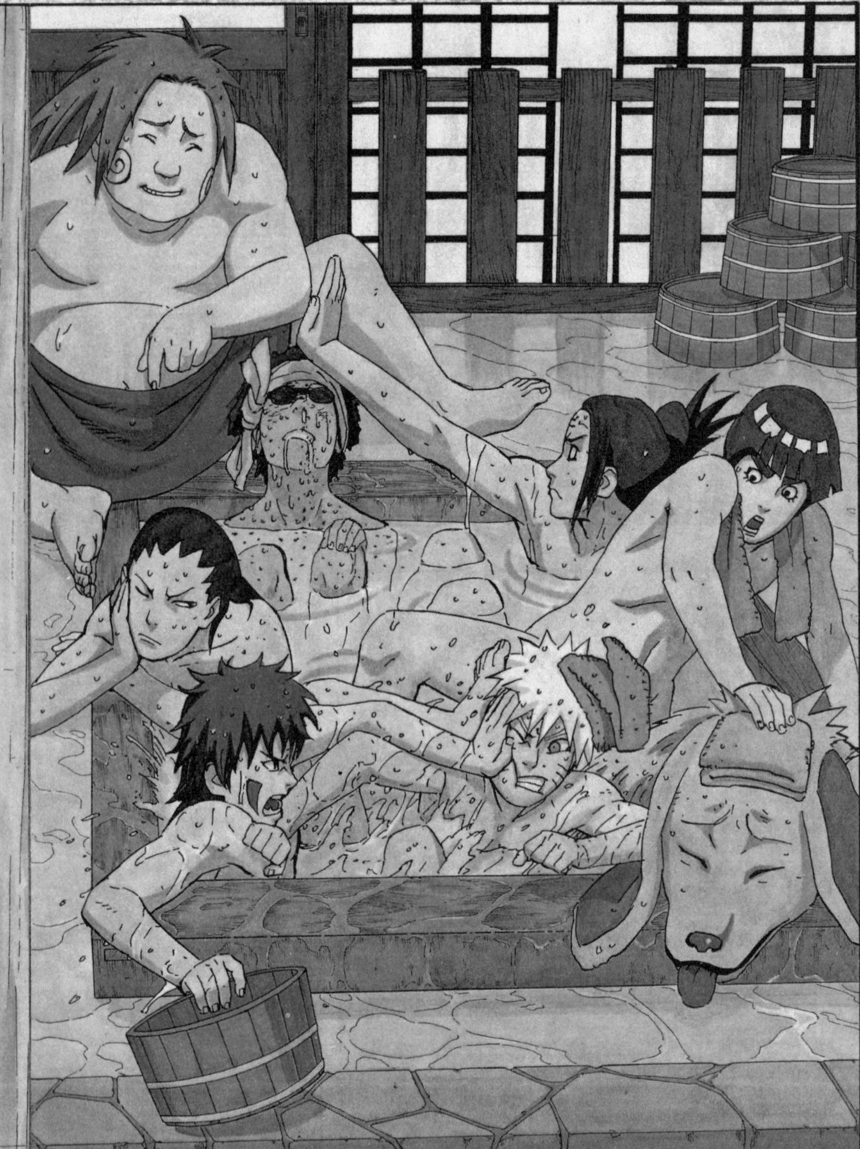

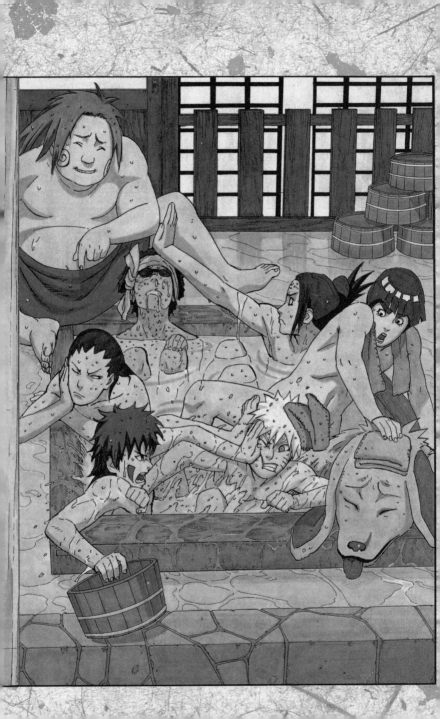

# Number 541: Raikage vs. Naruto?!

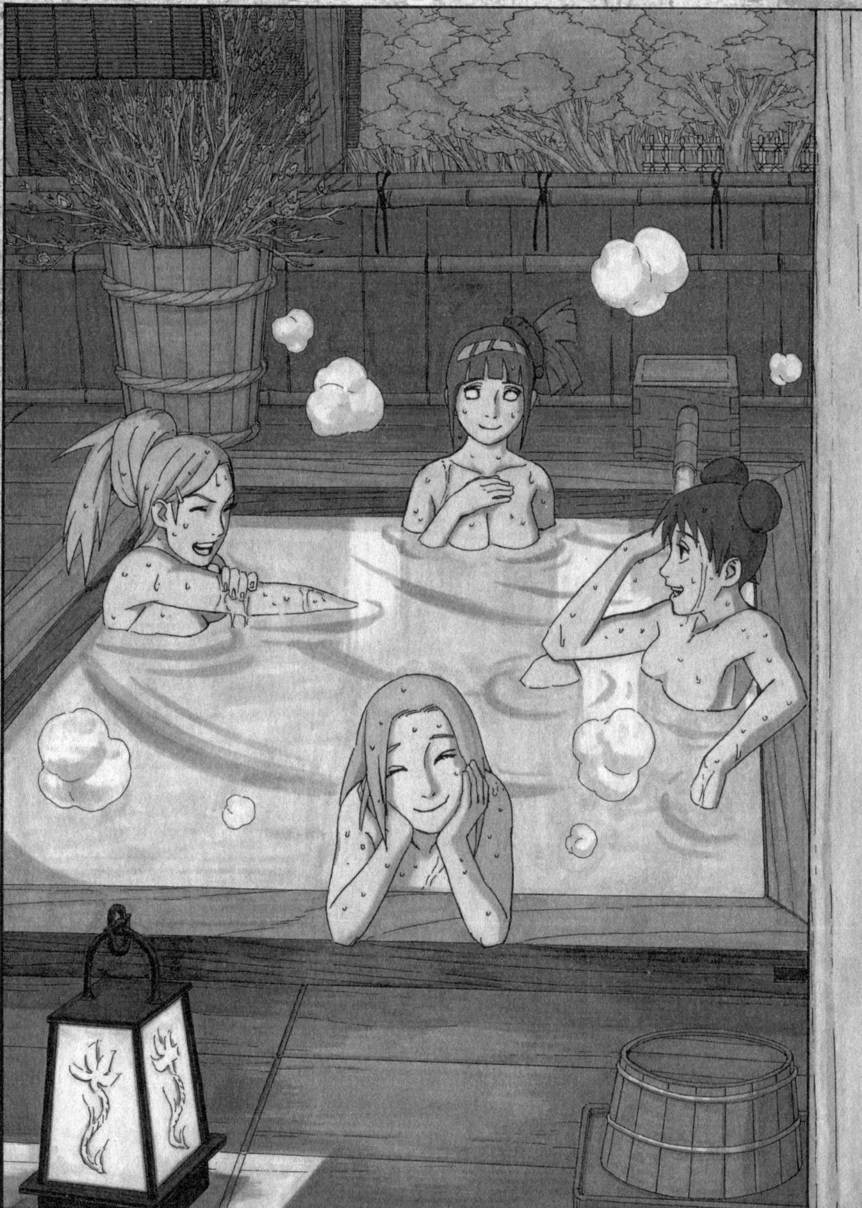

# NARUTO

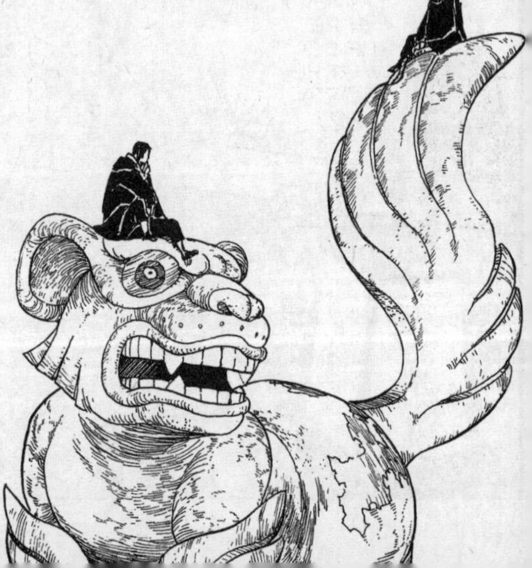

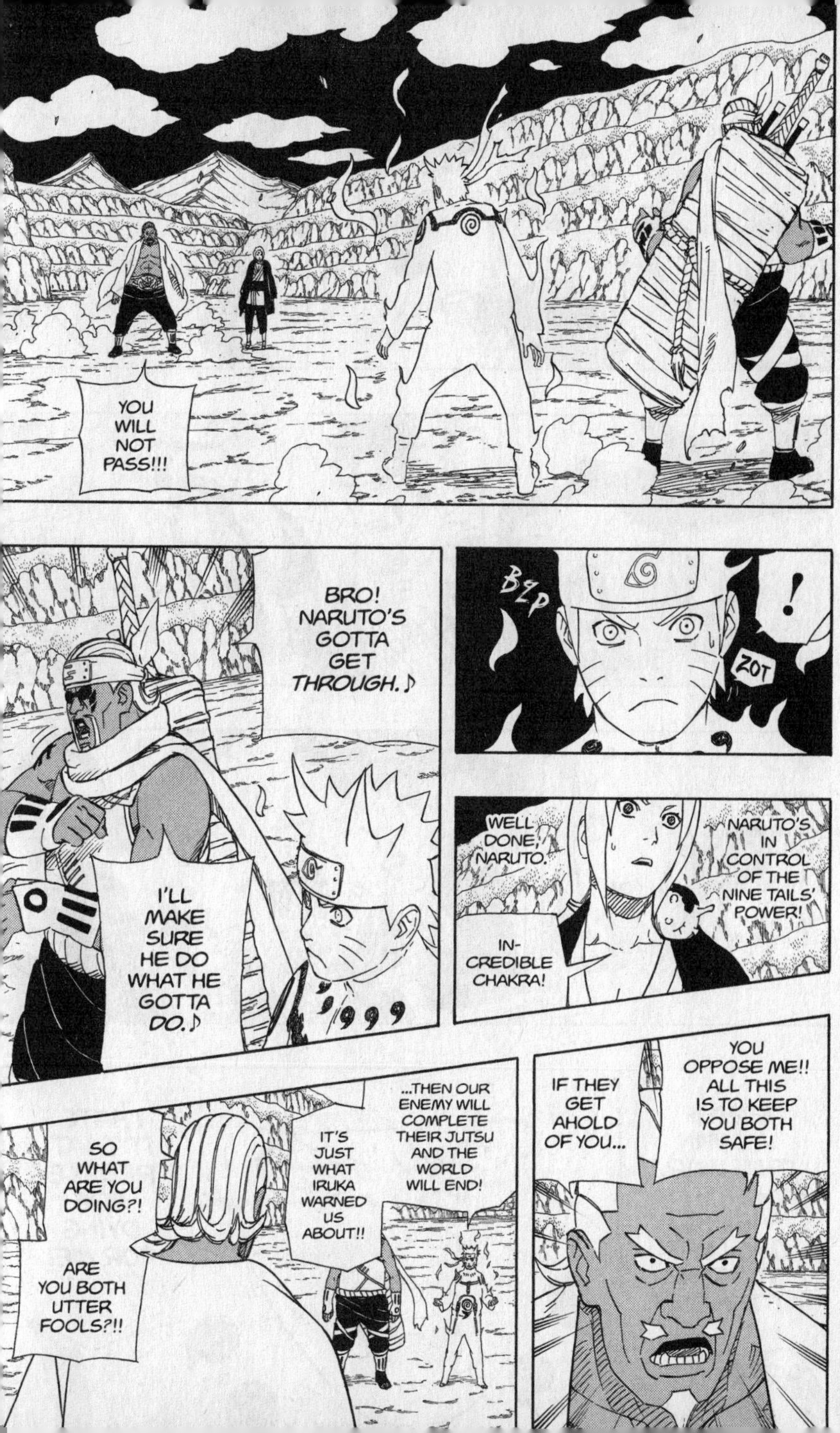
YOU WILL NOT PASS!!!
BZP
!
ZOT
NARUTO'S IN CONTROL OF THE NINE TAILS' POWER!
WELL DONE, NARUTO.
IN-CREDIBLE CHAKRA!
BRO! NARUTO'S GOTTA GET THROUGH.♪
I'LL MAKE SURE HE DO WHAT HE GOTTA DO.♪
YOU OPPOSE ME!! ALL THIS IS TO KEEP YOU BOTH SAFE!
IF THEY GET AHOLD OF YOU...
...THEN OUR ENEMY WILL COMPLETE THEIR JUTSU AND THE WORLD WILL END!
IT'S JUST WHAT IRUKA WARNED US ABOUT!!
SO WHAT ARE YOU DOING?!
ARE YOU BOTH UTTER FOOLS?!!

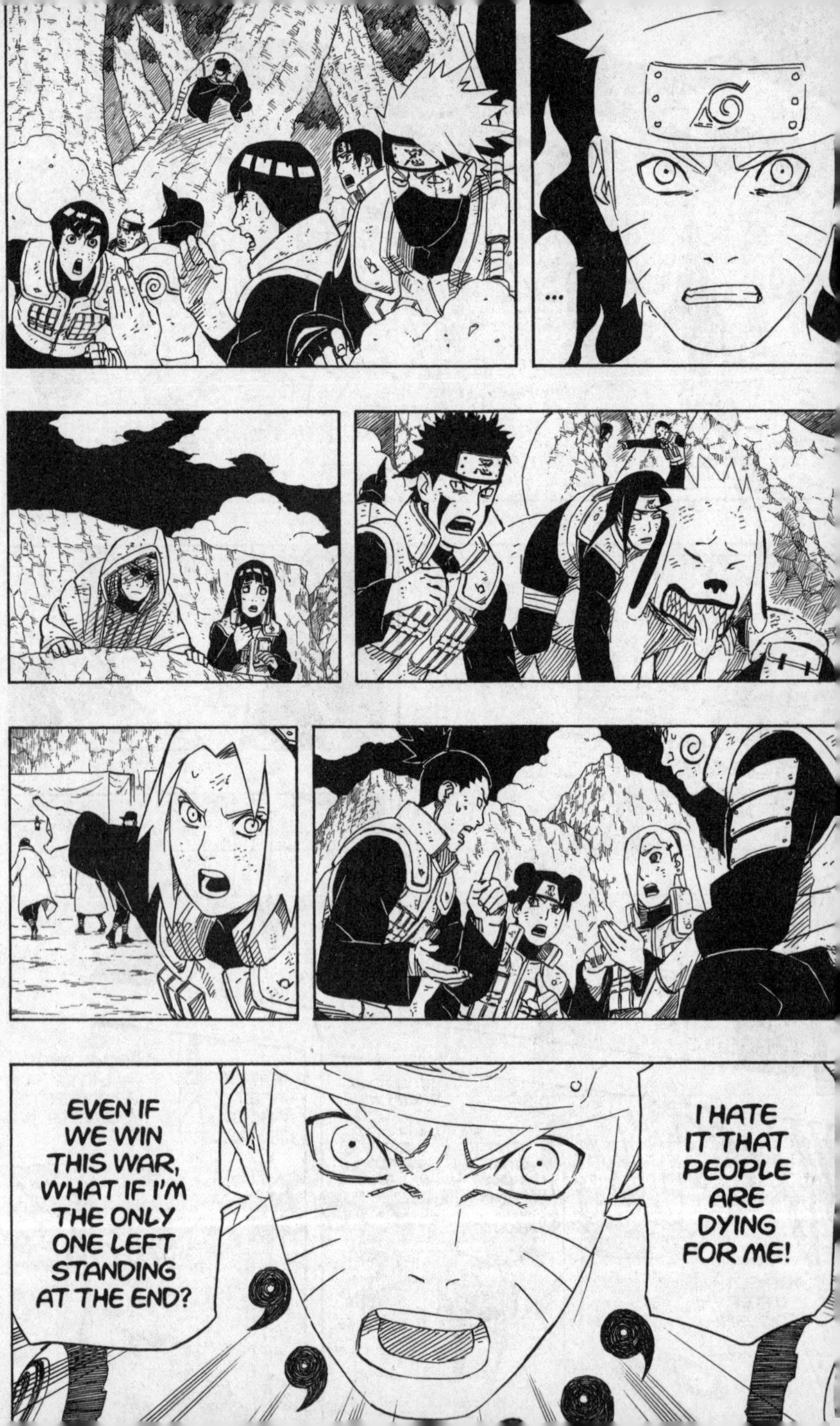
...
I HATE IT THAT PEOPLE ARE DYING FOR ME!
EVEN IF WE WIN THIS WAR, WHAT IF I'M THE ONLY ONE LEFT STANDING AT THE END?

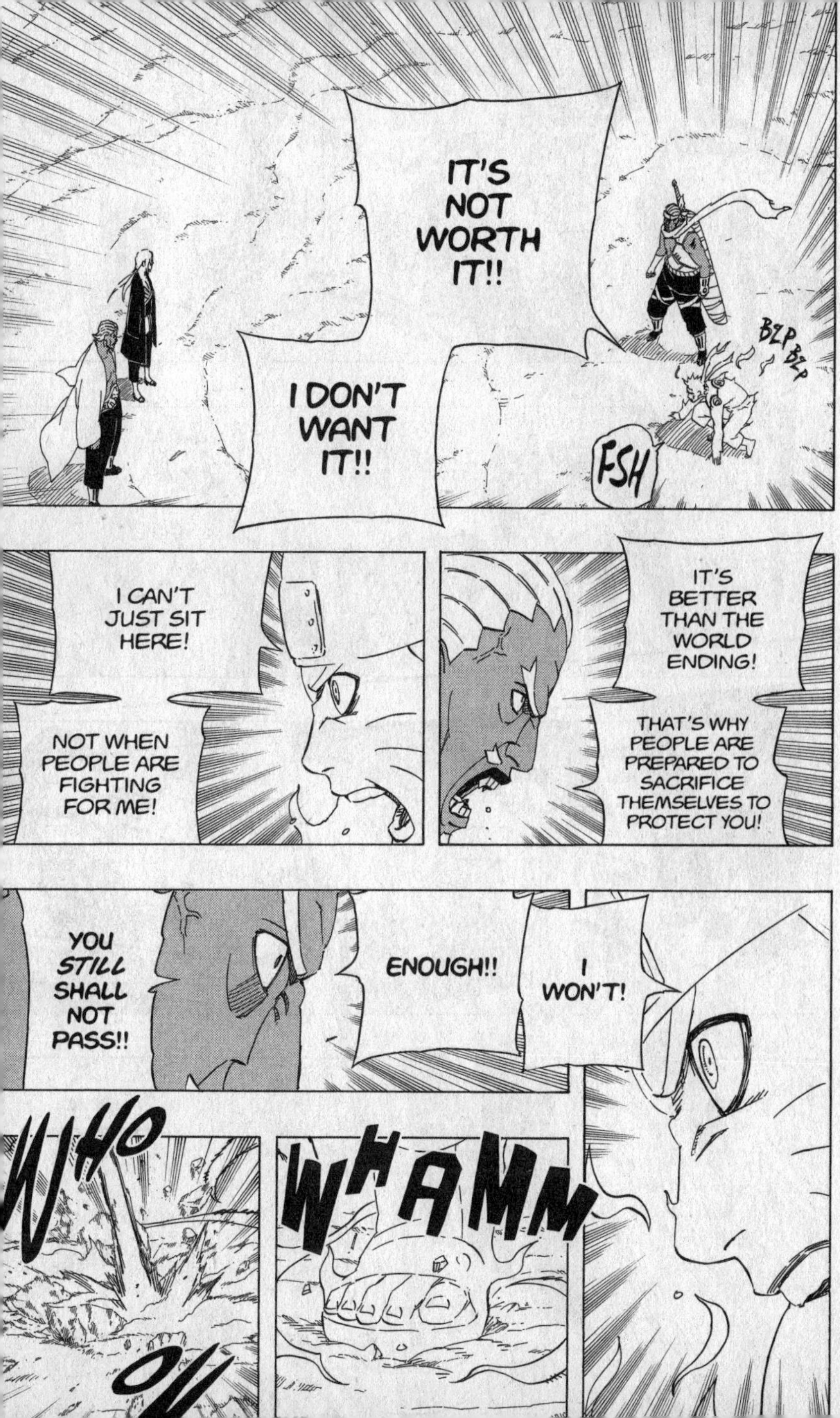

IT'S NOT WORTH IT!!
BZP BZP
I DON'T WANT IT!!
FSH
IT'S BETTER THAN THE WORLD ENDING!
THAT'S WHY PEOPLE ARE PREPARED TO SACRIFICE THEMSELVES TO PROTECT YOU!
I CAN'T JUST SIT HERE!
NOT WHEN PEOPLE ARE FIGHTING FOR ME!
I WON'T!
ENOUGH!!
YOU STILL SHALL NOT PASS!!
WHAMM
WHOOM

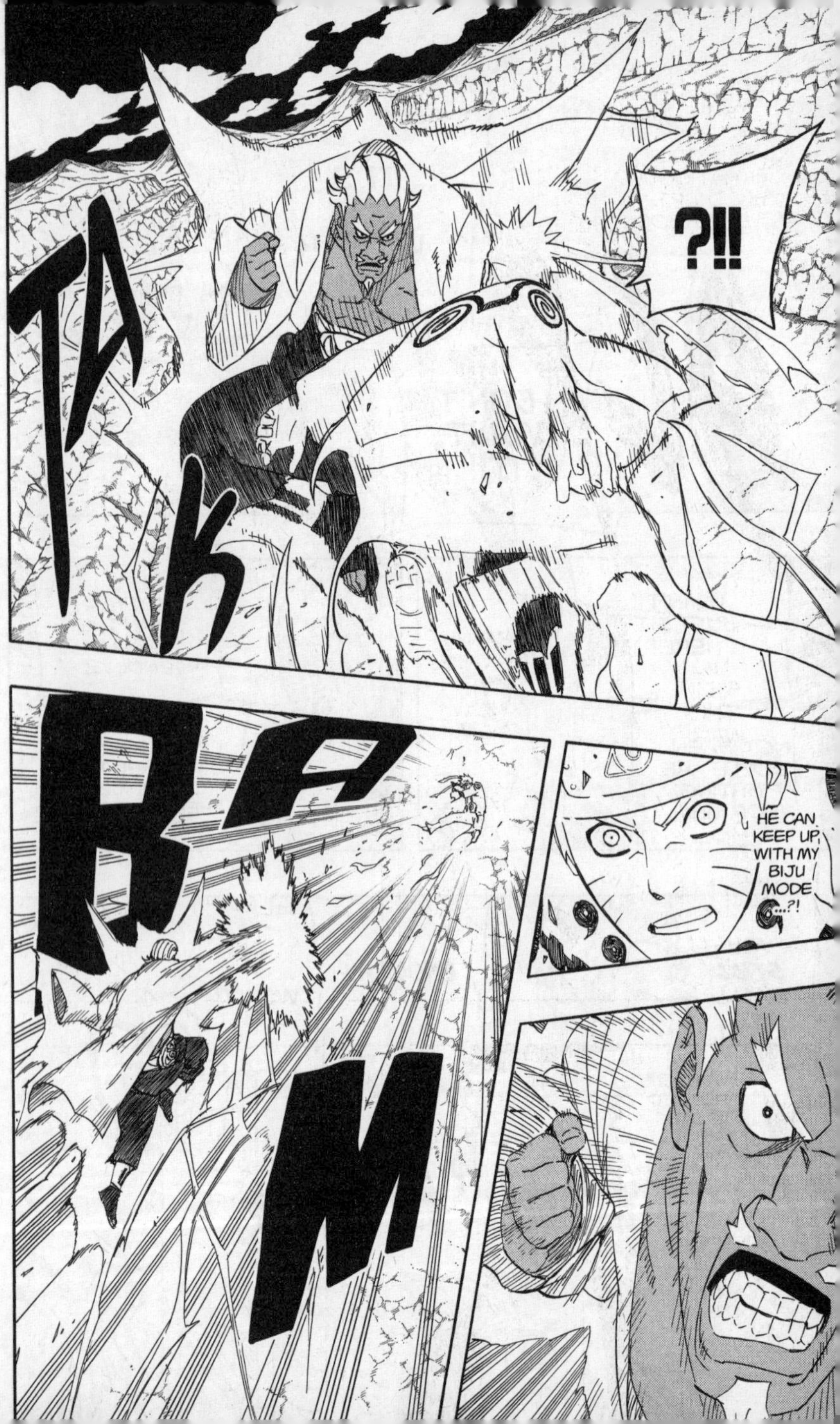
?!!
TAK
HE CAN KEEP UP WITH MY BIJU MODE...?!

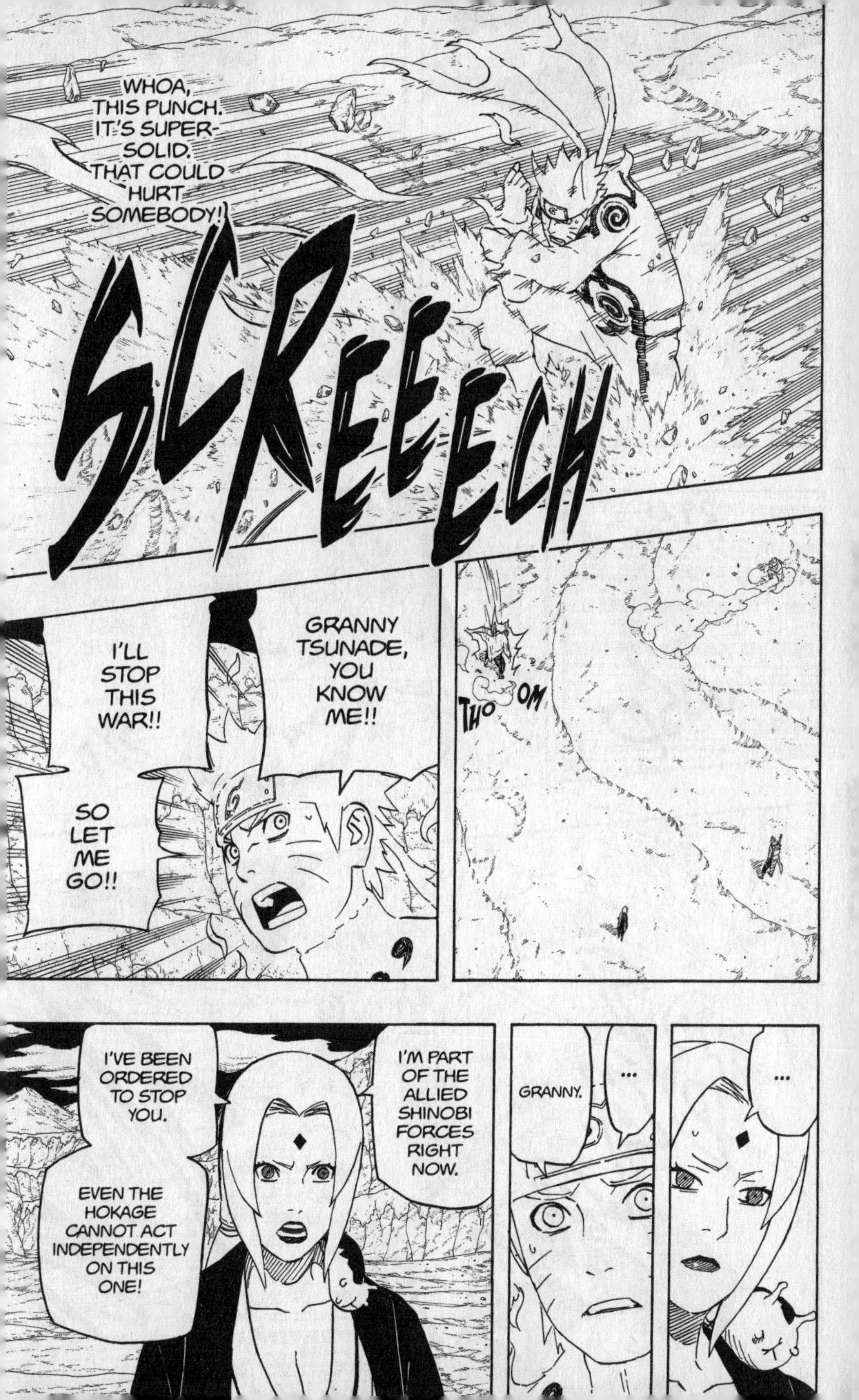
WHOA, THIS PUNCH. IT'S SUPER-SOLID. THAT COULD HURT SOMEBODY!!
SCREEECH
THOOM
GRANNY TSUNADE, YOU KNOW ME!!
I'LL STOP THIS WAR!!
SO LET ME GO!!
...
...
GRANNY.
I'M PART OF THE ALLIED SHINOBI FORCES RIGHT NOW.
I'VE BEEN ORDERED TO STOP YOU.
EVEN THE HOKAGE CANNOT ACT INDEPENDENTLY ON THIS ONE!

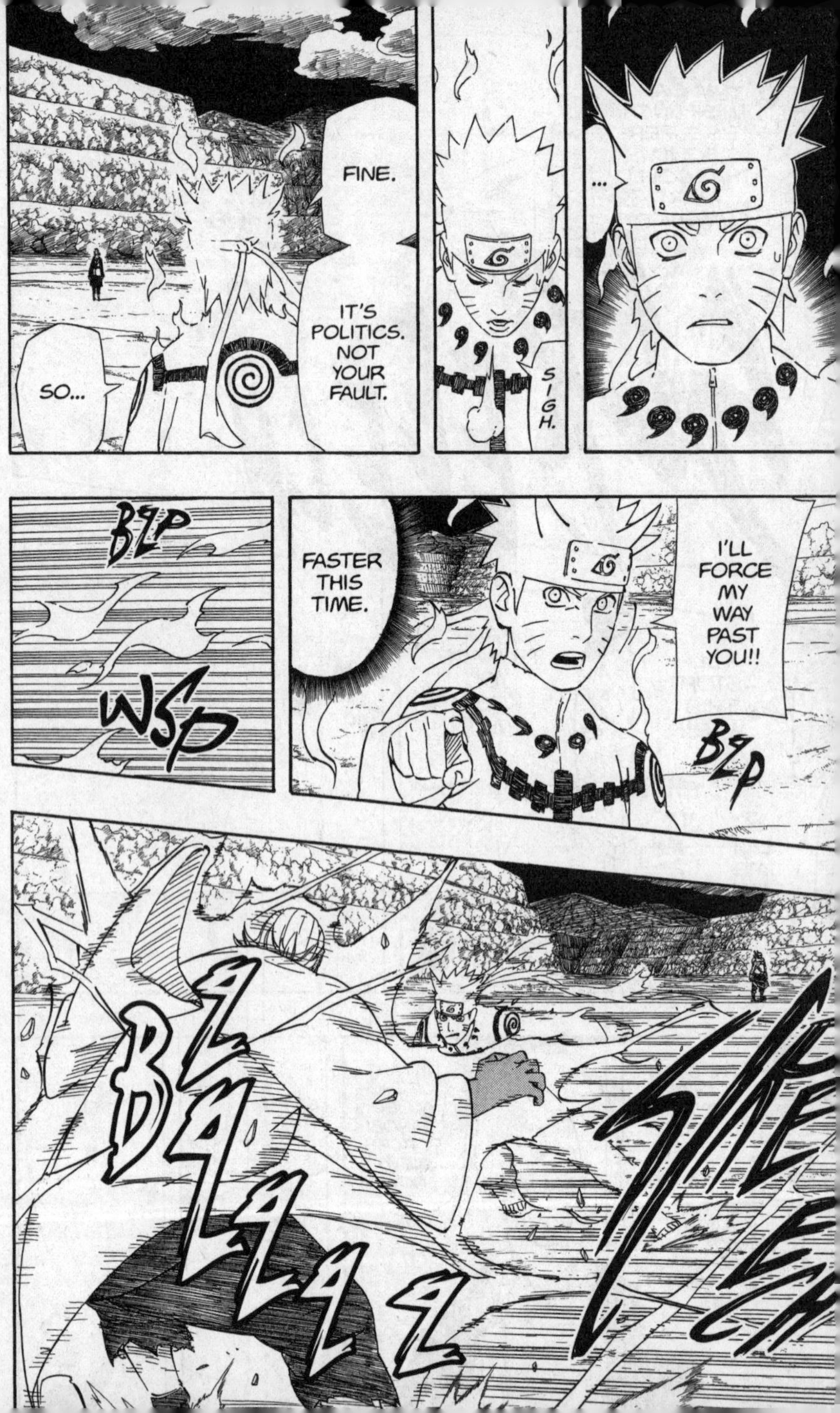
...
SIGH.
FINE.
IT'S POLITICS. NOT YOUR FAULT.
SO...
I'LL FORCE MY WAY PAST YOU!!
BZP
FASTER THIS TIME.
BZP
WSP

READ THIS WAY

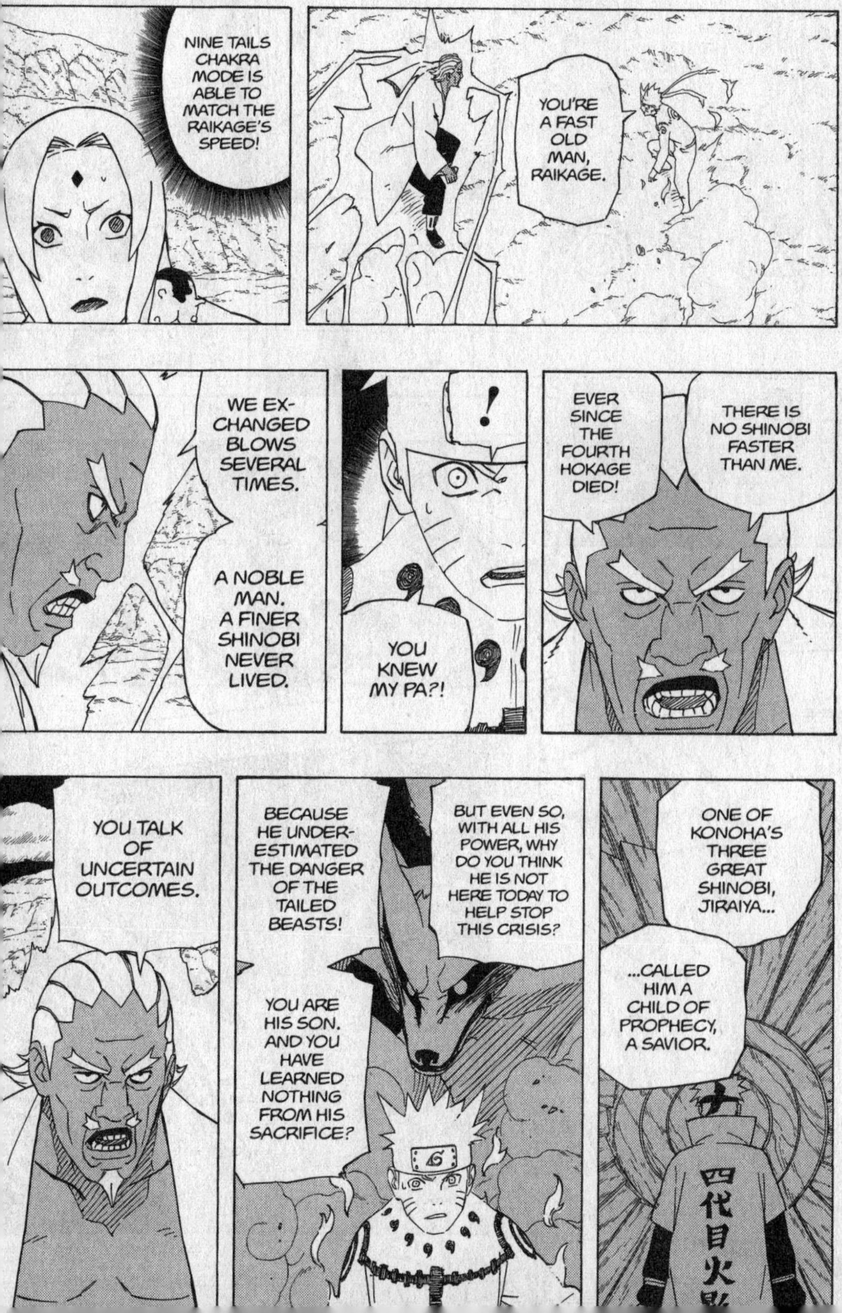

YOU'RE A FAST OLD MAN, RAIKAGE.
NINE TAILS CHAKRA MODE IS ABLE TO MATCH THE RAIKAGE'S SPEED!
THERE IS NO SHINOBI FASTER THAN ME.
EVER SINCE THE FOURTH HOKAGE DIED!
!
YOU KNEW MY PA?!
WE EXCHANGED BLOWS SEVERAL TIMES.
A NOBLE MAN. A FINER SHINOBI NEVER LIVED.
ONE OF KONOHA'S THREE GREAT SHINOBI, JIRAIYA...
...CALLED HIM A CHILD OF PROPHECY, A SAVIOR.
四代目火
BUT EVEN SO, WITH ALL HIS POWER, WHY DO YOU THINK HE IS NOT HERE TODAY TO HELP STOP THIS CRISIS?
BECAUSE HE UNDERESTIMATED THE DANGER OF THE TAILED BEASTS!
YOU ARE HIS SON. AND YOU HAVE LEARNED NOTHING FROM HIS SACRIFICE?
YOU TALK OF UNCERTAIN OUTCOMES.

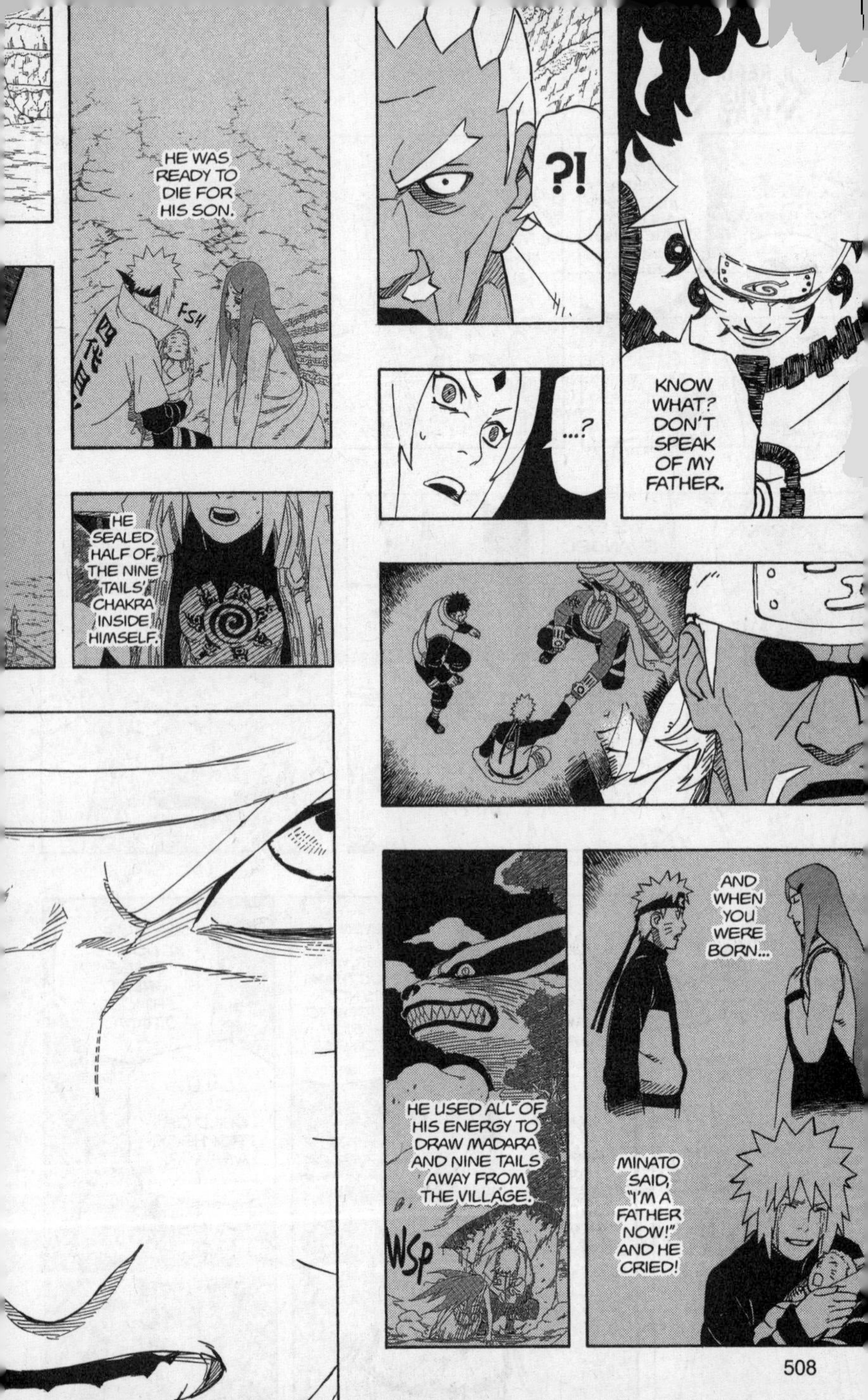
KNOW WHAT? DON'T SPEAK OF MY FATHER.
?!
...?
AND WHEN YOU WERE BORN...
MINATO SAID, "I'M A FATHER NOW!" AND HE CRIED!
HE USED ALL OF HIS ENERGY TO DRAW MADARA AND NINE TAILS AWAY FROM THE VILLAGE.
WSP
HE WAS READY TO DIE FOR HIS SON.
FSH
HE SEALED HALF OF THE NINE TAILS' CHAKRA INSIDE HIMSELF.

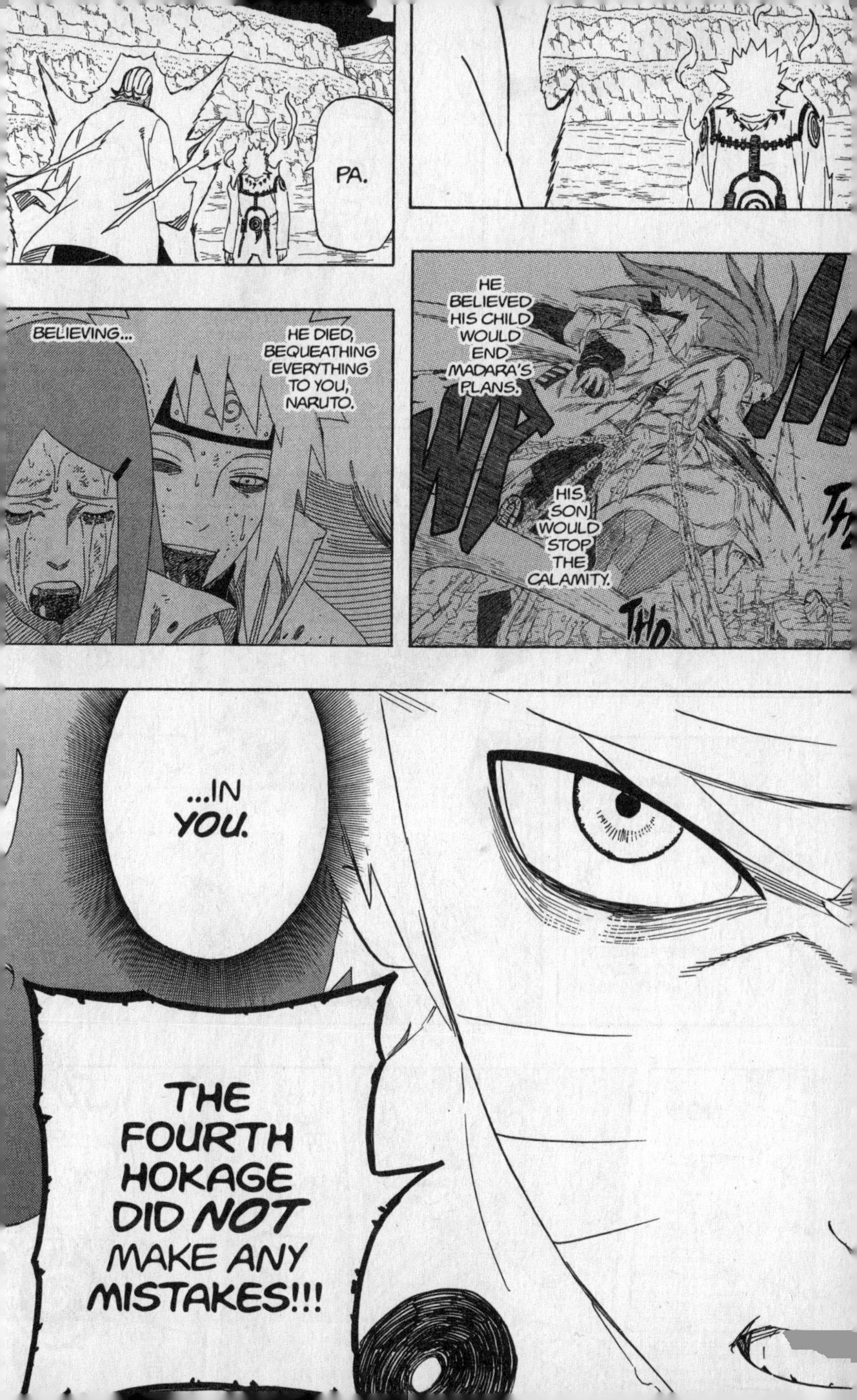
PA.
HE BELIEVED HIS CHILD WOULD END MADARA'S PLANS.
HIS SON WOULD STOP THE CALAMITY.
THD
HE DIED, BEQUEATHING EVERYTHING TO YOU, NARUTO.
BELIEVING...
...IN YOU.
THE FOURTH HOKAGE DID NOT MAKE ANY MISTAKES!!!

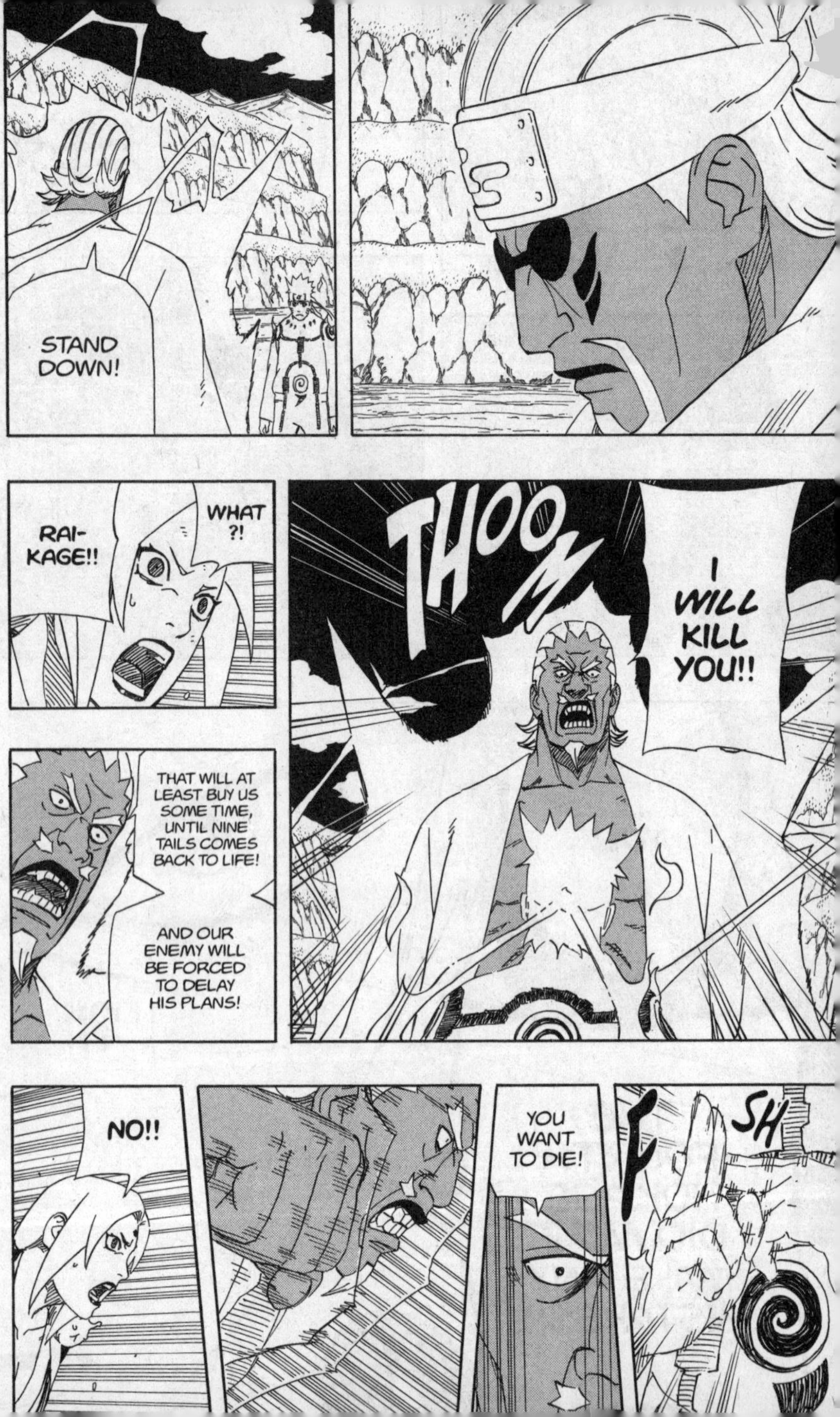
STAND DOWN!
THOOM
I WILL KILL YOU!!
WHAT ?!
RAI-KAGE!!
THAT WILL AT LEAST BUY US SOME TIME, UNTIL NINE TAILS COMES BACK TO LIFE!
AND OUR ENEMY WILL BE FORCED TO DELAY HIS PLANS!
FSH
YOU WANT TO DIE!
NO!!

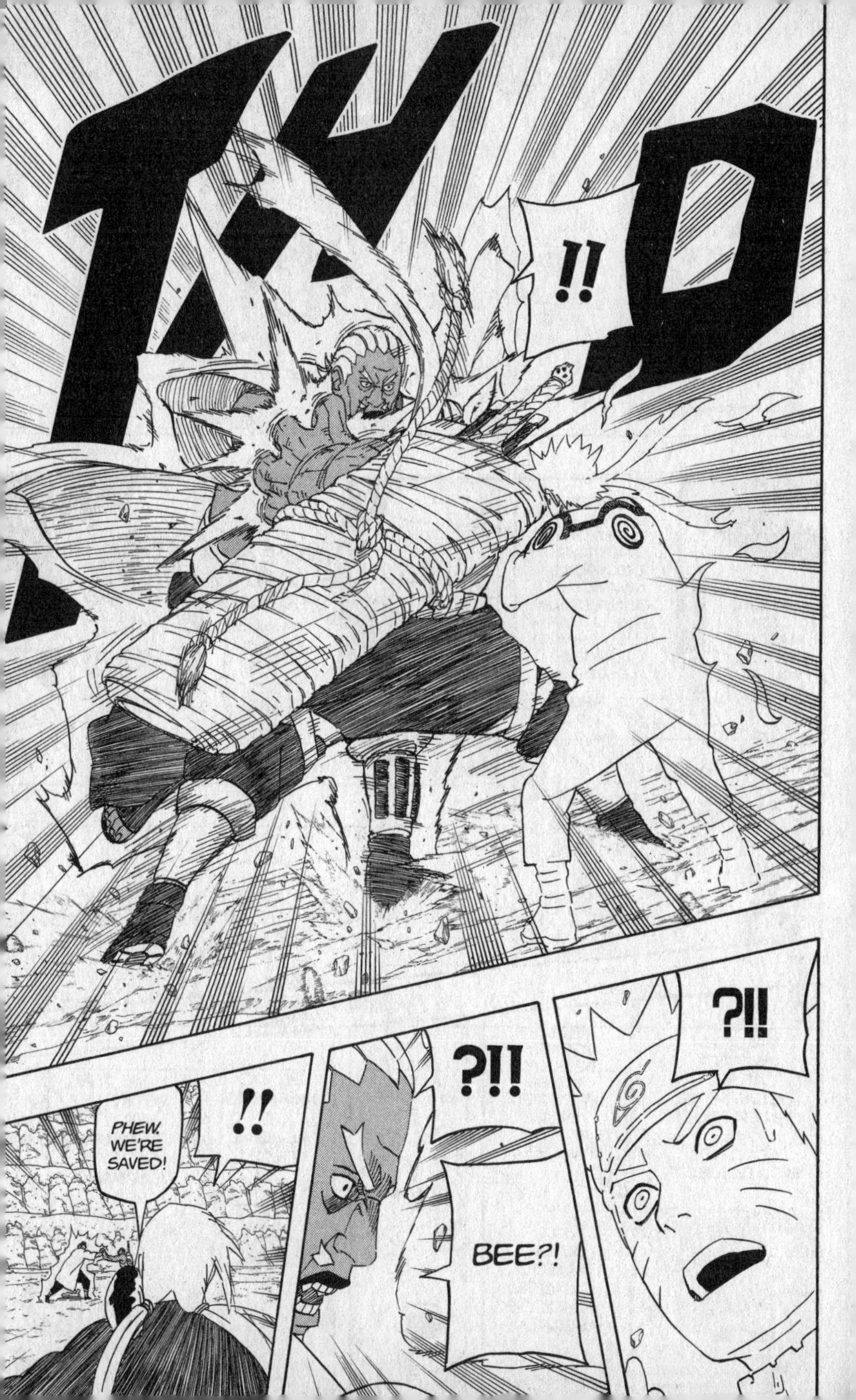
!!
?!!
?!!
BEE?!
!!
PHEW. WE'RE SAVED!

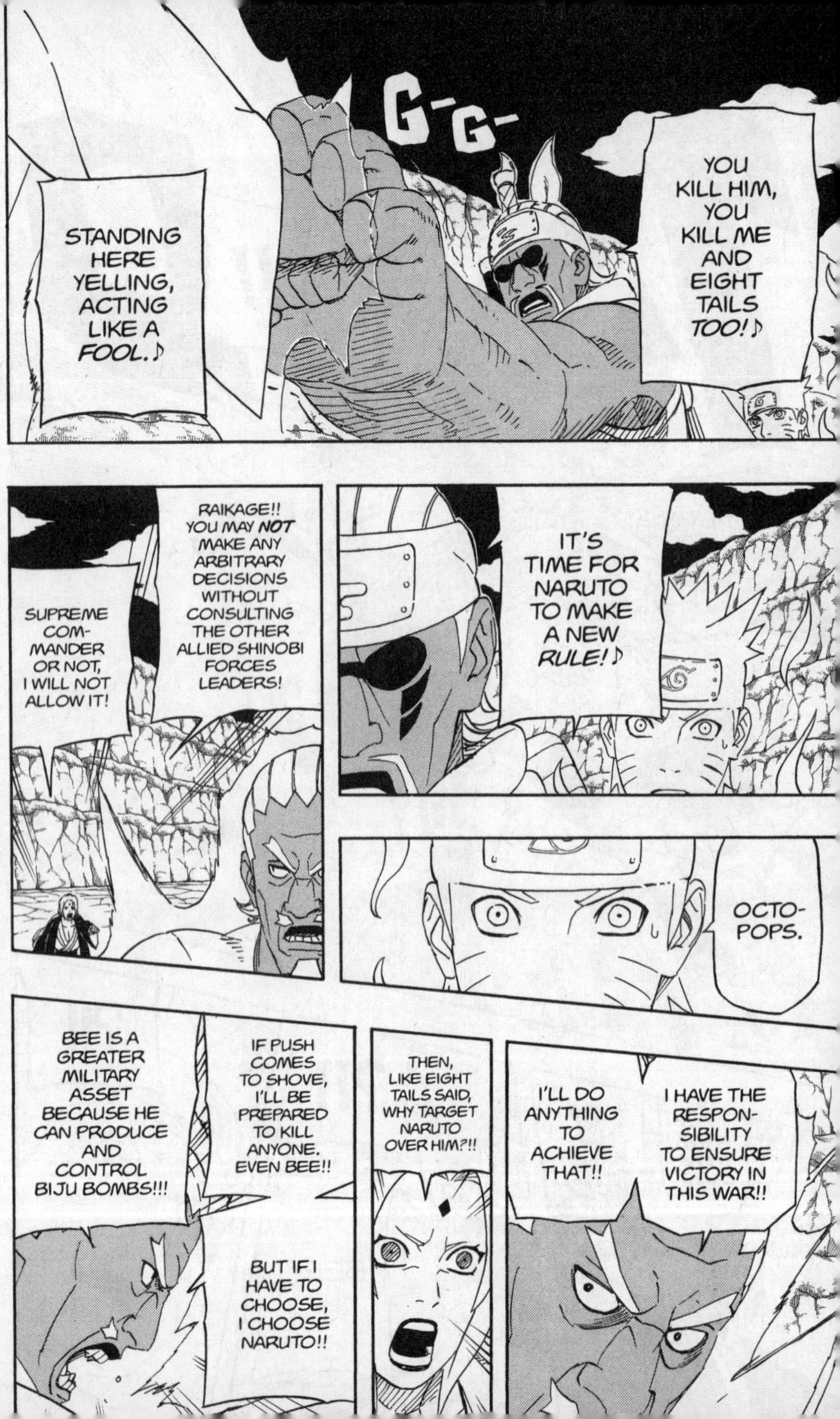
YOU KILL HIM, YOU KILL ME AND EIGHT TAILS *TOO!*♪
G-G-
STANDING HERE YELLING, ACTING LIKE A *FOOL.*♪
IT'S TIME FOR NARUTO TO MAKE A NEW *RULE!*♪
OCTO-POPS.
RAIKAGE!! YOU MAY ***NOT*** MAKE ANY ARBITRARY DECISIONS WITHOUT CONSULTING THE OTHER ALLIED SHINOBI FORCES LEADERS!
SUPREME COMMANDER OR NOT, I WILL NOT ALLOW IT!
I HAVE THE RESPONSIBILITY TO ENSURE VICTORY IN THIS WAR!!
I'LL DO ANYTHING TO ACHIEVE THAT!!
THEN, LIKE EIGHT TAILS SAID, WHY TARGET NARUTO OVER HIM?!!
IF PUSH COMES TO SHOVE, I'LL BE PREPARED TO KILL ANYONE. EVEN BEE!!
BEE IS A GREATER MILITARY ASSET BECAUSE HE CAN PRODUCE AND CONTROL BIJU BOMBS!!!
BUT IF I HAVE TO CHOOSE, I CHOOSE NARUTO!!

READ THIS WAY

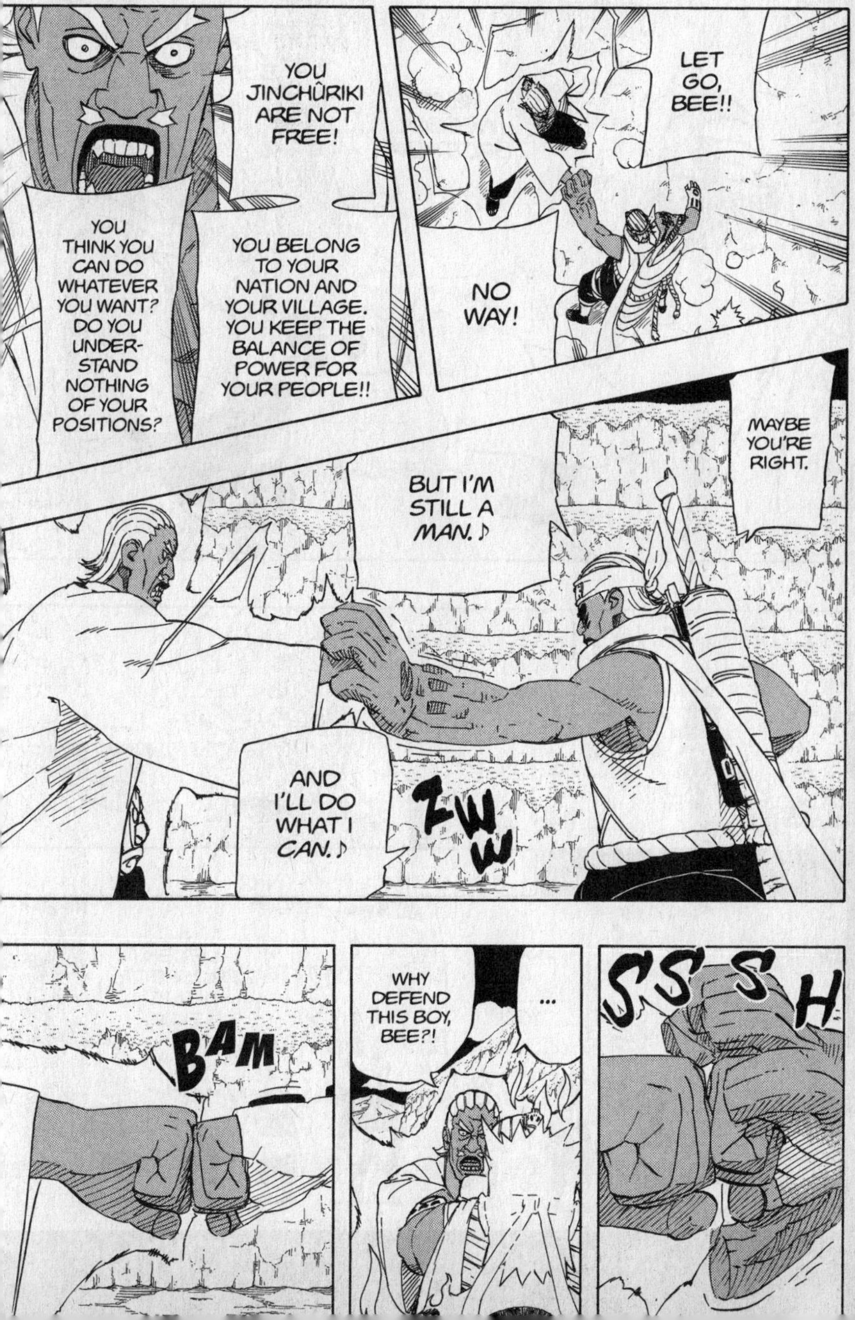
LET GO, BEE!!
NO WAY!
YOU JINCHÛRIKI ARE NOT FREE!
YOU BELONG TO YOUR NATION AND YOUR VILLAGE. YOU KEEP THE BALANCE OF POWER FOR YOUR PEOPLE!!
YOU THINK YOU CAN DO WHATEVER YOU WANT? DO YOU UNDER-STAND NOTHING OF YOUR POSITIONS?
MAYBE YOU'RE RIGHT.
BUT I'M STILL A MAN.♪
AND I'LL DO WHAT I CAN.♪
ZWW
SSSH
...
WHY DEFEND THIS BOY, BEE?!
BAM

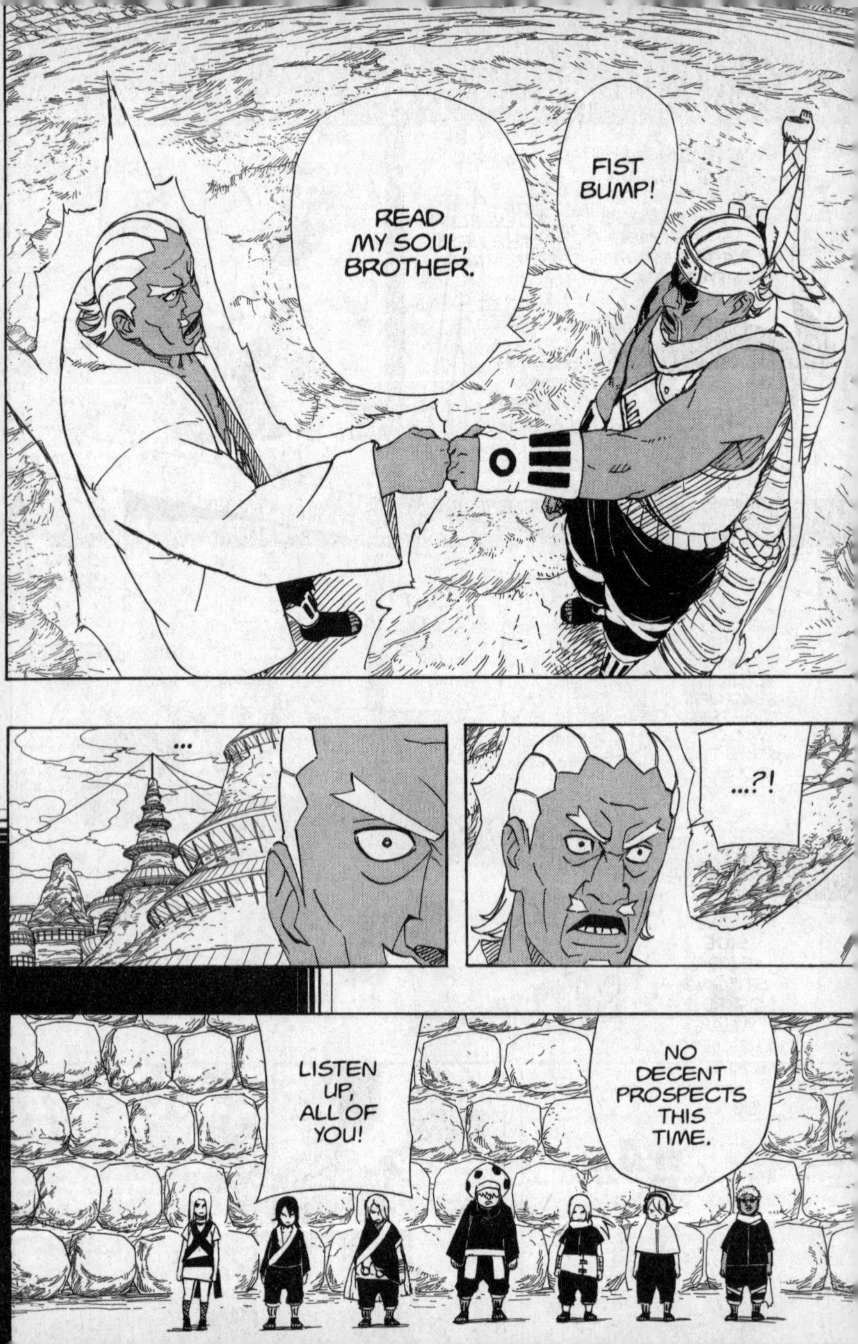
FIST BUMP!
READ MY SOUL, BROTHER.
...?!
...
NO DECENT PROSPECTS THIS TIME.
LISTEN UP, ALL OF YOU!

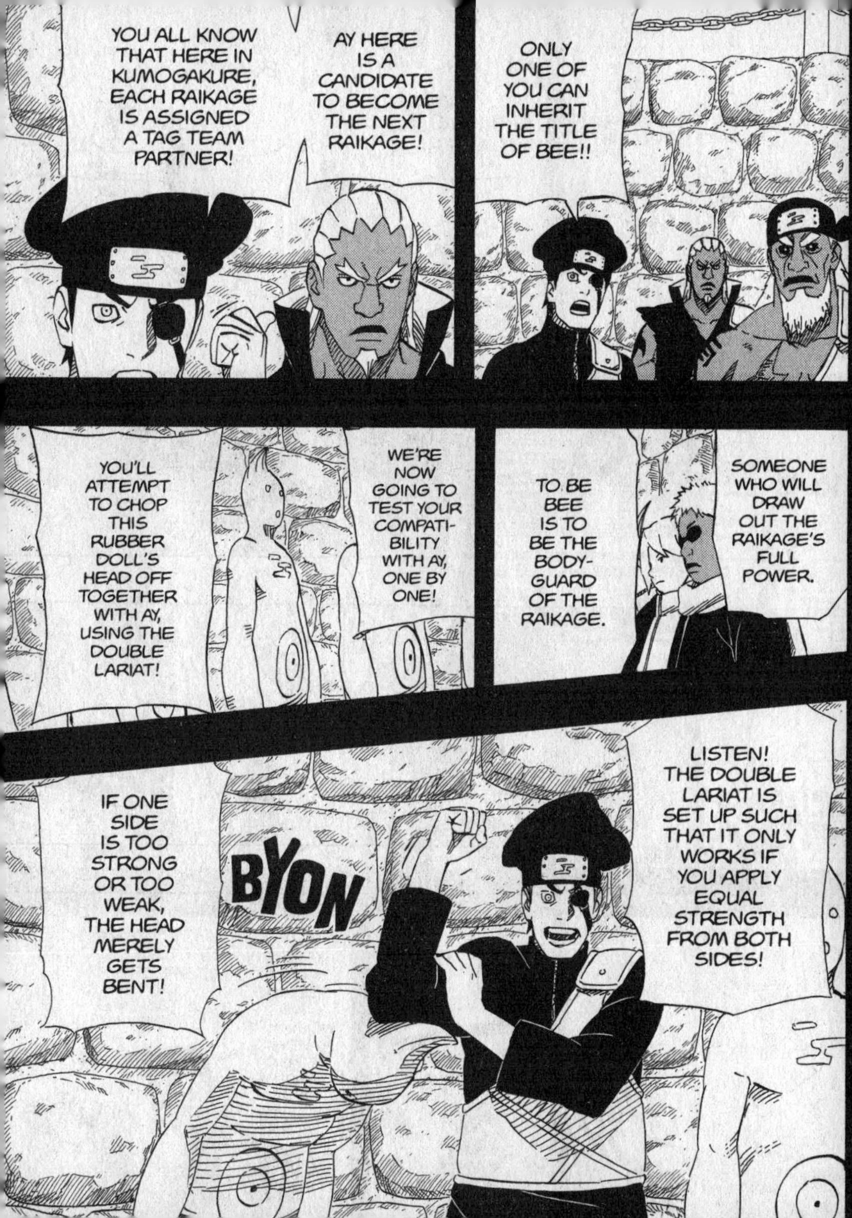
ONLY ONE OF YOU CAN INHERIT THE TITLE OF BEE!!
AY HERE IS A CANDIDATE TO BECOME THE NEXT RAIKAGE!
YOU ALL KNOW THAT HERE IN KUMOGAKURE, EACH RAIKAGE IS ASSIGNED A TAG TEAM PARTNER!
SOMEONE WHO WILL DRAW OUT THE RAIKAGE'S FULL POWER.
TO BE BEE IS TO BE THE BODY-GUARD OF THE RAIKAGE.
WE'RE NOW GOING TO TEST YOUR COMPATI-BILITY WITH AY, ONE BY ONE!
YOU'LL ATTEMPT TO CHOP THIS RUBBER DOLL'S HEAD OFF TOGETHER WITH AY, USING THE DOUBLE LARIAT!
LISTEN! THE DOUBLE LARIAT IS SET UP SUCH THAT IT ONLY WORKS IF YOU APPLY EQUAL STRENGTH FROM BOTH SIDES!
BYON
IF ONE SIDE IS TOO STRONG OR TOO WEAK, THE HEAD MERELY GETS BENT!

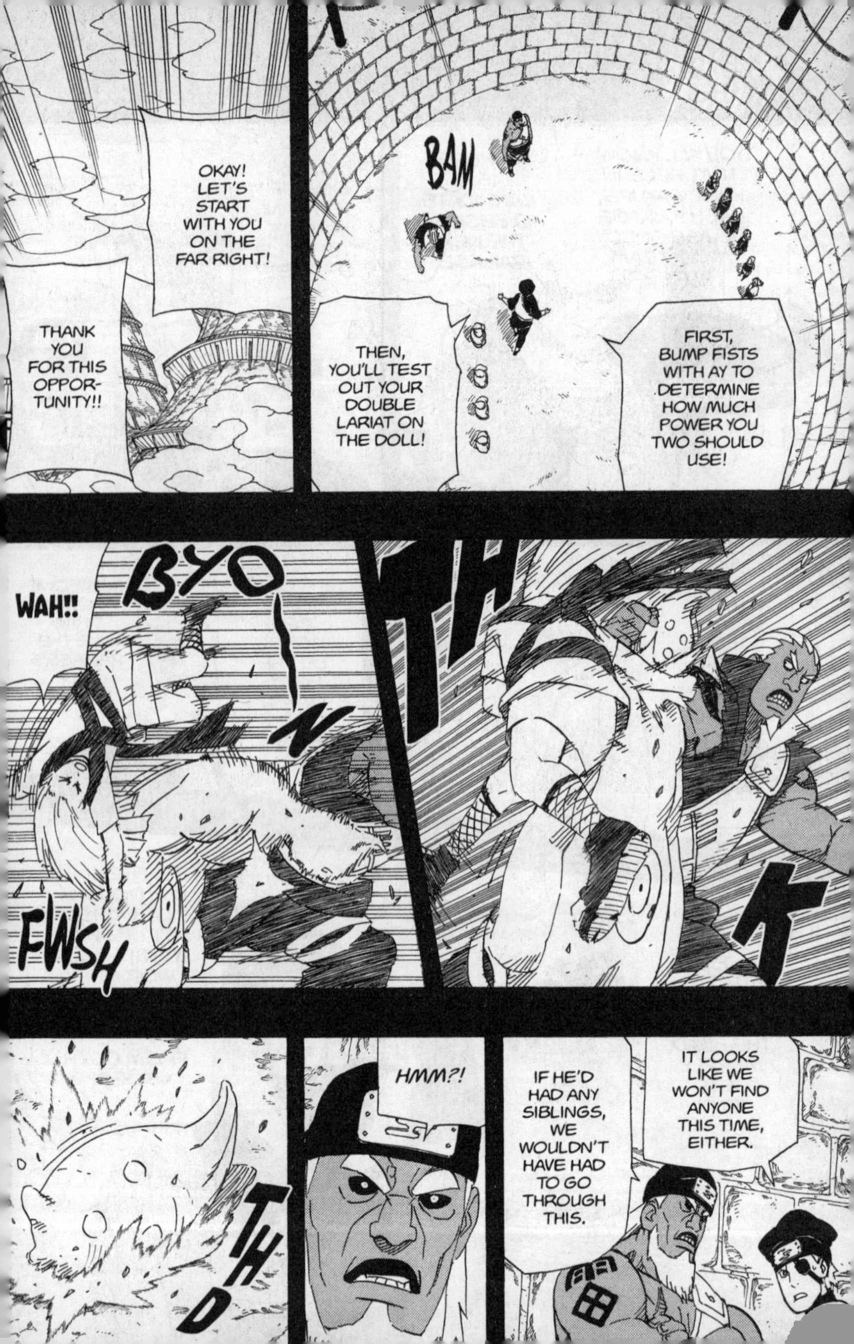
BAM
FIRST, BUMP FISTS WITH AY TO DETERMINE HOW MUCH POWER YOU TWO SHOULD USE!
THEN, YOU'LL TEST OUT YOUR DOUBLE LARIAT ON THE DOLL!
OKAY! LET'S START WITH YOU ON THE FAR RIGHT!
THANK YOU FOR THIS OPPORTUNITY!!
TH
K
BYO-I-N
WAH!!
FWSH
IT LOOKS LIKE WE WON'T FIND ANYONE THIS TIME, EITHER.
IF HE'D HAD ANY SIBLINGS, WE WOULDN'T HAVE HAD TO GO THROUGH THIS.
HMM?!
THD

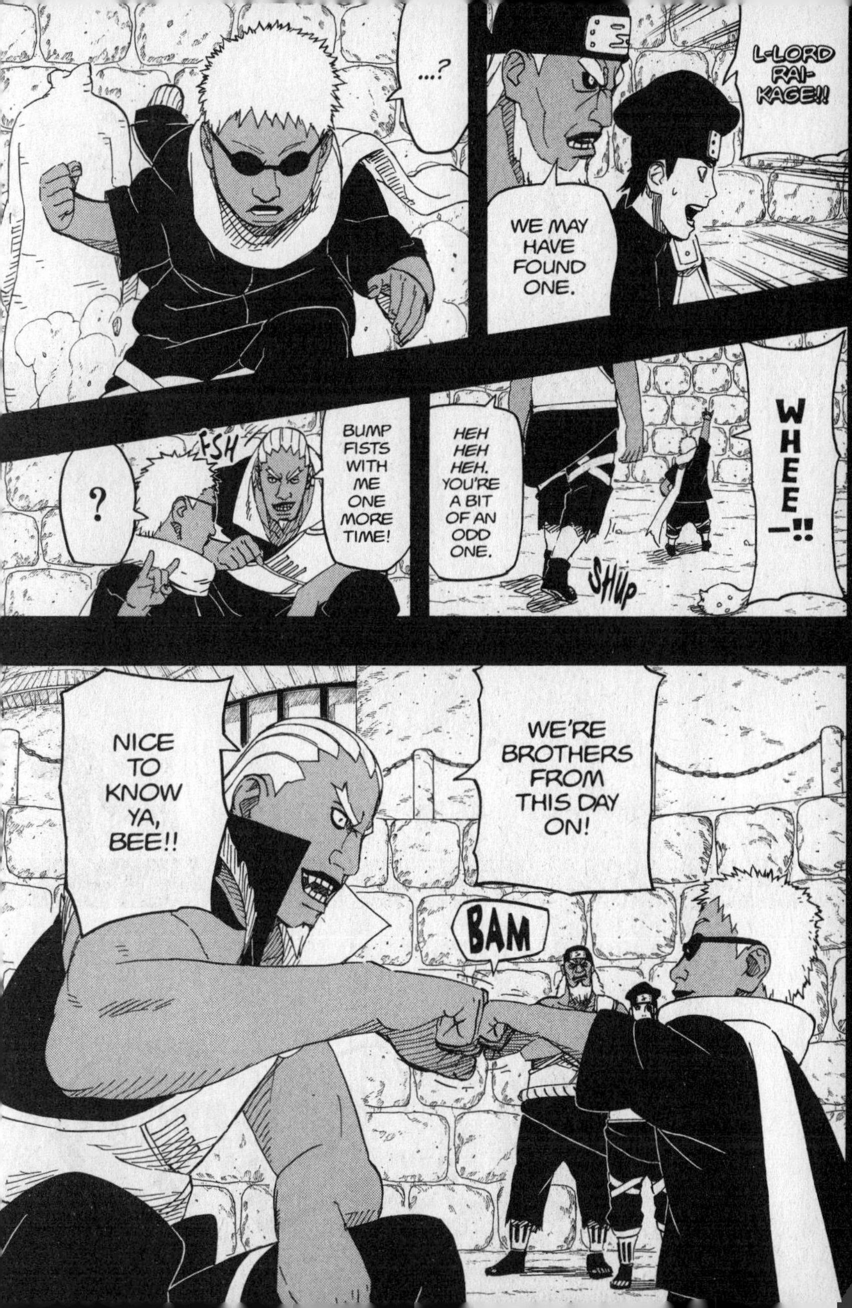
L-LORD RAI-KAGE!!
WE MAY HAVE FOUND ONE.
...?
WHEE—!!
HEH HEH HEH. YOU'RE A BIT OF AN ODD ONE.
SHUP
BUMP FISTS WITH ME ONE MORE TIME!
FSH
?
WE'RE BROTHERS FROM THIS DAY ON!
NICE TO KNOW YA, BEE!!
BAM

NARUTO

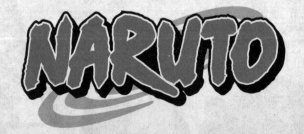

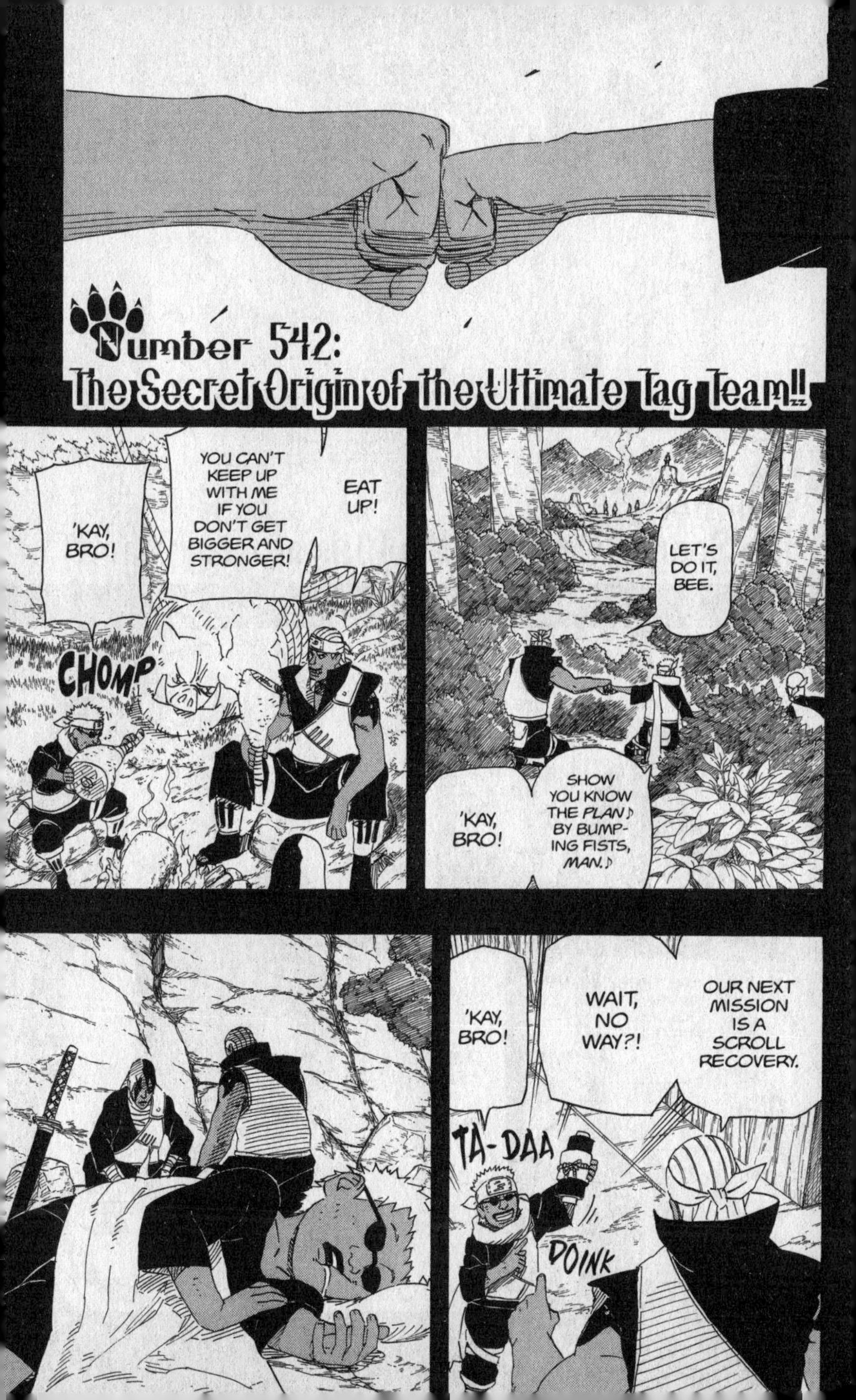
Number 542:
The Secret Origin of the Ultimate Tag Team!!
LET'S DO IT, BEE.
SHOW YOU KNOW THE PLAN♪ BY BUMPING FISTS, MAN.♪
'KAY, BRO!
EAT UP!
YOU CAN'T KEEP UP WITH ME IF YOU DON'T GET BIGGER AND STRONGER!
'KAY, BRO!
CHOMP
OUR NEXT MISSION IS A SCROLL RECOVERY.
WAIT, NO WAY?!
'KAY, BRO!
TA-DAA
DOINK

# Number 542: The Secret Origin of the Ultimate Tag Team!!

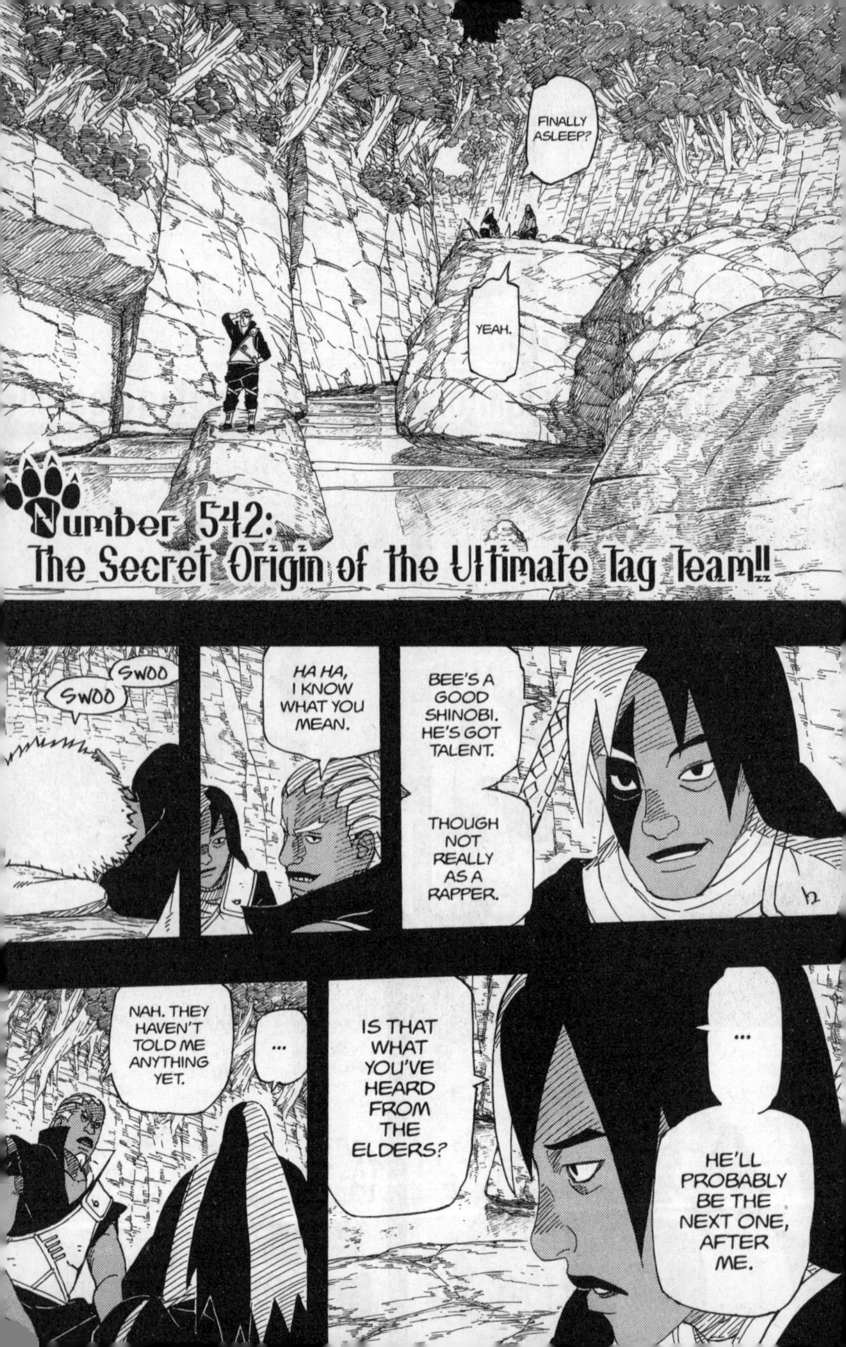
FINALLY ASLEEP?
YEAH.
Number 542: The Secret Origin of the Ultimate Tag Team!!
BEE'S A GOOD SHINOBI. HE'S GOT TALENT.
THOUGH NOT REALLY AS A RAPPER.
HA HA, I KNOW WHAT YOU MEAN.
SWOO
SWOO
...
HE'LL PROBABLY BE THE NEXT ONE, AFTER ME.
IS THAT WHAT YOU'VE HEARD FROM THE ELDERS?
...
NAH. THEY HAVEN'T TOLD ME ANYTHING YET.

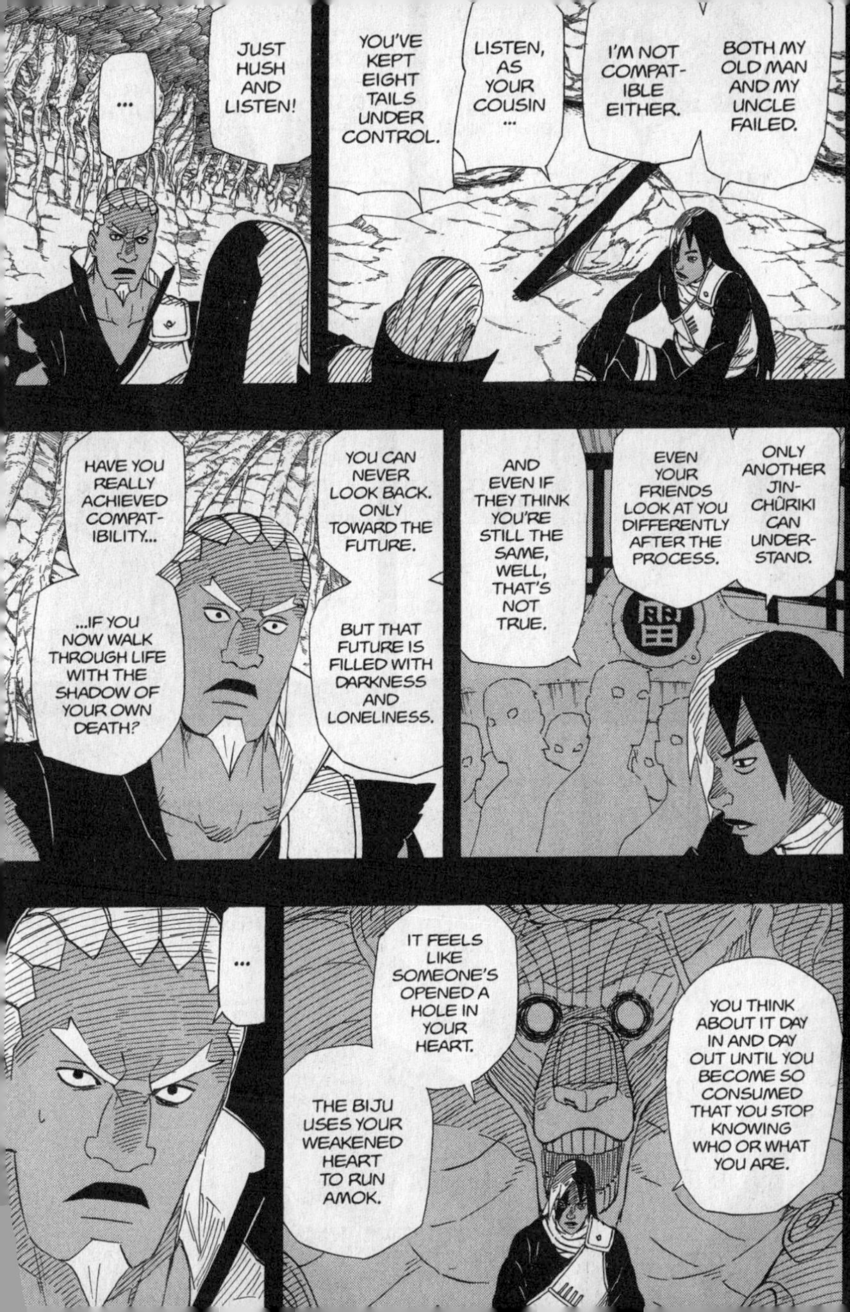
BOTH MY OLD MAN AND MY UNCLE FAILED.
I'M NOT COMPATIBLE EITHER.
LISTEN, AS YOUR COUSIN ...
YOU'VE KEPT EIGHT TAILS UNDER CONTROL.
JUST HUSH AND LISTEN!
...
ONLY ANOTHER JINCHŪRIKI CAN UNDERSTAND.
EVEN YOUR FRIENDS LOOK AT YOU DIFFERENTLY AFTER THE PROCESS.
AND EVEN IF THEY THINK YOU'RE STILL THE SAME, WELL, THAT'S NOT TRUE.
YOU CAN NEVER LOOK BACK. ONLY TOWARD THE FUTURE.
BUT THAT FUTURE IS FILLED WITH DARKNESS AND LONELINESS.
HAVE YOU REALLY ACHIEVED COMPATIBILITY...
...IF YOU NOW WALK THROUGH LIFE WITH THE SHADOW OF YOUR OWN DEATH?
YOU THINK ABOUT IT DAY IN AND DAY OUT UNTIL YOU BECOME SO CONSUMED THAT YOU STOP KNOWING WHO OR WHAT YOU ARE.
IT FEELS LIKE SOMEONE'S OPENED A HOLE IN YOUR HEART.
THE BIJU USES YOUR WEAKENED HEART TO RUN AMOK.
...

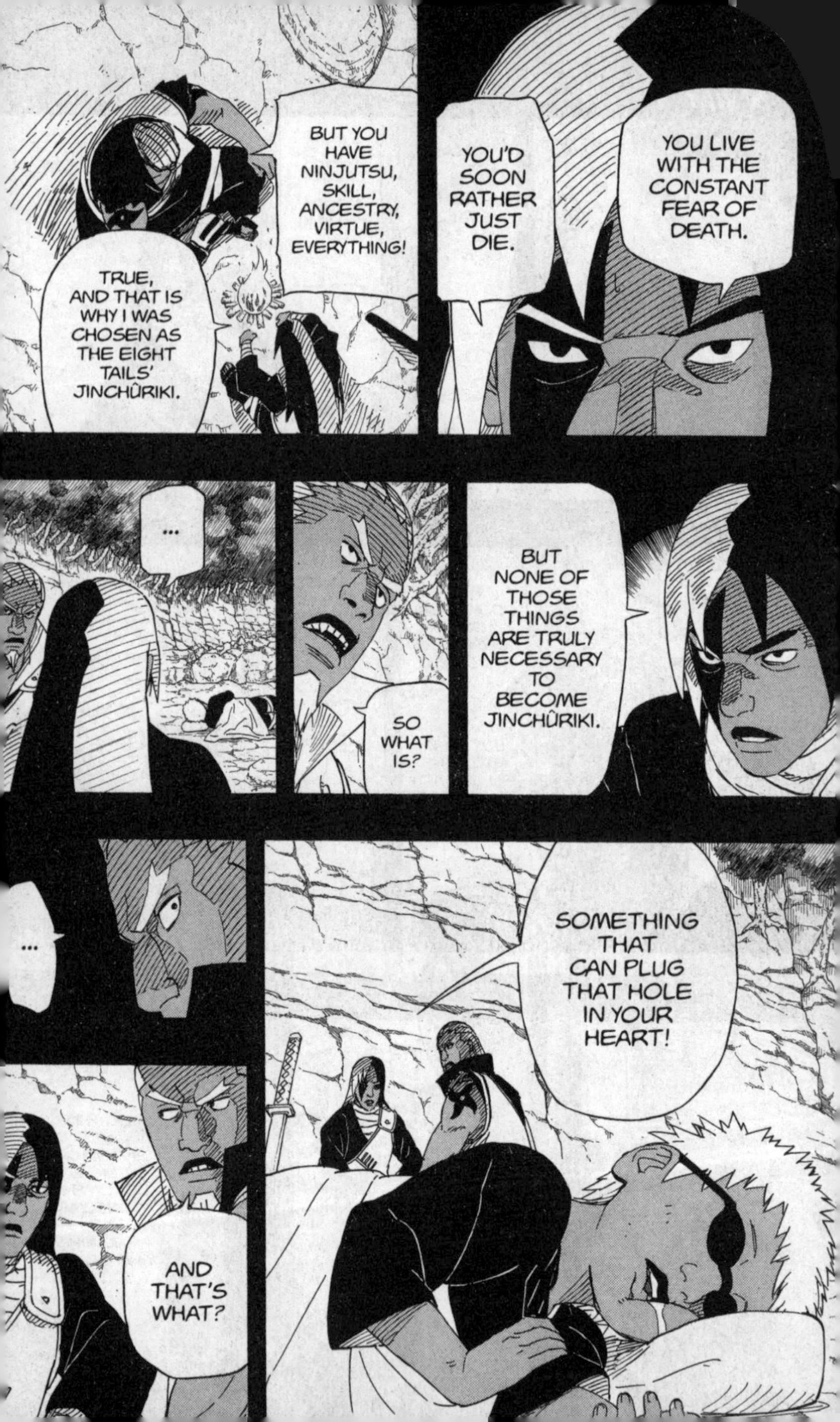
YOU LIVE WITH THE CONSTANT FEAR OF DEATH.
YOU'D SOON RATHER JUST DIE.
BUT YOU HAVE NINJUTSU, SKILL, ANCESTRY, VIRTUE, EVERYTHING!
TRUE, AND THAT IS WHY I WAS CHOSEN AS THE EIGHT TAILS' JINCHÛRIKI.
BUT NONE OF THOSE THINGS ARE TRULY NECESSARY TO BECOME JINCHÛRIKI.
SO WHAT IS?
...
SOMETHING THAT CAN PLUG THAT HOLE IN YOUR HEART!
...
AND THAT'S WHAT?

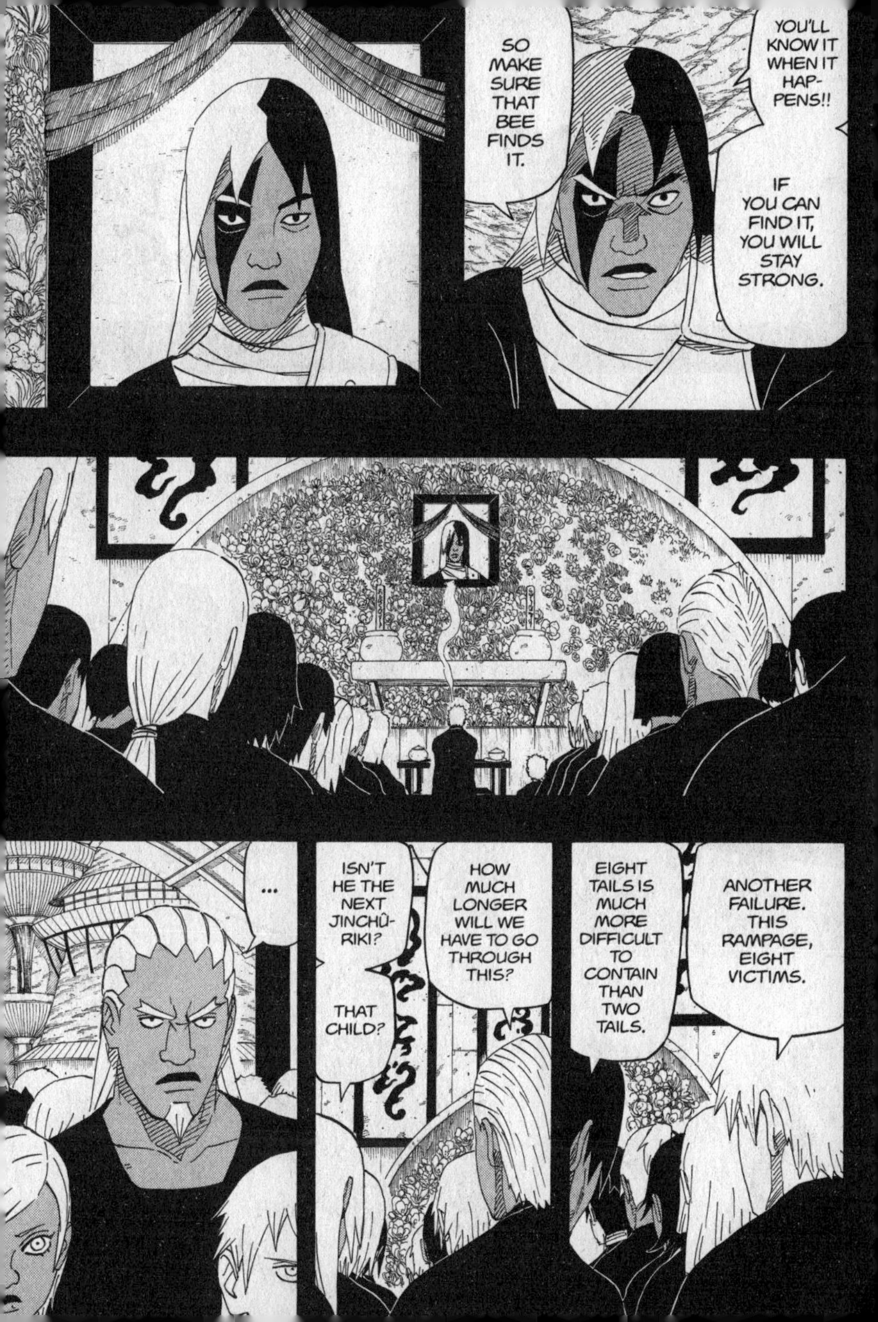
YOU'LL KNOW IT WHEN IT HAP-PENS!!
IF YOU CAN FIND IT, YOU WILL STAY STRONG.
SO MAKE SURE THAT BEE FINDS IT.
ANOTHER FAILURE. THIS RAMPAGE, EIGHT VICTIMS.
EIGHT TAILS IS MUCH MORE DIFFICULT TO CONTAIN THAN TWO TAILS.
HOW MUCH LONGER WILL WE HAVE TO GO THROUGH THIS?
ISN'T HE THE NEXT JINCHÛ-RIKI?
THAT CHILD?
...

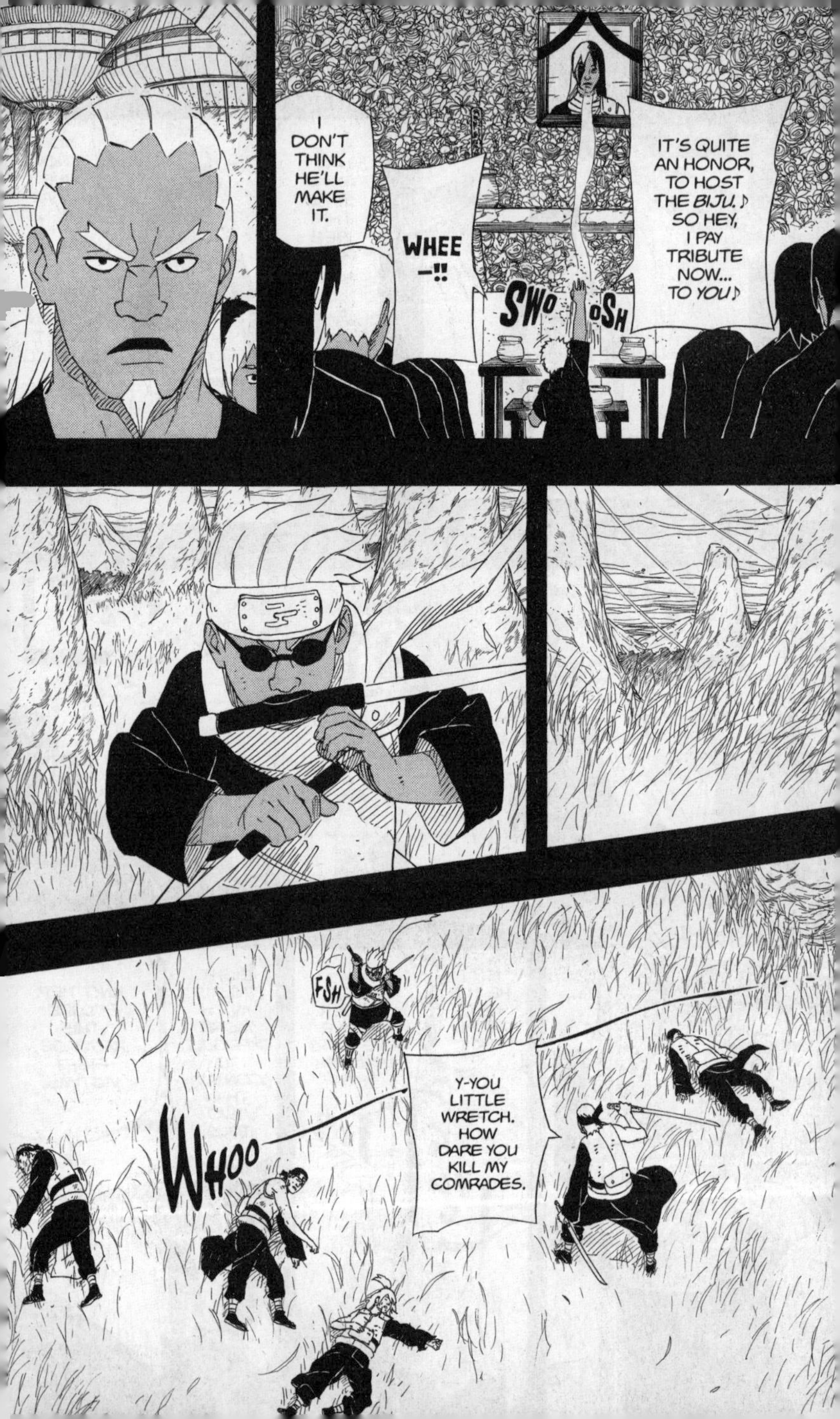
IT'S QUITE AN HONOR, TO HOST THE *BIJU.*♪ SO HEY, I PAY TRIBUTE NOW... TO *YOU*♪
SWOOSH
WHEE—!!
I DON'T THINK HE'LL MAKE IT.
FSH
Y-YOU LITTLE WRETCH. HOW DARE YOU KILL MY COMRADES.
WHOO

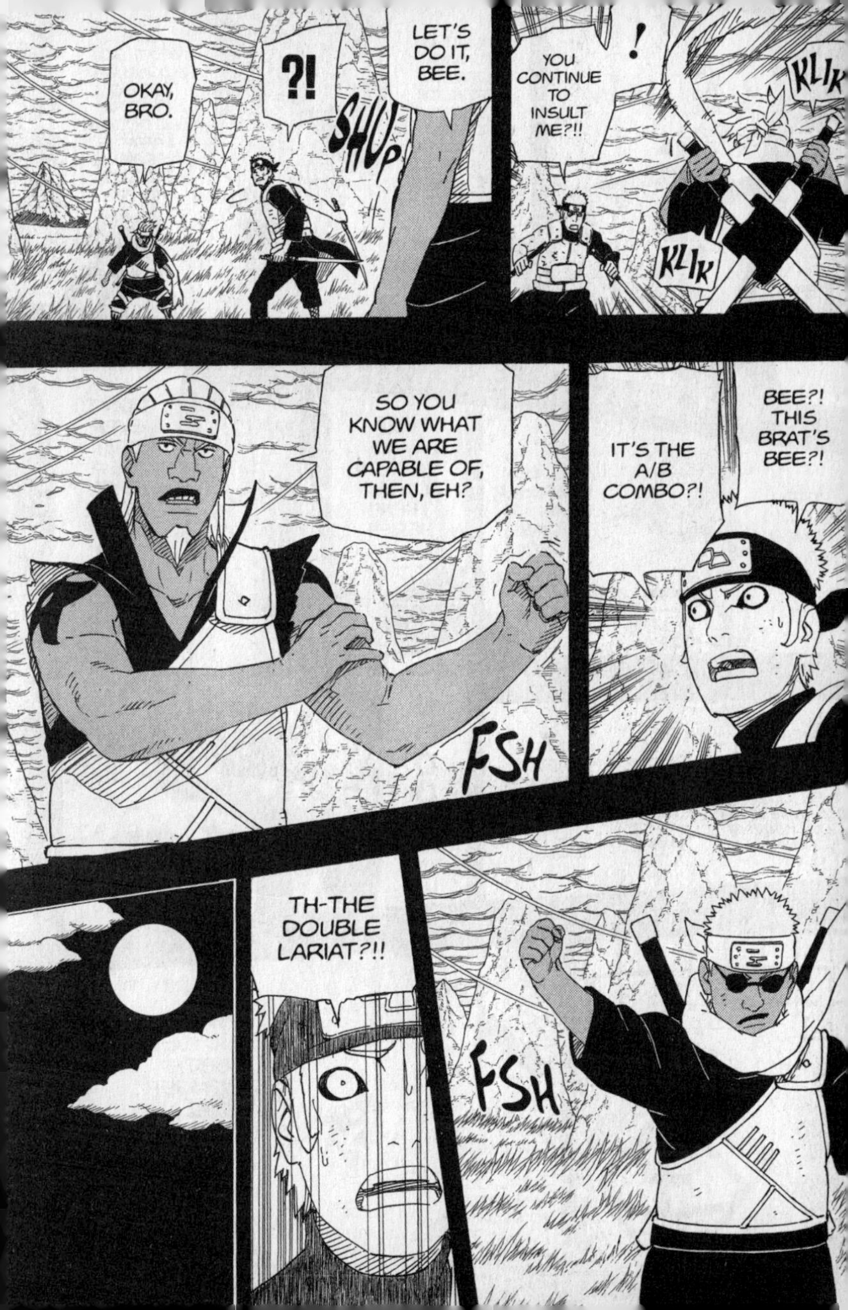
!
YOU CONTINUE TO INSULT ME?!!
KLIK
KLIK
LET'S DO IT, BEE.
?!
SHUP
OKAY, BRO.
BEE?! THIS BRAT'S BEE?!
IT'S THE A/B COMBO?!
SO YOU KNOW WHAT WE ARE CAPABLE OF, THEN, EH?
FSH
FSH
TH-THE DOUBLE LARIAT?!!

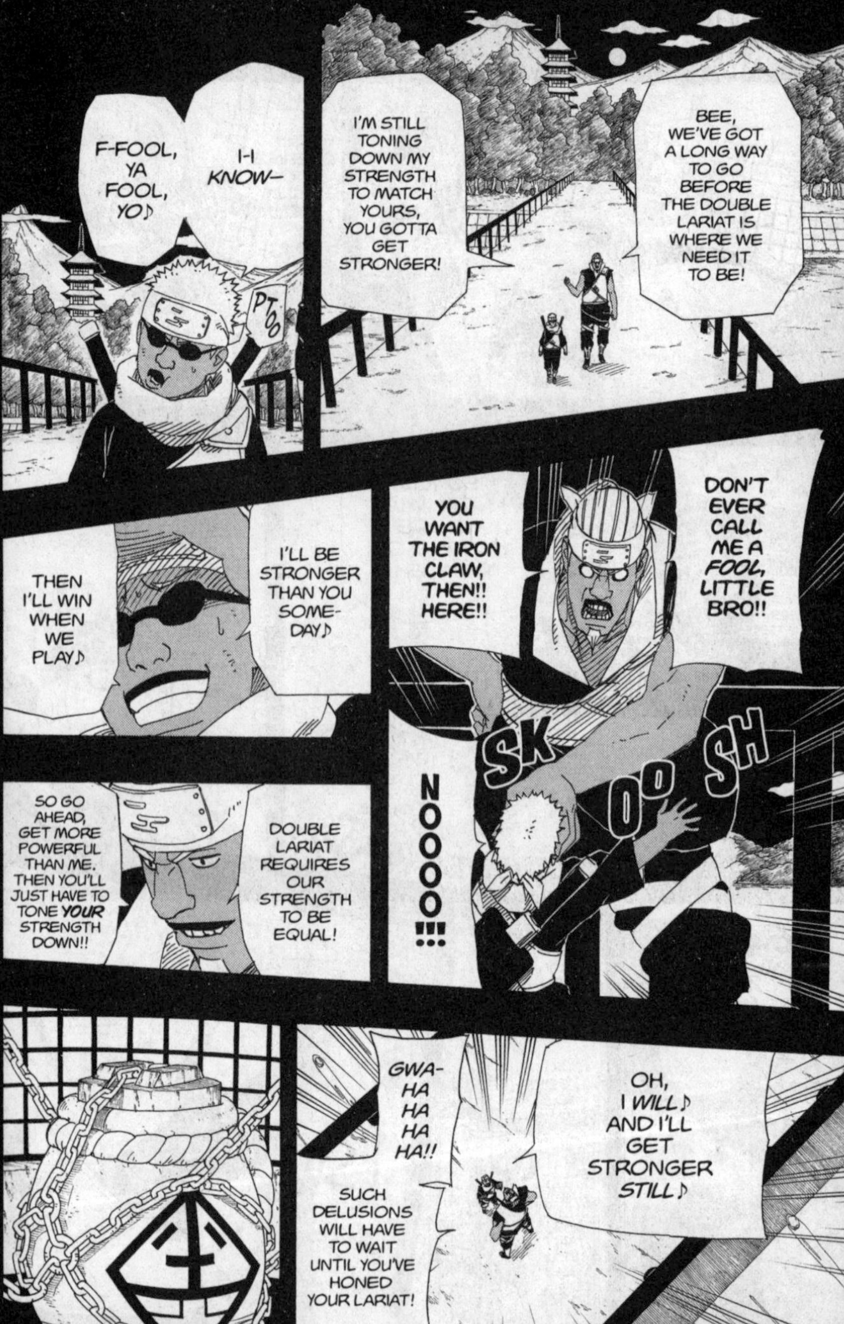
BEE, WE'VE GOT A LONG WAY TO GO BEFORE THE DOUBLE LARIAT IS WHERE WE NEED IT TO BE!
I'M STILL TONING DOWN MY STRENGTH TO MATCH YOURS, YOU GOTTA GET STRONGER!
I-I KNOW–
F-FOOL, YA FOOL, YO♪
PTOO
DON'T EVER CALL ME A *FOOL*, LITTLE BRO!!
YOU WANT THE IRON CLAW, THEN!! HERE!!
SKOOSH
NOOOOO!!!
I'LL BE STRONGER THAN YOU SOME-DAY♪
THEN I'LL WIN WHEN WE PLAY♪
DOUBLE LARIAT REQUIRES OUR STRENGTH TO BE EQUAL!
SO GO AHEAD, GET MORE POWERFUL THAN ME. THEN YOU'LL JUST HAVE TO TONE *YOUR* STRENGTH DOWN!!
OH, I *WILL*♪ AND I'LL GET STRONGER *STILL*♪
*GWA-HA HA HA HA!!*
SUCH DELUSIONS WILL HAVE TO WAIT UNTIL YOU'VE HONED YOUR LARIAT!

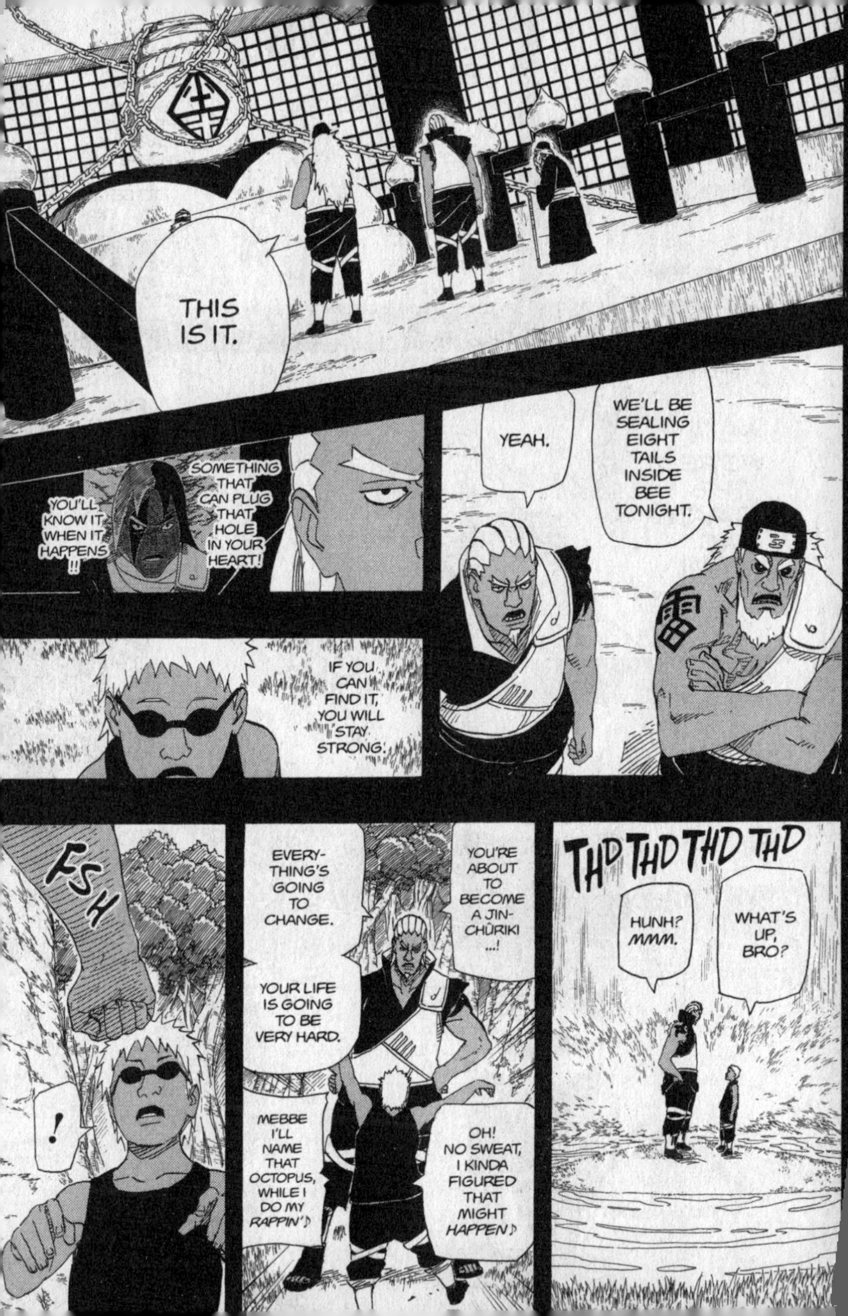
THIS IS IT.
WE'LL BE SEALING EIGHT TAILS INSIDE BEE TONIGHT.
YEAH.
SOMETHING THAT CAN PLUG THAT HOLE IN YOUR HEART!
YOU'LL KNOW IT WHEN IT HAPPENS!!
IF YOU CAN FIND IT, YOU WILL STAY STRONG.
THD THD THD THD
WHAT'S UP, BRO?
HUNH? MMM.
YOU'RE ABOUT TO BECOME A JINCHŪRIKI...!
EVERYTHING'S GOING TO CHANGE.
YOUR LIFE IS GOING TO BE VERY HARD.
OH! NO SWEAT, I KINDA FIGURED THAT MIGHT HAPPEN♪
MEBBE I'LL NAME THAT OCTOPUS, WHILE I DO MY RAPPIN'♪
FSH
!

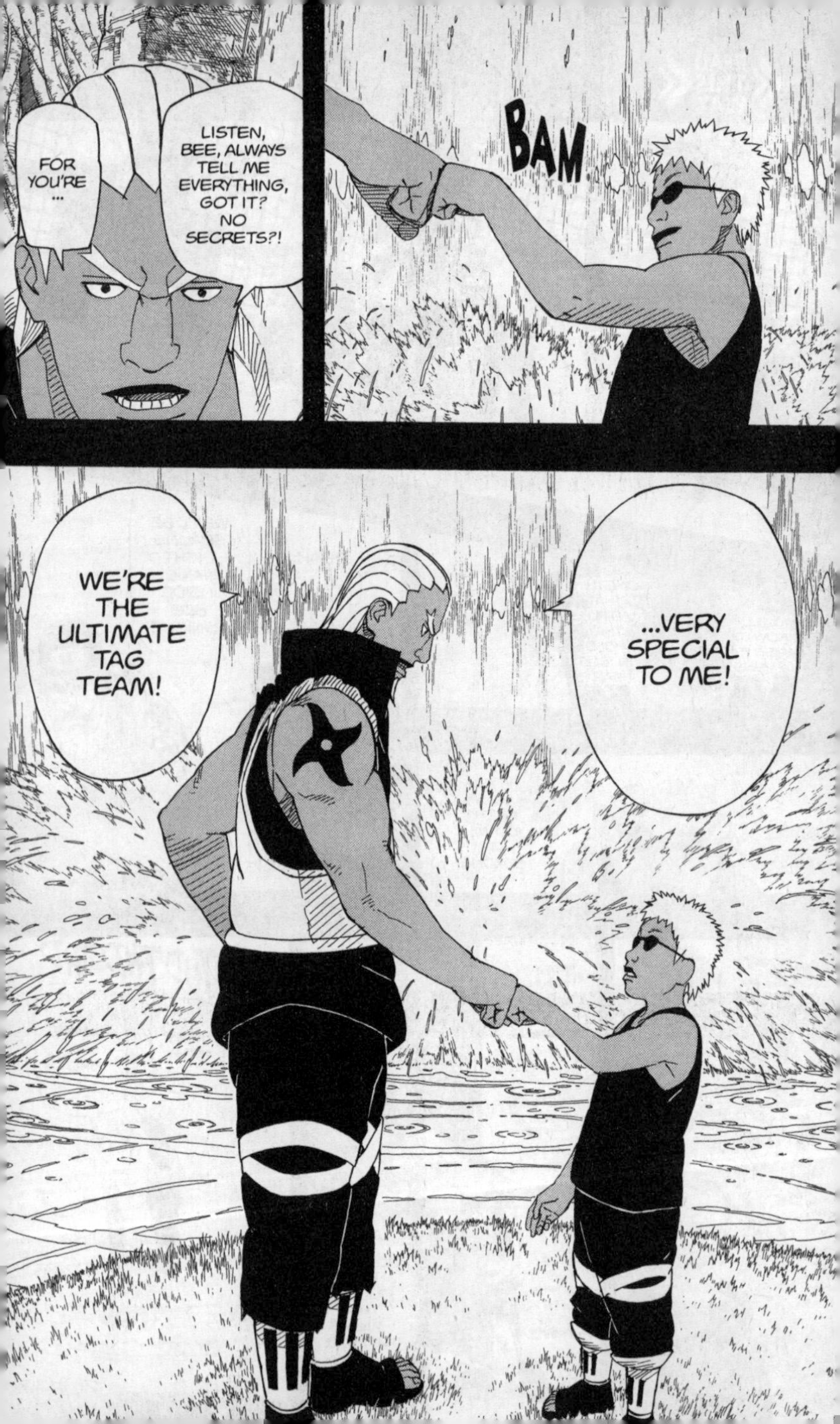
BAM
LISTEN, BEE, ALWAYS TELL ME EVERYTHING, GOT IT? NO SECRETS?!
FOR YOU'RE ...
...VERY SPECIAL TO ME!
WE'RE THE ULTIMATE TAG TEAM!

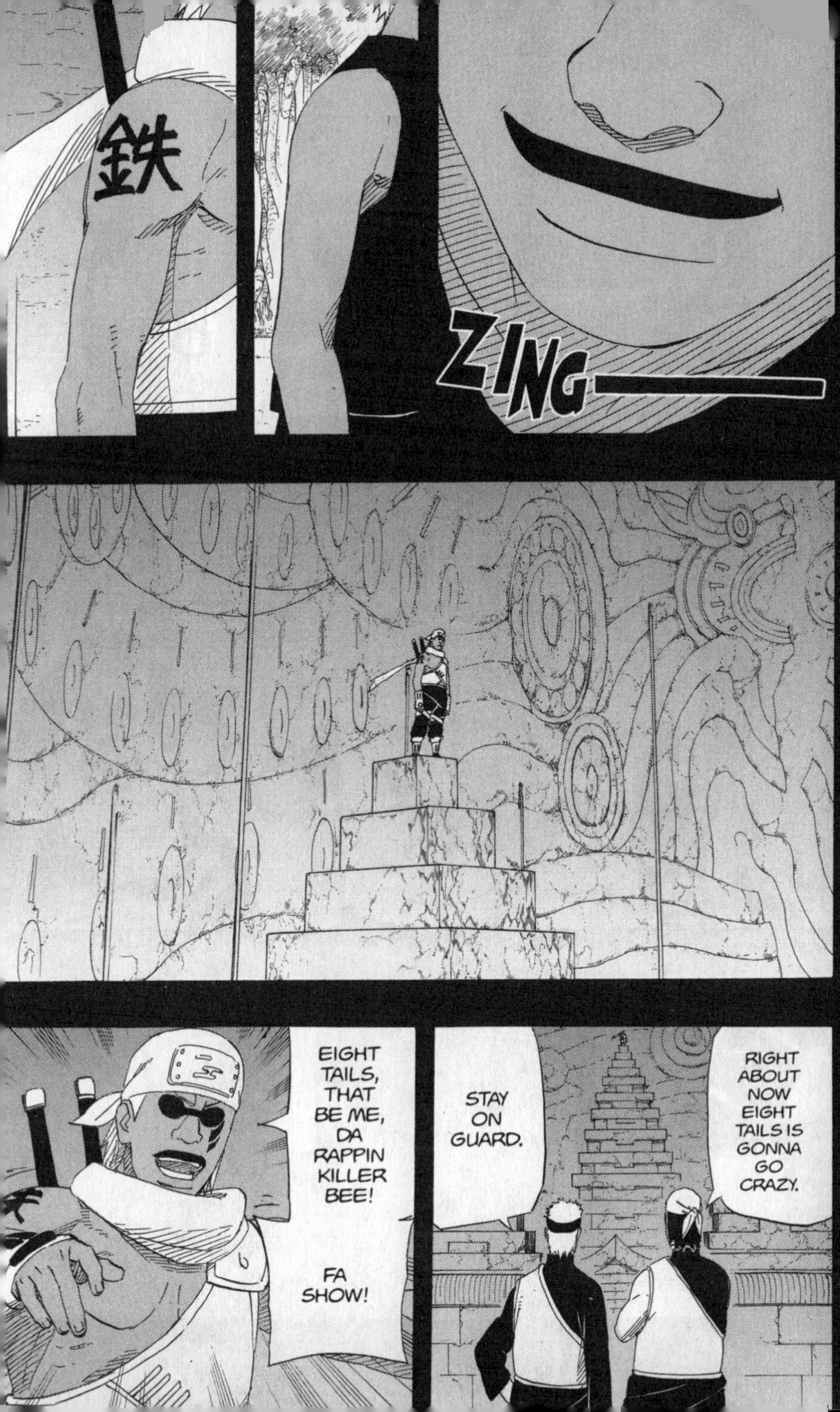
ZING
鉄
RIGHT ABOUT NOW EIGHT TAILS IS GONNA GO CRAZY.
STAY ON GUARD.
EIGHT TAILS, THAT BE ME, DA RAPPIN KILLER BEE!
FA SHOW!

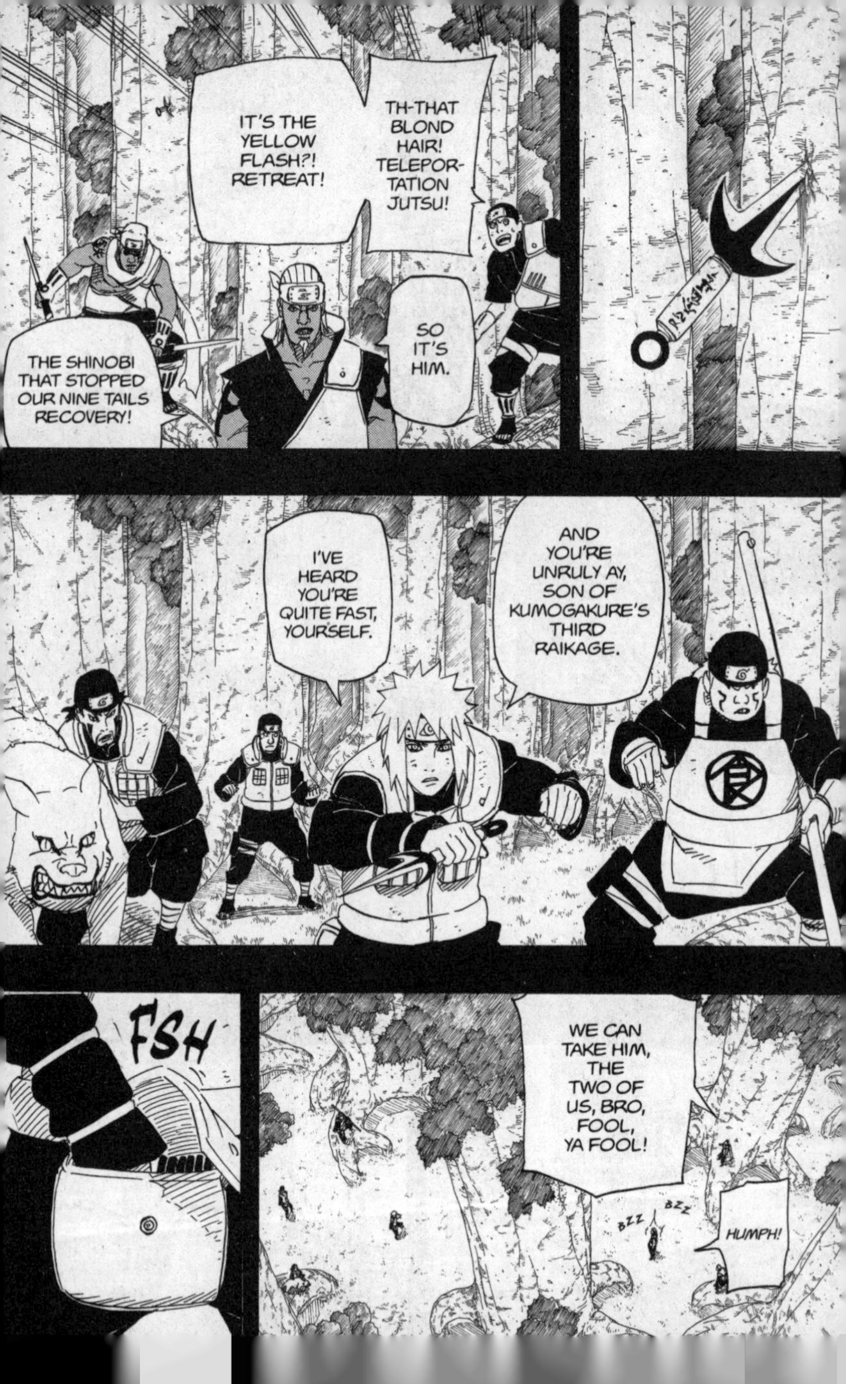
TH-THAT BLOND HAIR! TELEPORTATION JUTSU!
IT'S THE YELLOW FLASH?! RETREAT!
SO IT'S HIM.
THE SHINOBI THAT STOPPED OUR NINE TAILS RECOVERY!
AND YOU'RE UNRULY AY, SON OF KUMOGAKURE'S THIRD RAIKAGE.
I'VE HEARD YOU'RE QUITE FAST, YOURSELF.
WE CAN TAKE HIM, THE TWO OF US, BRO, FOOL, YA FOOL!
BZZ
BZZ
HUMPH!
FSH

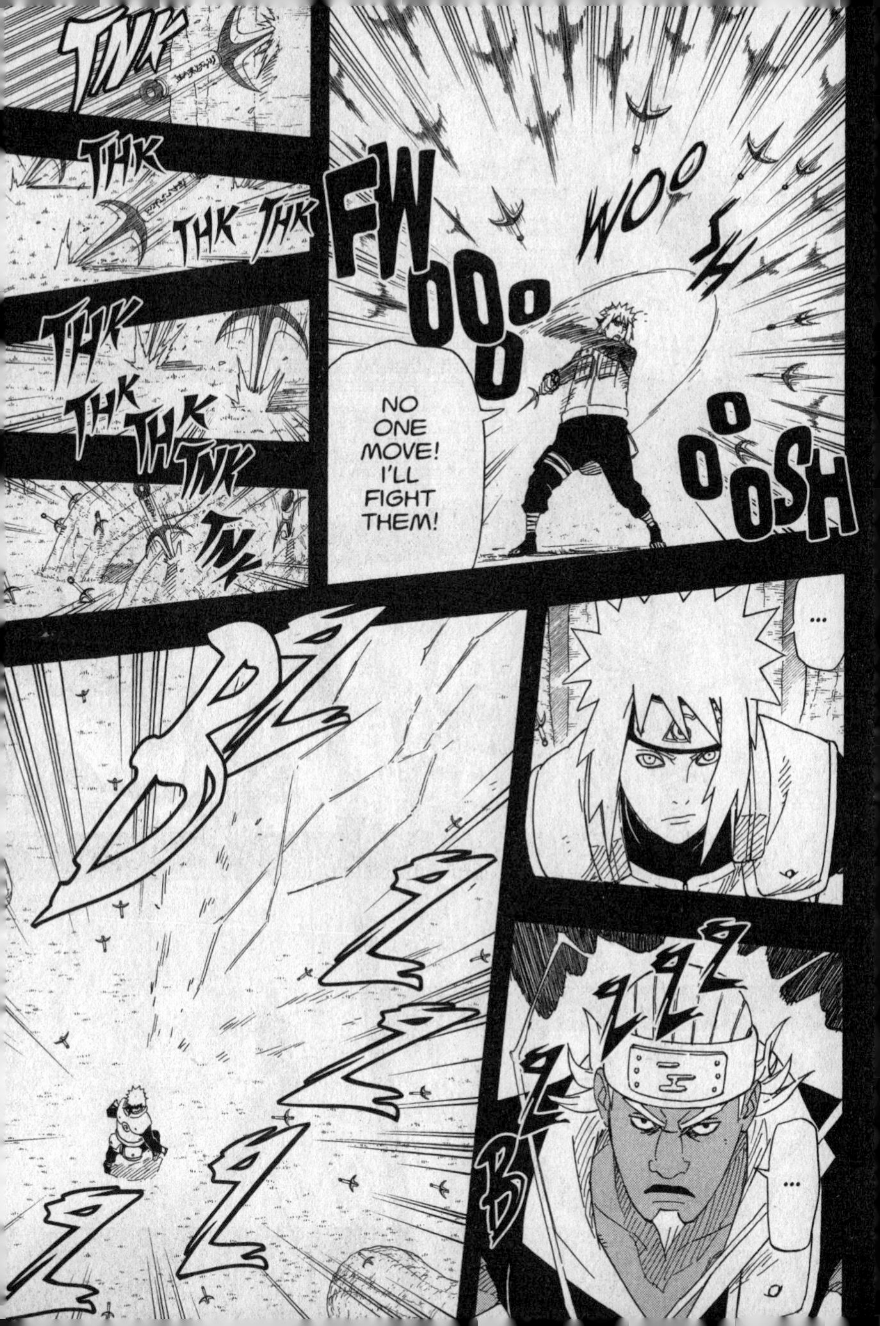
WOOSH
FWOOOO
OOOSH
NO ONE MOVE! I'LL FIGHT THEM!
TNK
THK
THK THK
THK
THK THK
TNK
TNK
...
BZZ
...
BZZ

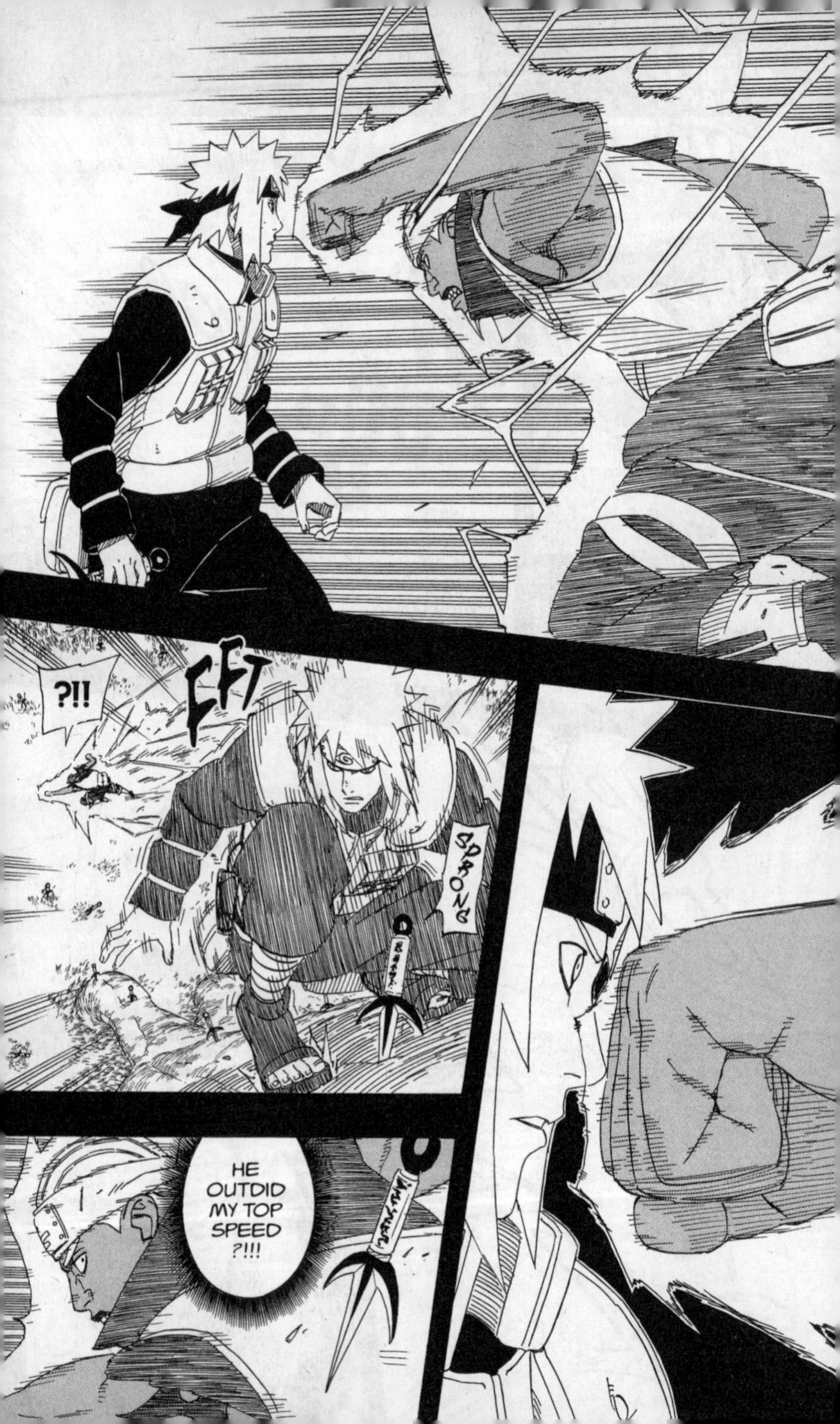
?!!
EFT
SPRONG
HE OUTDID MY TOP SPEED ?!!!

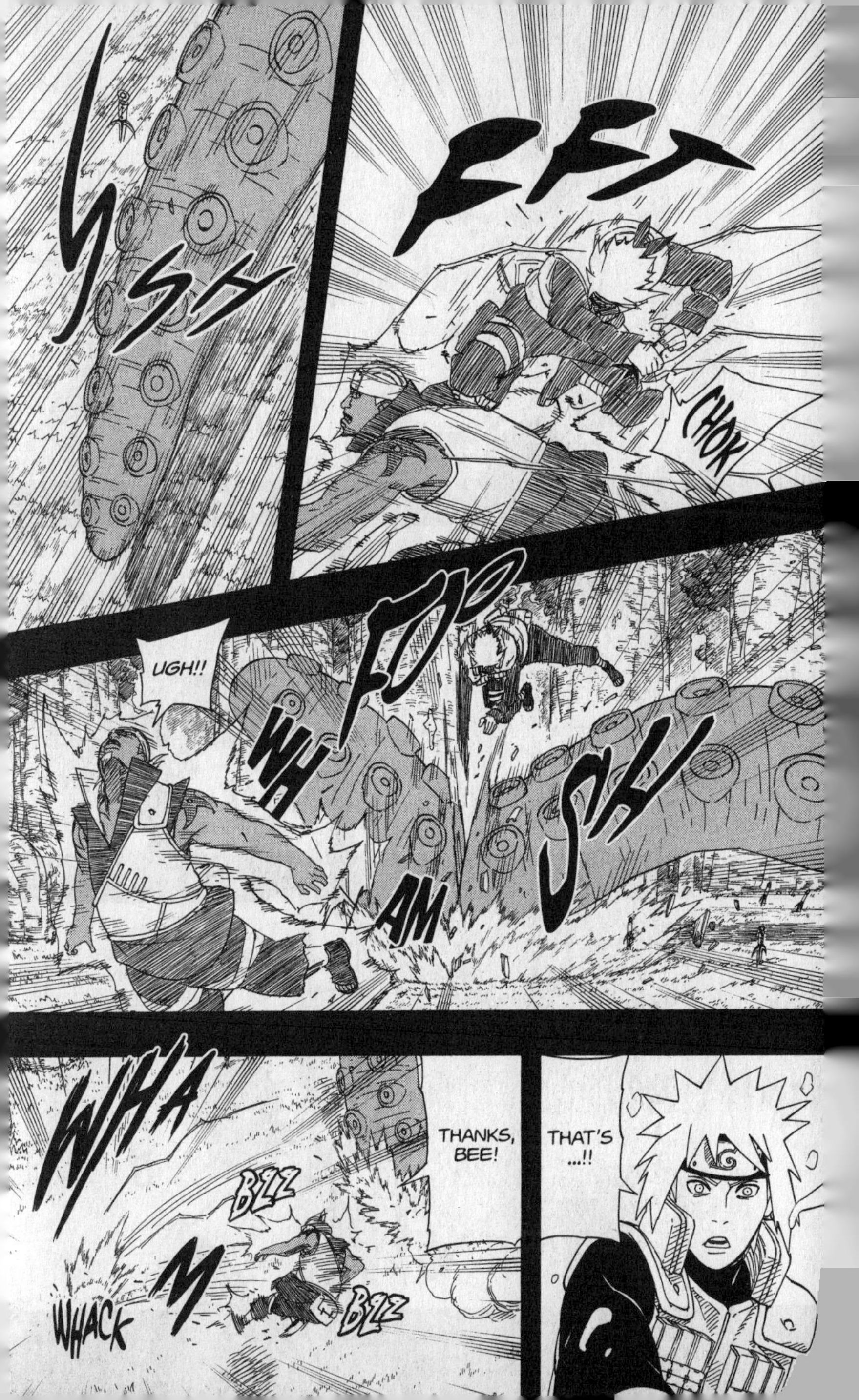
FFT
CHOK
SYSH
FO
SH
UGH!!
WH
AM
THAT'S ...!!
THANKS, BEE!
WHA
M
BZZ
BZZ
WHACK

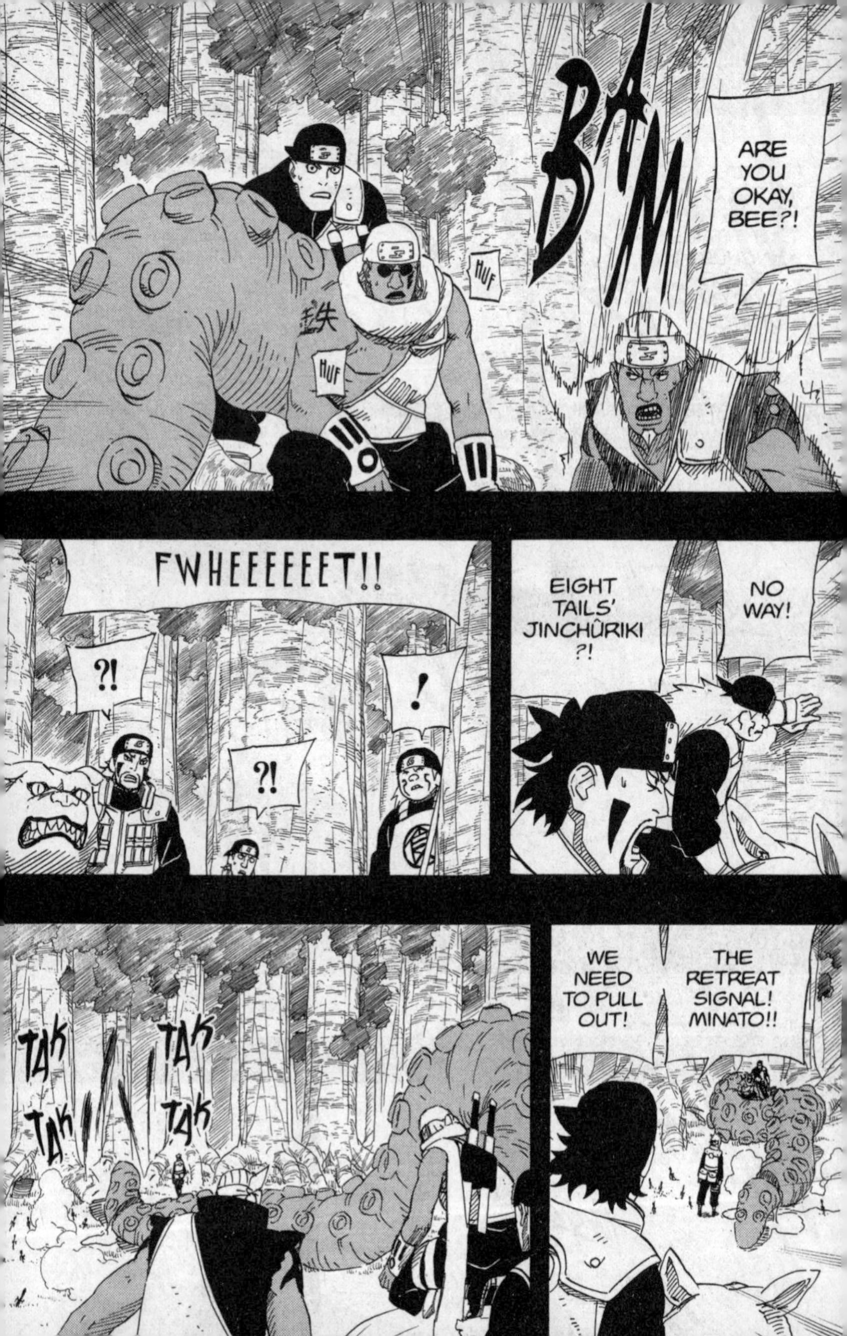
ARE YOU OKAY, BEE?!
BAM
HUF
HUF
NO WAY!
EIGHT TAILS' JINCHÛRIKI?!
FWHEEEEEET!!
!
?!
?!
THE RETREAT SIGNAL! MINATO!!
WE NEED TO PULL OUT!
TAK
TAK
TAK
TAK

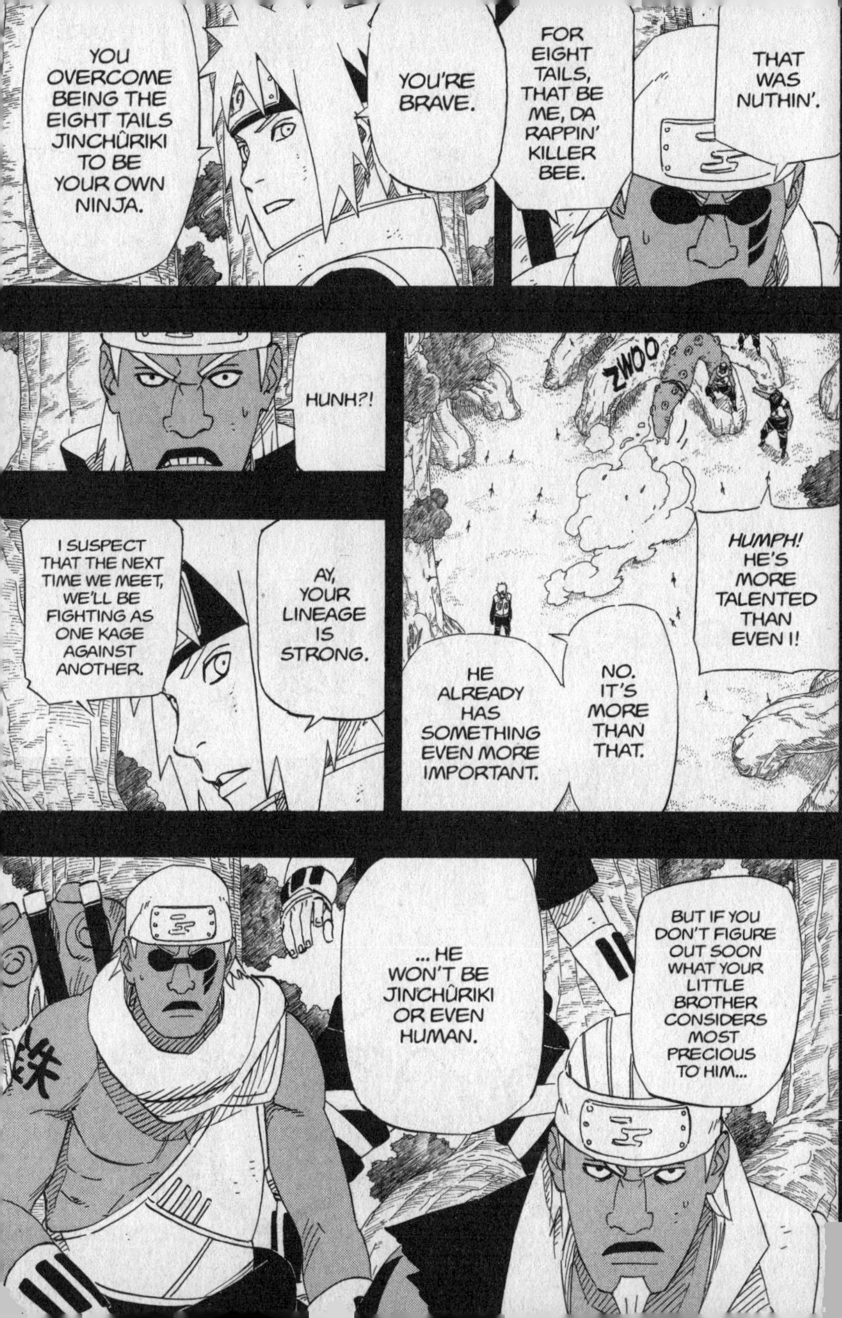
THAT WAS NUTHIN'.
FOR EIGHT TAILS, THAT BE ME, DA RAPPIN' KILLER BEE.
YOU'RE BRAVE.
YOU OVERCOME BEING THE EIGHT TAILS JINCHÛRIKI TO BE YOUR OWN NINJA.
ZWOO
HUMPH! HE'S MORE TALENTED THAN EVEN I!
NO. IT'S MORE THAN THAT.
HE ALREADY HAS SOMETHING EVEN MORE IMPORTANT.
HUNH?!
AY, YOUR LINEAGE IS STRONG.
I SUSPECT THAT THE NEXT TIME WE MEET, WE'LL BE FIGHTING AS ONE KAGE AGAINST ANOTHER.
BUT IF YOU DON'T FIGURE OUT SOON WHAT YOUR LITTLE BROTHER CONSIDERS MOST PRECIOUS TO HIM...
... HE WON'T BE JINCHÛRIKI OR EVEN HUMAN.

NARUTO

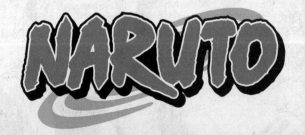

# Number 543: Truer Words

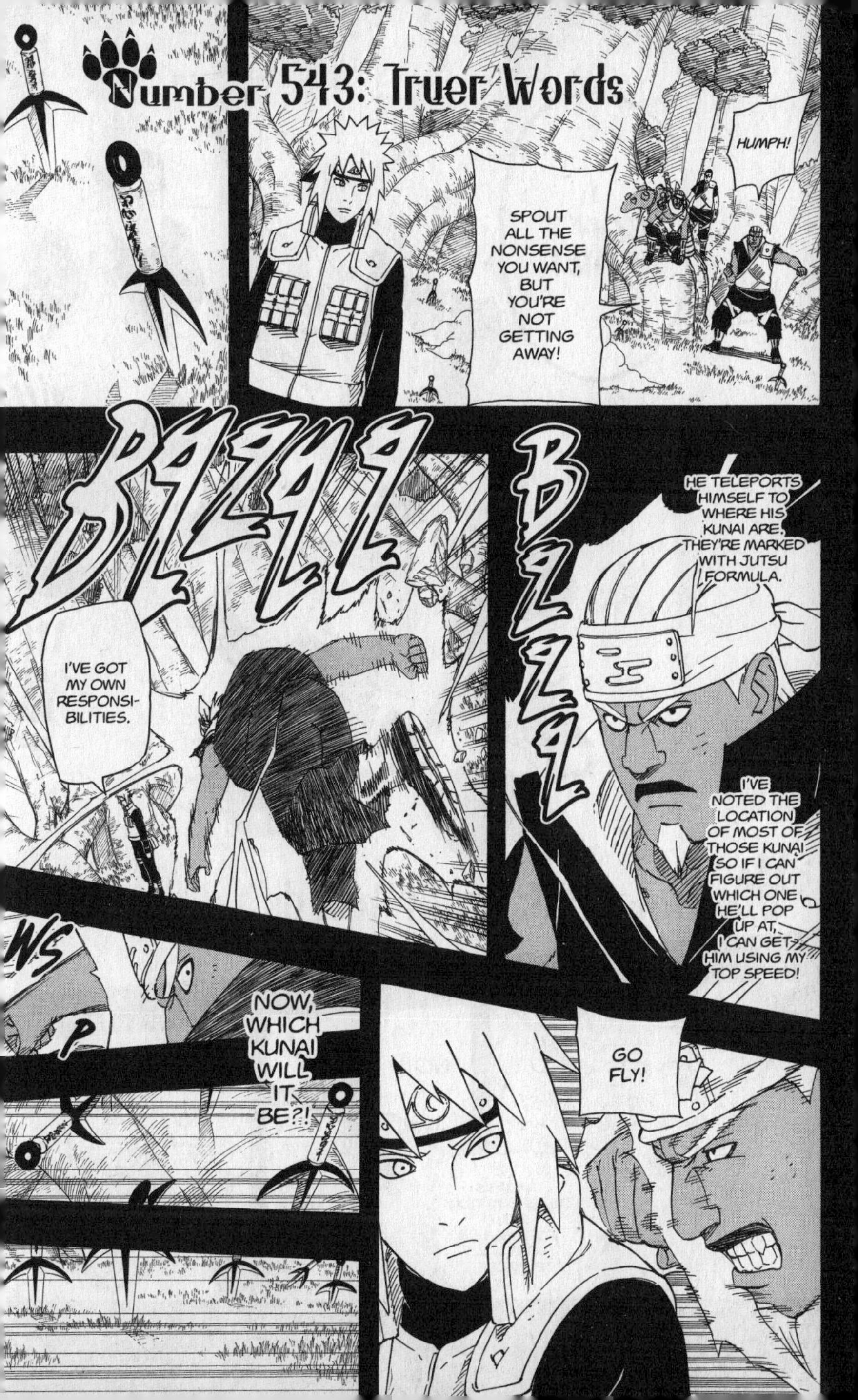
HUMPH!
SPOUT ALL THE NONSENSE YOU WANT, BUT YOU'RE NOT GETTING AWAY!
HE TELEPORTS HIMSELF TO WHERE HIS KUNAI ARE. THEY'RE MARKED WITH JUTSU FORMULA.
I'VE NOTED THE LOCATION OF MOST OF THOSE KUNAI SO IF I CAN FIGURE OUT WHICH ONE HE'LL POP UP AT, I CAN GET HIM USING MY TOP SPEED!
I'VE GOT MY OWN RESPONSI-BILITIES.
GO FLY!
NOW, WHICH KUNAI WILL IT BE?!

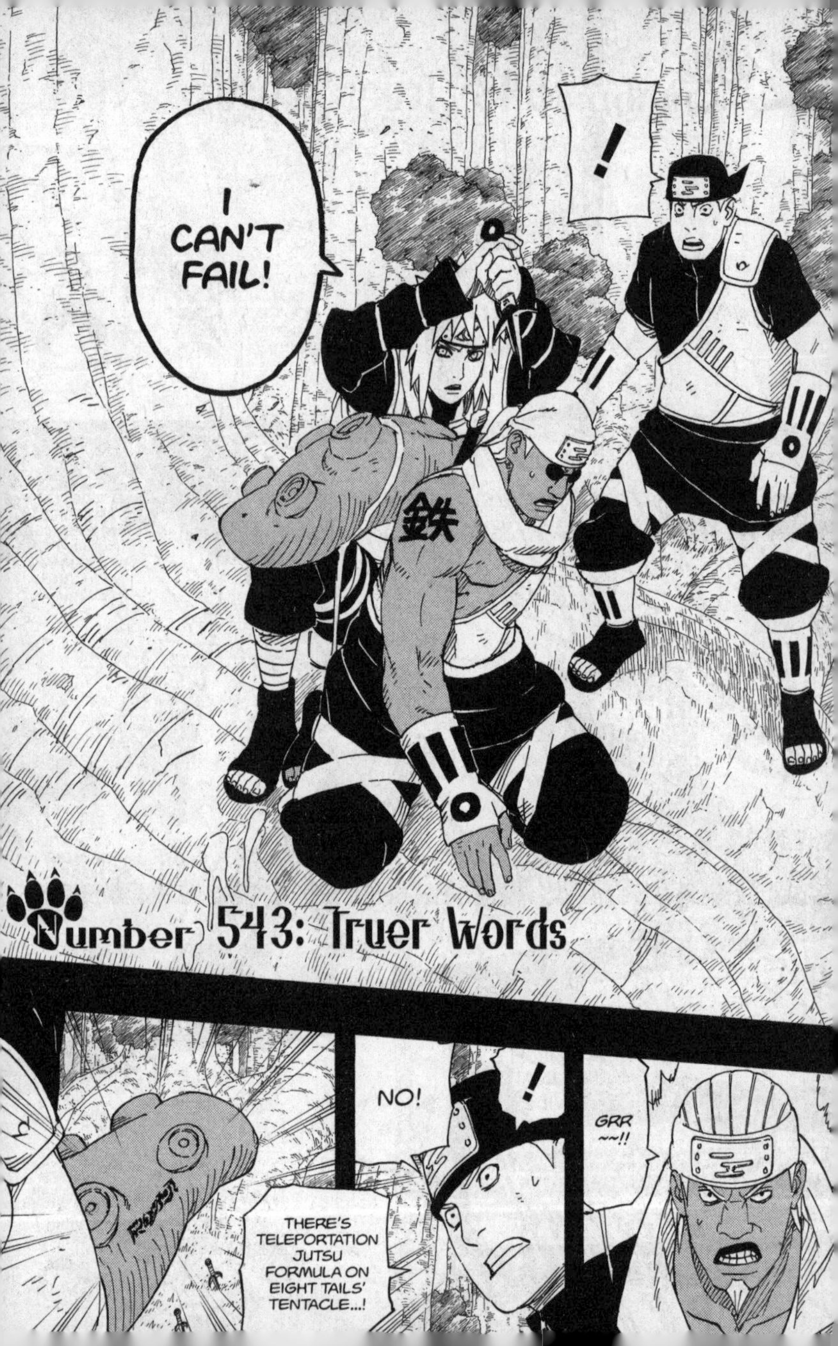
!
I CAN'T FAIL!
Number 543: Truer Words
GRR ~~!!
!
NO!
THERE'S TELEPORTATION JUTSU FORMULA ON EIGHT TAILS' TENTACLE...!

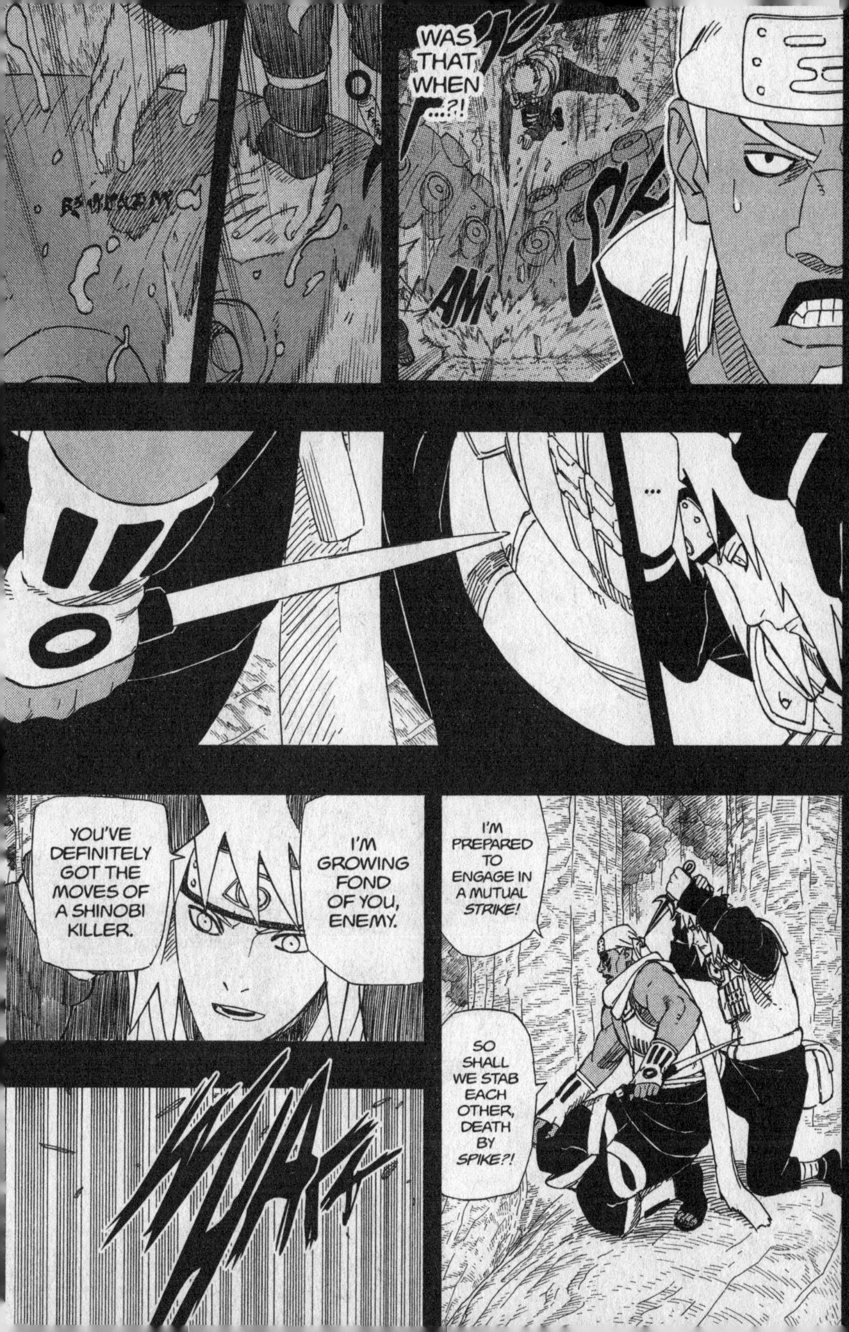
WAS THAT WHEN ...?!
...
I'M PREPARED TO ENGAGE IN A MUTUAL STRIKE!
SO SHALL WE STAB EACH OTHER, DEATH BY SPIKE?!
I'M GROWING FOND OF YOU, ENEMY.
YOU'VE DEFINITELY GOT THE MOVES OF A SHINOBI KILLER.

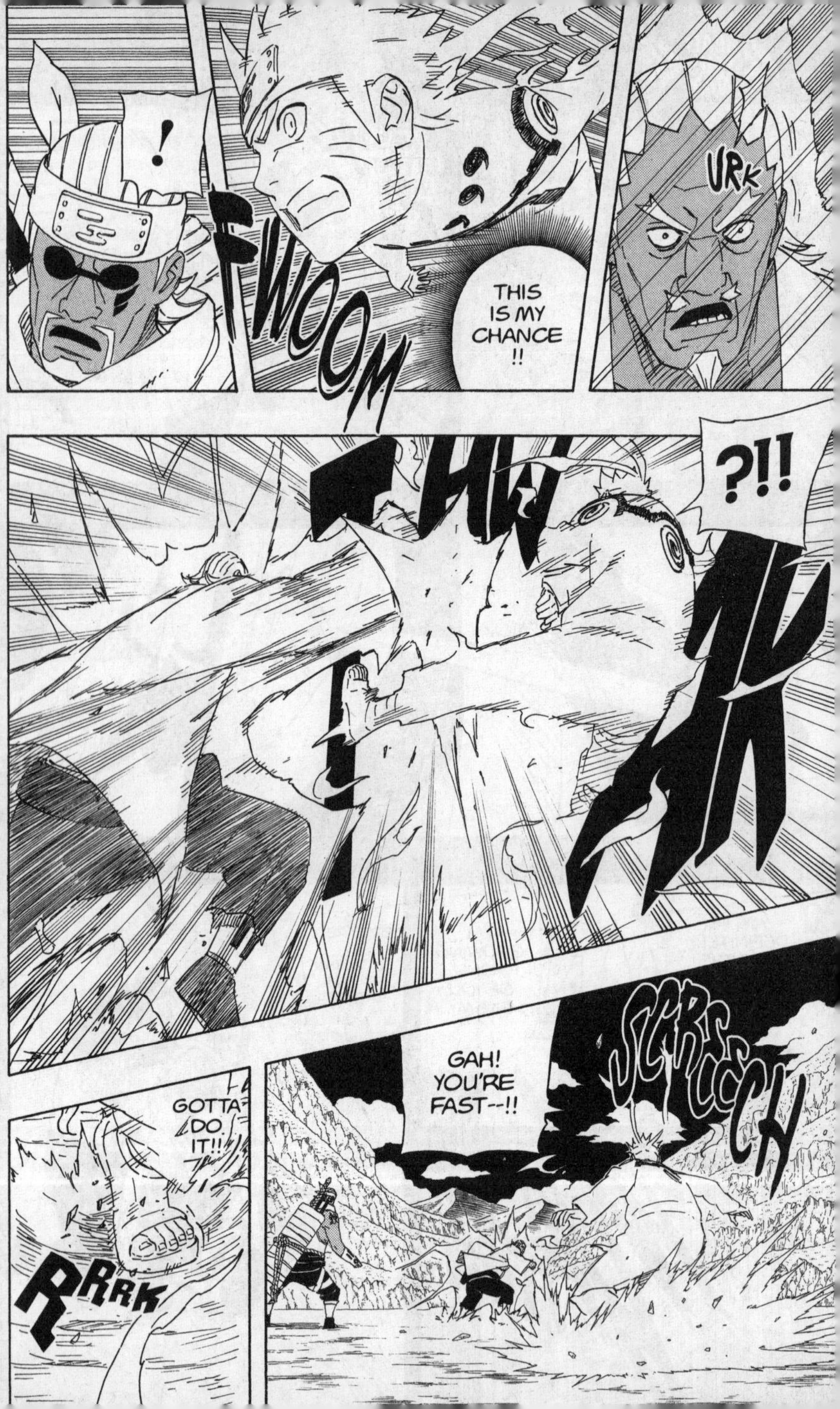
URK
THIS IS MY CHANCE !!
FWOOM
!
?!!
SCREECH
GAH! YOU'RE FAST--!!
GOTTA DO IT!!
RRRK

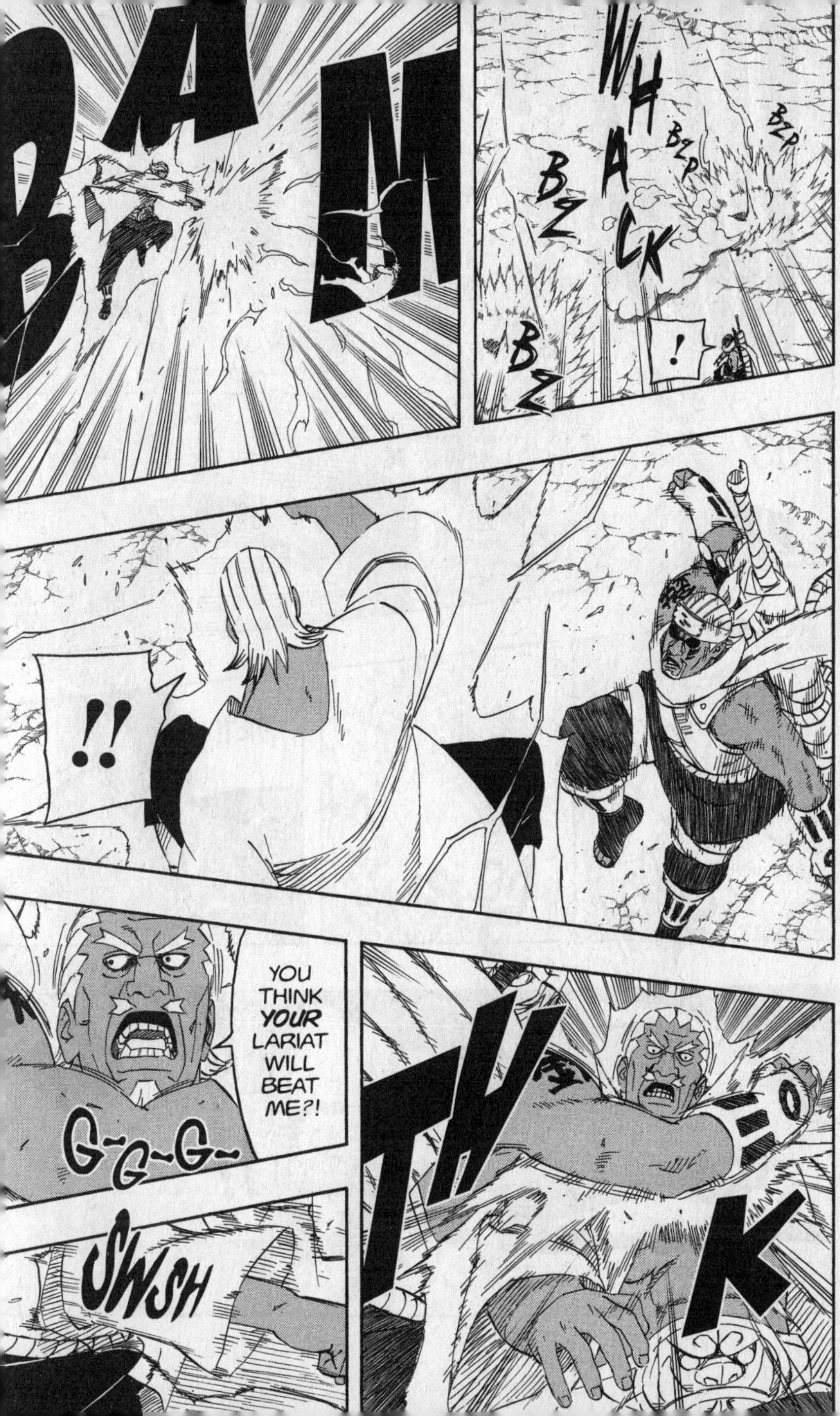

WHACK
BZP
BZP
BZZ
BZZ
!
BAM
!!
THK
YOU THINK *YOUR* LARIAT WILL BEAT ME?!
G-G-G-
SWSH

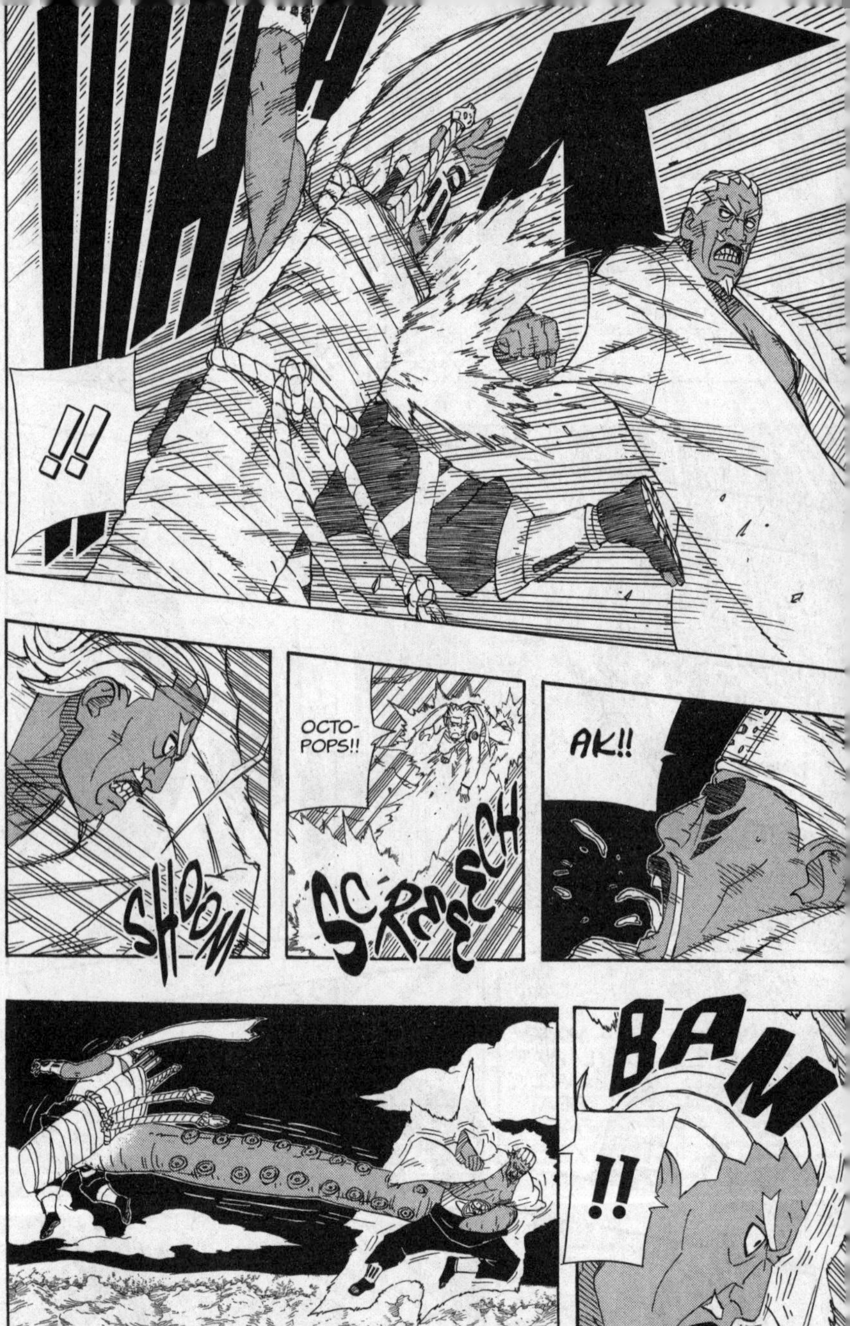
!!
AK!!
OCTO-POPS!!
SCREEECH
SHOOM
BAM
!!

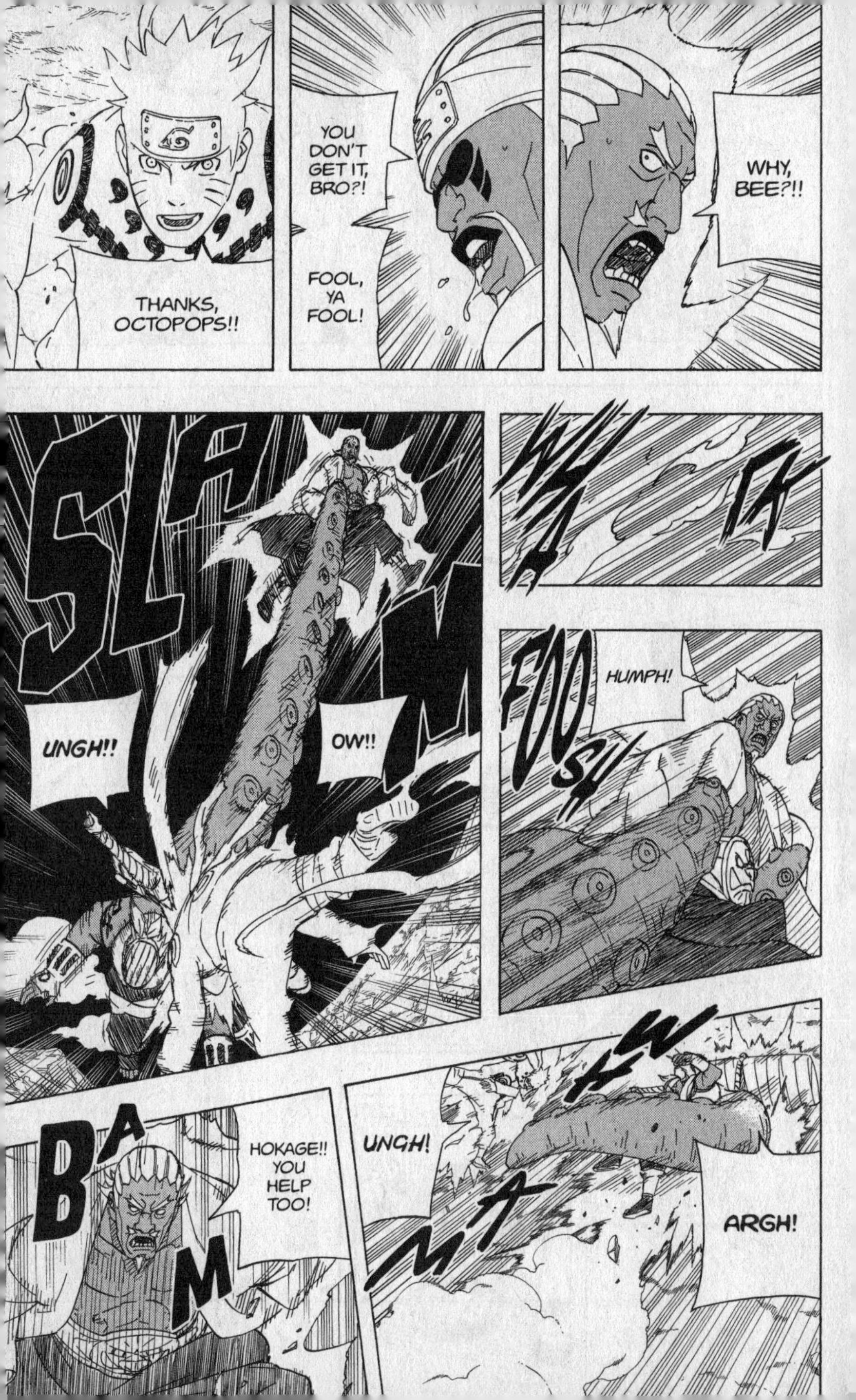
WHY, BEE?!!
YOU DON'T GET IT, BRO?!
FOOL, YA FOOL!
THANKS, OCTOPOPS!!
FOOSH
HUMPH!
SLAM
OW!!
UNGH!!
WHAM
ARGH!
UNGH!
BAM
HOKAGE!! YOU HELP TOO!

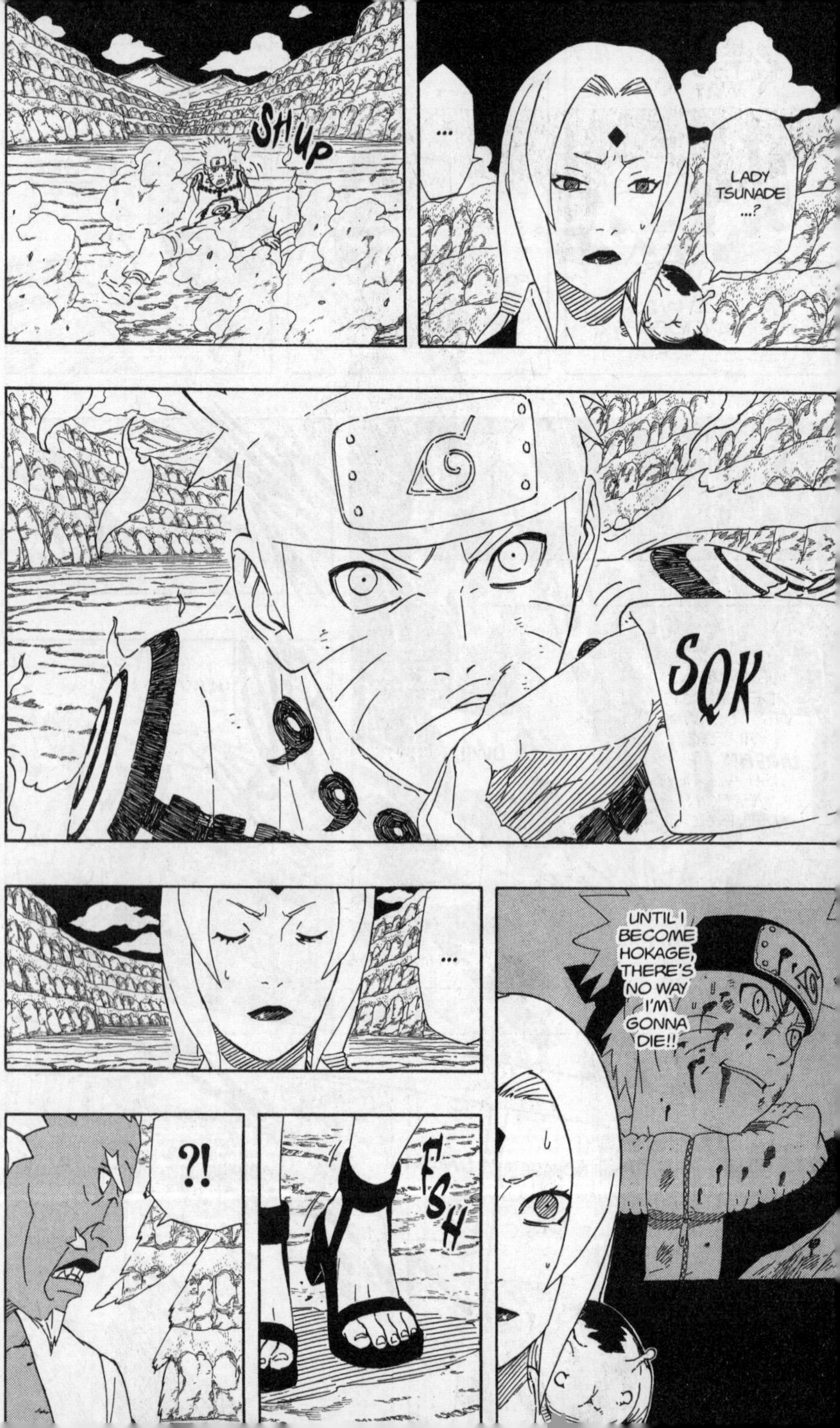

LADY TSUNADE ...?
...
SHUP
SQK
...
UNTIL I BECOME HOKAGE, THERE'S NO WAY I'M GONNA DIE!!
FSH
?!

READ THIS WAY

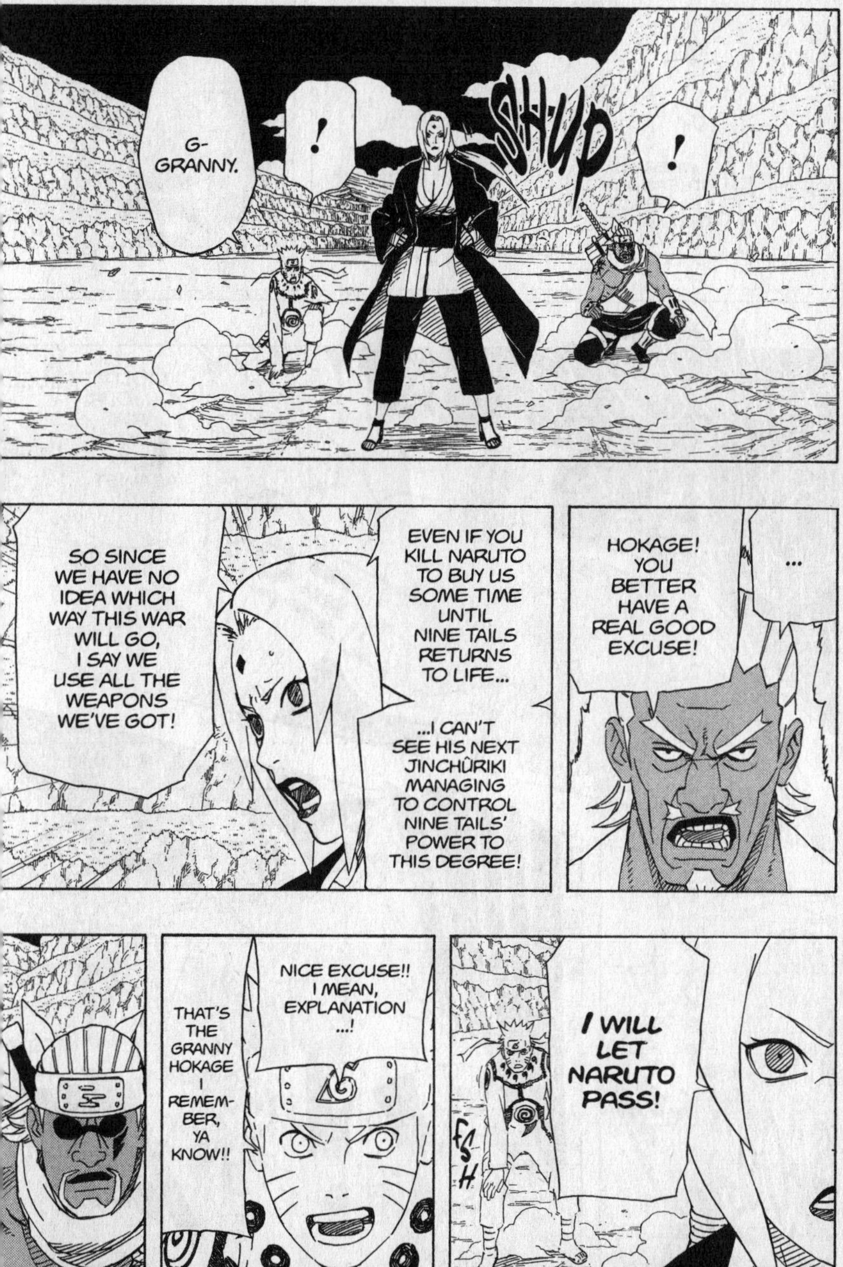
!
SHUP
!
G-GRANNY.
...
HOKAGE! YOU BETTER HAVE A REAL GOOD EXCUSE!
EVEN IF YOU KILL NARUTO TO BUY US SOME TIME UNTIL NINE TAILS RETURNS TO LIFE...
...I CAN'T SEE HIS NEXT JINCHÛRIKI MANAGING TO CONTROL NINE TAILS' POWER TO THIS DEGREE!
SO SINCE WE HAVE NO IDEA WHICH WAY THIS WAR WILL GO, I SAY WE USE ALL THE WEAPONS WE'VE GOT!
I WILL LET NARUTO PASS!
FSH
NICE EXCUSE!! I MEAN, EXPLANATION...!
THAT'S THE GRANNY HOKAGE I REMEMBER, YA KNOW!!

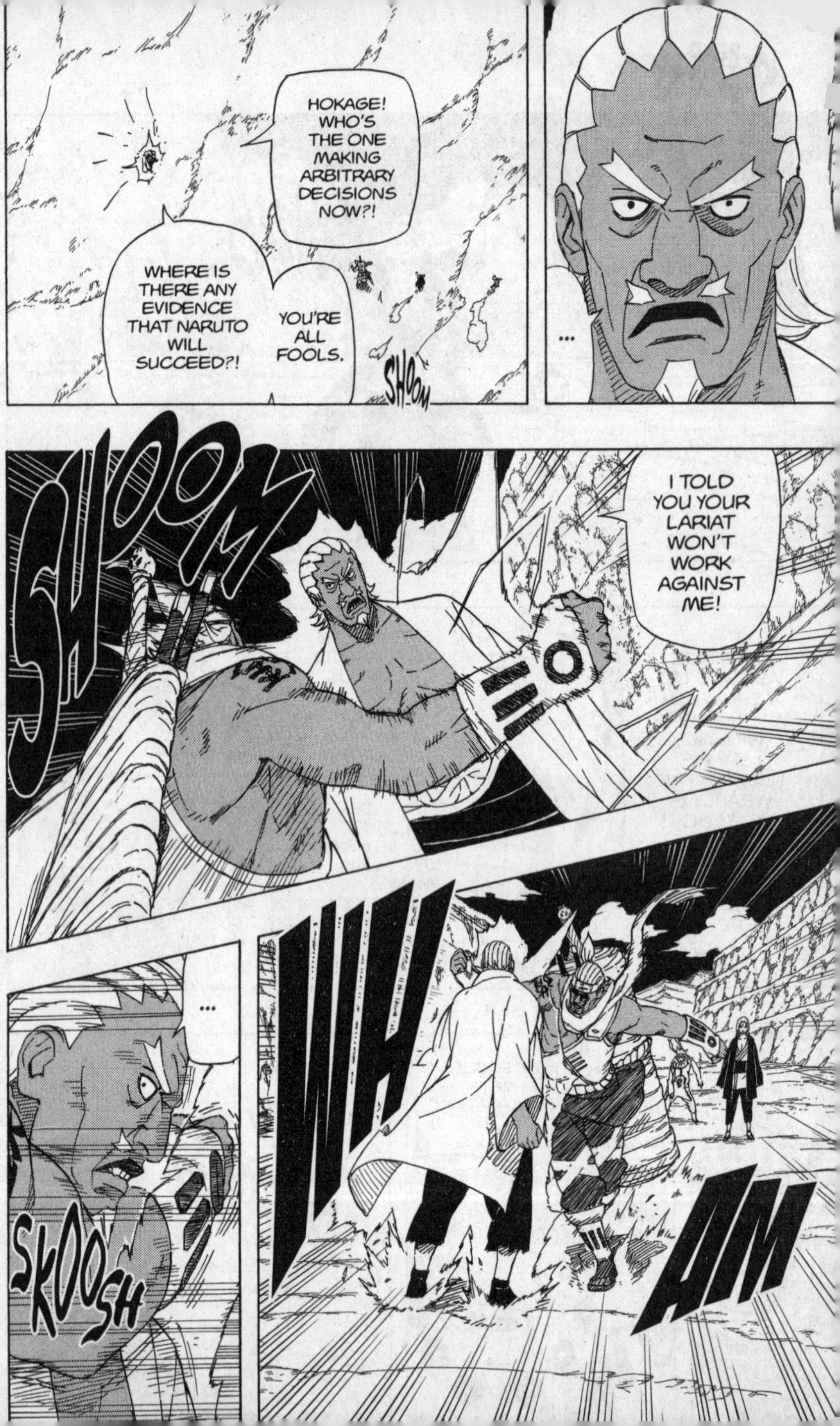
...
HOKAGE! WHO'S THE ONE MAKING ARBITRARY DECISIONS NOW?!
YOU'RE ALL FOOLS.
WHERE IS THERE ANY EVIDENCE THAT NARUTO WILL SUCCEED?!
SHOOM
SHOOM
I TOLD YOU YOUR LARIAT WON'T WORK AGAINST ME!
WHAM
...
SKOOSH

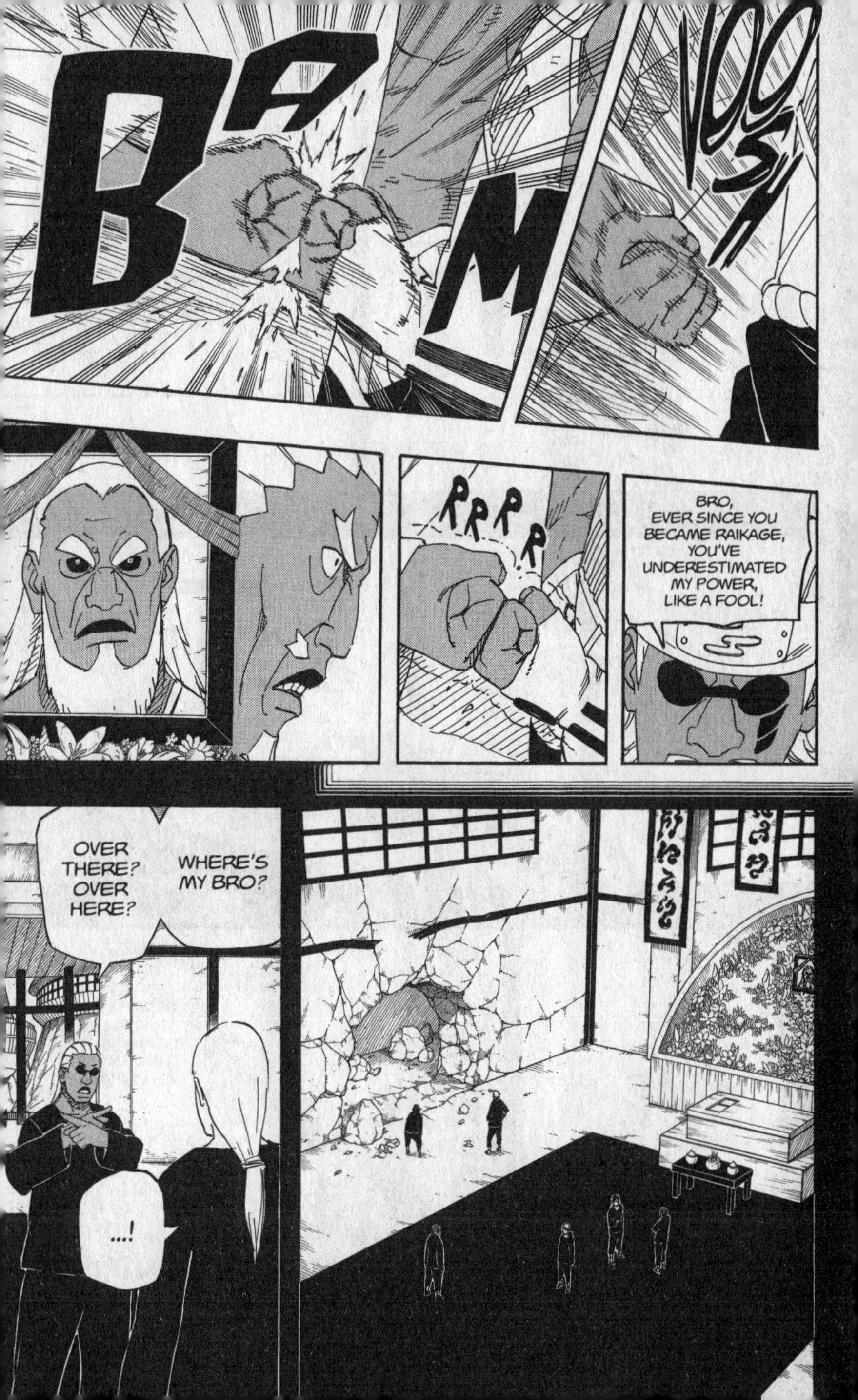
VOOSH
BAM
BRO, EVER SINCE YOU BECAME RAIKAGE, YOU'VE UNDERESTIMATED MY POWER, LIKE A FOOL!
RRRR
WHERE'S MY BRO?
OVER THERE? OVER HERE?
....!

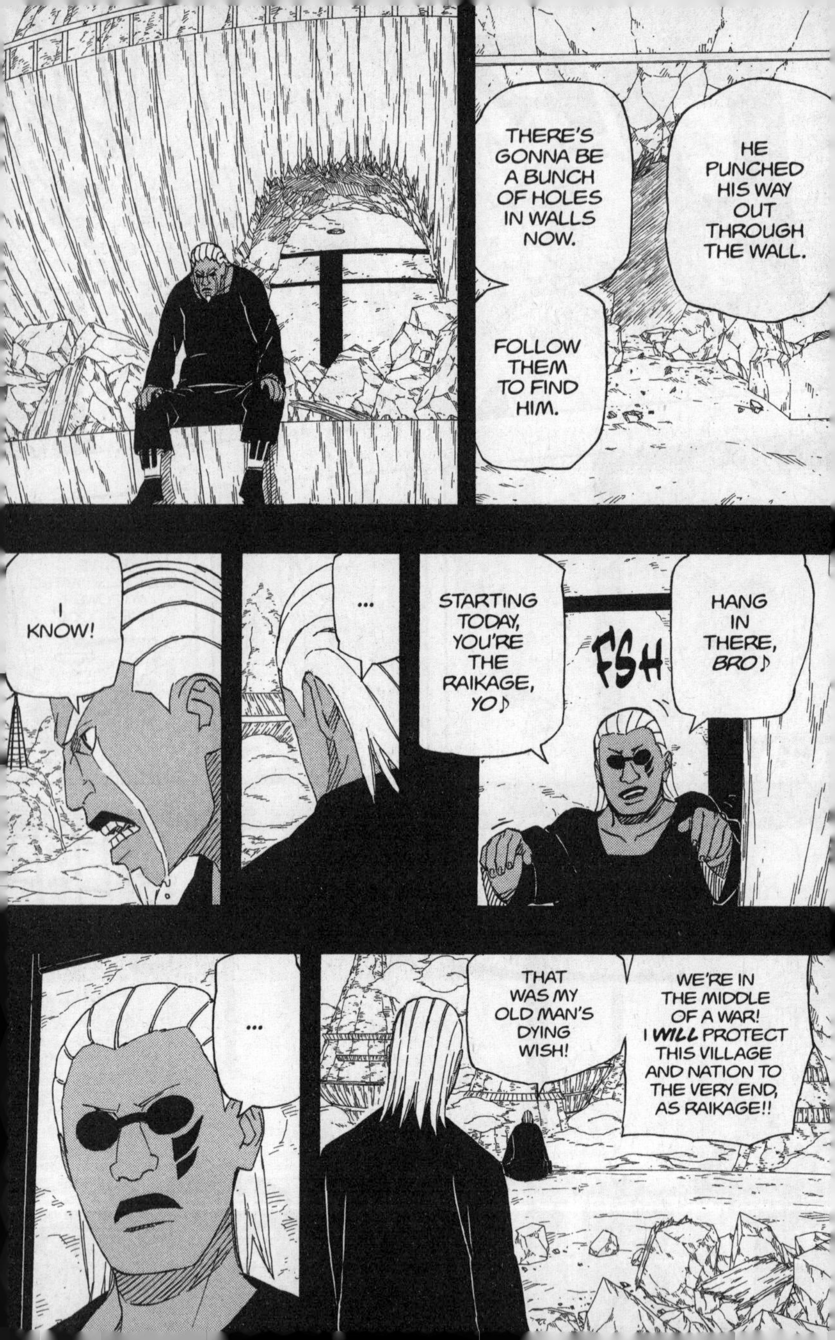
HE PUNCHED HIS WAY OUT THROUGH THE WALL.
THERE'S GONNA BE A BUNCH OF HOLES IN WALLS NOW.
FOLLOW THEM TO FIND HIM.
HANG IN THERE, *BRO*♪
FSH
STARTING TODAY, YOU'RE THE RAIKAGE, *YO*♪
...
I KNOW!
WE'RE IN THE MIDDLE OF A WAR! I ***WILL*** PROTECT THIS VILLAGE AND NATION TO THE VERY END, AS RAIKAGE!!
THAT WAS MY OLD MAN'S DYING WISH!
...

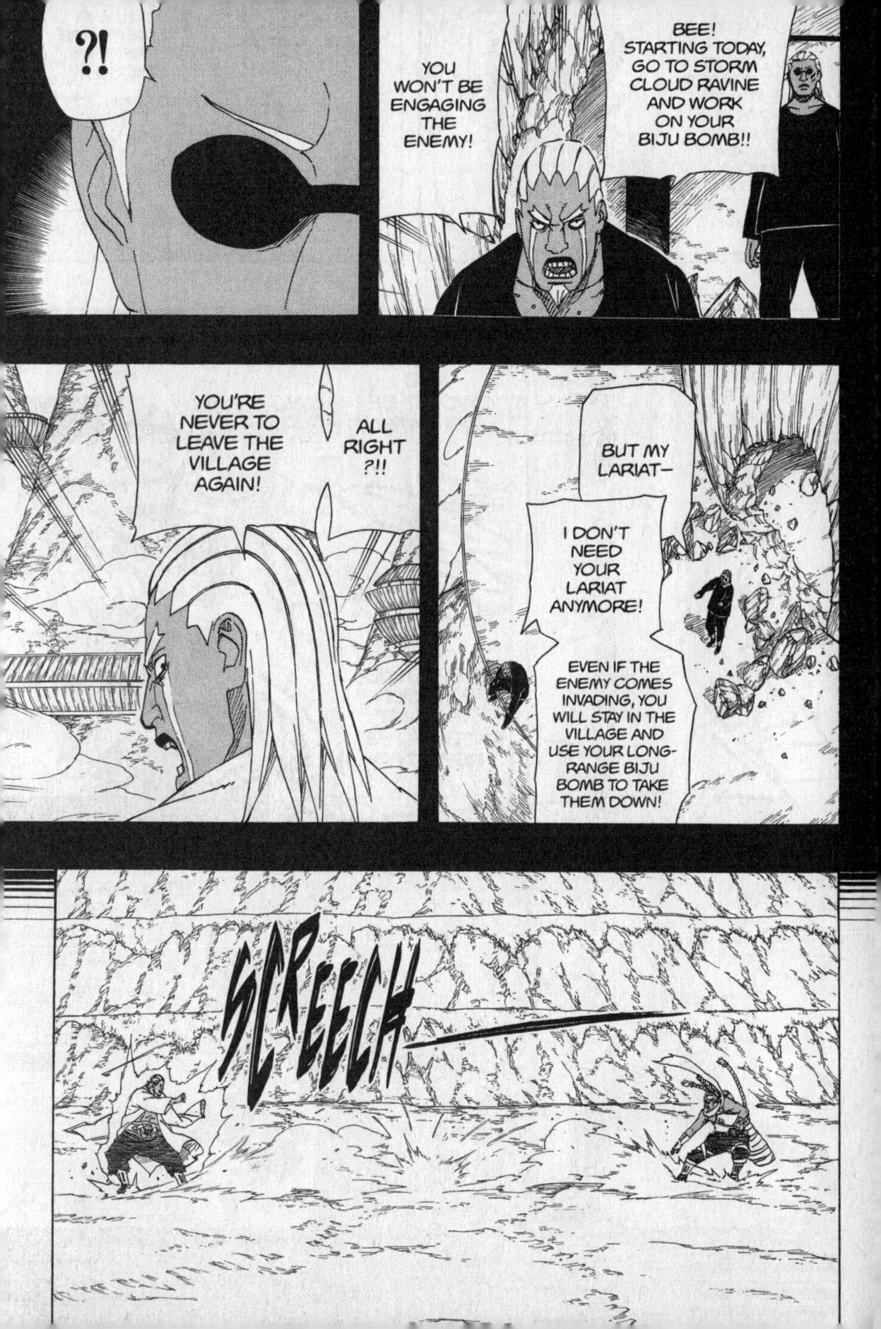
BEE! STARTING TODAY, GO TO STORM CLOUD RAVINE AND WORK ON YOUR BIJU BOMB!!
YOU WON'T BE ENGAGING THE ENEMY!
?!
BUT MY LARIAT—
I DON'T NEED YOUR LARIAT ANYMORE!
EVEN IF THE ENEMY COMES INVADING, YOU WILL STAY IN THE VILLAGE AND USE YOUR LONG-RANGE BIJU BOMB TO TAKE THEM DOWN!
YOU'RE NEVER TO LEAVE THE VILLAGE AGAIN!
ALL RIGHT ?!!
SCREECH

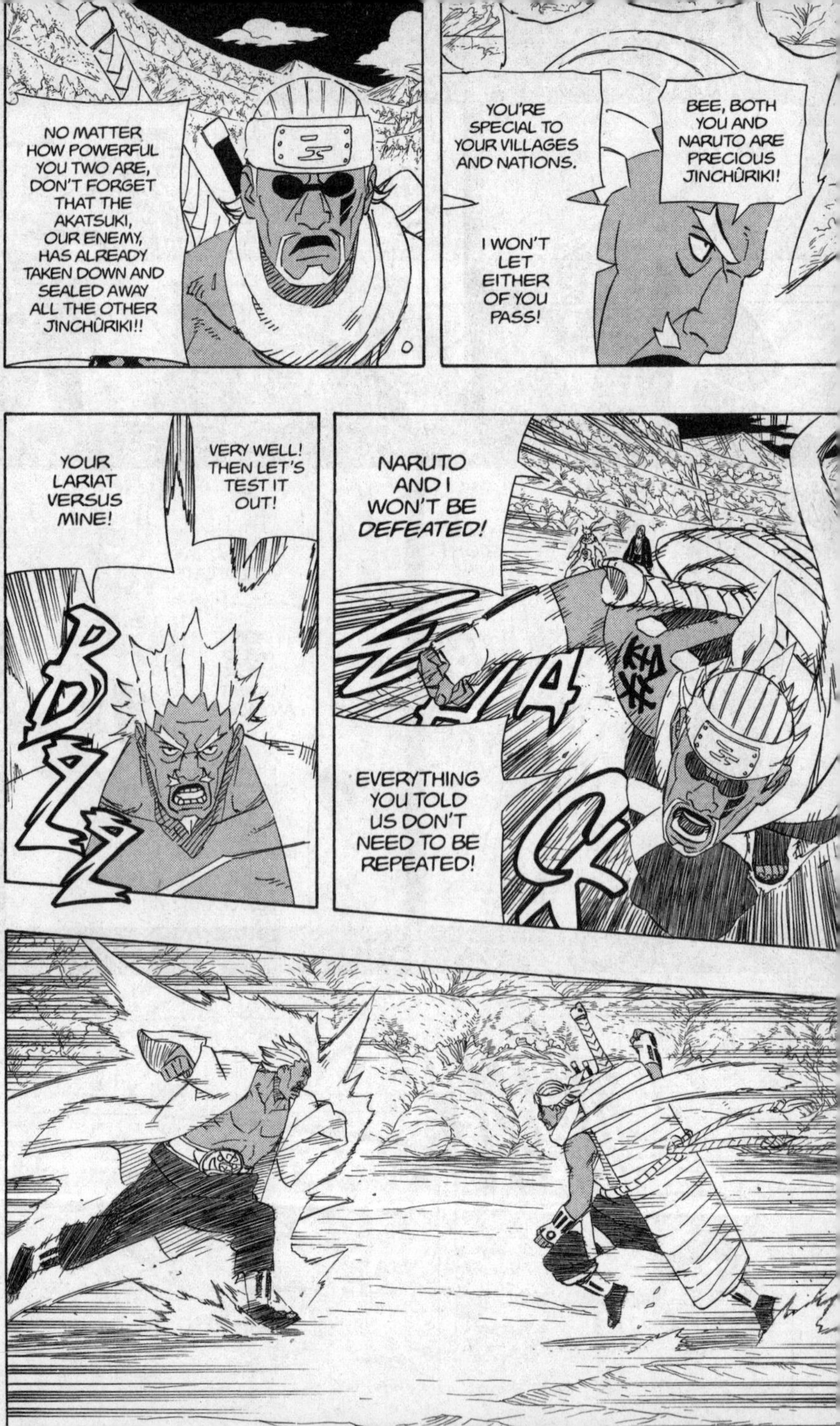
BEE, BOTH YOU AND NARUTO ARE PRECIOUS JINCHÛRIKI!
YOU'RE SPECIAL TO YOUR VILLAGES AND NATIONS.
I WON'T LET EITHER OF YOU PASS!
NO MATTER HOW POWERFUL YOU TWO ARE, DON'T FORGET THAT THE AKATSUKI, OUR ENEMY, HAS ALREADY TAKEN DOWN AND SEALED AWAY ALL THE OTHER JINCHÛRIKI!!
NARUTO AND I WON'T BE *DEFEATED!*
EVERYTHING YOU TOLD US DON'T NEED TO BE REPEATED!
VERY WELL! THEN LET'S TEST IT OUT!
YOUR LARIAT VERSUS MINE!

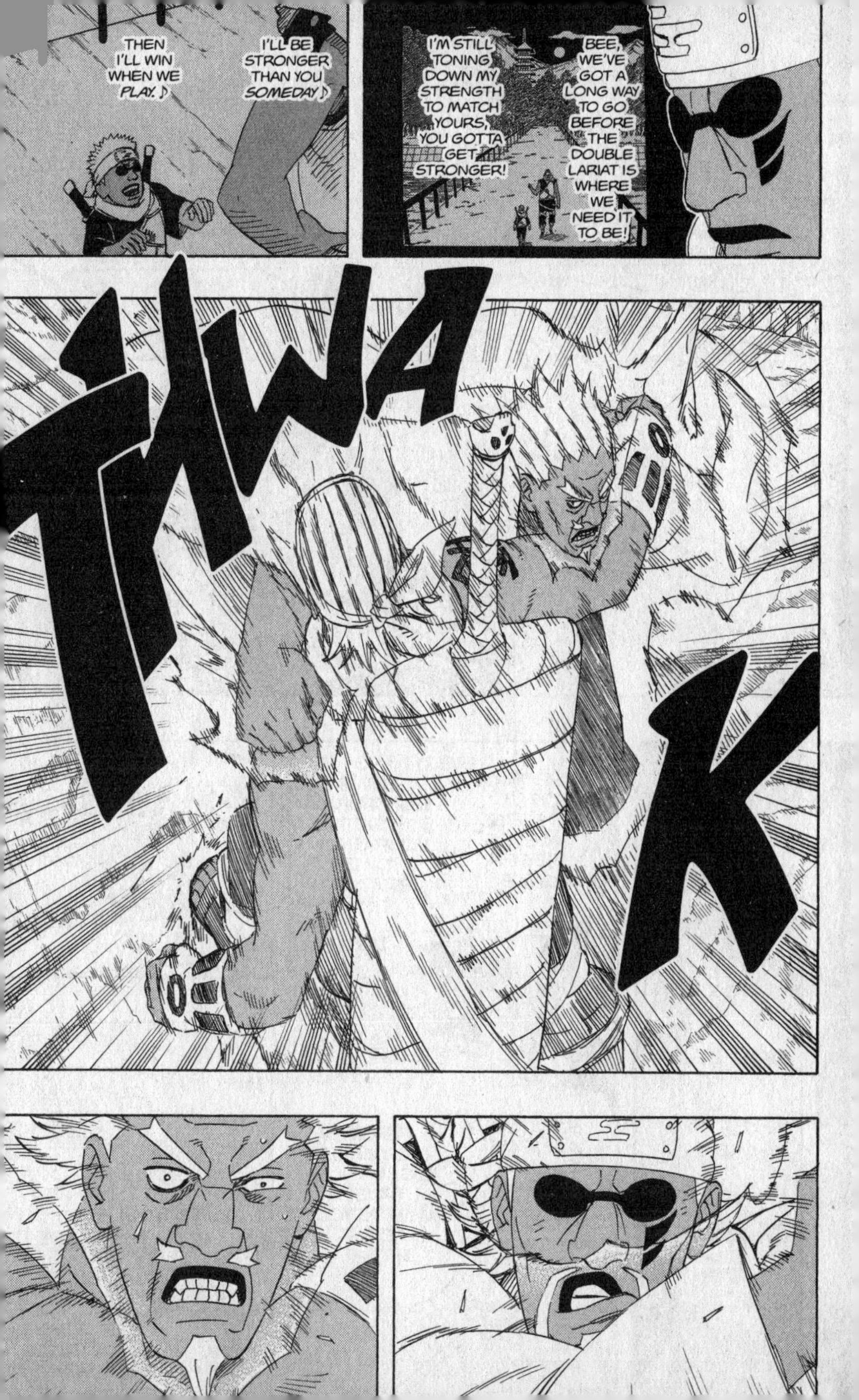
BEE, WE'VE GOT A LONG WAY TO GO BEFORE THE DOUBLE LARIAT IS WHERE WE NEED IT TO BE!
I'M STILL TONING DOWN MY STRENGTH TO MATCH YOURS, YOU GOTTA GET STRONGER!
I'LL BE STRONGER THAN YOU *SOMEDAY*♪
THEN I'LL WIN WHEN WE *PLAY*.♪
THWAK

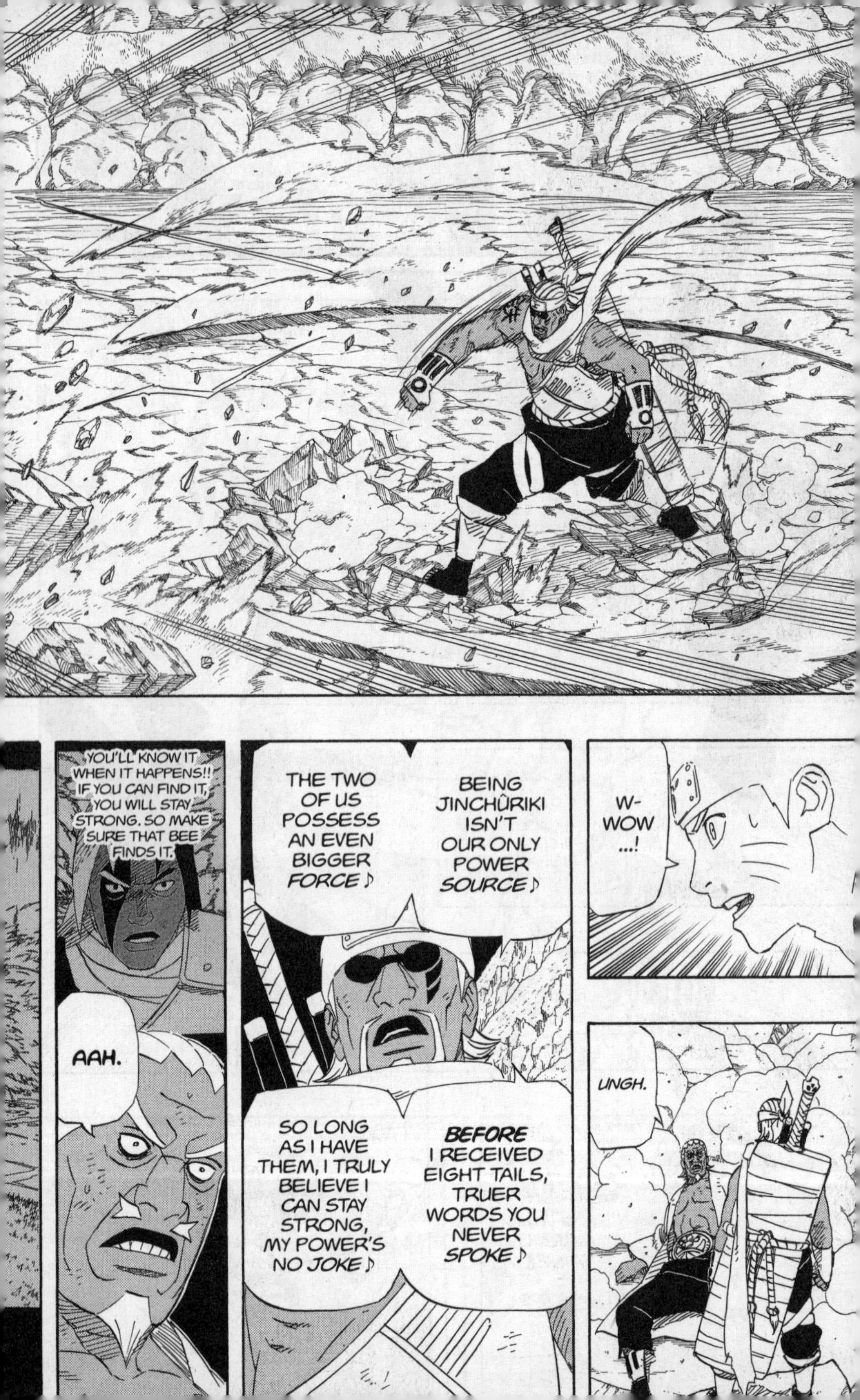
W-WOW ...!
UNGH.
BEING JINCHÛRIKI ISN'T OUR ONLY POWER SOURCE♪
THE TWO OF US POSSESS AN EVEN BIGGER FORCE♪
BEFORE I RECEIVED EIGHT TAILS, TRUER WORDS YOU NEVER SPOKE♪
SO LONG AS I HAVE THEM, I TRULY BELIEVE I CAN STAY STRONG, MY POWER'S NO JOKE♪
YOU'LL KNOW IT WHEN IT HAPPENS!! IF YOU CAN FIND IT, YOU WILL STAY STRONG. SO MAKE SURE THAT BEE FINDS IT.
AAH.

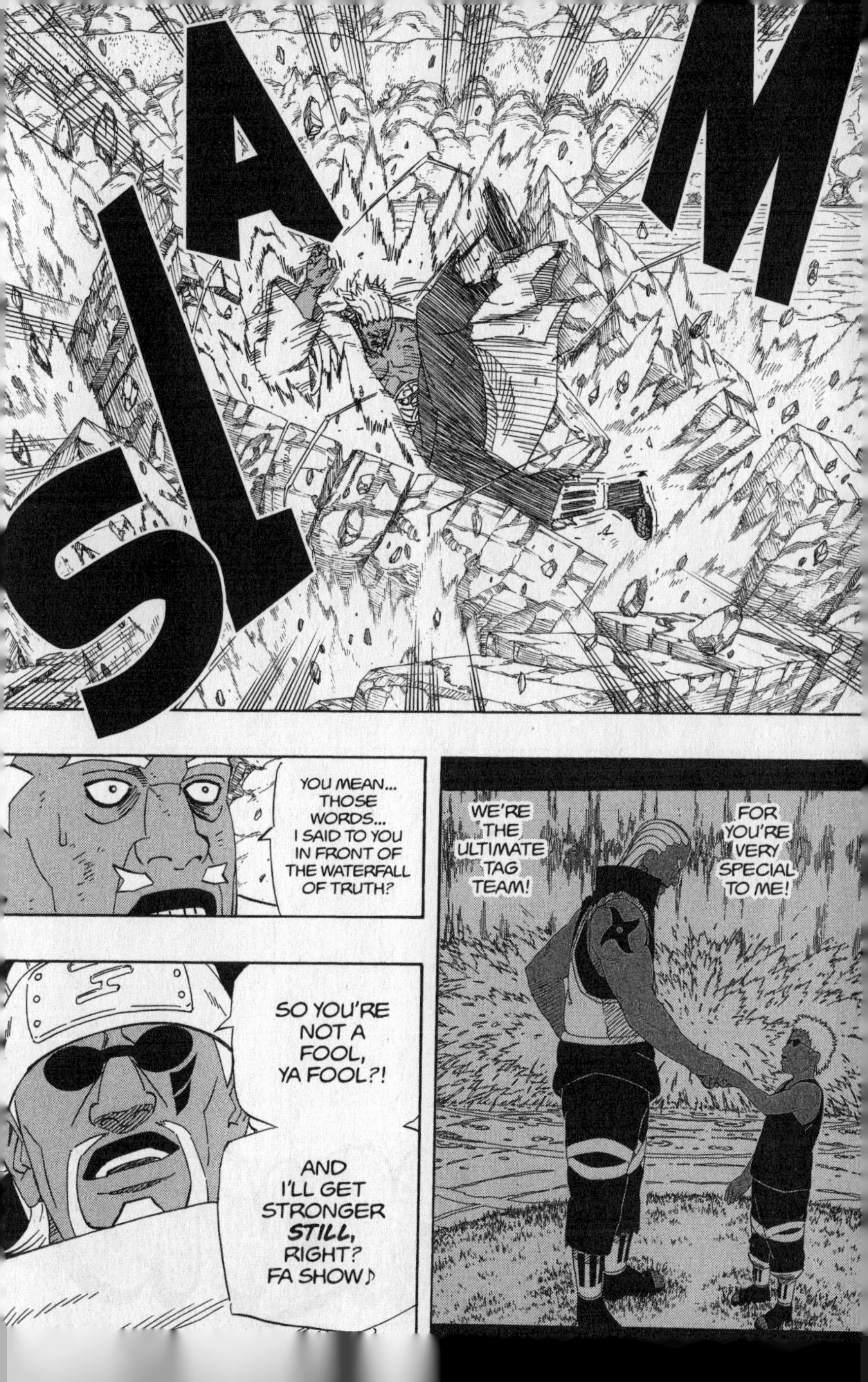
SLAM
FOR YOU'RE VERY SPECIAL TO ME!
WE'RE THE ULTIMATE TAG TEAM!
YOU MEAN... THOSE WORDS... I SAID TO YOU IN FRONT OF THE WATERFALL OF TRUTH?
SO YOU'RE NOT A FOOL, YA FOOL?!
AND I'LL GET STRONGER STILL, RIGHT? FA SHOW♪

NARUTO

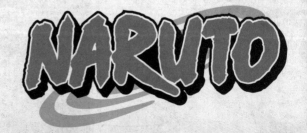

# Number 544: Two Suns!!

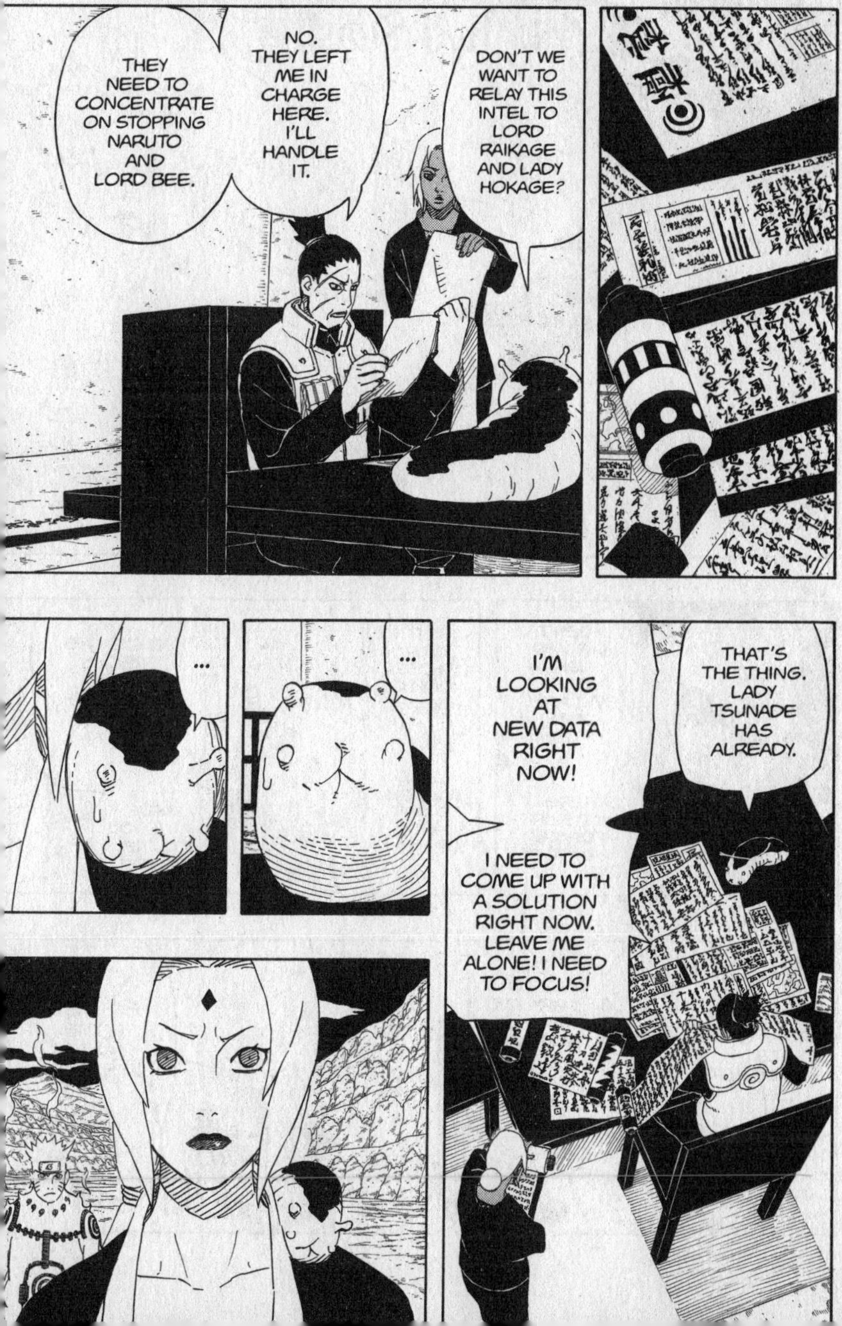
DON'T WE WANT TO RELAY THIS INTEL TO LORD RAIKAGE AND LADY HOKAGE?
NO. THEY LEFT ME IN CHARGE HERE. I'LL HANDLE IT.
THEY NEED TO CONCENTRATE ON STOPPING NARUTO AND LORD BEE.
THAT'S THE THING. LADY TSUNADE HAS ALREADY.
I'M LOOKING AT NEW DATA RIGHT NOW!
I NEED TO COME UP WITH A SOLUTION RIGHT NOW. LEAVE ME ALONE! I NEED TO FOCUS!
...
...

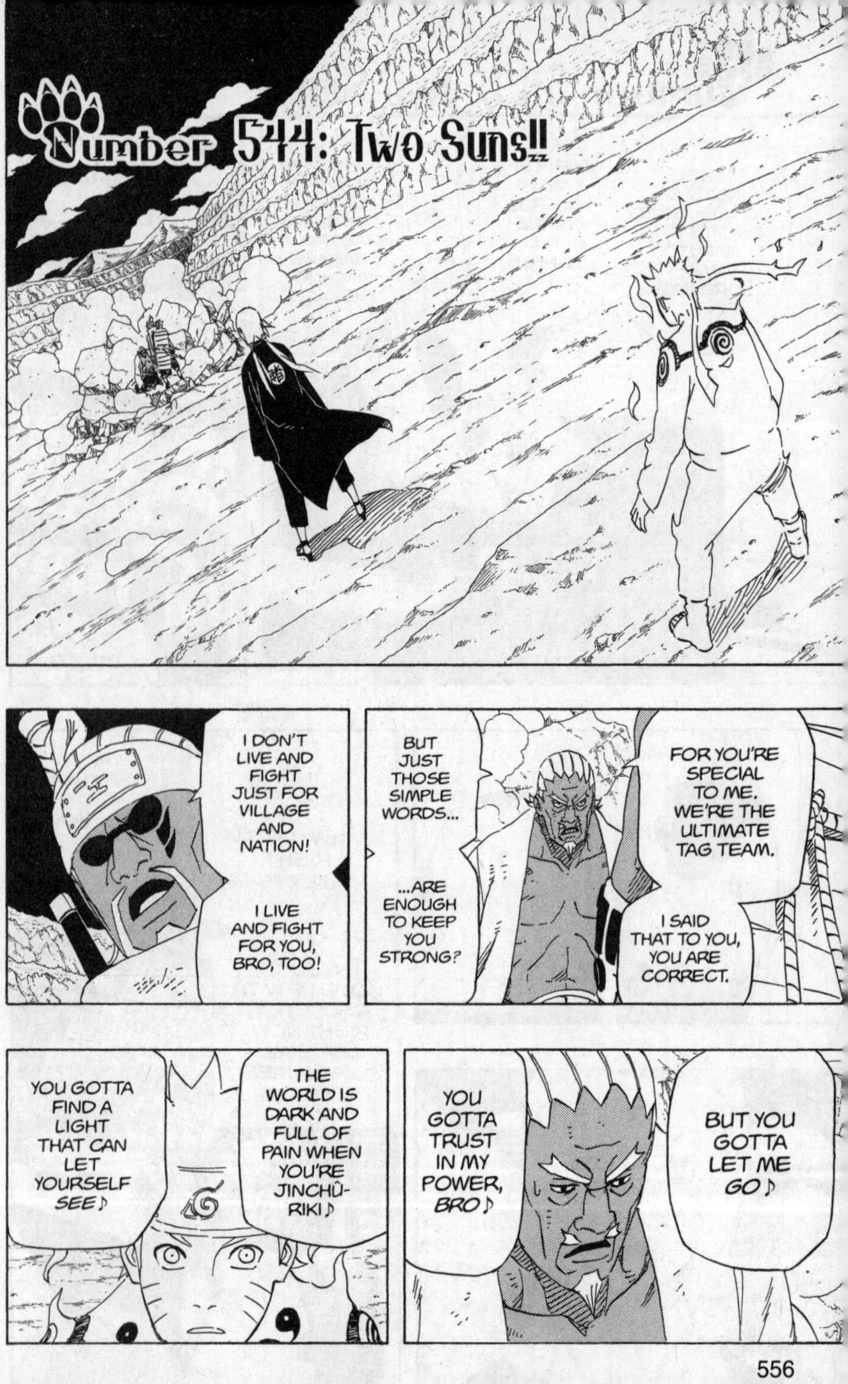
Number 544: Two Suns!!
FOR YOU'RE SPECIAL TO ME. WE'RE THE ULTIMATE TAG TEAM.
I SAID THAT TO YOU, YOU ARE CORRECT.
BUT JUST THOSE SIMPLE WORDS...
...ARE ENOUGH TO KEEP YOU STRONG?
I DON'T LIVE AND FIGHT JUST FOR VILLAGE AND NATION!
I LIVE AND FIGHT FOR YOU, BRO, TOO!
BUT YOU GOTTA LET ME GO♪
YOU GOTTA TRUST IN MY POWER, BRO♪
THE WORLD IS DARK AND FULL OF PAIN WHEN YOU'RE JINCHÛ-RIKI♪
YOU GOTTA FIND A LIGHT THAT CAN LET YOURSELF SEE♪

READ THIS WAY

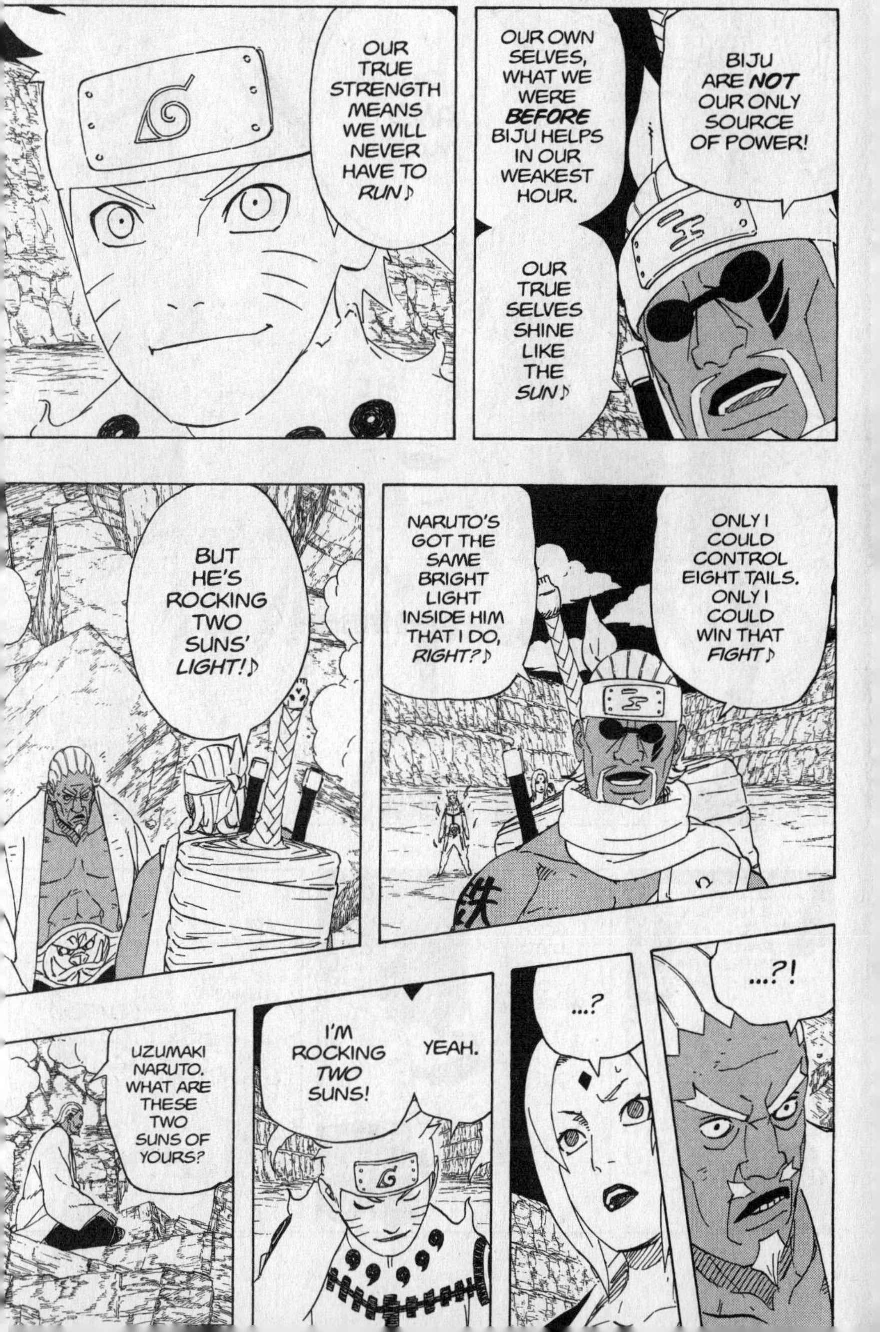
BIJU ARE NOT OUR ONLY SOURCE OF POWER!
OUR OWN SELVES, WHAT WE WERE BEFORE BIJU HELPS IN OUR WEAKEST HOUR.
OUR TRUE SELVES SHINE LIKE THE SUN♪
OUR TRUE STRENGTH MEANS WE WILL NEVER HAVE TO RUN♪
ONLY I COULD CONTROL EIGHT TAILS. ONLY I COULD WIN THAT FIGHT♪
NARUTO'S GOT THE SAME BRIGHT LIGHT INSIDE HIM THAT I DO, RIGHT?♪
BUT HE'S ROCKING TWO SUNS' LIGHT!♪
...?!
...?
YEAH.
I'M ROCKING TWO SUNS!
UZUMAKI NARUTO. WHAT ARE THESE TWO SUNS OF YOURS?

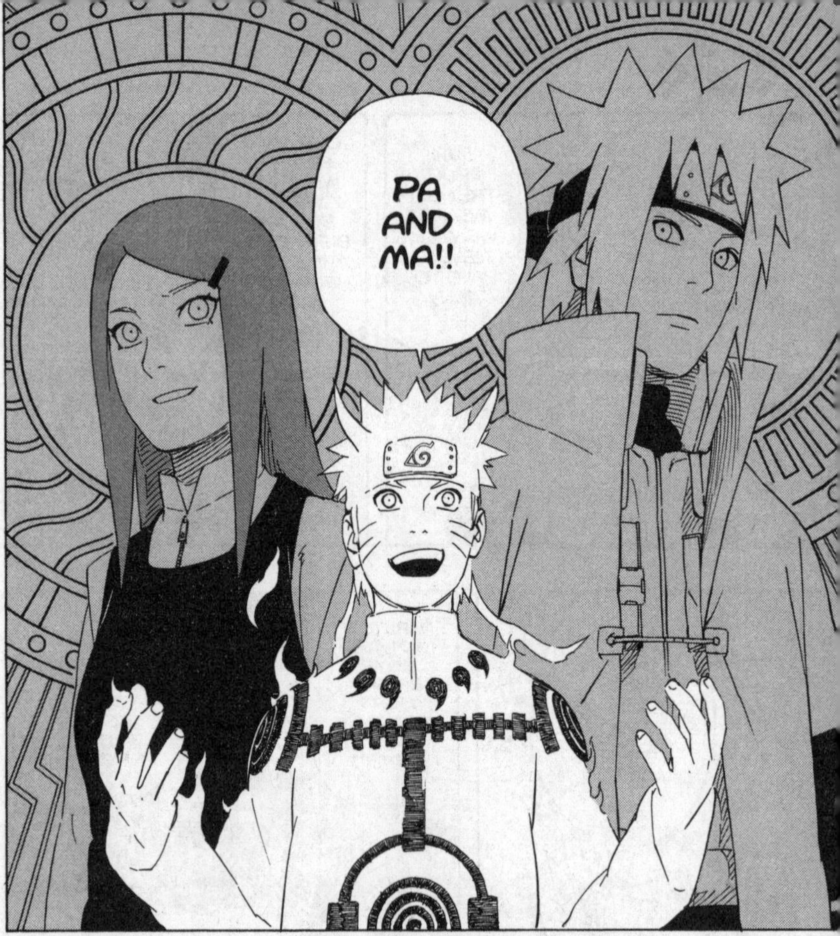
PA AND MA!!

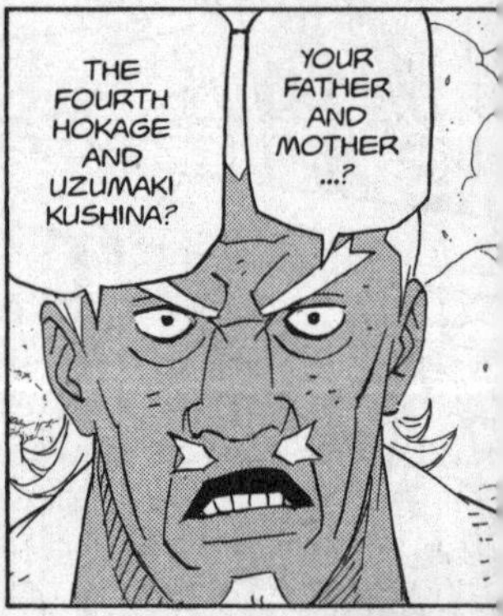
YOUR FATHER AND MOTHER ...?
THE FOURTH HOKAGE AND UZUMAKI KUSHINA?

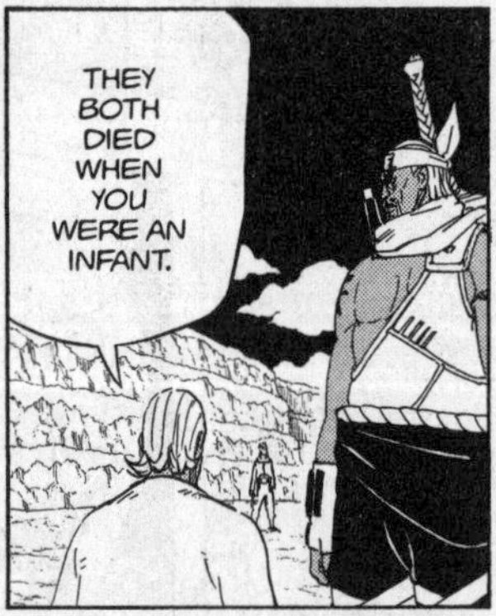
THEY BOTH DIED WHEN YOU WERE AN INFANT.

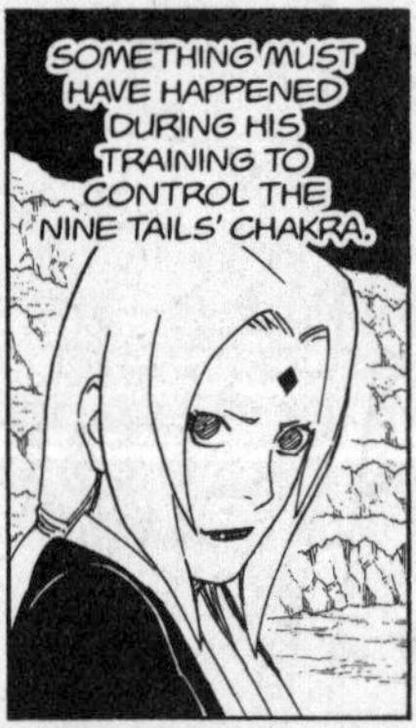
SOMETHING MUST HAVE HAPPENED DURING HIS TRAINING TO CONTROL THE NINE TAILS' CHAKRA.

READ THIS WAY

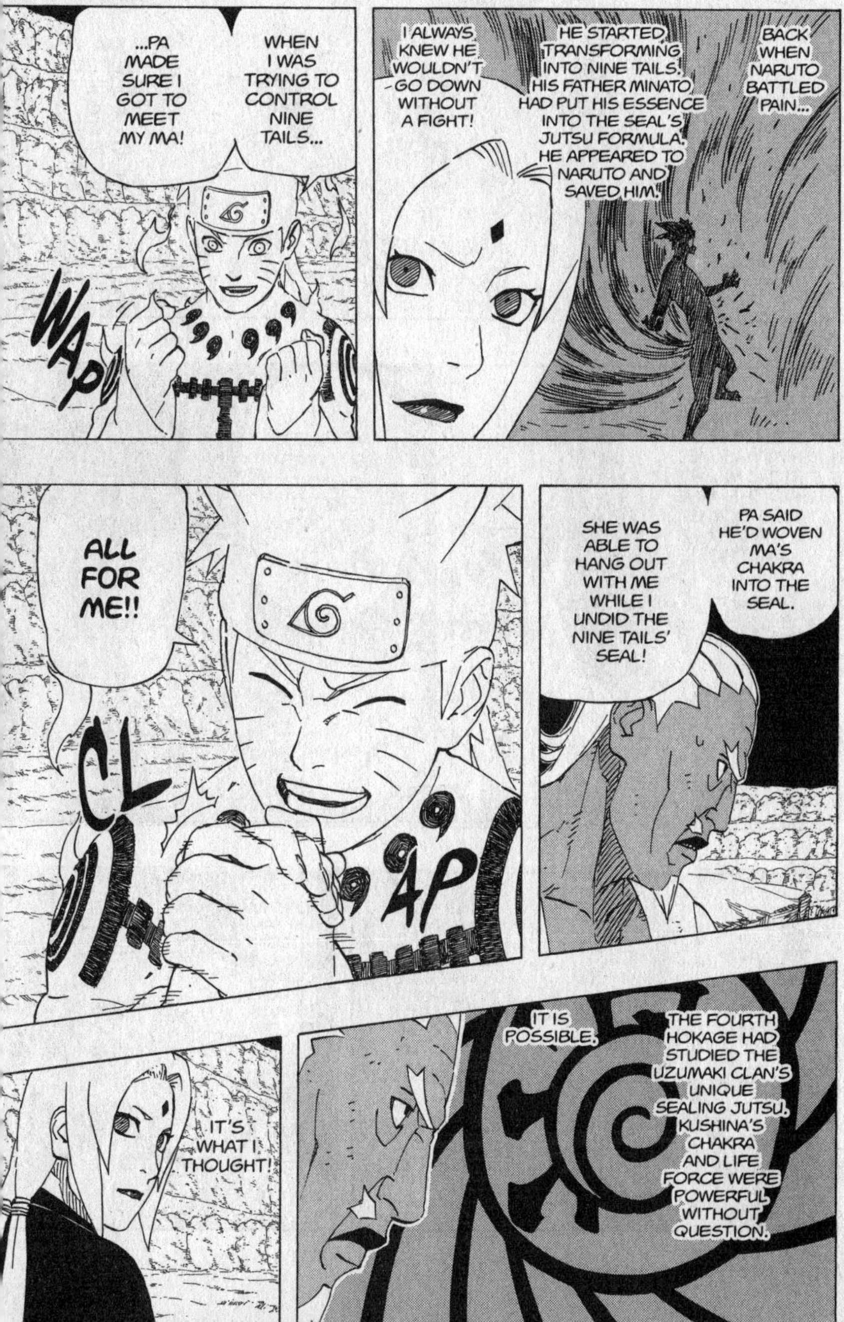
BACK WHEN NARUTO BATTLED PAIN...
HE STARTED TRANSFORMING INTO NINE TAILS. HIS FATHER MINATO HAD PUT HIS ESSENCE INTO THE SEAL'S JUTSU FORMULA. HE APPEARED TO NARUTO AND SAVED HIM.
I ALWAYS KNEW HE WOULDN'T GO DOWN WITHOUT A FIGHT!
WHEN I WAS TRYING TO CONTROL NINE TAILS...
...PA MADE SURE I GOT TO MEET MY MA!
WAP
PA SAID HE'D WOVEN MA'S CHAKRA INTO THE SEAL.
SHE WAS ABLE TO HANG OUT WITH ME WHILE I UNDID THE NINE TAILS' SEAL!
ALL FOR ME!!
CLAP
IT IS POSSIBLE.
THE FOURTH HOKAGE HAD STUDIED THE UZUMAKI CLAN'S UNIQUE SEALING JUTSU. KUSHINA'S CHAKRA AND LIFE FORCE WERE POWERFUL WITHOUT QUESTION.
IT'S WHAT I THOUGHT!

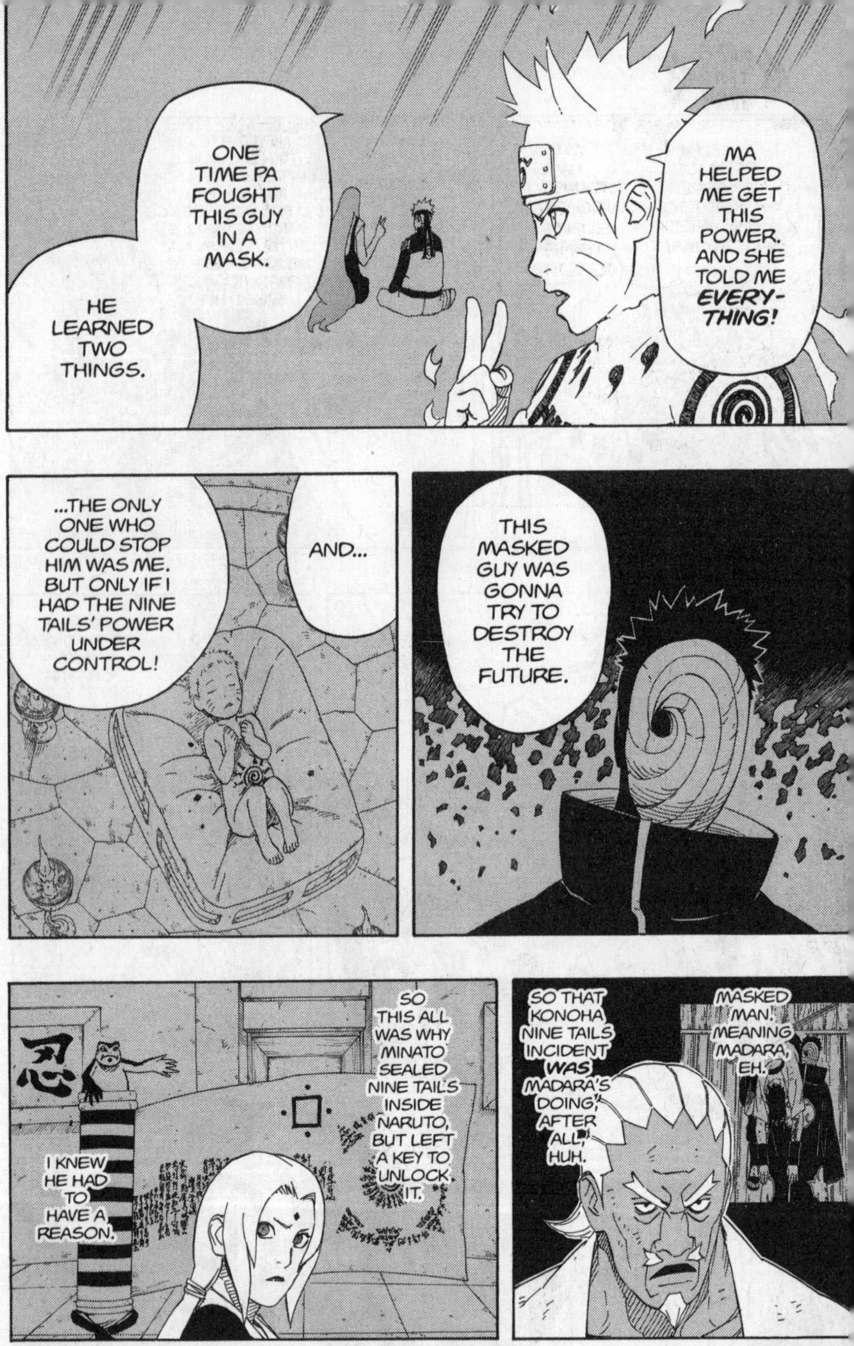
MA HELPED ME GET THIS POWER. AND SHE TOLD ME EVERYTHING!
ONE TIME PA FOUGHT THIS GUY IN A MASK.
HE LEARNED TWO THINGS.
THIS MASKED GUY WAS GONNA TRY TO DESTROY THE FUTURE.
AND...
...THE ONLY ONE WHO COULD STOP HIM WAS ME. BUT ONLY IF I HAD THE NINE TAILS' POWER UNDER CONTROL!
MASKED MAN. MEANING MADARA, EH.
SO THAT KONOHA NINE TAILS INCIDENT WAS MADARA'S DOING, AFTER ALL, HUH.
SO THIS ALL WAS WHY MINATO SEALED NINE TAILS INSIDE NARUTO, BUT LEFT A KEY TO UNLOCK IT.
I KNEW HE HAD TO HAVE A REASON.

READ THIS WAY

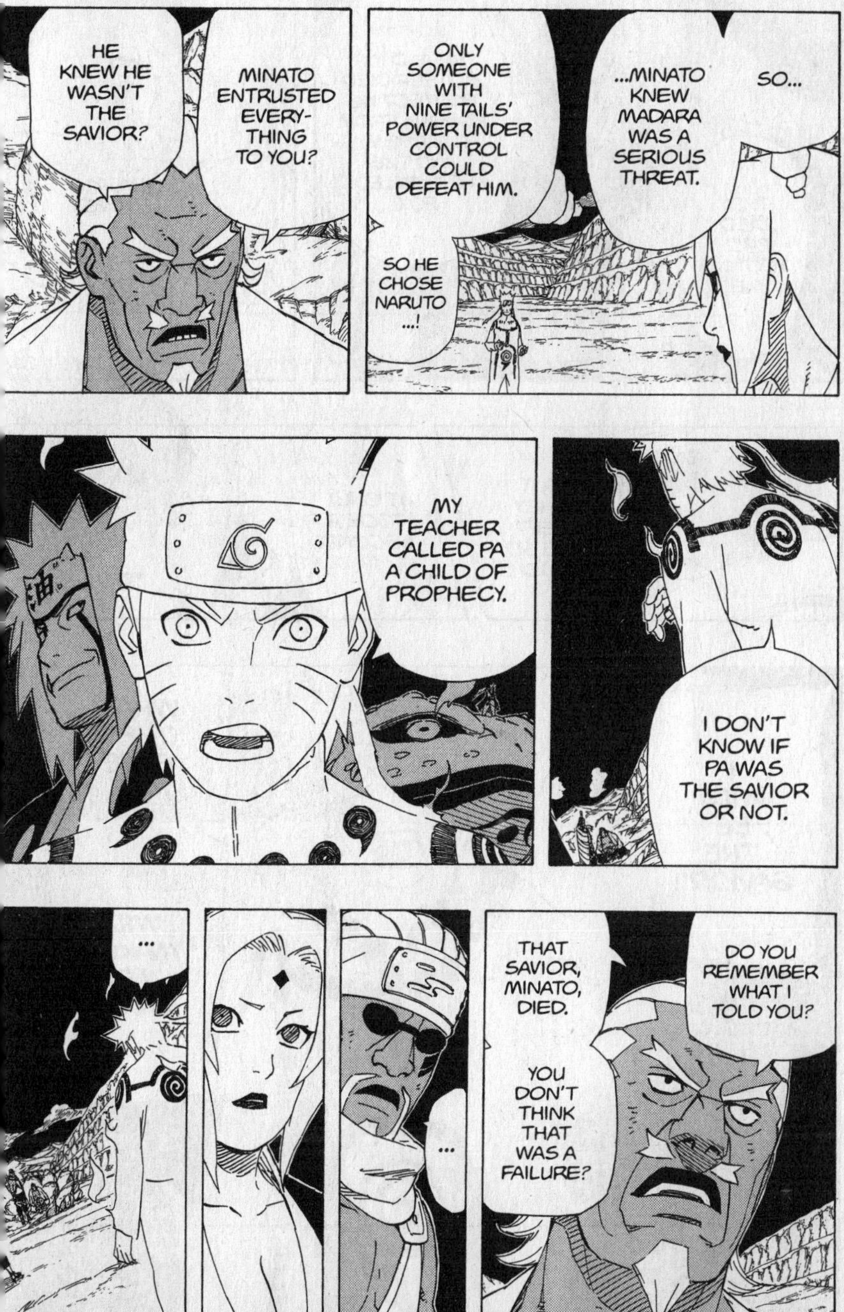
SO...
...MINATO KNEW MADARA WAS A SERIOUS THREAT.
ONLY SOMEONE WITH NINE TAILS' POWER UNDER CONTROL COULD DEFEAT HIM.
SO HE CHOSE NARUTO ...!
MINATO ENTRUSTED EVERY-THING TO YOU?
HE KNEW HE WASN'T THE SAVIOR?
I DON'T KNOW IF PA WAS THE SAVIOR OR NOT.
MY TEACHER CALLED PA A CHILD OF PROPHECY.
DO YOU REMEMBER WHAT I TOLD YOU?
THAT SAVIOR, MINATO, DIED.
YOU DON'T THINK THAT WAS A FAILURE?
...
...

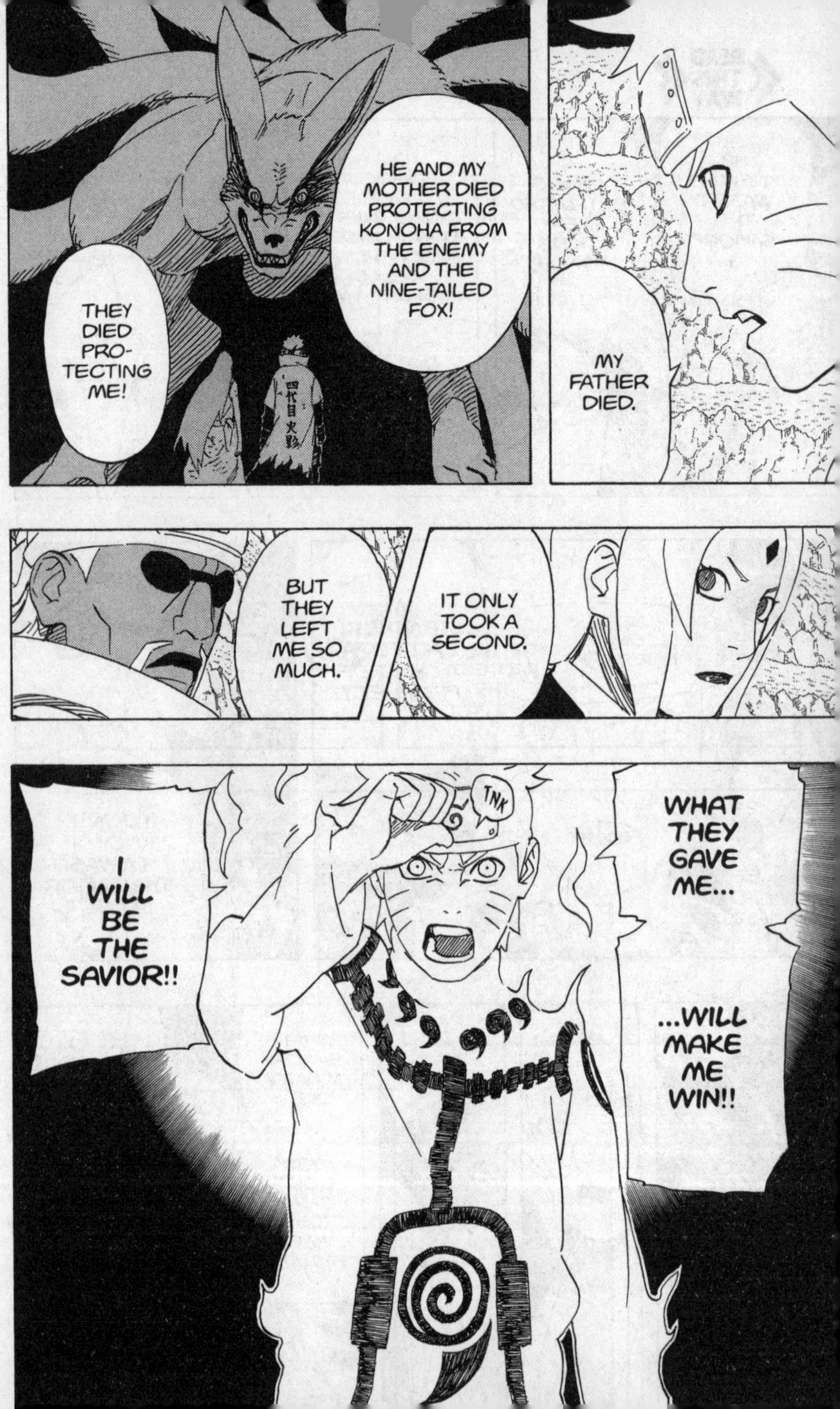
MY FATHER DIED.
HE AND MY MOTHER DIED PROTECTING KONOHA FROM THE ENEMY AND THE NINE-TAILED FOX!
THEY DIED PROTECTING ME!
IT ONLY TOOK A SECOND.
BUT THEY LEFT ME SO MUCH.
TNK
WHAT THEY GAVE ME...
...WILL MAKE ME WIN!!
I WILL BE THE SAVIOR!!

READ THIS WAY

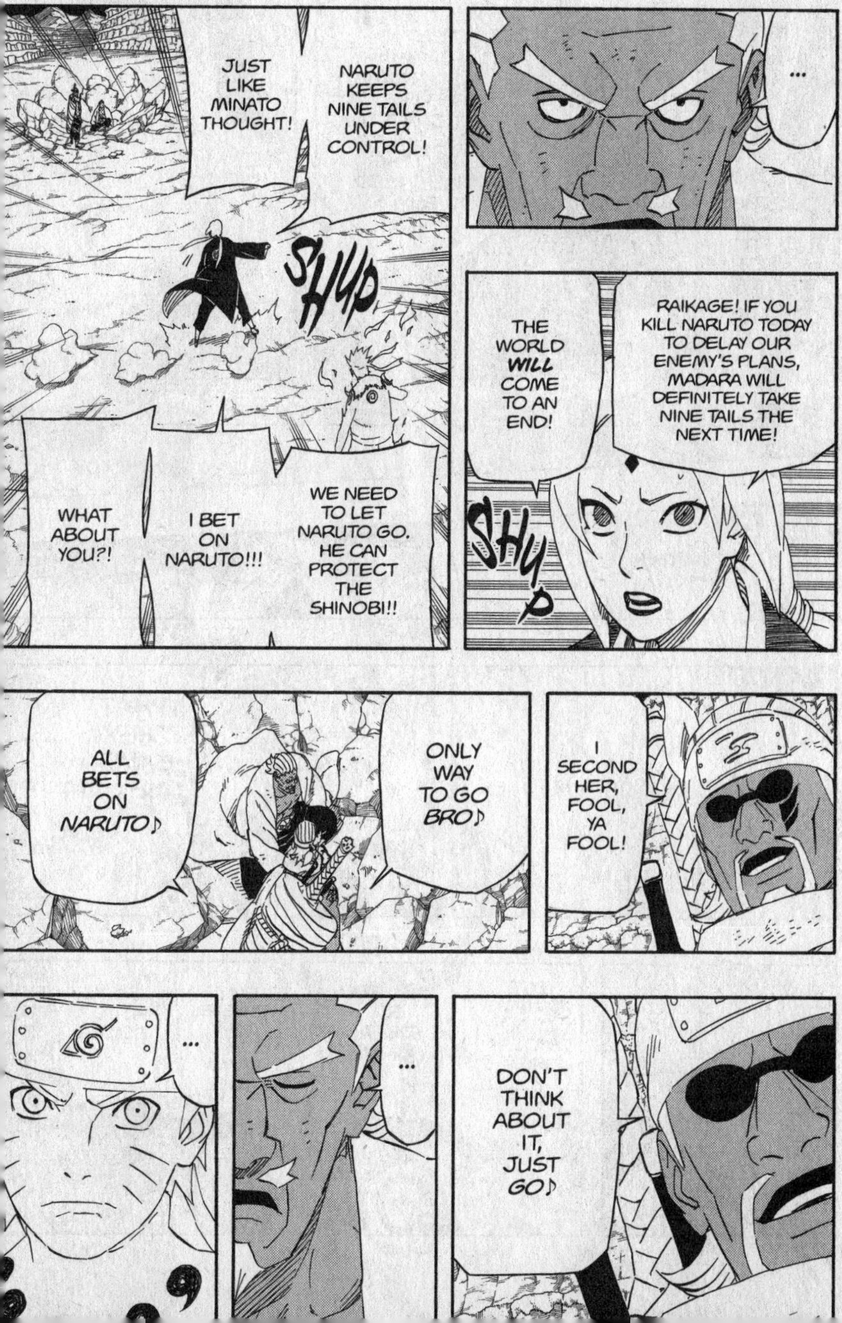
...
RAIKAGE! IF YOU KILL NARUTO TODAY TO DELAY OUR ENEMY'S PLANS, MADARA WILL DEFINITELY TAKE NINE TAILS THE NEXT TIME!
THE WORLD WILL COME TO AN END!
SHUP
NARUTO KEEPS NINE TAILS UNDER CONTROL!
JUST LIKE MINATO THOUGHT!
SHUP
WE NEED TO LET NARUTO GO. HE CAN PROTECT THE SHINOBI!!
I BET ON NARUTO!!!
WHAT ABOUT YOU?!
I SECOND HER, FOOL, YA FOOL!
ONLY WAY TO GO BRO♪
ALL BETS ON NARUTO♪
DON'T THINK ABOUT IT, JUST GO♪
...
...

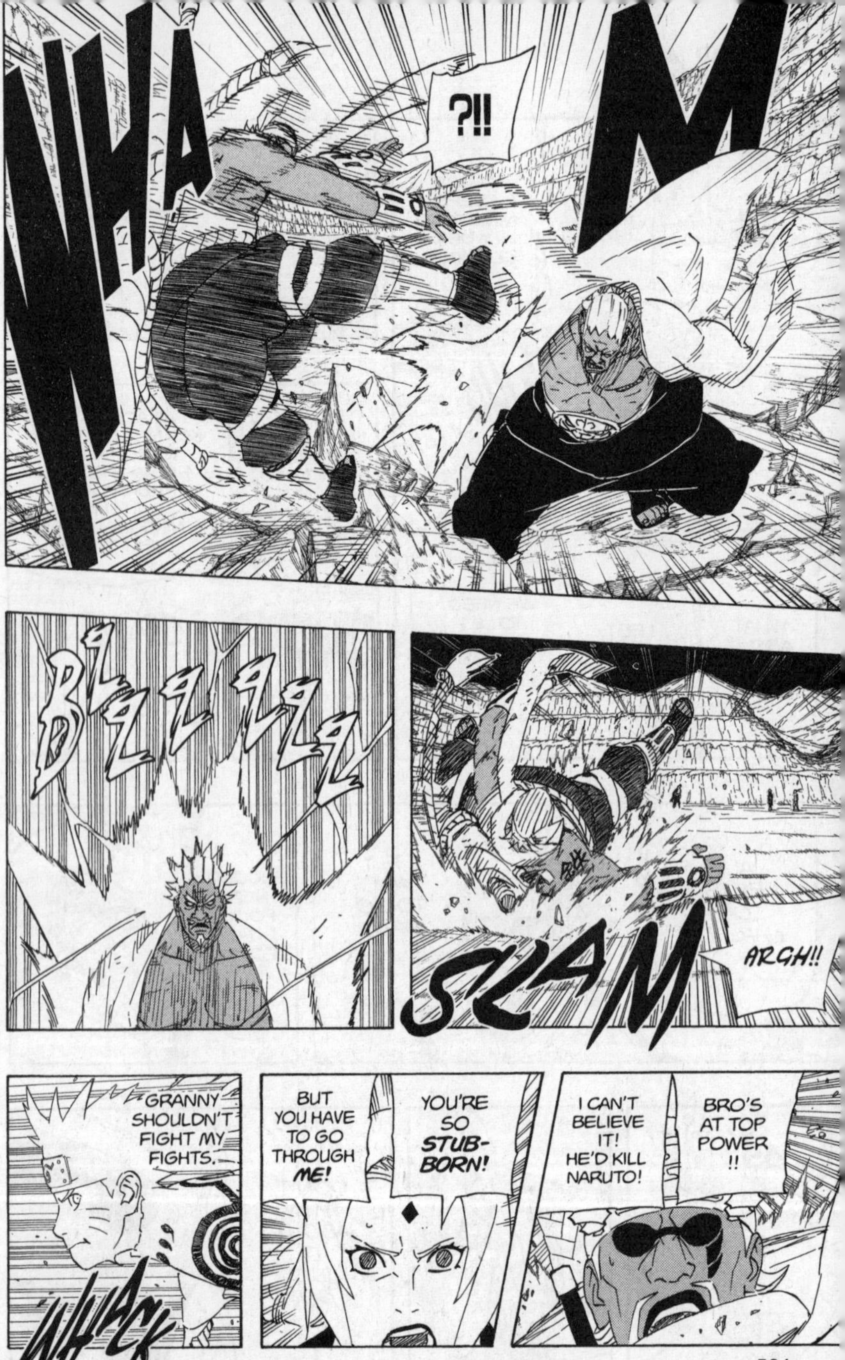
WHAM
?!!
SLAM
ARGH!!
BZZZZZZ
BRO'S AT TOP POWER !!
I CAN'T BELIEVE IT! HE'D KILL NARUTO!
YOU'RE SO ***STUB-BORN!***
BUT YOU HAVE TO GO THROUGH ***ME!***
GRANNY SHOULDN'T FIGHT MY FIGHTS.
WHACK

READ THIS WAY

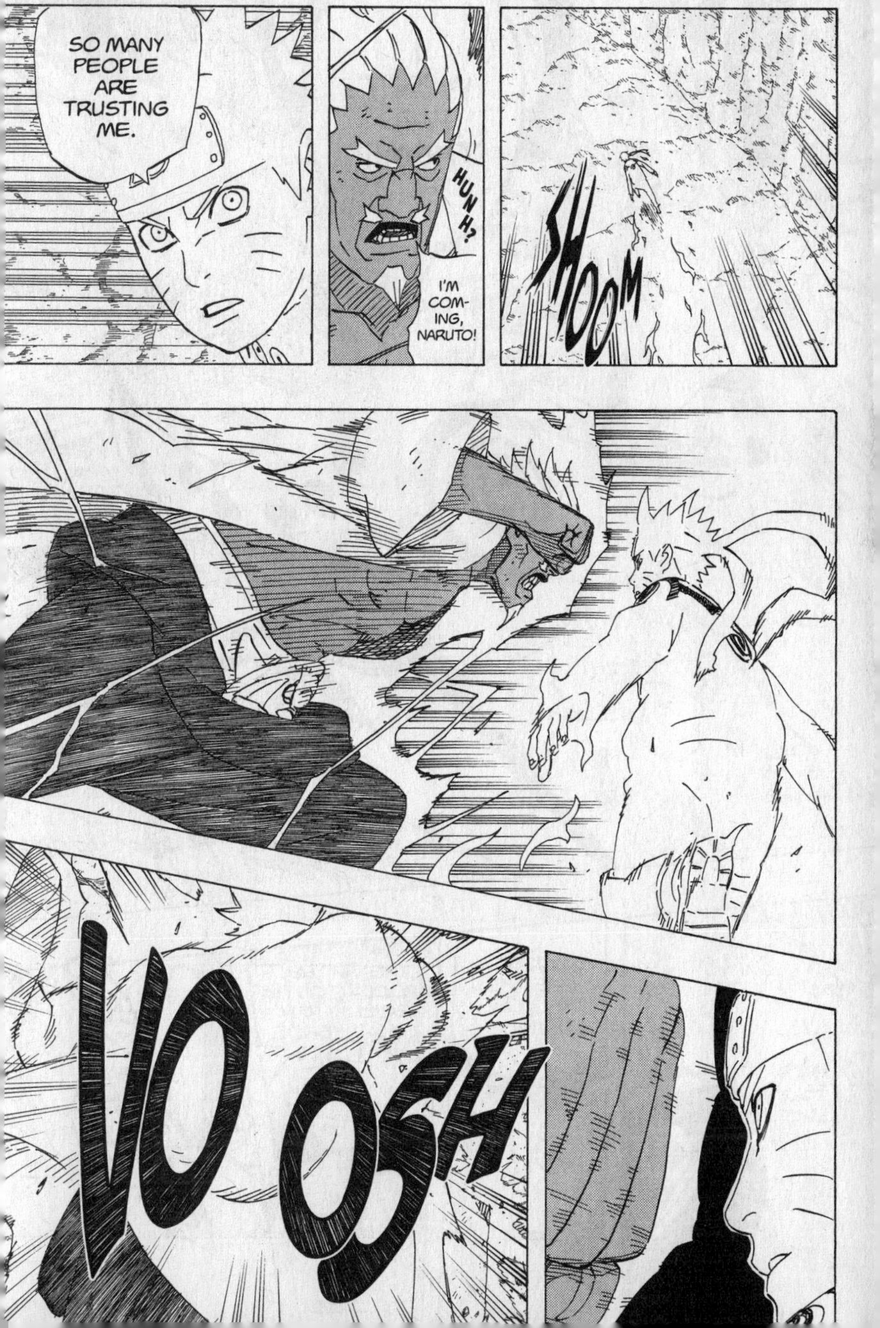
SHOOM
HUNH?
I'M COMING, NARUTO!
SO MANY PEOPLE ARE TRUSTING ME.
VOOSH

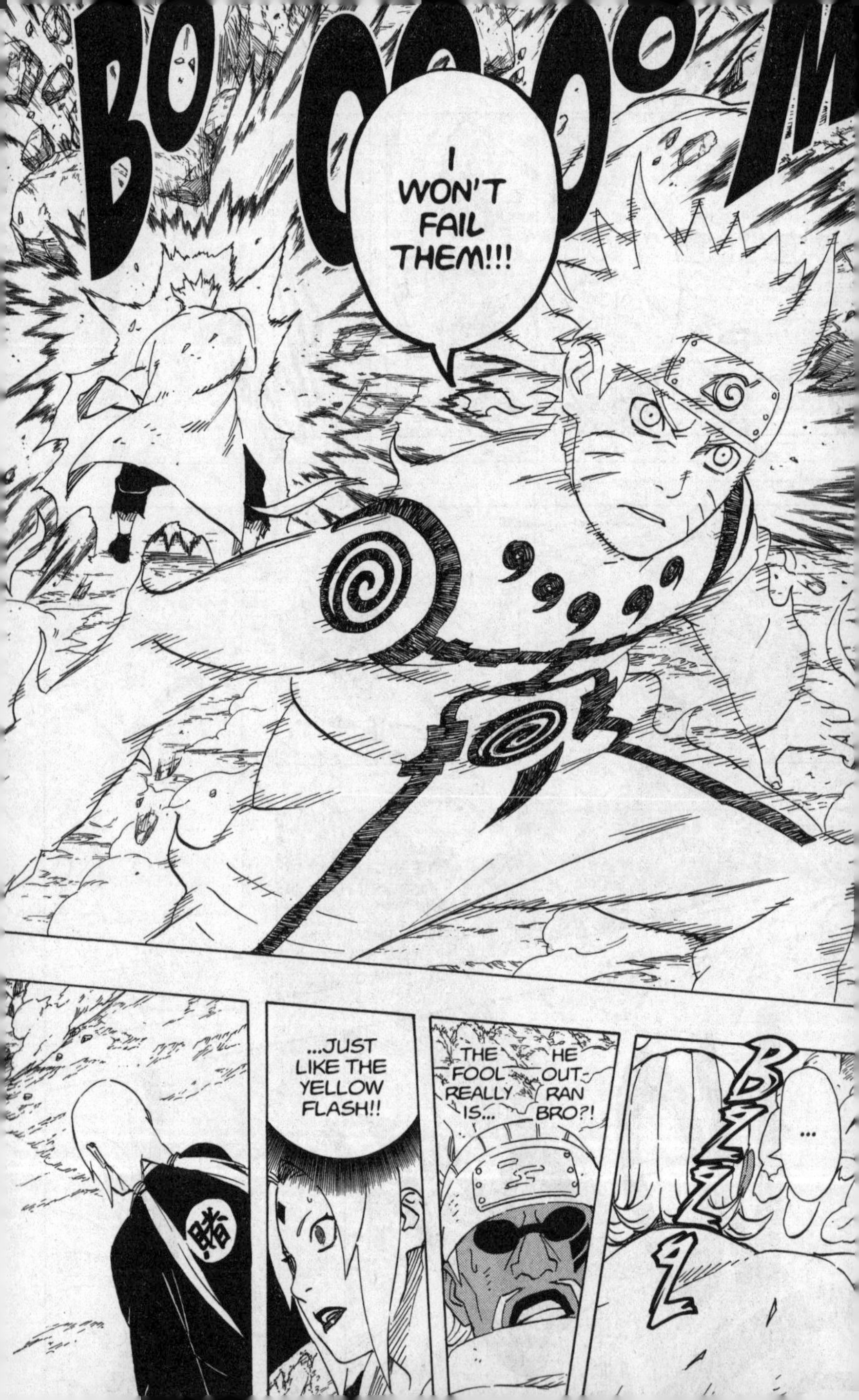
BOOOOOM
I WON'T FAIL THEM!!!
...
HE OUTRAN BRO?!
THE FOOL REALLY IS...
...JUST LIKE THE YELLOW FLASH!!

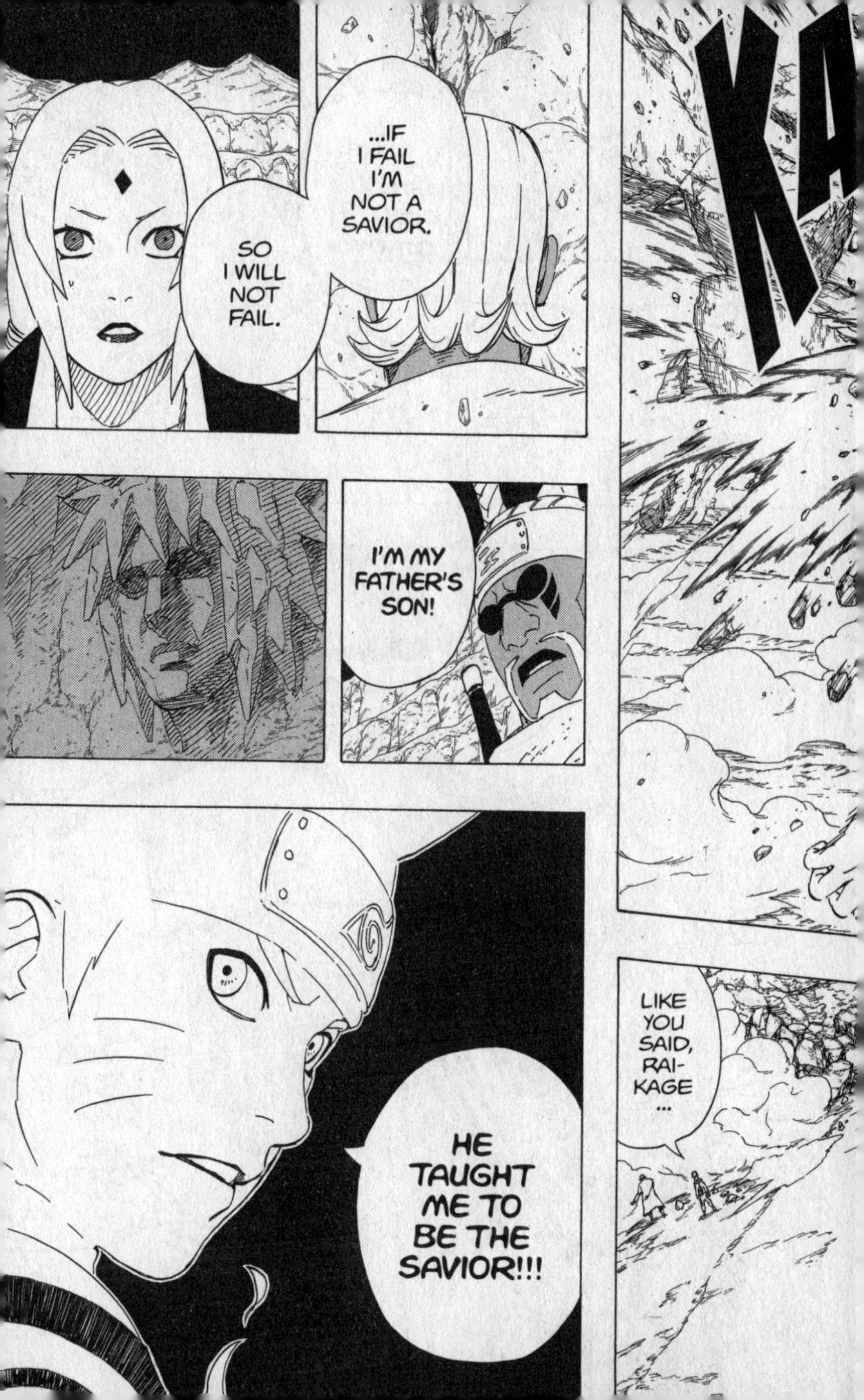
KA
...IF I FAIL I'M NOT A SAVIOR.
SO I WILL NOT FAIL.
I'M MY FATHER'S SON!
LIKE YOU SAID, RAI-KAGE ...
HE TAUGHT ME TO BE THE SAVIOR!!!

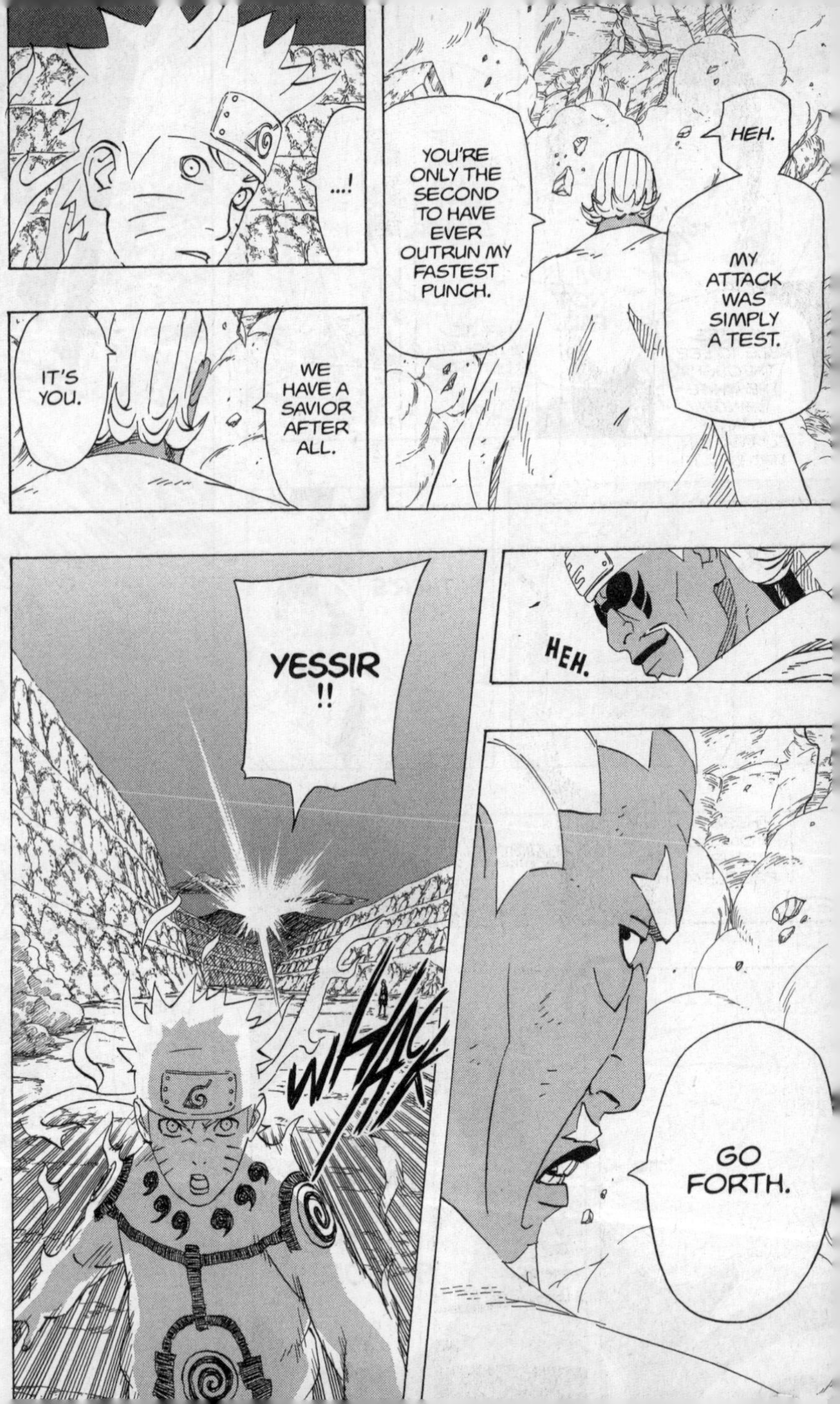
HEH.
MY ATTACK WAS SIMPLY A TEST.
YOU'RE ONLY THE SECOND TO HAVE EVER OUTRUN MY FASTEST PUNCH.
...!
WE HAVE A SAVIOR AFTER ALL.
IT'S YOU.
HEH.
GO FORTH.
YESSIR!!
WHAK

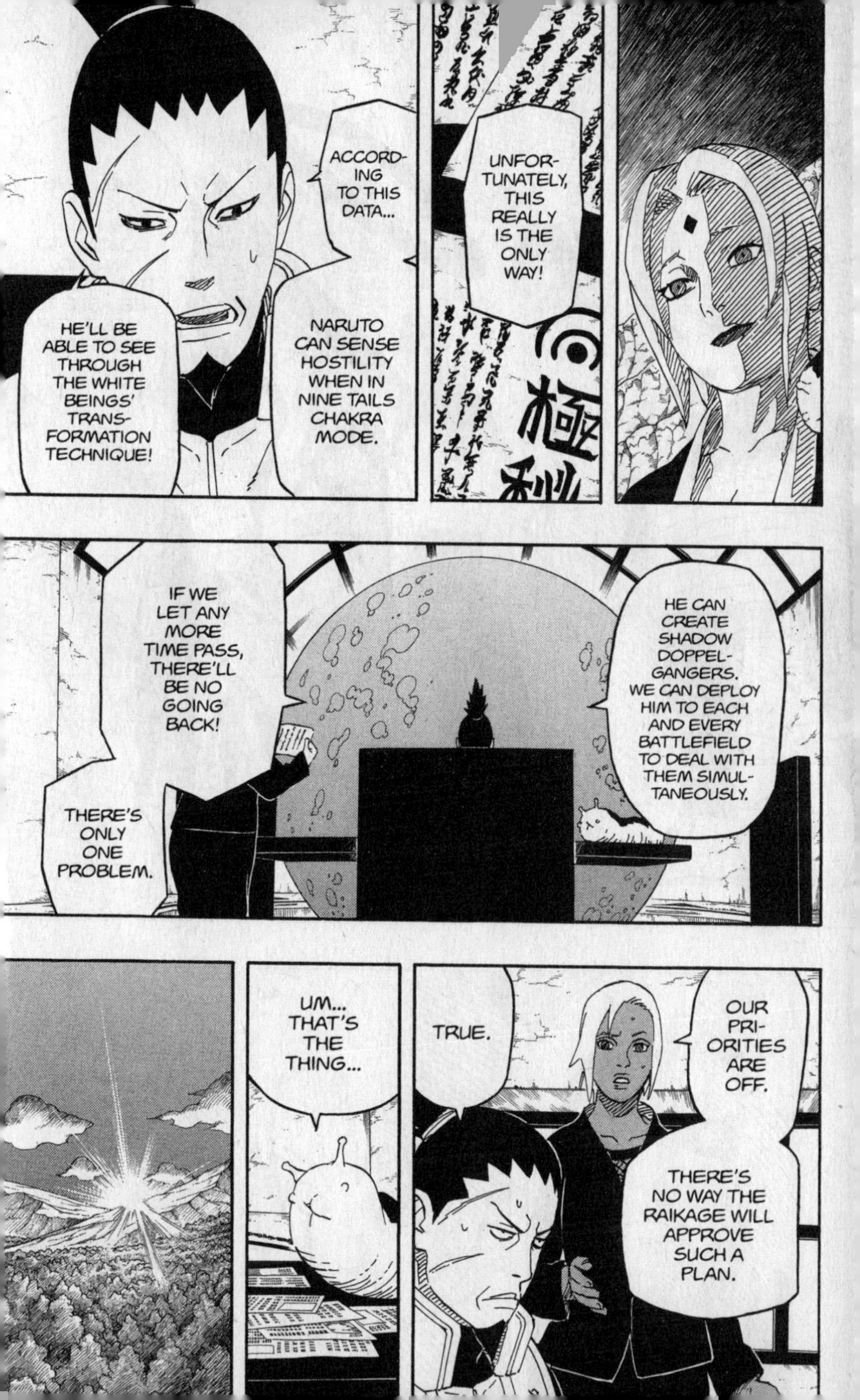
UNFORTUNATELY, THIS REALLY IS THE ONLY WAY!
ACCORDING TO THIS DATA...
NARUTO CAN SENSE HOSTILITY WHEN IN NINE TAILS CHAKRA MODE.
HE'LL BE ABLE TO SEE THROUGH THE WHITE BEINGS' TRANSFORMATION TECHNIQUE!
HE CAN CREATE SHADOW DOPPELGANGERS. WE CAN DEPLOY HIM TO EACH AND EVERY BATTLEFIELD TO DEAL WITH THEM SIMULTANEOUSLY.
IF WE LET ANY MORE TIME PASS, THERE'LL BE NO GOING BACK!
THERE'S ONLY ONE PROBLEM.
OUR PRIORITIES ARE OFF.
THERE'S NO WAY THE RAIKAGE WILL APPROVE SUCH A PLAN.
TRUE.
UM... THAT'S THE THING...

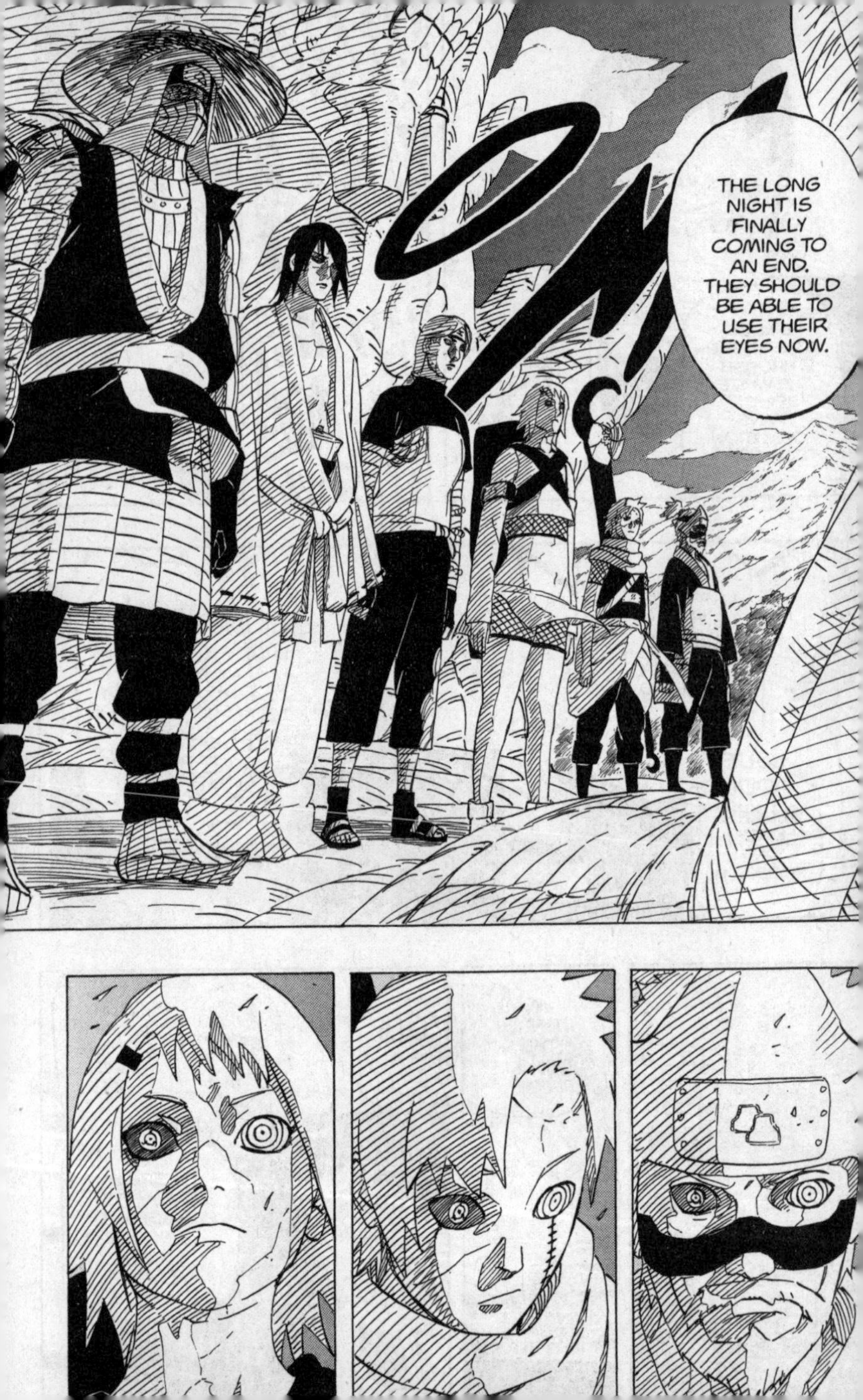
THE LONG NIGHT IS FINALLY COMING TO AN END. THEY SHOULD BE ABLE TO USE THEIR EYES NOW.

SIX NEW PAINS. ALL JINCHÛRIKI.

I JUST ADDED A LITTLE SOMETHING.

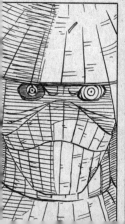

## IN THE NEXT VOLUME...

### THE BATTLEFIELD

Kabuto's hold over his army of undead minions tightens as he senses that he's losing power over the stronger members of his Immortal Corps, including Nagato Pain. Sasuke's brother, Itachi, may have the best chance of breaking Kabuto's hold. But he's still not completely in control of his actions, which means Naruto may have to take him down once and for all.

**NARUTO 3-IN-1 EDITION VOLUME 20 AVAILABLE OCTOBER 2017!**

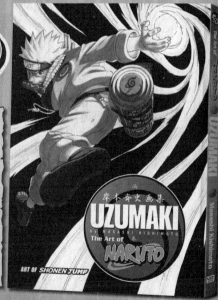

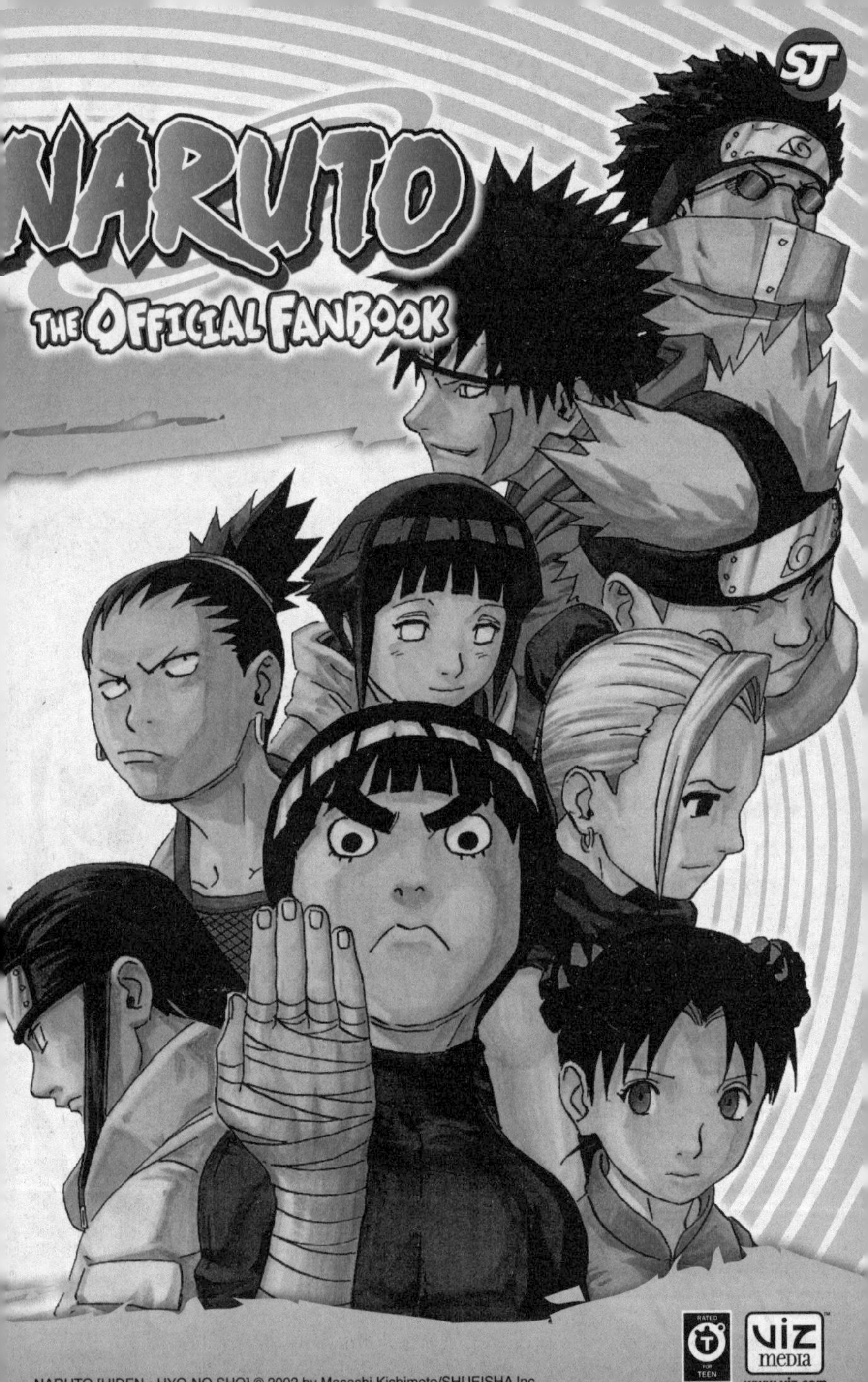
SJ
NARUTO
THE OFFICIAL FANBOOK
RATED T FOR TEEN
ratings.viz.com
viz media
www.viz.com